ENCYCLOPEDIA OF
AFRICAN HISTORY

BOARD OF ADVISORS

ENCYCLOPEDIA OF AFRICAN HISTORY

VOLUME 3
P–Z INDEX

Kevin Shillington, Editor

Fitzroy Dearborn
An Imprint of the Taylor & Francis Group
New York • London

Published in 2005 by
Fitzroy Dearborn
Taylor & Francis Group
270 Madison Avenue
New York, NY 10016

10 9 8 7 6 5 4 3 2

Library of Congress Cataloging-in-Publication Data
    Encyclopedia of African history / Kevin Shillington, editor.
        p. cm.
      Includes bibliographical references and index.
      ISBN 1-57958-245-1 (alk. paper)
      1. Africa—History—Encyclopedias. I. Shillington, Kevin.

    DT20.E53 2004
    960'.03—dc22   2004016779

CONTENTS

LIST OF ENTRIES A–Z

(with chronological sublistings within nation/group categories)

VOLUME 1

VOLUME 2

P

PAICGC: *See* **Guinea-Bissau: Cabral, Amílcar, PAICG, Independence, 1961–1973.**

Pan-African Technical Organizations and Associations

There is a wide range of inter-African organizations that can be classified under a number of headings, including the all-embracing Organization of African Unity (OAU) with its many subsidiary agencies. The United Nations (UN) and its various agencies in Africa include a range of regional offices. Economic organizations such as the African Development Bank and regional groupings such as the Economic Community of West African States or the Southern African Development Community, and intercontinental organizations with their affiliates such as the Franc Zone, the Commonwealth, the Lomé Convention, or the Organization of Islamic Conference also exist. Such organizations provide technical and professional advice and assistance at a number of levels, often to the range of smaller, more specific-purpose African technical organizations and associations that are dealt with here.

There are more than 100 continental or regional African organizations working at various levels of technical cooperation. They cover the following fields: agriculture, forestry, and fisheries including such activities as locust control or crop research; aid, development, and economic cooperation ranging from mapping to drought control; river basin development organizations; arts and culture; education; finance and economic research; government and politics; labor; law; medicine and public health; the media; religion; science and technology; social sciences; trade and industry; and transport and tourism.

It is not easy to give appropriate weighting to the importance of these organizations; their performance must depend upon the quality of personnel, available cash resources, and the level of cooperation provided by member countries that, in turn, may be adversely affected by political or other problems in the region. The more successful such organizations are often those with a precise, relatively narrow objective such as locust control rather than more wide-ranging objectives such as regional economic cooperation.

A number of organizations deal with water control, whether river basins and their management or drought control. At the technical level the Inter-African Committee for Hydraulic Studies, founded in 1960 with headquarters at Ouagadougou in Burkina Faso, works to bring about cooperation in water sciences such as hydrology, climatology, and urban sanitation. The Permanent Inter-State Committee on Drought Control in the Sahel working in collaboration with the UN combats the chronic drought of the region and is assisted by the Club du Sahel, based in Paris, which is a forum for donor countries that was formed in 1976 following the great Sahel drought of 1973–1974. The Intergovernmental Authority on Development, founded in 1986, coordinates measures in the Horn region to combat drought and desertification and its programs cover food security, desertification control, environmental protection, and water resources management. In 1996 its members decided to widen its scope so as to cover economic and regional integration and conflict resolution. Six states are members: Djibouti, Eritrea, Ethiopia, Kenya, Sudan, and Uganda.

Water and its control presents many problems on a continent where large areas are subject to drought or flooding and a number of river basins affect three or more countries. The Gambia River Basin Development Organization, formed in 1978 by Senegal and Gambia and later joined by Guinea (1981) and Guinea-Bissau (1983), is principally concerned with the agricultural and power potential of the river. The Mano River Union, on the other hand, was conceived in terms of fostering greater economic integration between its members (Guinea, Liberia, and Sierra Leone) although the civil wars in Liberia and Sierra Leone during the 1990s retarded its development. Two other river basin authorities are the Organization for the Development of the Senegal River (members: Mali, Mauritania, and Senegal) and the Organization for the Management and Development of the Kagera River Basin, whose member states are Burundi, Rwanda, Tanzania, and Uganda. There is also the Lake Chad Basin Commission, whose purpose is to regulate and control the waters of the lake for its riparian states—Cameroon, the Central African Republic, Chad, Niger, and Nigeria.

A number of organizations deal with aspects of development training such as the Centre africain de formation et de recherche administrative pour le développement based in Tangier, Morocco, or the Centre on Integrated Rural Development for Africa at Arusha, Tanzania.

Several of these inter-African organizations date from the immediate preindependence era of the 1950s when closer cooperation and union were seen as important political weapons in the nationalist struggles for independence and some, such as the Afro-Asian Peoples' Solidarity Organization (formed in 1957), linked the peoples of the two continents in their search for genuine independence at that time. The Pan-African Youth Movement, with headquarters in Algiers (founded in 1962), was created to promote youth participation in socioeconomic and political development at a time when politically oriented youth movements were appearing in different parts of the continent and were closely associated with independence struggles. Other organizations, such as the Association of African Tax Administrators, the African Bar Association, and the Association for the Taxonomic Study of the Tropical African Flora have far more precise professional objectives.

Finance and economic research institutions cover monetary studies, insurance, and banking. The International Confederation of Free Trade Unions–African Regional Organization, formed in 1957, has affiliates in 36 African countries, while the Pan-African Employers' Federation, founded in 1986 and based in Nairobi, exists to link African employers' organizations and represent their interests at the UN, the International Labor Organization, and the OAU.

The emphasis of many of these interregional organizations, understandably, is upon trade, industry, transportation, and common infrastructure as member countries attempt to reconcile limited resources, huge size and distances, and small populations with their need for greater continental cooperation.

GUY ARNOLD

See also: **African Development Bank; Commonwealth, Africa and the; Economic Community of West African States (ECOWAS); Lomé Conventions, the Organization of African Unity (OAU) and Pan-Africanism; Southern African Development Community; Trade Unions: Postcolonial.**

Further Reading

Arnold, Guy. *The Third World Handbook*, 2nd ed. London: Cassell, 1994.

Europa. *Africa South of the Sahara* (annual), London: Europa, 1997. (This annual handbook includes a comprehensive list of inter-African organizations.)

Pan-Africanism: *See* Blyden, E. W.; Du Bois, W. E. B. and Pan-Africanism; Organization of African Unity (OAU) and Pan-Africanism.

Pass Laws: *See* South Africa: Segregation, Political Economy of.

Peacekeeping: Postcolonial Africa

Peacekeeping in Africa began with the United Nations (UN) intervention in the Congo between 1960 and 1964 via the ONUC. This mission exemplified many of the problems that have bedeviled peacekeeping operations on the continent ever since. It was plagued by a frequently altered mandate, often driven by events on the ground; a lack of human, logistical, and financial resources; and the meddling of external actors. ONUC moved rapidly from peacekeeping to peace enforcement and finally to war fighting, and lost its impartiality in the eyes of all the Congolese factions. It was a traumatic episode for both the United Nations and Africa and for some twenty years colored their perceptions toward peacekeeping.

Released from the strictures of the Cold War, the United Nations became emboldened by the successes–of limited scope operations in Namibia (UNTAC) and the first mission to Angola (UNAVEM I). As a consequence it once again became involved in a large-scale peacekeeping operation on the African continent, this time in Somalia in 1992. Just as in the Congo thirty years earlier, Somalia embroiled the UN in the complexities of a collapsing state. This operation was afflicted by the persistent problems affecting all United Nations peacekeeping operations: lack of funding, the absence of readily available forces, and an overdependence on the resources of the United States. Coupled with confused mandates and a breakdown in communication and confidence between the UN and the United States, this led to disaster and ultimately to an effective withdrawal of the United States from UN peacekeeping operations.

This change of U.S. policy as announced in Presidential Decision Directive 25 in May 1994, with its restrictions on the commitment of U.S. funds and resources to the UN, had immediate and disastrous consequences in Rwanda. Here the United Nations mission (UNAMIR) sent to monitor an unstable peace accord between the Rwandan government and the Rwandan Patriotic Front, ended up as spectators to possibly the worse case of genocide since 1945. The UN and the broader international community have been accused of deliberately downplaying the events in Rwanda to avoid involvement. Whatever the reasons, the impotence of the UN and its endorsement of the heavily criticized French Operation Tourquoise did much to undermine its credibility in Africa.

The debacle in Somalia and catastrophe in Rwanda (together with events in the former Yugoslavia) have led to a devolution of peacekeeping responsibilities from the global to the regional levels. This can be interpreted as a function of Africa's general international marginalization, and it has forced the states of Africa to look to their own resources and capabilities when it comes to peace support operations and conflict resolution. African states have had some experience of mounting such operations, and African troops have made important contributions to UN peacekeeping operations both on the continent and elsewhere. However, the results from those purely African operations have been mixed. In 1982, the Organization of African Unity (OAU) sent its Inter-African Force (IAF) into the conflict in Chad, ostensibly in support of the government of Goukini Ouaddei. Its mandate was open to misinterpretation by all sides and it was short of all manner of resources. The OAU openly announced its determination to avoid another Congo, and those contributing countries that actually sent troops were operating to individual political agendas not always compatible with the avowed aims of the IAF. The result was that the IAF became a mere onlooker to the overthrow of the government by the forces of Hissene Habre. The OAU has not attempted anything on this scale since.

Perhaps the most "successful" African peacekeeping organ is ECOMOG, the military arm of ECOWAS. It was first constituted as a cease-fire monitoring force for deployment in the Liberian civil war in August 1990. However, a failure to obtain the consent of all the warring parties, and the perception by Charles Taylor and his National Patriotic Front of Liberia that the Nigerians, principle contributors to ECOMOG, were

in fact trying to prop up Samuel Doe's government, led to ECOMOG becoming embroiled in the conflict itself. On many occasions in the ensuing seven years ECOMOG appeared to act as just another faction in the civil war and its deployment exacerbated tensions between the Anglophone and Francophone members of ECOWAS. It was only when the latter were persuaded to use their influence on the faction leaders and contribute to ECOMOG that some sort of resolution was found to the Liberian crisis. In the meantime it had spawned a related conflict in neighboring Sierra Leone, where ECOMOG's efforts in support of the Kabbah government have met with limited success against the Revolutionary United Front rebels. In Guinea-Bissau an ECOMOG force was deployed in February 1999 to police a cease-fire between pro- and antigovernment factions and to replace Senegalese troops sent in to support the government. However, this failed to prevent a resurgence in the conflict in May 1999.

The United Nations now effectively limits itself to endorsing local peacekeeping operations such as ECOMOG in Liberia and Sierra Leone and the Inter-African Mission to Monitor the Implementation of the Bangui Accords. This African initiative to resolve a conflict between the government and mutinous soldiers the Central African Republic led to the deployment of African forces with French logistical support. Its mandate was to supervise the disarming of the various factions and facilitate a political solution. It resembled the more traditional style of peacekeeping operation and has now evolved into the United Nations Mission to the Central African Republic.

The capacity of African states to mount peacekeeping operations is limited by the available resources. In terms of manpower and equipment, Africa lacks the tools for the task. Despite the efforts of organizations such as the OAU, ECOWAS, and the Southern African Development Community, the political structures necessary to support peacekeeping operations remain threadbare. Much is expected of postapartheid South Africa, but its forces are in transition and large question marks hang over their effectiveness. The future of ECOMOG is also in doubt due to domestic pressures leading to a possible reduction of Nigeria's commitments. Some external help has been forthcoming; the United States has a training program known as the African Crisis Response Initiative, and has agreed with Britain and France to coordinate their assistance to Africa. All have contributed significantly to recent African peacekeeping exercises such as Blue Hungwe (1997) in Zimbabwe and Blue Crane in South Africa (1999). Nevertheless it is safe to say that much more significant external help will be required for the foreseeable future if African peacekeeping efforts are to stand any chance of success.

GERRY CLEAVER

See also: **Liberia: Civil War, ECOMOG, and the Return to Civilian Rule; Rwanda: Genocide, 1994; Somalia: Independence, Conflict, and Revolution.**

Further Reading

Durch, William J. (ed.). *U.N. Peacekeeping, American Policy, and the Uncivil Wars of the 1990s.* London: Macmillan, 1997.

Magyar, Karl. P., and Earl Conteh-Morgan (eds.). *Peacekeeping in Africa: ECOMOG in Liberia.* London: Macmillan, 1998.

May, Roy, and Oliver Furley (eds.). *Peacekeeping in Africa.* Aldershot, England: Ashgate, 1998.

Prunier, Gerard. *The Rwanda Crisis: History of a Genocide.* London: Hurst, 1995.

Vogt, M. A., and A. E. Ekoko (eds.). *Nigeria in International Peacekeeping 1960–1992.* London: Malthouse Press, 1993.

Peasant Production, Colonial: Cash Crops and Transport

During the colonial period in Africa, the most important economic activity was agriculture. Agricultural production was organized around cash crops, which were introduced by colonial regimes all over Africa not only to generate revenue to run the colonies but also to provide raw materials for industrial production in the metropolitan countries. Cash crops were produced by peasant farmers who owned small farms and who used traditional implements, such as hoes and cutlasses.

African farmers specialized in a wide variety of cash crops depending on the climatic conditions of the area. For example, cotton was important in the savanna regions of Uganda, Tanzania, Malawi, the Sudan, Mali, Burkina Faso, Senegal, and northern Nigeria. Groundnuts, first planted in Senegal in about 1820 as a food crop, became its chief export during the colonial period. With the coming of the railway to Kano in 1911, groundnut production soared, and by 1920 it had become the major export of northern Nigeria.

The most important recurrent cash crops during the colonial period were palm oil, cocoa, coffee, tea, pyrethrum flowers, and rubber. Oil palm was prominent in Zaire and in the rain forest of West Africa, especially Côte d'Ivoire and Nigeria. Cocoa was an important crop in Ghana, Nigeria, Cameroon, Kenya and Ethiopia, with Ghana and Nigeria being the world's top two producers during the colonial period. The coffee produced in West Africa was mostly of the robusta type, which is of lower drinking quality than other types and is primarily used for making instant coffee. Most of the coffee in Kenya, Uganda, and Ethiopia is the arabica type and is arguably the highest quality coffee produced anywhere in the world. Kenya was also the center of a flourishing tea industry.

Smallholders in cash crop production in Africa have not only used household labor, but also migrants. In some instances, migrants have been instrumental to the expansion of particular cash crops, as evidenced by the contribution of Akwapim migrants of southern Ghana to the growth of the cocoa industry in Ghana. Migrant farmers were also responsible for the phenomenal expansion of the cocoa industry in southwestern Nigeria in the 1940s and 1950s.

Plantation agriculture has been relatively insignificant in tropical Africa. During the colonial period plantation production was limited to only rubber, sisal, and tea, and there was substantial peasant farmer production of these crops as well. In the late colonial period, smallholders were responsible for most of the expansion in tea production and a significant part of the growth of rubber production—especially in Nigeria, which emerged as the largest producer in the region in the 1960s. European farmers in Rhodesia, Kenya, Angola, and other areas of white settlement have also produced export crops such as tobacco, pyrethrum, and coffee. In some instances—notably, that of coffee—production did not differ greatly from that on plantations. From these crops, too, there was substantial expansion by African smallholders after World War II in areas such as Kenya, where previous restrictions were removed and positive encouragement provided. Production of palm oil presents a mixed picture. In the late colonial period, exports of palm oil from the former Belgian Congo, which came about equally from European plantations and outlying groves, had caught up with exports from Nigeria, where smallholder production was dominant.

Cash crop production in colonial Africa had some important characteristics. First, it was possible to expand crop production with only minimal capital investments and without any significant change in the already available technology. Second, in colonies that developed cash crops, there was a significant increase in the standard of living and in the capacity of the colonial government to generate revenue for the development of infrastructure, such as roads and railways. Third, the emphasis on cash crops led to a decline of food production and a rise of food prices. Furthermore, the production of cash crops was not costless; it had an opportunity cost in terms of other economic production or leisure time lost. Production of cash crops such as cocoa in Nigeria and Ghana involved considerable investments of time and energy.

The colonial administrations in Africa created a transport system as an integral part of the colonial economy. The establishment of a transport network is arguably one of the truly revolutionary consequences of the colonial period. The transport system served three purposes: (1) it was designed to facilitate the movement of cash crops from the interior to the coastal ports; (2) it enhanced the capacity of the colonial governments to control the subject population; and (3) it expedited the flow of European manufactured goods into the interior at much lower prices.

The majority of the colonies strove to fund an inexpensive single-track railway from the coast to the interior. The British began railway construction in Lagos and Freetown in 1896 and Sekondi in 1898. The French began railway construction in Dakar in 1880 and in Conakry, Abidjan, and Cotonou in 1900. The majority of these railways, however, were not completed until after World War II. In French Africa, railway construction was given considerable impetus after World War II with the inauguration of the Investment Fund for Economic and Social Development (FIDES). The French colonial administration had realized that some of its territories did not have the resources to finance a transport network. For example, in the case of railways, the substantial expenditure that was earmarked could not be met only out of railway budgetary allocations. In the French colonial territories, new ways of financing these projects were thus created in the FIDES.

Under the first FIDES plan, which covered the period 1947–1954, expenditure on infrastructure amounted to 55.5 per cent of the total in French West Africa and to 53.7 per cent in French Equatorial Africa. As was stated in the 1954 report of the Commission du Plan des Territoires, which introduced a revised transport policy, the economies of the various territories had benefited from improvements in the transport sector financed through the FIDES. This was especially true of port improvements (e.g., at Abidjan, Dakar, and Conakry), and of railway development, the outstanding example of which was the completion in 1954 of the single-track Mossi line between Bobo-Dioulasso and Ouagadougou in Burkina Faso.

The FIDES was principally maintained out of grants from the French government, as well as contributions from the various territories, although most of the latter were also indirectly provided by the French Treasury in the form of long-term loans at a nominal rate of interest. Nevertheless, some of the expenditure incurred under the transport development plans laid a rather heavy burden on the territories concerned, in particular the outlay on certain very costly large-scale road projects that proved to be overambitious and whose economic impact was certainly not commensurate with their cost.

In Middle Africa the colonial powers had deemed it imperative to renovate the existing transport system in order to facilitate the exploitation of the area. They opined that only by constructing railways could European goods be sold profitably in the interior of Middle Africa. It was also necessary to transport the produce of the interior to the coast. To this end, the building of the line from Matadi to Kinshasa in Congo Free State was begun in 1889. This line linked the vast natural communication system of the Zaire River with the sea, and also incorporated the Kongo people effectively into the colonial economy. The construction of this line exerted a heavy toll on the Kongo people as the government compelled all those who could to work. In addition, large numbers of contract workers were brought in from Nigeria and Sierra Leone.

In East Africa, the British government's main concern was to have a better channel of communication with the Upper Nile. Pursuant to this the British began the Mombasa-Uganda railway in 1895. In contrast to the Congo railway, which passed through fairly thickly populated areas, the Mombasa-Uganda railway generally traversed relatively uninhabited land. Large numbers of Indian laborers were contracted to work on the railway; its completion in 1901 facilitated the development of a cotton-exporting industry in East Africa.

The Germans also embarked upon railway construction in East Africa. The first line, from Tanga to Usumbara, which began in 1893 and was completed in 1905, was only about 80 miles long. The next line, which was more elaborate, had more far-reaching consequences than the first. This second line, which began in 1905, started out in Dar es Salaam and had reached Morogoro by 1907 and Tabora by 1912, and by 1914 had reached its terminus on Lake Tanganyika. In order to get financing for these large railway projects, the colonial administration in German East Africa resorted to making people grow cash crops and pay high taxes.

Although the railways did open up the interior of Africa to European trade, they had some significant shortcomings. First, none of the railways of one colony were connected with those of any other (unless it was to link a land-locked country to a seaport) so there was no transcontinental African railway system. This inadequacy underscores the fact that European colonial powers were not interested in promoting interregional trade within Africa. Each railway was simply constructed to link the colony's port with its hinterland, and to incorporate each colony more completely into the colonial framework of the metropolitan country.

This same principle is also reflected in the attitude of the colonial governments to road construction. With the arrival of automobiles and trucks, colonial governments began to build feeder roads to connect with the railways, but not trunk roads to the seaports. New areas in the interior that did not have access to the railways could now grow export crops that were taken by truck to the railways. For the most part, trucks were African owned, and because they were cheaper and faster, they threatened the monopoly of the railways. Consequently, the colonial governments charged high license fees.

One significant result of railway and road construction was the growth in the population of port cities such as Mombasa, Dakar, and Lagos. Large numbers of people moved to these port cities in search of education and better economic opportunities. The inability of the colonial governments to cater to the social and economic needs of the growing population of the port cities would generate social unrest and make these cities important centers of political agitation throughout the colonial period.

EZEKIEL WALKER

See also: **Railways.**

Further Reading

Anthony, Johnston, Jones and Uchendu. *Agricultural Change in Tropical Africa.* Ithaca, N.Y.: Cornell University Press, 1979.

Berry, Sara. *No Condition Is Permanent: The Social Dynamics of Agrarian Change in Sub-Saharan Africa.* Madison: University of Wisconsin Press, 1993.

Afigbo, Ayandele, Gavin and Omer-Cooper. *The Making of Modern Africa*, vol. 2. London: Longman, 1986.

Peasant Production, Colonial: Food, Markets: West Africa

European colonialism in West Africa started after the abolition of the slave trade, which led to the transitory period of "legitimate" commerce as a precursor to conquest and imposition of colonial rule. The main impact of this period beside the creation of the colonies was the expansion of agricultural production and exports of vegetable oils, which were demanded in increasing quantities in Europe for processing into soap, lubricants and candles. By the 1880s Senegal was exporting an average of 29,000 tons of groundnuts a year, and Lagos in Nigeria (still a major slave port in the 1850s) an average of 37,000 tons of palm kernels.

Thus, the initial stage in the imposition of colonial rule was mainly coastal based, where most of the European (particularly British, French, German and Portuguese) trading ports were established in areas like Senegal, Gambia, Gold Cost, Lagos, and the Niger Delta. These centers became the operational basis of the different colonial frontiers and tariffs, transportation, and communication (i.e. rail, road, telegraphic, and postal) systems and set the bases for the establishment of colonial West Africa. These coastal colonial enclaves were at St. Louis, Freetown, Lagos, and Monrovia.

In West Africa the colonial governments took advantage of the long history of trading contacts with the coastal peoples in the imposition of colonial rule (and a colonial cash economy). In fact, by 1960, West Africa was practically partitioned as the colonies of France, Britain, Germany, and Portugal. What followed was the establishment of the various colonial state formations of the different European nations.

The production of cash crops, either on the farms of the small African producers or in the few plantations that existed in French West Africa, determined the role of the majority of West Africans involved in agricultural production under colonial rule. Cash crops such as palm products, groundnuts and cotton had been exported before the imposition of colonial rule, fetching very low prices. The peasants produced just enough to pay taxes and to satisfy their immediate needs for imported textiles, utensils, and foodstuffs (like sugar and flour). The only exception were the producers of cocoa and coffee, which fetched high enough prices to affect their existing socioeconomic activities.

Although the process of colonial imposition went on at different phases, it nonetheless led to the mobilization and harnessing of African producers of exportable commodities needed in Europe. Food crop production was a desultory result of neglect and increased demand, with little rise in production as a direct consequence of the growth of cash economies based on the production and export of agricultural produce. Thus, in Gambia, production of groundnuts was done at the expense of rice cultivation, so that the colony had to import rice. The same was true of Senegal (in 1911) and Guinea, when production of groundnut and rubber led to shortages of rice produced locally, resulting in the inflation of prices of domestically produced rice, which eroded the gains from the sale of the export commodities (groundnut and rubber). Similarly, in the Gold Coast in 1930, imported foodstuffs like fresh fish, rice, maize, beans, salted and fresh meat, edible oils, spices, and fresh vegetables, which could have been produced locally, cost the colony up to £200,000 (Crowder 1968, p.384). Even though Capet estimated that in French West Africa "the main foodstuffs grew by an average of about 50% between 1947 and 1954" (Hopkins 1982, p.245), this was the exception rather than the rule. Even then, the marginal growth in food production was generally insufficient to satisfy increases in demands as a result of expansion in export crop production, mining activities, and the growth of urban centers.

The emergence and growth of new administrative headquarters—which were also important commercial centers—in colonial West Africa had a great impact on the region. For example, in the case of northern

Nigeria, the various administrative centers, like native authority, provincial, regional, and national capitals or headquarters, were in most cases in railway stations (or on a railway line), motor vehicle stopping points (or linked to a nearby road), and seaports, which led the rise and growth in trade in foodstuffs to these centers of colonial urbanization.

The colonial cash economy created two types of markets in Africa. One was the market for export-import commodities under the control of the foreign firms or traders, with their local retailing agents as buying and selling representatives. The other market type was the locally grounded trading outlet, which adapted to the new opportunities and realities of colonial rule. The import-export markets were mainly for the purchase of export commodities and the sale of imported manufactured goods, controlled mainly by European firms. This trade was an addition to the age-old commodity trade for internal consumption, dominated by the selling and buying of foodstuffs (Crowder 1986, p.299).

The markets in foodstuffs, as adjuncts of the internal trade system, were organized on precolonial models that were adapted to fit the new colonial order. These involved local markets centered around large towns or settlements, as the center of a local district, division, and provincial administrative unit. There were also natural and regional market centers, which specialized in the supply of certain types of products. These were strategically located on major transportation lines (railway, roadway, and seaways), linking areas of diverse demand in the regional colonial economy of West Africa. This trade was wholly in the hands of the local traders, with the only exception being when it involved the importation of foodstuffs from overseas. A unique aspect of this local trade in foodstuffs is that it was also dominated by the commissioned agents (such as the African middlemen) of the foreign trading firms, who purchased export commodities on their behalf. In Nigeria, the old merchants among the Hausa, Yoruba, Igbo, and Kanuri, traders mainly of kolanuts, cattle, and palm oil, became also the main agents of the foreign firms in the purchase of groundnuts, gum arabic, hides, and—most likely—cocoa for export. This is in addition to a network of overland trade across the colonially imposed borders between British and French colonies.

The trade in staple foods produced and consumed locally by African producers referred to as "peasants" or "petty commodity producers" was marketed in an organized pattern predating colonial rule. The commodity for sale passed through middlemen to the local market, from where the rural population could obtain it. These local markets were also the source of supplies for various traders and agents who supplied the urban centers.

Wholesalers distributed commodities to different consumers. This marketing system was also organized as an interstate trade, particularly in commodities produced from different ecological zones. However, the general direction of the trade was along northern-southern lines. For example in Nigeria, the northern traders from the savanna took cattle, groundnut oil, and cereals to the south and from the south brought forest-belt commodities like kola nuts, fruits, and palm oil to the north.

The small-scale producers of raw materials in West Africa—indeed, most of Africa—were exploited through the imposed cash economy, in which they were paid just enough to pay their taxes, which sustained the colonial state. This was succinctly put forward by Governor Clifford's report to the Nigerian council in 1923:

> The vast majority of the indigenous population are still independent of the outside world for all their essential supplies. They can and do spin their own thread, weave their own garments, provide their own foodstuffs and even when the necessity arises, forge their own tools and make their own pottery. For them imports from Europe are still in the main, luxuries with which if needs must, they can wholly dispense; and the sole exception to this in prewar days was imported spirits, of European manufacture. (Crowder 1986, p.347)

Twenty years later, with regards to the whole of British West Africa, the Leverhulme Trust Commission reported that "all Africans are to a very large extent, and very many of them wholly outside the system of money economy which dominates the economic life of Europe and the rest of the world" (Crowder 1986, p.347). A reflection of this aspect of colonial rule was also reported in French West Africa. In Senegal, families who had been involved in the export of groundnuts to Europe for over seventy years reverted to the production of foodstuffs for their consumption in 1932. As a result millet, manioc, and taro were substituted for imported rice, home-grown tobacco replaced imported varieties, honey was gathered in place of sugar, and local soap and perfumes were produced again (Crowder 1986, p.347).

The extent of the involvement of African peasants as producers of raw materials, wage earners, and traders under colonial rule depended on factors such as the nature of colonial rule itself, the value of commodity production in quantity and quality, transportation, taxation, and the marketing system. All these variables determined the extent of their involvement and cash returns which accrued to them as the most important level of measuring social value and material relevance in the new, colonially imposed, cash economy.

IBRAHIM MAINA WAZIRI

Further Reading

Afigbo, A. E. "The Establishment of Colonial Rule, 1900–1918." In *History of West Africa*, vol. 2, edited by J. F. Ade Ajayi and Michael Crowder. London: Longman, 1974.

Berstein, Henry. "Agrarian Structures and Change: Sub-Saharan Africa." In *Rural Livelihood: Crises and Responses*, edited by Henry Berstein, Ben Crow, and Hezel Johnson. Oxford: Oxford University Press, 1992.

Boahen, Adu A. "Africa and the Colonial Challenge." In *General History of Africa*, vol. 7, edited by Adu Boahen. Paris: UNESCO, Calif.: Heinamenn, 1985.

Crowder, Micheal. *West Africa under Colonial Rule*, 4th ed. Benin City: Ethiope, 1976.

Flint, J. "Economic Change in West Africa in the Nineteenth Century." In *History of West Africa*, vol. 2, edited by J. F. Ade Ajayi and Micheal Crowder. London: Longman, 1974.

Hogendon, J. *Nigerian Groundnut Exports: Origin and Early Development*: Zaria, Nigeria: Ahmadu Bello University Press, 1978.

Hopkins, A. G. *Economic History of West Africa*, London: Longman, 1982.

Oliver, Ronland, and Anthony Atmore. *Africa since 1800*, 4th ed. London: Cambridge University Press, 1996.

Saul, S. John, and Roger Woods. "African Peasantries." In *Peasants and Peasant Societies*, edited by Teodor Shanin. Harmondsworth, England: Penguin, 1971.

Waziri, Ibrahim Maina. "Colonial Export Trade in Borno: A Case Study of the Impact of Selected Commodities in the Emergence and Growth of a Cash Economy 1902–1945." Ph.D. diss., University of Maiduguri, 1996.

Peasant Production, Postcolonial: Markets and Subsistence

One of the most intriguing aspects of the African economic crisis in the new millennium is the apparent exit from the world market and return to localized subsistence farming in much of rural Africa. This has been the culmination of a long process of neglect, and even deliberate undermining of small-scale producers dating back to the colonial period, especially in the settler colonies. The collapse of national markets for both subsistence and export crops, however, was mainly exacerbated by the structural adjustment policies that African states implemented under pressure from multilateral agencies and foreign governments in the 1980s and 1990s. As a direct consequence of this policy of rolling back the state, ending the provision of supportive services in production and marketing, peasant commercial farming all over Africa was destroyed.

American development anthropologist James Ferguson (1999) has described the resulting state of "global disconnect and abjection" in the midst of accelerating integration among Zambian workers and peasants, but other Africans have suffered the same fate. Indeed, the process of globalization under capitalism has always been based on policies that favored capital intensive farming over more sustainable peasant production, but the reversal suffered by peasant farmers and unskilled workers since the advent of a neoliberal agenda in world economic management since the late 1970s has been as dramatic as the increased integration and deterritorialization of economic and cultural life for the global elites, including those who mismanage Africa's economies.

Experiments with laissez-faire capitalism date back to the colonial period. Between the end of World War II and the first decade of African independence, the benevolent colonialism of a declining Europe and the developmental policies of the independent states both tried to promote peasant farming. This period of rural development, coinciding with a battle for the hearts and minds of the world's poor during the Cold War and the Green Revolution in Asia, as well as World Bank involvement in aid to peasant farmers, played a significant role in containing communism.

The 1960s was a United Nations Development Decade, and saw many African nations gain independence. The two processes were well coordinated by UN agencies, as former African colonies, marked as less developed countries, were integrated into the global market as national economies and not European dependencies. What followed was ambitious economic planning, massive infrastructure projects funded by foreign aid and rapid but short-lived growth in certain sectors of the economy, such as import substitution industries. Local funding for the industrialization and infrastructure construction came from peasant agriculture, except in mineral-rich countries like Gabon and Zambia. This exploitation of the peasantry through price controls and government buying agencies was not very popular with the farmers and was an example of the "urban bias" that some economists blamed for the African crisis.

After the 1970s oil crisis and the unmanageable debts accumulated during this period, African governments sought the support of the International Monetary Fund (IMF) and World Bank in their attempts to stabilize their declining economies. The economic liberalizations that were demanded as conditions for accessing IMF and World Bank support led to the collapse of peasant farming in most countries in the 1990s.

Peasant farmers in countries like Côte d'Ivoire, Ghana, or Kenya who still earned cash incomes from export crops (e.g., coffee or cocoa) were also affected by the collapse of commodity prices. The cash revenues from export crops are insufficient for peasant farmers to pay their children's school fees or even to buy adequate food for their families. As a result, famines have been common in those parts of rural Africa that were once prosperous from the production of tea, coffee, cotton, and other export crops. In East Africa for example, producers of the high quality

Kenyan coffee begun to uproot coffee trees and plant beans, bananas, and other food crops. The latter were for the local market and did not earn foreign exchange, but were not subject to the control of urban elites and corrupt marketing agencies.

As it was in the colonial days, the export crops such as flowers and vegetables for European supermarkets now occupy the best land owned by local and foreign companies or capitalist farmers. Supportive services previously under government departments have been privatized, and infrastructure, irrigation, extension services, and credit have been channeled in support of exports whose earnings enable such countries to service their foreign debts.

Food crops like millet, sorghum, or maize grown by peasant farmers have been steadily denied access to supportive services, with the result that peasant farmers are no longer able to produce substantial harvests for the market and merely grow enough for local consumption and trade. In part this collapse of peasant farming has been caused by unfair competition from the heavily subsidized farmers in the European Union and the United States. Transnational monopolies that produce genetically modified and patented food crop varieties have also been aggressive in taking a share of the market away from small-scale producers.

The collapse of the cashew farming industry in Tanzania and Mozambique is a striking example of World Bank intervention on the side of global business. The case of how World Bank advisors and local ruling elites destroyed the Mozambican cashew nut processing industry is a good example of what has befallen peasant farming in Africa. As a study by Joseph Hanlon has revealed, the World Bank and IMF forced Mozambique to allow the free export of unprocessed nuts if India was prepared to pay a higher price than local industry. As predicted, once the factories in Mozambique closed, the Indian price plummeted to less than half the earlier price. It might be true that there was underinvoicing on the part of corrupt traders who reported export prices well below the real price in order to put the difference in foreign bank accounts (and not paying local taxes on the difference). Nevertheless, nearly all of the cashew factories closed, and 8500 of 10,000 cashew processing workers became unemployed. Despite claims by the World Bank that this intervention would bring higher earnings, both peasants and workers have suffered. There was no world market for raw African nuts since virtually all unprocessed cashew nuts were bought by India, which has excess processing capacity. Mozambican cashew processing factories were closed, precisely because of the World Bank–imposed liberalization of the trade in cashews—a policy that, in essence, held that it was better to export the nuts to India than to process them

locally. The Mozambican and Tanzanian cashew nut producers unable to sell their nuts found themselves facing the threat of famine as a result of being pushed out of the market by unfair competition from the more politically powerful transnational elites and their lobbies.

Having become disconnected from the market, Africa's peasants, especially able-bodied young men and women, have increasingly resorted to migration as a way of escaping the grinding poverty that has gripped rural Africa. If current demographic trends continue, rural-to-urban migration and attempts to legally or illegally enter the fortress economies of Europe and America will increase because the African peasant farming sector is no longer able to provide for the basic reproduction needs of the population.

OWEN SICHONE

See also: **World Bank, International Monetary Fund, and Structural Adjustment.**

Further Reading

Berry, Sara. *No Condition is Permanent: The Social Dynamics of Agrarian Change in Sub-Saharan Africa.* Madison: University of Wisconsin Press, 1993.

Chachage, C. S. L. "Forms of Accumulation, Agriculture and Structural Adjustment in Tanzania." In *Liberalized Development in Tanzania,* edited by Peter Gibbon. Uppsala, Sweden: Nordiska Afrikainstitutet, 1995.

Egwu, Samuel G. *Structural Adjustment, Agrarian Change and Rural Ethnicity in Nigeria.* Uppsala, Sweden: Nordiska Afrikainstitutet, 1998.

Ferguson, James. *Expectations of Modernity: Myths and Meanings of Urban Life on the Zambian Copperbelt.* Berkeley and Los Angeles: University of California Press, 1999.

Mkandawire, Thandika, and Naceur Bourenane (eds.). *The State and Agriculture in Africa.* Dakar, Sengal: CODESRIA Books, 1987.

Peasantry: *See* South Africa: Peasantry, African.

Pedi Kingdom, and Transvaal, 1822–1879

The Pedi Kingdom emerged from the Maroteng paramountcy of Sotho-speaking peoples in the Leolu Mountains of the northeastern Transvaal in the early nineteenth century. Pedi oral tradition establishes their origins as an offshoot of earlier Kgatala ironworkers, who likely monopolized metal tools and weapons for hunting and agriculture. In the 1820s, during the upheavals of the *difaqane* (the violent period of Zulu state formation), the Maroteng survived a severe attack by the Ndwandwe, who had fled the fighting in the Zulu heartland. This event reconfigured the Maroteng into the new Pedi polity. The Pedi founding statesman Sekwati (1824–1861) then consolidated the kingdom by amalgamating subordinated chiefdoms through careful diplomacy. Thereafter, despite suffering repeated assaults from neighboring African and white communities, the Pedi rose to great power until their conquest by British imperial forces in 1879.

The unique Pedi political economy consisted of a centralized state, agropastoralism and hunting (which later developed into raiding), and the region's earliest example of migrant labor. Sekwati forged political links with the outside colonial societies of Boer and British settlers. This facilitated the development of Pedi migrant wage labor to distant urban centers such as Port Elizabeth long before conquest or the imposition of taxation. Migrant workers' earnings were crucial for the acquisition of firearms and thus the long-term military power of the Pedi. Indeed, they enabled the Pedi to fend off an attack in 1838 from the competing Swazi kingdom to the west. Moreover, after they repelled an attack by King Mpande's Zulu in 1851, the Pedi established cordial relations with that kingdom through diplomatic overtures and a symbolic gift of skins and ostrich feathers. Pedi society, while highly stratified and dominated by the Maroteng royal house, was flexible and accommodated newcomers through marriage and conquest. The Pedi polity was not strictly a unitary kingdom, but rather a federation where cohesion was maintained through political marriages arranged between subordinate chiefs and wives from the royal family. There remained, however, tensions between the core of the Maroteng people and neighboring chiefdoms that paid allegiance to other states such as the Swazi. The social hierarchy consisted—in descending order—of the royal lineage (bakgomana), Pedi commoners (balata), incorporated foreigners (bafaldai), and captive slaves (mathupya). The paramount and royal family governed in conjunction with commoners through an advisory cabinet of leading chiefs, state councils and the pitso, an obligatory public meeting for all male citizens.

The arrival of Boer settlers in 1845 presented the Pedi with political and military challenges. Sekwati gave a cautious welcome to the Boer leader, A. H. Potgieter, and the three hundred families that accompanied him. The Pedi were apprehensive of these white settlers who, having left the British-dominated Cape, had recently vanquished Mzilikazi's powerful Ndebele, and commanded considerable firepower. Nevertheless, Sekwati and Potgieter concluded an ambiguous peace treaty. The Boers, on the one hand, claimed the treaty gave them full ownership and title to a large area of Pedi lands. The Pedi, on the other hand, believed the treaty only entitled the settlers to use the land as clients. The Boers then sought to enforce their claims

by demanding taxes and labor, most often in the form of inboekselings (captive or indentured child labor) from the Pedi. In 1847, the tenuous interdependence that Sekwati and Potgieter had achieved collapsed after a dispute over the division of spoils from a joint raiding party. Matters deteriorated further when Boers from Natal established the Volksraad Party as a rival to Potgieter. The Volksraad Boers then gained a spurious title to Pedi lands from their new allies (and Pedi foes), the Swazi. In 1852, the Boers, emboldened by their alliance, sent a commando against the Pedi settlement of Phiring. The Pedi suffered heavy losses, but survived the siege, and retreated to Thaba Mosega in the Leolu Mountains. An 1857 treaty then established the Steelpoort River as the boundary between the Pedi and Boers.

During the 1860s, despite internal upheavals, the Pedi withstood further encroachments and established themselves, for a time, as the most formidable force in the eastern Transvaal. Following Sekwati's death in 1861, his son and heir, Sekhukhune I (1862–1883), was embroiled in civil conflict over the throne with his rival brother, Mampuru. While Sekhukhune prevailed, Mampuru fled, found refuge with Pedi adversaries and harassed the kingdom. Nevertheless, in part because of their formidable arsenal of guns, the Pedi routed a powerful Swazi attack in 1869. This intimidated the Boers and facilitated peaceful relations with them. Pedi society was, moreover, influenced by the arrival of Christian missionaries of the Berlin Missionary Society (BMS). Sekwati had permitted them access to the kingdom in 1861, in the hopes of strengthening his diplomatic relations with colonial governments.

Pedi relations with white society in general, and local missionaries in particular, soured through the 1860s and 1870s. Sekhukhune was suspicious of white motives, and wary of Alexander Merensky, the local BMS missionary who pressed the paramount to change Pedi society. Merensky had, after all, converted the king's brother, Johannes Dinkwanyane, to Christianity, and encouraged many people to abandon Pedi customs and polygamy, thereby undermining Sekhukhune's authority. In 1864, Sekhukhune attacked the BMS converts, and distanced the Pedi from Merensky, who was by then perceived to be a supporter of the Boers.

The 1870s was the final decade of complete independence for the Pedi. Boer settler society, which had consolidated in the Zuid Afrikaansche Republiek (ZAR) under President T. F. Burgers, increased pressure on the Pedi for land, taxes, and labor. A treaty recognizing Sekhukhune's authority did not specify territorial boundaries, thus leaving the Pedi open to Boer depredations. Moreover, the ZAR perceived the Pedi as a threat because of the increased numbers of people and firearms within the kingdom. Contrary to common arguments, however, the Pedi were not the aggressors in the ensuing war in 1876. Although the Pedi were not vanquished in this conflict, Sekhukhune sued for peace and submitted to a fine of cattle in reparations. Negotiations, however, were complicated by the British imperial factor. Under the British confederation scheme for South Africa, Sir Theophilus Shepstone was dispatched to annex the ZAR in 1877. Shepstone, fearing unfounded rumors of a Pedi alliance with the powerful Zulu kingdom, then demanded the cattle fine to be paid in full. As with the ultimatum presented to the Zulu a year later, Shepstone's demand was impossible for Sekhukhune to fulfill, and thus calculated to precipitate conflict. British imperial forces under Sir Garnet Wolseley's command invaded in October of 1878 and finally conquered the kingdom by September of 1879. The British then broke up the Pedi and relocated them to two distant reserves, thus ending the independent kingdom.

ARAN S. MACKINNON

See also: **Boer Expansion: Interior of South Africa; South Africa: Confederation, Disarmament and the First Anglo-Boer War.**

Further Reading

Agar-Hamilton, J., *The Native Policy of the Voortrekkers 1836–1858*. Cape Town: University of Cape Town Press, 1928.

Bonner, P., *Kings Commoner and Concessionaires*. Cambridge: Cambridge University Press, 1982.

Bryant, A. T., *A History Of The Zulu And Neighbouring Tribes*. Cape Town: Struik, 1964.

Cope, R. *Ploughshare of War: The Origins of the Anglo-Zulu War of 1879*. Pietermaritzburg: University of Natal Press, 1999.

De Kiewiet, C. *British Colonial Policy and the South African Republics, 1848–1872*. London: Macmillan, 1929.

———. *The Imperial Factor in South Africa*. Cambridge: Cambridge University Press, 1937.

Delius, P. *The Land Belongs to Us: The Pedi Polity, the Boers and the British in the Nineteenth Century Transvaal*. Berkeley and Los Angeles: University of California Press, 1983.

Elphick, R., and H. B. Giliomee (eds.). *The Shaping Of South African Society, 1652–1840*, rev. title, 2nd edition. Cape Town: Longman, 1989.

Etherington, N. *Preachers, Peasants and Politics in South East Africa, 1835–1880*. London: James Curry, 1978.

Marks, S., and A. Atmore. *Economy and Society in Preindustrial South Africa*. London: Longman, 1980.

Marks, S., and R. Rathbone (eds.). *Industrialisation And Social Change in South Africa: African Class Formation, Culture And Consciousness, 1870–1930*. London: Longman, 1982.

Merensky, A. *Erinnerungen aus dem Missionsleben in Transvaal, 1859–1882*. Berlin: Berlin Mission Society Press, 1899.

Monnig, H. *The Pedi*. Pretoria: University of the Witwatersrand Press, 1967.

Omer-Cooper, J. *The Zulu Aftermath*. London: Longman, 1966.

Preston, A. (ed.). *The South African Journal of Sir Garnet Wolseley*. Cape Town: Oxford University Press, 1973.

Schapera, I. *Western Civilization and the Natives of South Africa: Studies in Culture Contact*. London: Longman, 1934.

———. *Government and Politics in Tribal Societies*. London: Longman, 1946.

Thompson, L. *African Societies in Southern Africa*. London: Longman, 1969.

Peul: *See* Fulbe/Fulani/Peul: Cattle Pastoralism, Migration, Seventeeth and Eighteenth Centuries; Fulbe/Fulani/Peul: Origins.

Permanent Settlement, Early

The archaeologist Gordon Childe suggested that humankind went through a series of evolutionary stages in its sociocultural development. A committed Marxist, Childe saw human social development in terms of revolutionary events; his "Neolithic Revolution," he argued, saw the emergence of agricultural and settled societies, and the beginnings of class/wealth differentiation. It is now recognized that developed agriculture was not a prerequisite for permanent sedentism; ethnographically, historically, and archaeologically there are many examples of settled communities whose occupants maintained hunting-, gathering-, and fishing-based economies (Hayden 1990).

The benefits of sedentism rather than cyclic mobility are clear; living a settled life permitted the accumulation of personal goods and the large-scale storage of foodstuffs; but sedentism would have been possible only with access to a dependable and predictable resource base and, in arid climates, the availability of water. In settling down, one radically reduces one's economic options, and the potential risk of social stress is increased; when this happens, it becomes attractive to resume a mobile, economically specialized way of life. Transhumant pastoralism can be a response to such crises (Mace 1993); flexibility, and a sliding scale of socioeconomic options, would be the key to survival.

The Nile Valley plays an important role in the emergence of sedentism in African Holocene prehistory; there is no archaeological evidence of sedentism prior to the beginning of the Holocene in Africa (see, e.g., the late Pleistocene site of Wadi Kubbaniyah, near Aswan). During periods of extreme aridity, as are witnessed throughout the Holocene, this zone, with its dependable water supply and fertile alluvial land, would have been an attractive refuge for desert-dwelling peoples. During the middle Holocene, the Nile valley became home to an extensive population concentration, and the earliest archaeological signs of permanent settlement in Africa are to be observed in and around the river margins.

The earliest occupation at the site of Merimde Beni Salama in the Nile Delta, dating from around

8000BCE, has yielded evidence of a small, semi-sedentary community of broad-spectrum hunting-gathering-fishing peoples who lived in oval huts that contained hearths and pottery water jars sunk into the ground. The uppermost strata at this site, dating from around 4300BCE, show an increase in settlement size; now huts were built from mud brick strengthened with straw and plastered, roofs were probably thatched with reeds or rushes, and the huts were arranged in rows. The presence of large grain storage bins indicates a new socioeconomic emphasis, and it is estimated that this village supported a population of some 1300–2000 people (Hassan 1988).

Southward, in the Fayyum Depression, we have evidence of a rather more ephemeral occupation centered around a shrinking lake from around the seventh millennium BCE. The earliest "Fayyum B" occupations were essentially seasonal hunter-gatherer camps, but by the time of the "Fayyum A" occupations, during the sixth to fifth millennia BCE, the economic emphasis shifted more toward the exploitation of plant resources. Large grain storage silos are present, but it is clear that the inhabitants of these sites still exploited a wide range of resources. There is no evidence for permanent structures associated with these sites, but it is possible that the dwellings were ephemeral—rather like tents—and were built from perishable materials (Wenke, Long, and Buck 1988). The largest Fayyum site, Kom, dating from around 4700BCE, yielded evidence of hearths, granary pits and (probably) ephemeral structures. It has been noted, however, that the full annual complement of economic resources is present at this site, and it is possible that it served as a permanent refuge for children and the elderly, while the remainder of the population switched between seasonal, smaller camps. It has been suggested that the Fayyum developments represent something of a "halfway house" between mobile and fully settled societies (Hassan 1988).

Moving southward along the Nile and into the Western Desert, the sites of Bir Kiseiba and Nabta Playa—dating from around 7000BCE—exhibit signs of incipient social complexity. These desert margin sites seem to have been continuously occupied, and have yielded evidence of small, planned dwellings, large storage pits arranged in arcs, and large stone wells that would have been needed for watering cattle. Debate rages about the status of the faunal remains here; it remains a contentious question as to whether domesticated elements are present. At the least, it may be possible that the storage facilities represent some form of social control, and it has been variously estimated that these sites were home to 14 "family units" (Wendorf, Schild, and Close 1984, pp.425).

The desert zones should not be thought of as a wasteland in terms of human settlement; during wetter periods these areas furnished a range of economic resources. Outlying *Steinplätze* (stone place) encampments were probably satellite functionally specialist sites of the villages; the rock shelter of Ti-n-Torha, Libya, was probably home to a small population of herders at around 7000BCE, and the site of Dakhleh Oasis has yielded evidence of small, circular huts. It is certainly clear that during the eighth millennium BCE the desert zones were much wetter than today, were probably crossed by numbers of dependable watercourses, and were home to sedentary groups of hunting-gathering-fishing peoples. The most striking evidence for these communities is witnessed in the southern reaches of the Nile Valley around Khartoum, Sudan.

During the 1940s, archaeological research in Khartoum uncovered evidence of a culture with a highly distinctive ceramic technology. The peoples who inhabited this settlement clearly relied extensively on fishing (a large number of net weights and bone harpoons were recovered), but also hunted game and gathered wild grasses from around the fringes of the desert margin. With an eye toward the European intellectual archaeological tradition, the excavator Anthony Arkell (1949) proposed the term *Khartoum Mesolithic* for this culture. Here was a settled community with pottery and storage technology (from c.7000BCE), yet without evidence of agriculture. Further work has indicated that seasonal, semipermanent specialist settlements were also of great importance at this time; some were specialist hunting stations, while others were dedicated fishing stations. The wide distribution of the distinctive "wavy line" pottery form and bone harpoon points in contemporary settlements across the Sahara (even as far west as Niger) led John Sutton (1977) to propose a hypothetical "Aqualithic" culture sphere, a notion no longer accepted by archaeologists.

It is certainly true that hunter/gatherer/fisher settlements were a feature of northern Africa during the wet, warm early Holocene period. In northern Kenya, for instance, settlements with similar ceramics and bone harpoon points have been found around the shores of Lake Turkana (e.g., Lowasera, Lothagam), and it is clear that these settlements supported quite a number of inhabitants (Stewart 1989). It is clear that it was the economic wealth of the lake margin environments, with a variety of ecozones available for exploitation, which permitted a largely settled lifestyle without the need for a dependable (and work-intensive) agricultural base.

Further archaeological research by Arkell in the Khartoum area uncovered evidence of a later settlement, with a different ceramic tradition, but with a developed agricultural resource base. Again, following on from the European archaeological tradition, Arkell named the culture the *Khartoum Neolithic* (Arkell 1953). Khartoum Neolithic sites, which span the period of 5000–3000BCE, were characterized by extensive reliance on stock keeping and the emergence of a degree of social complexity, although it is clear that many outlying settlements continued to serve discrete, specialist economic roles. In broadly contemporary contexts in eastern Sudan (the Atbara region), the site of El Damer has yielded evidence of houses and burials, and large quantities of pottery; again the economy was based primarily on aquatic resource exploitation, and the use of pottery allowed for storage of foodstuffs (Haaland 1997).

Away from the main Nile Valley axis and the Western Desert, evidence for early settlement is sparse. In eastern Africa, apart from the lake-margin communities discussed above, major permanent settlements are not a feature until at least the early Iron Age, for thousands of years mobile pastoralism remained the preeminent economic strategy. Toward the south of the continent, mobile hunter-gatherer economies predominated until at least the first millennium CE. Of late, however, new data has emerged from the Sahel and tropical rain forest zones of West Africa that bear comparison with the northeastern African picture.

Coastal shell midden sites from the Mauretanian Atlantic coast, dating from the sixth millennium BCE, bear witness to an intensive scale of aquatic resource exploitation, and it is probable that some form of permanent settlement was associated with these sites. Inland, although the archaeological data is sparse, it is clear that essentially a transhumant pastoralist strategy emerged during the third millennium BCE in response to increasing aridity in the Sahara. The settlement sites of the Tichitt Lake Plain and the Agadez basin (Mauritania) were clearly sited with access to water in mind. Cattle pens and granaries were associated with these sites (dating from around 1500BCE), and some evidence of socioideological development, going hand in hand with the process of "settling down," is witnessed by discrete tumuli cemetery groups and cattle burial (McIntosh and McIntosh 1988). Southward, into the tropical rain forests of Ghana, the Kintampo culture, dating from around 2000BCE, represents evidence of an early sedentary society. The Kintampo sites, which are recognizable by assemblages of clay "cigars," ground-stone axes, and decorative items (evidence for an associated "luxury" economy), include Ntereso, with its rectangular houses and post holes; Boyasi, with its granite house foundations; and Mumute, with its large, developed water cisterns.

It is clear from the overview presented above that the earliest sedentary communities in Africa were centered along the Nile Valley axis, and to some extent in the marginal desert zones during wet periods in the middle Holocene. Although these data may be indicative of patterns of archaeological fieldwork over the last 50 years, it is clear that the proximity of water was a clear prerequisite for permanent settlement, and a dependable economic resource base with storage systems (including pottery) was an absolute necessity. It is also important to note that the earliest settlements were not agricultural per se, but were homes to broad-spectrum hunter-gatherer-fisher peoples who maintained a degree of economic flexibility and continued to maximize their options by using the complete range of their ecozonal resources. This is why we see central, permanent settlements and outlying functionally specialized satellite seasonal sites. From a social aspect, the settling-down process saw the emergence of more structured social roles and enhanced ideological outlooks, probably linked to the development of rigidly defined gender roles (Haaland 1997). It is clear, at least in the Nile Valley, that the successful earliest village economies of the area formed, for all intents and purposes, the basis of the civilization that came later.

NIALL FINNERAN

See also: **Iron Age and Neolithic: West Africa; Stone Age (Later); Urbanization and Site Hierarchy: West Africa: Savannah and Sahel.**

Further Reading

Arkell, A. *Early Khartoum.* Oxford: Oxford University Press, 1949.

———. *Shaheinab.* Oxford: Oxford University Press, 1953.

Haaland, R., "The Emergence of Sedentism: New Ways of Living, New Ways of Symbolising." *Antiquity* 71 (1997): 374–385.

Hassan, F. "The Predynastic of Egypt." *Journal of World Prehistory* 2 (1988): 135–185.

Hayden, B. "Nimrods, Piscators, Pluckers and Planters: The Emergence of Food Production." *Journal of Anthropological Archaeology* 9 (1990): 31–69.

McIntosh, S., and R. McIntosh, "From Stone to Metal: New Perspectives on the Later Prehistory of West Africa." *Journal of World Prehistory* 2 (1988): 89–133.

Mace, R. "Transitions between Cultivation and Pastoralism in Sub-Saharan Africa." *Current Anthropology* 30 (1993): 235–240.

Stewart, K. *Fishing Sites of North and East Africa in the Late Pleistocene and Holocene.* Oxford: British Archaeological Reports International Series 521, 1989.

Sutton, J. "The African Aqualithic." *Antiquity* 51 (1977): 25–34.

Wendorf, F., R. Schild, and A. Close (eds.). *Cattle-Keppers of the Eastern Sahara: The Neolithic of Bir Kiseiba.* Dallas: Southern Methodist University Press, 1984.

Wenke, R., J. Long, and P. Buck. "Epipalaeolithic and Neolithic Subsistence and Settlement in the Fayyum Oasis of Egypt." *Journal of Field Archaeology* 15 (1988): 29–51.

Phelps-Stokes Commissions

The Phelps-Stokes Fund was established in 1911 by a bequest of Miss Caroline Phelps Stokes, a New York philanthropist. The fund was set up principally for the education of blacks in Africa and in the United States. Dr. Anson Phillips Stokes, one of the trustees of the fund, chaired its educational committee, while Dr. Thomas Jesse Jones served as the educational director of the fund. The latter had formerly served on the U.S. Bureau of Education in Washington, D.C., where he was involved in the production of two volumes on the education of blacks in 1917. He later served at the Hampton Institute, dubbed "the most successful institute for Negro education in the world," as director of its research institute.

Through the activities of the Phelps-Stokes Fund, the education of American blacks came to be used as a blueprint for the education of blacks in Africa. In this regard, the educational experiments undertaken at the black institutions of Hampton and Tuskegee served as an example of an "appropriate" education for colonial Africans. The Southern industrial and agricultural institutions of Hampton and Tuskegee were originally set up as a compromise to the Southern labor problem following the emancipation of slaves. Industrial education became the cornerstone of the education system that was offered to the freed slaves, which aimed at prevention of racial conflict. The rural educational applications of the American black South were extended within America by such educational agencies as the General Education Board, the Jeanes and Slater Funds, and the United States Department of Agriculture. They were extended to the African soil primarily by the Phelps-Stokes Education Fund. Thus, the Phelps-Stokes education commissions were influenced by the education principles that Samuel Chapman Armstrong had developed at Hampton, and those of Booker T. Washington and Principal Mouton at Tuskegee.

The membership of the Phelps-Stokes Education Commissions attested to the cooperation of colonial governments and missionary societies in America and Europe. Members included Dr. Henry Stanley Hollenbeck, who had served as a missionary in Angola, Mr. and Mrs. Arthur Wilkie of the Church of Scotland Mission in Calabar, Nigeria, and Leo Ray, an accountant and specialist in industrial education. Ray had also supervised the technical training of "Negro" soldiers during World War I, and now served as the first commission's secretary. Dr. C. T. Loram, chairman of the South African Native Affairs Commission, and former chief inspector of native education in Natal, was included in the second commission. Hanns Vischer, secretary and member of the newly formed Advisory Committee on Education in Tropical Africa at the colonial office in London, and Mrs. Vischer also served in the second commission.

Only two of the members of the first commission also served in the second. These were Dr. Thomas

Jesse Jones and Dr. James Emmanuel Kwegyr Aggrey, the latter of the famed Achimota College in Gold Coast (Ghana). Dr. Aggrey's inclusion had been suggested by Dr. Paul Monroe, a professor at Columbia University and member of the board of trustees of the Phelps-Stokes Fund. "The Great Aggrey," an individual of outstanding ability, had just completed a professional teaching qualification. He went on to exert significant influence on the activities of the Education Commissions, and left an indelible mark on subsequent developments in African education.

The first of the two Phelps-Stokes Education Commissions carried out its activities in western, southern and equatorial Africa from July 15, 1920 to September 10, 1921, and in particular visited Sierra Leone, Liberia, Gold Coast, Nigeria, Cameroon, Belgian Congo, Angola, South Africa, and the British territories. The second, instituted at the suggestion of colonial governments, concentrated its efforts in eastern, central, and southern Africa from January 5, 1924 to June 19, 1924, traveling to Kenya, Uganda, Tanganyika, Zanzibar, Nyasaland, Rhodesia, South Africa, and the trust territories. The goal of the education commissions was to ascertain the necessary requirements for improvement of the education of blacks in Africa.

The commissions invoked the Jeanes idea, which was based on the view that Africans were a mainly rurally oriented and agriculturally based people; it was named after Anna T. Jeanes, who had donated money to pay for the teachers of rural schools. Jeanes education went beyond the basics of formal teaching, and sought to facilitate an overall change in the socioeconomic makeup of African communities. It sought to do this by encouraging the emphasis of the African environment in the teaching of skills and trades as well as by promotion of the African way of life; African institutions, customs, stories, and songs; and the use of drills and games as a teaching method.

The most far-reaching of the commissions' recommendations were centered on the teaching of industrial education and agriculture as the core basis of colonial African education. Hence, less emphasis was placed on the "literary" or "bookish" education of Africans, as it was considered to be irrelevant to their needs. It was also seen to be alienating Africans from their predominantly rural lifestyle. Instead, institutions that promoted manual work and taught "practical" subjects were upheld as a good illustration of appropriate African education. The education philosophy espoused by the commissions sought to promote African traditions and aimed to foster African appreciation of these. Appropriate education of women was considered to be paramount to the adoption of a holistic and rurally oriented education system. It was on the basis of this that domestic science in its widest sense was envisaged as an appropriate education for women. Women's education was to include hygiene and sanitation, the care of infant life, simple remedies for common ailments, and the nursing of the sick. Concerns about health and the spread of disease, advances in medicine (and, notably, the discovery of new vaccines) influenced the inclusion of hygiene in the curriculum.

In both formal and informal ways, African education was to reflect more closely the needs of a mainly rural populace. In this regard, much emphasis was placed on the importance of the village school. Teacher training was to form an integral part of this holistic view of African education, and in this regard mobile schools were started using both the teachers and extension workers to bring the school closer to the community. In eastern and central Africa for example, model Jeanes settlements or model villages were set up that served as examples to the rest of the community; in Zimbabwe, home visits by social workers, nurses, and family welfare educators were a part of the plan.

The commissions made valuable observations regarding the status and future prospects of the Western education of Africans—in particular, mission education, the education of women and girls, and the role of agriculture and indigenous skills training. The activities of the commissions culminated in the publication of two reports. The first, published in 1922, was titled *Education in Africa: A Study of West, South and Equatorial Africa by the African Education Commission, under the Auspices of the Phelps-Stokes Fund and Foreign Mission Societies of North America and Europe*. The second report, entitled *Education in East Africa*, was published in 1925.

LILY MAFELA

See also: **Education.**

Further Reading

King, K.J. *Pan-Africanism and Education: A Study of Race, Philanthropy and Education in the Southern States of America and East Africa*, Oxford: Clarendon Press, 1971.

Lewis, L. J. *Phelps-Stokes Reports on Education in Africa*. New York: Oxford University Press, 1962.

Phelps-Stokes Fund. "Education in Africa: A Study of East, Central and Southern Africa, Second African Education Commission under the Auspices of the Phelps-Stokes Fund, in Cooperation with the International Education Board, 1923–24." 1925.

Phelps-Stokes Fund. "Report of the Education Commission in West, South and Equatorial Africa, July 15th, 1920–September 10, 1921." 1922.

Phiri Clan: *See* **Maravi: Phiri Clan, Lundu and Undi Dynasties.**

Plaatje, Sol T. (1875–1932)
South African Nationalist

A dominant figure among modern African political and cultural leaders in South Africa, and a talented linguist and writer, Sol Plaatje was instrumental in the founding of the African National Congress, serving as its first general secretary. He did much to publicize the grievances of Africans in South Africa.

Sol Plaatje was born on the farm Doornfontein, located in the Boshof district of the Orange Free State, then an independent Boer Republic, on October 9, 1876. His parents, Johannes and Martha Plaatje, were both Barolong, connected to RoloNg royalty and to the Lutheran Berlin Missionary Society (BMS) station at Pniel. Following the breakup of his family, Plaatje was educated and confirmed at Pniel by Reverend and Mrs. Ernst Westphal of the BMS. As a young man, he studied and learned eight languages, both European and African, as well as music and English literature.

Plaatje moved to Kimberley in 1894, where he first worked for the postal service and associated with other educated Africans. He voted in the Cape election of 1898 and became a clerk-interpreter in the magistrate's court at Mafeking, the headquarters of the Bechuanaland Protectorate. Plaatje lived in Mafeking during the town's 217-day siege in the Boer War in 1899 and 1900, and produced the only known diary of an African during the war, in which he criticized Colonel Baden Powell's treatment of Barolong and other Africans under his control.

Early in the new century, Plaatje became the founder and editor of a series of African-language newspapers in the northern Cape Colony: *Koranta es Becoana*, launched in Mafeking in 1901 as the first Setswana-English weekly; and later, in Kimberley, *Tsala ea Becoana* (1910) and *Tsala ea Batho* (1912). In these newspapers Plaatje defended Africans against the inequities of colonial rule, urged policies of unity and reform by governments in South Africa, and promoted cultural life and literature among his Setswana readers.

During the formation of the Union of South Africa by Dutch-Afrikaans and English-speaking whites in 1908–1909, and in its early years after 1910, Plaatje opposed discrimination against black Africans and encouraged their unity across ethnic lines. He played a crucial role in the 1912 formation of a new African political movement, the South African Native National Congress (SANNC), which became the African National Congress (ANC) in 1923. Plaatje assumed a key leadership role within the SANNC, as its first general secretary. In this capacity he served on deputations formed to protest the Natives Land Bill of 1913 and its mandatory restrictions on African land ownership, appearing before the authorities in Pretoria and London. Plaatje remained in Britain from 1914 to 1917, composing works that ranged from his *Native Life in South Africa* (1916)—a lengthy analysis of racial conditions in his homeland that appealed to the British public to eliminate South Africa's land segregation, which he blamed for the destruction of the African peasantry—to his *Sechuana Reader* (1916), a collection of Tswana proverbs.

Plaatje returned home at a time when social and economic unrest had spread to African workers. He and other SANNC leaders opposed the industrial strikes of 1918 as a form of political protest. During the worldwide influenza epidemic, Plaatje contracted a serious heart condition. Nonetheless, he led a new SANNC deputation to London seeking the extension of voting rights to educated Africans. Plaatje made public speeches and conferred with officials. During his interview with Lloyd George on November 21, 1919 Plaatje requested property and voting rights, reminding the prime minister of the loyalty shown by the union's Africans to the empire during World War I. Lloyd George promised only to meet with his fellow prime minister, Jan Smuts, who rejected Plaatje's proposals.

After a delay, Plaatje journeyed to North America, touring Canada and the United States from 1920 to 1922. There he received treatment for his heart condition and spoke to large audiences in New York City and Detroit. He befriended W. E. B. DuBois, and toured other cities and the South, where he met Booker T. Washington's successor at Tuskegee. He left America, having created bonds between his movement and those of African Americans, especially the National Association for the Advancement of Colored People.

Back in South Africa, Plaatje grew disillusioned by numerous failed attempts to redress African grievances and by continued ethnic divisiveness among the union's African population. Fearing enactment of a more restrictive color bar by the pact alliance of the Labour and National Parties, Plaatje worked unsuccessfully for Smuts's reelection in 1924. The election of the government of J. B. M. Hertzog by white voters, and its subsequent Native Bills, did not encourage him. While protesting these new segregationist proposals, Plaatje urged his followers to adopt a program of moral regeneration.

During the final decade of his life, Plaatje increasingly withdrew from political concerns and devoted himself to cultural and literary activities. He gathered the proverbs and folklore of his fellow Batswana, developed a phonetic orthography for their language, translated four of William Shakespeare's plays into it, and worked on a new Setswana dictionary. In 1930, he published a historical novel, *Mhudi*. The first of its

kind by an African writer in southern Africa, it depicted the era of the *difaqane* and the Great Trek from the standpoint of the Sotho-Tswana population on the High Veld and included strong female characters.

Despite his weakening heart, Plaatje continued to work hard in his final months, touring as far north as the Belgian Congo in 1931, where he was warmly received. Plaatje was stricken with influenza in Johannesburg in May 1932 and died of it the following month. No violent revolutionary, Plaatje sought to expand the old Cape liberalism as a vehicle for African advancement. As a highly cultured and accomplished individual, Plaatje sought to lead by example, including his interethnic marriage and espousal of the British democratic principles and the rule of law. The ANC of his era was highly reflective of his philosophy.

LOUIS W. TRUSCHEL

Biography

Born in the Orange Free State in 1876 and educated by German missionaries. He worked as a postal employee in Kimberley and court interpreter in Mafeking, including its lengthy siege during the Boer War. As a journalist, Plaatje opposed racial and ethnic segregation in South Africa. Playing a major role in the formation and early leadership of the African National Congress, he appealed to the British to improve political conditions for Africans in South Africa in deputations to London in 1914, and again in 1919. He established contacts with black leaders in the United States in the early 1920s. His literary career involved his creation of a new orthography for Setswana and production of the first African historical novel in South Africa, *Mhudi* (1930). Disillusioned with his limited political successes, he died of influenza near Johannesburg in 1932.

See also: **Dube, John Langalibalele; Jabavu, John Tengo; South Africa: African National Congress; South Africa: Peace, Reconstruction, Union: 1902–1910; South Africa: Segregation, Political Economy of.**

Further Reading

Comaroff, J. L. (ed.). *The Boer War Diary of Sol T. Plaatje; an African at Mafeking*. London: Macmillan, 1973.

Plaatje, Sol. *Mhudi: An Epic of Native Life a Hundred Years Ago*. London: Heineman, 1978.

———. *Native Life in South Africa before and since the European War and the Boer Rebellion*. London, 1916.

Willan, Brian. *Sol Plaatje, South African Nationalist, 1876–1932*. Berkeley and Los Angeles: University of California Press, 1984.

———. (ed.). *Sol Plaatje: Select Writings*. Johannesburg: Witwatersrand University Press, 1996.

Plague: *See* **Egypt: Mamluk Dynasty (1250–1517): Plague.**

Plantations and Labor, Colonial

Plantations created more than a century ago by Europeans continue to dominate the current affairs of those African territories in which they were established. The term *plantation* has been invoked to describe agricultural units of varying size; both small cocoa plots belonging to African peasants and large landed areas worked by slaves in nineteenth century Sokoto have been categorized as plantations. Plantations in Africa produced for the export market, and the combination between management and labor was heavily influenced by racial considerations.

Generally, plantations were created in areas with significant white settler populations, although plantations did flourish in colonies without a settler element. Kenya and Zimbabwe (formerly Southern Rhodesia) are examples of the former, while Cameroon epitomizes those territories with a vibrant plantation culture in the absence of a large European population. In places like Zimbabwe and Kenya, corporate plantations existed alongside large-scale farms owned by individual settlers, while the plantations in Cameroon were in 1947 formed into a quasi-government entity, the Cameroons Development Corporation.

Plantations were often created through a combination of administrative, tax, and land instruments that provided generous allowances and conditions for plantations, typified by the "White Highlands policy" in Kenya. Thus, for example, land commissions were set up in Cameroon, Kenya, and Zimbabwe with the aim of creating "native reserves," but these worked largely to reserve the best lands for white-owned plantations. The work of these land commissions was accompanied by laws such as the Land Apportionment Act of 1930 in Zimbabwe, which formalized the allotment of the best lands to plantations. In the early 1900s the Unilever Corporation was given enormous concessions in the Congo with respect to leasehold and freehold rights over almost one million hectares, but the Firestone Rubber plantations in Liberia were probably the most (in)famous in Africa. At the beginning of the twentieth century, nine million acres had been taken over in Zimbabwe, and by the start of World War II plantations covered more than 800 square miles in southwest Cameroon. In between these dates, plantations were built up in German East Africa (particularly in Tanganyika) and Portuguese Mozambique, while Unilever also acquired plantations in Nigeria and Gabon. Creation of plantations raised the question of labor supply, especially as Europeans were unwilling to provide manual labor.

Plantations are associated with "modernizing" or "developing" the areas in which they were established, though political considerations also played a key role in the concept. Plantations were the most significant avenue for promoting European colonialism and Western capitalism in Africa. They were sources of raw materials for European industry; avenues through which European currencies could be introduced; practical schools for instructing Africans in European agricultural and technical methods; and instruments for forging a wage-labor market in colonial Africa. In many respects, the link between plantations and African labor was the most critical.

Plantations were created by expropriating African lands, and native Africans became workers on these plantations—sometimes on the same lands they formerly occupied and cultivated. Plantation agriculture in Africa was characterized by the extensive use of cheap, often unskilled, labor that was obtained by various methods, with some element of compulsion central to all. Initially, it was military force that compelled Africans to work on plantations, but colonial governments included recruitment of labor for European enterprises among the duties of African chiefs. The need to pay taxes in cash to colonial regimes and the desire to purchase European imports forced Africans to work on plantations.

Plantations required a cheap, regular, and docile workforce. Cheap labor took several forms and became inseparable from exploitation and the abuse of labor. Plantation enterprises were loath to pay decent wages; consequently, both money and real wages were low. Similarly, laborers put in very long hours in a day's work. Further, feeding and housing laborers formed part of the contractual arrangements between laborer and plantation, but the quantity and quality of the food supplied were poor and the standard of housing was poor.

Colonial control facilitated labor's exploitation and conditions resembled slavery. Plantation labor involved the migration of large numbers of male workers. The indigenous population of the plantation zones was unwilling or unable to meet the needs of the plantations for large amounts of labor due to the demographic and socioeconomic features of these precolonial African societies. Populations were small, and planter interests resorted to importing labor from within and without the plantation colonies. Generally, women had been responsible for agricultural production in precolonial societies, but their labor services were not heavily demanded by the plantations; nonetheless, women found employment doing light duties on tea estates.

The period 1890–1945 marked the zenith of exploitation of African labor, and conditions during the economically depressed 1930s and World War II were particularly harsh. However, there were attempts at reform affecting the plantations. Labor departments were set up by colonial regimes and trade unions emerged in response to increased labor agitation between 1930 and 1945. The demands of Africans for economic and political change often targeted the plantations, yet there was no consistency in African politics in plantation areas. There emerged in Cameroon a conservative political movement based on the Cameroons Development Corporation Workers Union, while in Kenya, Mozambique, and Zimbabwe more radical forms of nationalism developed in which land reform was central.

RICHARD A. GOODRIDGE

See also: **Zimbabwe (Southern Rhodesia): Colonial Period: Land, Tax, Administration.**

Further Reading

Berman, Bruce, and John Lonsdale. *Unhappy Valley: Conflict in Kenya and Africa.* London: Currey, 1992.

Epale, Simon. *Plantations and Development in Western Cameroon, 1885–1975: A Study in Agrarian Capitalism.* New York: Vantage Press, 1985.

Goodridge, R. A. "'In the Most Effective Manner'? Britain and the Disposal of the Cameroons Plantations, 1914–1924." *International Journal of African Historical Studies* 29, no. 2 (1996): 251–277.

Loewenson, Rene. *Modern Plantation Agriculture: Corporate Wealth and Labour Squalor.* London: Zed Books, 1992.

Pokot: *See* **Nilotes, Eastern Africa: Southern Nilotes: Kalenjin, Dadog, Pokot.**

Policing, Colonial

Before World War I, pioneer colonial administrators received paltry amounts of funds, which made policing the young colonial states difficult. This slowed colonial occupation, since expanding and maintaining colonial influence required substantial policing, which was not affordable. In Nyasaland, Harry H. Johnston was sent to found a colonial administration with his own salary and £10,000 a year. With this, he could just barely afford an armed force of 70 Indian soldiers under two British officers. When Captain Lugard set up a colony in Northern Nigeria, he had little over £100,000 for a territory of approximately ten million people. His police force consisted a regiment of a West African frontier force consisting of 2000 to 3000 African soldiers under about 120 European officers. Forces of this size always had to be used with the greatest caution. One serious defeat, or even a successful ambush, could have wiped out the entire police force of most early colonial governments.

When the colonial government adopted a policy to recover the costs of occupation through taxation, the necessity for efficient policing became evident. Open revolt from the natives necessitated reinforcements of the established small groups of forces. In nearly every territory of every colonial power, only a serious military crisis brought forth reinforcements and forced up grants-in-aid to a level that permitted some rough policing of the whole territory. By 1900 for instance, Nyasaland's £10,000 grant-in-aid had risen to £100,000 and Uganda's from £50,000 to £400,000. The policing situation in most colonial territories showed a comparable development five to ten years after the start of colonial rule.

By 1914, metropolitan grants-in-aid to colonial establishments were virtually extinguished. The result was that a great burden was placed on colonial officers, and policing the colonial state became an administrative nightmare. For instance, because he could not provide the capital outlay represented by the period of grants in aid in more conventional colonies, King Leopold employed an ill-controlled and barbarous native soldiery to levy arbitrary amounts of tribute for the benefit of the state and the concessionaire companies in which it held interests. This was a doomed undertaking and his personal rule in the Congo sank to such appalling depths of misadministration that he was forced to surrender his private empire to the Belgian government in 1908.

Throughout tropical Africa, the termination of grants-in-aid more or less coincided with the bringing of all but the most remote of the peripheral areas under civil administration. With the opening up of the hinterland to trade through expanded communications, the "pacification" through military patrols in the early colonial states was rolled back to the areas that had not been opened up for trade.

In the early stages of colonial history, every occupying power inevitably made both friends and enemies, depending on whether the local communities felt advantaged or humiliated by the colonial occupation. Consequently, before any occupying power could train a local police force, it needed native allies and was prepared to accord substantial privileges to those who would play this part. Policing thus became an important factor in gaining and executing the sense of gain and loss in the minds of the natives in relation to the fortunes of colonial expansion.

The first one-third of the colonial period throughout tropical Africa was a period when colonial powers were concerned first and foremost to making their own territories self supporting, with policing options being conditioned by shifting economic foci of the early colonial stations.

Policing options in the colonial states changed in the years preceding World War I. Colonies throughout

Sub-Saharan Africa began to assume the forms they would retain until the eve of independence. Since the period of emancipative nationalism had not began, and the period of resistance by traditional communities was over, police and military garrisons consisting almost entirely of African troops under European officers were adequate to deal with any small emergencies.

Between World War I and World War II the idea that the colonial powers had an obligation to go beyond policing, institute just governments, and carry the colonial peoples forward economically and politically had currency. This policy was more aggressively pursued after World War II, creating great changes in the social and political structures of the colonies—changes that ushered in the period of nationalism and lay the groundwork for the road to independence.

In North Africa, two currents of virtually no significance elsewhere in the continent determined the course of events. The first was the direct political and military conflicts between European states, and the second was the growth of Arab nationalism. The British protectorate in Egypt had become a nominally independent monarchy, though British troops remained in occupation to guard the Suez Canal, much to the displeasure of Egyptian nationalist party, the Wafd. The British troops were withdrawn under the Anglo-Egyptian Treaty of 1936 to a narrow zone on either side of the Suez Canal. Egypt was also to become a vital base for the British troops in their campaigns of 1940–1943. In 1943 Britain used its troops to impose and maintain a Wafd government. But internal disintegrations and corruption of the Wafd saw a group of young army officers inspired by colonel Gamel Abdul Nasser institute a military government. Nasser continued working with the British until 1957, when the British and French used the Israeli invasion of Egypt as a reason to send in troops to police the Suez area. International opinion briefly forced out the British and French, making Nasser a hero of the anticolonialist movement throughout Africa and Asia.

In Algeria, France's biggest interest in North Africa, a force of close to half a million troops was employed to counter Algerian resistance. By 1958 it was clear that the military occupation had failed to keep down the Algerian revolt; a cease-fire was negotiated in 1962, and the right to self-determination was granted.

MICHAEL WAINAINA

See also: **Algeria: War of Independence, 1954–1962; Egypt: Nasser: Foreign Policy: Suez Canal Crisis to Six Day War, 1952–1970; Johnston, Harry H.; Nigeria: Lugard, Administration and "Indirect Rule"; Stanley, Leopold II, "Scramble."**

Further Reading

Roland, O., and J. Fage. *A Short History of Africa*, 6th ed. London: Penguin, 1962.
Kyle, K. *The Politics of Independent Kenya.* Contemporary History in Context Series, general editor Peter Caterall. New York: St. Martin's Press, 1999.

Polisario and the Western Sahara

In 1884, Spain occupied Rio de Oro and Vila Cisneros, proclaiming a Spanish protectorate over the Western Sahara coast. In 1900, a Franco-Spanish agreement settled the frontier between the Spanish Sahara and French-occupied Mauritania. In 1956, when it gained its independence from France, Morocco at once laid claim to all the Spanish possessions in northwest Africa, as well as Mauritania. The following year, "irregular" Moroccan forces raided the most heavily populated areas of the Spanish Sahara. Both France and Spain intervened militarily to put down these Moroccan incursions.

Mauritania became independent in 1960, and in 1964 and again in 1966 informed the United Nations Special Committee that it wanted to take part in direct talks with Spain over the future of Western Sahara. In 1965, however, the people of Rio de Oro (the southern part of the Spanish Sahara) pledged loyalty to King Hassan of Morocco, while at the United Nations Morocco expressed the hope that its claim to the Spanish Sahara would be settled peacefully. In December 1967 the UN called upon Spain to hold a referendum on the future of Spanish Sahara. A UN resolution of 1973 called on Spain to grant independence to the Spanish Sahara; the resolution also recognized that both Morocco and Mauritania had "claims" to the territory.

Spain established a tripartite administration for the territory with Morocco and Mauritania, and announced that it would cease to administer the Spanish Sahara on February 28, 1976. Several nationalist

The Western Sahara conflict. Training camp of Polisario near Rabouni, Algeria, 2001. © Sebastian Bolesch/Das Fotoarchiv.

groups had emerged by that point, each seeking an end to Spanish rule, leading Spain to declare a state of emergency in the territory in 1972. The most significant of these groups was the Popular Front for the Liberation of Saguia al-Hamra and Rio de Oro (Polisario). Algeria decided to arm and support Polisario, mainly on the grounds that it did not wish to see the emergence of an enlarged and more powerful Morocco. In 1975 King Hassan of Morocco launched the peaceful Green March of 350,000 Moroccans across the border into the Spanish Sahara to emphasize his country's claim. The marchers, however, were halted by Spanish troops at El Aaiun.

On February 27 1976, the day before Spain was to withdraw, Polisario proclaimed the Saharan Arab Democratic Republic (SADR) and turned to Algeria for support. Spain now handed over "rights" in its former colony to Morocco and Mauritania and withdrew from the territory, leaving a situation ripe for conflict. The war that followed was to be popular in Morocco and came at a time when Hassan's popularity at home was on the wane. It would almost cripple Mauritania, which was far too poor to sustain a long military campaign. After suffering an initial defeat by Moroccan forces at Angala in January 1976 (before the Spanish had departed) Polisario turned to guerrilla tactics. It also made the tactical decision to concentrate its war efforts upon its weaker opponent, Mauritania, first. It was able to inflict such damage upon the Mauritanian military and economy that in July 1978 a coup was mounted against President Ould Daddah. After his fall, the Mauritanian government withdrew from the conflict and gave up its claims to the Spanish Sahara. Morocco at once moved its forces to occupy the whole territory, and the war became a struggle between the Moroccan army and the Polisario guerrillas.

By 1980 the Polisario had 10,000 troops, with half engaged in guerrilla warfare and half in camps in Algeria at any one time. Its primary tactic was to mount hit-and-run attacks upon centers of population. By 1982 Morocco controlled the main centers of population, as well as the huge phosphate mines at Bou Craa; it then embarked upon the construction of defensive sand walls, which were designed to deny Polisario access to the populated regions of Western Sahara. By 1984 these extended over 600 kilometers to the Mauritanian border.

The war continued throughout the 1980s, with both sides using increasingly sophisticated weapons. Various efforts by the UN and the Organization of African Unity (OAU) to find a formula for peace came to nothing. In 1988 Morocco and Polisario did accept a UN plan for a cease-fire and referendum, but this broke down in 1989 and the war was resumed. Other UN efforts were aborted, mainly because of Morocco's insistence that the referendum should include Moroccans that had been settled in Western Sahara since 1976, as opposed to only those who had been living there at the time of independence. (In 1975 there had been a population of only 75,000, and by the mid-1980s about 10,000 of these had been killed).

During the 1990s the territory was in a state of uncertain peace marked by outbreaks of war. Morocco insisted upon its claim, while the United Nations and Polisario demanded that the referendum be held. In 1990 Algeria, which wanted to forge a good relationship with Morocco, began to withdraw support from Polisario. In 1993 Morocco included its "Saharan Provinces" in its general elections and the UN secretary general, Boutros Boutros-Ghali, postponed the referendum until 1994; it was then again pushed back to 1995. Further delays and fighting occurred throughout 1995; the referendum was again deferred and the secretary general of Polisario, Mohamed Abdelaziz, said that Polisario would continue the struggle, whatever the result of the referendum.

Morocco's principal strategy was to stall on the referendum while entrenching its power in Western Sahara; the longer it managed to do this, the more it reduced the effectiveness of Polisario. In 1996, the UN again extended the mandate of MINURSO (the UN Mission for the Referendum in Western Sahara) while setting no new date for the referendum. Voter registration remained blocked. The UN secretary general declared that the differences between the two sides were irreconcilable. Meanwhile, MINURSO reduced its military and police components in the territory. Morocco continued its delaying tactics and persuaded ten states in the OAU to withdraw their earlier recognition of Polisario by offering them financial assistance.

The referendum was again set, this time for December 1998, after Morocco had agreed to accept lower figures for voters eligible to take part and for the number of troops it could place in the disputed territory. Yet at the same time the Moroccan prime minister, Abellatif Filali, claimed that the referendum would merely reaffirm Moroccan sovereignty over Western Sahara, which, he said, would always be an integral part of the Moroccan kingdom. At the end of the year the referendum was once more deferred, this time until mid-1999; from then until the present, the situation has remained essentially unchanged, with the UN unable to schedule a referendum on Western Sahara's status, as the two sides continue to disagree on who is eligible to take part in such a vote.

GUY ARNOLD

See also: **Morocco: International Relations since Independence.**

Political Elites and Patronage: Postcolonial Africa

Patron-client relations undoubtedly remain at the heart of all postcolonial African political systems, whatever the nature and the official ideology of the regimes concerned. In a former dictatorship like Zaire, where Mobutu's clique was acknowledged to have largely cut itself off from the rest of the population, empirical studies show that redistributive clientelistic networks reached relatively low down the social strata. In contemporary Zambia, or Benin—two countries generally considered as relative success stories of political transition—it is evident that a particularist relationship among high-ranking officials, myriads of middlemen, and the population matter much more politically than universalistic, institutionalized regulations. Under civilian as well as military regimes, it appears obvious that accumulation of wealth and patronage remain crucial for any ambitious politician.

Several aspects must be distinguished when one studies patron-client networks in postcolonial Africa. It is essential to understand that the ties between the privileged and their dependents are of a particularistic nature. They also involve exchanges (admittedly unequal) and not just pure domination or exploitation. Furthermore, they durably tend to strengthen vertical cleavages and solidarities, meanwhile preventing the emergence of class antagonisms and favoring factional struggles. Finally, they are decisively informal, constantly renegotiable, and therefore largely inimical to the development of genuinely institutionalized patterns of relationships.

Particularist Loyalties

In Sub-Saharan Africa, prestige and influence are intimately linked to the number of clients one claims to have. Pressure from modern political competition compels political leaders to continuously widen their support base. They endeavor to constitute themselves as "big men," controlling as many networks as they can. Patrons' legitimacy derives from their ability to nourish the clientele on which their power rests. Political elites try to establish principles of reciprocity, based on the model of kin and family relations, but these loyalties are much less solid and depend almost entirely on the extent to which the clientelistic networks are properly resourced. In the absence of an institutionally autonomous and relatively impartial state, affording protection to the country's "citizens" (whatever their origins and social position), it is imperative for ordinary people to maintain links with those who have power by playing on ties of clientelism. This long-lasting trend prevents the development of more neutral and impersonally organized relationships

associating individuals directly with the state, and where everyone would be treated according to the same standards. On the contrary it maintains deeply particularistic ties which are much more evanescent, uncertain and open to instrumentalization.

Asymmetrical Reciprocity

Although there are strong inequalities within clientelistic relations, patrons suffer considerable constraints. In fact, the maintenance of their status is entirely dependent on their capacity to meet the expectations of their dependents, who in turn must satisfy their own clients. The acuteness of apparent inequalities is reduced by the need to be seen as a redistributor on a scale appropriate to one's standing. When rooted in clientelistic ties, social relations are inevitably based on personalized bonds of mutually beneficial reciprocity. The demands of such networks may frequently force patrons to act against their own immediate economic self-interests in order to meet the obligations on which their social rank and political authority depend. That is why, despite the undeniably large gap between elites and the populace, leaders are never wholly dissociated from their supporters. They remain directly bound to their supporters through a myriad of clientelistic networks staffed by dependent brokers. A powerful figure will see his authority all the more reinforced as his reference group identifies with him and he incarnates all its hopes. One would be wrong to consider that this type of relationship amounts to a simple manipulation, for the evidence shows that it partakes much more profoundly of a sort of common heritage, within the framework of complex networks which are interwoven from the top to the bottom. The exercise of power rests firmly on commonly recognized terms. Even if patron-client relations remain unequally biased in their favor, patrons can easily suffer "the blackmail of the ruled"—that is, the obligation of personalized and vertical redistribution to which they must submit in order to anchor their position across the different social strata which provide support.

Vertical Cleavages

If relations between leaders and followers, rulers and ruled, are to be understood in terms of asymmetrical reciprocity, then solidarities, mobilization, political linkages tend to be more vertical than horizontal. This is not a denial that African sociopolitical systems are far from egalitarian but simply emphasizes that most political actors are simultaneously dominant and dominated, one of the links in the many chains of dependence. Often torn by internal disputes, faction leaders are forced to cultivate relationships with those below them in order to gain support in their power struggle with one another. This argument thus casts serious doubts on the validity of those interpretations which conceive of African societies from an excessively dichotomized angle, emphasizing divisions between "high" and "low" politics, elites and masses, ruling classes and populace. Taking advantage of power is not necessarily inadmissible but it is still necessary to live up to the expectations of one's supporters in a satisfactory way as regards redistribution. Political leaders enjoy relative legitimacy only in accordance with the credit granted by the populations. For those at the very bottom of the social system, the material prosperity of their betters is not itself reprehensible so long as they too can benefit materially from their association with a patron linking them to the elites. Even if it had achieved the economic means of its hegemonic ambitions, any elite that became a ruling "class," thus cutting itself from the rest of society, would rapidly lose prestige, influence and, thereby, legitimacy. Within the existing African political culture, patrons generally have closer links with their clients than with rival leaders. At the opposite end of the social scale, ordinary people will always relate more directly with their local Big Man than with their economic peers elsewhere in the country.

Informal Transactions

South of the Sahara, the nature of the relations between the rulers and the ruled is determined by practices that have little to do with the formal structures of power. It is crucial to understand that the foundations of political accountability are both collective and extrainstitutional: they rest on the informal links between "big men" and their respective networks. This may be considered as nefarious to the macrodevelopment of African countries since it makes political and economic activities quite unpredictable. There are, however, good reasons as to why it is not likely to disappear. Indeed, a system of such profound uncertainty and opaqueness, which depends on subtle and constantly fluctuating ties of loyalty, provides ample opportunity for the instrumental use of properly cultivated social relations. African states would undoubtedly benefit from more regulated relations, but the main political and economic elites are able to use the absence of transparency as a most valuable resource. Such is the efficacy of the existing system that it has survived unscathed all generational and social change—adapting as it goes along to the demands of modernity.

Despite the current political "democratic transitions" on the continent, it is far from clear that this complexion of political transactions has been modified. For instance, voting is indelibly linked to the anticipation of the direct particularist benefit that elections offer. Contrary to teleological presuppositions, political life in postcolonial Africa remains essentially a question of infranational identity representation. The debate is hardly tied to choices of society that would be presented through competing formations to enlightened "citizens." Elites, intermediaries, and common inhabitants first of all perceive themselves according to ethnoregional reading grids, or factional ones in the event of needing to enter into coalitions. There is no reliable evidence that this type of particularistic leadership, based as it is on clientelistic transactions, is waning on the continent, although it might be markedly weakened by the scarcity of resources from which the elites are currently suffering. On the contrary, it could be argued that the present economic crisis in Africa reinforces, rather than undermines, the logic of vertical and personalized patronage.

JEAN-PASCAL DALOZ

Further Reading

Barnes, Sandra T. *Patrons and Power: Creating a Community in Metropolitan Lagos.* Manchester: Manchester University Press, 1986.

Chabal, Patrick. *Power in Africa: An Essay in Political Interpretation.* Basingstoke, England: Macmillan, 1992.

Chabal, Patrick, and Jean-Pascal Daloz. *Africa Works: Disorder as Political Instrument.* Oxford: James Currey/Bloomington: Indiana University Press, 1999.

Daloz, Jean-Pascal (ed.). *Le (non-) renouvellement des elites en Afrique subsaharienne.* Bordeaux: Centre d'Etude d'Afrique Noire, 1999.

Jackson, Robert H., and Carl G. Rosberg. *Personal Rule in Black Africa.* Berkeley and Los Angeles: University of California Press, 1982.

———. "Le 'Big Man' en Afrique: esquisse d'analyse du politicien entrepreneur." *L'Année sociologique* (1992).

Médard, Jean-François. "The Underdeveloped State in Tropical Africa: Political Clientelism or Neo-Patrimonialism?" In *Private Patronage and Public Power: Political Clientelism in the Modern State,* edited by Christopher Clapham. London: Frances, 1982.

Political Identity

The colonization of Africa by the major European powers in the late nineteenth century was caused by many factors—political, economic, and nationalistic. Colonial hegemony brought on by colonization was partly constructed on the idea of race difference; the assumption was that blacks were inferior and needed new tools and ideas to uplift themselves. The advent of anthropology helped to provide many middle- and upper-class Victorians with scientific justification for believing that they had a divine duty to "civilize" Africans. The idea of race was made respectable by reports of missionaries and gentlemen explorers and travelers of the nineteenth century. Once colonial rule was established, class and race became inseparable.

Race constituted a group identity that had certain predetermined advantages. Nowhere was this manifest more than in the settler colonies of South Africa, Algeria, Kenya, and Zimbabwe. Wages, residential locations, as well as access to education and health care facilities were determined by one's race. While the foundation for a segregated South African society was laid in the decades before and immediately after the dawn of the twentieth century, it was the victory of the Nationalist Party in the 1948 election that led to the adoption of apartheid—racial segregation—as the official government policy. As a result, the South African apartheid regime classified all the people in South Africa into the following "racial" categories: Caucasian, Asian, Colored, and Black. Each race had its own place in the society. The significant point to note here is the way the apartheid regime defined and constructed the idea of race for the purpose of control of the majority by the minority. Furthermore, it is also instructive that the regime created a distinctively capitalist nation whose economy was based officially on racial oppression and exploitation. In Algeria the victorious French armies imposed French civic codes on the Muslim society. In British colonial Kenya, the Devonshire Declaration of 1923 upheld the view that Kenya was primarily an African country, but the British had the authority to hold and govern the country in trust for the Africans. This view was the cornerstone of the principle of British Trusteeship mandate by which it justified its governance of the country until Africans would be "guided" to independence. In all these cases Africans were dispossessed and considered in the new milieu to be inferior to Europeans. Colonialism was a system that buttressed race, thereby exerting pressure on all Europeans in the colonies to maintain a pretense of race preeminence and class snobbery so as not lose face in front of the Africans.

Besides race, ethnicity was another critical group identity in the colonial plan and scheme of governance. Ethnicity represents a sense of collective identity that rests on claims of common descent, shared attributes such as language and cultural traditions, territoriality, and political organization. In the context of most African societies ethnicity was not unchanging identity. Before the onset of colonialism ethnic groups in Africa were involved in fruitful mingling and migration. In the process ethnic identity went through constant redefinition, as some communities split and were either absorbed by the dominant groups or simply moved away into new terrain to assume new identity. What is important in the history of evolution and development of most ethnic groups in Africa is not how they are, but how they came to be. Most communities operated on the notion that their continuity and long-term survival depended less on its purity or single origin than on its ability to accommodate and assimilate diverse elements. Ethnicity, then, may represent one of the most accessible and easiest levels of discourse on the complex issue of identity in both colonial and postcolonial Africa, but it is not the most accurate, nor is it explanatory.

With the onset of colonialism and the institutionalization of the colonial state, African societies were forced to exist within defined boundaries and borders of the artificial construct of nation-state. The construction of the borders of the African colonial state was so arbitrary that some communities, clans, and even lineages were torn apart and placed under different nation-states. In the same vein, many and varied societies, with little in common, were lumped together, given new names, and depicted as ethnic groups. Ethnicity in the colonial system became relational markers of differences between groups. It served the colonial state as its premier instrument of divide and rule. Ethnicity was used to emphasize differences in culture, economy, and politics among the various communities. Terms that were hitherto merely expressive of ethnic identity became transformed into stereotypical prisms of ethnic differences. Indeed, the colonial state nurtured and promoted ethnic schism by privileging myths in which some communities were adulated as superior and enlightened, while others were dismissed as indolent and inferior. This sowed the seeds of rivalry, hatred, and destruction that flowered in the postcolonial period. In essence, the colonial state nurtured ethnic and racial parochialism for the purpose of maintaining order by emphasizing difference. Individual identities were sacrificed at the altar of group identities, race and ethnicity.

African elites have confronted the variables of race and ethnicity in many different ways, both in the colonial and postcolonial periods. While colonial powers promoted Western education and developed health care facilities, these developments occurred against the backdrop of African political marginalization and cultural disinheritance. Some of the Africans who had acquired Western education attacked racist ideas and presented significant historical evidence on the consequences of African civilization and contributions to human progress. In the French colonies this critique of colonialism and race coalesced into the Negritude movement. Spearheaded by Leopold Senghor of Senegal, the movement emphasized pride in African culture, but not the dismantling of the colonial system.

However, in some cases, particularly after World War II, the critique of preferential treatment based on race led to the formation of nationalist movements, which challenged and sought to change the status quo. The African elite found out that the colonial pecking order prevented them from assuming certain positions in the colonial public service, denied them access to state resources, and confined them to eternal subjugation. Since racism endowed the settler with class/race cohesion, the African elite mobilized the masses in their determination to dismantle colonialism. In essence, the African elite viewed colonial oppression and exploitation as situations reinforced by race difference. Africans were united by their common desire to attain independence. In the course of struggle for independence ethnicity was temporarily suppressed, and they rose above ethnic parochialism in the determination to present a united and formidable front against the colonial state. The attainment of independence and dismantling of colonial rule signaled the end of race as a dominant factor in the domestic politics of postcolonial African countries. The paradox, though, is that no sooner had the independence been won than ethnicity resurfaced as a destructive force in African politics. The end of colonial rule unleashed forces of cultural, ethnic, economic and national intolerance with untold suffering to the citizenry. The critical issue in postcolonial Africa has been the persistence of ethnicity as a potent force in national politics.

The African elite inherited the colonial state structures intact. The institutions of governance had been anything but democratic. Furthermore, few political parties were developed on the basis of interests that transcended ethnic interests. The African elite and leadership focused more on using the inherited state apparatus and structures to accumulate wealth and reward their cronies and less on democratizing the political institutions for better governance. As a result, the elite perpetuated the colonial state's authoritarianism, as well as an agenda of divide and rule by using ethnicity to rally members of their ethnic groups in support of self-centered narrow political and economic interests. Thus, ethnicity in the postcolonial period has been used within the wider political field as an instrument in the exercise of power and accumulation of wealth, as well as a mechanism for rallying members of an ethnic group to support their elite in their struggles on the national stage.

In the wake of weak economies and fragile institutions, the competition for access to state resources has intensified ethnic tensions leading to military coups, political instability, and incessant civil wars. Ethnicity has become the crushing burden that most postcolonial African states have to contend with. This is not to imply that ethnic conflicts were nonexistent in Africa before European colonization. Nothing could be further from the truth. The contention is that the intensity of ethnic conflicts that have characterized most African countries in the postcolonial period have been destructive and severe in the extreme. Also, the unbridled competition for access to state resources within the boundaries of the nation-state is a unique phenomenon that can be partly attributed to colonialism, since the boundaries of the nation-state are fixed. Power struggle and competition for resources usually takes place within the defined boundaries of the nation-state. When rivalry gets out of control the stability of the state is compromised. And in cases where members of an ethnic group have been split and live in two or three adjacent nation-states, the turmoil spills over to those countries as well. Furthermore, when the state collapses or its institutions are mobilized by the elite and directed against members of a rival group the consequence is usually catastrophic in terms of human lives lost and the number of people who are displaced from their homes. Indeed, Africa has the largest number of refugees. The situation in the Great Lakes Region of Africa best exemplifies the intricacies of the legacy of colonialism, ethnicity, power struggle, competition for resources, and international economic interests in postcolonial Africa.

GEORGE ODUOR NDEGE

See also: **Ethnicity; Martial Races, Political Élites and Patronage: Postcolonial Africa.**

Further Reading

Boahen, A. Adu. *African Perspectives on Colonialism.* Baltimore: Johns Hopkins University Press, 1987.

Clapham, Christopher. *Africa and the International System: The Politics of State Survival.* Cambridge: Cambridge University Press, 1996.

Chretien, Jean-Pierre. *The Great Lakes of Africa: Two Thousand Years of History.* New York: Zone, 2003.

Davidson, Basil. *The Black Man's Burden: Africa and the Curse of the Nation State.* New York: Random House, 1992.

Magubane, Bernard M. *The Making of a Racist State: British Imperialism and the Union of South Africa, 1875–1910.* Trenton, N.J.: Africa World Press, 1996.

Mamdani, Mahmood. *When Victims Became Killers: Colonialism, Nativism, and Genocide in Rwanda.* Princeton, N.J.: Princeton University Press, 2002.

Ottaway, Marina. *Africa's New Leaders: Democracy or State Reconstruction.* Washington D. C.: Carnegie Endowment for International Peace, 1999.

Wilmsen, Edwin and Patrick McAllister. *The Politics of Difference: Ethnic Premises of a World Power.* Chicago: University of Chicago Press, 1996.

Political Parties and One-Party States

One of the most important political acts undertaken by the first generation of postcolonial African leaders was the establishment of single-party political systems to replace the hastily constructed, ill-suited, and largely untested multiparty political systems bequeathed by the departing colonial powers. These single-party systems ranged from Chama Cha Mapinduzi, a mass mobilizing party created by Julius Nyerere, the former socialist leader of Tanzania, to the Workers Party of Ethiopia, a vanguard party created by Mengistu Haile Mariam, the former Marxist leader of Ethiopia, and the Kenya African National Union (KANU), the sole ruling party of capitalist-oriented Kenya that was created by former President Jomo Kenyatta, and strengthened by his successor, Daniel arap Moi. Regardless of their political ideology, nearly all African leaders exhibited authoritarian tendencies that inevitably resulted in the creation of single-party political systems.

African leaders offered numerous rationales to justify the establishment of political monopolies over their respective political systems. The first justification was that single-party systems were reflective of traditional African political systems as they existed prior to the imposition of direct colonial rule. According to this argument, explains J. Gus Liebenow, the single-party system was not to be perceived as a "temporary aberration" from a universal norm of multiparty democracy, but rather as a "modern adaptation of traditional African political behavior" (1986). Unlike the divisive nature of Western multiparty systems in which one party emerges dominant and the others are marginalized, the concept of single-party democracy was heralded as conducive to promoting the traditional African norm of seeking consensus in which every participant has the right to voice his or her opinion—though women were normally excluded from decision-making during the precolonial era—and decisions are made only when agreed upon by all present.

A second rationale for creating single-party systems was the imperative of responding to existing and potential crises. African leaders argued against "wasting" scarce resources on competitive politics when their countries were confronted with crises of development (How can we quickly develop our society?), crises of administration (How do we quickly educate the required leaders?), and, most important, crises of governance (How do we quickly satisfy rising popular demands for the fruits of independence?). Just as unity was crucial to the attainment of independence, as those who led the nationalist struggles during the 1950s argued, so too was unity important once that independence had been achieved. Equally important, African leaders feared that multiparty systems would foster the fragmentation of ethnically diverse African societies, and therefore perceived the single-party system as one of the most important tools for transforming colonially inspired, artificial states into true nations.

A third rationale, especially offered by African leaders from the Marxist tradition, underscored the vanguard role that single parties were expected to play. Drawing upon the Leninist concept that the "masses" of individual African societies needed to be led by an "enlightened elite," the single party was envisioned as serving to protect and promote Marxist revolutions on the African continent. The single party was particularly oriented toward the future evolution of African societies, especially in terms of ensuring industrial development and the promotion of basic human needs such as guaranteed access to adequate food, shelter, and health care.

The nearly 30-year experiment with single-party rule achieved few positive results. Even in the most benevolent of examples, such as Nyerere's *ujamaa* experiment in Tanzania, the country made significant strides in promoting mass literacy and the provision of basic human needs only at the expense of a failed overall economy that witnessed an annual average decline of 7 per cent in agricultural output. One of the primary reasons for this failure was that the initially voluntary villagization program, the centerpiece of the *ujamaa* ideology in which peasants were grouped together in new communal villages, ultimately became coercive in nature. Many peasants were forced to move from their traditional lands to village projects that were either poorly conceived or simply inappropriate for farming practices. If the state inevitably became coercive and therefore counterproductive to the goal of development in the most benevolent of single-party systems, one has only to imagine its impact on the development of the most authoritarian single-party systems such as the Marxist-inspired tyranny created in Mengistu's Ethiopia.

The most notable problem associated with the single-party experiment was that it led to a stagnation of ideas. For example, although Kenyan legislative candidates were allowed to run against each other under the unified banner of KANU, they were not permitted to question either the capitalist domestic ideology or the foreign policy of the Kenyatta regime. Candidates could debate the instrumental aspects of carrying out party-approved policies, but were unable to offer alternatives to misguided policies. In this and other cases, African leaders who felt they "knew best" restricted the range of political debate to such a degree that the single party ultimately became a means for maintaining control rather than a dynamic tool for promoting change and development.

The downfall of single-party communist systems throughout Eastern Europe and the former Soviet Union at the end of the 1980s sent shock waves throughout single-party political establishments of the African continent. The rejection of single-party rule in its intellectual heartland ensured that African leaders could no longer justify the continuation of this model on the African continent. "If the owners of socialism have withdrawn from the one-party system," proclaimed Frederick Chiluba, the leader of the Zambian prodemocracy movement and future president of Zambia, "who are the Africans to continue with it?" Equally important, authoritarian leaders could no longer use Cold War rhetoric as the means for ensuring superpower attention and therefore the financial and military support necessary to prevent opposition movements from taking power; the former Soviet Union had ceased to exist and a new Russian regime preoccupied with domestic economic restructuring had largely withdrawn from African politics, while the United States and its Western allies were increasingly prone to link African support for democratization and economic liberalization to future commitments of foreign assistance and preferential trade agreements.

The emergence of a Western consensus in favor of promoting democratic principles coincided with the rise of increasingly vocal and powerful African prodemocracy movements. Popular protests and demands for political reform often emerged due to the intensification of government-sponsored political repression and human rights abuses throughout the 1980s. This trend peaked in 1991 when a total of 86 popular protests were recorded in 30 African countries. Protestors were emboldened by the adoption of continent-wide human rights norms confirmed by the ratification of the African Charter of Human and Peoples' Rights by the majority of African countries at the beginning of the 1990s. Protesters were also driven by the severe deterioration of African economies that made it increasingly difficult for individual families already perilously close to abject poverty to acquire basic foodstuffs and other necessities of day-to-day living.

The convergence of these domestic and international trends resulted in renewed scholarly interest in the emergence and consolidation of multiparty democracy in Africa. Reminiscent of the optimism expressed by modernization theorists during the 1950s and the 1960s, the liberal democratic tradition at the end of the 1980s was reinvigorated by the emergence of prodemocracy movements that fostered dozens of experiments in multiparty democracy throughout the African continent. An initial euphoria surrounded what some scholars optimistically referred to as the rebirth of political freedom throughout Africa, making transitions to multiparty democracy the most studied topic among Africanists within the field of political science during the 1990s.

The best example of this scholarly trend is Michael Bratton and Nicolas van de Walle's *Democratic Experiments in Africa: Regime Transition in Comparative Perspective* (1997), which offers the first comprehensive analysis of all democratic transitions which took place between 1989 and 1994. According to their study, truly competitive multiparty elections during the five-year period (1985–1989) preceding the fall of the Berlin Wall were held in only five African countries: Botswana, Gambia, Mauritius, Senegal, and Zimbabwe. From 1990 to 1994, more than 38 countries held competitive multiparty elections. Most important, 29 of the multiparty contests of the 1990–1994 era constituted founding elections in which "the office of the head of government is openly contested following a period during which multiparty political competition was denied." South Africa's founding election of April 26–29, 1994, serves as one of the most heralded examples of African democratic transition. For the first time, voters of all races cast ballots in free and fair elections that ushered in South Africa's first multiracial, multiethnic, and multiparty democracy.

However, numerous scholars nonetheless remain wary of the long-term impact of multiparty politics and the literal explosion of opposition parties throughout the African continent. In the extreme, scholars are particularly critical of the role of foreign powers in promoting multiparty democracy as a form of neocolonialism that is contributing to the recolonization of the African continent. According to Claude Ake (1996), for example, the adoption of multiparty political systems in many cases has fostered what he refers to as the "democratization of disempowerment"—a process whereby multiparty elections allow for the rotation of self-interested elites of different parties while the vast majority of the population remains disempowered from the political system. As Ake argues, the critical aspect of true democracy is not multiparty elections but the assurance of "popular" (mass) participation within African political systems. It is precisely for this reason that the multiparty experiments of the 1990s and beyond will serve as the cornerstone of debates over the viability of democracy in Africa.

PETER J. SCHRAEDER

See also: **Banda, Dr. Hastings Kamuzu; Nkrumah, Kwame; Tanzania (Tanganyika): Chama Cha Mapinduzi (CCM), One-Party Politics; Zambia: Second Republic, 1973–1991.**

Further Reading

Ake, Claude. *Democracy and Development in Africa.* Washington, D.C.: Brookings Institution, 1996.

Bratton, Michael, and Nicolas van de Walle. *Democratic Experiments in Africa: Regime Transition in Comparative Perspective.* Cambridge: Cambridge University Press, 1997.

Ihonvbere, Julius O. "From Movement to Government: The Movement for Multi-Party Democracy and the Crisis of Democratic Consolidation in Zambia." *Canadian Journal of African Studies* 29, no. 1 (1994): 1–25.

Liebenow, J. Gus. *African Politics: Crises and Challenges.* Bloomington: Indiana University Press, 1986.

Lijphart, Arend. *Electoral Systems and Party Systems: A Study of Twenty-Seven Democracies, 1945–1990.* New York: Oxford University Press, 1994.

Sisk, Timothy D., and Andrew Reynolds (eds.). *Elections and Conflict Management in Africa.* Washington, D.C.: United States Institute of Peace, 1998.

Widner, Jennifer A. *Economic Change and Political Liberalization in Sub-Saharan Africa.* Baltimore: Johns Hopkins University Press, 1994.

Political Systems

Any attempt to study African political systems confronts three problems: historical scope, comparability, and generalization. Is it possible to study politics from the precolonial period to the contemporary? How does one compare systems across such wide expanses and such diverse historical periods? On what basis can one generalize from the incomplete knowledge we have of the various parts of the continent? One way forward is to approach the question from a clear conceptual perspective.

Africa has often been regarded as "traditional" or "timeless," a world where nothing changes. Yet all political systems are dynamic, even when they appear to evolve very little; they need to respond to environmental and other historical challenges or crises (disease, invasion, migration, slave trading, etc.). It is thus quite pointless to seek here a description of a notional "single" African political system, one that would encompass the range of historical experience of the continent since the beginning of time.

Finally, how is it possible to generalize about such a huge continent, the north of which is often more commonly associated with the Middle East, the west with slave trading, the east with the Indian Ocean, and the south with white settlement? The short answer is that the only profitable way of discussing such diverse regions is to focus squarely on how arrangements of power contrast with those found elsewhere. Hence, this essay attempts to account for African political systems in firmly comparative terms. Politics in Africa is in no way unique—even if today it appears to be historically singular—and it can readily be related analytically to that of Europe or Asia.

This article is in two parts. The first gives a brief overview of some key moments in the history of the continent, among which migration, European expansion, slave trading, colonial conquest, and decolonization loom large. The second is an attempt to show how a properly grounded historical knowledge of African political systems helps us to understand what is happening today on the continent.

Overview

Underlying the evolution of the continent as a whole is the question of demography. Until the colonial "revolution," which significantly lowered the death rate, population growth in Africa had been very slow. Thus, for most of their history, the peoples of the continent have sought to adjust their ways of living in order to match a relatively limited population with the large availability of space. Socioeconomic and political developments were thus predicated on the politics of survival rather than growth. The simplest response to a crisis was to move elsewhere, to occupy land as yet not settled by others. It has been argued that Africa's slender population density made possible a way of life in which technical and scientific innovation was largely superfluous. Although this argument can easily become a caricature of an unchanging or "timeless" Africa, there is no doubt that local conditions led to the widespread system of small and relatively self-contained political communities for the greater part of the continent's history.

Up to the fifteenth century, when the Portuguese "discovered" the continent, Africa's political evolution was primarily affected by the movement of people. Such migrations had two main effects: the first was that culture, technique, and tools were shared over time; the second was that migrants, even where they asserted political dominance, were eventually assimilated into those people they encountered. Africa was thus not a land of splintered and discrete entities, but one in which the migration of people constantly affected existing social and political cultures and where modes of cultivation or husbandry were influenced by such exchanges.

The most important of these movements was the systematic drive by Bantu people toward the west and south of Africa, colonizing land, creating new communities, and adapting to their environment wherever they settled. Despite the pronounced differences of languages and cultures to be found in Africa today, there is thus much shared "common" history. This has obviously had a bearing on the sociopolitical systems that developed before colonial rule.

A second significant factor in the continent's history was the expansion of Islam from the Middle East and North Africa, also toward the west and south of the continent. The spread of this religion had distinct societal effects, of which literacy and changes in political structures figure prominently. Islam brought with it not just a belief system, but a way of life tied to commerce and a certain notion of social order. It was also able to accommodate existing sociocultural traditions, thus rooting itself quite effectively among the peoples who adopted the faith. There was thus a distinct Islamic sociopolitical environment to be found in large swathes of western, eastern, and central Africa.

Equally, it is useful to understand that Africa was, with the exception of a few groups like the Pygmies and Khoisan, a continent of continually shifting regional and sometimes long-distance commerce. Until the Sahara became a desert, and even afterward, trade between North Africa and the Middle East with the rest of the continent was significant. Exchange with Asia, as far afield as China, had also been recorded long before the Europeans landed on the continent's shores. Africa was, in this respect, well connected to other parts of the world.

Contact with the Europeans, initiated by the Portuguese in the fifteenth century, added a new dimension to Africa's evolution but did not result in a wholesale "revolution," as is sometimes alleged. Other than in the few areas (the islands of Cape Verde and São Tomé, a number of coastal towns, or the Zambezi colonies) where the Europeans (or, more likely, their mixed-blood offspring) settled, the main effect of their presence was to divert commerce and influence economic activity. Undoubtedly, the most serious changes were wrought by the (infamous) Atlantic slave trade. Although domestic slavery existed long before that period, the demands from the New World resulted in a pattern of trade from western and central Africa wholly or partly dominated by slaving during at least three centuries.

The impact of the slave trade on African political systems was complex, but three main points should be stressed. First, commerce in human beings became economically profitable for a large number of the continent's societies. Some raided their enemies to obtain slaves, others exchanged them for diverse products, and still others delivered them to the coast. Given the value embodied in slaves and the duration of the Atlantic (and the later Indian Ocean) trade, commerce in that single commodity made many rich. Those who controlled the trade, inevitably the chiefs or kings, had a ready supply of wealth with which they consolidated their power and extended their reach. Conversely, those who suffered slavery (either through raid, defeat or poverty) belonged to societies prone to economic weakness and disintegration.

Second, while it is impossible to minimize the horrors of such slave trade, it is important to stress that its effects on the continent were not as all-consuming as has sometimes been argued. Estimates suggest that around 10 to 13 million Africans were transported between the fifteenth and nineteenth centuries. Such numbers undoubtedly had a serious impact on those African societies that supplied most of the slaves. However, given a pattern of economic activity in which production was geared to assert power rather than promote growth, it is unclear how much long-term damage the trade inflicted. Furthermore, it is wrong to assume that the slave trade displaced all other commercial activity. Africans continued throughout the period to exchange goods (from salt to ivory or gold) with the rest of the world. Thus, the abolition of the slave trade had a differentiated impact on the various societies involved in it. Some undoubtedly collapsed from the lack of revenue, but others adapted readily by expanding the trade of other goods.

Third, the scale of the slave trade undoubtedly led to an increase in the level of sociopolitical disruption endured by Africans on the continent. Not only was there an incentive to obtain slaves during several centuries, thus prompting raiding and warring, but there was strong competition to control their supply to the coast. The demands of the trade brought about violence and cruelty on a scale greater than had hitherto been known. Furthermore, when the trade declined and was finally abolished, there was inevitably an increase in the number of slaves available to African rulers. This resulted in an expansion of the use of slavery for domestic production, thus affecting the ways in which the economy of some societies would develop in the nineteenth and twentieth centuries. Since the colonial powers were committed to the abolition of slavery, the colonial "peace" turned out to be problematic for some political systems in place.

Partly because of the impact of the abolition of the slave trade, but also for a host of internal factors, the nineteenth century proved a particularly chaotic period for many African societies. The transition to what the Europeans called "legitimate" commerce had differentiated effects on the continent, although the search for profitably tradable goods such as ivory put a premium on force and violence. The greater use of firearms only compounded the problem. A large section of East Africa suffered from the aftereffects of the *mfecane* (the aggressive northward migration of Ngoni peoples from Southern Africa), based as it was on military might and oppressive force. As a consequence ancient kingdoms from southern Mozambique to the Great Lakes regions either suffered or engaged in aggressive military action.

As trade from the Indian Ocean increased steadily throughout the century, distinct communities reacted differently. The kingdom of Bunyoro, for example, was perhaps the chief example of a centralized political structure that maximized its opportunities from trade and conflict. Buganda, by contrast, was unable to resist the force of such commercial and military intrusion and disintegrated in the nineteenth century. Whatever the case, the movement of population and developing commerce provided challenges that some could meet and others could not. While the development of mining, for instance, would benefit a number of Africans in the long term, reliance on the trade of slaves or ivory ended abruptly as the "Scramble" for Africa gathered momentum.

In West Africa, the most important event probably was the wave of jihads that swept the northern part of the region in the first part of the nineteenth century. Of these, the 1804 jihad led by Usuman dan Fodio (1754–1817) was undoubtedly the most consequential, as it united Hausaland into the Sokoto Caliphate and provided a highly sophisticated and efficient political structure for the region which was congenial to economic development. The Western savannah also experienced other, less successful, jihads but the long-term consequence of these movements was to turn the greater part of West Africa (with the exception of the coastal areas) into comparatively modern, centralized states well able to negotiate on a level of equality with the European "explorers" who arrived in greater numbers as the century progressed.

In southern Africa the disruptive influence of the Boers' trek northward and the Ngoni's aggression on their neighbors provided opportunities for local modernizing chiefs to transform their fledging political community into viable kingdoms. The Tswana, Swazi, and Sotho peoples came to be aggregated into greater political entities due in large measure to the political acumen of some of their leaders. Moshoeshoe, originally one of many minor Sotho chiefs, eventually brought together a large proportion of his nation and, through a combination of shrewd diplomacy and enlightened politics, created and defended the kingdom of Lesotho. His use of missionaries both as legitimating European influence and as intermediaries with the outside world eventually ensured that his realm came under British protection and thus escaped Boer conquest.

There were obviously wide variations in the manner in which nineteenth century African societies met the acute internal and external challenges that faced them. Broadly, however, it can be argued that political trends during that period were toward centralization and modernization. True, many areas of central and southern Africa suffered grievously either from the consequences of violence (in what is today the Congo and Angola region) or disease (particularly virulent in eastern Africa). But it would be wrong to portray the nineteenth century, as often it was done during the colonial period, as a time of universal savagery and dereliction. In every part of the continent there were successful and thriving societies that had successfully managed the transition from slave trading and adapted to the new demands of the increasingly present world economy.

It is customary to distinguish nineteenth-century Africa as being politically composed of state and stateless peoples—that is, to make a distinction between those societies in which patterns of authority were centralized and structured and those that were diffuse and informal. Although this contrast can easily become reductive, it does have explanatory merit as there was

indeed a clear difference between these two types of political communities. In Nigeria, for example, there could be no greater contrast than between the Sokoto Caliphate and the Igbo peoples of the coastal areas. The one was in every respect a highly developed state structure, complete with bureaucracy and armed forces, presiding over the destiny of a large population and controlling a vast economy. The others were small-scale village based communities, where politics remained tied to kinship and where the power of the local chief, *primus inter pares*, was sanctioned by a council of elders, reflecting as it did the primacy of older adults over the young.

Clear as this distinction is in terms of patterns of authority, it would be wrong to deduce from it that economic dynamism and innovation was the preserve of the former while the latter were stagnant, autarkic, and "traditional" political communities. The reality was indeed far from this cliché so favored by the Europeans, who loved the pomp and pageantry of the West African emirates. Indeed, in many instances it was the stateless peoples who proved most deft at adapting to the developing trade with European traders and most resilient in the face of the increasingly hostile imperial challenge. This should come as no surprise given their active involvement in procuring and trading slaves in the three previous centuries. Moreover, these communities had long been involved in regional, and even long distance, commerce much before their northern neighbors had consolidated into powerful Islamic states. Finally, it was precisely these societies that proved to be the most difficult to "pacify" after the onslaught of colonial conquest.

Thus, contrary to colonial myth, African societies in the nineteenth century were evolving quickly. It was the suddenness, arbitrariness, and violence of the "Scramble" that introduced into the political equation a number of new and unpredictable variables to which, ultimately, most of these communities could find no satisfactory answer. Indeed, the European will to conquer could scarcely have been anticipated by Africans based on their previous experience. Nor could it have been achieved without the introduction of modern weapons, of which the Maxim gun was the key.

The colonial conquest of the continent had three important consequences for the evolution of African political systems. First, it created boundaries around given territories regardless of existing historical and sociopolitical realities. At a stroke it cut across or reordered precolonial political structures. Second, it established a colonial state, the main attributes of which were that it was coercive, bureaucratic, and unaccountable to the people over whom it presumed to rule. Third, it facilitated the development of an imperial economy in which the colonies were simultaneously open to the world capitalist system and beholden to the economic requirements of the metropolis.

African Political Systems, Historical and Contemporary

Understanding politics in contemporary Africa demands that we identify the nature of the changes—but also, and crucially, the continuities—between the pre- and postcolonial periods. It has long been argued that the colonization of the continent resulted in the wholesale destruction of precolonial African political structures and the restructuring of power around the norms and practices of the bureaucratic colonial political order. What we now know of the history of post-colonial Africa suggests that such an interpretation was quite simply erroneous. It is not just that the political practices to be observed in contemporary Africa belie the simplistic view that independence made possible the Westernization of political systems; it is also that the assessment of the true impact of colonial rule was misjudged.

The colonial powers had neither the ambition nor the means to establish in Africa working models of their own political institutions. Nor, paradoxically, were they as zealous as they proclaimed to be in eradicating precolonial political structures. In simple terms, the imperial rulers administered their colonies as cheaply and effectively as they could. Although different colonial powers had distinct political traditions—from Britain's parliamentary conventions to Portugal's authoritarianism—they went about the business of managing the colonies in surprisingly similar fashion. Where it was possible to use African political systems, as in most of Muslim West Africa, they did so. Where it was necessary to impose some hierarchical structure on stateless societies, as in the coastal areas of that same region, they appointed colonial chiefs. In practice, therefore, the behavior of the local colonial administrator (British district officer, French *commandant de cercle* or Portuguese *chefe de posto*) had broadly similar consequences for the political development of the colonies.

Despite the admittedly massive differences between the political institutions inherited by the nationalists after decolonization, there has been a quite remarkable convergence in the political evolution of independent Africa. Although in the first long decade and a half (1960–1975) after independence it seemed that the colonial legacy had enabled the establishment of self-standing Western political institutions in Africa, the economic crisis unleashed in the 1970s by the sharp increase in oil prices revealed that this analysis of the patterns of authority and power on the continent had been superficial. Put very simply, what that crisis made

manifest is the extent to which nationalist euphoria had masked the continuities between the pre- and postcolonial eras. Contemporary politics on the continent had to be analyzed in greater historical depth.

What had in fact occurred is what is best described as the Africanization of politics—that is, the process by which the new African rulers redesigned the political structures inherited at independence, reshaped their architecture and redefined the parameters guiding political action. Although the modalities of such Africanization differed substantially according to the nature of the political system put in place after decolonization, what is significant for political analysis are the evident similarities. Indeed, the widespread notion that the colonial heritage, as well as the vagaries of decolonization, were decisive for the formation of the postcolonial political "order" turned out to have been vastly exaggerated. In retrospect, what is striking is that the Africanization of politics had similar systemic effects everywhere.

In essence, what took place amounted to the overlapping of two apparently discordant political logics. On the one hand, there was an ostensible strengthening of the political institutions as they emerged out of the decolonization process, whether peaceful or violent. On the other, there developed a new disposition of political priorities that was frequently at odds with the newly constructed formal structures. The supposed democratic and pluralist organs of political representation set up in most African countries at independence rapidly gave way to the one-party state: the development of a single, not plural, political logic.

In retrospect, what became clearer over time is that there was a more important political process at work than the narrowing of formal politics at the top. Indeed, the Africanization of politics entailed the emergence of neopatrimonialism, the central characteristic of which is the resort to personalized and vertical ties of solidarity as the backbone of the operative political system. The concept of neopatrimonialism is used here to refer to the juxtaposition of an apparently "traditional" patrimonial political logic and "modern" formal state institutions derived from the Western experience. The reasons why the one-party state became the norm in Africa is not, as has been widely argued, primarily because postcolonial governance required cohesion and unity—which it obviously did. It is fundamentally because politics at independence became patrimonial rather than institutionalized. What is meant is that, despite their Western appearance, African political systems operated differently. At the core of the formal political order there developed a logic of patronage which relied almost entirely on networks of personalized and vertical relations between rulers and ruled, elite and populace. The stuff of politics became more and more informal.

The Africanization of politics thus entailed the overriding dominance of a system that bore little relation to that defined by the tenets of the constitutional order. The one-party state was thus nothing more than the logical evolution of the reshaping of the political structure inherited at independence. In a neopatrimonial system, political accountability rested on the extent to which the patrons were able both to influence and meet the expectations of their followers according to well-established norms of reciprocity. The quest for political legitimacy thus required the fulfillment of particularistic obligations that had nothing to do with the emergence of a public sphere transcending infranational identities. Elections, the measure of accountability in Western polities, became in Africa one of the many instruments of factional mobilization.

While most political leaders at independence were new rather than "traditional" elites, the parameters of the neopatrimonial system that they put in place owed a great deal to what might be called "traditional" principles of legitimacy. Among those, the most significant had to do with a system of accountability in which the legitimacy of political leaders was perceived by all (from top to bottom) to rest on their ability to provide for their own personal constituents. Political representation, in other words, was seen to occur when patrons met their obligations in respect of their clients.

Although such a neopatrimonial system worked well in many countries after independence, it was inherently unstable. First, the situation of relative economic well being—useful colonial assets and stable export prices— was shattered by the world economic crisis in the 1970s. As revenues declined and debt increased, African patrons began to run out of means. In a situation where the search for resources became ever more difficult, political competition increased. Since in the African neopatrimonial system access to governmental assets is paramount, struggles for power intensified and violence rose.

Second, the neopatrimonial system as it developed in postcolonial Africa was essentially inimical to economic development as it took place in the West, or later in Asia. This is because it failed to foster, and in many ways totally undermined, economic growth—the prime basis for sustainable development. Political legitimacy was based on the maintenance of a situation in which patrons had simultaneously to uphold the image of substance that their station required and to feed the networks on which their position depended. Thus, they could scarcely defer consumption and expenditure for the longer-term purpose of "national" economic growth. For this reason, African states as well as entrepreneurs rarely invested in economically productive activities.

African political systems today exhibit three intriguing characteristics that deserve careful analysis, if only because they go against prevailing expectations. They are increasingly informal, they appear to "retraditionalize," and they have failed to spur sustained economic development.

The first trend—the apparent informalization of contemporary African politics—is best explained by reference to the notion of identity and the relation between the individual and his or her community. Western political systems rest on the assumption that citizens are discrete, autonomous, and self-referential individuals who cast their votes according to overtly political criteria. The reality in Africa is different: the individual cannot be conceived outside of the community from which he or she hails, however geographically distant he or she may be from it. The political system thus operates according to criteria that embody this core "communal" dimension. The individual is less the self-conscious citizen than someone whose behavior accords to the multiregistered (and sometimes contradictory) logics that guide his or her place within the community. These belong essentially to the realm of the informal, meaning here only that they are not encompassed within the legal and constitutional order that is the official political norm in all African countries.

The manner in which power is understood and exercised helps to explain why politics in contemporary Africa diverges from that of the West. Briefly, the state in Africa is not much more than a relatively vacuous shell, useful insofar as it permits the control of the resources it commands but politically feeble because it is neither institutionalized nor functionally differentiated from society. Similarly, there is no self-standing civil society because vertical ties remain infinitely more significant than horizontal (professional or functional) links. Finally, African political elites behave according to the norms of political legitimation and representation inherent in the neopatrimonial system. They use their (official) position to fulfill their (unofficial) obligations to their clients and to meet the demands on which their power and standing as rulers rest.

The second paradox is that much of what is happening in contemporary Africa seems to reinforce the notion that the continent is moving backward, or that it is in some ways retraditionalizing. What is meant here is that what we see in Africa confounds expectations of modernization. Both the ways in which Africans appear to define themselves and the manner in which they behave fail to conform to what social scientists expect of modernization. This notion of retraditionalization, as it were, emphasizes the extent to which Africans function simultaneously on several different registers, from the most visibly modern to the most ostensibly traditional, in their everyday lives. The failure to understand the apparently contradictory nature of politics in Africa is itself very largely the result of a Western analytical convention that tends to assume a dichotomy between the realms of the modern and of the traditional. The African elites, however, operate in a world that combines both—a world congruent with the beliefs of the rest of the population. One example will illustrate the point. Based on empirical evidence, it is clear that what is apparently illegal (for example, smuggling or the embezzlement of state funds) is often seen as legitimate by those who benefit from it. In other words, neopatrimonial political accountability allows for actions that in the West would be seen as corrupt.

The third, and final, question about Africa's path to modernization is the absence of development. The evidence is disquieting. Although there were in the early 1960s a number of African countries (like Zambia) with a gross domestic product per capita equal to some of their Asian counterparts (like South Korea), the situation today is radically different. The erstwhile Asian Tigers have surged ahead while even the most prosperous African states (Gabon, Nigeria, or Côte d'Ivoire) have failed to achieve anything like sustainable economic growth. If the external constraints—falling world prices, debt, and structural adjustment—that have constrained Africa's economies are clear enough, they cannot in and of themselves account for such disparities in development.

It is becoming more obvious, therefore, that the very organization of African political systems must itself be considered to be (at least) partly responsible for this state of affairs. On reflection this is not surprising. Neopatrimonialism rests on notions of political legitimacy that favor the redistribution of resources from patrons to their clients. If the principal source of revenues is the export of primary or agricultural products, if insufficient attention is devoted by government to the development of such exports, and if the world prices for these commodities tend over time to decrease, then income falls. In the absence of coherent policies to generate growth from other economic assets, resources diminish overall. External borrowing obviates such shortfalls in the immediate future, but the burden of debt soon cripples the economy. This, with only a few notable exceptions like Botswana, is what has happened everywhere in Africa.

Indeed, neopatrimonialism may well have reached its limits or, rather, it may now have been changed into a political economy of disorder. Where the search for short-term economic gain is paramount, political leaders find that their legitimacy as "big men" is conditional upon their ability to obtain resources by any and all means necessary. The informal sector has always been of singular importance in Africa. There are now indications that it may well be the exploitation of the resources engendered by disorder (corruption, civil strife, war, smuggling, dealing in illegal substances) that have become the more substantial marketable activities available. Thus, the primacy of communitarian and clientelistic political imperatives, which may make good sense at the microlevel of individuals and communities, leads assuredly to massive economic inefficiency and, possibly, to terminal damage at the national level. For this reason, we are likely to witness an increase in informal practices, both domestically and internationally. This will obviously impinge strongly on the future evolution of African political systems.

PATRICK CHABAL

See also: **Colonial European Administrations: Comparative Survey; Colonialism: Impact on African Societies; Community in African Society; Democracy: Postcolonial; Identity, Political; Law and the Legal System: Postcolonial Africa; Organization of African Unity (OAU) and Pan-Africanism; Political Élites and Patronage: Postcolonial Africa Political Parties and One-Party States.**

Further Reading

Austen, Richard. *African Economic History*. London: James Currey, 1987.

Bates, Robert. *Markets and States in Tropical Africa*. Berkeley and Los Angeles: University of California Press, 1981.

Callaghy, Thomas. *The State-Society Struggle*. New York: Columbia University Press, 1984.

The Cambridge History of Africa, 8 vols. Cambridge: Cambridge University Press, 1975–1986.

Chabal, Patrick, *Power in Africa: An Essay in Political Interpretation*. Basingstoke, England: Macmillan, 1994.

———. (ed.). *Political Domination in Africa: Reflections on the Limits of Power*. Cambridge: Cambridge University Press, 1986.

Chabal, Patrick, and Jean-Pascal Daloz. *Africa Works: Disorder as Political Instrument*. Oxford: James Currey, 1999.

Clapham, Christopher. *Africa and the International System: The Politics of State Survival*, Cambridge: Cambridge University Press.

Curtin, Philip. *Economic Change in Precolonial Africa*. Madison: University of Wisconsin Press, 1975.

Fieldhouse, David. *Black Africa, 1945–1980*. London: Allen and Unwin, 1986.

Iliffe, John. *Africans: The History of a Continent*. Cambridge: Cambridge University Press, 1995.

Mudimbe, Valentin. *The Invention of Africa*. Bloomington: Indiana University Press, 1988.

UENSCO General History of Africa, 8 vols. London: Heinemann, 1981–1993.

Wilks, Ivor. *Asante in the Nineteenth Century*. Cambridge: Cambridge University Press, 1975.

Young, Cawford. *The African Colonial State in Perspective*. New Haven, Conn.: Yale University Press, 1994.

Population and Demography

The demography of Africa in precolonial times remains largely unknown. Since the pioneering study of

William Brass and colleagues (1968), the detail and scope of the demographic data available has improved markedly across the continent. Independence granted new states opportunities to more closely examine population issues in national development planning. Specialized demographic surveys were initiated in several countries in the 1970s, while others participated in the World Fertility Survey in the early 1980s. Large, centrally funded programs (such as those by the World Bank) continue to dominate data collection.

Currently, Africa's population and demography broadly can be characterized by uneven population distributions, rapid population growths, and high rates of population mobility. Africa's population reached over 803 million by 2000, and 1.5 billion by 2025. The population structure is youthful, with a "bottom-heavy" population pyramid. Approximately 45 per cent of the continent's population was under the age of 15, while only about 3 per cent was over 64 (Sadik 1990). This has wide implications for health care, education, and employment.

Africa's population is also characterized by high fertility and high mortality, especially among infants and mothers. The total fertility rate is the average number of children a woman will bear during her reproductive years, usually between the ages of 15 and 49. Women in Africa on average give birth to six children over this period of their lives. Explaining Africa's high fertility is difficult, but it reflects various influences including attitudes toward children, infant mortality patterns, marriage customs, and family planning. However, there is considerable variation by region, socioeconomic status, and rural or urban place of residence. For instance, Doenges and Newman (1989) identified a belt of markedly lower fertility rates in central Africa stretching from southwest Sudan through the Central Africa Republic into Zaire.

Other zones of low fertility, or what has been termed "impaired fertility," have high incidences of gynecological disorders and pelvic inflammatory diseases such as gonorrhea, syphilis, and schistosomiasis. African children also have the world's lowest life expectancy at birth, about 49 years for boys and 52 years for girls. With the AIDS epidemic in Africa still in its infancy, its implications for Africa's demographic future is debatable. Infection with HIV (the virus that causes AIDS) has brought about zero or even negative population growth rates in many African countries. AIDS is the number one cause of death in Africa, and in Botswana, Lesotho, Namibia, South Africa, Swaziland, Zambia, and Zimbabwe, 20 per cent of the population or higher is infected with HIV (Stephenson 2000). To date, Africa is affected by two distinct strains of the HIV virus: HIV-1 and HIV-2. HIV-1 is particularly concentrated in central Africa (Uganda,

Rwanda, eastern Zaire, northwest Tanzania, and the Lower Conga River basin), while HIV-2 is found primarily in West Africa, especially in Mali, Côte d'Ivoire, and Guinea-Bissau. The two strains have different demographic effects. HIV-2 affects older age cohorts, while HIV-1 is most prevalent among those aged 15 to 49, with young women aged 15 to 20 having the very highest rates of infectivity, so more seriously impacts birthrates and infant survival.

Birth and death rates are higher in Africa than in any other region of the world. This places most African countries in the second stage of the demographic transition model, a "high expanding stage," which signifies declining death rates but consistently high birthrates. If Africa follows the European countries' four demographic stages associated with their level of economic development, then the continent will witness substantially falling birthrates. However, in some regions of Africa, such as Sub-Saharan Africa, death rates have been rising, primarily from AIDS (Brown and Halweil 1999).

A crude death rate in Africa of 13 per thousand in 1990 remained high, especially in eastern, western, and central Africa. Mortality levels in Africa have declined substantially over the years, converging toward the levels associated with more developed countries. This is attributed to improvements in health, sanitation, and nutrition standards, massive vaccination campaigns against measles, small pox, and other diseases, and increased efforts on the part of the World Health Organization and the International Red Cross. The rate of infant mortality (infant deaths between birth and age one) reached 96 deaths per thousand in 1990. This rate is relatively high compared to the average rate of 10 per 1,000 in more developed countries. Malnutrition, disease, and poverty are the most common causes of infant and child (between birth and the age of five) mortality.

Contemporary population distributions reflect disparate natural environments and historical processes of development. For example, the slave trade depleted regions such as parts of West Africa's Middle Belt, while other regions such as Nigeria's Jos Plateau served as defensive refuges from the slave trade and became more densely populated as a result (Stock 1995). While little is known of precolonial population distribution, the imposition of colonial rule, which visibly marked the landscape with new cities, administrative and trade centers, certainly reshaped Africa's population distribution.

Currently, Africa is characterized by uneven population distributions. The population of Africa is still predominantly rural. Overall, less than one-third of the population resides in urban centers, while in some countries, such as Rwanda, 94 per cent of the population of 7.9 million live in the rural areas. Population densities also vary widely, ranging from 273 people per square kilometers in Rwanda to 29 people per square kilometer in Zimbabwe. Areas of high or low population density seldom, if ever, correspond to national units. For instance, one major zone of dense settlement is the West African coastal belt stretching from Dakar, Senegal to Libreville, Gabon, while the arid-semiarid region of southwestern Africa represents a sparsely population region. These spatial distributions coincide with various environmental and developmental issues (urbanization levels, industrialization, and agricultural development), and sociopolitical characteristics (oppressive regimes, ethnic disputes, and resettlement schemes). For example, the West African coastal strip contains most of the region's urban, economic, and political centers. These uneven population distributions are also evident on small scales. For example, in Tanzania, the sparsely settled, environmentally hazardous central region is surrounded by dense population clusters. These clusters exist on the fertile slopes of Mount Kilimanjaro in the north, on the shores of Lake Victoria in the northwest, on the shores of Lake Malawi in the southwest, and in the economic center of Dar-es-Salaam on the east coast. Government policy on resettling people into cooperative, nucleated settlements (Ujamaa villages) has also had its impact.

Population growth is a function of birth or fertility, mortality, and net migration. In Africa, migration data is often difficult to track, so birth, fertility, and mortality rates are used primarily to gauge net changes in population. With a growth rate of 3 per cent per year, population is growing faster in Africa than any other region in the world, and it almost doubles the world average of 1.6 per cent. A 3 per cent annual rate of growth can result in a country doubling its population in just over 23 years. Ethiopia and Nigeria are predicted to attain the (particularly high) population growth rates of 177 per cent and 124 per cent, respectively (United Nations 1998). Africa's rapid population growth rate is often linked with various problems, including damage to ecosystems or food shortages. However, it is debatable whether population growth is the primary cause of these problems.

Africa's rapid population growth stems from high fertility, with an average birthrate of 43 per thousand and relatively high but declining mortality over the past 30 years, about 13 per thousand in 1990 (Sadik 1990). Regional differences persist, with high rates of population growth in western and eastern Africa (3.3 and 3.2 per cent, respectively), and relatively low rates in central Africa (2 per cent in 1990). Intraregional, intracountry, and rural-urban differences in growth rates are substantial. For instance, in northern African states, population growth rates ranged from 2.3 per cent in Libya to 3.1 per cent in Algeria in 1990

(Joffe 1992). Africa has one of the lowest proportions of its population living in urban areas (34 per cent in 1990) but the rate of growth of the urban population is by far the highest among the regions of the world (5 per cent in 1990). This rapid urban growth results from high natural increase combined with accelerated in-migration to towns. Africa's rural population has been increasingly steadily at about 2 per cent per year, making it the fastest growing of all the world regions except South Asia.

Oral history indicates that Africans have been highly mobile from early times. Major large-scale migrations have occurred over several centuries, including the Bantu colonization of the southern half of the continent over five millennia, and the exodus of Ndebele from South Africa to Zimbabwe in the mid-nineteenth century. Ancient local-scale circulations include pastoralists moving between seasonal pastures to access adequate water and fodder for their animals. Long-established migration streams can impact on modern population distributions. For example, since the fourteenth century reign of Emperor Mansa Musa of Mali, West African Muslims have been traveling to Mecca and other holy places of Islam. Many West Africans have settled permanently along the entire savanna corridor once followed by most pilgrims from Nigeria through Chad and Sudan to the Red Sea. The pilgrimage route has served as a cultural conduit along which innovations such as new crops, farming techniques, and architectural styles have spread, both eastward and westward. Pilgrims seldom completed the journey in less than three years, often worked along the way, and stayed in their own neighborhoods in the larger towns. This ancient overland pilgrimage exemplifies the complex relations among population movements, distributions, and growths.

Contemporary Africa continues to have high rates of mobility on various scales—regional, national, and international. While official statistics on migration are sketchy and sometimes deficient, Africa is estimated to contain about half of the world's total international migrants (Ricca 1989). Several theories aim to explain Africa's high rates of mobility, and the resultant differential effects on source areas and destination areas. Two prominent forms of migration include flow of labor migrants to colonial (then postcolonial) centers of economic development and flight of refugees from politically or ecologically distressed areas. In central Africa, oil in Gabon and the copper and diamond mines of Zaire are major attractions, while in southern Africa, Zambia's copper and the economic force of South Africa (particularly the Witwatersrand region) have been the major "pull" factors. Ecological changes occurring because of colonial policies also affected local population movements. Diseases as well as people migrated along the transportation corridors, creating environments where disease vectors could proliferate.

Africa has the largest concentration of refugees in the world. The volume has continued to grow over the past four decades, and the vast majority of these refugees are women and children. The flow of refugees has been very uneven, both spatially and temporarily, but the current refugee crisis is especially problematic for countries such as Malawi, Mozambique, Sudan, Guinea, Ethiopia, Kenya, Zaire, Tanzania, and Burundi. For instance, the estimated one million Mozambican refugees in Malawi in 1992 equaled one-fifteenth of Mozambique's population and one-eighth of Malawi's. Difficulties in measuring actual numbers of refugees are compounded by competing definitions of what a refugee is. Refugees can escape to safe havens within or outside of their country of origin for a wide range of reasons including religious, ethnic, or political persecution; economic deprivation and famine; external aggression or occupation, or foreign domination.

CAMILLA COCKERTON

Further Reading

Brass, William, Ansley J. Coale, Paul Demeny, Don F. Heisel, Frank Loramer, Anatole Romaniuk, and Etienne Van de Walle. *The Demography of Tropical Africa*. Princeton, N.J.: Princeton University Press, 1968.

Brown, Lester R., and Brian Halweil. "Breaking Out or Breaking Down." *World Watch* 12, no. 5 (1999): 20–25.

Doenges, C., and J. Newman. "Impaired Fertility in Tropical Africa." *Geographical Review* 79, no. 1 (1989): 99–111.

Joffe, George. "The Changing Geography of North Africa: Development, Migration and the Demographic Time Bomb." In *The Changing Geography of Africa and the Middle East*, London: Routledge, 1992.

Ricca, S. *International Migration in Africa: Legal and Administrative Aspects*. Geneva: International Labor Office, 1989.

Sadik, N. *The State of World Population 1989, Investing in Women: The Focus of the 90s*, New York: UNFPA, 1990.

Stephenson, Joan. "Apocalypse Now: HIV/AIDS in Africa Exceeds the Experts' Worst Predictions." *Journal of the American Medical Association* 284, no. 5 (2000): 556–560.

Stock, Robert. *Africa South of the Sahara: A Geographical Interpretation*, New York: Guilford Press, 1995.

United Nations, *Demographic Yearbook*, New York: Department of Economic and Social Affairs, Statistical Office, United Nations, annually.

Port Harcourt

A British colonial creation, Port Harcourt was established on the Niger delta in Nigeria in 1913 to serve European commercial, administrative, and industrial needs. Its origins are rooted in the 1909 discovery of coal in the Udi Hills, near Enugu. Although the name Port Harcourt was said to have been given after a British Marine Department navigator, Mr D. L. Harcourt, who was allocated land in the area in 1911, many believed that the town was named after Lewis Harcourt (later Viscount Harcourt) who served as secretary of state for the colonies at the time.

The city was organized and administered according to European models, and by European personnel. It was the British Railway Department that built the port and the city, and laid the solid foundation that gives the town the distinction of being one of West Africa's few well-planned cities. The residential areas, which are separated from the industrial and commercial areas, are the government reserved area, accommodating the city's expatriates and the Nigerian upper class; the section for the middle-class population; and some squatter settlements. Accommodation has remained a serious problem in the city.

Port Harcourt was populated primarily by culturally diverse rural immigrants. Apart from the Ijo, Efik, and Ibibio, the initial immigrants that flooded the city were the Igbo. Other immigrants were the Hausa, Yoruba, and Edo of Nigeria. There were also Europeans, Americans, and Asians. The city witnessed a rapid increase in population because of its commercial and industrial potentials. Today the city's population is estimated at 288,900.

Port Harcourt's population was predominantly working-class, made up of traders of all categories—market women, venders in market stalls, and the larger importers and contractors who competed fiercely with foreign firms. There were three major markets in the city, but the largest and most popular was the Port Harcourt Main Market, located at the center of the town.

Since it was established, Port Harcourt has played a significant economic role in Nigeria because of its connection to the railway, the harbor, the airport, and the oil industry. A major port expansion was completed in 1960, with eight berths and seven transit sheds. Inland water services were provided between the city and some major riverine communities. By 1965, Port Harcourt was the site of the second largest harbor in Nigeria, serving as the principal distribution point for eastern and parts of northern Nigeria's exports and imports.

The city is also the site of the great eastern terminus of the Nigerian Railway. The Eastern Railway line, which passed through Enugu in 1916 and the northern cities of Makurdi, Jos, and Kaduna in the 1920s, linked the two regions and helped in the transportation of coal from Enugu, palm produce from the Igbo hinterland, and groundnuts and other products from the north to the terminus and the port. In 1969, a link line to the NNPC Refinery at Alesa-Eleme was constructed to move petroleum products to other parts of the country.

Today the city has one of the three major international airports in the country, the Port Harcourt International Airport, Omagwa, commissioned in 1979. Since opening it has acted as a gateway for aircraft billed to central, eastern, and southern Africa in addition to several parts of Europe, including Rome, Amsterdam, and London. The airport is the second busiest airport in Nigeria.

A major factor in the economic importance of Port Harcourt was the discovery of oil at nearby Oloibiri in 1956 by Shell–British Petroleum. In 1958, the company transferred its African headquarters from Owerri to Port Harcourt, and by 1963, nine oil and natural gas fields had been established. The development of the industry led to advent of more oil marketing companies in Port Harcourt, such as Mobil, Texaco, African Petroleum, Total, Agip, National, Unipetrol, and Independent. Consequently, the city witnessed an industrial upsurge. The Trans-Amadi industrial estate, built after the 1957 Saville Report, provided industrial plots that the government leased out to expatriate and indigenous investors as an incentive. A tire plant, an aluminum sheet factory, a glass industry, a cement paints industry, and an enamelware factory were in operation by the early 1960s, in addition to already established concerns such as the Nigerian Tobacco Company and breweries. In 1984, the first gas recycling plant was established at nearby Obrikom/Omoku.

Port Harcourt has also played an important role in the field of trade and commerce. With the establishment of the city, European merchants and mercantile firms penetrated the hinterland and flooded the local markets with their merchandise. The railway, harbor, and airport facilitated movement of people and goods. The solid commercial foundation laid by the early immigrants into the city has made Port Harcourt the scene of intense commercial activity, a situation that continues today.

The colonial government that established Port Harcourt was so preoccupied with its own economic interests that it paid little or no attention to the provision of social facilities and services. The city did not have a secondary school until 1932, when Rev. L. R. Potts-Johnson established the Enitonna High school, a coeducational, nondenominational institution. Between 1942 and 1962, seven secondary schools and one industrial training school were established in Port Harcourt. In 1975 the University College of Port Harcourt, which was affiliated with the University of Lagos, was established. It was upgraded to a full university, the University of Port Harcourt, in 1977. In 1980, the first technical university in Nigeria, the Rivers State University of Science and Technology, was established at Port Harcourt by the state government.

Investments were made also in the field of health. The Port Harcourt General Hospital, established in 1916, has since been improved upon with modern structures, equipment, and facilities to meet the health demand of the city's teeming population. The Port Harcourt School of Nursing was commissioned in November 1970, and the School of Midwifery was established in March 1972. In October 1974, the School of Health Technology–Port Harcourt came into existence. All these facilities have helped to improve the health condition of the city's population.

Port Harcourt's economic importance has placed the city at the center of both the intra- and interregional politics and conflicts that have characterized recent Nigerian history. The question of who controls Port Harcourt, given its oil economy and position as a major national and regional economic center, has been a crucial issue in colonial and postcolonial Nigerian politics. At the city's inception, political resources were monopolized by the European minority. The Igbo of Eastern Nigeria took over between the mid-1940s and the outbreak of the civil war. Their numerical and financial strength placed them at a vantage to monopolize seats in the municipal, regional, and federal governments, and therefore determined who would represent the interests of Port Harcourt residents. Port Harcourt has had a role of special significance in the political development of the Igbo. The city housed the administrative headquarters of the Igbo State Union, which was transferred from Lagos; it was their economic center, and the residence for a large number of Igboland's most prosperous and influential citizens. Port Harcourt adequately served the interests of the Igbo entrepreneurs because it gave them direct access to the sea for their waterborne international commerce.

Igbo hegemony over Port Harcourt was challenged by the Ijo separatists, who in 1958 presented a case before the Willink Commission for the creation of a Rivers State with Port Harcourt as its capital and with the exclusion of the Igbo. Their desire was met at the eve of the Nigerian civil war, when the federal military government, under the States Creation Decree of May 27, 1967, created twelve states that included Rivers State (capital: Port Harcourt) and East Central State (capital: Enugu; the only Igbo state). It is widely believed that the oil politics and petroleum diplomacy that centered around Port Harcourt were instrumental in the outbreak of the civil war.

The postwar reconciliation between the Rivers and East Central States, especially as regards the issue of "abandoned property," was embedded in Port Harcourt politics. The Igbo claimed they owned about 92 per cent of buildings in Port Harcourt. They were denied access to these properties until November 1971, when the Rivers State government released a mere 1,000 "abandoned" houses to their Igbo owners.

The political focus has shifted to an intrastate issue between the Ikwerre-dominated upland people and the

Okrika-dominated riverine population. Port Harcourt is not only the capital city of Rivers State but also the only city there. The Ikwerre called for a Port Harcourt state that would exclude the Okrika, which came to pass in 1997, when Bayelsa state was created out of Rivers State.

GLORIA IFEOMA CHUKU

See also: **Nigeria: Biafran Secession and Civil War, 1967–1970; Nigeria: Lugard, Administration and "Indirect Rule."**

Further Reading

Alagoa, E. J., and T. N. Tamuno (eds.). *Land and People of Nigeria: Rivers State*. Port Harcourt, Nigeria: Riverside Communications, 1989.

Etuk, Effiong M. *This Is Port Harcourt: A Comprehensive Survey of Port Harcourt from the Blight of Biafra Including Bonny etc.*, 1st ed. Port Harcourt, Nigeria: Goodwill, 1961.

Ogionwo, W. *The City of Port Harcourt: A Symposium on Its Growth and Development*. Ibadan, Nigeria: Heinemann, 1979.

Tamuno, Tekena N. "Patriotism and Statism in the Rivers State, Nigeria." *Journal of Royal African Affairs* 71, no. 284 (1972): 264–281.

Wolpe, Howard. "Port Harcourt: Ibo Politics in Microcosm." In *Nigeria: Modernization and the Politics of Communalism*, edited by R. Melson and Howard Wolpe. East Lansing: Michigan State University Press, 1971.

———. *Urban Politics in Nigeria: A Study of Port Harcourt*. Berkeley and Los Angeles: University of California Press, 1974.

Portugal: Exploration and Trade in the Fifteenth Century

When Portugal commenced its voyages of exploration down the African coast during the fifteenth century it had already freed itself from Muslim rule. At that time the economic reward from exploration and finding a direct sea route to the east were attractive. The area beyond Portugal offered richer fishing opportunities. The Portuguese had an appetite for gold, which had been reaching Mediterranean ports through trans-Saharan trade. Portugal employed technological innovations available at the time to make the voyages possible. Innovations in navigation and sailing, and improvements in navigational tools like the compass, astrolabe, and quadrant were significant. The caravel also allowed fast coastal and shallow water travel.

Portuguese expansion in Africa dates back to 1415 and the capture of the thriving Muslim city of Ceuta on the Moroccan coast. From the North African coast, the Portuguese acquired valuable information on trans-Saharan trade, and the prospect of outflanking the Muslim merchants and trading directly with the Africans on the coast proved attractive to Portuguese merchants. During their voyages down the African coast, the Portuguese used the Atlantic islands as strategic and forward-looking positions. In 1420 the Portuguese settled at Madeira and also began colonizing the Azores, which they had reached in the 1340s. Sugar cane planted in the Madeira from the middle of the fifteenth century brought prosperity to the island. Sugar came to dominate the Canaries, and by 1460 the Cape Verde islands had been colonized.

The organized Portuguese exploration down the African coast under the patronage of Prince Henry the Navigator moved slowly. The Portuguese reached Madeira in 1418 and passed the reefs of Cape Bojador in 1434. Arguin was reached in 1443, and two years later the Portuguese built a fort there in the hope of diverting some of the inland African trade between Mali and Morocco, but this proved a failure. By 1444–1445, the Portuguese had passed beyond the desert and reached more fertile areas, where the population was predominantly black. Although Portugal failed to develop the inland trade, it started to capture Africans on the coast.

In 1441, Antam Goncalvez captured a few slaves and took them to Portugal. This violent capture of Africans later turned into regular trade between Africans and Europeans. By 1460, the Portuguese had reached the area of Sierra Leone. Between 1460 and 1469 the Portuguese colonized and developed Cape Verde into a base for holding slaves as well as a trading base for the adjacent mainland of the Upper Guinea Coast. A number of Portuguese settled on the upper Guinea coast to trade. They took African wives and entered into alliances with local rulers and traders. This led to the creation of a new society of private European and mixed-race traders living with Africans and known as Lacandos. Official and unofficial Portuguese policy toward the region was focused on reducing the power of African rulers and maintaining a system of order needed for the flourishing of peaceful trade.

In 1469, a merchant from Lisbon named Fernao Gomes was given a five-year monopoly of the trade beyond Cape Verde, on the condition that he explord a hundred leagues of coastline each year. In 1471 two of Gomes's captains reached the gold-rich area of the Gold Coast. The availability of gold fulfilled in part the Portuguese aim for exploration, and when Gomes's contract expired, King John I of Portugal took direct control of the work of exploration.

In December 1481, the Portuguese crown sent Don Diego d'Azambuja to build a castle in El Mina on the Gold Coast. Despite the opposition from the local chief, the castle was constructed. The castle was the first true European building on the coast designed to protect Portuguese trade against other Europeans and to store gold and other trade goods for transportation to Europe. The gold trade in El Mina developed steadily, and from 1487 to 1489 an average of 8,000 ounces a year was shipped to Lisbon. From 1494 to 1496, the figure rose to 22,500 ounces.

The Portuguese had no commercial interest in the area between the Volta and Benin. They traded in slaves and pepper, but the pepper trade declined after the Portuguese reached India. The Portuguese sent many of the slaves to the Gold Coast, where they were used in mining activities. By 1475, the Portuguese had passed the equator and in 1483 Diego Cao reached the mouth of the Congo River. Here the Portuguese encountered a well-organized state where the ruler, Nzinga Nkuwu, shared rule with provincial and district chiefs. Nzinga Nkuwu sent an embassy to Portugal in 1490 that returned with technical help and missionaries. During this period there was a certain amount of cultural borrowing. In fact, Nzingu Nkuwu was baptized as Joéo I.

In 1490, the island of Sâo Tomé was colonized by Portuguese sugar planters who used a labor force composed of convicts and racial minorities. In 1487 Bartholomeo Dias rounded the Cape of Good Hope and on May 20, 1498 the Portuguese navigator Vasco da Gama arrived in Calicut, India, after a voyage of 9,500 miles from Lisbon. Gama stopped at some of the city-states on the East African coast, such as Mombasa and Malindi, but most of the trade goods the Portuguese had to offer were unsuitable for tropical trade.

Gama's successful voyage to India achieved the primary Portuguese objective of finding a sea route to the east, and after the direct contact with Asia, Africa became a secondary concern for the Portuguese. Portuguese interest in Africa was to be challenged by the European powers of Holland, England, and France. These Europeans did not respect the Treaty of Tordisellas (1494), which had divided the world between Portugal and Spain.

EDWARD REYNOLDS

Further Reading

Ajayi, J. F., and M. Crowder (eds.). *History of West Africa*, vol. 1, 3rd ed. London: Longmans, 1985.

Thornton, John. *Africa and Africans in the Making of the Atlantic World*. Cambridge: Cambridge University Press, 1998.

Vogt, John. *Portuguese Rule on the Gold Coast, 1469–1682*. Athens, Ga.: University of Georgia Press, 1979.

Walter, Rodney. *A History of the Upper Guinea Coast, 1545 to 1680*. Oxford: Oxford University Press, 1969.

Predynastic Egypt: *See* Egypt, Ancient: Predynastic Egypt and Nubia: Historical Outline.

Press: Northern Africa

The first printing press was brought to Egypt in 1798 as part of the arsenal of Napoleon's expeditionary force in Egypt. The French produced a newspaper, *Le courier de l'Egypte*, and a scientific journal, *La decade egyptienne*, for the instruction of the French troops. The press also printed proclamations addressed to the Egyptian nation for the purpose of political indoctrination. The brief French regime in Egypt, therefore, introduced some of the techniques characteristic of modern mass communication.

A printing press was resumed at Cairo in 1805, producing an official journal, *Jurnal al-Khidiwi*, in 1822. This journal was superseded by *al-Waqa'i' al-Misriyya* in 1828, which printed material for military personnel. It was discontinued in the 1850s, but reappeared in 1865 when the Egyptian ruler, Isma'il Pasha, began his reforms of Egyptian cultural institutions. The press became an instrument of public education, particularly in journals such as *Wadi al-Nil*, which was published by an official from the Bureau of Schools, and *Rawdat al-Madaris*, edited by Rifa'a Rafi' al-Tahtawi. In the 1870s privately owned journals were printed, such as *al-Ahram*, founded by the Taqla family of Syria in 1876.

Journalists led the cultural renaissance of nineteenth- and twentieth-century Egypt. The expansion of the press and educational institutions occurred simultaneously, in both cases influenced by European models. The result was the development of a more functional use of Arabic in place of the rhymed prose (*saj'*) of existing Arabic literature. The new literary form of the political essay was developed in Egypt by the leaders of the national parties that formed in opposition to British colonial rule. Mustafa Kamil and Ahmad Lutfi al-Sayyid edited the journals *al-Liwa'* and *al-Jarida*, representing the ideological positions of the *Watani* and *Umma* parties. The political essay was perfected by professional journalists in the interwar period, notably by Muhammad Husayn Haykal, 'Abbas Mahmud al-'Aqqad, and Ibrahim al-Mazini. Beside the anticolonial movement, journalists were involved in causes such as socialism and feminism, the latter beginning with the appearance of the journal *al-Fatah* in 1892. Journalists also played a part in democratic politics after 1922; for instance, the journals *al-Siyasa*, *Misr*, and *al-Balagh* represented the ideological positions of the Liberal-Constitutional, Watani, and Wafd Parties. In content, the cultural renaissance adapted Arabic to the expression of foreign concepts through the redefinition of words such as *watan* and *umma*, to represent the nation, as well as concepts such as justice, liberty, socialism, and feminism. Perhaps the most important impact of the press upon the Arabic-speaking societies of northern Africa was this redefinition of identity and the community.

The other states of northern Africa adopted the innovations of the Egyptian journalists. In Tunisia an official journal, *al-Ra'id al-Tunisi*, appeared in 1861 and was published regularly after 1873 when the reformist prime minister, Khayr al-Din, encouraged the publication of articles on educational, social, and political reform. After 1881 the French protectorate supported journals such as *La Petite tunisien* and *La Tunisie-francaise*, which argued in favor of gradual constitutional reform. The first nationalist arguments were made in the Arabic-language journals *al-Hadira* (1888), *al-Zahra* (1890), and *Sabil al-Rashad*, the last of which appeared in 1895 and was edited by 'Abd al-' Aziz al-Tha'alibi. In the prewar period these Tunisian journals were influenced by the Egyptian, Islamic reform journal, *al-Manar*. However, during the first massive demonstrations against colonial rule in 1911, Tha'alibi's Arab-language journal, *Tunisien*, showed the impact of Egyptian, nationalist journalism. After the First World War the Young Tunisians formed the Destour Party, led by Tha'alibi, who was succeeded by Habib Bourguiba. Like his predecessor, Bourguiba's career began with the publication of a journal, *L'Action tunisienne* in 1932, and then a party, the Neo-Destour, in 1934. Journalism and political associations were inseparable, at least in the formative period of northern, African nationalism.

The Algerian press was at first influenced by Tunisian and French metropolitan politics. The journals *Le Rachidi* and *L'Etendard algerien* provided the platforms for the formation of the Young Algerian movement in 1912, which was modeled on the example of the Young Tunisian movement. After World War I, the Young Algerian leader Emir Khalid published political essays in the journal *al-Iqdam*. The French colonial administration responded by suing the journal in the colonial courts. Another Young Algerian leader, Ferhat Abbas, argued for assimilation of Algerians into French Algeria in *Taqqadum*, *La Tribune*, and *Le Trait d'Union*. He also edited *La Republique al-gerienne*. At the same time a more radical nationalist program was popularized in journals published in France, *Iqdam nord-africain* and *El-Oumma*, which began the movement that took the name *Parti du Peuple Algerien* in 1937. An independent Arabic press appeared in 1924 with the publication of the journal *al-Shihab* by the Islamic reformer and educator 'Abd al-Hamid Ben Badis. This journal was influenced by the Islamic reformism of *al-Manar* and therefore was part of the larger cultural renaissance in northern Africa and the Middle East. The press of the *Front de Liberation National* followed this trend, publishing the journal *al-Mujahid* that popularized the idea of an Islamic and Arab, Algerian nation, alongside the guerrilla war against the French.

In Morocco the press was at first private, with the appearance of *al-Maghrib* in 1889. After the French occupation in 1912, the radical nationalist journals of northern Africa were banned by the French authorities. The nationalist press appeared in 1933 with the publication in Fez of *L'Action du Peuple*, a moderate journal countenanced by the French authorities. An Arabic journal, *al-Hayat*, appeared first in Tetouan in the Spanish zone. The *Plan de Reformes* of the nationalist party was penned and published by the editors of the nationalist journals in 1934. Afterward, the national movement and journalism were centered in Rabat, with the publication of the French-langauge *L'Action populaire* and the Arabic *al-Atlas* and *al-Maghrib* in 1937. At this time a new element was introduced into the North African press when Spain's General Francisco Franco attempted to undermine French power in Morocco by broadcasting radio transmissions into the French zone.

The new medium of radio made the press available to a broader spectrum of society in the postwar years. Although it had emerged privately in the 1920s, radio only became popular in Egypt after it was adopted as an instrument of public education by the government after 1952. The revolutionary regime used radio to communicate the socialist and Arab nationalist message through the programs *With the People* and *Voice of the Arabs*. The results were successful, with the broadcasts reaching 85 per cent of the Egyptian population. Moreover, the unifying image of the Arab nation had an impact across the Arab-speaking population of northern Africa. This increased the legitimacy of the medium and the message. In Algeria the National Liberation Front (FLN) broadcast the revolutionary cause through *Radio-Algerie libre*, a crucial factor in mobilizing resistance as well as instilling a renewed nationalist ethos within the Algerian people.

The media expanded rapidly with the national movements against European colonialism. Therefore, the power of the media to educate or influence public opinion was something already appreciated by the political leaders in northern Africa at the time of independence. The printed press, however, was limited in its utility by social conditions. The relative impoverishment of northern Africa meant that there was only an elite market for newspapers. In the mid-twentieth century only 13 per cent of the Arabic dailies in Egypt were able to survive without subsidies, state or private, and among the small number of profitable papers it was necessary to put the courting of popular opinion (the small number of literate readers) before impartial news reportage. The other inhibiting factor was literacy, which was restricted to little more than 10 per cent of the population in northern Africa at the time of World War I and remained so in Morocco, Algeria, and Libya until the 1960s. Since then literacy has increased rapidly with the social and cultural reforms of the independent states; for instance, by 1980 literacy rates in Algeria and Egypt were at 42 per cent, Libya's were higher at 56 per cent, while Morocco lagged at 29.5 per cent. Radio and television were mediums that did not rely on literacy, but the new mediums were developed in the postcolonial setting, in which governments attempted to monopolize or censor the message.

The newspaper *al-Ahram*, the oldest independent paper in Egypt with a reputation for news reportage, was transformed into Gamal Abdel Nasser's mouthpiece after the press was nationalized in 1960. The editor of *al-Ahram*, Muhammad Hasanayn Haykal, provided Nasser with a means to influence public opinion through his weekly editorials. After the defeat of Egypt in the 1967 war with Israel the editorials appeared to argue for a reevaluation of socialist policies and a return to a more "open society." Nasser exploited the "open society" to attack the military establishment through Haykal's editorials. The episode did not reestablish the autonomy of the press; it simply reasserted presidential power.

In the other states of northern Africa even the principle of press freedom was ignored as newspaper, radio, and television were employed by governments as media for educating the population in "correct" political attitudes. Libya's official press policy was to embody the revolutionary social, economic, and political objectives of Muammar Gaddafi. After Tunisian independence in 1956, Bourguiba's *L'Action* was transformed into the official journal, *al-Amil*, of the ruling Neo-Destour Party, while radio was placed under the control of the Ministry of Information in 1957. Journals representing opposing views or groups were suppressed. Upon Algerian independence in 1962 there were a multitude of French and Arabic papers and radio stations, all of which were placed under the supervision of special committees of the ruling FLN party. In 1962 *Al-Chaab* became the first national daily, printed in French and later in Arabic. In 1963 an edict nationalized the daily journals of Algiers, Constantine, and Oran. In 1964, after the coup that brought Houari Boumedienne to power, the government took complete control of the press by establishing a new French-language daily, *El-Moudjahid*, to communicate the official Arab, socialist ideology.

Morocco, uniquely, has had a liberal policy toward print, radio, and televised media. It was the first country to have a national news agency, l'Agence Maghreb Arabe Presse, which was begun as a private initiative but became a public establishment in 1977. In Tunisia, Libya, and Algeria the news agencies were state owned from the start and therefore monopolized subscriptions to foreign wire services. The result was state censorship of news reportage. In Egypt the private press has been relatively free, having access to foreign wire services. Nevertheless, the national news agency reportage has served as an indicator of the government-endorsed point of view, which independents have tended to cautiously follow. *Jeune Afrique*, a Tunisian journal, was able to remain politically independent only by remaining in exile after 1956. It put itself beyond the reach of the state censors by publishing first in Rome, and later in Paris. Satellite television broadcast by Arab communities in Europe has had a similar impact in the late twentieth century, because northern African governments have little power to control the reception of satellite broadcasts. In the 1980s the press across northern Africa recovered some autonomy when Egyptian politics was democratized after the assassination of Anwar Sadat in 1981. The removal of Bourguiba in 1987 had a similar impact in Tunisia. In Algeria the government adopted a new press policy in 1982, encouraging the expression of free opinion. This had an impact on the demands for political reform that were voiced during the demonstrations of 1988, which led in turn to the experiment in democratic reform in the 1990s. At the same time, the government's criticism of the press and subsequent attacks upon journalists during the Algerian civil war reflect the fragile condition of the press in postcolonial northern Africa.

JAMES WHIDDEN

See also: **Egypt: Printing, Broadcasting; Journalism, African: Colonial Era; Media as Propaganda.**

Further Reading

Ainslie, Rosalynde. *The Press in Africa: Communications Past and Present*. London: Victor Gollancz, 1966.
Aouchar, Amina. *La Presse Marocaine dans la lutte pour l'independence*. Casablanca: Wallada, 1990.
Ayalon, Ami. *The Press in the Arab Middle East: A History*. Oxford: Oxford University Press, 1995.
Freund, Wolfgang S. *La Presse ecrite au Maghreb: realites et perspectives*. Hamburg: Deutsches Orient-Institut, 1989.
Kattani, Zayn al'Abidin. *Al-Sahafa al-Maghribiyya, nash'atuha wa tatawwuruha*. Rabat: Ministere de l'Information, 1969.
Laroui, Abdallah. *Les orignes sociales et culturelles du nationalisme marocain 1830–1912*. Paris: Maspero, 1977.
Rugh, William A. *The Arab Press, News Media and Political Process in the Arab World*. London: Croom Helm, 1979.
Ziadeh, Nicola A. *Origins of Nationalism in Tunisia*. Beirut: Librairie du Liban, 1962.

Press: Southern Africa

The press in southern Africa dates to the beginning of European colonialism, with the earliest newspaper appearing at Capetown in South Africa in 1800. In 1824, the *South African Journal* was launched, defying British colonial restrictions on nonofficial newspapers. Media-government relations in the region have been contentious ever since.

Colonial states' efforts to gain and exploit economic and political domination, and Eurocentric cultural, religious and social influences, set the parameters for press development in the region well past independence. The colonial press in southern Africa almost exclusively represented the interests of governments, missionary societies, and settler communities. Many early papers began as official newsletters of the British colonial authorities. For example, the Bechuanaland Protectorate government produced a Tswana/English newsletter, *Naledi ya Batswana*.

By the early twentieth century, most commercial southern African newspapers catered to small, urban-based, white settler populations, publishing in Dutch and Afrikaans (South Africa), Portuguese (Angola and Mozambique), German (Namibia), and English (South Africa, Zambia, Zimbabwe, Malawi, Lesotho, Swaziland, and Botswana). With the spread of British colonial rule and white settlers, new papers emerged that were designed to serve whites but also increasingly came to be read by literate Africans. A good example was the *Rhodesia Herald* (Salisbury). Throughout the twentieth century, English-language newspapers from South Africa—especially *The Star*, *Rand Daily Mail*, *Sunday Times*, and *Bantu World*—enjoyed a small but significant African readership throughout the region.

The earliest African-language (vernacular) newspapers appeared during the colonial era, generally produced by Christian missions, who viewed the printed word in many forms—not just in the Bible translated into vernacular languages—as a tool for education as well as the winning and holding of converts. In Botswana, for example, a Tswana-language press has existed in some form since 1856, when the monthly Wesleyan Mission *Molekude wa Bechuana* first appeared. Missionary newspapers helped set the stage for growth of a more news-oriented Tswana press in the twentieth century. In 1901, the first newspaper published and edited by Batswana, *Koranta ea Becoana*, appeared.

Most African-language newspapers from Botswana, Swaziland, and Lesotho were absorbed into a larger South African "African Press," and it was not until the 1950s, at the threshold of independence, that a more nationalist African press reemerged in these territories.

In West Africa during the 1930s and 1940s, anticolonial nationalist opposition grew increasingly articulate in strongly worded editorials in indigenous newspapers. Colonial states imposed a vast array of legal restrictions to slow or stifle development of independent African newspapers. Restrictive press laws and court rulings proliferated and spread to eastern and southern African territories in the 1950s. All newspapers had to be registered with colonial governments in order to lawfully publish.

The key factor in the rise of a second wave of African newspapers in the region was anticolonial nationalism and formation of political parties pressing for independence. Some parties and national liberation movements published their own newsletters, such as the African National Congress's *Sechaba* and SWAPO's *New Era* in Namibia.

Clandestine radio was more effective than the printed press as a vehicle for launching and expanding nationalist movements. Gripped by fears of rising Soviet and Chinese subversion and propaganda, and based on their interpretation of events leading up to the Congo crisis, colonial governments and white minority regimes were, by the 1960s, cracking down on the small African presses and setting up their own government newspapers.

South Africa (particularly after 1948 and the rise of formal apartheid) and Southern Rhodesia (after the 1965 Unilateral Declaration of Independence) imposed the most elaborate, complex, and stifling array of press restrictions. Penalties grew increasingly severe as white minority regimes were pressed during the 1970s and 1980s. The ultimate sanction was outright banning of a publication or jailing of editors. Many chose exile.

Government-run newspapers persisted in many African states long after the end of colonial rule. With independence, many pronationalist newspapers became mouthpieces of the new governments they had helped bring to power. Private papers were steadily brought within the range of government influence, if not outright control.

Following Zimbabwe's independence in 1980, the *Herald* and *Chronicle*, the two largest national newspapers, which had been oriented to the white minority and had been under partial South African ownership, were placed under the guidance of an ostensibly autonomous Mass Media Trust (ZMMT). Government influence over management of the ZMMT and outright purchase of South African shares resulted in these newspapers' eventual transformation into what were virtually government publications. Independent-minded editors were forced out, Ministry of Information news directives were applied, and any semblance of press freedom had ebbed away by 1990.

In the name of national unity, development, and nationalism, new leaders were reluctant to abide any press criticism. Critics were treated as subversives who jeopardized development. Structures of colonial control over information and free expression were well-suited for authoritarian one-party regimes, and were thus retained and even extended. Indirect measures to control the independent press included withdrawal of government advertising and denial of foreign exchange allocations to "uncooperative papers" for purchase of newsprint, presses, and spare parts.

More of an explanation than lack of press freedom is needed to account for this pattern. In a number of cases, incoming postindependence governments inherited official newspapers and continued them, not only for political reasons but for economic ones as well. Some new states, such as Botswana, with a small, mostly illiterate population scattered across a wide territory, lacked a mass readership, commercial advertising base, or production and distribution facilities to make a viable private national newspaper possible. Only two decades after independence did the necessary elements of commercial press viability begin to reach critical mass. Independent private newspapers did not take root in Botswana until the mid-1980s, and then only as weeklies. All four major papers today are based in Gaborone, the capital, and primarily target English-literate, urban-based readers and the small commercial sector.

The press played pivotal roles in the so-called second wave of independence that rolled across many African states in the late 1980s and 1990s—notably Zambia and Malawi, where mass movements pressing entrenched authoritarian regimes for democratic changes were led or strongly aided by newly established private newspapers.

In the early 1990s, these pressures for democratic reforms were rewarded by unprecedented media freedom and an explosion of new independent newspapers. In Malawi, the most dramatic example, the number of private newspapers grew from 1 to 30 by 1994. In Zambia, under incoming President Frederick Chiluba, some of this heady press freedom lasted only as long as it took some of the new publications to criticize the new regime. In 1995, the offices of the *Post* were raided and its editor jailed.

Although political pressures on independent newspapers in southern Africa eased considerably during the 1990s, today most find themselves in constant struggles for viability, if not outright survival; economic constraints continue to directly affect production and distribution. Despite the end of apartheid and a more democratic political order, many alternative South African newspapers are facing severe economic problems. Many are folding, while mainstream newspapers are increasingly falling into the hands of global media conglomerates and experiencing a new kind of external control.

Economic stagnation and decline does not allow for the development of a viable commercial business sector interested and able to purchase advertising space, chief major revenue source of most private newspapers. Outside of South Africa, there are virtually no commercial daily newspapers in the region today.

External financial support, be it from global media conglomerates or nongovernmental organizations interested in the promotion of democracy via freedom of expression and media pluralism, are responsible for keeping some of the major private weekly newspapers afloat in Namibia (the *Namibian*) South Africa (the *Weekly Mail*) and elsewhere across the region. The Media Institute of Southern Africa (MISA) based in Windhoek, Namibia, is investing foreign donor support to develop programs aimed at training and organizing southern African journalists, commercial media owners, and other African media professionals. MISA provides economic, managerial, and even political support.

Across the region, private newspapers still have to negotiate not only economic and educational barriers but also increasingly intolerant government censors. Even in states with relatively high degrees of press freedom (Botswana, Namibia, and South Africa), self-censorship, fears of court actions, threats, and violence are all too commonly a part of southern African journalists' daily work environments, stunting their professionalism, credibility, and independence.

A growing number of fledgling southern African newspapers are taking advantage of recent advances in information technology to become economically and politically sustainable. Some, such as the *Independent* in Zimbabwe and *Mmegi* in Botswana, are posting weekly editions in cyberspace, and networking with regional and international media pools, such as the Pan-African News Agency and press freedom groups (MISA, Reporters sans Frontieres, Index on Censorship, Article XIX) to improve news flows, ease government pressures on their operations, and gain support for national media reforms.

Western research on the postindependence press in Africa focuses strongly on the issue of press freedom, usually conceptualized in Western terms or not defined at all. A counterconceptualization that gained much currency in Africa during the postindependence era, "developmental journalism," emphasizes the responsibility of the press to support government policies rather than adopting a fourth-estate critic-watchdog mission, especially in the reporting of news.

JAMES J. ZAFFIRO

See also: **Journalism, African: Colonial Era; Media as Propaganda.**

Further Reading

Barton, Frank. *The Press of Africa.* New York: Africana, 1979.

Eribo, Festus. "The Elusive Press Freedom in Angola." In *Press Freedom and Communication in Africa*, edited by Festus Eribo and William Jong-Ebot. Trenton, N.J.: Africa World Press, 1997.

Hachten, William, and C. Anthony Giffard. *The Press and Apartheid.* Madison: University of Wisconsin Press, 1984.

Jackson, Gordon S. *Breaking Story: The South African Press.* Boulder, Colo.: Westview Press, 1993.

Kasoma, Francis P. *The Press in Zambia: Development, Role and Control of National Newspapers in Zambia, 1906–1983.* Lusaka: Multimedia, 1986.

Mwase, Ngila, R.L. "The Media and the Namibian Liberation Struggle." *Media, Culture and Society* 10, no. 2 (1988): 225–237.

Parsons, Neil. "The Tswana Press: An Outline of Its History since 1856." *Kutlwano* (Gaborone), no. 8 (1968): 4–8.

Press Freedom in Zimbabwe, Harare: Willie Musarurwa Trust, 1993.

Switzer, Les, and Donna Switzer. *The Black Press in South Africa and Lesotho.* Boston: G. K. Hall, 1979.

Tomaselli, Keyan, and P. Eric Louw, *The Alternative Press in South Africa*, London: James Currey, 1991

Tomaselli, Keyan, Ruth Tomaselli, and Johan Muller. *Narrating the Crisis: Hegemony and the South African Press.* Johannesburg: Richard Lyon, 1987.

Walsh, Gretchen. *The Media in Africa and Africa in the Media: An Annotated Bibliography.* London: Hans Zell, 1996.

Zaffiro, James J. "Mass Media, Politics and Society in Botswana in the 1990s and Beyond." *Africa Today* 40, no. 1 (1993): 7–26.

Press: Tropical Africa

The birth of the press in tropical Africa dates to 1801, when black settlers in Sierra Leone began publishing a simple broadsheet called *The Royal Gazette and Sierra Leone Advertiser.* From this humble beginning the independent African press has gone on to play an important role in articulating a critique of racism and colonialism throughout much of Africa during the colonial era. In the initial decades after independence African rulers of one-party states tightly controlled the press in the name of nation-building. However, as many nations began moving toward democratization during the 1990s, the continent has witnessed a revival of an independent press.

The first newspapers in tropical Africa appeared in regions of heavy European influence. An English journalist in South Africa established the *Cape Town Gazette*, the continent's first settler paper, in 1800. The following year repatriated Africans in the West African settlement of Sierra Leone published their first paper. However, publication of these early papers was sporadic, and the first periodical that could be compared to a modern newspaper was the *Liberia Herald*, first published by Charles L. Force in 1826. Force had emigrated to Liberia from Boston, where the Massachusetts Colonization Society had given him a printing press. Though Force died shortly after the publication of his first issue, his paper was renamed and relaunched in 1830 by another American émigré. The reconstituted paper continued publishing until 1862. During its three decades in operation the *Herald* was a vociferous opponent of the slave trade, and frequently published articles popularizing the accomplishments of famous Africans. Its last editor was the West Indian pan-Africanist Edward Blyden.

The early press in West Africa found its audience in the Westernized, literate, urban African peoples of the coastal communities. From its bases in Liberia and Sierra Leone, the West African press spread to other regions of English influence. In 1874 several newspapers were founded in Gold Coast, and in 1890 the first daily paper in West Africa appeared in Lagos, Nigeria. Though these papers often contained criticism of colonial policy, their staunch support of Western over indigenous African culture is reflected in the *Liberian Advocate's* motto "Christian Liberia: the open door to heathen Africa."

West Africa was also home to the first newspaper to be published in an African language. In 1859 Anglican missionaries in Abeokuta began producing a newspaper in Yoruba. Though the paper ceased publication after its equipment was destroyed in 1867, this was the first of many similar ventures in vernacular publishing that would be launched by Christian missionaries. By 1900, limited-circulation papers were being published from mission stations in many colonies, including Uganda, South Africa, and Cameroon. Their efforts helped to spread literacy, and eventually fostered a mass readership for newspapers.

While the press in Anglophone West Africa remained in African hands, the rapid expansion of colonial rule after 1880 inspired the creation of a number of new papers published by and for the growing white settler communities. In South Africa the press expanded in tandem with the rapid growth of the mining industry after 1867. In East Africa the first newspaper arrived with the construction of the Uganda railway at the end of the nineteenth century. British settlers in Kenya published the *East African Standard* after 1910, which was conspicuous for its racist prosettler views. The publishers of the *East African Standard* also introduced similar papers into neighboring Uganda and Tanzania.

Outside of Anglophone Africa there were few African newspapers before the 1930s. In the new French territories of West and Central Africa, low levels of literacy, and the high cost of importing publishing equipment, discouraged the spread of an indigenous press. The only papers of note in French West Africa appeared in the older colony of Senegal, where periodicals such as *Le Rèveil du Sènègalais* (founded in 1885) catered to a largely white, urban, merchant community. In the Belgian Congo, official opposition to local initiatives discouraged the development of an indigenous press until the eve of independence. In these regions missionaries produced the only newspapers, usually in local languages.

Before the 1930s, African newspapers tended to cater to an educated class that aligned itself with the colonial order. There were incidents of short-lived papers publishing strident attacks on colonial administrations. But these were sporadic, and they enjoyed little circulation or influence. In West Africa the moderate tone of the press changed dramatically in 1935 when the Nigerian journalist Dr. Nnamdi Azikiwe moved to the Gold Coast to take over publication of the *Africa Morning Post*. Azikiwe had spent nine years living and working in the United States, and his experiences there had radicalized his approach to journalism. Working with I. T. A. Wallace-Johnson, a West Indian Marxist who had worked for a Communist newspaper in Paris, Azikiwe turned the sleepy Gold Coast paper into a champion of African rights. While their predecessors had published well-reasoned appeals for constitutional reform, Azikiwe and Wallace-Johnson employed fiery, inflammatory language to inveigh against the iniquities of the colonial system. When he was prosecuted for libel in 1937 Azikiwe moved to Lagos, where he became the editor of the *West African Pilot*. In Gold Coast and in Nigeria his controversial editorials resonated with urban audiences, and soon inspired journalists throughout the region to copy his style.

Journalism in Francophone Africa also experienced an important change in tone during the 1930s. By the late 1920s, there were several small African papers outside of Senegal, many of which were in the colony of Dahomey. These and other fledgling newspapers in the region received a boost in the early 1930s, when Africans in Senegal were allowed to elect representatives to the French National Assembly. Though confined to Senegal, the election campaign inspired interest and discussion throughout the region. Political associations began disseminating their messages through party-sponsored periodicals. However, the political aspirations of these papers remained much more conservative than those of their English-speaking neighbors. It was not until after World War II and the formation of the interterritorial Rassemblement Démocratique Africaine party that journalists in French West and Central Africa began demanding independence. The 1950s saw a dramatic rise in the number of nationalist newspapers in French Africa, and many of the future leaders of Francophone nations, such as Félix Houphouët-Boigny of Côte d'Ivoire, and Léopold Senghor of Senegal, published their own papers during the final decade of colonial rule.

When most African states achieved their independence during the 1960s, the newspapers of the victorious political parties became important organs for disseminating official information. In the former French territories the colonial power provided equipment and technical expertise to the new regimes. The independent press, which in many colonies had played an important role in the liberation movements, soon found itself falling under the control of the new postcolonial regimes. Anxious to consolidate their power, and concerned with the fragile nature of their multiethnic nations, the leaders of independent states discouraged the existence of an independent press in the name of nation-building. The poverty of many of the new states of Africa also meant that there was little capital to support an independent press. Therefore, until 1990 journalism in most African countries consisted of one state produced national newspaper. Typical of these party papers was *Fraternité Matin*, a government tabloid published in Côte d'Ivoire that routinely trumpeted the accomplishments of the leader and former journalist Houphouët-Boigny.

With independence, many of the settler-owned newspapers were taken over by African governments. While minority rule continued in South Africa and Rhodesia, the press remained in the control of the large newspaper syndicates. However, in both countries the press remained heavily censored. With independence in 1980 the *Rhodesian Herald* became a state newspaper and was renamed the *Zimbabwe Herald*. Though democracy brought a freer press to South Africa in 1994, many of the strict laws governing the press remained in effect.

In 1990, the end of the Cold War inspired many African nations to begin taking steps toward democratization, and the independent press in Africa immediately began to revive. Throughout the continent new independent newspapers began appearing. Most of these papers positioned themselves in opposition to the ruling regimes and attracted readers by exposing the corruption of government officials. Papers like Cameroon's *Le Messager* established a reputation for fearlessly criticizing public figures. However, these new journalists have faced considerable opposition from entrenched regimes. Since 1990 journalists have been imprisoned, tortured, and murdered in dozens of countries throughout the continent.

JAMES BURNS

See also: **Azikiwe, Nnamdi; Journalism, African: Colonial Era; Media as Propaganda.**

Further Reading

Ainslie, Rosalynde. *The Press in Africa: Communications Past and Present*. New York: Walker, 1967.

Azikiwe, Nnamdi. *Suppression of the Press in British West Africa*. Onitsha, Nigeria: African Book Company, n.d. (1946?).

Barton, Frank. *The Press of Africa: Persecution and Perseverance*. London: Macmillan, 1979.

Eribo, Festus, and William Jong-Ebot (eds.). *Press Freedom and Communication in Africa*. Trenton: Africa World Press, 1997.

Faringer, Gunilla L. *Press Freedom in Africa*. New York: Praeger, 1991.

Tomaselli, Kenyan, and Ruth Tomaselli (eds.). *The Press in South Africa*. London: James Currey, 1989.

Pretoria

In 1855, the purchase of two farms by President Marthinus Pretorius in the Apies River Valley to accommodate a permanent building for the South African Republic's Volksraad (colonial legislative assembly) heralded the establishment of South Africa's administrative capital. Named after its founder's father, Andries Pretorius, a *voortrekker* leader, over the next half century Pretoria acquired a population of 50,000 as well as the infrastructure of a modern city: a Dutch Reformed church (1857); public schooling (1859); postal services (1864); a telegraph (1877); railway links (1893); electric lighting (1892); a daily newspaper (1898); waterborne sewage (1904); and electric tramways (1910). The planting of the 70,000 Jacaranda trees that still constitute the city's most attractive feature began in and around its 350 public parks in 1888.

Throughout most of its history, Pretoria's status as the bureaucratic headquarters of government, as well as its especially discriminatory boundary demarcation, ensured that it was the only major South African city to be predominantly white. It was the first to institutionalize racial hierarchy: a law prohibited blacks and "coloreds" (those of mixed blood) from using pavements until 1925. During the twentieth century it became a major industrial center, beginning with such pioneering enterprises as the Eerste Fabrieke distillery, a munitions factory founded during the Anglo-Boer war, and an iron furnace established in 1918. Pretoria's significance as a manufacturer was confirmed in 1928 when an Afrikaner nationalist government decided it should be the site for the state-owned Iron and Steel Corporation; the steelworks began operations in 1934. During the 1960s, Pretoria became the hub of South Africa's transportation and defense industries, as well as Africa's largest producer of barbed wire. The civil service, heavy industry, and a huge complex of military bases just south of the city shaped the city's social and cultural character decisively. A modestly paid and partly transient population of officials (their livelihoods protected by racial job preservation) created a demand for cheap housing and prompted the construction of the apartment block neighborhoods that define Pretoria's white suburbs. Notwithstanding the existence from 1930 of a full-fledged local university, Pretoria's high culture was to be dominated by national institutions headquartered in the city as well rival genres of imperial and nationalist monumental architecture: since 1949, Gerard Moerdijk's Voortrekker Monument has balefully confronted Herbert Baker's Union Buildings (1913) from its hilltop perch across the Apies River Valley. As with its cultural life, from the 1940s, municipal politics chiefly reflected the preoccupations of apartheid's main beneficiaries, blue-collar and lower-middle-class Afrikaners; they ensured National Party predominance in Pretoria parliamentary and municipal elections until a black challenge to local bus segregation prompted a swing to the conservative right in 1989.

Contrasting with the social conformity of a white community largely composed of functionaries in and out of uniform, Pretoria's black inhabitants represented a livelier historical vein of social dissent. One of the first of the African National Congess's campaigning successes occurred in the city when a local leader, S. M. Makgatho, organized a civil disobedience offensive against segregated pavements. The 20,000 freehold black landowners recorded at the time of the 1913 Land Act constituted a substantial layer of middle-class leadership. They lived mainly in the northwest suburb of Lady Selborne as well as the inner city ghetto of Marabastad, childhood home of the writer Es'kia Mphahlele. These and other "black spots" began to be subjected to clearances from the 1940s (after two decades of white agitation), and dispossessed African landowners, together with their tenants, were resettled in Atteridgeville (est. 1939) and Mamelodi ("mother of melody," est. 1953), respectively east and west of the city, each secluded from the outlying white suburbs by belts of heavy industry. During and just after World War II, political activism by a local multiracial branch of the Communist Party drew upon the broader social tensions that underlay the Marabastad municipal compound riots of December 1942 and the two-week 1947 Atteridgeville bus boycott. Slum clearances and the harsh imposition after 1945 of municipal pass laws more or less extinguished a militant trade union movement, but the African National Congress (ANC) remained busy in Lady Selborne, supported as it was by finance from Chinese traders, and making a brave showing during the Defiance Campaign as well as mobilizing black Pretoria's contribution to the 1957 Witwatersrand bus boycott. By the 1960s, however, most of its notables were gone. Designated for white occupation, Lady Selborne had become a demolition zone by 1963. Meanwhile, African communal politics shifted its fulcrum to the more regulated municipal townships: in 1963 a local branch of the Pan-Africanist Congress attempted to mount a military uprising from its bases in Atteridgeville's secondary schools. A parallel sabotage campaign by local Umkhonto we Sizwe adherents ended with the arrest of its participants in 1964. During a succeeding period of apparent political docility, secondary industrialization spurred by the introduction of car assembly lines and the expansion of black tertiary education facilities (Medunsa, Vista and UNISA) around the city supplied new seedbeds for political activism. Trade unions and student movements were in the vanguard of a sustained insurrectionary rebellion in Mamelodi and Atteridgeville between 1984 and 1990. The cultural accompaniments to local political assertion included Mamelodi's emergence as South Africa's jazz capital.

Postapartheid Pretoria remains a government city, but that feature itself has accelerated its social transformation: given the pace of affirmative action within the public bureaucracy, Pretoria's middle class of black professionals is the largest in the country. In 2000, a reconfiguration of its municipal boundaries to incorporate Centurion to its south and the commuter dormitories of Ga-Rankua and Mabopane to the north tripled its population (to around two million) and ensured the future ascendency of the ANC in municipal politics as long as it can hold the loyalty of Pretoria's industrial workers and junior officials. Reborn as an African city, in 2000 it was re-christened Tshwane, the Northern Sotho name for the fertile valley in which Marthinus Pretorius built his parliament.

TOM LODGE

See also: **South Africa.**

Further Reading

Dauskardt, R. P. A. "Local State, Segregation and Transport Provision: The Atteridgeville Bus Boycott, 1947." *South African Geographical Journal* 71, no. 2 (1989): pp.109–115.

Grobler, J. E. H., "The Marabastad Riot." *Contree*, no. 32 (1992): 24–31.

Hattingh, P. S., and A. C. Horn, "Pretoria." In *Homes Apart: South Africa's Segregated Cities*, edited by Anthony Lemon. Cape Town: David Philip, 1991.

Horn, A. C. "The Identity of Land in the Pretoria District, 19 June 1913." *South African Geographical Journal* 80, no. 1 (1998): 9–22.

Jaffee, Georgina. "Beyond the Cannon of Mamelodi." *Work in Progress*, no. 41 (1986): 4–10.

Lodge, Tom. "Political Organisations in Pretoria's African Townships." In *Class, Community and Conflict: South African Perspectives*, edited by *Belinda* Bozzoli. Johannesburg: Ravan, 1987.

Mokgatle, Naboth. *The Autobiography of an Unknown South African.* Berkeley and Los Angeles: University of Calfornia Press, 1971.

Mphahlele, Ezekiel. *Down Second Avenue.* London: Faber, 1979.

Nel, B. F. "Pretoria." In *Standard Encyclopaedia of Southern Africa*, vol. 9. Nasou, 1973.

Production and Exchange, Precolonial

Production, whether purely for subsistence or as a means of generating surpluses for exchange for other products, is a fundamental element of any society's economy. The level and types of inputs and the eventual distribution and consumption of goods, services, and materials, as well as the division of labor and the manner in which production is organized and time is allocated, can all vary widely from one society to another and in relation to differences in social and political organization.

Scholars attempting to distinguish production systems in different societies frequently talk in terms of their "mode of production." The concept derives from the work of Karl Marx, but has been elaborated by various anthropologists and historians, most notably those aligned with the French school of structural Marxism. There are two components to a mode of production—*the forces of production* and *the relations of production.* The former refers to the range of raw materials, technologies, and labor employed within a particular system's approach to the appropriation of nature. The latter refers to the ways in which surplus is extracted and distributed among different sections of the community, and thus encapsulates different modes of exchange.

The reconstruction of precolonial African modes of production and their associated exchange systems relies on a combination of written and oral historical sources, archaeological evidence, and inferences drawn from colonial ethnographies and modern anthropology. Archaeological data have played a particularly important role, partly because they provide tangible evidence for the technologies employed, raw materials exploited, and produce exchanged by different societies at different times in the past, but also because of their ability to greatly extend the time depth of our knowledge of the continent well beyond that available from historical sources alone.

Anthropological studies of the social basis for trade and exchange also make it possible to infer the existence of a particular mechanism, such as tribute payments or market exchange, from other evidence concerning the prevailing pattern of social organization. As the American anthropologist Karl Polanyi observed, exchanges can take many forms, ranging from simple reciprocal exchanges between close kin, through prestige gift exchange and the collection and redistribution of tribute to commercial, market trading. Not only are these different modes of exchange, the social relations that exist between exchange partners in these different systems are normally markedly different and they can also generate different spatial patterns.

Virtually all known modes of production, with the notable exception of the variants of industrial capitalism, were represented among precolonial African societies. In broad terms, archaeological research indicates that prior to approximately 8,000 years ago, all African societies relied on wild resources for their food supply, through a combination of gathering, hunting and, where appropriate, fishing. From at least 20,000 years ago, there is evidence that certain items were being exchanged between individuals who, given the distances involved, probably belonged to different social groups. Tools made of obsidian from sources around Lake Naivasha and Mt. Eburru have also been recovered from Middle Stone Age contexts at Muguruk and Songhor in western Kenya some 190 kilometers away, suggesting a much longer history of exchange.

The existence of exchange networks may also have played a significant role in the emergence of food production among many foraging societies. The earliest evidence on the continent comes from sites on the dry, drought-prone steppes of the Egyptian Western Desert, especially those at Nabta Playa and Bir Kiseiba. By approximately 8000BCE and possibly up to a millennium earlier, inhabitants of these areas were deliberately herding wild cattle, and even digging wells so as to extend their grazing areas into drier areas. Well-laid-out villages with semipermanent architecture and storage pits appear for the first time, indicative of population growth and increased sedentism. Analysis of the faunal assemblages from these sites also suggest that the herds were being exploited for their milk and blood rather than their meat. The remains of a wide spectrum of wild plants recovered from these sites, including the progenitors of domesticated sorghum and millet, point to the continuing importance of gathering in these economies.

Similar evidence for localized groups of specialized herders, hunters, fishers, and incipient cultivators has been documented at various points across the Sahara to its western edges around Dhar Tichitt in Mauritania. Although these clusters range quite widely in date, and appear to have been associated with different phases of climatic amelioration and deterioration, they share a number of characteristics. In particular, it appears that the exploitation of these semiarid regions, and the ability to survive quite long periods of climatic deterioration, were greatly facilitated by the existence of reciprocal exchange links between groups with different subsistence strategies. This not only enhanced food security, but even seems to have encouraged increased sedentism and population growth.

For the most part, production among these and other early farming communities would have been geared toward the reproduction of the lineage or some other similar kin-based group. Land and its produce would have been collectively owned and held in trust for future generations, and labor divided principally on gender lines. Nevertheless, through their control over symbolic resources (such as the means of propitiating ancestors and/or the spirits) and access to the kin group's surpluses for payment of bridewealth, elders would have exercised considerable power and authority over junior members of the domestic group. Most craft production, such as potting, woodworking, bark cloth (and later textile) manufacture also appears to have been organized at the household level, principally for domestic consumption. Exchange, in the form of barter or gifts of both locally produced and exotic items such as beads, nevertheless took place for both economic and social reasons.

One significant exception seems to have been metal production, principally of iron and copper, and there is copious evidence to suggest the emergence of regional specialization in this craft at a relatively early date. One of these areas was in Buhaya, in northwestern Tanzania, where evidence for ironworking has been dated to at least 500BCE, and perhaps earlier. Analytical studies of the slag, iron objects, and smelting furnaces from archaeological sites in this area suggest a very capable understanding of the technology and chemical processes required to obtain low-grade steel—an invention that predates the European invention of forced-draught furnaces by roughly two millennia. Such was the scale of production, the concomitant demand for charcoal, and the associated expansion of agriculture and settlement that the surrounding landscape had become sufficiently degraded by the year 500 that iron production virtually ceased and large swaths of countryside were depopulated. Only after a lapse of several centuries was there a resurgence in iron smelting and an associated rise in population.

West Africa was another important center of iron production, especially during the mid- to late second millennium CE. One area that has received extensive study is the Bassar region of Togo, where a combination of archaeological, historical, and ethnographic research has provided a detailed picture of the growth of the industry from the late thirteenth century onward, the organization and social relations of production and the symbolism of iron manufacture. The number and size of slag heaps and the number of smelting furnaces attributable to the fifteenth–eighteenth centuries, in particular, suggest a massive increase in the rate of production over this period, perhaps by as much as 300–600 per cent compared with earlier periods, probably attributable to the rise during the same period of the neighboring states of Gonja, Mamprusi, and Dagomba, and the demand for iron tools and weapons that this precipitated. Three other factors may also have contributed to the rise in prominence of the Bassar region, however—the exhaustion of wood supplies for charcoal in neighboring areas, the quality of the ore used by Bassari smelters, and the region's access to preexisting long distance trade routes. Such was the vibrancy of the industry that it managed to flourish even during the nineteenth century in the face of increasing competition from European imports, and at the time of German contact in 1890 villages across the area were still differentiated according to the distinct specializing of their inhabitants in either charcoal making, smelting, or smithing.

Copper artifacts were also important commodities from a relatively early date, especially across central Africa, where sources of the raw material are common. On present evidence, the earliest examples from the region, such as the Kipushi copper mine in northern Zambia and its smelting furnace, remains from Naviundu Springs near Lubumbashi, all date to around the fourth and fifth centuries. By the eighth century, copper mining and smelting was common. However, unlike iron, copper was used almost exclusively either as currency, jewelry, or for similar ornamental purposes rather than for tools. It was probably because of the nonutilitarian and ceremonial associations of copper that items such as bracelets, beads, wire, rings, ceremonial axes and various types of ingots were all traded widely and often occur as grave goods. As well as indicating the considerable geographical extent of the regional trade networks, an interesting feature of the copper artifacts is that they exhibit much greater formal standardization than in the previous centuries, which would imply an increasing tendency toward their use as currency, of which the X-shaped ingots are the best known. The fact that some of the richest burials are those of children and young adults also suggests that social status was inherited rather than achieved and, as later historical sources indicate, that copper was regarded as a sign of rank.

Almost without exception, the establishment of farming communities across the continent witnessed an intensification of production and exchange. As a consequence, this often led to the emergence of craft specialists, or, as in West Africa, distinct craft castes, who became reliant on the exchange of products for their livelihood. In many parts of the continent, there was also a shift in the relations and organization of production from kin- and age-mate based systems to tributary, mercantile, or slavery modes, or some combination of these. In turn, this facilitated the accumulation of surpluses by certain individuals or groups, typically members of the ruling elite, and the emergence of social ranking. At the same time, the expansion of trading networks needed to satisfy the demand for prestige goods increasingly drew African societies into contact with other parts of the world, thereby helping integrate local production with the Red Sea, Indian Ocean, Atlantic Ocean, and Mediterranean Sea mercantile systems.

Of these, the Red Sea was probably the first to emerge as a major shipping route, linking the Mediterranean world with that of the Indian Ocean. At Ras Hafun on the Somali coast, the remains of two sites ranging in date from the first to the fifth century, with quantities of pottery of Egyptian, Mesopotamian, and Iranian origin as well as a few examples of Mediterranean and South Asian manufacture, indicate the importance of the route at least since Roman times. The recent discovery of a shipwreck containing Roman/Byzantine amphorae off Assarca Island, Eritrea, dated to between the fourth and seventh centuries, and ongoing excavations at the third to sixth century port of Berenike, on the Egyptian coast, provide additional confirmation of the importance of this route. These and related discoveries also confirm the historical value of the first-century manuscript known as the *Periplus of the Erthryean Sea*, which provided mariners with topographic information and sailing instructions concerning these seaboards, as far south as central Tanzania. Later texts, and especially the tenth-century accounts by the Arab geographer Al-Mas'udi, contain additional detail, particularly concerning the range of commodities being traded.

From these sources, and the results of numerous archaeological excavations at sites along the Swahili coast, it is evident that a wide range of manufactured goods, including glazed ceramics from the Gulf, Chinese porcelain and Indian earthenware as well as glass and copper artifacts were being imported. Beads—made of glass, shell, carnelian, and other types of stone, in various sizes and types—were also a common trade item, many of them probably originating in India. Cotton cloth was imported from India, and silk from China. As demand for textiles grew, however, they were also produced from locally grown cotton, as attested to by the large number of spindle whorls discovered on sites along the Indian Ocean coast. In exchange for imported goods, the documentary sources suggest that ivory, mangrove poles, tortoise shell, ambergris, gold, and slaves were among the major exports. As far as one can tell, the main sources of slaves were from communities living inland and from the islands of Pemba and Zanzibar, many of whom were used to drain the swamps of southern Iraq during the ninth century. The primary source of gold was the Zimbabwe Plateau, where thousands of ancient mine workings have been recorded. This particular trade was especially instrumental in the emergence of the Zimbabwe state in the thirteenth century, and the corresponding rise in prominence of the Swahili trading port of Kilwa on the southern Tanzanian coast. The exchange and manufacture of ivory products, such as bangles, is also attested, particularly at the eleventh century site of Bambandyanalo near the Shashe-Limpopo confluence and Ingombe Ilede, but also at a number of sites fringing the Kalahari, including that of Mosu 1 on the edge of the Makgadikgadi Pans (Botswana).

Access to the Red Sea and Indian Ocean trade also played an important part in the rise of the Axumite kingdom in the Ethiopian highlands, which flourished between the first and tenth centuries. Archaeological and textual evidence indicates that the principal imports were iron, precious metals, textiles, glass, and a wide range of ceramics. Exports included ivory, obsidian, gold, rhinoceros horn, various exotic live animals and slaves. The importance of long-distance, external trade to the Axumite economy is also attested by the presence of a local monetary system. Axum was the first state in sub-Saharan Africa to mint its own coinage, with the earliest known examples dated to the third century. The system appears to have been closely modeled, in terms of weights, forms, and standards, on that employed in the Byzantine world, with which the kingdom had well-established links.

Long-distance trade was also critical to the economies of a number of West African states in both the forest and savanna zones. Although extensive regional exchange systems had existed well beforehand, the direction, level and intensity of trade began to change toward the end of the first millennium CE with the expansion of the trans-Sahara caravan routes. Settlements situated near the forest-savanna or desert-savanna ecotones, such as Begho (Ghana) and Kong (Côte d'Ivoire) in the south and Tegdaoust (Mauritania) and Timbuktu and Gao (Mali) in the north, flourished precisely because of their geographical position and the opportunities this offered to access and control the movement of raw materials and products from a variety of ecological zones. As on the east side of the continent, the principle exports were raw materials, including gold, slaves, kola nuts, and ivory, which were exchanged for a variety of finished goods. Rock salt, extracted using slave labor from various mines deep in the Sahara, such as those at Idjil (Mauritania) and Taghaza (Mali), was also taken south and used to acquire goods from the forest zone. Aside from the stimulation of production, the expansion of trade in the first millennium had a number of social consequences, including facilitating the spread of Islam and the creation of groups of specialized traders, who often had their own residential areas within the major towns.

After 1500, the trans-Saharan trade began to decline in importance, largely because of increased competition from European traders who had begun to explore Africa's Atlantic seaboard. The Portuguese were the first to establish permanent trading stations along the coast, the fort at Elmina (Ghana) being perhaps the best known of these. Excavations here and at a number of other sixteenth- through eighteenth-century towns, trading posts, and villages between the Senegal and Niger deltas, have provided a wealth of information that supplements the various documentary sources concerning the range of imports, their regional distribution and the economic and social impacts of this trade. Of these, the increase in warfare and raiding from the mid-seventeenth century, following the advent of the Atlantic slave trade and all its other associated consequences, were the most profound and far reaching. The demographic changes initiated by the introduction of new food crops, especially maize and cassava, also contributed to the transformation of West African societies during this era of contact. Nevertheless, participation in this trade also offered novel economic and political opportunities, enabling certain communities to increase their wealth and power at the expense of their neighbors, and the overall impression gained from the different sources is one of considerable cultural dynamism, entailing a combination of innovation, continuity, and resistance to foreign interference. Factors which in many ways could be said to have characterized exchange and production over the millennia throughout Africa.

PAUL LANE

See also: **Gold: Production and Trade: West Africa; Iron Age (Later): East Africa: Salt; Sahara: Trans-Saharan Trade.**

Further Reading

Barros, P. L. de. "Bassar: A Quantified, Chronologically Controlled, Regional Approach to a Traditional Iron Production Centre in West Africa." *Africa*, no. 56 (1986): 148–174.

Brooks, G. E. *Landlords and Strangers: Ecology, Society, and Trade in Western Africa, 1000–1630.* Boulder, Colo.: Westview Press, 1993.

Connah, G. *African Civilizations.* Cambridge: Cambridge University Press, 1987.

Gray, R., and D. Birmingham (eds.). *Pre-Colonial African Trade.* London: Oxford University Press, 1970.

Horton, M. C. *Shanga: The Archaeology of a Muslim Trading Community on the Coast of East Africa.* London: British Institute in Eastern Africa, 1996.

Koponen, J. *People and Production in Late Precolonial Tanzania.* Uppsala, Sweden: Scandinavian Institute of African Studies, 1988.

Mitchell, P. J. "Prehistoric Exchange and Interaction in Southeastern Southern Africa: Marine Shells and Ostrich Eggshell." *African Archaeological Review* 13, no. 1 (1996): 35–76.

Schmidt, P. R. "Archaeological Views on a History of Landscape Change in East Africa." *Journal of African History* 38 (1997): 393–421.

Shaw, T., P. Sinclair, B. Andah, and A. Okpoko (eds.). *The Archaeology of Africa: Food, Metals and Towns.* London: Routledge, 1993.

Stahl, A. B. "The Archaeology of Global Encounters Viewed from Banda, Ghana." *African Archaeological Review* 16, no. 1 (1999): 5–81.

Professions, Africans in: Colonial

Professions can be defined as salaried intellectual work requiring formal training and certification beyond a level of secondary education. The core professions that fall under this definition in Africa during the colonial era include: lawyers, medical doctors, certified teachers, engineers, ministers of religion, journalists, and higher-level clerks. Some professions were not monolithic, but incorporated wide variations in training, income, and status; for this reason, lower-level clerks, interpreters, teachers, clerics, and catechists may be excluded. Also excluded are non-Western professions such as scholars of Islam and traditional healers or "native doctors," who were rarely counted as professionals by colonial authorities. During the later colonial period more professions were added, such as nurses, social workers, dentists, pharmacists, and accountants. Most professionals were male; the only significant areas of professional employment for African women in the colonial period were nursing (including midwifery), teaching, and social work.

The professions were most developed in areas which saw the most extensive degree of Westernization and social change. Professionals tended to be concentrated in urban areas, and particularly in administrative and trading centers. Their rise was also linked to the establishment and development of local institutions to provide training and certification, though some students went to Europe or the United States for training throughout the colonial period.

In Egypt, Muhammad 'Ali Pasha established a system of schools to train a new professional elite, including administrators, military officers, engineers, veterinarians, doctors, midwives, and translators, from the 1820s onward. The Abu Za'hal Hospital was reported to have trained 420 medical students by the time of its move to Cairo in 1837, where it became the Qasr al-Aini Medical School. Muhammad 'Ali Pasha also sent students to Europe for training. By the end of the Pasha's reign in 1848 the nucleus of an indigenous professional elite had been established.

French settler colonialism ensured that the new professions emerged more slowly in the Maghrib. In Morocco, a steady trickle entered the professions from the time of Mawlay Hassan (1873–1994) on. In Tunisia, Franco-Arab schools formed a rudimentary school system beginning in the late nineteenth century, with the Sadiqiyya College at its apex. These schools began educating a new Tunisian elite that thereby gained access to professions; the future nationalist leader Habib Bourguiba is an example. In Algeria the Muslim *évolués* demanded improved educational opportunities after World War I. Some went to study in France, while others went to modern Islamic schools in Egypt or elsewhere. By 1955, 25,000 Muslims were said to be working in the "liberal professions" in the Maghrib, the majority being in Morocco and Algeria. Meanwhile, in Libya the indigenous professional elite

remained of negligible proportions throughout the relatively brief period of Italian colonialism.

The first Africans in the professions in West Africa appeared in the 1850s. They were drawn from Westernized Creole communities in Liberia and Sierra Leone, supplemented by members of the indigenous Gold Coast elite. Some settled in Lagos, where they formed the nucleus of the new professional class there. Eight of nine African medical doctors to practice in Nigeria before 1900 were from Sierra Leone, while the first African lawyer in Nigeria returned from the Gold Coast in 1886. As late as 1921 there were still only 73 persons classed as professionals in Southern Nigeria, a third of whom were "native foreigners." In Northern Nigeria, the professions hardly developed at all before independence. By 1955 there were only 150 barristers and 160 physicians in the whole country, almost all of whom were Yoruba or Ibo. However, there was a growing number in professions such as teaching and nursing, as well as in engineering, surveying and other technical areas.

In the French territories of West Africa, as in the Belgian Congo, the colonial authorities were generally hostile or indifferent to the development of an independent professional class. However, training was provided for employment in the government service. By 1945 the École William Ponty (1903) had granted 2,800 teacher training certificates, while the École Medicine De L'Afrique Occidental Français in Dakar (1918) had graduated over 400 "medical aids" (called "doctors" but unable to practice outside the government service), as well as some midwives. African lawyers were rare in the French speaking territories, though a few were able to train in France before World War II.

The first African doctor in South Africa began practicing in the early 1880s, and the first barrister in 1910. However, the numbers in all professions grew only slowly before World War II. Although there were 48,714 listed as in professional or technical employment in South Africa by 1960 (the vast majority being nurses or teachers), both their training and salary scales were adversely affected by segregation and apartheid policies so that most had only a tenuous claim to professional status.

In East Africa, Makerere College offered a form of medical training to the Bugandan elite from 1913; by 1956 there were 48 Ganda doctors. African physicians in other East African territories also tended to be products of Makerere, including most of the 14 Africans practicing medicine in Tanganyika by 1961. Even so, Makerere graduates were not fully accredited as doctors by the colonial authorities until 1963. The legal profession was even less developed; the first African lawyer in Kenya did not begin practice until 1956, while there were fewer than ten African lawyers in Tanganyika by the time of independence.

Finally, in British, Portuguese, and Belgian central and equatorial Africa, the virtual exclusion of Africans from secondary education until almost the end of the colonial period ensured that the professions were almost nonexistent there before the 1960s.

Although the professions were numerically insignificant in many parts of Africa throughout the colonial period, this did not prevent those who did acquire professional status from becoming the nucleus of a new social and political elite. Almost everywhere the nationalist movements that agitated against and ultimately overthrew colonial rule were led by members of the professions. Ultimately, their historical importance lies in this role.

ALAN GREGOR COBLEY

See also: **Colonialism: Impact on African Societies; Colonialism, Overthrow of: Thirty Years War for Southern African Liberation; Colonialism, Overthrow of: Nationalism and Anticolonialism; Colonialism, Overthrow of: Northern Africa; Colonialism, Overthrow of: Sub-Saharan Africa; Colonialism, Overthrow of: Women and the Nationalist Struggle.**

Further Reading

Cobley, Alan G. *Class and Consciousness: The Black Petty Bourgeoisie in Politics and Society in South Africa, 1924–1950.* Westport, Conn.: Greenwood Press, 1990.

Kilson, Martin. "The Emergent Elites of Black Africa, 1900–1960." In *Colonialism in Africa 1870–1960,* vol. 2, *The History and Politics of Colonialism 1914–1960,* edited by L. H. Gann and Peter Duignan. Cambridge: Cambridge University Press, 1970.

Lloyd, Peter C. *Africa in Social Change,* rev ed. Harmondsworth, England: Penguin, 1972.

Toledano, Ehud, R., "Social and Economic Change in the 'Long Nineteenth Century.'" In *The Cambridge History of Egypt,* vol. 2, *Modern Egypt, from 1517 to the End of the Twentieth Century,* edited by M. W. Daly. Cambridge: Cambridge University Press, 1998.

Zachernuk, Philip S. *Colonial Subjects: An African Intelligentsia and Atlantic Ideas.* Charlottesville: University Press of Virginia, 2000.

Prophetic Movements: *See* Religion, Colonial Africa: Prophetic Movements.

Ptolemaic Dynasty: *See* Egypt, Ancient: Ptolemaic Dynasty: Historical Outline.

Punt and Its Neighbors

The name Punt occurs in ancient Egyptian sources to identify a region in eastern Africa that existed as a distinct entity for a thousand years, *c.*2500–1170BCE, during which time the Egyptians traded with Punt to obtain myrrh, incense, gold, ebony, other rare woods, and animals. Originally, the mention of aromatics had suggested that Punt was located in the Middle East. But then came the discovery of the panorama of the land of Punt among the sculptured scenes in the memorial temple of Queen Hatshepsut (*c.*1470BCE), which included giraffes, baboons, rhinos, and palm trees, all indicating an East African setting.

Expeditions to and from Punt moved along the Red Sea. A port of the Middle Kingdom period (*c.*1900BCE) at Mersa Gawasis has inscriptions about ships visiting Punt, while the vessels sent by Queen Hatshepsut are portrayed as sailing over a sea full of various species of Red Sea fish. At a much later period, there is a description of rain falling upon the "mountain of Punt," which drained into the Nile to augment the Nile flood. This indicates a location for Punt in the eastern Sudan, running south into northernmost Eritrea and Ethiopia, from the coast of the Red Sea inland, westward, toward the Nile south of the Fifth Cataract and the Atbara. This corresponds to the presence of various kinds of frankincense and myrrh trees on the borderlands of Sudan, Ethiopia, and Eritrea, and to that of ebony in northwest Ethiopia and Eritrea bordering on northeast Sudan.

The great mercantile expeditions to Punt were usually sent at times of Egyptian greatness and prosperity, when the pharaohs could stage such enterprises. Hence our most explicit records come from the height of the Old, Middle, and New Kingdoms, respectively. The earliest of these was that sent by Sahure (Fifth Dynasty), *c.*2450BCE, in the Old Kingdom or "Pyramid Age." Then we have expeditions sent through the Red Sea port at Mersa Gawasis (ancient Sawaw) under Mentuhotep III, *c.*1975BCE, in the Eleventh Dynasty, and under Sesostris I, *c.*1920BCE (Twelfth Dynasty) in the Middle Kingdom. In the New Kingdom, there is the famous expedition celebrated in sculptured scenes by Queen Hatshepsut (Eighteenth Dynasty, *c.*1470BCE), and the report of another such under Ramses III (Twentieth Dynasty), the last of its kind, *c.*1170BCE. As the texts of Queen Hatshepsut make clear, the aim of such expeditions was to establish a direct link with the suppliers of the exotic products desired, to cut out middlemen (and thereby cut down on costs) and obtain significant quantities of merchandise. At other times, the trade was carried out, stage by stage (doubtless through many such middlemen) down the Nile into the Egyptian domain. During the New Kingdom at least, the inhabitants of Punt sometimes took the initiative, by sending their own modest-sized trading expeditions north up the Red Sea coast, directly to Egypt's Red Sea port at Sawaw, where they would trade with the Egyptian officials, who then sent on the products so obtained westward through the desert valley of Wadi Hammamat to the Nile at Koptos, for transit to the royal capitals at either Memphis or Thebes.

From the Egyptian sources it is clear that Punt was a large area divided up among various groups ruled by local chiefs; there was no centralized "kingdom" of Punt. Pile houses were in use, and cattle herding was practiced. The reason for the dissolution of Egypt's links with Punt in the twelfth century BCE is unknown at the time of this writing. It has been suggested that South Arabian trade up to Palestine may have eclipsed it, or that climatic changes played some part.

The Egyptian records also permit a glimpse of other named regions and groups in eastern Africa, especially in the later second millennium BCE. Thus, between Punt and Egypt's Nubian empire (to the Fourth Cataract) there existed an area called 'Amaw, a source of gold that was outside Egyptian control, but traded through Punt. 'Amaw probably occupied an area of the northeast Sudan between the Nile (from Abu Hamed to the Fifth Cataract) and the Red Sea mountains behind Sudan's Red Sea coast from north of Ras Shagara south to near Suakin. Between Egypt's border at the First Cataract, along the Nile south to the Second Cataract (and reaching into the Eastern Desert), was Wawat (Lower Nubia, in modern terms). The Nile Valley from the Second to the Fourth Cataracts (and adjoining Eastern Desert) was Kush (Upper Nubia), a name that could also be used to include Kush and Wawat together. These formed, at times, the two provinces of Egypt's Nubian domains. Kush was also a kingdom in its own right at various periods, most visible from the first millennium BCE onward (the kingdom of Napata).

A much-discussed entity is Irem. It seems most likely that this ancient chiefdom (or even kingdom) was based in the Nile Valley from about Berber to Khartoum but reached north across the Bayuda desert routes toward the Nile. The wells on some such routes were disputed by Irem, and Sethos I and Ramses II of Egypt, in the thirteenth century BCE Irem repeatedly resisted Egyptian domination. The area of Medjau was probably that of the Red Sea hills between Wawat and the Red Sea, a land populated by Bedouins and marked by desert wells; Medjau is often compared with modern Beja. Finally, Kenset, also mentioned in ancient texts, may be the desert region west of the Nile, opposite Wawat. Parallel with the Nile, in Nubia, there is a line of lesser oases that may have fallen within its general limits.

K. A. KITCHEN

See also: **Egypt, Ancient, and Africa; Egypt, Ancient: Old Kingdom and Its Contacts to the South: Historical Outline; Kush; Nubia: Relations with Egypt.**

Further Reading

Herzog, Rolf, *Punt,* Gluckstadt: Augustin Verlag, 1968.

Kitchen, K. A. "Further Thoughts on Punt and its Neighbours." In *Egyptological Studies,* edited by M. A. Leahy and W. J. Tait. London: Egypt Exploration Society, 2000.

———. "The Land of Punt." In *The Archaeology of Africa: Food, Metals and Towns,* edited by D. O'Connor. "Egypt, 1552–664 BC" and "Appendix, the Toponyms of Nubia." In *The Cambridge History of Africa,* vol. 1, edited by J. Desmond Clark. Cambridge: Cambridge University Press, 1982.

———. "Punt and How to Get There." *Orientalia* 40, no. 2 (1971): 184–207.

Qalawun: *See* **Egypt: Mamluk Dynasty: Baybars, Qalawun, Mongols, 1250–1300.**

Qayrawan

Arab armies sweeping across North Africa from bases in Egypt began entering what is today Tunisia in the mid-seventh century (*c.*640–650), moving through the steppe regions that separated the coastal plain from the mountains. The first commanders set up military encampments at a site called al-Qarn (the hill), which afforded protection from enemy attack and was also safe from the floods that periodically devastated the area. The founding of the city of Qayrawan, a few miles to the southeast, is traditionally attributed to Uqba ibn Nafi, a veteran soldier appointed governor of the province of Ifriqiya (the Arabized form of the Latin "Africa") in 670. Qayrawan served as a garrison city for Uqba's bedouin troops and became the first permanent Arab administrative center in North Africa. It contained the first major mosque west of the Nile Valley (named, after its builder, Sidi Uqba), and was the point from which Islam and Arab rule spread farther west, into Algeria, Morocco, and Spain, as well as south, into and across the Sahara. Qayrawan's links with Tunisia's earliest Muslims made the city a place of pilgrimage—a popular local belief equating three visits to Qayrawan with one to Mecca—and clothed successive generations of its religious dignitaries, the *ulama*, with great prestige.

For more than a century after its founding, nearby Berbers subjected it to attacks. These were, at first, acts of resistance to the conquest, but they continued even after the Berbers' conversion to Islam. On a number of occasions, the hostile Berbers occupied Qayrawan. The later forays were frequently inspired by ideas advocated by the Kharajis, a Muslim sect that emphasized the equality of all believers regardless of racial or familial background. This doctrine proved particularly appealing to many Berbers, who believed that, despite their embrace of Islam, Arab rulers sent to Qayrawan from the east discriminated against them, and the Sunni religious establishment of the city held them in low esteem.

In 800, the Abbasid caliph in Baghdad named Ibrahim ibn Aghlab governor of Ifriqiya. Ibrahim stabilized the situation and laid the groundwork for his descendants to assert their independent control over the province, acknowledging the caliph's spiritual, but not political, authority. The Aghlabids turned Qayrawan into a major commercial center through which goods from Sub-Saharan Africa passed en route to markets in the Middle East. Revenues earned from taxing commerce and agriculture, along with booty taken in their conquest of Sicily, enabled the Aghlabids to enrich the city with religious monuments and to undertake large-scale public works projects. During their era, Qayrawan became a center of Muslim intellectual life. Among the important scholars and thinkers who resided there were Malik ibn Anas, the founder of one of the four legal schools of thought recognized throughout the Muslim world, and Asad al-Furat and Imam Sahnun, jurists who synthesized Malik's work and wrote commentaries on his teachings. The Aghlabids built a royal suburb, Raqqada, which acquired a reputation for luxury and decadence, in striking contrast with the austere religious atmosphere of Qayrawan. The dynasty's excesses fueled a wave of unrest that culminated in its overthrow by the Fatimids, Shi'i Muslims who seized power in Ifriqiya in the early tenth century. When the Fatimids captured Egypt and moved their capital there in 969, they designated the Zirids, an allied Berber community, as their lieutenants in Ifriqiya. Like all of their predecessors since the Arab conquest, the Zirids used Qayrawan as their capital, but spent considerable amounts of time at Mansuriya, another royal suburb added to the city by the Fatimids.

In the years after the Fatimids' departure, the growing power of the Almoravid Berber confederation in western North Africa produced a shift in trans-Saharan trade routes toward Morocco, causing a reorientation of Ifriqiya's commercial activity from Qayrawan to cities on the Mediterranean. This setback was aggravated by the advent of the Banu Hilal, a group of Arab bedouin dispatched to Ifriqiya by the Fatimids to punish the Zirids for their insolence in acting as independent sovereigns. The Banu Hilal defeated the Zirids at the Battle of Haidaran, northwest of Qayrawan, in 1052, and captured and sacked the city itself five years later. The Zirid rulers retreated to Mahdiya, a coastal stronghold. In the centuries that followed, Tunis, with its Mediterranean focus, eclipsed Qayrawan as the province's center of political and economic gravity— so much so that the name Tunisia replaced Ifriqiya as the standard designation for the entire area. Nonetheless, Qayrawan's role as a religious center continued long after its political and economic power had dissipated.

Not until the early eighteenth century did Qayrawan again figure prominently in political affairs. Husayn ibn Ali, the founder of the Husaynid Dynasty (1705–1956), sought refuge there in the midst of a civil war instigated by his nephew Ali. The latter's forces besieged Qayrawan between 1735 and 1740, finally capturing and executing not only Husayn, but many of the city's prominent citizens who had approved of sheltering him. Qayrawan was a leading center in the 1864 revolt in southern and central Tunisia brought on by the imposition of heavy taxes on rural regions by the central government in Tunis. Qayrawan was also one of the few Tunisian cities where efforts, albeit unsuccessful ones, were made to resist the French occupation in 1881. The *ulama* of Qayrawan saw it as their task to safeguard the city's rich Islamic heritage against foreign, non-Muslim encroachment.

After Tunisian independence, Qayrawan was the scene of the first serious demonstrations against President Habib Bourguiba's secularizing policies, which aimed at circumscribing the power of the ulama. His 1961 exhortation that Tunisians ignore the practice of fasting during the month of Ramadan because of its deleterious effect on the economy produced particularly strong resentment in the city. Two decades later, in the waning days of Bourguiba's presidency, Islamist groups formed to reverse what they regarded as Tunisia's abandonment of Islamic values and traditions enjoyed considerable support in Qayrawan.

KENNETH J. PERKINS

See also: **Maghrib.**

Further Reading

Despois, Jean. "Kairouan: Origine et évolution d'une ancienne capitale musulmane." *Annales de Géographie* (1930): 159–77.

Idris, Hady Roger. *La Berbérie orientale sous les Zirides, Xè–XIIè siècles*, 2 vols. Paris: Adrien-Maisonneuve, 1962.

———. "Contribution à l'histoire de l'Ifriqiya. Tableau de la vie intellectuelle et administrative à Kairouan sous les Aghlabites et les Fatimites (4 premiers siècles de l'Hégire) d'après le *Riyad En Nufus* de Abu Bakr al Maliki." *Revue des Etudes Islamiques*, no. 9 (1935): 105–178, 273–305; no. 10 (1936): 45–104.

———. "Al-Muizz ben Badis, grandeur et décadence de la 'civilisation Kairouanaise.'" *Les Africains, sous la direction de Ch.-A. Julien et al.* 12 (1978): 223–251.

Monchicourt, Charles, "Etudes Kairouanaises." *Revue Tunisienne* (1931): 309–338; (1932): 79–91, 307–343; (1933): 57–92, 285–319; (1934): 33–58; (1936): 187–221, 425–450.

Talbi, Mohamed, *L'Emirat aghlabide, 800–909: histoire politique*. Paris: Adrien-Maisonneuve, 1966.

R

Rabih ibn Fadl Allah

Rabih Fadl Allah (1845–1900), known as Rabih Zubayr, was of Hamaj origin born in an undesirable quarter of Khartoum, *Salamat al-Basha*, who sought his fortune from the slave trade in the upper Nile.

Rabih joined the slaving empire of Zubayr Pasha Rahma Mansur in the Bahr al-Ghazal and rose to prominence as his chief lieutenant by military skill and organizational abilities. He led Zubayr's personal army in its conquest of Darfur in 1874 until the incarceration of Zubayr in Cairo by the Khedive and the execution of his son and heir by Egyptian forces under Gessi Pasha in 1879. Rabih rallied the remnants of Zubayr's slave soldiers, and armed with rifles, muskets, and a few cannons welded them into an army personally loyal to him. He first plundered the Azande country, where he established a sultanate from 1880 to 1884 before moving westward with his *basinqir* (slave troops) to distance himself from the Egyptian army in the Bahr al-Ghazal. Rabih swept through Dar Banda in 1882 and the following year occupied Dar Kuti and Dar Runga until defeated by the forces of the Sultan of Wadai. He retired to Dar Kuti and Dar Runga, where he systematically enlisted the population into his slave regiments or sold them and their ivory for firearms and ammunition. In 1892 his army of 20,000-armed basinqir destroyed the neighboring state of Bagirmi and occupied the rich agricultural region between the Chari and Logone Rivers. The previous year his chief lieutenant, Muhammad al-Sanusi, had massacred the French mission of Paul Crampel coming up the Ubanghi under auspices of the Comité de l'Afrique Française that was to open relations with the sultans of the Sudanic states before crossing the Sahara to Algeria. He had no wish to provoke the French, and, consistent with his policy to remove himself from any authority other than his own, he marched northwest into Borno. Between 1884 and 1896 his basinqir defeated the armies of Borno, destroying its capital at Kukawa. By 1896 Rabih was the ruler of Borno from his capital at Dikwa, south of Lake Chad, and for the first time in his career he settled there as a sultan of a Sudanic kingdom to plan further conquests in the west (to Kano and Sokoto), with which he most likely would have succeeded if not for the appearance of the French.

French policy in Africa was neither consistent nor formulated in Paris, but shaped by the colonial caucus in the Chamber of Deputies, commercial interests, and the geographical and scientific societies all organized by the Comité de l'Afrique Française to promote France overseas. More decisive in French African policy were not the civilians in Paris but the ambitious French officers in the Western Sudan, the *officiers soudannais*. They were men of action equipped with modern arms and modest intellect who raised insubordination to a heroic art in order to lead the patriotic expansion of France through the Sahara and into the Sudan to the exasperation of timid civilians more concerned with the eastern frontier of France than acquisitions of light soil in Africa. Although Rabih had plundered central Africa since 1880, he had not come to the attention of the French until 1893. Thereafter his whereabouts, alive or dead, remained unclear until 1896 when Emil Gentil, a naval officer with an insignificant rank, *ensigne de vaisseau*, left Brazzaville to establish a French presence on the Lower Chari River and Lake Chad. Gentil was not alone. At the turn of the century, France, Britain, and Germany were active sending expeditions into the African hinterland to occupy the spheres delimited to them on the map of Africa in Europe before any interloper might poach unsecured territory. Imperialism in Central Africa was a race along the spokes of a wheel of empire; its hub was Lake Chad, whose shores were ruled by none other than Rabih Zubayr.

Two other French expeditions had been launched to consolidate French claims in the Sahara and Sudan and then to rendezvous with Gentil to secure Lake Chad. The Central African mission, led by Captain Paul Voulet and Lieutenant Charles Chanoine, marched eastward from Say on the Niger in January 1899, cutting a swath of blood and destruction across Hausaland that equaled the ravages of Rabih's basinqir. Lieutenant Colonel Klobb, sent in haste to stop their slaughter, was killed by orders from Voulet, and the brutality continued as they advanced on Zinder until their *tirailleurs* (Africans, mostly from Senegal, recruited to serve in the French West African army) mutinied and shot both Voulet and Chanoine. The remnants of this ill-fated mission were reorganized, and managed to struggle on to Lake Chad to join the Foureau-Lamy Mission on February 18, 1900.

The Comité de l'Afrique Française organized another *missionaire scientifique*, ostensibly led by the experienced Saharan explorer Fernand Foureau. In fact the expedition, under the command of Major François Lamy, bore a philanthropic facade in order to break the historic independence of the Tuareg, press on to Lake Chad, and rendezvous with Voulet and Gentil to overwhelm any African opposition. Lamy and his tirailleurs defeated the Tuareg but did not subdue them. His determined but much diminished contingent met the remains of the Voulet Central African Mission on the eastern shore of Lake Chad to march south, where the combined expedition established a camp on the right bank of the Chari opposite Guelfi on February 24, 1900. They crossed the Chari to capture Kusseri, Rabih's stronghold at the confluence of the Chari and Logone rivers 50 miles (80 kilometers) south of Lake Chad. On April 20, Emil Gentil arrived at Kusseri as the French administrator. His expedition was weary, decimated by disease, and Rabih Zubayr had massacred its advance guard under Henri Bretonnet in the Niellim Hills in July 1899. But by April 1900 the French *rendevous de Tchad* was complete.

The loss of Kusseri was the beginning of the end for Rabih Zubayr. Gentil authorized Major Lamy to take command of the three French missions and destroy Rabih Zubayr. The battle began at dawn on April 22, 1900. The *tirailleurs* attacked Rabih's stockade at Lakhta three miles from the walls of Kusseri and ended in the early afternoon when the severed head of Rabih Fadl Allah was brought to the dying Lamy to be carried on a stick through Kusseri. His body was thrown into the Chari. Commandant Lamy is largely forgotten, for the capital of colonial Chad in his name was replaced by Ndjamena in 1973 to commemorate the great spreading tree that provided the shade for the original fishing village of Am-Djamina across the river from Kusseri.

Rabih is still remembered. To some his implacable opposition to the French is heroic, but to the Africans of southern Chad his rule is a tragic tale of depopulation and devastation along the banks of the Chari and in Bagirmi and Borno. Not unlike Voulet and Chanoine in Hausaland, Rabih in Chad was known as *Le Maudit—* the Accursed.

ROBERT O. COLLINS

Further Reading

Hallam, W. K. R. *The Life and Times of Rabih Fadl Allah*. Ilfracombe, Australia: Arthur H. Stockwell, 1977.

Porch, Douglas, *The Conquest of the Sudan*. New York: Alfred A. Knopf, 1984.

Santandrea, Fr. S. *A Tribal History of the Western Bahr el Ghazal*, Bologna: Verona Fathers, 1964.

Urvoy, Y. *Histoire de l'empire du Borno*. Paris: Chevalier, 1949.

Railways

Africa's rivers to its coasts are not navigable throughout the year, and early on did not provide access to the areas that European imperialists wanted to reach; railways were built to facilitate annexation and exploitation. In northern, western, and eastern Africa, imperial conquest and defending territorial claims against European rivals were the primary motives for railway building. Farther south, conquest was achieved largely without railways, which did help support imperial territorial claims but were built primarily to facilitate the exploitation of mineral resources. In central and parts of southern Africa, anticipation of profit from minerals attracted private finance. Reality did not always meet expectation, leaving some lines only partially built or financial failures, while inadequate planning meant that some lines were unable to achieve their intended purpose.

The imperial state financed construction in cases where it was considered essential to retain control or the prospects of financial returns were too low to attract purely private finance. In East Africa, imperial governments built the line from Mombasa to the Kenya-Uganda border, and later beyond the frontier and the line from Dar es Salaam to Lake Tanganyika. The lines helped to establish "effective occupation," protecting British and German claims against possible encroachment by the French, Portuguese, or one another, and facilitated rapid troop movements into the interior as needed for defense or suppressing African unrest.

In Algeria and elsewhere in North Africa the French awarded concessions for strategically essential railway construction, sometimes involving British capital. Many people involved had grandiose schemes for lines across the Sahara to connect with lines in French West African colonies, but ultimately the government had to subsidize rail operations heavily. In Ethiopia the Italians also built railways for military purposes, but not necessarily successfully. Defeat by Menelik II at Aduwa in 1896 was largely a consequence of the railway having only been completed to Saati.

In North Africa, railways came to link areas farther from the coast, serving commercial as well as strategic purposes and joining the French colonies by rail. Post-conquest mineral development was facilitated by the existence of railways but had not been a motive for their construction. The same was true elsewhere: Gold Coast's line to Tarkwa, built to aid the conquest of Ashanti, also supported gold mining there. Lines without mineral traffic required continued government support, while a lack of initial planning frequently required substantial reorganization between the time of the two world wars and later. Any local traffic they generated was minimal and had little impact on railway or government revenues, though some wider economic development did result. Substantial mineral traffic, by contrast, made it possible for railways to be profitable and to carry agricultural produce at acceptably low rates.

This was the case farther south, where the Cape government built lines connecting the Kimberley diamond fields to Cape Town, Port Elizabeth, and East London to facilitate the importing of machinery and other goods. The East London connection was built only to satisfy demands by Europeans in that area to link their port to a valuable hinterland. Revenues from mineral traffic effectively subsidized agricultural traffic, which was able to expand and continue to make a significant contribution to the economy. Natal agriculture benefited similarly from the rail link between Durban and the Transvaal, which neither needed nor substantially used the route.

The shortest railway between the Transvaal and the coast was to Lourenço Marques (Maputo), and was preferred by President Paul Kruger. After the Second South African (Boer) War, poor port facilities, rate manipulation on the Cape line, and cheaper European freight rates to Port Elizabeth meant that the Portuguese line did not attract substantial amounts of Transvaal traffic. It was only by linking railway traffic to permission to recruit Mozambican labor for the Rand gold mines that the Portuguese were able to redress the balance. Recruiting rights had been negotiated with the Chamber of Mines in 1897, but a modus vivendi confirming those rights, guaranteeing rail traffic, and giving Mozambique a preferential trade position in the mining area was reached in 1901. A formal agreement was signed in 1909 and, modified over the year, continued to operate—primarily in South Africa's favor—until shortly after Mozambique's independence.

The British South Africa Company (BSAC) was required to build a railway line to the northern (unspecified) border of the area it was to administer and exploit. To bypass the Transvaal and as part of a vain attempt to get Bechuanaland included in chartered territory, Cecil Rhodes of the BSAC built the line through the protectorate to Bulawayo and on to Salisbury (Harare) to connect to the line through Mozambique to Beira, with a branch to Victoria Falls through the Wankie coal fields. The failure of Rhodesia's Second Rand to materialize drew the line to Broken Hill (Kabwe), but difficulties in separating zinc and lead ores there meant that the railway companies and chartered were only rescued from severe financial difficulties by reaching an agreement to link to the rich copper mines of Katanga (Shaba) in the Belgian Congo. From 1911 on, the line to Beira carried virtually all Katanga traffic. In 1928 two other lines became available.

The Benguela Railway was begun in 1904 with the intention of providing the shortest route from Katanga to the coast. World War I and opposition from Jan Smuts in South Africa delayed completion until 1928, by which time the Congo's own Bas-Congo to Katanga (BCK) line joined the mines to the navigable Kasai River. There copper was loaded on barges, shipped to Léopoldville (Kinshasa), loaded on trains, and taken around the rapids of the Lower Congo River to Matadi seaport. Politics and the need for BCK profits ensured its preference over the more direct Benguela route. Rhodesian Railways continued to benefit because of Katanga's reliance on Wankie coal to smelt copper ores.

Smaller lines in various places served as feeders for the main lines or navigable rivers, while others were started from the coast but never completed. Economic realities and political demands determined the structure and use of Africa's rail network, ultimately leaving many African countries better connected to the outside world than to their neighbors.

SIMON KATZENELLENBOGEN

See also: **Ghana, Republic of: Colonial Period: Economy; Kenya: East African Protectorate and the Uganda Railway; Nigeria: Colonial Period: Railways, Mining, and Market Production; Peasant Production, Colonial; Rhodes, Cecil J.; Senegal: Colonial Period: Railways; Smuts, Jan C.; South Africa: Gold on the Witwatersrand, 1886–1899.**

Further Reading

Brant, E. D. *Railways of North Africa: The Railway System of the Maghreb: Algeria, Tunisia, Morocco and Libya.* Newton Abbot, England: David and Charles, 1971.

Katzenellenbogen, S. E. *Railways and the Copper Mines of Katanga.* Oxford: Oxford University Press, 197.

Katzenellenbogen, Simon. "The Miner's Frontier, Ttransport and General Economic Development." In *Colonialism in Africa 1870–1960,* vol. 4, *The Economics of Colonialism,* edited by Peter Duignan and L. H. Gann. Cambridge: Cambridge University Press for the Hoover Institution, 1975.

Katzenellenbogen, Simon E. *South Africa and Southern Mozambique: Labour, Railways and Trade in the Making of a Relationship*. Manchester: Manchester University Press, 1983.

Lunn, Jon. *Capital and Labour on the Rhodesian Railway System 1888–1947*. Houndmills, England: Macmillan, in association with St. Antony's College, Oxford, 1997.

Maggi, Stefano. "The Railways of Italian Africa; Economic, Social and Strategic Features." *Journal of Transport History* 18, no. 1 (1997): 54–71.

Ramgoolam, Seewoosagur: *See* Mauritius: Ramgoolam, Seewoosagur, Government of.

Ramphele, Dr. Mamphela Aletta (1947–)
South African Doctor, Activist, Intellectual, and Educationalist.

As a college student, Mamphela Aletta Ramphele met Steve Biko, the founder of the black consciousness (BC) movement, and worked closely with him on a range of the South African Students Organisation's matters. She was married (unsuccessfully) to an old friend, then resumed her relationship with Biko after she qualified as a medical doctor in 1972. While a medical intern in Durban and then Port Elizabeth, she worked as an activist in the BC movement, then set up and ran Zanempilo, a health center near King William's Town, while also working toward a commerce degree with the University of South Africa. She was hoping that her relationship with Biko would be regularized when she was banished by the state to a remote area near Tzaneen in the northern Transvaal. There, in September 1977, when pregnant with their child, she heard the terrible news of Biko's murder by the police. Their son Hlumelo was born shortly afterward. She subsequently had another son by a second husband, but that marriage, like her first, did not last long.

After Biko's death Ramphele slowly built a new life for herself in Lenyenye township, continuing her work with the rural poor of the district and setting up the Ithuseng Community Health Programme, which opened in 1981. She obtained diplomas in tropical health and hygiene and public health from the University of the Witwatersrand. After her banishment was lifted in 1983 she moved, first to Port Elizabeth in 1984 and then to the University of Cape Town, where she worked with Professor Francis Wilson on the Second Carnegie Inquiry into Poverty and Development in South Africa. She was formally appointed a research fellow at the university in 1986, where she collaborated with Wilson in the writing of *Uprooting Poverty: The South African Challenge* (1989), which won the Noma Award for Publishing in Africa. The two also coauthored *Children on the Frontline: A Report for Unicef on the Status of Children in South Africa* (1987).

Ramphele obtained a doctorate in social anthropology for a dissertation entitled "The Politics of Space: Life in the Migrant Labor Hostels in Cape Town," subsequently published as *A Bed Called Home* (1993). She also coedited and contributed to *Bounds of Possibility: The Legacy of Steve Biko* (1991), and edited *Restoring the Land* (1992), a book on the ecological challenges facing postapartheid South Africa. As South Africa entered a new political dispensation, this forceful woman began to serve on the boards of major corporations and nongovernmental organizations. She rose to become chairman of the board of the Independent Development Trust, and was a member of the boards of Anglo American, the Old Mutual Foundation, and the Open Society Foundation.

Dr. Stuart Saunders, vice-chancellor of the University of Cape Town, saw in Ramphele a possible successor, suitable for the new democratic South Africa about to be born. Appointed a part-time deputy vice chancellor in 1991, she mainly concerned herself with issues of gender and race. She began to argue that the staff profile should be fundamentally transformed to bring the university in line with the demographics of the country. In September 1996 she took over as vice chancellor of the University of Cape Town, the first black woman to hold such a post in South Africa, at a ceremony graced with the presence of Nelson Mandela, with whom she had had close relations for some years. She was critical of many BC positions, and remained an independent voice, refusing to join the African National Congress. She spoke out against corruption in government, and in December 1999 against the "culture of silence" that she saw as a threat to the consolodation of democracy.

At the time that she was appointed vice chancellor, Ramphele had never taught in a university, headed an academic department, or been a dean, and was now thrust into a position in which she was mainly dependent on white men. After serving an eight-month overlap period with Saunders, she showed her determination to transform the university. She got the budgetary council to agree to balance the budget and set aside considerable funds for special projects, which included rebuilding the library and promoting the African Gender Institute and the African studies program. In early 1999 she was elected chair of the South African Vice Chancellors' Association. By then she had received a number of honorary degrees, the first from Hunter College (of the City University of New York) in 1984. Once vice chancellor, she received an award from Princeton University in 1997; an honorary doctorate of medicine from

Sheffield University in 1998; and an honorary doctorate of law from the University of Michigan in 1999.

In May of 2000 Ramphele was appointed managing director for human resource development at the World Bank, where she manages development programs in the areas of education and health.

CHRISTOPHER SAUNDERS

Biography

Born near Pietersburg in the Transvaal (now in Northern Province) on December 28, 1947. Attended a local high school, then the University of the North, before moving to the University of Natal to study medicine. Qualified as a medical doctor in 1972. Currently holds a Ph.D. in social anthropology from the University of Cape Town and has received numerous honorary degrees. Since 2000 has served as managing director for human resource development at the World Bank.

Further Reading

Pityana, B., M. Ramphele, M. Mpumlwana, and L. Wilson, *Bounds of Possibility: the Legacy of Steve Biko.* Cape Town: David Philip, 1991.

Ramphele, Mamphela. *Across Boundaries: The Journey of a South African Woman Leader.* New York: Feminist Press at the City University of New York, 1996.

Ramphele, Mamphela. *Mamphela Ramphele: A Life.* Cape Town: David Philip, 1995.

University of Cape Town. *Monday Paper.* 1991–1999.

Wilson, Lindy. "The Story of Dr. Ramphele: The Tears and Joy." *Die Suid-Afrikaan*, no. 8 (1986).

Woods, Donald. *Biko.* New York: Paddington Press, 1978.

Ramses II
Egyptian Pharoah

The third ruler in Egypt's Nineteenth Dynasty, Ramses II reigned for just over 66 years in the thirteenth century BCE, from approximately 1279 to 1213. The Eighteenth Dynasty had extended Egypt's rule far south of its own border at the First Cataract, far up the Nile (through Nubia) to the Fourth Cataract, and also into the Levant, over Palestine, up the Mediterranean coast and into Syria. The sun-worshipping Akhenaten lost part of the Levantine possessions, and (with no heir of his own) the last Eighteenth Dynasty Pharaoh, Horemhab, appointed a military colleague to succeed him. This man, Ramses I, reigned only 16 months, but his strong-minded son Sethos I conducted war in the Levant and suppressed a revolt in Nubia; from him, Ramses II thus inherited the entire Nubian empire of his predecessors, and much of their Levantine holdings. Of military origin, the family hailed from the eastern delta area of Avaris on the main route to the Levant.

Ramses II (1290–1224 BCE). Head of black granite from Karnak, Egypt. Now in the Museo Egizio, Turin, Italy. Anonymous. © Erich Lessing/Art Resource, New York.

Ramses II is remembered primarily for his wars, his vast construction program, and his extensive family. The most famous of the wars were those conducted in the Levant, where the main opposition came from the Hittite Empire, based in Anatolia (now Turkey), which had taken over north Syria and laid claim to central Syria, the source of the rivalry with Egypt. Ramses II had achieved a superficial success there on his first campaign in year 4 of the reign (c.1276–1275 BCE). But close to the strategic center of Qadesh on the River Orontes, which Ramses intended to capture on his second campaign in year 5 (c.1275–1274 BCE), the Hittite king sprang a trap on him, from which the young pharaoh only narrowly escaped, at the notorious Battle of Qadesh. Pharaohs never admitted loss or defeat; thus, he celebrated his personal bravery in a florid literary and pictorial record, using the walls of Egypt's great temples as a canvas. Later wars in Syria were indecisive. Eventually, the two powers signed a treaty of lasting peace and became allies.

A prosperous reign of over six decades enabled Ramses to honor the gods with large new temples and spectacular additions to old ones in important cities. Elsewhere, there was hardly a temple that did not receive some refurbishment in his name. In the eastern delta, Ramses II built an entirely new capital city, planned to rival the traditional centers at Memphis (near modern-day Cairo) and Thebes (at modern-day Luxor). South of Egypt, a series of temples in his name lined the Nile Valley between the First and Fourth Cataracts.

In his long reign, Ramses II had eight principal queens that included Nefertari, Istnofret (mother to his successor), four princess queens (his own daughters), and two Hittite princesses. This takes no account of other consorts only briefly mentioned in the texts. He fathered approximately 50 sons and over 50 daughters.

The strong Egyptian belief in an afterlife often stimulated immense investment in elaborate tombs and funeral furnishings. Thus, Ramses II had his own great corridor tomb excavated deep in the rock in the Valley of the Kings at Thebes, and opposite his own tomb he created a huge underground mausoleum for the burials of many of his sons.

Under Ramses II, a traditional firm control over the Nubian Nile (First through Fourth Cataracts) was strenuously maintained by military means. In northern Nubia, just south of the First Cataract, Ramses as crown prince crushed a petty local revolt as part of his military training. Many years later, it was the pharaoh's regular state governor of these southern lands, the Viceroy of Nubia, who crushed other local revolts.

Otherwise, an enforced peace reigned. Egypt's interest in dominating the region was twofold: to mine the gold found in the eastern deserts between the Nile and the Red Sea, and to control downriver trade that brought goods northward from inner Africa. Taxes were also levied on the local chiefdoms along the Nile, both major (e.g., Irem) and minor, to the extent that (eventually) a proportion of the inhabitants may have moved southward, beyond Egyptian control, leaving fewer people to work the Nile-bank fields and bear taxation.

In Nubia as in Egypt, Ramses II emphasized the dominance of Egypt's gods and of himself as their representative and earthly manifestation. His own temple buildings in Nubia fall into three groups. First there are, in his father's last years and the early years of his own reign, the Beit el-Wali temple of Amun (state god of Egypt) and a temple at Quban for the local falcon god, south from the First Cataract. With these belong the temples at Aksha near the Second Cataract (for Ramses II as "Lord of Nubia"), at Amarah West and Napata (for Amun) between the Second and Third Cataracts, and below the Fourth Cataract, respectively. Second, there are the spectacular twin temples at Abu Simbel for the king (as Amun and Re) and Queen Nefertari (as the goddess Hathor), and the king as the sun god Re at Derr (all well north of Aksha). Third, there are two further temples to the king as Amun and Re, which were dedicated at Wadies-Sebua and Gerf Hussein, in northern Nubia. Thus was the ideology of royal supremacy stamped on the Nubian landscape in this reign.

K. A. Kitchen

See also: **Egypt, Ancient: New Kingdom and the Colonization of Nubia.**

Further Reading

Desroches Noblecourt, Christiane. *Le secret des temples de la Nubie.* Paris: Stock/Pernoud, 1999.

Kitchen, K.A. *Pharaoh Triumphant: The Life and Times of Ramesses II.* Warminster, England: Aris and Phillips, 1982.

————. *Ramesside Inscriptions Translated and Annotated, Translations,* vol. 2. Oxford: Blackwell, 1996.

Kitchen, K.A., *Ramesside Inscriptions Translated and Annotated, Notes and Comments,* vol. 2. Oxford: Blackwell, 1996.

Tyldesley, J. *Ramesses the Great.* London: Viking, 1999.

Rawlings, Jerry John (1947–)
Ghanaian Politician and Former Coup Leader

Considered by many as the leading figure of the "new generation" of African leaders, Jerry Rawlings was born in June 1947 to a Scottish father, who had been a chemist in Accra, Ghana's capital, and an Ewe mother. Rawlings attended the prestigious Achimota Secondary School, leaving in 1966 to join the air force the following year. Following his initial cadet training he was posted to the No. 1 Communication Squadron. At the time of a military mutiny that he led in May 1979, he had achieved the rank of flight lieutenant and was attached to the No. 4 Jet Squadron in Accra. There he had begun to identify with a group within the armed forces who considered that there was an urgent need for radical political change in Ghana.

The genesis for a growth of radicalism in the armed forces was the dramatic decline in Ghana's economic and political fortunes. Ghana achieved independence from Britain in 1957, but by 1977 real wages were estimated to have fallen to a quarter of their 1972 value and authoritarian, military-led governments had become the norm. In an economic world of shortages and a political world of unaccountable governments, black markets and corruption, a demand grew for fundamental changes. With the government decidedly unpopular for its denial of democratic rights, the ever-growing economic hardship, and corruption among the military leadership, the military ruler, General Ignatius Kutu Acheampong was replaced by his deputy, General Fred Akuffo. The new administration promised to hold multiparty elections, but public dissatisfaction had reached the point where there were demands not just for civilian government but for the punishment of Acheampong and his colleagues for their corruption and mismanagement.

It was chiefly a burning sense of outrage and injustice occasioned by such events, as well as a serious and prolonged decline in living standards, that led Rawlings to lead a small-scale armed forces mutiny on May 15, 1979. Although Rawlings was arrested, two weeks later, on June 4, a successful military uprising erupted that resulted in his release. Appointed head of state by the coup leaders, Rawlings sanctioned the executions for corruption of the three surviving former heads of state: Generals A. A. Afrifa, Akuffo, and Acheampong. While Rawlings claimed not to be personally in favor of such killings, he was aware that the anger of the ordinary soldiers was barely under control. Consequently, had those judged guilty for Ghana's decline not been killed, Rawlings believed that the "entire officer corps would have ended up being eliminated because they [the ordinary soldiers] would have seen this as just another example of officers' solidarity, another conspiracy of the officer corps to protect itself" (quoted in Okeke 1982, 52).

Following a brief, intense, yet unsuccessful, period of attempted "house cleaning" to rid the country of corruption, elections were held in September 1979. An elected civilian government led by Hilla Limann, whose People's National Party was molded on the Convention People's Party of the late president Kwame Nkrumah, came to power. The incompetence and corruption of this regime contributed to its short life. In addition, its assiduous hounding of Rawlings helped to precipitate a further military coup, led by him on December 31, 1981. This time Rawlings said he wanted a revolution, something that would lead to an appreciably more just equitable order in Ghana, in which ordinary people would have a say in the formation and execution of government policies.

The second phase of Ghana's postcolonial history, from 1981, is a story of evolving political stability and growing economic steadiness. But the period is nonetheless intensely controversial, centering on the figure of Rawlings: nothing divides Ghanaians more than their opinions regarding their ruler of the last two decades. All would agree that he has been a pivotal, absolutely central, figure in the country's political and economic fortunes; but he is a hated figure for some, a hero to others. Yet even his greatest critics might well agree that his initially chaotic, then authoritarian, and finally democratic rule has managed to take Ghana through the uncertainties of the 1970s to the political balance and comparative economic equilibrium of the 1990s.

Ghana's dire economy improved under Rawlings's leadership. By 1985, two years after the commencement of a highly controversial economic "structural adjustment program," Ghana had become the International Monetary Fund's (IMF) star pupil in Africa, held up as a staunch exponent and regional showcase example of economic reform. As a reward, over the next decade Ghana received more than $9 billion (U.S.) in foreign loans, principally from the IMF and the World Bank. Primarily as a result of the economic reforms and foreign injections of funds, Ghana achieved significant growth between 1984 and 1993, with the economy growing by an average of 5 per cent annually. With the population increasing by about 2.6 per cent a year, annual real growth of around 2.5 per cent was a highly commendable achievement, one of the best in Africa at the time. Since then, however, progress has been less swift.

Initially it appeared that the second Rawlings government would institute a one-party system, but later its political focus changed: an early socialist orientation gave way to a concern to build local-level democracy with a "developmentalist" focus, with mixed results. Under pressure from both home and abroad, Rawlings set in motion a transition to multiparty national politics in 1990, which resulted in presidential and legislative elections in 1992 and again in 1996. Both presidential elections were won by Rawlings, and the parliamentary polls by his party, the National Democratic Congress. This characterized the progress from personalist rule with socialist pretensions to an increasingly stable pluralist democracy under Rawlings's leadership. Under the 1992 constitution, Rawlings could not serve for a third term; John Kufuor won the presidency in the 2000 election.

JEFF HAYNES

Biography

Born in Accra in 1947. Formally educated at Achimota School, before joining the air force, where his involvement in radical politics developed. Led armed forces mutiny in May 1979 and was imprisoned. Released soon after to lead successful military coup d'état in June of that year. Handed over power to elected civilian government in September 1979. Led a further successful coup in December 1981. Served as head of Provisional National Defence Council government from 1982 to 1992, during which he presided over growing economic and political stability. Elected president in elections in 1992 and 1996.

See also: **Ghana, Republic of: Achaempong Regime to the Third Republic, 1972–1981; Nkrumah, Kwame.**

Further Reading

Haynes, Jeff. "Ghana: From Personalist to Democratic Rule." In *Democracy and Political Change in Sub-Saharan Africa*, edited by John Wiseman. London: Routledge, 1995.

Ninsin, Kwame (ed.). *Ghana: Transition to Democracy*. Dakar, Senegal: CODESRIA, 1998.

Nugent, Paul. *Big Men, Small Boys and Politics in Ghana*. London: Pinter, 1995.

Okeke, Barbara E. *4 June: A Revolution Betrayed*. Enugu, Nigeria: Ikenga, 1982.

Pinkney, Robert. *Democracy and Dictatorship in Ghana and Tanzania*. Basingstoke, England: Macmillan, 1997.

Rothchild, Donald (ed.). *Ghana: The Political Economy of Recovery*. London: Lynne Rienner, 1991.

Shillington, Kevin. *Ghana and the Rawlings Factor*. Basingstoke: Macmillan, 1992.

Red Sea: *See* Egypt, Ottoman, 1517–1798: Nubia Slavery: Mediterranean, Red Sea, Indian Ocean.

Refugees

Refugees are people who are forced to leave their homelands owing to various reasons such as war, conflict, persecution, poverty, famine or environmental or social disintegration. The phenomenon of refugees reflects the major upheavals of modern times: World War I; the Russian Revolution (1917); the persecution of Jews under fascism and the horrors of World War II; the partition of India (1947); the partition of Palestine (1948); wars of liberation in Asia and Africa; the partition of Pakistan (1971); wars in Vietnam, Cambodia, the Middle East, the Horn of Africa, Afghanistan, and Central America; the breakup of the Soviet Union and Yugoslavia; foreign intervention in Kosovo (1999); and the widening economic disparities within and among nations. All of these have caused massive refugee movement.

In the mid-1970s, only 2.5 million people could claim refugee status, about the same number as in the 1950s and 1960s. By the mid-1990s, the world's refugee population had risen to an alarming 27 million. In addition, there are even more who are victims of mass expulsions, forcible relocation programs, and internal flight within their own countries. According to 1999 estimates, there are probably more than 50 million people around the world today who might legitimately be described as "displaced" or "uprooted." As many as another 50 million refugees have been resettled or repatriated since the end of World War II.

In order to understand and analyze the phenomenon of refugees in the modern world, it is important to examine the causes of these mounting sources of human suffering. What conditions do these vulnerable people face? And what needs to be done to avoid this human tragedy?

No continent is immune to the mass displacement of people for one reason or another. Statistics reveal that the overwhelming majority of refugees today come from poor, developing countries and that most of them end up in other parts of the same Third World. Some of the countries least able to financially cope with asylum seekers have been most accepting of them. This is particularly true of the refugee situation in Africa.

Africa today has a refugee population (according to the United Nations High Command for Refugees, or UNHCR) of over 7 million, in addition to some 15–18 million internally displaced. The vast majority of the refugees in Africa also come from the poorest countries on the continent such as Rwanda (2.2 million), Liberia (0.8 million), Somalia, Eritrea, Sudan, Burundi, Angola, Sierra Leone, Mozambique, Chad, Ethiopia, and Mali. Most of the African refugees are also accommodated by countries unable to financially cope with the burden, such as the Democratic Republic of Congo (Zaire; 1.7 million), Tanzania (0.9 million), Uganda, Sudan, Liberia, Kenya, Guinea, Ghana, Ethiopia, and Burundi.

The refugee problem in Africa is predominantly a phenomenon of the postcolonial epoch, with the exception of a few cases, such as Rwanda, which was torn by civil strife shortly before independence; the North African states of Algeria and Morocco; Tunisia, in its anticolonial struggles; and the Portuguese and minority ruled countries of southern Africa. Colonial oppression and liberation wars apart, the root causes of the refugee problems in Africa derive directly from the prevalent concrete conditions in independent African countries. This results partly from Africa's colonial heritage and the manner in which the states are organized. The policy of "divide and rule" followed by colonial powers did not lead to a reasonable measure of national integration, a situation that created a fertile ground for interethnic conflicts once the heterogeneous groups gained independence as political units.

The most spectacular example of the complex mix of reasons why people leave their homes could be found in Africa. In some places hunger and malnutrition alone have created refugee flows. Overpopulation is another. Ethiopia, for instance, made the news in the 1970s and 1980s for its large flows of refugees seeking relief from a vicious circle of famine and civil war. By the end of 1993, almost 230,000 Ethiopians lived outside the country—mostly in Sudan—and at least half a million were internally displaced.

Just as desperate, but perhaps more complex, is the plight of Somalia. Clan warfare forced approximately half a million Somalis out of the country by the end of 1993, with another 700,000 internally displaced. After surviving years of civil war in the Somali capital Mogadishu, a large number of people fled the country by boats crossing the Red Sea to Yemen through the town of Bosao early in 1999.

In the wake of the power struggle between the Hutus and the Tutsis, some 1.7 million Rwandans remained refugees in 1994. But despite the speed with which the crisis broke in April 1994, it had its roots in long-term trends. The hatred between the Hutus and the Tutsis was based on Rwanda's colonial history, the inequalities of its educational system, the ownership of its land, the control of its government, and other deep, long-standing tensions. Popular analysis of the disaster neglected to take most of those contributing stresses into account. The various tensions were compounded by class conflict between the Hutus and Tutsis. The underlying tension remains unresolved.

As a result of civil war since 1989 in the West African state of Liberia, more than 50 per cent of the country's 2.3 million people have been uprooted. Civil war in the neighboring state of Sierra Leone since 1997 led to massive refugee flows. Continuing civil wars in Angola, Mozambique, and the Sudan are taking a heavy toll of refugees. After about three decades of liberation war, Eritrea won its independence from Ethiopian occupation in 1993. However, new fighting erupted in 1998 between the two countries as a result of a border dispute creating new refugee flows. In North Africa, over 200,000 relatively unknown refugees from the war in Western Sahara have been living in camps in Southern Algeria.

In short, the refugee problem in Africa is indeed grave. Underdeveloped and burdened with the precarious task of welding numerous heterogeneous groups into viable modern states and confronted with both internal and external destabilizing forces, Africa is likely to have to deal with larger numbers of refugees unless urgent preventive and curative measures are taken.

In seeking durable solutions to the refugees' problems, the UNHCR has been attempting to facilitate the voluntary repatriation of refugees and reintegration into their country of origin or, where this isn't feasible, integration into their country of asylum or resettlement in a third country. Thus, by the end of 1997, the UNHCR offered emergency assistance to some 3.5 million refugees worldwide, particularly in Africa (and especially in Mozambique, Rwanda, and Burundi).

However, attempts at a solution should be realistic enough to tackle the root causes and underlying problems rather than mere symptoms. Africa undoubtedly has a serious and continuing refugee problem, but there are also a certain number of elements that indicate the way to a solution. The first is the existence and work of the Organization of African Unity (OAU), which provides a forum for African political leaders to tackle delicate and difficult questions—including that of refugees—in the spirit of the African tradition. The OAU Commission of the Fifteen on Refugees; the OAU Bureau on Refugees; and the OAU Mechanism for Conflict Prevention, Management, and Resolution of Conflicts in Africa (1993) have been making significant contributions.

The second positive element is the adoption by the OAU in 1969 of the OAU Convention on Specific Problems of African Refugees, which is the principal legal instrument in Africa dedicated to refugee issues. It represents a pragmatic response to the realities of social, political, and economic turmoil that have pervaded the continent since the beginnings of the decolonization process in the 1950s and 1960s. This convention rightly stresses the need for an essentially humanitarian approach to the problem of refugees.

The third positive element is the African Charter on Human and Peoples' Rights (the Banjul Charter) adopted by the OAU in 1981, which came into force in 1986. Among others, the Banjul Charter significantly advanced the status of refugee law on the continent. The most important advance relates to the granting of asylum. While the 1969 OAU Convention only imposed a duty upon member states to receive refugees, Article 12(3) of the Banjul Charter confers the right to seek and obtain asylum in other countries when persecuted. Further, under Article 12(5), "the mass expulsion of non-nationals is prohibited."

However, reforming the legal mechanisms must be viewed as only one facet of the comprehensive effort to solve the refugee crisis. Moreover, even a seemingly foolproof legal system can at best only alleviate, not resolve, the crisis. Attempts at solution should, therefore, be realistic enough to tackle the root causes and underlying reasons for refugeeism in Africa as elsewhere. Today's refugee policy mainly consists of responding to crises as they happen rather than trying to prevent them.

Once refugees have left their homes, no amount of money or assistance can fully restore their past lives. The real solutions are those that will enable people to avoid flight in the first place. It is ironic that emergency assistance is siphoning away the funds needed to prevent future emergencies. Without concerted action to improve the stability of countries and the security of individuals, the problems that produce refugees, particularly in Africa, will continue to recur. As events in Rwanda, Somalia, and elsewhere indicate, today's human rights violations are tomorrow's refugee problems. Therefore, resolving refugee problems will mainly depend on a range of human rights activities, including developing pluralistic political systems, strengthening civil societies and education, reinforcing legal and government structures, and empowering local grassroots associations. The agonizing problem of refugees in Africa deserves at least as much attention as the OAU has given to the problem of colonialism in earlier days. Ultimately, it is a political problem, one that requires a political solution.

K. MATHEWS

See also: **Rwanda: Genocide, Aftermath of; Rwanda: Genocide, 1994; Somalia: Independence, Conflict and Revolution.**

Further Reading

Bulcha, Mekuria. *Flight and Integration: Cause of Mass Exodus from Ethiopia and Problems of Integration in the Sudan.* Uppsala, Sweden: Scandinavian Institute of African Studies, 1988.

Cimae-, Inodep-mink. *Africa's Refugee Crisis.* London: Zed, 1986.

Gordenker, Leon. *Refugees in International Politics.* London: Croom Helm, 1987.

Loescher, Gill. *Beyond Clarity: International Coperation and Global Refugees Crisis.* New York: Oxford University Press, 1989.

Loescher, Gill, and Laila Monahan (eds.). *Refugees in International Relations.* Oxford: Oxford University Press, 1989.

United Nations High Command for Refugees (UNHCR). *The State of the World's Refugees: In Search of Solutions.* New Delhi: UNHCR, 1995.

Religion, Colonial Africa: Conversion to World Religions

Statistics on the growth of numbers of Muslims and Christians in Africa at the period of the consolidation of colonization (i.e., in the decade around 1900) are impressionistic rather than accurate. What is reasonably clear, however, is that in Sub-Saharan Africa during the first half of the twentieth century the pace of growth of Christianity outstripped that of Islam; numbers of Christians increased from around 10 million in 1900 to more than 250 million by the 1990s, while the total number of African Muslims grew from about 34 million to nearly 300 million over the same period. Many of Africa's Muslims live in North Africa, but a substantial minority live below the Sahara. The continent is predominantly Muslim above the tenth parallel, which cuts through the northern regions of Sierra Leone, Côte d'Ivoire, Ghana, Togo, Benin, Nigeria, Cameroon, the Central African Republic, Ethiopia, and Somalia. The same line roughly separates Muslim from non-Muslim in Sudan and Chad. Above the tenth parallel, Gambia, Senegal, Mali, and Niger are preponderantly Muslim.

During the colonial period in Africa (c. 1880–1960), conversion to Christianity and Islam was facilitated among Africans for various reasons. For many, conversion to Islam during this time was a manifestation of antipathy to European colonialism, an alternative modernizing influence opposed to the hegemony of the European Christian missionaries and their system of putative or actual enculturation. Islam provided converts with an alternative modernizing worldview, not defined by the colonial order and its foreign norms, but by a perceived "indigenous" religioculture that many Africans perceived as authentically closer to their existing cultures than the alien-imposed creed of Christianity. Conversion to Christianity, on the other hand, was seen by many Africans not only as a means to acquire spiritual benefits, but also to gain access to both education and welfare, which, during the colonial period, were under the almost exclusive control of the various Christian missions.

Various parts of the continent received greater proselytization from one faith or the other; rarely were the faiths in direct competition once the embedding of colonial administrations had established religious spheres of influence from whence Christian missionaries were strongly encouraged to refrain from proselytizing by the colonial authorities. This was because the introduced system of "indirect rule" relied greatly on good relations between colonial authorities and local Muslim rulers. The best example of a mutually beneficial relationship between Europeans and local Muslim rulers is probably to be found in northern Nigeria, where Lord Lugard's system of indirect rule (actually first developed in Uganda, following Britain's Indian colonial experiences) owed much of its success to the fact that it tampered hardly at all with preexisting sociopolitical structures and cultural norms. The local Fulani elite, albeit slave owners, become intermediaries with the colonial administration as a reward for putting down a Mahdist revolt in Satiru in 1906. While northern Nigeria emerged as a testing ground for the efficacy of the policy of indirect rule, the Fulani political leaders were able to enlarge their sphere of influence—and to convert more Africans to Islam—by extending their supremacy over groups of previously autonomous non-Muslims, especially those in what were to become Plateau and Borno States.

Conversion to Christianity was greatly facilitated by the existence of colonial regimes, not least because the Europeans themselves tended to see their presence in Africa as necessary to "civilize" African "pagans." While one kind of Christianity or another was rarely the "official" religion of European colonies in Africa, it was certainly the case that the faith's growth was encouraged by administrations in many, if not most, colonies, as it was regarded as a central facet of European civilization. As part of the claimed European mission in Africa was to enable Africans to one day run their own affairs, it was quite appropriate that Christian conversion would de facto be an integral facet of European rule.

However, until colonial rule was firmly established between approximately 1900 and 1920, Christian missions generally made relatively little headway. Nevertheless, the influence of the early missionaries was of importance. They were aware that teaching a love of Christ was insufficient on its own, realizing that many Africans regarded themselves as in need of material as well as spiritual assistance. It was therefore in the missionaries' interest to seek to improve material knowledge, skills, and well being via the potential African converts' ability to read, write, and have access to Western methods of health protection. In this way, Africans would develop into more useful members of Christian society. Over time a class of educated Africans emerged, people who owed their upward mobility to the fact that they had converted to Christianity and been able to absorb the benefits of a mission education.

Turning to Islam, the faith spread from North Africa southward from the seventh century, predating European colonialism by hundreds of years, while its diffusion was multidirectional. Over time, Islam strongly established itself (reflected in both sociopolitical organization and religiocultural developments) among many communities in much of western and, to a lesser yet still significant degree, eastern Africa. Attempts at mass Christian conversion in those areas in the late nineteenth and early twentieth centuries were, on the whole, singularly unsuccessful. Islam made much less progress during the colonial era in central southern and southern Africa. Its relatively late arrival from the north came up against the rapid spread of European Christianity from the south in the last decades of the nineteenth century; as a result Islam's influence was minimized.

Islam followed preexisting trade routes, such as the North African and Indian Ocean ways; conversion was also by jihads (holy wars) during the nineteenth century and into the twentieth prior to World War I. In the late nineteenth century, the wider Muslim world experienced the slow demise of the Ottoman Empire and the near contemporaneous emergence of Saudi Arabia as champion of Wahhabist reformist ambitions. The growth of the Sufi brotherhoods and their reformist rivals were two developments in African Islam more or less contemporaneous with the consolidation of European rule; others were the extension of Muslim networks throughout much of Africa and beyond, and the introduction of new modernizing ideas. Many Muslims joined Sufi brotherhoods to further their own commercial networks, and were often receptive to the reformist ideas of the Wahhabiya and of pan-Islamic ideals in the context of urbanization and the development of ethnically oriented Muslim associative groups. Sufi brotherhoods prospered under colonial rule in many areas, including Senegal, Mauritania, Northern Nigeria, Tanganyika, Sudan, and Somaliland.

JEFF HAYNES

See also: **Nigeria: Lugard, Administration and "Indirect Rule"; Religion: Islam, Growth of: Western Africa; Religion, Colonial Africa: Missionaries; Sudan: Mahdist State, 1881–1898.**

Further Reading

Boahen, A. Adu. *African Perspectives on Colonialism*. London: James Currey, 1987.

Etherington, Norman. "Missionaries and the Intellectual History of Africa: A Historical Survey." *Itinerario* 7, no. 2 (1983): 116–43.

Haynes, Jeff. *Religion and Politics in Africa*. London: Zed/ Nairobi: East African Educational, 1996.

Lapidus, Ira. *A History of Islamic Societies*. Cambridge: Cambridge University Press, 1988.

Oliver, Ronald. *The African Experience*. London: Weidenfield and Nicolson, 1991.

Stewart, C. C. "Islam." In *The Cambridge History of Africa*, vol. 7, *From 1905 to 1940*, edited by A. Roberts. Cambridge: Cambridge University Press, 1986.

Religion, Colonial Africa: Independent, Millenarian/Syncretic Churches

There are three major ideological sources for what have commonly been called African Independent Churches. These Christian movements, which have an exclusively African membership and the appearance of freedom from white control, could have originated from a combination of mission Christianities and ideas from African traditional religion; selected elements from within mission Christianities resulting in a different emphasis; or, counterestablishment Christian movements in Europe and the United States. Initially, scholars placed emphasis on the first explanation, arguing that Christian Independency was syncretistic in a pejorative sense—a confused mixing of ideas. This thesis, which was often advanced by theologians who had a stake in defending religious boundaries, has been discredited. Increasingly, explanations have focused on the second and third sets of ideological sources.

What has often been called the Ethiopian or separatist type of Independency took wholesale from the mission churches from which it seceded. Movements such as the Native Baptist Church founded in Lagos in 1888 or the Wesleyan-derived Ethiopian Church, founded in Pretoria in 1892, did not challenge the doctrine, theology, or organizational structures of their mission church "parents." In fact, they often clung to them with great loyalty. Their separation was more a protest against white missionary arrogance, which had hardened in the imperialist age, and a desire to have a degree of synthesis with African culture and aspiration. Perennially short of resources, even if they did link up with African American churches, these separatist movements remained a minority option attractive to more politically minded black Christian elites.

The other major type of Independent Christian movement, often known as Zionist, Aladura, or spirit churches, is also selected from mission Christianities. Although their characteristic religious enthusiasm might resemble African traditional spirit possession, it derived in part from missionary revivalism. Thus, the Zimbabwean *Vapostori* (Apostolic) movements founded by the Shona prophets Johanne Maranke and Johanne Masowe in the 1930s were influenced by Dutch Reformed Church and Methodist revivalism, respectively, while their members' "exotic" white robes and staffs derived from Catholic and Anglican sources. The robe-wearing Aladuras of West Africa likewise drew much from their Anglican heritage.

The third source of Independency was counter-establishment Christianity. This wave of mission activity had its social sources in late-nineteenth-century North America and Europe, and it reflected the aspirations of the proletariat and the petite bourgeoisie, who had been sidelined by industrial society. It was also a protest against the privilege and secularization of establishment churches and an increasingly "established" nonconformity. Counterestablishment Christian movements were often millennial, believing in the imminent return of Christ and the commencement of a thousand years of peace and justice. The urgency of this adventist message gave the movements a strong missionary impulse. The Chicago-based Zionists arrived in South Africa in 1904 to help spawn a host of southern African Zionist movements. Another millennial movement was Elliot Kamwana's Kitawala, an Africanized version of Watchtower, which he founded in Malawi in 1908. His message of future black liberation in contrast to the present-day excesses of forced labor, taxation, and the rule of chiefs was one of the more politically explicit variants of Independency, which the colonial authorities found unsettling.

The most vital strand of counterestablishment Christianity was Pentecostalism, which rapidly evolved into a global movement at the turn of the twentieth century. Its apostolic message of adventism, divine healing and emancipation by the Holy Spirit combined with mainline missionary revivalism to animate South African Zionism, Zimbabwean apostolic Christianity, and the West African Aladura Church into movements of baptism and witch cleansing.

The causes and motivations for Independency are as diverse as its ideological sources. First, the movement was clearly Protestant, having little effect in Catholic or Islamic areas. Separation on the grounds of truth was a defining feature of Protestantism, and once Africans had their own vernacular versions of scripture, they found ample reasons for contesting the missionary message, polygamy being a prime issue.

The second major factor was the pressure from African traditional religion. Contrary to early scholarly explanation of Independency, it did not adopt aspects of African traditional religion as much as compete with it, engaging with the same material and existential issues such as health and healing, purity, and protection from evil. Pioneer missionaries had spent much time with the sick, their often imprecise medicine not so dissimilar from that of the traditional healer. As missionary medicine became professionalized and secularized in the mission hospital, so did African Christian prophets institute movements of healing in the villages. In west central Africa there is a centuries-old cyclical pattern of societal renewal. Simon Kimbangu's millennial movement of witch cleansing and the destruction of fetishes, founded in the 1920s, stood within this tradition, though its conceptualization of evil went further, collapsing all traditional cults into the category of demonic.

Finally, Independent Christianity must be integrated into a spectrum of popular Christianities. Missionaries were always overstretched, taken up with building, administration, and Bible translation, with the result that evangelization was often left to African catechists and evangelists. In the early decades of the twentieth century, movements of mass conversion moved at such as pace that even missionary supervision was not possible. It was at this juncture that the Independent Church prophet often took on the missionary's task. Some of these African leaders, such as the Grebo Episcopalian William Wade Harris, did not even view their mission as schismatic. Many of Harris's converts initially joined the Catholic Church in the Côte d'Ivoire and the Methodist Church in the Gold Coast, with the formal Harris Church only emerging subsequently. It is noteworthy how Christian Independency took strong root during the Great Depression of the 1930s, when mission Christianity was shrinking, along with its health and educational services.

While Independent Churches continued to multiply throughout the 1940s and 1950s, these were often small-scale movements born out of schism with larger ones. The last major movement was the Lumpa Church of Alice Lenshina, founded in Zambia, one of the last colonies to be thoroughly missionized. The 1950s were more important for institutionalization of the major movements. Bible colleges, the ownership of buildings, bureaucratization, and the implementation of routine meant that Independency became more like the missionary movements it was so critical of a generation earlier.

DAVID MAXWELL

See also: **Kimbangu, Simon, and Kimbanguism; Religion, Colonial Africa: Missionaries; Religion, Colonial Africa: Prophetic Movements; Religion, Colonial Africa: Religious Responses to Colonial Rule; Religion, Postcolonial Africa: Independence and Churches, Mission-Linked and Independent; Religion, Postcolonial Africa: Neo-Pentecostalism; Zambia: Religious Movements.**

Further Reading

Campbell, James, T. *Songs of Zion: The African Methodist Episcopal Church in the United States and South Africa.* Oxford: Oxford University Press, 1995.

Fields, Karen. *Revival and Rebellion in Colonial Africa.* Princeton, N.J.: Princeton University Press, 1985.

Hastings, Adrian. *The Church in Africa 1450–1950.* Oxford: Clarendon Press, 1994.

Iliffe, John. *A Modern History of Tanganyika.* Cambridge: Cambridge University Press, 1979.

MacGaffey, Wyatt. *Modern Kongo Prophets: Religion in a Plural Society.* Bloomington: Indiana University Press, 1983.

Maxwell, David. "Historicizing Christian Independency: The Southern African Pentecostal Movement ca 1908–1960." *Journal of African History* 39, no. 2 (1999).

Peel, John, D.Y. *Aladura: A Religious Movement among the Yoruba,* London, 1968.

Sundkler, Bengt. *Bantu Prophets in South Africa.* London: Lutterworth Press, 1948.

Religion, Colonial Africa: Indigenous Religion

Understanding indigenous religion at any time in African history is difficult for several reasons. First, its practitioners usually passed their traditions orally from one generation to the next and kept no written records of their beliefs and practices. Second, when we do have written accounts of African religious beliefs, they are often seen through the prism of either Christianity or Islam. Christian missionaries, in particular, were interested in understanding the locals' beliefs in order to communicate better their own religion to their would-be converts. African religious belief systems, then, are almost always in the shadow of one of the two world religions that are practiced on the continent. A further complication is that scholars rarely study African

Fetish market in Benin, 1930s. © SVT Bild/Das Fotoarchiv.

religions in historical perspective, but rather use an anthropological or synchronic approach (Ajayi and Ayandele 1974; Magesa 1997). The result is that they are often seen as timeless and unchanging. Unfortunately, we currently have little understanding of historical changes in African religion.

By the colonial era, Islam had established itself as a significant religion in North, West, and coastal East Africa. Christianity, on the other hand, had just recently been introduced to most of the continent. The era of colonialism, then, was one in which three major religious traditions influenced the history of the continent. In some cases, the perceived parallels between Islam and African beliefs or Christianity and African beliefs eased conversion to the world religions. For example, in Ufipa, Tanzania, Fipa likened Fipa ancestors to Catholic saints (Smythe 1999). On the other hand, such congruence could also lead to conflict. Christian missionaries and African chiefs often vied for religious and political power in African societies because their sources for authority overlapped in multiple ways. For example, chiefs' rain-making abilities in southern Africa were threatened by the missionaries' claim that prayer to God brought the rain (Landau 1995, pp.23–27).

While not given equal attention in the literature, the importance of African religious beliefs during the colonial period cannot be overestimated. We know from incidences like the Maji Maji rebellion in southeastern Tanganyika, the Shona rebellion in colonial Southern Rhodesia, and the Mau Mau in colonial Kenya (Kibicho 1978, pp.380–382) that religious beliefs played a role in constructing anticolonial resistance. In Southern Rhodesia, for example, Shona rebelled against the British South Africa Company. One of the leaders of the rebellion was a spirit medium of one of the most eminent *mhondoro* (royal ancestors) (Lan 1985). Another lesser-known movement, the Nyabingi spirit cult, offered the most sustained challenge to British colonial power in Uganda (Hansen 1995). In most cases, these were not reactionary movements drawing exclusively on beliefs and ideology of the past, but they incorporated new elements as well. During the Maji Maji rebellion, for example, Bokero, the priest of a nature spirit, began to distribute water (*maji*) that would repel German bullets. While the appeal to medicine linked the movement to African beliefs in medicine that repelled evil, the attempt to conquer European military might with sacred water was new. As a result of these and other activities that colonial authorities deemed a threat to their power, much African religious activity was circumscribed during the period and driven underground (Vansina 1995, p.476).

The health of the community lay at the heart of African spirituality from early in the common era

(Magesa 1997, pp.66–71). This involved maintaining the health and reproductive capacities of the living, ensuring communication between the living and the ancestors, and protection of the land and living resources. During the colonial period, new political, economic, and spiritual authorities in African societies challenged the effectiveness of indigenous ideas to meet Africans' spiritual needs. Yet, these beliefs, throughout the colonial era, provided a means of dealing with individual and community fears and difficulties resulting from the morally bewildering colonial onslaught.

For example, the social and economic dislocation that occurred as a result of resettlement for transportation and taxation purposes, disease management, and labor migration all contributed to more heterogeneous communities where the fear of witchcraft was much greater. Africans believed that evil originated in witchcraft. It is not surprising, then, that as Africans faced rapid changes, fears of evil surfaced from time to time as witchcraft accusations. In colonial Northern Rhodesia, for example, the *mucapi* movement was popular among the Bemba in 1934 and caught the attention of the colonial authorities (Richards 1935). The *Bamucapi* (the witch-finders), according to Audrey Richards, wore European clothing, sold their medicine in Western-style bottles, used mirrors, and preached before administering medicine—all factors reflecting Western influence and power. At the same time, the Bamucapi called on the Bemba God and insisted that the medicine would only work if certain cultural taboos were kept. The syncretic nature of this witch-finder movement indicates that Bemba recognized dual sources of power. More important, though, the Bamucapi movement, while drawing on indigenous beliefs of evil and social alienation, marks a period of heightened personal and communal difficulty as the British colonial economy disrupted Africans' lives.

One of the phenomena of the colonial era that has continued into the postcolonial era is the creation of Christian churches under African leadership. Africans founded them throughout the continent. One of these churches, the Roho Church of Western Kenya, emerged in the 1930s. Like so many of these religious movements, it began with the prophetic and charismatic leadership of a missionary-trained man, Alfayo Mango. The Roho Church, like other religious movements that developed in Eastern Africa in the 1930s, emphasized the role of the Holy Spirit as a messenger from the sacred world, just as African ancestors were. In addition, in the early years of the church, evangelization often included church leaders' healing of the sick, which blended Luo and Roho practices of posesssion, singing, and sacrifice. Healing was a fundamental aspect of African indigenous beliefs and directly linked to reproduction. Frequently, an individual's conversion to movements like the Roho Church followed an illness and successful treatment by one of the church's members. Rather than signaling the demise of indigenous religions, these churches manifest the importance of these beliefs to Africans as well as the importance of local autonomy in African religion. It is also important to recognize, however, that these churches also had Christian roots, as demonstrated by their doctrine and use of the Bible (Hoehler-Fatton 1996).

By the end of the colonial period, half of Africans remained practitioners of their indigenous religions (Vansina 1995, p.475). Currently, whether official censes reveal it or not (Kibicho 1978, p.371) the number of Africans who practice African traditional religious beliefs—while members of a world religion or not—is substantial, and reflects the close link between culture and religion in African societies. That the records we have of the colonial period, predominantly written by foreigners, indicate a persistent maintenance of belief in ancestors, witchcraft, and the connection between spirituality and healing suggests the dynamism and durability of African indigenous religions.

KATHLEEN R. SMYTHE

Further Reading

Ajayi, J. F. Ade, and E. A. Ayandele. "Emerging Themes in Nigerian and West African Religious History." *Journal of African Studies* 1, no. 1 (1974): 1–39.

Hansen, Holger Bernt. "The Colonial Control of Spirit Cults in Uganda." In *Revealing Prophets: Prophecy in East African History*, edited by David M. Anderson and Douglas H. Johnson. London: James Currey, 1995.

Hoehler-Fatton, Cynthia, *Women of Fire and Spirit: History, Faith, and Gender in Roho Religion in Western Kenya.* Oxford: Oxford University Press, 1996.

Kibicho, Samuel G. "The Continuity of the African Conception of God into and through Christianity: A Kikuyu Case Study." In *Christianity in Independent Africa*, edited by Edward Fashole-Luke et al. Bloomington: Indiana University Press, 1978.

Lan, David. *Guns and Rain: Guerrillas and Spirit Mediums in Zimbabwe.* Berkeley and Los Angeles: University of California Press, 1985.

Landau, Paul S., *The Realm of the Word: Language, Gender, and Christianity in a Southern African Kingdom.* Portsmouth, N.H.: Heinemann, 1995.

Magesa, Laurenti. *African Religion: The Moral Traditions of an Abundant Life.* Maryknoll: Orbis, 1997.

Richards, Audrey. "A Modern Movement of Witch-Finders" *Africa* 8, no. 4 (1935): 448–461.

Smythe, Kathleen R. "The Creation of a Catholic Fipa Society: Conversion in Nkansi District, Ufipa." In *East African Expressions of Christianity*, edited by Thomas Spear and Isaria Kimambo. Athens, Ohio: Ohio University Press, 1999.

Vansina, Jan. "A Clash of Cultures: African Minds in the Colonial Era." in *African History*, edited by XXXX Curtin et al. New York: Longman, 1995.

Religion, Colonial Africa: Islamic Orders and Movements

Islam first came to Africa during the conquest of Egypt in the seventh century, from where it spread across North Africa toward what is now Mauritania. Two hundred years later, the religion had spread across the continent to the nomads of the central and western Sahara regions, and further east into the Horn of Africa; by the eleventh century, Islam had begun to travel southward into Sub-Saharan Africa. Spread sometimes through warfare but primarily through trade, Islam became the religion of many of Africa's great historical states, such as Mali, the Songhay empire, Ghana, the Hausa states, and Kanem-Bornu. Islam provided not only a religion, but also a linguistic and cultural framework that facilitated economic transactions and the exchange of political and social ideas. By the time the French invaded Algeria in 1830, ushering in the era of European colonialism in Africa, Islam was well established. During the colonial period, various Islamic orders and movements (often Sufi) served to articulate and organize political opposition to foreign rule and to provide followers with an alternative model of social organization.

One of the best examples of this is in the Sudan. In 1881, Muhammad Ahmad, a boatbuilder's son, declared himself to be the Mahdi ("divinely guided one") and began mobilizing supporters against what he viewed as the two primary enemies: Anglo-Egyptian control of the Sudan, and the orthodox 'ulama who supported the administration. The Mahdi advocated a return to the ways of the prophet Muhammad as the only means of solving Sudan's internal problems and denounced the visible manifestations of foreign rule (e.g., prostitution, gambling, and alcohol consumption). By 1882, the Mahdi had mobilized enough support to take control of most important parts of the country; in 1885, his forces succeeded in taking the capital city of Khartoum from an Anglo-Egyptian force under the command of British general Sir Charles George Gordon (who was then killed by the Mahdists). Shortly after taking Khartoum, the Mahdi also died, but his role as a political and religious leader was taken by the *khalifa* 'Abdullah, who vowed to continue upholding the late Mahdi's ideology and to expand the Mahdist state from its new capital at Omdurman. In accordance with the Mahdi's beliefs, the only law of the new state was the Shari'a. Though Britain invaded and occupied Egypt in 1882, it did not mount a campaign to retake the Sudan until 1897. In 1898,

at the Battle of Omdurman, the British, armed with modern military equipment, succeeding in devastating the Mahdist forces, and the Sudan was restored to Anglo-Egyptian control. Nonetheless, the Mahdi's short-lived state provides an excellent example of the ability of reformist religious leaders to mobilize resistance to foreign rule.

In Libya, the Sanusiyya brotherhood also called for a return to the essentials of Islam, organized resistance to colonization, and played an important role in state formation. The Sanusiyya brotherhood (a rather puritanical sect of Sufism) was established in 1837 by Sidi Muhammad Ibn Ali al-Sanusi with the goal of leading people back to the simple beliefs and lifestyles of the early years of Islam; in doing so, the movement built upon the teachings of the Moroccan jurist and Sufi shaykh Ahmed ibn Idris. Al-Sanusi alienated the orthodox 'ulama by asserting his right to *ijtihad* (individual judgment) and rejecting Islamic law based on the *ijma* (consensus) of the 'ulama. The Sanusiyya was also a missionary order in that it aimed at converting the non-Muslim inhabitants of the region to Islam, and it is a prime example of the new orientation of many rising Sufi orders in nineteenth-century Africa: rather than focusing purely on spiritual matters and the next world, these reformist Sufi orders instead redefined their focus as activism in this world. Led by a man known as the Grand Sanusi (a religious and political figure to whom many pledged personal allegiance), the Sanusiyyah brotherhood and their lodges (called *zawiyas*) spread throughout Cyrenaica (and to a lesser extent throughout Tripolitania) in the nineteenth century. In fact, the shaykhs of the zawiyas held enormous political and spiritual influence at this time and remained the de facto political leaders of Cyrenaica throughout the nineteenth century and during Italian colonization. The *zawiyas* provided material assistance and spiritual and political guidance to members. They thus helped create a sense of unity among their members and became a focal point for resistance to French influence from the south (during the Ottoman period) and later to Italian colonization. The Sanusiyyah leadership were the political spokespeople for Libya in negotiations with the Italians and with the British after World War II. The first (and last) king of Libya, Idris I, was the Grand Sanusi, or leader of the Sanusiyyah brotherhood at the time he was made king, which illustrates the importance and influence of the order. In short, the Sanusiyyah brotherhood helped foster religious and political unity, established a framework for organized resistance to colonization, and provided political and religious leadership, and its leader became the first political head of postindependence Libya.

In the late eighteenth and early nineteenth centuries, the Fulbe people mounted a series of jihads (holy wars) from Senegal to Cameroon. Like the other two movements mentioned, this movement was geared toward social and religious reform; unlike the Mahdiyya movement and the Sanusiyyah brotherhood, however, the Fulbe jihads were not directly tied to European colonialism. The most notable of the Fulbe jihads took place in northern Nigeria and was led by Usuman dan Fodio. Dan Fodio was among a generation of Islamic reformers in Africa who were influenced by the increasing presence of European influence (mainly missionaries and traders) and who sought to reform Islam in order to strengthen society and respond to political problems. Dan Fodio had served the Hausa *sarki* of Gobir and the sarki's son Yunfa. When dan Fodio became disenchanted with Yunfa's rule, he and a group of his supporters withdrew to the remote area of Gudu, where they were numerous enough to comprise a sizable fighting force. The result was the appointment of dan Fodio as *Sarkin Musulmi* (Commander of the Faithful) and the proclamation of jihad against the Hausa ruling elite. The movement gathered to itself not only religious reformers but also a variety of disenchanted groups: educated urban Fulbe, who opposed Hausa corruption; urban Hausa, who wished to free themselves from the domination of the Hausa ruling families; and rural Fulbe, who supported their urban kinfolk. The result was the formation of a number of Fulbe emirates under the nominal control of Usuman dan Fodio (later under his son Muhammad Bello and his brother Abdallah, ruling from Sokoto and Gwandu, respectively). The leaders of the new "state" (it lacked any real centralization and had no unified military or bureaucracy) then focused on spreading Islam from urban centers further into rural areas. The religious reformers then became themselves a ruling elite and their reformist zeal fizzled out; when British forces came to northern Nigeria, they used the Fulbe emirs in colonial government. The emirs taxed, policed, and administered justice to the Hausa subjects.

In Algeria in 1832, 'Abd al-Qadir, the emir of Mascara and the son of a well-known *marabout* (saint) began another jihad, this time against the French invasion and occupation of Algeria that had begun in 1830. Though perhaps a more overtly political movement than the Mahdiyya and the Sanusiyyah, the jihad of 'Abd al-Qadir succeeded in drawing numerous supporters and used Islam as a rallying point for opposition to foreign rule. The emir succeeded in forming his own state in western and central Algeria; in 1841, French forces began systematically crushing the new state. The net result of the French policy of total colonization in Algeria was the effective eradication of any real Algerian national identity by about 1870. When large-scale organized resistance to French colonization mobilized again after WWII, it was not explicitly religious

in nature and cannot properly be called an Islamic movement. Yet since independence was linked to the recovery of Algerian culture, including the reassertion of an Islamic identity, it must be mentioned here.

Other movements can be mentioned as well. Sayid Muhammad Abdille Hassan, another Sufi leader, organized groups of Somali tribesmen around himself and his reformist ideas in 1900; he succeeded in preventing European takeover until 1920. Shaykh 'Umar Tal used the reformist teachings of the Tijaniiyya Sufi brotherhood and called for jihad against non-Muslim states to found a vast centralized empire (the Futaanke or Tukolor empire) centered at Dingirai; in the process, Shaykh 'Umar came into conflict with the French on the Senegal River. (Though the military conflict was indecisive and the French remained in control of the river, Shaykh 'Umar continued his conquests in nearby areas.)

In addition to these political movements, there was also a vast amount of intellectual energy being expended in the late nineteenth and early twentieth centuries on how to best reform Islamic societies. Though not centered around any particular order, the writings of men like Jamal al-Din al-Afghani and Muhammad 'Abduh surely are excellent examples of calls for reform in response to western encroachment and internal political and social disorder. The activist Sufi orders, the less explicitly religiously oriented movements that used Islam as a way to mobilize support for secular political goals, and the intellectual movements toward reform are all testament to the ability of religious orders, leaders, and movements to rally support for social and political change in colonial Africa.

AMY J. JOHNSON

Further Reading

Evers, Eva Rosander, and David Westerlund (eds.). *African Islam and Islam in Africa: Encounters between Sufis and Islamists*. Athens, Ohio: Ohio University Press, 1997.

Hiskett, Mervyn. *The Course of Islam in Africa*. Edinburgh: Edinburgh University Press, 1994.

Levtzion, Nehemia, and Randall L. Pouwels (eds.). *The History of Islam in Africa*. Athens, Ohio: Ohio University Press, 1999.

Sanneh, Lamin O. *The Crown and the Turban: Muslims and West African Pluralism*. Boulder, Colo.: Westview Press, 1997.

Simone, T. Abdou Maliqalim. *In Whose Image?: Political Islam and Urban Practices in Sudan*. Chicago: University of Chicago Press, 1994.

Religion, Colonial Africa: Missionaries

Missions were an important physical presence in colonial Africa, both in terms of the number of white mission workers in the field (10,000 men and women in 1910) and the size of their landholdings: by the

1920s, missions owned 400,000 acres in colonial Zimbabwe, while the Church of Scotland's Kibwezi mission in Kenya held 64,000 acres.

Not surprisingly, many Africanist commentators have epitomized white missionaries as the spiritual arm of colonialism, echoing the traditional African saying, "In the beginning we had the land, and the missionaries had the Bible; now we have the Bible and they have the land." This view has been questioned by more recent research, which suggests, to the contrary, that where cooperation between mission and imperialism did occur (for instance, in western Zimbabwe in 1889–1890), this did not signify identical objectives. At partition, the goal of missionaries was, quite simply, to foster the Christian evangelization in Africa through the best means they could find.

However, the sheer scope of the enterprise, the rapidity with which colonial rule was established, and, for most of Africa, the dearth of official agencies on the ground served to deflect missions from this objective. In Sub-Saharan Africa, the provision of school education quickly became *a priority*, initially to enable potential converts to read the Bible (in the case of Protestants) or the Catechism (in the case of Roman Catholics). Postpartition economic development created a need for literate Africans, and in many parts of the continent the colonial state provided grants-in-aid to mission schools to facilitate this output. Education thus became a central mission concern, and represented the missions' major contribution to the colonial order. As late as 1945, 96.4 per cent of pupils in British tropical Africa were attending mission schools. Missionaries were also responsible for starting some of the pioneer secondary schools in Africa, destined to become cradles of black nationalism, such as Lovedale in South Africa and Achimota in Ghana. It has been claimed that, in acting as admittedly unwitting midwives to this process, missionaries made their major contribution to postcolonial Africa.

To a lesser extent they also pioneered the provision of health care, Albert Schweitzer's hospital at Lambaréné (Gabon) being the best known example. Up and down colonial Africa, the often rudimentary mission dispensary treated hundreds of outpatients, while women missionaries advised mothers on baby and child care.

The bulk of Christian conversion under the colonial order seems, ironically, to have stemmed from the work of black evangelists and catechists (rather than white missionaries) who often worked far away from mission stations. Their efforts were supplemented by those of the many black independent churches that emerged from the 1890s onward, starting in South Africa and Nigeria. The result was a series of largely spontaneous mass conversions in the first forty years of

the colonial period. It has been estimated that in 1950 there were at least 23 million Christians in Sub-Saharan Africa, a testimony to this work (though it should be noted that few inroads were made into Islamized areas). From this evangelization emerged the village Christianity that has become a significant feature of rural areas in postcolonial Africa.

Missions contributed in other ways to the colonial order by becoming, consciously and unconsciously, agents of acculturation. The "square" house, as opposed to the traditional "round" hut, became a symbol of "civilization" on the Cape's Eastern Frontier. To this could be added the strict isolation of black Catholic seminarians from the temptations of village life, the frequent censure of traditional dancing as immodest, and the condemnation of polygamy (properly, *polygyny*) as a sign of sexual license and/or the degradation of women by black males.

With few exceptions (such as the missionary poet Arthur Shearly Cripps, who believed that the receipt of grants-in-aid from colonial governments made them less effective champions of African interests), missions played a generally subservient and unquestioning role in the colonial order between the two world wars. J. H. Oldham, secretary of the International Missionary Council, epitomized this stance in his belief that the interests of colonial government, missions, and white settlers alike could be harmonized. A similar relationship developed in the Belgian Congo and Portuguese territories after Concordats were reached with Rome in 1908 and 1940, respectively; in both instances this enabled a particularly aggressive form of local mission work that prevailed up to the threshold of Vatican II in the late 1950s.

The post–World War II period was one of considerable strain, with black nationalists accusing white missionaries of being paternalistic at best and hypocritical accomplices of imperial oppression at worst. Relations were particularly sour in areas where there were large white settler communities, as expressed in the Kikuyu saying, "There is no difference between missionary and settler." In return, conservative missionaries accused nationalists of being power hungry, or of acting as tools of international communism. However, with the sole exception of the Congo, where missions were attacked by rebels in the postindependence civil war, the end of colonial rule in black Africa passed peacefully for white missionaries. And once the impediment of colonial rule had been removed, they found that they were more than welcome to stay on and continue to contribute to the development of the new states.

Meanwhile, the missionary movement itself was undergoing a kind of spiritual decolonization, typified by a more understanding attitude toward traditional religion; the incorporation of African forms into worship, including dancing and drumming; and, after a considerable interval, the Africanization of local churches, as exemplified by the consecration in 1951 of the first Anglican diocesan bishop in Nigeria since Samuel Crowther, and Pope Paul VI's appointing of Laurean Rugambwa as cardinal.

The so-called white south held out, seemingly disregarding the winds of change in black Africa. In South Africa, the English-speaking mission churches found themselves poised uncomfortably in the middle of a debate between black antiapartheid churchmen such as Desmond Tutu, and the Dutch Reformed Church, which held that racial separation had been ordained by God. It was only after the political crisis of the mid-1980s, and the publication of the Kairos Document calling upon churches to employ civil disobedience against the apartheid regime, that they began to respond more effectively.

MURRAY STEELE

See also: **Congo (Brazzaville), People's Republic of: Independence, Revolution, 1958–1979; Education in Colonial Sub-Saharan Africa; Religion, Colonial Africa: Independent, Millenarian/Syncretic Churches; Religion, Colonial Africa: Religious Responses to Colonial Rule; Zimbabwe: 1880s.**

Further Reading

Gray, Richard, *Black Christians and White Missionaries*. New Haven, Conn.: Yale University Press, 1990.

Hastings, Adrian. *The Church in Africa, 1450–1950*. Oxford: Clarendon Press, 1994.

———. *A History of African Christianity, 1950–1975*. Cambridge: Cambridge University Press, 1979.

Stanley, Brian. *The Bible and the Flag: Protestant Missions and British Imperialism in the Nineteenth and Twentieth Centuries*. Leicester, England: Apollos, 1990.

Religion, Colonial Africa: Prophetic Movements

During the colonial period in Africa (*c.*1880–1960), prophetic movements emerged in various geographic locations in response to changes (often encapsulated under the term *modernization*) galvanized by the novel presence of Europeans and their administrations. Evolving in response to some kind of social crisis, prophetic movements were founded by men and women claiming to have had a mystical experience that gave them the status of an authentic prophet to their followers. Reflecting this, such movements had clear millenarian hopes, in which a divinity would help its followers to improve their lot on earth. Followers of prophetic movements would normally reject established authority, especially if, like European colonial

power, it was not regarded as authentic. In such cases, there was a selective rejection and retention of aspects of traditional culture, with the rejection-retention balance corresponding to popular demands. Social solidarity expressed itself in membership of the prophetic group, which might offer healing and other, more material, advantages to followers, in addition to spiritual benefits.

Prophetic cults arose, employing local religious beliefs as a basis for anti-European protest and opposition, led by prophets and stimulated by colonialism and the social changes to which it had led. Of particular importance in the appeal of prophetic movements in Africa was their dual attraction as both a materialist and a spiritual healing force. The most tenacious elements of "traditional" religion were those that touched a common bedrock of African traditional religions which involved the individual's concern for divinatory and magicomedical assistance. The existence of prophetic movements in Africa during the colonial period also reflected continuing popular adherence to traditional religious ideas, symbols, and rituals, often juxtaposed to modernist accretions from the European intruders. The result was that hybrid religious beliefs developed, often developing into formal organizational structures. Prophetic movements in colonial Africa were an example of how religious beliefs are not static but continually develop and redevelop over time, melding religious and cultural resources in response to changing sociopolitical and economic conditions.

Prophetic movements were found among both Muslim and non-Muslim communities in colonial Africa. As the Muslim faith spread from its Middle Eastern heartlands from the seventh century AD, it was periodically "purified" by *jihad* (holy wars). Between the sixteenth and nineteenth centuries, from Mauritania to present-day Sudan, until the coming of the Europeans put an end to such forceful means of religious reform, there were jihads for religious purification purposes. This was the result of a militant tradition that had long emerged, involving a determination to found Islamic states by defeating non-Muslim rulers, converting populations to Islam, and ruling them according to the tenets of Shari'a law.

These jihads were finally brought to a close by the European conquest of Africa, though Islam continued to spread by way of the Sufi brotherhoods, founded by exemplary figures regarded by their followers as saints. The brotherhoods facilitated the provision of commercial opportunities and offered material assistance to new arrivals from rural areas to urban centers. As African societies rapidly urbanized during the colonial era, Sufi brotherhoods established for themselves a reputation as the single most important facilitator of credentials necessary for newcomers to the city. In the postcolonial period, Sufism came to represent a form of "uncaptured" Islam beyond the control of the reformist elites dominating state-controlled national Muslim organizations. For this reason they were widely targeted by state authorities and the 'ulama as examples of "corrupt" Islam.

While the Muslim faith ostensibly allows no reinterpretations of the fundamental tenets of belief, especially that Muhammad was *the* prophet of God and that there is but one God, other (albeit lesser) "prophets" have periodically emerged within Islam. The beginning of the Muslim thirteenth century in 1879 stimulated an intense period of jihad. Islamic literature had long prophesized the emergence of the "awaited deliverer" (the Mahdi) who would prepare the world for the end of time. At about this time there emerged a self-styled Mahdi in the Sudan, a man named Muhammad Ahmad ben Abdallah, who led a determined revolt against British colonizing power. Ultimately unsuccessful, Muhammad Ahmad died in 1885, but amid the political uncertainties following the partition of Africa, Mahdism retained a populist appeal that endured until after World War I.

Prophetic movements flourished away from Islamic areas, especially in many rural locales in eastern and southern Africa. Like Mahdism, they were not simply religious movements but tended to have overtly political aspirations linked to dissatisfaction with aspects of colonial rule. For example, in present-day Zimbabwe, erstwhile foes the Shona and the Ndebele combined forces to try to resist British domination in the 1890s. Spirit mediums, utilizing mystical "medicines" to try to enhance fighters' martial efforts, created a national network of shrines to provide an agency for the transmission and coordination of information and activities, a structure later reestablished during the independence war of the 1970s.

The use of various alternative forms of medicine also helped galvanize the anticolonial Maji Maji rebellion of 1905–1907 in German-controlled Tanganyika. The diviner and prophet Kinjikitili gave his followers treatment that was supposed to render them invulnerable to bullets and anointed local leaders with medicinal *maji* (water). This helped to create and develop solidarity among some 20 different ethnic groups, encouraging them to band together to fight in the common anti-European cause. In neighboring Uganda, the cult of Yakan among the Lugbara people in the north of the country also focused on the use of magic medicine, encouraging them in their short war against the British colonialists in 1919.

Prophetic movements were by no means exclusively led by men. Colonial era and postcolonial female prophets, such as Gaudencia Aoko (of Maria Legio in Kenya), Alice Lenshina (of the Lumpa Church of Zambia), and Alice Lakwena (of the Holy Spirit Church in Uganda) used the vehicle of religion to enhance their own personal (and by extension, their gender's) social position in one of the only means available in their male-dominated societies. However, the use of religion as a means of social enhancement for women was not a novel phenomenon in colonial Africa in the late nineteenth and early twentieth centuries. Dona Beatrice, the alleged incarnation of Saint Antony, was burned to death at Mbanza Congo (in present-day Angola) by the Portuguese as a heretic at the beginning of the eighteenth century. Her "crime," which later led to her proclaimed status as national heroine during the anticolonial war, was to preach an Africanized Christianity.

Prophetic movements during both the colonial and postcolonial periods were sometimes vehicles of ethnic solidarity. The Lumpa Church of northern Zambia; the Holy Spirit Church among the Acholi in northern Uganda; the followers of Manuel Antonio in northeast Mozambique; the Ovimbundu Church of Christ in the Bush in southern Angola; and Dini ya Msambwa among the Bukusu of western Kenya, led by Elijah Masinde, were all examples of ethnically orientated prophetic movements with political overtones.

JEFF HAYNES

See also: **Sudan: Mahdist State, 1881–1898; Tanganyika (Tanzania): Maji Maji Rebellion, 1905–1907.**

Further Reading

Allen, Tim. "Understanding Alice: Uganda's Holy Spirit Movement in Context." *Africa* 51, no. 3 (1991): 370–399.

Fields, Karen. *Revival and Rebellion in Colonial Central Africa*. Princeton, N.J.: Princeton University Press.

Haynes, Jeff. *Religion and Politics in Africa*. London: Zed/ Nairobi: East African Educational, 1996.

Lan, David. *Guns and Rain*. London: James Currey, 1985.

Lapidus, Ira. *A History of Islamic Societies*. Cambridge: Cambridge University Press, 1988.

Ranger, Terence. *Peasant Consciousness and Guerrilla War in Zimbabwe*. London: James Currey, 1985.

Religion, Colonial Africa: Religious Responses to Colonial Rule

Conversion to Christianity and Islam was facilitated during the period of European colonialism in Africa (*c.*1880–1960). During this time, conversion to Islam often became a symbol of anti-Europeanism, an alternative modernizing influence opposed to the hegemony of the European Christian missionaries and their system of putative enculturation. Islam provided its followers with an alternative worldview not defined by the colonial order and its norms. For many Africans, the primary perceived benefit of Christianity was the access to both the education and rudimentary welfare systems that it would provide. During the colonial period, such institutions were under the almost exclusive control of the various Christian missions, the Roman Catholic Church, and various Protestant churches.

Before the coming of the Europeans, Islam spread southward in Africa, from western Asia and North Africa, by proselytization, trade, and conquest. Between the sixteenth and nineteenth centuries, as Islam became Africanized, orthodox reformists, from Mauritania to present-day Sudan, sought to "purify" Islam. As a result, the faith spread, typically by converting African communities into constituent parts of Islamic states by defeating non-Muslim rulers, converting their people to Islam, and then ruling according to Muslim law.

During the late nineteenth and early twentieth centuries, many among Africa's Islamic communities opposed what they perceived as European-Christian rule; later, however, they learned to live with it and to benefit from it where and when they could. Earlier, jihads (holy wars) led by Muslim reformers aiming to purify what they saw as examples of corrupt Islam had erupted. They had led to widespread political, moral, and social reconstruction of Muslim societies in various parts of northern, western, and eastern Africa. During this period, the wider Muslim world also experienced the slow demise of the Ottoman Empire and the near contemporaneous emergence of Saudi Arabia as champion of Wahhabi reformist ambitions. Widespread growth both of Sufi brotherhoods and their reformist Wahhabist rivals were also contemporaneous with the emergence and consolidation of European rule.

In the context both of urbanization and the development of ethnically oriented Islamic associative groups, many African Muslims became receptive to the reformist ideas of the Wahhabiya. In addition, the spread of Pan-Islamic ideals around the time of World War I was of serious concern to British colonial rulers, who worried that, acting together, Germany and the Ottoman Empire would manage to recruit Muslim leaders and their communities as allies to their war efforts. In the long run, however, ethnic, religious, and regional divides prevented the emergence of a durable and robust Pan-Islamic movement in Africa.

Followers of African traditional religions appeared to exhibit to the Europeans all the worst aspects of a lack of appropriate religion and its civilizing influence in their lives. As a result, once religious challenges to their domination from Islam had been quelled, French and British colonial administrations preferred dealing with Muslims rather than with so-called pagans, as they recognized that the latter followed a relatively "civilized" religiocultural code. But this is not to imply that Muslim resistance to putative Christian hegemony

soon dropped away. From the 1890s until as late as the 1920s, Muslim resistance to European imperialism flourished in Sudan, Somaliland, Libya, and Morocco. Both Libya and Morocco were then in the first flushes of an Islamized militancy, following the recent founding of polities espousing a purity of Muslim values. In Morocco, it was the feeling that the Sultan had been compromised too far by successive European demands that led to Islamic resistance. In Somaliland, what focused Islamic militancy were the deprivations of Muhammad Abdallah Hasan (called by the British the "Mad Mullah"), which unleashed a reign of terror against local people who refused to join his Salihiyya brotherhood. The British were compelled to send four expeditions between 1900 and 1904 to attempt to quell the jihad, but Hasan retained his influence in the north of Somaliland until 1920.

If the situation involving Muslims and colonial administrations was, to some extent, the result of the inequality of the power attributes of each group, that regarding the Christian mission churches and the European authorities was based on a different range of relationships. There were differences in the nature of the association between missionaries and colonial authorities that probably escaped many Africans. Although these were differences of degree rather than anything more fundamental, there were various kinds of relationships between the Christian churches and the different colonial authorities, ranging from very good (in Northern Rhodesia and Nigeria, for example) to significantly worse (in Kenya, for example, where ownership of land was a burning political issue).

The Christian mission churches were perceived by many Africans to be in the vanguard of the advance of European dominance, yet frequently regarded with ambivalence because the Europeans not only brought desirable innovations—such as Western-style education and health care—but also took native people's land, often compelling them to work on their farms and plantations. During the colonial period the mission churches were in charge of education and health care provision in virtually all African colonies. This gave them both ideological and material power—the latter deriving from collection of school fees, grants, ownership of land and buildings, and so on, which was of obvious and great importance. In the face of the multifaceted changes—both domestic and international—of the times, it is hardly surprising that the ideas of many educated African Christians vis-à-vis European domination gradually underwent a sea change.

After some initial animosity, African responses to colonial rule and the advance of the mission churches in many parts of the region became generally favorable. While Europeans were perceived as de facto representatives of foreign cultural and political hegemony, to some Africans this was not unwelcome in itself. Many educated Africans, at least initially, regarded the Christian missionaries as welcome representatives of civilization and modernization. But African society began swiftly to polarize from the 1880s and 1890s as a result of the impact of European colonization and rule. On the one hand there was a small but growing educated and professional elite and, on the other, there was an overwhelmingly large traditional and illiterate group among Africans. The educated elite was subdivided between Christians and Muslims, the latter focused initially in the coastal regions of West and East Africa. The majority of educated Christians initially welcomed colonialism, while their Muslim counterparts were often more ambivalent. Sometimes educated African Christians, in tandem with European missionaries, put pressure on both the local administrations and the metropolitan governments in the 1880s to annex adjoining areas before other European powers could move in.

The West Indian Pan-Africanist Edward Blyden went so far to claim that West Africa had been "partitioned, in the order . . . of providence, by the European powers. . . . this partition has been permitted for the ultimate good of the people and for the benefit of humanity" (quoted in Boahen 1987, p.36). Largely as a result of their teaching at the hands of Christian missionaries, educated Christian Africans had been led to believe that Africa could only be "civilized" through the combined activities of Christianity, education, capitalism, and industrialization—in short, by a process of fundamental modernization directed by European Christians. Fifty years later, however, in 1936, I. T. A. Wallace-Johnson of Sierra Leone bitterly attacked the role of the mission churches for the way that they had used Christianity as the justification for a brutal ideology of domination, using force to subdue and convert pagans to Europeanized Christianity. He wrote:

> I believe the European has a god in whom he believes and whom he is representing in his churches all over Africa. He believes in the god whose name is spelt Deceit. He believes in the god whose law is "Ye strong, you must weaken the weak." Ye "civilized" Europeans, you must "civilize" the "barbarous" Africans with machine guns. Ye "Christian" Europeans, you must "Christianize" the "pagan" Africans with bombs, poison gases, etc. (Quoted in Furedi 1994, p.35)

Wallace-Johnson was by no means an extremist by the 1930s. Europeans were widely regarded no longer as the benign purveyors of civilization, but increasingly as the problem of Africa's future development rather than its solution. Scattered, often religiously motivated anticolonial actions (such as the Maji Maji rebellion and the founding of African Independent Churches), had occurred from around the time of World War I; they were to intensify from the mid-1930s on. One of the chief catalysts of a wider African nationalism, led for the most part by educated African Christians and Muslims, was the Italian occupation of Ethiopia in 1935; before then only a relatively small number of African nationalists had demanded a complete overthrow of the colonial system.

JEFF HAYNES

See also: **Maghrib: Muslim Brotherhoods; Religion, Colonial Africa: Independent, Millenarian/Syncretic Churches; Tanganyika (Tanzania): Maji Maji Rebellion, 1905–1907; Wallace-Johnson, I. T. A. and Radical Politics: West Africa: 1930s.**

Further Reading

Boahen, A. Adu. *African Perspectives on Colonialism*. London: James Currey, 1987.

Etherington, Norman. "Missionaries and the Intellectual History of Africa: A Historical Survey." *Itinerario* 7, no. 2 (1983): 116–43.

Furedi, Frank. *Colonial Wars and the Politics of Third World Nationalism*. London: I. B. Tauris, 1994.

Haynes, Jeff. *Religion and Politics in Africa*. London: Zed/ Nairobi: East African Educational, 1996.

Hastings, Adrian. "Church-State Relations in Black Africa, 1959–1966." In *The Church in a Changing Society*, edited by the Commission Internationale d'Histoire Ecclesiastique Comparée (CIHEC). Uppsala, Sweden: CIHEC, 1977.

Hastings, Adrian. *A History of African Christianity, 1950–1975*. Cambridge: Cambridge University Press, 1979.

Lapidus, Ira. *A History of Islamic Societies*. Cambridge: Cambridge University Press, 1988.

Oliver, Ronald. *The African Experience*. London: Weidenfield and Nicolson, 1991.

Stewart, C. C. "Islam." In *The Cambridge History of Africa*, vol. 7, *From 1905 to 1940*, edited by A. Roberts. Cambridge: Cambridge University Press, 1986.

Religion, History of

Traditional African religions use antiwitchcraft movements as a means to right social wrongs. During the Great Depression, for example, these movements were found throughout Africa. In east Africa, drought, locusts, and the Great Depression evoked fears of witchcraft in Nyasaland and Northern Rhodesia. Antiwitchcraft cults arose, drawing on traditional religious and cultural beliefs and values to offer hope to the generally poor population. In many parts of Africa there is a belief in an *otiose*, or neutral god, who has withdrawn from the day-to-day activities of the world and has left its working to lesser gods and spirits. This High God is unapproachable, and therefore lesser deities and spirits are approached to help with the concerns of the day. Thus, turns to magic and antiwitchcraft movements were logical moves for people faced with inexplicable disasters.

In common with people of other traditionally non-literate cultures, Africans see their traditional spiritual beings as either helpful or malevolent according to circumstances. The Yoruba of western Nigeria, for example, view the god Eshu as either a protective, benevolent spirit or as a spirit with an evil power that may be directed toward one's enemies, depending on the situation. These beings possess what is called *mana* (pure supernatural power).

Christianity, like Islam, found it had to work within the context of indigenous beliefs. By the twentieth century, Christianity had reached most of South Africa and was well entrenched in many of its areas; new mission societies blossomed. These societies propelled an expansion of Christianity not only in South Africa but also throughout most of Sub-Saharan Africa. Catholic missions, in particular, began a strong renaissance as colonialism was consolidated after the Congress of Berlin. In the colonial context, missions found that they were responsible for most education and health services in the colonies.

Any sect that wanted to spread in the continent had to adopt one of two methods used by Christianity and Islam. Christianity was successfully spread throughout Africa because the first missionaries indoctrinated young children. Later, as adults, these children passed on the new beliefs to their own offspring, thus creating a tradition from generation to generation. The spread of Islam was often initially accomplished by warfare and intimidation; those who resisted conversion were often harshly punished.

Christianity had been in Sub-Saharan Africa long before Muslims or Western missionaries arrived. Ethiopia was Christian by the fourth century and Monophysite Christianity had spread to Eritrea shortly after. With the coming of Islam by the eighth century, religion began to be used as an ethnic identity marker, with pastoralists often being Muslims and peasants often Christian.

Missionaries brought with them not only their version of Christianity but that of civilization as well. For missionaries, European civilization of the Victorian variety was at the top of the evolutionary ladder. It carried with it the notion of progress—namely, entry into the labor markets. In South Africa the Khoisan and Griqa peoples were among the first converted to Christianity. Missionaries then used these people to convert other groups to Christianity. Among the heroes of Christian conversion were two nineteenth-century Scottish missionaries, Robert Moffat and David Livingstone, who worked among the Tswana.

Often, converted African leaders used their power to persuade their people to become Christians. The Tswana convert King Khama III (who reigned from 1875 to 1923) established a theocracy. In the second half of the nineteenth century, missionaries made great progress among the Xhosa and Zulus. Missionaries usually preceded colonists and colonial administration; they also proved to be strong critics of both groups, and advocates for African rights.

At first, Christianity made its converts mainly from those on the margins, the poor and women. As colonialism progressed, however, the damage it did to the belief systems of African groups led many to turn to Christianity. Ironically, much of Christianity as the missionaries presented it helped undermine African indigenous systems. Missionaries favored individual salvation and accepted the stratification that capitalist labor markets engendered. Moreover, Christian ideology tended to support the colonial hierarchy and color bar. Many African Christians, however, used Christianity to attack the colonial system and its evils.

In Lesotho, for example, the Basotho used Christianity as a means to keep independent of South Africa. The people distinguished themselves from their neighbors and used Christianity to forge a new ethnic identity. The majority of Basotho profess to Roman Catholicism. Others have joined the Lesotho Evangelical Church, or the Anglican Church. There are also members of independent churches and Zionist sects. As elsewhere, people still hold traditional beliefs but merge them with Christianity.

Given that missionaries moved away from supporting black leadership in African missions—thus practicing their own form of segregation—many Africans turned to the independent churches. These generally began in rural areas and then spread to the cities. In 1892, for example, the Ethiopian Church, linked to the African Methodist Episcopal Church in the United States, began in South Africa. It had a "back to Africa" ideology that was an essential part of Ethiopianism. Ethiopianism was a Christian movement that emphasized African political solidarity and religious autonomy. Whites were troubled by the message of African independent churches, which were marked by a millenarian vision. Not surprisingly, they often sought to suppress these churches, which openly subverted the very foundations of colonialism and offered a new vision of reality.

In African religions, prophets tend to arise when foreign systems present a challenge to established beliefs. African religions have long had diviners who dream the future and serve as counselors for their peoples. Prophets have frequently been found in anticolonial movements as well as messianic ones in Africa. Their goal was and is a return to traditional African culture and religion. Many prophets used themes of the world ending and great disasters while taking up Christian ideas for their purposes. Nxele, for example, a nineteenth-century Xhosa prophet, preached the return of the dead on a day he foretold. These prophets also tended to be healers and miracle workers. Many African prophets founded churches that broke away from Christianity and opposed colonialism; these churches took on strong political tones and used African themes and symbols to convey their messages.

Islam has succeeded among pastoralists on the Horn of Africa while Christianity has been the religion of peasant farmers. Muslims are also well represented among the trades and commerce in towns. Under colonialism, Catholic and Protestant missionaries competed to convert Eritreans to their version of Christianity. They succeeded among the Kunama tribe and among some townspeople.

Islam had originally come into Sub-Saharan Africa as a commercial religion. Members of the ruling class had also been quick to grasp its advantages in organizing and centralizing their rule. In western Africa, for example, Islam had been spread by merchants who were content to adapt their practice of their religion to the social and political realities in which they found themselves. For the most part, these merchants lived in towns and adapted themselves to the religious practices of the "pagans" in the town. In these towns, merchants had great influence on the various kings and artisans with whom they came into contact and Islam spread in one form or other among the influential classes.

However, with the Moroccan occupation of the Niger Bend in 1591 the political and religious situation of the western Sudan changed dramatically. Ghana, Mali, and Songhay no longer controlled the western Sudan. The entire power situation changed, and Berber and Tuareg tribesmen—all Muslims—began to assert their power in the region. The pagan tribes found themselves pushed by stronger polities as the remnants of the great empires began to seek new power bases. Descendants of Moroccans settled in the Niger Bend; known as the Arma, they paid tribute to the Berbers and Tuaregs and were prominent in trans-Saharan trade. Some of the Arma were leaders in western African Islam. The Kunta tribe of Arabized Berbers, for example, was dominant in the salt trade to Timbuktu, and through the influence of Sidi Mukhtar (d.1811) had become so respected among the Muslims of the western Sudan that they mediated quarrels among the pastoral tribes, benefiting both commerce and urban society. Mukhtar owed his influence to a combination of personal and social factors. He was learned and holy, but also a leader of the Qadiriyah, one of the Muslim *tariqas* (brotherhoods). These brotherhoods passed on their own traditions of sanctity and learning. They had arisen in the eleventh century and continued to grow as a form of mystical Islam spread from the eastern areas of Islam.

Mysticism was compatible with Berber society in North Africa. In the eighteenth century another brotherhood, the Tijaniya, arose there. The tariqa entered the Sahara, arriving in western Africa by the beginning of the sixteenth century. The arrival of the tariqa signaled that the days of relative tolerance were coming to an end. Well-organized groups of devout Muslims who were both specifically trained and morally compelled to work toward a true Islamic society if people resisted their preaching, these tariqa preached the doctrine of jihad (holy war).

The Fulani found this doctrine appealing. They felt they were unduly taxed by the Hausa states. They resented the increasing wealth of these states. Muslim clerics among the Fulani felt a kinship with the Berber and Tuareg mullahs who preached jihad. In addition, the Fulani were related to the long Islamized Tukulor of Futa Jalon. Fulani clerics were renowned in the region and easily contacted members of their ethnic group who shared their grievances.

FRANK A. SALAMONE

See also: **Futa Jalon; Ibn Khaldun: History of the Berbers; Khama III; Maghrib: Muslim Brotherhoods; Missionary Enterprise: Precolonial; Monophysitism, Coptic Church, 379–640; Religion, Colonial Africa.**

Further Reading

Du Toit, Brian M. "Inculturation and African Religion: Indigenous and Western Approaches to Medical Practice" *Choice* 35, nos. 11, 12, 1893.

Hayes, Diana L. "Through the Eyes of Faith: The Seventh Principle of the Nguzo Saba and the Beatitudes of Matthew." *Journal of Religious Thought* 52, no. 2 (1996): 18–36.

Oduduyoye, Mercy Amba. "The African Experience of God through the Eyes of an Akan Woman." *Cross Currents* 47, no. 4 (1997): 493–404.

Okafor, Victor Oguegiofor. "Towards an Africological Pedagogical Approach to African Civilization." *Western Journal of Black Studies* 20, no. 3 (1996): 125–133.

Oosthuizen, G. C. "Indigenous Christianity and the Future of the Church in South Africa." *International Bulletin of Missionary Research* 21, no. 1 (1997): 8–11.

Redding, Sean. "Government Witchcraft: Taxation, the Supernatural, and the Mponda Revolt in the Transkei, South Africa, 1955–1963." *African Affairs* 95, no. 381 (1996): 555–579.

Salamone, Frank A. "Dancing in the Streets of Ibadan: The Krishna Consciousness Movement in Nigeria." *Eastern Anthropologist* 47, no. 1 (1994).

———. "The Plight of the Indigenous Catholic Priest in Africa: An Igbo Example." *Missiology* 23, no. 2 (1995).

Salzman, Todd. "Catholics and Colonialism: The Church's Failure in Rwanda." *Commonweal* 124, no. 10 (1997): 17–19.

Tidjani-Serpos, Noureini. "The Postcolonial Condition: The Archeology of African Knowledge: From the Feat of Ogun and Sango to the Postcolonial Creativity of Obatala." *Research in African Literature* 27, no. 1 (1996): 3–18.

Religion: Indigenous Beliefs: Sub-Saharan Africa

There are a number of widespread religious beliefs throughout Africa. There is, for example, a widespread belief in a supreme god; there is a belief in some sort of afterlife, as evidenced in myths and funeral ceremonies. Rituals form an important part of life; there are crisis rituals, rituals for life stages—indeed, rituals for every occasion. Rituals involve the entire person, body, and soul, in their performance.

Every traditional African religion has a concept of god. There are many different names for this supreme being, even within the same ethnic group. There are lesser deities and spirits, but the concept of one high god is indigenous to African religions. The high god is generally a distant one. Representations are made to help people comprehend god, but no one can actually see god or have contact with him or her. (In some African societies, god is perceived as both mother and father.) God is both intimately involved in creation and above it. Finally, evil comes from the spirits, not from God. God is considered to be all merciful and kindly disposed toward humans.

African beliefs attempt to link all the spheres of human existence: spiritual, psychological, physical, and political. The spiritual world is filled with minor spirits who control nature. Ancestors are a link with these spirits. Africans traditionally believe that spirits are found everywhere and cults are centered on where these spirits are found. Africans do not see anything contradictory about holding simultaneous beliefs in one God and numerous spirits. Spirits are involved in the daily lives of the living, and can cure the ills that beset everyday life.

Most precolonial African religions were animistic in one sense or another. They partook of what scholars call shamanism, totemism, or ancestor propitiation. Each of these were aspects, or institutions, within the broader religion. In fact, it is impossible to separate religion from other aspects of African life.

Shamanism, with its reliance on the ecstatic, often uses part-time practitioners who partake in the daily work of the community. Animism, in general, attributes importance to categories of supernatural beings. The individual members of a given group find themselves attached to particular locations or people.

Animism teaches that people can communicate with supernatural beings. Moreover, these beings can aid people in dealing with the realities of their everyday lives: procuring food, curing illness, and averting danger. These beings are real and have distinct personalities in the eyes of their devotees. Creator gods, however, tend to be distant and dealt with from afar.

Animistic spirits have an egoistic sense of rewarding those who remember them and take care to perform appropriate rituals. Similarly, they have no compunction about punishing those who fail to show proper respect. Their power is quite particularistic in common with ancestors. Spirits are intermediaries between God and people. The earth, for example, is often a female spirit: Mother Earth. Notably, in some African religions she is the spouse of God; in others, his enemy. Therefore, since a spirit possesses the earth, it is revered and cared for as God's gift. Since a spirit inhabits the earth, the earth is respected. There is an obligation to care for and to improve it as a sacred trust. Therefore, the Akan and Ashanti ask the earth's permission before digging a grave, or pouring a libation to the earth. The purpose is to make sure that a child will reenter the earth's womb. They also ask permission before tilling and swear oaths while touching the earth as a guarantor of truth.

Spirits also inhabit great waters. For example, Olokun is the owner of the sea to the Yoruba and the Benin in Nigeria. He lives in an underwater palace with a great entourage of human and fishlike attendants. In fact, the Yoruba make so many sacrifices and offerings that they are often called the essence of the Yoruba religion. Libation is common in Africa. Prayers accompany libation and sacrifices, for example, "Olodumare, ajuba gbogbo iku mbeleshe." (God, we give homage, we salute the ancestors that sit at your feet in counsel.)

People can pray at any time, and the act of prayer can substitute for sacrifice or offering. Prayers may be directed at God, to ancestors, or to other spirits. Usually, a priest or another official prays on behalf of the community or a family. Prayers can be made for a number of desires: food, a good life, health, the weather, assistance in dealing with life's problems. Some daily expressions are prayers such as, "God, give us rain;" "Oh, Great God"; and "God preserve you and keep you until you see your children's children."

In precolonial Africa, chiefs and other political leaders had a spiritual basis for their powers. Their communication with ancestors and enlistment of ancestors in their cause provided a continuity to life. People expected their leaders to protect them from natural and supernatural evils, to fight witchcraft and wizardry, and to enlist diviners and others to aid in that protection.

Similarly, the connection between control of the supernatural and spiritual power meant that those who were most powerful controlled those who were weakest. Witchcraft was often a tool of the powerful while it was the least powerful who suffered under witchcraft control. People often used diviners to help weed out witchcraft.

As in many African societies, the most respected doctor among the Zulus is the diviner, or *isangoma* (the word means "someone who wanders about the mountains and who lives on roots," a clear description of what those seeking to become a diviner did). The diviner is also known as an *isanusi*, an "unraveler." A diviner is also an herbalist, with an extensive knowledge of roots and herbs to aid in curing diseases. Diviners are generally chosen by the spirits, and then undergo lengthy initiations.

In most of Africa, there are several methods of divining. There are thumb, stick, and bone divinations. Each method depends on receiving a positive or negative answer from the spirits. The person may hear voices calling him to a particular location or giving him other instructions. Additionally, the chosen one may act strangely, avoiding certain foods and manifesting other signs of spirit possession.

Religion in Africa embraces all aspects of human life. There is no clear separation among the spheres of life; it is a holistic and humanistic concept. There is a clear understanding that good and evil are opposites and that doing good is its own reward.

FRANK A. SALAMONE

See also: **Religion, Colonial Africa: Indigenous Religion; Religion, Postcolonial Africa: African Theology, Indigenization.**

Further Reading

Abimbola, Wande. *Ifa: An Exposition of Ifa Literary Corpus.* Ibadan, Nigeria: Oxford University Press, 1976.

Ardagh, Philip. *African Myths and Legends.* New York: Dillon, 1998.

Barnes, Sandra (ed.). *Africa's Ogun.* Bloomington: Indiana University Press, 1989.

English, Parker, and Kibujjo M. Kalimba (eds.). *African Philosophy: A Classical Approach.* Englewood Cliffs, N.J.: Prentice Hall, 1996.

Magessa, Laurenti. *African Religion: The Moral Traditions of an Abundant Life.* Maryknoll, Orbis, 1997.

Peek, Philip M. (ed.). *African Divination Systems.* Bloomington: Indiana University Press, 1991.

Religion: Islam, Growth of: Western Africa

The growth of Islam in West Africa predominantly follows a north-south pattern whereby the earliest conversions were in the Sahara, followed by the inhabitants of the Sahelian fringe of the desert, and then in the savanna and forest zones. Yet this is also something of a simplification, as Islamic conversion also appears to have varied according to socioeconomic group. Initial converts were frequently nomads, exposed to Muslim

Mosque on the Niger River. Sekoro, Mali, 1976. Photograph © David C. Conrad.

influence through their acting as guides for Muslim trans-Saharan traders, for example. Local rulers and merchants might also be early converts to Islam as frequently were town dwellers, with the last group to adopt Islam being the bulk of the population, the sedentary agriculturists, for whom, it has been suggested, the greatest upheaval was involved in abandoning traditional religion and practices in favor of the new faith of Islam.

Arabic historical sources record that the first contacts between Muslims and the inhabitants of West Africa began in the ninth century. These first contacts were primarily undertaken by Ibadi merchants. The Ibadis were a Kharidjite group who, though Muslim, held differing beliefs from the orthodox Sunni Maliki tenets that prevail today in both North and West Africa. All trace of Ibadi beliefs in West Africa have now disappeared, but one possible indicator of their former influence in the region persists: certain features in the so-called Sudanese style of architecture, which have parallels with the architecture of the Mzab and other Ibadi strongholds in North Africa, and include the staircase minaret and the three-tiered mosque structures. This could, however, also be due to similarities in the construction material used in the two areas, *banco* (liquid mud) and palmwood, a factor that limits both architectural expression and building technology.

Ibadi contacts were on a small scale, as would have been conversions to Islam in the ninth century. Evidence for Islam is scarce and confined to the northern Saharan fringe at sites such as Essuk/Tadmekka in Mali. After this point in time the popularity of Islam gradually grew, and both the Arab historical sources and archaeological evidence indicate that the local Muslim community expanded in the urban centers of the Sahel. Mosques and Muslim burials are found dating from the late tenth and eleventh centuries onward at sites such as Gao in Mali, and Tegdaoust and

Koumbi Saleh (reputedly the trader's town attached to the capital of the empire of Ghana) in Mauritania. Local rulers, as in Ghana and Gao, began to convert to Islam, even if the bulk of the population remained animist. Muslim functionaries were employed to administer local kingdoms and treasuries, and access to literacy via Arabic was an accompanying benefit of royal conversion to Islam.

Over the following two to three centuries, conversion to Islam gradually grew, becoming entrenched in the urban environment. Similar patterns are evident farther to the east in Kanem-Borno, centered around Lake Chad, for example. Here, an early Ibadi influence also appears to have been of significance but is little understood, although by the late eleventh century the ruler of this state had, according to tradition, become a Muslim.

Away from the Sahel, Islam was spread by indigenous Muslim merchants and clerics rather than Arab or Berber merchants, as had tended to be the case in the former area. Among the most successful of these disseminators of Islam were the Mande merchants (sometimes also referred to as Dyula or Wangara), who succeeded in spreading Islam throughout the Savannah and forest of West Africa from their homelands on the Middle Niger, beginning in the late fourteenth century. Trade rather than missionary zeal appears to have provided their impetus as they sought gold and kola nuts to take north with them. In so doing, many Mande established settlements in the regions in which they traveled. Mosques were built and conversions to Islam among the local population occurred, mirroring processes that had taken place several centuries earlier in the Sahel. The impact of the Mande was felt in Northern Ghana, where sites such as Begho indicate their former presence, and also in Burkina Faso and the Côte d'Ivoire.

Possible Mande influence on the growth of Islam in West Africa has also been suggested for Nigeria, where the Hausa began to convert to Islam from the mid-fourteenth century on. Besides a potential Mande influence on Islamization, the seven original Hausa city states, the *Bokwoi* of Daura, Zaria, Biram, Kano, Rano, Katsina, and Gobir were also under the sway of Kanem-Borno, their neighbor to the north, and Songhay, with Gao as its capital, to the west. Initially, following the pattern noted elsewhere, the influence of Islam was restricted to the court circle, but by the sixteenth century it appears that Islam dominated in the cities of Hausaland while paganism was still tolerated in the countryside. In fact, perceptions of the lax Islam of Hausaland and the continuation of traditional religion in its rural areas were to have severe implications for the inhabitants of the region. This came in the form of the Fulani jihad (holy war), begun as a reaction against their perceptions of the impurity of Hausa Islam in the

early nineteenth century. Hausa forces were to sweep across much of the savanna of West Africa during this century. Powerful military and religious leaders such as 'Uthman dan Fodio created vast empires on the ruins of Hausa and other states, and a more orthodox Islam was preached and practiced.

Yet the impact of the Fulani jihads, though profound in terms of increasing conversion to Islam, often by coercion, did not wholly succeed in eradicating the special characteristics often apparent in West African Islam. The blending of traditional and Muslim religious beliefs and practices continued, and indeed, continues, to be a feature of Muslim practice in many areas of West Africa.

TIMOTHY INSOLL

See also: **Fulbe/Fulani/Peul; Hausa Polities: Origins, Rise.**

Further Reading

Hiskett, M. *The Course of Islam in Africa.* Edinburgh: Edinburgh University Press, 1994.

Insoll, T. "The Archaeology of Islam in Sub-Saharan Africa: A Review." *Journal of World Prehistory*, no. 10 (1996): 439–504.

Levtzion, N. *Ancient Ghana and Mali.* London: Methuen, 1973.

Levtzion, N., and J. F. P. Hopkins. *Corpus of Early Arabic Sources for West African History.* Cambridge: Cambridge University Press, 1981.

Lewicki, T. "The Ibadites in Arabia and Africa." *Cahiers d'Histoire Mondiale*, no. 13 (1971): 3–130.

Trimingham, J. S. *Islam in West Africa.* Oxford: Clarendon Press, 1959.

———. *A History of Islam in West Africa.* London: Oxford University Press, 1962.

Religion, Postcolonial Africa: African Theology, Indigenization

One of the most significant recent developments within African Christianity has been the mushrooming of African independent churches (AICs). There are now thought to be more than 20,000 of these new congregations. Their growth has been swift in a number of countries, including Nigeria, Kenya, Ghana, Liberia, Malawi, Zimbabwe, and South Africa. From small beginnings, some have now reached an impressive size. Among them are Benson Idahosa's Church of God Mission in Nigeria, which has more than 2,000 branches; others, including Andrew Wutawunashe's Family of God Church and Ezekiel Guti's Zimbabwe Assemblies of God Africa (both in Zimbabwe), and Mensa Otabil's International Central Gospel Church and Bishop Duncan-William's Action Faith Ministries (both in Ghana), have also grown swiftly.

African independent churches offer a distinctive reinvention of an externally derived innovation, moulded and adapted to offer spiritual rebirth, potentialities for material improvements, and the growth of a new community spirit among followers. Regarding their theology, while adhering to the Bible as an unimpeachable theological source, many such churches also preach the effectiveness of experiential faith, the centrality of the Holy Spirit, the spiritual gifts of glossolalia and faith healing, and the efficacy of miracles. Their worldview is also often informed by personal conversion as a distinct experience of faith in Christ as Lord and Savior (being "born again" in the sense of having received a new spiritual life), and in helping others have a similar conversion experience. Rather than relying on foreign donations, as many of the former mission churches still do to some degree, most AICs are primarily reliant on members' donations for their upkeep.

Members of AICs often have a strongly moralistic worldview: lying, cheating, stealing, bribing (or being bribed), adultery, and fornication are frowned upon. Because members of the churches conceive of a clear division between what is right and what is wrong, they tend to be opposed to public corruption. There is a strong sense that the well-being of society is highly dependent upon good standards of personal morality. The nature of social interactions within some of the AICs also helps to reorient traditional gender relations and, in the process, transform sexual politics. While some of the churches continue to promote a doctrine of female submissiveness, many do not. This appears to be one of the main attractions of such churches for young urban women in Lagos, the capital of Nigeria. It is particularly in the spheres of marriage, family, and sexuality that one finds doctrines and practice in some AICs transforming gender relations quite dramatically.

Millions of Africans have joined AICs in recent years because of the intensity of the prayer experience they offer; the attraction of a simple and comprehensible message that seems to make sense out of the chaos that many perceive all around them; a moral code that offers guidance and the resuscitation of community values; and a sense of group solidarity exemplified in the way that individual followers often call each other "brother" and "sister." In addition to spiritual and social objectives, members of AICs often also seek material goals. For some, the hope of prosperity is one of the churches' main attractions, leading to charges that their message of hope is little more than a mindless and self-centred appeal to personal material well-being.

Although it would be misleading to try to standardize all these churches, some things are generally clear. First, such churches often function as an alternative for those seeking a religious and social experience that the former mission churches often appear unable to offer. Most AIC members formerly belonged to the Roman Catholic Church or one of the various Protestant denominations. Second, many of their followers are young people. Third, regarding their theology, while there is a need for more research, it is clear that the faith gospel of "health and wealth" is central to many, perhaps most. In Lagos, Nigeria, for example, AIC members run their own catering companies, hospitals, kindergartens, and record companies. Employment is offered first to coreligionists because they are considered likely to be honest and to work hard.

The faith gospel was originally an American doctrine devised by the media evangelists in the 1950s and 1960s. Yet much of Africa's traditional religion has always been concerned with fertility, health, and plenty. It is by no means clear to what extent such a gospel is still an identifiably American doctrine or whether it has now been thoroughly Africanized. The class make up of the AICs is diverse: they do not simply minister to the poor, the middle classes, or some other identifiable societal group, but find adherents from among all social classes. Another key theological feature is the understanding of spirits in the churches. Like the notion of "health and wealth," spirits are an essential part of African religious culture. It is by no means clear what the relationship is between this traditional thinking and the demonology of Western Pentecostalism.

The members of AICs are often concerned with social issues, involving a communal sharing of fears, ills, jobs, hopes, and material success. Earthly misfortune is often perceived to be the result of a lack of faith; God will reward true believers. Such believers appear to estimate that people's redemption is in their own hands (or rather in both God's and the individual's hands), and that expectations that government could or should supply all or even most of people's needs and deal with their problems is misplaced.

AICs challenge the Christianity of the former mission churches both intellectually and materially. Such is the concern with the hemorrhaging of followers, that the mainstream Christian churches attack them on two fronts. On the one hand, AICs are accused of being little (if anything) more than Trojan horses of American fundamentalist churches. However, the fact that some AICs are patronized by wealthy foreign (especially North American) pastors probably helps confirm to many followers the desirable association between religion and personal prosperity. At the same time, the mainstream churches rush to incorporate glossolalia, faith healing, and copious biblical allusions into their services.

JEFF HAYNES

See also: **Religion, Colonial Africa: Independent, Millenarian/Syncretic Churches; Religion, Postcolonial Africa: Independence and Churches, Mission-Linked and Independent.**

Further Reading

Dijk, Rijk van. "Young Puritan Preachers in Postindependent Malawi," *Africa* 61, no. 2 (1992): 159–181.

Gifford, Paul. "'Africa Shall Be Saved': An Appraisal of Reinhard Bonnke's Pan-African Crusade." *Journal of Religion in Africa* 17, no. 1 (1987): 63–92.

Gifford, Paul. "Some Recent Developments in African Christianity." *African Affairs* 93, no. 4 (1994): 513–534.

Gray, Richard. "Popular Theologies in Africa." *African Affairs* 85, no. 4 (1986): 49–54.

Haynes, Jeff. *Religion and Politics in Africa*. London: Zed/Nairobi: East African Educational, 1996.

Lan, David. *Guns and Rain*. London: James Currey, 1985.

Mbembe, Achille. *Afriques Indociles. Christianisme, Pouvoir et Etat en Societé Postcoloniale*. Paris: Karthala, 1988.

Ter Haar, Ger. *Spirit of Africa*. London: Hurst, 1992.

Walshe, Peter. "South Africa Prophetic Christianity and the Liberation Movement." *Journal of Modern African Studies* 29, no. 1 (1992): 27–60.

Religion, Postcolonial Africa: Independence and Churches, Mission-Linked and Independent

The role of Christian churches, both mission-linked and independent, at the time of the drive to African independence in the 1950s and 1960s was the result of a number of discrete yet related factors. Whether the churches were early (principled) or late (opportunist) supporters of African independence depended on a number of issues, including, in the case of the mission-linked churches, the attitude of the European parent church and whether individual leaders of the local churches themselves welcomed independence.

The Catholic Church, controlled from the Vatican, was initially highly suspicious of the notion of African independence, as it was thought likely that some independent African countries, under the influence of the Soviet Union, would find communism attractive. However, the Church sought to make the best of a situation that was beyond its control, seeking—and generally obtaining—close ties with postcolonial governments in African countries where there were significant numbers of Catholics, such as Côte d'Ivoire, Togo, and Zaire (now the Democratic Republic of Congo-Kinshasa).

Following independence, the Catholic Church (the largest in Africa, at over 100 million baptized members), with its foreign historical, institutional, and financial links, was perceived with a high degree of suspicion by some African nationalist leaders, such as Ghana's Kwame Nkrumah. Elsewhere, such as with Félix Houphouët-Boigny of Côte d'Ivoire, the Catholic Church managed to maintain close ties with postcolonial leaders. This was because, in many cases, ideological, religious, and class affinities were pronounced and of greater practical import than the somewhat idealized conflict for power between whites and blacks that nationalist leaders officially portrayed as their main postcolonial struggle.

While many of the Protestant mission churches tended to be rather disinterested in African independence, some at least had a theologically derived worldview more liberal than that of the Catholic Church. As a result, Protestant churches generally became accustomed to the idea of African independence relatively quickly. In the postcolonial period, like the Catholic Church, they attempted to fit in with new political arrangements as best they could, not least by a process of swift Africanization of religious hierarchies.

Relationships among the various Protestant churches and postcolonial African leaders were diverse. This is because the mission-linked Protestant churches were not a unified force like the Catholic Church and, as a consequence, individually had much less spiritual and religious clout. In addition, whereas the Catholic Church possessed its own (albeit tiny) state—Vatican City—that aided its unity vis-à-vis both colonial authorities and African nationalists, the main Protestant mission churches (Anglican, Methodist, Presbyterian, and Lutheran) were in competition with each other, as well as with Catholicism and Islam. Protestant churches individually achieved close relations with some postcolonial administrations, such as that of the Kenya African National Union, yet sectarian divisions between them meant that they never individually had the same corporate significance as the Catholic Church.

Independent African churches were for the most part strong supporters of independence, as their leaders believed that the postcolonial era would facilitate their advance at the expense of the mission-linked churches. Such churches were often close to nationalist leaders, such as the African Methodist Episcopal Church (AMEC) in Zambia. The AMEC had some 50,000 members by the 1960s, and was renowned for its nationalist militancy. The growth of the AMEC, and of other independent churches in Zambia, was in part a reaction to the impact of a substantial white settler community and its links with the mission-linked churches. The latter had long been considered by most Africans to be part of the white establishment. The result was that nationalist leaders turned to African alternatives for both spiritual and organizational purposes. Kenneth Kaunda was both a local preacher and choir leader at the Lusaka branch of the AMEC in the 1950s, which gave him an opportunity to hone his political skills. Yet following independence in 1964, the AMEC refused to join with a number of other Protestant churches to form the United Church of Zambia, which later became more or less the state church. The significance of the AMEC and its role as a focal point for many nationalist politicians was that once independence was won, its political purpose came to an end as nationalist leaders sought to establish a church that could be counted upon to work closely with government.

Leaders of independent churches, like practically every other organization, religious and secular, quickly realized the necessity of cultivating close links with political leaders in the postcolonial era where the importance of the concept of *mange d'abord* ("eat first") propelled them into the hurly burly of political competition. Charged with such concerns, the Musama Disco Christo Church of Jehu Appiah, for example, was very close to Kwame Nkrumah, leader of Ghana, for a decade between 1957 and 1966. The Church of Africa was another church close to senior figures in Nkrumah's Convention People's Party government, while the F'Eden Church taught obedience to those in both secular and religious authority, counting among its followers several senior state figures. Over time in Ghana, such independent African churches have often retained their close links to senior politicians

Religious allegiance was sometimes an emblem of political factionalism and competition during the run up to, and immediately after, independence. This situation is illustrated by the experiences of Uganda in the 1950s and 1960s, when political rivalry between Protestants and Catholics was the main political issue. Conflict focused on the role of the Baganda people and their king in the political structure of the country, independent in 1963. The temporary exile of their *kabaka* (king), Mutesa—judged necessary by the British colonial authorities who were concerned (and rightly so) that he was a powerful symbol of nationalism—achieved what the British most feared: an upsurge of Baganda nationalism with Protestant overtones. Catholics felt discriminated against, and as a result they used the opportunity occasioned by the Kabaka's exile to organize themselves into a predominantly Catholic party, the Democratic Party in 1955, founded by a leading Catholic politician, Matayo Mugwanya. The Democratic Party was to lead the colony's first internally self-governing administration in 1961–1962, with the mainly non-Baganda Protestant Uganda Peoples' Congress (UPC) and the Baganda-led Protestant party, Kabaka Yekka (King Alone) taking over at independence in 1962, until Milton Obote seized power for the UPC alone. (Obote was overthrown by Idi Amin in 1971, but returned to power in 1980.)

Elsewhere, the political acumen of some Catholic politicians was illustrated in Congo-Brazzaville, where the priest-politician Foulbert Youlou led the country to independence in 1960. Three years later, however, he was deposed in a populist coup d'état led by a number of trade union activists. In neighboring Congo, where the Catholic Church was the largest, the withdrawal of the Belgian colonial administration in 1960 was the

signal for an all-out battle for political power. Representatives of the Catholic Church—identified by some Africans as a bastion of authoritarianism and racism—were notable victims of the outbreaks of violence. Dozens of Christian missionaries were killed during the civil war, which reflected the "overbearing manner in which missionaries had often behaved: 'You are as wicked as a priest' (Tu es aussi méchant qu'un pére) was commonly heard at the time" (Hastings 1979, p.136).

JEFF HAYNES

See also: **Houphouët-Boigny, Félix; Mutesa (Kabaka); Nkrumah, Kwame; Obote, Milton; Uganda: Amin Dada, Idi: Coup and Regime, 1971–1979; Uganda: Buganda Agreement, Political Parties, Independence; Zambia: Religious Movements.**

Further Reading

Etherington, Norman. "Missionaries and the Intellectual History of Africa: A Histroical Survey." *Itinerario* 7, no. 2 (1983): 116–143.

Hastings, Adrian. *A History of African Christianity, 1950–1975.* Cambridge: Cambridge University Press, 1979.

———. "Church-State Relations in Black Africa, 1959–1966." In *The Church in a Changing Society*, edited by the Commission Internationale d'Histoire Ecclesiastique Comparée (CIHEC). Uppsala, Sweden: CIHEC, 1977.

Haynes, Jeff. *Religion and Politics in Africa.* London: Zed/Nairobi: East African Educational, 1996.

Oliver, Ronald. *The African Experience.* London: Weidenfield and Nicolson, 1991.

Ter Haar, Ger. *Spirit of Africa.* London: Hurst, 1992.

Religion, Postcolonial Africa: Islam

There are a number of versions of Islam extant in Africa, both north and south of the Sahara. In both regions Africans have long belonged to Sufi brotherhoods; in addition, many ethnic groups, especially in West and East Africa, converted to Islam en masse before and during the colonial era, giving religious belief among such people an ethnic dimension. Some of them would also be members of Sufi brotherhoods, so the latter may also have an ethnic aspect. However, orthodox conceptions of Islam (nearly always Sunni in Africa) are the province of the religious elite, the *'ulama* (religious-legal scholars) who tend to look down on the "uneducated" followers of Sufi Islam who practice "degenerate" or "impure" versions of the faith.

Differing manifestations of Islam point to the fact that the faith in Africa in fact covers a variety of interpretations of what it means to be a Muslim. Outside the Arab countries of the north, Islam in Sub-Saharan Africa can be divided into distinct categories, corresponding to extant social, cultural, and historical divisions. The first includes the dominant sociopolitical and cultural

Hassan II Mosque. Rabat, Morocco. © Charlotte Thege/Das Fotoarchiv.

position of Islam in the emirates of northern Nigeria, the lamidates of northern Cameroon, and the shaykhdoms of northern Chad. In each of these areas religious and political power is fused in a few individuals; over time a class structure has developed based on religious differentiation. Second, there are the areas where Sufi brotherhoods predominate—generally in West and East Africa, and especially in Senegal, the Gambia, Niger, Mali, Guinea, Kenya, and Tanzania. Third, in a number of African states, Muslims, fragmented by ethnic and regional concerns, are politically marginalized as a bloc.

Such is the situation in a number of Sub-Saharan countries, including Ghana, Togo, Benin, and Côte d'Ivoire. In Sudan, on the other hand, it is the country's Muslim rulers of the National Islamic Front who seek to use Islam as an ideology of conquest and of Arabization, against southern Sudanese peoples, including the Dinka and the Nuer. The latter groups have fought a long civil war against the northern Sudanese Muslim-dominated state, aided by Iran, which has long wished to establish an Islamic state throughout the country. Even though northern Sudanese leaders claim that Islamic (*Shari'a*) law would not be introduced in non-Muslim areas of the country, it has become clear that their aim, involving forced conversion of Christians and "pagans" to Islam, is eventually to Islamize and Arabize the entire country; in effect, it is a putative policy of "ethnic cleansing." Culturally and religiously distinct southern Sudanese would regard such an objective as tantamount to an assault upon their way of life, even their very survival.

The campaign of the Sudanese state over the last few years to Islamize their country is but one manifestation of the growing importance of what is commonly, if unhelpfully, referred to as "fundamentalist" Islam or, better, "Islamism." In recent years of great religious and political importance in several North African Arab

countries, including Algeria and Egypt, and to a lesser but still significant extent in Tunisia and Morocco, Islamism is less influential in most Sub-Saharan countries with the exception of Nigeria. In that country, political and religious conflict between Muslims and Christians has in recent years become a serious issue; the country has also seen the emergence of various Islamist groups in recent years. Sufi Muslims have found themselves targeted by Islamists who regard Sufism as a primitive, degraded form of Islam in need of "purification."

Broadly speaking, there are two types of Islamist groups to be found in Sub-Saharan Africa. On the one hand there are the reforming groups, often influenced by Iranian or Saudi Arabian concepts of Islamic orthodoxy, which attract mostly the educated, who are intellectually convinced of the desirability of attaining a "pure" Islamic society. On the other hand, another kind of Islamic fundamentalism has also emerged, notably in Nigeria, in response to growing polarization between Christians and Muslims over the issue of which religion is to dominate in the country. This is an Islamism less concerned with the introduction and promulgation of orthodox Islamic purity than in championing the "rights" of Muslims in relation to those of Christians. Generally speaking, however, Islamism has made relatively little impact in much of Sub-Saharan Africa, unlike in the Arab north, because its aims (namely, the imposition of Islamic orthodoxy) are not welcomed by many of the region's Muslims, who are either followers of traditional Sufi Islam or who live in small Muslim communities where local Islamic norms predominate.

In the north of the continent there is a diversity among Islamists. Some groups propose (or practice) armed struggle to wrest power from government (in, for example, Algeria and Egypt), some believe in incremental change through the ballot box (in, for example, Morocco and Tunisia), while others seek to achieve their goals by way of a combination of extraparliamentary struggle, societal prozelytization and governmental lobbying (in, for example, Algeria and Egypt). However, despite differences in tactics, North African Islamist groups tend to share two broad ideas: that politics and religion are inseparable, and that *Shari'a* law must be applied to all Muslims, whether they accept it voluntarily or by force.

Islamist groups in North Africa recruit members and supporters from a range of professions and backgrounds; but they tend to come from lower middle- or middle–class backgrounds and are found predominantly among teachers, university students, graduates (especially from scientific and technical backgrounds), military and police officers, and shopkeepers. Many live in urban areas but have a recent history of a rural past. The arguments and appeals of the leaders are couched in theological language, but the chief concerns of followers are probably in some cases more prosaic: social and economic goals predicated upon fundamental political change. In other words, bolstering and strengthening the overtly theological and religious terminology are a range of basic political issues and socioeconomic grievances that account for the widespread political support in North Africa for Islamist groups' programs and policies. Islamist groups seek participation in what are essentially closed political and economic systems dominated by an often cohesive political and economic elite, including the upper echelons of the military.

Political parties with Islamist concerns have fought elections in a number of African countries in the 1980s and 1990s—for example, in Egypt, Algeria, Kenya, Morocco, Sudan, and Tunisia; several have registered a degree of electoral success. Islamists in these countries (with the exception, controversially, of Algeria) have gained seats in legislatures in recent times, and this has helped to sustain public support for their movements' aims and objectives. The effects of this have been twofold: on the one hand, pressure is kept up against the governing elites which may lead to further concessions, while on the other, Islamist victories help both to sustain the support of the existing followers while making it more plausible for others to add their weight to the fundamentalist campaign for change.

Islam has also been the rallying cry of a number of minority ethnic groups in several African countries in recent times. Whereas during the 1960s and 1970s regimes were apparently successful in subjugating ordinary Muslims' concerns by helping to exacerbate religious and ethnic divisions, by the 1980s increasing economic decline, growing political repression, and authoritarianism combined with international moves toward democratization and growing universal Muslim assertiveness to produce a number of popular Islamic groups that confronted orthodox religious leaders as well as their temporal rulers.

In Burkina Faso, Kenya, and Tanzania, popular Islamic groups have recently led opposition to one-party states when the systems they represent were already beginning to fracture as a result of both domestic and international pressures. In Burkina Faso the catalyst for Muslim opposition was the self-styled revolutionary military government of Captain Thomas Sankara, which grabbed power in a military coup in 1983. Muslims, about 30 per cent of the country's population, were galvanized into confrontation with the state because of its attempts to diminish the social and political status of Islam during a period of putative revolutionary transformation.

In Kenya, which is around 10 per cent Muslim (concentrated in the coastal, northeast and eastern provinces), opposition to single-party rule was linked to some groups' perceived economic marginalization. Certain non-Muslim ethnic groups (e.g., the Luhya, Kamba, and Kalenjin) were commonly regarded as benefiting disproportionately during the rule of the Kenya African National Union (KANU). The legalization of political activity in December 1991 was the catalyst for the emergence of popular Islam groups with strong ethnic connections. In February 1992, a senior KANU official warned mosque guardians not to allow their premises to be used for political meetings, as this would be illegal. Religious parties were not allowed to register for the 1992 elections, which prevented the newly formed Islamic Party of Kenya, led by Khalid Salim Ahmed Balala, from competing.

Although about a third of mainland Tanzania's population is Muslim, they are scattered among the country's numerous ethnic groups; the greatest concentrations are found in the coastal areas. In Zanzibar, 97 per cent of the population (about 650,000 people) are Muslim. As in Kenya, the general context of the emergence of Islamic-based opposition was the fracturing of the one-party system and the tentative beginnings of political pluralism. As in Kenya, Tanzania's Muslims argued that they were discriminated against economically. Yet until recently there appeared to be little tension between Tanzania's Muslim communities and the government, no doubt in part because Muslims enjoyed senior political positions, or between Muslims and Christians—a reflection of the almost unique social consensus achieved under the former president, Julius Nyerere.

JEFF HAYNES

See also: **Kenya: Islam; Nyerere, Julius; Religion, Colonial Africa: Islamic Orders and Movements.**

Further Reading

Birai, U. M. "Islamic Tajdid and the Political Process in Nigeria." In *Fundamentalisms and the State: Remaking Politics, Economics and Militance,* edited by M. Marty and R. Scott Appleby. Chicago: University of Chicago Press, 1993.

Haynes, Jeff. *Religion, Fundamentalism and Identity: A Global Perspective.* Discussion Paper no. 65. Geneva: UNRISD, 1995.

———. *Religion and Politics in Africa.* London: Zed/Nairobi: East African Educational, 1996.

Lapidus, Ira. *A History of Islamic Societies.* Cambridge: Cambridge University Press.

Lubeck, Paul. "Islamic Protest under Semi-industrial Capitalism Yan Tatsine Explained." *Africa* 55, no. 4 (1985): 369–389.

Mayer, Anne. "The Fundamentalist Impact on Law, Politics and Constitutions in Iran, Pakistan, and the Sudan." in *Fundamentalism and the State: Remaking Polities, Economies, and Militance* edited by M. Marty and R. Scott Appleby, Chicago: University of Chicago Press, 1993.

Religion, Postcolonial Africa: Neo-Pentecostalism

Pentecostalism is by no means only a postcolonial phenomenon. American missionaries bearing news of the "Apostolic Faith" arrived in South Africa only two years after what is commonly accepted as the beginning of the Pentecostal movement: the great outpourings of the Holy Spirit in the African Methodist Chapel in Azusa Street, Los Angeles. By 1920, missionaries from the earliest Pentecostal denominations in the United States, Canada, Sweden, Norway, and Britain were at work in Africa, proclaiming their distinctive "foursquare gospel" of justification by faith, sanctification by the spirit, divine healing, and the Second Coming. This missionary Pentecostalism often combined with revivalistic tendencies in mainline Christianity to stimulate the rise of a host of "spirit-" or "Aladura-" type independent churches in Southern and West Africa, but on the whole the Pentecostal denominations themselves remained relatively small.

It was not until the late 1970s that Pentecostalism took off. In part, the growth can be explained by the steadily increasing missionary input from the older Pentecostal denominations, such as the American and British Assemblies of God and the Pentecostal Assemblies of Canada. Some African pastors and evangelists broke away from these missionary movements to found their own churches, retaining part of the original name, such as Ezekiel Guti's Zimbabwe Assemblies of God Africa. The rise of Pentecostalism can also be traced to such ministries as Scripture Union and Campus Crusade, which targeted Africans in higher education. These African elites, joined by others with a similar Christian experience in higher education in the West, began ministries in cities among the educated middle classes, forming movements like the Redeemed Christian Church in Nigeria. The growing momentum of Pentecostalism caused still others to leave mainline churches to found new movements. Mensa Otabil, one of Africa's leading Pentecostals, left the Anglican Church to found the Ghana-based International Central Gospel Church in 1984.

These new movements were also catalyzed and shaped by a large variety of evangelical, charismatic and Pentecostal organizations, which, although different in theology and practice, agreed on the centrality of the born-again conversion experience. First, an interdenominationalism was fostered by parachurch bodies like Woman's Aglow, the Full Gospel Business Men's Fellowship International, and the Haggai Institute. Second, American Bible Colleges such as Gordon Lindsay's Christ for the Nations Institute in Dallas, provided new Pentecostal leaders such as Benson Idahosa (in Nigeria) and Nevers Mumba (in Zambia) with training, but also—and more important—with a vast pool of resources and international contacts. Finally, numbers were boosted by the teaching and proselytizing activities of Western-based charismatics and Pentecostals such as Reinhard Bonnke, Benny Hinn, John Avanzini, and Oral Roberts.

Some scholars have argued for the existence of a neo-Pentecostalism that distinguishes the newer movements from the older ones. The first marker of neo-Pentecostalism is its association with media technologies. Although other churches, particularly the Roman Catholic Church, have made good use of print media and religious broadcasting, Pentecostals have come to appropriate the electronic media with such a zeal that it is almost a defining characteristic. Audio- and videotapes, produced locally and internationally, now augment gospel tracts, Bible study guides, and Christian monthlies as tools of teaching and proselytism. Religious broadcasting is particularly strong in West Africa, though Pat Robertson's *700 Club* appears on television in numerous African countries, and gospel music is on the airwaves throughout the continent.

The strong reliance by African Pentecostals on literature and electronic media derived from America contributes to two other markers of neo-Pentecostalism: its supposedly global and homogenous character and its interdenominationalism. These tendencies are enhanced by the itineration of African Pentecostal leaders around born-again conventions and conferences in Europe, Asia, and America, and the activities of Western born-again leaders in Africa. African Pentecostals are proud to be part of a global born-again community. Their convention centers are decked out in the flags of other nations and many ministries include the label *International* in their name.

The final characteristic of neo-Pentecostalism is its embrace of the faith gospel. The older missionary-derived Pentecostal denominations often had a strong holiness strand that placed emphasis on the socially humble person and was suspicious of material success. More recent strains of African Pentecostalism have drawn from the teachings of Oral Roberts, T. L. Osborn, Kenneth Hagin, and Kenneth Copeland to argue that material success is a both a sign of faith and of God's blessing. This prosperity gospel is often accompanied by rituals of deliverance (exorcism) that liberate believers from the heritage of their ancestors, and the demands of their extended families to redistribute wealth and participate in acts of traditional commensality. The stereotype of the African Pentecostal who drives to church in a Mercedes dressed in the finest clothes and jewelry is often not far from the truth.

In some respects, the faith gospel both facilitates and legitimates the accumulation of young upwardly mobile middle-class Pentecostals and their leaders in a time of general economic decline. But contemporary Pentecostalism has a far greater force than this. As African states retreat in the face of demographic pressure on resources and the demands of structural adjustment programs, so have Pentecostals taken on welfare provision, providing education and heath care. Moreover, the Pentecostal community replaces the extended family or "tribe," helping the believer with access to jobs and accommodation and operating as a burial society in times of bereavement. The "puritan ethics" of sobriety and industry Pentecostalism engenders in believers makes them socially mobile, or at least keeps them from falling over the edge into poverty. Although Pentecostal leaders like Guti, Mumba, Otabil, and the late Benson Idahosa have accumulated through their church members and their international connections, their wealth is usually not despised by their followers, who view them as born-again "big men." They are seen as effective leaders, able to represent their movement to the authorities and dispense vast amounts of patronage such as jobs, bursaries, and travel abroad.

Although African Pentecostalism might initially look like American born-again Christianity, the faith gospel resonates with "traditional" culture. While the Pentecostal middle classes aspire to prosperity, the majority of believers in townships and villages seek security. The poor make offerings to their leaders in the hope of receiving protection from witchcraft and evil spirits, and to secure fertility, healing, employment, success in public examinations, and harmonious marriages. As such, Pentecostalism stands in the trajectory of African personal security movements. Moreover, as mainline churches become increasingly fixated upon the gospel of development, so do ordinary Christians flock to Pentecostal churches, which are more inclined to address traditional concerns of purity, empowerment, well-being, and longevity. Thus, in both its engagement with existential questions and its creation of religious communities Pentecostalism does not represent a radical disjunction with African Christian independency, but stands in continuity with it.

Given the high profile of some of Africa's "born-again" political leaders such as Gatscha Buthelezi, Daniel arap Moi, and Frederick Chiluba, the question arises as to whether Pentecostalism contributes toward the politics of authoritarianism and neopatrimonialism. In states such as Ghana and Kenya, where some of the historic denominations have distanced themselves from regimes with poor records of human rights, political accountability, and financial management, certain Pentecostal movements have filled the legitimacy gap in order to obtain respectability and recognition. In Southern Africa, the Rhema Church espoused the causes of the American Religious Right. And in Nigeria and Zimbabwe Pentecostal leaders have joined the dominant elite in a culture of corporatism and clientelism, their personalized bureaucracies mirroring those of secular "chiefs."

Yet Pentecostalism's relation to politics is far from clear cut. In many of its daily practices it contributes to a culture of democratic pluralism and egalitarianism. At the level of the local assembly the disciplined believer participates in a culture of pragmatism and competition. Here also, in an autonomous space free from the state, social relations are remade. Ethnic and class differences are repatterned through the language of Christian brotherhood. Women and youth are empowered through the spirit. The reliance of many pastors on local tithes and offerings makes them vulnerable to capture from below and hence sensitive to local political agendas. In the same way that independent prophets undermined the sacred legitimation of kings and chiefs, Pentecostals make a vicarious attack on contemporary politicians, demonizing the spiritual forces through which they lay claim to authority. Some Pentecostals even espouse an explicit political theology. Otabil is renowned for his message of black pride and self-reliance and his repudiation of neocolonialism.

But it is in the sphere of gender and generational politics that Pentecostalism is most significant. With its central concern of personal rebirth, Pentecostalism begins with the remaking of the individual and the renewal of the family. In the home, the man is domesticated. He ceases to drink, is no longer promiscuous, and focuses his energies on work and education. Beyond the family and the community, Pentecostalism's critique is directed first and foremost at other elements in the religious field, such as Islam and traditional religion, which it demonizes, and the historic mission churches, which it casts as "worldly." Here the state is often used instrumentally to gain an advantage over rivals through access to public broadcasting and authorization for proselytizing activities.

It is clear that, since the late 1980s, Pentecostalism has had a significant impact on African societies. Politicians treat Pentecostals with respect, and other elements in the religious field have innovated in response to the Pentecostal upsurge. Anglicans, Catholics, and Methodists have instituted charismatic renewal to acquire "gifts of the spirit" for themselves. In West Africa, Islam has cultivated transnational connections and rapidly adopted print and electronic media to compete with Pentecostal proselytism.

DAVID MAXWELL

See also: **Religion, Colonial Africa: Independent and Millenarian/Syncretic Churches; Religion, Colonial Africa: Missionaries; Religion, Postcolonial Africa: Islam; Religion, Postcolonial Africa: African Theology, Indigenization; Religion, Postcolonial Africa: Church and State Relations; Religion, Postcolonial Africa: Independence and Churches, Mission-Linked and Independent.**

Further Reading

Gifford, Paul. *African Christianity: Its Public Role*. London: Hurst, 1998.

———. *The New Crusaders: Christianity and the New Right in Southern Africa*. London: Pluto, 1991.

Gifford, Paul (ed.). *The Christian Churches and the Democratisation of Africa*, Leiden: E. J. Brill, 1995.

Meyer, Birgit. *Translating the Devil: Religion and Modernity among the Ewe of Ghana*. Edinburgh: Edinburgh University Press, 1999.

Maxwell, David (ed.). Special Issue on Pentecostalism, *Journal of Religion in Africa* 28, no. 3 (1999).

Religion, Postcolonial Africa: Church and State Relations

Four great historical forces have shaped the postcolonial church in Africa. The first is the dramatic shift in clerical leadership, from foreign missionary leadership to indigenous African leadership. The second is the pressure on the church to link the Christian faith to African culture (enculturation). The third is the challenge for the church to increase its role as an active moral force on African political and social life. The fourth is the challenge of the Islamic purists, who would like to impose the Shari'a (Islamic law) and their religious understanding about the nature of the state on their fellow citizens. In the face of all these challenges, the African Church has frequently sought to promote the common good.

At the time of political independence, many of the nationalists who had been exposed to Christian traditions wished the church well. The church, on the other hand, applauded the nationalists for promoting principles of justice, equality, and unity. Both church and state recognized each other as legitimate partners in the task of nation-building. This partnership came under stress as African societies were gradually subjected to racial autocracy, civil wars, and political and military tyranny. The political thinking of certain African political leaders had to be urgently challenged. The church opted to become a "watchdog" of the political scene, rather than a mere "lapdog," so to speak, and in so doing put African Christians at the center of African politics. Christians, the church insisted, were bound by their conscience to resist tyrannical government policies. Clerics such as Cardinal Bayenda of Brazzaville and Archbishop Luwum of Kampala lost their lives in the face of hostile Congo and Ugandan governments, respectively. In the Republic of Zaire, the government of Mobutu temporarily exiled Cardinal Malula and stripped him of the National Order of Leopard.

Marxist regimes, such as Seku Touré's in Guinea and Ethiopia under the Derg-military junta of Mengistu, attacked the clerical leadership. In such attacks Archbishop Tchidimbo of Conakry was imprisoned, in 1971, while Abuna Teoflos of the Ethiopian Orthodox church was murdered in July 1979. The Ethiopian government of the Ethiopian Progressive Revolutionary Democratic Front continued to interfere in the internal politics of the Orthodox Church. It was such intervention that led to the resignation in 1991 of Abuna Mekorious and the government's subsequent appointment in 1992 of Abuna Paulos Gebrehiwot as the fifth patriarch. Individual African clerics had been targets of attack, but in the cases of the Jehovah's Witnesses and Alice Lenshina's Zambia Lumpa Church, a whole church came under government attack. The Jehovah's Witnesses were threatened in Kenya and Malawi for their rejection of political party membership and refusal to salute the national flag. In Zambia, the Lumpa Church condemned worldly materialism, which precipitated a conflict with the Zambian government.

The church found itself in the center of Africa's two bloodiest civil wars. In Nigeria from 1967 to 1970, the church, especially the Christian leadership in Eastern Nigeria ("Biafra") supported the cause of "Biafra." The federal government of Nigeria declared many foreign clerics in Eastern Nigeria persona non grata. The federal government of Nigeria followed this with the seizure of mission schools. Similarly, the Republic of Sudan was engaged in a bloody civil war. The Sudan People's Liberation Movement, the most vigorous opposition to the Islamic State, had been supported by the Christian clerics, while the Christian leadership was also engaged in positive peace negotiation with the state. It would be too simple to portray the civil wars in Nigeria and the Sudan as purely religious conflicts, but the need to establish a democratic and secular state was a serious concern for the opposition factions in both states. Islamic purists in both states have been insisting that the Shari'a should become the social and political framework. Sudanese Christians have taken a stand against such a proposition in the south. In Nigeria, the Christian Association of Nigeria, under the leadership of the Catholic Archbishop of Lagos, Anthony Okogie, has actively sought to maintain the secular character of the Nigerian state. The Copts of Egypt have lived in a predominantly Muslim state, and have requested constitutional guarantees for their membership. In one such confrontation, President Anwar Sadat removed Pope Shenouda III of Alexandria and the patriarch of the see of St. Mark from his post in 1981 and exiled him to a desert monastery. Amnesty International and the Vatican protested his detention, and he was released in 1985.

The question of Muslim-Christian conflicts in Africa has raised issues of dialogue. In Nigeria, the government had instituted instruments for such a dialogue. The appointment of Cardinal Arinze of Nigeria as the Vatican's point man for Muslim-Christian dialogue shows the significance attached to this issue.

The church in Africa since political independence has stood steadfastly on the side of human rights. It soon became clear that the state theology of the apartheid regime of South Africa would be vigorously opposed. That decisive moment came with the leadership of Black liberation theologians such as Anglican Archbishop Desmond Tutu, Catholic Bishop P. F. J. Buthelezi, and Dutch Reformed Church clerk Allan Boesak. Apartheid was theologically delegitimized and declared a heresy. Meanwhile, many church leaders had become exile casualties of the tyrannical apartheid regime, such as the Anglicans Abrose Reeves, Trevor Huddleston, Gronville F. French-Beytagh, and Collia Witner, and the Catholic Archbishop Denis Hurley.

African church leaders have intensified their efforts as "watchdogs." Unfortunately, the involvement of certain Rwandan Hutu clerics in the genocidal onslaught of the Tutsi in 1994 has stained the recent record of the clergy in Africa. Yet the majority of the church leaders in Africa see their main duty to be that of protecting and nourishing Christian life in Africa. In promoting this mission of the church, the church leaders are joining African political leaders in their projects of development, reconciliation, and liberation. The church of Africa continues to invest heavily in educational, medical, and social services. The reconciliation capacity of the African church was exemplified in South Africa, where Archbishop Tutu was appointed to head the Truth and Reconciliation Commission. Pope John Paul's clarion call during his various visits to Africa for reconciliation and the restoration of constitutional order and democratic freedom is now the model to which the church in Africa aspires.

Religion, despite rising secularism, still speaks from the center of African societies, and as such the church will continue to have a voice in African political life. Even as the church focuses on the individual soul and transformation, that focus will always be based on Christian principles of justice and when necessary structural change. In that respect, Africans should expect more church-state confrontation. Christianity is one of among effective instruments of moral critique regarding African political life.

AUSTIN METUMARA AHANOTU

See also: **Religion, History of; Religion, Colonial Africa: Independent, Millenarian/Syncretic Churches; Religion, Postcolonial Africa: Independence and Churches, Mission-Linked and Independent.**

Further Reading

Ahanotu, Austin Metumara. *Religion, State and Society in Contemporary Africa: Nigeria, Sudan, South Africa, Zaire and Mozambique*. New York: Peter Lang, 1992.

Borer, Tristan Anne. *Challenging the State: Churches as Political Actors in South Africa, 1980–1994*. University of Notre Dame Press, 1998.

Fasholé-Luke, A., Richard Gray, Adrian Hastings, and Godwin Tasie (eds.). *Christianity in Independent Africa*. Bloomington: Indiana University Press, 1978.

Hansen, Holder. *Religion and Politics in East Africa* Eastern African Studies series. Ohio University Press: 1994.

Hastings, A. A. *History of African Christianity 1950–1975*. London: Cambridge University Press, 1982.

Okulu, Henry. *Church and Politics in East Africa*. Nairobi: Uzima Press, 1982.

The Kairas Document: Challenge to the Church: A Theological Comment on the Political Crisis in South Africa. Grand Rapids, Mich.: Eerdmans, 1986.

Sindima, Harvey J. *Drums of Redemption: An Introduction to African Christianity*. Westport, Conn.: Greenwood Press, 1994.

Renamo: *See* Mozambique: Renamo, Destabilization.

Resettlement of Recaptives: Freetown, Libreville, Liberia, Freretown, Zanzibar

The abolition of slavery by European powers in the nineteenth century led to a massive effort by the British and French to suppress the slave trade on the coasts of Africa. This antislavery campaign was marked by the resettlement of thousands of recaptive slaves on the west and east coasts of Africa. Sierra Leone was one of the earliest settlements of these "liberated slaves." These recaptives came to revive a troubled colony created in 1787 by the British to settle freed blacks from England, Nova Scotia, and Jamaica, who created a self-governing community in a site called "Freetown." But financial difficulties, the hostility of local populations (the Temne) and the ravages of the fever threatened the existence of this settlement.

It was only saved in 1791, when it was reorganized as property of the Sierra Leone Company, a joint-stock enterprise of British philanthropists. Ruled with a heavy hand by Zachary Macaulay, the company kept the colony alive. The company hoped to use these settlers to develop a commercially profitable venture. Unfortunately, it lost heavily and was forced to turn its undertaking to the

British government. In 1808 this settlement became a crown colony, an event that coincided with the abolition of slavery in Great Britain. Freetown became a convenient rehabilitation center for recaptive slaves who were being rescued by the British antislavery naval patrol in the Atlantic Ocean. The abolitionists transformed this settlement into a center for the radiation of Christianity and Western culture throughout West Africa.

The Church Missionary Society (CMS), created in 1799, was to carry out this "civilizing mission." The missionaries found recaptive slaves to be more receptive to the Christian gospel than the Nova Scotians and the natives, and these recaptives lived under missionary guidance. By massively converting to Christianity they began to emulate the Nova Scotian settlers in their assimilation of Western culture. These liberated slaves learned English, and progressively created a culture (Krio), which is a mixture of African and European experiences.

Another rehabilitation center for former slaves was being set up some 200 miles south of Freetown. In 1822, a small group of American blacks arrived in Liberia. Their voyage, organized by the American Colonization Society, was guided by the idea that free blacks and manumitted slaves in the United States might begin a new life on African soil, away from the discrimination and persecution they experienced in the United States. The beginning of the settlement of these freed blacks in "Liberia" (named for the freedom this establishment symbolized) was as difficult as in Sierra Leone. Diseases, poor leadership, and hostility from local populations almost provoked the extinction of these settlers. But they were saved by a young white Briton, Yehudi Ashmun, who assumed control of the settlement at the time the agents of the Colonization Society deserted their responsibilities. Ashmun forced the colonists to work together, organized a resistance against local tribal groups, and slowly put together a permanent community. When Ashmun departed in 1828, Liberia was established. But the political heat surrounding the issue of slavery in the United States made impossible any substantial financing of the Liberian venture by the U.S. government. This was complicated by the fact that few American blacks were interested in colonization unless it was in exchange for manumission, and as late as 1850, the Liberian settlement numbered less than 3000 individuals. By 1847, however, despite a faltering economy, political instability, and chronic troubles with local people, Liberia had become an independent African nation that, despite its weaknesses, instability, and troubles with the local population, symbolized the freedom many African nations aspired to after World War II.

The British action in Sierra Leone inspired the French in the Gabon estuary. They also created a "civilizing center" called Libreville (Freetown), which has its origins in the capture of a Brazilian slave ship (the *Elizia*, or *Ilizia*) by the French Naval Patrol. The *Elizia* had 300 slaves, who were taken to Senegal in 1846. In order to solve Gabon's chronic labor problem, 50 of these recaptives were resettled in the Gabon estuary in 1849. French authorities gave this project a political character, because the Libreville sought to become a center for the radiation of French culture and Christianity in the region. But early on this project faced difficulties, because the very existence of the village was threatened. Indeed, that same year, 17 of the recaptives, working in the hospital ship *l'Adour*, rebelled against the mistreatment they were receiving. These rebels broke their relationships with the French and created a separate village in the forest. After deserting, the Loango attacked Libreville itself in 1849, and the French authorities assisted by the Mpongwe repressed these aggressions. Despite the violent nature of the counteroffensive, 14 Loango managed to escape, but 3 were killed. Nonetheless, life was taking shape in Libreville. The Loango received food from French authorities and agreed to form unions among themselves. In 1850, however, the French naval officers suspended their food supply, leading to a revolt among the recaptives. They viewed the French action as despotic and even asked to be returned to Senegal. But French authorities adopted a reconciliatory approach and convinced them to stay. The change in the leadership of the Comptoir du Gabon created more problems for the Loango. Abuses of power multiplied and the Loango began abandoning the village of Libreville to live among the Mpongwe at the Louis, Glass, and Denis villages. Some of these Loango even became traders, while others worked as crewmen in ships trading with the Mpongwe. In 1851, Libreville was almost completely deserted, and those who decided to stay were mainly invalid inhabitants experiencing different kinds of social disorders. Libreville was a failure for the French administration, but its name was extended to Mpongwe villages as the French comptoir grew in the second half of the nineteenth century and became the capital of the French Congo, between 1885 and 1910.

While the combat against slavery on the west coast of Africa was carried out by both the French navy and the British antislavery squadron, in East Africa the abolition of slavery was solely a British crusade against a massive "asiatic evil." If, around 1850, suppression of the slave trade was well established and resettlement areas were being developed in West Africa, this crusade took more time to accomplish in East Africa. Even though it was a long and difficult enterprise, the British antislavery squadron became involved in the massive stopping of Arab dhows carrying slave cargoes between 1860 and 1897. But the main problem was the resettlement of recaptive slaves, a task given to the missionaries. Some of these slaves were resettled in Zanzibar, while the majority of them found new homes in Christian centers in the mainland. Among them there was, Bagamoyo and mainly Freretown.

Situated just outside Mombasa, Freretown was founded in 1874 by Sir Bartle Frere as a settlement for freed slaves. After a special mission to Zanzibar in 1872 to negotiate a much more effective treaty for the abolition of slave trade, he urged the CMS to provide a refuge for liberated slaves. The CMS station at Freretown, under the Reverend Salter Price, received its first 500 freed slaves in 1874, and by 1888 there were over 3000 settled there. It continued to receive freed slaves until the end of the nineteenth century, but because of its tendency to forcibly disrupt slave caravans this mission was a matter of contention with slave owners. The main mission of the CMS was to teach Christianity to the recaptives, who also received basic education from the missionaries and worked on the mission's plantations. Freretown became a center of the Christian missionary movement, and freed slaves were used as missionary agents throughout East Africa.

In Zanzibar, the end of the slave trade was more difficult to obtain because of the Sultan of Zanzibar's interest in this commerce. Nonetheless, the British and the sultan signed a treaty abolishing slavery in Zanzibar in 1873. Zanzibar became a British protectorate in 1890, and additional pressure was put on the Sultan Ali bin Said to abolish the legal status of slavery; he signed a decree to this effect in 1897. This decree was a major blow to slave traffic, and slavery progressively disappeared from the island. After the 1897 decree, slaves who wished to acquire freedom had to apply to the district court and would be issued freedom papers. European slavery commissioners were to oversee the emancipation process. Despite difficulties, a slow but steady number of slaves asked for freedom papers and this process continued throughout the twentieth century. But the majority of freed slaves became prostitutes. Drinking became widespread, and terrorism and banditry increased. Nonetheless, the work of emancipation was well underway, even though many slaves asked to return to slavery and others were simply reemployed by their former masters. Those who crossed to the mainland to work on the Ugandan railway or the Uganda transport department did so under the strict orders of a European caravan leader. These former slaves became "free laborers," and discovered new forms of hardship imposed by the capitalist colonial economy.

FRANÇOIS NGOLET

See also: **Sierra Leone: Origins, 1787–1808. Sierra Leone: Development of the Colony, Nineteenth Century.**

Further Reading

Beachey, R. W. *The Slave Trade in East Africa.* New York: Harper and Row, 1976.

Cassell, Christian Abayomi. *Liberia: History of the First African Republic.* New York: Fountainhead, 1970.

Clapham, C. *Liberia and Sierra Leone: An Essay in Comparative Politics.* London, 1976.

Fyfe, C. *A History of Sierra Leone.* London: Oxford University Press, 1962.

Mbokolo, Elikia. *Noirs et Blancs en Afrique Equatoriale.* Paris: La Haye-Mouton, 1981.

Morton, Fred. *Children of Ham: Freed Slaves and Fugitive Slaves on the Kenya Coast 1873 to 1907.* Boulder, Colo.: Westview Press, 1990.

Sheriff, Abdul. *Slaves, Spices and Ivory in Zanzibar: Economic Integration of East Africa Into the World Economy.* London: James Currey, 1987.

Resistance to Colonialism

By about 1890, the European colonial powers were united in their determination to conquer a then divided Africa. They not only agreed which parts of the continent each power should have, but also promised to help each other against African resisters. In contrast, African states generally stood alone, though there were a few isolated attempts at cooperation between Muslim rulers in parts of both West and East Africa. The result was that, while actual conquest was delayed by up to 30 years in some areas, most of the African continent was under some form of European administration by 1920. Even then, a few territories on the fringes of the Sahara—for example, in Morocco and Somaliland—had still to be fully "pacified."

Forms of African resistance to colonial rule were present from the beginning. Initial African military opposition to conquest is sometimes known as "primary resistance." It was usually organized by the precolonial state, however small, and it was, nearly everywhere, brief. Other examples of primary resistance included examples of state-building resistance. In these cases, leadership had to create a new political structure, and relevant examples include state-building attempts by 'Abd al-Qadir in Algeria, the Maji Maji revolt in Tanganyika, and later phases of the Shona and Ndebele rebellions in Rhodesia. Later, after World War II, the final victory for African independence had its roots in modern nationalism. This was a form of political organization, borrowed from the West or adapted from other non-Western countries (like India). The goal of African nationalists throughout the continent was to take over the colonial state and replace European rule by new frameworks of renewed and independent African political life.

The first phase of anti-European resistance in Africa lasted roughly from the late 1880s to the time of World War I. During this time, the existing West African states were defeated in battle or forced into submission. In 1890, after a brief campaign, Segu, the principal city in the Tukulor empire, fell to the French. Between 1891 and 1898 Samori Touré was driven back, despite skillfully fighting rearguard actions and seeking to maintain his supply of the precious modern arms and ammunition from European traders on the coast. However, in 1896 the European arms blockade became fully effective against Samori and, in 1898, he surrendered. The Mossi empire of Ouagadougou was overthrown by the French in 1896 and a powerful British force occupied Asante in the same year. In 1892, the British broke the power of the Ijebu kingdom, and between 1892 and 1894 the kingdom of Dahomey was occupied after a strong resistance. Buoyed by its greatly superior military capabilities, the British colonial government at Lagos was able to penetrate the whole of Yorubaland. In 1896 the Royal Niger Company defeated the Nupe army and entered the city of Ilorin. In 1897 the kingdom of Benin fell and the following year, Rabih ibn Fadlallah, who had recently established his power in Borno using rifles imported across the Sahara, was slayed by the French. Soon after this, between 1901 and 1903, a series of major battles around Kontagora, Yola, Kano, and Sokoto left the great emirates of northern Nigeria under the control of the British.

While the states of West Africa were collapsing, European powers, including Britain, France, and Germany, attempted to extend and deepen their domination in East and Central Africa. London sent a large Anglo-Egyptian force into the Sudan and broke the khalifa's power at the battle of Omdurman in 1898, while newly established Arab states, located in the eastern Congo basins, were destroyed by European invaders. The British managed to maneuver themselves into a dominant position in the interlacustrine kingdoms in the early 1890s and, by 1900, had managed to impose themselves over the chief state in the area, Buganda. On the coast of East Africa, anticolonial resistance was defeated by 1890. Later, during the 1890s, the Germans defeated both Isike, leader of the Nyamwezi people, and Meli, the Chagga chief. Further south, in Rhodesia, the Ndebele suffered a heavy defeat in 1893 and in 1898 the resistance of the Ngoni, west of Lake Malawi, was also broken.

In the 1890s and the early years of the twentieth century, as European colonial power developed and deepened, conversion to Islam became, for many Africans, a potent symbol of anti-European resistance. For many pagan Africans, Islam was an alternative modernizing influence in opposition to the hegemony of the European Christian missionaries and their system of putative, hegemonic enculturation. Islam provided its followers with an alternative modernizing worldview, not defined by the colonial order and its norms.

Conversions to Islam encouraged a particular kind of resistance to European rule across the Maghrib and the Sudanic belt: jihad (holy war). This development was further encouraged by the beginning of a new Islamic century and Islam-inspired resistance flourished in Sudan, Somaliland, Libya, and Morocco. Both Libya and Morocco were in the first flushes of an Islamized militancy at this time, following the recent founding of polities espousing Muslim values. In Morocco, it was a feeling that the Sultan had been compromised too far by successive European demands that led to Islamic resistance. In Somaliland, Islamic militancy was focused by the actions of Muhammad Abdallah Hasan (called by the British the "Mad Mullah"), who unleashed a reign of terror against local people who refused to join his Salihiyya brotherhood. The British sent in four expeditions between 1900 and 1904 to attempt to quell the jihad, but Hasan retained his influence in the north of Somaliland until 1920.

The effect of jihad was initially both to stiffen the resolve of Muslims to fight European encroachment, as well as to identify Islam more generally with a militant anticolonial stance. Aggressive European intrusion against various African peoples sometimes led to their mass conversion to Islam as a potent signal of continued resistance. In West Africa, for example, the Mandinka people converted en masse following French campaigns against them in the last two decades of the nineteenth century. In German East Africa, the bloody repression of the Maji Maji revolt of 1905–1907 led the persecuted Ngindo people to convert to Islam en masse. In addition to localized Islamic militancy there was also the threat of militant Pan-Islamism to worry the Europeans. Not only were there links between militant Islamists in the Sudan and in Northern Nigeria in 1900–1920, but also Pan-Islamic influences associated with the Ottoman Turks. At the outbreak of World War I, the Ottomans issued a call to jihad against the Europeans that circulated widely in North Africa and parts of Kenya and Mozambique, although without conspicuous numbers of African Muslims heeding the call. The crushing of the Ottomans during World War I, coupled with the apparently inexorable spread of European power, confirmed to many African Muslims that the Europeans could not be defeated by force and gradually they came to accept European rule.

In sum, by the early years of the twentieth century, preexisting African states had been destroyed throughout the region by the European invaders. However, the small European forces were not immediately capable of effectively occupying all parts of Africa. They were especially slow to change the more remote areas and the territory of small self-governing communities whose complex social and political organizations often baffled them. Once paralyzing blows had been struck to the major African states, colonial officials went out with small escorts over a large part of the continent ordering chiefs great and small to arrest opponents of the new regime; provide labor; collect taxes; change laws; abolish tolls; permit European mining or settlement; admit missionaries; grow certain crops; give land for railways; or protect telegraph lines—in short, to become agents of colonialism. Despite periodic strikes, mutinies, and riots, the conquest was over. The business of actually imposing their authority throughout Africa would take the new colonial rulers much longer.

Once colonial power was ensconced, generally by the advent of World War I, various forms of secondary resistance to colonial rule emerged. In many cases, such movements had a cultural dimension, often involving new, syncretistic religious movements. Many emerged in the first decades of the twentieth century as vehicles of anticolonial resistance and, in many cases, flourished in the context of growing and widespread dissatisfaction with many aspects of colonial rule. On occasion, erstwhile foes, such as the Shona and the Ndebele in Rhodesia, combined to resist British colonialism in 1896–1897. In this case cultural identification was an important facet of the rebellion's organization, with spirit mediums employing "medicines" to enhance the martial efforts of the fighters. The mediums created a national network of shrines to provide an agency for the transmission and coordination of information and activities; a structure later rejuvenated during the independence war of the 1970s.

Use of "medicine" also helped stimulate the anticolonial Maji Maji rebellion of 1905–1907 in German-controlled Tanganyika. The diviner and prophet Kinjikitili gave his followers "medicine" supposed to render them invulnerable to bullets. He anointed local leaders with the *maji* ("water"), which helped to create solidarity among about 20 different ethnic groups and encouraged them to fight together in a common anti-European cause. A further example comes from northern Uganda, where a cult known as Yakan among the Lugbara people, centering on the use of "magic medicine," helped stimulate their short, unsuccessful, anticolonial war in 1919. The list of such forms of secondary resistance could be extended, but the overall point is, one would hope, clear: various movements arose, often led by prophets and stimulated by anticolonialism and the social changes that the Europeans brought with them. Local anticolonial movements employed local cultural and religious beliefs as a basis for anti-European protest and opposition.

In conclusion, primary resistance came to an end in most of Africa before World War I, and modern nationalism did not find success until after 1945. The period in between—the 1920s and 1930s—was a time of various forms of resistance to European rule. This period can be labeled one of "secondary resistance," though it is an inconvenient category. This is because its forms were so varied, to the extent that it hardly deserves to be identified as a specific category. During the interwar decades, some resistance was organized around elite political parties like the West African National Congress or the African National Congress in South Africa. Other acts of protest (or resistance) included anticolonial cultural movements, strikes, riots, and mutinies. Additionally, peaceful opposition to colonial rule was expressed via the press or the political process.

These developments were encouraged by a process of modernization during the first 50 years of the twentieth century, almost revolutionary in its medium- and long-term effects. Urbanization was an important effect of this process, leading to mass migrations and gradual industrialization. Preexisting towns expanded and new urban centers grew. Abidjan, Takoradi, Port Harcourt, Lusaka, Nairobi, and many other towns and cities were founded as ports and harbors, administrative and mining centers, and as transportation—especially railway—focal points. Urban centers expanded swiftly. The population of Accra, for example, increased from about 18,000 in 1901 to nearly 136,000 only 50 years later; Nairobi's population more than doubled in little more than a decade in the 1930s from around 12,000 people to more than 25,000; while Casablanca's population rose a hundredfold from just over 2,000 to a quarter of a million people between 1910 and 1936.

Migrants flooded into the urban centers, while traditional communities were disrupted and consequently changed as a result both of gradual insertion into the modern world economy and via the effects of an increasingly centralized political environment. The overall result of population growth, urbanization, cultivation of cash crops, and new educational and employment opportunities, was that a new social order developed. Numerous Africans found employment in the modern economic sector, but often encountered poor working conditions. Especially after World War II, both strikes and anticolonial riots broke out (for example, in the Gold Coast and Kenya) that were widely regarded as expressions of emerging nationalism.

In sum, the variety of forms of African resistance to colonial rule developed over time from primary to secondary forms of African opposition to colonial rule. In the interwar decades, such secondary resistance is most easily identified by what it was not; it was neither primary resistance nor modern nationalism.

JEFF HAYNES

See also: **Colonialism.**

Further Reading

Curtin, P., S. Feierman, L. Thompson, and J. Vansina. *African History: From Earliest Times to Independence*. London: Longman, 1995.

Engels, D., and S. Marks (eds.). *Contesting Colonial Hegemony. State and Society in Africa and India*. London: German Historical Institute/British Academic Press, 1994.

Haynes, Jeff. *Religion and Politics in Africa*. London: Zed/ Nairobi: East African Educational, 1996.

Mamdani, M. *Citizen and Subject: Contemporary Africa and the Legacy of Late Colonialism*. Kampala, Rwanda: Fountain, 1996.

Manning, P. *Francophone Sub-Saharan Africa, 1880–1995*. Cambridge: Cambridge University Press, 1998.

Rathbone, R. *Nkrumah and the Chiefs: The Politics of Chieftaincy in Ghana, 1951–60*. Accra: F. Reimmer, 2000.

Réunion: Nineteenth Century to 1946

Originally known as Ile Bourbon, Réunion was first settled under the administration of the French Compagnie des Indes Orientales in 1664. The settlers were of European origin; their slaves, who at times outnumbered them by as many as three to one, were from Madagascar and eastern Africa. In the early eighteenth century, coffee was the principal crop, but disease and competition from the Caribbean islands led to the collapse of the coffee industry in the 1740s. By then France had established sovereignty over the neighboring island of Mauritius and diversification into food production for export to Mauritius led to renewed prosperity for Réunion, although in 1764 financial difficulties obliged the Compagnie des Indes to sell both islands to the French crown.

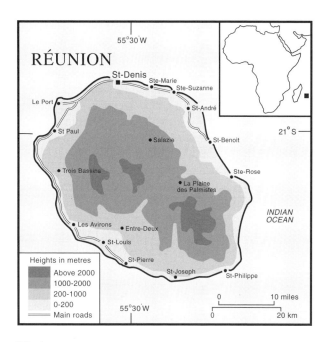

Réunion.

At the end of the eighteenth century the French revolutionary government established a colonial assembly in Réunion, granting the island a significant degree of autonomy. At the same time it attacked the privileges of the large landowners and in 1794 slavery was abolished. The island's economy depended almost entirely on slave labor, and this highly unpopular law was ignored locally. However, while proslavery sentiment united the island, the accompanying constitutional reforms that called for the integration of the island as a French department divided it, and a counterrevolutionary, proslavery group called for independence. The independence movement was eventually defeated, and with the reestablishment of slavery in 1802 the principal object of contention was finally removed.

Under the restoration, the administrative system of 1766 was reestablished, removing the local assemblies and thus significantly reducing the island's autonomy. Subsequent conflicts between the two representatives of the crown—the governor and the intendant—led to the suppression of the latter post in 1818 and a concentration of power in the hands of the governor. In 1825 the administration was reformed to restrict the powers of the governor, but although a general counsel was created, its 24 members were chosen by the king, and legislative and executive power both effectively remained with the governor.

Further changes in the 1830s granted more rights to the population: deputies sent to Paris were nominated rather than chosen, and a colonial counsel was established with 30 elected members; but renewed conflicts led to its disbanding under the Second Republic (1848–1852), and under the Second Empire (1852–1870) the autonomy of the colonies was further reduced; prospects of integration with France were rapidly disappearing. Although a general counsel, with 24 nominated members, was reestablished in 1854, their decisions were still not binding on the governor.

The most durable effect of the Napoleonic Wars had been to deprive Réunion of its market in Mauritius, which was lost to the British. However, France's loss of Mauritius also deprived the country of a source of sugar, and in Réunion large tracts of land were planted with cane; in some areas, previously untouched land came under cultivation, while in others coffee and food crops were replaced. Industrialization and a general improvement in techniques led to improved yields, but the emphasis on sugar meant that by 1848 Réunion had become a net importer of food.

By the early nineteenth century the population had increased to the point at which there was insufficient land to meet demand. If early settler families possessed large estates, more recent arrivals often found themselves with unworkable holdings hundreds of meters long but only a few meters wide. There developed a class of white settlers who, unable to exercise trades that were already the preserve of slaves or freed slaves, were obliged to move to higher ground where they eked out a meager existence on the fringes of society. The creation of a class of poor whites was exacerbated by the growth of the sugar industry, which was capital intensive and benefited from economies of scale. Land was increasingly concentrated in the hands of a few large estates, while the abolition of slavery in 1848 created another class of poor blacks almost overnight as former slaves abandoned the cane fields.

To provide more land, the interior of the island was opened up to settlers. Although there were restrictions on the amount of land that could be cleared, and on the steepness of slopes cultivated, these rules were not respected and the ensuing erosion was severe, exacerbating the poverty. In an effort to ease the labor shortage and meet the needs of the sugar industry, indentured laborers were imported from Madagascar, but abuses led to a ban on the recruitment of labor in Madagascar by 1859. Under an agreement with the British, Réunion turned to India, but again, abuses led to the British abrogating the agreement in 1885.

The period of prosperity, like the preceding ones, did not last. By 1860 sugar production was dropping: competition from other producers and a fall in prices were accompanied by disease, both of plants and laborers. As France acquired a new empire in Africa and Asia, Réunion was increasingly ignored; poor port facilities discouraged shipping, and the opening of the Suez Canal further isolated the island. By 1900, other crops were being introduced to reduce the dependence on sugar. Fragrance crops and spices—notably geranium, ylang ylang, vetiver, and vanilla—did well; tea, cotton, and tobacco were less successful, although tobacco was still an important crop for the local market.

The introduction of new crops demonstrated the islanders' resourcefulness in the face of neglect, as did the engineering works carried out at the same time. An artificial port in the west of the island was completed in 1884, and a 78-mile (125-kilometer) railway line linking St. Benoit to St. Pierre via St. Denis, including a tunnel more than six miles (ten kilometers) long, was a technical triumph.

Both World War I and the interwar period proved profitable for Réunion. Export crop (particularly sugar) prices rose, and sugar production peaked at 110,000 metric tons in 1940. But high population growth rates and extreme inequalities of wealth meant that when the slump came, as it did during World War II, the effects were severe. Sugar production virtually ceased, unemployment was extremely high, and famine threatened. During the prosperous years not only had investments in infrastructure ceased, but even basic

maintenance had been ignored. Poverty, malnutrition and disease were rife among the majority of the population, while the rich elite lived in comfort. The island was crying out for political and economic reform. It was considered that this could only be achieved by full integration with France as a department.

IAIN WALKER

See also: **Bourbon, Ile de France, Seychelles: Eighteenth century; Slavery, Plantation: East Africa and the Islands.**

Further Reading

Aldrich, R. and John Connell, *France's Overseas Frontier: Départements et Territoires d'Outre-Mer*, Cambridge: Cambridge University Press, 1992.

Beaton, Patrick. *Six Months in Reunion: A Clergyman's Holiday and How He Passed It.* London: Hurst and Blackett, 1860.

Harrison-Church, R. J. *The African Islands of the Indian Ocean: The Comoro Islands, Madagascar, Réunion, Mauritius And Seychelles.* London: Longmans, 1964.

Houbert, Jean, "Réunion Island: French Decolonisation in the Indian Ocean," *Journal of Commonwealth and Comparative Politics* 18, no. 2 (1980): 145–171.

Lavaux, C.. *La Réunion.* Paris: Éditions Cormorans, 1986.

Leguen, Marcel. *Histoire de l'ile de la Réunion.* Paris: L'Harmattan, 1979.

Mouat, F. J. *Rough Notes of a Trip to Reunion, Mauritius and Ceylon.* New Delhi: Asian Educational Services, 1984.

Scherer, A., *La Réunion.* Paris: Presses Universitaires de France, 1998.

Vergés, Françoise. *Monsters and Revolutionaries: Colonial Family Romance and Metissage*, Durham, N.C.: Duke University Press, 1999.

Réunion: 1946 to the Present

After World War II, Réunion was transformed into a French *departement* (ministry) in a law passed on March 15, 1946. This course of action appeared to be the best way to modernize the island's economic and social system, which at the time was still based on the old colonial structure. The economy was primarily dependent on the production and exportation of cane sugar, and society was sharply stratified into a few wealthy families (*les Grands Blancs*) and the rest of the population (*Ti Moun*), whose living and educational standards were low and who depended on the former for their subsistence

The local population favored full integration into the French Republic. This integration meant that main decisions concerning the island were to be made in France, according to the centralized nature of the French state. It also meant that French law, institutions, administration, public services, and public expenditures were to be transferred to the island in order to improve the local situation and bring about the social assimilation of the population.

As a result, public investments were made to renovate infrastructures, increase agricultural production, and diversify the economy. New roads were built, and extensive irrigation and electricity programs were set up. Productivity increased, allowing for more cane sugar exportation, and attempts were made to develop other products for local consumption, and thus reduce the dependence of the island on imported food.

However, this attempt, much like efforts at promoting industrial development, has remained limited. The island has generally continued to export agricultural products and import manufactured goods, which accounts for one of its major economic problems—namely, the deficit in its balance of trade. In fact, its economic growth for the last 20 years has mainly come from the development of tourism. The majority of the population works in the service industry, as opposed to agriculture or manufacturing.

The transfer of French public services to Réunion also resulted in the creation of a new social class, with living standards similar to those of France. At the same time, French social legislation was introduced to the island. Education and health services greatly improved. In 1954, 43 per cent of the population was literate; by 1999, that number had increased to 79 per cent. Similarly, infant mortality has greatly decreased from an estimated 149 deaths per 1000 live births in 1946 to 6.9 per 1000 in 1991.

However, despite the overall increase in the gross domestic product, social problems have remained acute, due partly to the high birthrate of the population (from 1946 to 1999 the population increased from 22,7000 to 717,723) and to a huge disparity in revenues. Réunion does not have enough qualified people to implement its economic and social development programs, and this has been the case since the 1950s. Approximately 20,000 French citizens have moved to the island to work. They have traditionally held the key posts in the private and public sectors, which accounts for lingering resentment and tension between them and the local population.

Indeed, unemployment has remained a major problem, especially for the young generation. More than 60 per cent of that population still depend for their living on social benefits. Moreover, the fact that most decisions concerning the island have for a long time been made in Paris, by individuals unfamiliar with local customs and circumstances, has made the implementation of many measures take longer than expected, and has increased resentment among the native inhabitants of Réunion.

Regionalist movements have emerged, calling for more consideration of, and respect for, the local culture. From 1958, the Communist Party, which previously approved transforming the island into a French departement changed its position. As the main opposition party, it asked for more political autonomy, considering that reform as the only way to achieve the quick development of the island. For a long time, its program of action remained unclear; the party did not offer any specific proposals until March 1981. During an extraordinary government session on March 29, 1981, the Communist Party stated that the current status of the island as a departement essentially denied the very existence of a Creole people with its own distinct personality, culture, language, customs and history. It proposed the creation of an island-based legislative assembly composed of locally elected officials that would be entrusted with significant governmental power and its own executive council.

In 1982, the Communist Party supported the French law on decentralization, which transformed Réunion into a *collectivité territoriale*—that is, a territory with its own financial resources and some political autonomy. This led to the creation of a regional council composed of 45 members, each elected for a five-year term. A law passed on August 2, 1984, outlined the role and duties of this body. It is entrusted with specific tasks and powers, especially the promotion of social, economic, intellectual and scientific development, education and local culture. It is assisted by a social and economic council and a committee for education, culture, and environment. The regional council can make proposals for modifying or adapting laws passed in France. It has independent financial resources, but also receives financial transfers from the French state.

VÉRONIQUE DIMIER

Further Reading

Leloutre, J. C. *La Réunion, Département Français*. Paris: F. Maspéro, 1968.
Sherer, A. *La Réunion*. Paris: PUF, 1998.

Rhodes, Cecil J. (1853–1902)
Founder, De Beers Mining Company

As a young man, Cecil John Rhodes, who would later become a mining capitalist, colonial politician, and imperial ideologue, was imbued with the racial pride and imperial enthusiasm of his times. He believed that the English were "the finest race in the world" and advocated the formation of a secret society to bring about British world domination. These ideas governed Rhodes's ambitions for the rest of his life, and between 1878 and 1888 he accumulated the wealth and power with which he hoped to realize them.

Building on already substantial holdings in Kimberley, Rhodes and his partner, Charles Rudd, formed the De Beers Mining Company, and opened that which would become the most highly capitalized mine in Kimberley and would enable Rhodes to monopolize diamond-mining in 1887 and 1888. At De Beers, Rhodes pioneered the migrant labor system and established "closed compounds" in which black workers were rigorously searched before and after being incarcerated for the duration of their contracts. These labor controls provided the model for twentieth-century southern Africa. Such draconian controls were made possible by imperial conquests in southern Africa, and Rhodes's election as a member of the Cape's parliament, after it incorporated Griqualand West in 1880.

Rhodes's earliest political involvement concerned the affairs of Basutoland and Bechuanaland; diamond interests undoubtedly shaped his regional perspective. Between them, Basutoland and Bechuanaland provided labor, food, and wood for Kimberley, while in Bechuanaland Afrikaner mercenaries threatened the route to the north. Imperial indecisiveness over these territories convinced Rhodes, by this time one of the wealthiest men in South Africa, of the need for a local power base. Aware of the growing political importance of the newly formed Afrikaner Bond, he championed a Cape subimperialism in partnership with Afrikaners.

The discovery of gold on the Witwatersrand in the South African Republic (SAR) in 1886 opened a new phase in the history of the subcontinent. Initially Rhodes underestimated its importance, and the inadequacy of his Rand holdings spurred him to look further north, where he hoped to find a "second Rand." Fearing Transvaal expansion across the Limpopo, he persuaded the British High Commissioner at the Cape to secure a treaty with the Ndebele king, Lobengula, ensuring imperial sovereignty over his kingdom. Shortly thereafter, on 30 October 1888, Rhodes's own agents, secured a concession granting them exclusive rights to exploit minerals in Lobengula's realm, in which they included Mashonaland. This greatly strengthened Rhodes against his rivals, and in October 1889 his newly formed British South Africa Company (BSAC) obtained a royal charter to "develop" a vast area of southern and central Africa. In 1890 his "pioneer column" occupied Mashonaland.

In 1888 and 1889, Rhodes's agents staked out the whole of present-day Malawi and Zambia for crown and company, securing mineral and land concessions for the BSAC. These treaties greatly increased Britain's bargaining position in the European scramble for Africa, and helped establish the modern frontiers of Angola, Malawi, Mozambique, Namibia, Tanzania, Zambia, and Zimbabwe.

It was, however, events in South Africa and Rhodesia that absorbed most of Rhodes's energies and finances. In Mashonaland, settlers soon realized the absence of gold, and in 1893 deliberately provoked war against the Ndebele. This was followed by a boom in BSAC shares and huge mining speculation, but by the end of 1894 it was evident that there was no "second Rand" north of the Limpopo, and Rhodes's policies toward the SAR hardened.

Until the mid-1890s, Rhodes's expansionist schemes were supported enthusiastically within the Cape Colony, where he became premier in 1890 and 1894. In 1894 he annexed Pondoland, the last independent African territory between the Cape and Natal, and in 1895 introduced the wide-ranging Glen Grey Act, an astute way of satisfying his disparate constituencies, introducing individual landholding for Africans and forcing out labor. Rhodes's railway between the Cape and the Transvaal was also popular with Cape Afrikaners, who hoped to sell their agricultural products on the Rand. When the SAR responded by raising tariffs on colonial produce and blocking the Vaal crossings, war between the two states was only narrowly averted. Despite this, Rhodes continued to enjoy the support of the Afrikaner Bond and was a leading exponent of a white South African nationalism within the British Empire.

Like many magnates with deep-level mining interests on the Rand, from the mid-1890s Rhodes found the SAR's policies increasingly costly. With the secret backing of Joseph Chamberlain, the British colonial secretary, he plotted its downfall. At the end of 1895 his lieutenant, Leander Starr Jameson, entered the Transvaal with a small band of armed followers, hoping to precipitate an armed insurrection. There was, however, no uprising, and the raiders were quickly arrested, tried, and sentenced to death, though they were released when Rhodes paid their fines. Rhodes was forced to resign from the premiership of the Cape, his Anglo-Afrikaner alliance destroyed. South African politics became increasingly polarized on ethnic lines. Rhodes was also forced to resign as managing director of the BSAC, as a parliamentary enquiry into the raid was enacted.

In Southern Rhodesia, the absence of the BSAC Police who joined Jameson facilitated an uprising by the Ndebele in March 1896. Three months later the Shona also rose. For a time the small white colony seemed doomed, and after the battle of Taba zi ka Mambo on July 5, Rhodes sought peace. In mid-October the Ndebele accepted his terms although the Shona uprising continued until 1898. By this time Rhodes had rejoined the board of the BSAC and regained political influence at the Cape, where he became president and patron of the Loyal Colonial League, founded in 1896 to promote British supremacy in South Africa. Together with the Cape newspapers, which he largely controlled, the league fomented war against the SAR.

Rhodes also led and funded a new grouping of Cape Progressives in the 1898 parliamentary elections, during which he announced that he favored "equal rights for all white men." He later reformulated this as "equal rights for all civilized men south of the Zambezi," in the hope of gaining African electoral support. To the same end he also funded the African newspaper, *Izwi la Bantu.*

Had he lived longer, Rhodes may well have recaptured his former position. He had a weak heart and was increasingly aware of his own mortality; his last years seem filled with almost frenzied activity, including four months under siege in Kimberley during the South African War. He also found time to write his eighth will, in which he established scholarships to Oxford University for young men (women were explicitly excluded) from the colonies and the United States, which he still hoped would be restored to the British Empire. In addition Rhodes left money for proimperial projects; it was used in the twentieth century to fund a variety of imperial causes.

In his lifetime, Rhodes acquired vast wealth and power, often by unscrupulous means, and justified it in terms of his imperial vision. Although he was revered by his supporters and his use of power was often tempered by his ability to empathize with and bestow patronage on those he dominated, in southern Africa his ventures accelerated the pace of capitalist and colonial expansion, and were accompanied by conquest and exploitation, sharp business practice and civil corruption, with long-term consequences for the subcontinent.

SHULA MARKS

See also: **Botswana: Bechuanaland Protectorate, Founding of, 1885–1899; Jameson Raid, Origins of South African War: 1895–1899; Kimberley and Diamond Fields; Kruger, Paul; Lewanika I, the Lozi, and the BSA Company; Rhodes, Jameson, and the Seizure of Rhodesia; South Africa: Gold on the Witwatersrand; 1886–1899; South African War, 1899–1902; Zambia (Northern Rhodesia): British Occupation, Resistance: 1890s.**

Biography

Born Cecil John Rhodes at Bishop Stortford in Hertfordshire, the son of an Anglican clergyman, in 1853. Joined his brother in South Africa at the age of seventeen, rapidly making his mark on the newly discovered diamond fields of Kimberley in Griqualand West. With funds accumulated in Kimberley, returned in 1873 to study at Oxford University, finally graduating in 1881, having spent the intervening years building up his fortune in Kimberley. With his partner, Charles Rudd, formed the De Beers Mining Company. Died on March 26, 1902 in Muizenberg, outside Cape Town. According to his request, was buried in the Matopos in Rhodesia on April 10.

Further Reading

Flint, John. *Cecil Rhodes.* London: Hutchinson, 1976.

Rotberg, Robert I., with Miles F. Shore. *The Founder: Cecil Rhodes and the Pursuit of Power.* New York: Oxford University Press, 1988.

Tamarkin, Mordechai. *Cecil Rhodes and the Cape Afrikaners: The Imperial Colossus and the Colonial Parish Pump.* London: Frank Cass, 1996.

Thomas, Antony. *Rhodes: The Race for Africa.* London: BBC Books, 1996.

Turrell, Robert V. *Capital and Labour on the Kimberley Diamond Fields.* Cambridge: Cambridge University Press, 1987.

Vindex [pseud. of John Verscholyle]. *Cecil Rhodes: His Political Life and Speeches, 1881–1900.* London: Chapman and Hall, 1900.

Rhodes, Jameson, and the Seizure of Rhodesia

The white seizure of Rhodesia (Zimbabwe) occurred swiftly between 1889 and 1893, but the pressures which led to this rapid sequence of events had been building up for some time. Disillusioned by their violent conflicts with the Boers, the Ndebele under King Mzilikazi had moved into the Matopos region in southwestern Zimbabwe in 1837. There they established a fluid state system in which some Shona peoples were incorporated some moved into a peaceable relationship of trade and tribute, and others, generally more distant from the heartland of the state, were periodically raided. Europeans were to treat this system as a quasi European-style state from which concessions and treaties, supposedly relating to the entire region of the modern Zimbabwe, could be secured. Alternatively, when it suited them, they saw the Shona peoples as "underdogs" in need of protection from the Ndebele. European interest was stimulated by the fabulous stories of rich gold-bearing regions that emanated from Central Africa. The German prospector Carl Mauch, who traveled in Zimbabwe between 1864 and 1870, brought out tales both of the Zimbabwe ruins and of gold-bearing reefs. Both Mzilikazi and his son and successor Lobengula (who ruled after a succession crisis in 1868–1870) had attempted to control, often with some success, the activities of white hunters, ivory traders, and prospectors, eager to make their fortunes in Central Africa. They were invariably sent off into Shona country. There had also been desultory efforts to secure mining rights from Lobengula as early as 1880.

International competition was relatively slow to develop, but by the 1880s it was clear that the Portuguese were attempting to establish their supposedly historic claims to a great band of south-central Africa, stretching from the Angolan Atlantic coast to that of Mozambique on the Indian Ocean. By that time, the extraordinary land hunger of the Boers was beginning to lead some of those in the Transvaal to cast covetous eyes across the Limpopo. Moreover, the Germans had unexpectedly arrived on the coasts of Tanganyika (Tanzania) and southwest Africa (Namibia) in 1884 and appeared to have further ambitions in the interior. Although Cecil Rhodes had exhibited little interest in the interior until the mid-1880s, he was then moved to act by a combination of these international rivalries, his megalomaniac vision of British rule stretching from the Cape to Cairo, and his belief that an outflanking movement against the Boers would ultimately help in the refederation of the entire southern African region. He may also have been influenced by dreams of riches that might help to redress his comparative failure to secure the best claims on the newly discovered Rand goldfields. The British acquisition of Bechuanaland (Botswana) in 1885, designed partly to deter the Boers from making contact with the Germans, gave Rhodes his opportunity. He called it his "Suez Canal to the interior," and he was soon sending representatives to Lobengula's capital in Bulawayo.

The rapid escalation of these tensions was all too apparent at Lobengula's court between 1887 and 1889. Various British figures, including John Smith Moffat (the son of the missionary Robert Moffat, who had been a friend of Mzilikazi), argued that a protectorate should be declared over Lobengula's territory. Other Britons, convinced that the Rand gold fields offered confirmation of vast riches in the interior, sought mining concessions. In 1888, a Boer representative called Pieter Grobler succeeded in persuading the king to sign a treaty that would have given the Transvaal a privileged relationship with the Ndebele. In the same year, Rhodes's three agents, Charles Rudd, Rochfort Maguire, and Francis Thompson, negotiated a concession from Lobengula that offered highly restricted prospecting rights in exchange for arms, ammunition, an annual subsidy, and a steamer for the Zambezi. The king later made several efforts to repudiate this concession. He soon recognized its dangers, attempted to exploit the divisions among the various concession-seekers, and sent two of his indunas as emissaries to London. However, Rhodes was able to neutralize all of Lobengula's efforts: he bought his rivals out and was so successful in manipulating politicians in London that he secured a royal charter, establishing his British South Africa Company, in October 1889. The geographical region covered by the charter was necessarily vague and it ultimately helped him to acquire the territories of both Southern and Northern Rhodesia (now Zimbabwe and Zambia).

Rhodes dispatched Leander Starr Jameson, an Edinburgh-trained doctor who had practiced in Kimberley, to persuade Lobengula not only to accept the charter, but also acquiesce regarding the arrival of white settlers in Mashonaland. Jameson used his medical skills to establish influence over the king by relieving some of the symptoms of his gout. Rhodes organized a "pioneer column" comprising fewer than 200 men, well armed with machine guns and equipped with a searchlight and a generator, to invade Mashonaland, supposedly under the terms of the concession. Each of its participants was heavily bribed with offers of fifteen mining claims and a farm. It set out in June 1890 and succeeded in peaceably skirting Matabeleland, largely because of the restraint of Lobengula. By September, the column had established a settlement at Fort Salisbury (now Harare) and its members spread out in search of their fortunes. Others of Rhodes's followers indulged in a sequence of aggressive acts against the Portuguese and African peoples that, in effect, established the modern northern and eastern boundaries of Zimbabwe.

The first administrator of the territory was a civil servant from India, Archibald Colquhoun, but he quickly fell out with Rhodes's representative Jameson, who duly replaced him in 1891. Jameson was profligate in his land grants and was largely incompetent as an administrator. The settlement soon suffered from excessive rains, dramatically high prices, failures to find the expected gold reefs, and many other problems. Moreover, the settlement's uneasy peace with the Ndebele could not last.

In July 1893, a Matabele *impi* (regiment) raided Shona people in the vicinity of the European border township of Fort Victoria. They pursued the Shona into the township and allegedly also attacked the servants of the whites. Jameson ordered the Ndebele out and threatened war. Rhodes (now premier of the Cape) concurred, particularly as the chartered company was passing through a period of severe financial difficulty and there was talk of further goldfields in Matabeleland. Jameson tempted the white settlers with more gold claims, farms, and the promise of extensive booty, particularly in the form of cattle, from the Ndebele. Jameson's men made effective use of the new maxim gun, and Lobengula's armies were soon defeated. There were few losses on the European side, except for Major Wilson's Shangani patrol, which was cut off and killed, thus becoming the major heroic icon of Rhodesian whites. The king himself died in flight, probably of smallpox, in 1894 and the whites added Matabeleland to their conquests. The territorial area of southern Rhodesia was now complete, acquired through a combination of duplicity, violence, and greed, together with the acquiescence of an imperial government that was anxious to keep others out.

JOHN M. MACKENZIE

See also: **Jameson Raid, Origins of South African War, 1895–1899; Rhodes, Cecil J.; Rudd Concession, 1888; Zimbabwe: 1880s; Zimbabwe (Southern Rhodesia): Ndebele and Shona Risings: First Chimurenga.**

Further reading

Galbraith, John S. *Crown and Charter: The Early Years of the British South Africa Company*. Berkeley and Los Angeles: University of California Press, 1974.

Rotberg, Robert I., with Miles F. Shore. *The Founder: Cecil Rhodes and the Pursuit of Power*. New York: Oxford University Press, 1988.

Samkange, Stanlake. *Origins of Rhodesia*. London: Heinemann, 1968.

Glass, Stafford, *The Matabele War*. London: Longman, 1968.

Phimister, Ian. *An Economic and Social History of Zimbabwe, 1890–1948*. London: Longman, 1988.

Rhodesia: *See* Zimbabwe (Rhodesia): Unilateral Declaration of Independence and the Smith Regime, 1964–1979; Zimbabwe: Second Chimurenga, 1966–1979.

Rinderpest and Smallpox: East and Southern Africa

Rinderpest probably entered Africa early in 1888, in cattle shipped from India to supply the Italian army in Eritrea. Once established, the disease moved southward through east and central Africa at an average speed of about 20 miles a day. Early in 1891 it was destroying herds in western Uganda and in the Maasai areas of Kenya and northern Tanzania; 18 months later it had reached northern Zambia. The Zambezi River formed a barrier that it did not cross for three years, but rinderpest eventually broke into Zimbabwe and Botswana in 1896, reaching Cape Town by the end of 1897. It was Africa's most spectacular, though not its worst, plague of modern times. Together with smallpox, drought, and civil strife it temporarily destroyed local economies and ripped the social fabric from Ethiopia to South Africa. The names given to it evoke the horror of watching prosperity and security disappear almost overnight. Maasai remember the time as *emutai* (wipe out); and with grim appropriateness the disease was called *masilangane* (let us all be equal) in the Cape.

Rinderpest is a viral disease of cattle and wild ungulates, like buffalo. It is transmitted only through immediate contact with infected matter. Animals that survive acquire permanent immunity. In its first appearance, rinderpest was extraordinarily virulent and sudden. Mortality varied, but in many areas it seems that nine out of ten infected cattle died. Fortunately, the pandemic soon burned itself out. Communities restocked with fresh animals from elsewhere, and by the early 1900s in Maasailand, for example, large herds were again in evidence. The method of direct-contact transmission also meant that some areas, where herds were widely dispersed or isolated from infection, would escape. The Nandi and Turkana herds in Kenya were unaffected, and the Lozi of western Zambia and the Nuer of the southern Sudan appear to have suffered lighter losses than their neighbors. Rinderpest returned periodically, either to new areas or to sweep up a new crop of susceptible animals in old areas.

For all its fury, however, rinderpest was neither Africa's worst threat to cattle nor its greatest veterinary challenge. That distinction belonged to endemic vector-borne diseases like East Coast Fever and trypanosomiasis, whose eradication required a greater degree of continuous expenditure and of ecological and political control than most states could muster; and to bovine pleuro-pneumonia, another directly transmitted disease with a long incubation period that made it much more difficult to detect in the dormant state. Pleuro-pneumonia had also entered Africa from outside several decades before rinderpest and had cut a swathe through the herds of southern and eastern Africa, moving from south to north. Rinderpest, however, could be controlled fairly simply once cheap and effective immunization techniques were developed. The first attempts were risky and crude, a matter of simultaneously injecting both the disease and its antidote. High losses created widespread opposition, but after 1930 safely attenuated vaccines were becoming available. They conferred reliable immunity and could be used repeatedly in mass inoculation campaigns. Rinderpest remained endemic and locally dangerous, but its worst days were over by 1950.

The impact of the rinderpest pandemic of the 1890s must be seen within a wider context. Disasters were common in African history, often caused by prolonged drought. The patient colonization of Africa by Africans has been an epic of human achievement and tenacity, largely unknown. To survive and prosper required careful planning, the accumulation of stores of inherited information and the establishment of complex mechanisms of exchange and reciprocity within and between small communities. The pandemic came as one more challenge, and it tested existing survival mechanisms to the limit. But rinderpest also came at a particular point in time. For almost everywhere in eastern and southern Africa, the 1880s and 1890s were decades of transition and uncertainty. While communities were able to draw on long experience of survival, they were also assimilating the differentiating effects of the mid-nineteenth-century expansion of long distance trade and, in the some regions, the ravages of increasingly destructive slaving and the dissolution of familiar forms of authority. Moreover, as rinderpest moved south in space, it crossed a line in time that separated those regions that had not yet faced colonial conquest from those that were either in the process of conquest or had already been shaped into colonial states. Response to rinderpest was thus partly shaped by the constraints and opportunities of different worlds. In Ethiopia, the famines of the late 1880s coincided with, and perhaps supported, the beginning of the rapid accumulation of state power in Shoa under King Menelik. In central Kenya, a land of small "stateless" communities, the need to rebuild the herds led many to take up arms as "auxiliaries" for colonial invaders rather than against them; but in Bunyoro in Uganda, rinderpest immediately preceded the beginnings of a prolonged resistance to colonial conquest that left the kingdom a wilderness for a generation. Much farther south, rinderpest destroyed what was left of the Ndebele herds, which had already been pillaged by Cecil Rhodes's "pioneer columns" of settlers and looters from South Africa, and perhaps played a role in the Chimurenga risings of 1897. South of the Limpopo River, rinderpest entered a world already partly reshaped by colonialism. Here state structures were already in place, though they proved equally ineffective at halting the disease or ameliorating its effects. In the north, one response to the loss of livestock was to raid for more; in South Africa the same impulse was interpreted, and was punished as stock theft. Survival in the south might be measured in the cash price of food rather than in the strength of social networks, and one option was to sell labor on an existing market, something that hardly existed in eastern Africa.

It was not so much rinderpest itself that wreaked havoc but its effect on the human and natural environment and the way in which it combined with other troubles (drought, smallpox, and colonial invasion) to disrupt and destabilize. The abrupt removal of one part of the ecosystem (cattle and some wildlife) and the disturbance of another (the human communities dependent on them) profoundly affected the functioning of the whole. In pastoral and semipastoral areas especially, settlement contracted, the bush encroached on cultivation, and pasture and grassland left ungrazed grew rank. Community management systems—in northeastern Tanzania and eastern Zambia, for example, which had previously organized production and kept disease and hunger at bay—broke down. In the long term, and in combination with other factors, this loss of control facilitated the spread of the tsetse fly and ticks, the vectors of trypanosomiasis and East Coast Fever.

Communities, families, and individuals coped as best they could. Pastoralists were the hardest hit— without cattle they might starve and their social systems would collapse—but almost everyone was linked to or dependent on livestock in some way, from plough cultivators in highland Ethiopia to transport riders in South Africa. Those who could fled to find food or fought others for what cattle remained. Reciprocities and obligations were discarded with the carcasses of the animals that sustained them. Cattle debts had to be written off or were collected by force. Families split up, and children and women were pawned.

Famine refugees spread smallpox, the second scourge. Smallpox was endemic in more densely settled areas, where it was kept in circulation by contact but also conferred immunity on those who recovered. Scattered populations, however, were highly susceptible. When population densities were sharply altered by an influx of susceptible refugees, as in Kenya Kikuyuland, or by the congregation of the poverty-stricken around what resources survived, as among the Herero in Namibia, smallpox became epidemic and overwhelmed the crude methods of vaccination (variolation) that had previously kept the disease in check in endemic areas. Smallpox finished what drought and rinderpest had begun. While the rinderpest destroyed the herds, smallpox then wiped out the herders and protectors. It was an invitation to further turmoil as the stronger preyed on the defenseless. Yet, in public disaster there is always private profit. Effective leaders in East Africa found new followers and strengthened their positions in what was soon to be a colonial world. In southern Africa, famine refugees made cheap and docile laborers on colonial farms and government projects.

The demographic and moral effects of the pandemics lasted long and struck deep. Explanations for disaster brought fears and suspicions to the surface, sharpening racial antagonisms in southern Africa and questioning the benevolence of power in the north. Apocalyptic visions seemed to have stayed south of the Zambesi, but in many areas missionaries made converts, more perhaps because they offered food and shelter than for their religious consolation.

The rinderpest pandemic was in some respects a forerunner of the droughts and famines of modern Africa. It was the first to be extensively reported by foreign observers. It shook belief in the predictability of the environment. It enriched some and ruined many. But Africans survived, and by their own efforts.

RICHARD WALLER

See also: **Drought, Famine, Displacement; Ethiopia: Famine, Revolution, Mengistu Dictatorship, 1974–1991.**

Further Reading

Dawson, Marc. "Smallpox in Kenya, 1880–1920." *Social Science and Medicine* 13B, no. 4 (1979): 245–250.

Giblin, James. *The Politics of Environmental Control in Northeastern Tanzania, 1840–1940.* Philadelphia: University of Pennsylvania Press, 1992.

McGraw, Roderick. *Encyclopedia of Medical History.* New York: McGraw-Hill, 1985.

Mugera, G. M., et al. *Diseases of Cattle in Tropical Africa.* Nairobi: Kenya Literature Bureau, 1979.

Pankhurst, Richard, and Douglas Johnson. "The Great Drought and Famine of 1888–1892 in Northeast Africa." In *The Ecology of Survival*, edited by Douglas Johnson and David Anderson. Boulder, Colo.: Westview Press, 1988.

Ranger, Terence. "Plagues of Beasts and Men: Prophetic Responses to Epidemic in Eastern and Southern Africa." In *Epidemics and Ideas*, edited by Terence Ranger and Paul Slack. Cambridge: Cambridge University Press, 1992.

Vail, Leroy. "Ecology and History: The Example of Eastern Zambia." *Journal of Southern African Studies* 3, no. 2 (1977): 129–155.

Van Onselen, Charles. "Reactions to Rinderpest in Southern Africa 1896–97." *Journal of African History* 13, no. 3 (1972): 473–488.

Waller, Richard. "'Emutai' Crisis and Response in Maasailand 1883–1902." In *The Ecology of Survival*, edited by Douglas Johnson and David Anderson. Boulder: Westview Press, 1988.

Waller, Richard, and Kathy Homewood. "Contesting Veterinary Knowledge in a Pastoral Community." In *Western Medicine as Contested Knowledge*, edited by Andrew Cunningham and Bridie Andrews. Manchester: Manchester University Press, 1997.

Rock Art, Saharan

In the Sahara, the Palaeolithic era (prior to 10,000BCE) ended with a long and arid climatic episode, the Postaterian Hyperarid Phase, during which all fauna and human life disappeared. However, toward 10,000BCE, rain returned and groups of nomadic hunter-gatherers reoccupied the desert. They practiced specialized hunting and collected local wild cereals, which led them to adopt a sedentary lifestyle. Around 5000BCE they embraced animal domestication. The economic and social disruptions provoked by this change found expression in the phenomenon of rock art in the Saharan region. Rock art also served to mark the territory of sedentary or semisedentary ethnic groups.

The development of Saharan rock art coincided with the start of an important wet fluctuation, the so-called Neolithic Wet Phase, which lasted from *c.*5000 to 3000BCE. Plains turned into semiarid steppes, making extensive pastoral exploitation with mobile herds possible. Saharan rock pictures are only found on well-sheltered overhangs, not in caves. The birth of this art was sudden. Since its earliest origins, some schools practiced a perfectly naturalistic style, executed through accomplished technical means. This absence of a "primitive" or "precocious" phase is usual in terms of art history and development. Perhaps this phase did indeed take place, but it is lost to contemporary scholars and archaeologists, as it was practiced on fragile or perishable materials such as wood, hide, or sand, which have disappeared.

Two main periods of Saharan rock art can be distinguished, delineated by a long arid episode between them. The ancient period corresponds to the Neolithic Wet Phase. This is the time of the finest engravings,

attributable to a school covering Rio de Oro, southern Morocco, the Saharan Atlas, Fezzan, and northern Tassili (generally speaking, a chiefly northern area) that is named Naturalistic Bubaline—*Naturalistic* on account of its realistic style, the aim of which was to faithfully reproduce the subject, and *Bubaline* because it abundantly pictures an extinct species, the giant buffalo (*Bubalus antiquus*). It mainly represents wild animals, but domestic cattle are artistically rendered as well. For the most part, the animal figures are accurately drawn, with a deep polished outline and sometimes a few internal details.

The ancient period also includes paintings that are mainly found in Tassili. These paintings fall under the rubric of the Early Bovidian school, which is primarily composed of works marked by depictions of livestock, and battle scenes involving bowmen. The figures in this school suggest a "negroid" type. Outside this category and region, Saharan rock art generally represents only Europoid types.

Another remarkable school of paintings of the ancient period is also confined to Tassili and its surroundings: the Round Heads school. It mainly represents figures, but in a schematic, original, expressionist style. They are involved in mysterious compositions that appear to religious, mythical, or symbolic connotations, including humans with animal heads, horned goddess figures, and figures floating in the air.

The Neolithic Wet Phase was interrupted throughout the Sahara by the Postneolithic Arid Phase, which lasted from *c.*3000 to 1500BCE. Populations took refuge in oases, or migrated into the fringes of the desert, the Maghrib or the Sahel. However, a last, minor wet fluctuation around 1500–1000BCE marked the beginning of the most recent period of Saharan rock art. It allowed a last extensive occupation of the massifs. New populations, from the Berber group, were then arriving in the central Sahara. One of them, the Iheren-Tahilahi group (the name refers to two important Tassilian sites) settled in the central and northern Tassili. This school of paintings (it belongs to the Final Bovidian in the art sequence) produced numerous paintings, finely drawn in a sophisticated, naturalistic style. It chiefly represents pastoral scenes, campsite scenes and lion hunting. The bow was then gradually being replaced by the throwing spear, as represented in the rock art.

This most recent period also includes engravings. They are mainly those of the Tazina school, chiefly spread throughout the same northern area as the ancient school of the Naturalistic Bubaline. Like the latter, the Tazina school almost exclusively carved animals, with a polished and well-finished outline, but the drawing had now turned schematic, accompanied by artistic stylizations.

To the south, in Air (Niger) and Adrar of Iforas (Mali), regions where no artistic school had yet emerged, this recent period saw the rise of the wall engravings of what has been termed the Libyan Warrior school. The engravings mainly represent armed warriors, crudely engraved in pecked lines, heavily decorated, shown in symmetrical front view and in a schematic style. A warrior often holds a horse by a leading rein, with the horse generally minimized. Riders are represented as well.

By this point, ideologies and lifestyles have changed, as reflected in the rock art. Pastoral scenes are lacking, women are generally not represented, and the most represented are dignitaries or warriors, who appear much magnified. This next period, already in the protohistoric age (prior to the keeping of written records in an area, but after that area has been mentioned in writings from other regions), is called the Horse Period. It is marked notably in the central Sahara, throughout Tassili and Ahaggar, by the Caballine school of painting. This school abundantly represents figures of a schematic aspect, often including "bitriangular" types (broad shoulders shown in front view, thin waist, ample skirt) with only a vertical line for the head. These Caballine figures often drive two- (sometimes three- or four-) horse chariots. These chariots are similar to the many ancient chariots used at this time throughout the Mediterranean region, and therefore allow dating of the Caballine school to later than 700BCE.

After the Horse Period, aridity intensified, leading to the so-called Actual Arid Phase. Saharan populations fragmented, again taking refuge in oases. A new domestic animal, which would prove very important to the Saharan economy, was introduced around the third or second century BCE: the camel. In rock art, the Camel Period is characterized by compositions in a technically impoverished style, as subjects grew more succinct, representing isolated figures or animals, signs, and writings. Indeed, an alphabetic writing system was used for inscriptions (called *libyco-berbers* or *tifinagh*). It was introduced approximately at the same time as the camel. This alphabet was only used in the Sahara for writing short messages, exclusively carved on the rocks, mainly by lovers. It is still currently used by the Tuaregs in Ahaggar and Air. The most recent paintings and engravings of the Camel Period have been made in modern time, and reflect modern innovations and developments, such as airplanes and guns.

ALFRED MUZZOLINI

See also: **Art and Architecture, History of African; Garamantes: Early Trans-Saharan Trade; Herding, Farming, Origins of: Sahara and Nile Valley; Stone Age (Later): Sahara and North Africa.**

Further Reading

Jelinek, J. "Tilizahren, the Key Site of Fezzanese Rock Art, Part I: Tilizahren West Galleries." *Anthropologie*, 23, no. 2 (1985): 125–165.

———. "Tilizahren, the Key Site of Fezzanese Rock Art, Part II: Tilizahren East, Analyses, Discussion, Conclusions" *Anthropologie* 23, no. 3 (1985): 223–275.

Mori, F. *The Great Civilisations of the Ancient Sahara*. Rome: L'Erma di Bretschneider, 1998.

Rock Art: Eastern Africa

The largest concentration of prehistoric rock art (both painted and engraved) in eastern Africa is found in and around the Ethiopian/Eritrean plateau; fewer rock art sites have been recorded to the south in Kenya and Tanzania, or to the west in Uganda and southern Sudan (Willcox 1984, pp.55–71). There is little academic consensus as to the dating and meanings of these paintings; direct scientific dating of pigment is still an experimental technique, and while some scholars suggest that these images embody a graphic language (Hassan 1993), other scholars see these images as codifying economic information, or even representing depictions of shamanistic-style trance states (Lewis-Williams and Dowson, 1988). Within the rock art corpus of eastern Africa there is a single image that keeps recurring, that of the cow, so it is probable that cattle were of more than a *secular* importance to the people who made these images.

Within the corpus of Ethiopian/Eritrean rock art, it is generally held that naturalistic representations of cattle are earlier than the more stylized, abstract images; occasionally this is borne out by a superimposition of styles. A particularly large concentration of rock art sites exists around the Eritrean capital (Asmara). Two phases of stylistic development are clearly recognized at these sites; on the one hand are naturalistic herding depictions with humans and (humpless) cattle juxtaposed, while the schematic (probably later) cattle images concentrate exclusively on the abstract depiction of a small bovid head with highly elongated horns (Graziosi 1964). The naturalistic images clearly show the socioeconomic relationship between human and beast; a rather "seminaturalistic" depiction at the site of Baahti Facada shows a pair of oxen yoked to a type of plough that can still be seen in these highlands today. The later stylized cattle paintings, however, could be seen as iconic representations; they are not faithfully depicting animals, rather conveying an idealistic conception of their identities.

A similar picture of naturalistic versus schematic depiction can be seen at the southern Ethiopian rock art sites. The earlier naturalistic forms again depict scenes of milking and herding; cattle, fat-tailed sheep, humans, and even dogs are all identifiable. The more stylized southern images are markedly different from those observed in the Eritrean sites; cattle may be rendered by pecking at the rock or by painting in outline. The stylized southern cattle outlines are often filled with paint or shapes—some of these marks have been interpreted as being cattle brands—and are associated with a bewildering variety of geometric shapes and symbols. It has been suggested that the rock art of these highlands shows clear affinities with rock art from Southern Arabia, indicating, perhaps, some form of prehistoric culture contact. Although this may be true to a small extent, it is clear that the distinctive rock art of the Ethiopian/Eritrean highlands belongs firmly in the African milieu.

Around the fringes of the Ethiopian/Eritrean highlands, broadly similar styles of naturalistic paintings may be observed. The site of Karin Heegan in northeastern Somalia has yielded a rich corpus of rock art; naturalistic herding scenes predominate, although there is a clear trend toward abstraction in the image of the cow (Brandt and Carder 1987). In Djibouti, a number of rock art sites have been located and described in detail. The naturalistic paintings here show cattle-herding scenes, camel caravans and hunting scenes (especially giraffe), but it can be problematic using such paintings for economic reconstruction; the artist's choice of subject material may have differed from the day-to-day diet of his contemporaries. It has been suggested that this art formed a socioideological role in these societies; during periods of climatic deterioration this art would have served as a central ideological focus for disparate social groups in the region.

Away from the Horn of Africa, the picture of eastern African rock art is rather more scant. Around Lake Victoria a number of rock art sites have been located and cataloged; at most of these sites abstract symbols and schematic cattle/human figures predominate, and many of these abstract forms bear comparison with the Ethiopian/Eritrean images (Chaplin 1974). Naturalistic (humpless) cattle depictions have been observed on Mount Elgon in northwestern Kenya; a number of petroglyphic representations have been noted at later prehistoric sites around Lake Turkana; and a few schematic painted (humped) cattle paintings have been discovered in southern Sudan. In north-central Tanzania a number of rock art images have been described which seem to bear comparison with southern African paintings; eland predominate (in naturalistic style), and highly schematic humans are also present. The antiquity of the Tanzanian paintings is attested to by the discovery of an ochre "pencil" that was associated with deposits at the site of Kisese 2 dating to around 17,000 years BCE (Masao 1982).

It is virtually impossible to physically date these images, and one is often left with the rather unsatisfactory method of attempting to link the images to associated (datable) archaeological material. Another problem is attempting to try and read meanings into this art; it is possible that on one level these images are purely aesthetic, while on another level they could subtly encode various social rules and ideological statements. It is clear that the most redundant motif in African rock art as a whole is that of the cow; this is no different in eastern Africa. This image is repeated both spatially and temporally over vast distances, and this cannot be a coincidence. It is clear that cattle played more than an economic role in the lives of the artists who painted these pictures.

NIALL FINNERAN

See also: **Art and Architecture, History of African; Cushites: Northeastern Africa: Stone Age Origins to Iron Age; Eastern Africa: Regional Survey; Neolithic, Pastoral: Eastern Africa; Stone Age (Later): Eastern Africa.**

Further Reading

Brandt, S., and N. Carder. "Pastoral Rock Art in the Horn of Africa: Making Sense of Udder Chaos." *World Archaeology*, no. 19 (1987): 194–213.

Chaplin, J. "The Prehistoric Rock Art of the Lake Victoria Region," edited and with additional material by M. A. B. Harlow. *Azania*, no. 9 (1974): 1–50.

Graziosi, P. "New Discoveries of Rock Paintings in Ethiopia." *Antiquity*, no. 38 (1964): 91–98, 187–190.

Hassan, F. "Rock Art: Cognitive Schemata and Symbolic Interpretation: A Matter of Life and Death." *Memoire della Societa Italiana di Scienze e del Museo Civico del Storia Naturale di Milano* 26, no. 2 (1993): 269–282.

Lewis-Williams, D., and T. Dowson. "The Signs of All Times: Entoptic Phenomena in Upper Palaeolithic Art." *Current Anthropology* 29, no. 2 (1988): 201–246.

Masao, F. *The Rock Art of Kondoa and Singida: A Comparative Description.* Occasional Paper no. 5. Dar Es Salaam: National Museums of Tanzania, 1982.

Willcox, A. *The Rock Art of Africa.* London: Croom Helm, 1984.

Rock Art: Southern Africa

Southern Africa has long been noted for the abundance, diversity, and beauty of its rock art. Recent research has opened up new insights into the well known hunter-gatherer (*San*) rock art and, moreover, identified pastoralist and agriculturalist traditions that have hitherto been overlooked. After three decades of intensive historical and ethnographic research, the hunter-gatherer traditions are among the best understood rock arts in the world. Numerous attempts have been made to divide southern Africa into hunter-gatherer rock art regions, but the results tend to reflect research interests

Rock and cave paintings of the San, Drakensberg, South Africa. © Markus Matzel/Das Fotoarchiv.

rather than empirically defined regions. Still, certain observations are valid.

A fundamental distinction exists between rock engravings (petroglyphs) and rock paintings (pictographs). These two techniques of execution are found in broadly defined, but overlapping, regions. By and large, the dominant technique of the central interior of southern Africa was engraving. A number of subtypes are distinguishable: pecked (or hammered), incised (or fine line), and scratched. All three techniques depend upon the removal of the outer patina of rocks so that the lighter interior rock shows through. Engravings are, with a few rare exceptions, found on rocks on low, open hilltops that rise above the plains, or sometimes on glacial pavements in riverbeds; they are not usually found in rock shelters.

Rock paintings occur on the walls and ceilings of rock shelters of the more mountainous periphery of the central plateau. On the plateau itself they occur sporadically in the few small shelters that do exist. The pigments used included various shades of ochre, manganese oxide, charcoal, and white clay. The media with which they were mixed is less certain, but antelope blood was historically recorded.

Generally speaking, the paintings of the Drakensberg (South Africa), the Malutis (Lesotho), and parts of Zimbabwe, such as the Matopos, are more elaborate, polychromatic, and detailed than those of the southern Cape mountains and of the Cederberg, respectively just inland from the southern and western coasts of South Africa. This difference may be partly, but not entirely, explained by the poorer preservation of the art in the southern and western ranges.

The age of this art is difficult to establish. The earliest date that has been reliably ascertained comes from southern Namibia and relates to five flat stones, or plaquettes, about the size of a hand. Radiocarbon dates obtained for charcoal in the same stratum as the painted stones suggests that they are possibly 27,000 years old, which would make them 10,000 years older than the generally accepted date for the French Upper Palaeolithic cave of Lascaux. The most recent southern African rock art was made about 100 years ago in the Drakensberg and its foothills. The images of southern Africa therefore represent one of humankind's longest art traditions.

Most of the subcontinent's rock art was made by hunter-gatherers. The early Dutch settlers named these hunter-gatherers *Bosjesmans*, the word that now takes the English form *Bushmen*. For many of the people themselves and their descendants, *bushmen* has become a distasteful term, though some wish to rehabilitate the word, imbuing it with the meaning "first freedom fighters." To avoid this controversy, many writers now prefer *San*, a word deriving from a pastoral Khoekhoe language. Unfortunately, its meaning is close to that of the term *vagabond*, though this does not seem to be widely known. The nonjudgmental, subsistence term *hunter-gatherer* is perhaps preferable because until comparatively recent times the makers of the art kept no domestic animals and, like other foragers, moved seasonally from place to place according to a carefully planned strategy.

For many decades, researchers who emphasized the "simplicity" and "primitiveness" of the art makers' way of life concluded that the images were "simply" idle art for art's sake. The argument is, however, circular. Researchers inferred an aesthetic imperative from the art and then used it to explain the making of the images. Since the late 1960s and early 1970s researchers have adopted a different approach. They have attempted to explore the significance of the images from the standpoint of authentic, not inferred, San beliefs and rituals.

Contrary to a long held view, many of the beliefs of the people who made the images are not lost. Apart from some valuable reports by early travelers and missionaries, the earliest and largest collection of hunter-gatherer ethnography was compiled in the 1870s in Cape Town by the Bleek family. Working with informants who had been brought to and imprisoned in Cape Town, Wilhelm Bleek and his sister-in-law Lucy Lloyd recorded over 12,000 pages of verbatim beliefs, myths, personal histories, and accounts of rituals in the (now extinct) Xam language. Along side these vernacular texts they prepared line-by-line English translations. Toward the end of Bleek's life (he died in 1875) he was able to show his informants, who by that time had been released from jail to live with him in his suburban home, copies of rock paintings and to note down their explanations.

As twentieth-century work with Kalahari hunter-gatherers confirms, the belief system of the artists centered on a spiritual realm that interpenetrated the material world. Access to this realm was afforded to those who mastered the appropriate ritual techniques. They "activated" a supernatural power, and it carried them into an altered state of consciousness. In this condition they healed the sick, went on extracorporeal journeys, made rain, and controlled the movements of antelope herds.

Imagery relating in diverse ways to these experiences and beliefs accounts for much of the art. In many regions, for instance, the eland was the most frequently depicted creature; it was believed to embody a great deal of power. It also referred to girls' puberty ceremonies, boys' first-kill rituals, and marriage observances. In some instances, images of eland became "reservoirs" of supernatural power on which people could draw in times of need. The ways in which these and other meanings (such as gender statements) are encoded in the art constitute a topic for continuing research.

J. D. LEWIS-WILLIAMS

See also: **Art and Architecture, History of African; Stone Age (Later): Central and Southern Africa.**

Further Reading

Garlake, Peter. *The Hunter's Vision: The Prehistoric Art of Zimbabwe.* London: British Museum Press, 1995.

Lewis-Williams, David. *Believing and Seeing: Symbolic Meanings in Southern San Rock Paintings.* London: Academic Press, 1981.

Lewis-Williams, David, and Thomas A. Dowson. *Images of Power: Understanding Southern African Rock Art.* Johannesburg: Southern, 1999.

Smith, Benjamin W. *Zambia's Ancient Rock Art: The Paintings of Kasama.* Livingstone, Zambia: National Heritage Conservation Commission, 1997.

Vinnicombe, Patricia. *People of the Eland: Rock Paintings of the Drakensberg Bushmen as a Reflection of Their Life and Thought.* Pietermaritzburg: University of Natal Press, 1976.

Wendt, Erich E. "'Art Mobilier' from the Apollo 11 Cave, South West Africa: Africa's Oldest Dated Works of Art." *South African Archaeological Bulletin*, no. 31 (1976): 5–11.

Rock Art: Western and Central Africa

Western and central African rock art is often overlooked in studies on the art and archaeology of the African continent. Although several research projects have been undertaken during the past century, they are widely scattered over this vast region that encompasses several ecological zones, from the savannas of Sub-Saharan West Africa to the tropical rainforest of the Congo River Basin. The known rock art of western and central Africa differs from the art traditions of northern and southern Africa in that narrative art with scenes involving human and animal figures is rare. Instead, the rock art is characterized by highly variable geometric forms, including lines and dots, and to a lesser degree by often strongly abstracted anthropomorphic and zoomorphic motifs. Recognizing this difference, J. Desmond Clark referred to southern central African rock art as the Central African Schematic Art Group. However, this term masks considerable differences in motifs within the rock art of central Africa, and obscures similarities with motifs in other regions of the continent, such as Sub-Saharan West Africa.

Western African rock art is known from the Sahel and savanna belts of Sub-Saharan West Africa, but has only rarely been reported from the forest zone to the south. Rock art in central Africa has been recorded along the periphery of the Congo River Basin. Broad similarities in the rock art of this region can be postulated, such as its focus on geometric forms, particularly rectangular and circular shapes, and stick figures. However, an immense range of motifs is encountered throughout the region, while techniques of manufacture, the locations of motifs at the sites, and the attributes of the sites themselves are also highly variable. Both pictographs (paintings, drawings, stencils, etc.) and petroglyphs (peckings, incisions, abrasions, etc.) are known from western and central Africa.

Pictographs resembling highly abstracted horse riders have been reported from the Gambaga escarpment of northern Ghana, the vicinity of Nambouanga in northern Togo, northeastern Nigeria, Aribinda in northern Burkina Faso, several sites in southern and central Mali, and west-central Angola. Stick figures and rectangular, circular, or triangular geometrics with or without interior subdivisions or exterior appendices occur throughout the region. Groups or lines of dots are known from southern and central Mali, northern Togo, and southeastern Burkina Faso. White and red dots and lines in a rock shelter in Mayombe in the Democratic Republic of Congo seem to have been regularly repainted within living memory. So-called saurian motifs are common in western and west-central Africa, having been recorded at numerous rock art sites in central and southern Mali, Gabon, and Angola. They resemble lizards or crocodiles viewed from above, or humans. To the south of the Congo River Basin a wide range of motifs of varying style and date are encountered, some resembling motifs of traditional sand painting. A number of rock shelters feature postcontact rock art. At the site of Cambambi in west-central Angola, for example, numerous zoomorphs, as well as horse riders and anthropomorphic figures with rifles, apparently in battle, have been recorded.

What is often called "naturalistic" rock art is rare in western and central Africa. The site of Birnin Kudu in northeastern Nigeria is often mentioned for its lively representations of bovids, primarily of domestic humpless cattle. More recently, narrative rock art has been identified in the Massif de Kita, in southwestern

Mali. At the site of Folonkono, a group of anthropomorphic figures holding bows, arrows, and other objects seems to move toward an elephant. These male figures are characterized by their protruding calves, buttocks, and bellies, as well as their elaborate headdresses. Two possibly female figures with similar characteristics are found at the rock shelter of Fanfannyégèné Donsoma. They hold sticklike objects in front of their bodies and seem to follow a male figure with bow and arrows. At present these motifs are the only known examples of narrative art in the region.

Pecked, incised, abraded, or polished petroglyphs are particularly well known from southern and central Mali and southern Burkina Faso, as well as from numerous sites in west-central and central Africa. Petroglyphs in Sub-Saharan West Africa include primarily circular cup marks of varying size and depth, oblong or spindle-shaped grooves in a variety of arrangements, and pecked motifs, some of which resemble saurians, bovids' heads, and rosettes. Circular grooves and cup marks combined into rosette shapes have been located in southwestern Burkina Faso, while incised triangular motifs are located at Aribinda in the north of the country. Petroglyphs resembling fish have been reported from Bamako (southern Mali), the vicinity of Akure (southwestern Nigeria), and Angola. Intricate combinations of rosette-like circular and linear forms have been recorded at Bidzar in Cameroon, together with cup marks and other motifs. A large number of petroglyphs, mostly pecked, have been located in the Ogooué valley in Gabon. While many of these petroglyphs are circular in form, comprising lines of circles, concentric circles or spirals, a number of triangular, zigzag, and saurian motifs are found as well. Saurian motifs are also encountered in the southeastern part of the Central African Republic. Additionally, petroglyphs have been reported from Côte d'Ivoire, Equatorial Guinea, the north of the Republic of Congo, and Angola, where concentric circles and other circular motifs prevail at the sites of Tchitundo-hulo in the south and Calola in the east of the country.

The dating of rock art and its attribution to particular groups of historically or archaeologically known peoples is generally difficult. In some cases the content of the motifs gives clues as to their age. Horses or firearms, for example, have been introduced to different regions of western and central Africa only recently and depictions of these are thought to date back no more than a few hundred years. Also, the technique of manufacture may give an indication as to the age of petroglyphs. Those that are thought to have been made with iron tools can be dated to after the introduction of iron use and production to an area, such as in the case of the Ogooué Valley in Gabon. In other cases rock art has tentatively been linked in date to archaeological

layers at rock art sites, such as in the Boucle du Baoulé of southwestern Mali, where the first rock art has been ascribed to Late Stone Age peoples. Such attributions remain hypotheses, however, since no direct relationship of the pictographs and petroglyphs to these layers can be proven. Only exceptionally have paint samples from rock art sites been dated, such as in the case of pictographs from Opeleva (Angola), which have yielded a date of about 1900 years old.

West Africa is exceptional in the presence of some direct ethnographic information on contexts of rock art making as well as the significance of motifs. Until recently, young grooms among the Marghi in northeastern Nigeria painted the walls of specific rock shelters during a preparation period for the *mba* marriage ceremony. The motifs, mainly stick figures and geometric forms, were said to represent humans, animals, weapons, and shields. In a number of instances, resonating rock slabs (so-called rock gongs) were struck by the young men during the ceremonies. Among the Dogon of central Mali, rock art was made or remarked in a variety of contexts, often associated with the fabrication of masks for a variety of funerary ceremonies. To a lesser extent rock art was made during circumcision, as well as in a range of nonritual contexts. The pictographs are mostly monochrome red, white, or black, but in some instances all three colors have been combined in polychrome paintings. The motifs are said to represent a variety of masks, humans, animals, supernatural beings, objects used during particular rituals, and tools. The extent to which Dogon rock art traditions are still alive today is unclear. Available information is restricted to the large rock shelter of Songo, where polychrome pictographs are currently remarked and added every three years, during a circumcision ritual. While this information gives invaluable insights into aspects of rock art making and use, it is likely that rock art in western and central Africa was made in a host of different contexts over time and space.

CORNELIA KLEINITZ

See also: **Art and Architecture, History of African; Stone Age (Later): Western Africa.**

Further Reading

Bayle des Hermes, Roger de. *Recherches préhistoriques en République Centrafricaine*. Paris : C. Klingsieck, 1975.

Carter, Patrick L., and Patricia J. Carter. "Rock Paintings from Northern Ghana." *Transactions of the Historical Society of Ghana*, no. 7 (1964): 1–3.

Fagg, Bernard E. B. "The Cave Paintings and Rock Gongs of Birnin Kudu." In *Third Pan-African Congress on Prehistory: Livingstone 1955*, edited by J. Desmond Clark. London: Chatto and Windus, 1957.

Griaule, Marcel. *Masques Dogons*. Paris: Institut d'Ethnologie, 1938.

Kleinitz, Cornelia. "Rock Art in Sub-Saharan Mali." *Antiquity* 75, no. 290 (2001): 799–800.

Millogo, Antoine K. "Archéologie du Burkina Faso. L'art rupestre." in *L'Archéologie en Afrique de l'Ouest. Sahara et Sahel*, edited by Robert Vernet. Saint-Maur, France: Éditions Sépia, 2000.

Oslisly, Richard, and Bernard Peyrot. *Les Gravures rupestres de la valleé de l'Ogooué (Gabon)*. Paris: Éditions Sépia, 1993.

Vaughan, J. H., "Rock Paintings and Rock Gongs among the Marghi of Nigeria," *Man*, no. 62 (1962): 49–52.

Willcox, A. R. *The Rock Art of Africa*. London: Croom Helm, 1984.

Roman Conquest: *See* Egypt, Ancient: Roman Conquest and Occupation: Historical Outline.

Roman Empire: *See* North Africa: Roman Occupation, Empire.

Rovzi: *See* Torwa, Changamire Dombo, and the Rovzi.

Royal Niger Company, 1886–1898

The Royal Niger Company occupies an important place in the history of the British colonial acquisition of Nigeria. Although it was chartered in 1886 and thereby obtained sovereign administrative authority over the areas of its commercial activity, a full assessment of the company must start in 1879.

That year, Sir George Taubman Goldie arrived on the Niger. Trade on that river was marked by bitter rivalry between a number of British and French companies. Goldie, a major shareholder in the smallest of the British companies and an astute business negotiator, persuaded the British companies to merge to form the United Africa Company in 1879, renamed the National Africa Company (NAC) in 1882. Goldie also persuaded Lord Aberdare, a British industrialist, influential politician, and president of the Royal Geographical Society, to become the chairman of the new company. Goldie himself took up the administration of the company in Nigeria. From then on, the story of Goldie becomes the story of the company. Against the French companies that had declined to join the merger, Goldie waged a relentless price war and eventually bought them out in 1884. The purchase made NAC the sole European trading firm in the lower Niger. The era of free trade was thereby ended, as the company went on to establish a monopoly hitherto unknown in the history of the Niger trade. In time the company established about a hundred trading stations on the Niger, employing a labor force of 1500.

Contemptuous of the local people, the company dictated the prices it paid for their produce, and sold imports to them. To impress and intimidate the local population, Goldie established a well-drilled constabulary force of 241 men equipped with sophisticated heavy artillery and machine guns, specially designed by the inventor Hiram Maxim in a way so that the shells ignited the thatched roofs of the native houses. Goldie also acquired twenty gunboats which could ply the Niger all year round. Between 1879 and 1886, most communities in the Lower Niger Valley were sacked for resisting the company's harsh monopoly.

Goldie was as much a businessman as an imperialist. His arrival on the Niger coincided with the era of mounting European imperialism in Africa. To him, British dominion over the Niger Basin was of supreme importance, key to gaining access to the rich west African interior. To preempt other European powers, by 1886 Goldie had foisted 237 "treaties of protection" on local chiefs in the area. The treaties were of doubtful legal validity, as they were extracted from the people mostly under duress. Largely as a result of the NAC's influence at the Berlin West African Conference of 1884–1885, Britain was recognized as the de facto power in the Niger region.

To cement its control of the Niger trade, the NAC sought a charter from the British government. This was granted, giving the company sovereign rights to levy customs duties, acquire and develop lands, and exploit the mineral and agricultural resources of the area under its jurisdiction. The company was renamed the Royal Niger Company (RNC). The charter enabled Britain to exclude other European powers from the area by creating a facade of effective administration at a minimum responsibility and cost to the British taxpayer.

Goldie took up the new responsibilities entrusted to his company with zeal, quickly enlarging the company's domain through exclusive treaties with the Yola, Adamawa, Borgu, Sokoto, and Gwandu. By 1892 Goldie had signed some 360 such treaties, which the British Foreign Office quickly ratified. The company then evolved a range of measures to exclude all other trading firms from the Niger trade and to silence its critics. Its employees were bonded to silence with £1,000 each, and some Christian missionaries were compromised through material benefits they received from the company. Duties levied on companies venturing into the RNC's domain were so excessive as to make such ventures uneconomic. Trade on the Niger was permitted only at designated "ports of entry," and the most lucrative oil markets were declared "closed ports" to other trading interests. Defiance of the regulations resulted in the confiscation of the offender's trade goods. Local traders received no exemption from the restrictions and so found themselves unwelcome strangers on the Niger, which had been their ancestral heritage.

The RNC represents a classic case of exploitation without redress. The company exploited its absolute monopoly to make profits far in excess of what it could have made in a free-trade situation. The company effected no positive social transformations in the area, building no roads, schools, nor hospitals. Until 1905, it stuck to the barter system of trade with the local people because this enabled it to exploit them fully. It spread terror and resentment all along the valleys of the Niger and the Benue Rivers. Having received the charter, the company became even more high-handed and vicious. The slightest local dissent against the company was visited with great venom. In 1888, half of Asaba, where the company had its administrative headquarters, was decimated, and Obosi was razed to the ground the next year, in both cases on the specious charge of the practice of human sacrifice. The soldiers lived off the people's livestock and food crops, and sexually assaulted their women. In 1897, led by Goldie himself, the company forces invaded Ilorin and Nupe. The pretext was to stop slave raiding in both kingdoms, but the actual aim was to keep the French and the Lagos government off the area.

However, the company's tactics boomeranged on the trade of the Niger. Many communities resorted to subsistence production to achieve self-sufficiency. Palm oil exports fell from 2,500 tons in 1886 to 1000 tons in 1888. But not all the communities could achieve self-sufficiency. The Brass people, situated on the margin of the saline delta water, depended on the Niger trade for their livelihood. After years of futile negotiations with the company for a fair trade deal, the people resolved to die in battle rather than in hunger. In 1895, they sacked the company's station at Akassa, and the company's reprisal action was predictably draconic. By the late 1890s mounting storms of protest against the company forced the British government to revoke the company's charter, effective December 31, 1899.

ONWUKA N. NJOKU

See also: **Delta States, Nineteenth Century; Lagos Colony and Oil Rivers Protectorate; Nigeria: British Colonization to 1914.**

Further Reading

Alagoa, E. J. *The Small Brave City State: A History of Nembe–Brass in the Niger Delta.* Madison: University of Wisconsin Press, 1964.

Cook, A. N. *British Enterprises in Nigeria.* London: Frank Cass, 1964.

Dike, K. O. *Trade and Politics in the Niger Delta, 1830–1885.* Oxford: Oxford University Press, 1956.

Flint, J. E. *Sir George Goldie and the Making of Nigeria.* London: Oxford University Press, 1960.

Rubber: *See* Liberia: Firestone.

Rudd Concession, 1888

Zimbabwe's rapid transformation into colonial Rhodesia in the late nineteenth century was due largely to the political and economic ambitions of Cecil Rhodes and his support from British officials, at home and in Southern Africa, who wished to expand the empire without incurring imperial expense or responsibility. The Rudd Concession, a mineral rights award from King Lobengula of the Ndebele, was the means toward this end, since it was utilized by Lord Salisbury's government, in 1889, as the convenient precondition for issuing a royal charter creating the British South Africa Company to function as an economic and governmental organization for much of south-central Africa.

During the height of the "Scramble" for African empire in the 1880s, British officials in London and Southern Africa, as well as Rhodes in Kimberley, feared expansionist activities by other Europeans in Zimbabwe—particularly the Portuguese, with their ambition to connect their Angolan and Mozambican colonies and the Transvaal Boers of Paul Kruger's South African Republic. The latter claimed to fall heir to an 1853 agreement between Piet Potgieter and Lobengula's father Mzilikazi, protecting Boer hunting and trade interests in Matabeleland. Another Transvaaler, Pieter Grobler, began to visit the Ndebele king on Kruger's behalf in 1886. During a later meeting, Grobler obtained from Lobengula a "peace and friendship" treaty dated July 30, 1887. The British feared this as the first step toward unwelcome Boer expansion in the north. Their concern was increased by a report from a close ally of Rhodes, Sir Sidney Shippard, the Bechuanaland commissioner, that Boer advances were imminent into gold-rich and fertile Mashonaland, a region adjacent to Lobengula's kingdom and partly subject to it. Alternatively, the Grobler agreement can be viewed as a cooperative effort, or even protoalliance, by two nineteenth-century leaders threatened by overseas imperialism.

Alarmed by the Grobler Treaty, the British sent an envoy to deal with Lobengula. John Smith Moffat, the son of the Reverend Robert Moffat of the London Missionary Society (LMS), brother-in-law of David Livingstone and a close confidant of Mzilikazi, was himself a former London missionary in Matabeleland who had joined the British colonial service in 1879 and became the assistant commissioner for the Bechuanaland Protectorate, stationed at Khama's capital of Shoshong. Lobengula, who trusted no Europeans like he trusted the Moffat family, signed the Moffat Treaty of February 11, 1888, by which he agreed not to alienate any of his domains without the consent of the British government. London then considered Matabeleland its colonial sphere of influence and warned away potential rival powers.

Salisbury's government, including its high commissioner in Cape Town, Sir Hercules Robinson, was now prepared for an act of "imperialism on the cheap" by supporting Rhodes north of the Limpopo. Grobler himself, and perhaps the supposed Boer threat as well, were soon eliminated as a result of an attack on Grobler's party by Ngwato warriors while crossing King Khama's country on his return from a visit to Lobengula in July 1888. Shippard reported the Grobler incident as an unfortunate accident, and Kruger sent no new representative north.

Rhodes sent his party of concession seekers north from Kimberley in August 1888, with a supply of liquor and £10,000 in gold sovereigns. This group was headed by Charles Dunell Rudd, an early business partner of Rhodes in the De Beers Mine. Rudd represented Griqualand West in the Cape Parliament during 1883–1988 and had recently gone to the Witwatersrand to foster Rhodes's interest in the gold fields. James Rochfort Maguire, the lawyer in the group, had met and befriended Rhodes in his days at Oxford University. Francis Robert "Matabele" Thompson was considered an old "Africa hand," despite his pathological fear of Africans.

Arriving at Bulawayo on September 20, 1888, they found a number of fellow Europeans present in Lobengula's capital, including missionaries, traders, and rival concession seekers. Urged by some of his warriors and advisors not to sign an agreement with whites, but by others—particularly *Induna* Lotshe Hlabangana—to strike a bargain with the Rudd party, Lobengula wavered for over a month. A letter of support from High Commissioner Robinson and efforts by the LMS missionary Charles D. Helm, and Shippard, who arrived in full uniform accompanied by a detachment of his troopers, persuaded Lobengula that Rudd and his associates represented Queen Victoria. The king—assured by Shippard that the British wanted only a political alliance and none of his land (as well as, apparently, by Rhodes's delegation that digging for minerals would be confined to a single location)— eventually agreed to the Rudd treaty, which was dated October 30, 1888.

Under its terms, Lobengula and his successors were to receive shipments totaling 1000 Martini-Henri rifles and 100,000 cartridges, a monthly payment of £100 in gold sovereigns, and an armed steamboat or an additional £500. In exchange, the king conferred on Rudd and his associates an exclusive mineral concession within his domain, "together with full power to do all things that they may deem necessary to win and procure the same."

Rudd hurriedly delivered his concession to Rhodes at Kimberley, who assumed ownership of it through his Central Search Association. Supported by an array of officials, financiers, political leaders, and even former rivals in Britain during the next year, Rhodes used the Rudd Concession as his crucial bargaining tool to obtain a royal charter creating the British South Africa Company (BSAC).

Lobengula's increasing skepticism, and efforts to nullify the concession during the months of the charter negotiations, including his repudiation of it in April 1889, and his massacre of Lotshe Hlabangana and his household in September, were to no avail. As detailed in its royal charter issued in October 1889, the powers of the BSAC extended far beyond the bounds of the Rudd Concession. The BSAC was designated as the effective government for a vast new British area on both sides of the Zambezi. Rhodes and its other directors were empowered to exercise the functions of government over an undefined area north of Bechuanaland for an initial period of 25 years. These included the military, diplomatic, and settlement actions necessary to establish colonial Rhodesia during the following decade. The settlement of neighboring Mashonaland in 1890 by the BSAC created white Rhodesia and sparked the 1893 Matabele War, Lobengula's death, and the conquest of his kingdom.

LOUIS W. TRUSCHEL

See also: **Kimberley and Diamond Fields; Rhodes, Cecil J.; Rhodes, Jameson, and the Seizure of Rhodesia; South Africa: Gold on the Witwatersrand, 1886–1899; Zimbabwe: 1880s; Zimbabwe (Southern Rhodesia): Ndebele and Shona Risings: First Chimurenga.**

Further Reading

Galbraith, John S. *Crown and Charter: The Early Years of the British South Africa Company.* Berkeley and Los Angeles: University of California Press, 1974.

Keppel-Jones, Arthur. *Rhodes and Rhodesia: The White Conquest of Zimbabwe 1884–1902.* Kingston, Ontario: McGill-Queen's University Press, 1983.

Rotberg, Robert I., with Miles F. Shore. *The Founder: Cecil Rhodes and the Pursuit of Power.* New York: Oxford University Press, 1988.

Rufisque: *See* **Senegal: Colonial Period: Four Communes: Dakar, Saint Louis, Gorée, and Rufisque.**

Rumfa, Muhammad (1463–1499)

Sarkin of Kano

Muhammad Rumfa was the *sarkin*, or chief, of Kano, one of the Hausa Bakwai, or true Hausa states. Rumfa sought the help of the famous Muslim teacher al-Maghili. Under Rumfa, a strong Islamic ruling tradition began. Kano became important in the trans-Saharan trade, famous for its cloth, dyeing pits, and Moroccan leather.

Rumfa is generally considered one of the greatest of the Hausa kings. Leo Africanus, for example, noted his power and the strength of his mounted knights. Rumfa initiated a number of reforms, which contributed to his strength. He intensified the influence of Islam and, therefore, the centralization of state power. He did so through enjoining the public celebration of the Id al-kabir, Islam's major festival, extending the city's walls, creating a council of state, building and protecting a public market, appointing eunuchs to positions of power, and introducing *purdah*. Moreover, Rumfa welcomed the coming of the Fulani and the special knowledge of Islam contained in their books of theology and grammar. Furthermore, Rumfa courted visiting scholars from the University of Timbuktu.

Through increasing the role of Islam, Rumfa could extend his trade ties and thereby increase the wealth of the state. Rumfa also found sanction for his various practices, part of his famous twelve reforms, such as taking women from conquered groups, putting them in his harem, and putting women in purdah. He also had the first-born virgin of families taken to his harem. These practices tied different families to him. Moreover, al-Maghili became his closest advisor for a number of years and directed his actions carefully to bring Kano into line with Islamic orthodoxy and strengthen its ties with North African kingdoms. Al-Maghili wrote *The Obligation of Princes* as a guidebook for Rumfa.

Rumfa became the benchmark against which other kings were judged. The power of Kano and its preeminence were established under his administration. He became the model for future leaders—especially the Fulani, whose jihad (holy war) led to successor states in the Hausa area.

FRANK A. SALAMONE

See also: **Hausa Polities: Origins, Rise.**

Further Reading

Ajayi, J. F. Ade. *Milestones in Nigerian History.* London: Longman, 1980.

Hodgkin, Thomas. *Nigerian Perspectives,* London: Oxford University Press, 1975.

Low, Victor. *Three Nigerian Emirates.* Evanston, Ill.: Northwestern University Press, 1972.

Rural Development, Postcolonial

National agricultural policies implemented in the postcolonial era have generally been based on ambitious objectives of increasing production and diversifying agricultural activities. In addition to agricultural development plans, national administrative institutions in charge of rural development have been put in place in many cases.

The rural development schemes of postcolonial African nations share some general characteristics, as they were shaped in the early years of independence. In the absence of contractors and adequate economic structures, the state played a determining role in the development process. The objectives of rural development, and the strategies implemented, were defined in a similar way for the entire nation. Technical training bodies were created, and economic organizations (cooperatives) were set up to execute tasks related to supply and commercialization. In most countries, attempts were made to involve more of the population in training schemes.

In the second decade after independence, a great number of varied development projects emerged. Sectoral projects sometimes involved only one cash crop. Integrated projects for agricultural development included nontechnical aspects of infrastructure development (such as road construction), as well as initiatives in the fields of health, literacy, and education. The projects were often designed under the assumption that, by mobilizing specific material means and tools, acquired via external funding, it would be possible to implement the technical plans and increase production. The era of project development was also characterized by a technocratic approach that disregarded traditional peasant production methods. The objectives of the project, its content, the systems of its structure, and its operations generally were defined without taking into account peasant reactions to new means of production.

The third stage of development was reached around the year 1980, marked by questioning of assumptions, and multiple orientations. Positive results were recorded for certain crops, such as cotton. In some areas, such as south Mali, production increases was noticeable and generally the result of the adoption of advanced, technical means of production. Producer organizations were set up and strengthened.

However, development projects were marked by several hindrances. The systems set up to popularize new development methods, and to familiarize the peasantry with said methods, are often expensive, and the mixed results they produce do not always justify the expense. In some cases, development aid has not always been profitable to rural populations but has, too often, contributed to strengthen the bureaucratic power of central state administrations. Several negative side effects have been traced to the implementation of new development systems, including degradation of the natural environment and decreases in fertility. The juxtaposition of autonomous projects has made consistent planning difficult. Coherent agricultural policies (i.e., those that would set up systems of exchange between zones with a surplus of a product and zones in need of that product) have been lacking.

Several factors distinguish recent rural development. Participation has become the key issue. The participation of peasants through associations and professional organizations, and the presence of clear and fair contracts for workers, are recognized as key to effectiveness and lasting development plans. Nationally based policies are prevalent. Governments, such as in Senegal and Burkina Faso, define policies for land management, for the funding of local development, for agricultural credit, and for research. However, such nationally based plans are often accompanied by actions by the state to disengage itself, by breaking up state and parastatal institutions into privately run bodies. New actors, especially nongovernmental organizations (NGOs), have appeared. They are generally viewed as a positive presence, and they have increased the amount of funding available for postcolonial agricultural development. NGOs tend to prefer organizational structures based on decentralized cooperation, and they generally employ for the local-level approach.

Finally, this most recent period of postcolonial development has been characterized by the revival, by the World Bank, of classical popularization methods known as *methods training and visits*, which have had remarkable results elsewhere in the world, such as Asia. New development policies are introduced and explained through several actions including support for research, reform of agricultural services, and structural adjustment programs.

GUY ZOUNGRANA

See also: **Development, Postcolonial: Central Planning, Private Enterprise, Investment; Peasant Production, Postcolonial: Markets and Subsistence; World Bank, IMF, and Structural Adjustment.**

Further Reading

Bates, R. H. "Essays on the Political Economy of Rural Africa." *African Economic History*, no. 14 (1985): pp.245–247.

Boserup, E. *The Conditions of Agricultural Growth.* London: George Allen and Unwin, 1965.

Conac, G., F. Conac, and C. Savonnet-Guyot (eds.). *Les politiques de l'eau en Afrique: Développement agricole et participation paysanne.* Paris: Economica, 1985.

De Wilde, J. C. *Expériences de développement agricole en Afrique Tropicale*, vol. 3, *Pays divers.* Paris: Maisonneuve et Larose, 1968.

Haubert, M. "Politiques agraires et dynamismes paysans: de nouvelles orientations ?" *Tiers-Mondes*, no. 128 (1991): 721–932.

Heiyer, J., P. Roberts, and G. Williams (eds.). *Rural Development in Tropical Africa.* London: Macmillan, 1981.

Lélé, U. *The Design of Rural Development: Lessons from Africa.* Baltimore: Johns Hopkins University Press, 1975.

Rwanda: To 1800

The early history of Rwanda (formerly Ruanda) often suffers in the telling due to a scarcity of archaeological evidence and the repetition of earlier, untested theories, some of which continue to be widely propagated. One thing that is certain is the centrality of both ethnicity and cattle to this history, and the indivisibility of these two from each other.

The original inhabitants of Rwanda were the Twa, formerly described as a pygmy race. They were forest dwellers who flourished as hunter-gatherers in the forests around the Virunga mountain range in the west of the country. Their numbers were reduced significantly as Bantu-speaking Hutu started arriving in the fifth century and began clearing forest for farming.

The Hutu, whose lifestyle was based around small-scale cultivation and animal husbandry, developed a mutually beneficial relationship with the Twa, with the latter providing the farmers with game and honey in exchange for crops such as bananas and corn. Hutu society was governed by a clan system with kings (*bahinza*) ruling over small groups of clans. The Hutu believed that the bahinza were also invested with magical powers, such as the ability to create rain or protect crops and livestock from disease. Their settlements were built around a hill or group of hills, providing an easy means of differentiating between clans and also a means of settling local disputes.

It is thought that the Tutsi began to arrive in this area in the early to mid-fifteenth century and their ancestry, while not certain, is likely to have been Lwo. The Lwo

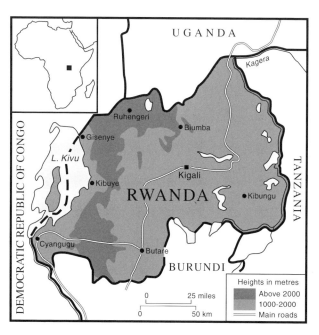

Rwanda.

were earlier migrants to the interlacustrine, or Great Lakes, region, formerly from southern Sudan. The Tutsi arrival used to be widely described as an invasion, in which they overran and subjugated the weaker Hutu. This tidy view of migration and conquest was popular for a long time, partly because it seemed to support wider theories of racial superiority that were especially prevalent among many nineteenth-century colonists; in reality, the first Tutsi arrivals would have been few in number and in no position to impose their will on any preexisting group of people, had they wanted to.

More certain than the origin of the Tutsi is the fact that by the end of the fifteenth century these pastoralists were arriving in ever greater numbers, straining the peaceful relations that had characterized early dealings between them and the Hutu farmers. Cattle in East Africa had long come to represent an obvious symbol of wealth and status. They were also that rare form of wealth that, in the absence of disease, is self-generating. With increasing numbers of cattle, however, comes the need for more land. As well as raising cattle pastoralists were traditionally soldiers too; used to taking other people's land when the need for more pasture arose. Farmers, on the other hand, were unlikely to be well versed in war and no match for an opponent that was. That said, the takeover was not entirely violent.

Many Hutu beliefs and traditions were adopted by the Tutsi, such as the principle of divine kingship and the powers over climate and agricultural production that were also attributed to him. The use of drums, allowing the king to make announcements across the land, was also of Hutu origin. At other times a fusion of the two traditions was reached, as with the *abiru*, or law-making council. The imposition of a nationwide Tutsi king (*mwami*) who was given lordship of all land was the last stage in the movement of power in favor of the Tutsi. At the same time, numbers of Hutu chiefs were brought into the new, Tutsi-controlled regime, becoming Tutsi in the process. From this point on it becomes more apparent that the terms Hutu and Tutsi were less about ethnicity and more about power and social status. Marriage, which was not uncommon between the two groups, was one further way to change one's social group.

This combination of land seizure and more peaceful means saw the Tutsi hegemony firmly in place by the sixteenth century. The relationship that now grew more definite between Hutu and Tutsi was known as *ubuhake*, a patron-client arrangement. Under this system, which came to control the lives of most people and became increasingly feudal, the (Tutsi) patron would give (or rather, lend) a cow or cows to a (Hutu) client. The client would then do the bidding of the patron by providing crops and performing military service in return for protection and the use of the cow and the

land. In this way land and cattle became the de facto tools of power, and they were both held by the Tutsi.

The downside to this arrangement, however, was the fact that at any time the patron could demand a client's entire stock of cattle as his repayment, and not just the one initially lent out. Such absolutism was open to extreme abuse, but as long as all cattle (that is to say wealth) remained in the hands of the few there was very little that those on the receiving end could do to reverse this situation. What had once been purely tribal groups now tended to appear increasingly as occupational and social delineations, especially when the opportunity to change class remained an option. The Twa remained somewhat outside of the equation; they kept to the forest and the hunting-foraging ways they had always known, as well as making pottery.

As the system of ubuhake grew in importance for the general population so did the power of the Nyiginya tribe who were eventually to extend their sphere of influence to cover an area roughly the size of the modern state of Rwanda. Over a period of several centuries, and starting from their homeland in the center of the country, they engaged in a series of policies, some diplomatic and others violent. In the seventeenth century, Mwami Ruganzu Ndori was responsible for huge extensions to the tribe's territory, the spoils of a series of invasions on independent Hutu land in the west and the north of the country. This was the land and the system that was firmly established at the start of the nineteenth century, and which proved too convenient to be ignored by later colonists.

EAMONN GEARON

See also: **Great Lakes Region: Growth of Cattle Herding.**

Further Reading

De Waal, Alex, and Rakiya Omaar. *Rwanda*, 2nd ed. London: African Rights, 1995.

Dorsey, Learthen. *Historical Dictionary of Rwanda*. Lanham, Md.: Scarecrow Press, 1999.

Fage, J. D. *A History of Africa*, 3rd ed. London: Routledge, 1995.

Lemarchand, René. *Rwanda and Burundi*. New York: Praeger, 1970.

Murphy, E. Jefferson. *History of African Civilization*. New York: Thomas Y. Crowell, 1972.

Prunier, Gérard. *The Rwanda Crisis 1959–1964: History of a Genocide*. New York: Columbia University Press, 1995.

Shillington, Kevin. *History of Africa*, New York: St. Martin's Press, 1989.

Rwanda: Precolonial, Nineteenth Century

It is often anachronistic to speak about precolonial times, as if the start of the colonial era had been expected. In the case of Rwanda, one might say this view would not be entirely inappropriate. Indeed, by the end of nineteenth century, the situation of the country had deteriorated so much that millenarianism was calling for a change, and the first few Europeans to enter the country were not unwelcome if they were kept at bay by the court.

Another objection to the use of the word *precolonial* to qualify history before the establishment of colonial rule would be to convey the impression that history started with colonial times. Historians such as Jan Vansina have demonstrated that oral traditions, when carefully used, are valuable historical sources, and he applied his methods to the history of Rwanda. Confronting the traditions, and putting them to the test of a confrontation with archaeological data whenever possible, has allowed Vansina to detect the emergence of kingdoms in the Great Lakes area in the seventeenth century.

One of them would take shape when a powerful pastoralist of Hima descent, Ruganzu Ndori, settled in Central Rwanda and increased its domination through gifts of cattle and military conquest. His ruling lineage, belonging to the Nyiginyia clan, strengthened its grip on this core area, and by the end of the eighteenth century was making an increasing use of military power to expand. The court, which was benefiting from the conquests, supported the efforts. By the beginning of the nineteenth century the Nyiginyia kingdom had extended its influence on what is now known as Rwanda, and even beyond. This influence, however, remained quite uneven depending on the areas, varied over time, and remained looser on parts of Western Rwanda, as well as on the Northern part of the country. Some small political entities remained governed by Hutu heads of lineages, for ritual motives, up to 1926.

During the nineteenth century, governance also varied, with an intricate system of control, taxation, and bondage being progressively imposed. Land, cattle and labor were increasingly used by the ruling class to tighten their grip on farming lineages. The wealth drawn to the top of society through this imposition resulted in increasing rivalries between powerful families at court, in an exacerbated class consciousness, and in a widening gap between rulers and ruled. This was especially the case in central Rwanda, where high fertility rates combined with the length of settlement to produce a land shortage that made it difficult for farmer lineages to maintain themselves. According to Vansina, by the middle of the nineteenth century a first distinction between Hutu and Tutsi had become institutionalized, referring to respective occupations within the army, and not to origins.

This distinction shifted progressively to the entire society, with farmers being called Hutu, and pastoralists Tutsi. It seems the link between denomination and origin had become more prominent by the end of the century, especially at court and under circumstances relating to political matters, with variations in their use in everyday life. This shift testified to the expansion of court customs as the result of military conquest. Studies on peripheral areas, such as Kinyaga, illustrate the dynamics of penetration of those customs. When the first Europeans entered mountainous Rwanda (1894, Götzen) in defiance of its military reputation, King Kigeri Rwabugiri had been reigning for almost thirty years. Wars had increased the wealth of rival families exerting power at court, but Rwabugiri had taken care to master their rivalries, with shifts in positions that involved periodical persecutions and executions. Under Rwabugiri, external wars and internal politics had intertwined to determine the dynamics of power.

Other circumstances combined with those dynamics to alter Rwandan society. Epidemics affected men and cattle. The loss of herds meant many small pastoralists were ruined and became Hutu agriculturalists. Wealth became even more concentrated in the hands of a few. Meanwhile, merchants were at the doorstep of the country, and some campaigns testified to the opening of the country to interactions meant to bring luxury goods to the court, in exchange for ivory and slaves. The last campaigns were directed at Ijwi Island. By the end of a century marred with increasing violence against the powerless and anarchy at court, rivalries between factions culminated in a coup after Rwabugiri's death. After his designated successor had been destroyed, young king Yuhi Musinga was put on the throne. By the time the German lieutenant von Ramsay proposed an alliance to the regent queen mother (1897) revolts were raging in the north, and she was happy to accept.

This was the start of the colonial era. The Germans, however, were very few and did little to interfere with internal matters. Intrigues went on, as did the influence of the diviners and other ritual practitioners. In this kingdom where violence was the usual tool for oppression, religious beliefs related to the person of the king and to fertility were indeed central, and justified the submission of the people. At the turn of the century, missionaries entered Rwanda. In the beginning, however, they got very little opportunity to interact with the powerful ones. In 1900, three Catholic missionaries were allowed to settle in Save, an area known as inhospitable. Rwanda had lost its splendid isolation.

DANIELLE DE LAME

See also: **Rwanda: To 1800; Rwanda: Colonial Period: German and Belgian Rule.**

Further reading

Chrétien, J. P. *The Great Lakes of Africa: Two Thousand Years of History*. New York: Zone, 2003.

Newbury, C. *The Cohesion of Oppression: Clientship and Ethnicity in Rwanda, 1860–1960.* New York: Columbia University Press, 1988.

Newbury, D. *Kings and Clans: Ijwi Island and the Lake Kivu Rift, 1780–1840.* Madison: University of Wisconsin Press, 1991.

Rwanda: Colonial Period: German and Belgian Rule

Germany's rule in Rwanda began in 1896, when the government of German East Africa founded a first military post in Usumbura, Urundi. From there German officers established relations with *Mwami* (King) Musinga of Rwanda. Musinga recognized German sovereignty, and the Germans reciprocated by exercising a kind of indirect rule. In view of their military weakness, they were wary of any military conflict with the ruling Tutsi. Throughout the German period the policy of indirect rule favored the Tutsi monarchy and continued in the vein of the precolonial shift toward annexation of the Hutu principalities and an increase in Tutsi chiefly power. Along with the soldiers, missionaries penetrated the country, and by 1904 the White Fathers had established five missions in Rwanda. Peaceful relations between Musinga and the Germans were disturbed around 1904–1905, when missionaries were attacked by several of Musinga's subchiefs, who opposed the influence of missionaries and ruthless Asian and European traders. The German administration in Usumbura reacted by issuing licenses to foreign merchants in March 1905, and by extending its network of military posts. During this affair it became clear that Musinga was more of a marionette to several competing court fractions and subchiefs than an absolute ruler. On account of their mwami-friendly treaties, these fractions considered the Germans to be

Tutsi dancers, Rwanda, 1958. © Lode van Gent/Das Fotoarchiv.

enemies that stood in the way of their ambitions. From 1907 onward Rwanda was no longer governed from Urundi, but from the new residence in Kigali. In the years between 1909 and 1912 several of Musinga's rivals as well as rebellious Twa groups were defeated by German forces. By 1914 missionary work was the only thriving European activity in Rwanda-Urundi with a total of 80 missionaries, while economic development was failing.

The German forces withdrew from Rwanda and Urundi in April and May 1916 to avoid the concentric attack of superior Belgian and British troops. The Belgian military conquest of Rwanda was made official by a League of Nations mandate in 1919. Between 1919 and 1926 the Belgians adopted a wait-and-see policy, supervising the Tutsi chiefly courts. From 1926 onward Governor Voisin took a series of reform measures. Nearly all political and economic power was concentrated in the hands of the Tutsi chiefs, which meant that the Hutu peasants were strictly controlled by a Tutsi chief with Belgian backing. Furthermore, *ubuletwa*, the hated forced-labor system, was enforced more intensively and introduced in places where it had not existed previously. With the help of the Belgians the Tutsi were able to gradually change traditional land rights in their favor, to the disadvantage of the Hutu. Thus the Tutsi chiefs could gain control of the traditional *ubukonde* Hutu landholdings in the northwest and southwest of Rwanda. This resulted in the individualization of economic resources and the destruction of the traditional collective folds of the ancient Rwandese society. Furthermore, the Belgians and Tutsi created the myth of a superior Tutsi "master race" and transformed this myth into administrative politics. The Hutu were told that they were inferiors who deserved their fate and, as a consequence, they started to hate all Tutsi regardless of their financial status. In November 1931 the Belgians deposed Musinga, who had never been sympathetic to them, and replaced him with one of his sons, who ruled as Mutara III Rudahigwa. He converted to Christianity, as did many of his Tutsi subjects, since Christianity was a prerequisite for the attainment of a higher social rank. The church, which monopolized the system of education, regarded the Tutsi as "natural-born chiefs" and gave them priority in education. This meant that the church could enhance its control over the future elite of the country. Hutu also graduated, but rarely found adequate employment.

World War II brought a vast expansion of the cash economy in which the Hutu had to share. The old clientship system, which was basically part of the nonmonetary economy, therefore became increasingly obsolete. In this stiffening atmosphere the church began to favor the growth of a Hutu counterelite. Many priests were now recruited from the Tutsi elite. They acquired new ideas of racial equality, colonial political devolution, and self-government. The white portion of the clergy had meanwhile shifted from conservative, upper-class Walloons to lower-class Flemish priests, who were sympathetic to the Hutu rather than to the Tutsi. With this backing the Hutu began to found periodicals and social associations. The ultraconservative Tutsi courts reacted by ousting progressive Tutsi chiefs, who had supported this development.

In 1957, two Hutu parties were created: the Mouvement Sociale de la Masse (MSM) by Grégoire Kayibanda and the Association pour la Promotion Sociale de la Masse (APROSOMA) by Joseph Gitera. In the same year, the Tutsi reacted with the formation of the Union Nationale Rwandaise (UNAR) which was strongly monarchist but anti-Belgian, and therefore received money from communist countries. To counter the UNAR the Belgians had released the liberal Tutsi chief Banakweri, who in September 1959 founded the Rassemblement Démocratique Rwandais as a liberal Tutsi party that, however, was trusted neither by monarchist Tutsi nor by the Hutu. In October 1959 the MSM had become the Mouvement Démocratique Rwandais/Parti du Mouvement et de l'Emancipation Hutu (PARMEHUTU).

By late 1959, tension had built considerably. When a PARMEHUTU activist was attacked by members of UNAR, false news of his death spread quickly. In the Hutu uprising which followed, Tutsi houses were burned and 300 people killed. Afterward, however, the Belgians arrested mostly Tutsi. This marked a serious break between the Belgians and their former protégés, since the former felt that they had protected a combination of backward traditionalists and communists. In the face of imminent chaos the helpless Belgians launched the idea of self-government on November 11, 1959. In the meantime, Hutu went on hunting down Tutsi and burning down their houses. Starting in early 1960, the colonial government began to replace most of the Tutsi chiefs with Hutu ones. The latter immediately organized the persecution of the Tutsi, which resulted in a mass exodus of 130,000 Rwandese Tutsi to the neighboring countries until late 1963. The communal elections in June and July 1960 were won by the PARMEHUTU. At the urging of the United Nations, Brussels organized a "National Reconciliation Conference" in Ostend, Belgium in January 1961. After its failure, the Belgians and PARMEHUTU leader Kayibanda arranged a legal coup to prevent any further interference by the UN. In Gitarama, Kayibanda's birthplace, the "sovereign" Democratic Republic of Rwanda was declared on January 28, 1961. On September 25, 1961, legislative elections were held. PARMEHUTU received 78 per cent of the votes,

UNAR only 17 per cent. Rwanda became formally independent on July 1, 1962.

REINHARD KLEIN-ARENDT

See also: **Rwanda: Genocide, 1994.**

Further Reading

Hertefeld, Marcel d'. "Mythes et Idéologies Dans le Rwanda Ancien et Contemporain." In *The Historian in Tropical Africa*, edited by Jan Vansina, Raymond Mauny, and Louis-Vincent Thomas, London: Oxford University Press, 1961.

Lugan, Bernard. *Histoire du Rwanda: De la Préhistoire à Nos Jours.* Paris: Bartillat, 1997.

Kamukama, Dixon. *Rwanda Conflict: Its Roots and Regional Implications.* Kampala, Rwanda: Fountain, 1993.

Louis, W. Roger. *Ruanda-Urundi 1884–1919.* Oxford: Clarendon Press, 1963.

Newbury, Catherine. *The Cohesion of Oppression: Clientship and Ethnicity in Rwanda, 1860–1960.* New York: Columbia University Press, 1988.

Prunier, Gérard. *The Rwanda Crisis 1959–1994: History of a Genocide,* London: Hurst, 1995.

Rwanda: Civil Unrest and Independence: 1959–1962

It is necessary, in order to understand the unrest that surrounded the revolution and the independence of Rwanda, to bear in mind the changes that took place during colonial times. Many changes had been taking place in Rwandan society at the eve of colonization. Primary among them was the hardening of social divisions, according to classifications that, in many areas of the country, took racial overtones and combined well with the European mentality of the times.

Administrators and missionaries were few, and relied, for their understanding of the country they wanted to govern, on information provided by those nearest and most useful to them, the people in power. Famines provided opportunities for reforms. The territory was put for the first time under a unified mode of governance, and the status of the chiefs, some newly appointed on the basis of their skills in reading and writing, became more rigid. Reports of the administration testify to confusion between the ruling class and the Tutsi people. Subsequent discriminations had as a consequence that the better positions in the high schools and in the administration were reserved for those qualified as Tutsi. The clergy, the administration, and the Rwandan chiefs acted hand in hand to maintain the newly acquired positions. Religious seminars still provided an opportunity for Hutu people to progress. They would, however, soon be dominated by the increasing influence of the Tutsi clergy.

This situation was prevailing mainly where the influence of the central institutions was the strongest, with the northern cultural pride of the Kiga Hutu people, who had never been fully assimilated, remaining untouched. This specificity was to play a role in focalizing the ethnic divides, giving its own connotations to a revolution that had more social overtones in central Rwanda.

After World War II, changes in European society at large were reflected in the social origins of the missionaries. Social commitments induced changes in attitudes toward, respectively, the Tutsi elite, and a rising modern Hutu elite that had promoted itself by seizing the new opportunities commerce, religious education, and ideological changes offered them. The "indigenization" of the clergy left Hutu and Tutsi to themselves, and the first ethnic tensions took shape within the Church.

A split also occurred between the Tutsi court and the traditionalists and the more modern Tutsi elite. The United Nations visiting missions in the country entrusted to Belgium provided both sides, but specially the party in power, with opportunities to voice their demands. Pressures for reforms forced the Rwandan king to abolish the *ubuhake* system of bondage resting on the gift of cows (this only linking, in different ways, a small fraction of the population), but kept the rights on the pastures in the hands of the Tutsi chiefs, making this reform merely apparent.

Hutu expectations and feelings of frustration were rising. Civil unrest and social claims taking ethnic overtones started as soon as 1955. The Catholic press had, for quite a time, provided the Hutu elite with a channel to express their claims and discontents. A target date for independence was fixed, but the introduction of democratic procedures prior to this was differently felt by the two groups of population, with the Hutu seeing the benefits they could reap from a majority rule. Their claims became increasingly articulated, and synthesized, eventually, in the Hutu manifesto forwarded to the governor general in March 1957. At the eve of the elections, the Rwandan elite was very much divided along ethnic lines, with only a few populist Tutsi mitigating the divide. Soon would the Tutsi elite claim a quick independence for Rwanda, and look for international allies, while the Hutu reaffirmed their fidelity to Belgium, who would lead them to democracy. The manifesto, published in papers that traveled down to the hills where more than 95 per cent of the people lived, changed the atmosphere dramatically.

In July 1959, King Mutara Rudahigwa of Rwanda died suddenly in Burundi, and different interpretations were given to his death. His successor was almost immediately designated, without any consultation of the Belgian administrator. From September onward, the respective interests were represented by different political parties, with, at their extremes, the most conservative ones. Tutsis founded the National Rwandan

Union (UNAR), and the Hutu, the Movement for the Emancipation of the Hutu people. As the UNAR was referring to tradition and fidelity to the *mwami* (king), the first Hutu attacks against Tutsi houses were done as a token of conformity. The Tutsi reaction was swift and violent, as the leaders were appealing to the mobs to avenge the chiefs. Belgian troops intervened to restore order. A special resident, Coloniel Logiest, inclined to favor the Hutu, was appointed. He had "emergency interim chiefs" appointed, almost all of them Hutu people.

The consequences of the November 1959 riots and their political aftermath were important and far-reaching. They put many Tutsi families, deprived of their lands, on the road of a long exile, and fed their resentments against Belgian authorities. This exile was going to prove itself not only a multiple individual tragedy, but also a national tragedy, as the events of the last decade of the twentieth century have shown. The elections were organized in a climate of violence and intimidation using the lines of personal clientelism. On January 28, 1961, the Hutu government proclaimed Rwanda a republic, and took the lead. The country gained its independence on July 1, 1962. The first republic did not break with the habits of previous times, paving the way for the coup led in 1973 by the northerners. However, this change of leadership did not bring an end to the essential problem faced by Rwanda—namely, deeply rooted social inequalities in a context of extreme poverty.

DANIELLE DE LAME

Further Reading

Lemarchand, R. *Rwanda and Burundi*. London: Pall Mall Press, 1970.
Linden, I., and J. Linden. *Church and Revolution in Rwanda*. Manchester: Manchester University Press, 1977.

Rwanda: 1962–1990

The origins of conflict in postindependence Rwanda may be traced to the colonial legacy of partition and intercommunal division, and the creation in Rwanda of a sectarian, one-party regime that depended for its survival on the exclusion or elimination of its opponents. Ethnicity, although generally considered a cause of conflict, has often been used to obscure the Rwandan conflict's core causes: authoritarian institutions and political cultures, and those external influences that have played a significant role in supporting authoritarian regimes.

The country's eight million (pre-1994) inhabitants are categorized typically as Hutu (84 per cent), Tutsi (15 per cent) and Twa (1 per cent). However, the current Rwandan government is seeking to eradicate categorization by ethnic grouping, and argues that Rwanda's ethnic groups—commonly perceived, most catastroph-ically, by many within those groups as mutually antag-onistic throughout history—are instead "three strands of the same rope," and of one common Rwandan nationality, Banyarwanda, determined most obviously by a shared language, Kinyarwanda. By this reckoning, the ethnic division of this nation was not inevitable, but was a deliberate policy of colonialism.

Rwandan independence in 1962 was achieved on the colonists' terms, via the Belgian-sponsored over-throw and exiling of those favored (but, by 1959, proindependence) Tutsis who previously had adminis-tered on the colonists' behalf. The accession to power of the hitherto downtrodden Hutu majority reinforced sectarian divisions, reinforced despite generations of intermarriage by a Rwandan citizen's compulsory identity card, upon which his or her ethnic category was displayed, as in colonial times. The idea that the majority Hutu population had been oppressed not by Belgium but independently by the Tutsi was embraced enthusiastically by the Party for the Emancipation of the Hutu (PARMEHUTU). It was led by Grégoire Kayibanda, who founded the Rwandan First Republic and become its president following the 1959–1962 "social revolution," during which an ethnic transfer of power was accompanied by the killing or exiling of over half a million Tutsi. Violent expulsions recurred during the 1960s and early 1970s, and the exclusion of those remaining Tutsi from employment, public life, and political, economic, or military power created a quasi-apartheid system of discrimination. A Tutsi re-quired a Hutu patron in government in order to gain ac-cess to state jobs or economic assets. The client-patron relations that existed during the colonial and precolo-nial periods were reproduced, but in reverse. Interethnic tension became the definer of the country's problems, and sectarian prejudice and exclusion key features of the state because deemed essential to the state's survival. Accordingly, some observers argue that 60 years of colonial and Tutsi rule, and 35 years of Hutu supremacy following the 1959 revolution (which consigned half the Tutsi population to exile), have fundamentally changed the nature of the relationships between them. Political conflict since independence, punctuated by intercommunal violence, has created distinct and mutually opposed Hutu and Tutsi identities, which are identifiably "ethnic." By this analysis, it is impos-sible to interpret recent events without recourse to these labels, as they are the labels used by the people themselves.

Fearful of betrayal, Kayibanda had surrounded himself with supporters and family members from southern Rwanda, distributing patronage dispropor-tionately to those he felt he could trust. As a result, erstwhile PARMEHUTU supporters from the north

and center of the country grew isolated from the presi-dent and distant from the levers of political and eco-nomic power he controlled. Crucially, Kayibanda failed to retain control over the army, allowing his chief of staff, Juvénal Habyarimana, to build a power base for family, friends, and allies drawn from the lat-ter's home region in Gisenyi, northwestern Rwanda. By the early 1970s, northern and central Rwandan Hutu were conspiring to topple the Kayibanda estab-lishment, claiming the president was unable to protect the country against attacks from without by *inyenzi* (cockroaches—small bands of exiles seeking his over-throw) or to guarantee peace and stability in the climate of sectarian revenge within. As a result, Habyarimana was able to seize power in a military coup on July 5, 1973.

The political tensions that led to the overthrow of Kayibanda, and the shift from an ethnic to a regional basis of distribution of patronage, weaken the argu-ment that conflict in Rwanda is and always has been ethnically driven. Habyarimana re-created a one-party state, ensuring political, military, and—by extension—economic power was concentrated in his own hands and those of a close inner circle largely composed of family members: the *akazu* (little house). His Mouve-ment Révolutionnaire National pour le Développe-ment (MRND) published its manifesto on July 5, 1975, the second anniversary of the coup; it made clear the regime's readoption of a quasi-apartheid agenda, which severely limited access to education and state employment for ethnic minorities, and promised a robust official response to any perceived internal threat to national security.

Also in 1975, Rwanda signed cooperation agree-ments in terms of aid, trade, and cultural exchanges with France, which marked the formal expansion of France's African sphere from its own former colonies to include Belgium's ex-colonial territories. Franco-Rwandan military cooperation was formalized in a military technical assistance accord which entailed an initially modest annual transfer of arms and military equipment from France to Rwanda.

Over 15 years, the tranquility and introspection of this "little Switzerland of Africa" concealed a harden-ing of its authoritarianism as it failed repeatedly to address the basic injustice upon which it was built: the forcible exclusion of up to 600,000 citizens on the basis of sectarian discrimination. The central, enduring issue of Rwanda's exiles resurfaced at regular inter-vals, when tolerance for those exiles in surrounding countries was strained. Habyarimana and the party he founded insisted that "the glass was full": densely pop-ulated, high birthrate Rwanda, with a population of eight million in 64,200 square kilometers, was too overcrowded to allow the exiles to return.

However, in 1986, Rwandan refugees were in the vanguard of the successful campaign by Uganda's National Resistance Movement (NRM) to overthrow President Milton Obote. The Rwandan exiles in Uganda were driven to support the rebellion in large numbers (eventually providing 3000 of the 14,000 troops of the National Resistance Army, or NRA) by Obote's mistaken efforts in 1982 to force potentially disloyal Rwandans back into Habyarimana's hostile Rwanda. A disproportionate number of the NRA's senior commanders were drawn from these Rwandans—notably, chief of staff Fred Rwigyema and intelligence chief Paul Kagame (now Rwandan president). Militarily experienced and aware of growing resentment of the prominence—perceived as dominance—of Rwandans in the new Uganda's army and administration, Rwigyema and Kagame represented a generation of exiles radicalized by combat and aware that, as Rwandans, they would always be stateless until their "right to return" was granted or seized. Accordingly, the Rwandan Patriotic Front (RPF) was founded in Kampala in December 1987, and although recruited initially from Rwandan exiles in Uganda, the RPF also attracted support from the significant Rwandan diaspora in Tanzania, Burundi, Europe, and North America. Rwandan exiles had sought advancement through education, and many, prosperous professionals, were prepared to bankroll the new movement.

On July 27, 1987, the Central Committee of the MRND again announced, despite growing international pressure, that it would not allow the immigration of large numbers of exiles. By the late 1980s, pressure on the Habyarimana regime was growing, compounded by a series of bad harvests and a drop in the international price of coffee, the country's principal export upon which the cash crop economy was over-reliant. The regime also displayed an inability or refusal to address the country's chronic poverty and frequent shortages. Crucially, the issues of underused and unexploited land (including large areas of undrained swamp), and primitive agricultural practices, went unaddressed, despite the availability of studies advocating workable changes.

Under pressure for democratization from Rwandan civil society and some of his foreign backers, Habyarimana allowed the creation of opposition political parties and renamed his MRND the National Revolutionary Movement for Development and Democracy. However, he banned the nascent RPF and detained opposition supporters who proved too critical of the regime. On September 7, 1990, Pope John Paul II visited the fervently Catholic Rwanda, and although the pontiff made no call for greater democracy or observance of human rights by his hosts, Habyarimana felt the unaccustomed glare of international attention

merited a general amnesty for prisoners, excepting those charged with subversion or endangering state security. This gesture had the practical benefit of freeing space in the country's prisons for the mass detentions which would follow the launching of the RPF's first offensive three weeks later, on October first.

MEL McNULTY

See also: **Uganda: Obote: Second Regime, 1980–1985.**

Further Reading

Hintjens, Helen M. "Explaining the 1994 Genocide in Rwanda." *Journal of Modern African Studies* 37, no. 2 (1999): 241–286.

Kamukama, Dixon. *The Rwanda Conflict: Its Roots and Regional Implications.* Kampala, Rwanda: Fountain, 1993.

Newbury, Catharine. *The Cohesion of Oppression: Clientship and Ethnicity in Rwanda* (1860–1960). New York: Columbia University Press, 1988.

Prunier, Gérard. *The Rwanda Crisis: History of a Genocide,* London: Hurst, 1995.

Rwanda: Genocide, 1994

During approximately 100 days from April 7 until mid-July 1994, the government of Rwanda carried out a systematic campaign of extermination of citizens whom it declared to be national "enemies." In massacres conducted throughout the country, at least 800,000 persons lost their lives. The targets of this killing were, initially, actual or potential political critics of the government, particularly prominent members of opposition parties, and their families, characterized as "political enemies." Subsequently all members of the Tutsi minority ethnic group, regardless of age, gender, or ideas, were demonized by the ethnically Hutu-dominated regime as "historical enemies." The killing, which began in the capital city of Kigali and then expanded into a government-directed nationwide genocide, took place in the presence of international witnesses—including diplomats, aid workers, and even United Nations (UN) peacekeeping troops—who failed to prevent it, despite numerous warning signals, and who failed to stop it once it was underway.

The context in which the identification of "enemies" and the formulation of plans to exterminate them coalesced was one of intense international pressure on Rwanda's authoritarian single-party regime to "open up" to multiparty democracy and to negotiate with an armed group of refugees who had attacked from neighboring Uganda and proclaimed their right to return. These two initially unrelated developments burst onto the scene nearly simultaneously in late 1990. Over the course of the next four years, the two became inextricably interconnected in the "official" discourse of a

Rwandan government that grew ever more paranoid, defensive and extreme. The government propagated the notion that the two were elements of a single complex conspiracy meant to destroy the nation and reestablish the oppressive exploitation of the Hutu majority by a small group of Tutsi aristocrats that had existed in Rwanda under seven decades of colonialism, from the 1890s to 1961.

The independent Rwandan government that promulgated these fearsome images, however, was itself directed by a small elite group known popularly as the *akazu* (or "the family," in the sense of the mafia). This small circle of close associates of then president Juvenal Habyarimana exercised tight, essentially unchallenged control over all things political, military, administrative, and financial. From late 1990, this control was increasingly challenged (or, in the eyes of the akazu, threatened) by members of newly established opposition parties and incursions of the armed refugee group, the Rwandan Patriotic Front (RPF).

Opposition party adherents aggressively pursued the building of their party membership and the securing of government posts, often through intimidation and violence. Several parties, both the mainstream Mouvement Révolutionnaire National pour le Développement and its major opponents, including the Mouvement Démocratique Républicain, concentrated resources in their youth wings, relying on them to both encourage and intimidate potential members. Party activists also worked to intimidate, undermine, or openly attack local-level administrators of competing parties, angling to gain political capital by rendering them ineffective. By mid-1992, persistent challenges by political opponents had paralyzed administration of many locales, leaving residents free to defy authority.

As Rwanda plunged into widespread civil disobedience and political violence, its president faced continued incursions by the RPF, which in early 1992 seized a solid foothold in the north of the country. This accomplishment gained the RPF enough international leverage to force Habyarimana to the negotiating table at a series of internationally brokered peace talks held in Arusha, Tanzania in mid-1992. In July of that year, he was pressured to accept a cease-fire. In August 1992, he signed the first of a set of agreements called the Arusha Accords. The accords laid out the a new structure for the Rwandan government, which ensured power-sharing with the RPF as well as with internal opposition parties.

Although outside Rwanda these concessions generated goodwill (and, more important, economic aid), inside the country they were greeted with scorn. Keenly aware of the political cost of negotiating peace, Habyarimana disavowed them at home even as he touted them to please international donors.

During 1993 the "double" processes of negotiating peace with the RPF, while quietly tolerating and even committing acts of political and ethnic violence, intensified. In February, the RPF violated the cease-fire and killed hundreds of civilians. This transgression destroyed an alliance that had been forged between the RPF and the Rwandan opposition, ripped apart opposition parties, and catalyzed a "Hutu Power" coalition.

Proponents of Hutu Power sought to foster anti-Tutsi fear and hatred in order to bridge political differences. New doubts about the RPF's intent predisposed many to listen to the anti-RPF and anti-Tutsi rhetoric churned out incessantly by a new, akazu-controlled radio station, Radio Télévision Libre des Milles Collines (RTLM), which began broadcasting in April 1993. The station targeted the young, who were attracted by its trendy music, fast-paced format, and facetious commentary. Many adults paid little attention to it.

This changed dramatically, however, in 1993, when political tragedy struck in neighboring Burundi. On October 21, Burundi's first democratically elected president, a Hutu, was assassinated by his country's Tutsi-dominated army. Rapidly, Burundi's painstakingly built Tutsi-Hutu political coalition shattered, replaced by widespread violence. This enormous tragedy was all the Rwandan Hutu Power movement needed to convince their countrymen that to cooperate with the Tutsi-dominated RPF was to deliver themselves to into the jaws of the beast.

Distrust, belligerent rhetoric about the Hutu need for preemptive self-defense against all Tutsis, stepped-up militia training, and secret arms caches abounded in late 1993 and early 1994. International peacekeepers of the United Nations Assistance Mission for Rwanda (UNAMIR), deployed to Rwanda in December 1993 to assist with the implementation of the Arusha Accords, soon reported evidence of clandestine arming of civilians. As the weeks passed, UNAMIR's reports on covert civilian defense activities became increasingly direct, specific, and urgent. The reports received minimal reponse from UN headquarters, however. International attention was focused on the peace accords.

On the evening of April 6, 1994, as President Habyarimana returned from peace talks in Tanzania, his plane was attacked with missiles fired from a location near Kigali airport. Everyone aboard the plane was killed, including Habyarimana, his chief of staff, and the Burundi president. The identity of the assassins is not certain as of this writing. Within hours of the attack elite military units, including the presidential guard, moved through the streets of Kigali, setting up roadblocks, blockading prominent members of the political opposition inside their homes, and evacuating important Hutu Power figures. Later in the night, joined by regular army units and members of youth militias, they began assassinating opposition leaders and their families.

By the morning of April 7, armed soldiers and militia members bearing lists of named "enemies," most of them Hutu political leaders who had refused to embrace Hutu Power, as well as some prominent Tutsis, trolled Kigali's middle-class neighborhoods, breaking into houses and killing their targets. Meanwhile, key Hutu Power and akazu members gathered to strategize as well as to propose their presidential selections. UNAMIR officers urged the Rwandan military (Forces Armées Rwandaises, or FAR) to restore calm, even as they coped with the kidnapping, torture and murder of UN soldiers by the FAR. UNAMIR also struggled to convince decision makers back at the New York headquarters of the UN to broaden its mandate, to enable the organization to respond effectively to the highly charged situation.

By the evening of April 7, and over the next few days, with UNAMIR troops present but under stringent orders restricting their ability to respond, the killing spread from the capital city to select regions of the countryside where Hutu Power had been particularly active and organized. RTLM announcers incited this expansion, urging listeners to locate "enemies"— specifically, Tutsis and their moderate Hutu "accomplices" who were characterized as clandestine agents of the RPF—and to "defend" themselves vigorously. Reinforcing this message was the news that the RPF had recommenced hostilities.

Initially, many Hutus, having heard that the first wave of killings had targeted Hutu politicians, feared for their lives. But by the end of the first week, with the aid of the radio, the interim government disseminated the message that Hutus were not the target, and should not allow differences among them to distract them from attending to the "real" enemy—namely, all Tutsis.

Thus, within days of Habyarimana's assassination, Rwanda was plunged into a complex series of interlocked crises. The small country faced an internal power struggle among opportunistic and extremist political patrons who were willing to order their clients to commit massacres so as to outmaneuver their rivals. It faced abandonment and apathy from an international community that opted to evacuate most foreign nationals, limit the mandate and reduce the size of the UNAMIR force, and even lobby the UN (unsuccessfully) for a complete UNAMIR withdrawal. This disinterested international response created a permissive environment in which the massacres expanded into a full-fledged genocide.

In the days and weeks that followed the evacuations, Tutsi civilians were killed in large-scale massacres at public sites such as churches and schools where they had gathered spontaneously, seeking protection, or had

been ordered to gather. In a pattern of killing that replicated itself in many locales, hundreds of Tutsi civilians were concentrated at a particular site, detained or "protected" by police and/or soldiers for several days, then attacked with grenades, followed by close-range assault by a civilian crowd armed with machetes, clubs, hammers, and an occasional gun. As the killings multiplied and expanded, Rwandans who steadfastly opposed them—including some police, military and regional administrative officials—were isolated, intimidated, undermined, dismissed, or killed. In the hands of a small group of extremists, notably Colonel Théoneste Bagosora, the state apparatus was mobilized to exterminate an entire minority group.

As this complex catastrophe unfolded on the hillsides of Rwanda, the UN and prominent governments of the world focused not so much on halting it, but instead on how to refer to it. If what had now become the systematic massacre of Tutsis was acknowledged to be a genocide, then the UN, as well as countries that had been signatories to the 1948 Convention on the Prevention and Punishment of Genocide, were legally bound to intervene. But apart from France (which had helped to arm and train the FAR, and launched the unilateral Operation Turquoise in late June) those governments with the means to lead a UN intervention distanced themselves from the crisis.

Humanitarian agencies, however, did mobilize to assist Rwandan refugees (one group fleeing the genocide, and the other fleeing the advance of the RPF) who escaped to neighboring countries. It was not until June that the UN Security Council agreed to characterize the Rwandan situation as genocide. By this time, it was generally too late: more than 80 per cent of all victims had been killed in the first six weeks of the crisis.

As the RPF advanced successfully against the FAR in May and June, more civilians continued to die. Hutu officials stridently called for the "patriotic" elimination of any Tutsis who had managed to survive earlier massacres. The RPF, as it gained ground, massacred Hutu civilians along its line of advance, as well as behind the line.

On July 4, 1994, after intense fighting hill by hill and street by street, the RPF seized Kigali. In response, the genocidal "interim" government fled northward, then westward into Zaire. As it fled, the defeated government broadcast over the mobile RTLM radio station that the fate all Hutus had feared, a "Tutsi takeover," had now occurred. Hutus needed to run for their lives to avoid slaughter. Terrified, traumatized and fearing retribution, one million Rwandans, nearly all of them Hutus, fled in the course of a few days. The humanitarian catastrophe that ensued from their flight was poignant and captured on world television. The corpse-strewn country that they left behind was not to capture the world's attention until later, as the full extent of what had occurred was only gradually acknowledged.

MICHELE WAGNER

Rwanda: Genocide, Aftermath of

Although the pursuit of justice has dominated the political agenda within Rwanda since the genocide of 1994, other objectives, including security and economic recovery, as well as the quest for revenge, regional power, and financial gain through plunder, have also driven decision-making processes, as various factions within the Rwandan Patriotic Front (RPF) government have competed among themselves since gaining power.

In mid-July 1994, after three months of intensive combat, the Rwandan Patriotic Army (RPA), under the brilliant leadership of General Paul Kagame, conducted a massive military sweep northward that pushed the former government and its armed forces (the Forces Armées Rwandaises, or FAR) over the border into neighboring Zaire. With this final campaign, the RPF emerged victorious from a four-year war and established a transitional government. The new leaders immediately announced plans to apprehend those who had supported the former government's genocidal program and bring them to justice.

Explicitly marking its difference from the xenophobic former regime, the Tutsi-dominated RPF declared its intent to pursue pan-ethnic cooperation and followed up rapidly by naming Hutu politicians to key posts, including the presidency (Pasteur Bizimungu), the prime ministry (Faustin Twagiramungu), and the ministries of interior and justice. These men had been prominent members of the political opposition to the prior government and had themselves been targeted for killing in the purges of April 1994. Hence, in the early days of the RPF government there prevailed a climate of optimism, and a hope that cooperation, determination, and a shared quest for justice would lead Rwandans to rebuild their war-torn nation.

Responding positively to these declarations were members of the Rwandan Tutsi diaspora living in other parts of Africa and abroad, many of whom had sacrificed young family members and financial resources to the RPF cause. In 1994–1995, Tutsis first trickled, then poured, back into Rwanda. For some, it was the first time they had stepped on Rwandan soil for several years. For others, particularly the younger generation, their main link to Rwanda had been from its role as the setting of their parents' narratives of the past. Many of the incoming refugees harbored romantic or patriotic notions of a heroic return to the homeland. In time these newcomers, referred to as "Tutsi returnees," would become a dynamic force in emerging economic and political developments.

The elation of homecoming, however, soon gave way to shock and grief as a sense of the immensity and the horror of what had occurred in the months of April through July 1994 began to emerge.

Rwanda was a country literally strewn with rubble and corpses. Village after village harbored hastily dug mass graves, unburied corpses, the ground-up debris of human bones, and living survivors suffering from serious physical and psychological injuries. There were displaced and wandering adults and children who had been separated from their families in earlier torrents of refugee flight. In addition to this shocking human damage, there was also widespread destruction of the physical infrastructure: broken water systems, mangled electric lines, dynamited and collapsed public buildings, and cratered roads. Everywhere there was evidence of extensive pillage.

The immensity of the destruction was overwhelming, but even more disturbing for those of new RPF-governed Rwanda was the response to this tragedy by the international community. It appeared to many living inside Rwanda that the world was much more concerned about their countrymen who now lived outside the country: the primarily Hutu refugees.

Since April, desperate individuals bearing chilling tales of escape and survival had begun to straggle across the borders into neighboring countries. Initially, the outflow was comprised of those fleeing politically and ethnically targeted killing, many of whom were Tutsi. By late April, with the renewal of military conflict and the successful advance of the RPF through eastern Rwanda, there were new, much larger refugee outflows composed mostly of Hutus. On the single day of April 29, 1994, more than 200,000 individuals fled across a bridge at the border between Rwanda and Tanzania. By May, more than 470,000 refugees had fled to Tanzania, where the largest of the several refugee camps in the region, Benaco, became almost overnight the largest refugee camp in the world.

As aid agencies scrambled to cope with the refugee crisis on Rwanda's eastern border, the axis of military activity inside the country shifted westward and then northward. Fleeing before the RPF's final advance on July 13 and 14, 1994, more than 10,000 persons per hour crossed over the northwestern border into Goma, Zaire. This unprecedented outflow was met with inadequate aid personnel and provisions. By July 26, 1994, the Rwandan refugees at Goma, weakened by dysentery, exhaustion, malnutrition, diarrhea, and cholera, were dying at a rate of 2,000 persons each day. The Goma crisis ultimately claimed 46,000 lives.

The tragic plight of the refugees, in whose midst mingled former government and army officials and extremist Hutu militiamen, riveted international attention—and infuriated RPF supporters. From the

RPF perspective, "the international community" (which it rhetorically constructed as a single entity) had in April 1994 turned its back on those in imminent danger of genocide, callously evacuating foreign nationals while leaving their Rwandan colleagues behind to die. United Nations (UN) troops were prevented from intervening to stop genocidal killing, and now in July engaged in a gripping televised drama of rescuing the killers. Meanwhile, no significant international assistance was flowing to Tutsi survivors of a genocide that had claimed an estimated 800,000 to 1,000,000 lives. Instead, donor governments called for reconciliation.

Security and justice, not reconciliation, were the RPF government's most immediate objectives in the second part of 1994. Pursuing these goals with the means available to a civilian government was new for the RPF, which until recently had relied on the enforcement tactics available to a guerrilla army. Allegations of RPF atrocities, including torture and summary executions, had proliferated both before and during the fighting of 1994. Now as a government, the RPF had to make the transition to utilizing other tactics. By late 1994, although clear evidence suggests that it continued to rely on familiar tactics of summary justice, the new government was beginning to make use of arrest as well. Indeed, mass arrests, including the rounding up of all Hutu men in market-day sweeps and nocturnal attacks, became commonplace by late 1994. By October, an estimated 10,000 detainees populated the nation's official jails and prisons. Two months later, the number of detainees had risen to 15,000. Unofficial detention sites—including private houses, latrines, and shipping containers—proliferated, although the number of "unofficial" detainees could not reliably be estimated.

As the new government's pursuit of justice grew increasingly aggressive, making flagrant use of summary, extrajudicial, and inhumane tactics carried out by soldiers empowered in the civilian sphere, its official policy of pan-ethnic cooperation began to erode. In March 1995, the Hutu chief prosecutor of Kigali fled the country under threat of death after he denounced human rights violations by the army. Also in March, a prominent Hutu governor (Dr. Jean-Pierre Rwangabo) was assassinated after he protested against mass arrests by soldiers of civilians against whom there was little or no evidence. In August, the three most prominent Hutu ministers, the prime minister, the minister of interior, and the minister of justice, were forced out of office. This erosion extended beyond the small circle of elite politicians into the broader society, in a political discourse that became prevalent in 1995: for every victim there is a killer, and with at least a million Tutsi dead, there were at least as many Hutu killers.

This discourse, which facilitated the generalization that most Hutus were murderers or accomplices to murderers, came to rationalize widespread callousness toward the extrajudicial detention and killing of Hutus. For example, in April 1995, in forcibly closing a cluster of camps of internally displaced people in southwestern Rwanda, RPA soldiers repeatedly fired on Hutu crowds over the course of six days. In the largest of the camps, Kibeho, which had housed 120,000 residents, international eyewitnesses, including UN soldiers assigned to bury the bodies, estimated 8000 dead—a figure later revised, under RPF pressure, to 2000. The official government death toll was 360, many of whom it claimed had died as a result of their own panic in a rainstorm-induced stampede.

Coinciding with the camp closures and an August 1995 expulsion of select refugees from Zaire, the arrest rate increased to 2,000 per month. This swamped the nation's jails and prisons, which had an official capacity of 12,250, but held 62,000 by the end of the year. Particular prisons, such as Gitarama, which housed 7,000 inmates in cellblocks built for a maximum capacity of 600, became notorious for neglect, illness, and death. Likewise, communal lock-ups, when filled far beyond their maximum capacity, became sites of suffocation. In 1995, at least 2,300 people died in government detention.

Despite aggressive political rhetoric emphasizing the pursuit of justice, as 1995 drew to a close not one of 62,000 detainees had been tried. Most detainees continued to be held without charge or judicial file. In its defense, the government explained that it lacked the resources to unblock its paralyzed judicial system and to create humane conditions in its prisons. It pointed out that its priority was to assist the genocide's Tutsi victims, not the Hutu killers, whose plight the humanitarian relief organizations had amply addressed. By the end of 1995, approximately $2.5 billion had been spent to support the refugee camps. In contrast, $572 million had supported programs inside Rwanda. Nevertheless, this callous response to the horrendous conditions in which primarily Hutu detainees who had never been charged were forced to exist convinced Hutus both inside and outside Rwanda that the Tutsi-dominated government was bent on revenge. Some two million refugees remained in camps outside Rwanda, unwilling to return home.

With so many of its citizens outside Rwanda, including most members of the former government and army, security became the dominant issue by 1996. Intelligence sources reported that in Zairian camps former soldiers and militiamen were rearming and training new recruits. Their intent, it was believed, was to conduct cross-border raids aimed at gaining a foothold inside the country—precisely the tactic used by the

RPF in its rebel days to force the then government into negotiations. Cross-border raids and RPA reprisals centered on the northwestern regions of Gisenyi and Ruhengeri, adjacent to the Goma camps. There, during the course of 1996, infiltrators killed at least 278 persons. The RPA responded with mass arrests, such as the detention of some 10,000 on a hilltop without food or water for several days in August. It also conducted search-and-cordon operations during which 600 persons, mostly civilians, died. Another element that became characteristic of this conflict was attacks on communal lock-ups, which involved tossing grenades or shooting into crowded jail cells.

By late 1996, the Rwandan government made the decision to stop the cross-border threat at its source. Under the guise of a Zairan rebel movement called the Alliance des Forces démocratiques pour la libération du Congo-Zaire (AFDL), the RPA launched series of attacks on Rwandan Hutu refugee camps inside Zaire. This attack quickly expanded into broader conflict in both Rwanda and Zaire.

Within Rwanda, the mass return of approximately 1.7 million refugees from both Zaire and Tanzania (which seized the opportunity to expel 500,000 Rwandans from its camps) in the two months between November 1996 and January 1997 fueled the existing conflict in the northwest and exacerbated the crisis within the prisons. By January 1997, arbitrary arrests and killings in the northwest had escalated into a daily occurrence. Large-scale massacres of unarmed civilians—such as those that took the lives of 1,853 civilians in the neighboring Ruhengeri villages of Nkuli and Nyamutera in early May, and another that took the lives of 120 persons inside a church in Karago, Gisenyi—seemed so strikingly reminiscent of the events of April 1994 that even the most optimistic Rwandans began to abandon hope of reconciliation. In prisons, the number of detainees rose from 83,000 in October 1996 to 130,000 one year later. With international assistance, the nationwide prison capacity was increased, but only to 17,000. Detainees continued to die at an exorbitant rate, about 3,300 per year. Although the judicial system had begun to function, only 320 detainees had been tried by the end of the year, of which one-third received death sentences. Their public executions commenced in early 1998.

Within Zaire, having attacked refugee camps with relative impunity, the RPA and the AFDL penetrated farther into the vast, resource-rich eastern part of the country, ostensibly to apprehend the fleeing ex-FAR, and ultimately to combat the army of the discredited Zairian dictator Mobutu Sese Seko. With careful military and political tactics, and allegedly at the cost of hundreds of thousands of civilian lives, the allied RPA/AFDL managed to seize control of lucrative mining regions, and ultimately the nation itself, which it renamed the Democratic Republic of Congo. In this way, by 1998, Rwanda, with a per capita gross domestic product of $190 and itself still struggling to recover from war, managed to conduct a protracted armed struggle within the borders of its enormous and resource-laden neighbor—a war which, as of this writing, has continued.

With input from an eclectic assortment of sources and partners, in 1998 Rwanda was actively engaged in rebuilding its economy and infrastructure several regions of the country. In July 2002, the presidents of Rwanda and the Democratic Republic of Congo signed a peace agreement. In October of that year, Rwanda pulled the last of its troops out of the Democratic Republic of Congo.

MICHELE WAGNER

S

Sa'adians: *See* Morocco: Sa'dians.

Sadat: *See* Egypt: Sadat, Nationalism, 1970–1981.

Sadiq Al-Mahdi: *See* Sudan: Sadiq al-Mahdi Regime, 1980s.

Sahara: Peoples of the Desert

The economic basis for life in the Sahara, although constantly changing in response to ecological crises and political tensions, has been traditionally twofold: pastoralism (in camels, goats, and sheep) and trade. Some oases support permanently sedentarized populations who practice oasis (irrigation) gardening; many of these settled farming peoples on oases formerly were subjugated peoples, who until recently gave tribute to nomadic noble and tributary groups.

The population of the Sahara is about 2.5 million, living in oases or in the moister highlands. The main population groups are Arab, Moor, Berber, and Tubu/Teda. Constant fluctuations in ethnic/cultural identities, however, make it most useful to consider these distinctions primarily as linguistic. The Arab-speaking peoples live mainly on the northern edge of the desert, major groups being the Bedouins of the Libyan Desert and the Chamba of Algeria. In the west (southern Morocco, Mauritania, and parts of Mali) the majority language is Hassaniyya, an Arabic dialect with a strong Berber influence. The Hassaniyya speakers called Moors are internally divided between the *bidan*, who traditionally had a higher social status, and vassals, with the *haratin* (freemen) or former slaves on oases, in the lower positions. The Moors constitute 30 per cent of Mauritania's total population, and the mixed Moor haratin make up 40 per cent. The term *Moor* derives from the people and country known in Roman times as Mauretania, which comprised the present country of Morocco with the Western Sahara and the coast of the present Republic of Mauritania as far as its capital, Nouakchott.

The Arabs conquered Egypt in 640BCE, but they made no effort before 670 BCE to penetrate farther west than Libya. North Africa was not subdued by the caliphate until the end of the century. In 712BCE a majority Berber army crossed into Spain. By 756BCE the Islamic state of Al-Andalus had been constituted in Spain by an Umayyad dynasty of Syrian descent. The newcomers, to whom the term *Moors* was now more broadly extended, included not only Berbers from northern Africa but also Syrians, Yemenis, and Jews. A further Berber invasion by the Almoravids lasted only half a century. In its turn it was overthrown by a new Berber group, the Almohads, in 1145. Thereafter the Christian kingdoms—first Portugal, and then Spain—slowly eroded Moorish power, culminating in the fall of Granada and the unification of present-day Spain in 1492. In the following year all Jews who would not convert to Christianity were expelled, followed by the expulsion of the Moors in 1502. The Moors who were expelled from the kingdom of Granada first migrated to their ancestral homelands, of which Fez was the center. Thus, the relatively narrow original sense of the word *Moor* was extended over time, as a gloss, to designate peoples who were distinct but related in their connection with Saharan migrations and Islam.

Many Berber groups (Shluh or Tashelhayt, Tamazight, and Znaga) live on the desert edge in the north and west. One group, the Zwaya of the western Sahara, preserved their Berber language and the memory of their heroic past. By the fifteenth or sixteenth centuries, *zawaya* (or *zwaya*) became the name

1309

commonly given to those descendants of the Almoravids, the Berbers of the western Sahara, who yielded their status as warriors to the incoming Arabs of the Banu Hassan, preferring instead the pursuit of Islam. Out of the original genealogies of the Zanaga or Znaga (the Berber form of Sanhaja), many of which appear to have been matrilineal, developed the lineages of religious scholars who traced their ancestry back to the Prophet Muhammad and his companions, just as the Almoravids had claimed descent from the kings of the Yemen. In this way they established themselves and their clansmen and descent groups in a hierarchical Saharan society of Arab warriors, Berber clerics, and servile cultivators. The largest group of Berber-speaking peoples in the Sahara is the Tuareg, of which there are between one-half and one million. The Tuareg cover the region from the Niger River Bend in the west to the Azben (Air) highlands in present-day Niger in the east, with some small Tuareg groups living beyond these borders. They can be divided into the northern groups—namely, the Kel Ahaggar and Kel Ajjer (mostly in Algeria)—and the southern groups, consisting of the Kel Adrar near the Niger River Bend, the Ioullimmiden to their east, and the Kel Air or Kel Azben. Of these, the Ioullimmiden has the largest population.

Evidence from geology, archaeology, and rock art suggests that the Sahara before 8000 years ago was wetter; rivers flowed, and farming and fishing were practiced. Rock art portrays these activities, and also depicts cattle raising and charioteers. These latter are widely believed by scholars (Bovill 1956; Briggs 1960; Bates 1970) to be the Garamantes, referred to in Greco-Roman classical literature. Archaeological evidence such as artifacts like metals and beads in the tomb of an ancient Berber queen named Tin Hinan in present-day Algeria indicate the importance of early matrilineal ancestress culture heroines and trade with the Mediterranean and the Sudanic worlds. Heinrich Barth (1857), Camille Jean (1909), and Lord Francis Rodd (1926) provide secondary source material, which at times presents conflicting views of some early origins and migrations. But most authors agree on the existence, at an early date throughout North Africa, of proto-Hausa, Sudanic peoples much farther north than their present distribution, up into the Sahara. These people, the Gobirawa, were an aristocratic division of Hausa-speaking groups, and their domain was known as Gobir, located in and around the Air. In addition, there were also at that time some Sanhaja (western Muleththemin), in the region. Both these groups were in the region of Air before the arrival of the first Tuareg groups. Ibn Battuta's accounts, as well as those of Barth and Rodd, maintain that the Gobirawa were later either driven back into the Sudan region or became

servile groups of the more nomadic conquerors, incorporated into the Tuareg groups as tributary (*imghad*) groups.

Leo Africanus regarded both Ahaggar and Air Saharan massifs as inhabited by the Lemta groups. The migration of Lemta in late classical times is intimately connected with the history of the Air Tuareg. The Azgar represent the old Lemta stock in the northern part of the area. The central African histories of Leo Africanus placed them in Bornu in the early eras. The southern end of the area extending to the Sudan between Lake Chad and Damargu (Zinder, in present-day Niger) was lost to the Tuareg under progressive ethnic pressure from the east, driving the boundary of Tuareg westward and forcing the Lemta to find room in the west for their expansion. Some of the latter entered Air from the south; others went on to occupy Tademekka and drove the inhabitants westward. Rodd maintains that the Lemta movement was of long duration and directly involved the first invasion of Air by the Tuareg; it took place south and then west, and not, as Barth maintained, southeastward, directly from North Africa (Rodd 1926, p.359). Before these movements took place, Ahaggar was held by a Hawara group. Thus Air, first occupied by a group of Lemta from the southeast, was then invaded by another wave of Tuareg from the north, of Hawarid stock. Therefore, by the time of Leo Africanus, Air was largely already occupied by the same ethnic group as Ahaggar, and like the latter was described as held by the "Targa people."

It has been suggested that the first Tuareg to come to the Air massif of the Sahara were caravan traders attracted by the region's excellent grazing grounds. The invasions, however, cannot be dated precisely, but sources such as the *Agadez Chronicle* (a compilation of Arabic manuscripts kept by the current Sultan of Agadez) suggest that as early as the seventh century there were extensive migrations of pastoral Berbers, including the two important tribal groups of Lemta and Zarawa. The Zarawa reached the Lake Chad country, where the state of Kanem Bornu was created. At that time, pastoral Berbers also arrived in Air, where new states were created. The name of one of them, the Hausa state of Gobir, existed up to the twelfth century.

The Tubu (Teda) peoples inhabit the eastern part of the desert, in Kawar (Niger) and northern Chad; their name means "man from Tibesti." They are a nomadic and seminomadic people in the present-day states of Chad, Libya, Niger, and Sudan, and are divided into two main groups based on dialect: the Teda and the Dazaga. The Tubu/Teda reside above the eighteenth parallel of the African continent. Most Tubu/Teda are concentrated in the southeastern central Sahara, notably in the Tibesti massif in northern Chad, and frequent the Tenere region of the Niger Sahara for trading with the Tuareg; they are predominantly Muslim. Historically, they also lived on the northern edge; thus, they inhabited the Kufra Oasis until the nineteenth century, and had a strong presence in Fezzan (both in Libya). The Dazaga are closely related to the people to the south of the Sahara in language and culture.

The political history of these groups is the history of encounters between the Saharan region and its desert-side neighbors. Early kingdoms south of the Sahara, like Ghana in the west and the Zaghawa (nomadic peoples of Chad and points east) probably had a strong presence in the Sahara. The desert also served as a refuge for political and religious groups. Farther east, the new kingdoms south of the Sahara stretched across the desert. During the last half of the thirteenth century, the central Sahara, as well as Fezzan to the north, were ruled by the king (*mai*) of Kanem. In the eastern Sahara west of the Nile Valley, outside control was limited, and the Tubu/Teda clans ruled unchallenged. Only in the nineteenth century was the region brought into a more united framework, through a religious movement, the Senoussi Sufi brotherhood, which worked among the Bedouin from the 1840s and later led resistance movements against Turkish and French rule in parts of the Sahara.

SUSAN RASMUSSEN

Further Reading

Barth, Heinrich. *Travels and Discoveries in North Central Africa*, vols. 1–5. London: Longman, Brown, Green, Longmans, Roberts, 1857.

Bates, Oric. *The Eastern Libyans*. London: Frank Cass, 1970.

Bovill, E. W. "The Camel and the Garamantes," *Antiquity*, no. 30 (1956): 19–21.

Brett, Michael, and Elizabeth Fentress. *The Berbers*. Oxford: Blackwell, 1996.

Briggs, Lloyd Cabot. *Tribes of the Sahara*. Cambridge, Mass.: Harvard University Press, 1960.

Cornevin, Robert. *Histoire de l'Afrique*, vol. 1. Paris, 1962.

Jean, Lt. Camille. *Les Touareg du Sud-Est (l'Air), Leur rôle dans la politique saharienne*. Paris: Larose, 1909.

Rodd (Rennel of Rodd), Lord Francis. *People of the Veil*. Costerhut, Netherlands: Anthropological Publications, 1966.

Sahara: Salt: Production, Trade

The importance of salt in the history of the Sahara cannot be overestimated. It has been variously responsible for the growth of cities and the rise and fall of more than one empire, and a central component in the gold and slave trades as well as a vital element in the spread of Islam south and west across the continent. A daily intake of salt is as essential for life as is water; without either people cannot live more than a very few days. For the hunter-gatherer, whose diet contained significant quantities of meat and/or fish, the ingestion of additional salt was not necessary, as animals' flesh contains a sufficiency of sodium chloride. With the movement toward more sedentary lifestyles, made possible with the advent of crop cultivation, farmers had reduced access to meat and so a need arose for alternative sources of salt.

Salt has been produced in the Sahara for at least 2,500 years and, despite the lack of archaeological evidence to substantiate the claim, salt production is thought to significantly predate this. Such production has also always been widespread across the Sahara, and centers of production can be found from Mauritania to Sudan. The two major methods of production are mining and evaporation (both natural and artificial), which tend to occur in mutual exclusivity of one another. The widespread availability of salt across the Sahara has meant that since the demand existed, initially from the forests and savanna to the south where it was not readily available, there has been a need to produce it.

Where possible, salt is always first produced through mining; this is only possible if the salt is present in sufficient quantities and of the right constitution. The reason for the preeminence of mining is twofold: first, digging slabs of salt directly from the earth is by far the easiest means of production, and second, rock salt is of a higher quality than other kinds of salt (e.g. those produced through evaporation). There are even instances where coastal dwellers who had the means of processing salt through evaporation did instead pay for the importation of rock salt. A number of salt mines are justly famous for their antiquity and size. The earliest salt mine for which definite records exist is Idjil, in Mauritania, which has been active since at least the eighth century. Of equal renown is Taghaza, Mali, described by Ibn Battuta as an established center of

Timbuktu, arrival of a salt caravan. © SVT Bild/Das Fotoarchiv.

salt production by the mid-fourteenth century. The huts and the mosque of the settlement were, he notes, all made from blocks of salt. The town was destroyed in the sixteenth century and replaced by Taoudenni, in the same area to the north of Timbuktu, as the region's leading salt producer.

Evaporation is the other method of salt production widely employed across the Sahara. In several locations (for instance, Bilma, Niger) this is achieved through the "farming" of natural salt pans—large, circular briny depressions from which the salt is harvested as it is left behind following solar evaporation. Where such pans are not present other methods have been developed. In Manga, Niger, and Darfur, Sudan, evaporation takes place in conjunction with the filtration of saline-laden earth through ash. This residue is then subjected to partial evaporation and the remaining brine is boiled. This method of production is the least favored both because of the need for fuel (a scarcity in the desert) to aid the evaporation process and because the end product is of a generally poor quality.

Due to the impossibility of life without it, there is little doubt that salt was one of the earliest goods traded in and across the Sahara. Although as the trade developed it became instrumental in the growth of empires, it was also active on a small-scale local level, with individuals traveling relatively short distances in order to collect or produce as much as they required for their own use. Although archaeological evidence of the early salt trade is hard to come by, a 2,500-year-old account from Herodotus talks about the existence of a 450-mile "salt road" that connected the salt mines to the trading center at Timbuktu, that place in the Western imagination that marked the end of the known world and was known, if at all, through the stories of its unparalleled wealth.

The variety of goods that moved along the trade routes and were exchanged for salt is staggering: cowrie shells, ostrich feathers, glass, kola nuts, slaves, and gold. Prices that could be charged may seem hard to believe, and perhaps there is an element of hyperbole in some of the travelers' tales, such as salt being exchanged weight for weight with gold, but then again perhaps not. The introduction of the camel to the region had an enormous impact on the trade scene, with the distances that could now be traversed growing considerably. With a substantial increase in trading activity, a number of urban centers grew where previously there had just been a regular water supply.

Although other factors also had a role, the salt trade was at least partially responsible for the rise of such empires such as Ghana, Mandingo (Mali), and Songhai. Ghana established itself as being of some regional importance in about 650, and in its early history the rulers of the state decided to impose a tax on goods that passed through its territory, of which salt was one of the largest. The decision to charge a transit tax, which was only made when they felt strong enough to enforce it, quickly made them both rich and unpopular with merchants who, however, had little choice but to pay it. The Mandingo empire, which rose to prominence at the start of the thirteenth century, managed to do so by controlling the salt trade from Taghaza. In the Songhay Empire (c.1450–1590) salt was used for currency, resulting in the location of the salt mines being the kingdom's most jealously guarded secret. And in spite of the rise and fall of these individual kingdoms the importance of the salt trade itself was hardly diminished until well into the twentieth century, when various technologies conspired to overrun the ancient ways.

EAMONN GEARON

See also: **Sijilmasa, Zawila: Trans-Saharan Trade; Tuareg: Takedda and Trans-Saharan Trade.**

Further Reading

Adshead, S. A. M. *Salt and Civilization* New York: St. Martin's Press, 1992.
Bovill, E.W. *The Golden Trade of the Moors,* 2nd ed. London: Oxford University Press, 1968.
Kurlansky, Mark. *Salt: A World History.* New York: Walker, 2002.
Lovejoy, Paul E. *Salt of the Desert Sun.* Cambridge: Cambridge University Press, 1986.

Sahara: Trans-Saharan Trade

Studies of trans-Saharan trade from the development of the Iron Age in Western Africa to the end of the 1700s focus on the connectivity between northern Africa and the West African Sahelian societies of Ghana, Mali, and Songhay; the role of Islam as a unifying factor among African peoples north and south; and the discrete nature of the products traded, of which gold, slaves, and salt were the most notable.

The long run of relations between the peoples of the Sahara and those of the adjoining Sahel are characterized by periods of cooperation alternating with competition. In the background to human affairs lies the enlarging nature of the desert and the recoiling nature of the savanna and Sahel environments, beginning at the end of the post-Pleistocene pluvial, now dated generally at 3000BCE. Where sedentary black people had previously inhabited north to about 20 degrees latitude, Berber-speaking nomads progressively enlarged their domain at the expense of sedentary environments as desert life pushed south in a general desiccation of Africa between 15 and 25 degrees latitude. These

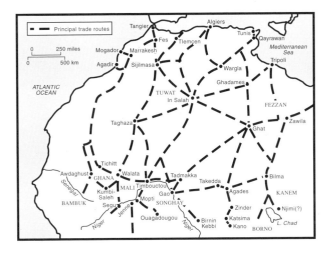

Trans–Saharan trade, ninth–nineteenth centuries.

environmental changes played in favor of the nomads, the enlargement of whose realms were further facilitated by the introduction of the camel, first to North Africa and then the entire Sahara, during late Roman times. Trade between the two broadly distinct African regions and peoples of North and West Africa, is thus set against a general framework of environmental change and more local social relations between adjoining peoples, nomad and sedentary Africans, at the moving southern margins of the desert.

Before Islam, trade between tropical Africa and North Africa across the Sahara was effectively non-existent. The largely unknown history of relations between black sedentary folk of the Sahel and Berber-speaking nomads of the Sahara was interrupted by the emergence of Islam, which penetrated partially and differentially throughout the Sahara and the Sahelian fringe of tropical Africa during an initial period of Islamization, which can be dated from the 660s to the emergence of the Almoravid Islamic movement in the 1030s. With the eruption of the Almoravid movement among the Sanhaja people of the southwestern Sahara, Islam became more codified and widespread among Saharan peoples. Islam is significant because it unified geographically and socially disparate peoples and unification furthered trade.

In the east, the route through Zawila became the primary conduit by which black African slaves were traded north, especially with Ifriqiya (Tunisia) and the eastern Islamic lands, for horses south. So it was that in the Chad Basin, Kanem arose as a slave-raiding state connected to North Africa and today's Middle East through Zawila and Tripoli. As first noted in the writings of Herodotus, the Libyan (Berber) peoples of the northern fringe of the Sahel raided for slaves among their neighbors still farther south, a practice that continued until the early 1900s.

In the west, the interest was on gold. In the earliest Islamic empire, the Umayyad, considerable progress was made tying the newly conquered Maghrib to Sudanic peoples trading in gold. Ghana, first identified in the Arabic sources in the 830s by al-Fazari and al-Khwarizmi, was the likely destination, although nothing is sure about places in western Africa at this early date. The last in 'Uqba's line, great-grandson 'Abd al-Rahman, final Umayyad (and first Abbasid) governor of the Maghrib (747–754), ordered wells dug along trade routes running south from Morocco to the Sudan. The last of these was about 16 days' south from the Draa River Valley.

The earliest routes across the Sahara from Morocco crossed territory, largely in Mauritania, covered by light grasses in which water was relatively plentiful. This route allowed connections between the Maghrib and the Senegal River to flourish, and may well have led to the conversion of the people north of the Senegal River and the intervening Sanhaja nomads of the western Sahara to Islam early on, before significant cross-desert relations began with Ghana. The end of this route landed caravaniers in Tarkrur, in the Senegal River lowlands. What was traded here is unknown, but the sedentary people of Takrur became the core of the modern Tukolor, as they have become known. The Takarir (people of Takrur) were Islamized as early as, or earlier than, the nomads to the north of them; they strengthened Islam outward from their far western homeland to other peoples north and east of them, and formed the core for the construction of modern Senegalese identity.

Equally early was a route from Ghana leading east to Gao and then northeast through the Air and Tibesti highlands of Niger and Libya to the Egyptian oases of Kharga and Dakhla. Described in early Arabic sources, this route was then prohibited by Ahmad ibn Tulun, the Abbasid ruler of Egypt between 868 and 884, perhaps because of its environmental hazards or because of raiders plundering camel loads of goods. It was, in any case, to Sijilmasa's benefit that the Ghana-Egypt route dried up.

The main trade route connecting Sijilmasa and Ghana ran due south from Morocco, from the Draa Valley to Awdaghust and then onward to Ghana. The route, more dangerous than the Mauritanian, was shorter: Ghana lay some 50–60 stages, or daily marches and stops, from Sijilmasa and some 10–15 stages south of Awdaghust. Eight stages passed through land without water. Caravans organized like fleets in the desert, composed of hundreds of camels bearing trade goods in both directions, are described in the medieval literature. These were sent out by Sijilmasa merchants on schedules with, as the tenth century writer Ibn Hawqal informs us, letters of credit of very high value. In 951, Ibn Hawqal estimated the revenue of the independent emir of Sijilmasa at approximately 400,000 dinars, half the annual income of the Maghrib. Undoubtedly, most of this value was in gold.

The King of Ghana extracted levies on salt and other goods coming in and going out of Ghana; he may have held the trade in gold nuggets (as opposed to gold dust) as a monopoly. Ghana, presumably at the site known as Kumbi Saleh in southeastern Mauritania (excavated by Mauny and others in 1949–1951 and 1970) was a break-in-bulk point in the trade in gold. Gold dust and gold nuggets, culled from placer deposits in the streams of the Guinea Highlands and particularly along the Bambouk gold fields in the upper Senegal River watershed, were brought to Ghana by black African traders, ancestors of the Juula (Dyula) merchant class, and traded in the Sahelian capital for salt, copperware, cloth, and spices brought south along the trade route. Slaves, ivory, cowrie shells (used as currency in the Sudan) and ambergis accompanied the movement of gold north, but in contrast with Kanem, far to the east, the trade in slaves out of Ghana appears to have been distinctly secondary to gold. However, al-Idrisi, writing nearly a century after al-Bakri, notes that Ghana (and Takrur and Silla, a city in the Senegalese lowlands converted to Islam by Takrur) raided people living in stateless societies to the south and sold them to Maghribi traders. Likewise, gold, some 18 days' distant, was from lands probably not directly controlled by Ghana, although clearly within its sphere of influence.

Salt—not gold—may lie at the urban genesis of Ghana some centuries before Ghana's connections with northern Africa over gold. Rock salt, absent throughout the Sahel and West Africa generally, is prevalent at a number of sites in the south central Sahara. The most prominent of these was Teghaza, in the center of the desert, toward which a caravan route was directed to pass and from which Maghribi traders carried slabs of salt south to Ghana.

By the thirteenth century, Ghana had passed into oblivion and the focus of trans-Saharan trade pushed east to Malinke-speaking chiefdoms incorporated into the Mali empire. By the early 1200s, the Soso, earlier a tributary people of the Soninke, ruled Ghana; they were defeated by a Malinke warrior destined for greatness, Sundiata Keita. One hundred fifty years after the emergence of the Almoravids, ancient Mali emerged as a second great empire of the western Sudan. New sources of gold in the Bure region in the upper Niger had opened up, favoring Mali's location in that area; the merger of its two parent chiefdoms,

Do (Daw) and Malal, may have yielded overwhelming strength.

Songhay was the last of the great empires of the western Sudan. In the late 1300s, Mali had been invaded by Tuareg raiders; the former allies of Mali sacked and held Timbuktu for a generation. As in the past, the nomads attacked along the edges of empire in a time of weakness but did not penetrate beyond the fringe of the desert. In this human ecotone arose Sunni 'Ali, who, with the help of Niger fishermen, chased out the Tuareg and established a new polity along the Niger Bend. His successor, Askiya Muhammad (r. 1493–1528), established Songhay power from the borders of modern Nigeria in the east to Senegal in the west. Songhay power, greatest in the 1500s, was eventually eclipsed by forces new and different to the dynamics of a realm of society and trade that had endured for 1000 years. In 1591, Timbuktu was invaded by Moroccans themselves, intruders from the Maghrib, who attempted to conquer the trans-Saharan trade for themselves in an attempt that petered out over 30 years of fragile control over Timbuktu. Timbuktu, however, came to radiate cultural strength as a city where Muslims—both Berber and Sudani—lived and worked together. By this time Europeans, previously entirely unknown in the western African scheme of things, had established footholds along the West African coast.

JAMES A. MILLER

See also: **Sahara: Salt: Production, Trade; Sijilmasa, Zawila, Trans-Saharan Trade; Tuareg: Traders, Raiders, and the Empires of Mali and Songhay; Tuareg: Takedda and Trans-Saharan Trade.**

Further Reading

Brett, Michael. "Islam and Trade in the Bilad al-Sudan, Tenth-Eleventh Century A.D." *Journal of African History*, no. 24 (1983): 431–440.

Garrard, Timothy. "Myth and Metrology: The Early Trans-Saharan Gold Trade." *Journal of African History*, no. 23 (1982): 443–461.

Levtzion, Nehemia. "The Sahara and the Sudan from the Arab Conquest of the Maghrib to the Rise of the Almoravids." In *The Cambridge History of Africa*, vol. 2, edited by J. D. Fage. Cambridge: Cambridge University Press, 1978.

Levtzion, Nehimia, and J. F. Hopkins (eds.). *Corpus of Early Arabic Sources for West African History*. Cambridge: Cambridge University Press, 1981.

Saifawa Dynasty: *See* Borno (Bornu), Sultanate of: Saifawa Dynasty: Horses, Slaves, and Warfare.

Salafiyya: *See* **Egypt: Salafiyya, Muslim Brotherhood.**

Salah al-Din/Saladin (1138–1193)
Sultan of Egypt

Saladin (Salah al-Din Yusuf Ibn Ayyub, 1138–1193), whose name means "bounty of religion," was born in Tikrit, Mesopotamia, in 1138 to Kurdish parents. His father was an official of the Seldjuk Turks. While still an infant, his parents moved to Ba'albak in Syria (now Lebanon) where his father served as commander of the garrison. They later settled in Damascus.

A devout Sunni Muslim, he left his theological career in 1164 when his uncle, Skirkuh, ordered the young Saladin to accompany him on a military campaign against the unorthodox Shiite Fatimid Caliphate in Egypt, and the occasional ally of the Latin Christian Kingdom of Jerusalem. In 1168, Shawar, the Fatimid Wazir of Egypt, sought the support of Nur ed-Din, then the Sultan of Damascus, against the Christian King Almaric of Jerusalem. Nur ed-Din sent Shirkuh and Saladin defeated all before them, entering Cairo on January 8, 1169. Three months later Shirkuh died, leaving his office to his commander and nephew, Saladin. Two years later, when the last Fatimid caliph, al-Adid, died, Saladin seized control of the government of Egypt and founded the Sunnite Muslim Ayyubid dynasty (1171–1250).

Even before the Egyptian campaign, Saladin had demonstrated his capacity to rule. He had been appointed by Nur ed-Din as chief of police in Damascus, where he supposedly levied a tax from the earnings of prostitutes. A contemporary account of Saladin attests to his resolve to be tough-minded, warning the thieves of Syria to "go softly" or Saladin would cut off their hands. Other accounts write of the austere piety of Saladin who, at his appointment, abandoned "wine-drinking" and "frivolity" so that he might "assume the dress of religion." When he succeeded Shirkuh as ruler of Cairo, he demonstrated his political aptitude, winning over the populace by distributing to the poor money amassed by his uncle. He methodically removed the Fatimid troops from Cairo, and ruthlessly suppressed any conspiracies against his authority that emanated from the palace.

When Nur ed-Din, sultan of Damascus, died in 1174, Saladin was summoned by its emirs to replace his ten-year-old son and heir, al-Salih, in the expectation that Saladin, in control of Cairo and Damascus, could erode the entrenched power of the Christian Franks in Palestine. Supported by the Damascene army, Saladin conquered Muslim Syria and northern Mesopotamia as far as Mosul. The caliph in Baghdad accepted his defeat and confirmed Saladin as sultan of Egypt and Syria. He could now mobilize his armies to surround Palestine from east and west. He was the only possible Muslim leader, the *mujahid,* to organize a jihad (holy war) against the Christian Franks.

On July 4, 1187, he defeated the forces of the Christian king of Jerusalem, Guy de Lusignan (*r.*1186–1192), and his allies at the Battle of the Horns of Hattin. The king and Renaud de Chatillon, Prince of Antioch (*r.*1153–1160), lord of the stronghold of Krak des Chevaliers, who had recklessly plundered Muslim caravans, were captured; Renaud was executed. On October 2, 1187, without pillage or looting, Saladin entered Jerusalem on the anniversary of Muhammad's ascent to heaven from the Dome of the Rock, ending 88 years of Christian control by the Franks. His humane treatment of the Frankish inhabitants was in sharp contrast to their treatment of the Muslims massacred in 1099 when the city fell to the Crusaders. His advisors urged him to demolish the Church of the Holy Sepulcher, but he simply closed it for three days, only to reopen it to pilgrims (for a fee).

Although he retained control of the interior of Palestine and the city of Jerusalem, Saladin ceded the important coastal towns between Acre and Jaffa to the Crusaders, who maintained a distinct advantage by their fleet, which dominated the Mediterranean. He failed to retain Acre, which fell to the Crusaders in July 1191 after the victory of the English king Richard I (the Lionhearted) and his allies at the Battle of Arsuf. He concluded an armistice with Richard in 1192 that demonstrated the extent of his achievements, for the Crusaders were left in control of the coastal castles along the shores of Palestine.

Saladin lived less than six years after his dramatic capture of Jerusalem. On March 3, 1193, he died in Damascus, where his tomb, adjacent to the Ummayyad Mosque, remains a place of pilgrimage. Deeply devout, he consolidated Sunni Islam in Egypt and the Middle East and revived the pilgrimage, the *Hajj,* to Mecca, but his authority rested in the army rather than the religious elite, the *'ulama.* Despite his confrontations with the Crusaders, his empire prospered from peace, his support of learning, and the revival of Indian Ocean trade. His last words record his career with modest brevity: "In the end I did go with my uncle. He conquered Egypt, then died. God then placed in my hands the power that I have never expected."

ROBERT COLLINS

See also: **Egypt: Ayyubid Dynasty, 1169–1250.**

Biography

Born in Tikrit, Mesopotamia in 1138. Gave up his theological career to accompany his uncle on a military campaign in 1164. Captured Cairo in 1169. Seized control of Egypt and founded the Sunnite Muslim Ayyubid dynasty in 1171. Conquered Muslim Syria and northern Mesopotamia after being named ruler of Syria in 1174. On July 4, 1187, defeated the forces of the Christian King of Jerusalem, Guy de Lusignan, at the Battle of the Horns of Hattin. On October 2, 1187, entered Jerusalem, ending 88 years of Christian control of the city. Died in Damascus on March 3, 1193.

Further Reading

Ehrenkreutz, Andrew S. *Saladin*. Albany: State University of New York Press, 1972.

Gibb, Sir Hamilton R. *The Life of Saladin: From the Works of 'Imam ad-Din and Baha' ad-Din*. Oxford: Clarendon Press, 1973.

Lane-Poole, Stanley. *Saladin and the Fall of the Kingdom of Jerusalem*, 1898. Reprint, London: Darf, 1985.

Salt: *See* Iron Age (Later): East Africa: Salt; Iron Age (Later): East Africa: Trade.

Samkange, Rev. D. T. (*c.*1893–1956)
Methodist Minister and Pioneer Black Nationalist

Mushore Samkange was born in about 1893 near the modern town of Chinoye, in northern Mashonaland. His father was a renowned hunter who, like many prominent traditional figures in the area, rejected Christianity when it arrived in the early years of the colonial occupation. However, Samkange became a Christian some time in his late teens after going out to work in Kadoma (Gatooma), and took the name Douglas Thompson in place of his traditional name.

Between 1922 and 1928, he served as a detached Methodist evangelist at the Hwange (Wankie) colliery. This was an important period in his career: he was operating at some distance from his home in one of the least hospitable parts of the country, and without local white supervision, ministering to a polyglot labor force. Samkange's many gifts here reached fruition. He became a Zimbabwean, rather than a Zezuru Shona, fluent in Sindebele, the language of western Zimbabwe; and an inspirational preacher fired by a determination to serve God and the needs of the poor and destitute. Not surprisingly, this propelled him toward the Christian ministry. In 1928, he was accepted as a candidate for ordination, and moved to Bulawayo, where he fearlessly attempted to bring both sides together in the 1930 Ndebele-Shona ethnic conflict. His leadership qualities were further recognized in his appointment as secretary of the new Native Missionary Conference set up in 1928, the first of many such positions he was to hold up to his death. In 1936, he was ordained and posted to the rural Kwenda mission in Mashonaland.

Samkanke was selected to attend the 1938 International Missionary Conference at Tambaram, Madras,

an experience that brought him into contact with Indian and other nonwhite Christians and opened his eyes to the prospect of an indigenized church in Rhodesia (Zimbabwe). These views were, on his return, to lead him into growing conflict with the more conservative elements of the white Methodist establishment in Zimbabwe, exacerbated by the enforcement of official policy requiring direct European supervision over mission education. However, unlike some his colleagues, like Esau Nemapare, he remained loyal to the missionary authorities to the end of his life.

His political activity began in April 1925, when he joined the very moderate Rhodesian Native Association, and together with Aaron Jacha helped to form the Southern Rhodesian Bantu Congress in 1938. The initial moderation of the congress was assailed by wartime radicalism, inspired in turn by events in the wider world and within the colony itself, and Samkange was chosen as president in July 1943. Under his leadership, the congress adopted a more critical stance. It mounted an attack on unpopular government policies—especially the use of compulsory black labor on wartime aerodrome construction, and the threatened destocking of cattle in the reserves. Prime Minister Huggins's plans to seek the amalgamation of the two Rhodesias and Nyasaland (respectively, Zimbabwe, Zambia, and Malawi) and to remove blacks from the common voters' roll also earned vehement Congress dissent. It also attempted—at that stage without great success—to build up a mass membership.

By the end of World War II, however, Samkange and the congress leadership themselves came under fire from a generally younger, more militant, generation of activists—like Charles Mzingeli and Benjamin Burombo—who were typically from a trade union background and often hostile to missionaries and their black "protégés." They believed that Samkange, with his missionary background, was inherently too acquiescent to adequately serve black political interests. The short-term result was a fatal weakening of the nationalist cause at a time when it could least afford it, as the divisions over the April 1948 general strike showed. Shortly after this, Samkange decided to stand down from the congress presidency, and at the beginning of 1949 a new generation of younger leaders, including his son Stanlake, took over.

The final years of his life were marked by further conflict with the colony's Department of Native Education, involving school standards and proper financial accounting at his Pakame Mission, during which the support of the Methodist authorities began to waver. In 1954 he surrendered his educational work and returned to evangelism in Bulawayo. His sudden death from a heart attack on August 27, 1956, occurred at a time when several friends had been urging him to reenter politics and give fresh impetus to the faltering African National (formerly Bantu) Congress.

Perhaps inevitably, D.T. Samkange has been dismissed by some as an essentially petit bourgeois figure, an elitist who was temperamentally unable to escape from missionary leading strings to respond to the many challenges of the mid-to-late 1940s. Terence Ranger's account has shown that, on the contrary, he was an important figure appearing at the transition point between the "participation" politics of the 1920s and the confrontationist politics of the late 1950s and early 1960s, one whose effectiveness as a leader was undermined by the factional nature of black Zimbabwe politics during and after World War II.

MURRAY STEELE

See also: **Zimbabwe (Southern Rhodesia): Urbanization and Conflict, 1940s.**

Biography

Entered the Nenguwo Institution (later, Waddilove), outside Marondera, in 1915, eventually becoming a teacher at Nenguwo. Married Grace Mano in 1919; his wife became an important personality in her own right, and a prominent and well-respected *Ruwadzano* (African Women's Prayer Union) leader. Their children included Stanlake, historian and writer, whose novel *The Mourned One* captures much of the spirit of Waddilove between the two world wars; and Sketchley, a leader of the NDP who died young in 1961. Named president of the Southern Rhodesian Bantu Congress in July 1943. Died suddenly, from a heart attack, on August 27, 1956.

Further Reading

Andrews, Charles F. *John White of Mashonaland*, 1935. Reprint, New York: Negro Universities Press, 1969.

Gann, Lewis. *A History of Southern Rhodesia: Early Days to 1934*, 1965. Reprint, New York: Humanities Press, 1969.

Ranger, Terence. *The African Voice in Southern Rhodesia, 1898–1930*. London: Heinemann/Evanston, Ill.: Northwestern University Press, 1970.

———. *Are We Not Also Men? The Samkange Family and African Politics in Zimbabwe, 1920–1964*. London: James Currey/Portsmouth, N.H.: Heinemann, 1995.

Vambe, Lawrence. *From Rhodesia to Zimbabwe*. London: Heinemann/Pittsburgh: Pittsburgh University Press, 1976.

Zvobgo, C. J. M. *The Wesleyan Methodist Missions in Zimbabwe, 1891–1945*. Harare: University of Zimbabwe Publications, 1991.

Sanhaja

The Berbers of North Africa and the Sahara were originally divided into three major ethnic groups, the Lowata, Sanhaja, and Zanata, and each group was subdivided into many smaller groups. For a long time the majority of the Berber groups remained independent, although all were somewhat influenced by the civilizations that flourished successively along the shores of the Mediterranean.

The Sanhaja Berbers inhabited the land mass of the Sahara between Mauritania and Ahagar as far north as the Sudan. By the ninth century, the Sanhaja Berbers had formed a loose confederation consisting of the Lamtuna, Masufa, and Godala in order to control the Saharan trade route originating from Zanata and terminating in Ghana in the south.

The arrival of the Sanhaja nomads in a predominantly agrarian area necessarily upset the whole western Sahara region. The pastoralist Sanhaja roamed the most suitable regions occupied by farmers. Under the rule of the king Telagagin and his successor Tilutan, the Sanhaja imposed their authority throughout present-day Mauritania.

Ghana, however, successfully resisted Sanhaja domination, and by the year 900, when internal strife broke apart the Sanhaja confederation, Ghana emerged as the dominant power. During the tenth century, certain Sanhaja chiefs were converted to Islam, with Audoghast becoming a principal commercial and religious center.

The overlordship of Ghana soon provoked the consummation of a united action by leaders of the Lamtuna, Godala, and Masufa. It was probably during this period that Tarsina, a Lamtuna, emerged as the first important Muslim Sanhaja ruler.

Although Audoghast maintained superficially friendly relations with the Soninke of Ghana, there were instances of constant friction between the Lamtuna and the Soninke. The Soninke waylaid caravans from the north as they approached Audoghast; in retaliation, the Lamtuna intervened in Ghana's internal affairs. The inability of the Sanhaja to establish a formidable and united opposition gave the Soninke enough time to gradually become the dominant power in the area. Ghana recovered some of the outlying districts that had earlier been taken from the Soninke, although no attempt was made to occupy Sanhaja, the capital city of Audoghast, until at least 1054.

Tarsina went on a pilgrimage to Mecca, ostensibly to justify his campaigns against the Soninke and others. Upon his death in 1023, his son-in-law Yahya ibn Ibrahim succeeded him; he, too, made a pilgrimage, in 1035, not as an act of religious devotion so much as a political gesture.

Ibn Ibrahim displayed an embarrassing ignorance of the doctrines of Islam. When he realized how deeply he had shocked the learned Abu Amran of Mecca, he implored his assistance in employing a theologian who would teach his people the religion. On the recommendation of Abu Amran, a pupil of Wajjaj Ibn Zalwi named Abd Allah ibn Yacin accompanied Yahya Ibrahim back to Audoghast. Ibn Yacin's mission was not immediately successful. Resistance to his teaching forced Ibn Yacin to relocate to an island in the Atlantic, where a *ribat* (fortified center for gathering) was built and maintained.

The ribat soon won a great reputation as a recruiting center for a jihad that attracted new followers, and a place of refuge for the Lamtuna. Ibn Yacin and his motley crowd of followers became known for their dress code and puritanical Islamic doctrines based on Sufism. Seclusion in a place surrounded by water encouraged spirituality and meditation; among the Sufis, a ribat is a place in which a man shuts himself up for the purpose of worship. When the disciples of Ibn Yacin swelled to one thousand, the preacher called them together and gave them a new name, El-Morabethin, or the Morabouts, and instructed them:

> Go under the protection of God and warn your fellow-tribesmen, teach them the law of God and threaten them with His Chastisement. If they repent and return to the truth and amend their ways, then leave them in peace; but if they refuse and persist in their errors and infidelity, let us invoke the aid of God against them and make war upon them until God decides the issue between us.

In 1042, Ibn Yacin and his followers, now known as the Almoravids, undertook a jihad against the pagan Godala and were successful in their campaigns. The offered alternatives of death or conversion to true Islam resulted in remarkable victories for the Almoravids. Ibn Yacin, however, did not allow his followers to indulge in looting or rape, two common "benefits" of warfare.

Wajjaj ibn Zalwi enjoined Ibn Yacin to return to Sijilmasa, where he found both sympathy and many eager followers. Wajjaj endorsed Ibn Yacin and threatened to expel from Islam those who refused to obey him. He even sent his own disciples and new adherents back into the desert, with strict orders to destroy anybody who opposed the teachings and religious observances of Ibn Yacin and the Almoravids.

Ibn Yacin carried out his master's instructions to the letter, such that within a short period of time most of the tribes of the western desert had accepted the new doctrine and were united under the banner of the Almoravids. Ibn Yacin soon had an army of 30,000 positively motivated men who were fanatical in their loyalty to the leader. The well-ordered army was intended to assist in spreading the orthodox religion to the pagan tribes of the north.

In 1056, Ibn Yacin set out to liberate the people of Dra'a in southern Morocco, who were under the oppression of the Emir of Sijilmasa. Ibn Yacin defeated the army of Sijilmasa, killed the emir, and occupied the capital city. He returned to Audoghast, leaving behind a garrison of his force to protect the newly liberated citizens against further abuses of power.

Ibn Yacin was, however, killed in 1057 while on one of his numerous battles. At his death, Ibn Yacin was one of the most remarkable characters in African history. He was a brilliant organizer, an empire builder and a patriot. The great movement that he established, led and inspired had, by 1057, spread across the whole of the western Sahara region, as well as the fertile northern districts of Sus, Aghmat, and Sijilmasa.

The leadership of the Almoravids passed into the hands of Abu Bakre ibn Omar, who eventually led the assault against the Soninke kingdom of Ghana in 1076, when Kumbi Saleh fell to the superior force of the Almoravids. Several Soninke were either killed or sold into slavery; many were forced to adopt Islam. The Kingdom of Ghana collapsed, leading to the emergence of the successor states of Tekrur, Diara, and Kaniaga. Sumanguru Keita of Kaniaga filled the void for a period before Mari Djata eventually assumed political dominance in the western Sudan. While Abu Bakre ibn Omar was in the western Sudan, Yusuf ibn Taclifin led a section of the Almoravids into the heart of the Maghrib, reestablishing Marrakech as an important commercial and clerical center. The Almoravids split into two factions when Yusuf ibn Taclifin refused to relinquish leadership of the movement to Abu Bakre ibn Cemar.

AKIN ALAO

Further Reading

Bovil, E. W. *The Golden Trade of the Moors*. London: Oxford University Press, 1958.
Trimigham, J. Spencer. *A History of Islam in West Africa*. London: Oxford University Press, 1962.

Sankara: *See* Burkina Faso (Upper Volta): Independence to the Present.

Sanusiyya: *See* Libya: Muhammad al-Sanusi and the Sanusiyya.

São Tomé and Príncipe, to 1800

The Gulf of Guinea islands of São Tomé and Príncipe were among the first territories colonized by Portugal in the late fifteenth century. In 1470 and 1471, the Portuguese navigators João de Santarém and Pedro Escobar discovered the then uninhabited archipelago. Not before the first contacts with the kingdom of Kongo in 1482 did São Tomé gain strategic importance for the Portuguese. They intended to create there a Christian European society, sustained by a sugar export economy

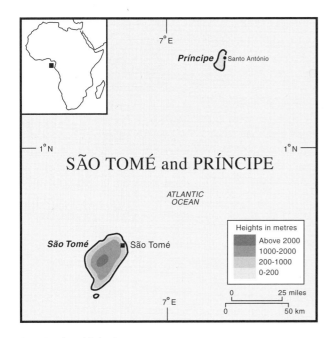

SÃO TOMÉ and PRÍNCIPE

ATLANTIC OCEAN

São Tomé and Principe.

that used African slave labor and would be an entrepôt for their navigation in the South Atlantic. However, the first Portuguese who settled in 1486 in the Northwest of São Tomé succumbed to the unhealthy tropical climate. Not before 1493 did the third feudal lord (*donatário*), Álvaro de Caminha, succeeded in establishing a colony in the northeast of the island. Apart from volunteers, many convicts and deported Jewish children, who had been separated by force from their parents, were transported to São Tomé. The colonization of Príncipe began in 1502 when this island was granted to the donatário António Carneiro.

The new colonists began to cultivate sugarcane on plantations where labor was provided by slaves from Benin, Gabon, Congo, and Angola. São Tomé was the first plantation economy in the tropics. Due to tropical diseases, the mortality rate among whites was very high. Therefore, only a few whites went voluntarily to São Tomé, since they were terrified of the dangerous tropical climate. Consequently, the Portuguese encouraged mixed unions between blacks and whites as a strategy to populate the islands. King Joéo II (r.1481–1495) ordered that a slave woman be given to every white settler. In 1515 these African women and their children were manumitted by royal decree. Another royal decree of 1517 determined that the male slaves, who had come with the first settlers and their offspring, were also manumitted.

Consequently, a group of free Creole blacks, locally known as *forros*, was created. In the early sixteenth century there were 1,000 settlers (mostly convicts), 2,000 slaves on the plantations, and some 5,000 slaves on São Tomé for the regional trade with Elmina. In

the 1530s the export of slaves from São Tomé to the Americas began. However, since 1520, sugar had become the most important factor of the flourishing economy. In the late sixteenth century, annual sugar production reached a peak of 12,000 tons. At that time, rich planters had up to 300 slaves.

Until 1522 the donatário exercised the civil and criminal jurisdiction over São Tomé. Subsequently, the local representative of the Portuguese crown was a governor appointed by Lisbon. In 1525 King João III (r.1521–1557) granted city rights to São Tomé town, including the right to have a city council with full legal and legislative powers for the entire island. The great Creole landowners controlled the city council. In 1548 the king granted the city council the right to exercise the powers of the governor whenever this office was vacant. As a result, local Creoles frequently assumed the office of governor.

From the beginning of the settlement, the evangelical project of the Catholic Church was an integral part of the archipelago's colonization. In 1534 the diocese of São Tomé was founded, the first in Sub-Sahara Africa, and it existed until 1677. The local clergy dominated by the Creole elite was plagued by internal conflicts and engaged in power struggles with the governor and the town council. The fragmentation of local political power among the church, the governor, and the municipality; the distance from the central government in Lisbon; the frequent power vacuum due to the early death of office-holders caused by tropical diseases; and the polarizing effects of a small and insular society facilitated all kinds of conflict. In addition, assaults by escaped slaves and slave revolts contributed to the political instability.

Slaves frequently fled into the mountainous and inaccessible interior of the island. There, the *maroons* (the Spanish term for runaway slaves) organized themselves into gangs that assaulted the plantations. From 1530, the local government waged a bush war against the maroons, who were finally defeated in the late seventeenth century.

The documented first slave uprising in São Tomé occurred in 1517. In 1595 the greatest revolt, led by a slave called Amador, threatened the city. Finally, the slaves were defeated and Amador was arrested and hanged.

The prosperity of the islands provoked several assaults by the English, French, and Dutch. From 1641 to 1648 the Dutch occupied São Tomé's fort, from where they controlled the local sugar and slave trade. At that time the sugar industry was already in decline, due to the increasing competition from Brazilian producers, the relatively poor quality of the local product, and the constant assaults by runaway slaves who later became known as *Angolares*. Finally, most planters migrated to Brazil, and the plantation economy virtually ceased to exist. Following the reduction of white settlers, the local Creoles mixed more frequently with Africans. By this time, the forro society and culture had been firmly established.

The direct and prolonged encounter of the dominant Catholic Portuguese culture and of the various African cultures resulted in the emergence of a distinctive Creole society with its own culture and languages. The islanders cultivated the former plantations that were not overgrown by tropical forest for subsistence and the provision of ships with food supplies. Meanwhile, most former slave markets were controlled by foreign powers, while only Gabon and Calabar continued to supply slaves to the archipelago. At the end of the sixteenth century, São Tomé had already lost its position as an entrepôt for the slave trade to Luanda. In the seventeenth century, the elite Creole families dominated the city council, competing for power with each other, the church, and the governor. Due to frequent political unrest, in 1753 the residence of the governor was transferred from São Tomé town to Santo António on Príncipe, which simultaneously reverted to the crown.

GERHARD SEIBERT

See also: **Kongo, Teke (Tio), and Loango: History to 1483; Portugal: Exploration and Trade in the Fifteenth Century; São Tomé and Príncipe, 1800 to the Present.**

Further Reading

Albuquerque, Luís de. *A ilha de São Tomé nos séculos XV e XVI. Biblioteca da expansão portuguesa*, Lisbon: Publicações Alfa, 1989.

Caldeira, Arlindo Manuel. *Mulheres, sexualidade e casamento no arquipélago de S.Tomé e Príncipe (Séculos XV a XVIII).* Lisbon: Ministério de Educação, 1997.

Garfield, Robert. *A History of São Tomé Island 1470–1655: The Key to Guinea.* San Francisco: Mellen Research University Press, 1992.

Hodges, Tony, and Malyn Newitt. *São Tomé and Príncipe: From Plantation Colony to Microstate.* Boulder, Colo.: Westview Press, 1988.

Tenreiro, Francisco. *A ilha de São Tomé. Lisbon: Junta de Investigações do Ultramar.* 1961.

São Tomé and Príncipe, 1800 to the Present

São Tomé and Príncipe had been a Portuguese colony since the mid-seventeenth century, but the local Creoles, known as *forros*, had exercised virtual control over local affairs. The move of the capital from Príncipe back to São Tomé in 1852 marked the beginning of the second colonization of the islands. The independence of Brazil in 1822, the abolition of the slave trade in the Portuguese territories in 1836, and the end of a long period of political instability in Portugal in 1852 contributed to the political conditions for the recolonization. The introduction of coffee in 1787 and cocoa in 1822, both from Brazil, made the production of new cash crops possible. Large-scale coffee and cocoa cultivation with slave labor began around 1850. Following the abolition of slavery in 1875, the Portuguese began immediately to recruit contract workers in Angola, and from the early twentieth century on also in Cape Verde and Mozambique. The newly liberated slaves, as well as the local forros and *Angolares* (runaway slaves) refused manual fieldwork on the estates, since they considered it beneath their status as free men. By 1890, cocoa production had surpassed that of coffee, thanks to increasing world market prices, and since then cocoa has always dominated the local plantation economy.

Before the second colonization of the archipelago, many lands had been in the hands of the *forros*. During the expansion of the plantations in the second half of the nineteenth century, the Portuguese planters gradually dispossessed the landholding Creoles through land purchase, fraud, and force. By 1898 the Portuguese owned 90 per cent of the land. By that time they had established the financial system, the administrative infrastructure and the communications for an effective colonization. Unable to regain their economic power based on agriculture, the educated forros sought employment in the colonial administration, from where they derived their social status. Unlike the sugar plantations in the sixteenth century, the cocoa plantations covered almost the entire archipelago at the end of the nineteenth century. In 1909, the cocoa production peaked, with 30,300 tons. Subsequently, however, dropping prices led to a decline of cocoa production. Cocoa exports decreased from 26,283 tons in 1921 to 9,234 in 1961. Since the 1930s the estates had been inefficient and unprofitable, and were unable to compete with the more efficient West African smallholders. The large estates that employed hundreds of workers constituted states within the state, as they maintained their own infrastructures. The recruitment of thousands of African contract workers from 1875 changed the demographic balance in favor of these immigrants. In 1900, the archipelago had a total population of 42,100, of whom 19,430 were natives, 21,510 contract workers, and 1,190 whites. Until the 1940s, the contract workers outnumbered the native Creoles. The workers lived in barracks within the estates, while the forros lived in the towns and dispersed communities. In 190, reports of the harsh living and working conditions of the plantation workers, as well as the fact that they were rarely repatriated, provoked a boycott of São Tomé cocoa by British chocolate manufacturers.

In response, the Portuguese improved the situation of the contract workers. Not until 1961, however, did the Portuguese formally grant equal status to the plantation workers.

In February 1953 the colonial government's attempt to break the forros' resistance to plantation labor resulted in their spontaneous uprising. At the order of Governor Carlos Gorgulho (1945–1953) the police, white volunteers, and contract workers put down the rebellion with excessive violence, killing numerous innocent people. The bloody event became known as the Massacre of February 1953, which later served to justify nationalist demands for independence. In 1960 a few elite forros in exile created the Comité de Libertação de São Tomé e Príncipe (CLSTP), which merely agitated within the diplomatic arena from abroad. The CLSTP, which had offices in Accra and Libreville, was plagued by constant personal conflicts and virtually ceased to exist in 1966. It was 1972 before the exiled nationalists reconstituted the CLSTP as Movimento de Libertação de São Tomé e Príncipe (MLSTP) and Manuel Pinto da Costa became its secretary general. Six months after the military coup of April 25, 1974, the revolutionary Lisbon government recognized the Libreville-based MLSTP as the sole and legitimate representative of the people. In March 1975 a conflict on the dissolution of the native troops placed a radical faction within the MLSTP in opposition to the moderate faction led by Pinto da Costa. With the support of the Portuguese government the latter successfully ousted the radicals from power. Meanwhile, the 2,000 Portuguese had departed due to the turmoil preceding independence depriving the country of trained personnel in virtually all sectors.

On July 12, 1975, São Tomé and Príncipe gained independence and constitutionally became a one-party state based on the Soviet model. Manuel Pinto da Costa became president and Miguel Trovoada the first prime minister. The MLSTP regime announced the diversification of the economy, including agriculture, the development of industrial fishing, and the promotion of tourism. In September 1976 the Portuguese-owned plantations were nationalized and subsequently regrouped into 15 large state-owned plantations. Externally, the regime favored political relations with Angola and the socialist countries, while it maintained economic ties with Western countries. Internally, the first years after independence were marked by constant orientation and power struggles within the party leadership that were accompanied by real and alleged coup attempts, increasing the repressive and authoritarian character of the regime. Following the threat of an alleged imperialist invasion, in March 1978 Angolan troops were sent to São Tomé to protect the regime. In August 1979 a population census, which was perceived by the forro population as an attempt to introduce forced labor, resulted in antigovernment riots. The next month Miguel Trovoada was accused of connivance in the census turmoil and detained without charge or trial for 21 months before he was released into exile to France. Following Trovoada's imprisonment the regime radicalized considerably, and Pinto da Costa reached the climax of his dictatorial powers. At the same time exiled opponents of the regime in Portugal and Gabon created three opposition movements. Although they were divided by personal and political quarrels, their agitation abroad worried the MLSTP regime, which was struggling with serious economic problems. Due to mismanagement and a lack of investments the cocoa output had decreased from 7,000 tons in 1979 to 3,400 tons in 1984. Equally, investments in the diversification of the economy proved to be a failure since they were ill-designed and poorly managed.

The consequent economic crisis forced the government to redefine its policies, as its socialist allies were unable to sustain the regime. From 1984 the regime gradually liberalized the economy, shifted away from its socialist allies, turned to Western countries for aid funds, and reconciled with the former dissidents. Between 1986 and 1990 the regime signed contracts with foreign and local companies for the private management of seven estates. The objective was to rehabilitate the plantations to increase cocoa output; however, the privately managed estates did not show the expected improvements. In 1987, the government signed an agreement on a structural adjustment program with the Bretton Woods institutions. The economic reform opened business opportunities for foreign investors and local politicians, but also created new possibilities for corruption. Unimpressed by the political change, in March 1988 a dissident group waged an amateurish invasion attempt to overthrow Pinto da Costa, but was easily overwhelmed. In December 1989 the MLSTP announced the introduction of a multiparty democracy. The political transition that occurred without unrest or violence culminated in the approval of a democratic constitution by a popular referendum in August 1990. In October the MLSTP transformed itself into the neoliberal Social Democratic Party (MLSTP/PSD). The following month, President Pinto da Costa withdrew his candidature for the presidency.

In the first free democratic elections, held in January 1991, the opposition Partido de Convergência Democrática—Grupo de Reflexéo (PCD-GR) swept the MLSTP/PSD out of office and formed a government headed by Prime Minister Daniel Daio. In March 1991, Miguel Trovoada, who had returned from exile the year before, was elected uncontested president. Since then, the struggle for power and funds have placed the president in conflict with successive governments creating continuous political instability. In April 1992, President

Trovoada dismissed Daio due to the alleged lack of consensus with the prime minister. Subsequently, Noberto Costa Alegre was appointed prime minister of a new PCD-GR government. In July 1994, President Trovoada discharged Prime Minister Costa Alegre, alleging a lack of institutional loyalty in some government actions. The early elections of October 1994 brought the MLSTP/PSD back to power. In August 1995 young officers staged a one-week military coup that was ended when the coup plotters returned to the barracks in exchange for a general amnesty. In July 1996 President Trovoada was reelected president. After serving the maximum two terms as permitted by the constitution, he stepped down. The election of 2001 was won by Fradique de Menezes, a wealthy cocoa exporter.

Free elections have been held regularly since 1991, but the country's public institutions have remained weak and inefficient, while corruption and other malpractice has flourished. Liberal democracy has not resulted in a sound economic policy and a flourishing market economy; attempts to boost cocoa production and to diversify agricultural exports have largely failed. Despite large amounts of foreign aid, there has been almost no real economic growth, while mass poverty and external debts have increased since 1991.

GERHARD SEIBERT

See also: **São Tomé and Príncipe, to 1800.**

Further Reading

Cadbury, William A. *Labour in Portuguese West Africa.* London, 1910.

Clarence-Smith, William Gervase. "The Hidden Costs of Labour on the Cocoa Plantations of São Tomé and Príncipe, 1875–1914." *Portuguese Studies,* no. 6 (1990): 152–170.

Eyzaguirre, Pablo B. "The Ecology of Swidden Agriculture and Agrarian History in São Tomé." *Cahiers d'Études Africaines* nos. 101–102 (1986): 113–129.

Foreign Office (London). *San Thomé and Príncipe.* Confidential handbooks prepared under the direction of the Historical Section of the Foreign Office, no. 126. London: Foreign Office, 1919.

Hodges, Tony, and Malyn Newitt. *São Tomé and Príncipe: From Plantation Colony to Microstate.* Boulder, Colo.: Westview Press 1988.

Seibert, Gerhard. *Comrades, Clients and Cousins: Colonialism, Socialism and Democratization in São Tomé and Príncipe.* Leiden, Netherlands: CNWS, 1999.

Tenreiro, Francisco. *A Ilha de São Tomé.* Lisbon: Junta de Investigaçãoes do Ultramar, 1961.

Torp, Jens Erik, L. M. Denny, and Donald I. Ray. *Mozambique, São Tomé and Príncipe: Politics, Economics and Society.* London: Pinter, 1989.

Sassou-Nguesso, Denis (1943–)

President of the Republic of Congo, 1979–92, 1997–

Denis Sassou-Nguesso was born in 1943 in the village of Edou. He claims that he was the last-born child of his father's six wives, and enjoyed a carefree childhood with a doting mother and stern father. Sassou also claims that his father enjoyed great local respect as a village headman and president of a local hunter's association.

Sassou was initiated into an Mbochi brotherhood at the age of ten, and left home shortly afterward to study at a regional school, 60 miles from his native village. Proving himself an able student, Sassou won a place at the Normal College for Teachers in Dolise (now Loubomo).

By his account, Sassou graduated first in his class, but was denied a place at the lycée in Brazzaville for lack of political connections. Instead, he was allowed to test for a place in a military training school, which he won. He first trained at Bouar, in the Central African Republic, and then at Cherchell, Algeria, after which he became a second lieutenant. Sassou served one year in Congo, and then undertook more advanced training at Saint-Maixent in France, where he gained a very favorable impression of that country and its military establishment. Upon his return, Sassou joined a paratrooper unit, which he later commanded as a captain in 1968.

Following the rise of Marien Ngouabi that same year, the military became increasingly involved in politics, and Sassou became a member of the National Revolutionary Council. When Ngouabi created the Marxist-oriented Congolese Worker's Party in 1970, Sassou was named a member of its Politbureau. As a military man and a nonintellectual, Sassou seems never to have been a committed Marxist, though he was far more ideological than his predecessor, Joachim Yhombi-Opango. In his military career, he was promoted to commander of the Brazzaville Military Zone, and then to chief of political security. In 1975, he was named minister of defense.

At the time of Ngouabi's assassination in March 1977, Sassou was perhaps the most influential figure in the army and the party, but he was outmaneuvered by Yhombi-Opango, who became the leader of the Parti congolais du travail's (PCT's) military committee and head of state. Sassou remained Defense Minister and was also named first vice president. Yhombi never fully consolidated his grip on power, and was forced to share real power with other military leaders, including Sassou. In February 1979 Yhombi's opponents organized a meeting of the PCT Central Committee in which he was ousted in favor of Sassou. Using classic Stalinist techniques, Sassou had soon purged his most important ethnic and military rivals from the party, of which he assumed supreme control. Sassou's rise was then interpreted as a return to strict Marxist-Leninist policies after the uncertain Yhombi interlude. As significantly, it represented a triumph of Mbochi officers over their Kouyou rivals.

In the first half of the 1980s Sassou's regime was buoyed by high world petroleum prices, which allowed him to undertake a massive expansion of the state sector and patronize his political cronies. Meanwhile, his Marxist and anticolonial rhetoric resonated well in Africa. Congo also benefited from substantial Soviet, Chinese, and Cuban aid in this period, even as French companies invested in the petroleum sector. After 1985, falling petroleum prices hit the Congolese hard, and Sassou's popularity waned. Meanwhile, his putatively Marxist orientation hurt him as the end of European communism loomed. At home, Sassou bloodily put down an attempted coup in 1987, and turned to more repressive measures in quelling public dissent.

By the end of 1990, public sentiment had turned completely against Sassou, and even his army chief of staff refused to stand in the way of a transition. He was forced to allow the convening of a sovereign national conference in 1991, which he did not succeed in controlling. The conference ended up wresting real power from him, though he remained as nominal head of state through August 1992. He competed in the presidential elections of 1992, but finished third. He then threw his support to Pascal Lissouba, who prevailed in the second round against Bernard Kolélas. Sassou remained head of a reformed, non-Marxist PCT. When Lissouba failed to award the PCT with a sufficient role in his new government, Sassou joined with Kolélas's party in the opposition in the assembly. Upon losing power, Sassou retrained his presidential guard, made up entirely of Mbochi kinsmen, as a personal militia.

Sassou spent much of the 1993–1996 period in quasi-exile in France, fearing for his security in Congo. In France he maintained close ties with officials in the various governments of Mitterrand and Chirac, as well as with French industrial leaders. Sassou made a triumphal return to Brazzaville in early 1997 to begin his presidential election campaign, scheduled for July. He also readied his militia for a posssible cancellation of the elections. In May, Sassou's campaign visit to the northern city of Owando, the hometown of Yhombi, then Lissouba's campaign manager, led to violent clashes. On June 5, 1997, Lissouba sent an armed detachment to Sassou's residence to arrest several of his associates said to have been implicated in this violence. At that point, Sassou's militia resisted these forces, and a civil war was soon underway. The war raged from June through mid-October, and was essentially stalemated. Sassou's forces only seized control of the presidential residence and other key installations after Angolan government forces joined the battle against government forces. Angola's critical intervention at this stage was probably motivated by issues related to its own civil war: Lissouba had allowed Angola's rebel

UNITA movement to set up an office headquaters in Pointe Noire in 1997, and appears to have allowed UNITA forces to operate from within the Congo. Most Congolese believe that Sassou received aid from official French contacts, executives in Elf-Aquitaine, and some regional leaders, particularly Gabon's president Omar Bongo. In early 1998 Sassou seemed to be consolidating his grip on power, but in December the opposition militia began to actively contest Sassou's forces in the south and center of the country. Sassou is fawning toward France in his autobiography, and Franco-Congolese relations have improved markedly since his return to power.

In March 2002, Sassou won the presidential election, initiating a seven-year term in office. Two other primary contenders for the office, former president Pascal Lissouba and former prime minister Bernard Kolélas, were excluded from the race by a residency law. Andre Milongo had left the race, claiming irregularities in the election process. When he took office, Sassou put in place a revamped constitution that grants him more power.

JOHN F. CLARK

See also: **Congo (Brazzaville), Republic of.**

Biography

Born in 1943 in the village of Edou. Studied at the Normal College for Teachers in Dolise (now Loubomo). After attending military training school, named captain of his paratrooper unit in 1968. Promoted to commander of the Brazzaville Military Zone, and then to chief of political security. Named minister of defense in 1975. President from 1979 to 1992. Lived in France from 1993 to 1996. Won presidential elections again in 1997 and 2002.

Further Reading

Clark, John F. "Elections, Leadership and Democracy in Congo." *Africa Today* 41, no. 3 (1994): 41–60.

Decalo, Samuel. "Congo: Revolutionary Rhetoric and the Overdeveloped State." In *Coups and Army Rule in Africa: Motivations and Constraints.* New Haven, Conn.: Yale University Press, 1990.

Decalo, Samuel, Virginia Thompson, and Richard Adloff. "Denis Sassou-Nguesso." *Historical Dictionary of Congo,* rev. 3rd ed. Lanham, Md.: Scarecrow Press, 1996.

Levine, Victor T. "Military Rule in the People's Republic of Congo." In *The Military in African Politics,* edited by John Harbeson. New York: Praeger, 1987.

Savimbi, Jonas (1934–2002)
Angolan Politician and Guerrilla Leader

Jonas Savimbi was born on August 3, 1934, the son of a railway station master and Evangelical Church pastor, in

Munhango, situated along the Benguela railway in Bié Province. He was a member of the Ovimbundu, who are the largest single ethnolinguistic group in Angola but do not represent an overall majority of the population. His movement, UNITA, was to draw heavily on this regional support base.

On May 18, 1958, Savimbi left for Portugal to pursue his studies in Lisbon at the Passos Manuel Secondary School, briefly pursuing medicine before abandoning his studies. The United Church of Christ provided him with a scholarship, but he never completed his studies as a doctor. He nontheless used the title *doctor* throughout his life.

In 1959, he met with other Angolan nationalist leaders, was detained for a short time by the Portuguese secret police, and then left for Switzerland, where he enrolled in the Legal Faculty in Lausanne. The following year he joined up with Holden Roberto's Angolan People's Union (UPA) movement. Subsequently he was appointed secretary general. Following the fusion of the UPA with the Angola Democratic Party (PDA) into a movement called the National Liberation Front of Angola (FNLA) in March 1962, almost immediately thereafter the FNLA declared itself the Government of the Republic of Angola in Exile (GRAE), and Savimbi was appointed its foreign minister.

In July 1964, Savimbi resigned from the GRAE, taking some colleagues with him; he claimed as his reasons for leaving the U.S. imperialist influence on the GRAE, the failure of the GRAE and the Popular Movement for the Liberation of Angola (MPLA) to unite, GRAE's Bakongo domination, and the singular lack of serious military effort to oust the Portuguese. He and eleven colleagues then departed for guerrilla warfare training in China. In March 1966, Savimbi began guerrilla operations in eastern Angola, taking advantage of the neighboring country of Zambia's independence in 1964 by using it as an external base. He also recruited supporters from refugees in western Zambia. Following a brief detention by Zambian authorities in 1967, Savimbi visited Cuba, returning the following year to Angola, where he led an armed struggle against the Portuguese colonial regime. There is evidence that at times he collaborated with the Portuguese in a secondary struggle against the MPLA, and herein were sown the seeds of future distrust in UNITA's dealings with the MPLA.

After the dictatorship of Caetano in Portugal was overthrown, Savimbi signed a cease-fire in June 1974. In January 1975, he signed the Alvor Accords, granting Angola independence, along with Agostinho Neto of the MPLA and Holden Roberto of the FNLA. The nationalist struggle in Angola was complicated not only by the existence of three nationalist movements but by becoming embroiled in the Cold War struggles of the time. Savimbi gained support from the United States,

South Africa, and China, and entered into an alliance with the FNLA in opposition to the MPLA with its Soviet and Cuban backing.

Following the collapse of the Alvor Accords, fighting between the contending nationalist movements ensued and Savimbi retreated to his base in Huambo in the central highlands. Then, in March 1976, under MPLA government attack, he began the "long march" to the south, mirroring the Chinese leader Mao Zedong's heroic feat, in UNITA mythology, with only 79 surviving the journey. He established his new base at Jamba near the Namibian border under the protection of the South African military shield. A long period of civil war ensued. The MPLA government of President Neto and later President dos Santos faced continuing armed opposition by UNITA and the FNLA.

With the newly elected U.S. president Ronald Reagan avowing a "roll-back" of communism globally, Savimbi successfully courted increased U.S. backing for his cause, visiting the United States in 1981 and again in 1986, at which time he was received in the Oval Office by President Reagan himself. Savimbi and UNITA rapidly eclipsed Roberto and the FNLA as the chief opposition force. Inside UNITA Savimbi maintained an iron rule by using his obvious charisma and by eliminating any potential leadership contenders.

Following a period of bitter armed conflict and civil war in the 1980s, heightened by the Cold War struggle, initial efforts at reconciliation began. In June 1989, at the Gbadolite summit, organized by President Mobuto Sese Seko of Zaire, Savimbi and dos Santos, head of the MPLA and president of Angola, met for the first time. Eventually, on May 31, 1991, the Bicesse Peace Accord was signed by the rival leaders in front of all the key international organizations. In September 1991 Savimbi returned to Luanda for his first visit after sixteen years of independence.

United Nations–supervised democratic elections were held in September 1992, but Savimbi refused to acknowledge that he and UNITA had lost the vote to dos Santos and the MPLA. He relaunched the war using troops and armaments hidden from the UN peace process mechanisms. There followed the two most destructive years in Angola's history. Savimbi's forces took the initiative, occupying most of the country, including the provincial capitals. Funding for his war effort came from control of diamond producing regions in the northeast of the country. The military initiative eventually swung back to the government and under pressure on the battlefield, and with international diplomatic pressure also, a new peace agreement was signed in Lusaka in November 1994.

Yet Savimbi never accepted the Lusaka agreement. He pretended to go along with it out of necessity, but he continually procrastinated in fulfilling the terms of the agreement and kept ensconced his core army and control of his territory. Dos Santos attempted to isolate Savimbi by closing off his potential external sanctuaries and re-supply bases. This led to military overstretch for dos Santos, who committed his troops in Congo Brazzaville and the Democratic Republic of Congo while facing simultaneous escalating military offensives inside Angola from UNITA from 1998 onward. Armed confrontations began in April, and by December 1998 the peace agreement officially broke down. Astutely Savimbi bought logistical access through Zambia from his diamond revenues, and purchased arms from the Ukraine and elsewhere to reequip his forces. In a parallel with what happened in 1992, Savimbi once again initially managed to seize the military initiative. The international community placed sanctions on UNITA, and the countries of the Southern African Development Community passed a resolution proposed by the government of Angola to declare Savimbi a war criminal in 1999. He was killed in battle on February 22, 2002.

BARRY MUNSLOW

See also: **Angola: Cold War Politics, Civil War, 1975–1994; Angola: Independence: Civil of War: Impact of, Economic and Social; Angola: Independence and Civil War, 1974–1976; Angola: MPLA, FNLA, UNITA, and the War of Liberation, 1961–1974; Angola: Peace Betrayed, to the Present.**

Biography

Born on August 3, 1934, in Munhango. Left for Portugal to pursue studies in Lisbon in 1958. Joined the Angolan People's Union (UPA) movement in 1960, then appointed Secretary general. The UPA and the Angola Democratic Party joined together to form the National Liberation Front of Angola (FNLA) in March 1962. The FNLA declared itself the Government of the Republic of Angola in Exile (GRAE), and Savimbi was appointed its Foreign Minister. Resigned from GRAE in 1964. Began guerrilla operations in eastern Angola in 1966. After the Caetano dictatorship in Portugal was overthrown, signed a cease-fire in June 1974. Signed the Alvor Accords granting Angola independence in January 1975. Signed the Bicesse Peace Accords on May 31, 1991. Refused to acknowledge his loss in the UN-supervised elections of 1992. Relaunched armed warfare, signed a new peace agreement in Lusaka in November 1994. Resumed armed confrontation in 1998. Declared a war criminal by the Angolan government in 1999. Mortally wounded in battle and died February 22, 2002.

Further Reading

Anstee, Margaret. *Angola, Orphan of the Cold War.* London: Macmillan, 1996.

Bridgeland, Fred. *Jonas Savimbi: A Key to Africa.* Edinburgh: Mainstream, 1986.

Brittain, Victoria. *Death of Dignity: Angola's Civil War.* London: Pluto Press, 1998.

Minter, William. *Apartheid's Contras: An Inquiry into the Roots of War in Angola and Mozambique.* London: Zed, 1994.

Tvedten, Inge. *Angola: Struggle for Peace and Reconstruction.* Boulder, Colo.: Westview Press, 1997.

Windrich, Elaine. *The Cold War Guerrilla.* New York, 1992.

Schreiner, Olive Emilie Albertina (1855–1920)
South African Novelist, Feminist, and Political Activist

Olive Emilie Albertina Schreiner was the author of *The Story of an African Farm*, hailed by many as South Africa's finest novel. She was born of German/English missionary parentage at the Wittenbergen Wesleyan mission station, located on the Cape's eastern frontier. Following the death of her younger sister she set aside her parents' faith in favor of a personal humanist philosophy characterized by a deep spirituality evident in much of her writing. Thus, from an early stage, Schreiner marked herself as an unconventional individualist woman in a conformist patriarchal society. At the age of 17, she entered employment as a governess in a frontier homestead, and embarked on an intensive program of self-education, during which she came under the influence of the Darwinist Herbert Spencer. A brief sojourn at the New Rush (Kimberley) diamond field in 1873 provided her with material for her first novel, *Undine* (published posthumously). On her return journey, she experienced for the first time the chronic asthmatic condition that was to become a lifetime affliction.

Started in 1874–1875, preparation of *The Story of an African Farm* occupied several years; like *Undine*, it was written during what time she could spare from her governess duties. On completion of her final draft, Schreiner decided to leave the mentally confining environment of the Cape frontier and seek professional training in Britain. Although she did not avail herself of an opportunity to take up a nursing course, her exposure to conditions in a London maternity hospital in 1881 seems to have contributed to her empathy with the cause of disadvantaged women. The publication of *African Farm* in 1883, initially under the pseudonym Ralph Iron, caused a literary sensation in London as well as South Africa, and brought her into contact with some of the leading intellectuals of the day. It won Schreiner the lifelong, and almost certainly platonic, friendship of Havelock Ellis, one of the two major figures in her life. The pattern of her future life was now set: she conducted a voluminous correspondence with friends and acquaintances, but the scale of purely literary work on which she intended to build her reputation was restricted by persistent ill health and a deep-seated reluctance to revise what she had written lest the original inspiration be lost.

The 1890s, spent mostly in South Africa, witnessed several changes in Schreiner's life. Her sympathy with the Boer Republics grew in response to the bullying tactics employed against them by Cecil Rhodes, Cape Colony premier (1890–1995), and organizer of the Jameson Raid; and high commissioner Milner, who eventually presided over the South African War. Her widely publicized pro-Boer views induced the authorities to place her under virtual house arrest during the final stages of the conflict. Prior to this, in 1894, she had quite suddenly decided to marry the Cape liberal politician Samuel Cronwright. Their marriage became strained due to her inability to give birth to a child. Her childlessness is reflected in the strong maternal feelings evident in much of her later writings.

Following the South African War, Schreiner laid aside the cause of the Boers, feeling they could defend themselves, and returned to the cause of women. *Woman and Labour* (1911) attacked the "sex parasitism" of upper-middle class housewives in Britain (and, by implication, in settler societies) who accepted male patriarchy in exchange for a cosseted and essentially idle existence. Her final years were focused on the quest for an environment in which she could work while her health continued to deteriorate. The outbreak of war found her stranded in Britain, isolated by an antiwar stance that alienated her from many former friends. Cronwright brought her back to South Africa after the war ended, and she died in her sleep at Wynberg, on the Cape, on the night of November 10, 1920.

Schreiner's political reputation has been somewhat affected by her attachment to her Social Darwinist views, which she espoused until about 1895. These views changed radically thereafter, influenced by her own intellectual development and growing antipathy to the hypocrisy of the imperialist "civilizing mission," exemplified by the activities of Rhodes inside and beyond the boundaries of South Africa. She was especially critical of the way white politicians abandoned the African cause to reach an agreement about South African union at the 1908 National Convention, and in the last year of her life was collecting money to defend an African National Congress leader who had been arrested for organizing a strike.

Her literary reputation rests on *The Story of an African Farm*, which faithfully captures the atmosphere of frontier life in the 1870s, with its white overseers and itinerant peddlers. It is remarkable also for its portrayal of strong women, a feature in her other literary work, and for its deeply passionate humanism. However, mention should be made also of her more mature, though unfinished, *From Man to Man*, in which her feminist message is most clearly conveyed in the bond—transcending race—between its main character and her errant husband's mixed race daughter. Also notable are her collections of allegories (*Dreams* [1890] and *Stories, Dreams, and Allegories* [1924]), which set out the essence of her philosophy that in all relationships, the strong should help and offer a helping hand to—and not oppress—the weak.

Her influence over later generations of southern African writers has been acknowledged, especially by Doris Lessing and Nadine Gordimer. The standard biography, by Ruth First and Ann Scott (1980), has helped rescue her reputation from the omissions evident in her husband's biography and edited collection of letters, and the curiosity, some of it prurient, about her sexual orientation and sexuality later commentators have exhibited at the expense of a more balanced assessment of her life and work. First and Scott's rather matter-of-fact approach fails, however, to capture the essence of Olive Schreiner, evident in her lifelong passionate commitment to the cause of the underprivileged, whether Boer, poor, black, or female.

MURRAY STEELE

See also: **Cape Liberalism, Nineteenth Century; Rhodes, Cecil J.; South African War, 1899–1902.**

Biography

Born at the Wittenbergen Wesleyan mission station, located on the Cape's Eastern frontier, in 1855. At 17, entered employment as a governess in a frontier homestead, and embarked on an intensive program of self-education. Started writing *The Story of an African Farm* in 1874–1875. Moved to Britain, and worked in a maternity hospital in London in 1881. *The Story of an African Farm* was published in 1883. Married the politician Samuel Cronwright in 1894. Published *Woman and Labour* in 1911. Died at Wynberg, on the Cape, on November 10, 1920.

Further Reading

Clayton, Cherry. *Olive Schreiner*. London: Prentice Hall/ New York: Twayne, 1997.

First, Ruth, and Ann Scott. *Olive Schreiner*. London: Andre Deutsch/New York: Schocken, 1980.

Schreiner, Olive. *From Man to Man*. London: Virago, 1982.

———. *The Story of an African Farm*. Harmondsworth, England: Penguin, 1971.

———. *Woman and Labour*. London: Virago, 1978.

Scramble: *See* **Zanzibar: Britain, Germany, "Scramble."**

Sebetwane: *See* **Lozi Kingdom and the Kololo.**

Segregation: *See* **South Africa: Segregation, Political Economy of.**

Segu: Origins and Growth of a Bamana Kingdom

Bamana peoples were present in the middle Niger region of West Africa as early as the twelfth century, and during the thirteenth century they were integrated into the Mali Empire. With the decline of Mali, Bamana chiefdoms regained their independence, which they largely maintained despite the rise of the Songhay empire to the northeast. After the sixteenth-century Moroccan invasion of Songhay, the Bamana raided northward to the city of Jenne in the Middle Niger Delta. Local oral tradition indicates that in the mid-seventeenth century the Bamana may have established an ephemeral chiefdom in the neighborhood of Segu under KalaJan Kulubali, a descendant of Barama Ngolo. However, it was not until the early eighteenth century (*c.*1712) that kingship (*mansaya*) emerged at Segu, when Mamari Kulubali developed a power base by reorganizing a men's association, or *ton*, that became the dominant force in society. Mamari became the ton's leader, received the name Biton, and from his position of power defeated opposing factions and began establishing Bamana Segu as an important state that expanded over the delta of the Middle Niger and held sway over important trade routes and commercial centers.

The city of Segu, which is located on the south bank of the Niger River in Mali, originally consisted of four

Bamana Hunter. Segu, Mali, 1976. Photograph © David C. Conrad.

Street Scene. Segu, Mali, 1976. Photograph © David C. Conrad.

villages: Sekoro (Old Segu), Sebugu (Segu Hamlet), Sekura (New Segu), and Segu-Sikoro (Segu under the Si Trees). Nine other towns, commercial centers run by Maraka traders, were located in the immediate vicinity and were also regarded as central to the larger Bamana state. The four great *boliw* of Segu, potent sacrificial altars in which resided the spiritual force essential to political power and the judicial process, were kept at the administrative center because they were controlled by the *faama*. The Bamana rulers of Segu, who imposed and maintained their authority through force of arms, were known by the military title *faama* in preference to the more benign *mansa*, which is the usual term for "ruler," "king," "chief," or "Lord."

One of the most eventful periods in Segu history was the period of transition between *c.*1757 and *c.*1766, which saw the demise of Kulubali power and the rise of the Jara dynasty. Biton Kulubali (*d.*1755) was succeeded by two sons: Cekoro was a leper whose despotic rule (*c.*1755–1757) led to his eventual assassination by members of the ton, who were known as *tonjonw*. Bakari ruled for a short time in 1757, but he was a Muslim, which complicated his relations with the non-Muslim tonjonw and made it impossible for him to rule effectively. Concluding that the governing style introduced by Biton was unacceptable and wishing to restore the previously egalitarian system of the ton, the tonjonw killed Bakari Kulubali along with the rest of Biton's family.

Ton Mansa Dembele then became the first of several former slaves elected to rule at Segu, but he insisted on living at Ngoin, about 7 kilometers from Segu. This and Ton Mansa's determination to build a canal to bring water from the Niger to Ngoin caused other ton members to fear the emergence of a new center of power. One source claims that Ton Mansa was ambushed by the ton members, and another says he died of infection from an arrow in the ear that was possibly shot by one of his own men.

The next slave chief to be elected was Kanubanyuma Bari (c.1760–1763), who was a Fula. He is said to have been particularly occupied with raiding his predecessor's territory for slaves, and was regarded with suspicion by Bamana tonjonw, who feared that his leadership meant too much Fula influence in the ton. Kanubanyuma died in mysterious circumstances, possibly helped along by his chief rival Kafajugu, who became the third successive slave chief to be faama of Segu (c.1763–1766). Kafajugu died after two or three years in power, and again there is disagreement about whether he died a natural death or was killed by another ton chief.

A period of uncertainty followed, when nobody dared to assume authority, the elder ton members due to prudence, and the younger ones because they were not sure if they had the necessary support. Ngolo Jara, who had once been a slave of Biton, was just one ton chief among many. It does not appear that Ngolo had any reason to believe that if he became faama his fate would be any different than that of his immediate predecessors unless he did something to forestall his rivals and enemies. Sources differ about how Ngolo outwitted his rivals and forced them to swear their allegiance to him and his descendants, but the entire sequence of events that transpired during the period of transition between the death of Biton and the rise of Ngolo contributed greatly to Segu's reputation as a place of treachery and intrigue.

Ngolo Jara established a dynasty, the Ngolosi (descendants of Ngol) that would rule Segu for nearly a century. During his reign, which lasted some 25 years, Ngolo successfully reasserted *Bamanafanga*, or power of the king, reorganized the army and political administration (putting his sons in command of each of the five central districts), placed important commercial towns under state protection, and expanded the Segu state through military conquest. The oral sources agree that Ngolo died while leading his army into Mossi country, apparently sometime before 1790. Ngolo had chosen his son Monzon to succeed him, but three of Ngolo's other sons wished to divide the power among themselves. This resulted in a civil war in which one of the brothers allied himself with the neighboring Barnana state of Kaarta. After a prolonged struggle against numerically superior forces, Monzon conquered Kaarta, overcame his brothers, and reestablished his power at Segu in 1794–1795. When the intrepid Scottish explorer Mungo Park passed by Segu in 1805, it was Monzon Jara who sent him a message assuring him protection as far as Timbuktu.

Monzon died in 1808 and handed over power to Faama Da, whom oral tradition recalls as being the "favorite son." According to some sources, the eldest son was Cefolo, who would normally have been next in line, but Da was by far the more accomplished in military matters, providing strong support for his father's exploits as well as leading successful campaigns himself. The tonjonw wanted to consider the elder Cefolo and several of Monzon's brothers for the succession, but Faama Da gained control of Segu and consolidated its territorial possessions. Upon Faama Da's death in 1827 his brother Cefolo finally took power (1827–1839). During the reign of Cefolo's successor Nyènèmba, the neighboring Fula kingdom of Masina staged a strong rebellion against Segu authority in 1839. Masina was subdued by Bakari Jan Koné, hailed by oral tradition as one of Segu's greatest heroes. Following the brief rule of Nyènèmba there were five more Ngolosi rulers of Segu: Kirango Ben (1841–1849), Naluma Kuma (1849–1851), Masala Demba (1851–1854), Torokoro Mari (1854–1859), and Ali Jara, who was in power when Segu was conquered in 1861 by the Tukulor army of Alhaj 'Umar Tal.

DAVID C. CONRAD

Further Reading

Bazin, Jean. "War and Servitude in Segou." *Economy and Society*, no. 3 (1974): 107–144.

Conrad, David C. (ed.). *A State of Intrigue: The Epic of Bamana Segu according to Tayiru Banbera*. Oxford: Oxford University Press, 1990.

Djata, Sundiata A. *The Bamana Empire by the Niger: Kingdom, Jihad and Colonization 1712–1920*. Princeton, N.J.: Markus Wiener, 1997.

Kesteloot, Lilyan. "Le Mythe et l'Histoire Dans la Formation de l'Empire de Ségou." *Bulletin IFAN*, no. 3 (1978): 578–681.

Kesteloot, Lilyan (ed.). *Lepopde Bambara de Segou*. 2 vols. Paris: L'Harmattan, 1993.

Park, Mungo. *Travels in the Interior Districts of Africa in 1795, 1796, and 1797* (1799) and *The Journal of a Mission to the Interior of Africa in the Year 1805* (1815). In *The Travels of Mungo Park*, edited by Ronald Miller. London: Everyman, 1960.

Roberts, Richard L. *Warriors, Merchants, and Slaves: The State and the Economy in the Middle Niger Valley, 1700–1914*. Stanford, Calif.: Stanford University Press, 1987.

Sena, Tete, Portuguese, and Prazos

In the fifteenth century, Swahili traders from Kilwa and Angoche used the Qua Qua River to gain access to the Zambesi; one of them met Vasco da Gama there on his epic first voyage in 1499. From river ports caravans were organized to the gold fairs on the edge of the Zimbabwe escarpment. The Portuguese, who established a trading factory at Sofala in 1505, became aware of the Zambesi route through the journeys of António Fernandes between 1511 and 1513, but they only began to establish trading establishments on the river after about 1540. At first they merely copied the established Swahili traders, settling at Sena and Tete from where trading caravans departed for Manica and Karanga country. Sena and Tete both became considerable towns, and many of the Muslims and Portuguese established large rural residences in their neighborhood.

Portuguese and Muslims also established themselves permanently at the gold fairs and at the courts of the Karanga rulers. At fairs such as Masapa and Luanze, they acquired jurisdiction over their own affairs and at court formed factions which competed for the support of the ruler. In 1561 a Jesuit mission was sent to Zambesia to try to convert the *monomotapa* (paramount Karanga chief), but the mission came to an abrupt end with the murder of one of its members.

In 1569, the Portuguese dispatched an army under a former viceroy of India, Francisco Barreto, to try to conquer the gold fields and the supposed silver mines. Most of Barreto's army, including the commander himself, died of fever. A second expedition, led by Vasco Fernandes Homen, reached Manica by way of Sofala but withdrew peacefully when it discovered the small scale of the mining operations. Although the Barreto/Homem expedition had failed in its main objective of conquering the mines, it had secured control of the Zambesi Valley and had eliminated, through massacre, most of the independent muslim traders.

Sena and Tete now became Portuguese captaincies and most of the Tonga chiefs (*fumos*) of the valley submitted to Portugal, paying tribute and offering services to the Portuguese captains. From about 1585 the trade of the Zambesi Valley and the High Veld was declared to be a monopoly of the captains of Mozambique, and they now sought once again to dominate the trade with the interior and to gain control of the main mining areas.

The opportunity came in the 1590s, when invading bands from north of the river, which may have formed part of the advancing Maravi chieftaincies, began to endanger the survival of the Karanga chieftaincies. The Portuguese and their armies of Tonga soldiers recruited in the valley succeeded in defeating the invaders and placing the monomotapa, Gatse Lucere, securely on his throne. In return the Portuguese demanded a cession of the mines, which was formally made to them in 1607.

Over the course of the next 30 years, various factions of the Portuguese fought to gain control of the Karanga chieftaincy. The captain, who held the trade monopoly, sent his soldiers; the local Portuguese traders raised their own armies to defend their settlements; and the Dominicans also intervened, trying to gain a dominant position for their order through the conversion of the Karanga ruling family. Briefly successful in 1629 when Mavura recognized his vassalage to Portugal, the Portuguese seldom cooperated with one another for long and their divisions led to their being driven out of the country and back to their river ports in 1631. The local Portuguese were able to raise forces among the valley Tonga. With these forces the Portuguese commander, Diogo de Sousa Meneses, overwhelmed the Karanga in a campaign in 1632 and secured control of most of northern Zimbabwe as well as the Low Veld as far as Sofala. The Karanga paramountcy now became tributary to the Portuguese, as did the chieftaincies of Quiteve and Manica.

Portuguese rule in the gold-bearing regions of the High Veld lasted 60 years. During that time the Portuguese established mining towns and fairs throughout the region, the most important being Dambarar, and subjected the chiefs and peasantry of the region to their overrule, levying tribute and labor services upon them. From the Portuguese crown the settlers sought titles for the lands they had conquered in the form of three life leases, which came to be called *prazos*. From their bases on the High Veld the Portuguese intervened in the southern kingdom of Changamire and became king makers—and, effectively, overlords—over most of the High Veld.

The collapse of Portuguese rule came in the years 1693–1695, when a series of successful wars were waged against them by Changamire Dombo, ruler of the Roswi. The Portuguese were driven from the High Veld, their towns and trading fairs were destroyed, and they were confined to the river towns of Sena and Tete and to the two coastal ports of Quelimane and Sofala.

During the eighteenth century the Roswi never allowed the Portuguese to trade directly with the High Veld but permitted two trading fairs—one in Manica and the other at Zumbo at the confluence of the Zambesi and the Luangwa Rivers. Here a prosperous Portuguese trading town grew up that soon exceeded both Sena and Tete in importance and profited by the gold trade of the Roswi and the newly discovered mining areas north of the river.

During the eighteenth century the Zambesi Valley and the Low Veld south to Sofala was controlled by the prazo families, many of them headed by women to whom the leases were granted. The larger and more prosperous prazos, like Gorongosa and Cheringoma, became powerful chieftaincies with private armies of *chicunda*, professional soldiers recruited and maintained by the *prazo senhor*. The wealth of the prazos came partly from the agriculture of the peasant population, but mostly from the trade with the inland fairs and the opening of new gold fields north of the river. Prazos were also owned by the religious orders, but some of these were secularized when the Jesuit order in Portugal was abolished in 1759.

Although the Zambesi towns were made municipalities in the 1760s, their prosperity began to decline in the second half of the century. Chronic banditry made the river route to Zumbo precarious, while in the 1790s a cycle of drought began that would lead to chaos in the Roswi state and ultimately to the abandonment of Zumbo and the collapse of most of the gold mining activity at the fairs.

MALYN NEWITT

See also: **Mozambique: Nineteenth Century, Early; Swahili, Portuguese and: 1498–1589.**

Further Reading

Axelson, E. *Portuguese in South-East Africa, 1488–1600.* Cape Town: Struik, 1973.

————. *Portuguese in South-East Africa, 1600–1700.* Johannesburg: Witwatersrand University Press, 1960.

Isaacman, Allen. *Mozambique: The Africanisation of a European Institution, the Zambesi Prazos, 1750–1902.* Madison: University of Wisconsin Press, 1972.

Mudenge, S. I. *A Political History of Munhumutapa.* Harare: Zimbabwe Publishing, 1986.

Newitt, Malyn. *A History of Mozambique.* London: Hurst, 1995.

Newitt, M. D. D. *Portuguese Settlement on the Zambesi.* London: Longman, 1973.

Rea, W. F. *The Economics of the Zambesi Missions 1580–1759.* Rome: Institutum Historicum, 1976.

Senegal: Nineteenth Century

The foundations of the independent republic of Senegal were established firmly in the later nineteenth century. Between about 1860 and 1900 the political, religious, and economic map of Senegal was changed completely by a series of Muslim movements and expanding French imperialism. Both Muslim reformers and Europeans sought to topple the traditional nobilities, whose leadership was rooted in slave raiding and trading, and they were both successful. Al-Hajj Umar Tal, a Muslim military leader who waged a jihad (holy war) in his native Senegal in the mid-1850s, served as a model for later religious reformers, with his attention focused on indigenous rulers and frequent pragmatic accommodation with colonial rule. Governor Louis Faidherbe, who served in Senegal from 1854 until 1865, launched aggressive military campaigns combined with treaty negotiations, a pattern followed by his successors. Thus, in the late nineteenth century, a new generation of local rulers from Senegal faced the challenge of working under a new and more powerful set of rulers, the French. Religious leaders, many of whom initially came into conflict with the colonial military, shifted their policy toward one of accommodation and cooperation. The colonial administration likewise had to deal with the new Muslim reform leaders to further their own economic agenda. The collaboration between religious and secular authorities has characterized Senegal ever since.

Senegal.

Following the model of Al-Hajj Umar Tal, Ma Ba launched a Muslim reform movement in 1862 in the northern Gambian region and eventually to Saloum in central Senegal. Ma Ba, while successfully defeating the traditional leaders, was defeated and killed by the French when he attempted to invade Sin in central Senegal in 1867. Ma Ba's followers included Lat Dior (Joor) who conquered Kajoor (Kayor) and Alburi N'Diaye (Njay) who seized Jolof in western Senegal. The French supported the existing rulers, with whom they had signed treaties, but the Muslim reform movements were too powerful and overthrew the traditional nobility. The French then had to deal with the new leadership. The interactions between the colonial rulers and the Muslim reformers were often ambiguous and cautious, but generally cooperative. Lat Dior soon came into conflict with the French over the colonial plan to build a railroad through Kajoor linking Dakar and Saint-Louis. For its French sponsors, the railroad was a means of dominating the still-independent Kajoor, first militarily and then commercially. In 1886, when Lat Dior attacked a French ally in eastern Kajor, he was killed in battle. Albury N'Diaye overthrew the old leadership of Jolof and ruled the state as a charismatic military and religious leader. When N'Diaye threatened to become too powerful, he was overthrown by the French.

Another Muslim reform movement erupted in eastern Senegambia in 1887. A Soninke cleric, Al-Hajj Mamadu Lamine Drame, who cited Umar Tal as his inspiration, launched his attack against pro-French rulers in the Upper Senegal Valley. The French intervened to support their allies and actively pursued Lamine throughout the region, killing him in late 1887. In the process they brought the entire valley under their control. By 1890, the area of modern-day Senegal, with the notable exception of the Casamance, was under firm French control. Groups in the Casamance resisted colonial rule until World War I.

The most important religious figure in modern Senegal, Amadu Bamba M'Backe, a follower of Lat Dior, established himself in the late 1880s in central Senegal and quickly attracted a loyal following as well as the attention of the colonial authorities. While evidence suggests Bamba's resistance was primarily spiritual and directed against traditional leaders, many of his followers hoped that an active struggle of resistance against colonial rule would develop. In 1895 the French, deciding to end any threat, deported Bamba to Gabon, only allowing him to return in 1902, by which time his stature had grown considerably, especially among the Wolof of central and western Senegal. Bamba would later encourage his followers, who formed the immensely influential Murid brotherhood, to cooperate with colonial authorities.

The greatest colonial presence was in the coastal region, especially near Saint-Louis at the mouth of the Senegal River and in the vicinity of Dakar and the Cap Vert Peninsula. In 1848, Saint-Louis and Gorée, off the Cap Vert Peninsula, were declared communes of France. In 1880, the commune of Rufisque and in 1887 that of Dakar were created. The French policy of assimilation was most fully enacted in the Four Communes, whose residents were considered French citizens rather than subjects, as in the rest of Senegal, and elected a deputy to the French Assembly. Saint-Louis served as the capital of Senegal as well as of the Federation of French West Africa until 1902, when the federation capital was moved to Dakar. Saint-Louis remained the capital of the colony. Senegal continued to occupy a privileged position within the French empire in West Africa throughout the colonial period.

It was during the later nineteenth century that Senegal's economy, previously based on the export of gum arabic and other agricultural products from the Senegal River region and coastal areas, became almost exclusively dependent on peanuts, introduced by the French in 1848. All areas of the colony, except the tropical Casamance, witnessed the rapid growth of peanut production for export, particularly in the central area of the colony. Religious authorities who controlled the peanut basin urged their followers to cooperate with colonial economic policy and grow peanuts, gaining the Muslim leaders colonial support for their religious activities. The economic fortunes of the desert-side river region declined while that of western and central Senegal rose considerably. The colony's entire infrastructure, especially railroad construction, was based on the transport of peanuts from the central peanut basin to the coast. Other areas of economic development were neglected in favor of peanut production. Senegal became a single-crop economy in the later nineteenth century and has remained so ever since.

ANDREW F. CLARK

See also: **Senegal: Faidherbe, Louis and Expansion of French Senegal, 1854–1865.**

Further Reading

Clark, Andrew F. *From Frontier to Backwater: Economy and Society in the Upper Senegal Valley (West Africa), 1850–1920.* Lanham, Md.: University Press of America, 1999.

Gellar, Sheldon, *Structural Changes and Colonial Dependency: Senegal, 1885–1945.* Beverly Hills: Sage, 1967.

Klein, Martin. *Islam and Imperialism in Senegal: Sine-Saloum, 1847–1914.* Stanford, Calif.: Stanford University Press, 1968.

Robinson, David. *The Holy War of Umar Tal: The Western Sudan in the mid-Nineteenth Century.* Oxford: Clarendon Press, 1985.

Senegal: Faidherbe, Louis and Expansion of French Senegal, 1854–1865

Louis Faidherbe served two terms as governor of Senegal, from 1854 to 1861 and from 1863 to 1865. He instituted a "forward policy" that certain critics labeled "peace or powder." He took decisive steps to advance eastward from Saint-Louis through the Senegal River Valley and the vast Sudan region to Lake Chad. He even dreamed of a French African empire stretching from the Atlantic Ocean to the Red Sea. He would create a firm basis for its future development culturally as well as politically and economically.

Faidherbe's career in Senegal had begun in 1852 as a subdirector of engineers. He participated in seizing Podor and constructing its fort, attacking Diman's capital, and reinforcing Bakel's defenses in 1854. He wrote *Les Berbères* (1859), began learning Wolof, Pular, and Sarakolé, and became interested in exploring the Niger River. Admiring Faidherbe's activities, major Bordeaux firms doing business with Senegal recommended him for Senegal's governorship.

Militarily, Faidherbe first sought to protect the gum trade along the Senegal River and quell the Moorish Trarzas who were raiding Wolof peasants living along the river's south bank. In February 1855 Faidherbe ordered his forces to expel Trarza military clans from Walo. War ensued with Walo, whose leadership rebuffed Faidherbe's plan to "liberate" them; in April Faidherbe had to fight the principal Trarza warrior clans. By the end of 1855 he overcame Walo, making it

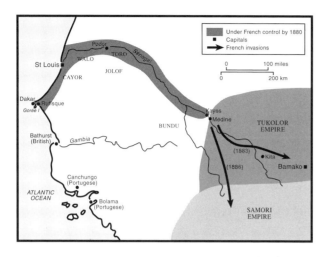

Senegal and the French, nineteenth century.

the first Sub-Saharan state dismembered and annexed by France.

In 1858, having warred and used divide-and-conquer tactics, Faidherbe made treaties with the Trarzas of southern Mauritania. The Trarzas agreed to respect French traders and commute the controversial "customs" charges into a fixed export duty of 3 per cent.

Faidherbe's endeavor to end all African controls over French navigation along the Senegal River, particularly the toll at Saldé-Tébékout in central Futa-Toro, brought greater hostilities. Conflict erupted with the traditional leaders of Futa-Toro and the Tukolor Muslim reformer and state builder, Al-Hajj Umar. In 1858-1859, Faidherbe forced the confederation of Futa-Toro to make peace on French terms, and divided the confederation into four client states of France.

Faidherbe's greatest adversary was Al-Hajj Umar, charismatic leader of the Tijaniyya in west Africa. Before Faidherbe's governorship, Umar had attacked the French because of their prohibiting the firearms trade in the Senegal Valley. Faidherbe gallantly led a small force in relieving Médine from Umar's three-month siege. In 1860, Faidherbe negotiated a demarcation line along the Bafing River with Umar's emissary, and provisionally agreed to send his own envoy to discuss future relations with Umar.

Faidherbe hoped that Umar, in return for political support and firearms, would permit France to erect a line of fortified trading posts from Senegal to a base for navigation on the Niger. With Umar's cooperation, Faidherbe envisioned pushing French trade and influence downstream and averting the monopoly that Britain, through its traders in the delta, threatened to establish over the Niger.

Returning as governor in 1863, Faidherbe sent Lieutenant Eugene Mage to contact Umar; eventually Mage negotiated a treaty with Umar's successor,

Ahmadu Tal. Ahmadu renounced holy war against France, and permitted French trade and exploration in his territories, while France allowed him to buy goods in Saint–Louis.

While fighting Umar, Faidherbe's forces had gutted the principal villages of Buoye, Kaméra, and Guidimakha. Thereupon Faidherbe made treaties with new client rulers in each state.

By 1859 Faidherbe gave attention to the kingdom of Cayor. He aimed to prevent its warriors' interference in the collection of peanuts by peasants and to open a trail featuring three small forts and a telegraph line linking Saint-Louis, Dakar, and Gorée via the coast. Faidherbe first tried peaceful means, but rebuffed by Damel (King) Biraima, he used force. When Biraima died, Faidherbe claimed that Biraima had agreed on his deathbed to France's demands. Biraima's successor, Macodu, would not recognize the treaty. Faidherbe declared war and sought to replace Macodu with Madiodio. However, Lat Dior rebelled. Faidherbe's replacement, Governor Jean Jauréguiberry, allowed Lat Dior to expel Madiodio and become ruler. Returning as governor, Faidherbe moved to restore Madiodio, who ceded more territory to France. As disorder still prevailed in Cayor, Faidherbe retired Madiodio and annexed the remainder of Cayor in 1865.

Faidherbe's military successes owed much to his ingenuity. In 1857 he organized the Senegalese Riflemen. He created two battalions of volunteers recruited as much as possible from Senegambia's free population. The first recruits were paid relatively well; served short, two-year terms; wore special, colorful uniforms; underwent looser discipline than European troops; and received traditional food.

Faidherbe labored in multifold ways in Senegal. He founded a school for the sons of chiefs, and lay schools for Muslims. He established scholarships for primary education in Saint-Louis and secondary education in France. He built small technical schools at Dakar, and opened a museum and newspaper at Saint–Louis. Faidherbe organized the Bank of Senegal; laid out Saint-Louis afresh as befitted a capital city; promoted the export of groundnuts; made valuable and detailed studies of the indigenous people; and founded Dakar, future metropolis of French Africa.

Faidherbe stood at the center of modern French imperialism. He initiated firm French control of the Senegal Valley, which became the springboard for further expansion in West Africa. By opening up Senegal's trade he provided the means for reaching the Niger Basin. His plan for railroad construction eventually materialized. His proposal, rejected by his superiors, for France and Britain, and France and Portugal, to mutually arrange exchange of territories in West Africa would have created the French Gambia Valley.

Faidherbe grappled sympathetically with Islam in West Africa; he used war and diplomacy to stop the westward push of the great Al-Hajj Umar. Faidherbe's policy of opposing Christian proselytizing Muslims caused a prestigious Francophile Muslim community and tradition in Senegal.

Faidherbe further affected West Africa. In Senegal his governorship distinguished priorities and discriminately allocated limited resources. Faidherbe started new public works and aided the peasants. His policies of non-French settlement and restricted assimilation into French citizenship became models for French West Africa.

ERVING E. BEAUREGARD

Further Reading

Abun-Nasr, Jamil M. *The Tijaniyya: A Sufi Order in the Modern World*. London: Oxford University Press, 1965.

Barrows, Leland C. "Faidherbe and Senegal: A Critical Discussion." African Studies Review 19, no. 1 (1976): 95–117.

Cohen, William B. *Rulers of Empire: The French Colonial Service in Africa*. Stanford, Calif.: Stanford University, Hoover Institution Press, 1971.

Hrbek, Ivan. "General Faidherbe and the French Colonial Policy in West Africa." *Archiv Orientalni: Journal of the Czechoslavak Oriental Institute, Prague* 49, no. 1 (1981): 1–17.

Robinson, David. *The Holy War of Umar Tal: The Western Sudan in the Mid-Nineteenth Century*. Oxford: Clarendon Press, 1985.

Senegal: Colonial Period: Railways

French railway construction in Senegal and its Sudanese hinterland was driven by the desire to conquer the Niger Valley, and later, to develop West African trade. The railway was built in three stages: a coastal railway between Dakar and the mouth of the Senegal River, a second railway between the Senegal and Niger Rivers, and finally, a third railway to link the first two. To reduce costs and speed up construction, the French built a narrow-gauge line with lightweight rail along a route that eliminated the need for tunnels and most bridges. To further reduce costs, the French relied on African labor to build most of the three lines and to operate them once they were finished.

The first segment connected Saint-Louis, the commercial city at the mouth of the Senegal River, to Dakar, with the best deepwater harbor in the region. In the spring of 1882, the government awarded a contract to the private construction firm Société des Batignolles. Using a combination of European, Moroccan, and Chinese labor, the firm laid 264 kilometers of rail near the coast, completing the Chemin de Fer Dakar–Saint-Louis in July 1885.

At the same time, the French government dispatched troops of the colonial marines to build a second railway from the Upper Senegal River to the Niger River. When low river levels forced them to unload prematurely in March 1880, the marines began building the Chemin de Fer Kayes–Niger near the village of Kayes. Progress was slow due to disease and poor planning, and by the time the National Assembly cut the project's funds in 1884, only 54 kilometers of the railway were finished. The 1890 conquest of Ahmadu Tall's empire at Segou revived interest in the railway, and after engineers completed a bridge over the Bafing River in 1896, the work proceeded rapidly. The first train reached Bamako in November 1904, and the tracks were completed to the Middle Niger Valley at Koulikoro during the following month.

The government immediately began to plan a link between the two railways, but military engineers and French merchants disagreed on the route and who should build it. Eventually a compromise was reached and in 1907, military engineers employed African laborers to start a new spur at Thiès, 70 kilometers east of Dakar. The following spring, a second construction site opened at Kayes, and by July 1909, the Chemin de Fer Kayes–Ambidédi extended the line 44 kilometers downstream from Kayes. Construction ceased during World War I, but resumed after the war and the two spurs were joined at Gouloumbo, 660 kilometers east of Dakar, on August 15, 1923. From that date on, the railway provided a year-round transportation link between the Middle Niger Valley and the Atlantic Ocean. Two years later, the government combined the two interior railways into the Chemin de Fer Thiès–Kayes–Niger, and took over the Chemin de Fer Dakar–Saint-Louis in May 1933 to form the Chemin de Fer Dakar–Niger.

The railway provided the administration with a potent tool for economic planning. Although ports like Kaolack and Rufisque were closer to the interior, the government adjusted shipping rates to promote the use of Dakar. During the 1920s, the government promoted rail shipments of peanuts for export, which favored the growth of Dakar while Saint-Louis stagnated.

Much of the original construction work was of poor quality however. In some places, rails had been laid directly on the ground without any ballast. Termites rapidly consumed untreated wooden ties, lightweight rail was prone to failure, and simple bridges and culverts washed out during the rainy season. Between 1923 and 1956, most of the original rails were replaced and the system was extended with feeder lines in Senegal from Louga to Lingéré in 1931 and from Diourbel to Touba in 1933. More ambitious plans were drafted to extend the railway to the Casamance region of Senegal, Segou, Timbuktu, and Algeria, but except for some grading in the Sahara during World War II, none of these plans materialized.

The railway employed Africans in construction as early as 1882 and in skilled positions such as locomotive drivers by 1900. During the 1920s thousands of forced laborers built the Chemin de Fer Thiès–Kayes, and by the end of World War II, nearly 8,000 Africans worked on the Chemin de Fer Dakar–Niger. Railway workers staged the first of many strikes in 1888, and some of their later actions presented a serious challenge to French authority. The 1938 strike at Thiès produced martyrs when government troops killed six strikers and injured more than one hundred others. The 1947–1948 strike mobilized more than 15,000 workers from French West Africa and shut down the railway for more than five months. By the time of the 1952 general strike, railway workers had a reputation for militancy and solidarity.

After World War II, the administration upgraded the railway by rebuilding the Kayes–Niger line, creating new technical training schools and introducing new equipment. The railway obtained its self-propelled diesel passenger cars in 1940 and diesel locomotives in 1947. In 1951, the last steam locomotives were shifted to freight switching, and by 1960, there were none left in service.

The railway contributed to the development of several towns in Senegal. Thiès was founded to house the main repair shops of the Chemin de Fer Thiès–Niger in 1923. Tambacounda grew at the intersection of the railway and the main overland route to the Casamance region. Kidira developed next to the bridge that carried the railway over the Senegal River into Mali. Other cities like Dakar, Kaolack, Diourbel, and Louga benefited from handling freight that was carried on the railway.

The railway also promoted close ties between Senegal and the French Sudan. At independence, those ties contributed to the decision to form the Mali Federation in June 1960. When the federation dissolved two months later, Senegal and Mali broke off diplomatic relations and severed the railway at Kidira. During the next three years, the Malian portion declined, and after the railway reopened in 1963, its usefulness was greatly reduced by increased competition from trucks and the railway from Abidjan to Ouagadougou. The Senegalese railway remained viable, and twice-weekly express trains still operate between Dakar and the Niger River.

JAMES A. JONES

See also: **Kenya: East African Protectorate and the Uganda Railway; Nigeria: Colonial Period: Railways, Mining, and Market Production; Railways.**

Further Reading

Church, R. J. H. "Trans-Saharan Railway Projects: A Study in Their History and Geographical Setting." In *London Essays in Geography: Memorial Essays to Rodwell Jones*, edited by Wooldridge and Stamp. London: Longman, 1951.

Jones, Joseph. *The Politics of Transport in Twntieth Century France.* Kingston, Ont.: McGill-Queen's University Press, 1984.

Riembau, Frédéric. *De Dakar au Niger.* Paris: Augustin Challamel, 1908.

Suret-Canale, Jean. "The French West African Railway Worker's Strike, 1947–1948." In *African Labor History*, edited by Peter C. W. Gutkind, Robin Cohen, and Jean Copans. Beverly Hills: Sage, 1978.

Senegal: Colonial Period: Four Communes: Dakar, Saint-Louis, Gorée, and Rufisque

The Four Communes enjoyed a distinct legal status during the colonial period, which set them apart from other townships in French West Africa. The Four Communes were ruled under French law and were considered full-fledged municipalities, with the right to elect a mayor and town council and to vote in elections for the Legislative Assembly, which sat in Saint-Louis, and for a deputy. Africans born in the Four Communes were considered French "citizens," distinct from the African "subjects" who made up the vast majority of the population.

The special legal status of the Four Communes was a product of history. In the eighteenth and early nineteenth centuries, Saint-Louis and Gorée were important French commercial settlements. They were considered part of the French Empire in 1848 when slavery was abolished and when their inhabitants were declared citizens for the first time. Legislation passed between 1872 and 1880 extended the privileged status of Saint-Louis and Gorée to Dakar and Rufisque, largely to accommodate the large resident population of French merchants in both towns. Dakar and Rufisque had close ties to Gorée, which was too small to accommodate the growing French merchant community. Legislation intended to make life comfortable for French residents had the unintended effect of creating political rights for Africans born in the townships (Johnson 1971). In the late nineteenth century the most prominent citizens were merchants of mixed ancestry, referred to as *métis*, who were Catholic. African merchants, artisans, fishers, and laborers, many of them freed slaves or migrants, made up the bulk of the local population. The vast majority of the population was Muslim. Saint-Louis was the largest city in Senegal in 1890, with a population of 25,000. Dakar grew rapidly after it became in capital of French West Africa in 1904 and the terminus of the railway and port system. By 1920 the population of Saint-Louis had declined to 20,000 and Dakar's had expanded to 37,000.

During the conquest of the interior the Africans of the Four Communes allied themselves with the French, even though the merchant community feared the consequences of French political power. French merchants moved into the interior after the conquest and took over the leading positions in the import-export trade. Africans from the Four Communes, who were now called *originaires*, were welcome as employees of French merchants or as clerks in the administration if they were literate in French. These were perceived as dead-end positions, because originaires could not serve as chiefs, despite the ambitions of some, because of their "citizen" status. Declining economic opportunities combined with political frustrations related to their anomalous legal status led to political activism. Galandou Diouf was the first African originaire to win a political office as the legislative councilor of Rufisque in 1907. Along with other political militants he encouraged fellow originaire Blaise Diagne to run for deputy in 1914. Diagne's candidacy was a response to French efforts to restrict originaire political activism outside of the Four Communes and to contest their status as "citizens."

Diagne was elected deputy only a few months before the outbreak of World War I. He used the issue of military recruitment in the Four Communes to win formal acknowledgment of the "citizenship" of originaires. They served in the French army during the war, not in colonial military units alongside African subjects. African citizens received higher pay and more benefits than ordinary African soldiers. They paid the "blood tax" of military service, but they received concrete political benefits for their service. After the war, Diagne created a political party, the Republican Socialist Party, which won a resounding victory in the legislative and municipal elections of 1919. In the immediate postwar period Diagne tried to consolidate his power by challenging the political influence of French merchants and by demanding that all Africans in Senegal receive the same rights as the citizens of the Four Communes. French colonial officials countered Diagne's demands by granting more authority to African chiefs in a new colonial Legislative Assembly. By 1923 Diagne felt obliged to reach a political compromise with French merchants, who were invited to join his party, and to accept the political realities that confined his power to the Four Communes.

From 1919 until his death in 1934, Diagne dominated politics in the Four Communes. In the later part of his career he formed close working relationships with French administrators and merchants, leading to charges that he had "sold out." His critics included former allies like Galandou Diouf, who formed a rival political party. Diagne's alliance with the colonial administration and French merchants meant that he was virtually invincible. When Galandou Diouf and Lamine Guèye protested that Diagne had received French aid in the elections of 1928, their complaints were dismissed with the comment that the originaires

were the "spoiled brats" of the French Empire. Diouf, who succeeded Diagne as deputy in 1934, found that his own power was hemmed in by the same mechanisms that the French had used to limit Diagne's ambitions. Galandou Diouf died during World War II and was replaced by Lamine Guèye, another prominent African "citizen" who was the last of the originaire politicians. The political credo of the citizens was their demand for equality with the French colonizers in Senegal.

African subjects resented the privileged political status of the originaires, which was based only on their place of birth. The political reforms that gave the vote to African subjects after 1946 prepared the way for the demise of the originaires. Léopold Senghor's defeat of Lamine Guèye in the elections of 1948 owed much to Senghor's status as a former "subject" and his ability to identify his cause with that of the rural majority. Lamine Guèye saw himself as the designated heir to the political leadership of Diagne, but most voters saw him as arrogant and out of touch. Since independence the special status of the Four Communes has disappeared, but the political tradition of elections and lively debate that they represented has continued to exert an influence on the political behavior of urban residents in postcolonial Senegal.

JAMES SEARING

Further Reading

Johnson, G. Wesley. *The Emergence of Black Politics in Senegal: The Struggle for Power in the Four Communes, 1900–1920.* Stanford, Calif.: Stanford University Press, 1971.

Lunn, Joe H. *Memoirs of the Maelstrom: A Senegalese Oral History of the First World War.* Portsmouth, N.H.: Heinemann, 1999.

Schachter, Ruth Morgenthau. *Political Parties in French Speaking Africa.* London: Oxford University Press, 1974.

Searing, James F. *West African Slavery and Atlantic Commerce: The Senegal River Valley, 1700–1860,* Cambridge: Cambridge University Press, 1993.

Senegal: World War I

World War I accelerated the process of economic and political change in the early twentieth century occurring in Africa, which was largely colonized by 1914. The war signaled the end of the final phase of French colonial expansion in Africa; it also caused the recruitment of French Africa's first great conscript army and the first concerted effort to exploit the colonial empire's resources on a massive scale. Because of its long tradition of colonial rule and its close ties to France, the colony of Senegal particularly felt the impacts of World War I. The influences, however, differed somewhat between the coastal Four Communes (Saint-Louis, Dakar, Rufique, and Gorée), where the colonial presence was most keenly felt, and the rural interior of the colony, where most of the residents lived.

By 1914, the entire colony of Senegal was firmly under French colonial control. Residents of the coastal Four Communes, regardless of race, were considered citizens, rather than subjects, of France. They had the right to elect a deputy to the French Assembly in Paris. In 1914, the African electors sent Blaise Diagne, a former colonial official, as their deputy to the National Assembly. Military conscription had first been introduced to French West Africa in 1912 in hopes that colonial troops would eventually take over the garrisoning of the colonies in order to release French contingents for service in Europe. The colonial troops could also augment French forces in Europe if necessary. The decree mandated compulsory military service for all African males between the ages of 20 and 28. With the outbreak of war in 1914, Diagne and residents of the communes insisted that urban residents should fight as voluntary enlistees in regular units at the side of their French co-citizens. However, very few *originaires,* as the residents of the Four Communes were known, actually served at all until Diagne pushed through the Law of October 19, 1915, which resulted in a massive recruitment drive. In return for assistance in recruiting Senegalese soldiers for the war effort, Diagne obtained confirmation of French citizenship of this urban minority, even if they chose to retain their status under Muslim law as well. When the originaires did begin to serve in larger numbers after the law passed, their privileged conditions antagonized their countrymen from the rural areas. Subjects residing outside the coastal communes were subject to involuntary conscription into colonial units, received less pay and endured harsher conditions.

In the rural areas of Senegal, war recruitment had a marked impact on domestic slavery, or involuntary servitude, which persisted after official abolition. Village chiefs were required to fill quotas for war recruitment, and often sent descendants of slaves to the posts to meet the requirements. The servants were freed if they enlisted in place of free-born men. Sometimes masters of people of slave descent promised their subordinates freedom if they enlisted. Other slave-descended men enlisted on their own to escape servitude. In some cases, serviles had to turn over their enlistment bonus, usually the sum of 200 French francs, the price of a male slave, to their owners. This payment insured the servile's freedom from his master.

War recruitment also influenced migration patterns throughout Senegal. Both free-born and servile-descent men migrated to other areas of the colony or to other colonies to avoid conscription. Many men and their families migrated into the central peanut basin of Senegal to escape recruitment. Desertion after enlistment was also very high, contributing to migration from areas firmly under colonial control to more rural remote regions. Returning veterans, especially those of servile descent, also migrated to other areas, especially the coastal region and peanut basin.

In 1918, France's manpower needs for the war became desperate, and Diagne agreed to become commissioner for the recruitment of African troops, with the rank of governor general, in exchange for a French pledge to improve social services in Senegal. Diagne conducted a sweepingly successful, but much criticized campaign across French West Africa, drawing more than 100,000 enlistments, while simultaneously insisting on veterans' benefits and other privileges to be won by fighting for France. Eventually, over 200,000 Africans from French West Africa fought for France, with about one-third coming from Senegal.

The intense war recruitment, combined with a mobilization of colonial resources to meet metropolitan needs, had a marked impact on Senegal's division of labor. Taxes were not reduced during the war, and even families with members serving in the military had to meet their financial obligations. Subsistence crops were requisitioned and paid for at prices below the free market price. Women took an increased role in agricultural production and herding in the rural areas to make ends meet. Government revenues declined during the war. The war effort also meant increased pressures on the land to produce and soil erosion became a serious problem for many areas of the colony during the war years.

Because it seriously disrupted economic links between Senegal and France, World War I marked the end of Senegal's most dynamic period of economic growth, which had begun in the late nineteenth century with a marked increase in peanut production and export. Even with increased migration to the peanut basin, the production of peanuts dropped precipitously after the outbreak of the war, largely in response to the deteriorating terms of trade and falling peanut prices on the world market. Throughout the colony, and even in the peanut basin, farmers abandoned the cash-crop production of peanuts for food crops to feed their families. Peanut exports dropped from over 300,000 tons in 1914 to 126,000 tons in 1918. The war also had a negative impact on the nascent industrial sector in Senegal. Most of the European personnel running the colony's banks and industries either left or were recalled to France, leaving the colony without an experienced entrepreneurial class until well after the war had ended.

ANDREW F. CLARK

See also: **Senegal: Colonial Period: Administration and "Assimilation"; Senegal: Colonial Period: Four Communes: Dakar, Saint-Louis, Gorée, and Rufisque; Senegal: World War II.**

Further Reading

Echenberg, Myron. *The "Tirailleurs Senegalais" in French West Africa, 1857–1960.* Portsmouth, N.H.: Heineman, 1991.

Johnson, G. Welsey. *The Emergence of Black Politics in Senegal: The Struggle for Power in the Four Communes, 1900–1920.* Stanford, Calif.: Stanford University Press, 1971.

Page, Melvin (ed.). *Africa and the First World War.* London: Macmillan, 1987.

Senegal: Colonial Period: Administration and "Assimilation"

When the French regained possession of their colonies in 1818, the colony of Senegal consisted of two coastal islands, Saint-Louis and Gorée, and several trading posts. When France agreed reluctantly to abolish the slave trade in the Treaty of Paris (1815), it deprived Senegal of its commercial base. The mixture of *metis* (those of mixed blood) and French traders who dominated the colony had to find a new source of wealth. After the failure of a colonization scheme, Saint-Louis thrust itself into the trade in gum, produced from acacia trees on the north bank of the Senegal River. Gorée lived off coasting trade until the development of peanut exports in the 1840s provided Senegal with the crop that was thenceforth the basis of its economy.

France depended on its relations with neighboring African states, to whom it made annual payments for the right to trade. In 1848, these relations were briefly disrupted by the French abolition of slavery. Fearing flight to the French towns, several African states cut off trade. In 1854, a new governor, Louis Faidherbe, decided to force a change in these obligations. In a three-year war, he forced the Moors to accept suppression of customs payments, occupied Walo, the kingdom opposite Saint-Louis, and established French hegemony over the Futa Toro, a kingdom that stretched along the Senegal River. Later, he occupied parts of Kajoor and forced the kings of Siin and Saalum to accept French posts. War in Europe and military defeat suspended the forward movement, and the French were forced to allow their major enemy, Kajoor's Damel, Lat Dior, to return to power. A decade later, Lat Dior objected to French plans to build a railroad for the export of peanuts from Kajoor. The railroad was built, Lat Dior was defeated and killed in 1886, and by 1891, almost all of Senegal was in French hands.

The 1880s and 1890s also saw the conquest of what became French West Africa. The federation was established in 1895 and received a definitive form in 1904.

Senegal, however, differed from the other colonies in two ways. First, Senegal was France's partner in the conquest. France conquered West Africa with an army of Africans, mostly of slave origin and largely recruited in Senegal. Dakar was the capital and Senegal provided the clerks, telegraph operators, riverboat captains, and railway workers. There was a Senegalese quarter in Bamako and Senegalese traders and officials through western and equatorial Africa. One Senegalese, Mademba Sy, was made *fama*, or king, of the Sansanding in the French Sudan.

The second difference is that the Four Communes, the old coastal towns, had a measure of self-government shared by no other colony in Africa. The colony had representatives to French parliaments the revolutions of 1789 and 1848, and then after the establishment of the Third Republic in 1871, won the right to municipal self-government, to an elected General Council, and to a representative in the French parliament. The General Council had control over part of the budget, though the lines of authority were regularly contested. The existence of African elected officials served to limit the arbitrariness that marked colonial rule elsewhere and softened many of the harsh edges. Senegal experienced much less brutality and discrimination. The deputy was French until 1902, when a métis lawyer was elected and then, in 1914, an African, Blaise Diagne. Up to this time, the rights of people in the Four Communes were not clearly defined, but Diagne made a condition of his support for military recruitment in World War I confirmation of the citizenship of his electors. Thus, they were not subject to the *indigenat*, the law code that ruled most of French Africa and had all of the rights of other French persons. The French often talked of assimilation as a goal, but only in Senegal—and mostly in the Four Communes—did much assimilation take place. After the war, the General Council was renamed the Colonial Council and was emasculated with the addition of a series of appointed chiefs who could be counted on to support the colonial government. Diagne, however, was regularly reelected until his death in 1934, when he was succeeded by another African, Galandou Diouf.

The rest of Senegal was divided into *cantons*, headed by chiefs recruited mostly from traditional ruling families. The cantons were grouped into *cercles*, each headed by a French administrator. Increasingly, however, real authority devolved on Muslim leaders called *marabouts*. The most effective resistance to the French conquest was from a series of Muslim reformers. Faidherbe realized early that if he wished to govern Senegal he had to find allies in the Muslim community. The most important was Bou-el-Mogdad, who was *cadi* of Saint-Louis and undertook several missions for Faidherbe. Not all of his successors agreed with Faidherbe's policy, but eventually it prevailed. The colonial state used Muslims as agents, built mosques, financed the pilgrimage of the most loyal to Mecca, and was sensitive to their religious sensibilities. As the superiority of French arms became evident, more religious leaders decided to yield the political sphere to the French. The most important of these was Malik Sy, a disciple of the *tijaniya* religious brotherhood. His major rival was Amadu Bamba, son of Lat Dior's former cadi. He founded his own religious order, the Mourides, which preached piety, submission, and hard work. The French feared his popularity and deported him twice, but with time accommodation prevailed. Mouride colonies spread peanut cultivation into east and south into areas hitherto used mostly by pastoralists. Mourides were recruited for the French army and the French, in turn provided money for the construction of a large mosque at Touba, the order's capital. Politicians from Diagne on generally sought Mouride votes and financial aid.

In 1946, the constitution of the Fourth Republic extended the vote to all parts of the empire. In the first election, socialist candidates Lamine Gueye and Leopold Sedar Senghor prevailed. A poet, grammarian, and former teacher of Greek and Latin, Senghor became known as the deputy for the peasants. In 1951, with Mouride support, he challenged Gueye and won. He served in the French parliament until 1958, when Senegal was given self-government and Senghor became its first president.

MARTIN A. KLEIN

Further Reading

Barry, Boubacar. *Senegambia and the Atlantic Slave Trade: Senegambia before the Colonial Conquest.* Cambridge: Cambridge University Press, 1998.

Cruise O'Brien, Donal. *The Mourides of Senegal: The Political and Economic Organization of an Islamic Brotherhood.* Oxford: Oxford University Press, 1971.

Johnson, G. Wesley. *The Emergence of Black Politics in Senegal: The Struggle for Power in the Four Communes, 1900–1920.* Stanford: Stanford University Press, 1971.

Manchuelle, Francois. Willing Migrants. Athens, Ohio: Ohio University Press, 1998.

Robinson, David. *Paths of Accomodation: Muslim Societies and French Colonial Authorities in Senegal and Mauritania.* Portsmouth, N.H.: Heinemann, 2001.

Senegal: Colonial Period: Economy

The colonial economy of Senegal, which was based on the export of peanuts, had its historical roots in the transition from slave exports to what historians have referred to as "legitimate commerce." In Senegal this transition was facilitated by the fact that exports of gum arabic were already important in the eighteenth century and expanded rapidly in the first decades of the nineteenth century. Although gum came from the Saharan region to the north, the expansion of gum exports intensified the grain trade between the desert and the savanna. French and African merchants based in Saint-Louis bought surplus savanna grain, establishing relations with African producers which were later used to encourage the adoption of peanuts as a new export crop. The crucial role was played by Wolof merchants and Wolof-speaking merchants of mixed European and African ancestry. French merchants dominated the gum trade, so the peanut trade represented a new opportunity (Searing 1993).

Wolof cultivators, from the aristocracy to ordinary peasants, welcomed the new trade. The price paid for peanuts was high, particularly when compared to the price paid for millet, which was the only commercialized agricultural product before the 1840s. Peanut prices were based on the price paid for peanuts in London and Marseilles, discounted by the import-export firms to cover their expenses. Although the price paid to producers was further reduced by the profits of merchants who bulked the crop for export, it was sufficiently attractive to begin an export boom that was only interrupted by the colonial conquest, by World War I, and by the Great Depression. Exports reached 82,000 metric tons in 1882, 140,000 metric tons in 1900, 280,000 metric tons in 1914, and 508,000 tons in 1930. The expansion of exports reflected the extension of peanut cultivation to new regions as the colonial infrastructure of railways and ports was completed in stages between 1886 and 1915. The peanut boom began in Kajoor in the 1870s. By World War I, peanut cultivation was expanding most rapidly in the Sine-Saloum region, where the railway reached Tambacounda in 1915.

Not all regions participated in the peanut economy. Wolof and Sereer peasants were most favorably located in relation to the railways and Atlantic ports. The peanut basin coincided with the territory of the Wolof and Sereer kingdoms, including the "frontier zones" in the east where many migrants settled in underpopulated lands. Patterns of labor migration in Senegal reflected the new economic realities. Long-term migrant laborers were almost invariably from homelands that were too distant from the railways and the ports to make peanut exports a viable source of income. Migrants who came to the coast for one or several farming seasons or who sought full-time wage labor were also more willing to migrate to distant colonies. Wolof and Sereer, by contrast, migrated over short distances within the peanut basin in search of new land and could seek out seasonal wage labor in the cities (Manchuelle 1997)

The export economy brought together European commercial firms and peasant household production.

The dynamics of the peasant household are crucial for understanding African participation in peanut farming. Households grouped husbands and wives with their children and other dependents that accepted the authority of the household head. The household head was responsible for feeding household members by providing his wives with the grain staple millet. In exchange his dependents could be called on to work on his fields four days a week, from early morning to mid-afternoon. In practice, male dependents spent more hours farming for the household head. Women's garden plots were located near the residential compound and women were tied up with labor intensive chores like pounding millet and separating peanut shells from the plant. This work was carried out in the compound, where cooking and child care took place. Women contributed more labor time to agriculture overall, but spent less time working on the large plots where millet and peanuts were cultivated. Household dependents who were considered adults were given their own plot of land to cultivate. In the colonial period young men grew almost nothing but peanuts, because cash from peanuts became the quickest means to accumulate the wealth required for marriage. Whether bride-price was paid in cash, as was common for the Wolof, or in cattle, as preferred by the Sereer, cash from peanuts became the major source of wealth for social transactions. The cash crop economy was integrated into the reproduction of the peasant household.

Historians have judged the cash cropping of the colonial era through its long-term outcome, which was bleak, as the peanut boom did not generate any self-sustaining process of development. Overreliance on one export had negative consequences, especially since the crop was processed in France (Cooper 1993). The peanut trade did not create a modern economy, but the social consequences were profound and have been underestimated. Slavery was still a vital institution in Wolof society at the beginning of the peanut boom. Many slaves ran away and were able to acquire land as migrant farmers working for peasant households. When they accumulated enough wealth to move on they could merge into other currents of migration. Slaves who stayed with their masters stopped working for them, and the influence of the runaways was a powerful check on exploitation. Cash cropping also encouraged young people to migrate to regions where they could acquire land and social independence.

One of the negative consequences of cash cropping was peasant debt, which took the form of advances of food and seed at the beginning of the rainy season. Peasants agreed to repay the loan with a fixed amount of peanuts at a fixed price. This price, well below the market price paid to peasants, disguised the interest on the loan, which ranged from 100 per cent to 300 per cent.

French administrators condemned these practices and began creating rural cooperatives around 1910 to provide cheaper loans of seed grain. During the Great Depression of the 1930s the cooperatives began purchasing some of the crop. Worries about low prices and peasant debt led the colonial state to intervene for the first time on a large scale. State management was a trend of the late colonial period that continued after independence, but the peanut export economy never recovered the vigor it had in the decades between 1880 and 1930.

JAMES F. SEARING

See also: **"Legitimate Commerce" and the Export Trade in the Nineteenth Century.**

Further Reading

Brooks, George. "Peanuts and Colonialism: Consequences of the Commercialization of Peanuts in West Africa, 1830–1870." *Journal of African History*, 16, no. 1 (1975): 29–54.

Cooper, Frederick. "Africa and the World Economy." In *Confronting Historical Paradigms: Peasants, Labor and the Capitalist World System in Africa and Latin America*, edited by Frederick Cooper, Allen Isaacman, Florencia E. Mallon, William Roseberry, and Steve J. Stern. Madison: University of Wisconsin Press, 1993.

Cruise O'Brien, Donal B. *The Mourides of Senegal: The Political and Economic Organization of an Islamic Brotherhood.* Oxford: Oxford University Press, 1971.

Klein, Martin. *Slavery and Colonial Rule in French West Africa.* Cambridge: University of Cambridge Press, 1998.

Manchuelle, Francois. *Willing Migrants: Soninke Labor Diasporas, 1848–1960.* Athens, Ohio: Ohio University Press, 1997.

Searing, James. *West African Slavery and Atlantic Commerce: The Senegal River Valley, 1700–1860.* Cambridge: University of Cambridge Press, 1993.

Senegal: World War II

World War II was an important watershed in the political history of Senegal. At the beginning of the war, Africans in the Four Communes (the so-called *originaires*) lost their privileged status as French citizens. The war gave rise to an upsurge in anticolonial activity, the outcome of which, just 15 years after the end of hostilities, was to be political independence.

The war in Senegal can be divided into three periods. During the first phase, from 1939 to 1940, some 100,000 Africans were called up in French West Africa, a significant proportion of whom came from Senegal. Although some desertions were reported, these do not appear to have been widespread, as African pledges of loyalty to France reportedly flooded in from throughout the colony.

The armistice of June 1940, which marked the beginning of the second phase of the War in Senegal, was greeted with dismay, particularly by African *assimilés* and *évolués* who did not understand why France had surrendered to Germany without a fight. Most *colons*, on the other hand, rallied to Vichy and colonial officials for the most part acquiesced in the change of regime, seeing their essential task as the maintenance of the colonial administration. Acts of resistance among the French population of Senegal were relatively rare. Pierre Boisson was appointed commissioner for the whole of French Africa on June 25, 1940, and arrived in Dakar in July to take up his post, in place of Léon Cayla. The latter, who had initially hesitated over whether to respond positively to overtures from Charles de Gaulle and Winston Churchill, was demoted to the governorship of Madagascar. The aim of the new administration, like its counterpart in metropolitan France, was the abolition of the republican regime and the restoration of the rights of custom and tradition. In fact, elections in the Four Communes, which was the only part of Senegal to enjoy full political rights, had already been suspended by decree on September 8, 1939. The Vichy administration went further, however, by establishing an authoritarian regime in which the use of forced labor increased and public order became the paramount consideration. Following the British attack on the French naval ship the *Richelieu*, which limped into the port of Dakar on July 8, and the bombardment of Dakar by a combined British and Free French force on September 23–25, Vichy propaganda against the British and the Free French intensified in French West Africa, and any manifestation of pro–Free French activity was repressed, particularly among Africans who risked imprisonment or death if found guilty.

This second phase of the war effectively came to an end on December 7, 1942, when, following the Allied invasion of North Africa, Boisson rallied French West Africa to General Darlan in Algiers. There was then a short interregnum before the Vichy regime formally ended and the Free French appointee as governor general, Pierre Cournarie, arrived in Dakar to take over from Boisson on July 17, 1943. The assassination of Darlan on Christmas Eve 1942 led to his replacement by General Giraud, who visited Senegal in January 1943, raising hopes of an improvement in political conditions in the territory. However, Giraud refused to receive a delegation of Saint-Louis évolués during his visit, thereby forfeiting any goodwill toward him that may have existed among the évolués of Senegal. Republican liberties were restored in March 1943, and this was followed by the rapid resumption of political activity, notably under the guise of "patriotic associations," which quickly split along racial lines as Africans sought to use the associations as a vehicle for the expression of their political grievances. A Bloc Africain was formed under the leadership of Lamine Guèye, to prepare the list of demands to be presented to René Pléven in Algiers by a delegation of Senegalese assimilés and évolués. Hopes of a rapid improvement in conditions were soon dashed, however. The new governor general's overriding concern was with production for the war effort: the "battle for groundnuts" intensified the pressure on farmers to increase production and the use of forced labor increased. At the same time, apart from the change of governor general, there was virtually no purge of Vichy colonial officials. Thus, despite the "return to republicanism," these were trying times for most Senegalese: political change was slow to come and the situation remained very difficult in economic and military terms. Prices were high, African wages and the prices paid to African farmers for their produce remained low, and few imported goods were available for purchase. Aware that Africans would have to be rewarded after the War for the sacrifices they were making for France, the provisional government organized the Brazzaville Conference in January 1944 to discuss the changes to the colonial regime that would be needed. However, no Africans were present, and the conference's main recommendations met with resistance from *colons* and colonial officials. It raised hopes among African assimilés and évolués, but its immediate impact in Senegal was limited.

At the end of 1944, the government general was confronted with the problem of the repatriation of some 12,000 French West African soldiers, many of whom had spent long periods as German prisoners of war (POWs). The first contingent of 1280 ex-POWs arrived in Dakar and was transferred straight to a military camp at Tiaroye, just outside Dakar. The soldiers were angry about the nonpayment of back pay and pensions, and refused to be sent home until their demands were met. On December 1, the African soldiers' "rebellion" was brutally repressed, leaving 35 of them dead and another 35 wounded. Measures were taken to avoid any further such incidents, but the way France treated returning soldiers who had served it loyally in Europe lived on in Senegalese folk memory and a film about the events, *Camp Tiaroye*, was made by the Senegalese filmmaker Sembène Ousmane in 1988.

The war had far-reaching effects in Senegal. France as the colonial power emerged from the war in a weakened position: the armistice of 1940 and the dependence of the colony on the Allied Forces after 1942 demonstrated the weakness of the French position, and American and Soviet anticolonialism at the end of the war further undermined French authority. Within the colony, the crisis within the colonial administration after December 1942; the economic and military pressures on the population; the ending of the Four Communes' special political position within the colony; the resumption of political activity along racial lines, which was symptomatic of a growing anticolonialism; and the mishandling of returning African soldiers were all signs that the old colonial order had changed permanently. In this respect, World War II can be considered the prelude to decolonization in Senegal.

ANTHONY CHAFER

See also: **Senegal: Colonial Period: Four Communes: Dakar, Saint-Louis, Gorée, and Rufisque; Senegal: Nationalism, Federation, and Independence; World War II: French West Africa, Equatorial Africa.**

Further reading

Chafer, T. "African Perspectives: the Liberation of France and its Impact in French West Africa." In *The Liberation of France: Image and Event*, edited by H. R. Kedward and N. Wood. Oxford: Berg, 1995.

Echenberg, M. "Tragedy at Tiaroye: The Senegalese Soldiers' Uprising of 1944." In *African Labour History*, vol. 2, edited by P. C. W. Gutkind, R. Cohen, and J. Copans. London: Sage, 1978.

Gardinier, D. E. "The Second World War in French West Africa and Togo: Recent Research and Writing." In *Proceedings of the Tenth Meeting of the French Colonial Historical Society*, edited by P. P. Boucher. 1984.

Ousmane, Sembène, dir. *Camp Tiaroye*. 1988.

Thomas, M. *The French Empire at War, 1940–45*. Manchester: Manchester University Press, 1998.

Topouzis, D. *Popular Front, War and Fourth Republic Politics in Senegal: from Galandou Diouf to L. S. Senghor, 1936–52*. Ph.D. diss.University of London, 1989.

Senegal: Nationalism, Federation, and Independence

The assimilationist tradition gave rise to a complex, third form of nationalism in Senegal, which had a profound effect on the postwar political development of the territory. Assimilation operates at a number of different levels, but in Senegal essentially referred to the fact that African residents of the Four Communes of Senegal (the so-called *originaires*) had, since 1916, had full French citizenship rights and, with the exception of the World War II years, they had also, since 1914, been represented in the French National Assembly by a black African *député*. A recurrent demand of the Senegalese French-educated elite throughout the twentieth century was for assimilation to be made a reality—not necessarily, as has sometimes been suggested, in the sense of wanting to become "Black Frenchmen," but in the sense of wanting full equality of rights with Europeans. However, assimilation also entailed a certain emotional attachment to, and cultural identification with, France. Thanks to the strength of this assimilationist tradition, postwar Senegalese nationalism was thus a complex phenomenon.

The first postwar legislative elections to take place in Senegal were the Constituent Assembly elections of 1945. At these elections, French citizens, which meant mainly the originaires, voted in the first electoral college for their député, while certain categories of subject (mainly those with a French education or who had fought for France) voted in the second college. Lamine Guèye, a longtime advocate of assimilation who had joined the French Socialist Party (Section Française de l'Internationale Ouvrière, or SFIO) and helped to found the Senegal section of the SFIO in 1938, was elected from the first college, while Léopold Sédar Senghor, whom he had chosen as his running mate, was elected from the second college. By the time of the Second Constituent Assembly elections in 1946, all inhabitants of the French colonies had become citizens of the French Union, as the empire was now to be called. Citizenship of the French Union did not, however, confer the same rights as French citizenship: for example, citizens of the former were not represented proportionally in the French parliament on the same basis as citizens of the latter and only certain categories of citizens of the French Union (mainly those who had voted in the 1945 election) were allowed to vote. On this occasion, as for the National Assembly elections in November 1946, there was a single electoral college, and Guèye and Senghor were elected on both occasions. However, Senghor quickly sought to distance himself from the straightforward assimilationism of Guèye and left the SFIO to found his own party, the Bloc Démocratique Sénégalais (BDS), in 1948. Despite its stated commitment to assimilation, Senghor felt that the SFIO leadership was only interested in the African empire to the extent that it delivered votes in Paris for the SFIO, and that it paid little heed to what was in Africa's best interests. It had, for example, voted against a single college for African elections and against equal pensions for French and African war veterans. In contrast to the SFIO, the power base of which was the Four Communes, the BDS was to be a mass party organizing throughout the territory. Senghor was no secessionist, however, and his new party aimed to work within the French Union for the restoration of African dignity and for the implementation of the 1946 constitutional commitment to a "Union based on the equality of rights and duties, without distinction of race or religion."

It should be noted that, in following this path, Senegal's political leaders isolated the territory from the mainstream of French West African politics. In 1946, the political leaders of the other territories of French West Africa had gathered in Bamako to create the interterritorial Rassemblement Démocratique Africain (RDA). Pressure from the SFIO minister for overseas France, Marius Moutet, meant that Guèye and Senghor did not attend the meeting. As a result, Senegal was never a lead player in French West Africa's first interterritorial political organization and, although the RDA, in the form of the Union Démocratique Sénégalaise (subsequently renamed the Mouvement Populaire Sénégalais, or MPS) led by Doudou Guèye, was present in the territory, it was always overshadowed by Senghor's BDS. In the 1951 and 1956 legislative elections, the BDS (subsequently renamed the Bloc Populaire Sénégalais, or BPS) easily defeated Lamine Guèye's Socialist Party, and the RDA, which swept the board in most of the rest of French West Africa in 1956, gained only one per cent of the vote in Senegal.

There were two main foci of the nationalist campaign during the first ten years of the Fourth Republic: on the political front, it was for Africans to be given a greater say over their own affairs, while on the socioeconomic front, trade unions demanded equal economic and social rights with Europeans: equal pay for equal work, the right to metropolitan family allowances, and the adoption of a new overseas labor code were key demands. The leitmotif of these demands was equality with Europeans, and Africans made important breakthroughs in each of these areas during this period: for example, the new overseas labor code was adopted by the National Assembly in 1952 following a five-year coordinated campaign by political parties and trade unions. These African successes, which promised greatly to increase the cost of colonial rule, and the deteriorating situation in Algeria, which provoked fears in France of a similar explosion in Black Africa, led the government to introduce the first major political reform in black Africa since the 1946 Constitution. This was the *loi cadre* (enabling act) of 1956. In the run-up to its adoption, a debate took place between African political leaders and in the wider nationalist movement over whether powers should be devolved to Africans at the level of the federation, the position favored by Senghor, or whether they should be devolved down to the constituent territories, as Houphouët-Boigny of Côte d'Ivoire wanted. This debate was of crucial importance to Senegal, because devolving powers to the federation would have kept the federation together and, given that the federal government was traditionally based in Dakar, Senegal could hope thereby to retain its dominant political position within the federation. Devolving powers to the territories, on the other hand, promised to marginalize Dakar. In the end, it was the Houphouët-Boigny proposals that were adopted, which led Senghor to accuse the French government of setting out to "balkanize" West Africa.

The elections to the new territorial assemblies established by the loi cadre took place on March 31, 1957. The BPS won a resounding victory, and Mamadou Dia became the African vice president of the new government council. (Senghor chose not to take a portfolio.) In an effort to promote territorial unity and cement support for the new African-led government, there was now a drive for political unity, as a result of which the BPS joined forces with Lamine Guèye's Socialists to form the Union Progressiste Sénégalaise (UPS), although neither the MPS nor the newly formed Parti Africain de l'Indépendance, which was committed to immediate African independence, joined. The UPS became the Senegalese section of the Parti du Regroupement Africain (PRA), which was a coalition of most of the non-RDA parties in French West Africa. The UPS quickly split, however, over strategy for the campaign for the constitutional referendum of September 1958. With the collapse of the Fourth Republic, Charles de Gaulle returned to power and called a referendum over the question of membership of the French Community, as the French Union was now to be called. Gaulle made it clear that a yes vote would ensure continued cooperation from France, while a "no" vote would mean immediate independence "with all its consequences." Senghor and Dia, fearing the economic consequences of an abrupt French withdrawal, called for a yes vote and were immediately denounced by a section of the party, which favored a novote and left to form the PRA-Sénégal. The result was a crushing defeat for those campaigning for a novote, since nearly 98 per cent of those voting voted yes. Radical nationalists who, out of a commitment to the Pan-African ideal, wanted to keep the federation together as a first step on the road to a united Africa and who campaigned for a no vote as the best way to hasten African independence, now found themselves politically marginalized. The position of the UPS was unassailable, and when its leaders decided, a little over a year later, to ask France for independence, it was on their terms—that is, through negotiation and in cooperation with France.

Following the vote, several French West African political leaders put forward their own proposals for a West African federation, but these plans collapsed in the face of opposition, notably from Houphouët-Boigny, who put pressure on neighboring territories not to join by playing on their fears that any such federation would be dominated by Dakar. In the end, only Sudan and Senegal remained committed to the idea, and they formed themselves into the Fédération du Mali in January 1959. It was as part of the Fédération du Mali that Senegal gained its independence on June 20, 1960. The federation did not last long, however. Historical differences, personal rivalries, and ideological disagreements led to its collapse before the end of the year, amid recriminations on both sides. Senegalese independence thus brought with it the collapse of Senghor's dream of an African federation.

TONY CHAFER

See also: **Senegal: Colonial Period: Four Communes: Dakar, Saint-Louis, Gorée, and Rufisque; Senghor, Léopold Sédar.**

Further Reading

Ajayi, A. D. E. and M. Crowder (eds.). *History of West Africa*, vol. 2, 2nd ed. Harlow, England: Longman, 1987.

Barry, B. "Neocolonialism and Dependence in Senegal." In *Decolonisation and African Independence: The Transfers of Power, 1960–80*, edited by P. Gifford and W. R. Lewis. New Haven, Conn.: Yale University Press, 1988.

Benoist, J.-R. de. *L'Afrique Occidentale Française de 1944 à 1960*. Dakar: Nouvelles Editions Africaines, 1982.

Crowder, M. "Independence as a Goal in French West African Politics, 1944–60." In *French-Speaking Africa: The Search for Identity*, edited by W. H. Lewis. New York: Walker, 1965.

Ly, A. *Les Regroupements politiques au Sénégal (1956–1970)*. Paris: CODESRIA/Karthala, 1992.

Vaillant, J. G. *Black, French and African: A Life of Léopold Sédar Senghor*. Cambridge, Mass.: Harvard University Press, 1990.

Senegal: Independence to the Present

Senegal achieved political independence from France in April 1960, first as part of the Mali Federation with the French Sudan, and then as a separate nation when the federation collapsed in August 1960. Lepold Sedar Senghor, a prominent intellectual and poet, was named the first president.

The country owed much of its political stability in the first two decades of independence to Senghor's presidency. The first two years were marked by a power struggle between President Senghor and Prime Minister Mamadou Dia, which ultimately resulted in the ascendancy of Senghor and the arrest and imprisonment of Dia. In 1963 a new constitution established a strong presidential regime, and an election shortly thereafter gave Senghor an overwhelming majority. Until the mid-1970s, Senegal was transformed into a virtual one-party state, with Senghor treated as the "father of the nation" and the ruling Parti Socialiste (PS) the only viable political organization in the country.

The new republic experienced difficult economic circumstances as a result of the Sahelian drought of 1966–1973, France's abandonment of colonial price supports in 1967, the rise of oil prices in the early 1970s, and worldwide inflation. Halfhearted efforts at diversification of the single-crop economy based on peanuts had to contend with entrenched political and religious interests as well as French dominance of Senegal's foreign aid. A marked decline in peanut prices in the mid-1970s and a resultant decline in production had a severe impact on the nation's economy. Population growth outstripped economic growth, and constant inflation contributed to a declining real per capita income.

When Senghor resigned in December 1980 in favor of his prime minister, Abdou Diouf, the country's political stability was threatened by worsening economic stagnation and deterioration. Yet Senegal, and especially its capital Dakar, became a center of culture. The country hosted the third Festival of Negro Arts in 1966 and produced some of the continent's most respected artists, including the filmmaker Ousmane Sembene and Senghor himself.

Abdou Diouf, labeled a brilliant technocrat during his term as prime minister, quickly set about instituting political and economic reforms after becoming president on January 1, 1981. He liberalized the political process by allowing an increased number of opposition parties. Fourteen political parties were recognized in the elections of 1983. Increased urban unemployment, rising inflation, and falling groundnut prices, in addition to strict structural adjustments imposed by the International Monetary Fund, caused an economic downturn. Diouf was also criticized for his intervention in an attempted coup against Dawda Jawara in Gambia in 1981. The coup was suppressed, Jawara was restored as leader, and Senegal retained a strong military presence in Gambia. The resulting Senegambian Confederation was beset by difficulties, mainly owing to Gambian fears of being absorbed into Senegal, and the federation was dissolved in 1989.

The 1983 elections, the first test for Diouf and his reforms, gave the ruling PS an overwhelming majority and the president an 82 per cent approval rating. Diouf continued to impose economic and political reforms, but a deteriorating economy and a growing separatist movement in the southern Casamance region posed serious problems for the government. Protests and strikes by university students, and then the police, in 1987 caused the government to crack down on opposition forces. However, Diouf retained the overwhelming support of the rural population as well as the traditional religious leadership, a powerful force in the country. In the 1988 elections, Diouf and the PS received 73 per cent of the popular vote, though the absentee voter rate surpassed 40 per cent. Charges of vote rigging and other irregularities sparked serious rioting in Dakar. The city was placed under a three-month state of emergency, and many opposition leaders were arrested, tried, and convicted, but amnesty was eventually granted to all political detainees. Diouf pursued further reforms and reshuffled his cabinet. Critics called for radical changes to make Senegal a genuine participatory democracy, whereas Diouf preferred incremental constitutional and electoral reforms. A series of drought years, spiraling inflation, and rapid population growth, especially in the Dakar region, thwarted efforts to improve Senegal's economic outlook after the elections.

In 1989, Senegal faced a serious crisis with its Arab-dominated neighbor, Mauritania. Long-standing hostility and border disputes between the two countries erupted into a massacre of Senegalese in Mauritania, and revenge attacks against Mauritanians in Senegal. In the aftermath of the killings several thousand Senegalese and Mauritanians were repatriated, property and assets were confiscated, and borders were closed. The two countries appeared on the brink of war, but the violence came to an end. Despite mediation efforts and the restoration of diplomatic ties, tensions remain high between the two countries.

In the 1993 elections, Diouf won with almost 60 per cent of the popular vote, and the PS again dominated the legislative elections. The elections were not marred by violence, but turnout was low. The religious authorities, who had always publicly supported Diouf and urged their disciples to vote for him and the PS, remained conspicuous in their silence during the 1993 elections. In 1994, the country suffered from the devaluation of the CFA franc by the French, which resulted in the most serious uprisings in the country since independence. Hundreds were arrested; chief among them were urban youth and some radical Muslims who called for an Islamic state and the imposition of Islamic law in Senegal. Radical Islam is not especially influential in Senegal, which is dominated by the traditional leadership of the Muslim brotherhoods, notably the Murids and the Tijaniyya, who wield enormous political and economic power.

Senegal's economic problems continued throughout the 1990s. The separatist movement in the Casamance strengthened considerably with a coup in neighboring Guinea-Bissau in 1998. Senegalese intervention in the Bissau rebellion was harshly criticized by many in the region. Diouf invoked a mutual defense treaty, and the goal of keeping an apparently democratically elected civilian president in power. It was also an opportunity for the government to weaken the Casamance resistance, which reportedly received arms through Bissau and sought refuge there. In late 1999, further outbreaks of violence in the Casamance were cause for concern. Although a peace treaty was signed between President Wade and the MFDC in 2001, it has not been followed with any sustained effort to end the conflict. The government has refused to discuss any form of autonomy or independence, and the rebels have not agreed to turn over their weapons.

While Senegal has suffered economic stagnation and deterioration, it remains one of the few democracies, however flawed, in Africa. The military has never threatened to overthrow the government and opposition parties, though weak and divided, do exist and contest elections. The country has largely avoided internal ethnic conflict among the various indigenous groups in the country. Over the past two decades,

Senegal has also peacefully resolved its earlier difficulties with its neighbors, Mali and Guinea-Conakry. It has contributed forces to ECOMOG for peace-keeping missions in West Africa and has also sent forces to United Nations peacekeeping missions. Senegal has remained on very good terms with its former colonial ruler, France, and plays an active role in francophone summits and organizations. Some would argue the ties to France are too close, but both Senghor and Diouf have reaped the benefits of close cooperation with France by securing relatively generous amounts of foreign aid. The United States and Western donor countries also have excellent relations with Senegal because of its democratic traditions and civilian government, making the country one of the largest recipients of Western foreign assistance in West Africa.

Senegalese society remains largely Muslim and family centered. Urban migration, especially to the Dakar vicinity, has disrupted life in many villages, especially in the Senegal River region, yet close ties are maintained between urban migrants and their relatives in the rural areas. While Dakar has the potential to provide excellent health and educational services, especially at the University of Dakar, economic and political upheaval often disrupt the facilities. A newly created university in Saint-Louis increased higher education opportunities, but most university graduates face unemployment. Health and educational services are sorely lacking in the rural areas where most of the population still resides and works in agriculture, mainly in peanut cultivation. AIDS has recently become a concern, but the country has not been as hard hit as some other African nations. The arts, most notably the cinema and performing arts, have thrived in independent Senegal. Dakar is a bustling cultural center with a national theater, several museums, and numerous cinemas, though recent economic troubles have diminished the city's cultural scene. Sports, especially soccer and basketball, are widely popular in Senegal, as is traditional wrestling. The country periodically hosts championship events.

The country faces enormous economic and demographic problems in the next century, yet a tradition of civilian democracy, as well as a thriving culture and dynamic society, support a cautiously optimistic view of the future.

ANDREW F. CLARK

See also: **Diop, Cheikh Anta; Diouf, Abdou; Négritude; Senegal: Casamance Province, Conflict in; Senghor, Léopold Sédar.**

Further Reading

Clark, Andrew F., and Lucie C. Phillips. *Historical Dictionary of Senegal.* Metuchen, N.J.: Scarecrow, 1994.

Diop, Momar Coumba. *Senegal: Essays in Statecraft.* Dakar: CODESRIA, 1993.

Gellar, Sheldon. *Senegal: An African Nation between Islam and the West.* Boulder, Colo.: Westview Press, 1995.

Vengroff, Richard, and Lucy Creevey. "Senegal: The Evolution of a Quasi Democracy." In *Political Reform in Francophone Africa*, edited by John F. Clark and David E. Gardiner. Boulder, Colo.: Westview Press, 1997.

Villalon, Leonardo. *Islamic Society and State Power in Senegal: Disciples and Citizens in Fatick.* Cambridge: Cambridge University Press, 1995.

Senegal: Casamance Province, Conflict In

The Casamance is the southernmost region of Senegal, lying along the Casamance River between Gambia and Guinea-Bissau, and extending eastward from the Atlantic Ocean to eastern Senegal. The name Casamance derives from the Portuguese corruption of Kasa Mansa (King of Kasa), the principal Portuguese trading partner in the area in the fifteenth century. The Portuguese influence remained strong even after the French conquered the area in 1903 and attached it to their colony of Senegal. Pockets of resistance remained through World War I. The French administered the province differently than other parts of Senegal because of its distance from the capital at Dakar, its location south of the British-controlled Gambia, and the historical and ethnic background of the people. The region was generally inhabited by non-Muslims belonging to distinct ethnic and linguistic groups, primarily the Jola, not found elsewhere in Senegal but who did live in Guinea-Bissau and French Guinea. Senegalese, both within the Casamance and elsewhere, have historically considered the area socially, politically, economically, and culturally different from other regions in Senegal. The nation of the Gambia separates most of the province from the rest of Senegal, reinforcing the sociocultural differences among ethnic groups living on either side of the Gambia River.

Several movements for greater autonomy for the Casamance emerged in the late 1960s and 1970s, primarily among the Jola living near the region's capital and largest city, Zigunchor. The war of independence in neighboring Portuguese Guinea at this time, and the large number of refugees who sought refuge in southern Senegal, also caused some tensions in the region, and between the region and the central government. With the independence of Guinea-Bissau in 1974, many of the refugees returned home, while others stayed in the province, increasing their calls for more autonomy for Casamance from the central government in Dakar. The Sahelian drought of the 1970s, which crippled the economy of the central peanut basin and the northern Senegal River region, encouraged development planners to see the relatively rain-reliable

Casamance as a major hope for the future. Tourism in the Casamance was also developed. Yet, to many people in the region, the benefits appeared to flow northward to the central government in Dakar. The collapse of the ill-fated Senegambian confederation in the 1980s, designed to merge Gambia into Senegal, contributed to an increasing sense of isolation and neglect in the Casamance.

Beginning in the 1980s, unrest escalated, only to be brutally crushed by Senegalese soldiers. Since 1982, the Movement of Democratic Forces of Casamance (Mouvement des forces démocratiques de Casamance, or MFDC), which, in extreme calls for secession and the creation of a separate Casamance nation, has dominated the military struggle. In December 1982, serious clashes in Ziguinchor between the rebels and Senegalese soldiers left over 30 people dead. With every crushed uprising, tensions mounted, with each side accusing the other of human rights violations and terrorizing civilians. The government's response has fluctuated between aggressive military campaigns and a series of diplomatic initiatives to isolate politically the most radical elements. The government of President Abdou Diouf has consistently refused any talk of independence or autonomy, viewing the issue as a threat to Senegal's territorial and sovereign integrity. The rebel movement has agreed to temporary cease-fires but has not endorsed any comprehensive peace settlement until moves toward independence begin.

Cease-fires in 1993, 1995, and 1996 all broke down. The renewal of MFDC attacks and reprisals by the army have continued since 1996, with little progress toward resolution. The Senegalese government has always been convinced that the fighters were seeking refuge in Guinea-Bissau and receiving arms through Bissau, permitting the rebels to continue the armed struggle and to refuse to negotiate. The people of the Casamance straddle both sides of the Senegal-Bissau border, including areas where the mangroves and swampy terrain provide ideal grounds for tactical guerrilla activity.

In late 1997, Senegal called on Guinea-Bissau to take serious action against arms smuggling from its territory into Casamance and to arrest suspected fighters living in Bissau. In December 1997 and January 1998, the Bissau government arrested over 20 people, including Bissau soldiers and civilians, and Senegalese civilians suspected in arms trading. The Senegalese government also stepped up detention of people in the Casamance. In January 1998, President Vieira of Guinea-Bissau fired the armed forces chief of state, Brigadier Asumane Mane, for suspicion of being involved in the smuggling of arms to separatist groups in the Casamance. There were some talks between rebels and the Senegalese government but these collapsed in mid-1998 when an armed uprising erupted in Guinea-Bissau.

The conflict in Casamance became closely inter-connected with events in Guinea-Bissau in mid-1998 and 1999. In June 1998, General Mane, who was dismissed earlier in 1998, led a mutiny of most of the Bissau army against the unpopular Vieira. Within a few days, the rebels, assisted by armed Casamance guerrillas in and from Senegal with whom they sympathized and overlapped in many cases, gained control of most of the country. Several thousand Senegalese troops were brought in to support Vieira and crush the rebels. The Senegalese government clearly saw the opportunity to eliminate, or at least dramatically weaken, the Casamance rebels and their supporters as well as their support system in both Casamance and Bissau. After several weeks of fighting, a cease-fire agreement was reached, Vieira remained in power, and Senegalese troops were withdrawn. However, in early 1999, fighting erupted again in Bissau. President Vieira was overthrown and a new military regime, under General Mane, took power.

In 2000, hopes for a peaceful resolution were renewed when Abdoulaye Wade was voted in as president, pledging to devote significant attention to ending the Casamance conflict. In 2001, his government signed a peace treaty with the MFDC. Unfortunately, the treaty signing has not been significantly followed up, while the separatist movement has undergone a series of leadership changes. The rebels' demands for total independence and the refusal to disarm, and the Senegalese government's unwillingness to discuss any change in the region's status within Senegal or to withdraw its large forces, pose formidable obstacles to a permanent peace.

ANDREW F. CLARK

See also: **Senegal: Independence to the Present: Senegal: World War I.**

Further Reading

Amnesty International. *Senegal: Climate of Terror in Casamance*, New York: Amnesty Press, 1998.

Clark, Andrew F., and Lucie C. Phillips. *Historical Dictionary of Senegal*. Methuchen, N.J.: Scarecrow, 1994.

Lambert, Michael. "Violence and the War of Words: Ethnicity v. Nationalism in the Casamance (Senegal, West Africa)." *Africa* 68, no. 4 (1988): 25–48.

Linares, Olga. *Power, Prayer and Production: The Jola of Casamance*. Cambridge: Cambridge University Press, 1992.

Senghor, Léopold Sédar (1906–2001)
Former President of Senegal and Poet

When Léopold Senghor was born in Joal on October 9, 1906, the alienation characteristic of colonial areas had begun to affect the interior of Senegal. Senghor later cried out poetically that it was "white hands which pulled the triggers that destroyed the empires" of traditional Africa, "white hands which cut down the black forest to make railroad ties." The advent of the Franco-Senegalese railroad propelled the Africans into a world of economic progress and a period of acute social change.

Senghor's first seven years, spent in traditional villages, were the only happy ones of his life until he rediscovered traditional Africa in books (in Paris) and formulated his theory of *Négritude*. Throughout the rest of his life he longed for "the paradise" of his African childhood, which kept him "innocent of Europe." Sent to a Catholic mission school by his father so that he might become "civilized," Senghor later wrote that he was "torn away from the mother tongue, from the ancestor's skull, from the tom-tom of my soul." Senghor was, nevertheless, a successful student.

When he was 13, Senghor felt "the calling" and began preparing to enter the Catholic priesthood; his assimilation of Western civilization was well under way. In 1922 at Dakar, the colonial capital of French West Africa, Senghor entered the seminary and plunged into Catholic theology and philosophy. He believed firmly in his calling, but his African pride made him protest against the racism of the Father Superior, who one day called Léopold's parents "primitives" and "savages."

Obliged to leave the seminary in 1926, the adolescent Senghor entered the public Secondary School of Dakar. In 1928 he obtained his high school degree with honors. Placing his faith in Senghor's intelligence, his classical languages teacher exerted much effort to persuade the colonial administration to grant Senghor a scholarship to do what no African had previously been allowed to do: pursue literary studies in France.

With the trip to Paris began Senghor's second uprooting, he boarded at the Parisian Lycée Louis-le-Grand, along with some of France's most brilliant students. From December 1928 on, his closest friend was Georges Pompidou, who would become president of France in 1969.

The French university education completed his "Frenchification," and his greatest ambition was to become a "black-skinned Frenchman." But it was not long before he realized that this was impossible and he reacted against assimilation, beginning his quest for "Africanness," or *Négritude*, as he put it.

The avant-garde Paris of the 1930s had begun a love affair with jazz, Josephine Baker (the African American singer), and African art. This fashion and a very popular Colonial Exhibition in the Parc de Vincennes reawakened Senghor's long-suppressed love of Africa. He rediscovered his "Childhood Kingdom" and his "pagan sap which mounted and which pranced and which danced." He pleaded that the "protecting spirits" not let his blood "fade" like that of an assimilated person, like that of a "civilized man."

He conscientiously sought to develop a scholarly foundation for this emotional return to Africa, plunging into the works of anthropologists and avant-garde anti-rationalist artists and thinkers. He also avidly read the works produced by the African Americans of the Harlem Renaissance. He followed them along the path that led to the flat rejection of cultural assimilation but simultaneously advocated political integration and civil rights. He would hardly depart from this path until 1958.

Secure in his newfound philosophy, Senghor appealed to God to forgive "those who have hunted thy children like wild elephants, and broken them in with whips, (and who) have made them the black hands of those whose hands were white." He had conceived of a new universal civilization: modern Western civilization would recognize its debt to African music and sculpture, and modern black civilization would assimilate European technological tools to hasten African progress: "New York! I say New York! let the black blood flow into your blood so that it might unrust your steel joints, as a life-giving oil." In 1948 the French philosopher Jean-Paul Sartre explained this Négritude phenomenon in a 50-page preface to Senghor's first major publication, *Anthologie de la Nouvelle Poésie Nègre et Malgache de Langue Francaise precedee de Orphee Noir par J.-P.Sartre* (*The Anthology of New Black and Malagasy Poetry in the French Language preceded by Black Orpheus by Jean-Paul Sartre*).

Three years prior, Senghor had added a political dimension to his budding academic and literary career. After World War II, Senghor (who had lived in France from 1928 on) was persuaded to return to Senegal to enter the political arena and run for a seat in the French parliament. French colonial policy had taken the route of token African representation, and Senghor became part of the African caucus in the Assemblée Nationale. Worldwide anticolonialism enabled Senghor and other Africans to obtain increasingly generous reforms, providing full French citizenship for all Africans in the French overseas territories. He successfully opened a small breach in the wall of the colonial system, which he then progressively widened. It was not Senghor's tactic to make a frontal assault on the French system; instead, he proceeded by obtaining increasing civil rights rather than by advocating independence. Until 1958 his quest was for full statehood, on the order of the incorporation of Hawaii into the United States.

Unlike his British colonial counterpart, Kwame Nkrumah of the British West African colony of the Gold Coast (which became independent Ghana in 1957), Senghor did not push for independence. Rejection of independence did not, however, mean that Senghor accepted complete assimilation into France. Instead, he advocated a new political federation linking Africa and France as equal partners. Nationalism for Senghor was an "outdated weapon . . . an old hunting gun." It was to be replaced by a multiethnic, intercontinental union of equals. Neither the European politicians who balked at the enormous cost of bringing African incomes up to European levels nor the African nationalists who wished to break away from their former master found his "Eurafrica" at all palatable. The winds of change bringing independence to dozens of former colonies were too strong to resist. By September 1960 Senghor bowed to "micronationalism" and became the first president of independent Senegal.

While president, Senghor developed his theory of African socialism, which borrowed some socialist ideas but refused to reject capitalism entirely. Although harshly criticized by radical Marxist economists, Senghor brought a relatively stable economy to his country. French investment continued to favor his efforts at development.

After 20 years as president of Senegal, Senghor retired in 1981. He wished to lead humanity to a "promised land" devoid of racism, economic inequality, nationalism, and war. In the course of that effort, the Académie Française, an association of France's most honored intellectual leaders (known as "the Immortals"), elected him the first black member in its almost 400 years of existence.

Senghor died at the age of 95 on December 20, 2001.

JACQUES LOUIS HYMANS

See also: **Senegal: Independence to the Present.**

Biography

Born in Joal on October 9, 1906. Entered a Catholic seminary to study for the priesthood in 1922; left the seminary in 1926. Moved to France to attend the Parisian Lycée Louis-le-Grand in 1928; remained in France after completing his education. Returned to Senegal in 1945. Became the first President of independent Senegal in 1960. After 20 years as president of Senegal, he retired in 1981. Died December 20, 2001.

Further Reading

Spleth, Janice. *Léopold Sédar Senghor*. Boston: Twayne, 1985.
Spleth, Janice (ed.). *Critical Perspectives on Léopold Sédar Senghor*, Boulder, Colo.: Three Continents Press, 1993.

Vaillant, Janet. *Black, French and African: A Life of Léopold Sédar Senghor*. Cambridge, Mass.: Harvard University Press, 1990.

Hymans, Jacques Louis. *Léopold Sédar Senghor: An Intellectual Biography*. Edinburgh: Edinburgh University Press, 1971.

Senghor, Léopold Sédar. *The Collected Poetry*, translated and with an introduction by Melvin Dixon. Charlottesville: University Press of Virginia, 1991.

Seychelles: 1770 to 1960

The granitic and coralline islands about a thousand miles north-northwest of Madagascar known as Seychelles, which were settled by France in the 1770s, never quite lived up to the promise of the geographical position that seemed to make them a key to the Indian Ocean. After capitulating to a British squadron in 1794, and doing so again whenever the Royal Navy reappeared, Seychelles still served as an intermittent base for French warships and privateers until the capture of the parent islands of Ile de France and Bourbon in 1810. Under the influence of the existing French colonial courts, Seychelles were used as secret depots in the illicit slave trade to those islands until the early 1820s. Slavery's abolition in the 1830s hit Seychelles hard; later political indications are that some old white families passed their resentment down through generations in the form of rhetorical anticolonialism.

A remote dependency of Mauritius under the British until it became a crown colony in its own right in 1903, with terrain ill-adapted to extensive sugar plantations and a hand-to-mouth economy but an admirable climate, Seychelles preserved at least the shell of its eighteenth-century social structure. The self-styled *grand blanc*, or landed white families, struggled to preserve estates of coconuts, coffee, and essential oils with unwilling African slave-descended labor. (They were much happier with the short-term tied labor of freed Africans captured from slave dhows by the navy in the 1860s and 1870s.) Colored families with land of their own looked to the British administration for support, which they sometimes received.

For a brief period in the 1850s, the Haitian example was spoken of by people of color, and revolution against the grand blanc was promised. But the vast ex-slave majority of the population had borrowed their former masters' surnames yet still knew their own place in a pyramid that was solidified by the Catholic Church and a structure in which French was the language of the propertied while all the rest were supposed to speak a Creole patois.

After 1903 there was a direct government attempt to bring Creoles (here meaning the black majority) into the social and administrative or even political mainstream by providing far better secondary education than had ever been open to anyone through the rival Catholic and Anglican Churches. The former was heavily oriented toward the propertied, and the latter had little means. King's College taught in English, was free from priestly influence, and was fondly remembered as a model even by grand blanc pupils long after its demise at the hands of a Catholic governor. One of its masters had been, as a young man, the post–World War II champion of the unprivileged Charles Evariste Collet, a black barrister and leading light of the League for the Advancement of Colored Peoples, while studying in Britain during the 1920s and 1930s, when he was bombarding the latterly receptive Colonial Office with savage depictions of the social pyramid in Seychelles.

Creoles bore the weight of taxation before World War II; and the jail, with its incorrigible thieves, received the hungry in almost the same proportion; the undernourished physical state of people at large was revealed when almost half the pioneers leaving for the army in East Africa during World War I died. A magistrate objected to flogging a starving young thief to please a planter, and disapproved of plantations' paying workers in tokens redeemable in drink at the plantation store. He was promptly diagnosed as a dangerous socialist by a leading planter and dismissed, then committing suicide.

Government proposals for social welfare schemes in the shape of community centers, resettlement schemes, and an ambitious education plan much opposed by the Catholic Church were held up by World War II. And postwar reconstruction ran into trouble when the Labour Party government sent the

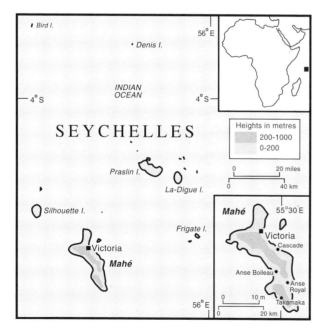

Seychelles.

Fabian Socialist Dr. P. S. Selwyn-Clarke to be governor of Seychelles; Selwyn-Clarke made Charles Collet his attorney general, with a Collet-inspired mandate to modernize law, society, and the taxation system. (Income tax had been evaded by those best able to pay it.) But since Collet turned out a poor lawyer and open to charges of venality himself, the campaign turned out very badly; and since he had not stooped to establishing any real party organization within his Seychelles Progressive Association, there was no political force to protect him from the consequences of his own actions or for him to fall back on.

After alarums and excursions in the mid- and late 1940s, while government tried dragging Seychelles into what British and a few Seychellois socialists thought the modern world should be, the political future fell back into the hands of propertied people represented by the powerful, well-organized Planters and Taxpayers Association, which dominated the new, elected Legislative Council. At the same time, the unfettered birthrate and restricted physical makeup of the islands meant that pressure on limited resources was only increasing. In 1958 the colony received grants-in-aid—with treasury control agreeable to few—after getting itself into a situation where it imported more than it exported and made up the difference by government expenditure on developmental works that, for the sake of maintaining the poor, were funded by grants from London and by drawing on revenue reserves that some landed proprietors regarded as more properly their own exclusive bank account.

DERYCK SCARR

See also: **Bourbon, Ile de France, Seychelles: Eighteenth Century; Colonialism: Ideology of Empire: Supremacist, Paternalist. Mauritius: Slavery and Slave Society to 1835.**

Further Reading

Scarr, Deryck. *Seychelles since 1770: History of a Slave and Post-slavery Society.* London: C. Hurst, 1999.

Seychelles: Independence, Revolution, Restoration of Democracy: 1960 to Present

Socialist sands having run out in Seychelles in the 1950s with the discrediting of Attorney General Charles Collet and Governor P. S. Selwyn-Clarke, there was a renewed sense at the government house ten years later that the clocks would not stand still. When people became interested in political issues, the police would have their hands full, reported Governor Sir John Thorpe. Flames from the admiralty fuel depot illustrated his point that advancement in social welfare

was essential for its own sake, and to prevent social conflict when actual hunger was rising under impact from the church's prohibition on family planning, the continued absence of significantly increased production, and the effective closure of East Africa to emigration as colonies there came to independence under, among others, Britain's desire to be gone from the region east of Suez.

What galvanized Seychelles in the 1960s was the Planters and Taxpayers Associations' assumption that internal self-government would devolve to them, if anyone. New political parties appeared amid cries from *petits blancs* and African spokesmen that "*grands blancs* [the landed white gentry] want to enslave us all over again." Alarmists, and people with their ears to the ground, heard cries for rebellion. To the British who were embarrassed by the fervor for continued close association with Britain among the Seychellois it all seemed very mild in comparison with the decolonizing processes in Africa; and in negotiations toward devolution of authority that ensued until independence in 1976, the record gives a strong sense that the Foreign and Commonwealth Office hardly took Seychelles very seriously nor imagined that much difficulty could arise there.

Continued close association with Britain was the policy embraced by the young emerging leader and first but short-term president of Seychelles, J. R. M. Mancham (*b.*1939), an English-educated lawyer and son of a leading merchant who was himself part French by descent from a pioneer family and part Cantonese. He was very conscious of Britain's desire to rid itself of colonies but unclear how independence could be sustained so close to doctrinaire Africa and with so little in the way of economic resources, but he was aware of the power vacuum around the present political elite of the Taxpayers. Mancham's Seychelles Democratic Party (SDP), with its emphasis on building a new Seychelles personality uncircumscribed by existing social divisions, set out to fill it with sound social comment satirizing church and the grand blancs. The SDP won every general election. Prosperity seemed to come in with an international airport and high global profile—even if prosperity's major tourist component brought the usual social problems.

Not merely consciousness of these questions, but a curiously atavistic and ahistorical glorification of a mythical French past, seemed to characterize the narrowly defeated rival Seychelles Progressive Party, led by the British-educated lawyer F. A. René (*b.*1935), who had declared for independence immediately upon his arrival 1963, uttering stereotypical railings against colonialism. Much of SPP's leadership in the 1970s came from educated young grands blancs who may have been drawing on the student movement in Europe and appeared to have been nourished at home on anti-British resentment traceable to the ending of slavery, among other things. Leninist undertones were not diminished by narrow electoral defeats in which boundaries played a large part. And a rhetorical reaching toward nonalignment in the immediate form of new African states was rewarded by armed support from Tanzania one Saturday night in June 1977 with the goal of removing the SDP's majority share in the coalition government, which, under British prompting, had taken Seychelles to independence on June 29, 1976 with Mancham as executive president and René as prime minister.

The British idea of a stabilizing coalition government with a majority for SDP had been a naive one, on the whole; and the coup was not bloodless, nor was the sequel to be without "disappearances" and assassinations in Seychelles and London, both before and after a failed mercenary countercoup from South Africa in 1981. Tanzanians in the Seychelles army put up a fairly poor show, but the mercenaries were not there to be killed, either. As a self-styled revolutionary under the Seychelles Peoples Progressive Front, Seychelles now had a totalitarian single-party regime, with President René sometimes speaking plaintively to his people about his need for personal guards and several of his erstwhile lieutenants leaving his government. And there were ten years of apparently ill-managed nationalized assets amid stark income inequality until the USSR's collapse in the early 1990s, coupled with pressure from the commonwealth and from France forced a return to multiparty elections in 1992 and 1993. René returned as president and his party won handsomely. Mancham and his party lost, but he preached national reconciliation.

DERYCK SCARR

See Also: **Colonialism, Overthrow of: Nationalism and Anticolonialism.**

Further Reading

Bededict, Marion, and Burton. *Men, Money and Women in Seychelles.* Berkeley and Los Angeles: University of California Press, 1982.
Hoare, Mike. *The Seychelles Affair.* London: Corgi, 1986.
Scarr, Deryck. *Seychelles since 1770: History of a Slave and Post-slavery Society.* London: C. Hurst, 1999.

Al-Shadhili: *See* **Abu Madian, al-Shadhili, and the Spread of Sufism in the Maghrib.**

Shaka and Zulu Kingdom, 1810–1840

Shaka Senzangakona, born probably in the latter half of the 1780s, presided over the emergence of the powerful Zulu kingdom during a period of unprecedented political, social, and environmental change in southeastern Africa. A controversial figure in both contemporary and present-day assessments, Shaka has been credited variously with being the "African Napoleon," a military genius, a founding statesman, a tyrant, and a potent myth. He is the central figure in historical interpretations that place an emphasis on the "Zulucentric" foundations of state formation in eastern and southern Africa in the early 1800s.

The Zulu kingdom emerged in the 1810s in what is now the KwaZulu-Natal region of South Africa. Bantu-speaking, Iron Age farming communities had established themselves in this fertile, well-watered region by about 300 and developed agropastoralism by about 1000. By 1800, the inhabitants had established numerous small communities that ranged in size from under a thousand to over several thousand people. Chiefdoms consisted of homesteads that were bound to the wider community through ties of kinship and marriage, and to the chief through clientage and the partial reciprocity of accumulated tribute.

In the early 1800s a number of factors combined to create the conditions for rising social stratification, and increased competition over natural resources and trade for these chiefdoms. Since the mid-eighteenth century, ivory trading with Europeans had been an important stimulus to generating wealth and power for some chiefdoms at the expense of others. Control over trade routes and the declining elephant population were crucial for the consolidation of political power. Moreover, a series of severe droughts and famines intensified the process of political amalgamation, whereby strong leaders, such as Shaka, sought to transform existing social relations between chiefs and people into militarized states to safeguard resources. Young men in the *amabutho* (circumcision age sets under the authority of the chief), which were previously schools for rites of passage into manhood, were employed in elephant hunting and also in military regiments needed to defend and expand control over hunting grounds, trade routes, and fertile land. This culminated in the formation of powerful, expansive military states that competed violently for control of territory. The genesis of the Zulu and other major states in southeastern Africa, therefore, is to be found in the conditions that created an increasing need to control trade, land, and labor.

It was in this context that Shaka rose to prominence. Following his obscure beginnings, which have since been mythologized, Shaka and his mother Nandi left his father Senzangakona's home. He later returned from exile and honed his skills as strategist and warrior, eventually taking over the minor Zulu chiefdom, a tributary of the Mthethwa paramountcy, in about 1816. A man of extraordinary skill, power, and ruthlessness,

Shaka moved quickly to exploit both political advantage and the innovative in-close spear fighting that proved successful in combat. During a conflict between the Mthethwa and the Ndwandwe chiefdoms, Shaka held back the subordinate Zulu from supporting the Mthethwa. This enabled Shaka to escape Mthethwa overlordship and to fend off and eventually rout the invading Ndwandwe after the Mthethwa were vanquished. Thereafter, Shaka sharpened his command over the young warriors of his regiments and the productive forces of society, thus transforming the Zulu kingdom into an efficient and formidable fighting force. The Zulu then consolidated their control of the region and its people and extended their hegemony north- and southward. They conquered much of KwaZulu-Natal, driving some chiefdoms away and enforced tributary relations over a society increasingly stratified between the Zulu kingdom and the remaining client chiefdoms.

This series of events, and Shaka's seemingly pivotal role in them, has been seen as the focal point for the explosive series of wars and migrations in the 1820s and 1830s referred to as the *mfecane*. It is now, however, generally acknowledged that European raiders, slavers, traders and settlers had (to varying degrees according to different interpretations) a significant influence on African societies and state formation in southeastern Africa. Thus, Shaka and the Zulu kingdom alone were not responsible for the widespread social and political dislocations that led to the rise of major African kingdoms in the region. Rather, it was the complex interplay of African societies with white labor raiders and traders in ivory and slaves that led African statesmen variously to defensive or aggressive strategies to consolidate their emerging kingdoms.

Following Shaka's rise to power, the Zulu intensified raiding, primarily for cattle, and expanded their domination by garrisoning Zulu warriors throughout the region. Yet this was a tenuous power, beset by internal dissent and external opposition. Deep-rooted divisions and inequalities emerged within the kingdom as the dominant Zulu ruling house enforced distinctions of ethnicity, status, and wealth between themselves and subjected peoples. Shaka and the Zulu aristocracy's increasing sensitivity to internal opposition was exacerbated by the resurgence of an external threat when the Ndwandwe attempted to invade in 1826. Tensions remained high despite the defeat of the Ndwandwe. Shaka resorted to extreme brutality with the massacre of Zulu political opponents during a period of mourning following his mother's death. Nevertheless, anxieties within the ruling house over Shaka's excesses culminated in his assassination in 1828 by two of his half brothers and his personal assistant. The kingdom was, however, well enough established to survive the crisis of succession, and Dingane, one of the assassins, succeeded Shaka as king.

Dingane consolidated his rule and legitimacy as king through some conciliatory gestures to his *amabutho* and the chiefs, but mainly through punitive violence against opponents and refugees returning from the upheaval of Shaka's rule. Through aggressive campaigns against neighboring chiefdoms, Dingane provided his warriors with the opportunity to acquire cattle, the mainstay of the Zulu society and economy. He, moreover, cultivated trade, established under Shaka, with the fledgling British settlement at Port Natal (Durban) to the south in order to acquire firearms and training for his men.

By the later 1830s, increasing white involvement with, and expansion into, the kingdom marked the decline of Zulu authority in the region. Frustrated with British efforts to halt the gun trade—and, more important, for their harboring a substantial number of Zulu malcontents—Dingane strictly limited their tenuous relations by the mid-1830s. It was, however, the arrival of the Boer voortrekker settlers under Piet Retief in 1837 that proved to be a more formidable challenge to the Zulu kingdom and led to Dingane's undoing.

Dingane, acutely aware of the expansionist predilections of the voortrekkers, put to death Retief and a party of his men who had negotiated a tentative cession of Zulu land for settlement. The Boers, under the new leader Andries Pretorius, then exacted a major reprisal against the Zulu at Ncome (Blood) River. Thereafter, relations between the Zulu and white encroachers remained unsettled. In a curious twist, the competing dynastic ambitions of Dingane's half brother Mpande converged with Trekker ambitions. In 1839, Mpande fled the kingdom, forged an alliance with the Boers, and with a combined force returned to defeat Dingane. This was a significant turning point for the Zulu kingdom. Although Mpande and his successors retained independence until 1879, his coronation by the Boers signaled that white intervention would play an increasing role in the compromised kingdom.

ARAN S. MACKINNON

See also: **Boer Expansion: Interior of South Africa; Mfecane; Natal, Nineteenth Century.**

Further Reading

Ballard, C. C. *The House Of Shaka.* Durban: Emoyeni, 1988.

Bryant, A. T. *A History of the Zulu and Neighbouring Tribes.* Cape Town: Struik, 1964.

Cobbing, J. "The Mfecane as Alibi: Thoughts on Dithakong and Mbolompo." *Journal of African History* 29, no. 3 (1988): 487–519.

Duminy, A., and B. Guest (eds.). *Natal and Zululand from Earliest Times to 1910.* Pietermaritzburg: University of Natal Press, 1989.

Edgecomb, D. R., J. P. C. Laband, and P. S. Thompson (eds.). *The Debate on Zulu Origins: A Selection of Papers on the Zulu Kingdom and Early Colonial Natal.* Pietermaritzburg: University of Natal Department of Historical Studies, 1992.

Fuze, M. M. *The Black People and Whence They Came*, translated by H. C. Lugg and edited by A. T. Cope. Pietermaritzburg: University of Natal Press, 1979.

Gluckman, M. "The Rise of a Zulu Empire." *Scientific American* 202, no. 4 (1963): 159–69.

Golan, D. *Inventing Shaka: Using History in the Construction of Zulu Nationalism.* Boulder, Colo.: Lynne Rienner, 1994.

Guy, J. J. "Analysing Pre-Capitalist Societies in Southern Africa." *Journal of Southern African Studies* 14, no. 1 (1987): 18–37.

Hamilton, C. *The Mfecane Aftermath: Reconstructive Debates in Southern African History.* Pietermaritzburg: University of Natal Press/Johannesburg: Witwatersrand University Press, 1995.

———. *Terrific Majesty: The Powers of Shaka Zulu and the Limits Of Historical Invention.* Cambridge, Mass.: Harvard University Press, 1998.

Marks, S. "The Nguni, the Natalians and Their History," *Journal of African History* 8, no. 3 (1967).

Marks, S., and A. Atmore (eds.). *Economy and Society in Pre-Industrial South Africa.* London: Longman, 1980.

Mfolo, T. *Chaka*, translated by D. P. Kunene. London: Heinemann, 1981.

Omer-Cooper, J. D. *The Zulu Aftermath: A Nineteenth Century Revolution in Bantu Africa.* London: Longman, 1966.

Peires, J. *Before and after Shaka: Papers in Nguni History.* Grahamstown, South Africa: Institute of Social and Economic Research, 1981.

Sharpeville Massacre: *See* South Africa: Sharpeville Massacre.

Shilluk: *See* Nilotes, Eastern Africa: Western Nilotes: Shilluk, Nuer, Dinka, Anywa.

Shoa: *See* Ethiopia: Shoan Plateau, Fifteenth and Sixteenth Centuries; Ethiopia: Muslim States, Awash Valley: Shoa, Ifat, Fatagar, Hadya, Dawaro, Adal, Ninth to Sixteenth Centuries.

Sidi Muhammad: *See* Morocco: Sidi Muhammad and Foundations of Essawira.

Sierra Leone: Origins, 1787–1808

Sierra Leone became a settlement with the arrival of a British naval vessel carrying 411 blacks on May 10, 1787. These people had experienced poverty and unemployment in Britain, where they had found little

Sierra Leone.

support from private charity and were usually ineligible for "poor relief" because they did not have a parish of settlement. They ended up migrating to Sierra Leone as a result of philanthropic endeavors by a group of British abolitionists including Thomas Clarkson, William Wilberforce. and Granville Sharp. These abolitionists were members of the Committee for the Relief of the Black Poor, which was concerned about the plight of black people in London in the aftermath of the American Revolution (a conflict in which many blacks had fought with the British forces). The abolitionists thought that blacks stood a better chance of independence in a free community based on Christian principles in Sierra Leone. The British government funded the initial expedition. The Sierra Leone settlement was augmented by two further waves of migrants. In 1792 some 1,200 blacks sailed from Nova Scotia to Sierra Leone. They relocated to West Africa because it seemed to offer better security, land, and independence. The third group of black settlers in Sierra Leone was maroons exiled from Jamaica after the Maroon War of 1795. Initially deported to Nova Scotia after the conflict was put down, they requested transfer to Africa. Some 550 maroons were consequently sent to Sierra Leone in 1800.

The Sierra Leone settlement began with high ideals. In 1787, Sharp wrote a constitution through which the settlers would be guided by the laws, customs, and traditions of Britain. He made provision for settlers to enact laws through common councils and to elect a governor plus a governing council. He suggested that the form of government should follow the old English system of frankpledge. The first settlers followed these instructions. They elected Richard Weaver as their first governor, and divided their settlement into tithings (groups of ten families) with a leader elected each year called a "tithingman." They named their original settlement Granville Town, after Sharp. Slavery and slave trading were not permitted. The early years of the Sierra Leone settlement, however, were beset by recurrent problems.

Arrangements for government were upset by more pressing difficulties of survival and working the land. Half of the original black settlers from Britain died on the voyage or within four months of arrival; various diseases—notably dysentery—claimed their lives. English seeds imported to Sierra Leone to establish viable agricultural production proved unsuitable. Conflicts arose between settlers and local Africans over access to land. In 1790, a native settlement near Granville Town was burned; in return, Africans razed that town to the ground.

By 1790 these problems led the British abolitionists, who had backed the enterprise to set up the St. George's Bay Company, to promote Christianity, commerce, and Western civilization in Sierra Leone. In 1791 the company sent out Alexander Falconbridge to refound the settlement. He established a new Granville Town near Fourah Bay and helped the settlers to plant crops, but he died in 1792. The arrival of the black loyalists from Nova Scotia compounded Sierra Leone's travails. John Clarkson, the brother of abolitionist Thomas Clarkson, was the naval lieutenant in charge of this wave of migrants. When the St. George's Bay Company changed its name to the Sierra Leone Company in 1792, he was appointed as its superintendent. But he found settlers in Sierra Leone were not as industrious as he had hoped; he also had to cope with quarrelsome councilors and pilfering from stores. Given enhanced powers as governor of the Sierra Leone Company in 1792, he worked hard to make the colony viable. But Clarkson was recalled to Britain by his company directors in 1793 because they were unhappy with his offer of free land to settlers, something that had been promised in Sharp's constitution.

Zachary Macaulay served as governor in 1794–1795 and again in 1796–1799. A former bookkeeper and manager on a Jamaican slave estate, he tried to rebuild Sierra Leone but faced difficulties. Rations and building supplies from Britain were inadequate. In September 1794 Sierra Leone was devastated by a two-week attack from a French naval squadron. After 1796, disputes between the settlers and the governor arose over the new policy of the Sierra Leone Company to charge quitrents, whereby settlers had to pay one shilling for every acre of land used. After Macaulay's return to Britain in April 1799 the Sierra Leone Company received a new charter from the British crown that effectively returned authority to the company and its governor. Dismayed at the erosion of representative government and upset by the quitrent issue and the free land that had been promised but not received, the Nova Scotians rose up against the Sierra Leone Company in 1800. The rebellion was crushed, and the company decided not to send any more blacks to West Africa. The company also became involved with quarrels with the Koya Temne (whose land had been sold to settlers). The Temne attacked the company's fort on Thornton Hill on November 18, 1801; the company's forces retaliated and destroyed many Temne settlements. In 1807 the Temne signed a dictated peace treaty with the British in which they renounced all claims to colony land.

On January 1, 1808, Sierra Leone became a crown colony. The British government, looking for a naval base in West Africa, hoped that a new constitutional arrangement would resolve some of the political and financial failure that had been endemic in the first 21 years of the Sierra Leone settlement.

KENNETH MORGAN

See also: **Sierra Leone: Development of the Colony: Nineteenth Century.**

Further Reading

Alie, Joe A. D. *A New History of Sierra Leone*. New York: St. Martin's Press, 1990.

Braidwood, Stephen J. *Black Poor and White Philanthropists: London's Blacks and the Foundation of the Sierra Leone Settlement, 1786–1791*. Liverpool: Liverpool University Press, 1994.

Fyfe, Christopher. *A History of Sierra Leone*. Oxford: Oxford University Press, 1962.

Kup, A. P. *Sierra Leone: A Concise History*. Newton Abbot, England: David and Charles, 1975.

Wilson, Ellen Gibson. *The Loyal Blacks*. New York: G. P. Putnam's Sons, 1976.

Sierra Leone: Development of the Colony, Nineteenth Century

January 1, 1808, marked the formal transfer of the colony of Sierra Leone from the ailing Sierra Leone Company to the British crown. British legislation abolishing slave trading also became effective that year, and the newly acquired colony became a depository for "recaptives" rescued from slave ships by the Royal Navy. The original group of emancipated slaves from Britain and the New World (settlers) numbered less than 2,000 in 1811. Nearly 40,000 "recaptives" (liberated Africans) had joined them by 1833, and more were to arrive in subsequent decades. Many of these new arrivals were found homes in small villages designed to emulate pastoral Europe, but the steep and thickly forested slopes of the Freetown Peninsula were never going to support an agricultural colony. Freetown's estuarine location and excellent natural harbor were better suited to commerce, and the liberated African population soon began to gravitate to Freetown to take up trading.

Freetown developed as an entrepôt for the Atlantic trade by tapping into the produce economy of its African hinterland. Principal exports in the early nineteenth century were timber and palm oil, later supplanted by rubber, hides, groundnuts, and palm kernels. British sovereignty was at first a positive factor in the colony's economic development. All traders engaging in "legitimate" commerce enjoyed military protection, and African rulers and merchants of the interior were courted by diplomatic missions financed by the British government. Yet, the growing prosperity of nineteenth-century Freetown also owed much to its African population. In an era when overland traders frequently ran the risk of theft, extortion, or worse, honest brokerage was highly prized. Having few alternative sources of income, settler and liberated African traders worked assiduously at building commercial networks in the hinterland. The growing population of Freetown also created opportunities in retail trade and food marketing, and successful merchants tended to invest in residential property rather than European securities. Commercial prosperity therefore generated urban growth, and this process continued as the city began to attract African immigrants from the hinterland. The most successful of these served as "landlords" (i.e. brokers, translators, and providers of accommodation) for traders from their home areas. African businesses competed on level terms with European firms based in the colony for much of the nineteenth century, and many Sierra Leone traders expanded their operations along the West African coast.

Freetown fostered many brilliant careers. For example, in 1828, a boy from Egba country in Nigeria was rescued from a slave ship and sent to Murray Town, near Freetown. Taking the name William Lewis, he began work as a fisherman after leaving the village school. He soon took up trading in the hinterland, exchanging European imports for foodstuffs destined for Freetown markets. In 1847, he bought a store in west Freetown, moving on to the city center in 1859. By 1870, Lewis was operating two ships, had served a term as vice president of the Freetown Mercantile Association, and had become a trustee of a new Wesleyan chapel. Samuel Lewis, one of his sons, was educated in Britain and called to the English bar in 1871; Queen Victoria knighted him in 1896 for political and legal services to the colony.

This example is also indicative of the cultural processes underpinning the colony's economic development. Most of the original settlers had embraced Christianity before arriving in the colony, but the liberated Africans reflected the diversity of Africa's peoples, languages, and cultures. Once deposited in the colony, recaptives faced a pressing need to find a common medium. With the encouragement of the colonial government, European missionaries set about building schools and churches in Freetown and the liberated African villages. Many liberated Africans soon embraced Protestantism and the cultural values of contemporary bourgeois Europe—especially the work ethic and esteemed notion of individual responsibility. This acculturation process did not elide their African heritage, however, but instead gave birth to a distinctive Krio (Creole) identity and culture. Krio culture was founded upon a lingua franca whose African grammatical structure was wedded to English, French, Portuguese, and African lexical elements. Krio Christianity also incorporated much traditional African ceremonial, and many of the mutual-aid associations supporting family and commercial life in the colony were organized on a distinctively African basis. The Krio social spectrum remained broad, covering both the descendants of the original settlers and the Akus. The latter were liberated Africans of Muslim Yoruba origin who built an Islamic community in east Freetown in partnership with Fula and Mandingo immigrants from the interior.

The colony also developed into a center of intellectual exchange. African inhabitants of the colony supplied information for the first systematic accounts of West African flora and indigenous African medicine to appear in print. Krio scholars also number among the pioneers of African-language analysis. Fourah Bay College (which offered university degrees from 1876 onward) took students from all over West Africa, and helped earn nineteenth-century Freetown the sobriquet "Athens of West Africa."

In the final analysis, however, the European agencies that had facilitated the early development of the colony proved to be a constraint. Freetown was first constituted as a municipality in 1799, but its offices soon withered as the colonial government assumed full executive powers. It was not reestablished until 1893, three years before a British Protectorate was declared over the territory adjoining the colony. Krios working in colonial administration had petitioned for greater self-government, but they now found their responsibilities diminished by racist legislation specifically designed to consolidate British colonial rule. Krio businesses also went into decline in this period. International demand for African produce was falling, and Krio retailers were also facing increasing competition from European firms and Levantine (Syrian) traders, both of whom tended to enjoy better credit facilities at European banks.

The nineteenth-century Sierra Leone colony exceeded all the expectations of Granville Sharp's philanthropic experiment of 1787. Its development was subsumed under intensified European colonialism at the close of the century. Yet it remains a testament to the energy and resourcefulness of ex-slaves forced to build a new society from the ground up.

RICHARD FANTHORPE

See also: **Freetown; Religion, Colonial Africa: Religious Responses to Colonial Rule; Religion, Colonial Africa: Conversion to World Religions; Resettlement of Recaptives: Freetown, Libreville, Liberia, Freretown, Zanzibar.**

Further Reading

Alldridge, T. J. *A Transformed Colony: Sierra Leone as It Was, and as It Is*. London: Seeley, 1910.

Fyfe, Christopher. *A History of Sierra Leone*. London: Oxford University Press, 1962.

———. "1787–1887–1987: Reflections on a Sierra Leone Bicentenary." Africa 57, no. 4 (1987): 411–421.

Fyfe, Christopher, and Eldred Jones (eds.). *Freetown: A Symposium*. Freetown: Sierra Leone University Press, 1968.

Porter, Arthur T. *Creoledom: A Study of the Development of Freetown Society*. London: Oxford University Press, 1963.

Sibthorpe, A. B. C. *The History of Sierra Leone*, 4th ed. London: Frank Cass, 1970.

Wyse, Akintola J. G. *The Krio of Sierra Leone: An Interpretive History*. London: C. Hurst in association with the International African Institute, 1989.

Sierra Leone: Christianity, Education, Krio Diaspora

The Sierra Leone colony was from the start a Christian enterprise. Granville Sharp's 1787 settlement was founded on Christian principles, as was the subsequent Sierra Leone Company venture. The settlers, originally from Nova Scotia, organized themselves into their own independent churches (Methodist, Baptist, and the Countess of Huntingdon's Connexion) under their own pastors, and used them as units of local government. They built their own churches and conducted their worship separately from that provided by the company's chaplain.

The colony was also seen as a base for Christian missionary outreach. After several abortive attempts in the 1790s, missionaries arrived in 1804 from the Church Missionary Society (CMS) founded in London in 1799, which took Sierra Leone as one of its chief stations. Making Freetown their base, they established a mission to the Susu people in the Rio Pongas country, a slave-trading center north of Sierra Leone, where their efforts were chiefly confined to educating the slave-traders' children. Meanwhile, at the request of the Nova Scotian Methodists, Methodist missionaries were sent to Freetown from London in 1811 by the Wesleyan Missionary Society (WMS).

After 1808, when the British Crown took over and Sierra Leone became a center for enforcing the campaign against the Atlantic slave trade, there was a steady influx into the colony of the recaptives taken from slave ships, liberated, and settled in villages round Freetown. They represented an obvious target for missionary work. In 1816 the CMS gave up the Susu mission and, encouraged by governor Sir Charles MacCarthy and with substantial government finance, embarked on an ambitious program to convert the recaptive population. The colony was divided into parishes with villages laid out as Christian villages, each sited around a stone-built church, parsonage, and school built by the villagers themselves. These parishes were under the control of missionary magistrates who combined secular with religious authority to preach their message. But the people had little need for such authority: lacking a common language and cut off from the religions of their homelands, they were eager to learn English and to listen responsively to preaching that offered a new life of salvation to match their new life of freedom.

Mortality was high among the early missionaries. The CMS could not recruit enough to carry on the work, and laypeople were eventually substituted. But the missionary impetus remained, supplemented by the pastors of the settler churches, which some recaptives preferred to join, seeing in the settlers a black reference group with whom they could identify. Moreover, recaptives, once converted themselves, would take those newly landed from the slave ships into their homes and instruct them in the faith of their new homeland. Thus the conversion of the recaptive community to Christianity was a joint enterprise in which government, CMS and WMS missionaries, settler pastors, and—above all—the people themselves collaborated with astonishing success. In 1834 the then governor could describe them, without too much exaggeration, as "a nation of Free Black Christians."

A Christian community required education in Christian schools. The Sierra Leone Company had provided a school in Freetown for the settler children, which the colonial government continued to maintain. It also accepted responsibility for educating recaptive children. The Liberated African Department, which supervised the care of the recaptives, financed schools and teachers. All the schools provided a Christian education, and every church had its school. The missionaries were the main educational agents, the WMS operating in Freetown, the CMS concentrating on the villages. People clamored for schools to educate their children, undeterred—indeed, growing more insistent—when the missions began charging fees. By 1840, over 8,000—about a fifth of the population—were in school (while in England only three-fifths of the population was literate).

The CMS opened a Christian Institution in Leicester village in 1814 to give a more advanced schooling and eventually train teachers. It closed after a few years, but in 1827 was reopened on a waterside site at Fourah Bay. (One of the first students was the later Bishop Samuel Adjai Crowther.) Still, it remained a small affair until 1845, when the CMS put up a substantial new building and turned it into an institution to train clergy as well as teachers. In the same year a fee-paying CMS Grammar School was opened in Freetown for the sons of the emergent bourgeoisie, offering an education similar to that provided in an English grammar school, and in 1849 a Female Institution (renamed in 1877 the Annie Walsh Memorial School), was founded for their daughters. The WMS opened a secondary school, the Wesleyan Boys High School, in 1874, and a Wesleyan Female Institution, run privately, opened in 1880.

The mid-nineteenth century was a period of prosperity in Sierra Leone, and the growing bourgeoisie, enriched by import-export trade, began seeking higher education for their children. Some sent them to Britain whence, from the 1860s, an increasing number returned qualified as lawyers or doctors. But there was also a demand for a local institution of higher education, and in 1876 the CMS turned Fourah Bay College (as it had been renamed in 1864) into a nondenominational university college, accepting students from any part of West Africa.

Compared to the enormous missionary outlay for education (provided ultimately by mission subscribers in Britain), government financing was minimal once the influx of recaptives ceased and the Liberated African Department closed. In the 1870s the government school was upgraded as a model school, and a school inspector was appointed (though during the economic depression of the 1870s education grants ceased altogether for several years). But not until the twentieth century, with the institution of an education department in 1909, did the government begin to undertake any serious responsibility for education.

The recaptives' children became known as *Creoles*, a word first used with this meaning in the 1830s (and today rendered *Krios*). Educated and socialized into a new lifestyle, within a generation they had transformed themselves into a cohesive community with their own Krio culture based on English models but adapted to their own ways. Their own distinctive religious practices were incorporated into Christian worship, while their speech evolved as the Krio language, giving the community its own identity. Not all were Christians. Some, who had been Muslims in their homelands before capture (perhaps 10 per cent of the population), retained their religion. Known as Aku, they settled together in East Freetown with their own mosques and Quranic schools. Nor did the the Krio community form one socioeconomic unit; differences

of wealth divided them by class, but they retained a common identity, conscious and proud of their own culture, which they articulated publicly through a flourishing newspaper press. Investment in house property gave the community stability. Moreover, at this period the government was ready to recognize their achievements and appoint those who were qualified to senior official posts. By the early 1890s nearly half of those posts were held by Krios.

The Krios' cosmopolitan culture suited the enterprising and was bounded by no frontiers. Economic opportunities within the Sierra Leone colony were limited, but the ambitious could seek their fortunes inland, trading for produce, or, more commonly, overseas. In 1839 a group of recaptives ventured down the coast to Badagry in the Yoruba country of what became Nigeria, whence many of them had been shipped as slaves, and settled there as traders. At their suggestion the CMS founded a Yoruba mission where some of them were employed as missionaries, attracting others to trade in the Yoruba hinterland where they became known as the Saro. A large Saro trading community grew up in Lagos where, as at home, they invested in house property. After Lagos became British in 1861, opportunities opened for the Saro in government service and as pastors and teachers. A grammar school had already opened in 1859 under a Saro principal. They did not only build churches in Lagos, though; Aku traders built the first mosque.

When the Niger was opened to steamship travel in the 1850s, Krio CMS missionaries of Igbo origin established a mission to the Igbo people, supervised by Bishop Crowther. Krio traders followed, trading on their own or as agents for European firms, along the Niger and in the rivers country. When British administration extended to Northern Nigeria, Krios flocked there to provide the necessary literate office staff. All along the coast they found opportunities as entrepreneurs, officials, professional men, and skilled craftsmen. In Gambia (where they were confusingly all called Aku) they formed the elite of Bathurst (Banjul), and in the Gold Coast (Ghana) they competed with the local elites. In Fernando Po (Bioko) there was a large Krio community of traders and cocoa planters. By the twentieth century the *Sierra Leone Weekly News* sold more copies abroad than in Freetown, linking together the far-flung diaspora whose families were also regularly linked by marriage, a Pan–West African community not defined by geography but by its distinctive culture.

CHRISTOPHER FYFE

See also: **Crowther, Reverend Samuel Ajayi and the Niger Mission; Religion, Colonial Africa: Missionaries.**

Further Reading

Cole, Patrick. *Modern and Traditional Elites in the Politics of Lagos.* Cambridge: Cambridge University Press, 1975.

Fyfe, Christopher. *A History of Sierra Leone.* London: Oxford University Press, 1962.

———. "1787–1887–1987: Reflections on a Sierra Leone Bicentenary." *Africa* 57, no. 4 (1987): 411–421.

Fyfe, Christopher, and Eldred Jones (eds.). *Freetown: A Symposium.* Freetown: Sierra Leone University Press, 1968.

Fyle, Clifford N., and Eldred D. Jones (eds.). *A Krio-English Dictionary.* Oxford: Oxford University Press, 1980.

Peterson, John. *Province of Freedom: A History of Sierra Leone, 1787–1870.* London: Faber and Faber, 1969.

Porter, Arthur T. *Creoledom: A Study in the Development of Freetown Society.* London: Oxford University Press.

Spitzer, Leo. *The Creoles of Sierra Leone.* Madison: University of Wisconsin Press, 1974.

Sumner, D. L. *Education in Sierra Leone.* Freetown: Government of Sierra Leone, 1963.

Wyse, Akintola A. *The Krio of Sierra Leone: An Interpretive History.* London: C. Hurst, 1989.

Sierra Leone: Temne, Mende, and the Colony

Temne (Atlantic language family) and Mende (southern Mande) speakers together account for approximately 60 per cent of the population of the Republic of Sierra Leone. In the nineteenth century their ancestors occupied much the same area of the Sierra Leone Guinea plain the Temne and Mende now inhabit. The early Portuguese traders encountered the Temne in the Sierra Leone estuary; the Kpaa Mende crossed the Jong/Taia River only in the early nineteenth century. Throughout the nineteenth century the Temne and Mende languages expanded at the expense of the coastal Bullom, Sherbro, Krim, and Vai. The Temne and Mende lived in villages, sometimes stockaded for defense, aggregated in larger political units, usually referred to as *chiefdoms*. These were of various origins, and of varying and changing boundaries and structures. In Temne, political authority often rested with lineages of Mande origin perhaps going back to the Mani invasions. In other polities, both Temne and Mende—as, for example the Gbinti under *Almami* Rassin Bundu—power had come to lie with more recently arrived Pular or Mande speaking Muslim religious or trading families (*juula*). Such juula families had earlier established themselves north of the Rokel as agents in the trade between the Upper Niger and the Atlantic. Elsewhere—for example, in Upper Mende—power lay with warrior leaders such as Nyagua or Kai Londo. Male secret societies, *ragbenle* in parts of Temne and *poro* in Temne, Mende, Sherbro, and Vai, played major social and political roles. The women's secret society *Sande/Bundu* had a social significance, and, in some Mende areas, political functions. Everywhere populations were mixed, multilingualism common, political boundaries permeable, and ethnic identities fluid.

The settlement at Sierra Leone was established in Temne territory in the late eighteenth century. From its earliest days Sierra Leone depended on trade. The staple food, rice, was imported from neighboring areas. Long-distance northern trade routes provided gold, hides, and ivory for export overseas. But bulkier commodities, traded by river, soon became much more significant. Until 1830, timber, particularly from Temne, predominated. After the forests were depleted, groundnuts, palm oil (and after 1850 palm kernels), and—later still—rubber replaced timber. North of the Rokel, juula played an important role in the export trade as well as in the interregional exchange of cattle for kola. Sierra Leoneans (Krio) were largely confined to heads of navigation towns such as Kambia and Port Loko. South of the peninsula, Sierra Leone traders were more significant and widely dispersed, though here too juula played an important part. The Sierra Leone government sought to promote trade and develop relationships with local societies. European and Sierra Leonean merchants established close relationships with juula living in Freetown. Emissaries were dispatched to major inland centers: the earliest was sent to Futa Jalon in 1794. Government also sought to extend its influence over Temne and Mende polities closer to the colony in order to keep the long-distance routes open and to promote the peace necessary for produce trade. In 1831, during a pause in the Temne-Loko war, Temne chiefs signed a treaty with the colony promising to refer disputes to the governor. Between 1830 and 1880 similar treaties were signed with Temne and Mende rulers in the coastal zone. Despite the efforts of T. G. Lawson, government interpreter from 1852 to 1888, the treaty system operated erratically and intermittently.

Major changes came in the 1880s. French advances in the Guinea rivers, acknowledged in the Anglo-French agreement of 1881, confined Sierra Leone's coastal control to the area between the Great Scarcies and the River Mano, which had been effectively established as the border with Liberia in 1879. In 1884 the dramatic expansion of the Samorian *Almamate* through Falaba and Biriwa Limba to the borders of Temne country threatened the hinterland. Governor Rowe declined to make the alliance with the Samori that many Krio wished him to do. The boundaries between Sierra Leone and French Guinea were left to be determined by the Anglo-French negotiations of 1889.

Within those boundaries, the Sierra Leone government became more assertive and more willing to use force. The spread of trade and the greater availability of firearms increased the reward available to military leaders as well as to traders. Rulers of Mende towns such as Bumpe, Tikonko, and Lago hired out mercenaries to competing families in Sherbro and Galinhas. The depression in trade in the mid-1880s sharpened competition for access to its reward and exacerbated tensions among European and Sierra Leonean traders and local Africans, as well as between competing African rulers. The Yoni Temne sought access to the waterside, first in the Rokel and later in the rivers leading to Yawri Bay. In 1887, the Yoni attacked Senehun, a Kpaa Mende town under Madam Yoko, an ally of Sierra Leone. The Colonial Office authorized a military expedition. Robari was captured, with Mende assistance, and a garrison installed. In 1889, a small party of colonial police drove the Makaia from Lago, again with African assistance, in this case from the Fula chiefs of Pujehun. In 1893 force was used to drive the remnants of the Samorian presence under Porekere from Upper Mende.

In 1890, the creation of a quasi-military frontier police, initially to patrol the road linking the towns at the heads of river navigation, consolidated effective control. The appointment of Governor Cardew in 1895 and the proclamation of the Protectorate Ordinance in 1896 signaled a further major transfer of authority from African rulers to colonial officials. Temne and Mende rulers believed that the ordinance traduced their sovereignty and destroyed their social and political authority. In 1898 the first collection of direct tax, undertaken by the hated frontier police, was met with violent resistance. In February, Bai Bureh of Kasse led a well-sustained attack on British positions in the north. In late April and early May, the Mende and Sherbro carried out a series of attacks on government posts, Christian missions, and European and Krio trading establishments. The so-called Hut Tax War shocked the colonial authorities. The first and fundamental reaction was to punish the rebels with military campaigns, during which large numbers of Temne and Mende were killed either in fighting or, after a form of judicial process, by hanging. Temne and Mende areas were then incorporated into the new Protectorate of Sierra Leone. The new communication system and the colonial fiscal regime disrupted long-standing links, particularly in the northwest to Futa Jalon and beyond. The new administrative arrangements were based on the "chiefdom" and largely ignored the wider alliances and broader hegemonies that had grown up in the course of the nineteenth century.

JOHN DAVIDSON

See Also: **Futa Jalon; Sierra Leone: Protectorate: Administration and Government.**

Further Reading

Abraham, Arthur. *Mende Government and Politics under Colonial Rule: A Historical Study of Political Change in Sierra Leone, 1890–1937.* Freetown: Sierra Leone University Press, 1978.

Denzer, La Ray. "Sierra Leone: Bai Bureh." In *West African Resistance: The Military Response to Colonial Occupation,* edited by Michael Crowder. London: Hutchinson, 1971.

Day, L. R. "The Evolution of Female Chiefship during the Late Nineteenth-Century Wars of the Mende." *International Journal of African Historical Studies* 27, no. 3 (1994): 481–504.

Howard, Allen M., and David E. Skinner. "Network Building and Political Power in Northwestern Sierra Leone 1800–1865." *Africa* 54, no. 2 (1984): 2–28.

Howard, Allen M. "Trade and Islam in Sierra Leone, 18th–20th Centuries." In *Islam and Trade in Sierra Leone.* edited by Alusine Jalloh and David E. Skinner. Trenton, N.J.: Africa World Press, 1997.

Ijagbemi, Adeleye. "The Rokel River and the Development of Inland Trade in Sierra Leone." *Odu,* no. 3 (1970): 45–70.

———. "Chiefs Warriors and the Europeans: Warfare and Diplomacy on the Rokel in the Late 19th Century." *Journal of the Historical Society of Nigeria* 10, no. 2 (1980): 13–34.

Jones, Adam. *From Slaves to Palm Kernels: A History of the Galinhas Country, 1730–1890.* Wiesbaden: Franz Steiner Verlag, 1983.

Wylie, Kenneth C. *The Political Kingdoms of the Temne: Temne Government in Sierra Leone, 1825–1910.* New York: Africana, 1977.

Sierra Leone: Protectorate: Administration and Government

The year 1787 was a landmark one in the history of Sierra Leone. The advent of the black poor, a freed slave settler group from Britain, necessitated the imposition of colonial rule on the territory. The Nova Scotians from Canada; maroons from Jamaica; and recaptives, or liberated Africans, who arrived later constituted a unique group of freed slaves who inhabited the colony of Sierra Leone. They were ruled by Granville Sharpe, a British humanitarian, the British-owned Sierra Leone Company, and later the British government, which colonized the settlement in 1808. At the time the British assumed control of the colony there were other indigenous residents in the settlement. They were the Temne, Mandingo, Susu, Mende, Fula, and Kru. The settlement was later called Freetown.

In order to implement swift administrative policies emanating from the governor and his council, the colonial government established villages around the newly proclaimed colony. Leicester Village was founded in 1809, Wilberforce and Regent in 1812, Gloucester in 1816, Charlotte in 1818, and York, Kent, Waterloo, and Hastings in 1819. Christian mission posts and schools were established in these villages.

The Church Missionary Society (CMS) was instrumental in aiding the colonial government with the education of children resident in the colony. The

Christian Institution at Leicester, where clergymen and teachers were trained, was transferred from that area. It was subsequently replaced by the CMS-administered Fourah Bay College, which was established in 1827. The CMS also founded a Grammar School for boys in 1845, and Annie Walsh Memorial School for girls in 1849.

Apart from the CMS, the Roman Catholic, Methodist, and Countess of Huntingdon's Connexion Churches, as well as Muslims, also operated schools in the colony and its environs peacefully. Literacy in Western education was important because the colonial administration wanted educated Africans to work as interpreters, clerks, supervisors, teachers, preachers, and noncommissioned officers in the military. The encouragement of religion and Western-style education in the colony was essential to the survival of the colonial administration. It was therefore not surprising that, by 1868, there were 95 elementary schools in Sierra Leone, supervised by the different religious denominations. The existing education ordinance applied to all educational institutions; there was to be regular inspection of all the government-assisted schools by the Department of Education.

By 1872, the governor of Sierra Leone, who resided in Freetown, was given full power and authority to establish ordinances not antithetical to the laws of England. The governor's Legislative Council was given power to establish courts and appoint officers for the proper administration of justice in Sierra Leone. In 1874, the Legislative Council consisted of the governor, lieutenant governor, chief justice, senior military officer, the colonial secretary, and an advocate of the settlement. An executive council was also established to advise the governor on policy matters.

The governor also had power to make grants of land, appoint judges and other officers of state, and impose fines on offenders. He had power to pardon offenders and suspend government officers, and to appoint a deputy in the event of his temporary absence from Sierra Leone. All government officers and others were to obey the governor. The governor was the head of government and commander in chief of the forces.

On August 31, 1896, a protectorate was proclaimed over the territory adjacent to the existing colony of Sierra Leone. Five districts were created for administrative purposes: Karene, Ronietta, Bandajuma, Panguma, and Koinadugu. Each district was placed under a district commissioner. Traditional rulers were renamed paramount chiefs under the direct supervision of the district commissioners.

Some of the traditional rulers did not favor the reduction of their powers, the slave clause in the proclamation, and the imposition of a house tax of five shillings. Led by Bai Bureh, the chiefs and their subjects engaged in warfare with the colonial administration. After the "Hut Tax War" of 1898, the colonial administration ruled both the colony and protectorate. An order in council of 1895 gave power to the Legislative Council to legislate for the protectorate.

Sierra Leone achieved representative government in incremental stages. In 1808, it was administered by a governor and his council, which served as both an executive and a legislative body. In 1821, the governor's council was increased to nine members. In 1863, two distinct councils—the Executive and the Legislative—were established. The Executive Council consisted of the governor, chief justice, queen's advocate, colonial secretary and officer commanding the troops. The legislative council consisted of the executive and minority of the members appointed by the governor with the approval of the secretary of state for the colonies.

Due to the activities of the British colonial administrators on the coasts of Africa, many Africans who were educated became exposed to political developments in countries like India and South Africa. The National Council of British West African was formed in 1920 by leading West African nationalists, whose activities led to constitutional improvements in the West African territories. Sierra Leone was granted a new constitution in 1924; for the first time there was protectorate representation in the Legislative Council. Three unofficial members were elected to the Legislative Council, which also consisted of 11 official members and 7 nominated unofficial members, of whom 3 were paramount chiefs.

More constitutional improvements were made in 1951. The Legislative Council was increased to 30 members, not including the governor. There were 7 official members and 7 unofficial members elected in the colony; the protectorate elected 14 members indirectly. While 12 of the protectorate members were elected through District Councils, the remaining 2 were nominated by the Protectorate Assembly. In 1952, some Sierra Leoneans were given cabinet positions for the first time.

In 1957, the Legislative Council was replaced by the House of Representatives, which consisted of 57 members. They included a speaker, 14 colony representatives, 25 protectorate representatives, and twelve paramount chief representatives. The constitution was replaced later by the 1961 independence constitution.

MICHAEL J. JUSU

Further Reading

A Figbo, A. E., et al. *The Making of Modern Africa*, 2 vols. London: Longman, 1990.

Barkindo, B., et al. *Africa and the Wider World*, vol. 3, *Africa since the Scramble*. Longman Nigeria, 1994.

Boahen, Adu (ed.). *General History of Africa*, vo. 7, *Africa under Colonial Domination 1880–1935*. UNESCO, 1985.

Foray, Cyril P. *Historical Dictionary of Sierra Leone*. Metuchen, N.J.: Scarecrow, 1977.

Oliver, Roland, and A. Atmore, *Africa since 1800*, new ed. Cambridge: Cambridge University Press, 2000.

Sierra Leone: Protectorate: Economy

The creation of the Protectorate of Sierra Leone in 1896 cut the port of Freetown off from the role it had once enjoyed as entrepôt for the trade of the Guinea Rivers, Futa Jalon, and beyond. Freetown's trade now derived from the protectorate itself.

Before the 1930s, Sierra Leone's major export was palm kernels, with a subsidiary role for palm oil, kola nuts, ginger, piassava, and, after 1945, coffee and cocoa. The volume of exports and the penetration of European firms were greatly enhanced by the building of the government railway. Begun in 1895, the railway reached Pendembu, close to the Liberian border, in 1908, and the spur line north from Bauya reached Makeni in 1914. The line ran through the area where export-oriented agriculture was most firmly established. Railway towns, often also administrative centers, supplemented the older river towns as nodes of the trading network.

European firms, hitherto confined to Freetown, Bonthe, and a few river towns, now established themselves along the line of rail; so did an increasing number of Lebanese traders. The first Lebanese (or Syrians, as they were called in Sierra Leone until the 1950s) arrived in Freetown in the 1890s. They came to dominate Freetown retail trade, thus generating the capital to exploit the opportunities the railway provided. Rather than compete directly with the European firms, the Lebanese supplemented them, penetrating where Europeans declined to go, gathering in produce and distributing imported goods. Lebanese also grasped opportunities European firms failed to see—notably, in the internal trade in rice, supplying the Freetown market by rail, and in the export of kola by sea to Gambia and Senegal.

Krio (Creole) traders were aware of the new opportunities, but were for the most part unable to sustain their position against Lebanese competition, most spectacularly demonstrated by the rapid retreat of Krio women kola traders in Sherbro in the years leading up to 1913. The Fula retained control of the cattle trade from the north to Freetown. They and other Muslim traders adapted their trading networks, moving to railway towns and later to the mining centers while maintaining their position in the rivers north of Freetown, largely ignored by European firms.

Commercial penetration was further enhanced by the development of the road network. The first roads were "feeder roads" for the railway, but also for the river towns, which were thus enabled to maintain their (diminished) position, particularly after motor launches were introduced in the 1920s. Trucks were first imported in 1916, but became a significant factor only in the late 1920s. Road and river transport provided a further opportunity for Lebanese entrepreneurship. The major increase in road building, the replacement of ferries by bridges, and the creation of an integrated road network came only in the late colonial period. River and rail transportion declined, and the railway finally closed in 1969. Africans, in particular the Fula, played a more and more significant part in trucking ownership and management.

An export trade and government customs revenues largely dependent on palm kernels were vulnerable to price movements. Like many other colonial economies, Sierra Leone suffered badly from the influenza pandemic of 1918, the slump of 1921, and the Great Depression of the 1930s. The 1921 downturn hit African firms that had managed to survive the first impact of the imposition of colonial rule. In the 1930s the European firms replaced European employees "up line" with Africans. Diminished returns did not destroy the export trade; exports of palm kernels attained their highest volume in 1936. Moreover, farmers responded to the pressures of the Depression years in a positive way. The agriculture department adopted policies more sympathetic to the needs of food-crop farmers than it did in earlier or subsequent periods. Production of rice expanded, and from 1934 to 1938, Sierra Leone was a net exporter of rice.

The major change produced by the Depression was the development of mining. Government provided the first stimulus by organizing a geological survey. Major deposits of iron were discovered in Marampa chiefdom in 1926, while diamonds were found in Kono in 1930. Smaller alluvial deposits of gold and platinum were identified. The low barriers of entry to alluvial mining enabled Africans as well as Europeans and Lebanese to participate in, and in some cases profit from, platinum and gold. The platinum deposits ran out quickly, and gold was largely exhausted by 1940. Iron and diamonds were the major contributors to mining exports in the longer term. But the high capital costs of mining (notably, the railway from the iron mine at Lunsar to the port at Pepel), and strong government support gave the major companies, Delco and SLST, a dominant role. Mining companies made little direct contribution to government revenue until after independence in 1961. They did employ substantial quantities of labor, and wages and other local spending stimulated economic activity and contributed to government revenue though import duties.

The strategic importance of Freetown's harbor in World War II promoted an expansion of the city that has continued ever since. From 1939 until 1956 demand for iron ore and other exports was buoyant, and prices high. Changes in Colonial Office policies after 1945 promoted public investment in infrastructure, education, and health services. The diamond rush of the 1950s to the alluvial deposits of the Sewa and Moa valleys, as well as to the SLST concession area in Kono, brought prosperity, together with a sharp increase in imports and in government revenue. The movement of young men to the diamond fields deprived agriculture of necessary labor and both food production and agricultural exports, now organized through the Produce Marketing Board, declined. The chaotic character of the diamond rush, much of which was formally illegal, promoted smuggling of diamonds through Liberia, often by Lebanese illicit buyers. The basis of the relative prosperity of the 1950s and 1960s turned out to be transitory. Iron mining declined, and the mines closed in 1974. Exploitation of diamonds became more and more destructive of the environment and of society, and effective government control of the diamond areas gradually diminished.

JOHN DAVIDSON

See also: **Freetown.**

Further Reading

Cox-George, N. A. Finance and Development in West Africa: *The Sierra Leone Experience*. London: Dennis Dobson, 1961.

Jalloh, Alusine. *African Entrepreneurship: Muslim Fula Merchants in Sierra Leone*. Athens, Ohio: Ohio University Center for International Studies, 1999.

Kaniki, Martin H. Y. "Economic Change in Sierra Leone During the 1930s." *Transafrican Journal of History*. no. 3 (1973): 72–95.

Laan, H. L. van der. *The Sierra Leone Diamonds: An Economic Study Covering the Years 1952–1961*. Oxford: Oxford University Press, 1965.

———. *The Lebanese Traders in Sierra Leone*. The Hague: Mouton, 1975.

Richards, Paul. *Coping with Hunger: Hazard and Experiment in a West African Farming System*. London: Allen and Unwin, 1986.

Saylor, Ralph Gerald. *The Economic System of Sierra Leone*. Durham, N.C.: Duke University Press, 1967.

White, E. F. *Sierra Leone's Settler Women Traders: Women on the Afro-European Frontier*. Ann Arbor: University of Michigan Press, 1987.

Zack-Williams, Alfred. *Tributors, Supporters and Merchant Capital: Mining and Underdevelopment in Sierra Leone*. Aldershot, England: Avebury, 1995.

Sierra Leone: Margai, Sir Milton: Independence, Government of
Doctor and First Prime Minister of Sierra Leone

According to colonial and historical records, Sir Milton Augustus Strieby Margai worked in most of the government hospitals in Sierra Leone. In fact, while working as a government medical doctor, he was involved in modernizing midwife service. He trained local instructors who taught the *sande* women about hygiene, delivery, child care, and literacy. He also prevailed on the women to include the literacy program in their initiation ceremonies. Consequently, he wrote a book (*Mavulo Golei*) that explained midwifery methods among the native women.

Margai retired from active government medical service in 1950 and established his own private practice in Bo; he was a well-reputed surgeon. During his free time, he engaged himself in politics, and he was listed as a Bonthe district council representative in the protectorate assembly in 1947. He was also a founding member of the first protectorate newspaper, *The Sierra Leone Observer* in 1949. Margai participated actively in the Protectorate Educational Progressive Union. A skillful politician, he was able to convince Etheldred N. Jones (Lamina Sanko) to merge his People's Party with the Sierra Leone Organization Society to form the Sierra Leone People's Party (SLPP) with the slogan "One country, one people"; Margai became the party's first chairman. He became leader of government business after the 1951 elections. There were six other members of his party who were given government departments to administer.

A tactful politician, Margai's rise witnessed an atmosphere of antagonism and acrimony between the Krio (Creole) educated elite and the protectorate politicians and chiefs. In 1947, when the colonial administration ushered in constitutional reforms that would give the protectorate assembly members a majority of the seats in the legislative council, the Krio community vehemently opposed the idea. Led by Bankole Bright, the Krio looked down on the illiterate chiefs, whom they described as savages and unfit to sit in the same legislative council. Margai rebuked the Krio faction, and the protectorate chiefs and educated elite united against them. With the introduction of the Stevenson's constitution in 1951, which provided for an African majority in the legislative and executive councils, it was not surprising to see the SLPP emerge victorious in the subsequent general elections. The party captured 41 seats (versus 9 for the opposition). The protectorate chiefs supported the SLPP overwhelmingly; in fact, it was widely believed that any political party that won the support of the populous protectorate would emerge as the winner. This was why the SLPP had an edge over the Krio opposition forces.

In 1954, Margai became chief minister. He held the post until 1957, when he was appointed premier. Due to personal problems between Margai and his younger brother, Albert (later, Sir Albert), the latter broke with the SLPP and formed the People's National Party (PNP). In 1959, Margai skillfully used tactful methods to win the support of the moderate Krio opposition elements and his brother Albert; they joined Margai's United Front coalition. The aim of the coalition was to proceed to London for the constitutional conference.

Margai rewarded the Krio opposition leaders C. B. Rogers Wright (leader of the United People's Party, or UPP) and G. Dixon Thomas with cabinet positions in his government. His brother Albert was appointed minister of agriculture. All of them then became members of the SLPP. The coalition was now ready to proceed to London for constitutional talks for Sierra Leone's independence.

In 1959, Margai was awarded a knighthood. The only opposition force remaining was that of Siaka Stevens, who formed the All People's Congress Party in 1960 with the slogan "Elections before independence." He tried to win the support of young men, women, and teachers in the urban areas.

The Sierra Leone constitutional conference was held in Lancaster House, London, in 1960 and a new constitution was drawn up for the country. The independence constitution provided for a governor general as head of state with ceremonial functions, and a prime minister, and a cabinet. Sierra Leone became independent on April 27, 1961, with Margai as prime minister. Sierra Leone also became the 100th member of the United Nations. Margai's cabinet was broadly based; Kandeh Bureh became minister of transport and communications, while Dr. John Karefa Smart was appointed minister of external affairs. Ahmadu Wurie was appointed minister of education, and Albert Margai minister of finance. G. Dixon Thomas, Mohammad Sanusi Mustapha, and paramount chief Madam Ella Koblo Gulama were also given cabinet position; Gulama became the first female cabinet minister of Sierra Leone.

Margai's ministership witnessed the visit of Queen Elizabeth II and the Duke of Edinburgh to Sierra Leone in 1961. Njala University College was established in 1963. Sierra Leone was a stable and progressive nation during Margai's tenure as prime minister. He died on April 28, 1964, a day after the third anniversary of Sierra Leone's anniversary. His brother Albert Margai succeeded him as prime minister.

MICHAEL J. JUSU

See also: **Sierra Leone: Christianity, Education, Krio Diaspora; Sierra Leone: Stevens, Siaka and the All People's Congress.**

Biography

Born December 7, 1895 at Gbangbatoke, Moyamba district. Attended the Evangelical United Brethren School, Bonthe and Albert Academy, Freetown. Subsequently attended Fourah Bay College, where he graduated with a Bachelor of Arts degree in 1921, becoming the first candidate from the protectorate to earn a degree at the institution. Entered King's College in England, where he graduated with a Master's degree in 1926. Set another record by becoming the first protectorate man to earn a degree in medicine, from the Armstrong School of Medicine. Appointed medical officer for Sierra Leone in 1928. Named prime minister of Sierra Leone upon its independence in 1961. Died on April 28, 1964.

Further Reading

Anene, Joseph C., and Godfrey Brown. *Africa in the 19th and 20th Centuries.* Ibadan University Press, 1981.

Fajana, A., and A. O. Anjorin. *From Colony to Sovereign State: An Introduction to the History of West Africa since 1900.* Nairobi: Nelson, 1980.

Foray, Cyril P. *Historical Dictionary of Sierra Leone.* Metuchen, N.J.: Scarecrow, 1977.

Mazrui, Ali (ed.). *General History of Africa,* vol 8: *Africa since 1935.* Calif.: Heinemann, 1993.

Webster, J. B., and A. A. Boahen. *The Growth of African Civilization: The Revolutionary Years. West Africa since 1800.* Hong Kong: Longman, 1980.

Wyse, Akintola. *The Krio of Sierra Leone.* London: C. Hurst, 1989.

Sierra Leone: Stevens, Siaka and the All People's Congress

Siaka Stevens (1905–1988) was cofounder of the United Mine Workers Union, which contributed to his appointment to Sierra Leone's Protectorate Assembly in 1946 to represent the workers' interests. He was elected to the Legislative Council in 1951, and in 1952 he was appointed minister of lands, mines, and labor. He won the 1957 general election to the House of Representatives as member for the Port Loko East constituency; an election petition, however, resulted in his losing the seat. He later became the deputy leader and secretary general of the Peoples National Party (PNP).

In July 1960, Stevens, who was a member of the PNP delegation to the London constitutional talks for Sierra Leone's independence, refused to sign the independence arrangement with Britain, citing the defense clause as a factor. He returned to Sierra Leone and launched his "elections before independence" movement as a protest against the United Front Coalition. The movement eventually crystallized into a formidable political party, the All People's Congress (APC), with Stevens as its leader.

The ruling Sierra Leone People's Party (SLPP) accused the APC leadership of attempting to sabotage the independence celebrations of 1961. Consequently, 43 APC leaders, including Stevens, were arrested and detained under a state of emergency act.

The 1962 general election returned Stevens as a parliamentary member for the Freetown West 11 constituency, and he was elected mayor of Freetown in 1964. The APC was in total control of northern Sierra Leone by 1966.

The APC campaigned for nonalignment and socialism, and advocated equal opportunity for all Sierra Leoneans irrespective of tribe, class, color, or creed. The party also expressed distrust of foreigners. The party's appeal to those on the lower rungs of the educational, social, and economic ladder was a clear manifestation of galvanizing mass support from the populace by using the bottom-to-top approach. This tactic was very successful, and the party eventually had a membership of thousands.

In the 1967 general election, Stevens retained his Freetown West 11 constituency seat. The general election gave the APC 32 seats out of 66 in the parliament. Although the election was won by the APC and Stevens was appointed prime minister by the governor general, the military commander Brigadier David Lansana disputed the results. The governor general and Stevens were put under house arrest on orders of the military commander. The latter was in turn arrested together with Albert Margai, outgoing prime minister and leader of the SLPP, on March 23 of the same year. The constitution was suspended and a National Reformation Council (NRC) was formed with Colonel Andrew T. Juxon-Smith as chairman. The NRC was in turn overthrown in April 1968 by junior army officers who formed the Anti-Corruption Revolutionary Movement.

Stevens was reinstated as prime minister in 1968, after the National Interim Council, headed by Brigadier Bangura restored the constitution. Before the end of the year, by-elections were held after most of the SLPP members of parliament lost election petitions. This led to the appointment of an all-APC cabinet. Due to subsequent provincial disturbances and the government's alleged discovery of a plot to overthrow the regime in 1971, a state of emergency was declared. Bangura was tried, found guilty of conspiracy to overthrow the government, and subsequently executed. Sierra Leone was proclaimed a republic in 1971 by Stevens, who became its first executive president. Meanwhile, another plot to overthrow the government was discovered in 1974, and the coup leaders were arrested, tried, and executed.

The SLPP boycotted the 1973 general elections due to widespread violence. APC thugs and stalwarts were accused of intimidating opposition party supporters. In fact, it became widely known that the APC was kept in power by election rigging and violence. After appointing Christian Kamara-Taylor as prime minister in 1975, Stevens was reelected president in 1976. In the 1977 general elections, the APC won 74 seats and the SLPP 15 seats. The constitutional referendum of 1978 gave Stevens's government approval for a one-party state. Consequently, the new 1978 constitution came into force, and SLPP members of parliament joined the APC party.

In July 1980, Stevens hosted the seventeenth summit meeting of the member states of the Organization of African Unity (OAU), representing 50 countries, in Freetown. This was followed by general elections in 1982 that were marked by large-scale violence and irregularities, which led to the cancellation of elections in 13 constituencies. By-elections were held on June 4, 1982.

Steven's new cabinet reflected ethnic balance between the Mendes and the Temnes. The new Finance Minister was Salia Jusu-Sheriff, former SLPP leader who crossed over to the APC in 1981. His presence in the cabinet was significant because many people began to view the APC as a true national party.

Some scholars believe that Siaka Stevens tried to open the ranks of the APC to people of all walks of life. His aim was to maintain ethnic balance, and he tried to solicit the support of the academics, clerics, businessmen and traditional rulers. While trying to extend an olive branch to those who opposed him, he was actually an unsympathetic leader. He also succeeded in molding the diverse ethnic groups into a unified nation. Cultural and regional tensions were minimized.

Other observers described Stevens as a unique man in African politics and an evil genius who should have made Sierra Leone better instead of destroying it, but his regime was all about politics and power. For political purposes, he actually took disastrous economic decisions, like the phasing out of the railway. Many people saw this as his determination to punish the Mende to the south and east, who persistently opposed the APC. The railway was to be replaced by an efficient network of roads, but road construction stopped at Kenema; Kailahun was left out completely. Stevens played a Machiavellian hand of politics to reduce wrong things in the state to trivialities or jokes.

The latter years of Stevens's reign saw Sierra Leoneans cautiously accepting the rule of the APC. Stevens actually dominated the ruling All Peoples Congress party. He retired from office in November 1985 and continued his role as chairman of the party. He died on May 28, 1988; by then the APC had endorsed Major General Joseph Saidu Momoh as the sole candidate for party leadership.

MICHAEL J. JUSU

Further Reading

Alie, Joe A. D. *A New History of Sierra Leone.* New York: 1990.

Cartwright, John R. *Politics in Sierra Leone: 1947–67.* Toronto: 1970.

Hayward, Fred M. "Sierra Leone: State Consolidation, Fragmentation and Decay." In *Contemporary West African States*, edited by Donal Cruise O'Brien, John Dunn, and Richard Rathbone. Cambridge: Cambridge University Press, 1989.

Sierra Leone: Momoh, Joseph Saidu: Regime, 1986–1992

Brigadier General Joseph Saidu Momoh, president Siaka Stevens's hand-picked successor, was first perceived as the person who would rescue Sierra Leone from the jaws of authoritarian rule and instill transparency and accountability in government. On the political front, Momoh introduced a political philosophy he called "constructive nationalism." According to this philosophy, Sierra Leoneans were to put the country above their own self-interests in all matters. However, even his own ministers did not practice this philosophy. Instead, they gave birth to an intraparty political club named *Ekutay* to further their own personal interests. At the height of the shift from authoritarian to democratic rule around the world, Momoh clung to the view that a one-party system was more appropriate in societies with multiethnic cleavages, such as Sierra Leone. In the end, however, he helped to pave the path toward multiparty democracy in Sierra Leone when he signed a new constitution in September 1991.

Momoh was inaugurated as president on November 28, 1985. In March 1986, Momoh's government announced that it had foiled an attempted coup; more than 60 people were arrested. Of these, 18 were later charged. In early April, Francis K. Minah, the first vice president, was arrested and charged with treason. A government reshuffle led to the appointment of a new finance minister and the creation of the Ministry for Rural Development and Social Services. In October 1989, Minah and 15 others were implicated in a plot to assassinate Momoh and overthrow the government. Minah and 5 others were executed, and the remaining 10 were sentenced to life imprisonment.

To combat corruption in the public sector, Momoh initiated several measures in 1987. In July, the first casualty of the measures, the minister of Agriculture, Natural Resources, and Forestry, was forced to resign for accountancy irregularities in the distribution of domestic sugar supplies. In August, a deputy minister and a number of senior officials in the civil service and the Bank of Sierra Leone were charged with financial corruption. During that same year, Momoh clamped down on the press by introducing severe penalties for the publication of "defamatory" articles. He also ordered government censorship and the inspection of private mail. In January 1988, the deputy minister of Development

and Economic Planning was forced to resign; he and five other people were later indicted for fraud. Prompted by accusations of official corruption, Momoh reshuffled his cabinet in November, leading to the removal of a number of ministers. At the January 1989 All Peoples Congress (APC) conference, Momoh was unopposed as secretary general of the party. An official code of conduct for political leaders and public servants was also adopted at the conference.

In the early part of 1990, popular support for the establishment of a multiparty system became widespread. This desire was first rejected by Momoh, who urged instead broad-based participation in the one-party system. However, by the middle of August, Momoh had bowed to both national and international pressures and announced an extensive review of the constitution. The APC central committee approved a number of proposed constitutional amendments, allowing Momoh to appoint a 30-member national constitutional review commission. In the latter part of 1990, the constitutional amendment to reduce the minimum voting age from 21 to 18 years was adopted.

The constitutional review commission submitted a draft constitution in March 1991. This provided for the restoration of a multiparty political system, and also stipulated that the president be elected by a majority of votes cast nationwide and by at least 25 per cent of the votes cast in more than one-half of the electoral districts. The president's tenure in office was limited to two five-year terms. In addition to appointing her or his own cabinet, the president was to have one vice president—not two, as in previous administrations. While accepting a majority of the proposals, the Momoh government rejected the call for the formation of an upper legislative chamber. Instead, the Momoh government opted for the establishment of a 22-member state advisory council to be made up of 12 paramount chiefs (representing each of the 12 districts) and 10 members appointed by the president. The government presented the draft constitution to the House of Representatives in early June and announced that the parliamentary term, which was due to expire that month, would be extended for one more year to compensate for the disruption caused by the conflict between the government and the Liberian-supported rebel forces of the Revolutionary United Front in the southern region of Sierra Leone. The government also declared that the general elections, initially scheduled for May, were to be postponed for one year to facilitate the transition to a plural political system.

In mid-July 1991, Musa Kabia, the minister of social affairs, rural development and youth, resigned from the cabinet due to disputes within the APC over the new constitution. Kabia and ten other members of the House of Representatives were temporarily suspended from the APC on the grounds that they had engaged in activities perceived to be contrary to the party's interests. The House of Representatives approved the new constitution in August; it was to be endorsed by a national referendum at the end of that month. Meanwhile, political activities by other parties besides the APC remained illegal until the new constitution became effective. By the time the constitution was published in March, about ten opposition movements had been created. When the national referendum was conducted between August 23 and 30, it was approved by 60 per cent of the voters, with 75 per cent of the electorate participating in the process. In September, the new constitution was formally adopted, yet the 1978 constitution remained officially in effect. By the latter part of 1991, many members of Momoh's administration, including the first and second vice presidents, had resigned from the government and the APC. In December, following legislation to provide for the registration of political associations, Momoh and his APC agreed with the leaders of the other registered political parties to cooperate in the establishment of a multiparty polity.

In the economic realm, two-thirds of the country's labor force employed in agriculture suffered the most from the nation's faltering economy during Momoh's regime. Poor producer prices, coupled with an international slump in demand for cocoa and coffee, cut into rural incomes. Momoh's promise to improve producer prices as part of a "green revolution" program went largely unfulfilled. Like its agricultural products, much of Sierra Leone's minerals were being smuggled out of the country. By 1989, the cost of servicing the country's debt had reached 130 per cent of its total exports.

Due to his administration's failure to improve the serious economic situation, Momoh's initial popularity declined precipitously in 1986. He was forced to implement economic austerity measures under the rubric of the structural adjustment program (SAP) recommended by the World Bank and the International Monetary Fund (IMF). The measures included the introduction of a floating exchange rate, the elimination of government subsidies on rice and petroleum, the liberalization of trade, and increases in producer prices with the hope that they could encourage self-sufficiency for those trading in rice and other food products.

In November 1987, Momoh declared a state of emergency, as workers in the public sector engaged in strikes precipitated by the government's inability to pay their salaries. He also announced measures to prevent the hoarding of currency and essential goods, and intensified his campaign against smuggling. Under the new measures, corruption was declared a criminal offense, and those accused of any crime could be tried in absentia.

By 1988, the IMF had withdrawn its support for the SAP on the grounds that Sierra Leone was ineligible for assistance because it had not made payment on its arrears. In 1989, the Momoh administration announced additional economic measures, including increasing the revenue from the mining sector and reorganizing unpredictable state-owned enterprises. This SAP, initially approved by the IMF, had to be postponed because the IMF was concerned about the government's failure to reduce expenditure and to control debt.

On April 29, 1992, Momoh's regime was ended when members of the armed forces seized a radio station in Freetown and occupied the presidential offices. The leader of the coup, Captain Valentine E. M. Strasser (age 27 at the time), subsequently announced that Momoh's government had been replaced by a five-member military junta. Momoh sought assistance from the Guinean government, which dispatched troops to Freetown. In the ensuing violence, more than 100 people were killed. On April 30, Momoh fled to Guinea, leaving Strasser to announce the establishment of the National Provisional Ruling Council.

ABDUL KARIM BANGURA

See also: **Sierra Leone: Stevens, Siaka and the All People's Congress; World Bank, International Monetary Fund, and Structural Adjustment.**

Biography

Born 1937 at Binkolo, near Makeni, in the Northern Province of Sierra Leone. Educated at the Government Rural School at Wilberforce; the West African Methodist Collegiate School and the Technical Institute in Freetown; the Nigerian Military Academy in Kaduna (winning the baton of honor as best cadet in 1962); and the Mons Officer Cadet School in Aldershot, England (winning the sword of honor for best overseas cadet in 1963). Commissioned as second lieutenant in the Royal Sierra Leone Military Force (RSLMF) in November 1963. Appointed commanding officer of the First Battalion of the RSLMF in 1969; deputy force commander in 1970; acting force commander in 1971; and force commander in 1972. In a cabinet reshuffle in 1975, appointed to the cabinet as minister of state. In 1985, recommended by president Siaka Stevens as his successor. On April 29, 1992, overthrown by the National Provisional Ruling Council, led by Captain Valentine E. M. Strasser.

Further Reading

Clapham, Christopher. "Sierra Leone: Recent History." In *Africa South of the Sahara*. Detroit: Gale Research, 2000.

Fyle, C. Magbaily. "Popular Islam and Political Expression in Sierra Leone." In *Islam and Trade in Sierra Leone*, edited by Alusine Jalloh and David E. Skinner. Trenton, N.J.: Africa World Press, 1997. Kurkowski, David C. (ed.). *Current Leaders of Nations.* Lansdale, Penn.: Current Leaders, 1990.

Musa, Sorie. *Sierra Leone Digest 1993.* Washington, D.C.: Sierra Leone Institute for Policy Studies, 1993.

Weeks, John. *Development Strategy and the Economy of Sierra Leone.* New York: St. Martin's Press, 1992.

Sijilmasa, Zawila: Trans-Saharan Trade

Trans-Saharan trade dates back to antiquity. We know from numismatic evidence that from the end of the third century, an irregular gold coinage was issued at Carthage, and by the end of the fourth century there was a significant, if not regular, trans-Saharan gold trade. The solidus, a coin first issued in 312, provided the standard used for weighing gold dust in West Africa from then until now. The trade was evidently flourishing before the Arab conquest, but it is with the arrival of Arab traders and Islam that this trade became based in new Islamic centers of commerce that were built in the mid-eighth century.

There were essentially two routes or systems of routes crossing the Sahara by the mid-eighth century. The most important connected the Maghrib to Ghana, where Muslim merchants sought gold, slaves, ivory, and ostrich feathers. The westernmost route went directly to Audaghust, and a more eastern route went to Ghana by way of the salt mines of Teghaza, halfway across the desert. Both routes converged at Sijilmasa in the Tafilelt Oasis in southeastern Morocco. A second system of routes crossed the central Sahara connecting Ifriqiya (Tunisia) and Tripoli to the kingdom of Kanem. A subordinate route, running west from the Fezzan to Tadmekka and Gao and east to Egypt, where it entered the Fatimid city of al-Qahira (Cairo), intersected the north-south road at Zawila. Both of these hubs, Sijilmasa and Zawila, were established as new Islamic cities in the middle of the eighth century.

Before Sijilmasa became an urban center it served as a seasonal gathering place for Berbers at least as early as 500. It became a city when Sufriya Kharijite Muslims settled there after their failed revolt against the central authority of Islam. For the first 200 years Sijilmasa was an independent city-state under the control of the Berber Bani Midrar. Its position at the head of the trade routes crossing the Sahara placed it in an ideal position to control the flow of West African gold into the Muslim world. Control of the city-state became the object of intense competition between the Fatimids of Ifriqiya and the Umayyads of Cordoba, who alternately controlled Sijilmasa in the tenth century, either directly or through client Berber communities. This competition is vividly reflected in the gold

Trekking caravan. © Knut Mueller/Das Fotoarchiv.

currency struck by these two regimes, alternately in greatest quantities when they controlled the routes passing through Sijilmasa. The increasing need for gold by them and other Muslim regimes beginning to strike dinars (gold coins) in the tenth century made the Sijilmasa trade system the dominant one from this time on.

The other crucial commodity was salt. The rise to predominance of the route through Teghaza coincided with the advance of the Almoravids (from modern Mauritania) who conquered Sijilmasa in 1054–1055. Until then, much of the salt exported to the Sudan came from Awlil, on the Atlantic coast, within the sphere of the Bani Gudala. When that tribe revolted against the Almoravids, the salt route that they controlled became more isolated from the network in the central Sahara under Almoravid protection. That network traded gold in the north for manufactured goods and food products which they exchanged for salt in the desert, which they in turn traded in the south for more gold.

For the next 250 years, under the Almoravids, Almohads, and Merinids, the city flourished as a provincial capital within a much larger empire and a broad economic network from the Ebro River (Spain) to the Niger. In 1393, the Merinid sultans lost control of Sijilmasa in a civil war. The period following the civil war is the least known in Sijilmasa's history. The sixteenth-century Arab writer Leo Africanus describes the city in decline, and it was neglected by the Moroccan Saadian dynasty. In the seventeenth century the Alaouite dynasty refortified the garrison of Sijilmasa and extended its rule over Morocco.

Tradition dates routes going through the central Sahara at least as far back as those in the west. The kingdom of Fezzan goes back to antiquity; it is the Phasania referred to by the Roman author Pliny. Herodotus recounts the Garamantes driving horse-drawn chariots from this region against the "Ethiopians" as far south, perhaps, as Kanem.

But again, it is with Islam that a sustained economic network is established. The city of Zawila was founded in the late seventh or early eighth centuries. It first appears in Arab sources when the Ibadi Kharijite Berbers of Zawila were defeated by the Abbasids in 761–762. Yet the city remained a center for the Ibadi sect for a long time. By the start of the tenth century, Zawila was still an important Ibadi town, now in the hands of the Berber dynasty of the Bani Khattab. That dynasty controlled Zawila until the last of its rulers was killed in 1190 by a Mamluk commander of the late Ayyubid regime in Egypt.

If gold was the driving commodity in the Sijilmasa trade system, in Zawila it was slaves. Authors of the late twelfth century describe Zawila as a city of modest size but with numerous, flourishing bazaars, specializing in the slave trade. Recent scholarship confirms that the Fezzan region was the largest avenue for slave traffic into the Maghrib and Egypt through the nineteenth century.

The north-south route from the Fezzan to Kamen/Bornu continued to flourish beyond the decline of Zawila. The kingdom of Kanem maintained relations with the Hafsid dynasty of Tunis into the sixteenth century. The rulers of Bornu did likewise with the Ottoman province of Tripoli into the nineteenth century.

Islam was vital in the beginning of both Sijilmasa and Zawila. The Kharijite Berbers in both hub cities not only traded with Sub-Saharan Africa but also brought their version of Islam with them. Kharijism was predominant among Muslims in the trade centers south of the Sahara until at least the late eleventh century. A shared ideology on both sides of the desert undoubtedly made the arduous journey across the Sahara less daunting.

RONALD A. MESSIER

See also: **Ibn Khaldun: History of the Berbers; Kanem: Slavery and Trans-Saharan trade; Maghrib; Slavery: Trans-Saharan Trade.**

Further Reading

Austen, Ralph A. "The Mediterranean Islamic Slave Trade out of Africa: A Tentative Census." In *The Human Commodity: Perspectives on the Trans-Saharan Slave Trade*, edited by Elizabeth Savage. London: Frank Cass, 1992.

Devisse, J. "Trade and Trade Routes in West Africa." In *UNESCO General History of Africa 3, Africa from the 7th to 11th Century*, edited by Muhammad Fasi, M. El Fasi, and Ivan Hrbek. Berkeley and Los Angeles: University of California Press, 1988.

Ehrenkreutz, Andrew S. "The Year 414/1023–4 in the Commercial Life of Zawila." In *Studies in Near Eastern Culture and History*, edited by James A. Bellamy. Ann Arbor, Mich.: Center for Near Eastern and North African Studies, 1990.

Garrard, Timothy F. "Myth and Metrology: the Early Trans-Saharan Gold Trade." *Journal of African History*, no. 23 (1982): 443–461.

Levtzion, N., and J. F. P. Hopkins (eds. and trans.). *Corpus of Early Arabic Sources for West African History.* Cambridge: Cambrigde University Press, 1981.

Lewicki, Tadeuz. *Études Maghrébines et soudanaises.* Warsaw: Éditions Scientifiques de Pologne, 1983.

Lightfoot, Dale, and James Miller, "Sijilmassa: The Rise and Fall of a Walled Oasis in Medieval Morocco." *Annals of the Association of American Geographers* 86, no. 1 (1986): 78–101.

Martin, B. G. "Kanem, Bornu, and the Fazzan: Notes on the Political History of a Trade Route." *Journal of African History* 10, no. 1 (1969): 15–27.

Messier, Ronald A. "Sijilmasa: Five Seasons of Archaeological Inquiry." *Archéologie Islamique*, no. 7 (1997): 61–92.

Sirikwa and Engaruka: Dairy Farming, Irrigation

The Sirikwa culture flourished between the twelfth and fifteenth centuries, and disappeared by the eighteenth century at the latest. To judge from material remains, the settlement area of the Sirikwa extended throughout the western highlands of Kenya between Mount Elgon in the northwest and Lake Nakuru in the southeast. The Southern Nilotic Kalenjin groups living in this region today refer to the Sirikwa as their ancestors.

The Sirikwa culture may well represent a development from the local pastoral neolithic (the so-called Elmenteitan Culture), as well as a locally limited transition from the Stone Age to the Iron Age. Thus far, however, only a few iron remains have been found.

The main archaeological sites lie on Hyrax Hill near Nakuru in Kenya. Hyrax Hill comprises a series of prehistoric sites that date back to the Stone Age. The Sirikwa sites are characterized principally by shallow round depressions, the so-called Sirikwa holes (better termed "Sirikwa hollows"), which have a diameter of 30 to 40 feet (10 to 20 meters) and an average depth of 7.9 feet (2.4 meters). These depressions always lie on hillsides; they show the outline of an entrance of some sort, always pointing downhill, one side of which is always flanked by low rubbish mounds with a height of about one meter. Other features of these sites are potsherds in the Sirikwa/Lanet style, crude obsidian implements, bone tools, domestic faunal remains, and structures indicating remains of houses. The depressions occur in groups of five to one hundred. Surrounded by wooden fences or stone walls, they served as cattle enclosures; small farmsteads, encompassing two or three buildings, were situated on the perimeter of the enclosure and could only be entered through the latter. The enclosures both kept the flocks together and protected them from cattle raids.

The Sirikwa culture is documented mainly by evidence from archaeology and oral history. Excavations at Hyrax Hill over the last 60 years have yielded little in the way of grain remains, while grindstones and mortars are lacking entirely. Isolated botanical samples like food plants and medicinal plants, which were found at the beginning of the 1990s near Hyrax Hill, provide no indication of a real agrarian-based culture. Instead, archaeologists have found a series of animal remains, mostly of cattle, sheep, and goats, leading to the conclusion that cattle raising was the economic mainstay of the Sirikwa. Pollen analyses indicate that wild plants such as fruits, nuts, berries, and tubers were also gathered as dietary supplements. Small-scale agriculture, however, must have been carried out in the wetter regions of Nandi and Kericho, for here mortars, grindstones, and the remains of longer-term dwellings have been found.

The Sirikwa certainly were not the first Highlands people to raise cattle, sheep, and goats, but they were the first to pursue an elaborated economy based on the production of milk and fresh meat. They did not lead nomadic lives, but founded new settlements every few years, which explains the great number of depressions over such a large area. A settlement would probably be abandoned when the rubbish mound at the entrance to the enclosure became too large, or when the grazing lands needed recovery.

In the seventeenth and eighteenth centuries these cattle-raising techniques were given up, presumably because of an increase in large-scale cattle theft, against which the traditional defensive measures were ineffective. The Maasai in particular are said to have acted as cattle thieves. The Sirikwa must have responded to this threat with more mobile cattle-raising techniques.

Engaruka is situated in Northern Tanzania, on the floor of the Rift Valley near the base of the escarpment; archaeological sites occur in great number, particularly along the Engaruka River and at the northern tip of Lake Eyasi. This mainly savanna area, characterized by dust and thornbushes, offers little opportunity for conventional agricultural techniques. From the crater highlands, however, rivers flow down to the bottom of the Rift Valley—some only seasonally, others, such as the Engaruka River, throughout the year. Between the fourteenth and seventeenth centuries these wild rivers, gushing naturally out of clefts in the escarpment, were regulated in stone channels by levelling, diking, and regular maintenance. A few of these channels had a length of several kilometers and ran along the base of the escarpment and through the foothills of the mountains.

The channels were further subdivided to supply small, leveled fields, which were laid out in gridlike form. These fields were delimited by stonewalls, which helped to prevent erosion of the soft and dusty ground. Archaeologists have identified these formerly irrigated sites over an area of at least 5000 acres (2000 hectares). The abandoned fields and irrigation facilities

point to a highly specialized and integrated agricultural economy. The main crop was sorghum, grains of which have been found in village fireplaces at old Engaruka. In addition, a few cattle, goats, and sheep were kept. Excavation at Engaruka has revealed seven large villages, which were built on the hillsides in series of terraces, just above the highest fields and channels. Several thousand people must have lived there.

In approximately 1700, Engaruka was abandoned, probably because economic success brought about a population increase which led to overexploitation of land resources. The gradual drying out of the natural water supply, caused in part by deforestation over the centuries, may have been another factor contributing to this exodus. The agricultural system of Engaruka has been copied by several contemporary ethnic groups of the East African savanna; thus the irrigation systems described above can be found today among the Sonjo and Marakwet of southern Kenya.

REINHARD KLEIN-ARENDT

See also: **Iron Age (Later): East Africa.**

Further Reading

Kyule, David M. "The Sirikwa Economy: Hyrax Hill." *Azania*, no. 32 (1997): 21–31.

Leakey, Mary D. "Report on the Excavations at Hyrax Hill, Nakuru, Kenya Colony, 1937–1938." *Transactions of the Royal Society of South Africa* 30, no. 4 (1945): 271–409.

Robertshaw, Peter. "Engaruka Revisited: Excavations of 1982." *Azania*, no. 21 (1986): 1–27.

Sassoon, Hamo. "New Views on Engaruka, Northern Tanzania." *Journal of African History*, no. 8 (1967): 201–17.

Sutton, John. "Hyrax Hill and the Sirikwa: New Excavations on Site II." *Azania*, no. 22 (1987): 1–37.

———. *A Thousand Years of East Africa.* Nairobi: British Institute in Eastern Africa, 1990.

Six Day War: *See* Egypt: Nasser: Foreign Policy: Suez Canal Crisis to Six Day War, 1952–1970.

Slave Trade: Arms, Ivory, and (East and Central Africa)

The trade in ivory, slaves, and firearms in East and Central Africa displays strong parallels in respect to the persons and the ethnic groups involved, as well as in commercial structures and trade mechanisms.

Ivory was supplied from the nearer and farther hinterland of the coastal strip stretching from Somalia to Mozambique. Hubs for this trade were Mozambique Island and Kilwa in the south, and Mombasa, Zanzibar, and the Lamu Archipelago in the north. When exactly the ivory trade in Eastern Africa began is not known;

estimates reach from Greek antiquity to the tenth century. Until the end of the eighteenth century, the southern trade route ran from the hunting areas in Zambezia and Malawi to Portuguese-controlled Mozambique Island. At the beginning of the nineteenth century, Kilwa became the main export center for ivory. By the end of the seventeenth century a well-organized system underlay the trade, in which Europeans, Arabs, the Swahili, and Indians figured as wholesale buyers of the ivory. In this they cooperated with the Yao and Makua peoples of Malawi and Mozambique, who also did the elephant hunting. The latter transported the tusks from the regions west and south of Lake Malawi to Kilwa and Mozambique Island, where they were conveyed to farther destinations, particularly Zanzibar.

The more northern centers like Pate and Lamu were probably supplied, even in pre-Portuguese times, with ivory primarily from the area between the Tana and Juba Rivers. In the seventeenth and eighteenth centuries, Lamu, Pate, Siyu, and Mombasa were the principal competitors for control of the ivory trade. The Oromo retained a role as middlemen; the Arabs and Swahili in the coastal towns were thus dependent on them. In about 1860, however, the Sultan of Zanzibar succeeded in uniting under his control the whole coastal strip from southern Somalia to Kilwa, and consolidating the ivory export business at Zanzibar. While the Oromo retained their supremacy over the ivory trade routes in the hinterland, they increasingly had to deal with competition from the Pokomo. In the 1867–1869 war with the Somali, the Oromo suffered a severe defeat and were completely driven out of the ivory trade. Arabs and the Swahili filled the gap, with the Swahili in particular now acting as middlemen between the hunters in the hinterland and the Arabs on the coast.

The ivory trade experienced a particular boom in the 1840s. The main beneficiary of this boom was the Sultan, who profited handsomely through taxation of imported and exported ivory that passed through Zanzibar. Until that time, the Indian subcontinent had been the main buyer for ivory. However, in the 1840s more and more North American and European vessels began anchoring at Zanzibar; the industrial revolution in America and Western Europe had also engendered a fashion revolution, which required ivory as the raw material for billiard balls, piano keys, and carvings.

At the beginning of the nineteenth century the ivory routes, particularly in the south, were increasingly used for slave trading. Starting in about 1770, the demand for slaves grew rapidly owing to the expansion of plantation economies on the French islands in the Indian Ocean, and later in Zanzibar and Pemba. At first it was mainly the French traders who appeared as slave buyers and the Portuguese as slave suppliers. The slave expeditions and trade were increasingly financed by coastal Arabs, Indians, or Swahili, with Zanzibar functioning as both distributor and consumer. The Yao, Makua, Bisa, Ngindo, and Nsenga were significant victims of the slave trade; they were sold as the captives of slave expeditions, as prisoners of war, as debtors or even as items of barter during times of famine. Ironically, the Yao and Makua themselves came increasingly to be the main slave hunters and dealers in the hinterland. Arabs brought the human booty across Lake Malawi to coastal settlements like Kilwa, Lindi, or Mikindani. The slave routes from Lake Malawi to the coast connected the southern end of the lake with Mikindani, the northern end with Kilwa, and proceeded straight across the lake to Lindi.

During the 1880s, the penetration of these territories by the English became more and more pronounced. Although at Zanzibar their antislavery policy had considerable success, the southern slaving routes from Malawi and Mozambique still remained largely intact and supplied a whole chain of smaller harbors between Kilwa and Sofala. Modern sources estimate that, even at the time of the intensification of British antislavery pressure (c.1875), 2,000 to 4,000 slaves were smuggled from these small coastal deposit centers Zanzibar and overseas. Ultimately, however, the political and military pressure upon slave hunters and dealers on the part of colonial administrators and missionaries intensified to such a degree that by the turn of the century the slave trade was virtually extinguished.

The consequences of the slaving expeditions for the regions affected are still controversial. Certainly it resulted in the depopulation of whole areas and in disturbances in the ivory trade. The actual numbers of people sold and the effects on the economy of the region are difficult to assess; they have, however, frequently been exaggerated. Between 1862 and 1875 slave exports from Kilwa presumably amounted to something between 10,000 and 20,000 annually, mostly to Zanzibar and Pemba. In the 1860s and 1870s some 20,000 to 30,000 people were enslaved annually on the East African coast.

From the beginning of the nineteenth century, the coastal strip between Mogadishu and Lamu became another focal point for the slave trade and the slave economy. At that time Lamu became a grain exporter and supplier to the growing populations of Zanzibar and Pemba. Slaves were therefore needed for cultivation, and were imported from southern Tanganyika; some of these were re-exported to Arabia. When in the 1880s the slave trade was suppressed, many areas could no longer be cultivated. Slaving expeditions aimed at the peoples in the hinterland of Kenya and southern Somalia were relatively rare because of their low population density, and presumably because preying on well-organized peoples like the Oromo or the Masai was too dangerous.

The spread of firearms in East and Central Africa was due, on the one hand, to African internal factors, such as elephant hunting, slave trade, endemic wars, and the characteristic love of self-display on the part of African despots. External factors also played a role. For instance, in the second half of the nineteenth century the weaponry of the European and North American armies underwent a process of modernization, creating a surplus of now-obsolete weapons. Large quantities of these firearms were delivered to eastern and central Africa—first muzzle-loaded weapons, then the breech-loaded, and, finally, repeating rifles.

In the eighteenth and nineteenth centuries, large numbers of firearms reached Mozambique and Zambezia via French merchants. The customers were chiefly the Makua and Yao, who increasingly used guns for elephant hunting; the guns were paid for with ivory and captured slaves. The armament of the Makua in particular constituted an increasing threat to the Portuguese colonial power in Mozambique from the second half of the eighteenth century on. This threat resulted in several armed clashes and produced many casualties and brought the trade between the Portuguese and the Yao to a standstill. Nonetheless, starting in 1787 the Portuguese authorities allowed selling guns to the Makua, a measure that can only be explained by the immense profits gained through the exchange of firearms for slaves.

From the beginning of the nineteenth century firearms were also common in the territories of present-day Tanzania, Uganda, and Kenya. Here, too, Europeans (both private dealers and, later, colonial administrators) were involved in the trade with Zanzibar as one of the main transshipment centers. The trade shifted increasingly to East and Central Africa owing to the breakdown of the South African market, which had been supplied by the Portuguese, and to Muslim revolts against the advance of the European powers in East Africa. In the 1880s firearms were so common in East Africa that missionaries and administrators foresaw great danger for the stability of the region. By that time presumably 80,000 to 100,000 firearms annually were finding their way into the interior via the East African seaports. In 1890 the import of firearms to Africa was restricted by the Treaty of Brussels. Despite this prohibition firearms continued to flow into East Africa, brought inland mainly by Arab traders in exchange for ivory and slaves, and financed by Indian businessmen at the coast. Only at the end of the 1890s did this trade die out in the English, Belgian, and German territories, through rigorous controls and the collapse of the Arab hegemony on the coast.

REINHARD KLEIN-ARENDT

See also: **Slavery: East Africa: Eighteenth Century; Zanzibar: Trade: Slaves, Ivory.**

Further Reading

Alpers, Edward A. *Ivory and Slaves in East Central Africa: Changing Patterns of International Trade to the Later Nineteenth Century.* London: Heinemann, 1975.

Campbell, Gwyn. "The East African Slave Trade, 1861–1895: The 'Southern' Complex." *International Journal of African Historical Studies* 22, no. 1 (1989): 1–26.

Martin, Esmond B., and T. C. I. Ryan, "A Quantitative Assessment of the Arab Slave Trade of East Africa, 1770–1896." *Kenya Historical Review Journal* 5, no. 1 (1977): 71–91.

———. "The Slave Trade of the Bajun and Benadir Coasts." *Transafrican Journal of History* 9, no. 1 (1980): 103–132.

Ylvisaker, Marguerite. "The Ivory Trade in the Lamu Area, 1600–1870." *Paideuma*, no. 28 (1982): 221–231.

Slave Trade: Arms, Ivory, and (Southern Africa)

Ivory is known to have been exported from southern Africa since at least the tenth century. An Arab chronicler of that time, al-Masudi, reported keen competition for the high-quality ivory obtained from towns as far south as Sofala on the central Mozambique coast, the tusks being transported by sea to China and India. Coins from Fatimid Egypt found at some of these towns provide evidence that the trade continued through the eleventh century; Ibn Battuta records that large quantities were still exported from Kilwa and Sofala in the thirteenth century. There is evidence to suggest that some of this ivory came from the far interior. Cowrie shells and glass beads made in Fatimid Cairo and southeast Asia (which could have been obtained in exchange for ivory) are found at Schroda in the Limpopo Valley, as well as the northern Botswana sites at Matlapaneng on the Okavango Delta and Nqoma in the Tsodilo Hills. These sites all produced ivory, much of it presumably for trade.

Around the end of the fourteenth century, Islamic traders began to move up the Zambezi; a number of trading centers arose where gold, tin, ivory, hides, salt, and sometimes slaves were sold for cloth, glass beads, and other items of great value in the interior. These centers, called *ferias* by the Portuguese who occupied them at the beginning of the siuxteenth century, continued to be the main foci of trade until the mid-eighteenth century. An impression of the volume of ivory exported can be obtained from later reports on Delagoa Bay (Maputo) where 22,500 kilograms were shipped between 1721 and 1729; it is estimated that by 1770 this increased to 45,400 kilograms annually. A century later, one trader bought 18,000 kilograms on the Zambezi in a single year.

European consumption of ivory increased dramatically during the first half of the nineteenth century as a consequence of the wealth created by industrialization; billiards and pianos became passions of the rich, for which ivory was required to make the balls and keys. To meet this demand, from the 1860s through the 1880s about 8,000 kilograms were exported annually from the comparatively small area west of the Okavango Delta, and another 36,000 kilograms annually from eastern Botswana. This ivory was sent out mainly through Durban, Port Elizabeth, and Cape Town. By 1890, elephants were all but extinct in southern Africa, and the ivory trade came to an end.

Trade in slaves also developed early, perhaps in association with that in ivory; al-Masudi mentions slaves, but it is unclear if he included the southern African port of Sofala in his brief account. In any case, captives would have been obtained comparatively near the points of export and would have been few in number relative to other regions until late in the eighteenth century. Portuguese accounts suggest that from the 1790s to about 1830 perhaps on average 1,000 slaves were taken annually from Zambezia and sent out through Quelimane (some 400 kilometers north of Sofala). This should be balanced against records indicating that in the first decade of the nineteenth century—shortly before slave exports from Mozambique reached their peak—the value of exported ivory was more than twice that of slaves; by this time, the value of exported gold was less than that of ivory or slaves. And during the 1720s, when ivory exports from Delagoa Bay were robust, a total of only 288 slaves passed through that port. It is widely accepted that the slave trade through southern Mozambique reached its peak in the early 1800s, but its scope and consequences for native peoples is strongly debated.

At the Cape, the situation was quite different. Slaves were imported, rather than exported, almost from the founding of the colony in 1652—first from Mozambique, Madagascar, and southeast Asia, and then from India. In addition, many indigenous Khoisan-speaking peoples were enslaved—initially those within the Cape colony itself, and then, after Britain abolished the practice in 1807, those captured on the frontier. To aid in the latter process, peoples of mixed European and Khoisan parentage, who came to be called *griqua*, *bergenaar*, and *kora*, were enlisted as procuring agents in association with their extensive interior trade.

In the far northern part of the subcontinent, from the vicinity of Victoria Falls through the Okavango Delta to the Atlantic mouth of the Kunene, slaving was reported by the first Europeans to reach the area from the south in the mid-nineteenth century. Indeed, native oral histories indicate that the trade had begun a quarter century or so earlier. The Portuguese, with Chokwe and Mbwela associates operating from Benguela and Luanda, were the principal agents of this trade, but they were often supplied by local providers, including Khoisan-speaking peoples. It must be stressed that slaves were never taken here in quantities comparable to those in other parts of southern Africa, and many were used to resupply labor shortages within Angola itself. There was also a small trade to the south, but this was miniscule compared with that of the rest of the region.

Although all European colonial administrations took steps at various times to ban or limit the conveyance of firearms to natives, guns were closely tied to the expansion of the ivory and slave trade. Arms, gunpowder, shot, and lead were sold at the *ferias* in the eighteenth century. Toward the end of that century, griqua and other frontier peoples were heavily armed by Europeans at the Cape for the express purpose of hunting for ivory and raiding for slaves. On the northern margins, gunpowder was in such abundant supply by 1850 (obtained through links to Angolan Portuguese) that Cape traders found their stocks of little value in exchange for ivory unless they increased the supply of guns. Firearms were, of course, also used to further the expansion of their owners both in territory and in trade. Competition for power and wealth in the combined markets for ivory and slaves, abetted in the nineteenth century by an abundance of arms, led to profound demographic displacements throughout the subcontinent and to the strengthening of those native polities that were in a position to control local terms of trade. Most other peoples were either absorbed into those polities or subjugated to them.

EDWIN N. WILMSEN

See also: **Cape Colony: Slavery; "Legitimate Commerce" and the Export Trade in the Nineteenth Century; Slavery, Colonial Rule and.**

Further Reading

Eldredge, Elizabeth, and Fred Morton (eds.). *Slavery in South Africa: Captive Labor on the Dutch Frontier.* Boulder, Colo.: Westview Press, 1994.

Hamilton, Carolyn (ed.). *The Mfecane Aftermath: Reconstructive Debates in Southern African History.* Johannesburg: Witwatersrand University Press/Pietermaritzburg: University of Natal Press, 1995.

Miers, Suzanne, and Michael Crowder. "The Politics of Slavery in Bechuanaland: Power Struggles and the Plight of the Basarwa in the Bamangwato Reserve, 1926–1940." In *The End of Slavery in Africa*, edited by Suzanne Meirs and Richard Roberts. Madison: University of Wisconsin Press, 1988.

Miller, Joseph. *Way of Death: Merchant Capitalism and the Angolan Slave Trade, 1730–1830.* London: James Curry, 1988.

Ross, Robert. *Cape of Torments: Slavery and Resistance in South Africa*. London: Routledge and Kegan Paul, 1983.

Slavery in African Society

Slavery is an age-old institution in many African cultures. It usually involves the acquisition and maintenance of men, women, and children, often nonkinsmen of the host society, in involuntary servitude by capable individuals. The existence of slavery in Africa can hardly be dated precisely, but it can be easily attested to by the varied appellations for it in different societies in the continent. In Nweh society in Cameroon for example, a slave is called *efueht* (pl. *befueht*) and slavery is known as *lefueht* (Fomin 1996). The people of Nso, also in Cameroon, refer to a slave as *kwan* (pl. *akwan*) and slavery as *vikwan*. And we find these appellations wherever slavery was deeply rooted in the continent.

Despite these varied appellations, the notion of slavery and the perception of slaves by owners can be discussed in two broad perspectives: that of the centralized polities and that of the noncentralized societies. In the centralized polities, they were perceived as acquired members of the host states. Here slavery was therefore a means of recruiting and integrating outsiders into the corporate group in the state-building enterprise. In the noncentralized societies, where kinship was the basis of nationhood, slaves were perceived as outsiders in the affairs of the corporate group of the freeborn (Fomin 2002). Thus, while the slaves remained permanently on the margin of corporate life in noncentralized societies, they lived in a continuum (Miers and Kopytoff 1977) from being outsiders to insiders in the centralized states. Both types of polities acquired slaves largely from purchase, capture, gifts, and pawns, and in some cases through procreation. The polemic of acquisition and perception of slaves in Africa is, however, not as hairsplitting as that of the origin of slavery.

The origin of slavery in African society was never uniform. In some polities, slavery evolved from indigenous servitude in a process referred to by some scholars as institutional continuity. That is, from voluntary to involuntary servitude, the distinction in origin between slavery per se and voluntary servitude is in the procurement of slaves. The slave was procured involuntarily, but the freeborn went into servitude voluntarily and could theoretically terminate it at will. But the circumstances that led them into servitude—hardship, abject poverty, and insecurity—could hardly be corrected within a brief servitude. Thus servitude preceded slavery in many African societies, especially in the centralized kingship system where servitude was an integral part.

Some societies developed slavery in the process of taking part in the trans-Saharan, transatlantic and trans–Red Sea slave trade. They either played the role of middlemen as in the case of many West African coastal societies (Austen 1995) or intermediary forest states, which provided sojourns and markets for slave dealers from the far hinterlands. In this transaction, they developed slavery without a previous system of indigenous servitude. The societies that built their slavery system in this way can be identified today with the history of separate slave settlements. These distinct slave settlements were not farm settlements but parallel communities to those of the freeborn (Fomin 2002).

Slavery in African society was really the product of interactions between indigenous practices and extraneous influences. By the eighteenth century the impact of these foreign influences on the organization and functioning of slavery had reached their zenith in Africa. The trans-Saharan slave trade, though much declined by the eighteenth century, had left great and lasting impact on the continent. The transatlantic trade that had been going on for over 200 years had deeply penetrated the continent and involved many societies in a capitalist slave business and its ramifications. It was from the reckless and callous transatlantic system that some coastal societies built a slavery system in which slavery was essentially an economic venture.

The Arabs, who were the main torch bearers of the spread of Islamic faith in Africa, had dominated the much older trans-Saharan trade (Lavers 1994) and their merchants-cum-clerics tied enslavement to conversion. They used their slaves in a variety of purposes and left an Islamic oriented slavery system in many societies in the Sahel and Sudanic Africa. Along the Indian Ocean coast of Africa, Arabs used slaves in the eighteenth and nineteenth centuries to run clove plantations but did not seem to have reduced them to absolute chattels. Slaves were considered persons with recognized minimum privileges (Lovejoy 1993).

Despite these foreign influences, slavery in Africa still maintained its essential indigenous values. It was largely benign and more a social and political, rather than an economic, institution in many centralized states. Slave owners in centralized states also exploited slave transactions for wives, concubines, soldiers and retainers. Slaves performed many economic services for their masters, but no economic activity in the centralized states was reserved for slaves. It was in some noncentralized societies that slaves had specific jobs that were reserved for them alone.

Many African societies had inherent cultural values that ensured the general benignity of slavery and also worked in favor of its decline in the continent. The cruel sacrifice of slaves in rituals is known (Lovejoy 1983), but it was the exception rather than the rule. The rapid integration of slaves into the corporate life and the freedom that slaves had in their own affairs made the lot of slaves generally less irksome in Africa.

E. S. D. FOMIN

Further Reading

Austen, R. H. "Slavery and Slave trade on the Atlantic Coast: The Duala of the Littoral." *PAIDEUMA*, no. 41 (1995): 127–52.

Fomin, E. S. D. *A Comparative Study of Societal Influences on Indigenous Slavery in Two Types of Societies in Africa*. New York: Edwin Mellen Press, 2002.

Lavers, John E. "Trans-Saharan Trade before 1800: Toward Quantification." *PAIDEUMA*, no. 40 (1994): 243–60.

Lovejoy, Paul E. *Transformation in Slavery: A History of Slavery in Africa*. Cambridge: Cambridge University Press, 1983.

Miers, Suzanne, and Igor Kopytoff. *Slavery in Africa: Historical and Anthropological Perspectives*. Madison: University of Wisconsin Press, 1977.

Slavery, Atlantic Basin in the Era of

The Atlantic basin in the era of the slave trade was characterized primarily by shifting commodity exchange pursued within civil society over a period of three centuries, climaxing in the eighteenth century.

Prior to the rise of "legitimate" trade relations during the nineteenth century, West Africans exported numerous commodities including elephant ivory, wood timber, color dyes, vegetable gum, beeswax, and food spices. Gold and leather were especially prominent exports. In Gambia, for instance, the Portuguese purchased between 5,000 to 6,000 gold doublons annually from 1456, while Senegambia produced a record total of 150,000 leather hides in 1660. Throughout the eighteenth century, the vegetable resin gum marketed in Senegambia became central to the Atlantic trading system because of its importance as raw material for the booming textile industry.

The central export commodity in the Atlantic basin, however, became slaves. According to recent estimates calculated by David Eltis (1987) around 5,595,477 slaves were exported from the five major regions of West Africa to the New World between 1662 and 1867. The Bight of Benin accounted for 33 per cent of these human exports; the Bight of Biafra, 30 per cent; the Gold Coast and Sierra Leone, 13 per cent apiece; and Senegambia, 11 per cent. This export business peaked at certain times, with the heaviest exports taken from the Bight of Benin in the 1690s through 1730s; Senegambia and Gold Coast from the 1720s through 1740s; Sierra Leone in the 1760s and 1770s; and the Bight of Benin again in the 1770s and 1780s. Such estimates of slave exports have been hotly debated for a generation—calculations of slave exports from Senegambia between 1681 and 1810 range from 304,330 (Curtin 1969) to 361,090 (Eltis 1987) to 500,000 (Barry 1998), and will no doubt continue to do

so. Revisionist historians have also begun to turn their attentions toward slave revolts against slavery, emanating out of high concentrations of labor power in domestic units and coastal slave factories, as recorded in 1756 and 1785 in Senegambia. Although new research and old debates will continue, most historians agree the slave trade increasingly dominated the export business of West Africa in the Atlantic basin during this era.

The major cause of this slave trade expansion was the rise in demand for slave labor in the Americas. Eltis (1987) estimates that some 10,247,500 slaves were forcibly removed from Africa and dispersed throughout the Atlantic basin between 1451 and 1870. Around 2 per cent went to Europe, the Atlantic islands (Maderia, the Canaries, and the Azores), and São Tomé. Most ended up in Brazil and the West Indies, which accounted for 39 per cent and 37 per cent, respectively, of all slave imports. Around 16 per cent went to Spanish America and 5 per cent to British North America. These slaves were mainly taken from west Africa prior to the eighteenth century, and from then onward increasingly from west central Africa. Along with demand for slave labor, the emergence of popular consumer tastes for the fruits of empire played a central role in slavery's expansion. Annual sugar consumption among Britain's growing middle classes and wage-earning proletariat rose from 6 pounds per head in 1710 to 23.2 pounds per head in the 1770s.

West Africa also imported goods from Europe during this era. Such goods included dozens of types of textiles during the seventeenth century. Textiles accounted for one-half to three-quarters of all goods sent to West Africa from Rouen and Le Havre in the eighteenth century. The Gold Coast absorbed around 20,000 meters of European and Asian cloth annually by the early to mid-seventeenth century. Metal goods, whether raw as iron bars and copper *manillas* (horseshoe-shaped ingots) or in the worked form of knives, swords, copper basins, and bowls, were important imports. Senegambia imported a record 150 tons of European iron every year by the last half of the seventeenth century. Then there were nonutilitarian goods such as jewelry, mechanical toys, and alcoholic beverages. Guns and gunpowder accounted for about one-fifth of cargoes shipped from Britain to Africa during the zenith of the slave trade in the eighteenth century.

The first major merchants in the Atlantic basin were sponsored by European state authorities through their policies of mercantilism. The Portuguese were the leading European power in West Africa throughout the fifteenth and sixteenth centuries, the Dutch in the seventeenth century, and the English and French during the eighteenth century. State interests were represented by chartered companies that were guaranteed trading monopolies. The Netherlands was represented by the Dutch West India Company (formed in 1621); the French by the Compagnie des Indes Occidentales (1664), the Compagnie du Senegal (1673), and the Compagnie du Guinee (1684); and the English by the Royal African Company (1672). Despite their official patronage, these companies proved of limited effect because of their unattractiveness to capital investment, stuffy bureaucracy and poor staffing, unrealistic production targets, and stiff opposition.

Private traders and independent merchants were among the harshest critics of these mercantilist policies. Their success can be appreciated from the rise of slave entrepôts rimming the Atlantic basin. Old Calabar, in the Bight of Biafra, was dominated by British merchants, whose adaptation of the local institution of debt bondage or "pawnship" underpinned the region's burgeoning involvement in the transatlantic slave trade from the 1740s onward.

Slave ports on the slave coast included Little Popo, Agoue, Great Popo, Jakin, Porto-Novo, Badagry and Lagos, but the principal one was Ouidah. This port became prominent in the last part of the seventeenth century and continued to be so until the mid-nineteenth century, with slave exports amounting to 14,000–15,000 slaves annually from the 1640s through the 1720s.

The merchant activities in these slave ports commercially threaded the Atlantic basin. In 1750s coastal western Europe, Liverpool assumed the lead in slave trading, with its ships carrying over half the slaves exported from Africa, while Nantes carried over 10,000 slaves annually across the Atlantic accounting for over half of all French shipping. Slave merchants in both slave entrepôts were also landowners, manufacturers, tradesmen, and other commercial citizens. But slave trading required increasing specialization so that, by the 1750s, 50 merchants dominated the trade in Nantes, while Liverpool's trade was dominated by about 10 firms with a dozen partners by the 1780s.

During the eighteenth century, these shifting merchants of slave trading contributed to the establishment and consolidation of slave entrepôts in the eastern coastal regions of the Americas. Between 1698 and 1707, private traders delivered 34,157 slaves through Bridgetown, Barbados, and 37,522 slaves through Port Royal, Jamaica. Over 110,000 African slaves were landed and marketed at Sullivan's Island, near Charleston, South Carolina, during the eighteenth century. Portuguese merchants shipped slaves from Luanda and Benguela in West Central Africa to Rio de Janeiro in Brazil and from Ouidah to Bahia. An average of eighteen ships sailed from Bahia to the slave coast annually in the eighteenth century.

Trading between Europeans and Africans in the Atlantic basin was facilitated by the emergence of Afro-Portuguese *lancados* and *tangomaos*. By the 1520s, these unofficial traders were working western and west central Africa. They often originated from the Cape Verde islands, married local women, and formed their own settlements. These mixed traders and agents acted as important commercial and cultural links. They were significant in the Southern Rivers area of Senegambia, dominating trading circuits from Casamance to Rio Grande and active as far as Gambia in the north and Rio Pongo in the south. These traders included Abee Coffu Jantie Seniees, a leading African merchant on the Gold Coast in the late seventeenth century, and merchant princes John Jabes and John Konnywho. It is generally agreed they played a crucial role in commodity exchange relations in the Atlantic basin during the era of the slave trade.

The impact of the Atlantic basin on West Africa during the era of the slave trade was immense. The forced labor of African slaves in the Americas transformed nature into commodities for popular consumption. British industrial and commercial dominance rested on the received goods of empire—especially the slave plantation complex of the New World. The role of west African and west-central African slave labor was critical to this process of extended primitive accumulation.

Despite continuing echoes of imperial benevolence or the region's insufficient incorporation, it is difficult to deny the tremendous transformative impact of the Atlantic complex upon West African peoples. Commercial disputes and wars were directly linked to the slave trade. Although John Thornton (1998) claims that the Dahomey wars during the eighteenth century had "more conventional diplomatic, cultural, and even ideological goals," we cannot overlook the broader context of heavy firearm imports from the British as well as the Bight of Benin region serving as the prime slave exporting region in eighteenth-century West Africa. More generally, without the external demand and presence of imperial powers, it is hard to see what forces in West Africa could have transformed traditional social relations of slavery, labor, and gender to the same extent as the area's incorporation into the Atlantic basin. Whether the result was the development of continental underdevelopment, West African enclave development arresting external-domestic economic links (Hopkins 1973), or Senegambian regional economic regression (Barry 1998), this transformative impact was overwhelmingly destructive.

JEFFREY R KERR-RITCHIE

See also: **Slavery: Atlantic Trade: Effects in Africa and the Americas; Slavery: Atlantic Trade: Transatlantic Passage.**

Further Reading

Barry, Boubacar. *Senegambia and the Atlantic Slave Trade.* Cambridge: Cambridge University Press, 1998.

Berlin, Ira. "From Creole to African: Atlantic Creoles and the Origins of African-American Society in Mainland North America." *William and Mary Quarterly*, 3rd Series, vol. 53, no. 2 (1996): 251–288.

Blackburn, Robin. *The Making of New World Slavery: From the Baroque to the Modern 1492–1800.* London: Verso, 1997.

Curtin, Philip. *The Atlantic Slave Trade: A Census.* Madison: University of Wisconsin Press, 1969.

Eltis, David. *Economic Growth and the Ending of the Atlantic Slave Trade.* Oxford: Oxford University Press, 1987.

Hopkins, A. G. *An Economic History of West Africa.* New York: Columbia University Press, 1973.

Law, Robin, and Kristin Mann. "West Africa in the Atlantic Community: The Case of the Slave Coast." *William and Mary Quarterly*, 3rd series, vol. 56, no. 2 (1999): 307–333.

Lovejoy, Paul E., and David Richardson. "Trust, Pawnship, and Atlantic History: The Institutional Foundations of the Old Calabar Slave Trade." *American Historical Review* 104, no. 2 (1999): 333–355.

Morgan, Philip D. *Slave Counterpoint: Black Culture in the Eighteenth Century Chesapeake and Lowcountry.* Chapel Hill: University of North Carolina Press, 1998.

Thorton, John. *Africa and Africans in the Making of the Atlantic World, 1400–1800.* Cambridge: Cambridge University Press, 1998.

Slavery: Atlantic Trade: Transatlantic Passage

The transatlantic passage, also known as the Middle Passage, was one of the most horrendous continuous phenomena in human history. It lasted for three centuries, peaking in the eighteenth century, a period within which the largest number of Africans was sent across the Atlantic into slavery in the Americas. The number of Africans who were captured, sold, and brought to the Americas and resold into chattel slavery defies quantification because of the manner of their capture and the survival rate in crossing the Atlantic as well as the difficulty in retrieving exact figures from ship logs. Estimates of Africans who survived the transatlantic passage into enslavement during the eighteenth century, however, are put around 6,133,000.

Along the African coast, Europeans built fortresses that were holding ports for Africans sold to slavers. These forts were open bleeding wounds on the body of Africa from which millions of men, women, and children began the forced voyage westward across the Atlantic in chains. Slave-buying middlemen who lived along the coast procured the captured Africans. They were put in dungeons in the slave castles awaiting either the arrival of slave ships, or for the numbers to reach the maximum capacity the slave ships could transport. The waiting period varied from a few days to months, while the Atlantic crossing took between three to six weeks, sometimes even longer depending on

Fort Elmina, in Ghana. Built by the Portuguese in the fifteenth century and later owned by the Dutch and the English, the fort held Africans before shipment to the slave markets of the Americas. © Friedrich Stark/Das Fotoarchiv.

weather conditions. Shipwrecks were common, which meant some slaves and sailors never completed crossing the voyage.

The arrival of slave ships at the slave fortresses from European ports signaled the last days for the captured and sold Africans in their homeland. Before being forced into the holds of the ships, their heads were shaved. They were branded by impressing on their bodies the owner's initials using fashioned red-hot pieces of silver or iron. The Portuguese baptized their slaves in compliance with the laws that required all slaves being brought to Brazil be christened. On the day of departure, after being fed, slaves were chained in pairs by ankles and embarked. Once aboard the slave ship, they were stripped naked, with the justification that nudity would ensure cleanliness and health during the long voyage ahead. The women and men were, therefore, separated and women and boys, in some cases, were allowed to stay on deck protected only by a tarpaulin from the elements during the voyage.

The slave ships were custom-built for the transportation of humans across the Atlantic. The holds of the ship contained the slave holds that were divided horizontally into shelves and fitted with chains. Each slave hold could be less than four feet in smaller ships and seldom not taller than five and one-half feet in larger ships. This meant the slaves could hardly sit upright or had no room to shift and move their bodies freely. For the duration of the voyage, they lay on their backs or sides on the raw wooden shelves in chains for weeks on end. In good weather, slaves were brought up onto the deck in the morning to exercise by singing and dancing. Whipping was used to force those who refused to be cooperative. The slaves were often used to satisfy the sexual proclivities of sailors and those who refused were often severely beaten and raped more brutally. The slaves were constantly and closely monitored, as revolts were common. It is estimated that 20 per cent of slave ships experienced slave revolts during the transatlantic crossing.

Meals consisted usually of rice, farina, and horse beans served twice a day—breakfast around ten in the morning and another meal at about four in the afternoon. Each slave was given a ration of half a pint of water twice a day. Buckets of salt water were passed around, with which the slaves could wash their hands after meals. Food consumption was monitored closely to hinder those who would starve themselves to death. Those who refused food were severely whipped and forced to eat by holding a shovel of hot coal near the lips so that the mouth was scorched and burned or food was forced down the throat by a mouth-opening speculum. Disease and death filled the holds of the slave ships.

While slavers wanted the slaves to arrive at the American ports alive and healthy, the conditions under which slaves made the Atlantic crossing were so deplorable that many lost their lives. "Tight packers" and "loose packers," two terms that describe how slavers loaded their ships and the conditions under which the slaves made the voyage, seemed not to affect the death rate of the slaves significantly. It is estimated that the total mortality rate of all slaves during the crossing was about 24 percent and that men died at a higher rate, 19 per cent, when compared to 14.7 percent of women. Children and older people died at the same rate as men. The mortality rate per slave ship was used to gauge pay to captains and ship surgeons, so the records were manipulated in favor of higher slave survival rates. Insurance claims for lost slave lives also involved a distortion of figures, and even the murder of slaves.

The barbarism and horrors included the practice of throwing sick slaves overboard, as exemplified by the massacre on the slave ship *Zong*. The ship left Africa in September 1781 with 440 slaves, arriving two months later in the Caribbean with 380 alive, but most of those were sick or dying. Since insurance compensation excluded sick slaves or those killed by illness, 78 slaves were chained together and thrown overboard into a watery mass grave. Later, in Liverpool, England, an insurance claim for a total of 132 drowned slaves was made. While the transatlantic passage of the eighteenth century ensured a constant flow of slaves and wealth to slave masters, slavers, and others involved, it deprived Africa of a considerable amount of human resources. The exposure of the horrors endured during the passage contributed to efforts to end the transatlantic slave trade.

LEONARD GADZEKPO

See Also: **Slavery: Atlantic Trade: Effects in Africa and the Americas; Slavery, Atlantic Basin in the Era of.**

Further Reading

Equiano, Olaudah. *The Interesting Narrative of the Life of Olaudah Equiano, Written by Himself*, edited by Robert J. Allison. Boston: Bedford Books of St. Martin's Press, 1995.

Craton, Michael. *Sinews of Empire: A Short History of British Slavery.* New York: Anchor Books, 1974.

Curtin, Philip D. *The Atlantic Slave Trade: A Census.* Madison: University of Wisconsin Press, 1969.

Dow, George Francis. *Slave Ships and Slaving.* Port Washington, N.Y.: Kennikat Press, 1969.

Lovejoy, Paul E. *Transformation in Slavery: A History of Slavery in Africa.* Cambridge: Cambridge University Press, 1983.

Rawley, James A. *The Transatlantic Slave Trade: A History.* New York: W. W. Norton, 1981.

Reynolds, Edward. *Stand The Storm: A History of the Atlantic Slave Trade.* Chicago: Ivan R. Dee, 1993.

Walvin, James. *Slavery and the Slave Trade: A Short Illustrated History.* London: Macmillan, 1983.

Slavery: Atlantic Trade: Effects in Africa and the Americas

The transatlantic slave trade was a global economic system of forced migration that shipped approximately 12 to 15 million Africans to the Caribbean, North America, and South America. The Atlantic trade in human cargo from Africa began during the 1450s, peaked during the 1780s, and then gradually declined until a rise during the 1850s, followed by an eventual termination of the practice after 1900. However, between 1600 and 1800 the transatlantic slave trade, at its height, impacted Africa culturally, demographically, socially, and politically.

The plantation economic system based on slave labor that developed in the Caribbean during the late sixteenth century and eventually spread to South and North America drove the demand for African labor occasioned by the transatlantic slave trade. Sugar was one of the early cash crops instrumental in the development of these plantation systems.

The techniques of sugar production and the use of slave gang labor on plantations were first developed in the Levant during the twelfth century. The use of slave labor for sugar production then spread to the Mediterranean when Italian states, like Genoa and Venice, began to promote sugar plantations on islands including Cyprus, Sicily, and Crete. The techniques of sugar production and slave gang labor eventually spread to southern Spain and Portugal, where they were co-opted by the Portuguese. Despite the proliferation of sugar plantations based upon slave gang labor, it was not until the end of the fifteenth century that West Africa became a primary market for slaves.

The spread of sugar production coincided with Portuguese exploration of the coast of West Africa. The Portuguese developed sugar plantation systems based upon slave gang labor on islands like São Tomé and Príncipe, using African labor from adjacent sources, and eventually spreading into the Caribbean and South America. By the early sixteenth century, sugar production was developed on the island of Hispaniola. From there, it would spread to other islands in the Caribbean and eventually to Brazil. In Brazil, sugar production would take off by the late sixteenth century on a scale far superseding its Atlantic roots.

Centered around the production of cash crops like sugar, these plantation economic systems were highly labor-intensive, requiring a constant supply of cheap labor. Europeans initially tried Native Americans as labor sources. These proved unsuitable for various reasons, as did indentured European servants. African slaves, however, were found to be a much more practical and cost effective solution to the labor demands of the plantation system.

Many of the slaves came from the Senegambia region, Upper Guinea Coast, Gold Coast, and the Bights of Benin and Biafra in western Africa. Slaves were also taken from the Angola and Mozambique regions in west central Africa. The regionalization of the source populations of Africans was felt in the New World as well. For example, large numbers of Yoruba slaves came out of the Bight of Benin during the nineteenth century and ended up in Brazil. This had an effect on the strong influence of Yoruba religions in the area of Bahia in Brazil. The effect of African culture was also seen in language and social customs throughout the New World. The predominance of the gullah language, spoken among descendants of slaves on the South Carolina coast in the United States, is a reflection of this.

The effects of the slave trade varied according to the regions and also through time, but there are some generalizations that describe the impact of the slave trade as a whole upon Africa. Europeans preferred young males for work on plantations in the Caribbean and the Americas. This consequently had a demographic effect upon African populations targeted as labor sources as the number of males within a society were reduced. The depopulation of young African males led to the development of skewed sex ratios. In some areas targeted for the slave trade, like the Loango area of Angola, female-to-male ratios shifted on the order of two females to one male. Conversely, in the Americas the result was a sex ration among slaves heavily skewed toward males over females. For Africa as a whole, the slave trade reduced the population of Africa between 1600 and 1800 and led to virtually no population growth, particularly for the time period 1700 to 1800.

The European market preference for African males led to social and cultural changes as well. With depopulation of African males some areas experienced an increase in the scope of polygyny. With a dearth of young males, African social systems adapted. For example, in the Luanda region of Angola, some men were able to acquire more wives than would have been possible before the depredations of the slave trade. The increase in polygyny, however, weakened some societies, particularly in west central Africa, that were based upon matrilineal descent. For instance, in some cases, instead of property being handed down to the son of a man's sister, as would be the case in a matrilineal society, it would go to his progeny from slave women instead.

The onset of the transatlantic slave trade in some areas led to alterations in systems of justice. With the pressure for human commodities occasioned by the trade, some areas witnessed an increase in sanctions for crimes that resulted in enslavement. For example, the Aro traders of the town of Aro Chukwu in the Niger Delta became powerful through the manipulation of an oracle that helped to decide disputes and mete out justice in the region. During the era of the slave trade an accusation of adultery or theft would usually result in a pronouncement of enslavement.

The slave trade targeted communities that were least able to organize politically against encroachment from slave raiders. In areas where many communities were not able to organize centrally, on a large scale, coupled with a lack of large, strong centralizing powers, slave raiding proliferated. The transatlantic slave trade led to more political violence and instability as so-called warlord states, like the Ibangala in west central Africa and the Bambara state of Segu in the savanna region of West Africa, arose organized around slave raiding as the primary economic function. As slave trading intensified and target communities increased their ability to defend themselves or moved further away, slave raiding increased and led to more political violence. Some African polities, like Oyo and Dahomey in the Bight of Benin and Ashante on the Gold Coast, were able to enhance their political status to some degree by becoming involved in the slave trade as conduits. However, in case of Oyo and Dahomey their inability to completely dominate the market in the bight of Benin contributed to instability and furthered slave raiding among the Aja speakers of the area. Although Ashante was eventually able to dominate the slave market on the Gold Coast after the 1750s, the period of instability that accompanied the consolidation process led to intensified slave raiding in the area. Once Ashante was established, moreover, slave raiding stopped within its borders but was now carried to its neighbors.

Politically, African slaves were able to organize and resist enslavement only in areas where the European control or population was weak. As a result, there were more maroon societies in the Caribbean and South America. However, in North America, maroon societies were difficult to maintain and as such were not as pervasive as in the Caribbean and Latin America.

Culturally, the involvement of African communities in the transatlantic slave trade also led to the increase of servile populations among slave-catching societies. Although Europeans preferred young males, within the African domestic slave market the preference was for young females. Consequently, with the maturation of the transatlantic slave trade African slavery increased to the point where, for Africa as a whole, as much as 10 per cent of the population would have been in servile status. This figure was almost equal to the number of slaves living in the New World.

The increase in African slavery was concomitant with a transformation in its utility. In many social formations in Africa the slavery transformed from an institution of marginality rooted in concepts of lineage or kin to a central institution where slaves' importance was in the economic product of their labor. For example, with the official close of British involvement in the transatlantic slave trade, slaves became more important in production on plantations for commodities like palm oil, rice, and kernels. States like Ashante and Dahomey in West Africa were able to adapt to the close the slave trade by shifting to slave based production of commodities.

The economic system of slave gang labor used for the production of commodities was at the core of the transatlantic slave trade. This economic system had its roots in the Mediterranean and the Levant before being transferred to the New World. However, the difference between the Old World origins of sugar and slavery was in the scope of the enterprise. The transatlantic slave trade was on a much larger international scale, involving far-flung geographic regions like Africa, Europe, the Caribbean, and the Americas. In addition, the products of slave labor were produced for an international market that drove demand to new heights.

OPOLOT OKIA

See also: **Anti-Slavery Movement; Slavery: Atlantic Trade: Transatlantic Passage; Slavery: Mediterranean, Red Sea, Indian Ocean.**

Further Reading

Barry, Boubacar. *Senegambia and the Atlantic Slave Trade.* Cambridge: Cambridge University Press, 1998.

Inikori, Joseph, and Stanley Engerman (eds.). *The Atlantic Slave Trade: Effects on Economies, Societies and Peoples in Africa, the Americas and Europe.* Durham, N.C.: Duke University Press, 1992.

Lovejoy, Paul E. *Transformations in Slavery: A History of Slavery in Africa*, 2nd ed. Cambridge: Cambridge University Press, 2000.

Manning, Patrick. *Slavery and African Life: Occidental, Oriental and African Slave Trades.* Cambridge: Cambridge University Press, 1990.

Meillassoux, Claude. *The Anthropology of Slavery: The Womb of Iron and Gold.* Chicago: University of Chicago Press, 1991.

Miller, Joseph. *Way of Death: Merchant Capitalism and the Angolan Slave Trade, 1730–1830.* Madison: University of Wisconsin Press, 1997.

Northrup, David (ed.). *Trade without Rulers: Pre-Colonial Economic Development in South-Eastern Nigeria.* Oxford: Oxford University Press, 1978.

Thornton, John. *Africa and Africans in the making of the Atlantic World, 1400–1800.* Cambridge: Cambridge University Press, 1998.

Slavery: Atlantic Trade: Opposition, African

The slave trade took at least 12 million people, and affected many millions more in Africa. As such, it involved a great deal of violence and brutality and, not surprisingly, resistance as well. Resistance took many different forms depending on the social relations within African society. At some points, the African elite took actions that resisted or restricted the slave trade; at others, it fell to religious leaders, or occasionally the common people, to act. In addition to the resistance coming from those who ran society or sought to change it, there was an ongoing and not unexpected resistance from the people who were recently enslaved, both before and after their embarkation on slave ships.

The majority of Africans who were enslaved and sold to the Atlantic slave trade were captives in wars. Where the attackers were Europeans whose principal motive was enslavement, such as the earliest Portuguese sailors along the coast of Senegambia in the mid-fifteenth century, or the armies led by Portuguese officers who conducted wars in Angola in much of the seventeenth century, the connections are fairly clear. Likewise, it is obvious that the occasional punishment of rogue European slave shippers who sought to attack African coastal points from time to time throughout the period represented resistance to the slave trade. However, most wars that resulted in the enslavement of Africans were between African powers, or civil wars in which all participants were African. Since it was well known that the prisoners taken in wars of all sorts would be enslaved, all who participated in a war might be said to be resisting enslavement, as they defended their territory against attackers or sought victory to avoid enslavement.

Resistance against direct European aggression was rare, however, because for the most part the trade with European dealers was conducted peacefully under

African law supervised by African state officials. But there were times and places where the traders violated these rules, and African leaders sought to curb this disorder. For example, during the early years of the trade, King Afonso I of Kongo (1509–1542) protested against the illegal enslavement of people within his country by unruly elements acting with the support of Portuguese merchants. In 1526, he issued a series of strong restrictions on the activities of the Portuguese and established a system of inspections to insure that all those people sold as slaves were legally enslaved. This concern for legal and orderly enslavement represented a stream of central African concerns about the trade, including, protests made by Queen Njinga Mbandi of Ndongo (1624–1663) and Garcia II of Kongo (1641–1661).

The second most common way in which people were enslaved was through banditry, or the illegal use of force, usually by small armed gangs that operated through kidnapping or highway robbery. Clearly, all attempts on the part of African states to rid themselves of such banditry can count as suppression of the slave trade, such as took place, for example, when King Alvaro XII of Kongo ordered the men of Mbwa Lau, a bandit, to desist from their activities and lay down their arms.

Ultimately, even the orderly use of state authority to supervise the slave trade causes sufficient larger social disorder that might lead to protests from a lower level in society. The institution of slavery, for example, is a concept that takes as a starting point unequal opportunities, wealth, and authority, and states that accept it as an item of law, as African states did, can expect that the sort of social pressures that operated against such inequalities would apply to slavery and the slave trade. Mandinga slaves working on estates in Sierra Leone in the 1780s, for example, revolted against their masters and built armed camps to protect their freedom, even though they were not in immediate danger of being sold into the Atlantic trade.

The Islamic reform movement of Nasr al-Din (1673–1677), known locally in Senegambia as the Tubenan, grappled with the larger issues of exploitation within societies as well as the linkage between such issues and the Atlantic slave trade. Nasr al-Din and his disciples preached against the misrule of the authorities by arguing that kings were made for the people, not vice versa. Even though Nasr al-Din owned slaves himself and did not oppose slavery in principle, he did oppose the sale of Muslim slaves to Christians, and thus the Atlantic branch of the trade. While this might be seen simply as a form of chauvinism on the part of the Islamic al-Din, it also recognized the link between the greed of rulers, their disregard for what was accepted in Islam as the fundamental rights of

subjects, and the Atlantic slave trade. The Tubenan, in addition, was a popular movement, and the rank and file followers of Nasr al-Din probably sought to put an end to war and enslavement in general.

Most movements that followed Nasr al-Din's drew at least partially on his ideology. The movement in Futa Jallon (after 1726) was torn between a recognition of the evils of the slave trade and a desire to sell slaves in order to purchase munitions to protect their reforms or defend their country. A more principled resistance developed in the movement in Futa Tooro led by Abd al-Qadir after 1776, which opposed warfare and the resulting enslavement as well as the sale of Muslims to Christians. In a celebrated letter to English traders, Abd al-Qadir threatened those who would seek to buy slaves in his country with death and confiscation of goods.

In other cases, social resistance to war might lead to resistance that affected the slave trade as well. The Christian reform movement led by Dona Beatriz Kimpa Vita in Kongo from 1704 to 1706, for example, ostensibly addressed only the problem of civil war, which in Beatriz's view was caused by the greed of rivals to take the Kongo throne. But it was obvious to most Kongo in her day that enslavement and deportation was a natural and frequent outcome of such wars, and that stopping the wars would also lead to an end of enslavement. The fact that war and enslavement were entangled with each other, and that war had many other negative impacts as well as enslavement of some of the participants, makes it hard for modern annalists to separate social movements with more general aims from resistance to the slave trade in general.

The most obvious and unambiguous forms of resistance to the slave trade were those made by the recently enslaved, beyond the obvious ones that arose from their participation in war. There were often revolts in the barracoons on the coast, for example, especially in the Gold Coast area, and these, in turn led to frequent shipboard revolts, of which the largest number took place in the eighteenth century. These revolts of people who were unarmed, in environments where they were unlikely to have any effective assistance from anyone else, were often violent and desperate, even though only a tiny fragment ever succeeded in long-term freedom for the rebels. Because many of the slaves were enslaved by armies and had recent military experience, often having served together, they were better able to cooperate and to see military options. Recent research has shown that as many as 1 in 15 slave ships faced some sort of violent resistance, which reached proportions that they caused or threatened loss of life or loss of a ship. This was frequent enough that slave ships carried complement and weapons sufficient to suppress rebellion, and took fairly elaborate security measures against them. English shippers, for example, commonly included slaves from another part of Africa on ships whose cargo was to be made up of people from a particular part of the coast, called "guardians." Gold Coast slaves were purchased to oversee those from the slave coast; Sierra Leoneans guarded slaves from the Bight of Benin. Even when guardians were not deliberately purchased, sometimes interethnic differences spoiled or diverted revolts.

Given the great differences in social origins and motivations of the various Africans involved in the slave trade either as participants or victims, it is difficult to discern a single pattern. The trade cannot be simply delineated in terms of Europeans against Africans, nor was it generally marked by direct invasion. Rather, it was a complex outgrowth of African politics crossing with European economic demands that led to changes in both. The resistance that is easiest to discern is that of the enslaved people themselves against their enslavers, but under conditions that made armed resistance difficult, and even hopeless.

JOHN K. THORNTON

Slavery: Atlantic Trade: Abolition: Philanthropy or Economics?

The first major achievement of the antislavery movement lay in the campaign to end the British slave trade. Analysis of this topic has shifted between explanations that emphasize either the moral arguments and effective propaganda of the abolitionists as the key to success, or the economic considerations relating to the slave trade and the British Caribbean as a more compelling reason for the demise of the British slave trade. The historiographical debate on philanthropy, economics, and abolition reveals the arguments made with regard to the abolition of the British transatlantic slaving. Though economic conditions in Britain and the West Indies were much more at the forefront of the debate than anything specifically linked to Africa, the impact of abolitionism clearly affected Africans in an important way.

Before World War II, the chief explanation given for the abolition of the British slave trade lay in the humanitarian work of the antislavery campaigners. Sir Reginald Coupland, the leading advocate of this point of view, traced the abolitionist campaigns both inside and outside the British Parliament after the formal campaign against the slave trade began in London in 1787. He argued that the statutory ban on the British slave trade 20 years later was a moral triumph for saintly Christian evangelicals and Quakers, clustered around the Clapham Sect and the leadership of William Wilberforce in the Commons. According to

this interpretation, humanitarianism triumphed in 1807. Philanthropic individuals had thus achieved a striking success in organizing a moral campaign to eradicate what was seen as an evil blot on British national life.

A challenge to these arguments came with the publication of the Trinidadian Eric Williams's *Capitalism and Slavery* in 1944. Williams presented a strong case for the economic reasons why Britain abolished its slave trade. Aimed as a direct counterpoint to Coupland's ideas, *Capitalism and Slavery* adapted material from a previously published book by Lowell Ragatz to argue that the British West Indian plantation economy was in serious decline after the Seven Years War. The causes of decline included soil exhaustion on sugar estates, interruptions to the marketing of sugar during the American War of Independence, and planter indebtedness during the period of 1793–1807. Williams also argued that the late-eighteenth-century British economy was undergoing a shift from mercantilism to industrial capitalism, with an accompanying change from an emphasis on slavery to free wage labor in the empire: thus Britain abolished its slave trade primarily for economic reasons.

The arguments supporting either philanthropy or economics as the prime movers behind early British abolitionism have continued since *Capitalism and Slavery* was published. In the late 1960s, Roger Anstey argued that Williams had not provided systematic statistics to support his case, and that little evidence was produced in the parliamentary debates over slave trade abolition to suggest that economic matters were paramount in the minds of politicians. In his book *The Atlantic Slave Trade and British Abolition* (1975), Anstey traced the sources of antislavery ideas and provided a novel explanation for the passing of the Abolition Act in 1807. Much abolitionist thought was pervaded by an emphasis on Christian benevolence and a belief in God's providence. These beliefs drew antislavery campaigners to single out the slave trade as an act of national wickedness. The difficulties of war with revolutionary and Napoleonic France delayed the progress of the campaign against the slave trade in Parliament but a turnaround in fortunes occurred in 1806–1807, when the newly formed coalition ministry (the Ministry of All the Talents) resolved first to restrict the supply of slaves to foreign territories in wartime and then to abolish the British slave trade altogether. According to Anstey, a particular and fortuitous set of politicoeconomic circumstances impelled the British to abort their slave trade in the national economic interest.

The most direct attack on Eric Williams's views about the abolition of the British slave trade came in Seymour Drescher's *Econocide* (1977). Marshaling an impressive array of statistical evidence, Drescher argued that the British slave trade met its demise at a time of propitious economic circumstances for the British Caribbean economy. Soil exhaustion was a temporary phenomenon; so, too, was planter indebtedness. Evidence on the profitability of sugar plantations showed them still making profits on average even during difficult wartime periods. At the turn of the nineteenth century, Britain was expanding its plantations in the British Caribbean into newly acquired territories such as Trinidad and British Guiana. Moreover, British West Indian trade comprised as significant a share of total British foreign commerce as it had in the 1770s. For these reasons, Drescher argued, the abolition of the British slave trade must be seen as an act of economic suicide.

The implication of this conclusion, of course, was to return the arguments over philanthropy and economics full circle to a position favorable to Coupland's emphasis on the primacy of humanitarianism. Recent work on the campaign to abolish the British slave trade has pointed to the sheer effectiveness of the philanthropic campaign in the diffusion of its oral, visual, and written propaganda, and to the popularity of this crusade as evidenced by the number of signatures appended to petitions presented to Parliament on this issue. In the years 1787 to 1792, for instance, approximately 1.5 million out of 12 million people in Britain signed antislave trade petitions, a higher proportion than for any other reform issue of the time. Barbara Solow and Stanley Engerman's 1987 collection of essays reassessing *Capitalism and Slavery* reached a consensus that serious economic decline did not occur in the British Caribbean economy in the late eighteenth century. But the notion that the British abolished their slave trade for economic reasons is not yet dead and buried as a possible interpretation. Recent research has shown that a serious economic crisis occurred in the British imperial economy between 1803 and 1807, and that sugar prices in Jamaica (and hence the profits to planters and merchants) were declining steeply from 1793 through to 1807. Given the longevity of the debate over philanthropy, economics, and British abolitionism, these new findings suggest that the arguments will continue.

KENNETH MORGAN

Further Reading

Anstey, Roger. *The Atlantic Slave Trade and British Abolition 1760–1810*. London: Macmillan, 1975.
Coupland, Reginald. *Wilberforce: A Narrative*. Oxford: Oxford University Press, 1923.
Ragatz, Lowell Joseph. *The Fall of the Planter Class in the British Caribbean, 1763–1833: A Study in Social and Economic History*. New York: Octagon, 1963.
Solow, Barbara L., and Stanley L. Engerman. (eds.). *British Capitalism and Caribbean Slavery: The Legacy of Eric Williams*. Cambridge: Cambridge University Press, 1987.
Williams, Eric. *Capitalism and Slavery*. Chapel Hill: University of North Carolina Press, 1944.

Slavery, Abolition of: East and West Africa

The impact of the abolition of the Atlantic slave trade on the spread of slavery in East and West Africa has been an issue of great intellectual interest and debate. The crux of the matter is how the abolition of the Atlantic slave trade, rather than bringing to an end of the institution of slavery, instead produced an increase in the internal slave trade, and the continuation of slavery as an institution.

The abolition of the Atlantic slave trade left East Africa almost completely unaffected. It is instructive to note that, from the onset, Arabs dominated slave trade in the Indian Ocean region. While Europe and North America were increasingly responding to the dictates of industrial capitalism, and the humanitarian climate and political exigencies of their own milieu, the Arab world was marked by in mercantilism, labor-intensive enterprises, and the harem culture. The Europeans and the Arabs, having different agendas, moved in opposing directions. By 1840, Seyyid Said, the Arab ruler of Oman, wishing to exploit the resources—especially the potential slave resources—of East Africa, decided to transfer his court from his capital, Muscat, to the island of Zanzibar, off the coast of present-day Tanzania. The increasing cultivation of cloves and other crops meant the intensification of demand for African slaves. Zanzibar became the largest producer of cloves in the world, primarily because of the expansion of slavery in East Africa. To meet the labor needs of the plantations, as well as to feed the large slave markets in the Middle East and Arabia, Seyyid Said undertook a large-scale procurement of slaves. With Seyyid Said's protection and Indian financial assistance, Arabs organized caravans and penetrated almost every portion of East Africa. Their slaving activities reached the Great Lakes region of Central Africa and beyond, and they established "colonies" for the collection of ivory and slaves. The Arabs, through their slaving activities, ravaged large areas of East and Central Africa. In the upper regions of the Congo River, for instance, the Arabs raided villages, taking the population for slaves. The demise of slavery in East Africa was not helped by the fact that the British abolitionists entered compromise treaties with Zanzibar that allowed for a gradual, rather than an immediate, end to the slave trade. The gradualist approach allowed Arabs to carry on slave trading within their domain with impunity, and to smuggle slaves to the north through the interior slave routes.

The impact of the abolition of the Atlantic slave trade on the spread of slavery in West Africa was uneven. The major theme that dominates historiography of West Africa between the fifteenth and the nineteenth centuries is the Atlantic slave trade. The histories of Old Oyo Empire, the Aro hegemony, Asante, the Niger Delta states, and Old Calabar are all tied up with the slave trade. The rise and decline of these states had much to do with slave trade. During the era of the abolitionist movement, the British naval squadron stationed on the west coast was usually able to rescue about 3,000 slaves a year. As there was still a demand for slaves in some regions of the Americas (such as Brazil, which did not abolish slavery till 1888), it was not unexpected that the African coastal middlemen, who were profiting from human traffic, would resort to all kinds of stratagems to continue their slave trading activities. For instance, they were provided with hiding places in the numerous creeks any time they sighted the British naval squadron. Internally, West Africa had a number of slaveholding societies that depended on slave for economic and political ends. The slave plantations at Akpabuyo in Old Calabar and the Sokoto Caliphate–run plantations in Hausaland, for example, required slave labor (slave plantations in Hausaland, which were of the absentee landlordism variety, metamorphosed into serfdom). Slave laborers were also required as potters in long distance trade. In the Niger Delta states, slaves were used as paddlers of war and trading canoes. With increased patroling of the west coast, the population of slaves in some societies increased so much that the servile population outnumbered that of the indigenes. The successful take off of the "legitimate commerce" in West Africa owed much to the use of slave labor. Decades into the operation of the "legitimate commerce," slave labor was still in great demand and in use. Indeed, slavery and the slave trade survived into the second decade of the twentieth century. For instance, between 1906 and 1912, 63 slave-dealing cases were heard at the police court in Calabar, Nigeria. Out of this figure, there were 44 convictions and 19 acquittals. In the same period, Oba Native court in Calabar Province of Nigeria heard 13 similar cases, convicting 11 and acquitting 2.

In the final analysis, it is reasonable to state that the impact of the abolition of the Atlantic slave trade on the spread of slavery in East and West Africa owed much to the political, social and economic situations in the individual African societies in question, as well as the external political and external climate. As a result of the interplay of the internal African factors and the external influences, slavery and the slave trade survived into the twentieth century.

PAUL OBIYO MBANASO NJEMANZE

See also: **Anti-Slavery Movement; Slavery: Atlantic Trade; Slavery in African Society.**

Further Reading

Anderson, J. D. *West Africa and East Africa in the Nineteenth and Twentieth Centuries.* London: Heinemann, 1972.

Anene, Joseph C., and Godfrey N. Brown (eds.). *Africa in the Nineteenth and Twentieth Centuries.* Ibadan, Nigeria: Ibadan University Press, 1966.

Claphan, Christopher. *Liberia and Sierra Leone: An Essay in Comparative Politics.* Cambridge: Cambridge University Press, 1976.

Coupland, Sir Reginald. *The British Anti-Slavery Movement.* London: Buthermouth, 1933.

Hawks, Hugh (ed.). *The Abolitionist: Means, Ends and Motivations,* 2nd ed. D.C. Heath, 1972.

Hopkins, A. G. *An Economic History of West Africa.* Harlow, England: Longman, 1973.

Inikori, J. E. (ed.). *Forced Migration: The Impact of the Export Slave Trade on African Societies.* London: Hutchinson University Library, 1982.

Munro, J. Forbes. *Africa and the International Economy 1800–1960: An Introduction to the Modern Economic History of Africa South of the Sahara.* London: J. M. Dent and Sons, 1976.

Njemanze, Paul Obiyo Mbanaso. "A Century of African-American Experience in Nigeria, 1839–1939," Ph.D. Diss., University of Calabar, 1992.

Slavery: Mediterranean, Red Sea, Indian Ocean

Slavery existed in many ancient and medieval societies. Ancient Egypt acquired slaves from Nubia, from the Red Sea coast, and probably from the Horn of Africa. There were some black slaves in ancient Greece and Rome, but not many. Some slaves were also probably traded back and forth in the Indian Ocean trade. In fact, many early trade routes saw slaves moving in different directions. None of these slave trades ever achieved the numbers that marked the Atlantic trade, and it is unlikely that slaves were the major item of trade on any of these routes until the eighteenth century.

The slave trade into the Middle East and Mediterranean was stimulated by the introduction, toward the beginning of the common era, of the camel, which facilitated desert pastoralism and trade across the desert. It was also encouraged by the appearance of Islam in the seventh century. This was not because Islam encouraged the slave trade, but rather because Islam prohibited enslavement of other Muslims and allowed only the enslavement of captives taken in a just war. It also strictly delineated the characteristics of a just war.

Nevertheless, the Islamic conquests initiated a period of great prosperity. Wealthy Muslims sought concubines, servants, and eunuchs to guard their harems. Rulers sought male slaves who could be trained as soldiers. Forbidden to enslave their fellow Muslims, they looked outside the Muslim world. The majority of slaves were women, who became wives, concubines, and servants.

Christians faced similar restrictions. They also had a concept of just war and were prohibited from enslaving their fellow Christians. One result was that Christians and Muslims raided each other, and took prisoners on the seas. Both also sought slaves from societies that were neither Christian nor Muslim, and both traded with each other for slaves as for commodities. Slaves were used by both Christians and Muslims in the Mediterranean.

Until the fifteenth century, the most important sources of slaves for the Mediterranean and the Middle East were Slavic eastern Europe and the Caucasus. There was also a constant trade in slaves to the Mediterranean and the Middle East from Africa. The opening of trade and the conversion of some African states to Islam created trading partners capable of providing slaves. African slaves were more numerous in North Africa, but were found in all of the Muslim states of the region and in Christian cities and kingdoms bordering the Mediterranean. African states desired both the products and the knowledge of the Middle East, Europe, and India. To acquire these products, they often raided non-Muslim peoples and sold them to Arab traders.

Slaves crossed the Sahara with the camel caravans that maintained commercial contact between North and West Africa. Most of them were women. These crossings were usually on foot, the camels being used to carry goods. A considerable number also went into the Sahara, where the oases had a significant demand for slave labor, in large part because of the high slave-mortality rate. Some Saharan communities, such as the Ghadames, became important centers of the trade. In the Sahara, slaves tended date trees, mined for salt and copper, and worked as herders and servants. Others went to North Africa or were sold to other Mediterranean societies. In North Africa, they were sought not only as concubines and servants, but also as cultivators and laborers. Slave labor was particularly important in desert-side areas. Because Islam encouraged manumission, many of them became *haratin*, or freed slaves, with a client relationship to their former owners. It is difficult to make a precise statement on the number of slaves who crossed the desert, but Ralph Austen has estimated 3.5 to 4 million over a 12-century period.

The trade across the Sahara followed a series of fixed routes between wells and oases where the caravans stopped to replenish their water supplies. The nomads encountered throughout the desert could either act as protectors and guides for the caravans, or, if they were not paid and appeased, could attack the caravans.

Many caravans perished because wells had run dry, because they got lost, or because they were attacked by nomadic tribes.

There were a series of major routes. In the medieval period, the most important was the so-called Gold Road that led from Sijilmassa in southern Morocco to Awdaghust and Ghana. With the fall of Ghana, the southern terminus shifted first to Walata and then to Timbuktu. From Timbuktu, caravans could also go north to Ghadames and Tunis or Tripoli. Routes from northern Nigeria went through Agades and usually to Tripoli.

The Nile above Aswan was marked by cataracts and was difficult to use for transport. The Sahara in that area was also very dry. Thus, much of the trade from Ethiopia and the southern Sudan moved via the Red Sea or across it. This was a much easier route. Slave trade has taken place on the shores of the Red Sea since ancient Egyptian times; the area was a modest source of slaves for the Hellenistic empires and Rome. In more recent centuries, the Christian kingdom of Ethiopia and the Muslim kingdoms of Sennar and Darfur have all used and sold slaves. At the end of the eighteenth century, Darfur alone was sending 5,000 to 6,000 slaves a year to Red Sea ports. The slaves were generally a product of raids on and wars against people farther south who had not converted. As with the trans-Saharan trade, they were mostly women, though from time to time the demand for African soldiers was strong. Slaves were sometimes taken along on the pilgrimage to Mecca and sold there to pay the pilgrims' expenses.

Trade in the Indian Ocean goes back to at least the beginning of the common era. Almost half of the year the winds blew out from central Asia; the other half they blew in, making navigation easy. Most of the sailors were Arabs, whose boats were called *dhows*. On this route, slaves were secondary to gold, ivory, spices, and metal goods. When slaves were traded, they were traded primarily to the Middle East. Many went to the Persian Gulf, where some were used as pearl divers. Some slaves also went to India and even farther east to Indonesia or China. Both the Indian continent and East Asia had high population densities and were generally able to get slaves from local sources.

In the ninth century, slaves known as Zanj were brought to lower Mesopotamia to work salt pans and dredge irrigation canals. They revolted in what was probably the largest slave uprising in Arab history. The successes of the rebels may have discouraged similar large-scale use of slave labor, but some slave exporting persisted to Mesopotamia, Persia, the Persian Gulf, and India. Slaves also moved between various Asian societies. In India, there were ex-slave communities as early as 1100. Slaves were used as soldiers and several became generals. An Ethiopian ex-slave named Malik Ambar even became the ruler of an Indian state in the early seventeenth century.

In the seventeenth century, with the colonization by the Dutch of South Africa and Mauritius and by the French of the Ile de Bourbon (now known as Réunion), and then the occupation by the French of Mauritius, there was a sharp increase in the demand for slaves. All three areas had a very low population density and could only be put into production if labor were acquired. The two French islands developed a plantation economy and had large slave majorities, replicating the experience of the West Indies. In the Cape the farms were small, but slaves provided most farm and urban labor and were a majority of the population. Both expansion and the high mortality of slaves meant that demand for slaves was great in all three colonies. While some slaves for these areas came from India and Indonesia, most were purchased in Madagascar or on the coast of East Africa. Kilwa, and the Portuguese settlements in Mozambique became particularly important sources of slaves. This stimulated a penetration of the interior and the development of slave sources there, which grew dramatically in the nineteenth century with the development of a plantation economy on Zanzibar and the East African coast. Madagascar was both an exporter of slaves and then, as the Merina kingdoms became more powerful, an importer. The Dutch also used slaves in the East Indies, but few were brought in from Africa because there were well-developed slave markets in South East Asia.

Over the course of 12 centuries, the slave trade in the Mediterranean, Red Sea, and Indian Ocean probably involved the forcible removal of over eight million slaves from their African homelands. Due to high rates of manumission and intermarriage, the progeny of these slaves have generally blended in to the population, creating few groups that today are of distinct African descent.

MARTIN A. KLEIN

Further Reading

Austen, Ralph. "Marginalization, Stagnation and Growth: The Trans-Saharan Caravan Trade in the Era of European Maritime Expansion, 1500–1900." In James D. Tracy (ed.). *The Rise of Merchant Empires*. Cambridge: Cambridge University Press, 1990.

———. "The Mediterranean Slave Trade out of Africa: A Tentative Census." *Slavery and Abolition*, no. 13 (1992): 214–248. Clarence-Smith, William Gervase (ed.). *The Economics of the Indian Ocean Slave Trade in the Nineteenth Century*. London, 1989.

Manning, Patrick. *Slavery and African Life*. Cambridge: Cambridge University Press, 1990.

Savage, Elizabeth (ed.). *The Human Commodity: Perspectives on the Trans-Saharan Slave Trade*. London, 1992.

Slavery: Trans-Saharan Trade

Contact between the peoples who live north and south of the Sahara Desert dates back to approximately 1000BCE. Tentative at the beginning, trade between these peoples became systematic and sophisticated over the centuries, especially following the introduction of the camel by the Romans in the first century. This animal, so well suited physiologically and physically to the inclement Saharan environment, revolutionized the trade. By the eleventh century, a network of caravan trade routes across the desert had emerged. In general, the importance of the routes shifted from west to east according to political changes in the Sahara and the western Sudan.

During the Carthagenian and Roman eras in North Africa, the main exports from the western Sudan were precious stones, elephant tusks, and ostrich feathers. The Romans had other sources of gold and slaves, such as Britain and the Balkan countries. In the seventh century, the Arabs emerged as the dominant power in North Africa and spearheaded the spread of militant Islam. The trade across the Sahara entered a new period of sustained growth characterized by swelling demand for slaves in the Muslim cities of North Africa and the Levant, where slaves were used as domestic help, laborers, and soldiers in state armies.

One of the earliest sources of direct evidence of slave export from the western Sudan across the Sahara comes from ál-Yakub, a ninth-century Arab writer who observed that Berber traders from Kawar brought back black slaves from Kanem to Zawila, the capital of Fezzan. In the twelve century, Ibn Battuta witnessed a trans-Saharan caravan of 600 black women slaves. Although Ghana's foreign trade was dominated by gold, many merchants from the Maghrib still went there to buy slaves. Kumbi had a famous market kept fully supplied through raids on its southern neighbors. On his much publicized pilgrimage to Mecca in 1324, Mansa Musa's entourage included about 500 slaves. He returned to Mali with 30 Turks to serve as royal slaves. Leo Africanus described how Muslim traders from North Africa traversed the Sahara to Borno kingdom to trade horses for slaves. Their arrival sent the Borno king raiding neighboring kingdoms for slaves to exchange for the horses. On that occasion, the traders had to wait for a year until the king procured a sufficient number of slaves to exchange for their horses. Slaves continued to serve as the single most important export of Borno across the Sahara well into the nineteenth century.

From the seventh century on, raids between Christians and Muslims became characteristic of cross-Mediterranean warfare. These produced slave harvests, and became a favorable source for the Muslims of southern Spain. Black slave soldiers in the army of Almoravid Seville were noted for their bravery. Christian recrudescence in the Mediterranean in the twelfth century led to the capture of a growing number of blacks of western Sudanese origins. In the wake of the Crusade, Italian merchants of Venice and Genoa established sugar plantations on a number of Mediterranean islands. Initially the plantations were supplied with labor, especially slaves, from central Europe, the steppes of Asia, and Africa. From the eleventh century on, the European and Asian sources all but dried up, as the Slavic peoples became Christianized and no longer sold to Muslims, and as the Turkish peoples embraced Islam and were thereby exempted from enslavement. As was to be the case in the Americas, Africa became the main source of labor for the plantations. North African trans-Saharan merchants intensified their drive for Sudanese slaves.

Due to a lack of firm statistical data, it is difficult to provide a satisfactory assessment of the number of slaves siphoned across the Sahara from the Sudan, and also the impact of the population hemorrhage on the communities involved. It has been estimated that, during the Middle Ages, a total of 2 million slaves were exported across the Sahara. Lewicki has guestimated that between 12 and 15 million slaves passed through Cairo in the sixteenth century. Since a substantial proportion of these passed through Tripoli and Algiers, they were probably brought across the Sahara.

Given their conjectural nature, it is best not to make much out of these numbers. A few million slaves were likely transported from the Sudan across the Sahara to North Africa and the Levant by the end of the eighteenth century. The absence of black populations in North Africa and the Levant may well underscore the relatively small scale of the trans-Saharan slave trade. But it should be borne in mind that, unlike in America and the Caribbeans, the African slaves were denied the power and the opportunity to reproduce.

The popular tendency to assess the impact of the slave trade with an emphasis on numbers tends to ignore and underplay the miseries and the indignities to which the victims were subjected, as well as the societal dislocations the slave-induced raids and wars caused. Many Sudanese Muslim states raided non-Muslim or nominally Muslim communities at will for slaves, inevitably causing devastation and the disruption of normal life. The sale of consumer—often perishable and meretricious—goods in exchange for virile labor could not have brought any tangible benefits to the slave-exporting communities. And no meaningful economic progress could be made when the most virile segment of the population was constantly skimmed off. Moreover, the capture and sale of slaves created a climate of fear and nurtured a culture of violence, as stronger states preyed upon weaker ones. The system not only brutalized and dehumanized the enslaved, it robbed the slavers themselves of sensitivity to human suffering.

Two features of the trans-Saharan trade appear more repulsive than those of the transatlantic. First, the overwhelming majority of the slaves were young women, the most reproductive segment of society. A large proportion of the remainder were male children under 15 years of age. Second, a large number of the male slaves were made eunuchs through gelding. In North Africa and the Levant, the keeping of large harems by the higher classes in the society provided a steady demand for males who could be trusted with nubile women. The main centers of demand were Cairo, Baghdad, Beirut, Mecca, Medina, Jeddah, and Smyrna. At first these centers were supplied from the Balkans, Asia, and then the western Sudan. But from the eleventh century until the end of trade in the nineteenth, the western Sudan became the main source of supply. Thus by the seventeenth century, the most famous of all the harems in the Near and Middle East, the Ottoman Sultan's Seraglio at Constantinople, was staffed entirely by gelded Africans. Castration centers existed in the Mossi country, in Damagaram (Niger Republic), in Borno (Northeast Nigeria), and, especially Baghirmi (Chad Republic).

In comparison with their counterparts in the Americas and the Caribbean, much ado has been made of the relative leniency of slave owners in North Africa and the Near East. Greatly trusted because they could not produce progeny, slave eunuchs rose to high positions of state authority. However, it must be remembered that castration was an excruciatingly painful operation. Extensive hemorrhage which could not be stopped by traditional cauterization was rampant, and produced high mortality rates.

The journeys across the Sahara were one of the most hazardous enterprises in the world. All the travelers, both free and enslaved, faced severe privations and physical dangers. Sandstorms were a common occurrence and sometimes built up pyramids of sand that could bury alive an entire caravan. They could also obliterate caravan routes, causing travelers to lose their way. Whirling sand particles sometimes covered valuable oases, smote the eyes, and blistered the skin. The temperatures fluctuated wildly: in the day they could get up to 110°F, occasioning acute thirst and asphyxiation; at night they could drop to as low as 20°F. Not surprisingly, many caravan routes were found to be strewn with hundreds of human and animal skeletons. To these problems posed by nature were added those caused by marauding bands. The desert-dwelling nomads, especially the Berbers, often lived off the pillage of travelers crossing the Sahara.

In addition to these general perils, there were others to which slaves alone were exposed. While the traders were clothed and mounted on camels and horses, the slaves traveled naked and barefoot, and were chained around their necks and burdened with heavy loads on their heads. The hot sand and rugged tracks blistered their bare feet, while the severe heat in the day and the cold in the night took heavy tolls on them. Naturally, the slaves were the first to suffer from exhaustion and fatigue. Those who became too incapacitated to continue the trek were abandoned after whipping had failed to get them to their feet. When a caravan ran short of food and water, the slaves were the first to be excluded fom such rations. Not surprisingly, the mortality rate among them was quite high, estimates varying widely from 20 to 90 per cent.

ONWUKA N. NJOKU

See also: **Africanus, Leo; Berbers: Ancient North Africa; Borno (Bornu), Sultanate of: Saifawa Dynasty: Horses, Slaves, Warfare; Carthage; Ibn Battuta, Mali Empire and; Kanem: Slavery and Trans-Saharan Trade; Mansa Musa, Mali Empire and; North Africa: Roman Occupation, Empire; Sahara: Trans-Saharan Trade; Sijilmasa, Zawila: Trans-Saharan Trade; Tuareg: Takedda and Trans-Saharan Trade.**

Further Reading

Ajayi, J. F. A., and Ian Espie (eds.). *A Thousand Years of West African History.* Ibadan, Nigeria: Ibadan University Press/Lagos: Thomas Nelson, 1965.

Boahen, A. Adu. *Britain, The Sahara, and the Western Sudan, 1788–1861.* London: Oxford University Press, 1964.

Bovill, E. W. *The Golden Trade of the Moors.* London: Oxford University Press, 1958.

Fisher, A. G. B., and H. J. Fisher. *Slavery and Muslim Society in Africa.* London: C. Hurst, 1977.

Gordon, Murray. *Slavery in the Arab World.* New York: New Amsterdam, 1989.

Klein, M. A. (ed.). *Breaking the Chains: Slavery, Bondage, and Emancipation in Modern Africa and Asia.* Madison: University of Wisconsin Press, 1993.

Law, R. C. C. "The Garamantes and Trans-Saharan Enterprise in Classical Times." *Journal of African History,* no. 8 (1967): 181–200.

Meillassoux, Claude. *Anthropology of Slavery.* Chicago: University of Chicago Press, 1991.

Rodney, W. "Jihad and Social Revolution in Futa Jallon in the Eighteenth Century." *Journal of African History* 4, no. 2 (1968): 269–284.

Savage, Elizabeth (ed.). *The Human Commodity: Perspectives on the Trans-Saharan Slave Trade.* London: Frank Cass, 1997.

Slavery: East Africa: Eighteenth Century

The East African slave trade in the eighteenth century was composed of two elements: a traditional slave trade toward the mostly Muslim countries on the northern rim of the Indian Ocean, and the slave trade to the Mascarenes Islands.

Since the start of recorded commerce in the first centuries CE, slaves had been exported alongside luxury commodities like gold and spices, from East Africa to countries on the northern and eastern rims of the Indian Ocean, and even as far as China. African males were valued for their strength, and many were employed as soldiers and laborers, while female slaves (possibly more numerous than males) were most frequently sold into harems. Many young boys became eunuchs. Most East African slaves initially originated from the Somali and Ethiopian hinterland, though the slave export frontier quickly expanded south down the East African coast as far as Sofala and to the Comoro Islands and Madagascar. However, expansion south was limited by distance from the main slave markets, which lay on the northern rim of the Indian Ocean, and by the monsoons (upon which maritime shipping largely depended) that extended south of the equator only as far as northern Madagascar and the northern entrance to the Mozambique Channel.

Muslims and Hindus originally from Arabia and the Indian subcontinent dominated the trade. Indians, with strong links to family enterprises, chiefly on the northwest coast of India, largely financed Arabs and Swahili traders. Europeans, who entered the region from the close of the fifteenth century, commenced exporting slaves to their colonies. The Portuguese exported predominantly Mozambique slaves to their Indian colonies, the Dutch exported Malagasy slaves to Batavia and to Cape Town where, by 1834, an estimated 12 per cent of the slave community was of Malagasy origin, and the British shipped occasional cargoes of East African and Malagasy slaves to the New World. However, in comparison to the predominantly Muslim trade to the north, the number of slaves exported by Europeans was small and irregular.

The structure of the slave traffic, and of trade in general in the western Indian Ocean, was radically altered in the eighteenth century with the development by the French, from the 1730s, of a major plantation economy and military base on the Mascarene Islands of Réunion and Mauritius. This established a new and major market for slaves. Although some were drawn from the Swahili coast, the major markets were Mozambique and Madagascar, which together accounted for over two-thirds of total slave imports, Madagascar alone accounting for about 45 per cent of the 160,000 slaves imported into the Mascarenes from 1610 to 1810.

As slaves could only be exported in the nonhurricane season from March to October, those collected in the other months were stockpiled on the coast. In contrast to East Africans, Malagasy slaves gained a reputation for being difficult and uncoopertive. Many preferred to commit suicide rather than leave Madagascar because they feared that Europeans were going to eat them, and there were numerous cases of revolt aboard ship; in one instance in 1784, over 600 slaves were suppressed only after the loss of many lives, both European and Malagasy. Once on the Mascarenes, they frequently fled, either attempting to sail back to Madagascar or forming maroon communities in the mountains.

The traditional northern slave trade helped form the material basis for the rise along the Swahili coast of a number of small city-states, and in western Madagascar of the Sakalava dynasties. The Mascarene demand for slaves helped boost foreign trade in Mozambique, which was also a major center for the export of ivory. However, French traders in the region turned increasingly to the east coast of Madagascar, the nearest and cheapest source of slaves and an area where Muslim middlemen were not entrenched. Mascarene demand for slaves and provisions directly stimulated the rise of the Betsimisaraka and Merina polities in Madagascar. Slave exports to European traders (North Americans and Réunionnais) had formed one of the chief economic activities of the European pirate community in Madagascar from approximately 1685 to 1720. On the northeast coast, where pirates intermarried with women of leading local families, their offspring founded the Betsimisaraka federation, which between 1795 and 1816 launched maritime slave raids, each comprising up to 500 outrigger canoes, 23 to 33 feet long, and each with a crew of 30, against the Comoros and East Africa. The federation also stimulated trade with the central highlands of Madagascar, the chief source of Malagasy slaves for the Mascarenes. By the early nineteenth century, up to 2,000 slaves were being exported annually from Antananarivo to the east coast by French traders, in exchange for cloth, muskets. and gunpowder. At the same time, the Betsileo under Prince Masoandro traded to their south for slaves, whom they shipped north to Imerina, at the rate of 400 to 500 per annum, in return for cattle and cloth. The fight over control of this trade was a major cause of the Merina civil wars of the second half of the eighteenth century and the emergence of the Bezanozano as major middlemen. It also underpinned the rise of Imerina, when Andrianampoinimerina, one of the most powerful Merina warlords, emerged toward the 1790s as king of Imerina after consolidating control over the major slave routes to the coast.

The development of Malagasy states, notably the Sakalava and the Merina kingdoms, resulted in an expansion of both slavery and the slave trade in Madagascar. Domestic slavery had hitherto been limited in scope because of the lack of large plantations or industries. However, the emergence of states resulted in increased demand for servile labor to produce food for, and service the personal needs of, ruling elites. This trend was particularly marked in the central highlands from the mid-eighteenth century, with the development of a labor-intensive state managed system of hydraulic rice cultivation. The slave export trade laid the foundations for the emergence there of a powerful Merina state that from 1817, in alliance with the British, attempted to forge an island empire.

GWYN R. CAMPBELL

See also: **Asians: East Africa; Bourbon, Ile de France, Seychelles: Eighteenth Century; Mauritius: Slavery and Slave Society to 1835; Seychelles; Slavery: Mediterranean, Red Sea, Indian Ocean; Slavery, Plantation: East Africa and the Islands**

Further Reading

Alpers, E. A. "The French Slave Trade." Historical Association of Tanzania paper no. 3. Historical Association of Tanzania, 1967.

———. *Ivory and Slaves in East and Central Africa to the Later Nineteenth Century*. London, 1975.

Lovejoy, Paul E. *Transformations in Slavery: A History of Slavery in Africa*. Cambridge: Cambridge University Press, 1983.

Toussaint, Auguste. "Le trafic commercial entre les Mascareignes et Madagascar de 1773 à 1810." *Annales de l'Université de Madagascar* (1966).

Toussaint, Auguste, *La route des îles—contribution à l'histoire maritime des Mascareignes*. Paris, 1967.

Slavery, Plantation: East Africa and the Islands

It was only toward the end of the eighteenth century that eastern Africa and the islands began to be incorporated into the world economic system. Plantation economies began to emerge in the Mascarene Islands (composed of Mauritius, Réunion and Rodrigues islands) toward the end of the eighteenth century, leading to a massive expansion in the slave trade from East Africa to these islands. In East Africa itself, plantation agriculture emerged rather later, in the nineteenth century.

During the early years of French settlement in the Mascarenes, plantation agriculture had not been encouraged, as the French East India Company had instructed governors to concentrate on growing provisions. Several factors led to the development of plantation agriculture. Coffee cultivation succeeded beyond expectations on Réunion (then known as Bourbon island). Sugar became the preferred crop in Mauritius. Slaves also worked on indigo plantations.

According to Daniel North-Coombes, the suspension of the French East India Company's charter in 1769 is considered to be the main factor contributing to the emergence of plantation agriculture in Mauritius. This development paralleled the expansion in trading activity and benefited from it. Many merchants were also owners of sugar estates. The island was in need of exportable products. Coffee cultivation never expanded at the same pace as sugar or with coffee production in Reunion. Spice cultivation was also attempted by Pierre Poivre and others, but it never succeeded, partly due to the indifference of the settlers. Settlers in Réunion however, established clove plantations which was successful for a short period of time. Indigo cultivation was again attempted by Cossigny and others and by 1790, it was the principal export crop.

Sugar cane cultivation, which was later to be the sole export crop, did not expand, as it could not compete with the West Indies. Most sugar on the island was used in the production of spirits and *argamasse*, which was a paste made up of chalk and sugar, which was used for rooftop construction. Spirits were used extensively in the slave trade in the Western Indian Ocean region, as a gift as well as a method of payment. During the American War of Independence, there was a decrease in spirits export from France to the Mascarenes, which stimulated a rise in the production of locally produced rum. The 1790s was thus marked by an increase in sugar cane cultivation and an increase in the number of sugar mills.

There was a decline in the indigo cultivation and production, chiefly due to the availability of cheap and high-quality indigo from Bengal. Indigo growers in Mauritius switched to sugarcane cultivation. The acreage devoted to sugarcane cultivation jumped from 422 hectares in 1789 to 5,000–6,300 hectares by 1803. Another crucial factor in the expansion in sugarcane cultivation was the Haitian Revolution in 1791. French planters in Mauritius reacted to this revolution by shifting from producing cane-distilled spirits to manufacturing sugar. Statistics give the clearest evidence of this: sugar production jumped from 300 tons in 1789 to 3,000 tons in 1803; by that point, it was the most important crop in Mauritius.

Slavery was the dominant labor system in Mauritius. Slave labor was used for every type of work, even those which could be performed by plows or animals. No labor-saving devices were employed. At the end of the eighteenth century, the number of slaves on the island doubled, from 33,823 in 1787 to 65,367 in 1807. This was directly linked to the rise of commercial agriculture and the rise in the slave trade even though, in 1794, the Colonial Assembly had banned slave trading.

The slave population was sustained by continuing imports, both legal and illegal. It has been estimated that 62,387 slaves were brought between 1773 and 1810, alone although this figure is today considered conservative.

We have little detailed information on the conditions affecting slaves during this period. One early account came from Bernandin de St. Pierre who stated that slave owners did not respect the clauses of the Code Noir (the "Black Code" governing slaves and slave owning) and slaves had no right of redress. According to M. J. Milbert (1812), however, most slave owners were "humane." Even he was forced to admit, however, that the Code Noir was not respected.

Owners neglected their slaves particularly in times of crisis. Famine was a permanent threat as supplies did not arrive on a regular basis, and natural disasters, such as cyclones, were frequent. Slaves probably supplemented their rations with crops they grew or cattle and poultry they bred. Their movements outside their plantations were restricted. The slave diet was made up almost entirely of manioc and other starchy foods, and was short on mineral salts, protein, and vitamins. Epidemics contributed to the already weak health of slaves, and to a higher mortality rate. There were also abdominal diseases. The poor state of health was further aggravated by the absence of adequate provision for health care. Only a few plantations had hospitals for sick slaves, and even fewer were staffed by qualified by medical practitioners. Natural healing methods were used by "herbal" doctors, older Malagasy, and Indian slaves.

Slavery was threatened when the French Revolution occurred, and in 1794 slavery was abolished in French colonies. The French colonists in Mauritius and Réunion, particularly the plantation owners, sent away the two representatives of the French government, Baco and Burnel, who had come to implement the abolition laws. The islands became semiautonomous until the advent of "imperial" rule under Napoleon I. The revolutionary period had brought about one positive development, a relaxation in emancipation laws, and a larger number of emancipations seem to have occurred. These laws were, however, tightened again when Governor Decaen took over in 1803. Plantation slaves were not numerous among the emancipated however; most freed slaves were women who had worked as domestic servants. In 1810, the British took over Mauritius. With the entry of Mauritian sugar into the British market, sugarcane cultivation increased, and thus so did the system of plantation slavery.

VIJAYA TEELOCK

See also: **Bourbon, Ile de France, Seychelles: Eighteenth Century; Mauritius; Seychelles.**

Further Reading

Milbert, M. J. *Voyage Pittoresque a l'ile de France.* Paris: A. Nepveu, 1812.
North-Coombes, D. M. *Labour Problems in the Sugar Industry of ile de France or Mauritius 1790–1842.* M.A. thesis, University of Cape Town, 1978.

Sherif, A. *Slaves, Spices and Ivory in Zanzibar*. London: James Currey, 1987.

Slavery, Colonial Rule and

By the time of the "Scramble" for Africa, all the colonial powers had outlawed slavery in their own countries, and its suppression was one of the justifications for their conquest of the continent. African slavery was widespread and took many forms, some more exploitative than others. Slaves were farmers, porters, canoe men, miners, trusted trading agents, soldiers, privileged officials (royal slaves), and concubines. There were slaves consecrated to deities, and slaves earmarked for human sacrifice. Some were treated as junior kinsmen or wives and never sold. Others, usually first-generation or "trade" slaves, were worked hard and lived miserable lives. In some areas slaves formed over half the population and performed all the manual labor. Everywhere they were an important capital investment, and item of trade. They were also status symbols, since a man's prestige depended on the number of his dependents. Slavery thus served economic, political, social, and religious purposes.

During the wars of conquest, the colonial powers were short of manpower and resources, and heavily dependent on African allies and auxiliaries. To keep their allegiance they often allowed them to keep prisoners of war. They also returned runaways belonging to their allies, and liberated those of their enemies. Sometimes they even appointed chiefs and gave them the arms with which to raid and enslave their neighbors. They also "freed" or hired slaves to use as soldiers, policemen, porters, and laborers. Once established, however, it was in the interests of the colonial rulers to end slave raiding and large-scale trading, as well as the export of slaves. In most areas these were outlawed.

Slavery, however, was a different question. The new rulers needed the cooperation of African elites, the main slave owners, to keep the peace, to serve in the lower ranks of administration, and to develop the economy. They believed that Africans were inherently lazy and that if slaves were freed the economy would languish and owners would rebel. They thus faced a dilemma. They had to attack, or seem to attack, slavery to placate Western public opinion. However, to prevent their colonies from being a drain on the metropoles, they needed to keep slaves in place and working until they could introduce other forms of labor and social control. Each colonial power solved the problem differently, and their policies changed over time, depending on the extent of their control, the local economic situation, the amount of scrutiny exerted by humanitarian groups in the metropole, and the degree of international interest. The British, with the lion's share of the continent and the most active antislavery lobby, adapted a system developed in India. Slavery had to be outlawed in actual colonies, so, as the empire expanded, they established protectorates in which they simply did not recognize it as a legal status. Slaves could remain with their owners, but those who left could not be forced to return. This was acceptable to humanitarians, who believed African slavery was "benign," and could be allowed to die out as the supply of new slaves was cut off with the imposition of peace, the outlawing of the slave trade, and, in some colonies, the freeing of persons born or imported after a set date. Moreover, slaves would not be suddenly deprived of their livelihood, and good masters would not lose their labor. This policy was applied differently everywhere. In Zanzibar and the Kenya coast, for instance, Swahili/Arab owners whose slaves left were compensated, whereas in Northern Nigeria slaves had to ransom themselves. Elsewhere there was no compensation, and often no set ransom. Slaves were simply not encouraged to leave or helped to reestablish themselves, and sometimes fugitives were returned to their owners. Whether slaves could leave depended on whether they could get access to land, wage labor, or other means of livelihood, and, sometimes, on whether they could get a sympathetic hearing in a native or Muslim court or before a European official.

The French adopted a variation of this policy, officially not recognizing slavery, but in practice supporting it. However, the departure of large numbers of discontented slaves in the Sudan from 1905, and the failure of their efforts to stop the exodus, led administrators to change their policy. Henceforth they refused to recognize slavery, but did not interfere with slaves who chose to remain with their owners. In Morocco, however, they did not explicitly outlaw slavery until 1925, while in Mauritania and the Sahara the laws were not enforced and slavery, and even small-scale slave trading, remained a fact of life until the end of colonial rule. The Portuguese outlawed slavery completely in 1878 but did not enforce the laws; and it continued, together with an active slave trade supplying "contract labor" to São Tomé and Príncipe, well into the twentieth century. The Germans in Tanganyika recognized slavery but eroded it by official manumissions. In Cameroon they passed laws against it, but only sporadically enforced them, and even slave trading continued for many years. The Italians in Somaliland outlawed the slave trade in 1903–1904 as the result of the revelations of a journalist, and declared that all slaves born after 1890 were free. The Spanish ended slavery in Fernando Po in 1859 to avoid having to return fugitives from the Portuguese island of São Tomé, and to open the way to recruiting contract labor. They did little in their other colonies, however, and in 1926 they excluded Spanish Morocco from the provisions of the Slavery Convention. The Belgians in the Congo never recognized slavery, but often used freed slaves for their own purposes.

Although colonial policy and laws set the context in which slavery was gradually eroded, the more important factors in its demise were the economic and political changes that accompanied colonial rule, and the initiatives of the slaves themselves. As wars and raids ended, and as new forms of transportation were introduced, so the need for slave soldiers and porters declined. Economic development helped slaves to depart by offering them new opportunities for wage labor or independent peasant production. It also provided owners with new forms of investment, new trade goods, and new status symbols. In some cases colonial taxation policies added to the expense of keeping slaves. Forced labor policies had a leveling effect, as freemen and slaves were both conscripted. Famine and the disruptions of World War I also eroded the institution in some areas.

Slaves played a key role in their own emancipation. Thousands departed spontaneously, or renegotiated their terms of service with their former owners. Scholars are divided as to whether more departed or stayed. Much depended on their prospects of finding other employment and on their level of discontent. In some areas, such as Nkanu in Southern Nigeria, masters retained control far into the colonial period through their ownership of land and the monopoly of ritual functions. They even used slaves for human sacrifice in the early 1920s. In contrast, in parts of Northern Nigeria, many thousands of slaves went home during the disorders of conquest. Others decamped when the railway offered them access to the market as independent producers. Possibly the majority remained in place but renegotiated their relations with their owners.

Prospects of achieving freedom varied with the sex, age, and location of the slave. Men fared better than women; they were more likely to find jobs or be able to set themselves up independently. Women, when freed, were usually consigned to or sought the care of a male protector. In some cases slave children were sent to Western schools, and they and their descendants became more prosperous than the descendants of their former masters. Some owners were ruined. Others prospered—particularly chiefs who managed to retain control over land and "traditional" labor services. The fate of royal slaves, whose prosperity depended on resisting emancipation, has only begun to be investigated.

Humanitarian organizations, principally the British Anti-Slavery and Aborigines Protection Society, brought the issue before the League of Nations in 1922. This resulted in the Slavery Convention of 1926, which bound signatories to end slavery "in all its forms" as circumstances permitted. The League of Nations also appointed three slavery commissions, which met in the 1920s and 1930s. Each of them asked the colonial governments for reports on their antislavery policies. In response, administrations reviewed their laws and practices, and the British, in particular, revised them to ensure that slaves knew they had the right to claim their freedom. By the end of colonial rule, slave raiding had disappeared in all but the remotest areas. Slave trading had been reduced to small-scale underground traffic, and slavery was no longer legal anywhere. In some areas, however, the descendants of slaves still suffered discrimination in matters of marriage, inheritance, access to land, and the performance of religious rituals.

SUZANNE MIERS

See also: **Anti-Slavery Movement; Brussels Conference and Act, 1890.**

Further reading

Brown, Carolyn A. "Testing the Boundaries of Marginality: Twentieth Century Slavery and Emancipation Struggles in Nkanu, Northern Igboland, 1920–29." *Journal of African History* no. 37 (1996): 51–80.

Cooper, Frederick. *From Slaves to Squatters: Plantation Labor and Agriculture in Zanzibar and Coastal Kenya 1890–1925.* New Haven, Conn.: Yale University Press, 1980.

Klein, Martin A. *Slavery and Colonial Rule in French West Africa.* Cambridge: Cambridge University Press, 1998.

Lovejoy, Paul E., and Jan S. Hogendorn. *Slow Death of Slavery: The Course of Abolition in Northern Nigeria, 1897–1936.* Cambridge: Cambridge University Press, 1993.

Miers, Suzanne, and Martin A. Klein. *Slavery and Colonial Rule in Africa.* London: Frank Cass, 1998.

Miers, Suzanne, and Richard Roberts. *The End of Slavery in Africa.* Madison: University of Wisconsin Press, 1988.

Smallpox: *See* Rinderpest and Smallpox: East and Southern Africa.

Smith, Ian: *See* Zimbabwe (Rhodesia): Unilateral Declaration of Independence and the Smith Regime, 1964–1979.

Smuts, Jan C. (1870–1950)
Politician

Jan Christiaan Smuts was a scholar, scientist, and soldier, and white South Africa's leading statesman. He played a prominent role in the confrontation between Britain and the South African Republic (SAR), which culminated in the South African War (1899–1902). As attorney general he played a prominent part in the negotiations before the war, and helped frame the republic's strategy. After the capture of Pretoria in 1900, he joined the Boer commandos, leading troops a thousand miles into the Cape Colony in the following year.

Smuts showed an exceptional aptitude for war. He emerged from it physically robust, with added authority among Afrikaners and a formidably anti-British reputation. He displayed his soldierly skills again in World War I, when he put down civil war in South Africa, helped capture southwestern Africa from the Germans, and led imperial troops in eastern Africa. In 1917 he joined the imperial and then the British war cabinet. War developed Smuts's sense of masculinity, and perhaps his arrogance and sense of invincibility.

Nevertheless, Smuts thought of himself as a man of peace and a lawgiver. In May 1902, convinced the Afrikaners faced annihilation, he helped persuade the Boer commanders to sign the peace treaty with the British at Vereeniging in the Transvaal. He believed that reconciliation between the "white races" was crucial if white supremacy was to be maintained, and drafted the clause in the treaty that ensured that decisions about an African suffrage would be left to colonists; the exclusion of the majority African population from citizenship in the act unifying South Africa in 1910 was the inevitable result.

Throughout his life Smuts opposed extending political rights to Africans. His views on native policy never rose beyond notions of "trusteeship," paternalism, and segregation, while his actual native policy was mostly pragmatic and short-term. His relations with Indians were not much better. Despite declaring in 1943 that segregation had "fallen on evil days," Smuts retained his opaque views on race and his incapacity to provide vision and leadership on this, South Africa's most crucial issue, throughout his life.

After the South African War, Smuts played a major role in Transvaal politics, securing the region's self-government from Britain in 1906. In 1910 he was the architect of the union. In the Transvaal and then in the union, he held key ministerial posts under the premiership of his comrade-in-arms and confidante, Louis Botha, and established their racially exclusive legislative and constitutional frameworks.

Despite his blinkered vision on matters of race, after 1910 Smuts was acclaimed as an internationalist. He helped refashion the modern British Commonwealth, establishing the notion of dominion status during and immediately after World War I, and assisting in the birth of the independent Irish state in 1921.

He was present at the 1919 Paris Peace Conference, representing South Africa with Botha. There he argued in vain for a magnanimous peace and opposed the punitive reparations imposed on Germany, recognizing its threat to European peace and social order. Largely

responsible for establishing the framework of the League of Nations in 1918–1919, in 1945–1946 he participated in the discussions that set up the United Nations, and both suggested and drafted its human rights charter.

Nor did he ever forget his intellectual activities; during the South African War he had reputedly carried Immanuel Kant's *Critique of Pure Reason* and the New Testament in Greek in his knapsack. A busy minister, between 1906 and 1911 he wrote a philosophical treatise, *An Enquiry into the Whole*, based partly on his unpublished manuscript on Walt Whitman written at Cambridge University. This in turn formed the basis of his *Holism and Evolution*, published in 1926, in which he attempted to synthesize Darwinian science and metaphysics. Highly regarded by contemporaries, it attracts few admirers today; nevertheless, it paved the way for Smuts's presidency of the prestigious British Association for the Advancement of Science in its centenary year in 1931. By this time he was widely extolled for his capacity to synthesize knowledge across a range of scientific disciplines. A champion of South African science, he understood its importance in promoting white nationhood.

Smuts's reputation was always more lustrous internationally than at home, where his political life in the interwar years was far from distinguished. Succeeding Botha as premier in 1919, he was soon outflanked by the more extreme nationalism of J. B. M. Hertzog's Afrikaner National Party, and forced into an alliance with the party of mining capital that had supported him during the war. In office, he ruthlessly suppressed black millenarians at Bulhoek in the eastern Cape in 1921, striking white mineworkers on the Rand in 1922, and the Bondelswartz people in Namibia in the same year. In 1924, he was ousted from power. In 1933 he accepted office under Hertzog, despite the differences between them, especially over the Commonwealth connection, and to the dismay of more liberal members of his party who saw in it the betrayal of any hope of a more progressive racial policy.

Smuts's hour came again with the outbreak of World War II, when he persuaded the parliament, by a majority of 13 votes, to join Britain against Nazism, and became Prime Minister. He built up South Africa's defense forces, oversaw the dispatch of South African troops to North Africa and the Middle East, and visited the front on several occasions, frequently advising Winston Churchill on war strategy. Despite this, he lost the all-white South African elections in 1948 to Afrikaner nationalists using the slogan of apartheid. The election results came as a shock to Smuts. Not only did he underestimate nationalist sentiment; he also failed to take the precaution of altering the constituency boundaries that greatly favored rural areas.

He died two years later; the nationalists remained in power until 1994.

Revered in his lifetime, especially in Britain and the Commonwealth, in South Africa Smuts was reviled by nationalists as the "handyman of empire," and by white workers as a "lackey of capitalism"; in the apartheid era he was largely forgotten. His belief in white supremacy and refusal to accept South Africa's majority black population as fellow citizens greatly tarnished his image, while the speeches and writings that struck his contemporaries as profound frequently appear overblown or even banal. Nevertheless, in recent years, as white South Africans have once more faced the wider world, his life is attracting renewed attention.

SHULA MARKS

See also: **South Africa: Africa Policy; South Africa: Afrikaner Nationalism, Broederbond and National Party, 1902–1948; South Africa: Gandhi, Indian Question; South Africa: Peace, Reconstruction, Union: 1902–1910; South Africa: Segregation, Political Economy of; South Africa: World Wars I and II; South African War, 1899–1902.**

Biography

Born near Malmesbury in the Cape Colony. A scholarship took him to Cambridge, where in 1894 he was the first candidate to achieve distinction in both parts of the law tripos simultaneously. Secured the Transvaal's self-government from Britain in 1906. In 1910, was the architect of the union. Held key ministerial posts under the premiership of Louis Botha. Held the presidency of the British Association for the Advancement of Science in 1931. Named premier in 1919, and ousted from power in 1924. Reinstated as prime minister with the outbreak of World War II. Lost the all-white South African elections in 1948 to Afrikaner nationalists. Died in 1950.

Further Reading

Hancock, W. K. *Smuts: I: The Sanguine Years, 1870–1919.* Cambridge: Cambridge University Press, 1962.
———. *Smuts: II: The Fields of Force, 1919–1950.* Cambridge: Cambridge University Press, 1968.
Hancock, W. K., and Jean van der Poel (eds.). *Selections from the Smuts Papers, vols. I–IV, 1886–1919.* Cambridge: Cambridge University Press, 1966.
———. *Selections from the Smuts Papers, vols. V–VII, 1919–1950.* Cambridge: Cambridge University Press, 1973.
Friedman, Bernard. *Smuts: A Reappraisal.* London: George Allen and Unwin, 1975.
Millin, Sarah Gertrude. *General Smuts.* 2 vols. London: Faber and Faber, 1936.

Soba and Dongola

Upon the collapse of the Kushite state in the fourth century CE, political power was usurped by the Nubians. By the sixth century they were divided into three states, Nobadia, Makurra, and 'Alwa. Faras, the capital of Nobadia, had been an important town for millennia, in contrast to Soba (Soba East) and Dongola (now termed Old Dongola to distinguish it from the modern city 120 kilometers to the north), the capitals of 'Alwa and Makurra, respectively. Although a bark stand inscribed with the name of Taharqo (690–664BCE) was found at Dongola, and a granite statue base, a Hathor headed capital and two criosphinxes, one inscribed with Meroitic hieroglyphs, have been found at Soba, both these towns seem to be new foundations dating to the earlier years of the Nubian kingdoms.

The earliest structural evidence for occupation at Dongola is the massive defensive wall built on the prominent hill overlooking the Nile, which has been dated to the early sixth century on the evidence of associated pottery. At Soba, remains of circular timber huts can be dated to about the same period. There is a complete absence at both sites of pottery and other artifacts of earlier periods; we must assume that the Kushite monumental sculptures and inscribed blocks were brought to these sites from elsewhere.

Dongola occupies an excellent defensible position from which it dominates the Nile, making it ideally situated to control riverine traffic. It is also at the point where trade routes from Darfur in the west and Kordofan to the southwest join the Nile. Immediately to the north of the town is the fertile Letti Basin, an old palaeochannel of the Nile. The reasons for the choice of the site at Soba are less easy to ascertain. It lies on the right bank of the Blue Nile, 22 kilometers upstream from the confluence of the Blue and White Niles at present-day Khartoum. The featureless countryside at Soba does not appear to especially favor this site above many others in the vicinity, and the adjacent Wadi Soba is not a significant feature of the landscape. Although Wallace Budge, who excavated on the site in 1903, claimed to have found traces of a defensive wall and gate, further study has failed to substantiate this claim.

An historical outline of Dongola is available partly from the Arab sources who mention it frequently, usually in the context of Arab attacks on the town, and partly as a result of the extensive and ongoing excavations by the Polish Mediterranean Research Center on the site that were begun in 1964. By contrast, Soba, far to the south, is rarely mentioned by Arab sources and has seen much less extensive excavation.

Although defense seems to have been of primary importance to the early inhabitants of Dongola, large churches were, by the later sixth century, constructed outside the walls in the plain to the north. The sense of security that this implies was rudely shattered in 652, when an Arab army laid siege to the town and destroyed at least one of these churches. However, when the conflict ended, the town developed to the north, eventually covering an area 2.8 by 0.9 kilometers in extent, though much of this may not have been densely occupied. The most dominant structures in the town were churches and monasteries. The grandiose churches, frequently demolished and rebuilt on an ever greater scale, reflect the considerable vitality of the town and of the Kingdom of which it was the capital. Dating from its heyday in the Classic Christian period (85–1100) is the throne hall of the rulers, an impressive two-story building approximately 10 meters in height; fine houses also date from this period.

According to Ibn Selim el Aswani, who visited 'Alwa around 970, 'Alwa had "fine buildings and large monasteries, churches rich with gold and gardens." In the eleventh century, Abu Salih noted that in the town was "a very large and spacious church, skillfully planned and constructed . . . called the Church of Manbali." Excavations in the 1980s by the British Institute in Eastern Africa uncovered the remains of three of these churches, two of which are of a size and style directly comparable with the finest churches known at Dongola. Clearly both towns followed the same artistic traditions, although it is unclear whether one was directly influenced by the other, and if so which was the dominant partner in this cultural exchange. Five churches have been excavated at Soba as well as a large palatial structure, which in view of its close physical proximity to the three churches was perhaps the residence of the archbishop of Soba, or of the king. Reused within the building was the marble tombstone of a king of 'Alwa, David, who reigned probably from 99 to 1015. Soba appears to have attained its greatest extent in the early medieval period, when it covered 2.75 square kilometers. Later it was more nucleated, though perhaps with an equally large population.

The demise of Dongola went hand in hand with a general impoverishment of Makurra, brought about by incessant attacks from the north beginning in the late twelfth century that caused considerable destruction to a number of the major buildings, perhaps exacerbated by earthquake damage. In 1317 the throne hall was converted into a mosque and in 1323 the first Muslim ruler ascended the throne. Before the end of that century the city was abandoned as the capital of Makurra, with the transfer of the royal court to the northern town of Derr. We have much less information on the collapse of 'Alwa and the destruction of Soba. However, excavations within one of the major churches suggested that that building was already occupied by squatters during the twelfth century; rich Christian graves were being plundered at about that time. When the traveler David Reubeni passed through the town in 1523 the fine buildings were long gone; he described the inhabitants as living in crude huts.

DEREK WELSBY

See also: **Nubia.**

Further Reading

Godlewski, Wlodzimierz. "Old Dongola: The Early Fortifications." *Cahier de Recherches de l'Institut de Papyrologie et d'Egyptologie de Lille* 17, no. 2 (1997): 175–179.

Martens-Czarnecka, Ma_gorzata. "New Mural Paintings from Old Dongola." *Cahier de Recherches de l'Institut de Papyrologie et d'Egyptologie de Lille* 17, no. 2 (1997): 211–225.

Welsby, Derek A. *Soba: Archaeological Research at a Medieval Capital on the Blue Nile.* BIEA Memoir no. 12. London: BIEA, 1991.

———. *Soba II: Renewed Excavations within the Metropolis of the Kingdom Of Alwa.* BIEA Memoir no. 15. London: BIEA, 1998.

Żurawski, Bogdan. "The Cemeteries Of Dongola: A Preliminary Report." *Cahier de Recherches de l'Institut de Papyrologie et d'Egyptologie de Lille* 17, no. 2 (1997): 195–209.

Sobhuza I: *See* Swaziland: Sobhuza I, Foundation of Ngwane Kingdom.

Sobukwe, Robert and the Pan-Africanist Congress

The Pan-Africanist Congress was an antiapartheid political organization founded in 1959 and led by Mangaliso Robert Sobukwe, who was born in 1924 in the Eastern Cape town of Graaff-Reinet. Sobukwe's background was quite modest, but he was able to gain admittance to Fort Hare, at that time (the late 1940s) South Africa's premier African university.

At Fort Hare, Sobukwe was exposed to a wide range of political ideas and organizations, the most important being the African National Congress (ANC) Youth League. At the time, the Youth League was under the dynamic leadership of Anton Lembede. The Youth League, which was formed in 1942, would prove to be a crucial factor in shaping the resistance to racial inequity. It would provide the political start for many future leaders, including Nelson Mandela, Walter Sisulu, and Oliver Tambo, as well as Sobukwe himself. The Youth League differed from the main body of the ANC in that it argued that African solidarity must be the basis of action against repression. Although the Youth League clearly stated that it welcomed cooperation with other racial groups, it felt that the liberation of Africans had to be led by Africans themselves. In 1948, the year that the National Party formally introduced apartheid, Sobukwe and his classmates founded a branch of the Youth League at Fort Hare.

Shortly after the Fort Hare chapter joined the larger Youth League, the organization developed its Program of Action in 1949. This policy was designed to encourage a much more direct confrontation with government repression than the ANC had undertaken in the past. This policy was implemented with the Defiance Campaign of 1952, when large-sccale refusal to honor pass laws began. Although these protests were successful in raising consciousness among Africans and their sympathizers, there were those among the ANC that were unhappy with the way the organizations' leadership had coordinated their activities so closely with Asian activists. In addition to problems with coordination with Asians, there were misgivings among some ANC members over the influence of some whites, especially those in the Communist Party. According to Sobukwe's biographer, Benjamin Pogrund (1991), many Africans were uncomfortable with the South African Communist Party's close ties to the Soviet Union, which caused local communist activists to modify their positions according to directives from Moscow.

Those ANC members who were unhappy with the direction of their organization were known as the "Africanists." The area where Africanist sentiment was strongest was the Orlando community of greater Johannesburg. The initial leader of the Africanist faction was Potlako K. Leballo, but Robert Sobukwe would eventually become their leader when he moved to the area after gaining a position as an instructor of African Languages at the University of the Witwatersrand.

The acrimony between the Africanists and the ANC mainstream increased throughout the 1950s. The Freedom Charter movement, which was based on a union of all South Africa's communities, was dismissed by Africanists as a deviation from the 1949 Program of Action. The friction of the two cliques finally erupted in 1958, when Leballo was expelled from the ANC by Transvaal President Nelson Mandela and Africanist members were met with force at an ANC meeting that year.

The Pan-Africanist Congress (PAC) held its inaugural meeting in April 1959. At that meeting Robert Sobukwe was elected president and Potlako Leballo was elected secretary general. The PAC differentiated itself from the ANC not only by emphasizing African nationalism and leadership; it was also more internationalist in its orientation, stressing a desire for an eventual continent wide African state. The PAC also received messages from Presidents Sekou Touré of Guinea and Kwame Nkrumah of Ghana, who expressed support for the PAC's vision of a United States of Africa.

Less than a year after its founding, the PAC would initiate an antipass protest that would lead to the Sharpeville Massacre, an event that would display the brutal repression of apartheid before the world. On March 4, 1960, Robert Sobukwe called on the PAC membership to go without their passes to police stations and demand their arrest. When a large crowd of protesters appeared before the police station in Sharpeville, the police reacted by opening fire, killing 69 and wounding 180. Among the casualties were 40 women and 6 children. Although the nationalist government under Prime Minister Verwoerd tried to justify the shooting with claims of violence on the part of demonstrators, investigation would eventually prove that the protesters were unarmed, and were primarily shot in the back while fleeing the police.

The African population of South Africa was naturally outraged by the Sharpeville Massacre, and both the ANC and PAC sponsored strikes and other actions to express their dissatisfaction with the apartheid government. The government, in response, declared a state of emergency and eventually banned both the PAC and ANC. Additionally, the PAC leadership was sentenced to hard labor. Sobukwe was given a sentence of three years. In response to continuing repression of the minority government, the PAC organized an armed unit commonly known as Poqo.

The fallout from Sharpeville devastated the leadership of the PAC. After finishing his prison term, Sobukwe was forced to spend the rest of his life under strict security-force supervision until his death from cancer in 1978. Potlako Leballo was able to move to Maseru in Lesotho after his release from prison in 1962; here he established the PAC in exile. The PAC headquarters were then moved to Dar es Salaam in 1964. Once in Tanzania, the PAC set about the business of trying to develop an effective fighting force for the struggle against apartheid, but the organization found itself caught up in conflicts among factions, which resulted in deadly violence. The major split involved David Sibeko, the PAC's observer to the United Nations, and the supporters of Leballo.

Leballo and his supporters wanted to maintain the emphasis on armed struggle, while Sibeko began to move toward negotiated settlement. This rift was exacerbated by the large influx of military recruits as a result of the Soweto uprising of 1976. Sibeko would eventually be assassinated in 1979.

With the lifting of the ban on the PAC, ANC, and South African Communist Party in 1990, the PAC once again became an openly functioning political organization. It also posted candidates in the open elections of 1994, in which it won five seats in the parliament.

ANTHONY CHEESEBORO

See also: **Luthili, Albert; Mandela, Nelson; South Africa: Sharpeville Massacre.**

Further Reading

Gerhart, Gail. *Black Power in South Africa: The Evolution of an Ideology.* Berkeley and Los Angeles: University of California Press.

Leeman, Bernard. *Lesotho and the Struggle for Azania Africanist Political Movements in Lesotho and Azania: The Origins and History of the Basutoland Congress Party and the Pan Africanist Congress*. London: University of Azania, 1985.

Pogrund, Benjamin. *Sobukwe and Apartheid*. New Brunswick, N.J.: Rutgers University Press, 1991.

Socialism in Postcolonial Africa

In the immediate postcolonial period, the language of socialism was attractive to nationalist elites and emergent intellectuals in Africa as a means of further distancing themselves from the colonial powers (and the "imperialist system") from which they had now won their independence. Often this reflected the sincere belief that a socialist system promised a more just and humane society than any other likely alternative. It could also seem, in light of the apparent strength and rising ascendancy of the Soviet and Chinese models, to offer an effective growth strategy and a convincing rationale for the kind of "developmental state" thought necessary on the Left (and even, at the time, on the Right) to realize socioeconomic transformation.

In many of its earliest expressions the goal of socialism in Africa intersected with the ideological discourse of *African socialism*; this term came to summarize a claim (now much discredited) that there is a socialism distinctive to Africa, one that springs, quite spontaneously, from egalitarian cultural predispositions and communal social practices antedating European penetration of the continent. These predispositions and practices were said to have survived the impact of colonialism and to provide the basis for giving a promisingly collectivist tilt to the policies of postcolonial governments.

Sometimes these notions reflected the cultural-nationalist preoccupations of certain members of the first generation of successful African nationalists, less eager to advance a deeply critical analysis of their own societies than to develop an indigenous alternative to left-wing discourses (Marxism, for example) they considered too Eurocentric or too potentially divisive. Leopold Senghor of Senegal best exemplified such a tendency, perhaps, though it should also be noted that this perspective was, from the very earliest days of African independence, viewed with suspicion by other putatively socialist leaders like Kwame Nkrumah of Ghana and Sekou Touré of Guinea. These leaders employed a rather more universalistic, if still hazily defined, "progressive" discourse in outlining their own (ultimately unrealized) left-populist and anti-imperialist goals.

More often, the rhetoric of African socialism was adopted quite cynically by opportunistic elites, on the rise everywhere in Africa, to give a veneer of progressiveness and apparent concern for popular aspirations to their otherwise self-interested and increasingly capitalist policies. By means of this ideological rationale these elites sought to mask the workings of new class structures and continuing imperial linkages that a more rigorous socialist discourse might more readily have revealed to popular scrutiny. A particularly notorious example of this more manipulative use of the concept was the Kenyan government's "Sessional Paper #10" on "African Socialism and its Application to Planning in Kenya" (1965), which, substantively, had almost nothing to do with any recognizably socialist intention. It was not long before the Kenyan leadership itself began to rationalize its policies in much more straightforwardly capitalist terms. And certain other much-touted variants on African Socialist themes (the "humanism" of Zambia's Kenneth Kaunda, for example) also proved to have little or no genuine socialist content.

Probably the most sincere and well-developed of all variants of African socialism was the philosophy and practice of *ujamaa* (familyhood) generated by Julius Nyerere in Tanzania. Suspicious, in part on religious grounds, of Marxism and "class struggle," Nyerere nonetheless evinced a high moral tone, a certain skepticism as to the bona fides of Western economic interests and strategies, and a genuine concern for the fate of the mass of the population in his impoverished country.

As Nyerere sought to balance his perspective against his own deepening awareness of the profound contradictions inherent in modern African society, he produced a series of widely quoted analyses of rural questions, education, leadership, and democracy. In policy terms, he sought to curb elite aggrandizement and encourage equality, to make foreign investment serve positive social ends, and to encourage a new pattern of collective life for rural dwellers. Nyerere was to sustain his eloquent critique of capitalist-induced global inequalities until his death in 1999. In Tanzania, however, his project—which intersected in practice with weak administrative capacities, all-too-authoritarian political methods and only rather mildly social-democratic interventions in the economy—was not successful, either economically or in terms of realizing socialist ideals.

There had always coexisted in postcolonial Africa a more Marxist socialist current, however. This had contributed to the leftward inflection of radical populism in nations such as Algeria, where an interesting form of collectivism and autodetermination was briefly attempted in the rural areas, for example. It was to resurface in the rejection of Nyerere's ideas by a later generation of socialists, many of them linked to the liberation movements and postliberation governments of Southern Africa, such as Mozambique's FRELIMO, led by President Samora Machel. Deeply suspicious of western capitalist dictates and anxious to address the needs of its impoverished population, FRELIMO found in Marxism an alternative to the vague nostrums of African socialism and a possible guide to realization of the collectivist aspirations that had developed in the course of the movement's armed struggle against the Portuguese. This led to a heightened role for the state in the economy and an attempted practice of egalitarianism in class, gender, and racial terms.

Unfortunately, once in power (after 1975), Frelimo failed to avoid the authoritarian and vanguard practices, the stiff intolerance toward cultural diversity, and the economic strategies, top-down and technocratic, that had come to characterize the "Marxist-Leninist" brand of Marxism elsewhere. Moreover, before it could even hope to correct such mistakes and root its Marxism more firmly and effectively in the concrete realities that presented themselves on the ground, socialist Mozambique also found itself (like its counterpart regime in another former Portuguese colony, Angola) besieged by apartheid South Africa's ruthless destabilization policy in the region. In the end, Frelimo would abandon its progressive perspectives under South African and American pressure and capitulate to the new global economic orthodoxy of neoliberalism. Meanwhile, several other regimes (those of Ethiopia and Zimbabwe, for example) that presented themselves in socialist terms in the 1980s seemed, unlike Mozambique, merely to manipulate Marxist rhetoric in the attempt to legitimate their high-handed political methods and/or to sustain aid flows from the east in the last years of the Cold War.

Socialists on the continent came, therefore, to look for the immediate vindication of their hopes in the antiapartheid struggle in South Africa. There the principal liberation movement, the African National Congress, was linked both to the South African Communist Party and to a highly mobilized and radicalized network of mass organizations on the ground (including the country's vibrant trade union movement) and seemed to promise both a clearer version of socialist theory and a more effective socialist practice than elsewhere. Many of the ANC's preliberation formulations emphasized the need to impose a strong measure of social control upon the workings of the market and over a capitalist economy that was very much more developed in South Africa than elsewhere on the continent. Much was heard of the prospects for nationalization, and for economic strategies designed to produce "growth through redistribution." Yet the difficulties of confronting the post–Cold War global economic power structure were soon apparent and, in combination with the increasingly self-interested ambitions of at least some among the ANC leadership,

produced a markedly neoliberal postapartheid development project, one premised on "global competitiveness," the centrality of foreign investment, and the rule of the market.

Some sharp debates did continue over the likely efficacy of such a policy package to provide economic growth sufficient to redress the extreme inequalities that still characterize South Africa. But that country was, in any case, merely part of a broader pattern. Given the global and continental defeat/failure of regimes and movements that presented themselves as socialist, and faced with the hegemony of neoliberal orthodoxy worldwide, the language of socialism had, by century's end, lost a great deal of its credibility on the continent. At the same time, there are those in Africa who argue that any such setback may prove only temporary. Global capitalism shows no more sign of producing socioeconomic transformation in Africa than it has heretofore, and the costs of ongoing socioeconomic crisis for the continent are mounting. In this context, the claims of the social over those of the marketplace, and of the leftist developmental state over those of capital, may yet reassert themselves as crucial dimensions of emerging popular-democratic demands in Africa. If so, the analytical categories and political practices linked to socialist critique and practice (albeit freer, one hopes, of authoritarian propensities and of the often narrowly economic and statist orthodoxies that characterized such initiatives in the past) will ultimately have to be revived in Africa.

JOHN S. SAUL

See also: **Cold War, Africa and the; Guinea: Touré, Ahmed Sekou, Era of; Mozambique: Frelimo and the War of Liberation, 1962–1975; Nkrumah, Kwame; Nyerere, Julius; South Africa: African National Congress; Tanzania (Tanganyika): Arusha Declaration.**

Further Reading

Friedland, William H., and Carl G. Rosberg (eds,). *African Socialism.* Stanford, Calif.: Stanford University Press, 1964. Revised as Carl G. Rosberg, and Thomas M. Callaghy (eds.), *Socialism in Sub-Saharan Africa: A New Assessment.* Berkeley: University of California Institute of International Studies, 1979.

Keller, Edmund J. and Donald Rothchild (eds.). *Afro-Marxist Regimes: Ideology and Public Policy.* Boulder, Colo.: Lynne Rienner, 1987.

Machel, Samora. *Samora Machel: An African Revolutionary: Selected Speeches and Writings,* edited by Barry Munslow. London: Zed, 1985.

Munslow, Barry. *Africa: Problems in the Transition to Socialism.* London: Zed, 1986.

Nkrumah, Kwame. *Neo-Colonialism: The Last Stage of Imperialism.* London: Thomas Nelson, 1965.

Nyerere, Julius. *Freedom and Socialism/Uhuru na Ujamaa,* Dar es Salaam: Oxford University Press, 1968.

Ottaway, David, and Marina Ottaway. *Afrocommunism.* New York: Holmes and Meier, 1981.

Saul, John S. *Recolonization and Resistance: Southern Africa in the 1990s.* Trenton, N.J.: Africa World Press, 1993.

———. *Socialist Ideology and the Struggle for Southern Africa.* Trenton, N.J.: Africa World Press, 1990.

Young, Crawford. *Ideology and Development in Africa.* New Haven, Conn.: Yale University Press, 1982.

Soga, Tiyo (1829–1871)
Xhosa Missionary, Writer, Translator and Composer

The first African from South Africa to become an ordained missionary, Tiyo Soga was an important transitional figure who left a significant body of writings. He was born close to the Mgwali River, a tributary of the Tyumie, in what is now the Eastern Cape, in the heart of the old eastern frontier or, as it became known, the Ciskei.

Soga went first to a United Presbyterian Church of Scotland mission school at Chumie, and then to the Free Church of Scotland secondary school at Lovedale, which he entered in 1844, three years after its establishment. During the War of the Axe (1846–1847) between the western Xhosa and the British, he fled with his mother to the Kat River Settlement, but by then the principal of the Lovedale school, the Rev. William Govan, had recognized Soga's potential. Govan arranged to take him to Scotland for further education. In Glasgow he was taught at the Free Church Seminary, and baptized in May 1848. In October that year he returned to South Africa as a catechist. He then worked at the mission stations of Uniondale and Igqinbigha, where he ran into criticism from fellow Xhosa speakers because he had not been circumcised and for collaborating with the colonists. When war broke out again between the Xhosa and the British in December 1850, Soga again sided with the colony, and fled to Grahamstown. At the suggestion of the Rev. Robert Niven, who had been his superior at Uniondale, he left in June 1851 for Scotland, now to train for the ministry. After theological study, he was ordained a minister in December 1856. The following February, on the eve of his departure for South Africa, he married a Scotswoman, Janet Burnside.

The couple was the victim of racial prejudice when they arrived back in South Africa, but they soon went inland, to the area of Soga's birth, and on the Mgwali River he established a new Presbyterian mission among the western Xhosa, in what was now the high commission territory of British Kaffraria. His return took place in the aftermath of the Xhosa cattle killing, and he saw in its tragic consequences—large numbers of Xhosa left starving and uprooted from their homes—new opportunities for expanding mission work. And partly as a consequence of the changed circumstances, he was successful as a missionary at Emgwali, amassing a large congregation. Soga built a number of schools and outstations and a large church building, for which he collected over £600 from white supporters. He established a reputation as a fine preacher, equally at home with both the English and Xhosa languages. He kept a journal, and began writing occasional articles, some of them published in *Indaba*, the English-Xhosa periodical produced at Lovedale.

In 1865 Soga developed chronic throat trouble, yet he never took adequate rest from his demanding job. In 1867, Sarili, head of the Gcaleka (eastern) Xhosa, who had in 1864 been allowed to return to a portion of the lands from which he had been ejected after the cattle killing, asked for a missionary. Soga reluctantly left Emgwali in 1868 to establish the new mission east of the Kei River. He chose a site on the Tutura River, the later Somerville, and there lived in a mud hut while he sought to build up the new mission. He soon grew despondent as he encountered much opposition from Sarili, who continued to see mission work as the vanguard of colonial penetration, and the Gcaleka. He also grew increasingly ill, and suffered from depression as he battled to make converts. A new mission church was opened in April 1871, but in June on his way to establish an outstation he was trapped in a damp hut for some days and fell ill. He did not recover, and died in August of that year.

In 1866, Soga had completed the Xhosa translation of the first part of John Bunyan's *Pilgrim's Progress*, which became a classic of Xhosa literature and was to be published in a number of editions. He also composed a number of popular hymns in Xhosa, and translated a large part of the four Gospels for the Xhosa Bible. When he died at the early age of 42 there was an outpouring of grief in the colony, for he had become a revered figure.

In the eight articles that he had published in *Indaba*, and in other writing, Soga expressed his pride in being African and called on Africans to work together to promote the interests of their "nation." It was on the basis of such writing that Donovan Williams, a recent biographer and editor of Soga's writing, has argued that he was "the progenitor of black nationalism in South Africa" and a contributor to ideas of black consciousness and *Négritude*. The new generation of educated Africans who would pass through Lovedale in the 1870s—men such as Elijah Makiwane and John Tengo Jabavu—did see in Soga a role model, but there is no evidence that they or others drew on his ideas, and Williams's claims rest largely on a small body of writing, much of which remained unknown or forgotten until Williams himself rescued it. What is clear is that Soga was a man who was able to reconcile the two worlds in which he found himself. On the one hand, he retained a deep affection for Scotland and its culture; on the other, he remained proud of his Xhosa and African heritage, rejected criticism of African culture as barbarous and any idea that it would be replaced entirely by Western culture. He urged his children to be proud of the African side of their ancestry. He was the first African in South Africa to grapple with such dilemmas on paper; in this, John Knox Bokwe in the later nineteenth century and Sol T. Plaatje in the early twentieth would follow in Soga's footsteps.

CHRISTOPHER SAUNDERS

See also: **South Africa: Missionaries: Nineteenth Century.**

Biography

Born in 1929 close to the Mgwali River, a tributary of the Tyumie, in what is now the Eastern Cape. Upon the recommendation of a missionary teacher, moved to Scotland to study, where he was baptized in 1848; returned thereafter to South Africa. Left in June 1851 for Scotland again, to train for the ministry. After theological study, was ordained a minister in December 1856. The following February, on the eve of his departure for South Africa, he married a Scotswoman, Janet Burnside. From 1865 on, developed chronic throat trouble. Left Emgwali in 1868 to establish a new mission east of the Kei River, choosing a site on the Tutura River (Somerville). Died in 1871.

Further Reading

Chalmers, J. A. *Tiyo Soga: A Page of South African Missionary Work.* Edinburgh, 1877.

Cousins, H. T. *Tiyo Soga: The Model Kafir Missionary.* London, 1897.

De Kock, Leon. *Civilising Barbarians: Missionary Narrative and African Textual Response in Nineteenth-Century South Africa.* Johannesburg: Wits University Press, 1996.

Saayman, W. A. *The Christian Mission in South Africa.* Pretoria: University of South Africa Press, 1991.

Williams, D. *The Journal and Selected Writings of the Reverend Tiyo Soga.* Cape Town: A. A. Balkema, 1983.

———. *Umfundisi: A Biography of Tiyo Soga 1829–1871.* Lovedale, Lovedale Press, 1978.

Sokoto Caliphate: Hausa, Fulani and Founding of

From the fifteenth to the seventeenth centuries, centralized states emerged around the walled cities that had become important commercial centers in Hausaland (present-day northern Nigeria). The most prominent of these states were Kano, Katsina, Zazzau, Zamfara, Kebbi, and Gobir. The Hausa states were also the home of many immigrants of diverse ethnic origin.

The pastoralist Fulbe (Fulani in the Hausa language), who had spread from Futa Toro across much of the West African savanna, were among the most significant of these groups.

Although Islam had grown (at least in urban areas) from the faith of a small circle of merchants and scholars to the generally established religion of the various Hausa states, by the end of the eighteenth century indigenous religious rites were still commonly practiced. Within the Torodbe community, which produced many of the Fulani *mallams* (learned Muslims) in Hausaland, this syncretism was often equated with being an infidel, and many Torodbe agitated for the creation of Muslim states in which rulers would uphold the *Shari'a* (Islamic law). However, Shehu 'Uthman dan Fodio, who became the spiritual leader of the Sokoto jihad (holy war), initially refused to become embroiled in political disputes. Hence, in the early 1780s, while he was an adviser at the court of the Sarkin Gobir Bawa, there was little reason to believe that he would lead a movement against the Gobir government. Yet, as it became clear that the Hausa rulers were unwilling to dispense with the non-Muslim religious practices that buttressed their authority, 'Uthman began to sanction the establishment of autonomous Muslim communities throughout Hausaland.

His support among the Fulani was, however, uneven. Many of the Torodbe doubted 'Uthman's mission of reform, while others were comfortable enough at court to dislike the prospect of change. Many, however, supported the movement because their income was dependent upon the whims of their wealthy Hausa hosts since farming, trades, and commerce were seen as detracting from the pursuit of a religious life. Likewise, many of the Fulanin Gidda (settled Fulani) were unmoved by religious criticisms of a political and economic order though which they had become relatively successful. However, many Fulanin Gidda, who were desirous of more political power, also joined the jihadist movement. Conversely, the non-Muslim Baroji (pastoral Fulani), who were spread throughout Hausaland, remained largely separated from town life and maintained a symbiotic relationship with the Hausa peasantry. Nevertheless, *jangali* (cattle tax), forced military service, and restrictions on the use of water and grazing land often led the independent clan leaders to rise in sympathy with Usman.

Although the Sokoto jihad was waged primarily by Fulani-led independent armies, it also attracted many of the Hausa peasants, who were oppressed by slavery, excessive taxation, governmental corruption, and the imposition of customary rights that entitled the aristocracy to the pick of their daughters as well as their beasts of burden. Consequently, when 'Uthman taught of an Islam in which fellow Muslims would not be enslaved and government would be administered with social justice, he was also articulating Hausa discontent.

By the turn of the century there had been an alarming increase in the number of 'Uthman's followers in Gobir. In 1803, Sarkin Gobir Yunfa summoned 'Uthman to the palace and made an attempt on his life. The failure of this assassination attempt was ascribed to divine providence and, in the tradition of the Prophet Muhammad, the shehu, accompanied by his brother Abdullah and his son Muhammad Bello, resorted to flight. Still, it was not until Yunfa declared war on the Muslims in 1804 that the jihad began and 'Uthman became "commander of the faithful." In the military encounters that followed, however, Abdullah and Bello made most of the critical decisions.

In 1804 at Tabkin Kwatto, the shehu's followers, relying almost entirely on archers, defeated the numerically superior Gobirawa. Next, they attacked Alkalawa, Gobir's capital, but were defeated, losing over 2,000 of their best men. The shehu's forces then retreated to Zamfara, which they ultimately conquered. From Zamfara the jihadists moved to Gwandu, in southern Kebbi. The Gobirawa, aided by the Tuareg and the dissident Kebbawa and Zamfarawa, attacked Gwandu. The town was poorly fortified, but the hilly terrain was extremely difficult for the Gobirawa's heavy cavalry and Tuareg camel corps. The result was complete victory for the shehu's archers.

The flagbearers of the shehu invaded Zazzau in 1805. When the Sarkin Zazzau's son and heir, Makau, was surprised by the reformers on his way to a ceremonial prayer ground outside the city walls, he was forced to flee and the city of Zaria fell without a struggle. In 1806, after Kebbi and Zamfara had been subdued in the west, Bello proceeded to Katsina to reinforce the shehu's supporters there. A combined force of Fulani, Zamfarawa, and Kanawa defeated the forces of the Sarkin Katsina at Dankama. By 1807, the great city of Kano had also been captured. With the Kano, Zazzau, Katsina, Kebbi, and Zamfara firmly in the hands of the reformers, Gobir was completely surrounded. In 1808, Bello captured Alkalawa and Sarkin Gobir Yunfa was slain with all of his followers by his side.

With the fall of Gobir all of the Hausa states had become emirates of the caliphate, which was ultimately headquartered at Sokoto. However, other emirates had also been created: in the north, Ahir and Adar; in the south, Yauri, Gombe, Adamawa, and Bauchi; in the west, Gurma; and in the east (in areas formerly controlled by Bornu), Hadejia and Katagum. Consequently, when Bello became "commander of the faithful" upon the death of the shehu in 1817, the empire was divided, with Yauri and Gurma, in addition to most of Kebbi and its former provinces, becoming Abdullah's western sultanate of Gwandu. The bulk of the empire fell to Bello; his eastern sultanate included the former states of Gobir and Zamfara, which along with parts of Kebbi had been merged to form the metropolitan sultanate of Sokoto, as well as Kano, Katsina, Zazzau, Bauchi, Adamawa, Daura, Hadejia, and Ahir.

During this early period of expansion, the emirates of the newly formed Sokoto caliphate were relatively autonomous, polytheism persisted among the peasantry, and there were also unsubjugated non-Muslim enclaves within the caliphate's borders. Nevertheless, this vast empire, which stretched from Bornu in the east to Songhay in the west, united all of the Hausa states for the first time in their history, replacing their individual indigenous religious underpinnings with a common Islamic superstructure.

LAMONT DEHAVEN KING

See also: **'Uthman dan Fodio.**

Further Reading

Hiskett, Mervyn. *The Sword of Truth: The Life and Times of the Shehu Usman dan Fodio.* New York: Oxford University Press, 1973.

Johnston, Hugh Anthony Stephens. *The Fulani Empire of Sokoto.* London: Oxford University Press, 1967.

Last, David Murray. *The Sokoto Caliphate.* New York: Humanities Press, 1967.

———. "The Sokoto Caliphate and Borno." In *The UNESCO General History of Africa,* vol. 6, *Africa in the Nineteenth Century until the 1880s.* edited by J. Ajayi. Berkeley and Los Angeles: University of California Press, 1989.

Last, David Murray, and M. A. al-Haji. "Attempts at Defining a Muslim in Nineteenth Century Hausaland and Bornu." *Journal of the Historical Society of Nigeria* 2, no. 3 (1965): 231–240.

Martin, B. G. *Muslim Brotherhoods in Nineteenth Century Africa.* New York: Cambridge University Press, 1971.

Usman, Yusufu Bala. "The Transformation of Political Communities: Some Notes on the Perception of a Significant Dimension of the Sokoto Jihad." *In Studies in the History of the Sokoto Caliphate,* edited by Yusufu Bala Usman. Zaria, Nigeria: Ahmadu University Press, 1979.

Waldman, Marilyn Robinson. "The Fulani Jihad: A Reassessment." *Journal of African History* 6, no. 3 (1965): 333–355.

Sokoto Caliphate, Nineteenth Century

The Sokoto caliphate was situated mostly in present-day northern Nigeria and parts of southern Niger. It was founded as a result of the Fulani jihads (holy wars) in the first decades of the nineteenth century. By 1808 the Hausa states had been conquered, although the ruling dynasties retreated to the frontiers and built walled cities that remained independent. The more important of these independent cities included Abuja, where the ousted Zaria dynasty fled; Argungu, in the north, the new home of the Kebbi rulers; and Maradi, in present-day Niger, the retreat of the Katsina dynasty. Although

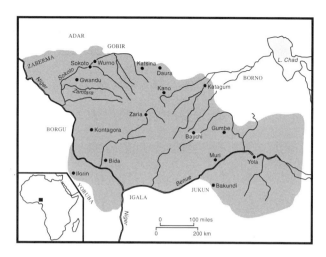

Sokoto empire, nineteenth century.

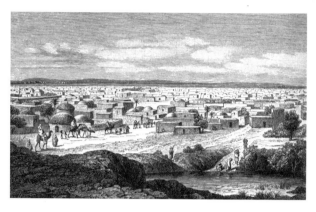

View of Kano, Sokoto, Nigeria, 1850s; sketch by Dr. Heinrich Barth. © Das Fotoarchiv.

the Borno *mai* was overthrown and Birni Gazargamu destroyed, Borno did not succumb. The reason, primarily, was that a cleric, Al Kanemi, fashioned a strong resistance that eventually forced those Fulani in Borno to retreat west and south. In the end, Al Kanemi overthrew the centuries-old Sayfawa Dynasty of Borno and established his own lineage as the new ruling house.

The new state that arose during 'Uthman dan Fodio's jihad came to be known as the Sokoto Caliphate, named after his capital at Sokoto, founded in 1809. The caliphate was a loose confederation of emirates that recognized the suzerainty of the commander of the faithful, the sultan. A dispute between Muhammad Bello and his uncle, Abdullahi, resulted in a nominal division of the caliphate into eastern and western divisions in 1812, although the supreme authority of Bello as caliph was upheld. The division was institutionalized through the creation of a twin capital at Gwandu, which was responsible for the western emirates as far as modern Burkina Faso and initially as far west as Massina in modern Mali. When 'Uthman dan Fodio died in 1817, he was succeeded by his son, Bello. The eastern emirates were more numerous and larger than the western ones, which reinforced the primacy of the caliph at Sokoto.

The allegiance sworn by Fulani elites and recognized by the caliph in the form of sending flags, as symbols of recognized powers and rights, constituted the elementary framework of the caliphate's leadership. It was these families that were to provide the Fulani aristocracy of the different emirates. The system of Wazirs, who served as a direct link between the caliph and the emirates, was initiated by 'Uthman dan Fodio already during his reign. Regular correspondence between the caliph and the emirates enabled a relatively unified policy for most of the century.

By the middle of the nineteenth century, there were 30 emirates and the capital district of Sokoto, which itself was a large and populous territory although technically not an emirate. All the important Hausa emirates, including Kano, the wealthiest and most populous, were directly under Sokoto's administration. Adamawa, in present day Cameroon, which was established by Fulani forced to evacuate Borno, was geographically the biggest, stretching far to the south and east of its capital at Yola. The influence of the caliphate reached the southern bank of the Niger when Ilorin became part of it in the 1830s. It was the Yoruba Oyo's cavalry, based in Ilorin and largely composed of Muslim slaves, that initiated this move when it swore allegiance to Sokoto following a series of internal clashes after 1817.

The caliphate remained divided into two major parts: former Islamic lands, composed mostly of Hausaland, and those lands on the peripheries that did not have an Islamic tradition, thus making their integration into the caliphate more difficult. As a result of the jihad, Islam was entrenched in Hausaland in the form of the Shari'a's introduction. However, the former Hausa society never fully abandoned its earlier approach to religion. The frontier states of Bauchi or Adamawa, for example, presented continuous problems up to the 1850s. An additional persisting internal problem of the caliphate was succession disputes. Although these were most often settled in the emirates themselves, there were open revolts defying the caliph's authority in Kano, for example.

Recent research, especially by Paul Lovejoy and Jan Hogendorn (1993), has called attention to slavery. Unlike in the earlier history of the region, when slaves were often used as currency, they now played an increasingly important role in the economic production of the caliphate. The percentage of slaves in the total population in several states was estimated at around 50 per cent by several European travelers, such as

Clapperton and Barth in the 1850s. It is estimated that by the 1890s the largest slave population of the world, about two million people, was concentrated in the territories of the Sokoto Caliphate. The use of slave labor was extensive, especially in agriculture. The growth of small plantations (*rinji*) occurred around the newly established core cities and commercial centers, like Zaria, Kano, and Gwandu. In the later period of the caliphate, slave settlements (*tungazi*) were established in Nupe, a phenomenon that attracted much attention from European visitors and traders and would eventually provide the *casus belli* for European conquest starting in 1897. While the rinji functioned as a small, private owned estate, the tungazi concentrated a dense population in small region of scattered villages. The agricultural sector produced goods like sorghum, millet, and shea butter. The most important aspect of the caliphate's economy was, however, its textile industry, also based on the slave labor of cotton plantations. In addition, the salt and livestock trades became more prominent by the late nineteenth century.

'Uthman dan Fodio's jihad created the largest empire in Africa since the fall of Songhai in 1591. By the middle of the nineteenth century, when the Sokoto Caliphate was at its greatest extent, it stretched 1,500 kilometers, from Dori in modern Burkina Faso to southern Adamawa in Cameroon. In present-day Nigeria, it covered the Nupe lands, Ilorin in northern Yorubaland, and much of the Benue River Valley. The jihad, and subsequently the states of the Sokoto Caliphate, influenced the political and social development of the region significantly. In addition, 'Uthman dan Fodio's jihad provided the inspiration for a series of related holy wars in other parts of the savanna and the Sahel that led to the foundation of Islamic states in Senegal, Mali, Côte d'Ivoire, Chad, the Central African Republic, and Sudan. The immediate states of the caliphate functioned as the most important polities in the nineteenth century and played a major economic role in agriculture, the labor movement, and the reinstitutionalization of slavery. They were also a key element in the arguments of the British for conquering the caliphate in the first years of the twentieth century.

LÁSZLÓ MÁTHÉ-SHIRES

Further Reading

Last, Murray. " 'Injustice' and Legitimacy in the Early Sokoto Caliphate." In *People and Empires in African History: Essays in Memory of Michael Crowder.* edited by J. F. Ade Ajayi and J. D. Y. Peel. London: Longman, 1992.

Lovejoy, Paul E. "The Characteristics of Plantations in the Nineteenth-Century Sokoto Caliphate (Islamic West Africa)." *American Historical Review*, no. 84 (1979): 1267–1292.

Lovejoy, Paul E. *Transformations in Slavery: A History of Slavery in Africa.* Cambridge: Cambridge University Press, 1997.

Lovejoy, Paul E., and Jan S. Hogendorn. *Slow Death for Slavery: The Course of Abolition in Northern Nigeria, 1897–1936.* Cambridge: Cambridge University Press, 1993.

Miles, William F. S. *Hausaland Divided—Colonialism and Independence in Nigeria and Niger.* Ithaca, N.Y.: Cornell University Press, 1994.

Soldiers, African: Overseas

Virtually every colonial power in Africa maintained a standing African army for internal security. Colonial forces cost only a fraction of their European counterparts and helped reduce the overall cost of colonial rule. France, Britain, Belgium, Portugal, and Germany all maintained such armies, but only Britain and France employed African soldiers overseas in significant numbers.

Although these African soldiers have often been described as mercenaries, many were coerced into joining colonial armies. This was particularly true in France's colonial African army, the Tirailleurs Sénégalais. Meaning "sharpshooters" or "riflemen," the *tirailleurs* were a branch of France's greater overseas colonial forces known as the Troupes de Marine. Created by Napoleon III in 1857, the Tirailleurs relied almost entirely on lottery-based conscription to select recruits in West and Equatorial Africa. French recruiters justified the practice under the doctrine of assimilation, which obliged service to France in return for the "civilizing" benefits of empire.

Over the course of World War I, approximately 170,000 Africans of the Tirailleurs Sénégalais served on the battlefields of France. They fought in segregated units until 1917, when mounting casualties and mutinies in French units forced French commanders to split them up among units. With casualty rates approaching 17 per cent, approximately 29,000 Africans died in France during the conflict. France again relied on conscripted tirailleurs when threatened by the Germans during World War II. Approximately 200,000 Africans served in the regular, Vichy, and Free French forces, and roughly 25,000 died during the war. During the German invasion of 1940, approximately 15,000 of the tirailleurs were taken prisoner when France fell. The Nazis executed many of these men in retaliation for France's decision to garrison the Rhineland with African troops in the 1920s. Tirailleurs stationed in French Equatorial Africa comprised a large part of General Charles de Gaulle's French forces that fought in North Africa, Italy, and France later in the war, and French generals continued to rely on them into the 1950s, when 18,000 Africans fought in France's failed effort to keep Vietnam within the empire.

In comparison, Britain was much less willing to use African soldiers overseas. While the French doctrine of assimilation justified conscription, Britain's governing ideology of indirect rule was much more restrictive. Under the terms of Frederick Lugard's Dual Mandate, Britain committed itself to protection of "less advanced" African "tribes." Christian missionaries argued that Britain had no right to involve Africans in foreign wars, and colonial officials worried that military service would breakdown the "tribal" units that were the cornerstone of indirect rule. Thus, African soldiers in Britain's combat units had to be volunteers, and only noncombatant military laborers could be conscripted. In reality, however, British recruiters often relied on African chiefs and headmen to coerce recruits into joining the army.

While the Tirailleurs Sénégalais were drawn from all of French Africa, Britain's colonial African forces were divided into the Royal West African Frontier Force (RWAFF), the King's African Rifles (KAR) in East Africa and the Northern Rhodesia Regiment. Settlers opposed arming the African population and succeeded in keeping the South African and Rhodesian armies all-European. This opposition helped ensure that Britain did not use African combat soldiers in Europe during World War I, and the only Africans in the European theater during the conflict were longshoreman from the South African Native Labour Contingent. Conversely, Britain sent roughly one-fifth of its approximately 500,000 African soldiers overseas during World War II. Faced with isolation in Europe and the loss of extensive territory in the Far East, British generals relied heavily on African manpower. The Axis threat silenced temporarily the moral arguments against embroiling Africans in foreign wars. The African Auxiliary Pioneer Corps and the South African Military Labour Corps provided frontline labor and military garrisons in the Middle East. Assuming that Africans were natural jungle fighters, British generals also committed three and a half infantry divisions of the RWAFF and KAR to fight the Japanese in Burma in 1944. Overall, approximately 15,000 African soldiers were killed during the war. The relative success of the African forces, coupled with the loss of India in 1948, convinced British military planners to send African soldiers back to the Middle East and Southeast Asia in the 1950s. In 1951, members of the KAR and the Northern Rhodesia Regiment fought communist guerrillas in Malaya, while the East African Pioneers ran Britain's bases in the Suez Canal.

There has been considerable debate over the impact of overseas service on African veterans of both colonial armies. On the whole, these men had training, experience, and wealth that set them apart from their civilian peers. Many had interacted freely with European comrades and were far less tolerant of racial discrimination. During World War I, the Tirailleurs fought in part because they expected political and social equality in return for their service. They were profoundly disappointed when they returned home, but Blaise Diagne, the first African to sit in the French Chamber of Deputies, did convince the French government to give them exemptions from forced labor, and hiring preferences for civilian jobs. After World War II, most French African veterans had the right to vote. As 5 per cent of the total electorate, they became a potent political force in the last decades of the colonial era. Britain, on the other hand, did not make similar concessions to its African ex-servicemen and instead followed a policy of "reabsorption" that sought to reintegrate veterans into rural African society with a minimum of disruption. Although former members of the RWAFF did play a leading role in riots in the Gold Coast in 1948, for the most part, veterans were largely absent from nationalist and anticolonial movements in the British colonies. British combat veterans were a much smaller percentage of the population than in the French colonies and, on the whole, were limited to seeking economic concessions rather than political change.

TIMOTHY PARSONS

See also: **World War I: Survey; World War I: North and Saharan Africa; World War II: French West Africa, Equatorial Africa; World War II: North Africa; World War II: Sub-Saharan Africa: Economic Impact.**

Further Reading

Brelsford, W. V. (ed.). *Story of the Northern Rhodesia Regiment.* Lusaka, Zambia: Government Printer, 1954.

Clayton, Anthony. *France, Soldiers and Africa.* London: Brassey's Defence, 1988.

Echenberg, Myron. *Colonial Conscripts: The Tirailleurs Sénégalais in French West Africa, 1857–1960.* Portsmouth, N.H.: Heinemann, 1991.

Lawler, Nancy Ellen. *Soldiers of Misfortune: Ivoirien Tirailleurs of World War II.* Athens, Ohio: Ohio University Press, 1992.

Parsons, Timothy. *The African Rank-and-File: Social Implications of Colonial Service in the King's African Rifles, 1902–1964.* Portsmouth, N.H.: Heinemann, 1999.

Solomonid Dynasty: *See* Ethiopia: Solomonid Dynasty, 1270–1550.

Somalia: Pastoralism, Islam, Commerce, Expansion: To 1800

Although pastoralism played a large part in the economy of Somalis and other related peoples, Somalis, being also coastal people, had always traded with other peoples in the vicinity of the Red Sea, the Gulf of

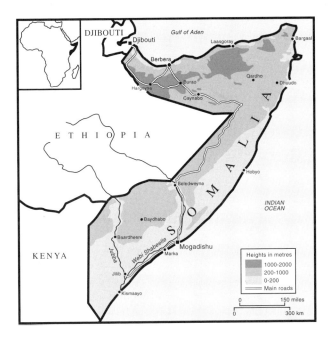

Somalia.

Aden, India, and as far east as what later became Indonesia, especially after the spread of Islam to those parts of Asia. Thus, the same Somalis who had been characterized as mostly nomads had always practiced varied economic activities, depending on the layout of the land. On the coast, they were traders, seafarers, and entrepreneurs, although still without an emperor or a highly centralized government; in the interior, they practiced animal husbandry and agriculture where conditions permitted.

Culturally, as Cushites, they had a monotheistic religion whose central deity was the *waaq* (sky god), as well as spirits of two types: good spirits called the *ayaan* or *ayaana*, and evil spirits called the *busho* or *bushi*. Thus, it was easy for them to espouse the monotheistic religions that sprouted from the Semitic Middle East. It may be surmised that the first religion to arrive from the Middle East was Judaism, judging from its survival among the Falasha of Ethiopia. This was to be followed by Christianity, and centuries later by Islam. However, nothing has survived among Somalis that has much in common with Judaism. Likewise, no noticeable vestiges of ancient Christianity remain among Somalis, except for a ceremony in which people make crosses on their foreheads when making a pilgrimage to one of the holiest Somali saints, Shaykh Yusuf al-Kownin (literally, "he of the two worlds"). Shaykh Yusuf al-Kownin invented a system of vulgarizing the reading of Arabic, and thus the Qu'ran, still in use today.

There is no exact date for the arrival of Islam among Somalis; however, given the proximity with Arabia,

and the fact that Muslims first arrived in the area during the lifetime of the Prophet Muhammad himself, it can be estimated that Islam arrived in the seventh century. However, the period between the tenth and fourteenth centuries corresponds to an era in which Muslim sultanates such as Ifat, known later as Adal and based in the Northern city of Zeilah (itself one of the most ancient coastal towns in northeast Africa), developed and prospered. By the fourteenth century, Muslim Somalis were an expanding people and were propagating the Muslim faith to their non-Muslim neighbors, notably the Oromo.

Somalis not only spread Islam, but also contributed to Islamic literature and jurisprudence. For example, Imam al-Zayla'i al-Hanafi, from the city of Zayla' (Zeilah), produced *Tabyin al-haqa'iq*, a well-known six-volume work, used in particular by the Hanafi school of Islamic jurisprudence. His student, Fakhr Abdalla ibn Yusuf ibn Muhammad ibn Ayub ibn Musa al-Hanafi az-Zaila'I, also wrote a reference work for Islamic jurisprudence in the fourteenth century (Hersi 1984, p.134). In addition, Somali scholars from Zeilah were among the top scholars and teachers in Yemen from the thirteenth to the fifteenth centuries (Hersi 1984, p.132). Other Somali literati wrote a number of religious eulogies, or *manaaqib*, in praise of various saints. Thus, Somalis, far from being a mostly oral society, were a society with scholars who wrote not in their own tongue, Somali, but in Arabic, the liturgical language.

Under Islam, the various Muslim city-states prospered by trade and Somalis built sizable cities. By the fourteenth century, Somali clans, such as the Ajuuraan clan, had migrated to the southern areas of today's Somalia, wresting control from the Oromo and Bantu-Swahili peoples in the interior of the south. In 1331, the famous Arab traveler, Ibn Battatu, visited the port cities of Zeilah in the north and Mogadishu in the south. He described the populations of these cities as Berbers, who spoke the Berber language (medieval Arabs knew Somalis and Afars as Berbers).

Eventually, the growing importance and prosperity of Ifat would warrant fearful reactions from the Christian Amhara-Tigrean highlanders. Thus, from 1415 to 1543, there was continuous warfare and rivalry between the Christians and Muslims of the Horn. In 1415, Negus Yeshaq, king of the Christians, invaded Zeilah and killed its ruler; Yeshaq's court jester would compose a victory poem, which gives us the first recorded occurrence of the word *Somali*. In 1530, Somalis and Afars, under the command of Iman Ahmed Gurey (known to the Christian Amhara-Tigreans as Gragne), would conquer all of the Christian highlands except for a few hilltops, as is well chronicled by Shihad Ad-Din, in his *Futuh al-Habash* (*The Conquest*

1403

of Abyssinia). However, by then the Portuguese had rounded the Cape of Good Hope and found the way to India; they would come to the rescue of the Christian king. Armed with superior cannons, they burned and sacked prosperous coastal cities such as Berbera, Zeilah, Brava, and Mogadishu, in their efforts to appropriate for themselves the Indian Ocean trade. Their efforts would disrupt the ancient trade between Africa and Asia, and throw the coastal Somali towns into a downward spiral of decline.

By the eighteenth century, Somali migrations had changed the demographics of most of the southern areas, especially along the coastal Benadir region, which includes the formerly Swahili cities of Mogadishu, Merca, and Brava. As a result, we have today the coastal Benadir people who speak a variety of Somali known as Coastal Somali, which is a kind of a creole or "contact" language, after their Swahili tongues disappeared completely save in the locality of Brava; and, around Kismayo, there is the tiny Bajuni community that still speaks a language of Bantu origin. In the interior, to the west of Benadir Coast, Somalis made contact with populations of Oromo origin that had preceded the Somalis in the area, as well as other peoples—notably, leftovers from the Oromo expansion, such as Bantu agriculturalists and hunter-gatherers, the latter being the most ancient inhabitants of the southern areas. The admixture of Oromo populations and migrating Somalis gave rise to today's Maay people, as well as other minority groups such as the Jiido, Garre, Dabarre, and Tunni, whose languages, despite strong Somali influence, still lack the sounds from the pharynx that are characteristic of the Somali language.

MOHAMED DIRIYE ABDULLAHI

See also: **Arab and Islamic World, Africa in; Islam: Eastern Africa; Religion, History of.**

Further Reading

Cassanelli, Lee V. *The Shaping of Somali Society: Reconstructing the History of a Pastoral People, 1600–1900.* Philadelphia: University of Pennsylvania Press, 1982.

Castagno, Margaret. *Historical Dictionary of Somalia.* Metuchen, N.J.: Scarecrow Press, 1975.

Diriye Abdullahi, Mohamed. *Culture and Customs of Somalia.* Westport, Conn.: Greenwood Press, 2001.

———. *Parlons somali.* Paris: L'Harmattan, 1996.

———. "Le somali, dialectes et histoire." Ph.D. diss., Université de Montréal, 2000.

Hersi, A. "The Arab Factor in Somali History." Ph.D. diss., University of California–Los Angeles, 1977.

Lewis, I. M. *Pastoral Democracy: A Study of Pastoralism among the Northern Somali of the Horn of Africa.* London: Oxford University Press, 1961.

Loughran, John, Katheryne Loughran, John Johnson, and Said S. Samatar (eds.). *Somalia in Word and Image.* Washington, D.C.: Foundation for Cross-Cultural Understanding, 1986.

Samatar, Said S., and David Laitin. *Somalia: A Nation in Search of a State.* Boulder, Colo.: Westview Press, 1987.

Somalia: Nineteenth Century

As the nineteenth century came into view, Somalis were, as they had always been, "a race of fierce and turbulent republicans" (Burton 1987), which meant that they did not have a centralized form of government. In the interior, pastoral clans, structured along a set of alliances and obeying a set of common laws known as *heer*, were engaged in a pattern of transhumance, still in existence today.

However, these same clans would, when needed, raise a pastoral parliament, or *guurti*, to discuss issues of common concern to the clan or group of clans. Complimenting the heer was another set of rules that the Somalis obeyed: Islamic law. The practice of Islamic law was in the hands of the *wadaad*, the man of religion, immune from the feuds of the clan warriors, the *warranle*. These two sets of laws held also sway over city folk who in most cases, except for some families in on the Benadir coast, were also members of the clans mostly through birth, but also sometimes through marriage and adoption.

Along the coasts and occasionally in the hinterland, nineteenth-century Somalis had many cities and villages. Some of the cities were actually city-states with a governor, a corps of law-enforcement officials consisting of soldiers, and a *qadi*—a judge with a stipend. The inhabitants of these coastal cities and villages were able mariners who sailed their own boats to the Arab world and India. The main raison d'être for these cities since ancient times had been commerce, both with the countryside and with the outside world in the Red Sea, the Gulf of Aden, and the Indian Ocean, and as far east as what later would become Indonesia. Among the exports were frankincense and myrrh, the trade of which dates back to the time of the ancient Egyptians. Additionally, at some during the Greco-Roman era, the coastal towns were entrepôts for precious products from India, especially cinnamon; in turn, the country was named "terra cinnamore," though no cinnamon cultivation is known among Somalis.

During trade time, which coincided with the cool winter months, northern coastal towns such Zeilah and Berbera would be transformed into teaming cosmopolitan towns, as Somalis, Afars, and flocks of sailor-merchants from Yemen, Oman, the Persian Gulf, and India mingled with the locals. From the interior would arrive camel caravans laden with coffee from the Highlands of the Amhara-Tigreans and the Oromo, Somali ghee (clarified butter); ostrich feathers, Arabic gum, and ivory. Other produce exported notably in the northern coastal cities for millennia were such famous goods as frankincense and myrrh, whose trade had already given the land the name Terra Aromatica ("the land of aromatic plants") in ancient times. The imports brought in by both Somali and foreign boats were usually rice, clothing, and dates.

In the south, trade was similar, except that textiles were an important export industry until the textile export trade was killed in the nineteenth century by cheap American cotton clothing, from slave- produced cotton; this was variously known as Wilaayaati (in Arabic, "the States") and Maraykaani ("American").

In the nineteenth century, while most Somalis lived just as they had done centuries before, politically the era of strong city-states and sultanates such as Zeilah and Mogadishu was over. In 1875, Ismail Pasha, the Egyptian *khedive* (viceroy), in a scheme to carve out an Egyptian empire in Northeast Africa, took control of the northern ports, with British encouragement; his troops even went inland to capture the city-state of Harrar, one of the most historic Muslim cities in the region. However, the Egyptians evacuated their Somali possessions in 1885, and in 1887, Emperor Menelik of Ethiopia attacked Harrar, defeating its defenders in a way reminiscent of past Muslim-Christian wars in the region. In the south, the Omanis of Zanzibar came to have a rather nominal suzerainty over Mogadishu. All in all, the major events of the nineteenth century were the arrival of spy-explorers from the main Europeans and the expansionism undertaken by the Amhara-Tigreans, encouraged by the armaments provided to them their Christian brethren; this would lead to a division of the Somali lands and the beginning of the colonial era for Somalis.

With the opening of the Suez Canal in 1867, Britain became more interested in the northern Somali coasts, especially after the British established Aden in Yemen as a coal station for their ships bound for India and the Far East and an outpost for monitoring the region after the defeat of the Mahdist revolt in the Sudan. Britain then added the northern region, called the British Protectorate of Somaliland, to its dominions so it could supply its Aden garrison with fresh mutton meat from the Somali coast. In the south, Italy, with British acquiescence and assistance, established its colony of Italian Somalia whose consolidation would end in the beginning of the twentieth century, because Britain was more afraid of Germany and France.

Other Somali areas were carved between Emperor Menelik, who saw Europeans as his coreligionists and sought help from by arguing that his kingdom was an island surrounded by Muslims. In the end, he was able to acquire, with Europeans arms, a large tract inhabited by Muslim Somalis, Afars, and Oromos, as well as other non-Muslim peoples. Britain also occupied another region inhabited by Somalis and Oromos in the extreme south and incorporated into its colony of Kenya. The British would call that southernmost Somali region the Northern Frontier District so that it could be designated a special region, under different regulations, whose aim was to halt the advance of Somalis and Muslims in the region. In the extreme North, France set up its French Somali Coast Colony, in a territory inhabited by Somalis and Afars, including the ports of Tadjoura and Obock.

As the twentieth century dawned, Somalis were living under five regimes; this division of Somali territories would give birth to the sentiments of a divided nation that became known as Somali irredentism.

MOHAMED DIRIYE ABDULLAHI

Further Reading

Burton, Richard. *First Footsteps in East Africa* (1856). Reprint, New York: Dover, 1987.

Cassanelli, Lee V. *The Shaping of Somali Society: Reconstructing the History of a Pastoral People, 1600–1900*. Philadelphia: University of Pennsylvania Press, 1982.

Diriye Abdullahi, Mohamed. *Culture and Customs of Somalia*. Westport, Conn.: Greenwood Press, 2001.

———. *Parlons somali*. Paris: L'Harmattan, 1996.

Hersi, A. "The Arab Factor in Somali History." Ph.D. Diss., University of California Berkeley and Los Angeles, 1977.

Hess, Robert L. *Italian Colonialism in Somalia*. Chicago: University of Chicago Press, 1966.

Lewis, I. M. *Pastoral Democracy: A Study of Pastoralism among the Northern Somali of the Horn of Africa*. London: Oxford University Press, 1961.

Samatar, Said S., and David Laitin, *Somalia: A Nation in Search of a State*. Boulder, Colo.: Westview Press, 1987.

Somalia: Hassan, Muhammad Abdile and Resistance to Colonial Conquest

On April 7, 1864, Muhammad Abdile Hassan was born at Kob Faradod, about 180 miles southeast of Berbera. At an early age he became interested in the teachings of the Prophet Muhammad and, in 1897, became an Islamic teacher. Muhammad Abdile quickly established a reputation as a religious scholar and gained the honorary title of *shaykh*. In 1891, he embarked on a long journey that took him to Harrar and Mogadishu, two centers of Islamic learning. In 1894, Muhammad Abdile made his *hajj*, or pilgrimage, to Mecca, where he joined the fundamentalist Salihiya sect of the Ahmadiya brotherhood.

The following year he returned to Berbera, and established a Qu'ranic school. Apart from preaching strict adherence to precepts of Islam, Muhammad Abdile condemned the growing influence of the colonial powers and Western missionaries. Such attitudes gained few adherents among Berbera's Somalis, who belonged to the more liberal Qadariyah order. After leaving Berbera in frustration, he moved to the interior and settled among the Dolbonhanta people. At Bohotleh, his teachings found a more receptive audience. Muhammad Abdile's influence also spread to the Darod clan, which inhabited parts of Ethiopia and British and Italian Somaliland. By April 1899, his followers numbered about 3,000. He claimed he was the *Mahdi*, or chosen one, who would unify the Muslims and lead them to victory over the Western infidels.

As his power and authority grew, Muhammad Abdile became increasingly critical of British colonial rule. British officials feared that he wanted to establish a presence in southeastern British Somaliland in preparation for a military campaign against them. Reports of Muhammad Abdile's mystical and supernatural powers provoked further suspicion among the British, who named him the "mad mullah." After occupying Burao, a village between Bohotleh and Berbera, Muhammad Abdile declared a jihad (holy war) against the British infidel and their Somali supporters. In early 1900, his dervish followers launched numerous attacks in British Somaliland and the Ogaden region of eastern Ethiopia, which caused trade in both areas to come to a halt.

To end dervish marauding, the British mounted four military expeditions. The first occurred in 1901, and involved some 15,000 Ethiopians, 1,000 Somalis, and 200 Anglo-Indian troops. After two encounters with the British, Muhammed Abdile withdrew to the friendly Majeerteen Sultanate. In February 1902, the British assembled a 2,300-man force that the dervishes attacked at Galcaio. Heavy losses forced the British to retreat to Bohotleh.

The third expedition, launched in January 1903, involved a two-pronged attack. Some 5,000 Ethiopians left Harrar, moved down the Webi Valley, and repulsed a dervish attack at Beledweyne. A 1,900-man British column landed at Obbia and proceeded inland while another 2,000-man British column marched southwest out of Berbera. However, fatigue and logistics problems forced the British to retreat to the region between Bohotleh and Berbera. Meanwhile, the dervishes occupied the Nogal Valley.

In January 1904, the British deployed nearly 8,000 troops who occupied Galcaio and then scored a victory over the dervishes at Jidbali by killing at least 1,000 of them. The survivors retreated to the Majeerteen Sultanate and eventually to Illig, from where they were expelled by a 500-man British force.

On March 3, 1905, with his forces in disarray, Muhammad Abdile and Giulio Pestalozza, the Italian consul at Aden, concluded a peace agreement known as the Ilig Accord. For more than three years, there was an uneasy peace, frequently interrupted by dervish raids, in northern Somalia. In September 1908, however, Muhammad Abdile launched a series of attacks in British and Italian Somaliland and in the Ogaden. On November 12, 1909, the British colonial government received orders from London to evacuate the interior and concentrate its forces in coastal towns. The withdrawal accelerated the growth of dervish influence throughout British Somaliland.

British and Italian strategy concentrated on facilitating local opposition to the dervishes. In December 1910, for example, the Warsangeli (in British Somaliland) and the Majeerteen (in Italian Somaliland) concluded a defense pact against Muhammad Abdile. Subsequent Warsangeli-Majeerteen military operations drove the dervishes out of Italian Somaliland. Muhammad Abdile's followers fled to British Somaliland and occupied Bohotleh. In January 1913, he moved his headquarters to a fortress in Taleh, where he remained for the next seven years.

The outbreak of World War I afforded Muhammad Abdile the opportunity to improve relations with Addis Ababa. With the British occupied elsewhere, he received scores of Muslim Ethiopian leaders. In April 1916, the Ethiopian Emperor, Lij Iyasu, announced his conversion to Islam, which raised the prospect of an alliance between Ethiopia and Muhammad Abdile. To achieve this goal, the two leaders explored the possibility of a marriage compact. Although the Ethiopian emperor sent a mission to Taleh to get the bride, the scheme floundered after Christian elements in Ethiopia deposed Lij Iyasu, who fled into the Danakil country.

After the war, however, the British government decided to renew military operations against the dervishes. In October 1919, London approved an operation that included the 700-man Somaliland Camel Corps, a 700-man composite battalion (the 2nd and 6th Regiments of the King's African Rifles), a 400-man half battalion (the 1st and 101st Grenadiers of the Indian Army), a 1,500-man irregular Somali tribal levy, and 300 *illaloes* ("scouts"—though these men were actually intelligence agents). In support of this ground force, the British deployed the Royal Air Force's Z Unit, which had 12 aircraft and 6 spare machines. The king's ships *Odin*, *Clio*, and *Ark Royal* also were active off the Somali coast.

The expedition, which lasted 21 days, ended on February 12, 1920, when British forces occupied the dervish stronghold at Taleh. Muhammad Abdile and a small group of his followers eluded capture by fleeing into the Ogaden. A 3,000-member British tribal levy pursued the dervishes and, in late July, reached Muhammad Abdile's camp near Gorrahei on the Fanfan River. Once again, he escaped and went to the Imi region at the headwaters of the Shebelle River.

Suffering from pneumonia, Muhammad Abdile died sometime between November 1920 and January 1921.

THOMAS P. OFCANSKY

Further Reading

Beachey, Ray. *The Warrior Mullah: The Horn Aflame 1892–1920*. London: Bellew, 1990.

Gray, Randal. "Bombing the 'Mad Mullah'—1920." *Journal of the Royal United Services Institute for Defence Studies* 125, no. 4 (1980): 41–46.

Hess, Robert L. "'The Mad Mullah' and Northern Somalia." *Journal of African History* 5, no. 3 (1964): 415–433.

———. "The Poor Man of God: Muhammad Abdullah Hassan." In *Leadership in Eastern Africa: Six Political Biographies*, edited by Norman R. Bennett. Boston: Boston University Press, 1974.

Jardine, Douglas J. *The Mad Mullah of Somaliland*. London: Herbert Jenkins, 1923.

Jennings, J. Willes. *With the Abyssinians in Somaliland*. London: Hodder and Stoughton, 1905.

Sheik-Abdi, Abdi. *Divine Madness: Mohammed Abdulle Hassan (1856–1920)*. London: Zed, 1992.

Silberman, Leo. "The 'Mad' Mullah: Hero of Somali Nationalism." *History Today* 10, no. 8 (1960): 523–534.

Somalia: Independence, Conflict, and Revolution

The modern history of Somalia began in the 1880s, when Britain, France, Italy, and Ethiopia occupied Somali-inhabited territories in the Horn of Africa. Britain established the colony of British Somaliland in the north, while Italy occupied the southern region, which came to be known as Italian Somaliland. The French established a colony around the port of Djibouti on the Red Sea, and Ethiopia occupied the Ogaden region in the interior. In 1960 British and Italian Somaliland merged and gained independence as the Somali Republic. The French colony became the independent nation of Djibouti in 1975 while other Somali areas were incorporated by Ethiopia and Kenya. Somalia has never given up its claims to those territories and has supported local rebel movements seeking to unite all Somali under one flag.

Somalia has been unique in that it is the only country in Africa that is ethnically and culturally homogenous. Virtually all citizens speak the same language, claim the same ethnicity, and follow the same religion (Islam). Many thought that the country had a solid foundation for political stability, but this was not to be the case.

Somalia was a parliamentary democracy until 1969, when the president was assassinated in a military coup led by Mohamed Siad Barré, who became the head of a new socialist state. Siad Barré also continued the irredentist policies of his predecessors by demanding the incorporation of all Somali speakers in a "Greater Somalia." By the mid-1970s, a single-party state had been created. Henceforth a combination of factors set Somalia on its tragic course toward catastrophe. These included the authoritarian character of Barré's government, compounded by the narrowing of the political base of the regime in terms of clan support; a number of wars with Kenya and Ethiopia (particularly, the disastrous war with Ethiopia in 1977 and 1978 over the Somali dominated Ogaden region of Eastern Ethiopia and the resulting influx of thousands of refugees from Ogden); and a regional arms race fueled by the superpower rivalry of the Cold War leading to increasing militarization of the country.

As economic, social, and political conditions deteriorated in the 1970s and early 1980s, traditional clan loyalties came to the fore, thus fragmenting the Somali nation. In the aftermath of the Ogaden war, many clans, having for a long time felt themselves deprived, especially in view of the preeminence in government of Siad Barré's southern Marehan (Darod) clan, began to assert their traditional clan autonomy by resisting the government. By 1988, the country was in the throes of a civil war. In May 1988, the northern-based Somali National Movement (SNM) launched a military campaign by capturing the northwestern town of Burao. The government reacted in the most savage way, butchering the northern Ishaak clan members and their livestock. Hargeysa, Somalia's second largest town, was virtually razed by government forces. As many as 50,000 people lost their lives in the fighting and an estimated 500,000 were driven from their homes; some 370,000 fled to Ethiopia.

In central Somalia, a movement drawing its main support from the Hawiye clan, the United Somali Congress (USC) also took up arms against Barré's government, forming an alliance with the SNM and the Ogaden-based Somali Patriotic Movement in 1990. After much fighting, in January 1991 Barré's army crumbled and he fled from Mogadishu, the capital. A large quantity of heavy weaponry fell into the hands of the victorious factions.

The USC, which took control of Mogadishu after the fall of Barré, was itself divided into several factions based on different subclans of Hawiye. The two main rival factions—one headed by General Mohamed Farah Aidid, who had led USC's military operations against Barré's government, and the other headed by Ali Mahdi Mohamed—soon became engaged in violent conflict. From 1991, Somalia was torn apart by battles among rival militias and by widespread looting and banditry in the absence of a central government. Rival factions seized or fought over different regions of the country. And at a conference in Burao in May 1991, the SNM proclaimed an independent state in the northeast known as Somaliland, the region formerly administered by Britain until independence. Even though many efforts at mediation were undertaken, the crisis in the country only deepened. From November 1991, a four-month-long war between the forces of Aidid and Ali Mahdi led to the killing of an estimated 25,000 civilians in and around Mogadishu. The city's estimated 500,000 inhabitants were left without even the most basic services.

The international community's collective conscience was sufficiently stirred by the human suffering in Somali, thus leading to the United Nations' involvement, which evolved through three different phases: the period of the first United Nations Operations in Somalia (UNOSOM-I) through much of 1992; the joint UN-U.S. Operation Restore Hope from December 1992 to May 1993; and UNOSOM-II from May 1993 to March 1995. The basic objectives of these operations were apparently humanitarian—that is, to protect aid workers and to ensure that food and medicine reached those in need without being intercepted by warring factions.

In mid-March, a national reconciliation conference held in Addis Ababa, Ethiopia, agreed to the establishment of a 74-member Transitional National Council as the supreme authority in Somalia with a mandate to hold elections within two years. The agreement, however, was violated and fighting between pro-Aidid and pro-Mahdi factions escalated. The UN forces were withdrawn from Somalia early in 1995. Although Operation Restore Hope and UNOSOM-II saved lives (as had the earlier UNOSOM-I), they also caused unnecessary loss of life and destruction, and were heavily criticized. Most of 1995 and 1996 witnessed intensification of faction fighting. General Aidid himself died in fighting on August 1, 1996. His son, Hussain Aidid, replaced him.

In December 1996 representatives of some 26 Somali factions, except the SNA, held protracted negotiations in Sodere, Ethiopia, and in January 1997 agreed to the formation of a 41-member National Salvation Council (NSC) with an 11-member executive committee and a 5-member joint chairmanship committee to act as interim government to draft a transition constitution and organize a national reconciliation conference etc. However, the Aidid faction rejected the agreement. International mediations efforts nonetheless continued. In December 1997, some 26 Somali factions signed an accord in Cairo establishing an end to all hostilities and for the eventual formation of a transitional government charged with holding general elections within three years A national reconciliation conference was to be held in Somalia in February 1998, but it was repeatedly postponed.

In August 2000, senior authority figures, including clan elders, named Abdulkassim Salat Hassan president. A transitional government was set up, with the aim of making peace among the various warring factions. However, as the three-year deadline approached, Hassan's administration had made little progress toward the goals of unification and peace.

KAY MATHEWS

See also: **Somalia: Barré, Mohamad Siad, Life and Government of; Somalia: 1990 to the Present.**

Further Reading

Lewis, I. M. "*A Modern History of Somalia: Rhetoric and Reality.*" London: Zed, 1988.

Omar, Mohamed Ossman. "*Somalia: A Nation Driven to Despair.*" New Delhi: Somali Publications, 1996.

Samatar, A. I. "Destruction of State and Society in Somalia: Tribal Convention." *Journal of Modern African Studies* 30, no. 4 (1992).

Thakur, Ramesh. "From Peace-keeping to Peace-Enforcement: The UN Operation in Somalia." *Journal of Modern African Studies* 32, no. 3 (1994).

United Nations. "*The United Nations and Somalia 1992–1996.*" New York: United Nations, 1998.

Somalia: Barré, Mohamed Siad, Life and Government of
Former President of Somalia

Mohamed Siad Barré (*c.*1910–1995), was born to a nomadic family that raised camels, sheep, and goats. His birthplace was a nomad settlement in the countryside of what is today the town of Shilaabo in the Somali region of Ethiopia (Greenfield). He had no formal schooling at all, like most Somalis of his time. When he reached adolescence, he left his nomadic settlement to seek a career in the colonial police in Italian-ruled Somalia. When the Italians were forced out of Somalia by the British forces during World War II and their colony was placed under a British military administration, he succeeded in being retained and sent to a training camp in British Kenya.

After Somalia was restored to an Italian trusteeship by the United Nations in 1950, Barré became head of the Special Branch of Police, an intelligence agency, the main aim of which was to spy on Somalis agitating for independence. In 1960 Barré and all the junior officers from the colonial police were promoted to senior commanding officers, in a bid to outrank young officers from British Somaliland, who had actually graduated from prestigious British military academies. This catapulted Barré into the position of second in command of the newly created army of the Somali Republic. After the death of General Daud in 1965, Barré was confirmed as chief of staff of the Somali army.

On October 16, 1969, President Abdirashid was assassinated; five days later the army staged a coup d'état. The officers agreed on Barré as a transitional compromise figure, seeing him as an older individual who would be easy to manipulate, and easy to dispose of later.

A group calling itself the Supreme Revolutionary Council (SRC) arose, with Barré as chair president of the Somali Republic, now renamed in the same leftist fashion as the Somali Democratic Republic. However, cognizant of their lack of experience in civilian rule, the junta appointed a 15-member Council of Secretaries to run the different ministries and departments of the government.

On January 1970, draconian laws of security were introduced and the NSS, which would become a feared organization, was created. With the NSS and its laws in place, the freedoms of press, expression, association, and the right to form a trade union or initiate a strike were made punishable by death.

On April 20, 1970, General Jama Ali Korshel, the first vice president of the SRC, was arrested and charged with plotting a coup. This was the beginning of Barré's consolidation of power into his hands and those of his close followers. A few months later, General Mohamed Ainanshe, the vice president of the SRC; General Salad Gabeyre, another senior SRC member; and army officer Major Abdulqadir Dheel would be accused of treason, tried, and the executed by firing squad on July 23, 1972.

Barré's Machiavellian tactics even extended to foreign policy: He adopted an anti–United States stance, ordered American aid workers out of the country, and accused Washington of imperialism. In turn, the Soviet Union rewarded him with more armaments, and more assistance in setting up and training security agencies. To appease the Soviets, who wanted to see a worker's party in place, Barré created the Somali Socialist Revolutionary Party in 1976; its members were hand-picked from government security agencies and government-controlled organizations.

In 1977, sensing that his popularity was waning, Barré sent the army into Ethiopia's Somali-inhabited region, which was easily captured with help from the Somalis therein; Barré thus increased his popularity. However, the victory was short-lived. The Soviets, the regime's main ally and major arms supplier to the Somali army since the 1960s, instead threw their support behind Ethiopia, now ruled by a regime committed to a more genuine version of communism than was Barré's veneer of socialism (behind which was a naked clan dictatorship). To help Ethiopia, the Soviets mounted their largest military campaign since World War II, airlifting a huge arsenal of weapons and thousands of troops, mostly from Cuba and South Yemen, into Ethiopia. After the Somali army withdrew from Ethiopia, a group of officers, led by Mohamed Shaykh Osman, a Majeerteen, organized a coup against the regime; it failed, and most of the ringleaders, all from the Majeerteen, except for one, were executed.

Unluckily for Barré, by 1980 the majority of the Somali population had no more tolerance for his repressive methods and clan hegemony. In 1982, the northern Isaaq clan, through a newly created guerrilla movement, the SNM, started active resistance against the regime. After the destruction of northern towns and villages in 1988, Barré's grip became tenuous, with much of the northern countryside in the hands of the SNM. Eventually, active resistance spread to the south, as the Hawiye clan confederation established another armed front, the USC. By 1990, Barré was bogged down with the war in the north, and faced southern insurgents at his door, and his MOD alliance of clans falling apart as the Ogaden region shifted, becoming actively oppositional.

Barré, now senile and suffering from multiple ailments, had become a captive to his own followers and greedy family members. His fall came in early 1991, when his hilltop palace barracks was stormed; he fled with his family from the popular uprising in Mogadishu, led the USC to the west of the city first and finally to the Gedo region that he had carved out for his clan, the Marehan, in the southwest; and made his new headquarters at Bardera. It was in Bardera that an Italian journalist found him in March 1991, living in squalid conditions and vowing to fight until death.

There he would contemplate a comeback, and his forces actually launched several counterattacks against General Aidid's forces; finally Barré's forces were defeated, and he was driven out of Somalia and into exile on April 28, 1992.

He first fled to Kenya, and then later to Nigeria, where he died on January 1995, never to be judged for his crimes by a nation in which he created such deep rifts that it remains divided today, more than a decade after his fall from power.

MOHAMED DIRIYE ABDULLAHI

Biography

Born in the Somali region of Ethiopia, *c.*1910. No formal education. Enrolled in the Italian and British colonial police forces and received police training in British Kenya and in Italy. Worked as a policeman, chief of a police station, and head of a special branch of the police during the colonial period. Transferred to the newly created army of the Somali Republic in 1960, and became second in command. Appointed chief of the army after the death of General Daud. The coup of October 1969 brought him to the presidency of the Somali Republic. His regime became increasingly repressive after 1970; popular resistance movements fought it from 1979 until he was toppled on January 1991. Fled first to Kenya with his family, and then to exile in Nigeria, where he died in 1995.

Further Reading

Galaydh, Ali K. "Notes on the State of the Somali State." *Horn of Africa Journal* 11, nos. 1–2 (1998): 1–28.

Ghalib, Jama M. *The Cost of Dictatorship: The Somali Experience*. New York: Lilian Barber Press, 1995.

Greenfield, Richard. "Siad's Sad Legacy." *Africa Report*, March–April 1991.

Lefebvre, Jeffrey A. *Arms for the Horn: U.S. Security Policy in Ethiopia and Somalia, 1953–1991*. Pittsburgh: University of Pittsburgh Press, 1991.

Lewis, I. M. *Blood and Bone: The Call of Kinship in Somali Society*. Lawrenceville, N.J.: Red Sea Press, 1994.

Nigro, Vincenzo. "Intervista con l'ex presidente della Somalia." *La Republica*, March 17, 1991, p.17.

Somalia: 1990 to the Present

At the beginning of the 1990s, Somalia was a country deep in turmoil; the regime that had caused so much anguish and destruction was experiencing its death throes. Most of the country was caught up in the popular rebellion, with only Mogadishu still a stronghold of the regime. On January 27, 1991, the regime collapsed.

The fall of the regime did not, however, bring peace and stability—especially in southern Somalia. Instead a power vacuum developed and the capital city became essentially a place without government, filled with roving clan militias, looters, and people bent on revenge killings. Soon after, in a unilateral move, Ali Mahdi, a politically obscure merchant, at the behest of a coalition known as the Manifesto Group, proclaimed himself president of Somalia. The Manifesto Group consisted of 1960s-era politicians, merchants, and ex-officers—mostly from the south—who had played no part in the active resistance against the regime.

In the south, Ali Mahdi's self-proclamation, seen as a kind of coup d'état, had two immediate effects. First, it caused a deep split in the USC guerrilla movement, which had waged war in the south against the regime; it drew its members from the Hawiye clan. More important, the USC's military man, General Aidid, who had actually coordinated most of the fighting in the south against the regime, rejected Ali Mahdi's claims. Although both belonged to the Hawiye clan, they differed in subclan affiliation. Additionally, another rebellion faction, led by Colonel Jess, leading a largely Darod Ogaden guerrilla, and based in the extreme south, also rejected Ali Mahdi's claims.

Neither Ali Mahdi nor Aidid was willing to make a compromise in order to bring peace to Mogadishu. It has been said that Aidid was an arrogant soldier who saw Ali Mahdi, a civilian, as someone who could be easily cast aside. Unluckily for Aidid, Ali Mahdi's clan was not so willing to let go of Ali Mahdi, one of their own. With each of the two now relying exclusively on militia members of his subclan, and the honor of each subclan in question, a new and deadly civil war started again in Mogadishu.

Meanwhile, events unfolded differently in the north. The notable difference was the immediate intervention of community and clan elders after of the fall of the regime. Additionally, the guerrilla movement that had started the fight against the regime in earnest and actually brought the regime to its knees in the first place, the SNM (located in the north and drawing most of its members from the Isaaq clan), went along with population consensus and the wishes of the elders; thus, instead of the guerrilla leadership dictating a political program for the people of Somaliland, community leaders and clan elders from all the northern clans—even from those that had fought on the side of the regime, took the unprecedented step of formally constituting themselves as a permanent sovereign assembly, the *Guurti* ("senators"; previously, the word meant "a committee of wise men chosen to tackle communal issues," a kind of a pastoral parliament).

After several congresses, the assembly of northern community leaders declared formally that the unratified political amalgamation that they had with Somalia since 1960 was being overturned. In further conferences, the northern leaders established permanent peace, and constitutional structures for their region, which now had all of the attributes of statehood: a bicameral parliament, a constitution, a flag, and a currency. Unknown to them, by forging a bicameral parliament based in part on tradition and in part on Western democratic ideals, the elders of Somaliland had started what might has termed as a unique indigenization of democracy in Africa.

From 1991 to 1992, constant battles raged between several militia groups in the south. In Mogadishu, the urban war between the factions of Ali Mahdi and Aidid destroyed large parts of Mogadishu and killed many people; it also rendered impossible the use of Mogadishu's airport and seaport. In the deep south, to the west and south of Mogadishu, other ferocious battles were fought between a coalition led by Aidid and Mohamed Siad Barré's loyalists attempting a comeback, and led by Barré's son-in-law, Said Hersi (alias General Morgan). The battles over the riverine areas, inhabited mostly by the agropastoral Maay and other minorities, disrupted the fragile cycles of sowing and harvesting in the riverine areas of the south; the result was the famine that was viewed around the world, unfolding on television screens in 1992. Most of the deaths from that famine occurred in and around

Baidoa, dubbed "the city of death" by Western nongovernmental organizations. As a result, on December 3, 1992, the United Nations authorized a humanitarian international intervention led by the United States with the aim of bringing humanitarian assistance to the famine-stricken populations of the South.

After an initial stage dubbed Operation Restore Hope and essentially coordinated by the U.S. intervention force, the United Nations Operations in Somalia (UNOSOM) began. However, in essence the whole operation remained in the hands of American policy makers, since the head of UNOSOM was Admiral Howe, a retired U.S. officer. At the same, all the top decisions were being coordinated by Howe and the head of the U.S. contingent.

The operation turned ugly when Howe adopted a militaristic approach. One of the main reasons that the operation went wrong was because Aidid's faction and those of his ally, Jess, were especially targeted for disarmament while at the same time, General Morgan's forces were allowed to occupy the port city of Kismayo in the southern extremity of the country, previously held by Jess's forces. Thus, another urban war followed in Mogadishu, in which this time the combatants were intervention forces and Aidid's supporters— especially after Howe placed a bounty on Aidid's head.

The new urban war proved to be as disastrous as the previous one; helicopter gunships would fire into Somali crowds; missiles would strike civilian sites. In the end, the international intervention forces became another faction involved in the civil war in deed, if not in intent. Thousands were killed by indiscriminate fire from the intervention forces. The mostly Western forces were comprised of young men with no cultural preparation for an African and Muslim environment. Charges of atrocious acts, including unwarranted shootings, rape, and child molestation, have been levied against Western forces.

The final act that brought about the end of UNOSOM would be the October 3, 1993, raid to capture Aidid and his lieutenants. The operation, prepared in secret by Howe and the head of the American contingent without consulting the other international forces, did not go as planned. The U.S. soldiers on the mission fought what was termed the biggest firefight that U.S. Army forces had engaged in since Vietnam. When the smoke cleared, 18 U.S. soldiers had died, but so did thousands of Somalis caught in indiscriminate fire from the U.S. side. Four days later, U.S. president Bill Clinton ordered troops out of Somalia by March 1994, effectively spelling the end of international intervention there, which would finally be terminated in 1995.

During the international intervention and after, several conferences were held to bring peace and civil governance to Somalia. To date more than a dozen conferences have been held since the collapse of the regime, but none of them has succeeded in providing a national government, making Somalia a country without a government since the fall of the Barré regime in January 1991. Of course, all of the territory of the Somali Republic of 1960 is not without governance: there is Somaliland (the north), which, though it has not been recognized by the international community, has not only given itself a government but has embarked on an ambitious road of reconstruction and democratization, with assistance from only a few nongovernmental organizations. In May 2001, voters in Somaliland overwhelmingly endorsed a new constitution for their country, declaring Somaliland as a sovereign nation, further diminishing any hopes of restoring the Somali Republic of 1960. Municipal elections followed in 2002, as did presidential elections in 2003.

In the south, after the different factions had drawn themselves into a military and political stalemate, the next stage was the consolidation of fiefdoms and the establishment of some order in some areas. In the northern areas, adjacent to Somaliland, Colonel Abdullahi Yusuf of the Majeerteen clan established a regional state called Puntland; this regional state drawing on the experience of Somaliland established a regional parliament composed of elders; however, Puntland, unlike Somaliland, is claiming to be only a regional state of Somalia with its own local administration. In turn, the experience of Puntland would inspire the inhabitants of the riverine areas, the Maay and other minorities. After having first organized a resistance movement against other factions occupying or fighting over their areas, the Maay people's Rahanwein Resistance Army established the second regional state of Somalia in 2002. Unluckily, after some initial success in establishing a semblance of order at the local level, fighting between local factions in both of these regional states broke out in 2002 and 2003. As for Mogadishu, it is still a divided city controlled by several factions and has no local government of its own. Other areas, such as Kismayo and parts of the central regions, also remain controlled by factions that have been unable to produce any local administrations, and are not immune to the attempts of annexation by other warlords.

From recent events, it is evident that war and chaos are not yet over, and they seem unfortunately likely to continue in such a way as to forbid the establishment of one central authority in Somalia proper any time soon; as for Somaliland, it is at this moment a de facto state with a firmly established central administration that collects taxes and pays its civil servants. It has been even described as one of the safest countries in Africa. Thus, the Somali Republic of 1960 has been reduced to two regions: one without the rule of law, and the other enjoying all the attributes of a state, as well as civil peace, but without international recognition—a fact that is impeding the republic's development, as it is neither able to get into international investment nor receive any bilateral aid.

MOHAMED DIRIYE ABDULLAHI

See also: **Somalia: Barré, Mohamad Siad, Life and Government of; Somalia: Independence, Conflict, and Revolution.**

Further Reading

Diriye Abdullahi, Mohamed. *Culture and Customs of Somalia.* Westport, Conn.: Greenwood Press, 2001.

———. *Fiasco in Somalia: US–UN Intervention.* Occasional Paper no. 61. Pretoria: Africa Institute of South Africa, 1995.

Lewis, I. M. *Blood and Bone: The Call of Kinship in Somali Society.* Lawrenceville, N.J,: Red Sea Press, 1994.

Songhay Empire, Gao and Origins of

The origins of the Songhay empire are intimately linked with the fortunes of Gao, its capital city. The empire, the largest of the three great West African empires of the later Iron Age, flourished between the mid-fifteenth and late sixteenth centuries, but the foundations were laid some hundreds of years earlier. Today, the Songhay are the dominant ethnic group in the vicinity of Gao and their fortunes are intimately associated with the River Niger, especially in the area known as the Niger Bend, encompassing eastern Mali and northwestern Niger. Songhay origins are unclear, but according to tradition they developed from contact among different groups: hunters, farmers, and fishers.

According to oral tradition and local historical sources written in Arabic—notably, the *Tarikh es Soudan* and *Tarikh el Fettach*—the proto-Songhay left their homelands in the Bentiya/Kukiya region south of Gao and traveled north, establishing a settlement in the vicinity of Gao in about 690. The whereabouts of this settlement (if such a migration took place) have been much debated. Archaeological research has indicated that the area around Gao has been almost continuously occupied since the late Stone Age (*c.*5000–1000BCE). Although it is difficult to be precise about ethnicity based upon archaeological evidence, it would appear from the material recovered that it was a settlement occupied by the Songhay from the first.

Following the foundation of the city, it rapidly grew in size and prosperity. This affluence was based upon trade, which was initially interregional in focus. Starting in the late eight or early ninth century, these local trade networks were supplemented by trans-Saharan trade routes directed to North Africa, but indirectly continuing much farther within the Muslim world and beyond.

Local trade was in commodities such as foodstuffs, pottery, beads, copper, and iron. Trans-Saharan trade predominantly followed a pattern in which finished items were imported from the north and raw materials were exported from the south.

Both the Arab historical sources and the archaeological evidence indicate the importance of trade to the inhabitants of Gao. Ivory, gold, and slaves were the dominant commodities exported, providing labor and materials that fueled the Muslim world economy. In return, glazed ceramics from Al-Andalus (Islamic Spain), Egypt, and Tunisia were carried south by camel caravan, along with glass vessels, glass, and semiprecious stone beads, items of metalwork, cloth, paper, cowrie shells, and spices. Gao also benefited from control of the salt trade. Salt was mined in the Sahara, sent to centers such as Gao, and from there was traded onward throughout the savanna and forest zones to the south. The importance of the trade in salt to the inhabitants of Gao is indicated by an observation recorded by the Arab historian, Yaqut, writing in the early thirteenth century, who noted that "'the King's treasure-houses are spacious, his treasure consisting principally of salt'" (cited in Levtzion and Hopkins 1981, 174).

By the late eleventh century, Gao had developed into a major urban center, and was composed of a variety of different quarters. Archaeological research has uncovered parts of the city, and the traders town, Gao Ancien, was found to contain buildings constructed out of fired brick, finished with colored plaster, with the whole area surrounded by an enclosing dry-stone wall. Neighboring this was a local Songhay settlement, which contained less trade-related evidence and where architectural styles also differed, with building in mud, and round houses rather than buildings employing the right angle constructed. Some 6 kilometers to the east of Gao was a further settlement, Gao-Saney, where the remains of a royal cemetery dating from the twelfth century was uncovered (including ready-carved tombstones imported from Islamic Spain) next to a large habitation mound, or tell. This site functioned as a residential area, a place of burial, and a manufacturing center, and indicated the considerable size of the population in the area.

Islam was gradually accepted by the population of Gao, a process starting possibly as early as the ninth century. The first historical reference to the acceptance of Islam by a ruler of Gao is by Al-Muhallabi who, writing in the late tenth century, recorded that, "their king pretends before them to be a Muslim and most of them pretend to be Muslims too" (cited in Levtzion and Hopkins 1981, 174). This suggests that Islam had not penetrated very deeply. By the eleventh or twelfth centuries, the historical sources are more equivocal in asserting that the ruler and part of the population of Gao were Muslims, and this is supplemented by archaeological data, such as dated Muslim tombstones, mosques, and trade-related evidence of contacts with the Muslim world.

As already noted, the prosperity generated by the local and long-distance trade was to lay the foundations for the Songhay empire. Until the mid-thirteenth century, Gao was an independent Songhay kingdom, ruled by the Za or Dia dynasty. But by the middle of the thirteenth century, its increasing affluence was to attract the attention of its powerful neighbor to the west, the empire of Mali, which extended control over the Gao region. Gao was, however, a remote province and periodically asserted its independence; one such rebellion, in about 1275, led to the rise of the Sonni dynasty, which replaced that of the Za. The rebellion was short-lived and Mali reasserted its control, but eventually lost its eastern provinces, of which Gao formed a part, at the beginning of the fifteenth century. Songhay military strength was built up and this was accompanied by territorial expansion. The period of empire had begun.

TIMOTHY INSOLL

See also: **Mali Empire: Decline, Fifteenth Century.**

Further Reading

Insoll, T. *Islam, Archaeology and History, A Complex Relationship: The Gao Region (Mali). Ca. AD 900–1250.* Oxford: Tempus Reparatum, 1996.
———. "A Cache of Hippopotamus Ivory at Gao, Mali; and a Hypothesis of its Use." *Antiquity*, no. 69 (1995): 327–336.
———. "Iron Age Gao: An Archaeological Contribution." *Journal of African History*, no. 38 (1997): 1–30.
Insoll, T., and Shaw, T. "Gao and Igbo-Ukwu: Beads, Inter-Regional Trade and Beyond." *African Archaeological Review*, no. 14 (1997): 9–23.
Levtzion, N., and J. F. P. Hopkins. *Corpus of Early Arabic Sources for West African History*. Cambridge: Cambridge University Press, 1981.

Songhay Empire: Sunni Ali and the Founding of Empire

Founded by the Sunni dynasty, Songhay was the last of the three great empires of the Western Sudan. Under Sunni Ali (*r.*1464–1492), Songhay became an empire, totally eclipsing Mali, which had been in decline by the early fifteenth century.

Much of Sunni Ali's reign was taken up by wars of conquest. The Sonni dynasty had built up a powerful army of horsemen and war canoes with which Suleyman Dandi had extended Songhay territory upstream along the Niger bend. Soon after his accession to the throne,

Sunni Ali turned his attention northward and marched on Timbuktu, which had been captured by the Tuareg in the last days of Mali. Sunni Ali was repeatedly successful in his wars. In 1468, he brought the city under his control. Some of the leading families of the city had exerted very little energy in defending themselves when the Tuaregs took and city and Sunni Ali. Probably they saw the Tuareg as a useful Muslim ally against Songhay overlordship. After the conquest of Timbuktu Sunni Ali treated the *qadis* and *'ulama* harshly. Scholarship in Timbuktu undoubtedly suffered in Sunni Ali's time. This action, perceived as a lack of respect for Islam, earned Ali harsh criticism from the Muslim clerics and writers.

Next, Sunni Ali's army moved into the turbulent Mossi region and pushed the Mossi to the south of the Niger in the late 1480s. However, he failed to subdue the Mossi, and pushed on across the Niger and conquered the Hausa state of Kebbi.

Sunni Ali's army was repeatedly successful in war. Certainly, he was a formidable military general who extended the Songhay empire deep into the desert in the north and as far as Jenne in the southwest, and pushed the Mossi back south of the Niger in the late 1480s, but never subdued them.

Sunni Ali devised a new method of administration. He divided his conquests into provinces, appointing the former rulers as governors over some, and his military officials over others. He appointed a special governor, the *tondifari* (governor of the mountains), for the troublesome Mossi region. He also appointed a *hi-koy* (chief naval officer) for his fleet.

Sunni Ali's raids on the Muslim educational and religious center of Timbuktu and his high-handed treatment of the clerics, coupled with his pursuit of the Tuareg, led to his being harshly criticized by Arabic historians. They portrayed him as a ruthless tyrant and oppressor, in contradistinction to Askia Muhammed.

In spite of the criticism of the Muslim clerics and 'ulama, Sunni Ali is remembered in Songhay oral tradition as a great conquering hero and founder of the Songhay Empire. He died in 1492 and his heir was quickly ousted in a power struggle by one of his generals, Muhammad Ture, a devout Muslim of Soninke origin. Muhammad Ture then took the title Askiya and is better known as Askiya the Great.

EDMUND ABAKA

See also: **Mali Empire: Decline, Fifteenth Century.**

Further Reading

Boahen, A. Adu. *Topics in West African History*. London: Longman, 1986.
Bovill, E. W. *The Golden Trade of the Moors*, 2nd. ed. London: Oxford University Press, 1970.

Davidson, Basil. *Africa in History*. New York: Touchstone, 1995.
Shillington, Kevin. *History of Africa*. New York: St Martin's Press, 1995.

Songhay Empire: Ture, Muhammad and the Askiya Dynasty

As founder of the Askiya dynasty, Muhammad Ture (Askia Muhammad, 1493–1528) strengthened the administration of the empire and consolidated Sunni Ali's conquests. By promoting Islam and going on a pilgrimage to Mecca, Muhammad Ture put Songhay on the map of the Islamic world.

Drawing on Sunni Ali's conquests, Muhammad Ture extended the Songhay empire into the desert, drove back the Tuareg of the southern Sahara, and captured the salt-producing center of Taghaza in the north. By that conquest, he maximized Songhay's benefit from trans-Saharan trade. Ture also sent an army as far west as Takrur, and fought off the Middle Niger raiders, the Mossi and the Dogon. In the east, Muhammad Ture's armies conquered the Hausa states of Gobir, Katsina, and, eventually, Kano. These conquests brought Songhay into the broader trading network of trans-Saharan trade.

After the wars of expansion, Ture strengthened the administrative system set up by Sunni Ali. He divided the empire into four vice royalties, each under a viceroy or governor, usually chosen from the royal family or a trusted servant. In terms of central administration, Muhammad Ture established a council of ministers composed of the *balama* (commander-in-chief), *fari-mundya* (chief tax collector), *hi-koy* (navy chief), *korey-farma* (minister responsible for foreigners), *warrey-farma* (minister in charge of property), and *hari-farma* (minister in charge of fisheries).

Unlike his predecessor, Muhammad Ture recognized the importance of Islam as an important ideology for purposes of state formation and development. He used Islam to reinforce his authority, unite his far-flung empire, and promote (trans-Saharan) trade. Soon after his accession, Ture displayed his concern for the faith by going on a pilgrimage to Mecca. While in Cairo, he persuaded the Caliph of Egypt to recognize him as the "caliph" of the whole Sudan.

On his return from Mecca, Muhammad Ture revived Timbuktu as an important educational and Islamic center. This spread the fame of Songhay far and wide, and Muslim scholars and clerics were attracted to the city for educational pursuit as well as for trade. He bestowed honors and favors on the *'ulama* and clerics of Timbuktu. Not surprisingly, while seventeenth-century Timbuktu writers excoriated Sunni Ali as a tyrant, they showered praise on Askia Muhammad. This is not to say, however, that many of the people converted to Islam.

Songhay derived government revenue from several sources. Muhammad Ture raised revenue for administration from tribute from vassal states, taxes on peasants, and contributions from his generals. The state also derived substantial revenue from royal estates in the Niger floodplain and the Songhay heartland that were possibly worked by slaves. The brisk trans-Saharan trade yielded substantial revenue. The items of trade included gold (a major impetus for the trans-Saharan trade) and kola nuts from the southern forest, and captives (mostly from raids into Mossi territory south of the Niger Bend) for sale as slaves in Muslim North Africa. From North Africa, Saharan salt, luxury goods, cloth, cowrie, and horses for the military were imported into the Songhay empire. Cloth from local Sudanese cotton—and, in towns like Jenne, Timbuktu, and Gao, woolen cloth and linen from North Africa— was also part of the trade.

After a 35-year reign, Muhammad Ture, who was old, blind, and infirm, was deposed by his children in 1528 and sent into exile to the Island of Kankaka on the Niger, but later returned home, and died in 1538.

The successors of Muhammad Ture did not have the courage, devotion to duty, and competence that he had demonstrated as ruler. They were involved in feuds and fratricidal struggles for the throne. Ture's successor, his son Musa, was assassinated in 1535 for his cruelty. Askia Bankouri, who succeeded him and exiled his uncle Muhammad Ture from Gao, was in turn deposed in 1537. Askia Ismail, the next ruler, not only brought back Muhammad Ture from exile but also proved to be a capable ruler. Unfortunately, he died after two years on the throne.

Fortunately for Songhay, Askia Daud, who succeeded Ismail, ruled for a long time (1530–1584), succeeded in suppressing turbulence, and imposed a long period of peace and stability. However, the Moroccan Sultan Al-Mansur invaded Songhay ten years later, at a

Sankoré Mosque. Timbuktu, Mali, 1984. Photograph © David C. Conrad.

time when Songhay was once more wracked by dynastic disputes, leading to a weakening of the court. Al-Mansur's first attempt in 1584 failed, but a more elaborate and better-planned invasion in 1591 succeeded and brought the Askiya dynasty to an end.

EDMUND ABAKA

Further Reading

Boahen, A. Adu. *Topics in West African History*. London: Longman, 1986.

Bovill, E. W. *The Golden Trade of the Moors*, 2nd. ed. London: Oxford University Press, 1970.

Davidson, Basil. *Africa in History*. New York: Touchstone, 1995.

Hanwick, John. "Songhay, Borno, and the Hausa States, 1450–1600." In *History of West Africa*, vol. 1, 3rd ed., edited by I. F. Ado Ajayi and Michael Crowder. London: Longman, 1985.

Songhay Empire: Moroccan Invasion, 1591

The year 1591 witnessed the fall of the last of the great empires of the western Sudan. The uniqueness of the fall of Songhay is not just that it was shot down at the peak of its glory, but that the collapse was a product of direct military aggression from North Africa. This unprecedented military adventure marked the first time a North African country would attack one in West Africa.

The primary reason for Morocco's hostilities against Songhay was due to economic interest. El-Mansur, the ruler of Morocco, coveted and sought to control the salt mines and gold deposits within Songhay's territory, which was erroneously believed to still be in abundance at the time of the attack.

The first attempt at invading Songhay was a failure. This was due to inadequate preparations for the expedition. However, in December 1590 a more carefully planned military campaign was embarked upon, with an impressive army of musketeers, many of whom

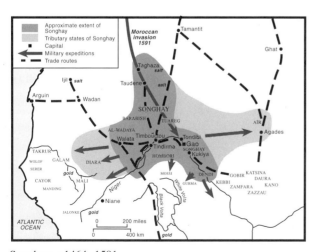

Songhay, *c.*1464–1591.

were renegade mercenaries from Spain. Commanded by Judah Pasha, the Moroccan army was very well equipped with the most sophisticated firearms of the time. Consequently, when both troops clashed at the battle of Todibi in 1591, the Songhay soldiers were forced to succumb to the superior firepower of their invaders. With the defeat of Songhay at Tondibi, Moroccan forces went on to capture other important cities such as Gao, Timbuktu, and Jenne.

The first consequence of Moroccan conquest was the establishment of a protectorate over a substantial part of what used to be the Songhay empire. Songhay thus became a province of Morocco, with Judah Pasha acting as the governor. The nonrealization of Al-Mansur's fortuitous ambition, and his consequent loss of interest in Songhay, resulted in the lack of effective administration of the territory and subsequent breakdown of law and order. By 1615, there was evidence of increasing internal weakness and confusion. Many of the former dependencies seized the opportunity to declare their independence as the empire disintegrated into small insignificant states. Among such states are those of the Tuaregs, Bambarra, Fulani, and the Hausa. The western Sudan never again had a political unit as large as the Songhay Empire.

Furthermore, the conquest and the rebellions which it occasioned took a heavy toll on the population of the western Sudan. Many lives were lost; some were sold into slavery and others taken to Morocco. There was a general displacement of the population. The breakdown of law and order, coupled with the general insecurity that pervaded the territory had grave economic effects. Agriculture suffered a setback, and this occasioned a period of famine. There was concomitant plundering of economic crops and valuables. In addition, trans-Saharan trade seriously declined because of the series of attacks connected with the invasion. The various routes were rendered unsafe, as pillaging of caravans and activities of brigands became a frequent phenomenon along trans-Saharan trade routes. This eventually led to a shift in trade traffic from the western routes linking Songhay to Marrakech and Fez to the eastern routes from Hausaland and Bornu to Egypt and Libya.

Again, none of the successor states had enough resources to support large-scale commercial activity. The Moors drained Songhay of the available gold. Moreover, there was the lure of the European presence along the Atlantic coast of the western Sudan that provided a better alternative to the cataclysmic state of affairs in Songhay and was not conducive to profitable economic activity. The totality of all these factors was a considerable decline in the volume of trade and loss of wealth in the Western Sudan.

In the realm of religion, Islam suffered a temporary setback. The Moroccans showed no enthusiasm for the promotion of religion, or for providing for the security and welfare of its agents. The Muslim scholars who did not welcome the Moroccan onslaught were regarded as foes and dealt with harshly. Their libraries and wealth were confiscated, while those found to be against them were exiled to Morocco. Prominent among such Muslim scholars were Ahmed Baba, the illustrious Timbuktu historian, Umar bin al Hajj Ahmed, Abdal al-Rahman bin Mahmud bin Umar, and many members of the Aquit family, who had previously enjoyed power and influence in Timbuktu as a result of their Islamic learning. Furthermore, the destruction of their libraries, and their deportation had a calamitous effect on Islamic learning in the region. The exiling of these renowned scholars, who had been the pride of Sankore University at Timbuktu, meant the death of learning and a gradual extinction of the scholarly reputation of Timbuktu.

Nevertheless, development in the post-Moroccan period suggests that Songhay's defeat at Tondibi did not inaugurate a completely dark chapter in the sociopolitical life of West Africa. Politically, there was a shift of force from the Sahel region and the savanna to the forest region of West Africa. In the religious sphere, the collapse did not mean the end of Islam. The fleeing Muslims, especially the Fulani group, dispersed all over West Africa, spreading Islam southward to places like Futa Jalon. Islam was therefore carried at a grassroots level; the stage was set for the eighteenth and nineteenth century jihads (holy wars) in West Africa.

C. W. N. OGBOGBO

See also: **Morocco: Ahmad al-Mansur and the Invasion of Songhay.**

Further Reading

Awe, Bolanle. "Empires of the Western Sudan: Ghana, Mali and Songhai." In *A Thousand Years of West African History*, edited by J. F. A. Ajayi and I. Espie. Ibadan, Nigeria, 1965.

Boahen, Adu. *Topics in West African History*. London: Longman, 1976.

Bovill, E. W. "The Moroccan Invasion of Sudan." *Journal of African History*, no. 26 (1926) and no. 27 (1927).

Hunwick, J. "Ahmed Baba and the Moroccan Invasion of the Sudan." *Journal of the Historical Society of Nigeria*, nos. 2–3 (1962): 311–328.

Sonni Ali: *See* Songhay Empire: Sunni Ali and the Founding of Empire.

Soshangane, Umzila, Gungunhane and the Gaza State

The Gaza state was the result of a military conquest carried out around 1821–1845 in southern Mozambique. In the third generation of rulers, the kingdom succumbed to a military campaign organized by the Portuguese government in 1894–1895 against the last king, Ngungunyane (Gungunhana).

There were numerous lineage-based states in Southern and Central Mozambique previous to 1821, including a few larger ones that may have had some 20,000 to 40,000 inhabitants. South of the Save River most of these belonged to what was to become the Tsonga linguistic group. The populations north of the Save included remnants of earlier Shona states like Manyika, Vumba, Uteve, and Madanda or were Portuguese subjects like most Shona. All were shaken by attacks made by the founder of the Gaza state, Soshangane (*r.*1821–1858) and some of his Nguni competitors during the period known as the *mfecane.* In Mozambique south of the Zambezi this period may be dated to around 1821–1840.

The name *Gaza* is derived from Mangwa Gaza, the name of the grandfather of Soshangane and the founder of a chiefly sublineage of the Nqumayo or Ndwandwe clan who seems to have resided close to a southern outlier of the Libombo range in present day South Africa. The first king, Soshangane, Mangwa Gaza's grandson, known in Mozambique after 1840 under variants of the name of Manukuza (Manukhuse, Manikhosi, and, in Portuguese, Manicusse). He seems to have initiated warfare in southern Mozambique in Tembe in 1821 and operated in association with a fellow subchief of the Ndwandwe kingdom, Zwangendaba Jere, until 1827 or 1829. The emigration or flight of Zwangendaba (1829), the defeat of Nqaba Msane (c.1835–1836), and finally the crossing of the Zambezi by the sucessor of Ngwane Maseko in 1839 at the Lupata Gorge left the area between the Nkomati and the Zambezi to Gaza. Soshangane sent armies composed of soldiers recruited from the Tsonga south of Save (known as Landins on the Zambezi), often under the command of one of his older sons, to obtain the subjection of chiefs and collection of tribute during the dry period (July–September). The Sena in the Portuguese *prazos* south of the Zambezi were under double tributation to Gaza and the Portuguese crown (c.1845–1894).

The rapid expansion and stabilization of the political system was made possible by age corporations or regiments called *butho* into which all males were integrated irrespective of their origin; royal and aristocratic houses to which individuals and chiefs were attached in addition to allegiance to the Gaza king. Many positions in the new state offered some chance of security, rank, and promotion, and remuneration from the spoils of war.

The state suffered a succession crisis in 1859–1862 because influential personalities at the court selected as successor Mawewe, a young man with little experience in government activity. At least three brothers and a sister senior in age rebelled or fled north but were killed. Mawewe then attempted to take over the areas formerly administered by them, which may have amounted to almost half the kingdom's territory. He did not manage to eliminate his brother Muzila, who was an experienced politician and war leader who had participated in warfare and administration at least since 1845. Muzila sought refuge with the Afrikaner in Zouthpansberg and formed an alliance with a refugee Tsonga chief, Magude Khosa, and elephant hunters (which included the governor of Lourenço Marques) and managed to shift the balance of power in his favor after winning two battles in the second half of 1861. He moved into the Limpopo Valley, but had to retire to the headwaters of the Buzi River, north of the Save, in the face of a Swazi incursion. It took his troops several campaigns to fight back the Swazi and he stayed north of the Save for the remainder of his reign. Muzila governed from Mussapa, or Mussurize, in the borderland between Mozambique and Zimbabwe and sucessively had residences at both sides of the border near modern Chipinge and Espungabera.

Major economic changes took place in Muzila's reign, which ended in 1884. The hunting of elephants on a large scale survived only in the north. In the south and center of the kingdom income from work in the South African mines, plantations, and railway-building projects permitted import, the payment of tribute, and payment of bride-prices. Muzila maintained diplomatic relations with the Ndebele, the Afrikaner of the Transvaal, the British in Natal, and the Portuguese on the coast. He intervened militarily among the Venda in 1869.

Ngungunyane (port Gungunhana) succeeded in late 1884 and was officially installed in 1885. In 1889, possibly in order to avoid the effects of a possible massive influx of miners near Macequece (Manica) and in order to consolidade his hold in the South, Ngungunyane shifted his capital, always called Mandl-hakazi, and central aristocracy to the south. Between 1889 and 1895 he moved the capital several times within a range of 12 kilometers in the modern districts of Mandlakazi (Manjacaze) and Chibuto.

Immediately after his accession, contacts with the Portuguese were taken up; these were manipulated during the scramble for this area in 1889–1892. Gaza lost part of its territory in the frontier settlements of 1890 and 1891. Ngungunyane tried to counterbalance Portuguese and British interests, but this was ultimately unsuccessful and in 1895 the kingdom was conquered by the Portuguese, who were reluctant to accept an autonomous chief who supported chiefs re-belling against their rule in the southern Lourenço Marques district. Ngungunyane was exiled to the

Azores in 1896, together with his son, an uncle, and a rebel chief, one of two such chiefs who had triggered off the campaign against the Gaza state. Ngungunyane died in the Azores in 1906, followed by his son and presumptive heir Godide in 1910.

The Gaza kingdom had the most important of its two centers in the present Gaza province of Mozambique, but also extended into part of the Maputo, Inhambane, and Manica provinces and, around 1840–1884, also northeastern South Africa and southeastern Zimbabwe. The Mozambique Company, which administered the area north of 22 degrees south, substituted and punished chiefs loyal to Gaza in 1896. In the south the destruction of the Gaza state took several phases between 1896 and 1900.

The post of senior military commander had gone, around 1886, to Magigwane Khosa, descended from the assimilated indigenous population of the Limpopo Valley and not one of the members of the Nguni aristocracy. Magigwane commanded a royalist revolt from March to August 1897 organized under the idea of forcing the Portuguese to return the exiled king. Magigwane was killed by the Portuguese in the last phase of the revolt, when he and others tried to escape to South Africa. There a number of refugees settled. The Gaza state system was dismantled by the Portuguese, and male age groups ceased to be named in 1897.

GERHARD LIESEGANG

Further reading

Liesegang, Gerhard. *Ngungunyane: A figura de Ngungunyane Nqumayo (ca.1845–1906), Rei de Gaza de 1884 a 1895 e o desaparecimento do seu estado.* Coll. Embondeiro no. 8. Maputo, Mozambique: Arpac, 1996.
Newitt, Malyn. *A History of Mozambique.* London: C. Hurst, 1995.
Pelissier, R. *Naissance du Mozambique.* Orgeval: Pélissier, 1984.

Soudan Français: *See* **Mali (Republic of): Colonial Soudan Français.**

South Africa: Missionaries: Nineteenth Century

The roles missionaries played in creating South African society have long been controversial. Some observers consider missionaries to have been agents of colonialism; others aver that missionaries were benign humanitarians. Missionaries were not a monolithic group and did not form a unified movement. Converts and missionaries forged the meaning of Christianity and missions, and this meaning varied greatly across time and place.

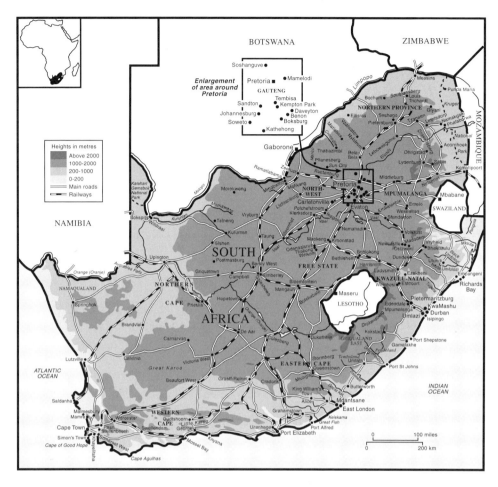

South Africa.

Before the end of the eighteenth century there was very little missionary activity in South Africa. The white Christians showed little inclination toward converting non-Christians: slaves, the Khoisan, and Africans. The evangelical revivals in the late eighteenth and early nineteenth centuries inspired Protestants in northern Europe and North America, including many future missionaries to South Africa, to spread Christianity throughout the world. The London Missionary Society (LMS) and the Moravians began work among the Khoi in the Western Cape in the late eighteenth century. The LMS also worked in the Northern Cape among the Griqua and the Tswana and attempted work among the Xhosa. By the 1850s, missionaries from the United States, Germany, Scandinavia, France, and the United Kingdom, representing various denominations, worked throughout South Africa. These early missionaries were clergymen and laity, often from the middle or working classes, who were sometimes accompanied by their wives and families.

The missionaries' primary goal was to convert people to Christianity. They associated conversion with "civilization" and encouraged Africans to adopt Western clothing, housing, gender roles, and labor patterns. Missionaries challenged African practices such as polygyny, dancing, beer drinking, and initiation ceremonies. Some people converted because they desired the resources and shelter of the mission, because they were marginal in their own society, or because Christianity offered useful spiritual insights. People who were in great cultural, economic or political distress, such as the Mfengu and the Khoi, often converted to Christianity as they adapted to South Africa's changing social order. Many African Christians were converted as the result of the preaching of other Africans. One of the most important of these early proselytizers was the Xhosa councilor Ntsikana.

By the mid-nineteenth century, missionaries worked among the major African polities of southern Africa, including the Zulu, Ndebele, Xhosa, and Tswana. However, in areas where African polities were intact, missionaries usually had limited success. Even when few people became Christians, Africans saw missions as valuable resources. Some leaders, such as Moshoeshoe of the Sotho, used missionaries as intermediaries in their dealings with Europeans. Missions became important sites for disseminating Western education and technologies, such as plow agriculture, irrigation, and medicine.

Missionary perspectives on colonialism varied greatly. Some early missionaries, such as the Moravians, were quietists. The LMS missionaries, especially Dr. Johannes van der Kemp and John Philip, vigorously protested the abuses to which Africans, Khoi, and slaves were subjected. By the mid-nineteenth century, many missionaries were frustrated by the slow pace of conversion and asserted that Christianity would never gain a foothold as long as African polities retained their independence. Thus, many missionaries went from being critical of colonial policies to supporting colonial rule.

The defeat of African polities and the industrialization of South Africa had a profound impact on missions. Missionaries established work in mining compounds and the locations of South Africa's growing cities. As people throughout the region migrated to South Africa for work, some became Christian and spread the religion when they returned home. When Indian indentured servants and immigrants came to Natal and the Transvaal, several Christian missions made work among Indians their special focus. The number of mission societies in South Africa increased steadily. By the 1860s, the Dutch Reformed Church, the Church of England, and the Roman Catholic Church began mission work. Thirty years later, diverse groups such as the Salvation Army and African American missions of the African Methodist Episcopal Church and the National Baptist Convention worked in South Africa. Most societies began sending single women to work as missionaries, in addition to the male missionaries. These women, including nuns and deaconesses, made African women the primary focus of their work. Many missions added social service work and education to evangelizing. Missionaries provided most of the schools and hospitals for Africans.

Mission perspectives on race relations generally became more conservative throughout the century. The early missionaries usually believed that all Christians, black and white, were equal in faith. They abhorred aspects of indigenous culture, but did not believe that nonwhites were inherently inferior to whites. As the century progressed, missionaries absorbed the racial ideologies developing in the West and tended to support the racial inequality and segregation that was developing in South Africa. Some missionaries believed that Africans were racially inferior to whites; others argued that segregation protected Africans from injurious colonial influences. Still others maintained that Africans should play a subservient role in the economy of the region. The missionaries usually accommodated themselves to the racial order.

African Christians, often independent of missionaries, made their religion an important part of their identity. In many communities there were stark divisions between non-Christian "traditionalists" and Christian "progressives." In the Eastern Cape, the "progressives," called "school" Africans, often became peasant farmers. Africans educated in mission schools such as Lovedale formed an influential elite that included teachers, ministers, clerks, lawyers, and doctors. Members of the elite ran newspapers, established agricultural, educational, and political associations, and assiduously defended Africans' rights. Many Africans framed their protest against European rule in terms of Christianity. African Christians also adapted the religion to suit their spiritual needs. African women formed prayer groups (*manyanos*) that became an important element of their experience of Christianity. Some Christians, such as the Pedi, formed independent communities. A group of Africans, frustrated by the racial prejudice and paternalism in the church, broke with missions and formed their own African-led churches. These Christians called their churches "Ethiopian," in reference to Psalm 68:31, "Ethiopia shall soon stretch out her hands unto God."

By the beginning of the twentieth century, over 30 missionary societies worked in South Africa. Most of the people working to promote Christianity, however, were Africans. Missionary influence was profound, resistant to easy categorization, and continually negotiated and shaped by African Christians.

MODUPE G. LABODE

See also: **Religion, Colonial Africa: Conversion to World Religions; Religion, Colonial Africa: Missions.**

Further Reading

Brederkamp, Henry, and Robert Ross (eds.). *Missions and Christianity in South African History*. Johannesburg: Witwatersrand University Press, 1995.

Chidester, David. *Religions of South Africa*. London: Routledge, 1992.

Chirenje, J. Mutero. *Ethiopianism and Afro–Americans in Southern Africa, 1883–1916*. Baton Rouge: Louisiana State University Press, 1987.

Cochrane, James. *Servants of Power: The role of English-Speaking Churches in South Africa, 1903–1930*. Johannesburg: Ravan Press, 1987.

Comaroff, Jean, and John Comaroff. *Of Revelation and Revolution*, vol. 1. Chicago: University of Chicago Press, 1991.

Comaroff, John L., and Jean Comaroff. *Of Revelation and Revolution* vol. 2. Chicago: University of Chicago Press, 1997.

Du Plessis, J. *A History of Christian Missions in South Africa*. London: Longmans, Green, 1911.

Etherington, Norman. *Preachers, Peasants, and Politics in Southeast Africa, 1835–1880*. London: Royal Historical Society, 1978.

Gaitskell, Deborah. "Devout Domesticity? A Century of African Women's Christianity in South Africa." In *Women and Gender in Southern Africa to 1945*, edited by Cherryl Walker. Cape Town: David Philip/London: James Currey, 1990.

Hodgson, Janet. *Ntsikana's "Great Hymn": A Xhosa Expression of Christianity in Early 19th Century Eastern Cape*. Cape Town: Centre for African Studies, 1980.

Majeke, Nosipho. *The Role of the Missionaries in Conquest*. Johannesburg: Society of Young Africa, 1952.

Meintjes, Sheila. "Family and Gender in the Christian Community at Edendale, Natal, in Colonial Times." In *Women and Gender in Southern Africa to 1945*, edited by Cherryl Walker. Cape Town: David Philip/London: James Currey, 1990.

Ross, Andrew. *John Philip (1775–1851): Missions, Race and Politics in South Africa*. Aberdeen: Aberdeen University Press, 1986.

South Africa: Confederation, Disarmament and the First Anglo-Boer War, 1871–1881

Closer association as a mechanism for imposing order, enhancing security, and thus bringing about a keenly desired reduction in military expenditure had been placed on the imperial agenda for South Africa by Sir George Grey in the late 1850s. The diamond discoveries of the late 1860s and the subsequent annexation of Griqualand West (1871) provided some momentum, but it was the arrival of Lord Carnarvon at the Colonial Office in April 1874 that saw it reinstated as an immediate objective of imperial policy. Carnarvon had presided over the formation of the Canadian confederation in 1867, bringing together two different white communities. He now took on the more intractable task of uniting Boer and Briton, with the added complication of a third—black—population.

His primary motivation has been the subject of some debate. The pioneer historian C. W. de Kiewiet noted his concern about the Boer treatment of Africans in the Transvaal, and his belief in a uniform native policy to reduce the risk of black revolt. Robinson and Gallagher have stressed the strategic importance of South Africa as a keystone of imperial communications. Norman Etherington (1975) and others have discussed the central role of Natal official Sir Theophilus Shepstone, an early visitor to Carnarvon's Colonial Office, who acted as a spokesman for Natal settlers concerned at the possibility that interior white communities might divert their labor supplies and thus threaten their own farming activities; while Benyon has credibly suggested that, in the initial stages at least, the interests of British imperialism and Natal sub-imperialism ran conjointly. Whatever its motivation, Carnarvon's eventual grand design for Southern Africa was breathtakingly ambitious: in addition to existing British colonies and Boer republics, and surviving independent black polities in South Africa, it envisaged control of the whole coastline between the southern borders of Angola and Mozambique, plus (possibly) the inclusion of modern Botswana and western Zimbabwe.

Following his discussions with Shepstone, Carnarvon embarked on a campaign to "sell" confederation in South Africa, in advance of a conference scheduled for 1875 but later postponed to August 1876. The Natal settlers were favorable, if rather apprehensive about possible Cape domination. Cape Colony politicians had major reservations about the likely dilution of their recently acquired self-governing status, plus likely additional financial burdens, and stayed away from the conference. The Orange Free State attended, but would not discuss it; while no one remembered to invite the Transvaal, an oversight that was to have important consequences. In the following month, Carnarvon appointed Shepstone special commissioner, with wide-ranging powers to execute his scheme in South Africa. Upon arrival, Shepstone selected the Transvaal as the likeliest prospect: it was virtually bankrupt; its president, Thomas Burgers, was deeply unpopular; its northern area had reverted to black rule; and the Pedi to the east and the Zulu to the southeast threatened its security.

Burgers's failure to defeat the Pedi gave Shepstone the opportunity to intervene in January 1877, and to formally annex the whole territory, claiming that his action had the support of the majority of Boers. Shepstone's assumption was not immediately challenged, and Carnarvon pushed through the parliament the (enabling) South Africa Act (1877), which provided the framework for a future confederation: Section 55 gave the crown an oversight of legislation affecting non-white people. A new high commissioner and governor of the Cape, Sir Bartle Frere, arrived and gave further impetus to confederation: in February 1878, he was able to get rid of the skeptical Cape premier Sir John Molteno on a technicality and replace him with the more amenable Sir Gordon Sprigg.

Meanwhile, Frere played a leading role in a concerted attempt to consolidate imperial interests by disarming and demilitarizing more powerful black communities on the fringes of, or adjacent to, areas of white settlement. He was able to exploit rumors of a possible black invasion, founded on reports of laborers returning with guns from the diamond fields, and African rulers importing weapons from the coast. White anxieties stemmed from the (incorrect) news at the end of 1876 of a Pedi victory over the Boers, and a threatened black incursion into the Cape's eastern frontier. The scare provided an opportunity for a number of actions launched in the later 1870s to demilitarize and/or break up potentially "dangerous" black polities, on the pretext that they were engaged in a concerted antiwhite conspiracy. Frere identified the Zulu monarch Cetshwayo as its head, and provoked a war in 1879 designed to smash the Zulu regimental system. Prior to this, and assisted by other black communities on the frontier, in 1877 the Cape government broke up Sandile's Gcaleka Xhosa, and by 1884 had extended its frontier to the Umtata River. It also enforced legislation passed in 1878 allowing its magistrates in Lesotho (then under Cape administration) to order the surrender of guns. The resulting Gun War (1880–1881) cost the Cape authorities £3 million and induced it to return Lesotho to the Imperial government at the end of 1883.

The breakup of the Zulu kingdom in 1879, and Sir Garnet Wolseley's defeat of the Pedi in November of that year, removed major black threats against the Transvaal Boers, who had become more and more antagonistic to British rule. However, influenced by Bartle Frere and Lanyon, the British administrator of the Transvaal, the imperial government had dismissed their leader Paul Kruger and his colleagues as unrepresentative, as well as irredeemably hostile, and even Gladstone's new government, formed in April 1880, allowed itself to be persuaded by the "men on the spot." Exasperated, Transvaal Boer leaders declared their independence at Paardekraal (December 1880); an outbreak of violence, after British authorities seized a Boer wagon, led to the First Anglo-Boer War (1880–1881). This comprised three main engagements, of which the most significant in exposing the deficiencies of British military strategy was that at Majuba Hill (February 26, 1881). Ironically, Gladstone, fearing a wider conflict between Boer and Briton, had already decided to give a limited independence to the Transvaal, an objective achieved in the Pretoria Convention (August 1881). Its main feature, an assertion of British suzerainty, was to be the subject of intense controversy a generation later.

By this stage, confederation was already dead: in June 1880, Sprigg's motion in favor of it was withdrawn, after it received a hostile reception in the Cape Assembly. Closer association was now to be delayed for more than a generation; its outcome, the 1910 Act of Union, took place in an environment greatly different from that of Carnarvon's day.

MURRAY STEELE

See also: **Kimberley, Diamond Fields and.**

Further Reading

Davenport, Trevor, and Christopher Saunders. *South Africa: A Modern History*. Basingstoke England: Macmillan/New York: St. Martin's Press, 2000.

De Kiewiet, Cornelius. *The Imperial Factor in South Africa: A Study in Politics and Economics* (1937). Reprint, New York: Russell and Russell, 1966.

Etherington, Norman. "Labour Supplies and the Genesis of the South African Confederation in the 1870s." *Journal of African History* 20, no. 2 (1975): 235–253.

Goodfellow, Clement. *Great Britain and South African Confederation, 1870–1881*. Cape Town: Oxford University Press, 1966.

Schreuder, Deryck. *Gladstone and Kruger: Liberal Government and Colonial "Home Rule," 1880–85*. London: Routledge and Kegan Paul, 1969.

South Africa: Gold on the Witwatersrand: 1886–1899

The search for Transvaal gold began in the 1860s with initially promising finds at Lydenburg, Pilgrim's Rest and Barberton following over the next decade. By 1885, hope for success in the eastern Transvaal faded and the search shifted westward to the Witwatersrand. There, after initial prospecting success in 1886, major gold reserves were considered well proven by the early 1890s. Many of the people financing early developments on the Rand were using profits gained from the battle between Cecil Rhodes and Barney Barnato that put De Beers Consolidated in control of Cape diamond mining. Investors included friends and associates of Rhodes, such as Alfred Beit as well as Barnato himself. Others among a small investment community whose interests intertwined included friends of President Paul Kruger, such as Sammy Marks.

In the De Beers struggle Rhodes had been helped by the Rothschild family, which also invested in the Transvaal. Only a relatively small number of financiers, individuals, and banks, were prepared to face the high risks of mining investment. Those who did tended to operate on an international scale without regard to national boundaries, or to which of the imperial powers claimed a particular territory. British capital dominated the Transvaal, followed closely by German banks and individuals who found the Rand much more promising than the minerals of Germany's own colonies.

Rhodes himself, involved in various grandiose schemes and fearing a repeat of earlier eastern Transvaal disappointments, went late to the Rand. His company, Consolidated Gold Fields, secured claims in the

Stock exchange, Johannesburg, Transvaal, South Africa, *c*.1890s. © Das Fotoarchiv.

less promising western Rand, and it was only dividends on Consolidated Gold Fields holdings of De Beers Consolidated shares assigned to the company by Rhodes that enabled the company to survive and pay its own dividends until the 1930s when, employing new technology, substantial gold reserves were located at great depth beneath a thick layer of rock.

The Rand gold reserves were extensive, but of very low grade, particularly as alluvial and weathered deposits closer to the surface were worked out and the search for gold extended to ever greater depths. Lingering doubts about the mines' longer term viability were put to rest with the widespread use of the MacArthur-Forrest cyanide process for separating the very fine particles of gold from the surrounding rock. Deep-level mining inevitably required increased investment, and in turn efforts to reduce operating costs to protect profitability. Because the price of gold was fixed on world markets, higher production costs could not be passed on to purchasers. Mining companies also had no control over the cost of the machinery or "mine stores" consumed in mining operations—most significantly, dynamite. Efforts to minimize costs faced a major obstacle in the dynamite monopoly, part of Transvaal president Kruger's concession policy intended to promote industrial development and ensure Transvaal control over key aspects of the country's economy.

The dynamite monopoly was initially granted to Edouard Lippert, a cousin of Alfred Beit whose interests were not primarily in mining. The operation of the concession initially caused considerable difficulties, including charges of corruption. Because the quality of explosive that the domestic industry was able to produce was very poor, virtually all the dynamite needed in this period was imported, with a high protective tariff adding to the cost. The dynamite monopoly was one of the bones of contention between the Kruger government and the mining industry that was used as a justification for the Jameson Raid of 1895 and the [Second] South African [Boer] War in 1899. In the very complex personal, political, and financial interests and pressures leading to those events, the monopoly was a factor whose importance can easily be exaggerated.

The Jameson Raid has also been seen as a reflection of conflict between the interests of the owners of deep level mines and those of the outcrop companies. While these companies did undoubtedly have different priorities, it is important to remember that most individual mine owners had interests in both outcrop and deep level operations, making it necessary to look to personal and perhaps political considerations to explain why a particular individual supported the raid or not. The simple distinction between outcrop and deep-level interests also does not take account of the group system of mine ownership. Although separate companies were floated for individual mines, they were grouped together under the primary ownership of one or another of six holding companies. The group structure made it less difficult to bring together the relatively massive amounts of capital required while overlapping mine ownership among groups ensured that within any group mines of varying depth and grade of ores helped even out cost and profit differentials, helping minimize risk as much as possible.

Railways were essential for the success of mining as the cheapest way to carry imported machinery and supplies into the interior from coastal ports. The Cape government had already linked the Kimberley mines by rail to Cape Town, Port Elizabeth (the closest to the mines), and East London, more than meeting the needs of the mines and satisfying the demands of the different port cities for whom the mines were a potentially profitable hinterland. From Kimberley the line reached the Transvaal border in 1895; here Kruger held it up to allow the completion of the shorter link to the coast at the Mozambique port of Lourenço Marques (now Maputo). Kruger preferred this line primarily because the greater part of its length was within the Transvaal, but also because its terminal port was outside direct British control. Close relations between Mozambique and the Transvaal went back to 1875 and included preferential trading ties. Both railway lines were completed in the course of 1895, followed by a third line from the Natal port of Durban. Manipulation of rates on the Cape routes and the fact that European shipping was considerably cheaper to Port Elizabeth than to Lourenço Marques meant that the railway to the Portuguese port did not benefit as much as it might have by virtue of being the shortest route to the coast. This disadvantage was ultimately offset by the importance of Mozambique labor for the Transvaal mines.

Rand mine owners sought to minimize capital requirements by using labor-intensive mining methods. As labor costs were the only significant factor of production over which they had any effective control at all it was generally regarded as essential for the industry's future to keep wages as low as possible while at the same time trying to convince African workers to accept longer contracts. The Rand, like most African mineral areas, was higher in altitude, relatively cold, and therefore relatively less populated. To attract African workers, the more profitable mines offered higher wages and shorter contract periods than those available either from farmers who were also competing for African labor or from mines with higher operating costs and narrower margins.

The desire to halt the resulting wage spiral was a major factor in the formation of the Transvaal Chamber of Mines in 1889. African men were more interested in satisfying whatever need they had to earn wages during those times of the year when they were not heavily involved in their own family's agriculture, and preferred shorter contracts and high wages. Efforts to fill the mining industry's demand for African workers was, particularly until 1895, also limited by the restrictions the Transvaal government imposed on the areas in which the chamber's recruiting agents were allowed to operate. President Kruger, contrary to many claims made about him, was not opposed to the mining industry, but did have to balance its demands against those of his primary constituency, Boer farmers.

Some workers came to the mines independently. Many others were under contract to labor "touts"—generally merchants and others with strong local contacts—who used debt, false wage and working-conditions promises, and bribery of officials to convince (entrap) men to agree to accept a contract. Touts paid the men much less than they received from the mine owners. In trying to establish recruitment on a more solid basis, the chamber began looking outside the Transvaal. Efforts in German Southwest Africa and Angola met with little success, but in Mozambique the result was very different. Mozambicans had been traveling to various parts of southern Africa, including the Kimberley diamond mines, for many years. Apart from a desire to travel and earn higher wages than those paid in Mozambique, for many Mozambicans migrant labor enabled them to escape the harsh labor regime imposed by the Portuguese.

In 1897 agreement was reached with the Portuguese for the RNLA to recruit in Mozambique. Success was limited because touts continued to operate independently and because most of RNLA's agents had been touts with highly unfavorable reputations. Nonetheless, by 1899 a pattern of migration was well established. Mozambicans were well on their way to becoming the most important single group of African workers on the Rand. The outbreak of war in 1899 disrupted but did not completely stop either the flow of migrants or mining itself.

SIMON KATZENELLENBOGEN

See also: **Jameson Raid, Origins of South African War: 1895–1899; Kruger, Paul; Labor, Migrant; Railways.**

Further Reading

Crush, Jonathan. *South Africa's Labor Empire: A History of Black Migracy to the Gold Mines.* African Modernization and Development series. Boulder, Colo.: Westview Press, 1991.

Duffy, James. *A Question of Slavery; Labour Policies in Portuguese Africa and the British Protest.* Oxford: Oxford University Press, 1967.

Harries, Patrick. *Work, Culture, and Identity: Migrant Laborers in Mozambique and South Africa.* Portsmouth, N.H.: Heinemann/London: James Currey, 1994.

Jeeves, Alan H. *Migrant Labour in South Africa's Mining Economy: The Struggle for the Gold.* Kingston, Ont.: McGill-Queen's University Press/Johannesburg: Witwatersrand University Press, 1985.

Johnstone, Frederick A. *Class, Race and Gold: A Study of Class Relations and Racial Discrimination.* International Library of Sociology. London: Routledge and Kegan Paul, 1976.

Katzenellenbogen, Simon E. *South African and Southern Mozambique: Labour, Railways and Trade in the Making of a Relationship.* Manchester: Manchester University Press, 1982.

Wilson, Francis. *Labour in the South African Gold Mines 1911–1969.* African Studies series no. 6. London: Cambridge University Press, 1972.

South Africa: Peasantry, African

Although much of what would later become the Republic of South Africa was conquered, claimed, or settled by whites between the 1830s and the 1880s, most blacks living in these territories did not feel the full effects of conquest until some decades later. In fact, African-run farms generally thrived until the 1880s, producing more tax revenue and food for market than European-owned farms did during this period. In later decades, however, the diamond (from 1870) and gold (from 1880) revolutions, as well as growing white settler control over the region's governments, ultimately created a situation in which Africans were increasingly unable to live off the food they grew on their own farms. As a result, most Africans were forced to rely on wage labor to make up the difference.

Until the 1830s, white settlement in southern Africa was almost entirely confined to the area of the the present-day Western Cape province. Over the course of that and the following decade, however, whites consolidated their control over the Ciskei in the Eastern Cape province, and pushed their settlements and land claims into what were to become Natal, the Orange Free State, and the Transvaal. In due course, in all these regions, the consequences for Africans were largely similar: the loss of the great majority of their land, confinement to increasingly overcrowded reserves, and growing dependence on wage labor. Nevertheless, some areas felt these consequences sooner than others. Consequences also varied within each area: some households prospered while many others suffered greatly, and men and women, old and young, felt the effects differently.

The prosperity of African agriculture between the 1830s and 1880s varied according to the balance of power between settlers and Africans in each region. Whites held the upper hand in some areas because of their relatively large numbers, military strength, proximity to agricultural markets, and familiarity with the land. This was certainly the case in much of the Ciskei, and in the immediate hinterland of such towns as Durban, Pietermaritzburg, Bloemfontein, Pretoria, and Potchefstroom. Here, in the nearby towns, white farmers found ready markets for their agricultural produce and were able to evict Africans from their lands, forcing them into reserves. The reserves, in turn, were inadequate for the Africans' needs, especially in the context of war and, often, famine. The white farmers' access to markets allowed them to acquire cash with which to pay farm workers real cash wages. Such wage labor offered many of these African households virtually the only means for survival, but it also came to mitigate some of the harsher effects of conquest. Some young African men were able to accumulate enough cash to pay bride-price to marry several wives, gain access to larger plots of land, and expand their cattle herds.

African agriculture was much stronger in most of Natal, the Orange Free State, and the southern and central Transvaal. In these places few white farmers had the know-how with which to farm their lands as well as Africans could, the labor with which to work the lands, or the means to pay for such labor. Neither did most whites have the military power with which to evict Africans from their lands wholesale and coerce some of them into returning as mere agricultural laborers. The result was that most Africans became tenant farmers on white-owned lands, paying taxes to the state in cash and rent to the landowners in cash, kind, or labor. African agriculture was prosperous enough in these areas for most African households to meet these demands by selling their surplus instead of turning to wage labor. Meanwhile, even though reserves existed, they were not yet overcrowded because so many Africans still lived outside them. For Africans, little changed in the way of residence patterns and means of subsistence. They produced more taxes and marketable produce than their white counterparts and managed to avoid becoming the agricultural workforce that white farmers wanted so desperately.

The situation was much freer for African farmers in the eastern, northern, and western fringes of the Transvaal. The government of the South African Republic might claim authority over these lands, and white settlers might claim ownership of some of them, but none of these claims carried much weight with the Africans who lived on the lands. Indeed, for all intents and purposes most Africans of the Transvaal borderlands were as independent as those in still nominally independent areas such as the Transkei, Zululand north of the Thukela River, and in what are now Lesotho, Swaziland, and Botswana. Migrant wage labor from these areas was limited and strictly voluntarily, much of it going to the diamond mining city of Kimberly in the 1870s, which, most notably, enabled Africans to accumulate guns that would allow them to fend off white armies. For its part, Lesotho became a major grain exporter, finding Kimberly a ready market.

The effects of European conquest on African agriculture varied not only from region to region, but also within each region according to religion, class, gender, and generation. Consider, for example, the plow, a major technological innovation adopted by many African farmers during this period. For the still-tiny Christian minority, the plow was both cause and effect of a whole host of social transformations they were experiencing. The plow gave males a central role in cultivation, which had been a strictly female domain in most southern African societies up to this point. Along with the connections and cultural capital that Christianization brought with it, the plow enabled a small minority of Christian landowners to prosper even when the vast majority of their African neighbors were struggling.

Nevertheless, the adoption of the plow and the accumulation of wealth in the form of livestock and access to land, by both Christian and non-Christian Africans, did not benefit all Africans. Women still did the greater part of agricultural labor, such as planting, weeding, and harvesting, even in plow-using households, and reproduction and maintenance of the household likewise remained female tasks. It tended not to be prosperous, married men who did the plowing, but rather young men, whether adult sons or hired hands. It was also the young, unmarried men who undertook migrant wage labor when times were tough. Indeed, generational tensions increased during the nineteenth century: in order to maintain control over the labor of youths for a longer time, elders increasingly delayed giving their sons enough cattle to pay bride-price, marry, and set up their own households. As a result, young men came to see the wages of migrant labor as a means to gaining independence. As much as the situation varied within a household, it varied even more between those households that were getting richer and those that were getting poorer.

The conditions that allowed many African farmers to prosper between the 1830s and 1880s changed drastically with the South African mineral revolution. The diamond and gold booms (especially the latter) from the 1870s and 1880s created huge nonagricultural populations who needed food and had the cash with which to pay for it. White farmers now had access to enough capital to allow them to evict their African tenants, make technological improvements, and hire (mainly African) wage labor. The evicted Africans were forced into reserves, which became overcrowded during this period if they were not already. Deforestation, overgrazing, and soil exhaustion on ever smaller plots of land left African farmers increasingly unable to meet their subsistence needs, not to mention pay the taxes they owed. The only alternative was migrant labor on the farms, in the mines, in the towns, and on the railroads.

It was not only purely economic factors that forced African farmers to become wage laborers; racist legislation contributed to the process as well. Large tracts of government-controlled land were thrown open for purchase by whites only. Settler-dominated legislatures passed laws designed to put pressure on landowners (especially absentee landowners) to evict their African tenants. This movement reached its climax in 1913, when the South African government passed the Natives Land Act, which limited African land ownership, whether communal or freehold, at first to 7 per cent and later to 13 per cent of South African territory. Outside these lands, Africans were not only prohibited from being landowners, according to the law, but neither could they be tenants or share-croppers.

Nevertheless, though the mineral revolutions and racist legislation dealt a serious blow to African farming, its subsequent decline was gradual, and in some senses it continued to survive through the twentieth century. In the poorer parts of South Africa that were the farthest from markets, white landowners ignored laws against African tenancy or sharecropping well into the 1930s, if not later. In the reserves, the boom in migrant labor around the turn of the century relieved pressure on the land and allowed for some accumulation and improvement. Migrant labor thus bought something of a reprieve for African agriculture from the early to mid-twentieth century. However, the situation in the reserves has been in sharp decline ever since. The "influx control" system under apartheid hindered and delayed for decades the resulting tendency toward urbanization, making urbanization since the fall of apartheid far more rapid and traumatic than it might otherwise have been.

MICHAEL MAHONEY

See also: **Kimberley, Diamond Fields and; Lesotho (Basutoland): Peasantry, Rise of.**

Further Reading

Bradford, Helen. "The Rise of the Male Peasantry: A South African 'Case Study,' 1850–1886." Paper presented before the Biennial Conference of the South African Historical Society, University of the Western Cape, July 11–14, 1999.

Bundy, Colin. "The Emergence and Decline of a South African Peasantry." *African Affairs* 71, no. 285 (1972): 369–388.

———. *The Rise and Fall of the South African Peasantry*, Berkeley and Los Angeles: University of California Press/London: Heinemann, 1979.

Jeeves, Alan H. and Jonathan Crush (eds.). *White Farms, Black Labor: The State and Agrarian Change in Southern Africa, 1910–1950*, Portsmouth, N.H.: Heinemann, 1997.

Lambert, John. *Betrayed Trust: Africans and the State in Colonial Natal*. Durban, South Africa: University of Natal Press, 1995.

Van Onselen, Charles. "Race and Class in the South African Countryside: Cultural Osmosis and Social Relations in the Sharecropping Economy of the South-Western Transvaal, 1900–1950." *American Historical Review* 95, no. 1 (1990): 99–123.

South African War, 1899–1902

The South African, or Anglo-Boer, War of 1899–1902 is a crucial event in South African history, for it both completed the British imperial conquest of modern South Africa and lay the foundations for the construction of a segregationist union state in 1910. In the most extensive colonial war of late-Victorian "new imperialism," British forces crushed territorially based Boer (Afrikaner) settler republicanism after a mutually costly and wasteful struggle. Thereafter, Britian turned to reconstruction and reconciliation with its former radical nationalist enemy, winning over reliable Boer collaborators who would uphold Britain's vital imperial interests in South Africa. The price of accommodation between white colonial society and the British Empire was paid by disenchanted black inhabitants, many of whom had hoped in vain for improved rights in the wake of Britain's victory.

The origins of the war lay in the 1886 discovery of gold in Boer republican territory and its impact on the balance of power in late-nineteenth century South Africa. While the agrarian Boer republics had hitherto been weak and of little consequence, within little more than a decade the Witwatersrand mines of the South African Republic (Transvaal) had become the world's largest single source of gold, tilting South Africa's economic center of gravity from the coastal British colonies of the Cape and Natal toward an increasingly nationalist, republican Boer state. Transvaal strength posed several grave problems for British interests. It opened the door for pro-Boer imperial rivals to wield commercial and political might in a customary British sphere of influence, and to challenge the Royal Navy's strategic command of the Southern African seaboard. However, the South African Republic government under Paul Kruger was tied to a conservative landowning oligarchy that enjoyed the income provided by the mines but was otherwise fairly cool toward their modernizing industrial order. The Boer ruling class would tolerate no liberalizing dilution of its monopoly of power through an enfranchisement of mining-based British *Uitlanders* (foreigners) on the Witwatersrand, a political reform demanded by Britain as a strategy to engineer a more proimperial political structure. Increasingly, some disgruntled mining capitalists concluded that the long-term success and efficiency of the gold mines as a British interest could only be secured by the removal of the Transvaal regime. For many imperial politicians and officials, it was also becoming quite intolerable for a great power to be defied by a tiny African settler state run by upstart Dutch farmers.

After the 1895 Jameson Raid, a botched plot hatched by some conspiring capitalists and gambling imperial politicians to unseat the Kruger government, every strategic eventuality led toward war. As diplomacy ran into the sand at the end of the 1890s, force was the only option left to a blustering Britain and a cornered Transvaal, now in a military alliance with its sister republic, the Orange Free State. To preserve republican independence, the anti-imperialist Boers declared war on Britain in October 1899. In seizing the initiative, their command hoped to knock back the British before the arrival of reinforcements to strengthen their fragile garrison position. The Boer hope lay in surprise, and the forcing of a negotiated peace.

Metropolitan observers who anticipated a rapid and easy war of conquest received a devastating shock. In the opening stage of hostilities, Boer armies struck deep into British colonial territory, inflicting several major defeats on badly organized and ineptly led British troops and creating a great domestic fuss over the failings of imperial power. But the Boer offensive was not a showcase for decisive generalship either. Failing to exploit their initial gains, republican command became bogged down in pointless diversions, giving the British time to feed in massive reinforcements, to regroup, and to adapt more effectively to the trying conditions of the vast South African countryside.

Under more competent leadership, British forces began to turn the tide early in 1900, launching a concerted assault to take the Boer states. By June, their heavily outnumbered enemy had been pushed back and, unable to stop their territories from being overrun, retreating Boer field armies began to disintegrate under pressure. With the Transvaal and Orange Free State State in his pocket, Britain's commander in chief, Lord Roberts, now considered the war at an end.

However, a dedicated core of younger generation republicans was still committed to the struggle. Encouraged by defiant Boer women, mounted forces under resourceful leaders like Louis Botha, Jan Smuts, and Christiaan de Wet reinvigorated the Boer effort through sure-footed irregular warfare. For nearly two years of guerrilla war, dispersed commandos kept the occupying imperial army on the run, lashing out with running attacks and sabotage. To cut Boers off from the lifeline of support and subsistence thrown out by their farming population, the British commander, Lord Kitchener, resorted to general doctrines of colonial wars of conquest against rural opponents. In the second half of the war, the imperial army instituted a sweeping scorched-earth policy, destroying crops and livestock and torching thousands of farms. Displaced women

and children were bundled into concentration camps while thousands of African refugees, also uprooted by scorched-earth tactics, were driven into segregated black camps. Appalling internment conditions produced high mortality rates and, when hostilities ended, some 28,000 Boers and at least 20,000 Africans had perished, mainly from disease.

Britain's unflagging determination to crush Boer republicanism and the enormous imperial resources used to achieve this end eventually whittled away the will and means of even the most diehard (or *bittereinder*) leaders to continue fighting. Their position was also worsened by two other crucial factors. Numerous Boers had lost faith in their cause, and were either laying down their arms or turning out for the British Army as collaborating National Scouts, fighting their erstwhile compatriots. The war therefore fractured Boer society. Second, African and "colored" (mixed-blood) inhabitants were increasingly resisting Boer authority and assisting the British war effort. With the conflict threatening to eliminate the very Boer existence it had been launched to defend, Boer military leaders yielded and made peace in May 1902. Although the republican states had to surrender their independence, Britain funded generous postwar reconstruction, which culminated in the creation of a white imperial dominion, the Union of South Africa in 1910.

By the end, Britain had put almost 450,000 soldiers into the field, and the Boers about 70,000 combatants. Some 22,000 imperial troops and 7,000 Boer soldiers perished. To this can be added a further toll of black casualties as a consequence of hostilities. It had never been a simple Anglo-Boer War, and both sides made considerable use of blacks as labor and as combat auxiliaries. The Boers pulled well over 10,000 men into the servicing of commandos, while the British engaged more than 100,000 black people in their war effort, as many as 40,000 of whom bore arms. In this sense, the contest was a true South African War, its political and social reach such that the neutrality of the majority black population in a supposed "white man's war" was never anything other than fiction.

BILL NASSON

See also: **Jameson Raid, Origins of South African War: 1895–1899; Kruger, Paul; Smuts, Jan C.; South Africa: Gold on the Witwatersrand, 1886–1899; South Africa: Peace, Reconstruction, Union: 1902–1910.**

Further Reading

Comaroff, John L. (ed.). *The Boer War Diary of Sol T. Plaatje: An African at Mafeking.* London: Fontana, 1973.
Labuschagne, Pieter. *Ghostriders of the Anglo-Boer War (1899–1902): The Role and Contribution of Agterryers.* Pretoria: UNISA Press, 1999.

Nasson, Bill. *Abraham Esau's War: A Black South African War at the Cape, 1899–1902*, Cambridge: Cambridge University Press, 1991.

————. *The South African War 1899–1902*. London: Arnold, 1999.

————. *Uyadela Wen 'osulapho: Black Participation in the Anglo-Boer War*. Johannesburg: Ravan Press, 1999.

Pakenham, Thomas. *The Boer War*. London: Weidenfeld and Nicholson, 1979.

Pretorius, Fransjohan. *Life on Commando during the Anglo-Boer War 1899–1902*. Pretoria: Human and Rousseau, 1999.

Reitz, Deneys. *Commando: A Boer Journal of the Boer War*. London: Faber, 1929.

Warwick, Peter (ed.). *The South African War: The Anglo-Boer War 1899–1902*. London: Longman, 1980.

South Africa: Peace, Reconstruction, Union: 1902–1910

In 1902, a bitter and costly war between Britain and the Afrikaner Republics in South Africa ended in victory for the imperial forces. On May 31, a treaty was signed at Vereeniging, which brought the republics under imperial rule as the Transvaal and the Orange River Colony. The British conquest of the Afrikaner republics created the framework for the construction of the new form of state in South Africa sought by mining capital since the 1890s. Now in control, the British held unprecedented power to intervene in South African society and shape its future. Under the British flag, white supremacy would be assured, property rights secured, mining costs reduced, and black labor controlled.

Although in their wartime propaganda the British claimed to be fighting for the rights of both black and white British subjects, many Africans who had supported the imperial army soon found their hopes betrayed, as the British quickly restored the racial hierarchy, which had eroded during the war. This was already signaled in Clause 8 of the Treaty of Vereeniging, which left any decision about a black franchise to self-governing white colonists. The exclusion of the majority African population from South African citizenship in 1910 was the inevitable result. Africans hopes of having their land restored were equally disappointed. A threatened jacquerie was quickly quelled and Africans disarmed. The pass laws, inaugurated in the 1890s at the behest of the mining industry, were more efficiently administered, and taxes more systematically collected.

Even before the war was over, Sir Alfred Milner, the British high commissioner, had appointed a closely knit circle of young men from Oxford, dubbed the "Milner kindergarten," to join him in "reconstructing" the Afrikaner republics. Initially their role was to establish an efficient bureaucracy in the new crown colonies, set up municipal government, address the most obvious prewar grievances of the mining houses and restore order in the countryside.

The mining industry was at the heart of Milner's plans for economic and political reconstruction. In 1902, shortages of investment finance and African labor had resulted from overheated speculation and the decision of the Chamber of Mines to reduce black wages drastically during the war. In response to the crisis in profitability and labor shortage, between 1903 and 1907, the industry succeeded in importing some 60,000 indentured Chinese workers on three-year contracts.

The importation of Chinese labor had far-reaching consequences for the future of labor relations and white politics in South Africa. African bargaining power was undermined and the use of unskilled white workers to fill the labor shortage was also preempted. In response to the clamor of white workers, the "color bar" that reserved work defined as skilled for whites and relegated "unskilled" work to others was greatly extended. This prevented Chinese and Africans from being recognized and paid as skilled workers, and gave the mine magnates a powerful incentive to employ cheap black labor at the expense of white unskilled labor. Milner may have wanted South Africa to be a "white man's country," but the white men had to be "the right kind of Englishmen," those who would maintain racial purity and pose no challenge to property, stability, and order.

The policy deeply divided English speakers, and unified nascent Afrikaner opposition to the Milner administration, giving their political organization Het Volk (which emerged between 1903 and 1905) an anticapitalist thrust that enabled it to attract non-Afrikaner support. Thus, the importation of Chinese labor jeopardized what have conventionally regarded as Milner's political objectives in South Africa: the securing of imperial supremacy through an immigration policy which would ensure a British majority in any future election and an Anglicization policy which would swamp Afrikaners in the Transvaal and the Cape.

Milner's plans to restructure the countryside were equally contradictory. He hoped British immigrants would stimulate capitalist agriculture among Afrikaner rural populace, and draw South African support for the empire. Despite imperial efforts, however, agricultural settlement was largely a failure. Only some 1200 settlers were established on the land as a result of these schemes, largely in the Orange River Colony (ORC). Most became as dependent as the Boers on sharecropping, forced labor, and state subsidies.

The dissatisfaction aroused by Milner's policies and a postwar slump spurred demands for increased political representation. In March 1905 the British government agreed to a new constitution, but this quickly proved inadequate. With the accession to government of the British Liberal Party, it was scrapped. Campbell-Bannerman, the new prime minister, who had referred during the war to British "methods of barbarism," swiftly conceded to the demand for self-government and white adult male suffrage, and in 1906 and 1907, the Transvaal and ORC were granted self-governing constitutions based on white adult male suffrage. This persuaded Generals Jan C. Smuts and Louis Botha, the leaders of Het Volk, of the "magnanimity" of the British government and opened the way for their collaboration with the imperial authorities.

In the elections that followed, the Afrikaner parties led by the Boer generals won handsomely, despite the many class and gender divisions that had emerged during and after the war within the Afrikaner community. Their support came from their wartime followers, as well as a literate intelligentsia, to whom the language issue and a sense of ethnic identity were of particular importance. In the decade after the war, this intelligentsia was responsible for a flurry of nationalist poetry, sermons, and historical writing, while a group of Afrikaner women began building new philanthropic institutions, designed in part to reconstitute the Afrikaner moral order.

This was all the more necessary because after the war another wave of indigent, unskilled, and barely literate whites had flocked to the new industrial centers, where they faced competition both from organized, skilled, and largely English-speaking labor, and from equally poor, unskilled, and illiterate black workers who still had some access to land. Unemployed and to some extent unemployable, "poor whites" constituted a major problem of social control for government and a volatile constituency for political mobilization whether by Afrikaner nationalists or English-speaking socialists.

As early as 1900, with the war still raging, the high commissioner had begun to enunciate a new language and education policy for the conquered territories, and in 1901 he brought a leading educationist to South Africa to restructure education in both of the ex-republics and to undertake the Anglicization of the children in the camps. This undoubtedly fueled demands for autonomous Christian National Schools in which Dutch would be taught and the religion of the Dutch Reformed Church fostered.

It was as a propagator of the Dutch (and later Afrikaans) language that the ORC leader, General J. B. M. Hertzog, most distinguished himself from the nationalism of Botha, Smuts, and Het Volk in the late 1900s, seeing in language a way of unifying a fractured community.

For Botha and Smuts, language was less crucial. In 1906, the importance of non-Afrikaner support and the centrality of the gold mining industry on the Rand led them to accept the primacy of the English language. They appealed for "reconciliation" between the white "races," in a common white South African nation in a unified South African state. Although this call was not new, it was given urgency by the exigencies of politics in the postwar Transvaal, and the need to restore white supremacy in the face of the threat from black resistance during and immediately after the war.

The appointment of the South African Native Affairs Commission (SANAC) in 1903 to provide a blueprint for a unified "native policy" in the different British colonial states was a further indication of the centrality of "native policy" in the reconstruction of South Africa. Rejecting overt coercion or forced labor, the commission recommended a series of policies on land and the franchise that were subsequently to be elaborated by the South African state under the general rubric of *segregation*, a new word that crept into official discourse at this time.

If SANAC foreshadowed the unification of the South African colonies, the outbreak of a poll tax rebellion in Natal in 1906, and the brutality of its suppression, hastened the movement for unification, which was already being advocated by the major interests in South Africa, if for different reasons. Local politicians hoped a more powerful nation-state would curb the imperial intervention while the British, like the mining capitalists, saw the advantages of "closer union" in the interests of building a unified economic infrastructure and a common "native policy." After Milner's departure, members of the "kindergarten" began maneuvering for closer union behind the scenes, encouraged by his successor as high commissioner, Lord Selborne; they saw this as the best way of retaining South Africa within the empire.

Electoral victories by Afrikaner parties in the Transvaal, the Orange Free State (as it became under self-government), and the Cape Colony in 1907–1908, provided a major impetus, and by the middle of 1907, the Het Volk leaders were collaborating with their political opponents and the "kindergarten" over union. By 1908, the Transvaal delegation to the National Convention that was called to discuss a nationwide constitution had a carefully agreed-upon position that incorporated the demands of Het Volk, the mining industry, and the "kindergarten."

The draft constitution that emerged, with subsequent amendments recommended in the colonial parliaments, was given legal force by the British parliament as the Act of Union in 1909. It provided for a sovereign central bicameral legislature, based on a first-past-the-post constituency model, but with considerable weighting in favor of rural areas. The legal equality of the Dutch and English languages was similarly safeguarded, with both languages being entrenched by a clause that prevented any change without a two-thirds majority of both houses sitting together.

Natal's preference for federalism was given short shrift in favor of unification, and the Cape property-based but nonracial franchise, while also protected by a two-thirds majority, was restricted to that province. The Cape's support for the extension of its franchise was overruled, as was Natal's attempt to introduce suffrage for women. A delegation of black political leaders and the ex-prime minister of the Cape, the liberal W. P. Schreiner, attempted to persuade the British government to veto the "color bar" in the constitution, but in vain. It was to take another 20 years before white women were enfranchised, and another 80 before Africans could enter parliament.

There were those who wished for the immediate incorporation of the High Commission Territories of Basutoland, Swaziland, and Bechuanaland, imperial-controlled enclaves that were resented by more ardent colonial nationalists. A combination of African resistance and British humanitarian opposition added to imperial caution over the inclusion of the High Commission Territories, however. In any event, a schedule to the Act of Union setting out the conditions for their ultimate transfer served over the years to ignite South Africa's demands for incorporation—and to frustrate them. Southern Rhodesia, still under chartered company rule, also had observers at the National Convention. When, in 1923, the British South Africa Company charter lapsed, Southern Rhodesians decided in a referendum to remain outside the union.

The British government, like the majority of whites in South Africa, supported the new union. Nevertheless, as an editorial in the *Times* asserted in 1909, "A handful of leaders may fashion a state but they cannot create a nation." Reconciliation among Afrikaners, let alone between English-speakers and Afrikaners, was extremely fragile. Blacks were almost completely excluded from the new nation-state. Nevertheless, the self-governing white community underpinned by black labor, as envisaged by Cecil Rhodes and Alfred Milner, was now a reality. Initially created by disparate and contradictory interests, and constantly reshaped by the contest between them, the new socioeconomic and political dispensation nonetheless lasted for much of the century.

SHULA MARKS

See also: **Rhodes, Cecil J.; Smuts, Jan C.; South African War, 1899–1902.**

Further Reading

Denoon, Donald. *A Grand Illusion: the Failure of Imperial Policy in the Transvaal Colony during the Period of Reconstruction, 1900–1905*. London: Longman, 1973.

Hancock, W. K. *Smuts*, vol. 1, *The Sanguine Years*. Cambridge: Cambridge University Press, 1965.

Krikler, Jeremy. *Revolution from Above, Rebellion from Below: The Agrarian Transvaal at the Turn of the Century*. Oxford: Oxford University Press, 1993.

Le May, G. H. *British Supremacy in South Africa, 1899–1907*. Oxford: Oxford University Press, 1965.

Marks, Shula, and Stanley Trapido. "Lord Milner and the South African State." *History Workshop.* no. 8 (1979): 50–82.

Odendaal, André. *The Beginnings of Black Protest Politics in South Africa to 1912*. Cape Town: David Philip, 1984.

Thompson, L. M. *The Unification of South Africa 1902–10*. London: Oxford University Press, 1960.

South Africa: Gandhi, Indian Question

When Mohandas K. Gandhi (1869–1948) arrived in South Africa in 1893 there were approximately 62,000 Indians in South Africa distributed among the self-governing British colonies of Natal and the Cape, and the Boer republics of the Transvaal and the Orange Free State (OFS). Of this total, 42,000 were in Natal, and 15,000 and 5,000 in the Cape and the Transvaal, respectively. There was only a handful of Indians in the OFS. Most of the Natal Indians were either indentured laborers on five-year contracts working on sugar plantations and industries, or ex-indentured individuals engaged in the free labor market and petty trade. A much smaller percentage of the immigrants was made up of traders, among whom about a dozen rose to establish substantial commercial enterprises. Those in the Transvaal and the Cape were traders or workers. There was enormous cultural, religious, and linguistic diversity among the immigrants as they came from at least three widely separated regions on the Indian subcontinent.

The London-trained barrister came to the country to help settle a dispute between two Indian business partners, but was to become directly involved in South African Indian politics until he finally left for India in 1914. Gandhi's role can be conveniently divided into two phases: before and after 1906.

In the period before 1906, Gandhi's organizational efforts went toward protecting the interests of the Indian commercial elite through the Natal Indian Congress (NIC; founded 1894) and the British Indian Association (founded 1903) in the Transvaal. Such interests were accommodated by loosely structured bodies before Gandhi came, but they lacked an efficient organizer, and a spokesperson proficient in the English language. In Gandhi, the commercial elite found such a person with whose views they agreed. Gandhi's use of "Indianness" was an attempt to place the rights of the subcontinent's immigrants within an imperial framework. He started the *Indian Opinion* in 1903 to promote "Indian-ness" among the divergent groups of the immigrants, and to propagate the idea that as British subjects, the Indians in South Africa enjoyed equality within the empire. In thus connecting Indian South Africans to India and Britain, he hoped to influence developments by means of polite constitutional protests. This strategy failed to halt anti-Indian laws in Natal. In the Transvaal, the British imperial authorities yielded to segregationist tendencies in the interest of Boer-Briton amity after the South African War (1899–1902). Indeed, the white authorities moved inexorably toward restricting the influx of Indians (who numbered over 149,000 in 1911) into South Africa.

In the period after 1906, Gandhi combined his moral and ethical beliefs with political considerations. The search for justice, Gandhi argued, required strict adherence to *satya* (truth) and *ahimsa* (nonviolence); and duty called for sacrifice and faith in God. These were the broad principles on which he launched the *satyagraha* (truth force) campaign in 1906 in the Transvaal. When that campaign went into effect in 1907, he had the support of some 3000 resisters, including the commercial elite.

By 1909, however, Gandhi lost the support of members of the merchant class for most of whom the political rather than the moral imperative was always more important. They found his approach idiosyncratic and his endeavors to widen the campaign inimical to their interests. They increasingly withdrew their political and financial support. By the end of April 1913, the NIC repudiated his leadership, though a formal split was to occur only in October 1913 after which Gandhi formed a new political organization, the Natal Indian Association.

Long before the split occurred, however, Gandhi had successfully appealed to prominent individuals in India for funds. Among his supporters was Gopal K. Gokhale, who as member of the Imperial Legislative Council had considerable influence in India and England. His visit to South Africa in 1912 did much to enhance Gandhi's leadership role. But Gandhi recognized that he would need allies in South Africa to make an impression on a government more firmly united on the Indian question after political unification had been achieved in 1910. Until 1911, the small Transvaal Chinese community joined Gandhi. But he did not seek support from among the African and "colored" (mixed-blood) leadership because, as he explained later, he did not want to confuse issues that affected the "children of the soil" with those of immigrant communities.

With the erosion of support, Gandhi reached out to the ex-indentured Indians in Natal. As individuals who considered themselves South Africans rather than Indians, their concerns revolved around the lack of educational facilities and interstate travel restrictions.

But Gandhi was wary about widening the scope of the campaign to include unrealizable goals. He bided his time with provisional settlements after 1911. His foremost adversary in the government, Interior Minister Jan C. Smuts, was counting on Gandhi losing support.

A series of developments was to help revive the campaign, however. The Cape Supreme Court decision delivered by Justice Searle in March 1913 ruled that all marriages contracted under Hindu and Muslim rites were invalid. Gandhi moved quickly to capitalize on the issue by getting Indian women involved. In June 1913 he resolved "to do something for the indentured men" and decided sometime thereafter to embrace the three-pound tax issue that directly affected the indentured and ex-indentured Indians. When in September 1913 Gandhi formally resumed the campaign, the three-pound tax became an important part of the movement. His trusted supporters lobbied the indentured Indians working on the mines to strike. By the end of October, the number of strikers had risen to 5000. Then, for reasons that are not entirely clear, some 15,000 Indian workers in the coastal sugar districts joined the strike. Services and industries in many parts of Natal were paralyzed. Gandhi was determined to take the campaign to the government. In November he marched with over 2,200 strikers from Natal into the Transvaal in defiance of the law. A general strike of white railway workers had compounded the government's problems, and Smuts decided to reach an agreement with Gandhi. Gandhi agreed to the settlement despite misgivings. The Gandhi-Smuts agreement was formalized in the Indian Relief Act of 1914.

It was a significant victory for Gandhi and his supporters. Yet there were many who were displeased with the settlement because it did not go far enough in establishing the inherent rights of the South African Indians. His legacy continued directly and indirectly in the 1920s and 1930s, most notably in the continued use of the imperial framework as a basis of the South African Indian politics. Gandhian ideas also inspired resistance to apartheid in the decades ahead.

SURENDRA BHANA

See also: **Smuts, Jan C.**

Further Reading

Bhana, Surendra. *Gandhi's Legacy: The Natal Indian Congress, 1894–1994*. Pietermaritzburg: University of Natal Press, 1997.

Gandhi, Mohandas K. *Collected Works of Mahatma Gandhi*. 12 vols. New Delhi: Government Printer, 1958–1964.

———. *Satyagraha in South Africa*. Ahmedabad: Navajivan, 1928.

———. *The Story of My Experiments with Truth*. Boston: Beacon Press, 1993.

Swan, Maureen. *Gandhi: The South African Experience*. Johannesburg: Ravan Press, 1985.

South Africa: Colored Identity

Contrary to international usage, in South Africa the term *colored* does not refer to black people in general. It instead alludes to a phenotypically diverse group of people descended largely from Cape slaves, indigenous Khoisan peoples, and other blacks who had been assimilated to Cape colonial society by the late nineteenth century. Being also partly descended from European settlers, "coloreds" are popularly regarded as being of "mixed race" and hold an intermediate status in the South African racial hierarchy, distinct from the historically dominant white minority and the numerically preponderant African population.

There are approximately three and a half million colored people in South Africa today. Constituting less than 10 per cent of the population and lacking significant political or economic power as a result of a heritage slavery, dispossession and racial oppression, coloreds form a marginal group in South African society. There is, moreover, a marked regional concentration of colored people, with approximately two-thirds resident in the Western Cape and about one-third in the greater Cape Town area.

Although colored identity crystallized in the late nineteenth century, the process of social amalgamation within the colonial black population at the Cape that gave rise to colored group consciousness dates back to the period of Dutch colonial rule. It was, however, in the decades after the emancipation of slaves in 1838 that the various components of the heterogeneous black laboring class integrated more rapidly and developed an incipient shared identity based on a common socioeconomic status. The emergence of a full-fledged colored identity was precipitated in the late nineteenth century by the sweeping social changes that came in the wake of the mineral revolution. It was especially the incorporation of large numbers of Africans into Cape society that drove acculturated colonial blacks to assert a separate identity in order to claim a position of relative privilege to Africans on the basis of their closer assimilation to Western culture and being partly descended from European colonists.

Because of their marginality and the determination with which the state implemented white supremacist policies, the story of colored political organization has largely been one of compromise, retreat, and failure. The most consistent feature of colored political history has been the continual erosion of the civil rights first bestowed upon blacks in the Cape Colony by the British Administration in the mid-nineteenth century. The process of attrition started with the franchise restrictions of the late nineteenth century. A spate of segregationist measures in the first decade of the twentieth century further compromised the civil rights of colored people. The most significant were the exclusion of coloreds from the franchise in the former Boer republics after the Anglo-Boer War and the denial of their right to be elected to parliament with the implementation of union in 1910. In the 1920s and 1930s the economic status of coloreds was undermined by the pact goverment's civilized labor policy and a number of laws designed to favor whites over blacks in the competition for employment. Furthermore, in 1930 the influence of the colored vote was greatly diminished by the enfranchisement of white women only. It was during the Apartheid era, however, that coloreds suffered the most severe violations of their civil rights. The most important of these measures were their classification under the Population Registration Act of 1950, the prohibition of mixed marriages, their removal from the common voter's roll in 1956, the forced relocation of tens of thousands of colored families under the Group Areas Act of 1950, and the segregation of public facilities under the Separate Amenities Act of 1953.

Because their primary objective was to assimilate into the dominant society, politicized coloreds initially avoided forming separate political organizations. By the early twentieth century, however, intensifying segregation forced them to mobilize politically in defense of their rights. Although the earliest colored political organizations date back to the 1880s, the first substantive colored political body, the African Political Organization (APO), was established in Cape Town in 1902. The APO dominated colored protest politics for nearly four decades, becoming the main vehicle for expressing this community's assimilationist aspirations as well as its fears at the rising tide of segregationism. The failure of the APO's moderate approach resulted in the emergence of a radical movement inspired by socialist ideology within the better-educated, urbanized sector of the colored community during the 1930s. The National Liberation League, founded in 1935 and the Non-European Unity Movement established in 1943 were the most important radical organizations. Prone to fissure and unable to bridge the racial divisions within the society, the radical movement failed in its quest to unite blacks in the struggle against segregation. Extraparliamentary opposition by colored political organizations was effectively quelled by state repression following the Sharpeville massacre of 1960 and only reemerged in the wake of the Soweto uprising of 1976.

From the late 1970s on, with the popularization of black consciousness ideology, the nature of colored identity became an extremely contentious issue as increasing numbers of educated and politicized people who had been classified as colored under the Population Registration Act rejected the identity. It was increasingly viewed as an artificial categorization imposed by the ruling elite as part of its divide-and-rule strategies. The growth of a mass, nonracial democratic movement through the 1980s and conflict over the participation of coloreds in the tricameral Parliament of the government of P. W. Botha from 1984 on intensified the controversy.

In spite of this, the salience of colored identity has endured. During the four-year transition to democratic rule under president F. W. de Klerk, political parties across the ideological spectrum made ever more strident appeals to colored identity for support. Postapartheid South Africa has, furthermore, witnessed a resurgence of "coloredism." This has been due partly to a desire to assert a positive self-image in the face of the pervasive negative racial stereotyping of colored people and partly as a result of attempts at ethnic mobilization to take advantage of the newly democratic political environment. It is also, however, to a significant extent due to fear of African majority rule and a hitherto unfounded perception that, as in the old order, coloreds are once again being marginalized. A common refrain among disaffected colored people is, "First we were not white enough and now we are not black enough."

MOHAMED ADHIKARI

See also: **South Africa: African National Congress; South Africa: Apartheid, 1948–1959.**

Further Reading

Adhikari, Mohamed. *"Let Us Live for Our Children": The Teachers' League of South Africa, 1913–1940.* Cape Town: UCT Press, 1993.

Du Pre, Roy H. *Separate but Unequal: The Colored People of South Africa—A Political History.* Johannesburg: Jonathan Ball, 1994.

Goldin, Ian. *Making Race: The Politics and Economics of Colored Identity in South Africa.* Cape Town: Maskew Miller Longman, 1987.

Lewis, Gavin. *Between the Wire and the Wall: A History of South African "Colored" Politics.* Cape Town: David Philip, 1987.

Van der Ross, Richard E. *The Rise and Decline of Apartheid: A Study of Political Movements among the Colored People of South Africa, 1880–1985.* Cape Town: Tafelberg, 1986.

South Africa: African National Congress

In January 1912, the inaugural conference of the South African Native National Congress (SANNC) was convened. Its purpose was to provide a platform for African opinion in South Africa and to create a vehicle through which to oppose discriminatory legislation being passed by the formed union of South Africa. No constitution was adopted by the congress until 1919, but this largely ratified the character and composition of the organization established in 1912. Then as later, its membership was confined to African men; it was subdivided into four provincial congresses; it sought and enjoyed the active support of chiefs; it aimed to overcome "tribal" divisions; it was unswervingly committed to nonracial ideals; and it confined its protests to constitutional channels, and at the most extreme, passive resistance.

The first major issue confronting the new congress was the Land Act that was hastily piloted through Parliament in 1913. This imposed territorial segregation and confined African land ownership to 7.3 percent of the union. It also banned African sharecropping in the Orange Free State. The Land Act struck hardest at African cultivators in the Free State, where sharecropping was widespread, and in the Transvaal, where only 3.5 percent of the land area was allocated to African reserves, and where chiefs had been trying to buy back land from which they had been previously dispossessed. In both provinces the congress campaign quickly attained the proportions of a mass movement. In the Transvaal, chiefs were particularly conspicuous in raising money to finance two delegations sent to petition the British Government in 1914 and 1918. The Eastern Cape, which was exempt from the provisions of the Land Act and also enjoyed the Cape African franchise, held aloof from these campaigns and, in 1919, formed its own separate political organization, the Bantu Union.

At the outbreak of World War I in 1914, the SANNC resolved to suspend agitation until hostilities were over. However, from 1917 on inflation rocketed and urban living conditions went into steep decline. Unrest mounted in towns and industries all over the Union—above all, on the Witwatersrand. Strikes punctuated the period of 1918 to 1920, culminating in the massive African miners strike of February 1920. SANNC members were prominent in all of these as well as in a major antipass campaign in 1919. Membership in th SANNC soared, as the congress experienced its most militant phase prior to 1950.

Militancy subsided in the early 1920s, in step with falling prices, recession, and the building of more African housing in the towns. In addition, the liberal Joint Council movement co-opted former radicals from the African elite. SANNC activity flickered on fitfully, mainly in the Transvaal and Western Cape.

At its 1925 conference the SANNC changed its name to the African National Congress (ANC). A brief resurgence of activity occurred after Josiah Gumede, the leader of one of the congress factions in Natal, was elected the organization's national president. He became radicalized by two trips to the Soviet Union in 1927 and 1928. Gumede played a leading role in the League of African Rights, which was sponsored by the

Communist Party of South Africa in 1928. This earned him the opprobrium of more conservative congress leaders (including the chiefs, who were rapidly losing influence) who succeeded in ousting him in April 1930, and electing in his place Pixley Seme.

Under Seme, the ANC became moribund and riddled with factions. Rival leaderships confronted each other in all of the provinces. This, along with the Great Depression, which struck South Africa in the early 1930s, virtually extinguished all political activity. In the Western Cape these divisions were ideological between radicals (B. Ndobe) and conservatives (J. Thaele). In the Transvaal such ideological differences were overlain by ethnic rifts between S. P. Matseke's Pedi/Kgatla group and S. Makhatho's multiethnic caucus. Despite numerous efforts at reconciliation, this paralyzing split was not closed until 1943.

The publication of the Herzog Bills in 1935, which stripped Cape Africans of their franchise, finally galvanized the ANC into action. At its 1936 annual conference, Seme was replaced as secretary general by the Reverend James Calata, who embarked on a program to revive dormant branches. In 1937 the Transvaal provincial congress received an injection of new purpose and new blood with the formation of the Transvaal Coordinating Committee for the Revival of the ANC, in which several communists were prominent. The ANC now took back center stage from the All African Convention (founded in 1935), which had, for a time, threatened to eclipse it. An important factor facilitating the revival of the ANC in the Orange Free State and the Transvaal were the electoral campaigns now permitted for the newly formed Native Representative Council. Additional stimulus was provided by accelerated industrialization and urbanization in the late 1930s and 1940s, and the reemergence of African trade unions, which coalesced into the Council for Non-European Trade Unions in 1941.

These advances were consolidated by the election of A. B. Xuma as secretary general in 1940. Under his leadership provincial splits were gradually resolved, the Cape was brought back into the ANC as an active member and national membership gradually inched up, to reach around 5000 by 1945, over half of which was concentrated in the Transvaal. In 1943 Xuma introduced a new constitution that gave women full membership and abolished both the Upper House of Chiefs as well as racial restrictions on membership. The central objective that this proclaimed was full participation for Africans in the government of South Africa. By 1949 the shift of direction was complete. By that stage the young radicals of the Youth League (formed in 1944) and the CPSA were on the point of gaining control of the congress, the Programme of Action that committed the ANC to mass action had

been passed, and the relatively cautious Xuma was about to be replaced. The era of mass nationalism was about to dawn.

PHILIP BONNER

See also: **Dube, John Langalibalele; Matthews, Z. K.; Plaatje, Sol T.**

Further Reading

Bonner, P. L. "The Transvaal Native Congress 1917–1920: The Radicalization of the Black Petty Bourgeoisie on the Rand." In *Industrialisation and Social Change: African Class Formation, Culture and Consciousness 1870–1900*, edited by S. Marks and R. Rathbone. London: Longman, 1982.

Rich, P. B. *State Power and Black Politics in South Africa 1912–1951*. London: Macmillan, 1996.

Walshe, P. *The Rise of African Nationalism in South Africa, 1912–1952*. Berkeley and Los Angeles: University of California Press, 1971.

Willan, B. *Sol Plaatje: South African Nationalist, 1876–1932*. London: Heinemann, 1982.

South Africa: Industrial and Commercial Workers Union

Trade unions were imported to South Africa by immigrant workers from Britain, Australia, and elsewhere. These took the form of often racially mixed craft unions in the Cape, and racially exclusive craft and mining unions on the Witwatersrand. In 1922 white miners on the Witwatersrand went on strike, and began the "Rand Revolt" to prevent African workers being employed to perform deskilled parts of white miners' jobs. Until World War I, African workers remained almost wholly unorganized, apart from piecemeal efforts by the communist Industrial Workers of Africa during and immediately after the war. In 1924 the Industrial Conciliation Act was passed by the new Pact government, which granted formal recognition and statutory bargaining rights to white, "colored," and Indian worker, but excluded most Africans from its terms.

The Industrial and Commercial Workers Union (ICWU) was formed in January 1919, through the joint endeavors of Albert Batty, a trade unionist of English extraction, and Clements Kadalie, a mission-educated Nyasa immigrant. Kadalie was its first secretary. The ICWU recruited its membership from the mainly "colored" workforce of Cape Town's docks and railways. Both sectors were ripe for unionization. Wartime inflation had bitten deep into wage packets and employers repeatedly refused compensatory wage rises. In December 1919 the ICWU launched a strike that lasted 14 days and brought out 2,000 men. Although the strike was broken, it secured modest increases in wages and won the esteem and support of Cape Town's black working class.

In July 1920 a conference was convened in Bloemfontein with the aim of establishing a national black labor organization. Representatives from the ICWU and from the Bloemfontein, Port Elizabeth, and East London unions attended. A new federation was formed, but soon foundered on disputes over who should occupy the leadership positions. Up until 1923, the ICWU was a Cape organization. At its January 1923 conference it resolved to extend itself nationwide, after which it set up a new branch in Bloemfontein. Only in 1924 did it embark on serious expansion. Between June and November Kadalie undertook a tour of the Union, establishing 12 new branches in his wake, the most important of which were in Durban and Johannesburg.

A major shift in the composition and distribution of the ICWU occurred in 1926–1927. In March 1926 it claimed 171,760 members. By January 1927 membership had risen to 571,760. The main expansion occurred in the Transvaal and Natal, although several new branches also opened in the Orange Free State. The Cape branches went into a correspondingly steep decline. A second, related change can also be noticed that overlapped with the first. Until 1926, the ICWU had a discernible urban bias. In late 1926 and 1927 the major thrust of its expansion was centered among the increasingly impoverished farm labor populations of the Highveld and Natal. These contributed the vast bulk of its new members, which swelled to between 100,000 and 200,000 strong in 1927. It was at this time that the ICWU also achieved its greatest territorial spread, extending to every corner of South Africa, and even into Southern Rhodesia. The ICWU thus became the first mass movement of blacks to have arisen in South Africa.

The strategy and tactics of the ICWU shifted markedly over this period. The early 1920s were years of rising unemployment and declining prices, a context that did not favor the use of the strike weapon. In 1923 and 1924 South Africa's government implemented "civilized labor" policies whereby Africans were displaced from central and local government employment in an effort to reduce levels of white unemployment. African artisans and clerical workers were particularly hard hit by these measures. They flooded into the ranks of the ICWU, with many assuming leadership positions.

One key to the ICWU's success in these years was the public meeting. Here ICWU leaders pilloried government officials often in abusive and derisive terms, much to the delight of their audiences, who relished "a taste of freedom" and returned again and again. ICWU offices also took up legal cases, either on an individual or collective basis. The Natal provincial leader A. W. G. Champion was particularly adept at mounting such legal actions through which he secured the abolition of the night curfew for Africans in Durban, the ending of the compulsory disinfecting of Africans entering Durban, and a variety of other gains. Similar tactics won fleeting successes in staying the evictions of farm laborers in Natal and the Transvaal, and this again massively boosted the ICWU's rural support.

Apart from lawyers and rhetoric, the ICWU had few weapons at its disposal. Even in the urban areas most non-mineworkers were migrants, and were rarely concentrated in sufficient numbers in any one sector of employment to permit orthodox trade union organization. On the mines and farms, systems of surveillance and control were sufficient to contain and crush any incipient worker organization. The ICWU reacted to these constraints in two related ways. The first was to recruit generally, and not according to occupational sector, and to mobilize around broader political issues such as the abolition of passes. The second was to seek external sources of support. The first of these was the Cape Federation of Labor Unions; this was replaced in 1925 by the South African Communist Party (SACP). Late in 1926 the communists were expelled for criticizing ICWU leaders' corruption and inaction, and their place was taken by a group of white Johannesburg liberals led by Ethelreda Lewis, who secured the ICWU its affiliation to the International Federation of Trade Unions, which Kadalie visited in 1927. Kadalie returned from that tour having secured the services of a Scottish trade union organizer, William Ballinger. Ballinger soon fell out with Kadalie, who now formed the breakaway Independent ICWU in 1928, which again turned to the SACP.

The third tactic of ICWU leaders was to encourage yearnings for freedom, which sometimes assumed almost millenarian form. This was especially evident in the countryside, where labor tenants often believed the ICWU would deliver land. More generally, ICWU leaders often preached the general strike, which they had no idea of how to accomplish, in what can be described as millenarian syndicalism.

The ICWU collapsed and fragmented in 1928. The IICWU remained active in Johannesburg, East London, and Bloemfontein until 1931. Thereafter it faded gradually away, although its memory remained potent among African workers and political activists for another two decades.

PHILIP BONNER

See also: **Religion, Colonial Africa: Independent and Millenarian/Syncretic Churches; South Africa: Mining; South Africa: World Wars I and II.**

Further Reading

Bradford, H. *A Taste of Freedom: The ICWU in Rural South Africa 1924–1930.* Johannesburg: Ravan Press, 1987.

Wickens, P. L. *The Industrial and Commercial Workers' Union of Africa*. Cape Town: Oxford University Press, 1978.

South Africa: Afrikaner Nationalism, Broederbond and National Party, 1902–1948

The year 1902 represented the lowest point in Afrikaner fortune, following the surrender of the Boer commandos and the Treaty of Vereeniging, which extinguished the republics of the Transvaal and the Orange Free State. High Commissioner Milner's subsequent Anglicization policy, designed to cement the imperial connection, seemed to threaten the very essence of Afrikanerdom. Ironically, Milner's policy had the contrary effect of provoking a popular movement for the protection of the Afrikaner language, culture and religion.

Aided by the magnanimity of the new Liberal government in Britain, Louis Botha's moderate nationalist Het Volk party won power in the Transvaal whites-only election of 1907, on a platform of Anglo-Afrikaner reconciliation. J. B. M. Hertzog's more radical Orangia Unie party won a parallel victory in the Orange River Colony's (also whites-only) election of 1908. The decade closed with the formation of the Union of South Africa, hailed as a landmark in the process of British/Afrikaner reconciliation.

Meanwhile, the Afrikaner community was experiencing considerable social and economic change that was to bring into existence a more radical, less accommodating nationalism based on a continued animosity toward British imperialism, anxiety about nonwhite economic competition in urban areas, growing concern among middle-class Afrikaners about the condition of Afrikaner "poor whites," and a continued determination to foster Afrikaner language and culture.

In political terms, this led to Hertzog's secession from the governing South African Party (SAP) and the formation of his Nasionale Party (National Party, NP) in January 1914 with the slogan "South Africa First." The NP won increasing electoral support and came to power in alliance with the (white racist) Labour Party in 1924. Hertzog's first premiership (1924–1929) witnessed some reduction in hostility toward British imperialism, helped by contemporary movement toward imperial devolution. Further attempts to advance the cause of Anglo-Afrikaner reconciliation brought about the fusion of the NP with General Jan C. Smuts's SAP in 1934 to create the United Party, but also witnessed the reemergence of radical nationalism in the form of D. F. Malan's Gesuiwerde Nasionale (Purified National) Party.

In social terms, Afrikaner nationalism embraced a policy of strict racial segregation that brought it into alliance with white labor in the mid-to-late 1920s, and further developed the white protectionist racial pattern of South Africa's industrial system. In the cultural sphere, it helped to engender institutions parallel to those of the English-speaking establishment, such as the Voortrekkers, an Afrikaner Boy Scouts movement. The Federasie van Afrikaanse Kultuurverenigings, formed in 1929, coordinated this wide range of voluntary associations. Given the high incidence of church attendance among Afrikaners, the Dutch Reformed Church exerted a powerful influence; its theologians were beginning to refine the Biblical defense of racial separation later expressed in Dr. Gert Cronje's *A Home for Posterity* (1945) and *Justifiable Race Separation* (1947). Work on an Afrikaans Bible and dictionary was completed, and in 1925, Afrikaans became an official language, alongside English. In economic terms, the interwar period witnessed the continued urbanization of Afrikaners and the development of *volkskapitalisme*, the mobilization of Afrikaner capital and the endeavor to bring Afrikaner employers and workers together in what Dan O'Meara (1983) calls a "national capitalism," challenging the grip of "international capitalism" and its imperialist backers.

The Afrikaner Broederbond (AB) played what some commentators, such as J. H. P. Serfontein (1978), have regarded as a commanding role in the mobilization of radical Afrikaner nationalism, articulating the various political, economic, and social institutions of Afrikanerdom within the Purified National Party. Started in 1918 by working-class Afrikaners in English-speaking Johannesburg, the AB became a secret society with an exclusively male membership open only to "pure" Afrikaners recommended by existing members. Its enemies declared that it was a sinister organization aimed at dominating South Africa through a process of infiltration into key areas; its friends declared it was merely a cultural body. Nevertheless, the AB seems to have played an important political role, both directly and indirectly. O'Meara has demonstrated its success in helping the Purified Nationalists establish themselves in what became their Transvaal power base in the mid 1930s.

The ten years leading up to the Nasionale Party victory at the polls in 1948 witnessed further developments of these trends in Afrikaner nationalism, launched by the 1938 Great Trek centenary celebrations, which extreme nationalists had effectively hijacked. However, a new influence, from Nazi and fascist Europe, was to shape nationalistic Afrikaner thinking on race issues, leading to a greater emphasis on race separation and "purity." Several future leaders, such as Hendrik Verwoerd, P. J. Meyer, and Nico Diederichs, had studied in Germany before World War II, and the term *Volk* began to appear regularly in the party's political lexicon. In an extreme form it was expressed by the

Ossewa Brandwag (Ox-Wagon Sentinel), a paramilitary organization that had emerged in the wake of the Trek centenary and blended Nazi and Great Trek symbols. Although divided among themselves politically, radical nationalists were united in their determination to end the imperial connection, and some were not averse to the prospect of a German victory to secure this aim.

However, the imminent collapse of Nazism in Europe led to a gradual reassembly of Afrikanerdom behind Malan's restyled Herenigde (Reunited) Nasionale Party, and a refiguring of nationalist philosophy into a "Christian Nationalism," emphasizing the place of Afrikaners as a people placed by God in southern Africa. From this emerged the policy of apartheid, which became the official policy of the Reunited National Party at the end of the war. In preparing for the 1948 election that brought him to power, Malan decided to highlight apartheid as a solution to South Africa's racial "problems." He was helped by the growing threat posed to white workers by an increasingly urbanized and skilled black labor force. The result of the election was nevertheless a surprise to those who thought Smuts's United Party would win again: the Reunited National Party and its allies secured a majority of eight seats over the UP and its allies, helped by Afrikaner working class voters in six key urban seats, and were to remain in power continuously for the next 46 years.

MURRAY STEELE

See also: **Afrikaans and Afrikaner Nationalism, Nineteenth Century; South Africa: Apartheid, 1948–1959; South Africa: World Wars I and II.**

Further Reading

Beinart, William. *Twentieth Century South Africa.* Oxford: Oxford University Press, 1994.

Davenport, T. R. H. *South Africa: A Modern History*, 4th ed. London: Macmillan/Toronto: University of Toronto Press, 1991.

De Klerk, Willem. *The Puritans in Africa: A Story of Afrikanerdom.* London: Rex Collings, 1975.

Moodie, T. Dunbar. *The Rise of Afrikanerdom: Power, Apartheid and the Afrikaner Civil Religion.* Berkeley and Los Angeles: University of California Press, 1975.

O'Meara, Dan. *Volkskapitalisme: Class, Capital and Ideology in the Development of Afrikaner Nationalism, 1934–1948.* Cambridge: Cambridge University Press, 1983.

Serfontein, J. H. P. *Brotherhood of Power: An Expose of the Secret Afrikaner Broederbond.* Bloomington: Indiana University Press, 1978.

Sparks, Allister. *The Mind of South Africa.* London: Heinemann/New York: Alfred A. Knopf, 1990.

Stultz, Newell. *The Nationalists in Opposition, 1934–1948.* Cape Town: Human and Rousseau, 1975.

Thompson, Leonard. *The Political Mythology of Apartheid.* New Haven, Conn.: Yale University Press, 1985.

Vatcher, W. H. *White Laager: The Rise of Afrikaner Nationalism.* London: Pall Mall Press/New York: Praeger, 1965.

Wilkins, Ivor, and Hans Strydom. *The Broederbond.* New York: Paddington Press, 1979.

South Africa: World Wars I and II

South Africa's participation in the first and second world wars is marked by striking similarities. Although geographically far removed from the central theaters of fighting, South Africa quickly entered both conflicts on the side of Great Britain. In each case the decision to support Britain was controversial and contested within South Africa's Afrikaner community. In both wars South African troops fought in campaigns throughout Africa and in Europe. When the conflicts ended the same South African leader, Jan C. Smuts, championed high-minded ideals for promoting international peace while maintaining harsh forms of racial segregation and discrimination at home.

Of the two conflicts, World War II, along with the rise of Nazism in Germany, played the more decisive role in influencing internal developments in South Africa and setting the stage for the climactic human rights struggle between the proponents of apartheid and the advocates of racial equality. Further, World War II spurred South Africa's second industrial revolution, diversifying the economy, expanding the exploitation of the country's African population, and generating growing labor unrest.

At the outset of World War I in 1914, South Africa was led by Prime Minister Louis Botha and Minister of Defense Smuts. Both had been Afrikaner commanders who fought the British during the Boer War (1899–1902), but at its end they had emerged as supporters of reconciliation with Britain and English-speaking white South Africans. Consequently, when fighting broke out in Europe they agreed to a British request to seize German South West Africa (today Namibia).

This action provoked a potentially serious rebellion of Afrikaners still bitter against Britain. Although a number of their influential leaders, including the commander of the armed forces, joined the uprising, Botha reacted swiftly and defeated the rebels. He then assumed command of the campaign in South West Africa, capturing the colony in 1915. British appreciation for this assistance increased when Smuts assumed command of the campaign in East Africa in 1916 and drove the Germans south from the Kenyan border. Later, South African troops fought in Europe.

South Africa's armed forces were made up not only of white soldiers but included both "Colored" and African units. Some joined out of patriotic reasons, others because of government pressure or reward, and many to escape the drought in the northern Transvaal. Although they often faced dangerous situations, these forces were restricted to noncombatant activities. The attitudes of South Africa's leaders were both racist and paradoxical: While arguing that Africans were incapable of fighting in modern wars, they feared the future ramifications of military training for large numbers of Africans.

Among Africans the war provoked a variety of responses. For some in the working class and peasantry, resentful at their economic exploitation, the war offered opportunities for the expression of anti-British sentiments and even consideration of revolts. Others saw the war foreshadowing millenarian visions that would lead to African liberation, while many viewed it as simply a white man's conflict. The Western-educated leaders of the South African Native National Congress (SANNC), predecessor of the African National Congress (ANC), however, supported Britain from the outset. They hoped that in recognition Britain would intervene with the South African government to address black grievances.

At the war's end SANNC leaders, such as Sol Plaatje, pressed their demands for reforms in South Africa as well as their hopes for an African voice in colonial adjustments, but they were largely ignored by the British government. Instead, London claimed it could not interfere in the internal affairs of a self-governing dominion. Smuts, on the other hand, found himself a respected figure among Allied leaders at the Paris Peace Conference. His proposals for the League of Nations strongly influenced the views of U.S. President Woodrow Wilson. Yet Wilson radically transformed Smuts's mandate program, insisting that it include the former German colonies in Africa and thereby preventing South Africa's annexation of southwest Africa.

The beginning of World War II in 1939 brought Smuts back to power in South Africa. During the early interwar years he had served as prime minister, but he joined a coalition government with Afrikaner nationalists during the Depression. They now opposed "England's war" and advocated neutrality. With Smuts determined to support Britain, the government split. By 80 to 67, Smuts prevailed. South Africa declared war on Germany, and he again became prime minister.

Deep divisions within the Afrikaner community took on a contemporary character. Beyond traditional resentment against Britain, Hitler's Nazi ideology proved attractive to many. A number of Afrikaner intellectuals had studied in Germany during the 1930s and later emerged as architects of apartheid. Before the war, fascist-type organizations had sprung up in South Africa, the most significant being the Ossewabrandwag, or Ox-Wagon Sentinels. Hoping for a German victory, they undertook subversive activities and some of their leaders were interned.

Other Afrikaners supported Smuts and joined his volunteer army, which fought in Ethiopia, North Africa, and Italy. Again racial prejudice prevented Africans and "colored" troops from serving in combatant roles. Still, almost half of the soldiers killed were black.

At home, war transformed the economy and accelerated social upheavals already under way. Although gold mining retained its leading position, manufacturing surged as South Africa was forced to produce many goods it had previously imported. Union organizing among African workers and rapid urbanization accompanied industrial expansion. Urban migration exacerbated overcrowding in African areas and led to the creation of new shantytowns on the outskirts of South Africa's cities.

The ANC responded to these changing conditions, and the South African government's continued determination to deny blacks their most basic rights, with increasing militancy. After Britain and the United States issued the Atlantic Charter, with its democratic statement of war aims, the ANC formed a committee that demanded the right of self-determination be applied in Africa.

During the war, the ANC Women's League and the ANC Youth League were formed. The former organization saw its special objectives as organizing women in the struggle for African freedom and equality while addressing social issues that affected women. The latter organization, which included a new generation of leaders such as Nelson Mandela, Walter Sisulu, and Oliver Tambo, pressured the movement to adopt more radical tactics. Petitions had failed to move the government; the time had arrived for organizing mass actions such as boycotts, strikes, and civil disobedience.

At war's end Smuts was again a respected figure within the British Commonwealth and contributed significantly to the drafting of the United Nations charter's preamble. At home, however, his politics were about to be swept aside as South African history approached a decisive turning point. Despite his segregationist policies, many Afrikaners viewed Smuts as a moderate on racial questions and too closely associated with Britain. In 1948 they rejected his leadership for that of the hard-line proponents of apartheid found in the National Party. At the same time the advocates of racial equality, led by the ANC, sought new methods of mobilizing the African population in the struggle for justice and democracy.

BRIAN DIGRE

See also: **Plaatje, Sol T; Smuts, Jan C.; South Africa: African National Congress; World War I: Survey.**

Further Reading

Furlong, Patrick. *Between Crown and Swastika: The Impact of the Radical Right on the Afrikaner Nationalist Movement in the Fascist Era.* Hanover, N.H.: Wesleyan University Press/University Press of New England, 1991.

Grundlingh, Albert. *Fighting Their Own War: South African Blacks and the First World War.* Johannesburg: Ravan Press, 1987.

———. "'Non-Europeans Should Be Kept away from the Temptations of Towns': Controlling Black South African Soldiers during the Second World War." *International Journal of African Historical Studies* 25, no. 3 (1992): 539–560.

Meli, Francis. *A History of the ANC: South Africa Belongs to Us.* Harare: Zimbabwe Publishing, 1988.

Nasson, Bill. "War Opinion in South Africa, 1914." *Journal of Imperial and Commonwealth History* 23, no. 2 (1995): 248–276.

Roth, Mirjana. "If You Give Us Rights We Will Fight: Black Involvement in the Second World War." *South African Historical Journal*, no. 15 (1983): 85–104.

Sparks, Allister. *The Mind of South Africa.* New York: Alfred A. Knopf, 1990.

Thompson, Leonard. *A History of South Africa.* New Haven, Conn.: Yale University Press, 1990.

South Africa: Segregation, Political Economy of

Racial discrimination in South Africa in the years following union in 1910 and preceding the institution of apartheid in 1948 was enforced through a policy of segregation. Although implemented to varying degrees throughout the new country, the policy of segregation generally separated races to the benefit of those of European descent and to the detriment of those of African descent. Segregation policies affected the rights of Africans to own land, to live or travel where they chose, and to enjoy job security. While segregation was not as sweeping or inclusive as apartheid, neither was it an informal system of discrimination. Segregation policies were implemented through a series of laws passed to limit increasingly Africans rights during the first half of the twentieth century, and they were enforced through the power of the state, often with great brutality. Although sometimes viewed as more benign than apartheid, segregation nevertheless shaped South African society in fundamental ways that still affect the country into the twenty-first century.

Segregation policies attempted to protect white political and economic interests while at the same time drawing Africans increasingly into the country's economy as the chief source of labor. Throughout the twentieth century, whites represented no more than 10 per cent of the South African population, yet they controlled the majority of the country's economic resources. Key to this development was the use of African labor at very low wages and under extremely strict control. One of the first pieces of legislation to emerge from the new South African government aimed to restrict African employment to menial and unskilled jobs was the 1911 Mines, Works, and Machinery Ordinance. Under this legislation, Africans were excluded from most skilled categories of work in the mines, in effect "reserving" those jobs for whites. In the same year, the Natives' Labour Regulation Act set down the conditions under which Africans could work: they were to be recruited in the rural areas, fingerprinted and issued with a "pass" allowing them to enter the cities, and if they broke their employment contract or stayed in the urban areas beyond the length of the contract they were to be arrested and forced to do hard labor for up to two months. As Africans increasingly protested and resisted these oppressive terms of employment through union organization and industrial strikes, the South African government responded with the Industrial Conciliation Act of 1924, restricting African rights to organize or to negotiate their terms of employment. Under this act, "pass-bearing" African males could not be considered under the legal term *employee*, thus excluding them from all rights of labor representation, mediation, or organization. Under segregation, African workers were limited to unskilled jobs, were punished if they quit their jobs, and were robbed of their rights to protest these conditions.

Not surprisingly, Africans tried to avoid such terms of employment and it was necessary for the South African government to take drastic measures to force Africans into the wage workforce. Key to these efforts were restrictions on Africans' ability to earn their own livelihood, as they had before white occupation, on their own farms. Heavy taxes on African farmers had been introduced by the British prior to 1910, including taxes on dogs, on huts, and even on heads in an effort to force them into employment on the mines or white farms. African farmers had responded to these pressures by increasing their agricultural production and successfully participating in the commercial sale of their crops in competition with white farmers. Thus in 1913, the South African government passed the Natives' Land Act, restricting African ownership of land to designated areas comprising 6 per cent of the country's total land area. Although the government justified the act by arguing that these lands approximated African landholdings prior to white occupation, and even increased the percentage of land up to 13 per cent in 1936, most land reserved for Africans was of poor quality and could not meet the needs of the growing African population. As the productive capacity of this land waned and taxation proved unrelenting, Africans were increasingly forced into work on white farms, in factories, and in the growing mining industry.

The impact of segregationist policies became most apparent in the cities, as white municipalities struggled to deal with the steady influx of Africans seeking work to support their families. While the system of labor contracts and passes encouraged and often forced Africans to return to the rural areas at the completion of their contract, many stayed in the cities rather than return to sure poverty and starvation. In 1923, the government passed the Urban Areas Act to establish a uniform policy toward urban Africans. The government had agreed that Africans should remain in the cities only to "minister to the needs of the white population." Under this act, employed Africans were restricted to segregated townships or locations where they could rent accommodation provided by the municipality. Africans coming to town to seek work could stay for only limited periods of time and were returned to the rural areas or imprisoned if they remained without work. The right to live in town was precarious and opportunities for advancement were circumscribed by segregationist limitations on land ownership and business licenses.

As segregation became increasingly broad, affecting Africans in the rural areas, urban areas, and at the workplace, the government sought to create a more comprehensive system of rule throughout the country. In 1927 the Native Administration Act was passed, giving the department of native affairs control over all matters pertaining to Africans. In effect, this act separated all policies concerning Africans from the rest of the government. Under this act, the government ruled by decree rather than by law in the African rural areas (deemed tribal reserves) and established separate administrations in these areas, staffed by bureaucrats and appointed chiefs. As Africans increasingly lost the right to reside in the cities and were pushed into the reserves, these policies left most under despotic rule. In 1936, the few political rights left to Africans under a color-blind voter franchise in the Cape province were removed under the Representation of Natives Act. Although Africans were allowed to elect a limited number of white representatives, by 1936 they were substantially segregated in the political as well as economic aspects of South African society.

The impact of segregation was devastating for Africans. The rural areas quickly became unable to support the African population and as Africans sought work elsewhere they were forced into a system of migrant labor, moving between workplaces where they had no rights back to rural homes where they could not survive. By the close of the segregation era, African workers and politicians increasingly and aggressively demanded greater rights, staging strikes, protests, and boycotts. Laying the foundations for the apartheid era, segregation systemized discrimination and strengthened the African resistance that would both intensify under apartheid.

NANCY L. CLARK

See also: **South Africa: Apartheid, 1948–1959.**

Further Reading

Ballinger, Margaret. *From Union to Apartheid: A Trek to Isolation*. New York: Praeger, 1969.

Dubow, Saul. *Racial Segregation and the Origins of Apartheid in South Africa, 1919–1936*. New York: St. Martin's Press, 1989.

Hindson, Doug. *Pass Controls and the Urban African Proletariat*. Johannesburg: Ravan Press, 1987.

Lacey, Marian. *Working for Boroko: The Origins of a Coercive Labour System in South Africa*. Johannesburg: Ravan Press, 1981.

Rich, P. B. *White Power and the Liberal Conscience: Racial Segregation in South Africa and South African Liberalism 1921–1960*. Manchester: Manchester University Press, 1984.

Simon, H. J., and R. E. *Class and Colour in South Africa, 1850–1950*. Harmondsworth, England: Penguin, 1969.

South Africa: Industry, Labor, Urbanization, 1940–1946

Between 1940 and 1946, South Africa underwent a massive economic and social transformation as the result of the country's participation in World War II. Prior to the war, the South African economy was based primarily on agriculture and mining, with the majority of the population, both white and African, still living in the rural areas. Most manufactured goods were imported from Europe and the local population worked on farms or in the mines on a racially segregated basis. During the war, factories expanded to fill the need for many goods, including military supplies, drawing workers into the cities from all over the country. As Africans and whites alike were employed in the new factories, the racial lines between workers became a source of great contention and South Africa experienced serious labor strikes and industrial action. By the end of the war, manufacturing had become the country's most productive economic sector, nearly half of the population was living in the cities, and competition for jobs between African and white workers worried the white electorate. While the war spurred tremendous economic growth, it also challenged the country's strict segregationist policies in the workplace and in the expanding cities.

As the demand for goods expanded during the war, South Africa's factories responded by more than doubling production. The number of factories grew, but most of the increase in production came about as a result of the expansion of existing factories. All sorts of goods were produced, including blankets, ploughs, dishes, and clothing, as well as supplies fo the army in the form of ammunition, helmets, trucks, and boots. The greatest growth was experienced in the industries producing machinery, vehicles, and tools, which had been cut off from the European suppliers during the war but were crucial for all of South Africa's industries. During the war, imports in the machinery category were cut by more than half and the local factories had to make up the difference, with heavy manufacturing accounting for nearly one-third of all factory production by the end of the war. At war's end, manufacturing had become the most productive segment of the economy, eclipsing the mining industry for the first time in South African history since the discovery of diamonds and gold.

While production swelled, the factory workforce grew by 50 per cent, mostly as a result of the expanded recruitment of African workers. Prior to the war, Africans had been prohibited from skilled and even semiskilled jobs, relegated to menial work and legally categorized as temporary workers. The growth of factory production, however, required workers who were trained to use complicated machinery for the mass production of goods. With more than 200,000 white males serving in the military, employers sought out women war workers to fill some skilled jobs but also increasingly relied on Africans without always paying them at the higher skilled rates. During the war years, from 1939 through 1945, the number of African males working in industry grew by nearly 70 per cent, while the number of women, both white and black, grew by 50 per cent. By comparison, white male employment in industry grew by only 30 per cent as many men joined the military. By the end of the war, Africans constituted over 50 per cent of the industrial workforce outside of the mining industry, for the first time in the country's history.

Changes in the South African economy began to affect the face of South Africa's cities, as increasing numbers of rural dwellers were drawn into the urban areas seeking work. A combination of opportunity in the cities with the expanding numbers of jobs in the war factories, and devastation in the countryside as South Africa experienced one of the worst droughts in its history, succeeded in driving nearly a million more South Africans into the cities during the war. Both Africans and whites moved to the urban centers, and for the first time Africans began to outnumber whites there. The massive influx of Africans created serious problems due to the myriad legal restrictions limiting African entry and residence in the cities. Africans were prohibited from entering cities without proper documentation and could live only in specially designated townships, or locations, controlled by the local municipality. Since the strict enforcement of these laws during the war would have overwhelmed the police and seriously impeded the war effort, the government relaxed most restrictions for the duration of the war. The result was the growth of the urban African population under trying conditions, with little accommodation or

services provided. Africans were forced to find shelter anywhere and "squatter" camps (a collection of impromptu shacks without proper sanitation or running water) emerged around the major industrial centers. One of the largest, in Orlando near Johannesburg, with more than 20,000 residents, resisted government clearance and eventually became the basis for the later township of Soweto. While the government and the local authorities were unwilling to recognize that African workers were becoming part of the permanent urban population, Africans themselves took matters into their own hands and created their own urban communities.

Africans increasingly organized to resist their appalling conditions of work and standard of living throughout the war years. Boycotts against the high bus fares charged African workers continued in the Johannesburg townships for most of the war years and after. Strikes and industrial disturbances rose to an all time high during the war, despite strict government emergency regulations prohibiting strikes. In 1941, the African Mineworkers' Union was formed for the first time, organizing the migrant workers who repeatedly staged work stoppages for higher wages. The union gained some wage increases during the war, and staged its most dramatic action in 1946, when 60,000 workers went out on strike. And in 1943, the African National Congress established a Youth League, led by young leaders such as Nelson Mandela and Walter Sisulu who were intent on invigorating the organization and organizing forceful popular protests against government segregation and discrimination. The inequities of life at the workplace and in the residential areas intensified during the war years and prompted serious efforts at resistance and political change.

The impact of the war years was dramatic. While the country experienced massive growth in national production, jumping nearly 80 per cent during the war, South Africa also became more divided than ever. Africans found a government unwilling to relent on the implementation of segregation and, more ominously, a growing sector of the white community that sought to further entrench segregation under the concept of apartheid. The economic and social transformation of the country frightened a large segment of the white population that welcomed growth and prosperity but rejected any recognition of African rights. Nevertheless, the integration of Africans into South Africa's economic and social life during the war years would prove impossible to reverse and African demands for greater rights would not go unanswered.

NANCY L. CLARK

See also: **South Africa: African National Congress; South Africa: World Wars I and II; World War II: Sub-Saharan Africa: Economic Impact.**

Further Reading

Clark, Nancy L. *Manufacturing Apartheid: State Corporations in South Africa.* New Haven, Conn.: Yale University Press, 1994.

Hancock, W. K. *Smuts,* vol. 2, *The Fields of Force.* Cambridge: Cambridge University Press, 1968.

Lewis, Jon. *Industrialisation and Trade Union Organisation in South Africa, 1924–55: The Rise and Fall of the South African Trades and Labour Council.* Cambridge: Cambridge University Press, 1984.

Martin, H. J., and Neil D. Orpen. *South African Forces, World War II,* vol. 7, *South Africa at War: Military and Industrial Organization and Operations in Connection with the Conduct of the War, 1939–1945.* Cape Town: 1979.

Van der Poel, Jean (ed.). *Selections from the Smuts Papers,* vol. 6, *1934–1945.* Cambridge: Cambridge University Press, 1973.

Webster, Eddie. *Cast in a Racial Mould: Labour Process and Trade Unionism in the Foundries.* Johannesburg: Ravan Press, 1985.

South Africa: Capitalist Farming, "Poor Whites," Labor

In South Africa, the late-nineteenth-century discovery of diamonds and gold, and the ensuing industrialization, did not provide all white settlers with wealth. By the early 1900s, perhaps as many as one in four Afrikaners lacked the skills and resources necessary to compete in a capitalist economy. Nonpropertied whites in the rural Cape, who had slid further into penury in the nineteenth century, remained on the margins of the industrial boom. In the interior republics of the Transvaal and the Orange Free State, Boer small landholders struggled to move from subsistence farming to market profitability. Many "poor whites," as they became known, experienced near-famine conditions after British troops devastated Afrikaner agriculture during the Anglo-Boer War (1899–1902). While some poor whites sought menial work in the emerging urban mining centers, the majority still labored on farms. Although poverty was long endemic to agrarian settler society in South Africa, "poor whiteism" in the early twentieth century was seen as a new social phenomenon in a rapidly industrializing world.

Poor whites lagged behind during a time of accelerating capitalist transformations. In agriculture, capitalizing farmers expanded yields to meet the food needs of burgeoning towns, evicting by-owners, their white sharecroppers and labor tenants, in order to use all available acreage for staple-crop production. Squeezed from the land, poor whites were now expendable, as large-scale white landowners discharged their employees when machinery made labor-intensive tasks obsolete. Seeking employment and a better life, landless Afrikaners drifted to cities, where they were alienated from far more affluent English-speaking immigrants.

In rural and urban areas, poor whites were often stigmatized, ridiculed by some landowners as lazy and feckless; *poor white* became a derogatory term. Commercial farmers favored low-paid and reputedly more productive African labor. Employers' preference for Africans also shaped an industrial sector now dependent on the extraction of precious minerals and metals. Unlike farming, mining was not subject to seasonal hazards such as cattle diseases, drought, or summer floods. Its main product, gold, commanded a ready market in overseas financial centers. Poor whites learned that in the diggings, as in capitalist farming, the bosses relied on machines and black workers.

In the years immediately after the union of South Africa in 1910, the continuing degradation of poor whites posed a paradox in the hardening racial hierarchy, challenging government native policies that stressed the inferiority of Africans. Such state attitudes underpinned the landmark 1913 Native Lands Act, which confined chiefdoms to small, barren reserves and drove increasing numbers of Africans into labor migrancy and urban employment. Early advocates of racial segregation, particularly Afrikaner politicians and clergy of the Dutch Reformed Church, were alarmed by the mingling of poor whites, "coloreds," and Africans in city slums. Race mixture, according to Boer general Jan Smuts, a leader in the union government's reigning South African Party, took place in the shared environment of squalor and threatened to spawn a labor movement that could unify working whites and blacks. Facing common deprivations and restrictions on upward mobility, poor whites and blacks could have created an alliance. Yet to a large extent, poor whites advocated racial segregation, to conform with the belief that their cultural and racial superiority would advance their economic interests.

It was against the background of the poor white problem that the Pact government came to power in 1924. The Pact was a two-party alliance of the Nationalist and Labour Parties, prompted by the discontent of Afrikaner landowners and working-class whites against what they saw as the antilabor and antifarmer regime of Smuts. The Labour Party, organized by protectionist-minded white trade unionists, sought votes from white workers in mining and related industries. The Nationalists represented a range of white farming interests, but primarily the Afrikaner rural electorate. These two parties shared a main objective—namely, safeguarding white South Africa, which included rescuing poor whites from indigence. Fulfilling its pledge, the Pact government initiated the "civilized labor" policy to replace black workers with whites (and some "coloreds") wherever possible—usually at a higher wage.

The Pact encouraged the development of secondary industries to create employment for rural whites migrating to urban areas. However, out of the 72,000 positions created between 1926 and 1928, only a small fraction went to poor whites; most new jobs were filled by skilled Europeans who were encouraged by the white government to emigrate to South Africa. In the late 1920s, the mining industry and the Pact frequently clashed over compliance with "civilized labor" guidelines as the mine owners, facing a falling rate of profit since World War I, undertook to keep their operations capital intensive and their workforce black, cheap, and tractable.

Nonetheless, a powerful bloc of Afrikaner nationalists in the government maintained the "civilized labor" policy as a means to uplift poor whites. In 1928 Pact officials, along with concerned private organizations, sought to broaden their understanding of "poor whiteism." Supported by a grant from the Carnegie Corporation of New York, the Carnegie Commission on Poor Whiteism included representatives from the union government, the University of Cape Town, and the Dutch Reformed Church. The Commission's report focused on five areas: sociology, economics, public health, psychology, and education. Its members determined that destitute whites had few employment qualifications other than for jobs held by unskilled Africans who were willing to work for lower wages. At the onset of the Great Depression in the early 1930s, Pact officials extended the "civilized labor" policy to public relief projects such as road building, demanding that local government employ only poor whites, despite protests from small-town authorities that the regular African road workers were far more productive.

By the late 1930s and 1940s, the expansion of manufacturing enterprises and a swelling state bureaucracy, dominated by Afrikaner nationalists, increasingly provided work for poor whites. The protected status of whites in the labor market solved the problem of "poor whiteism" in the 1940s, and foreshadowed the strategies of apartheid-era politicians who seduced the white vote, in part, by entrenching a regime built upon sheltered white employment and repression of black labor.

BEN CARTON

Further Reading

Beinart, William, Peter Delius, and Stanley Trapido (eds.). *Putting a Plough to the Ground: Accumulation and Dispossession in Rural South Africa 1850–1930*. Johannesburg: Ravan Press, 1986.

Bradford, Helen. "Highways, Byways and Cul-de-Sacs: The Transition to Agrarian Capitalism in Revisionist South African History." *Radical History Review: History from South Africa* 46, no. 7 (1990): 59–88.

Iliffe, John. *The African Poor: A History*. Cambridge: Cambridge University Press, 1987.

Marks, Shula, and Richard Rathbone (eds.). *Industrialisation and Social Change in South Africa: African Class Formation, Culture and Consciousness 1870–1930*. London: Longman, 1982.

Morrell, Robert (ed.). *White but Poor: Essays on the History of Poor Whites in Southern Africa 1880–1940*. Pretoria: University of South Africa, 1992.

South Africa: Apartheid, 1948–1959

In its 1998 report, South Africa's Truth and Reconciliation Commission declared apartheid "a crime against humanity." This system of racial oppression and exploitation is sure to be remembered as one of the most monstrously inhuman systems of government to operate in the twentieth century.

After winning the 1948 election, D. F. Malan's National Party (NP) government set about tightening South Africa's racial order. Measures introduced between 1948 and 1959 amounted to a more rigid, systematic implementation of earlier segregationist policies. For instance, the policy of racialized political exclusion and black disfranchisement was taken further. After some dubious constitutional, judicial, and political machination and maneuvering the NP government was eventually able in 1956 to disfranchise "colored" (mixed-race) voters at the Cape.

Racialized spatial separation was also advanced. A key measure was the 1950 Group Areas Act, which provided for demarcated urban areas to be set aside for particular racially defined groups. In this decade urban policy became geared increasingly toward limiting the African presence in urban areas. The 1952 Native Laws Amendment Act was designed to tighten influx control by restricting the right of permanent urban residence to Africans who fulfilled certain strict conditions relating to place of birth and duration of residence and employment in a particular urban area. The act also made stronger provision for the expulsion from urban areas of Africans who were deemed surplus to labor requirements. Restrictions on African labor were further tightened during the 1950s. The government strengthened the racial division of labor through industrial conciliation legislation, which gave the minister of labor effective powers to reserve specific jobs for particular race groups, thereby denying people of color entry into certain skilled positions. There were also measures prohibiting mixed-race trade unions, outlawing strikes by African workers, and withholding official recognition for African trade unions.

The segregation of education became more rigid in the 1950s. The Bantu Education Act of 1953 provided for a system of schooling for Africans that would be under strict central state control and would introduce a racially differentiated syllabus geared to prepare Africans for subservient, menial roles. The 1959 Extension of University Education Act brought apartheid to the tertiary sector. The measure served to tighten the segregation of universities, and to ethnicize the sector by providing for the establishment of separate universities for specific ethnic groups.

Few areas of basic human activity and social life were left untouched by apartheid. Laws passed in 1949 and 1950 prohibited either marriage or sexual relations between whites and persons of color. Mixed sports clubs were banned, as were sporting contests between whites and blacks. Most places of entertainment were almost entirely segregated. And the 1953 Reservation of Separate Amenities Act required that racial segregation be implemented in a whole range of public facilities: toilets, elevators, public transportation, post offices, beaches, and park benches (but not shops). Although seemingly absurd, these "petty apartheid" laws could have tragic consequences. There were, for instance, cases where an ambulance would arrive at the scene of an accident and refuse to convey an accident victim to hospital if the victim's color was wrong for that particular ambulance.

While much of the apartheid system amounted to a tightening of previous segregation policies, there was one significant new departure—the development of the bantustan/homeland system. The first step was taken with the passing of the 1951 Bantu Authorities Act, which set up a three-tiered authority structure in the reserves at tribal, regional, and territorial levels, with government-appointed chiefs in effect becoming the state's administrative agents in the reserves. Then the 1959 Promotion of Bantu Self-Government Act proclaimed the existence of eight African "national units," each of which was presumed to be ethnically and culturally distinct. These units would have their territorial base in the reserves and would gradually gain greater powers of self-government, perhaps even independence.

The bantustans would come to serve a number of functions in the greater apartheid order. They were part of a divide-and-rule strategy whereby the African majority was deemed to comprise a set of ethnic minorities. This was an attempt to undermine the broader African nationalist movement. According to official ideology the bantustans were also supposed to provide a "political home" for all Africans—a place where they could exercise political rights—thereby weakening the African claim to the vote and citizenship rights in greater South Africa. At the same time the bantustans would become dumping grounds for Africans considered surplus to labor requirements in white urban and rural areas.

Apartheid was never to be a smoothly functioning system. That it functioned at all was due much to four key pillars on which it rested. The first was the system of racial classification. If people were to be separated along racial lines every person's racial identity

had to be clearly defined. Under the 1950 Population Registration Act, everybody was designated as a member of one for four racial groups—white, African, "colored," or Asiatic. Second, apartheid policies required tougher repressive measures to quell growing opposition. One such measure was the 1950 Suppression of Communism Act, which enabled the minister of justice to use a very broad definition of communism to declare opposition organizations unlawful. Third, apartheid depended on an expanded bureaucratic apparatus. After H. F. Verwoerd become minister of native affairs in 1950, his department took on a new importance. Its staff expanded, and its administrative style became more centralized and authoritarian. Fourth, apartheid's defenders made vain attempts to offer ideological justification for the system. In the 1950s crude notions of white superiority and black inferiority were articulated in defense of white domination (known as *baaskap*). Other justifications rested on rigid ideas of racial difference, seemingly ordained by scripture and science—ideas that assumed a strict correlation between physical and cultural difference.

Although apartheid appeared to be a well-planned program of racialized social engineering, recent research suggests that the NP government was not following a master plan. During the 1950s the future direction of apartheid policy remained a matter of debate within NP circles, between those who wanted total, vertical separation, and the pragmatists who saw that total apartheid could not be implemented without ending the economy's dependence on cheap black labor. In the end, the pragmatists won, and apartheid policy makers were left to continue grappling with the fundamental contradiction in the system—between the insistence on racial separation and the necessary exploitation of cheap black labor. This contradiction would prove unable to resolve, and would lead to the ultimate collapse of apartheid.

PAUL MAYLAM

See also: **South Africa: Afrikaner Nationalism, Broederbond and National Party, 1902–1948; South Africa: Defiance Campaign, Freedom Charter, Treason Trials: 1952–1960; Verwoerd, H. F.**

Further Reading

Bonner, Philip, Peter Delius, and Deborah Posel (eds.). *Apartheid's Genesis 1935–1962*. Johannesburg: Ravan Press/ Witwatersrand University Press, 1993.

Kenney, Henry. *Power, Pride and Prejudice: The Years of Afrikaner Nationalist Rule in South Africa*. Johannesburg: Jonathan Ball, 1991.

Maclennan, Ben. *Apartheid: The Lighter Side*. Cape Town: Chameleon Press, 1990.

O'Meara, Dan. *Forty Lost Years*. Johannesburg: Ravan Press/Athens, Ohio: Ohio University Press, 1996.

Posel, Deborah. *The Making of Apartheid 1948–1961*. Oxford: Clarendon Press, 1991.

South Africa: Homelands and Bantustans

The establishment of "homelands" for various African communities was a device to divert internal opposition to apartheid and a failed attempt to convince the international community that South Africa was addressing, on its own terms, the demands for emancipation of its majority population. It provided for the bogus fragmentation of the population into a collection of ethnically distinct "minorities." Only the white population had political rights in the Republic of South Africa. The indigenous peoples were deemed not to be South Africans at all, but "nationals" of self-governing "Bantustans." Africans living and working in "white South Africa" were regarded as "temporary sojourners" (migrant workers) always at risk of deportation to a "homeland" that many had never even seen.

The idea was first conceived by Afrikaner intellectuals in the 1940s; they would later establish a think tank called the South African Bureau for Racial Affairs (SABRA). It was based on the notion of separate territories for Africans (the reserves), which had provided much of the ideological justification for segregation. In 1947, the Sauer Commission outlined the National Party's "color policy." The existing limited African representation in Parliament (indirectly by whites) was to be curtailed further, and the advisory Native Representative Council would be abolished. There would be an *eie* (own or native) system of government and administration, based on local councils comprising of the "chief" and his acknowledged *indunas* (officials or councilors), and eventually, larger councils "for each of the [African] ethnic groups and chief sub-groups." Although the commission prevaricated concerning the ultimate destiny of the new councils, the aim was to grant "each race in its own homeland . . . the inalienable right to self-assertion and self-determination."

The implementation of the policy is particularly associated with H. F. Verwoerd (minister of native affairs, 1950–1958 and prime minister, 1958–1966). The Bantu Authorities Act of 1951 provided for the abolition of the Native Representative Council and the establishment of individual "tribal authorities," based on the government's own ethnological surveys, as the foundation of a tiered system of local councils to be topped by "territorial authorities" for different "ethnic units."

The further extension of the policy faced formidable obstacles. Whites, who benefited from a plentiful supply of cheap African labor, feared the possible expulsion of their workers and servants to rural reserves. Second, the scheme was justified by the notion of "separate development," which implied the economic development of the reserves, which had become impoverished and functioned primarily as labor reserves. Third, the plan involved securing the agreement of rural African communities at a time when African leaders were calling for an end to racial discrimination. Last, many whites feared the ceding of territory to "independent," and potentially hostile, "Bantu statelets" on South Africa's borders.

The first problem was avoided when the government continued to allow Africans with established residential rights to remain in segregated townships in the cities. The development issue was more problematic. In 1956, the government rejected the recommendations of its own Tomlinson Commission for extensive economic development in the reserves. Verwoerd judged the Tomlinson plans too expensive. Moreover, he prohibited investment by outsiders in the reserves, wanting to maintain a black/white political division between the reserves and the rest of the country. It was also feared that new industries in the reserves would threaten the established industrial centers and undermine the privileged position of white workers. Under Verwoerd, development was limited: the state financed agrarian improvement schemes geared toward subsistence production; the Bantu Development Corporation was to subsidize indigenous development; and "border industries" were to be constructed in "white areas" adjacent to reserves, to employ Africans who would commute daily. SABRA leaders argued against Verwoerd's policies and even called for negotiations with African leaders.

The African National Congress opposed Bantu authorities and the majority of rural African communities refused to accept the new scheme, despite an intensive official propaganda campaign and increasing administrative pressures. Many chiefs were deposed, and they and others were sent into internal exile on the grounds of "agitation." Some communities were threatened with the withdrawal of state support for local services, while others were promised new services subject to their compliance. The scheme of course provided opportunities for some to accumulate local economic and political power, while others succumbed to official threats. In some areas, there were violent uprisings and Bantu Authorities were restored by force. "Mobile units" of police were deployed causing significant casualties; thereafter, "punishment arrangements" were instituted, including imprisonment and death sentences by the score.

As prime minister, Verwoerd pushed through the Promotion of Bantu Self-government Act of 1959, presenting the homelands scheme as the only alternative to majority rule, against the background of decolonization elsewhere in Africa. The indirect African representation in the parliament was ended. In 1963, amid increased state repression following the Sharpeville crisis, the Transkei was the first territorial authority to be granted "self-government."

The program of mass removals was a particularly lamentable aspect of the policy. Once labor requirements had been met, Africans were removed from white-owned farms. Others were uprooted from their homes in a campaign to eliminate "black spots" from areas deemed to be "white," or became caught up in rezoning exercises in efforts to consolidate the often fragmented homeland territories. Unemployed individuals and families, especially the elderly, always remained at risk of being "endorsed out" of the cities. Around two million people were removed to the dumping grounds of apartheid, housed in scarcely planned rural slums with few facilities, no access to productive land, and little prospect of waged employment locally.

Under Verwoerd's successors, B. J. Vorster and P. W. Botha, the homelands adventure continued. By 1984, Transkei, Bophuthatswana, Ciskei, and Venda had accepted "independence," and there were six other "self-governing" homelands; all these territories were eventually incorporated into the "new South Africa" in 1994. Homeland governments failed to secure international recognition and were regarded as illegitimate by the majority of Africans. Although external investment was permitted from the late 1960s on, the dominant source of capital was the billions of rands transferred by Pretoria. Yet, with ever increasing population pressures, homeland economies remained starved of investment, most people depending upon the remnants of smallholder agriculture and remittances from migrant workers. As homeland elites competed for control of the capital transfers and the inflated bureaucracies they financed, the scene was set for financial and political corruption. The political history of the homelands is marked with emergencies, effective dictatorships and one-party governments, coups and countercoups.

Yet government based on ideas of "tribe" and chieftaincy had a certain residual legitimacy among those who became resigned to operate within the new dispensations. In the past, ethnicity was often involved in the defense of rural resources against white encroachment; it could now be mobilized to compete for control in the new local states. Rival ethnic claims often led to violent competition over scarce economic and infrastructural resources. In KwaZulu, Chief Mangosuthu Buthelezi, the most successful exploiter of the system, invoked Zulu symbols and emphasized Zulu cultural renewal; while he secured popular support for his Inkatha movement, he refused to accept independence, which gave him considerable purchase with Pretoria, anxious for him to take this path. Ironically, General Bantu Holomisa, who seized power in Transkei (allegedly with Pretoria's connivance), announced in 1989 that he planned a plebiscite on Transkeian reincorporation into South Africa.

ROBERT MCINTOSH

Further Reading

Beinart, William. *Twentieth Century South Africa*. Oxford: Oxford University Press, 1994.

Delius, Peter. "Migrant Organisiation, The Communist Party, the ANC and the Sekhukhuneland Revolt, 1940–1958." In *Apartheid's Genesis, 1935–1962*, edited by Philip Bonner, Peter Delius, and Deborah Posel. Johannesburg: Ravan Press/Witwatersrand University Press, 1993.

Evans, Ivan. *Bureaucracy and Race: Native Administration in South Africa*. Berkeley and Los Angeles: University of California Press, 1997.

Lazar, John. "Verwoerd versus the 'Visionaries': The South African Bureau of Racial Affairs (Sabra) and Apartheid, 1948–1961." In *Apartheid's Genesis, 1935–1962*, edited by Philip Bonner, Peter Delius and Deborah Posel. Johannesburg: Ravan Press/Witwatersrand University Press, 1993.

O'Meara, Dan. *Forty Lost Years: The Apartheid State and the Politics of the National Party, 1948–1994*. Athens, Ohio: Ohio University Press/Randburg, South Africa: Ravan Press, 1996.

South Africa: Mining

Over many years, mining transformed the rate and nature of South African economic growth. Initial capitalization of gold mining drew heavily on overseas capital and, to a lesser extent, existing diamond companies. Between 1887 and 1934, 60 per cent of gold investment was external, but the trend reversed in the 1940s, helped by wartime exchange controls and expanding domestic financial corporations. Domestic investment in gold rose, with 55 per cent of dividends remitted locally by 1950, 69 per cent by 1960. South Africa's 1932 departure from the gold standard stimulated gold price rises that bolstered capital investment in mining and manufacturing. In 1941, the gold price was set at $35 per fine ounce. Fixed prices, limited mechanization, and labor shortages checked expansion, although state subsidies kept marginal mines viable. New capital raised by the mines was only £5 million from 1940 to 1945, but grew to £370 million in the period 1946–1959.

Gold production expanded by 84 per cent in the 1950s as major new mines were developed in the Orange Free State and Far West Rand. Foreign investment increased in the political stability of the 1950s and 1960s. The floating of gold in 1968 saw its price leap, reaching $150 in 1973 and averaging $613 in

1980. In the 1970s, gold doubled its share of gross domestic product from 10 to 22 per cent and state profits from gold rose from 1 billion to 10 billion rand. Capital investment in the 1980s targeted mechanization and new technologies of extracting gold from waste ore, helping to extend the life of old mines, but production fell as price swings destabilized the economy through fluctuating revenues and exchange rates, while rising inflation limited expansion. Mine employment fell from 534,255 people in 1986 to 473,685 in 1990, and further price falls and sales of gold reserves by some countries in the 1990s fueled mine closures and large-scale retrenchments.

Industrialization and overseas demand fueled increased output of minerals such as coal, platinum, and uranium. The Anglo-American Corporation, South Africa's largest gold producer and biggest company, also helped develop these sectors. Coal production tripled between 1930 and 1960, as low production costs based on large reserves and cheap labor aided capitalization. Exports rose from 1.3 to 44 million metric tons from 1970 to 1985 due to new technologies, construction of a port at Richard's Bay, and electrified railways, mechanization, removal of price controls, and new markets. Antiapartheid sanctions hit uranium exports but platinum production boomed in the 1980s, outstripping coal in exchange earnings. De Beers dominated world diamond production and marketing, but local output declined; still, the company's value rose 300 per cent from 1960 to 1985 and control of new mines in Botswana enabled De Beers to weather an industry crisis from 1978 to 1985. Overall, mining's share of GDP fell steadily, relative to manufacturing from the 1940s: in 1972 it comprised only 10 per cent, although this grew to 18 per cent by 1979 with rising prices.

The gold mines' workforce was overwhelmingly African and migrant in nature. It fluctuated in size—from 394,000 people in 1940; to 437,000 in 1960; 377,000 in 1980; and 474,000 in 1990—and was drawn chiefly from Mozambique, Lesotho, and Malawi. Foreign workers comprised 60 per cent in 1960, 80 per cent in 1973. Thereafter, the share of local labor grew, rising to 61 per cent in 1986, a shift stimulated by labor shortages, temporary withdrawal of Malawi labor in 1974, and Mozambique's independence in 1975. Real wages of African miners had remained static from 1910 to 1973, but the mines were then forced to offer higher wages to attract local workers. Helped by rising gold prices and increased productivity the average real wage of African miners tripled in the 1970s contributing to the stabilization, and thus eventual unionization, of the workforce.

The coercive nature of mine recruitment and workplace control made organizing on the mines hazardous.

African miners, unable to openly organize until 1982 and with their strikes illegal until the 1970s, faced enormous obstacles such as state and employer hostility, low wages, debilitating diseases, and high rates of work accidents (9,000 deaths from 1973 to 1985). They were forced to live in regimented compounds (98 per cent lived in single-sex hostels in 1985) that fostered horizontal divisions in the working class and interethnic tensions, though the high concentration of workers aided interaction. Job "color bar" legislation such as the Mines and Works Act of 1911/26 reserved privileged occupations for a small stratum of white artisans who in 1984 received five times the wages of African miners, and whose union spurned cooperation with blacks.

Sporadic unsuccessful attempts by unionists, communists, and African National Congress (ANC) radicals to organize African miners between 1918 and 1940 finally were realized in 1941, when the African Mine Workers' Union was formed. In 1946, the refusal of the state and the Chamber of Mines to recognize the union or extend wage rises granted to other blacks to miners precipitated a major strike involving at least 75,000 workers. The strike was savagely repressed and the union smashed, but its impact helped reinvigorate African politics. Further intermittent organizing campaigns and isolated strikes took place, and in 1972–1973 a strike wave sparked rapid union growth, but it was not until the 1982 formation of the National Union of Mineworkers (NUM) that miners effectively were unionized. Led by Cyril Ramaphosa and tolerated by the Anglo-American Corporation, NUM grew rapidly to 250,000 members in 1986. Behind this growth was the union's skilful organizing, and the liberalization of labor laws after the Wiehahn Commission in 1979 recommended abolition of job reservation (not extended to the mines until 1987). NUM gained support by vigorously championing miners' safety and health, and representing them after disasters such as the 1986 Kinross accident. It won wage increases but these barely kept pace with inflation, forcing the union in 1987 to call the longest and largest strike in South African history, involving 340,000 workers for three weeks, which was violently repressed. NUM allied itself closely with the UDF, joined COASTU, and adopted the ANC's Freedom Charter. The union's militancy and political stance brought it into conflict with both the Chamber of Mines and the state.

Mining played a crucial part in the economic life in the South from the 1940s through the 1980s, contributing to gross domestic product and capital investment in manufacturing, and nourishing the growth of cities such as Johannesburg and Welkom. Its profits were achieved at the expense of mineworkers, but in the 1980s they organized and became an integral part of democratic forces that dismantled apartheid. In the 1990s mining retained a major role in the economy, earning 42 per cent of export income in 1995.

PETER LIMB

See also: **Mining; Mining, Multinationals, and Development; South Africa: Gold on the Witwatersrand, 1886–1899.**

Further Reading

Chamber of Mines of South Africa. *Statistical Tables 1990–93.* Johannesburg: Chamber of Mines of South Africa, 1991–1994. Annual reports.

Crush, Jonathan, Alan Jeeves, and David Yudelman. *South Africa's Labor Empire: A History of Black Migrancy to the Gold Mines.* Boulder, Colo.: Westview Press/Cape Town: David Philip, 1991.

Frankel, S. Herbert. *Investment and the Return to Equity Capital in the South African Gold Mining Industry, 1887–1965: An International Comparison.* Cambridge, Mass.: Harvard University Press, 1967.

Innes, Duncan. *Anglo American and the Rise of Modern South Africa.* London: Heinemann, 1984.

James, Wilmot. *Our Precious Metal: African Labour in South Africa's Gold Industry, 1970–90.* Cape Town: David Philip, 1992.

Jones, Stuart, and André Müller. *The South African Economy, 1910–90.* Basingstoke, England: Macmillan, 1992.

Kanfer, Stefan. *The Last Empire: De Beers, Diamonds, and the World.* London: Hodder and Stoughton/New York: Farrar, Straus and Giroux, 1993.

Leger, Jeffrey. "From Fatalism to Mass Action: The South African National Union of Mineworkers' Struggle for Safety and Health." *Labour, Capital and Society* 21, no. 2 (1988): 270–292.

Moodie, T. Dunbar, with Vivienne Ndatshe. *Going for Gold: Men, Mines, and Migration.* Berkeley and Los Angeles: University of California Press/Johannesburg: Witwatersrand University Press, 1994.

O'Meara, Dan. "The 1946 African Mineworkers' Strike." *Journal of Commonwealth and Comparative Politics* 12, no. 2 (1975): 146–173.

Wilson, Francis. *Labour in the South African Gold Mines 1911–1969.* Cambridge: Cambridge University Press, 1972.

South Africa: Rural Protest and Violence: 1950s

With the election of D. F. Malan's National Party in 1948 and the subsequent implementation of numerous apartheid laws, the 1950s became a decade of intense protest against white minority rule in South Africa. In urban areas, the African National Congress (ANC), which was transforming itself from a moderate African elite organization into a broad-based liberation movement, orchestrated the famous Defiance Campaign of passive resistance to unjust laws. In rural areas, where the ANC was just beginning to make significant contacts in the 1950s, African people protested against apartheid laws that were adversely affecting their lives, albeit usually in a less focused and organized manner.

There were a number of common grievances that motivated rural protest at this time. The Bantu Authorities Act of 1951 sought to set up a system of self-government for rural and ethnically defined African homelands. Many African traditional leaders were co-opted into this system and given sweeping new powers over their subjects. Legitimate chiefs that refused to participate in this system were deposed by the government and replaced by men who often had tenuous claims to traditional leadership. Under this new system, chiefs were frequently seen as corrupt lackeys of the apartheid state. In order to shape the homelands into viable self-governing territories, a host of often ill-conceived betterment and rehabilitation schemes were imposed on rural people, such as resettlement and the culling of livestock to reduce overgrazing. Such programs were usually resented by rural Africans, to whom cattle represented a traditional form of wealth; they perceived the programs as just another way to reduce self-sufficiency in order to increase the number of migrant workers.

Rural people also came to despise the Bantu education plan, which replaced mission schools with government ones designed to reinforce the subordinate position of black people in South African society. Chiefs were also resented, because their duties involved enforcing the Bantu education system. In addition, many Africans were removed from the cities and white-owned farms and forcibly moved to rural homelands, where they became a radicalizing influence.

The protest methods used by rural Africans involved cutting fences; setting fires on common land; refusing to cooperate with, or even threatening, officials from the Native Affairs Department; raising grievances at public meetings; and boycotting cattle-dipping stations, white-owned stores, and local councils. Frequently, tensions boiled over into violence that was often directed against local African people, who were seen as agents of the state. In all these cases, the state security forces intervened aggressively to suppress resistance, and numerous people were imprisoned and even executed for their part in these disturbances. Examples of major peasant uprisings in this period occurred in the western Transvaal in 1957–1958, Sekhukuniland (in northern Transvaal) in 1958–1959, KwaZulu/Natal in 1958–1959, the Pondoland and Thembuland areas of Transkei (in today's Eastern Cape) in 1959–1962, and Ciskei (also in today's Eastern Cape), which was almost constantly in a state of alarm.

In Sekhukuniland, among the Pedi people, an organization called Khuduthamaga ("Red and White Tortoise") feared that chieftaincy was becoming an instrument of Bantu Authorities and attempted to reinforce the local belief that "a chief is a chief by the people." However, as historian Peter Delius (1996) points out, this underground organization did not attempt to democratize chieftaincy, as it was a traditionally hereditary institution. The subordinate place of women and young people in Pedi society was not challenged. Rebels in this area labeled anyone who approved of Bantu authorities as "rangers" (named after the African agricultural assistants of white government officials). Sometimes, people who were perceived as agents of Westernization, such as prominent Christians, teachers, and traders, were included in this category.

Rural communities became polarized and a belief spread that the so-called rangers were using witchcraft to undermine traditional values and advance their own interests. The long established fear of witches in the area contributed to the outbreak of violence. By May 1958, nine men had been killed, many had been injured, and the property of rangers had been destroyed. During this uprising the police, who would later grossly exaggerate the conspiratorial nature of Khuduthamaga, arrested 300 people, of whom 21 were eventually placed on death row. Notably, beginning in the 1960s, this area became a fertile recruiting ground for the ANC's Umkhonto we Sizwe (Spear of the Nation), which initiated an armed struggle against the apartheid state.

In Pondoland, where there had been a long history of independence from government, the Mpondo people strongly resented the implementation of Bantu authorities and Bantu education plans. Toward the end of 1959, violence broke out in the town of Bizana when the chairman of the district authority and an open supporter of Bantu authorities, Saul Mabude, failed to attend a public meeting on this issue and an angry crowd burned his house. The security forces began to terrorize the people of Eastern Pondoland, who in turn formed themselves into an alternative governing structure called the Hill Committee and informed Botha Sigcau, the paramount chief, that he was the "bootlicker of [H. F.] Verwoerd," the South African prime minister. It is interesting that people in the area also referred to this movement as *iKongo*, which was a Xhosa version of the word *congress* and seems to suggest that ANC influences were gaining popularity. Initially, the Hill Committee invited government officials to hear their list of grievances, but when they were ignored, they began to attack policemen, chiefs and anyone suspected of supporting Bantu authorities. The most famous incident of the Pondoland Uprising occurred at Ngquza Hill in June 1960, when police fired on a Hill Committee gathering that was displaying a white flag of truce. At least 11 people were killed, 30 were wounded, and 21 were arrested. At the commission of inquiry into this massacre, the Mpondo people demanded an end to Bantu Authorities; relief from taxes; dismissal of their paramount chief; and representation in the South African parliament. The uprising was subdued by force; thousands were imprisoned and 20 sentenced to death. However, assassinations of unpopular chiefs and councilors continued up to 1969. The exact role of the ANC in this rural rebellion seems to have been ambiguous as Chief Albert Luthuli, the ANC president, urged the rebels to stop fighting while at the same time some members of the ANC Youth League participated in the violence.

TIM STAPLETON

See also: **South Africa: Homelands and Bantustans.**

Further Reading

Delius, Peter. *A Lion among the Cattle: Reconstruction and Resistance in the Northern Transvaal*. Johannesburg: Ravan Press, 1996.

Redding, Sean. "Government Witchcraft: Taxation, the Supernatural, and the Mpondo Revolt in the Transkei, South Africa, 1955–1963." *African Affairs*, no. 95 (1996), 249–270.

Stapleton, T. J. *Faku: Rulership and Colonialism in the Mpondo Kingdom*. Waterloo, Wilfrid Laurier University Press, 2001.

Switzer, Les. *Power and Resistance in an African Society: The Ciskei Xhosa and the Making of South Africa*. Madison: University of Wisconsin Press, 1993.

Truth and Reconciliation Commission (South Africa). "Briefing Document for Commissioners and Committee Members, Lusikisiki Public Hearings, March 10–12, 1997." Truth and Reconciliation Commission, 1997.

South Africa: Defiance Campaign, Freedom Charter, Treason Trials: 1952–1960

The Defiance Campaign was launched jointly in June 1952 by the African National Congress (ANC) and the South African Indian Congress (SAIC). This civil disobedience campaign set out to mobilize mass defiance of discriminatory laws, targeting in particular pass laws, stock limitation laws, the Bantu Authorities Act, the Group Areas Act, the Separate Representation of Voters Act, and the Suppression of Communism Act. The organizers of the campaign called on volunteers to court arrest by deliberately breaking these unjust laws. The strategy was to disorganize the state and cripple the criminal justice system by filling the courts and prisons to overflowing thus making segregation unenforceable.

The Defiance Campaign did not achieve its main objectives. First, it drew responses mainly in the Transvaal and the Eastern Cape. There were not many more than 8,000 arrests for offenses relating to the Defiance Campaign of which about 6,000 occurred in the Eastern Cape. Second, although it was firmly the intention that protests be peaceful there was violence, mainly as provoked by the police. Police action in Port Elizabeth on October 18, 1952 resulted in a riot that claimed 11 lives and on November 9, 1952, 10 people were killed when police opened fire on a meeting in East London. Third, state repression of the Defiance Campaign was swift and effective. In November of that same year 52 black leaders were banned from attending meetings or leaving their districts of residence. Another 50 leaders were arrested and charged with launching the Defiance Campaign. Two new laws, the Public Safety Act and the Criminal Laws Amendment Act introduced harsh new measures for civil disobedience. The Defiance Campaign ground to a halt by mid-November 1952.

Despite these shortcomings, the Defiance Campaign was nevertheless of great significance for the development of the antiapartheid movement. It gave the ANC a great deal of publicity and drew international attention, especially at the United Nations. The Defiance Campaign also initiated the ANC into the politics of populism. The willingness of volunteers to defy the law openly and to confront the authorities head on changed the image of the ANC as the preserve of educated and more affluent Africans. Urban working-class people were drawn into the organization, swelling its membership from a mere 7,000 before the campaign to about 100,000 by the end of the 1950s. The Defiance Campaign, in addition, helped to cement solidarity against apartheid across racial lines because it was not just an African initiative but was carried out in partnership with the SAIC and drew support from white communists and some liberals.

The conviction that interracial cooperation was the most effective way of fighting white supremacism led to the formation in 1953 of a broad nonracial front against apartheid, the Congress Alliance. It consisted of the African National Congress, the South African Indian Congress, the Colored People's Congress, and the Congress of Democrats, which housed radical and liberal white supporters. In 1955 the South African Congress of Trade Unions and the Federation of South African Women joined the Congress Alliance.

Considering ways of carrying the struggle forward in the light of problems encountered during the Defiance Campaign and of harnessing the mass support the Congress Alliance was attracting, it was decided that the alliance should convene a congress of the people, at which a freedom charter for a democratic South Africa should be adopted. The idea was for organizers to canvass the South African people as widely as possible for their grievances and demands, that these be assimilated and then drafted into the freedom charter, to be adopted at a congress representative of the South African nation.

The Congress of the People was eventually held at Kliptown, near Johannesburg, on June 26, 1955, by a gathering of about 3,000 elected delegates from a wide range of organizations that supported the Congress Alliance. Key leaders such as Albert Luthuli, president of the ANC, and Yusuf Dadoo, president of the South African Indian Council, could not attend because they were serving banning orders. Busloads of delegates and supporters from various parts of the country were prevented from reaching Kliptown by police roadblocks. Surrounded by an armed cordon of police, this momentous meeting was convened and the freedom charter adopted.

The freedom charter affirmed that South Africa belonged to all its people, both black and white. It called for the scrapping of all forms of racial discrimination, the institution of a democratic system of government, and equal protection for all before the law. The charter demanded equal access to education, social security, and employment. It also asserted a need for a fairer distribution of wealth through the nationalization of industry, mines, banks, and the redistribution of land. The last-mentioned demand was an indication of the influence of Communist Party radicals within the Congress Alliance.

The Congress of the People had a sequel in the form of the marathon Treason Trial that lasted from December 1956 through to March 1961. In an attempt to intimidate the Congress Alliance and to neutralize its leadership, the police spent a year and a half after the Kliptown Congress collecting what it considered incriminating evidence and then on December 5, 1956, swooped down on homes all over South Africa, arresting 156 leaders and organizers of the movement on charges of high treason. The prosecution charged that the freedom charter was a communist document, that the ANC planned the violent overthrow of the state, and that the plot was inspired by international communism. These charges were ludicrous and were exposed as such in court proceedings. After a year, charges were withdrawn against 61 of the accused; as time passed, charges against others wwere dropped, and the remaining 30 accused were finally acquitted in March 1961. Although the state did succeed in disrupting the liberatory movement in the late 1950s and neutralizing a large part of its leadership, it failed, however, to intimidate the movement. This succeeded only in strengthening solidarity within the Congress Alliance, publicizing its cause internationally and elevating it in the eyes of the broad mass of the people.

MOHAMED ADHIKARI

See also: **Luthuli, Albert; Mandela, Nelson.**

Further Reading

Holland, Heidi. *The Struggle: A History of the African National Congress.* London: Grafton Books, 1989.

Karis, Tom, and Gwendolyn Carter (eds.). *From Protest to Challenge: Documents of African Politics in South Africa*, vol. 3, *Challenge and Violence, 1953–1964*. Stanford, Calif.: Hoover Institution Press, 1977.

Lodge, Tom. *Black Politics in South Africa since 1945*. Johannesburg: Ravan Press, 1983.

Luthuli, Albert. *Let My People Go*. London: Collins, 1962.

Mandela, Nelson. *Long Walk to Freedom: The Autobiography of Nelson Mandela*. Randburg, South Africa: Macdonald Purnell, 1994.

Meli, Francis. *South Africa Belongs to Us: A History of the ANC*. London: James Currey, 1988.

Suttner, Raymond, and Jeremy Cronin. *Thirty Years of the Freedom Charter*. Johannesburg: Ravan Press, 1986.

South Africa: Apartheid, Education and

Apartheid-era education policy was based on a need to preserve and promote the cultural and economic interests of the Afrikaner nationalists who came to power with the victory of the National Party in 1948. Yet it is also important to recognize that it was also an attempt to apply many of the principles of modernization and centralized state planning to South Africa.

When the party unexpectedly came to power it did not initially have a blueprint for education. It was only after a hastily convened conference on Christian National Education (CNE) that guidelines emerged. That policy represented a blend of Dutch traditions from the nineteenth century and the educational legacy of the prisoner-of-war camps in the South African War (1899–1902). It emphasized the significance of the more fundamentalist and xenophobic Afrikaner cultural traditions. Those local traditions were blended with aspects of the "pillarization" policy, which sought to address issues of religion and ethnic identity in the Netherlands during post–World War II reconstruction and the American innovations regarding school governance and management. Borrowings from the "culture contact" school of social anthropology were also significant.

These elements all proved to be most influential in shaping policy at this time. While there was no formal blueprint for white education beyond the vague and informal CNE document of 1948, the official government commission of enquiry into native education in South Africa, the Eiselen Report (1951), soon set out the direction of policy for the Bantu education plan. Two years later, the recommendations passed into legislation in the form of the Bantu Education Act (1953), which was to be the basis of segregated educational transformation for the next 20 years. Legislation was also passed to segregate universities and institutions of higher education along racial lines.

The education policy under apartheid sought to privilege Afrikaners by promoting Afrikaans language schools in place of the bilingual (English and Afrikaans) schools, which had been dominant since the establishment of the union of South Africa in 1910. White children were to go to separate English-language and Afrikaans-language schools, and the curriculum was to reflect a Calvinist and patriarchal outlook. "Poor whites" were to be "rescued" through the mechanism of schooling. In regard to the provision of schooling for the rest of the population, apartheid policy sought to end the "liberal" influences of missionary education and to promote the secularization of schooling, the mass expansion of rural education at the lower levels, and a degree of vocationalization of the curriculum under the control of separate educational authorities responsible for each "racial" group. That control was eventually extended to the various Bantustan authorities.

In the 1950s, these policies were crafted by the minister of native affairs (and later prime minister) Hendrick Verwoerd, and the chief architect of the Bantu education plan, the anthropologist Werner Eiselen. Through the Eiselen Commission they promoted the view that had been advocated since the 1920s by the Phelps Stokes Commission on *Education in Africa* (1922–1924) and the Native Economic Commission (1932), which favored the adaptation of education to the variety of cultural and economic circumstances, or so-called needs, of the various ethnic communities in South Africa. Just as schooling for Afrikaners was to prepare them for life in the Afrikaans community, so was Bantu education to prepare black youths for a life in the countryside "among their own people," where they would not come into economic and political conflict with whites. Critics were quick to point out that such educational differentiation in the context of rapid urbanization, industrialization, and racial discrimination in the wider society and in industry simply meant that education was being politicized as part of an overall effort to avoid any kind of competition between whites and blacks in the social, political, or economic spheres, and as such to the advantage of the white community.

During the 50 years of apartheid dominance (from 1948 to 1994) it is possible to identify two major phases of educational policy. The first, referred to above, is to be associated with the period of "grand apartheid" (from the 1950s to the mid-1970s); the second is associated with the era of the reform and modernization, as apartheid was put on the defensive in the 1980s.

During the era of grand apartheid there was a massive expansion of education. Nearly all white children, including the "poor whites," who were a source of great anxiety to the government, were provided with places at high school, and the number of university students increased dramatically. New Afrikaans language universities were established for the new urban white working class. There was also a dramatic expansion of black education, particularly at the primary level, and a mass education system was put in place, but the differentials in state support and finance between black and white education highlighted by South African Institute of Race Relations and United Nations Educational, Scientific, and Cultural Organization reports in the 1960s, as well as the opposition from political organizations like the African National Congress and the Unity Movement, were to provide a major indictment of government policies by the 1970s.

By 1976, apartheid was in deep crisis and the massive youth uprising that began in Soweto schools demonstrated that questions of educational provision and policy were a central aspect of the political problem. Language issues sparked the crisis, but it had deep roots in resistance politics and the black consciousness movement. This marked the beginning of an intensification of the war of resistance that had been launched in the 1960s. In response, the National Party launched a slate of reform policies relating to labor legislation, constitutional transformation, and urban renewal. In addition, an important set of recommendations for educational reform were introduced in the 1980s, in the form of the Human Sciences Research Council report on the provision of education in the RSA (the De Lange Report) and the Department of National Education's *Educational Renewal Strategy* report (1989). Although these were in large part still constrained by the racist parameters of apartheid policy and a lack of political will for reform on behalf of strong sections of the political establishment, they did mark a significant shift toward international norms in educational policy development.

During the 1980s there were massive increases in the finances for black education, attempts to reform the school curriculum in favor of an emphasis on work preparation, and decisive shifts in policy to place the control of school governance in the hands of local authorities and parental groups, but most of these reforms were unacceptable to the majority in a context where politics and educational policy were seen to be closely linked. The Peoples' Education movement took up the banner on behalf of the United Democratic Front to pursue the cause of radical change in education as part a total democratic transition. The call for peoples' history as an aspect of that curriculum demonstrated the desire for a new kind of school knowledge that would reflect the experience of the majority of South Africans. The transition to democratic rule in 1994 marked the end of apartheid education, but it will be many years before the legacy is erased. Policies to promote access to educational institutions for greater numbers of children and adults, for a new curriculum, and for anew form of school governance are currently being implemented.

PETER KALLAWAY

Further Reading

Cross, Michael, and Mkwanazi (eds.). *Resistance and Transformation*. Johannesburg: Ravan Press, 1992.

Hartshorne, Ken. *Crisis and Challenge: Black Education 1910–1990*. Cape Town: Oxford University Press, 1992.

Hyslop, Jonathan. *The Classroom Struggle: Policy and Resistance in South Africa 1940–1990*. Pietermaritzburg: University of Natal Press, 1999.

Kallaway, Peter (ed.). *Apartheid and Education: The Education of Black South Africans*. Johannesburg: Ravan Press, 1984.

———. *Education and Politics in Apartheid South Africa: New Perspectives on the History of Education, 1948–1994*. New York: Peter Lang/Cape Town: Maskew Millar/Longman, 2002.

Malherbe. *Education in South Africa*, vols. 1 and 2. Cape Town: Juta, 1924 and 1974.

Nkomko, Mokabung. *Pedagogy of Domination*. Trenton, N.J., 1990.

South Africa: Sharpeville Massacre

In 1960, Sharpeville was an African township of 21,000 people situated between Vereeniging and Vanderbijlpark, two industrial and mining towns in the southern Transvaal. At the time this area was one of the strongholds of the newly formed Pan-Africanist Congress (PAC).

In December 1959, the African National Congress (ANC) announced its intention of holding a series of single-day "antipass" marches beginning on March 31, 1960. In keeping with its stress on militant mass action and keen to make its presence felt, the PAC preempted this initiative by announcing that it would launch a sustained antipass campaign on March 21. It called upon its supporters to leave their passes at home on this day and to present themselves en masse, but peacefully, at police stations for arrest. The southern Transvaal and the Western Cape were the only regions where there was a significant response to the PAC's campaign. These were both areas where ANC organization was weak and where antipathy to pass laws ran especially deep.

The PAC's call drew a ready response from the residents of Sharpeville because the pass laws were a particular source of frustration to them. Rents were high because this was one of the newer townships and was relatively well serviced with running water, sanitation, and other amenities. Residents from the nearby area of Top Location, where rents were much lower, had in the previous year been forced to move to Sharpeville. As many as 5,000 Top Location residents who could not afford the higher rentals were moved to the reserves creating deep feelings of resentment among friends and relatives left behind. Also, there was a particularly high level of unemployment among younger work seekers. Influx control prevented them from going to the Witwatersrand to look for work.

On the morning of March 21, a crowd of about 5,000 gathered at the Sharpeville police station. At nearby Evaton, 20,000 protesters assembled at the police station, and 4,000 residents from the townships of Bophelong and Boipatong marched on the Vanderbijlpark police station. In Vanderbijlpark the protesters were dispersed by a police baton charge and in Evaton by low-flying jets. At Sharpeville the police were caught off guard by the size of the crowd; they refused to arrest pass offenders and reinforcements were called in. A stand-off ensued between 300 armed but nervous policemen and the crowd, the mood of which, according to eyewitness accounts, was not overtly hostile.

At 1:15 P.M. a scuffle broke out at the gate of the police station; a police officer was pushed to the ground, the crowd surged forward to see what was happening, the fence was trampled, stones were thrown, and it appears that inexperienced constables panicked and opened fire. No order to fire was given, and the firing did not stop when the crowd turned to flee. Sixty-nine people were killed; of these, 52 were shot in the back. A further 180 peeople were wounded.

At Langa in Cape Town two people were killed when police dispersed a crowd of 6,000 late that afternoon. Subsequent raids and brutality by police toward Langa residents resulted in two largely spontaneous marches by protesters to the Caledon Square police station in the center of Cape Town. On both occasions—the first a march by 5,000 on March 25, and the second a march by 30,000 five days later—bloodshed was averted when the protesters dispersed peacefully.

The Sharpeville shootings represent a dramatic turning point in South African history. The shooting was universally condemned and resulted a sharp escalation in the international campaign to pressurize the South African government into abandoning apartheid policies. There was a massive flight of capital forcing the South African government to impose currency controls. Calls for economic sanctions against South Africa within the United Nations were, however, vetoed by Britain and the United States. South Africa's isolation intensified as it was expelled or forced to withdraw from a number of international bodies including the British Commonwealth.

Strikes, "stayaways," mass marches, and various forms of social unrest throughout the country followed the massacre. After an initial moment of indecision, when the pass laws were temporarily suspended, the National Party government responded with harsh repression. On March 30, a state of emergency was declared and as many as 2,000 dissidents were arrested. The ANC and PAC were banned when the National Party government, with the support of its main opposition, the United Party, passed the Unlawful Organizations Act on April 8. The crisis impressed upon the liberatory movement the limitations of nonviolent protest. Unable to operate legally within the country, both the ANC and the PAC went underground and embarked on armed resistance. They established military wings, Umkhonto we Sizwe (Spear of the Nation) and Poqo (Standing Alone) respectively. Both organizations also moved to set themselves up in exile.

The wave of bombings and sabotage by Umkhonto we Sizwe and the seemingly nihilistic, antiwhite violence of Poqo of the early 1960s did not seriously challenge white control of the state. The government used this threat as an opportunity to put into effect draconian security laws that virtually destroyed African nationalist resistance within the country. The political quiescence that followed was an important ingredient in the ensuing decade of rapid economic growth as foreign capital flowed back into the country.

The Sharpeville Massacre has remained a symbol of the brute force that lay behind apartheid and has always held deep symbolic meaning for the liberatory movement. March 21 was commemorated annually as a day of mourning and defiance and was accompanied with stayaways, strikes, and protest marches. Indeed, on the 25th anniversary of the Sharpeville massacre, at one such protest in the Langa township near Uitenhage in the Eastern Cape, 20 people were killed when police opened fire on marchers. The significance of the Sharpeville massacre to the African nationalist cause was demonstrated by Nelson Mandela on December 10, 1996, when he went to Sharpeville to pay tribute to those who had fallen in the struggle. There he formally announced the signing of South Africa's new democratic constitution. In the "new" South Africa, March 21 is a public holiday celebrated as Human Rights Day.

MOHAMED ADHIKARI

See also: **Luthuli, Albert; Mandela, Nelson; South Africa: African National Congress; South Africa: Apartheid, 1948–1959.**

Further Reading

Gerhart, Gail M. *Black Power in South Africa: The Evolution of an Ideology.* Berkeley and Los Angeles: University of California Press, 1978.
Kgosana, Philip. *Lest We Forget.* Johannesburg: Skotaville Press, 1988.

Lodge, Tom. *Black Politics in South Africa since 1945*. Johannesburg: Ravan Press, 1983.

Pogrund, Benjamin. *Sobukwe and Apartheid*. Johannesburg: Jonathan Ball, 1990.

Reeves, Ambrose. *Shooting at Sharpeville: The Agony of South Africa*. London, Victor Gollancz, 1960.

South Africa: Soweto Uprising

During the 1960s, the South African apartheid state reached the height of its power. Once it had weathered the Sharpeville crisis at the beginning of the decade, it was able to take advantage of years of rapid economic growth to strengthen considerably the country's security apparatus. It was a difficult decade for the black liberation movement as well. The African National Congress (ANC) and Pan-Africanist Congress (PAC) had been banned, and their key leaders imprisoned, forcing the organizations to operate either in exile or underground.

During the 1970s, however, the once firm grip of the apartheid state began to weaken. There were two significant developments in this decade. One was the growth of the black worker movement. The other was a rising tide of black assertiveness and militancy, instilled in part by the black consciousness movement and gaining full expression in the Soweto uprising of 1976.

Black worker organization had been largely stifled by the state security clampdown in the 1960s. But there was a revival in the early 1970s. In 1972 there were strikes by dockworkers in Durban, and by bus drivers in Johannesburg, the latter winning a one-third pay raise. In the same year the trade union wing of the black consciousness movement was established, with the launching of the Black Allied Workers Union—though worker organization would not turn out to be a successful field for the black consciousness movement.

A crucial year in the revival of black workers' militancy was 1973, a year best remembered for the Durban strikes. These began in January at a brick factory where workers demanded a 100 per cent increase in their minimum wage, which then stood at a paltry 8.97 rand per week. Two thousand workers came out on strike at this factory. The strike soon spread to some of Durban's textile factories, where wages were also appallingly low. Here an intransigent management refused to negotiate and called in the police, forcing the strikers back to work. By the end of 1973, 100,000 workers had gone on strike in Durban alone. It appears that much of the strike action had been largely spontaneous. It had not been orchestrated by a trade union or by any prominent leaders. This made it difficult for the authorities to impose a clampdown because there were no particular individuals or organizations that could be targeted.

The Durban strikes had a significant impact. They were a catalyst for further strikes around the country—in Johannesburg and East London in particular. Short-term gains were achieved. Some employers conceded significant wage increases to avert strike action, but others dug their heels in, displaying the authoritarian management style so common in South Africa at the time. The government passed legislation granting black workers the right to strike (albeit a severely curtailed right). The strikes gained considerable press publicity, which served to highlight the miserable conditions of black workers. This was particularly embarrassing for foreign companies revealed to be paying starvation wages to their South African workers. However, the most important consequence of the 1973 strikes was that they gave momentum to the revival of the black trade union movement. A number of unions were established, such as the National Union of Textile Workers, launched in Durban in 1973. By the middle of 1976, 75,000 African workers belonged to 25 trade unions. In 1979, 11 of these unions affiliated themselves with the newly established Federation of South African Trade Unions (FOSATU). One significant feature of the FOSATU was their concern with concentrating on workplace issues and, for the most part, their desire to steer clear of larger political campaigns. However, this stance did not prevent workers from becoming drawn into the 1976 Soweto uprising.

On June 16, 1976, Soweto school students embarked on a mass demonstration: a march to protest against the government's imposition of Afrikaans as a medium of instruction in African schools. The police opened fire, killing a 13-year-old boy, Hector Petersen. At least 25 Soweto students (and probably more) were killed as a result of police action on that day. What began as a peaceful demonstration escalated into a rebellion, marked by a series of attacks on the symbols of state power—particularly police vehicles and government buildings in black townships. Within a week the rebellion had spread to other parts of the Transvaal. On June 21, there was a mass student march in Atteridgeville near Pretoria. In August there was an uprising in the Cape Town townships of Guguletu, Langa, and Nyanga. Student calls for a worker "stayaway" in the same month met with an 80 per cent response from workers in Johannesburg. In September there were student-led marches in the center of Johannesburg and Cape Town. Acts of rebellion also occurred in the eastern Cape and Natal. At least 160 communities around the country were affected by the uprising. Over a period of about 16 months from June 1976, about 700 people were killed as a result of the rebellion, and at least half of the deaths were in Soweto.

Education was clearly a key issue in the revolt. While the government edict on Afrikaans-medium instruction had sparked the protest, there was massive popular anger toward the Bantu education system, which entailed a grossly inequitable allocation of resources between black and white schools. Such was the level of anger that at least 350 schools were damaged or destroyed during the rebellion. A school boycott between August and December 1976 brought Soweto schools to a standstill. There were other issues and targets. Black policemen, viewed as apartheid collaborators, were attacked. Liquor outlets were damaged, with children complaining that drink made their elders oblivious to wider problems.

It was very much a rebellion driven by the youth. The Soweto Students' Representative Council played a key organizational role. There is no evidence that other political concerns (the ANC, the PAC, or the black consciousness movement) were significantly involved in the revolt, but the black consciousness movement had undoubtedly inspired a new mood of assertiveness and militancy among many black people. Workers were drawn into the struggle during August and September, at a time when the trade union movement was wary of broad political campaigns. The relationship between trade unionism and community struggles would become an important issue within the liberation movement over the next 15 years.

The Soweto uprising was accompanied and followed by massive government repression. There were numerous arrests and detentions. In October 1977, a few weeks after the murder of Steve Biko while in police detention, the government banned organizations linked to the black consciousness movement. In the short term, the apartheid state regained a measure of control. However, the 1973 strikes and the 1976 uprising mark a watershed phase in the history of the liberation movement. These events gave a new momentum to the liberation struggle and so hastened the collapse of the apartheid system.

PAUL MAYLAM

See also: **South Africa: Sharpeville Massacre; Trades Unionism and Nationalism.**

Further Reading

Brooks, Alan, and Jeremy Brickhill. *Whirlwind before the Storm*. London: International Defence and Aid Fund, 1980.

Du Toit, D. *Capital and Labour in South Africa: Class Struggle in the 1970s*. London: Kegan Paul International, 1981.

Friedman, Steven. *Building Tomorrow Today: African Workers in Trade Unions 1970–1984*. Johannesburg: Ravan Press, 1987.

Hirson, Baruch. *Year of Fire, Year of Ash: The Soweto Revolt: Roots of a Revolution?* London: Zed, 1979.

Institute for Industrial Education, *The Durban Strikes 1973*, Durban and Johannesburg: Institute for Industrial Education/ Ravan Press, 1974.

Lodge, Tom. *Black Politics in South Africa since 1945*. London: Longman, 1983.

Ndlovu, Sifiso. *The Soweto Uprisings: Counter–Memories of June 1976*. Johannesburg: Ravan Press, 1998.

South Africa: Africa Policy

When the unification of the four states in South Africa was being planned in 1908–1909, Jan C. Smuts and Louis Botha hoped that the new union might include the High Commission territories of Basutoland, Bechuanaland, and Swaziland. Britain in effect vetoed this, but a schedule to the South Africa Act, creating the union of South Africa, provided that they might at some future time be incorporated. Successive South African governments made proposals for such incorporation, sometimes for Swaziland and at others for all three territories. But it was never to happen, because of the policies of racial segregation pursued by successive South African governments and because it was known that the people of the territories wished to continue under direct British rule rather than fall under the control of Pretoria.

Smuts in particular had an imperial vision of a greater South Africa, stretching as far as the Congo. Ideas of obtaining southern Mozambique from the Portuguese came to naught, as did his hopes of incorporating South West Africa and Southern Rhodesia. In World War I, South Africa sent troops into German South West Africa, and Louis Botha and Smuts took over the territory, which they then ruled as if it were a part of South Africa. But at the end of the war the president of the United States, Woodrow Wilson, would not let any ally take over ex-German territory, so instead of being included in South Africa as a fifth province, southwest Africa became a C-class mandate under the League of Nations, though ruled by South Africa as if it were an integral part of South Africa itself. This disappointment was followed by another in 1923, when the white voters of Southern Rhodesia voted against joining South Africa, preferring to rule themselves separately under nominal British control. At the end of the World War II, Smuts again tried to incorporate southwest Africa: local leaders were consulted and he went to the new United Nations (UN) in New York to put the case for annexation. But again he was thwarted, for the UN rejected the case he made and insisted the territory not be annexed but instead fall under the new system of "trust territories."

Smuts's dreams of a greater South Africa failed to materialize, but South African influence did, of course, extend far beyond its borders. Many whites from South Africa settled in southwest Africa and the Rhodesias and close ties were established with the Portuguese regimes in Angola and Mozambique. The last South

African leader to propose a form of incorporation of the High Commission territories was H. F. Verwoerd, in the context of his Bantustan scheme. In the early 1960s, however, he had to accept that Britain would lead them to independence instead, but he continued to refuse to deal with any of the new decolonized nations under black governments. Verwoerd rejected a request by Abubakr Balewa of Nigeria to visit South Africa in 1962, for example, as well as Kenneth Kaunda's later offer of diplomatic relations. Verwoerd's successor, John Vorster, was more pragmatic. He not only met Leabua Jonathan of Lesotho in 1966 and Seretse Khama of Botswana in 1968, but agreed to establish diplomatic relations with the government of Dr. Hastings Banda of Malawi, who made a state visit to South Africa in 1971. Such relations meant accepting a black ambassador in Pretoria, which at the time was seen as a remarkable breakthrough. But Vorster's policy—successively called "outward looking," "dialogue" and "détente"—was based firmly on the idea that there was no question of any other government influencing the policy of apartheid, and he rejected the Lusaka Manifesto of April 1969, even though it agreed to recognize South Africa as an independent African state and supported peaceful means for change in South Africa, because it seemed to be interference in South Africa's domestic affairs.

Vorster realized that the 1974 coup in Portugal would transform the situation in southern Africa and increase pressure on the white regimes of Rhodesia and South Africa. He therefore stepped up attempts to establish contacts with leaders of other African countries, hoping such contacts might deflect international criticism of apartheid. He secretly visited the Côte d'Ivoire in September 1974 and in February 1975 he went to Liberia and met President Tolbert. But nothing substantial came of these visits, and South Africa's intervention in Angola in October 1975, when units of the South African Defence Force drove north almost to the capital, Luanda, brought an abrupt end to such efforts. It also alienated Dr. Kaunda of Zambia, who had met Vorster in a railway carriage at Victoria Falls in August 1975 in an effort to bring about a settlement in the Rhodesian conflict.

The South African forces withdrew from Angola in early 1976, but by then a sizable Cuban force was in place and the MPLA in place as the new Angolan government. The SWAPO, the Namibian liberation movement, was able to establish bases in southern Angola. South Africa's willingness to negotiate with the Western Contact Group in 1977–1978, and its agreement to the western plan for a transition to independence in Namibia, won it some credit from other governments in the region, which persuaded the SWAPO leadership to support the plan, which was then given UN backing. But the South African government's refusal to allow the implementation of the agreement produced years of bitterness and frustration, which added to the anger Africans felt at the brutal repression inside South Africa in the aftermath of the Soweto uprising of 1976.

At a conference in Johannesburg in November 1979, P. W. Botha set out a plan for a "constellation" of southern African states to meet and defeat what he set out as a Marxist challenge to control all of southern Africa. But within months Robert Mugabe had come to power in Zimbabwe and made clear that he would have no formal ties with racist South Africa. He joined the Front Line States (FLS) instead, a grouping designed to free South Africa's neighbors of dependence on it, and to coordinate action against it. From the FLS emerged the Southern African Development Coordinating Conference. Some of the states in that grouping agreed to allow guerrillas from South Africa to train and establish bases on their territories; others, such as Zimbabwe, merely allowed an African National Congress (ANC) office to operate. But it was to challenge any support for the ANC and its armed wing MK that Botha embarked on his policy of destabilization.

Destabilization took many forms. The most obvious was retaliatory raids for MK operations in South Africa: alleged MK bases in Maputo were bombed from the air, and attacked from the ground in Maseru and Gaborone. ANC and MK officials were the target of assassination attempts, some of them successful. South African mercenaries participated in a coup in the Seychelles in 1981, using weapons obtained from the South African Defence Force (SADF). Economic might was used to prevent any other black-ruled neighbor emerging as a new power in the region. Destabilization was seen in its most brutal and overt form in the repeated raids by the SADF into southern Angola, and the military occupation of part of that country from 1981 to 1985. South African military intervention in that country climaxed with the battle of Cuito Cuanavale in 1987–1988 (the largest land battle in Africa since World War II), in which the South African army and air force sought, unsuccessfully, to defeat a combined Angolan-Cuban-SWAPO force.

Such pressure was exerted on Mozambique that its president, Samora Machel, was driven to sign the Nkomati Accord, which spoke of noninterference in each other's affairs, with Botha in March 1984. Mozambique consequently expelled MK guerrillas, but elements in the SADF continued to supply arms to the Renamo rebels fighting the Frelimo government, and many suspected that South Africa had a hand in the October 1986 downing of the Mozambique aircraft that crashed just within South Africa when preparing to land at Maputo, resulting in Machel's death.

It was in 1988 that South African policy changed, as the wishes of the Department of Foreign Affairs won out against those of the military. Destabilization was replaced with negotiation, and a new policy in which friendly relations with neighboring countries was sought so that South Africa could be projected as an African country. In September of that year, for example, P. W. Botha and Chissano, Machel's successor, reaffirmed their commitments to the Nkomati Accord. The change of policy was seen most clearly with the signing in New York in December 1988 of a tripartite agreement with Angola and Cuba, providing for the withdrawal of the Cuban forces from Angola and the withdrawal of South Africa from Namibia, as part of the long-delayed implementation of the UN plan for that territory. This agreement also meant also that the MK had to relocate from Angola. As it became clear that South Africa was going to allow Namibia to move toward independence, relations with its neighbors continued to improve. By 1993 the constitutional negotiations in South Africa itself had led to the decision that South Africa should withdraw from Walvis Bay and allow its reincorporation in the new Namibia. With the coming into office of the government of Nelson Mandela in 1994, the transformation in relations with other African countries was completed: South Africa joined the Southern African Development Community and the Organization of African Unity, and established full diplomatic relations with all its neighbors.

CHRISTOPHER SAUNDERS

See also: **Angola: MPLA, FNLA, UNITA, and the War of Liberation, 1961–1974; Namibia: SWAPO, Freedom Struggle; Smuts, Jan C.; South Africa: Apartheid, 1948–1959; South Africa: Peace, Reconstruction, Union: 1902–1910; South Africa: Capitalist Farming, "Poor Whites," Labor.**

Further Reading

Barber, J., and J. Barrattt. *South Africa's Foreign Policy: The Search for Status and Security, 1945–88.* Cambridge: Cambridge University Press, 1990.

Chanock, M. *Britain, Rhodesia and South Africa, 1900–45: The Unconsummated Union.* Totowa, N.J.: Frank Cass, 1977.

Davies, R., and D. O'Meara. "Total Strategy in Southern Africa: An Analysis of South African Regional Policy since 1978." *Journal of Southern African Studies,* no. 11 (1985).

Hyam, R. *The Failure of South African Expansion, 1908–48.* London: Macmillan, 1972.

Jaster, R. S. *The Defense of White Power: South African Foreign Policy under Pressure.* New York: Ford Foundation, 1988.

Johnson, P., and D. Martin. (eds.). *Destructive Engagement: Southern Africa at War.* Harare, Zimbabwe: SAPEM, 1986.

Moorcraft, P. L. *African Nemesis: War and Revolution in Southern Africa.* London: Brassey's, 1990.

Nolutshungu, S. *South Africa: A study of Ideology and Foreign Policy.* London, 1975.

South Africa: Antiapartheid Struggle: Townships, the 1980s

Although the Soweto Uprising, which began on June 16, 1976, had been effectively suppressed by late 1977, small-scale resistance to the apartheid regime continued throughout the late 1970s and early 1980s and fed into the next major resistance, the insurrection of 1984–1986. This, more than any other single event, precipitated the downfall of apartheid.

In the late 1970s, Africans in a number of townships formed civic organizations in order to address local grievances, and many individual school and consumer boycotts took place. Then, in August 1983, hundreds of local resistance groups came together under the umbrella of the United Democratic Front (UDF), launched in Mitchell's Plain, Cape Town. The UDF led national campaigns against a number of different government policies, including the new tricameral system of government itself, from which Africans were excluded. By 1984 resistance to the new constitutional system was fueled by an economic recession, caused in part by the fall in the gold price from 1983. The recession in turn increased unemployment, and as the rand collapsed against other currencies, interest rates were pushed up to over 20 per cent. With inflation soaring, rents for the small township houses were ratcheted up, beyond the means of many to pay.

In keeping with the Community Councils Act of 1977, Africans were put in charge of local matters in a number of townships, especially on the Witwatersrand. But they were elected to their positions on very low polls, for most blacks saw them as collaborators with the apartheid system, and many of the new councillors used their positions to enrich themselves. When they increased rents, they became one of the prime targets of local resistance. As pass laws and influx control broke down, millions of people poured from the countryside into the cities, leading to large new squatter settlements, especially on the east Witwatersrand and on the Cape Flats outside Cape Town. In September 1984, opposition to rent rises combined with protest against the new tricameral parliament then being inaugurated, and young men clashed with the police on the East Rand. Councillors were killed in Sebokeng and Sharpeville townships. The army was called in, and the insurrection had begun. It quickly spread to most urban centers in the country, as well as to many small villages. It reached its apogee in 1985, when the police found it difficult to control many parts of the country.

As a result, a state of emergency was declared in July 1985, giving the police even greater power than they already had. The state of emergency was renewed, and extended to the entire country, the following year. Though the state tried to pin the insurrection on the UDF, and charged some of its leaders with treason for provoking it, it was in fact spontaneous protests that sparked off the greatest crisis to face the apartheid state.

Resistance took many forms. One of the most striking images from that time is of crowds of young people running and singing in the streets, or *toyi toying* (dancing in a particular style) at funerals. T-shirts of the banned African National Congress, or even of the Communist Party, began to be worn openly. Speeches often began with the slogan *Amandla Ngwethu* (the power is ours) and the word *Viva*, taken over from resistance in the ex-Portuguese colonies. The red Communist Party flag was unfurled in public at the funeral of the martyred teacher and local community leader Matthew Goniwe, one of the UDF leaders assassinated by security forces in 1985. Unarmed protestors sometimes picked up stones to throw; on occasion guns were used—some homemade, others (usually AK-47s) brought into the country by members of Umkhonto we Sizwe (the armed wing of the ANC), or by gangsters.

In what became a typical pattern, the police would open fire on demonstrators, and some would be killed. Their funerals would then become occasions for mass public protest, otherwise forbidden, and more people would be shot, leading to more funerals. Government officials and structures were prime targets, as were schools in the despised Bantu education system. In the townships, little education took place in the 1980s, as school boycotts became routine. In some townships, informal "people's courts" were set up to administer rough justice. The most notorious method of dealing with "collaborators" was the use of the "necklace": a tire would be placed around the neck of the victim and set afire.

In response to the resistance, security forces (the police and army) began using "extralegal" methods, including the assassination of activists and the use of "dirty tricks," such as using informers to lure activists to their deaths. In one notorious incident in 1985, police in Cape Town hid on the back of a lorry and waited for stones to be thrown at them, then emerged and opened fire, killing three youths. More information about such atrocities came to light when witnesses, victims, and perpetrators gave evidence about them to the Truth and Reconciliation Commission in the late 1990s. A significant number of the over 25,000 people who were jailed in the first year of the state of emergency in the mid-1980s were tortured.

By late 1986, through such drastic means, the state had managed to bring the resistance movements in the townships under control, although Umkhonto we Sizwe continued its operations, and sporadic acts of resistance continued. The suppression had been at enormous cost to the country, however: sanctions had been imposed by its main trading partners, and even more serious had been the refusal of international banks to roll over short term loans. Apartheid was the target for international action as never before. The insurrection led the government to think of what would happen if there was another similar act of resistance, perhaps on a larger scale, in the future. Those in the ruling National Party who argued that in the long run such resistance could not be suppressed and that a political solution was therefore needed were ultimately victorious over the hard-line "securocrats" who did not believe in "concessions." It was at the height of the insurrection of the mid-1980s that government officials began talking to the jailed Nelson Mandela, and other contacts with the African National Congress in exile from 1985 on helped lead to the breakthrough to a negotiated settlement in 1990.

CHRISTOPHER SAUNDERS AND REMDANI MOSES
RALINALA

See also: **Madikizela-Mandela, Winnie.**

Further Reading

Cobbett, W., and R. Cohen (eds.). *Popular Struggles in South Africa*. Trenton, N.J.: African World Press, 1988.
van Kessel, I. *"Beyond Our Wildest Dreams": The United Democatic Front and the Transformation of South Africa*. Charlottesville: University Press of Virginia, 2000.
Price, R. *The Apartheid State in Crisis*. Berkeley and Los Angeles: University of California Press, 1991.
Seekings, J. *Heroes or Villains? Youth Politics in the 1980s*. Braamfontein: Ravan Press, 1993.
———. *The UDF: A History of the United Democratic Front in South Africa, 1983–1991*. Cape Town: David Philip, 2000.

South Africa: Antiapartheid Struggle, International

The international campaign against apartheid in South Africa was one of the largest and most successful people's campaigns of the twentieth century; it made apartheid a global political issue, and it forced reluctant governments to impose sanctions against South Africa.

Chief Albert Luthuli, president of the African National Congress, was awarded the Nobel Peace Prize in 1960. That year, he also called for an "economic boycott of South Africa," which he said would cause suffering, but would be "a price we are willing to pay. In any case, we suffer already." In 1962, the United Nations General Assembly backed Luthuli and called for an economic boycott.

Isolation was already beginning. India had banned trade with South Africa in 1946. South Africa was forced to withdraw from the United Nations Educational, Scientific, and Cultural Organization in 1955, from the British Commonwealth in 1961, and from many other international bodies in the 1960s. The first consumer boycott was of students closing accounts with Barclays Bank in Britain in 1969. But the international campaign against apartheid got off to a slow start; the first actual trade embargo was an Arab oil boycott in 1973, though Iran continued to supply oil to the apartheid state.

It was only the massacre of school children in Soweto in 1976 that caused enough revulsion to trigger a serious international campaign. In 1977 the two most important sanctions were imposed: the United Nations Security Council imposed its first-ever mandatory sanctions against a UN member—an arms embargo against South Africa, and the British Commonwealth began organizing a sports boycott.

Throughout the 1980s, President Ronald Reagan of the United States and Prime Minister Margaret Thatcher of Britain led vociferous campaigns against sanctions, which initially blocked further governmental and UN actions. But the repression of township uprisings led to a wave of antiapartheid activity, with popular opinion repeatedly overriding government reluctance. Progressive governments started a wave of action: Sweden and Ireland banned the import of South African fruit, then Denmark banned all imports, and the lead was followed by all Scandinavian countries. The British Commonwealth agreed to sanctions packages, and in 1986 the U.S. Congress overrode President Ronald Reagan's veto to the approval of new sanctions.

It was public pressure that forced international professional, sporting, and governmental bodies to exclude South Africa. Consumer boycotts grew in Europe and the United States; actions were also taken by hundreds of local governments to refuse to buy South African products and then to refuse to deal with banks and other companies that still traded with South Africa.

States and city councils, as well as the United States, began to withdraw their large accounts from banks active in South Africa. The response came in August 1985, when at first a few and then all major U.S. and European banks refused new loans to South Africa and even refused to roll over old ones. There was also a rush to quit by U.S. and European companies; the UN Economic and Social Council estimated that 500 transnational corporations withdrew from South Africa, including big names like IBM, General Motors, and Coca-Cola. The chairman of the British Barclays Bank, whose subsidiary was the largest bank in South Africa, admitted that "political pressures on Barclays . . . to withdraw from South Africa finally became irresistible."

Sanctions took a long time to work, but, in different ways, four sanctions proved critical: those on oil, arms, sports, and banking. South Africa successfully broke most sanctions, but only at a very high cost. In 1979, the Shah of Iran was overthrown, and the new government of that nation joined the oil embargo, which suddenly became effective; breaking the embargo cost South Africa $25 billion, admitted former president P. W. Botha.

The arms embargo was tightly enough enforced to stop South Africa from buying the most modern weapons systems. In July 1987, South Africa invaded southern Angola and tried to capture the strategic town of Cuito Cuanavale. In previous invasions, South Africa had depended on air superiority to limit casualties on the ground; this time the Soviet-supplied Angolan air force and antiaircraft defenses were so superior that South Africa lost several planes that it could not replace. Without air cover, South Africa was forced to withdraw; the military was no longer invincible and South Africa quickly started negotiations over Namibian independence.

White South Africa was sports mad, and the sports boycott was the most damaging psychologically because it constantly reminded white South Africa of its increasing isolation and of the cost of maintaining apartheid. By the late 1980s South Africa was banned from 90 per cent of world sport.

The 1985 ban on loans had little practical impact. New investment had dried up in 1977 and South Africa responded to the 1985 loan ban by refusing to make repayments on old loans. But the political impact was huge, because it showed the business community that it could no longer remain above politics; within a year, South African business leaders were publicly calling for the release of the jailed ANC leader Nelson Mandela.

Although sanctions were undoubtedly the main, and most effective, form of international action against apartheid, there was also international support for both major liberation movements, the African National Congress and the Pan-Africanist Congress. The UN General Assembly had repeatedly called on member states to provide "moral, political and material assistance" to the liberation movements. The Soviet Union and eastern European countries provided extensive training as well as arms and other material support; most of the independent southern African states (Angola, Zambia, Zimbabwe, Mozambique, Lesotho, and Tanzania) allowed one or both of the liberation movements to set up bases for raids into South Africa, supporting a low-level armed struggle inside the country as well as several spectacular raids, such as one on the heavily guarded Sasol oil-from-coal plant in 1980.

Yet it was sanctions and the inability to control the uprisings in the townships, not the "armed struggle," that eventually convinced the white rulers to accept change. On February 7, 1994, outgoing president F. W. de Klerk admitted that "one of the main problems was the effect on our economy of the international sanctions campaign spearheaded by the ANC."

JOSEPH HANLON

Further Reading

Commonwealth Secretariat and the Independent Expert Study Group on the Evaluation of the Application and Impact of Sanctions against South Africa. *South Africa: The Sanctions Report, Prepared for the Commonwealth Committee of Foreign Ministers on Southern Africa*. London: Penguin, 1989.

First, Ruth, Jonathan Steele, and Christable Gurney. *The South African Connection: Western Investment in Apartheid*. London: Temple Smith, 1972.

Hanlon, Joseph, and Roger Omond. *The Sanctions Handbook*. London: Penguin, 1987.

Harker, Joseph (ed.). *The Legacy of Apartheid*. London: Guardian Newspapers, 1994.

Kasrils, Ronnie. *"Armed and Dangerous": My Undercover Struggle against Apartheid*. Oxford: Heinemann, 1993.

Orkin, Mark (ed.). *Sanctions against Apartheid*. Cape Town: David Philip/Catholic Institute for International Relations, 1989.

South Africa: Transition, 1990–1994

By the late 1980s a stalemate had been reached in South Africa. The mass movement for democratic change, increasingly grouped behind the African National Congress (ANC), had provoked a near-insurrection in the mid-1980s and had survived the especially brutal repression of the latter part of the decade. However, it could not expect to overthrow the apartheid state easily. As for those in command of that state, they could, up to a point, contain mass opposition, but they could not hope to stabilize the situation sufficiently to reassure nervous investors, or to placate the growing international distaste for their racist project. Important, in particular, were greater tensions within both Afrikanerdom and the ruling National Party (NP) itself. The new Afrikaner business class (a principal beneficiary of NP rule over the years) had, together with its English-speaking counterparts, begun to sense that the historical marriage between the twin structures of capitalist exploitation and racial oppression, so long a profitable (if contested) one, was no longer viable economically or politically.

The NP, led ultimately by F. W. de Klerk, who succeeded P. W. Botha to the presidency in 1989, increasingly understood that it would be necessary to deal with the ANC. Indeed, a certain rapprochement with the latter had begun from the mid-1980s, through meetings abroad of members of the Afrikaner and business elites with ANC representatives, and through more secretive conclaves of NP leaders with the imprisoned Nelson Mandela. Nonetheless, de Klerk's announcement, in February 1990, of the lifting of the ban against the ANC, the Pan-Africanist Congress, and the South African Communist Party (SACP), and the release of Nelson Mandela after 27 years in prison came as something of a shock to most observers.

The following four years were turbulent ones. It was clear that in the ensuing negotiations de Klerk, despite his repeal of some of the most offensive of apartheid legislation, would seek to retain the initiative and as much as possible of white minority privilege, his NP still holding the reins of state power throughout the period and only slowly moving toward acceptance of a more democratic outcome. The state's military and police apparatuses continued to harass opponents while also backing the brutal undertakings of Chief Mongosuthu Buthelezi of KwaZulu and his Inkatha Freedom Party (IFP), which moved to manipulate Zulu nationalism to advance its own interests and to render difficult the consolidation of the ANC as a national political force. Levels of violence rose precipitously, particularly in Natal and the East Rand. Meanwhile, among whites, de Klerk's victory for his reform strategy in a whites-only referendum in March 1992 consolidated the NP's central place in the negotiations—though some further on the right threatened civil war, forged bizarre alliances with corrupt Bantustan leaders, and/or argued for creation of a separatist white *Volkstaat*.

For its part, the ANC continued to consolidate itself at the head of the forces pressing for change, but negotiations between the two chief protagonists remained intermittent, and progress was slow. The initial Convention for a Democratic South Africa, created in 1991 as a forum for negotiations, broke down on several occasions. But mid-1992 witnessed a massacre at Boipatong and the shooting of demonstrators at Bisho in the Ciskei, as well as a massive trade union–led general strike in support of meaningful change. Both parties central to the process now sensed the need to guide a volatile situation toward compromise, their respective elites having developed a mutual vested interest in a smooth transition under their own joint control. The Record of Understanding they signed in September 1992 produced more serious negotiations at Kempton Park in 1993. Their intentions further focused by the massive outcry that followed the assassination of popular SACP leader Chris Hani by white extremists, the negotiators soon produced guidelines for a transition premised on the holding of national elections in April 1994, the appointment of an Transitional

Executive Council to help supervise the interim period, and an agreement on a set of constitutional guidelines designed to structure the final constitution-making process after the elections.

In the end, this "interim constitution" had not compromised the ANC's position of one-person, one-vote within a unified South Africa, although the ANC did agree to a Government of National Unity for five years that would guarantee cabinet representation for all parties, with significant support, and also conceded a measure of (rather guarded) federalism. Details regarding amnesty and compensation, as well as the further fleshing out of the important draft bill of rights, would remain for the new parliament (which would also sit as constitutional assembly) to address. Meanwhile, the IFP, despite boycotting the final stages of the negotiations, entered the electoral process, albeit at the very last minute and in part because of the overthrow of other Bantustan leaders in the Ciskei and Bophuthatswana. General Constand Viljoen's white separatist Freedom Front did the same, thereby splitting the white right and further undermining it.

The ANC had thus achieved its long-term goal of creating a democratic political system—a historic accomplishment of staggering proportions that the world quickly and vocally acknowledged as such; so too did the vast majority of African voters. While Buthelezi was ultimately awarded a negotiated victory in the violent and chaotic provincial election in KwaZulu-Natal, and while the NP, with considerable black support, took the Western Cape, the ANC won seven of nine provinces and an overwhelming national majority of 62.6 per cent of the 20 million South Africans who voted. Although short of the two-thirds majority that would have enabled it unilaterally to rewrite the constitution (had it been so inclined), the ANC now dominated the government, and its leader, Nelson Mandela, became the first president of a democratic South Africa on May 10, 1994.

Less publicly noted was the framing of these constitutional negotiations and electoral politics by what was, in effect, a second set of negotiations, a much more informal process that found the ANC, during the transition, reassuring various international capitalist actors (the bourgeoisies of both South African and international provenance, Western governments, and the World Bank and International Monetary Fund) of the modesty of its claims—which had sometimes seemed to be rather more radical in exile—to challenge the existing economic status quo. The road to a successful political-cum-constitutional transition was eased, both locally and internationally, by this increasing domestication of the ANC to the requirements of global capitalism. Some, perhaps too charitably, have

suggested that the ANC had little room to maneuver in this arena. Yet the fact remains that, by 1994, the movement/party had bound itself to an economic strategy with doubtful promise of changing for the better the material conditions of the mass of South Africans in the postapartheid period.

JOHN S. SAUL

See also: **Buthelezi and Inkatha Freedom Party; Mandela, Nelson.**

Further Reading

Bond, Patrick. *Elite Transition: From Apartheid to Neoliberalism in South Africa*. London: Pluto Press/Pietermaritzburg: University of Natal Press, 2000.

Davenport, T. R. H. *The Birth of a New South Africa*. Toronto: University of Toronto Press, 1998.

Friedman, Steven, and Doreen Atkinson (eds.). *The Small Miracle: South Africa's Negotiated Settlement*. Johannesburg: Ravan Press, 1994.

Marais, Hein. *South Africa: Limits to Change: The Political Economy of Transition*. London: Zed/Cape Town: University of Cape Town Press, 1998.

O'Meara, Dan. *Forty Lost Years: The Apartheid State and the Politics of the National Party, 1948–1994*. Johannesburg: Ravan Press/Athens, Ohio: Ohio University Press, 1998.

Saul, John S. *Millennial Africa: Capitalism, Socialism, Democracy*. Lawrenceville: African World Press, 2001.

Waldmeir, Patti. *Anatomy of a Miracle: The End of Apartheid and the Birth of the New South Africa*. London: Penguin, 1997.

South Africa: 1994 to the Present

Following the 1994 election, the African National Congress (ANC) entered power with a massive parliamentary majority and a mandate to construct a new South Africa. The party was immediately constrained by a number of factors—notably, the negotiated commitment to a Government of National Unity (GNU) and the "sunset clauses" that entrenched significant numbers of Afrikaner bureaucrats in their previous posts. Although Nelson Mandela had hoped that the Democratic Party, the Freedom Front and the Pan-Africanist Congress (PAC) would agree to be members of the GNU, only the Inkatha Freedom Party (IFP) and the National Party (NP) took up positions within the coalition administration. F. W. de Klerk and Thabo Mbeki were appointed as deputy presidents.

The GNU worked more effectively than many had predicted. Eventually, however, the tensions proved too great and in May 1996, F. W. de Klerk announced the NP's withdrawal from the coalition. Two months later, Bantu Holomisa left the ANC government and joined forces with Roelof Meyer of the NP to form the United Democratic Movement (UDM). Meanwhile, Mandela began the slow process of handing over power to his deputy. Increasingly, Thabo Mbeki handled day-to-day administration in the South African government as Mandela traveled overseas.

Although Mangosuthu Buthelezi was appointed minister for home affairs in the GNU, he continued to campaign for international mediation to settle the question of KwaZulu-Natal's autonomy. During 1995 the situation remained tense, with a number of deaths occurring from ANC-IFP local conflicts. Eventually, a peace of sorts was struck between the ANC and the IFP. The IFP retained a role in government following the collapse of the GNU in 1996. On a number of occasions when Mandela and Mbeki were visiting other countries, Buthelezi served as acting president.

The ANC faced many challenges in power, the most significant being in the area of economics. It quickly became apparent that the Reconstruction and Development Plan designed by the ANC when they were in opposition was overambitious: nationalization was abandoned, the targets of the house-building program were not met, and new jobs were not created in anything like the numbers required. Meanwhile, the government continued to pay the interest payments on the apartheid debt; this amounted to 20 per cent of the national budget. No new European or American version of the Marshall Plan was forthcoming to assist the establishment of the "Rainbow Nation." In mid-1996, the government introduced a neoliberal policy titled Growth Employment and Redistribution (GEAR). Inspired by the World Bank and South African business, the GEAR policy promised privatization, wage flexibility, deficit reduction and cutbacks in public spending. Despite GEAR, South Africa experienced the aftershocks of the East Asian economic crisis and the rand continued to tumble in value. Unemployment remained high and growth consistently failed to match the government's ambitions.

Mandela concentrated upon reconciliation as the key theme of his presidency. He visited or played host to many of his ex-enemies, demonstrating an important element of forgiveness while also neutralizing political opposition. The most famous of Mandela's gestures toward reconciliation was his appearance at the Rugby World Cup Final in June 1995 wearing a Springbok shirt. This had a profound impact upon many fanatical Afrikaner rugby supporters.

In February 1996, the ANC launched the Truth and Reconciliation Commission (TRC). In essence, the TRC was dominated by the concept of "forgiveness without forgetting." Gillian Slovo acknowledged, "The TRC was never supposed to be about justice; it's about the truth." Unlike comparable investigatory bodies in Latin America, the TRC possessed judicial powers to grant individual amnesties. In order to attain these amnesties, applicants were required to provide a full

confession. For more than two and a half years, the TRC held hearings throughout South Africa; the five-volume report of its findings was published in October 1998. The report, which constituted an alternative history of the country, revealed aspects of National Party and ANC activity of which neither party could be proud.

South African society had been transformed by the collapse of apartheid in the early 1990s. The transparency of the first ANC government and South Africa's newfound freedom of the press tended to promote an unfair picture of a rapid deterioration in standards. Although cases of corruption were exposed in the lower echelons of the government these were relatively small in comparison to the corruption of the last National Party administrations.

Crime was a much more serious problem. Although the murder rate had increased dramatically during the early 1990s, the South African and international media were preoccupied by the political struggle and had not focused on crime. Following the 1994 election and the ensuing decline in political violence, crime became the subject most associated with South Africa in the global imagination. Johannesburg was regularly portrayed as the most dangerous place on earth. The reasons for the crime wave were manifold: a discredited, under-funded, corrupt police force; the influx of international crime and drug syndicates; the number of demobilized and thereafter unemployed soldiers; and the abundance of weapons in South Africa.

South Africa's second majority-rule general election was held in June 1999. The ANC won 66 per cent of the vote and secured 266 seats in the parliament. The leading opposition parties were the Democratic Party (9.55 per cent; 38 seats); the IFP (8.6 per cent; 34 seats); the New National Party (7 per cent; 28 seats); and the UDM (3 per cent; 14 seats). Thabo Mbeki succeeded Mandela as president of South Africa.

JAMES SANDERS

See also: **Buthelezi and Inkatha Freedom Party; Mandela, Nelson; South Africa: African National Congress; South Africa: Antiapartheid Struggle: Townships, the 1980s; South Africa: Apartheid, 1948–1959.**

Further Reading

Adam, Heribert, Frederik van Zyl Slabbert, and Kogila Moodley. *Comrades in Business: Post-Liberation Politics in South Africa.* Cape Town: Tafelberg, 1997.

De Klerk, F. W. *The Last Trek: A New Beginning—The Autobiography.* London: Macmillan, 1998.

Sampson, Anthony. *Mandela: The Authorised Biography.* London: Harper Collins, 1999.

Toase, F. H., and E. J. Yorke. *The New South Africa: Prospects for Domestic and International Security.* London: Macmillan, 1998.
Truth and Reconciliation Commission (TRC) of South Africa. *Truth and Reconciliation Commission of South Africa Report.* 5 vols. Cape Town: TRC, 1998.

Southern Africa: Regional Survey

Early hominids probably appeared in southern Africa about one million years ago, but the processes by which *Homo sapiens* emerged remain obscure. Early *Homo sapiens* fossils from the eastern Cape have been dated to around 100,000 years ago, marking the origins or the Stone Age. The early (Acheulian) and middle (Mesolithic) Stone Age periods saw a progressive development of more sophisticated stone tools and a widening of the techniques of food gathering and scavenging and therefore the range of diet. These early humans probably learned the controlled use of fire in order to adapt their environment to their needs. With the later Stone Age, probably beginning somewhere between 17,000 and 20,000 years ago, we begin to recognize characteristics of familiar southern African peoples such as the San (the so-called bushmen) and, later, the Khoi. These people were hunting more successfully, using spears and arrows with fine stone blades and tips. They appear to have created more sophisticated social organization, as well as producing the leisure time to indulge in forms of religious ritual, some associated with deaths and burials, as well as decoration such as ostrich eggshell beads and cave paintings. Indeed, cave paintings and rock engravings constitute some of the artistic glory of the human past in southern Africa. They are to be found in many parts

of South Africa, Zimbabwe, and some of the adjacent states, in both abstract and naturalistic styles.

Some of the later rock paintings offer evidence of the arrival of pastoralists and cultivators. People of larger stature appear herding sheep or cattle, while cultivators are shown using iron axes to chop down trees. The first pastoralists, herding sheep and goats and then later cattle, were pre–Iron Age and are often seen as the origins of the Khoi community. Their earliest sites come from eastern Botswana and southwestern Zimbabwe, but they soon spread down to the western Cape and elsewhere. From an early period, the Khoi and San peoples intermingled, both in economic and social terms. Their lives often became closely intertwined and they established symbiotic systems of mutual exchange. This is why, in modern times, they came to be known as Khoisan.

Iron Age communities seem to have been established in the region about 1,800 years ago. These peoples were the ancestors of the Bantu-speaking inhabitants of southern Africa, arriving in the region via western and eastern streams of migration. It is clear from linguistic and other evidence that many of these Bantu speakers mingled with the hunter-gatherers and pastoralists who preceded them. Moreover, their modes of production were never exclusive. Many Iron Age peoples continued to hunt and forage, particularly in times of want, though hunting may also have come to develop wider social and ritual connotations in this period. It is also clear that the conventional gender divisions of labor (women as gatherers, agriculturalists, and basket makers; men as clearers of the land, hunters, iron workers and sometimes potters) do not always hold up. Some crafts (but never, it would seem,

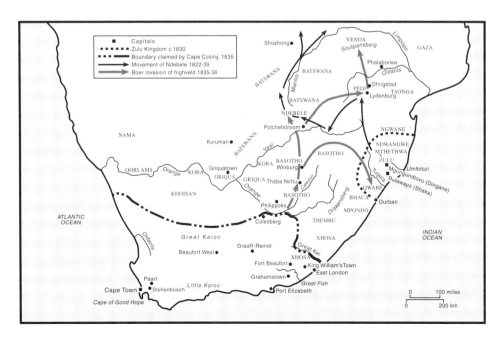

Southern Africa, *c.*1800–1840.

iron production) were interchangeable, and hunting could be so labor-intensive as to involve women and children as well as men.

The shift from the early to the later Iron Age took place about 1,000 years ago. This period is symbolized by the evidence of new pottery styles in many parts of southern Africa, together with the development of larger communities with obvious class distinctions, the ownership of larger cattle herds, and evidence of trade, including long-distance trade to the East African coast.

Two principal forces can be identified as influencing this period of relative transformation. One is the undoubted growth in the numbers of cattle, which offered opportunities for a step change in elite power and influence. Systems of clientship could be established through the circulation of cattle in bride-price and also in loan arrangements to subsidiary peoples. This new class of chiefs, who extended their power beyond that of just the extended kin, was also able to arrogate to itself power over trade. Much of this trade was with the East African coast, where Muslim communities (originally from the Persian Gulf and South Arabian areas) had established significant commercial towns as far south as the Mozambican coast, trading gold and ivory, and to a lesser extent copper and skins from the interior. The Save and Limpopo Rivers now became important trade routes, and southern Africa was beginning to be pulled into the international economy.

Significant trading sites appeared in the Limpopo Valley, and the important towns of Mapungubwe (in the modern northern Transvaal), Manekweni (in Mozambique), Great Zimbabwe (in central Zimbabwe), and Ingombe Ilede (at the junction of the Zambezi and Kafue Rivers, in what is now southern Zambia) flourished at different times between the eleventh and fifteenth centuries. All these sites reveal wide social distinctions between elites and common people, symbolized by their respective living areas, by the wealth of the goods associated with the ruling groups, their diets, and possession of trade goods. Crafts had reached a high state of excellence, with fine pottery, impressive soapstone sculptures, bone tools, and artifacts suggesting that one of the skills of the people was weaving. The existence of large quantities of cattle bones at Great Zimbabwe illustrates the access the elite had to plentiful quantities of meat.

Evidence of long-distance gold and ivory trading is confirmed by the presence of a fifteenth-century Islamic coin at Great Zimbabwe, as well as of Persian and Chinese pottery, traded across the Indian Ocean, at many sites. Hundreds of mine workings, for both gold and copper, are known throughout the Zimbabwean and Transvaal Highveld and were clearly exploited by Iron Age miners. After the decline of Mapungubwe and the fall of Great Zimbabwe (perhaps as a result of

an environmental crisis), other cultures, still involved in trade, appeared in Zimbabwe. The Butwa state (and there is now greater evidence of a state structure), with its ruling Torwa dynasty, was established in southwestern Zimbabwe with its capital at Khami, near present-day Bulawayo. Another was that of the Mutapa ruler established close to the Zambezi Valley, with trading connections to the Muslims and also to the newly arrived Portuguese.

While these trading cultures and states are prominent through their notable sites, the great majority of Iron Age peoples in southern Africa continued to live in smaller-scale societies, represented by extended kin groups, with a tendency for groups to break away and establish new political organizations. By now the distinction—marked by linguistic, social, and economic differences—between the Tswana peoples in the west, with their related Sotho peoples settled farther east, and the Nguni groups of the east coast, in what is now Swaziland, Natal, and the Eastern Cape, had become apparent. The Tswana economy was based more heavily upon pastoralism. They lived in larger communities in order to exploit rare water sources in their more arid region.

The Nguni had a mixed agricultural and cattle economy, and were settled in smaller communities in the river valleys for their better-watered lands. To the north, the extensive Shona subgroups, some of them associated with the Zimbabwe culture or with Butwa and Mutapa, were settled throughout Zimbabwe and parts of Mozambique. Other Bantu speakers such as the Ovambo, the Herero, and the Tsonga lived in what are now Angola, Namibia, and Mozambique.

The Islamic presence on the East African coast was joined in the early sixteenth century by that of the Portuguese. Bartolomeu Dias first rounded the Cape in 1488 and was followed within a few years by Vasco da Gama, who reached India. During the succeeding century, the Portuguese (who avoided the Cape as a region of storms) established settlements in Angola and Mozambique and even penetrated the Zimbabwean Highveld, established trading posts to attempt to tap the gold resources of the region. But they never fully succeeded in overcoming opposition from Muslim traders and their alliances with African chiefs in the region were not always successful, leading to violence and revolt. This attempt to divert the trade of the interior of southern Africa failed and by the end of the seventeenth century, they had been swept off the Highveld and even their coastal positions had become highly precarious. However, the Portuguese established south Atlantic connections between Africa and their major colony in Brazil. Slaves were taken to South America and crops from that region, such as cassava and maize, were introduced to the subcontinent.

These crops, originally designed to feed the slaves, proved popular in Africa and soon came to be grown in many parts of the region. In the later sixteenth century we have evidence from sailors from a number of ship-wrecks (Dutch, English, and Portuguese) who survived the experience and subsequently reported on their observations of African peoples and their crops, mainly on the eastern coasts of what is now the Cape and Natal. From them we learn of the settlements and social organization of the Nguni peoples, and also of the rapid spread of maize into these areas. Meanwhile, at the Cape itself, many ships were calling in the late sixteenth and early seventeenth centuries to take on fresh water and to trade with the Khoisan inhabitants. Sheep, cattle, ostrich feathers, shells and seafoods were traded for metal goods and beads, sometimes for liquor. Most of these ships were English and some of the Khoisan traders even picked up elements of the English language.

In 1652, however, a more permanent settlement was established by the Dutch. The Dutch East India Company (DEIC) decided that it needed a station where its ships could be replenished on the long jour-ney to the East Indies. In 1657, seven "freeburghers" were permitted to settle permanently in order to create a more fully developed agricultural economy. They were the first of many, including Huguenot and Moravian Protestants fleeing from persecution in France and Germany. Cape Town began to develop as a significant port, the first Western-style township in southern Africa, though it took some time to reach the size of Mapungubwe in the far interior.

The Dutch introduced slaves to the Cape. Although they decided not to enslave the local population so as not to inhibit trade, they brought slaves from elsewhere in Africa (notably Madagascar) and from the East Indies. By the early eighteenth century, there were some 1,779 settlers and 1,107 slaves at the Cape. By this time, further settlements had been founded at Stellenbosch (1679) and Drakenstein(1687). Moreover, though the DEIC had tried to restrain the settlers, ex-pansion was now so rapid that townships appeared much farther inland, at Swellendam (1745) and Graaff-Reinet (1785). By the end of the eighteenth century, Dutch settlers, by then often known in Dutch as Afrikaners, had penetrated territory up to 600 miles from Cape Town itself.

Dutch and other European people, who themselves had often come from regions of intensive settlement, developed an extensive system in which farmers re-quired at least 3,000 *morgen* (over 6,000 acres) of land. Khoisan peoples were subjected to intense frontier violence, and by the end of the eighteenth century had either been cleared from the land or had become virtual serfs of the Dutch farmers. By the 1770s, Cape settlers and migrants (the "Trekboers") were already beginning to show signs of unrest as regarded DEIC rule. They were also beginning to encounter Bantu-speaking peoples on the Cape frontier and began a long succession of so-called Cape/Xhosa Wars that were to be endemic for another hundred years.

By this time, the DEIC was in decline. Although DEIC administrations attempted to regulate the fron-tier, they had little success. With the outbreak of the Napoleonic wars, the Cape was highly vulnerable and it was taken by the British (1795–1802) and again, permanently, in 1806. This was an era of evangelical activity, and missionaries now became an important medium of social and economic transformation, both in the colony and on its frontiers.

This ferment of ideas and legislative and adminis-trative activity stimulated a great deal of opposition among the Afrikaner community (the British now called them "Boers," or farmers). In 1833, slavery was abolished throughout the British Empire, but it may have been other discontents, particularly in the regula-tion of employment, the use of English, and mission-ary activity among the Khoi and other black people that caused many Boers to decide to leave the colony. From 1835 on a number of Boer columns, the Voortrekkers, headed for the interior, and after a period of dispersed political activity in a series of small re-publics, these coalesced into the Transvaal (later the South African Republic) and the Orange Free State.

During this period of extraordinary white expan-sion, in which the political outlines of the modern South Africa were laid down, dramatic events had also been taking place in the interior of southern Africa. From about the 1790s on, processes of centralization occurred among the northern Nguni peoples. A ruler called Dingiswayo of the Mthethwa people began to create a larger state structure, which was later ex-panded further by Shaka of the Zulu. A considerable debate as to why this should have happened has con-sidered the roles of population growth, environmental pressures upon limited grazing territory, slave trading, and particularly the ivory and cattle trades associated with the southern Mozambiquan port of Delagoa Bay, as well as the innovative military tactics and charis-matic leadership of these rulers themselves.

What became the Zulu state was forged out of re-peated conflict. These wars sometimes resulted in in-corporation, but more often in setting up waves of mi-gration that resulted in the dispersal of Zulu-type states throughout many parts of southern and central Africa. The Swazi state of Sobhuza to the north of Zululand, the Ndebele of Mzilikazi to the west, and the Gaza state of Soshangane in southern Mozambique were some of these. Other groups headed northward across the Zambezi, and established states, known as Ngoni, in Malawi, eastern Zambia, and Tanzania. When the Ndebele came into conflict with the Boers in the western Transvaal, they moved on into southwestern Zimbabwe. The Boers also came into conflict with the Zulu state when they attempted to secure land in Natal. In 1838 a Boer party under Piet Retief was killed by Shaka's successor Dingane and the Boers secured their revenge through their victory at the Battle of Blood River, which duly entered the Afrikaner mythology.

Other peoples affected by the *mfecane* or *difaqane* (or "crushing of peoples") included Sotho refugees who congregated in the mountains of Lesotho under the remarkable king Moshoeshoe. Further participants in the general violence of the interior were peoples of mixed race known as the Griqua. They were caught between the British trying to control the frontier and the ever land-hungry Boers establishing themselves in the trans-Orange region. Ultimately, they lost their lands.

Another zone of violence was the eastern Cape frontier. In 1820, the British had attempted to settle immigrants from England and Scotland around Grahamstown, but this move was of limited success. Frontier wars continued to break out in almost every decade to the 1870s and environmental problems and cattle diseases placed the Xhosa people under great pressure, culminating in the cattle killing of 1857, when a prophetess suggested that this was the only way that a new dispensation could be achieved. This frontier region was not fully conquered and annexed by the British until the 1890s.

While these events were occurring in the interior, the Cape economy had become more closely connected with international trade through the export of merino wool, various agricultural products, ivory, and wine. Cape Town became an even more important port as its significance in relation to the British Empire, including the new colonies in Australasia, southeast Asia and the Far East was enhanced. But the opening of the Suez Canal in 1869 and the greater use of steamships seemed about to reduce this role. By then, however, one of the most striking events in southern African history occurred, the discovery of diamonds just beyond the Cape Frontier. The British soon annexed the region and the frontier town of Kimberley became the powerhouse of the Cape economy.

The results of these events were revolutionary. A modern infrastructure of railway lines and ports was established, with Port Elizabeth and East London developing to circumvent the overloading of Cape Town. Banking and other financial institutions; brick making and building contracting; and social services like education and hospitals were all considerably developed. White migrants were enticed into the colony, and representative institutions were developed in an attempt to avoid political resentment against the colonial power.

But perhaps the greatest change was to take place in respect of black-white relations.

As the diamond mines were concentrated into fewer hands and their operations became larger in scale, the demand for unskilled labor grew. Africans were drawn to the mines in large numbers. But this migrant labor system developed a number of key characteristics. One was that the workers seldom became permanent urban dwellers; they were contracted for a period and then returned to what were supposedly their "tribal" areas. While at the mines they were kept in closed compounds, both to prevent them stealing diamonds and also so that they did not constitute a threat to the whites. Their wages were kept to the minimum. They were forced to buy their requirements from mine shops, at high prices, and often fell into debt. This system was later transferred on a much larger scale to the gold mines of the Witwatersrand.

The wealth generated by the diamond mines briefly ensured that the Cape was by far the most powerful of the four territories (two British and two Boer) of white-controlled southern Africa. In the 1870s, this encouraged British rulers to attempt to reestablish their power over the impoverished and little-developed Boer states. The British had attempted to exert control in the middle of the century, but had conceded sovereignty to the Boers in the early 1850s. In 1877, the British governor, Sir Bartle Frere, ordered the invasion of the Transvaal. It was duly annexed with very little struggle. But the British were soon involved in a much more serious war with the Zulu in an attempt to settle and "pacify" the northern Natal border. Initially experiencing reversals, the British finally defeated the Zulu at Ulundi in 1879, thereby removing a major threat from the Boers of the Transvaal. The latter now resisted the British occupation in what became known as the First Boer War. They defeated a British force at Majuba Hill in 1881 and the Liberal Party government in London resolved to withdraw. This event set the stage for the conflicts of the future.

The power balance in southern Africa was transformed not by force of arms, but by a new stage in the "mineral revolution." Gold had been known in various parts of the interior since the 1870s, but now vast gold reserves, though of low-grade ore, were discovered on the Witwatersrand near present-day Johannesburg. Within a very few years the South African Republic had become richer than the Cape. Once more there was tremendous urban growth and infrastructural development connected with this, and, from the British point of view, there was a real danger of the Boers establishing close connections with other powers—notably, the Dutch or the Germans. The last two decades of the nineteenth century saw the rapid completion of the white conquest that had begun with the arrival of the Portuguese in Central Africa and the DEIC at the Cape several centuries earlier.

The Germans acquired southwest Africa (Namibia) in 1884. This event, together with westward pressure from the Boers of the Transvaal, prompted the British to secure their control over the Tswana people of Bechuanaland (Botswana). The Portuguese attempted to assert claims to a band of territory across Central Africa from west to east, but were frustrated by the British in the shape of the so-called Cape imperialism of Cecil Rhodes and his British South Africa Company, chartered in 1889. In the course of the 1890s, Rhodes established tenuous control over Zimbabwe and Zambia, ambitious for further mineral resources and anxious to frustrate the expansionist designs of the Portuguese and the Transvaal Boers. Rhodes's company fought wars with a number of African states (notably, the Ndebele and the Ngoni), forming alliances with others, and coping with serious revolts such as that of the Ndebele and Shona in 1896–1897. Some gaps in territorial control—for example, between the Cape and Natal and between Natal and Mozambique—were now closed. Basutoland (Lesotho) came under imperial control in 1868, after attacks by the Boers, and efforts to hand it over to the Cape failed, largely as a result of Sotho resistance. Swaziland was heavily penetrated by concession seekers and was dominated by the Transvaal until coming under British control in 1903. Both these territories became closely tied into the economy of South Africa, contributing large numbers of migrant workers to southern African mines and towns. It may well have been the desire for more labor that led to the conquest of the Venda and Pedi peoples of the northern Transvaal in the 1890s.

Indeed, the insatiable labor demands of the mines drew almost all the peoples of southern Africa into their economic system. Migrant workers, initially stimulated by the desire to "earn a gun" and later by the taxation demands of colonial administrations, were drawn from the entire region. The Portuguese and other colonial authorities made arrangements for deferred pay to be given to migrants upon their return, and as a result these territories became economically dependent on the mines.

The diamond and gold mines also had profound effects for the lives of women throughout the region. Some were drawn to the urban locations, where they brewed beer (usually illegally), became prostitutes, and established small businesses such as laundries. In the rural areas, women found themselves forced to take on new responsibilities with respect to children, the elderly, and control of meager family finances because of the absence of the men at work. They also found themselves coping with the increasing environmental problems of the so-called African reserves, which were becoming increasingly overpopulated and (from the white point of view) overstocked, with the land heavily eroded, as well as suffering from soil exhaustion.

All of these effects, already beginning to become apparent by the beginning of the twentieth century, were to be massively exacerbated in subsequent decades.

The gold resources of Southern Rhodesia proved to be a disappointment, though they were still a significant element of that economy. White settlers grew maize and ranched cattle, but tobacco soon became the most significant agricultural product. By the early years of the twentieth century almost the entire region was pulled together by railway lines, connecting the main production centers to harbors on the coast. German southwest Africa and southern Angola were less affected by these economic forces. The Germans exercised a brutal control of their colony and suppressed revolts by the Nama (a Khoisan group) and Herero people with a ferocity bordering on genocide. Many Nama and some Herero fled into the modern Botswana.

Natal, and its leading port of Durban, had also been pulled into this system. The colony had coal reserves which were significant in the economic development of the subcontinent. It also had good agricultural land that, from 1860 on, was extensively cultivated for sugar. Since African labor would not accept low agricultural wages, Indian indentured laborers were brought from India, further adding to the ethnic diversity of the region.

There was, however, a disjunction between the economic integration of the region, the power of international capital and its associated companies, and the political arrangements of the separate territories. Moreover, the white population had grown considerably in these years. In the 1780s, there were probably little more than 20,000 whites in southern Africa. By 1870, there were at least a quarter of a million. By 1891 this had risen to 600,000, and by 1903 to over a million. At this time, the black population of the entire region would probably not have exceeded four million.

The years between 1895 and 1910 were devoted to the solving of this political and demographic "problem." The Jameson Raid (1895–1896), an attack upon the South African Republic allegedly in support of the mining companies and their white immigrant workers who lacked political and other rights, was a disaster. But it has often been seen as the first blow of the Anglo-Boer War, which followed between 1899 and 1902. These events were supposedly restricted to the white population, but in reality Africans were heavily involved. They played many roles in the war itself and were caught up in the sieges of Kimberley, Mafeking, and Ladysmith. Many of them lost their lives. Africans were also the principal losers of the war. In the Peace of Vereeniging, the British effectively abdicated any prospect of improving the lot of blacks in the former Boer republics and ultimately the British colonies, even though that was one of the propagandist reasons for going to war. In the reconstruction era, the migrant labor system and segregationist tendencies were confirmed. The arrival of 60,000 Chinese indentured laborers to the mines reduced any prospect of wage bargaining power. Moreover, as the whites moved toward political union, black rights were increasingly threatened.

This union was achieved in 1910, when the two British and two Boer territories came together in a single unified state. The effect of this was to place political power largely in Afrikaner hands, but economic power remained with the British and the London markets to which South Africa was tied. Africans were again the losers, for though certain reserved powers were retained by the imperial government, these were never put into effect.

By this time, a considerable African educated and professional elite had emerged, largely the product of missionary education. Africans had been seeking various modes of resistance, including the founding of independent churches, syncretic breakaways from the standard denominations. There had been a serious tax revolt, the Bhambatha rebellion, among the Zulu in Natal in 1906. Various organizations had been founded, among them one to protect the voting rights of blacks at the Cape. In 1912, many of these elite figures came together to found the South African Native National Congress (later the word *Native* was dropped) to work for black political rights and to lobby the imperial government in London to exercise its reserved powers.

These aspirations were soon frustrated. In the Native Land Act of 1913, the new union government set about a major redistribution of land that was to produce considerable dispossession, migration, and much suffering. This was masked by the events of World War I and received little or no publicity in Britain or elsewhere. In the aftermath of this war, in which the South African government (despite opposition from many Afrikaners) participated in campaigns in southwestern and eastern Africa, the principal problem seemed to be the disaffection of both white and black labor. African workers had struck on various occasions, and there was a major strike in 1919. In 1922, a major strike of whites on the Rand was suppressed with considerable brutality, and this helped to ensure that the expansionist designs of Jan Smuts (who wanted to create a United States of Southern Africa) were frustrated. The white Rhodesian settlers declined,

in a referendum of 1923, to join the union, and the British government refused to hand over the so-called High Commission territories (Bechuanaland, Swaziland, and Basutoland) or the territories in central Africa (now Zambia and Malawi).

The period between the two world wars saw a considerable tightening of white and settler controls. In South Africa, the right wing Afrikaner Nationalist Party began to assume power, partly because of the disaffection of white labor, partly because of the economic pressures of the great depression. African workers also began to unionize effectively for the first time, notably in the Industrial and Commercial Workers' Union, led by a Malawian Clemens Kadalie, but this union ultimately failed partly because it became disunited, and partly because of the repressive measures taken against it.

In Southern Rhodesia, the white minority, constituting only a small fraction of the total population, also used the depression era to consolidate its economic power—not least over the land. The Portuguese, British, and South African administrations continued to encourage white migration and settlement in this period, as they would continue to do after World War II. The Union Government in South Africa had also acquired the League of Nations mandate over southwest Africa. After World War II, the South African government declined to transfer this mandate into a United Nations trusteeship territory and the stage was set for international pressures and violent resistance in more modern times.

South Africa participated in World War II, despite major opposition from Afrikaner nationalists, the leaders of whom often felt sympathetic to the Nazi regime in Germany and were consequently interned. In 1948, the victory of the nationalists in a general election brought some of these men to positions of power. The South African government now embarked on its apartheid policies of full racial segregation. Although this was given a greater legislative underpinning than it had ever received before, it was in essence based upon earlier colonial policies, which had included separation upon the land, job reservation, and separate arrangements for education, health care, and so on. Now, all South African peoples were classified according to color, as white, colored (mixed race), Indian, and black, and separate facilities had to be made available to all of these groups. The nonracial franchise of the Cape (which had had property and income qualifications restricting it to a small elite) had been abolished in the 1930s, but now all Africans were theoretically attached to "homelands" or "Bantustans" based upon ethnicity. They supposedly came from these and were to return there at the end of a period of working in the allegedly white parts of the country. Thus Africans were rendered alien in their own state, and the idea was even linked to the prevailing ideas of decolonization at work in the colonial world: the Bantustans were to become "independent" under a form of self-rule.

Farther north, the British attempted to stave off majority rule by creating, in 1953, the Central African Federation, which brought together Zimbabwe, Zambia, and Malawi. The Portuguese argued that their African colonies were part of metropolitan Portugal and that independence was consequently unthinkable. They also continued to encourage white migrants to settle in Angola and Mozambique. The South African government also attempted to integrate Namibia, where diamond mining had become a significant economic activity, into a greater South Africa. But the Central African Federation, which was dominated by the white settlers of Southern Rhodesia, encountered serious black resistance. Declarations of states of emergency in 1959 signaled the start of the processes of decolonization. Zambia, Malawi, Botswana, Lesotho, and Swaziland all emerged as politically independent states in the course of the 1960s, at a time when the South African regime seemed to continue to be intransigent.

Guerrilla campaigns, however, became an increasing feature of resistance in southern Africa. The Portuguese faced major resistance in Angola and Mozambique, and South Africa found itself committing troops, particularly in southern Angola. Campaigns also developed around Zimbabwe in opposition to a white supremacist regime that had declared unilateral independence from Britain in 1965. The African National Congress also decided that only violent resistance could force the political pace in South Africa. Movement came rapidly once the Portuguese Est_do Nuovo regime in Lisbon was overthrown in April 1974. Portugal's African colonies became independent in 1975, although rebel movements, with South Africa support, continued to be active. Zimbabwe achieved independence in 1980. Attempts by the South African government to buy off rising internal opposition with minor "reforms" of the apartheid system in the 1980s met with what amounted to open rebellion in the townships. The government responded with further repression and a "state of emergency," but by the end of the decade a combination of mounting internal and external pressures forced the South African government to face the inevitable. South Africa withdrew from its occupation of Namibia, and after free elections Namibia became independent in 1990. That year Nelson Mandela and other political leaders were released from prison, bans were lifted on free political activity, and some apartheid legislation was repealed. After fully democratic elections in 1994, South Africa emerged as a black-ruled state under President Mandela.

Although the political arrangements had been transformed, and interracial tensions had, to a certain extent, been ameliorated by the Truth and Reconciliation Commission, under the chairmanship of Archbishop Desmond Tutu, the economic and class system changed very little. The gulf between the haves and have-nots remained very wide, which helped to explain the high levels of crime in South African society. AIDS had become a major scourge and many felt that the South African government, particularly under Mandela's successor, Thabo Mbeki, was doing insufficient work to counter this problem. However, some improvements took place in freer access to certain sectors of employment, to education, and to some health services.

Angola and Mozambique both faced internal civil wars until comparatively recently. Namibia was destabilized by the violence on its northern frontier, but also experienced some genuine economic advance. In Zimbabwe, old strains between the Shona and Ndebele people reemerged, and the government of Robert Mugabe dealt brutally with any hint of political dissidence in Matabeleland in the southwest or anywhere else in the country. Mugabe also embarked on policies to redress the unequal and wholly unfair distribution of land within the country, overturning decades of white occupation of much of the best land. But the violent methods he adopted had a damaging effect on the Zimbabwean economy, producing runaway inflation, very high unemployment, and famine. Fellow African rulers, such as Mbeki in South Africa and Sam Nujoma in Namibia elected to take a diplomatic approach to the problem and Mugabe's regime continued to inflict considerable suffering upon the people of Zimbabwe.

Four imperial systems—those of the Portuguese, the British, the German, and the local one of the expansionist Afrikaners—had carved up southern Africa among them, subjecting African peoples not only to rule by whites, but also to oppressive and dislocating connections with the international economy. Efforts to create larger political systems throughout the subcontinent were only partially successful, and a single major state, like that in Canada or in Australia, failed to appear. Nevertheless, the power of diamonds and above all gold created high levels of economic integration that surpassed political boundaries. But throughout all of this, Africans, with the exception of the Khoisan peoples, maintained their population levels, despite all the checks of war and disease, as well as their capacity to resist. After a long tradition of warfare and oppression against indigenous peoples, southern Africa now boasts no fewer than eight independent states.

But in the process considerable environmental change has occurred throughout the region. The great game resources that had previously covered all areas right down to the Cape have been beaten back and confined to a number of game reserves. Whereas humans and animals had formerly coexisted, people were generally removed from the game parks. Forests have also been cut down, providing timber for fuel, railway building, and the construction of towns. The concentration of Africans in overpopulated reserves has also had negative environmental effects. The African practice of moving their settlements and rotating their crops and pasture had been much more ecologically friendly. Alien botanical species have made a dramatic mark upon southern African land. Cities, towns, and denser human settlement have increased pollution levels, while mining has frequently scarred the landscape. Thus, the challenges facing the new states of southern Africa are environmental as well as economic and social.

JOHN M. MACKENZIE

See also: **Boer Expansion: Interior of South Africa; Cape Colony: British Occupation; 1806–1872; Difaqane on the Highveld; Humankind: Hominids, Early, Origins of; Iron Age (Early): Herding, Farming, Southern Africa; Jameson Raid, Origins of South African War: 1895–1899; Mandela, Nelson; Mfecane; Nonqawuse and the Great Xhosa Cattle-Killing, 1857; South Africa: Apartheid, 1948–1959; South Africa: Gold on the Witwatersrand; 1986–1899; South Africa: Homelands and Bantustans.**

Southern African Development Community

The Southern African Development Community is Africa's newest attempt at fostering development through collective self-reliance for a particular area—in this case, the nine southern African countries that were founding members (Angola, Botswana, Lesotho, Malawi, Mozambique, Swaziland, Tanzania, Zambia, and Zimbabwe) plus Mauritius, Namibia, and South Africa.

The organization was born in 1979 and formalized in 1980 as the Southern Africa Coordinating Conference (SADCC), out of economic and political necessities resulting from apartheid in South Africa. SADCC countries either shared common frontiers with South Africa or were geographically within range of South Africa's military power. Except for Malawi, they initially were staunchly opposed to the apartheid regime in South Africa, and in different practical ways helped South Africa's liberation movements in their efforts to bring down the apartheid government. They allowed South African liberation organizations, especially the African National Congress (ANC), to use their territories to train antiapartheid fighters or to launch military attacks against targets in South Africa. But the states were militarily very weak and economically too dependent on South Africa; their citizens were, for a large part, employed in South Africa. For some countries, the only way in which they could receive imports or export their products was via South African ports. Others (Angola and Mozambique) had internal armed challenges to their legitimacy, which South Africa exploited to undermine them. In response to increased antiapartheid military attacks during the 1970s, South Africa adopted the strategy of launching military attacks deep inside neighboring countries considered to be the source of such attacks. Swaziland, Angola, Lesotho, and Mozambique were forced by the new South African strategy to expel or prohibit antiapartheid groups from using their respective territories as staging grounds for armed incursions into South Africa.

The motivation behind the creation of SADCC was to reduce member countries' dependence on South Africa and on other powers outside the region. This was to be done by the SADCC members coordinating their economic activities in ways that would enhance their collective and individual strengths. They sought to accomplish that by assigning each country a different sector to develop and to collectively mobilize external funding for the respective sectors. The principal sectors that were earmarked for development were assigned to member countries as follows: Angola—energy; Botswana—agricultural research and animal disease; Lesotho—soil conservation and land utilization; Malawi—fisheries wildlife and forestry; Mozambique—transportation and communications; Swaziland—labor; Tanzania—industrial development and trade; Zambia—mining; and Zimbabwe—food security. The arrangements also put the secretariat in Botswana and made that nation the SADCC chair.

Transportation and communication were given priority because the region's infrastructure for these was either poorly developed or had been destroyed by civil wars. The principal accomplishments of the SADCC during its first decade of existence took place in this sector and it consumed around 64 per cent of the organization's total project portfolio. Of the greatest expense was the corridor of regional rail and transportation systems that were developed to link Maputo, Beira Nacala, Dar Es Salaam, and Lobito. SADCC's approach through sectoral development meant less competition among several countries in the region for limited external funds in the same sector.

In August of 1992, SADCC member states converted the organization from a loose entity based on conferences to a more formal regional integration organization and assumed the new name of the Southern

African Development Community (SADC). The objective was to harmonize trade and monetary policies among members with the eventual goal of establishing a common market. This change in status was a reflection of internal developments in South Africa with the prison release of Nelson Mandela, leader of the African National Congress, and the beginning of talks to establish majority rule. After the election of 1994 that formalized the transfer of power from the white minority to the black majority in South Africa, with Mandela now as that nation's president, South Africa was admitted as the SADC's 11th member. Sonn after, Mauritius followed suit and became the 12th member.

The SADC's mission has continued to expand since the 1992 changes and so has its prestige, especially with South Africa's membership. This was further enhanced in 1996 when Nelson Mandela took over from Botswana's President Sir Ketumile Masire as the organization's chairman. South Africa's membership adds significant weight to the organization in various ways. It has a market size of over 42 million, with a high consumption pattern. It has an economic, industrial, and scientific capacity that is unparalleled in Africa. Its military power and communication infrastructure is also the best in the region. In addition, when Nelson became chairman, his status and reputation as a leader of impeccable integrity around the world provided the SADC with exactly the type of image the organization needed at a time when Africa was perceived to be suffering from a leadership crisis. South Africa also became the coordinator of a new sector within the organization known as the Organ for Politics, Defense, and Security. South Africa and Botswana invoked this provision to intervene militarily in Lesotho to restore order and electoral integrity when in May of 1998 disputed elections led the Lesotho military to attempt a coup d'état. The new role of the SADC on political military matters signifies that member countries are no longer going to remain aloof while wars and conflicts destroy the fabric of their region and render difficult their economic objectives. Only time will tell how successful the organization's new mission will be.

MOSES K. TESI

Further Reading

Chazan, Naomi, et al. *Politics and Society in Contemporary Africa*. Boulder, Colo.: Lynne Rienner, 1992.

Clough, Michael, and John Ravenhill. "Regional Cooperation in Southern Africa: The Southern Africa Development Coordination Conference." In *Changing Realities in Southern Africa*, edited by Michael Clough. Berkeley: Institute of International Studies, University of California, 1982.

Gwaradzimba, Fadzai. "SADCC and the Future of Southern African Regionalism." *Issue* 21, nos. 1–2 (1993).

Southern Nilotes: *See* **Nilotes, Eastern Africa: Southern Nilotes: Kalenjin, Dadog, Pokot.**

Southern Rhodesia: *See* **Welensky, Roy; Zimbabwe (Rhodesia): Unilateral Declaration of Independence and the Smith Regime, 1964–1979; Zimbabwe (Southern Rhodesia): African Political and Trades Union Movements, 1920s and 1930s; Zimbabwe (Southern Rhodesia): Colonial Period: Land, Tax, Administration; Zimbabwe (Southern Rhodesia): Federation, 1953–1963; Zimbabwe (Southern Rhodesia): Nationalist Politics, 1950s and 1960s; Zimbabwe (Southern Rhodesia): Ndebele and Shona Risings: First Chimurenga; Zimbabwe (Southern Rhodesia): Urbanization and Conflict, 1940s.**

Soweto Uprising: *See* **South Africa: Soweto Uprising.**

Soviet Union and Africa

The African continent became a factor in Russian foreign policy for the first time at the end of the nineteenth century during two wars, the Italo-Ethiopian War (1895–1896) and the second Anglo-Boer War (1899–1902). In both cases, a strong anti-British sentiment among the public and a cautious but obvious anti-British stand of the government made the Russians consider first Ethiopia, and then the Boer republics, as potential allies against their common powerful enemy, Britain.

After the 1917 Bolshevik Revolution, the young Soviet state perceived Africa, as well as other parts of the colonized world, as its natural ally in its struggle for survival and social progress because of the revolutionary potential of the colonized peoples, and their presumed ability to undermine and disrupt the capitalist world. The Communist (Third) International (Comintern), a union of communist parties of the world founded in 1919 in Moscow and to a large extent expressing its interests, was deeply involved in the ideological debate on the "national and colonial problem," in spreading socialist—and with it Soviet—propaganda, and in preparation of cadres for both national and social revolutions. In 1928, the Red International of Labor Unions, which acted under the auspices of the Comintern, created the International Trade Union Committee of Working Negroes, which played an important role in Moscow's African connection. Several future leaders of anticolonialism in

Africa were educated in the Comintern's schools, Jomo Kenyatta and George Padmore among them.

South Africa occupied the central place in Comintern's African policy for it was the only country in Africa south of the Sahara that had a well-developed working class, a well organized labor movement, and a vibrant and vociferous communist party. The Communist Party of South Africa gave the Comintern its only direct link to politics in the region but it was mainly the Comintern's rigid control over the party that led to the latter's demise in the 1930s.

In 1943 the Comintern was disbanded, because during World War II the Soviet Union was more interested in maintaining relations with its Western allies than with the communist movement. In Africa this new line found a reflection in the opening of Soviet consulates in South Africa which existed from 1943 until 1956.

The Comintern's greatest contribution to the cause of African liberation may have been its slogan of the "independent native republic," its official goal for South Africa from the late 1920s until 1935. However, until the 1950s the Soviet stand against colonialism was inconsistent. The USSR rejected the mandate system of the League of Nations, but it did join this organization despite the fact that it condoned colonialism. The Soviet Union was the only big European power to denounce Italian aggression against Ethiopia in 1935–1936, but even after the war it explored possibilities of territorial acquisitions in Africa for itself.

After the war, from the mid-1950s on, the center of attention of the Soviet government in Africa moved from South Africa to other African countries. Soviet strategists and policy makers saw them as allies in the struggle against its opponents in the Cold War and as potential members of the socialist camp because, one after another, they declared their desire to be socialist or "to build socialism" after proclaiming their independence. This new approach led to an upsurge of direct Soviet involvement in Africa during the 1960s, 1970s, and early 1980s.

The most important aspect of Soviet policy at that time was its assistance to liberation movements. The Soviet Union initiated the Declaration of Independence of Colonial Countries and Nations, which was passed by the United Nations in 1960, and championed every case of anticolonial struggle on the international arena. It provided liberation movements with funds, consumables, vehicles, air tickets and stationery, and granted scholarships for the study in Soviet tertiary institutions. From the 1960s on it became instrumental in providing military assistance: arms, advisers, and relocation of guerrilla forces. This was particularly significant in the case of the MPLA, Frelimo, SWAPO, and the African National Congress. In the context of the Cold War, assistance and support were always offered to a particular allied party as a measure against the influence of other power—first and foremost the United States and China, which often led to fragmentation of nationalist movements.

The spirit of the Cold War dominated Soviet relations with independent African countries as well, first of all in the sense that the USSR attempted to create a chain of allies in Africa, as it did elsewhere in the world. Countries that embarked on the program of reforms that Soviet authorities considered to be directed at building socialism, or just expressed their wish to do so, as well as those that did none of these but had tried to cut their ties with the West were pronounced "countries of noncapitalist development" (or, later, "countries of socialist orientation") and put into the category of "revolutionary democracies" (as distinct from the "people's democracies" of Eastern Europe). At different periods different countries fell into this category including Ghana, Mali, French Guinea, People's Republic of Congo, Tanzania, and Somalia. Ethiopia, Angola, and Mozambique enjoyed special attention and received the most in economic and military aid from the USSR.

There is little doubt that, both before and after World War II, Soviet policy in Africa was to a large extent dictated and motivated by the interests of the Soviet state itself. It is equally obvious, however, that Soviet assistance and its confrontation with the West where Africa's colonial powers belonged did make a difference for the outcome of Africa's struggle for independence. Soviet aid, on the other hand, did not help to alleviate economic problems of independent African countries and in some cases exacerbated them, and its ideologized approach and virtually unlimited supply of arms contributed to internal conflicts.

After the end of the Cold War, the center of Soviet interests in Africa moved to southern Africa once again. Due to its leverage in the wake of the Cold War and its involvement in Angola and Mozambique, the Soviet Union and then the Russian Federation were able to play an active role in the Namibian settlement and in South Africa's peaceful transition to the majority rule. However, from the beginning of the 1990s on, Russia's interest in Africa and its role on the continent began to decrease.

IRINA FILATOVA

See also: **Cold War, Africa and the; Socialism in Postcolonial Africa.**

Further Reading

Cassen, R. (ed.). *Soviet Interests in the Third World.* London: Sage/RIIA, 1985.

Golan, G. *The Soviet Union and the National Liberation Movements in the Third World.* London: Unwin Hyman, 1988.

Kempton, D. *Soviet Strategy toward Southern Africa*. New York: Praeger, 1989.

Nation, R. C. and M. V. Kauppi. *The Soviet Impact on Africa*. Lexington Books, 1984.

Somerville, K. *Southern Africa and the Soviet Union: From Communist International to Commonwealth of Independent States*. London: Macmillan, 1993.

Soyinka, Wole K. (1934–)

First African Nobel Laureate

The 1986 Nobel Laureate for Literature, Wole Soyinka, is a frontline Nigerian scholar, writer, social and literary critic, and activist whose literary works span drama, poetry, and prose, though he is better known as a poet and playwright than as a novelist. And of these he is primarily a poet: the poet in him always emerges in his nonpoetry writings—hence the much talked-about "obscurity in his works that results from his avid use of images, condensed words, and elliptical syntax. Soyinka's writings may be described as "writerly" in the sense that they make demands on the reader, who always has to be on the alert mentally, working out all the cues that may lead to purposeful decoding.

As a writer, Soyinka is pragmatically rooted in his traditional Yoruba culture despite his universal outlook. He draws copiously from the Yoruba traditions and cultural practices for the material contents of his writings, and demonstrates the influences of his culture on his philosophy. Elements of traditional African religion permeate his works, especially the belief in pantheon of gods, goddesses, and spirits. Ogun, the god of iron, with his ambivalence of creativity and destructiveness, can be regarded as Soyinka's muse, his patron god. References to Ogun, whether explicit or implicit, are common features of his individual works and collections—for example, "Ogun Abibiman," *Idanre and Other Poems*, *The Interpreters*, and *The Road*.

But it is interesting to note that Soyinka is a product of both traditional African culture and Western culture (notably, of Western Christian religion and education) as demonstrated clearly in his family memoirs *Ake* (1981) and *Isara* (1990). Although he may not be a practicing Christian, biblical echoes punctuate most of his works. He creates Christlike figures and gives in-depth treatment to the theme of willing self-sacrifice, as demonstrated in *Death and King's Horseman* and *The Strong Breed*, among others. Soyinka shuns religious dogmatism, and ridicules religious hypocrisy, as shown in his *Jero Plays*.

Soyinka's exposure to Western education and culture has contributed immensely to the development of his philosophy of life, but he does not subscribe to simple oppositions like white versus black, present versus past, modernism versus tradition. Rather, he reflects different sides of these oppositions, depicting their positive and negative possibilities with a view to enabling the reader to synthesize them. With this he reveals the complexities embedded in human life. Such a motif is apparent in such works as *A Dance of the Forest*, *The Lion and the Jewel*, *Kongi's Harvest*, and other works. This compels the reader to judge the positive and the negative elements encapsulated in the past and the present, tradition and modernism, in order to derive a new vision enshrined in the complex pattern of seeming contradictions. The different cultures that meet in Soyinka produce in human a form of cultural symbiosis such that as a broad-minded literary scholar, critic, and activist he shuns the cutting off of any source of knowledge, whether Oriental, European, African, or Polynesian. It is on this principle that his universal eclecticism and a strong belief in the adaptability of human culture are anchored.

It is important to note that Soyinka's life cannot be divorced from his art and it can be said that he believes in art for the service of humanity. Indeed, Soyinka lives his art; the artist and the man in him coalesce to expose and condemn all forms of social, political, and economic ills in society. Soyinka evinces graphically his abhorrence of any form of the exploitation of individuals as well as oppression and victimization, especially at the hands of an entity of great power; this may have accounted for his being regarded as an antiestablishment figure. Soyinka's *The Man Died* contains his dehumanizing and harrowing prison experience with the oppressive agents of government. As metaphorically illustrated by his poem "Abiku," in which he assumes the mask of an *abiku*, foiling all attempts to change his nature and make him conform, Soyinka is not ready to condone any political repression of an individual's free will. He can be regarded as an iconoclast who does not subscribe to conventions that tend to violate the individual's will.

Soyinka returned to Nigeria in the 1960s, after studying at Britain's Leeds University, to take up the mantle of struggle against what he considered the forces of retrogression within the university, his primary constituency, and the larger society. He actively opposed various attempts of governments to erode the autonomy of the university system.

He was also a strong voice of opposition to the government of the Western Region, led by Chief Ladoke Akintola in the 1960s. The government was seen as institutionalizing corruption and disorder, as well as attempting to perpetuate itself in power through the massive rigging of elections. In the ensuing scenario, Soyinka was accused of holding up the region's broadcasting corporation at gun point, hijacking the recorded audiocassette of the premier's speech ready for transmission, and replacing it with another carrying the message that the premier should quit office. He was consequently arrested and charged, but the case could not be successfully proved against him.

Soyinka also carried his "crusade" to the road by being instrumental in the establishment of the Oyo State Road Safety Corps during the tenure of Major General David Jemibewon as the military governor of Oyo State of Nigeria. The Unity Party of Nigeria civilian administration of Chief Bola Ige took over the corps in the Second Republic and reinvigorated it before it was crippled by the National Party of Nigeria's federal government. But during the regime of General Babangida, the corps was resurrected as the Federal Road Safety Commission and the indefatigable Soyinka was appointed chairman of its governing board on February 18, 1988. As a practical demonstration of his belief in commitment and self-sacrifice, he declined any remuneration for his services as chairman.

A study of Soyinka's works and life will no doubt reveal undeniable consistency and harmony. He demonstrates unequivocally his basic concern for human beings, celebrating life and deprecating its opposites. Sarcasm and wit are also prominent features of his drama, and its often biting tone has earned Soyinka the accolade "the tiger on stage."

AYO OGUNSIJI

See also: **Achebe, Chinua.**

Biography

Born in Nigeria in 1934. Educated at Government College, Ibadan; the University of Ibadan; and Leeds University in Britain. Worked briefly with the British theater before returning to Nigeria in 1960 to begin a series of struggles against what he regarded as antiprogressive forces. A prolific writer, his numerous dramatic works, among others, include *The Road, The Lion and the Jewel, The Jero Plays, Madmen and Specialists*, and *Death and King's Horseman*. His prose works include *The Interpreters, Season of Anomie, The Man Died, Ake, Isara*, and *Ibadan*, the last three being "faction," a subgenre of literature that blends fact and fiction. Soyinka's collections of poetry include *Idanre and Other Poems, A Shuttle in the Crypt*, and *Mandela's Earth*. In addition, he has written many critical essays and delivered lectures on literature, culture, religion politics and so on—for example, *Art, Dialogue and Outrage* (1988) and *The Credo of Being and Nothingness* (1991). Soyinka has won many prizes and awards, the most prestigious being the 1986 Nobel Prize for Literature.

Further Reading

Adelugba, Dapo (ed.). *Before Our Very Eyes*. Ibadan: Spectrum, 1987.

Adeniran, Tunde. *The Politics of Wole Soyinka*. Ibadan: Fountain, 1994.

Gibbs, James, and Bernth Lindfors (eds.). *Research on Wole Soyinka*. Trenton, N.J.: Africa World Press, 1993.

Jones, Eldred Durosimi. *The Writing of Wole Soyinka*, rev. ed. London: Heinemann, 1983.

Maduakor, Obi. *Wole Soyinka: An Introduction to His Writing*. Ibadan: Heinemann, 1991.

Ogunba, Oyin (ed.). *Soyinka: A Critical Collection of Critical Essays*. Ibadan: Syndicated Communications, 1994.

Spain: *See* Morocco: Spain in Morocco and the Sahara, 1900–1958.

Spanish Protectorates: *See* Morocco: French and Spanish Protectorates, 1903–1914.

Sports: Postcolonial Africa

Sports in Africa have been characterized by widely uneven geographic distribution, as programs, facilities, traditions, and competitive results vary across nations. Organized sports developed more recently in several countries, including Botswana, Burundi, Rwanda, Somalia, and Sudan. Generally the strongest sporting programs emerged in former British and French colonies, from Algeria and Tunisia in the north to Nigeria and Cameroon in the west and Kenya and Tanzania in the east.

In the early decades of the twentieth century, organized sport in Africa was constrained by the political considerations of the European colonial powers. In much of Africa, colonial culture, including sports, played an intrusive role destroying many aspects of local or traditional cultural activity. Where local or traditional sports were less overwhelmed by colonial practices, local sports had a greater chance of surviving and developing alongside colonial sports. Local pastimes often lost standing, prestige, or meaning among generations influenced by, or oriented toward, national and international developments.

In countries with multiple ethnic, cultural, religious, and linguistic groups and marked differences between urban and rural areas, sports can contribute to national cohesion and a sense of commonality. In practical terms, sports networks also contribute to overcoming regionalism. Social scientists have suggested that for new African nations, international athletic activity served as an unofficial complement to the work of diplomats and government officials, bringing a certain international notice and prestige to their nations. Sport has been viewed as a means to develop international relationships and friendships with other countries and to achieve diplomatic recognition. It is also valued as a venue for developing trade relations.

Regional divisions and rivalries marked African competition prior to the 1960s. The Jeux Inter-Africains held in the Central African Republic in 1959 was only open to French-speaking participants. In 1960, the Jeux de l'Amitié, an event cosponsored by the French government and 16 former French colonies was held in Madagascar with participation from 800 athletes competing in 8 sports. The following year saw English-speaking athletes from Nigeria and Liberia take part in the games in Côte d'Ivoire. By 1963 the Jeux de l'Amitié in Senegal enjoyed the participation of 2,400 athletes from France and 24 newly independent African nations, including the English-speaking countries Gambia, Ghana, Liberia, Nigeria, and Sierra Leone. Notably, the 1963 games saw African women compete in an international competition for the first time.

From the Jeux de l'Amitié of 1963 arose the notion of Pan-African games open to every African nation except the apartheid state of South Africa, and Rhodesia, and in 1964 representatives from 22 countries met to elect a planning committee for the Jeux Africaines (All-Africa Games). The first All-Africa Games took place in Brazzaville in 1965, with competitions involving over 3,000 athletes from 30 independent African nations.

The planning committee for the All-African Games was succeeded in 1966 by the Supreme Council for Sports in Africa (SCSA). This body, recognized by the Organization of African Unity (OAU) in 1967, would play a crucial part in coordinating and promoting Pan-African sport and developing prominence in global arenas. The SCSA played a major part in the attack on racially segregated sport in Africa, devoting energy and resources to secure the expulsion of South African sports organizations from participation in the Olympics and membership in international sports federations.

Sports played a significant part in developments toward Pan-Africanism, and this contributed to the shift in sports from local to global prestige. Notably, the growth of regional athletic gatherings in the late 1950s, as well as the emergence of All-African games in the 1960s, occurred simultaneously with the supranational conjoining of African states across regional and linguistic barriers in attempts to pursue common economic and political goals. Sport was viewed as a means to develop and promote Pan-African unity through international contacts and pursuit of common goals, such as the struggle against apartheid.

The expansion of Soviet and African sports relationships began in the mid-1950s, influenced by Cold War geopolitics and the emergence of vital independence movements in Africa. Soviet diplomatic relations were first established with Egypt, Ethiopia, and Liberia, the only sovereign black states in Africa before the 1950s, though various attempts to play a role in developments in Africa were made by Soviet governments between 1920 and 1950. Beginning in 1961, the Soviet Union lobbied the International Olympic Committee (IOC) to adopt a resolution to assist the development of amateur sports in Africa, Asia, and Latin America. Under this resolution, finally adopted in 1973, the national Olympic committees of countries with well-developed sports programs would provide material aid along with training and skills sharing for countries lacking developed programs or facilities. This "Olympic solidarity" program was financed by the IOC, receiving one-third of the television revenues from the Olympic games.

From the 1960s through the 1970s the Soviet Union developed sports relations with more than 30 African countries. The major area of Soviet and African sports initiatives came in the delegation of Soviet coaches and sports experts to African countries. Institutes of higher physical education, such as the Algerian Institute of Sports Science and Technology, were founded and developed with assistance of Soviet specialists who provided most of the training. Assistance was also given in building and equipping the new sports facilities.

Crucial in the development of international recognition for national sports programs has been performance on the world stage of the Olympic games. The rise to Olympic prominence coincided with the emergence of major movements for African independence. A hundred Africans participated in the 1960 Rome Olympics, at which Abebe Bikila was the first black African to win a gold medal. Four years later in Tokyo there were 150 competitors from African countries. The emergence of African athletics to Olympic—and world—prominence was signaled at the 1968 Mexico City games, where 13 African athletes won 16 different medals.

An important aspect of African involvement in the international sports arena was related to the elimination of racist regimes in South Africa and Rhodesia. The 1964 vote of the IOC to ban South Africa from the Tokyo games provided an indication of the emerging global strength of united action by independent African nations. When the IOC invited South Africa to return for the 1968 summer Olympics in Mexico City, the OAU initiated a boycott of the games. Within weeks of the IOC announcement, all 32 members of the SCAS had committed to the boycott. This united African front against apartheid presented the most formidable opposition force ever to confront the modern Olympic movement.

Pressure was also placed on South Africa through attempts to curtail sporting contacts with other nations. The most prominent example of this came in response to a sporting tour of South Africa by the New Zealand rugby team in 1976. Both the OAU and the SCSA issued calls to boycott the upcoming Montreal Olympics if New Zealand were not asked to withdraw. The refusal to act by the IOC led to the withdrawal of 30 African nations from the 1976 Montreal Olympics in what was the largest sports boycott up to that time.

On the eve of the 1972 Munich games, Ethiopia, Ghana, Guinea, Kenya, Liberia, Sierra Leone, Sudan, Tanzania, and Zambia announced their plans to boycott the games over the inclusion of athletes from Rhodesia. Again, support was forthcoming from the Soviet bloc and African American athletes, and again the IOC reversed its decision. Rhodesia was finally expelled from the IOC in 1975.

Attesting to the growing power of African athletes as a political force following the boycott of the 1976 Montreal Olympic Games, the Soviet Union put substantial resources into avoiding a boycott of the 1980 Moscow games by African states. This included sending delegations to visit countries to encourage the participation of African athletes and ensure countries of the Soviet Union's commitment to struggles against apartheid.

Sports cooperation agreements were signed between the Soviet Union and individual African countries as well as with the SCSA. Agreements included commitments to exclude South Africa from international competitions, to fight racism, apartheid, and commercialism, and to strengthen the unity and democratization of the Olympics movement. African initiatives against apartheid brought the attention of the world. A variety of nations with differing backgrounds, economies, and politics were able to make common cause in the struggle against apartheid in South Africa.

Ongoing and expanding athletic successes at global sports events such as the Olympic and Commonwealth games have brought further attention to sports in Africa. Recently, much recognition has been won on the soccer pitch. Successful entries to recent World Cup championships—notably, Cameroon's in 1990 and Senegal's in 2002—have brought much notice to African soccer. While no African nation has hosted a World Cup since its inception in 1930, Morocco was runner-up to the United States in 1994, and there is growing support at the top levels of the Fédération Internationale de Football (International Football Federation) for an African nation to host an upcoming World Cup soccer match.

JEFF SHANTZ

Further Reading

Allison, L. *The Politics of Sport*. Manchester: Manchester University Press, 1986.
Baker, W. J., and J. A. Mangan (eds.). *Sport in Africa: Essays in Social History*. New York: Africana Publishing, 1987.
Martin, Paul. "South African Sport: Apartheid's Achilles Heal." *World Today*, no. 40 (1984): 234–243.
Nauright, John. *Sport, Cultures and Identities in South Africa*. London: Leicester University Press, 1997.
Ndee, Hamad S. "Sport, Culture and Society from an African Perspective." *International Journal of the History of Sport* 13, no. 2 (1996): 192–202.
Steenveld, Lynette, and Larry Stielitz. "The 1995 Rugby World Cup and the Politics of Nation-Building in South Africa." *Media, Culture and Society* 20, no. 4 (1998): 609–629.
Taylor, Trevor. "Sport and World Politics." *International Journal* 43, no. 4 (1988): 531–553.
Wagner, Eric A (ed.). *Sport in Asia and Africa: A Comparative Handbook*. New York: Greenwood Press, 1989.
Wright, Steven. "Are the Olympics Games?" *Millenium* 6, no. 1 (1977): 30–44.

Saint-Louis: *See* **Senegal: Colonial Period: Four Communes: Dakar, Saint-Louis, Gorée, and Rufisque.**

Stanley, Leopold II, "Scramble"

The name of Leopold II, King of Belgium (r.1835; 1865–1909), is closely associated with the "Scramble" for Africa, the formation of the Congo State, and Belgian colonial expansion. His father, Leopold I, initiated him into the operation of government and provided him with military training. Early on, Leopold II developed an interest in international affairs. He visited England and other parts of Europe and appreciated the contribution of their overseas territories to the accumulation of their national wealth; he also visited Egypt and the Ottoman Empire. He nourished an ambition to provide his country with reliable sources of raw materials and outlets for its industrial production and surplus population. His accession to throne in 1865 provided Leopold with the opportunity to achieve his dream. He had important assets—his charismatic personality, the prestige of his position as the king of a neutral country, the service of loyal collaborators at home and abroad, his personal wealth, and his reputation as a philanthropic and generous monarch—but he had to overcome tremendous obstacles, including the constraints of the Belgian constitution, the reluctance of his entourage, the indifference of the business leaders and the public regarding overseas expansion, and the rivalry between European powers.

One of the most successful strategies Leopold II used to dissimulate his intentions was the convocation of a geographical conference in Brussels (September 12–14, 1876) to examine the economic potential of Africa. He spoke of the creation of bases to serve as the points of departure of the campaign to eliminate slavery and the slave trade and to spread "civilization." The conference resulted in the creation of the International African Association (IAA), the objectives of which were purely scientific and humanitarian. The participants appointed Leopold II as the chair of its executive committee and encouraged the creation of national branches of IAA across Europe. Although the IAA was a Belgian organization, it also included English, French, and Dutch shares. The king undertook to recruit his collaborators, and in June 1878, he hired Henry Morton Stanley.

Stanley had a difficult childhood because of his illegitimacy, and he had experienced difficult working conditions in the workhouse, on the farm, and in Liverpool. His life history made him a brutal and quick-tempered man. In Liverpool, he worked on a ship called the *Windermere,* which took him to New Orleans in 1858. He ran away from the ship and started a new life in the city, working as a clerk in a warehouse. In 1865 he went to work in New York, first as a freelance reporter and later for the *New York Herald,* which made him a permanent roving foreign correspondent based in London. He became famous with his well-publicized expedition in search of Dr. David Livingstone in 1871 and his exploration of the Congo River in 1877, which was financed by the *New York Herald* and *Daily Telegraph.*

In June 1878, Stanley met King Leopold II who, unlike the British, showed interest in the Congo River Basin. Stanley convinced the king that the exploitation of the immense resources in the Congo Basin required the construction of a railroad. On November 25, 1878, Leopold II created the Committee for Studies of the Upper Congo to study the feasibility of the project. He hired Stanley for five years to build stations and communication networks and to sign treaties with native chiefs on behalf of the committee. But after some European governments objected to the committee's political character, the king dissolved it in November 1879 and replaced it with a new organization, the International Association of the Congo (IAC), using the flag of the defunct IAA in order to promote "civilization" and commerce. Although "international," the IAC was managed by Leopold II and his close collaborators, such as Banning and Lambermont. The king succeeded in acquiring political rights through a sovereign organization by extending its territorial base from "free cities" or stations (November 1882) to "stations and free territories" (February 1883), Free States of the Congo and "independent states" (November 1883), and the Confederation of Free Negro Republics and

the Congo Free State (January 1884). He also promised free trade for all in a state without customs duties and played off the European powers against each other. He granted the right of first refusal to France, in case of failure of his Congo project, in exchange for its recognition of the association's power in the Congo basin, thus minimizing Portugal's threat. In 1884 the United States and Germany granted recognition to the IAC as sovereign power. By June 1884, when he returned to Europe from the Congo, Stanley had concluded 450 "treaties" with native chiefs on the defunct committee's behalf. Leopold II chose Sir Francis de Winton, a Belgian army officer, to replace Stanley.

The increasing rivalry between the European powers, especially the competition among Portugal, France, and the IAC in Central Africa, led German chancellor Otto von Bismarck to convene, on November 15, 1884, a Berlin West African Conference to resolve the conflicts and establish a new modus operandi. One of the most significant decisions taken by the participants, in February 1885, was the recognition of the IAC as an independent and sovereign power and of King Leopold II as sovereign of the Congo Free State, responsible for the implementation of the Berlin Act in the conventional basin of the Congo. It was an important diplomatic victory for the king. The Belgian government lent to the Congo Free State its officers, officials, and diplomatic personnel. But the king's new duties were strictly personal and did not engage the responsibility of the Belgian government and parliament. The king was represented in the Congo by a general administrator, later replaced by a governor general. After 1884 Leopold II used Stanley mostly in public relations, except in 1887, when he gave him permission to lead the British-sponsored Emin Pasha Relief Expedition (1877–1890) in the southern Sudan in the secret hope to integrate Equatoria into the Congo. But the mission failed, to Leopold's great disappointment.

Trading companies that operated from Stanley Pool created trading posts along the Congo River and its tributaries and engaged in the trade of ivory and rubber. The effective occupation and administration of the Congo and the exploitation of its human and natural resources proved to be more costly than the king had imagined. By 1890, despite the financial aid and loans from the Belgian government, the authorities in Congo were faced with chronic cash shortage. The financial crisis forced the king to renounce free trade and to adopt a new economic policy based on the appropriation of the land (crown domain), state commercial monopoly over ivory and other products, and the imposition of customs duties. The king's decision was inspired from the Dutch experience in Java, where the government had granted the monopoly trading concession to a private company, gave bonuses to the supervisors to stimulate production, and imposed forced labor. The new system, later referred to as the "Leopoldian system," established bonuses on the quantity of ivory and wild rubber obtained by the state officials in the rain forest and established a "hostage-taking system" for defaulting natives. Forced labor was exacted from natives in violation of the Sixth Article of the Berlin Act. It resulted in atrocities and other human rights abuses committed against the local population between 1895 and 1908 by agents of rubber companies such as Anversoise and Anglo-Belgian Indian Rubber that were monopolist companies created by the state. These abuses were contained in a report published in 1904 by British consul Roger Casement. The publication of the report provoked an international anti-Congolese campaign animated from England by E. D. Morel, secretary of the Congo Reform Association, who coined the expression "red rubber" to describe the economic scandal in Congo. In July 1904 the king created a commission of inquiry to verify the accusations made by Casement and the Protestant missionaries based in Congo who provided Morel with direct evidence. The commission recognized that abuses were committed, which led to Belgian annexation of the Congo territory in 1908. Congo Free State thus became the Belgian Congo.

KALALA J. NGALAMULUME

See also: **Congo (Kinshasa), Democratic Republic of/Zaire: Belgian Congo: Administration and Society, 1908–1960; Congo (Kinshasa), Democratic Republic of/Zaire: Belgian Congo: Colonial Economy, 1908–1960.**

Further Reading

Academie Royale des Sciences D'Outre-Mer. *Le Centenaire de l'Etat Independant du Congo*. Recueil d'Etudes. Bruxelles: Academie Royale des Sciences d'Outre-Mer, 1988.

Anstruther, Ian. *I Presume: H. M. Stanley's Triumph and Disaster.* Gloucester: Sutton, 1988.

Morel, Edmund Dene. *King Leopold's Rule in Africa. London:* William Heinemann, 1904.

Stevens, Siaka: *See* Sierra Leone: Stevens, Siaka and the All People's Congress.

Stone Age, Middle: Cultures

In Africa, the "middle Stone Age" represents an ill-defined stage in early human development that, until recently, has received comparatively little attention from archaeologists. It saw the development of regional cultural traditions recognized in the first instance by variation in lithic technology, but also marking important developments in socioeconomic practice as well, by implication, as in conceptual ability and communication. The establishment of absolute dates for these developments is particularly problematic, since they are too old for the application of radiocarbon and too young for reliable use of potassium-argon and other methods used to date earlier stages of hominid evolution and development.

Consideration of the typological issues involved in the processes that led to the emergence and eventual replacement of recognizable middle Stone Age industries is best undertaken with reference to the numbered "modes" of lithic technology proposed by the late Sir Grahame Clark in 1969. In this system, the technology of the Acheulian core-tool complex was designated mode 2, while the fully backed microlithic technology of the late Stone Age represented mode 5. In Europe, there intervened mode 3, a technology where the form of a desired flake tool was predetermined by preparation of the core from which it was to be struck; it thus represented a shift from emphasis on core tools to flake tools, an increase in ability to visualize the desired end product, and greater economy in the use of raw material. There was also a greater number of distinct tool types, each intended for a particular purpose. These trends continued in Europe into the more specialized mode 4 industries of the Upper Palaeolithic, based on the production of numerous punch-struck blades from a single core, seen as ancestral to the Mesolithic mode 5 technology.

In much of Africa, Clark's homotaxial sequence holds true, but the stages are less well defined, especially in the Sub-Saharan regions. This may have been because the cultural developments leading to mode 3 initially took place south of the Sahara, whereas in Europe they were introduced at a later stage in their development. Also, many parts of Sub-Saharan Africa lack lithic raw materials suited to the production of mode 4 blades.

Despite the chronometric difficulties noted above, it is now possible to state that the African transition from mode 2 to mode 3 was an enormously drawn-out process that proceeded at different times and speeds in various parts of the continent. In general terms, it seems to have begun as far back as 400,000 years ago, but it was probably not until 100,000–150,000 years ago that mode 3 industries were ubiquitous throughout the habitable continent. At the other end of the scale, trends leading to the development of mode 5 began as far back as 100,000 years ago but were not complete in all areas until about 6,000 years ago or even more recently.

Complete single-site sequences through these lengthy processes are rare and the correlation required for the establishment of composite sequences is hampered both by variation in the pace of change and by the chronometric problems already discussed. The best overview of the rise of mode 3 at a single site is probably that investigated by Desmond Clark at Kalambo Falls on the border between Tanzania and Zambia, close to the southern end of Lake Tanganyika. Here the process seems to have followed the course characteristic of the more densely wooded terrain of the major river valleys and, insofar as their archaeology is known, the fringes of the equatorial forest. The flat, sharp-edged bifacial core tools of the Acheulian were initially gradually replaced by thicker, comparatively crude core axes characteristic of the transitional industries known as Sangoan. At Kalambo, these eventually gave way to foliate bifacial points characteristic of industries known as Lupemban. As greater emphasis was, in due course, placed on the flakes removed in the process of manufacturing such core axes, smaller unifacial tools came into vogue, their overall shape predetermined by core preparation as well as by subsequent trimming.

In more open savanna areas of the continent, development took a somewhat different course, although the end product was often remarkably similar. Massive discoidal cores appeared in the late Acheulian industries; their preparation involved processes closely analogous to those involved in the production of hand axes. Eventually, the making of handaxes ceased and the discoidal cores became progressively smaller and more varied in shape. In the savanna country of eastern and southern Africa these post-Acheulian cultural stages are often classed as proto-Stillbay and Stillbay, although this terminology masks a considerable amount of interregional variation.

Other regions lack relevant data, either because their human occupation was not continuous (as in much of the Sahara) or because insufficient research has been undertaken (as in parts of West Africa).

In recent years it has been recognized that these archaeological materials represent social and economic developments of the greatest importance. Increased diversity and specialization is probably attested to in the African archaeological record well before corresponding trends are apparent in other parts of the world. Specialization carries implications for concomitant cooperation and communication. Development of prepared-core techniques of stone-tool manufacture has major implications for reconstructing human ability for visualizing abstractions and thus for interest in spirituality. These, in turn, suggest that art and language may have been approaching the complexity attained among more recent populations.

Speech is often regarded by archaeologists as a single phenomenon that originated at a single time; increasingly this development has been linked in recent years with the emergence of *Homo sapiens sapiens*. Such a view must be a gross oversimplification. Human speech covers an enormous range, from simple communication of needs (as for food, warmth, or sex) to the expression of complex ideas and abstractions. If, as argued above, the latter was associated with the middle Stone Age, the former must have a far greater antiquity, probably extending back to the growth in cranial capacity that accompanied the initial emergence of humanity.

Parallels have been noted between the processes outlined above and the conclusions based on analyses of mitochondrial DNA in modern human populations that are interpreted as suggesting that anatomically modern people (*Homo sapiens sapiens*) may originally have evolved in Sub-Saharan Africa before spreading out to other continents. The time depth tentatively attributed to this process by geneticists is broadly analogous with that of the middle Stone Age.

The African middle Stone Age has thus been transformed from an archaeological backwater, so to speak, to an area of major importance for understanding the origins of modern humans on a worldwide front. In due course this will presumably provide an impetus for increased research activity within Africa. Already, innovations such as use of specialized bone tools, previously considered as restricted to the late Stone Age, have been demonstrated to be far earlier both in eastern Congo and in South Africa.

It is noteworthy that later developmental stages similarly appear to have been pioneered in Sub-Saharan Africa. True mode 4 industries are generally absent other than in restricted areas where suitable raw materials were available, such as parts of South Africa where blades form an important component of certain middle Stone Age assemblages, and certain Kenyan and Ethiopian highland regions where blade-based industries, as in Europe, precede those of mode 5. The development of mode 5 technology, based on the production of backed microliths, took place at widely disparate times (apparently more than once) in different regions of Sub-Saharan Africa. The earliest such event was in the southern coastal regions and elsewhere in South Africa, in the Howiesons Poort industry that may be more than 100,000 years old. Comparable technology was a gradual development with less than half this antiquity in the savannas and forest fringes of eastern Africa, but it was not until Holocene times that it became ubiquitous. These observations confirm that the conventional division between middle Stone age and late Stone Age has outlived its utility.

DAVID W. PHILLIPSON

Further Reading

Brooks, A. S. and C. C. Smith. Ishango Revisited: New Age Determinations and Cultural Interpretations. *African Archaeological Review* 5 (1987): 65–78.

Clark, J. D. *Kalambo Falls Prehistoric Site*, vol. 3, Cambridge, 2001.

———. The Middle Stone Age of East Africa and the Beginnings of Regional Identity. *Journal of World Prehistory* 2 (1988): 225–305.

Clark, J. G. D. *World Prehistory: A New Outline*. Cambridge, 1969.

Mellars, P., and C. Stringer (eds.). *The Human Revolution: Behavioural and Biological Perspectives on the Origins of Modern Humans*. Edinburgh, 1989.

Phillipson, D. W. *African Archaeology*, 2nd ed. Cambridge, 1993. See especially chapter 4.

Singer, R. J. and J. Wymer. *The Middle Stone Age at Klasies River Mouth in South Africa*. Chicago, 1982.

Stone Age (Later): Central and Southern Africa

The later Stone Age of central and southern Africa represents a continuation and amplification of behaviors first expressed by hunter-gatherers in the middle Stone Age, including increased regional specialization in technology, greater use—and survival—of organic materials, deliberate burial, and the systematic use of art. Later Stone Age tools first appear in central Africa about 40,000 years ago and continue to be made until about 100 years ago in regions still populated by hunter-gatherers. The historical and contemporary presence of hunter-gatherers in the Kalahari Basin and tropical forests of central Africa provide a link between the ethnographic present and the archaeological record which enables archaeologists to model social, ideological, and economic changes in the more recent later Stone Age. In particular, the southern African ethnographic record has been used to explain the social context of the region's later Stone Age rock art.

The transition from Middle to later Stone Age technologies takes place between 40,000 and 20,000 years ago. A shift occurs in techniques of producing stone tools with greater emphasis on smaller, more standardized flakes and blades used as inserts in handles and shafts of bone, horn, ivory, or wood. Small inserts or microliths were made in central Africa between 40,000 and 30,000 years ago, and slightly later in southern Africa between 30,000 and 20,000 years ago. The earliest evidence for microlithic technology comes from Matupi Cave on the edge of the Ituri forest in northeastern Congo. Pollen and animal remains from Matupi show that 40,000 years ago this region was drier and the cave was situated in a mixed habitat of forest and grassland savanna. Early evidence of microlithic technology is also found in west central Africa at the Shum Laka rock shelter in the highlands of Cameroon. The lowest deposits, dated to 31,000 years ago, provide evidence for a grassland environment.

Microlithic technology may have enabled hunter-gatherer communities to extract more types of food, and more efficiently, from a wider variety of habitats. A broadly based diet would have been an advantage during periods of climate change when availability of plant and animal foods would be unpredictable and pressure from other human groups may have grown. The increasingly dry and cool conditions that affected central and southern Africa 30,000 years ago may have stimulated the subsequent widespread adoption of microlithic technology but cannot explain the earlier origin of the later Stone Age. The lack of well-dated sites with preserved environmental data for this early period, especially in the tropical lowlands of the Zaire River Basin and the dry interior of southern Africa, makes any explanation of the development of the later Stone Age largely conjectural.

Around the eastern and southern fringes of southern Africa, the shift to microlithic technology had taken place about 22,000 years ago, as can be seen at sites in Zambia and South Africa. Between 20,000 and 12,000 years ago, regional differences emerge in the types, frequencies, and techniques of making microliths. North of the Zambezi, a distinctive tradition of microlith manufacture, the Nachikufan industry, develops in central and eastern Zambia. Small blades were trimmed to form narrow pointed inserts and some flakes were shaped into geometric forms such as crescents and triangles. Other characteristic tools include small scrapers and bored stones that may have been weights attached to digging sticks. Nachikufan-like assemblages also occur in northeast Zimbabwe.

In South Africa, the earliest recognizable expression of later Stone Age microlithic technology, called the Robberg industry after the area of its discovery on the southern Cape coast, dates to about 22,000 years ago. Unlike the contemporary Nachikufan, Robberg microlithic technology is less standardized, with few formally shaped inserts and few scrapers. Bone tools, pigment, and ostrich eggshell artifacts are found in Robberg sites, and the faunal record suggests the hunting of large migratory game on the plains of the highlands of far southeast Africa. Robberg sites are absent from the Karoo and Namibia, areas that are today scrubland and desert, respectively. Here, nonmicrolithic tool making continued until about 10,000 years ago. These hunter-gatherers may have been isolated from groups to the south and east or simply chose to retain a successful technology suited to the rigors of the region.

By 14,000 years ago, the prevailing cool dry climatic conditions ended, as warmer and wetter conditions returned to central and southern Africa. North of the

Zambezi, variants of the Nachikufan industry continued with no interruption to the microlithic tradition. In equatorial central Africa, a later Stone Age variant known as the Tshitolian, develops from a local middle Stone Age adaptation to a forest environment. Flared triangular microliths are among the distinctive artifacts of the Tshitolian, which includes larger hafted tools, possibly used as axes for felling trees or for wood-working. Sites in the heartland of the Tshitolian, the Kinshasha plain and northeast Angola, are poorly dated and rarely preserve organic remains because of acidic soils. Kalahari sands underlie this region and reflect previous northward incursions of the desert during arid phases from its current location in Botswana. South of the Zambezi, a break in the microlithic tradition occured between 12,000 and 8,000 years ago. Polished bone points took the place of microlithic arrowheads and large hand held scrapers made on coarse raw materials replaced small-hafted scrapers. A shift toward hunting smaller game is also part of the 4,000-year interlude known as the Oakhurst Complex in South Africa and the Pomongwe in the Matopos region of southern Zimbabwe. The Oakhurst is named after a southern Cape farm where the distinctive nonmicrolithic industry was first recognized. Regional variants are found across South Africa, including numerous undated open-air sites in the interior. Resettlement of the interior followed the end of the arid phase that had made this an inhospitable area for hunter-gatherers. The population of southern Africa as a whole rose about 13,000 years ago. Explanations for the shift from microlithic to nonmicrolithic technology from southern Zimbabwe southward stress climatic and demographic stimuli but there is no direct correlation between these forces and the preference for large over small scrapers or bone over stone points. The Oakhurst could be a social response to environmental changes and population growth analogous to those seen among living hunter-gatherers. Indirect evidence exists in Oakhurst for the formation of alliances between widely dispersed groups, seasonal gathering of large groups for ritual and social exchange and complex religious beliefs, reflected in deliberate burials with grave goods and the making of portable art.

By 8,000 years ago the nonmicrolithic traditions of southern Africa are replaced by microlithic assemblages characterized by highly standardized inserts, especially scrapers, blades, and flakes trimmed into a variety of geometric shapes. Where organic preservation is especially good, such as at the waterlogged site of the Gwisho hot springs in southern Zambia, there is evidence of the use of a variety of materials including wood and bark for tools, leather for clothing, and grass for bedding. From the Zambezi southward these microlithic industries are grouped into the Wilton Complex, named after two rock shelters in the Eastern Cape. The complex encompasses rapidly changing regional and chronological variants that span the period of the Wilton from 8,000 to 2,000 years ago. The return to microlithic technology takes place earliest in southern Zimbabwe about 10,000 to 9,000 years ago and at the same time in Namibia followed by a southward spread. This is a time of generally hot and dry conditions across central and southern Africa with the semidesert interior and its margins abandoned briefly between 6,000 and 4,000 years ago. Explanations for the dramatic reversal in tool-making traditions stress the interaction of environmental, demographic, and social trends, as in the case of the appearance of the Oakhurst. The readoption of microlithic technology may be part of wider strategy for coping with declining resources, which included increased reliance on extended social networks, and the clear demarcation of territorial rights through deliberate burial and highly visible rock art.

The rich archaeological record of the Wilton is the prehistory of indigenous hunter-gatherers and herders of southern Africa known collectively as the Khoisan. Pottery and sheep herding was introduced into the region about 2,000 years ago by herders moving south from Botswana. Cattle herding, ironmaking agriculturists followed, originating in central Africa. The later Stone Age hunter-gatherer way of life changed irrevocably, with some groups becoming acculturated into the new herder economy and others engaging in trade with agriculturists. Later Stone Age peoples no longer lived in a world of hunter-gatherers. The colonization of southern Africa by Europeans led to the final destruction of Khoisan communities. North of the Zambezi, the microlithic Nachikufan remained largely intact into recent centuries in northern and eastern Zambia, but the presence of pottery indicates interaction with farmer communities. In the forests of central Africa, hunter-gatherers of small stature—"pygmies"—today live in close contact with settled indigenous farming communities. Central African hunter-gatherers differ genetically from the Khoisan, and this reflects a long separation of the forest and savanna communities of the later Stone Age, a distinction that may have its roots in the middle Stone Age.

LAWRENCE BARHAM

Further Reading

Brooks, Alison, and Peter Robertshaw. "The Glacial Maximum in Tropical Africa: 22000–12000 BP." In *The World at 18000 BP*, vol. 2, *Low Latitudes*, edited by Clive Gamble and Olga Soffer. London: Unwin Hyman, 1990.

Deacon, Hilary J., and Janette Deacon. *Human Beginnings in South Africa: Uncovering the Secrets of the Stone Age*. Cape Town: David Philip, 1999.

Mitchell, Peter J. "Holocene Later Stone Age Hunter-Gatherers South of the Limpopo River, ca. 10,000–2,000 B.P." *Journal of World Prehistory* 11, no. 4 (1997): 359–472.

Phillipson, David W. *African Archaeology*, 2nd ed. Cambridge: Cambridge University Press, 1994.

Pwiti, Gilbert, and Robert Soper (eds.). *Aspects of African Archaeology: Papers from the 10th Congress of the Pan-African Association for Prehistory and Related Studies.* Harare: University of Zimbabwe Publications.

Wadley, Lyn. "The Pleistocene Later Stone Age South of the Limpopo River." *Journal of World Prehistory* 7, no. 3 (1993): 243–296.

Walker, Nicholas J. *Late Pleistocene and Holocene Hunter-Gatherers of the Matopos.* Uppsala, Sweden: Societas Archaeologica Upsaliensis.

Stone Age (Later): Eastern Africa

The criteria for defining the "late Stone Age" are technological rather than chronological. It should be remembered that the late Stone Age is not a time period, but represents instead an attempt to bring a broad three-age definition to the vast range of later prehistoric African stone tool industries. The later Stone Age at its simplest technological level of definition subsumes all lithic industries of a microlithic character. Microliths are small stone tools in a range of shapes, which are frequently backed (blunted) along one edge; this backing is believed to have facilitated the hafting of the tool to a wooden stock/handle; traces of mastic have only rarely been found on these backed edges.

Although the use of the term *later Stone Age* (hereafter, LSA) is broadly accepted, and commends itself by its simplicity, it ignores a great deal of stylistic variation; LSA technologies in certain parts of eastern Africa also include blade industries underlying these microlithic industries. The earliest microlithic industries in Africa are observed as far back as 70,000BCE (in the case of the enigmatic Howeison's Poort industry at Klasies River Mouth, South Africa), and nearer to our region at around 30,000BCE at Matupi cave, eastern Zaire (Phillipson 1993, pp.60–101); in many areas of Africa some populations still use microlithic stone tools in their everyday lives, yet one would recoil at the thought of defining the African modern world as the LSA. This is a vast temporal canvas on which to work, and emphasizes the unsuitability of the term *late Stone Age* as a chronological indicator.

The period during which LSA industries were fabricated fits in geologically with the later Pleistocene and Holocene periods. Paleoenvironmental data—derived mainly from lake cores—indicate a marked cool and dry period in eastern Africa (the hypothermal) at around 16,000BCE, which on a global scale was a phenomenon associated with the maximum extent of the ice sheets during the later Pleistocene. The onset of the Holocene at around 10,000BCE was marked in eastern Africa by the melting of the mountain glaciers and an increased rate of precipitation that led to an increase in size of local lake and river systems. A number of arid, cooler periods are noted throughout the Holocene, and these varied in duration and severity until the onset of neothermal conditions at around 3000BCE (Brooks and Robertshaw 1990). It should be noted that the region under consideration here offers a vast spectrum of ecological and raw material resources, and only a very generalized cultural outline may be presented here. It should be noted that there are still large gaps to be filled in the archaeological record, and the extant radiometric dates can only provide a bare chronological frame in which to work. Let us now consider the nature of cultural and economic change within eastern Africa during this period, starting in the north of the region with the relatively unknown Ethiopian/Eritrean highland/Rift Valley and Somalian sequences.

The key source for understanding the later Stone Age cultural succession in the Horn of Africa remains Desmond Clark's seminal 1954 work *The Prehistoric Cultures of the Horn of Africa*; it is a testament to the quality of this synthesis that it should still be of relevance today. Of late, new information from the present writer's research in the Aksum region has thrown new light on the LSA of the Ethiopian/Eritrean highlands; an LSA blade industry has been noted in stratified sequences dating to around 10,000BCE, and the makers of these industries were essentially hunter-gatherers who exploited plentiful animal resources in a highland zone that was probably wetter than today (Brandt 1986). At around 8000BCE a fully microlithic industry emerged in the area, essentially building on local cultural foundations; this industry was based almost exclusively on quartz, an ideal material for the fabrication of small, sharp-edged tools, and associated faunal evidence would seem to indicate a shift in preference toward smaller ungulates. Similar microlithic tool forms (generically termed "Wiltonian") have been noted at sites across highland Ethiopia and Eritrea, but these stone tool industries remain poorly understood, as does the emergence of the first pottery in this area, which is held to have occurred sometime after 4000BCE. We can only be imprecise because of the lack of good associated radiometric dates, and this problem applies additionally to evidence for plant exploitation, which is nonexistent until pre-Aksumite times (i.e. after 500BCE). Along the Rift Valley, and into the Red Sea coastal hinterlands, similar developments are noted; blade industries are recognized in southern Somalia—the Magosian industry, and in the north at Midhishi 2—and the Hargeisan, though the integrity of the former industry is at best dubious (Brandt 1986). It is possible that the earliest manifestation of an LSA industry in the Rift/lowland zone of Ethiopia is represented by material from Lake Ziway, dating to around 25,000BCE. In southern Somalia, microlithic industries are represented by the Eibian/Doian industry—dating from around 7000BCE—and in the north by the broadly contemporaneous "Wilton" industries. Economic evidence from Lake Besaka in the Ethiopian Rift points to a gradual shift away from hunting and fishing toward stock keeping by around 1500BCE (Brandt 1986). From a social orientation, perforated ostrich eggshell beads have been discovered at LSA sites in the lowlands, human burials were observed at Lake Besaka and Bur Eibe, and the region is home to an extensive concentration of rock art that was associated with LSA *sensu lato* stone tool–using populations.

Moving southward, the pioneer of LSA studies in the Kenyan Savanna and highland zones was the noted archaeologist Louis Leakey, who in the 1930s attempted to establish a rough chronology of technological development with old shore-lines on Rift Valley lakes. Leakey's excavations at Gamble's Cave yielded the "Upper Kenya Capsian" (latterly called Eburran) industry, the first LSA industry to be satisfactorily defined in this region. The recently excavated cultural sequence from Enkapune Ya Moto (Marean 1992) would appear to indicate that an LSA industry was in place by at least 14,000BCE, and that these early LSA industries were overlain by this morphologically distinctive Eburran industry. In many cases, the antecedents of the Eburran industry are poorly known, and many disparate underlying LSA industries have been observed at a number of sites in Kenya (e.g. Nderit Drift, Lukenya Hill). The Eburran would appear to be essentially a functionally specialized, mainly obsidian-based industry of hunting populations concentrated around the eastern Rift Valley in south central Kenya from around 11,000 to 7000BCE. Other microlithic industries in the area remain poorly defined, and are generically subsumed under that very loose term *Wilton*.

Evidence for a strikingly different economic strategy in the region at this time is witnessed by contemporary lakeside settlements around Lake Turkana in northern Kenya. These specialist sites, which include Lothagam and Lowasera, yielded wavy-line pottery akin to that witnessed at Khartoum Mesolithic sites in the central Nile Valley, and they date from somewhere between the ninth and fifth millennia BCE. Cultural remains at these sites included quantities of bone harpoon points, and faunal evidence points to economies based on extensive utilization of aquatic resources including a range of fish, crocodile, and hippopotamus (Stewart 1989).

Within Tanzania and Uganda the picture is somewhat sparse. Excavations at the rock shelters of Kisese and Nasera would seem to indicate early occurrences of microlithic industries as far back as 18,000BCE, based broadly on earlier local lithic traditions and associated with a hunting economy based on a wide range of fauna including large and small land game, birds, fish and reptiles. The sequence from the Ugandan site of Munyama Cave on an island in Lake Victoria would seem to indicate the emergence of a microlithic industry at around 13,000BCE.

A number of key points may be made from this generalized overview. Toward the south of our region, microlithic industries emerged between the eighteenth and fifteenth millennia BCE, much later than is observed south of the Limpopo. Into the Horn, these industries appeared later still and were frequently preceded by blade industries. All these microlithic industries subsume a wide range of variation in form and in raw material preference; these two factors are clearly linked.

Two key contemporary economic components may be noted: broad-spectrum generalist hunting-gathering economies of the highland and savanna zones, and specialist fishing settlements around the lake margins. Direct archaeological evidence for plant utilization in this region until at least 500BCE (northern Ethiopia) is exceptionally sparse; this could be a simple question of assuming negative evidence, or may point to problems concerning the preservation of African-origin cereals. It is certain that these peoples were, to a degree, beginning to manage their economic resources and plan their resource procurement strategies. Essentially, the foundations of the later eastern African agricultural economies were being built on these local protointensive, or "preadaptive," hunter-gatherer economies.

From a social aspect, the wide-ranging raw material procurement strategies in certain areas may point to the building of incipient trade/exchange links (Barut 1994); this would certainly be reflected in the widespread ornamental use of beads, and the cases of human burial and rock art representations may point to a deeper ideological sense in these hunter-gatherer peoples than we have given credit for. What remains clear is that a great deal more research on this fascinating period is required, with special emphasis on the retrieval of early plant material, well-dated cultural sequences, and integrated programs of palaeo-environmental research.

NIALL FINNERAN

See also: **Permanent Settlement, Early; Rock Art: Eastern Africa.**

Further Reading

Barut, S. "Middle and Later Stone Age Lithic Technology and Land Use in East African Savannahs." *African Archaeological Review*, no. 12 (1994): 43–72.
———. "The Upper Pleistocene and Early Holocene Prehistory of the Horn of Africa." *African Archaeology Review*, no. 4 (1984): 41–82.

Brooks, S., and P. Robertshaw. "The Glacial Maximum in Tropical Africa: 22,000–12,000 BP." In *The World at 18,000 BP*, edited by Clive Gamble and Olga Soffer. London: Unwin and Hyman, 1990.

Clark, J. D. *Prehistoric Cultures of the Horn of Africa.* Cambridge: Cambridge University Press, 1954.

Marean, C. "Hunter to Herder: Large Mammal Remains from the Hunter-Gatherer Occupation (Early Ovicaprine) at Enkapune Ya Moto Rockshelter, Central Rift Valley, Kenya." *African Archaeology Review*, no. 10 (1992): 65–128.

Phillipson, D. *African Archaeology*, 2nd ed. Cambridge: Cambridge University Press, 1993.

———. *The Later Prehistory of Eastern and Southern Africa.* London: Heinemann/New York: Africana, 1977.

Robertshaw, P. "Environment and Culture in the Late Quaternary of Eastern Africa: A Critique of Some Correlations." In *Prehistoric Cultures and Environments in the Late Quaternary of Africa*, edited by John Bower and David Lubell. British Archaeological Reports, international series no. 405 Oxford: British Archaeological Reports, 1988.

Stewart, K. M. *Fishing Sites of North and East Africa in the Late Pleistocene and Holocene.* British Archaeological Reports, international series 521. Oxford: British Archaeological Reports, 1989.

Stone Age (Later): Nile Valley

Long before the first human beings existed, the Nile River Valley was a major route by which Lake Victoria drained through the longest riverbed in Africa into the Mediterranean far to the north. From the highlands of equatorial Africa, where today Uganda, Kenya, and Tanzania are located, it eventually coursed through thick vegetation and swamps before reaching a series of rapids known as cataracts where ancient Nubia would in time emerge. Continuing its descent through arid lands where Upper Egypt would emerge, it eventually entered the delta that would become Lower Egypt before emptying into the sea. Long known for its unique importance to the unfolding of human evolution, Eastern Africa, including the Nile Valley, is equally important to the study of human prehistory.

Corresponding with an extended period of heavy rainfall widely known as the Mousterian Subpluvial between 50,000 and 25,000 years ago, mountains of Ethiopia's central plateau where Lake Tana is located captured so much water that for the first time this lake developed its own course of drainage into the Nile. After this second source for the Nile came into being, a distinction was eventually made between the so-called White Nile flowing from Lake Victoria and the so-called Blue Nile cascading from the mountains of Ethiopia. It is the river valley north of where the Blue and White Niles have their confluence that is the focus of this article about the late Stone Age of the Nile Valley.

In this particular area, the late Stone Age extends roughly from 30,000BCE to 5,500BCE. Alternatively, it is also known as the Upper Palaeolithic or late Palaeolithic stage in the cultural development of ancient Nubia and Egypt. The unfolding of late Stone Age cultural innovations in this valley, while pivotal to an understanding of prehistoric civilization in ancient Nubia and Egypt, also has relevance to our understanding of the emergence of civilization globally.

Though by the late Stone Age our ancestors were anatomically modern human beings, their subsistence remained centered on the foraging of wild plants and wild animals, also known as hunting, gathering, and fishing. Associated with contrasting environments, resources, and biodiversity within the valley, toolmaking evolved so as to reflect considerable variation from one Nilotic subregion to another. While relative changes in patterns of toolmaking during the late Stone Age were many, probably none was more important overall than the increasing emphasis placed on the manufacture of small stone tools classified as microliths. More specifically, the increased emphasis on greater reliance on microlithic blades and small projective points that were sometimes hafted on shafts represented a major technological advance during this stage of prehistoric subsistence and development.

As early as the middle Stone Age, the Nile Valley had been home to an array of coexisting cultures, as illustrated on the Kom Ombo Plain just south of ancient Egypt. However around 30,000 years ago, when the late Stone Age was beginning, the coexistence of different traditions near each other became more widespread. In large parts of Upper Egypt and Nubia people developed localized specialization in exploiting new plants and riverine foods with microliths as large mammals on which their ancestors had depended became increasingly scarce. Overall, all such specialization merely represented variation within a pattern of broad spectrum foraging that was the focus of subsistence throughout the valley.

In addition to the emergence of Sebilain, Silsilian, and Sebekian stonemaking or lithic traditions, by 17,000BCE the Fakhurian and two subtypes of the Idfuan, one of which was well represented at Wadi Halfan, were also apparent. Similar innovations also took place at the Dabarosa Complex, at some eight or so camps reflecting Gemaian culture in Upper Nubia, and at Ballanan sites in Lower Nubia. During the period from about 14,000 to 12,000 years ago, other innovations tied to the needs of particular subregions became apparent in traditions known as Qadan, Afian, and Isnan. While during this same period, Nubians at Jabel Sahaba manufactured bows and arrows, it was only some three to five millennia later that bows and arrows were manufactured in Europe.

Although foraging remained the dominant subsistence pattern throughout the valley's late Stone Age, some evidence points in the direction of indigenous experimentation with plant domestication in the Isna area as early as 16,000 years ago that may have been the earliest such activity in the world. Though any such precocious experimentation was not sustained here, during the still early period of between 11,000 and 9,000 years ago, other evidence points in the same direction. That Nilotic foragers did this is suggested by grinding stones used for plant preparation both in the Arkinian (10,580 years ago) and Shamarkian (8860 years ago) industries just north of the Second Cataract in the center of Nubia. Arkin 8 finds in northern Sudan are also outstanding for evidence of the most ancient house-like shelters ever discovered in the valley, in fact, the second most ancient ever discovered in Africa.

Between around 7000 and 6000BCE, when heavy rainfall enabled the Nile to deposit copious amounts of rich silt along its banks, residents of Nubia and Upper Egypt, whose numbers by this time were augmented by Saharan immigrants with a history of herding, used the changed environment both to expand herding and to supplement herding and foraging with farming. In these ways, indigenous herding and experimentation with farming in the valley as well as the Western Desert helped to establish the foundation of later civilization that would be based on agriculture.

There remains much to be learned about the transition from Epipalaeolithic lifeways like those at El Kabian and in Badari villages to Predynastic cultures that would follow, but at least in the south some important continuities are suggested at Bir Kiseiba and Nabta Playa in southwestern Egypt before 6000BCE and at Nubia's Catfish Cave around 5110BCE. While sustained agriculture associated with a truly Neolithic way of life, including settled farming communities, has been confirmed in the Nile Valley from only around 5,000BCE or in the early predynastic era, some indigenous antecedents already existed in Upper Egypt and in Nubia. In northern Egypt, in contrast, the predynastic era made its early appearance in Merimde Beni-Salama and Fayum A developments thanks largely to domesticates introduced from nearby southwestern Asia.

Alongside this north-south contrast, as the late Stone Age gave way to the succeeding predynastic period, some trends were shared throughout the valley. These included more toolmaking through polishing as well as earlier chipping methods, large increases in the proportion of microliths and composite tools manufactured, and the emergence of larger and more permanent communities relying more on farming than foraging and having considerable investment in storage facilities.

STEFAN GOODWIN

Further Reading

Hassan, Fekri A. (ed.). *Droughts, Food and Culture: Ecological Change and Food Security in Africa's Later Prehistory.* New York: Kluwer Academic/Plenum, 2002.

———. "Prehistoric Settlements along the Main Nile." In *The Sahara and the Nile: Quaternary Environments and Prehistoric Occupation in Northern Africa*, edited by M. A. J. Williams and H. Faure. Rotterdam: Balkema, 1980.

Hoffman, Michael A. *Egypt before the Pharaohs: The Prehistoric Foundations of Egyptian Civilization.* New York: Alfred A. Knopf, 1979.

Midant-Reynes, Béatrix. *The Prehistory of Egypt: From the First Egyptians to the First Pharaohs.* Oxford: Blackwell, 1999.

Wendorf, Fred (ed.). *Prehistory of Nubia.* Dallas: Southern Methodist University Press, 1968.

Wendorf, Fred, and Romuald Schild (eds.). *Prehistory of the Nile Valley (Studies in Archeology).* New York: Academic Press, 1976.

Wetterstrom, Wilma. "Foraging and Farming in Egypt: The Transition from Hunting and Gathering to Horticulture in the Nile Valley." In *The Archaeology of Africa: Food, Metals, and Towns*, edited by Thurstan Shaw et al. London: Routledge, 1995.

Stone Age (Later): Sahara and North Africa

During the early Stone Age, humans had reached the Sahara, but their remains in this region are few, and we know them almost exclusively through surface finds of diverse stone tools. These lithic assemblages have been given names borrowed from European prehistory: *Lower Palaeolithic* and *Acheulean*. These terms only point to typologic analogies, not to actual links with European groups. Some bones of *Homo erectus* accompany these finds.

However, toward the end of Palaeolithic times, a specifically African group was emerging: the Aterian. Its tools were smaller (5 to 10 centimeters), and still lacked blades; their exact function is unknown. It is clear that the Aterian moved in groups of nomad hunters. Remains of their campsites have been found from the Atlantic coast to the Nile Valley, in all regions of the Maghrib, and through the southern Sahara (Mauritania, northern Mali, Air, and southern Tibesti). Aterian sites are particularly numerous in the Mediterranean region Algeria, Morocco, and Mauritania. However, the cultural features they have in common are very few, except for a degree of homogeneity in lithic assemblages.

Two sites, Dar es Soltan and Temara (near Rabat, Morocco), have provided bones of Aterian individuals. Contrary to accepted opinion, which linked Aterians to Neanderthals, it was eventually discovered that these bones were attributable to the "modern" physical type *Homo sapiens sapiens*. The Aterian developed during several successive wet episodes between *c.*175,000 and 70,000BP. A long, severe arid episode, the Postaterian Hyperarid Phase, followed in the Sahara, which was devoid of fauna and humans until around 9000BCE.

It was only around 15,000BCE that other populations, called the epipalaeolithic, appeared in the

Mahgrib, characterized by new lithic traditions. The earliest epipalaeolithic group is the Iberomaurusian. They were initially given this name because they were thought to be linked with Iberian groups, though this theory has since been discredited. The main feature of the Iberomaurusian is a profusion of small blades, 2 to 5 centimeters long, that are often retouched on one edge. They equipped diverse multifunction tools, adapted to the needs of this group of seminomad hunter-gatherers. The remains of both men and women are marked by a distinctive practice, the meaning of which is unknown: the upper incisors were extracted at around 12 to 15 years of age. Their physical type is fairly uniform: the Mechta el-Arbi or Mechta-Afalou type, which refers to a tall, robust man, close to the European Cro-Magnon type, with which it was contemporaneous. Iberomaurusian sites are scattered in Algeria on the Mediterranean coast, and in Morocco along the Atlantic coast, as well as in the inland mountains. They are not found in the central Sahara, which was in this period still uninhabited

The end of the Iberomaurusians is obscure. They disappeared around 10,000–8000BCE, when the lithic tradition of the Capsian, also epipalaeolithic, took their place. One view as to the demise of the one group and rise of the other values lithic typology, setting it in the position of a major cultural feature for defining the identity of ethnic groups. This theory posits the Capsians as an ethnic group of newcomers, probably arriving from the Middle East, and driving out and replacing the Iberomaurusians. However, other scholars only describe a trivial evolution in the technology of stone tools within diverse ethnic groups, who were simply at approximately the same stage as far as lithic typology is concerned. The latter position was strengthened by systematic studies conducted by a Canadian team (Lubell, Sheppard, and Jackes 1984) on Capsian sites in the Constantine region (Algeria). They could show that, even if only lithic assemblages are taken into account, statistical differences between some layers with exclusively Capsian tools are larger than differences between Iberomaurusian and Capsian sets considered in bulk.

Besides small blades, the Capsian sets include genuine blades (about 5–10 centimeters long) and also geometric microliths (triangles, trapezes, crescents). The latter have small dimensions, often of 1 to 2 centimeters, and are finely chipped. Adornment objects, notably made from fragments of ostrich egg shell, are also found, sometimes decorated with geometric patterns.

The Mechta el-Arbi physical type is still frequent among the Capsians, but types similar to current Mediterranean people were increasing in number. Capsian sites date from 10,000 to 8000BCE and 5000 to 4000BCE. The sites are mainly found in southern Tunisia, the Constantine region, and the eastern Saharan.

Animal domestication and plant cultivation were still unknown, and therefore the Capsian were classified as a group still belonging to the epipalaeolithic. Southward, the Capsian assemblages are not found beyond the Saharan Atlas. However, toward 9000BCE the Saharan space, which the Postaterian Hyperarid Phase had cleared, became alive again. Rains were coming back, and the period 9000 to 6000BCE is known as the Great Wet Phase of the beginning of the Holocene era. Fauna and humans repopulated massifs and even the plains. Groups that used tools of the epipalaeolithic type, diverse and small in size, are now perceived throughout the great plains of the eastern Sahara, Tibesti, Tassili, Hoggar, Air, and around the large lakes of northern Mali. Groups of nomad hunters were living in the mountains, mainly hunting Barbary sheep.Throughout the whole southern Sahara and current Sahel, from the Sudanese Nile to Mauritania, the rains of the Great Wet Phase maintained an abundance of rivers and lakes, where sedentary populations of fishermen and hippopotamus hunters were active. This group, linked with sources of water, has been called Aqualithic.

As early as 8500BCE, pottery appeared at El Adam in the western Egyptian Desert and at Tagalagal in Air. The domestication of cattle occurred later, perhaps as early as 8000BCE at a site in the western Egyptian Desert, Nabta, but more certainly around 5500BCE in other Saharan regions.

The Neolithic replaced the Stone Age. Its earlier phase, characterized by the presence of pottery but still a lack of animal domestication, is called the Saharo-Sudanese Neolithic. Toward 6000BCE, the Great Wet Phase came to its end, and the vast Saharan areas gradually became the great desert we know today. However, between 5000 and 3000BCE, a last wet fluctuation called the Neolithic Wet Phase supported the continuing existence of a steppe, which allowed the rise of the earliest pastoral societies and the birth of Saharan rock art. The era of the ancient hunter-gatherers of the prehistoric times had come to an end.

A. MUZZOLINI

See also: **Rock Art: Saharan.**

Further Reading

Camps, G. *Les civilisations préhistoriques de l'Afrique du Nord et du Sahara.* Paris: Doin, 1974.

Gabriel, B. "Die östliche Libysche Wüste im Jungquartär." *Berliner geographische Studien no. 19.* Berlin: Institut für Geogr. der Technic. Univ., 1986.

Gautier, A."Prehistoric Men and Cattle in North Africa: A Dearth of Data and a Surfeit of Models." In *Prehistory of Arid North Africa,* edited by A. E. Close. Dallas: Southern Methodist University, 1987.

Lubell, D., P. Sheppard, and M. Jackes. "Continuity in the Epipalaeolithic of Northern Africa with Emphasis on the Maghreb." In *Advances in World Archaeology*, vol. 3. New York: Academic Press, 1984.

MacBurney, C. B. M. *The Haua Fteah (Cyrenaica) and the Stone Age of the South-East Mediterranean.* Cambridge: Cambridge University Press, 1967.

Phillipson, D. W. *African Archaeology.* Cambridge: Cambridge University Press, 1985.

Sheppard, P. J. *The Capsian of North Africa: Stylistic Variation in Stone Tool Assemblages.* British Archaeological Reports, international series 353. Oxford: British Archaeological Reports, 1981.

Wendorf, F., and R. Schild, "The Middle Palaeolithic of North Africa: A Status Report." In *New Light on the Northeast African Past*, edited by F. Klees and R. Kuper. Cologne: Heinrich Barth Institut, 1992.Wendorf, F., R. Schild, and A. E. Close, *Cattle-keepers of the Eastern Sahara: The Neolithic of Bir Kiseiba.* Dallas: Department of Anthropology, Southern Methodist University, 1984.

Stone Age, Later: Western Africa

The West African later Stone Age (hereafter, LSA) covers a wide variety of assemblages that include one or more of the following: microliths, large flake tools, core tools such as axes and picks (flaked or ground), bone tools, pottery, and remains of domesticated plants and animals. Generally speaking, sites with microlithic or Levallois flaked stone artifacts are earliest (from c.6,000 to 13,000 years ago), followed by the addition of pottery (between 4,500 and 6,000 years ago) and the appearance of domestic millet and cattle, sheep and goats in a number of sites in the northern half of Sub-Saharan West Africa (between 4000 and 3000 years ago). These three aspects of the LSA cannot be considered to be time-successive stages, as there is evidence for contemporaneous sites with and without food production, for example. Only in the past decade has it been realized that the adoption of new tool and subsistence technologies may have occurred in a complex mosaic fashion rather than along a simple advancing front. Thus, patterns of change and chronology cannot be extrapolated from one documented site to an entire region or beyond, as used to be common practice. Recent research focuses on documenting the range of sites within regions and describing variability in tool kit and subsistence. In the few areas where this kind of research is underway, a detailed picture of LSA lifeways has begun to emerge. For much of West Africa, however, our understanding of this period rests on a handful of excavations at sites widely separated in space and time.

The LSA developed against a backdrop of significant climate change. From 12,000 to 8000 years ago, conditions were much cooler and wetter than at present, and perennial rivers flowed in the Sahara. Between 8000 and 7000 years ago, there is evidence for a dry period, the intensity of which varied from region to region. Renewed wet conditions after 7000 years ago appear to be correlated with the spread of pastoralism in the Sahara. Another period of desertification began around 4500 years ago, and within two millennia, rainfall and vegetation zones had reached approximately modern positions.

Microlithic Late Stone Age

Early LSA assemblages typically contain a variety of small flake tools, with at least one blunted edge and a sharp edge that were probably hafted for use. Where good quality stone was available, these microliths occur in a limited number of standardized geometric shapes, such as crescents and trapezoids. In many places, however, the available raw material was a poor quality quartz, which may account for the high proportion of unstandardized small flakes at these sites. Both kinds of microlith may be present in a single assemblage. At a few sites, larger flake tools were made using a Levallois technique, and it is not clear what the relationship between large flake tool and microlithic tool users might be. Notably, there seems to be little effort to procure better quality stone through travel or exchange during this period. At Shum Laka in Cameroon, one of the few sites where raw material studies have been done, obsidian, though present within 5 kilometers of the site, does not increase in frequency through the many millennia of occupation, nor is it used to produce more standardized or more efficient tools with less waste.

All groups at this early period (6,000–13,000 years ago) were hunter-gatherers living in small bands whose archaeological traces are known mainly from rock shelters and caves. These groups likely recolonized northern West Africa from the south after the end (c.12,000 years ago) of a cold, hyperarid period that pushed the desert margin 500 kilometers south of its present location.

Ceramic Late Stone Age

Pottery first appeared in Africa in the central Sahara 9000 to 10,000 years ago. In West Africa, ceramics and ground stone axes were added to microlithic toolkits between 5,000 and 6,000 years ago. At some sites, large numbers of hoe- and pick-like core tools and axes are present. There have been various attempts to assign these microlithic and core tool assemblages to different "cultures" used by groups with different ways of life. Early researchers reasoned that the axes, for example, were for forest clearance, and the hoes for cultivation of yams. These large tool sites were thus assigned to the "Guinea Neolithic." More recent research emphasizes the co-occurrence of core and microlithic tools in many sites, with an increase in large tools through time. This may in fact be related to the cultivation of crops, such as yams, that are difficult to detect archaeologically. Although there is no hard evidence for domesticated plants during this period, the increasing exploitation of oil rich seeds and oil palm nuts around 5000 years ago at sites such as Bosumpra and Kintampo (Ghana) suggests subsistence intensification. At the important site of Shum Laka (Cameroon), however, a subsistence economy based on hunting forest hog and dwarf forest buffalo continued without apparent change after the introduction of pottery around 6000 years ago. For English-speaking archaeologists, this lack of subsistence change provides a powerful reason for not automatically identifying as Neolithic all sites with pottery. French-speaking archaeologists, in contrast, consider the ceramic LSA to be "Neolithic." It is not until around 4000 years ago that we have definite evidence for domestic plants and animals, a shift to greater sedentism in some areas, and increased involvement in regional and long-distance exchange.

Food Production and the Neolithic

Between 3000 and 4000 years ago, subsistence diversified in many northern regions of West Africa with the introduction of domestic livestock by herding populations moving out of the increasingly arid Sahara. Sites with domestic cattle and sheep or goat became concentrated in southerly, well-watered environs, such as the Tichitt Lake plain (Mauritania), the Tilemsi Valley (Mali), the floodplain of the Middle Niger (Mali), and the Lake Chad plain (Chad, Cameroon, northeastern Nigeria). Arrival of domestic livestock prior to the appearance of domestic plants (Pennisetum millet) is documented on the western margin of Lake Chad, where a pastoral economy that included hunting, fishing and collecting wild cereals was established five centuries before the appearance of domestic millet. Along the Middle Niger, several different, partly contemporaneous subsistence economies may have coexisted between 2,500 and 3,500 years ago, including semisedentary hunter-gatherer groups specializing in the exploitation of aquatic resources such as shellfish and fish; mobile hunter-gatherers; and agropastoralists with stock and domestic millet. Farther south, small sheep or goat appear approximately 3,600 years ago as new elements in a continuing hunting-gathering economy in the Kintampo region of central Ghana. The continued importance of wild resources long after the appearance of food production is a recurring pattern in West Africa.

A number of new trends accompany the shift to food production in West Africa. There is a rise in ornamentation as stone and shell beads, stone arm rings, bracelets, and pendants become common after 4,000 years ago. Trade and exchange networks expand, such that raw materials from sources 250–400 kilometers away are present at many sites. Labor specialization is suggested by the occurrence of stone-and-shell bead-working ateliers, as well as stone ax quarry sites, where roughouts were produced. Residential mobility decreases through time, attested by an increase in the quantity of domestic material deposited, the appearance of storage pits, and a shift in some areas from thatch or wattle structures to more durable wattle and daub, banco, and, on the Tichitt escarpment where it exfoliates naturally, stone. House groupings within hamlets and villages have been mapped in the Kintampo region (Ghana) and on the plateaus around Tichitt in southeastern Mauritania. In this latter area, some arrangements of dry-stone walled residential enclosures form very large aggregations of over 200 compounds.

The large range of settlement sizes at Tichitt has prompted hypotheses of centralized political organization and the existence of a vast site hierarchy. One of the difficulties in evaluating these interpretations is the lack of agreement by different researchers over the interpretation of chronology at these settlements. Additionally, the identification of the elites expected in a chiefdom or state has proven elusive at Tichitt, because imported "prestige" items are extremely rare in domestic contexts and no burials have yet been excavated. While big and small residential compounds do exist, differences in compound size are hard to interpret without information on which parts of the settlement were occupied contemporaneously. Some settlements may have been occupied for over a millennium. Additional research to resolve chronological issues will be necessary before the interpretation of sociopolitical organization at Tichitt can advance much farther. A similar set of issues hampers the interpretation of some quite extensive LSA sites in the Méma region of the Middle Niger. There, as in several other regions where burials have been excavated, lack of grave goods suggests that social stratification had not yet developed. However, a larger excavated sample may, in the future, change the current picture substantially and will do much to solidify current assessments.

SUSAN KEECH MCINTOSH

Further Reading

Grove, A. T. "Africa's Climate in the Holocene." In *The Archaeology of Africa: Foods, Metals and Towns*, edited by C. T. Shaw, P. Sinclair, B. Andah, and A. Okpoko. London: Routledge, 1993.

MacDonald, K. C. "Korounkorokalé Revisited: The Pays Mandé and the West African Microlithic Technocomplex." *African Archaeological Review*, no. 14 (1997): 161–200.

———. "The Late Stone Age and Neolithic Cultures of West Africa and the Sahara." In *Encyclopedia of Precolonial Africa*, edited by J. Vogel. Walnut Creek, Altamira Press, 1997.

MacDonald, K. C., and P. Allsworth-Jones. "A Reconsideration of the West African Macrolithic Conundrum: New Factory Sites and an Associated Settlement in the Vallée du Serpent, Mali." *African Archaeological Review*, no. 12 (1994): 73–104.

McIntosh, S. "West African Neolithic." In the *Encyclopedia of Prehistory: Africa*, edited by P. Peregrine and M. Ember. New York: Kluwer Academic/Plenum, 2001.

McIntosh, S., and R. "From Stone to Metal: New Perspectives on the Later Prehistory of West Africa." *Journal of World Prehistory* 2, no. 1 (1988): 89–133.

Neumann, K. "Early Plant Food Production in the West African Sahel: New Evidence." In *The Exploitation of Plant Resources in Ancient Africa*, edited by M. van der Veen. New York: Kluwer Academic/Plenum, 1999.

Shaw, C. T. "Hunters, Gatherers and First Farmers in West Africa," In *Hunters, Gatherers and First Farmers beyond Europe*, edited by J. V. S. Megaw. Leicester: Leicester University Press, 1977.

Stahl, A. "Intensification in the West African Late Stone Age: A View from Central Ghana." In *The Archaeology of Africa: Foods, Metals, and Towns*, edited by T. Shaw, P. Sinclair, B. Andah, and A. Okpoko. London: Routledge, 1993.

Sudan, nineteenth century.

Structural Adjustment: *See* World Bank, International Monetary Fund, and Structural Adjustment.

Sudan People's Liberation Army: *See* Garang, John, and the Sudan People's Liberation Party (SPLA).

Sudan: Turco-Egyptian Period, 1820–1885

Between 1820 and 1885, most of present-day Sudan was under Turco-Egyptian colonial rule. The annexation of the country to Egypt was begun in 1820–1821 by Muhammad 'Ali, the Ottoman viceroy of Egypt, and later completed by his grandson Khedive Isma'il. Muhammad 'Ali's primary motives in undertaking the conquest were to obtain black slaves for a new army and to find new sources of revenue to finance his projects in Egypt. It is also probable that he wanted to crush the survivors of the Mamluk massacre, who had established themselves at Dongola.

The invading force, under the command of Muhammad 'Ali's son Isma'il, occupied Dongola and scattered the Mamluks without serious opposition. Indeed, in his relentless march southward, Isma'il encountered no serious military resistance, except two pitched battles with the Shayqiya. The Funj, already weakened by internal strife and intrigue, capitulated without a fight. The last of their sultans, Badi VI, made the submission in person before Isma'il at Wad Medani. Meanwhile, after taking Dongola and the Shayqiya country, Muhammad 'Ali sent his son-in-law Muhammad Khusraw ad-Daramali, the Bey Daftardar, to Kordofan. At Bara, the Fur governor of the province, the Maqdum Musallim, was defeated and the Daftardar entered El-Obeid unopposed on August 20, 1821.

Having attained the military objectives of the conquest, Isma'il turned his attention to consolidating the conquests. The capital was moved from Sennar to Wad Medani and a rudimentary administration established. In late October 1822, however, he was assassinated at Shendi while en route to Cairo. The incident triggered widespread rebellion among the riverine Sudanese, who had already become restive because of an oppressive new tax system. The rebellion was eventually crushed, but at high cost in life and property.

As its position steadily grew stronger, the regime added new territories to the original conquests: Kassala and Suakin (1840), Equatoria (1871), Bahr al-Ghazal (1873) and Darfur (1874). A highly centralized bureaucracy, headed by a governor general or *hukumdar* directly answerable to Cairo, was developed to administer the country. Cairo also depended on the army to maintain its authority in the Sudan. The troops consisted of the *jihadiya*, of slave origin, and Shayqiya irregulars, who replaced the Turkish and Albanian irregulars of Isma'il's army. Both served the Turco-Egyptian regime with devotion and loyalty until the end of its tenure.

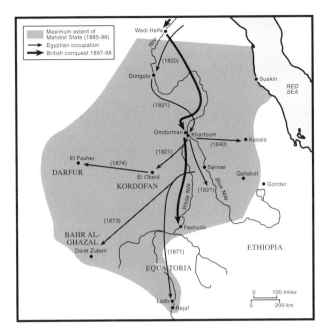

Sudan.

Their position consolidated, the Egyptians proceeded to exploit Sudan's natural resources. Considerable sums of money were spent on gold prospecting in the Fazughli area and around Jabal Shaybun in the Nuba Mountains, but nothing came of the search. In agriculture some success was achieved. From the early years of the conquest, Egyptian experts were sent to the Sudan to teach new methods to Sudanese farmers. The strategy paid off. The irrigation system was improved and new basin lands along the Nile were brought into use. The result was a marked expansion in the area of cultivable land available to the riverine communities. Pests, plagues, and locusts were effectively combated, and experiments with new crops led to the successful growing of sugarcane and cotton. Veterinary services were extended to the Sudan, as was expertise for the preservation of hides and skins. Coupled with the construction of watering and feeding places along the principal routes, these measures facilitated the export of cattle, camels, and hides to Egypt.

Livestock exports to Egypt were only part of the growing volume of trade between the two countries made possible by the improved security on trade routes. The Egyptian government was anxious to expand it in order to generate more revenue. Partly because of this, steamer services were introduced on the Nile and linked to the Egyptian railway system. Trade goods could now flow both ways with relative ease. The development of an electric telegraph system, with a network of up to 3,000 miles of telegraph line by 1880, further boosted trade since it improved contacts between merchants. Trade was aided also by the

construction of warehouses along the main trade routes to which goods bound for Egypt were first collected before shipping northward.

Much of the profits from this expanding economy went to the Egyptian state which, between 1821 and 1838, had an exclusive monopoly of Sudan's external trade. A small number of private traders—Sudanese, Egyptians and some Turks—prospered, too, through selling to and buying from the state trading company and participating in domestic commerce. After 1838, European traders entered the field and established themselves in Khartoum, where the presence of foreign consulates served to support and protect their commercial interests. The main attraction for them was ivory, readily available in abundance in the southern Sudan. The quest to obtain it inevitably led in 1839–1841 to the opening of the White Nile route to the south.

Traders and missionaries soon flocked southward to exploit the natural and human resources of the southern Sudan. The traders were the first to go. They organized regular commercial expeditions to the south in search of ivory and made handsome profits. Missionaries followed later and established a mission station for the Roman Catholics at Gondokoro in 1851; but death from fever and growing resentment and hostility among the Bari forced its eventual closure in 1860.

Bari hostility was partly the result of deteriorating relationship between the southerners and the traders caused by a set of interrelated circumstances. As nearby sources of ivory were depleted and the traders became increasingly dependent on intermediaries in their search for it, the Bari demanded higher prices for less tusks. At the same time, rivalry between Turkish officials and European traders and their unscrupulous manipulation of promising middlemen like Nyigilo destroyed Bari trust in both groups of intruders. This in turn undermined all efforts to establish a proper basis for a mutually beneficial commercial relationship. To compound the situation, the invaders adopted a hostile contemptuous attitude toward the southerners, regarding them as racially inferior. Henceforth, violent confrontation could hardly be avoided.

With ivory still much sought after but its search blocked by the stalemate that had developed between the invaders and the southerners, the traders began to acquire it by force. From zaribas (fortified bases) established away from the Nile stations they raided surrounding peoples for grain and cattle to exchange for ivory. The relationship between the southerners and the invaders had begun to fray into violence, which spread outward from the advancing frontier like a whirlwind. Trade and robbery had been fused together and a policy of divide and rule adopted to perpetuate it.

The extension of the trading frontier into the interior spurred demands for slaves to supply the domestic needs of the trading communities. Moreover, faced with rising expenditure, decreasing profits, and high credit interests, White Nile traders soon realized that slaves could be used as a form of payment to their employees to reduce the actual cost of their services. As in raids for grain and cattle, European traders took the lead in the taking of slaves. The result was that a secondary slave trade developed as a by-product of the ivory trade. By 1864 all traders on the White Nile combined the export of slaves with that of ivory and zaribas could be found scattered throughout Equatoria.

A similar sequence of violence and conflict was taking place about the same time in the Bahr al-Ghazal under the auspices of Arab traders. Like their counterparts on the White Nile, the Bahr al-Ghazal traders constructed zaribas from which they traded in slaves. But while the White Nile traders exported their slaves by way of the Nile, they channeled theirs overland through Darfur and Kordofan. The trade was so lucrative that large firms soon emerged whose powerful and wealthy owners became virtual rulers of the areas in which they traded.

Viceroy Muhammad Sa'id had begun to take steps to stop this ignominious trade, but it was only Khedive Isma'il who exerted the most concerted efforts toward that goal. In 1864 a river police force was established on the Nile at Fashoda to intercept vessels carrying slaves. A heavy capitation tax on personnel was also levied on the traders' employees as was a property tax on their zaribas. These measures reduced, but did not end, the White Nile slave trade. Isma'il then decided that annexation of the Southern Sudan was the answer to the problem. Consequently two expeditions, one under Muhammad al-Hilali and the other commanded by Sir Samuel Baker, were respectively dispatched to the Bahr al-Ghazal and Equatoria to extend khedivial rule there and to suppress the slave trade. Both expeditions met with failure. Hilali was killed by the most powerful of the traders in the Bahr al-Ghazal, al-Zubayr Rahma Mansur, in the inevitable conflict that ensued between the Turco-Egyptian forces and the traders. Baker lacked tact and statesmanship and quarreled with almost everyone: governor general Ja'afar Mazhar Pasha, the slave traders and the southerners whose interests he was supposed to protect. His only achievement was the establishment of a few isolated military garrisons.

Baker's successor as governor of Equatoria, Charles George Gordon, achieved some success in suppressing the slave trade. By declaring the collection of ivory a government monopoly, banning the importation of firearms and ammunition, and breaking up private armies, he put the traders out of business. Nonetheless,

they remained in Equatoria sulking at the antislavery policy and waiting to foment trouble at the earliest opportunity.

Meanwhile, after Hilali's death, Khedive Isma'il constituted Bahr al-Ghazal as a province and appointed Zubayr as its governor (December 1873). Zubayr eventually went on to defeat and occupy Darfur for Egypt (October 1874) before his unexpected incarceration in 1876 while on a visit to Cairo. The resulting anarchy in the province added to the serious problems facing the khedive in the Sudan. The treasury was collapsing, exhausted by expenditure on wars in Abyssinia and Darfur and the wadi Halfa railway project. Desperate measures imposed to increase revenue, including the suspension of all salaries, alienated government officials. To make matters worse, Gordon's zeal as governor general in continuing the antislavery policy pushed the traders to support rebellions that broke out in the Bahr al-Ghazal, Darfur and Kordofan.

Though all three revolts were suppressed, Isma'il was nevertheless the loser for he lost the all important struggle to avoid bankruptcy. In June 1879, bowing to European pressure, Sultan 'Abd al-Hamid II deposed him. Shortly thereafter, Gordon resigned as governor general of the Sudan. His successor was Muhammad Ra'uf Pasha, a man who had served under both Baker and Gordon. It was under his administration that the Mahdist Revolution broke out in June 1881.

KENNETH OKENY

See Also: **Egypt: Muhammad Ali, 1805–1849: Imperial Expansion.**

Further Reading

Gray, Richard. *A History of the Southern Sudan, 1839–1889.* London: Oxford University Press, 1961.

Hill, Richard. *Egypt in the Sudan, 1820–1881.* London: Oxford University Press, 1959.

Holt, Peter Malcolm. *A Modern History of the Sudan from the Funj Sultanate to the Present Day.* New York: Grove Press, 1961.

Holt, P. M. (ed.). *Studies in the History of the Near East.* London: Oxford University Press, 1973.

Ibrahim, H. A. "The Sudan in the Nineteenth Century." In *General History of Africa,* vol. 6, *Africa in the Nineteenth Century until the 1880s,* edited by J. F. A. Ade Ajayi. Paris: UNESCO, 1989.

Sudan: Mahdist State, 1881–1898

Literally, *Mahdi* means "the guided one." In Islam, it refers to one chosen and guided by God to restore the community to its pristine purity (as it existed in the days of the Prophet Muhammad). Mahdism is thus the Islamic equivalent of the Judeo-Christian expectation of a messiah, a "deliverer" who would restore the "golden age."

The Mahdist revolt in the Sudan was a by-product of Egyptian imperialism. Muhammad 'Ali, who governed Egypt (1805–1848) is known for his expansive Westernization policy, which overhauled the country's economy and society. A former army officer, he considered a new military the cornerstone of his reforms. An Albanian, Muhammad 'Ali initially considered Egyptians unreliable as his soldiers. Motivated by the need for conscripts for his military and by a general need for gold, he invaded the Sudan in 1820. Within a year, much of the Sudan was under Egyptian jurisdiction. In 1822, Khartoum was founded as the headquarters of Egyptian operations; in 1830, the first Egyptian governor of the Sudan was installed there. The military success did not yield the 20,000–30,000 conscripts Ali had anticipated. Many Sudanese died resisting the Egyptians; transportation difficulties resulted in the deaths of many thousands more before they reached Egypt; and of the 20,000 who reached Aswan, only 3,000 remained alive by 1824. The hopes for gold were similarly disappointed because the deposits had long been exhausted.

The Egyptians were more successful in improving agricultural productivity in the Sudan. But this was for Egypt's benefit. Not only did Egypt control all external trade, considerable quantities of Sudanese products were also sent there. The severity of the taxes imposed on the Sudanese was only matched by their disillusionment. The end of Ali's tenure in 1848 brought no relief to the Sudanese. Thus, over the years, Sudanese resentment deepened and became the basis of popular support for the Mahdist movement. The antislavery campaign of Ismail, who came to office in Egypt in 1863, was the last straw. Slavery had long been the basis of the economies of large portions of the Sudan, which meant that there was a powerful mercantile class with a vested interest in it. Matters were further complicated by the brutal methods employed to eradicate slavery, and Ismail's extensive reliance on Europeans for his Sudanese operations. For the Sudanese who were mostly Muslims, Egyptian overrule was thus hardly distinguishable from Christian domination.

By 1879, much of the Sudanese population had been totally alienated from the Egyptian administration. Muhammad Ahmad provided them the framework for the ventilation of their anti-Egyptian feelings. On June 29, 1881, Ahmad proclaimed himself the Mahdi. Although his movement was cast in religious idioms, its causal dimensions were complex.

Ahmad was born in 1844. His early formal education, like that of his peers in the Sudan, followed the basic Islamic pattern. By 1861, his religious interests had led him to a Sufi brotherhood, the Sammaniya. By 1870, when he settled at Aba, an island 160 miles south of Khartoum, Ahmad had become a highly regarded religious leader. Like other religious leaders, he urged a return to the ideal Islamic life; but he also preached that a holy war upon the Egyptians and their local agents was one of the means to this end. This way, Ahmad attracted a large following and forged the diverse strands of Sudanese disillusionment into a movement and ultimately into an army.

Ahmad's audacity in finally proclaiming himself the Mahdi was certainly encouraged by Egypt's financial and political difficulties, which reached a head with Ismail's deposition in June 1879. Cairo's inability to militarily contain this incipient revolt further emboldened Ahmad and rallied more Sudanese support to his camp. Thus, by 1882, when Britain occupied Egypt, the military initiative belonged to the Mahdi. In 1883, Khedive Tawfiq raised an impressive military expedition under William Hicks, a retired British colonel, to crush the Mahdist revolt. The ensuing conflict was disastrous for Egypt, which lost virtually all the soldiers, including Hicks, sent against the Mahdists. Britain immediately decided to evacuate the Sudan, a task entrusted to Charles Gordon, one of Ismail's former governors of the Sudan. Gordon arrived in the Sudan in 1884; he understood his mandate as one of military offensive against the Mahdi. Without adequate resources for this purpose, he was soon isolated and killed in Khartoum in January 1885. Gordon's death removed any immediate challenge to the Mahdist state, which now established its capital at Omdurman, a few miles from Khartoum.

In June 1885, the Mahdi himself died. He had earlier named three of his ablest subordinates as khalifa (successor), and was succeeded by one of them, Abdallahi. Fundamentalist in his enforcement of the Shari'a at home, the khalifa and his entourage saw themselves as the vanguard of a universalistic (Islamic) revolution. He therefore wrote letters to Queen Victoria of England, the khedive, the Ottoman sultan, and the Emperor of Ethiopia, inviting them to come to Omdurman, to submit and convert to Islam. This aggressive policy brought the Mahdists into conflict with internal dissidents in Darfur, Bahr al-Ghazal, and Equatoria, as well as with both Ethiopia and Egypt.

The European "Scramble" for Africa spread into the Sudan in the early 1890s with the Belgians from the Congo probing the Congo-Nile watershed. In 1895, France sent an expedition into Bahr al-Ghazal. Consequently, Britain, in 1896, instructed Horatio Kitchener, the commander in chief of the Anglo-Egyptian army, to occupy the Sudan. He went into action against the Mahdists in September 1896, and captured Dongola. It took another two years before the Mahdists were routed by the well-supplied Kitchener. In the final battle on September 2, 1898, at Karari, near Omdurman, about 11,000 Mahdists were killed and 16,000 wounded, against 48 dead and 382 wounded on the Anglo-Egyptian side. To fully avenge Gordon, Kitchener and his men exhumed the Mahdi and pulled out his fingenails. Meanwhile, the khalifa fled after the defeat of his forces; he was found and killed, along with his many supporters, in November 1899. Thus ended the Mahdist state.

EBERE NWAUBANI

See also: **Sudan: Turco-Egyptian Period, 1820–1885.**

Further Reading

Brown, C. "The Sudanese Mahdiya." In *Protest and Power in Black Africa*, edited by R. I. Rotberg and A. Mazrui. New York: Oxford University Press, 1970.

Collins, R. O. *The Southern Sudan, 1883–98: A Struggle for Control*. New Haven, Conn.: Yale University Press, 1962.

Collins, R. O., and R. L. Tignor. *Egypt and Sudan*, Englewood Cliffs, N.J.: Prentice-Hall, 1967.

Holt, P. M. *The Mahdist State in the Sudan, 1881–1898: A Study of Its Origins, Development and Overthrow*. Oxford: Clarendon Press, 1961.

———. *A Modern History of the Sudan: From the Funj Sultanate to the Present Day*. London: Weidenfield and Nicolson, 1961.

Holt, P. M., and M. W. Daly. *A History of the Sudan*, 4th ed. New York: Longman, 1988.

Shaked, H. *The Life Of The Sudanese Mahdi: A Historical Study of Kitab saadat al-mustard bi-sirat al-Imam al-Mahdi*. New Brunswick, N.J.: Transaction, 1978.

Sudan: Omdurman and Reconquest

In 1877, Khedive Isma'il, viceroy of Egypt, appointed Englishman Charles George Gordon governor general of the Sudan (conquered by Egypt in 1821 under Muhammad 'Ali). In order to fulfill the Anglo-Egyptian Slave Convention signed that year by Isma'il (which called for an end to slavery in the Sudan within three years), Gordon launched an energetic antislavery campaign. However, in closing the markets and imprisoning traders, Gordon's campaign set off an economic crisis in the country. Because the antislavery movement was led by a European Christian, it also generated much hostility, and many came to believe that the antislavery actions were un-Islamic.

By 1879, Isma'il's profligate spending had bankrupted Egypt and he was forced into exile; Gordon resigned his post that same year. By 1881, the administration of the Sudan had become lax, the government unable to deal with the looming threat of revolt in the countryside, and a man named Muhammad Ahmad, the son of a boatbuilder, had declared himself to be the *Mahdi* ("divinely guided one").

His supporters viewed the Mahdi as someone whose arrival heralded the end of an age of darkness and the beginning of a new era of enlightenment. The Mahdi, for his part, was a staunch opponent of both the orthodox *'ulama* (the learned scholars, whom he viewed as infidels for supporting government by foreign Christians) and the administration of the Sudan. The problems of the Sudan, he believed, could be solved only by a return to the ways of the Prophet Muhammad. Discontented elements in the Sudan allied themselves with the Mahdi, and a military campaign was launched to take control of the Sudan from what the rebels viewed as a corrupt and infidel administration. By 1882, the Mahdists had taken over most of the important parts of the Sudan; Khartoum fell to the Mahdi in 1885, and Gordon (who had been sent to save Khartoum) and his supporters were killed two days before the British-led military mission dispatched to rescue them arrived.

The Mahdi died shortly after taking Khartoum and political leadership fell to the *khalifah* (caliph) 'Abdallah, who viewed his mission as the expansion of the Mahdist state and Mahdist ideology from its new capital of Omdurman to the rest of the world. The khalifa's armies met with little success. The British were content to leave the Sudan to itself, even after Britain invaded Egypt in 1882. By the late 1890s, however, British officials had determined that the reconquest of the Sudan was a necessary, though not particularly appealing, step. This reluctant conclusion was forced upon Britain in part because of French efforts to obstruct the waters of the Nile. When it became evident that the British were not likely to withdraw from Egypt after 1882, the French, who were opposed to British control of Egypt, devised a plan to construct a dam on the waters of the Upper Nile near Fashoda; this, it was thought, would force Britain to withdraw from Egypt. The French launched their expedition under the command of Captain Jean-Baptiste Marchand in 1896, and the British realized that despite their nominal control of the Anglo-Egyptian Sudan, they were, in fact, powerless to stop Marchand's forces. Taking the Sudan back from the khalifa thus became a necessity in order to safeguard the waters of the Nile; popular British sentiment in favor of avenging the murder of Gordon and the dreams of those like Evelyn Baring (later Lord Cromer), the British consul general in Egypt, to establish British colonies from the Cape to Cairo, may have played roles as well.

In October 1897, Major General (later Lord) Herbert Kitchener was dispatched to head the Anglo-Egyptian forces in their reconquest of the Sudan; he began his march on the Mahdist capital on August 28, 1898. The Battle of Omdurman, which took place in a few short hours the morning of September 2, was the decisive battle in Britain's war against the Mahdist forces. It was also a demonstration of how effective and devastating modern military technology could be. The Anglo-Egyptian forces under Kitchener's command numbered some 25,000; their opponents fielded about twice that number. But Kitchener's troops were equipped with the new Maxim guns, an early machine gun capable of firing 600 rounds per minute. Kitchener's army was equipped with Maxim guns mounted both on carts and on nearby gunboats in the Nile, howitzers firing high explosive shells, and soldiers armed with new rifles featuring ten-round magazines; the Mahdist forces had only outdated gear (flintlock rifles, muzzle-loading cannons, spears, and swords). While historians have criticized Kitchener's planning and strategy, the use of modern weapons doubtless made the battle both short and devastating.

Kitchener deployed most of his forces in a semicircle around the village of Egeiga, on the west bank of the Nile, while a smaller contingent from the Egyptian Camel Corps was situated in the nearby Kerreri Hills. The Ansar (Mahdist forces) launched the first attack, advancing on Egeiga from both sides of Jebel Surgham (southwest of the village) and simultaneously sending forces against the Camel Corps in the Kerreri Hills. The advance of the Ansar was halted by machine gun and other fire, both from the land forces and from the gunboats on the Nile, and the Mahdist forces retreated. It was clear to Kitchener that his modern weaponry had inflicted heavy losses on the khalifa's armies. In the meantime, the Camel Corps was almost trapped in the Kerrari Hills by the initial Ansar advance, but supporting fire from the gunboats rescued the corps.

The second phase of the battle began with the Twenty-first Lancers advancing to the south in the direction of the city of Omdurman. Encountering some three hundred men, the Twenty-first Lancers viewed the moment as their chance for glory. They rode directly at their opponents, not realizing until it was too late that the force of 300 was but a small fraction of the khalifa's forces there. These warriors had been stationed on the crest of a shallow valley, and they concealed a much larger army below, an army of some 4,000 men. The Twenty-first Lancers rode directly into this army, a mistake that cost 22 lives, wounded 50 men and over 100 horses, the highest loss of any Anglo-Egyptian regiment in the entire battle (one member of the Twenty-first who survived was a young lieutenant by the name of Winston Churchill, who had also been supplementing his military pay by working as a part-time war correspondent). Several Anglo-Egyptian brigades then pushed to the southwest, following the khalifa's retreating armies toward Jebel Surgham; this was quickly followed by a more concentrated advance in a southerly direction designed both to clear the slopes of Jebel Surgham of Mahdist forces and to cut off possible routes of retreat to Omdurman. While the Camel Corps rejoined the main body of forces, the khalifa's armies succeeded in cutting off the First Egyptian Brigade, under the command of Hector Macdonald.

The final phase of the Battle of Omdurman began with the main body of Kitchener's army advancing upon Jebel Surgham, the First British Brigade reinforcing Macdonald's troops, and the First British and First Egyptian Brigades together holding off the attack by the Ansar northwest of Egeiga. This combined force, with the help of the Camel Corps, then turned their attentions to the west to defend themselves against an attack by the "green flag Ansar," led by Ali wad Ullu and Uthman al-Din. This combination of the assault by the Anglo-Egyptian forces to the southwest on Jebel Surgham and the successful repulsion of the attack in the northwest brought victory to Kitchener's forces. The khalifa's armies were forced to retreat behind the Kerreri Hills, were driven from Jebel Surgham, and the way south to Omdurman was left open for the victorious Anglo-Egyptian forces.

The Anglo-Egyptian casualties in the Battle of Omdurman were 48 killed and 382 wounded. The khalifa's armies were devastated: an estimated 10,000 were killed, another 15,000 wounded, and some 5,000 taken prisoner. The casualty rate for the Mahdist forces was thus about 50 per cent, which illustrates at once the courage and dedication of the warriors and the immense destructiveness of modern weaponry.

In addition to its devastating human toll, the Battle of Omdurman brought significant changes to the Sudan. Mahdism was virtually eradicated, the khalifa himself, who survived the battle, was hunted down and killed by British forces in 1899, and British control over the Sudan was firmly established. Though few realized it at the time, the devastation caused by modern weaponry in the Battle of Omdurman also eerily foreshadowed the destruction that would be caused by World War I less than 20 years later.

AMY J. JOHNSON

See also: **Religion, Colonial Africa: Islamic Orders and Movements.**

Further Reading

Beal, Clifford. "Omdurman." *Quarterly Journal of Military History* 3, no. 1 (1993): 34–45.

Churchill, Winston. *The River War: An Historical Account of the Reconquest of the Soudan*, edited by F. Rhodes. London: Longmans, 1900.

Clark, Peter. "The Battle of Omdurman." *Army Quarterly and Defence Journal* 107, no. 3 (1977): 320–334.

Ewald, Janet. *Soldiers, Traders, and Slaves: State Formation and Economic Transformation in the Greater Nile Valley, 1700–1885.* Madison: University of Wisconsin Press, 1990.

Featherstone, Donald F. *Omdurman 1898: Kitchener's Victory in the Sudan.* London: Osprey, 1993.

Gordon, Charles George. *The Journals of Major-Gen. C. G. Gordon, C.B. at Kartoum.* London: Darf, 1984.

Harrington, Peter, and Frederic A. Sharf (eds.). *Omdurman, 1898: The Eyewitnesses Speak.* London: Greenhill/Stackpole, 1998.

Holt, P. M. *The Mahdist State in the Sudan, 1881–1898.* Oxford: Clarendon Press, 1970.

MacGregor-Hastie, Roy. *Never to Be Taken Alive: A Biography of General Gordon.* New York: St. Martin's Press, 1985.

Neillands, Robin. *The Dervish Wars: Gordon and Kitchener in the Sudan, 1880–1898.* London: Murray, 1996.

Spiers, Edward .M. *Wars of Intervention: A Case Study. The Reconquest of the Sudan 1896–99.* Camberley, England: Strategic and Combat Studies Institute, 1998.

Spiers, Edward M. (ed.). *Sudan: The Reconquest Reappraised.* London: Frank Cass, 1998.

Steevens, G. W. *With Kitchener to Khartoum.* London: Greenhill, 1990.

Zilfu, Ismat Hasan. *Karari: The Sudanese Account of the Battle of Omdurman*, translated by Peter Clark. London: F. Warne, 1980.

Sudan: Condominium Period: Administration, Legacy in South

On September 2, 1898, an Anglo-Egyptian force led by General Herbert Kitchener defeated the forces of Khalifa Abdullahi at the battle of Karari, marking the end of the Mahdist state in the Sudan. Eight days later Kitchener went south to Fashoda to confront the French (Major Marchand and a small force) and to hoist the Egyptian and British flags. Symbolically, this began the long process of the occupation of the southern Sudan. Meanwhile, by the terms of the Anglo-Egyptian Convention of January 19, 1899 (commonly known as the Condominium Agreement), Britain and Egypt declared joint sovereignty over the Sudan. In reality, however, Egypt had only nominal authority, as real power was vested in a British governor general who. Moreover, all higher levels of the administration were occupied by British personnel, while Egyptians were confined to the lower ranks and after 1924 expelled from the country.

In the south, provincial administrations were set up in Upper Nile (Malakal), Bahr al-Ghazal (Wau), and Equatoria (Mongalla), with identical structure to that in the north: governors, inspectors (later called district commissioners) and *mamurs* (mostly Egyptians). The extension of government authority to the outlying districts was a slow process, however, and was not completed until 1928, when the last Nuer resistance was finally crushed. Because of the long period of pacification, the government tended to rely on periodic patrols rather than the establishment of effective administration, which would have required more staff and money as well as improved communications, all of which were lacking in the south. The government's preoccupation with northern affairs convinced some officials in the south of the need for a separate southern policy, but for such a policy to succeed it would have to rely on local funding and the use of southern, rather than external, labor. This, of course, called for the development of the southern Sudan.

Inevitably this raised the question of how compatible was such a goal with the presence of Muslim northern Sudanese in the south. To many British officials who deplored the spread of Muslim influence up the Nile, especially as it was associated with the Nilotic and East African slave trades, such a presence could hardly be positive. Until the formulation of Southern Policy in 1930, British officials' response to the problem of an Islamic south was neither consistent nor coherent. For governor general F. R. Wingate, who was still concerned about the threat of neo-Mahdist risings in the north, the main issue was internal security. Allowing the expansion of Islam to the south might threaten the still fragile British position there. It was this consideration that motivated him to accept Mongalla province governor R. C. R. Owen's proposal of 1910 for an English-speaking force (the Equatorial Corps), composed of southerners and Christian in outlook, to replace northern Sudanese troops in the south.

Also taken with security considerations in mind was the decision to promulgate the Passports and Permits Ordinance of 1922, which declared the southern provinces, Darfur and parts of Kassala and White Nile provinces as "Closed Districts," entry into which were forbidden to outsiders except with the permission of the governor general or his representatives. Despite restricting movement between north and south, the ordinance had no significant effect on the *jallaba* presence in the south due to the ambivalent attitude of the government on the issue. While some officials favored their expulsion and replacement by Greeks and Syrians, others worried that it might adversely affect southern development. Thus between 1924 and 1927 the number of jallaba in the south actually increased in spite of the passports and permits ordinance.

In administration, government practice was also at variance with policy. From the beginning government policy in the south was to work through native rulers. In practice, however, officials tended to limit, rather than support, the powers of traditional authorities. In the 1920s, once it was generally agreed to insulate the south from "harmful" Arab Muslim influences, they sought to bring practice into line with policy. The aim now was to devolve more power to the chiefs and to gradually replace northern officials with trained southerners. The expulsion of Egyptians from the Sudan and the shift in policy to native administration in the wake of the assassination of governor general Sir Lee Stack in Cairo in 1924 improved the chance for implementing the policy. Yet while efforts were made to institutionalize chiefs' judicial powers through the establishment of chiefs courts, not much of it was devoted to developing the executive functions of these courts. The result was that the district commissioner remained the locus of the administration while the courts became the means through which he communicated new rules or decisions to the people. Even the avowed goal of replacing northern staff with trained southerners suffered, too, because the 1924 crisis provoked an illiberal attitude toward education, which was heavily circumscribed in attempts to extirpate the educated elite. Furthermore, that the leaders of the first nationalist organization in the country, the White Flag League, and of the 1924 pro-Egyptian demonstrations that erupted following their expulsion, were southerners like Ali Abd al-Latif and Zein al-Abdin Abd al-Tam did not endear them to the British. As a result the south was neglected even further in the field of education and economic development, thus making it harder to fill the posts vacated by expelled northern officials.

In education there was even greater division of opinion within the government over the question of the proper role of mission schools in the development of southern education. The prospect of government education appeared dismal due to cost but also because, by requiring teachers from the north, it would undermine government policy in the south. By 1930, therefore, mission education with government financial assistance and supervision became the accepted policy for education in the south. But the folly of lack of government direct involvement in southern education soon became so glaringly apparent that mission monopoly of education simply had to be terminated by 1944.

Connected to education was the language issue: was Arabic or English to become the official language of the region? Once it decided, after 1926, to intervene in southern education and the Rejaf Language Conference (1928) determined group languages for the south, the government was forced to deal directly with the language question. The British foreign secretary, Arthur Henderson, took the final decision to approve English in late 1929. A program to implement it and other aspects of government policy in the south was drafted, and promulgated in January 1930 as the Southern Policy.

The Southern Policy was a comprehensive plan that reiterated much that had already been set in motion. It aimed at building units based on indigenous laws and traditional customs and beliefs. To promote that aim it was necessary to exclude the Arab and Muslim influences from the south. British officials were enjoined to familiarize themselves with local beliefs, customs and languages and to communicate in English whenever possible. Except in the Arabicized western district of Bahr al-Ghazal, the implementation of Southern Policy posed no serious problems.

Within a decade of its formulation, however, the Southern Policy was caught up in the maelstrom of rising northern Sudanese nationalism. To the emerging nationalists, Britain, by its Southern Policy, intended to amputate the south and attach it to Uganda. This seemed to be confirmed when in 1943 the Advisory Council for the Northern Sudan was formed, and southern Sudan excluded from its scope of discussion. A chorus of criticism followed.

Yet in fact, the prospect of a separate future for southern Sudan was fast receding. On April 3, 1944, the civil secretary, Sir Douglas Newbold, won the governor general's council's approval for a new Southern Policy. While not claiming to prejudice the future status of the southern Sudan, Newbold's proposed policy, by seeking to fund the economic and educational development of the south with northern money, would in fact bind the south to the north.

Increasingly, this appeared to his successor, Sir John Willy Robertson, to be the only viable alternative. Robertson's inclination toward union was more clearly revealed at the first Sudan Administrative Conference on April 24, 1946. When pressed on the matter by northern representatives, the chief justice, Charles Cumings, volunteered that there was no legal difference between the north and the south and that the conference's terms of reference obliged them to discuss the whole Sudan, both north and south. When southern governors concurred, too, Robertson issued a new policy for the southern Sudan on December 16, 1946 affirming the idea of union between north and south. British officials in the south were generally supportive of Robertson's decision, but when the third administrative conference failed to even consider the question of safeguards that they had pressed for to protect the south's integrity, they demanded a separate southern administrative conference be held in the south.

The result was the Juba Conference of June 12 and 13, 1947, which, however, could only consider whether and how southerners should be represented in the legislative assembly proposed to replace the advisory council. Although the future status of the south was now decided and efforts were made to prepare the southerners to participate as the equal partners in the Sudan of the future, it was by no means certain that the process of unification would be easy. Isolated from the north for nearly two decades, the south had developed its own distinctive identity as a "Christian-Afro-English" culture and hardly any sense of identification with the Sudan.

As the transition to self-government gathered momentum, there was no pretence of consulting southerners. In October and December 1952, the Umma Party, independents, and the National Unionist Party reached agreements with the Egyptian government on the Sudanese right to self-determination. This was followed on January 10, 1953 by the All Parties Agreement reaffirming self-determination. On February 12, 1953 the codominant powers signed the Anglo-Egyptian Agreement recognizing this right and prescribing steps to terminate the condominium. The south was neither represented nor consulted in these meetings. When combined with the wrenching process of Sudanization, in which of 800 positions vacated by the British, southerners got only 4 minor posts, the rising discontent inevitably boiled over into revolt on August 18, 1955.

KENNETH OKENY

See also: **Nilotes, Eastern Africa: Western Nilotes: Shilluk, Nuer, Dinka, Anyuak; Sudan: Mahdist State, 1881–1898.**

Further Reading

Collins, Robert O. *Land beyond the Rivers: The Southern Sudan, 1898–1918.* New Haven, Conn.: Yale University Press, 1971.
———. *Shadows in the Grass: Britain in the Southern Sudan, 1918–1956.* New Haven, Conn.: Yale University Press, 1983.
———. *The Southern Sudan in Historical Perspective.* Tel Aviv: Shiloah Center For Middle Eastern and African Studies, Tel Aviv University, 1975.
Daly, M. W. *Empire on the Nile: The Anglo-Egyptian Sudan, 1898–1934.* Cambridge: Cambridge University Press, 1986.
———. *Imperial Sudan: The Anglo-Egyptian Condominium, 1934–1956.* Cambridge: Cambridge University Press, 1991.
Holt, Peter Malcolm. *A Modern History of the Sudan from the Funj Sultanate to the Present Day.* New York: Grove Press, 1961.

Sudan: Condominium Period: Economy

At the beginning of the Anglo-Egyptian Condominium Period, the Sudan had largely fallen out of the world economy. The government of Khalifa Abdullahi was the product of a revolt against the old Turco-Egyptian state and naturally did not deal with those it considered oppressors. Not surprisingly, the new regime under the governor general, Lord Kitchener, was able to collect very little revenue during its first few years of existence. For example, in the year 1900, the condominium was only able to collect US $550 in taxes. This limited economic activity was further complicated by the continuing reality of armed resistance to Anglo-Egyptian rule in Sudan.

Although the Sudan was still unstable, the British, who dominated the condominium, began to investigate the possibility of economic projects in the Sudan very early in their tenure. In 1899, the government in Egypt sent a hydrological engineer, Sir William Garstin, to survey the Nile throughout Sudan. During this survey he observed the entire Nile system in Sudan, which includes the main Nile from Khartoum northward and, South of Khartoum, the Blue Nile to the east and the White Nile to the west. After he completed this task in 1904, Garstin released a report in which he said that the area south of Khartoum, the Gezira (Arabic for

"island") would be an ideal location for an irrigated agricultural project. He specifically said that the dam should be built on the Blue Nile at Sinnar, since the eastern half of the country is higher and this would cause the water to flow westward throughout the Gezira.

The major crop to be grown on the Gezira was long-staple cotton, the raw material for expensive cotton fabrics. By the late nineteenth century, Great Britain was no longer competitive with the newer textile industries in countries like Italy and India in the lower price ranges, and was being forced to focus on more expensive cloth; the result was a need for greater crop sources. The northern Sudan, which is ecologically quite similar to Egypt, was an ideal location for such an expansion. Obviously, the needs of British industrialists fit quite well with the condominium's desire for a revenue base.

Although the government was active in promoting the idea of an irrigated cotton plantation in the Gezira, the actual management of the project, which came to be known as the Gezira Scheme, was done by a private corporation, the Sudan Plantations Syndicate. The majority of the land in Gezira technically remained under Sudanese control, but in reality, the government strictly regulated how much land could actually be held by any one tenant in the scheme.

By the late 1920s, the Gezira would become the dominant engine in the Sudan's economy, generating the great majority of the nation's foreign exchange. The success of the Gezira, however, led to Sudan developing into a classic monocrop economy. This became readily apparent during the Great Depression, when the price of cotton fell precipitously. The amount of revenue generated by the Gezira was decreased 75 per cent from 1928 to 1938 and Sudan's prosperity correspondingly declined.

As a monocrop economy, the Sudan underwent very uneven development. The region between Khartoum and Sinnar saw massive infrastructure development. The great majority of Sudan's electrical power grid was placed in this area also. Outside of the Gezira region, development was much more spotty. There were major railroad lines built to Kassala and Port Sudan. Another significant railroad line was built to reach the southwestern cities of El Obeid, Wau, and Nyala. These southern railways were important because they facilitated the export of groundnuts from Kordofan. The southern Sudan was largely outside of the international export economy during the condominium, since significant portions of the region were not pacified until the late 1920s. Although gum arabic and groundnuts were important regional crops, cotton produced in the Gezira region remained Sudan's major source of revenue during the condominium.

Since cotton was so overwhelmingly important, the condominium government and the Sudan Plantations Syndicate sought to expand the area that could be brought under cotton cultivation. In the period after World War II, the condominium developed the Five Year Plan of 1946 to expand the area of irrigated agriculture to the Northwest of the Gezira. This expansion of the Sudan's cotton production was quite fortuitous because the price of cotton rapidly rose during the period from 1946 to 1953 from LE8,300,000 to LE46.340,000. In individual terms, the income of farmers increased from LE29 yearly to LE800. This sharp upswing in the economy coincided with a rapid increase in Sudanese nationalism, which eventually resulted in the cancellation of the Sudan Plantations Syndicate contract in 1950 and the introduction of Sudanese as the managers of the Gezira. This culminated in the appointment of Mekki Abbas as the Gezira's first Sudanese managing director in 1953.

As Sudan began to move toward independence in 1956, the price of cotton started to decline. This resulted in a complicated situation because the Sudanese naturally looked toward the Gezira cotton crop as the source of funding for expanded social services and education. The result was that by the early 1950s, there were plans to expand irrigated cotton agriculture to the Southwest in what became known as the Managil expansion. More important, this expansion once again reinforced the Sudan's overwhelming dependence on crop and would leave nation at the mercy of the changes in the world commodities market.

ANTHONY Q. CHEESEBORO

Further Reading

Cheeseboro, Anthony. "Integration and Change in the Gezira Scheme and the Sudan 1938–1970." Ph.D. diss., Michigan State University, 1993.

Holt, P. M., and M. W. Daly. *A History of the Sudan*. London: Longman, 1988.

Sudan: Civil War, Independence, Military Rule, 1955–1964

Sudan's transition to independence was marred by the outbreak of a nationalist uprising in the southern Sudan on August 18, 1955, which marked the beginning of the Seventeen Years Civil War (1955–1972). While the immediate cause of the revolt was an order to relocate Number 2 Company of the Equatorial Corps to the north, it was the result of overhasty political change. The southerners had not been represented at the talks between northern politicians and the Egyptian government that preceded the 1953 Anglo-Egyptian agreement. After the November 1953 elections, the administration of the region was speedily Sudanized between June and November 1954. Coming in the wake of outlandish election promises made by northern politicians, the results of Sudanization was a great disappointment for the southern elite. The newly formed Liberal Party began to cash in on the inevitable southern disaffection and to channel it into a demand for federation between the north and the south. Regarding such talk as foreign inspired, the National Unionist Party (NUP)–led government of Isma'il al-Azhari warned against sedition and secessionism, and threatened those southerners criticizing the government. When this was followed by the arbitrary and illegal imprisonment of a southern member of parliament, the summary dismissal of 300 southern workers in the Zande agroindustrial scheme, and the shooting to death of 6 of them at a demonstration against the management's action, whatever confidence the southerners still had in the administration disappeared overnight. By August 18, 1955, when the revolt broke out, a growing spirit of unrest had thus gripped southern Sudan. The British airlifted 8,000 northern troops to the south, in effect inaugurating the present-day military occupation of the southern Sudan by the north.

The northern faction in parliament was eager and determined to achieve independence, even if this meant bypassing the steps outlined in the agreement of 1953. When southern opposition threatened to block this, they inserted a clever ploy in the independence resolution to the effect that the claims of the southern members would be fully considered. The southern members dropped their opposition, and the Sudan became formally independent as a parliamentary democracy on January 1, 1956.

During the period of parliamentary rule (1956–1958), however, the government devoted little attention to the south. To gain southern support, the government relented on its refusal to allow discussion of a federal constitution. A 46-member constitutional committee, of which only three were southerners, was appointed in September 1956 to write a draft constitution. When the committee considered federation and the northern members rejected it as an expensive facade, the three southern members subsequently boycotted its meetings. The northern members continued their work and eventually produced a draft constitution that called for a centralized unitary system of government and a predominant role for Islam and Arabic over other religions and languages. By then, a more politically militant and better-educated group of southerners had been elected to parliament and formed themselves into a federal bloc. When this group walked out of parliament during discussions of the draft constitution, a new 40-member committee was set up to study it and report back to the assembly. No report, however, came from the committee as its work was paralyzed by disagreement between northern and southern members on the federal issue.

The parliamentary system was soon rendered unstable by the constant political bickering, maneuvering, and corruption in high places. In February 1956 Al-Azhari had formed a government of national unity, but five months later a new coalition made up of Umma and Peoples Democratic Party (PDP) ousted him from power. The two parties differed on many policy issues. By 1958 the coalition had reached the breaking point, and Umma politicians began talks with their NUP colleagues about the possibility of an Umma-NUP coalition. About the same time, a section of the PDP was also scheming to form a coalition with the NUP. Their contacts in Cairo, during October 1958, with President Abdel Nasser and Al-Azhari roused suspicion in the mind of prime minister Abdalla Khalil that the ground was being prepared for Egypt to play a much more influential role in Sudan's affairs. A small group of senior army officers shared the prime minister's misgivings as well and the possibility of a military takeover began to seem attractive. It was against this background that the army seized power in a bloodless coup d'état on November 17, 1958, a day after the agreement to form an Umma-NUP coalition government had been concluded.

The first year of army rule was preoccupied with struggles between competing military factions and personalities for control of the Supreme Council, the body for ruling the country. By December 1959, a relative degree of stability prevailed and the regime began to tackle pressing issues. In October 1959 they had resumed negotiations with Egypt on the utilization of Nile waters. On November 8, 1959 a new Nile Waters Agreement was concluded which divided a reasonable share of water between the two countries.

In the economic field, military rule brought some progress in the north. To sell the backlog of unsold cotton, the regime abolished the fixed price for cotton and allowed it to be determined by market forces. Within six months all accumulated cotton had been sold and the foreign exchange surplus rose. In agriculture, more land was cultivated, lending facilities were established and foreign investment in agro-industrial projects was encouraged. New industrial development projects were financed and constructed with bilateral economic assistance agreements.

But these economic achievements were concentrated in the north, while the south languished. There the regime's priority was to reverse the disintegrative effect of Southern Policy. The solution was to eliminate those aspects—language, culture, and religion—that set the south apart from the rest of the country. In pursuit of this objective, the Arabization and Islamization of the south was stepped up. Despite the vigorous and widespread protest that followed, the regime banned all religious gatherings outside church for prayers, and catechist teaching, while Muslims were free to pray anywhere and to proselytize. Missionaries on leave were refused reentry into the country. Governor Ali Baldo of Equatoria went so far as to order southerners to adopt Muslim names. In May 1962, the Missionary Societies Act was enacted which gave sweeping power to the authorities to regulate all missionary activities. On February 27, 1964 the government expelled all the remaining foreign Christian missionaries working in the south from the country.

Unaccompanied as it was by economic and educational development, Arabization and Islamization provoked resistance that was met by violent repression. In February 1962, under the leadership of Joseph Oduho, Father Saturnino Lohure, and William Deng, southern dissidents formed the Sudan African Closed Districts National Union (later transformed into the Sudan African National Union, or SANU), which called for the independence of the south, but only if federation was unattainable. For the next two years, the SANU tried in vain to convince the northern elite to accede to the southern demand for a federal system of government.

In September 1963, at a meeting convened by Oduho, former soldiers of the Equatorial corps who were resident in East Africa founded a guerrilla movement known as the Anya-Nya. Their ranks were swelled by an influx of students, officials, prison warders, policemen, and politicians fleeing the repression of the military regime. Military attacks began in Equatoria on September 19, 1963 and soon spread to the other southern provinces. Shocked into a sharper awareness of the seriousness of the southern resistance and its inability to impose a military solution, the regime eventually appointed a commission in September 1964 to investigate the causes of unrest in the south. Bereft of civilian support and divided over whether to employ force to suppress the opposition, the military was forced by massive demonstrations to step down from power on October 29, 1964. A transitional government led by Sir al-Khatim al-Khalifa took over, under an agreement to rule under the provisional constitution of 1956. Thus ended the first military dictatorship in Sudan's modern history. A second period of parliamentary democracy was set to begin in earnest.

KENNETH OKENY

See also: **Sudan: Condominium Period: Administration, Legacy in South.**

Further Reading

Alier, Abel. *Southern Sudan: Too Many Agreements Dishonored.* Exeter, Ithaca Press, 1990.

Collins, Robert O. *The Southern Sudan in Historical Perspective*. Tel Aviv: Shiloah Center for Middle Eastern and African Studies, Tel Aviv University, 1975.

Deng, Francis M. *War of Visions: Conflict of Identities in the Sudan*. Washington, D.C.: Brookings Institution, 1995.

Khalid, Mansour. *The Government They Deserve: The Role of the Elite in Sudan's Political Evolution*. London: Kegan Paul International, 1990.

Niblock, Tim. *Class and Power in Sudan: The Dynamics of Sudanese Politics, 1898–1985*. Albany: State University of New York Press, 1987.

Wai, Dunstan M. *The African-Arab Conflict in the Sudan*. New York: African Publishing, 1981.

Woodward, Peter. *Sudan 1898–1989: The Unstable State*. Boulder, Colo.: Lynne Rienner, 1990.

Sudan: October Revolution, 1964

The October Revolution of 1964 was an unprecedented period of hope and excitement in postindependence Sudan, but in the end it was a source of disillusionment. The hopes lay in the sense of failure attaching to Sudanese politics from independence in 1956. Sudan had then a liberal, democratic government, but politics proved extremely chaotic and gave rise to unstable coalitions. In an effort to resolve one such crisis, then prime minister Abdullah Khalil invited the army commander, General Ibrahim Abboud, to take power. Khalil intended this to be an interim measure to tackle the pressing problems, but once in power the army proved reluctant to retire to the barracks.

At first Abboud's regime had some success. Economic development accelerated with the Managil Extension to the cotton growing Gezira Scheme. Agreement was achieved with Egypt on the difficult question of sharing the Nile waters, and the inundation of Sudanese Nubia above the Aswan Dam. And the former politicians were quite well treated—at least initially.

By the early 1960s, however, the situation was beginning to sour. The troubles really started in southern Sudan, where there had been a mutiny shortly before independence, and where there was growing insecurity. Abboud decided to tackle the problem by a vigorous policy of coercion on the one hand and Islamization and Arabization of the region on the other. This brought new opposition, especially from the Western educated elements in the south, who were mainly Christian and English-speaking. Resistance in the south grew, and from 1963 there was a situation of civil war in the region.

Meanwhile, opposition was also growing in the northern Sudan. There was a feeling that it was time to return to the political freedom enjoyed at independence. This was backed by the activities of the Sudan Communist Party (SCP), one of the largest and best-organized communist parties in Africa or the Middle East. It took advantage of the repression to win new underground supporters in preparation for a confrontation with the government.

The opportunity came on October 21, 1964. Students gathered at the University of Khartoum to protest at the civil war in the south. There was a police ban on the protest, and when the students tried to carry on, two were shot by police and killed. This opened the way for fresh demonstrations, and soon the SCP in particular had called for strikes and mass demonstrations in the capital.

The military rulers debated how best to respond. Some wanted to take a hard line and confront the demonstrators, but others sought to avoid further confrontations. There were also doubts about the willingness of junior officers in the army to obey orders to repress the students and workers on the streets. On October 26, Abboud and his fellow senior officers agreed to stand down in favor of a new civilian government. They were allowed to retire, and Abboud moved first to Port Sudan and later to Khartoum, with few signs of animosity toward him.

Military rule had been ended by a broad coalition of civilian groups, and when the soldiers retreated the civilians decided to establish a transitional government rather than simply handing power back to the old party politicians. It was headed by an educationalist, Sirr al-Khatim al-Khalifa, and contained a wide range of groups, with the Western-educated intelligentsia of the Professionals' Front being the major one.

However, rifts soon opened in the new government. The Professionals' Front wanted a new constitution based on representation of occupational groups. In this way they hoped for a more progressive program than the old parties, with their uneducated rural followings, were likely to produce. But the parties, especially the Umma and the National Unionist Party (NUP) began to regroup, and put pressure on Al-Kahlifa's government by organizing more demonstrations. In 1965 Al-Khalifa was forced to return Sudan to the old geographical constituencies, which meant the success of the old parties once more, against the Professionals' Front and the Communists. Elections were held in 1965, and the old parties returned to share power.

However, the problem of the civil war in the south, which had triggered the October Revolution, was still unresolved. The Professionals' Front in particular had wanted the war ended before holding any elections, but the insistence of the old parties had defeated that idea, even though elections could not be held in areas of the south. In March 1965 a Round Table Conference was held in Khartoum with northern and southern representatives and international observers, but it proved inconclusive, with differences among northerners and southerners as well as between the two regions. Its failure saw the continuation of the war.

The aftermath of the October Revolution returned northern Sudan to a situation similar to that which had existed before Abboud's coup of 1958. No northern party was able to win a clear majority, and there was thus once more a succession of weak coalition governments, with little by way of policy to develop the country's resources. At the same time, there was no progress toward peace in the south, and governments in Khartoum intensified the conflict in unavailing attempts at military victory.

Given these circumstances there was little surprise when a further coup in 1969 brought Jaafar Nimeiri to power. Initially he was supported by the Communist Party, which saw an opportunity for progress following the frustration after the October Revolution. But it was only after a coup and countercoup of 1971, which saw the elimination of the communists from government and much destruction of the party, that peace could be made with the south in the Addis Ababa Agreement of 1972. It seemed like the end of the problem which had most directly triggered the October Revolution, but peace lasted only a decade, and Sudanese politics returned to the old ways of civil war in the south and party maneuvering in the north.

PETER WOODWARD

Further Reading

Bechtold, Peter. *Politics in Sudan*. New York: Praeger, 1976.

Hassan, Y. F. "Sudanese Revolution of 1964." *Journal of Modern African Studies* 5, no. 4 (1968): 491–509.

Holt, P. M., and M. W. A. Daly. *History of the Sudan: From the Coming of Islam to the Present Day*, 4th ed. London: Longman, 1986.

Niblock, Thn. *Class and Power in Sudan: The Dynamics of Sudanese Politics, 1898–1985*. London: Macmillan, 1987.

Woodward, Peter. *Sudan, 1898–1989: The Unstable State*. Boulder, Colo.: Lynne Rienner/London: Lester Crook, 1990.

Sudan: Nimeiri, Peace, the Economy

President Jafar Nimeiri had governed Sudan for three years, from 1969 to 1972, before peace was finally made in the south. Yet from the time of the coup which brought him to power, peace had been high on his agenda.

In his first two years in office Nimeiri was in a close alliance with the Sudan Communist Party, which had its own views on peacemaking in the civil war in the south. The minister appointed with responsibility for the region was a leading communist, Joseph Garang, and he had his own ideas on how peace should be achieved. Garang was not impressed by the existing group of southern politicians, or by the Anya Nya guerrillas. Instead, as a committed Marxist-Leninist, he believed that class analysis could be applied to Sudan, and the south was essentially an exploited periphery. His solution was therefore to link steps toward making peace with the adoption of a socialist program for the country and the region.

However, Garang's approach won limited support; and with Egyptian and Soviet backing, which reflected the foreign policy of the new regime, the war in the south was stepped up. But Garang's approach came to an abrupt end in the coup and countercoup of 1971. Following Nimeiri's return to power, Garang was arrested and swiftly executed.

Nimeiri then reversed various policies, including the approach to peace in the south. He turned to Abel Alier, a senior lawyer and pragmatic politician, who had a fresh and different approach to the south. Instead of seeking to promote socialism, quiet contacts with the Anya Nya were made, especially utilizing church contacts as intermediaries. Circumstances were more propitious within the Anya Nya as well; Joseph Lagu, its leader, had consolidated his control with aid from Israel via Uganda and Ethiopia; and he then came under pressure from Uganda in particular to move toward peace, and thus talks moved ahead quickly.

The eventual peace agreement was signed in Addis Ababa in 1972 and saw the creation of an autonomous southern region, later enshrined in the Permanent Constitution of 1973. In addition to peace in the south, it was tacitly agreed that Ethiopia's backing would see Sudan less favorable to the Eritrean Liberation Front; while Sudan's break with the Soviet Union, following the unsuccessful coup of 1971, brought recognition from the West.

Peace in the south also meant the ending of a severe drain on Sudan's economy. The economy had been affected not only by war, but the program of nationalization which had been encouraged by the Communist Party from 1969. But with the communists out of power, and with growing friendship among Sudan, the Western powers, and the Arab states (enriched by oil price rises after 1973), a new economic strategy was pursued.

The Arab states were keen to develop food supplies in the Arab world, and Sudan with large areas of fertile land, both naturally watered and irrigated from the White and Blue Nile Rivers, seemed a prime area for investment. The recycled oil money was to be invested in Sudan mainly through contracts handed out to Western companies. Thus there was a triangular process—with Sudanese land, Arab capital, and Western businesses—to try to make the country the "breadbasket of the Arab world."

There were some successes—most notably, the giant sugar producing Kenana scheme on the White Nile. Other projects were only partially successful, such as the attempt to develop textile factories; and some, like the brewery at Wau in the south, never functioned at all. But in the process a great deal of capital had flowed into Sudan, and some had corruptly flowed back out. The upshot was that by the end of the decade Sudan's balance of trade was heavily in deficit, and the country was sliding into debt and turning to the World Bank and the International Monetary Fund for assistance.

There was, however, still economic hope. After many years of exploration, in 1978 significant quantities of oil were established, especially around Bentiu in the south, and the oil company Chevron prepared to begin to extract it. At the same time Sudan and Egypt agreed that the long discussed Jonglei Canal would be built to carry White Nile water around the Sudd swamps in the south, thus reducing losses by evaporation, and making more water available for irrigation in northern Sudan and Egypt.

Instead of proceeding, both these schemes were halted by political developments. In the south there was a growing feeling that the region was being economically exploited, and that insufficient benefits were reaching the region. At the same time the south thought that the Addis Ababa agreement was failing. Nimeiri wanted to undermine the autonomy of the southern region by introducing a new regional program for the whole country. At the same time in the north he had forged "national reconciliation" with major Islamic groups in 1977; and as economic pressures worsened he introduced Islamic law in 1983. Opposition in the south to both political and economic policies was rising fast, and in 1983 southern units of the army mutinied and launched a new civil war that has continued up to the time of writing. Early targets of the rebels were the oilfield at Bentiu and the Jonglei Canal, both of which were successfully attacked. Reopening civil war once more also proved a huge drain on the indebted economy.

Nimeiri had thus taken Sudan from war, to peace and back to war again, at the same time leading the country through an economic experience of boom and bust from which it has never recovered. The importance of peace in southern Sudan for Sudan's economy had also been clearly demonstrated.

PETER WOODWARD

See also: **Sudan: Cotton, Irrigation, and Oil, 1970s.**

Further Reading

Alier, Abel. *Southern Sudan: Too Many Agreements Dishonoured.* Exeter, Ithaca, 1990.

Khalid, Mansour. *Nimeiri and the Revolution of Dis-May.* London: KPI, 1985.

Malwal, Bona. *People and Power in the Sudan.* London: Ithaca, 1981.

Sylvester, Anthony. *Sudan under Nimeiri.* London: Bodley Head, 1977.

Woodward, Peter (ed.). *Sudan since Nimeiri.* London: Routledge, 1991.

Sudan: Cotton, Irrigation, and Oil, 1970s

By the 1970s, Sudan had an economy that was heavily dependent upon the export of cotton from a series of irrigated agricultural areas in the north central area of the country dominated by the Gezira Scheme between Khartoum and Sennar. Although Sudan also exported other items such as gum arabic and groundnuts, cotton provided the great majority of the country's foreign exchange.

The Sudanese government had realized the vulnerability of its single-crop economy to international fluctuations in commodity prices, and in the 1960s it had attempted to avoid such a weak position by implementing a policy intensification and diversification in the Gezira Scheme. This policy eventually failed due to difficulties related to growing an extra crop (groundnuts in the Gezira), and the fact that there were physical limits to the amount of land that could be efficiently fertilized.

In addition to the basic weakness inherent in an economy based on a few agricultural exports, Sudan was burdened by a civil war between the majority Arabic speaking Muslims of the north and the practitioners of traditional religion and Christians in the south. This war had begun shortly before independence in 1956 and continued throughout the 1960s and into the 1970s.

It was in this atmosphere that Jafaar al-Nimieri came to power in 1969. Nimieri initially presented himself as a leftist and maintained close ties to the Sudanese Communist Party; after a communist-led coup attempt against him in 1971, however, he began to move into more of an Arab nationalist position. Nimieri's initial economic policy, the Five Year Plan of 1970, reflected the leftist direction early in his regime. The goals of the Five Year Plan were to increase Sudan's capacity to feed itself, and also increase the production of export crops. By the 1972, the initial emphasis on government coordination of the plan diminished, instead, the initiative in development was taken by wealthy merchants from Khartoum and Arabs from outside Sudan, especially those from the Persian Gulf region.

The increasing influence of wealthy investors in agriculture was important because it signaled a great increase in the level of mechanization in Sudanese agriculture. Although the initial impetus for mechanization stemmed from the government prior to Nimieri in 1968, mechanization gained momentum in the early 1970s. Mechanization was an attempt on the part of commercial farmers to increase their levels of productivity in both irrigated and rain-fed agriculture.

Although actual agricultural production remained in the hands of commercial farmers, the Sudanese government under Nimieri did return to its traditional role of facilitator of irrigated agriculture. During the 1970s a number of new irrigated agriculture projects came into being, the most significant being the Rahad Scheme on the Blue Nile that opened in 1973. Rahad was significant because unlike Gezira, it depended on pump, not gravity, irrigation. This would leave Rahad very vulnerable to the great increase in oil prices that would occur during the 1970s.

The Yom Kippur War with Israel and the oil embargo against the West in 1974 had the effect of clearly demonstrating the power of the oil producing nations within the Arab world. The government of Nimieri sought to take advantage of this new power by attempting to establish Sudan as the "breadbasket of the Arab World." Sudan secured loans and increasing levels of direct investment from oil rich Arab nations in its agricultural sector.

This investment ultimately would prove disappointing to Sudan. The heavy reliance on mechanization had the effect of making rural unemployment higher, and when costs of maintenance were considered, mechanization actually proved less efficient than human labor. Droughts in the western regions also exacerbated problems because it forced large numbers of workers to move to the east and compete for already scarce jobs. In addition to job loss, the rapid expansion of mechanized farming into regions of traditional rain-fed agriculture encouraged less than optimal soil management in an area that is very susceptible to soil erosion. The final major problem for the rapid expansion of mechanized farming in Sudan was the sharp increase in oil prices that came during the 1970s. This made it increasingly difficult for commercial farmers to use or maintain tractors, combines and pumping equipment. The result of these factors was that Sudan ended the 1970s with a sharply increased burden of debt.

The Nimieri period was very different from any other period in the history of the independent Sudan because for a short period, 1972–1983, it was actually possible for the national government to make substantive plans for the development of southern Sudan. When Nimieri first took office, the Sudan was still involved in the civil war. By February 1972, Nimieri had arranged for a conference between himself and the southern leaders in Addis Ababa, Ethiopia. The result was the Regional Self-Government Act for the Southern Provinces, which was ratified in March 1972. This act provided for a regional assembly and autonomy for the south. This was the basis for the longest period of peace that Sudan has experienced since independence. Once peace was achieved, it was possible to begin development plans for the south. The major hydrological project put forward at this time was the Jonglei Canal. This idea, which was first suggested by the British in 1901, was that a canal should be built between the Bahr al Ghazal and the White Nile; such a canal would allow for the movement of a greatly increased flow of water into the northern Sudan. Not surprisingly, the people of the southern Sudan were quite hostile to the idea and would eventually riot against the construction. The canal has yet to be built.

During the Nimieri period, there was the possibility of oil production in the south. The Chevron Corporation found oil in the Bentiu district of the Upper Nile Province. The response of the national government was to redefine boundaries so as to place Bentiu in the north, but southern politicians prevented this move. The national government responded by insisting that the pipeline deliver oil to the north. By 1983, the peace between the south and north had collapsed, Nimieri was deposed, and any chance of development in the south was once again gone.

ANTHONY Q. CHEESEBORO

See also: **Oil.**

Further Reading

Allen, Tim. "Full Circle: An Overview of Sudan's 'Southern Problem' since Independence." *Northeast African Studies* 2, no. 2 (1989).

Cheeseboro, Anthony. "The Influence of the Gezira on Later Development Plans." *Northeast African Studies* 2, no. 1 (1995).

Holt, P. M., and Martin Daly. *A History of the Sudan.* London: Longman, 1988.

Sudan: Sadiq Al-Mahdi Regime, 1980s

In 1969 General Jafar Nimeiri seized control of the Sudan government in Khartoum, determined to end the debilitating civil war in the southern Sudan. In February 1972 at Addis Ababa he agreed to grant autonomy to the southern Sudan in return for peace. Ten years later Nimeiri unilaterally revoked the Addis Ababa agreement to renew the civil conflict in the Sudan. By 1983 Nimeiri had dissipated in the Sudan and abroad the good will generated by the Addis Ababa agreement. He considered the south to be an impotent giant that he could manipulate to gain control of water and the newly discovered deposits of oil. He reorganized the administration of the southern regional government and ordered units of the former southern insurgents, the Anya-Nya, integrated into the Sudan army, to be relocated in the Northern Sudan where they would be immobilized by culture and climate. In March 1983 Nimeiri sent Colonel John Garang de Mabior to resolve the hostility over economic neglect, the dissolution of regional autonomy, and the dislocation of the troops. On May 16, the garrison at Bor rebelled, and fled to sanctuary in Ethiopia where John Garang consolidated the insurgency by founding the Sudan People's Liberation Movement and its military forces, the Sudan People's Liberation Army (SPLA). One month after the rebellion at Bor, Nimeiri promulgated his "September Laws" to apply the Shari'a to all Sudanese—Muslims and non-Muslims. Southern Sudanese of every ethnic, political, and religious persuasion renewed the war in 1983 that continues into the twenty-first century.

The resumption of war in the South was another failure by Nimeiri to govern. Disastrous economic decisions, famine ignored, foreign supporters disillusioned, and his arrogance by assuming the Islamic title of *imam* (leader) were dramatized by the execution in January 1985 of Muhammad Taha, a 76-year-old supporter of the regime who objected to the imposition of the Shari'a. During Nimeiri's visit to Washington, D.C., in late March 1985, the Alliance of National Forces for National Salvation organized massive demonstrations in Khartoum against the government that the army refused to suppress. On April 9, the army commander in chief, 'Abd al-Rahman Muhammad Siwar al-Dahab, announced the formation of a Transitional Military Council that would administer, with a civilian Provisional Council of Ministers, a transitional government for one year only. Nimeiri went into exile in Cairo.

The transitional government suspended the constitution, freed political prisoners, dismantled Nimeiri's moribund political apparatus, and promised to hold elections in April 1986. The prospect of democracy produced a plethora of political parties but the inability to hold elections in the southern war zone resulted in no clear majority that forced Sadiq al-Mahdi and his Umma party into a coalition government on May 15, 1986. He was 50, the great grandson of the *Mahdi*, and undisputed head of the Umma Party whose three years as prime minister demonstrated the ambiguity produced by his traditional Islamic heritage and his Western secular education and experience. His fragile coalition was overwhelmed by fundamental, irreconcilable issues—civil war in the South, the implementation of the Shari'a, and a stagnant economy that polarized the government and the Sudanese. After his first year Sadiq could not resolve the civil war without repealing the Nimeiri's "September Laws." Sadiq's search for consensus in 1987 failed when his facile rhetoric to implement a modified Shari'a deepened the divide between the Islamists of the National Islamic Front (NIF), led by Hasan al-Turabi, and the African non-Muslims, led by the southern Sudanese. Confronted by

organized NIF demonstrations in the summer of 1987, he declared a state of emergency on July 25. To remain in power he resorted to political manipulation in the Constituent Assembly that reelected him prime minister on April 28, 1988, in return for a national constitutional conference and greater participation in his government by the NIF, including its leader and his brother-in-law, Hasan al-Turabi. The religious issue, symbolized by the Shari'a, and economic stagnation could not be resolved without an end to the debilitating civil war. The Islamists were determined to the pursue the war in search of the new Islamic Sudan, a vision that was not shared by Sadiq's coalition partners—the professional associations, the trade unions, and the army, who pressed him throughout the summer of 1988 to end the war. In November he reluctantly agreed to seek a political agreement with the SPLA for a new constitution by March 1989 that would presumably return the Sudan to a secular state.

Faced with popular frustrations and the dissipation of his coalition if the peace process failed, Sadiq in February 1989, not unlike Numaryi in 1980, sought ever more support from Islamists and the NIF. This shift in the balance of power within his coalition government provoked a strong reaction from the military to bring a quick resolution to the civil war. The civilian opposition allied with the army. On May 1, the SPLA announced a cease-fire to which Sadiq did not respond, while in Khartoum his ambivalence about the Shari'a, fundamental to the Islamists and the NIF, provoked calls for his resignation in the Constituent Assembly and the complete abrogation of the "September Laws" of 1983. On June 30, 1989, the government of Sadiq al-Mahdi was overthrown in a coup led by Brigadier 'Umar Hasan Ahmad al-Bashir and his fellow officers of the Revolutionary Command Council of the Salvation Revolution to restore to the Sudan the lost values of Islam.

ROBERT O. COLLINS

See also: **Sudan: Mahdist State, 1881–1898.**

Further Reading

Africa Contemporary Record: Annual Survey and Documents, London, New York: Africa Research, Africana Pub. Co.1985–1990; Africa Confidential, London;

Kok, Peter Nyot. *Governance and Conflict in the Sudan, 1985–1995*. Hamburg: Deutsches Orient-Institut.

Lesch, Ann Mosely. *The Sudan—Contested National Identities*. Bloomington: Indiana University Press, 1998.

Sudan: Turabi's Revolution, Islam, Power

The Islamist movement, which has held power in Sudan since 1989, is more the product of Hassan al-Turabi's work than of any other individual. Turabi was born in 1932 into a family of Muslim holy men in the village of Wad Turabi, south of Khartoum. He had an Islamic education before going on to study law at the Universities of Khartoum and London and the Sorbonne in Paris, where he received his doctorate.

Turabi joined the Muslim Brotherhood while he was a student, and became a leading figure in the movement during the October Revolution of 1964, which overthrew Ibrahim Abboud's military regime. Turabi then led the small Islamic Charter Front in Parliament, where he campaigned for an Islamic constitution; however, Nimeiri's coup of 1969 forced him into exile.

After playing an active role in opposition, Turabi returned to Sudan in 1977 when Nimeiri sought "national reconciliation." It was from this time that Turabi led the Muslim Brotherhood in a policy of "entryism." He became attorney general, and many other Muslim Brothers moved into positions in government, the civil service, the armed forces, and the new Islamic banks. At the same time the Muslim Brotherhood actively recruited in schools and universities in particular.

The way forward for Turabi's Islamic revolution was not smooth. He was pleased when Nimeiri introduced Islamic law in 1983, but the two men later broke ties. However, since Nimeiri was overthrown in 1985, the break was politically useful for the Muslim Brotherhood; and in the democratic period from 1986 to 1989 it was active as the National Islamic Front (NIF). During that time it was in and out of the unstable coalition government of Prime Minister Sadiq al Mahdi.

In 1989, with the civil war in the south continuing since 1983, there were moves by the government toward peace with the Sudan People's Liberation Army (SPLA). These involved suspending Islamic law, and it is widely believed that it was this development that triggered the military coup of Omar al-Beshir on June 30 of that year. The NIF was then out of government, and Beshir and his fellow officers were known sympathizers with the party, even though as cover Turabi and others were briefly arrested.

In fact, Turabi took no formal position in government, but it was widely believed that he led the group of senior NIF figures who were the real power behind the soldiers. It was also clear that NIF supporters were taking over in many areas of the state. Up to 4,000 were dismissed from the armed forces, to be replaced, in senior positions at least, by Islamists. In addition, the Popular Defence Force was established, numbering up to 150,000, to defend the National Salvation Revolution, as the new rulers proclaimed their coup. At the same time, a number of new security networks were established, and there was a good deal of repression which has been widely documented by international human rights organizations and the United Nations.

The political system also was changed. Federalism was proclaimed; it grew to 26 states, though the NIF was alleged to remain in effective control. A "no-party" parliamentary system was established, though with multiple candidates, but in reality with limited powers. In 1996 Beshir was elected president, with a cabinet full of known NIF figures; Turabi became speaker of the National Assembly.

In civil society there was a sustained attack on those often referred to in Sudan as the "modem forces," many of whom were regarded by the NIF as secularists and leftists. The existing leaders of professional organizations and trade unions, who had been prominent in the democratic eras in Sudan, were vigorously persecuted. Many were detained and tortured without trial; thousands more chose to leave the country for exile abroad. In their places NIF people were promoted who were often far less qualified for their posts in such areas as civil service and education. The NIF also firmly controlled the media. At the same time, Islamic organizations were encouraged to emphasize the sense of Islamic renewal. NIF supporters were also favored in the economic system, and many were enriched at a time when overall the Sudanese economy continued on an accelerating downward path, worsened by the continuing war in the south.

In the early years of the regime Turabi himself pursued an international agenda. He traveled widely, promoting his call for an Islamic revolution; and in 1991 founded the Popular Islamic and Arabic Conference with himself as secretary general. Sudan was widely associated with the Islamist movement around the Middle East in particular, and was soon being connected with acts of Islamist terrorism, especially by the United States. The resulting international isolation of Sudan came to a head in 1995 with the attempted assassination of President Hosni Mubarak of Egypt in Addis Ababa, in which Sudan was implicated.

While Turabi's Islamic revolution was consolidating itself it remained clear that it was still not all-powerful. Initially it was hoped that the war in the south could be won, but in spite of intensifying the conflict the SPLA survived, and even reversed, initial setbacks. At the same time the ousted northern Sudanese politicians came together to form the National Democratic Alliance (NDA), which in time linked up with the SPLA. By 1997 the NDA was opening new fronts in eastern Sudan. Sudan's international isolation meant that there was considerable support for the NDA, especially from neighboring states that were concerned by Sudan's international Islamic agenda.

As a result, the Islamist government has publicly announced changes to its policy. Domestically it has moved toward a "managed" multiparty system; and internationally it has tried to be more conciliatory toward neighboring states. It has also announced its wish to negotiate with the SPLA and encouraged northern politicians to return to Sudan.

In 2000, President Bashir declared a state of emergency and dissolved parliament. Turabi was placed under house arrest in May 2001.

PETER WOODWARD

See also: **Islam in Eastern Africa; Sudan: October Revolution, 1964.**

Further Reading

El-Affendi, A. *Turabi's Revolution: Islam and Power in Sudan.* London: Grey Seal, 1991.

Lesch, Ann Mosley. *The Sudan: Contested National Identities.* Bloomington: Indiana University Press/Oxford: James Currey, 1998.

Sidahmed, Abdel Salam. *Politics and Islam in Contemporary Sudan.* Richmond, England: Curzon, 1997.

Somone, T. Abdou Maliqalim. *In Whose Image? Political Islam and Urban Practices in Sudan.* Chicago: Chicago University Press, 1994.

Sudan: Civil War: 1990s

Sudan's civil war pit the Muslim and Arabized north against the south, where Christians and followers of various African traditional religious beliefs live, and where the rebel Sudan Peoples' Liberation Army (SPLA) fought for more religious and political freedom. Under British colonial rule, the Southern Policy barred northern Sudanese from entering or living in the South. In 1946, a decade before Sudan became independent, this policy was reversed under the pressure of a growing Sudanese nationalist movement in the North. Movement between the two regions was allowed. When independence came in 1956, northerners hurried to resume all the activities that the Southern Policy had interdicted. Arabic was imposed as the only official language of administration and education, Muslim preachers flocked to the south, and northern merchants poured in to exploit southern resources. With large numbers of Arabs, who were better educated under colonialism, overwhelming the region, they managed to monopolize all the institutions in the south. The Arabs soon controlled the civil service, finance and banking, education, and security.

Southern fears of Arab domination, which they had expressed to the British before independence, were now confirmed. Southerners were aware that the objective of northern leaders in their drive for independence was not only to free Sudan of colonial domination, but also to establish an Arabized and Islamic culture throughout the country. This was obvious during preindependence negotiations on self-determination of the country in the 1950s. During the negotiations,

southerners were often excluded and did not become a part of the "Sudanized" administration. These and other measures taken against the south soon led to the development of a secessionist sentiment. This sentiment inspired an armed struggle in 1955 when southerners in the army mutinied in the southern town of Torit. Armed secessionist activity grew stronger after the organization of a guerrilla army known as the Anya Nya. The war between Anya Nya forces and the successive governments in Khartoum went on for 17 years (1955–1972) before it was ended through an accord signed in Addis Ababa, Ethiopia, between then president of Sudan, Jaafer Nimeiri, and the Anya Nya forces. The agreement granted the south autonomy, but had too many loopholes and Nimeiri was quick to take advantage of these weaknesses. He contravened the pillar clauses of the agreement, including the integrity of the autonomous government itself, without consulting with the southern leaders. For example, in the early 1980s, Nimeiri redesigned the north-south boundaries, planned to build a refinery in the north for exploitation of the southern oil resources, divided the south into smaller and weaker states, and finally declared the imposition of Shari'a Islamic law all over the country.

Nimeiri's policies angered the southerners, and although they had initially been strong supporters of Nimeiri for ending the first civil war, many people in the south organized into underground opposition groups. The period of relative calm brought by the Addis Ababa agreement and the serious attempts to pacify and unite the country through the autonomous status for the South were interrupted in 1983. A group of former Anya Nya officers who had been absorbed in the National Army mutinied in the southern town of Bor, and shortly afterward, the Sudan People's Liberation Army (SPLA) and its political wing, the Sudan People's Liberation Movement, were formed under the leadership of Colonel John Garang. A full-fledged second round of war between the North and the South ensued immediately, and with the Ethiopian and Libyan support for the SPLA, the latter made significant military gains against Nimeiri's government in1984.

This phase of the war revealed another face of the southern struggle. The SPLA claimed that it was not fighting for the secession of the south, but for liberation of the whole country and creating a new Sudan free from any discrimination based on race, ethnicity, religion, or cultural background. Although this stipulation was perceived by many southerners as a diplomatic tactic necessary to win the support of countries that opposed the breakup of Sudan (e.g., Libya), it appealed to other people that had also been economically neglected by the central government. Many nonsoutherners, including the Nuba of central Sudan, joined the SPLA.

SPLA military gains, the burden of war on the national economy, and the political achievements within the north as the SPLA's ideology gained some support among the northern opposition groups led to the fall of Nimeiri in 1985 through a popular uprising. A succession of governments have come to power since then, including the Transitional Military Council, the elected government led by Sadiq el Mahdi, and the present military regime of General Omar Hassan el Bashir, backed by the fundamentalist National Islamic Front (NIF). The latter came to power through a military coup on June 30, 1989.

Although the deposed and current governments had differing ideologies, they agreed on two things. First was their shared Islamist stand, and second their commitment to the military solution to the conflict in the south. They displayed no intention of entering into serious peace negotiations with the SPLA. The presently ruling military junta, in association with the NIF, pursues a policy of Islamization and holds very little respect for other faiths. Their religious zeal heightens their willingness to fight.

The year 1991 was a turning point in the history of the SPLA for two reasons. The first was the loss of its main supply lines and military bases in southwestern Ethiopia, following the collapse of Mengistu's Dergue government in May of that year. This event provoked the mass exodus of southern Sudanese refugees from their Ethiopian hiding places into southern Sudan where they fell prey to the bombing by the Khartoum government. They sought refuge in Kenya and Uganda. The second, and most debilitating, was the split in SPLA's ranks in August 1991. Formation of rival factions along ethnic lines led to militarization and polarization of the two largest ethnic groups in southern Sudan, the Nuer and the Dinka. John Garang (Dinka) controlled the SPLA mainstream and Riek Machar (Nuer) led the SPLA-Nasir. Leadership wrangles between the two men prompted them to reach for the ethnic card, and each started preying on the other's civilian population. The Khartoum government fanned the flames of these conflicts between southern rebel leaders, and the southern opposition was greatly weakened, causing the SPLA to lose military ground until 1997, when it regained its footing. Unfortunately, SPLA's military gains have not halted the ethnic clashes, nor have they prevented the continued raiding by the government and its militia on the southern civilian population. These raids were the cause of a major famine in the Bahr el Ghazal region, which led to the death of 60,000 people in 1998.

Since it resumed, the war has caused the death of two million southerners, according to the U.S. Refugee Committee. The bombing of civilians has driven one million southern refugees to the neighboring countries of Uganda, Kenya, Eritrea, Congo, Egypt, and Central African Republic and another three million southerners have fled to northern Sudan. About two million of the latter struggle to make a living in Khartoum. Displaced southerners complain of the lack of schools, place of worship, decent living spaces, and drinking water. Those living in the camps around Khartoum face more horrors. People are forced to renounce their faith and embrace Islam before they can receive food aid. Their churches and schools run by the churches are bulldozed down by the city under the pretext of violating zoning policies and are denied permits to build churches in the zoned parts of the city.

Since 1989, opposition parties have been banned and their leaders exiled. A tight security system ensures that all internal opposition is suppressed and ethnic and religious minorities are persecuted. The regime pursues a policy of forced Islamization of the country, strengthening the Islamic laws, and declaring the war in the south to be a holy war (jihad). As a result, leading opposition parties in the north joined the SPLA's call for change of the whole system of governance and the establishment of a pluralistic, secular state with equal rights for all citizens. It is the view of this opposition that referendum will resolve whether the "marginalized" groups want secession or a united Sudan with a federal structure. In 1995, the parties in exile formed a united opposition front with the SPLA, called the National Democratic Alliance (NDA), which is based in Asmara, Eritrea. This group seeks to overthrow the NIF government by all means, including the military option. John Garang was chosen to command the NDA forces.

The NIF, in its quest for governance, and in order to maintain it, have used all and any means at its disposal, including jihad against unbelievers, and in this process human rights appear to count for nothing. As long as the NIF is at the helm of state affairs in Khartoum, the production and reproduction of conflict in the Sudan with an inevitable spill over into neighboring countries will continue unabated.

Countries neighboring Sudan have also felt the pinch of Sudan's war, whether through the burden of hosting a large number of refugees or through economic upheavals. They have also been exposed to political destabilization created by Sudan's moral, material, and financial support to various rebel groups. Uganda in particular has been hit hard. The Lord's Resistance Army has for several years been headquartered on the government's side of the front line in Sudan. Their activities in the northern part of Uganda have forced the country to remobilize more than 3,000 of the soldiers who had been demobilized, and have stopped development efforts in the affected areas. Sudan rejects criticism about supporting rebel forces, claiming that it is self-defense against its neighbor's support of the SPLA.

Sudan also supports the operations of extremist Islamic groups within Ethiopia, Eritrea, and Libya in retaliation for support these countries have allegedly given to the SPLA. Recently, the regional conflicts of interest have openly been displayed in Congo with Sudan and its neighbors supporting different groups. Some of these countries have therefore decided to mediate in an effort to bring peaceful solution to Sudan's conflict. A regional group calling itself the Inter-Governmental Agency for Development (IGAD) was formed in 1989, consisting of Sudan and its eastern and southern neighbors, to negotiate a peaceful settlement of the conflict. One of the most significant steps taken by IGAD has been the initiative called the Declaration of Principles (DOP), reached in Asmara in 1995. It includes points accepted by all parties as common ground for a settlement such as abandoning the military means, unity of the country, pluralism, and the right of the southern people to self-determination through a referendum. However, Sudan has stalled the initiative by wavering between implementing and dropping the DOP.

Instead, the NIF government launched what it called a "peace from within" initiative. This was intended to achieve a peace agreement with the small breakaway factions of the SPLA, but without involving the northern opposition parties or the SPLA mainstream. "Peace from within" includes provisions for a referendum to determine the future of Sudan, but it is unacceptable to SPLA since it contradicts some of their key demands, besides the fact that it was agreed to and signed by representatives of a minority of the people of the south. As the war continues, it seems that political settlement is even further away, and a decisive military victory by one side is unforeseeable.

JOK MADUT JOK

See also: **Garang, John, and the Sudan Peoples' Liberation Party.**

Further Reading

Burr, Millard, and R. Collins. *Requiem for the Sudan: War, Drought and Disaster Relief on the Nile.* Boulder, Colo.: Westview Press, 1995.
Daly, M. W., and Ahmed A. Sakainga (eds.). *Civil War in Sudan.* London: British Academic Press, 1993.
Deng, Francis M. *War of Visions: Conflict of Identities in the Sudan.* Washington, D.C.: Brookings Institution, 1995.
Human Rights Watch Africa. *Civilian Devastation: Abuses by All Parties in the War in Southern Sudan.* New York: Human Rights Watch, 1994.
Nyaba, Peter A. *The Politics of Liberation in South Sudan: An Insider's View.* Kampala: Fountain, 1997.
Ruay, Deng Akol. *The Politics of Two Sudans: North and South.* Uppsala, Sweden: Norkiska Afrikainstitutet, 1994.

Suez Canal

The Suez Canal, crossing the isthmus that joins Africa and Asia, was formally opened in 1870. The canal at once assumed a strategic significance. In 1854 the Frenchman Ferdinand de Lesseps was given an act of concession by the Egyptian government to construct the canal. In 1856 a further concession was given to the Suez Canal Company to operate it. Construction of the canal began in 1859; it was completed in 1869. Shortly before his death in 1865, the British statesman Lord Palmerston warned that Britain should not try to control the canal or, he argued, it would become embroiled in 100 years of problems. His advice was to be ignored. The composer Giuseppe Verdi was commissioned to compose an opera to mark the opening of the canal, and composed *Aïda*, with a suitable Egyptian theme for the occasion. The concession to the Suez Canal Company was to run for 100 years. Initially only France purchased shares in the company.

The canal, 105 miles in length, cuts across the Suez isthmus to connect the Mediterranean Sea and the Red Sea. It provides the shortest sea route between Europe and the Indian Ocean, the Far East and the Western Pacific. The canal does not follow the shortest land route but uses several lakes, especially the Great and Little Bitter Lakes. The Suez isthmus and the Sinai Peninsula form the sole land link between Africa and Asia.

When Khedive Ismail of Egypt went bankrupt in 1875, Britain's prime minister, Benjamin Disraeli, purchased the 44 per cent of Canal Company shares then owned by Egypt, with the result that Britain and France shared a controlling interest in the Suez Canal Company. It was from this time onward, spurred by Disraeli's newfound interest in imperialism, that Britain came to regard the canal as the "lifeline" to its Indian Empire. Many of its subsequent policies (such as the occupation of Sudan at the end of the century) were motivated, in part, by a determination to control Egypt and the canal. In 1882, Britain began its occupation of Egypt, which would only come to a complete end just prior to the 1956 Suez Crisis.

During the next 70 years the canal was to be internationalized. In 1898, it was opened to all international shipping, but closed to Spanish warships for the duration of the Spanish-American War of that year. In 1905 it was closed to the Russian Navy during the Russo-Japanese War. In 1911–1912 it was closed to Italian ships during the Italo-Turkish War and it was closed to the Central Powers throughout World War I (1914–1918) as a result of the British presence in Egypt and its superior naval power. The canal was closed to the Axis powers during World War II (1939–1945), again due to the British presence in Egypt.

In 1949, Egypt was reinstated on the board of the Canal Company, from which it had been absent since 1875. It was agreed that Egypt would receive 7 per cent of the canal's profits. Following the first Arab-Israeli War of 1948–1949, Egypt closed the canal to Israeli shipping. By this time, growing nationalist agitation in Egypt was directed against the British, who still maintained a huge military base in the Canal Zone. Then came the Suez Crisis of 1956.

It was the height of the Cold War. President Abdel Nasser of Egypt wished to construct the Aswan High Dam to bring new land under cultivation and provide hydroelectric power for his country's rapidly expanding population and industries. In February 1956 the World Bank offered a loan of $200 million for the construction of the dam with the United States and Britain contributing a further $70 million, while Egypt undertook responsibility for all local costs. In September 1955, however, Nasser concluded an arms deal with Czechoslovakia that included the provision of Soviet tanks and aircraft. When this became known, U.S. Secretary of State John Foster Dulles objected to the deal, though Nasser refused to cancel it. In June 1956 the last British troops were withdrawn from the Canal Zone of Egypt to Cyprus. Egypt, meanwhile, launched propaganda attacks upon the West because of the formation of the Baghdad Pact. On July 20, 1956, the United States and Britain withdrew their offers to finance the dam and were followed by the World Bank. On July 26, in retaliation, Nasser nationalized the Suez Canal Company and claimed he would use the canal revenues to finance the Aswan High Dam.

Britain, France, and the United States protested and an international conference of was called in London under the chairmanship of Australia's prime minister Robert Menzies. Menzies subsequently went to Cairo in an attempt to persuade President Nasser to accept international control of the canal, but Nasser refused. A second London conference in September proposed that a Canal Users' Association be established, but this proposal was rejected by Egypt.

Britain, France, and Israel now entered into a secret agreement, and on October 29, Israeli forces crossed the border into Sinai and advanced on the canal. On October 30, Britain and France called on Israel and Egypt to cease warlike actions and withdraw from either side of the canal. Egypt was then asked to agree to an Anglo-French force being stationed at key points along the canal. Nasser refused. In the United Nations Security Council, Britain and France vetoed a U.S./USSR resolution calling for an Israeli withdrawal. On October 31,

Anglo-French air attacks were launched against Egyptian positions along the Canal Zone, and on November 5, Anglo-French forces landed at Port Said.

The UN General Assembly, which had already called for a cease-fire, adopted a Canadian resolution on November 4 to create a UN emergency force, and on November 6, under intense U.S. pressure, Britain's prime minister Anthony Eden called a halt to the invasion. The first UN units reached Egypt on November 15, and in December, the British and French forces were withdrawn and Israel withdrew from Sinai, except for the Gaza Strip and Sharm el-Sheikh on the Gulf of Aqaba, although it eventually withdrew from those two places in March 1957. Egypt, meanwhile, had blocked the canal by sinking old ships along its course; these were removed by a UN salvage operation and the canal was reopened in March 1957. From that time on, Egypt exercised full control over the canal.

From its opening, the canal became one of the most used shipping routes in the world. In 1884 the first widening of the canal took place. Oil became the principal commodity transported through the canal, and in 1913 northbound oil from the Gulf accounted for 213,000 tons; by 1966 that figure had risen to 166,000,000 tons. However, after the second reopening of the canal in 1975 (it was again closed during the 1967 Six Day War) the amount of oil transported through the canal declined: giant tankers had to go around the Cape; oil discoveries in Algeria, Egypt itself, the North Sea, and Mexico lessened demand in Europe for oil from the Gulf; while overland pipelines had replaced some of the need for sea transportation. Principal northbound cargoes apart from oil were ores, metals, fabricated metals, wood, and oil seeds; the main southbound traffic consisted of empty tankers (up to 175,000 deadweight tons), cement, fertilizers, fabricated metals, and cereals. Further works to deepen and widen the canal were carried out through the 1980s and 1990s, to enable it to handle the largest oil tankers.

The canal had again been closed as a result of the Six Day War of 1967 and was only reopened in 1975, though not to Israeli shipping, which was only allowed to use it after the 1979 Camp David Accords between Egypt and Israel.

The economic importance of the canal has to be seen from two points of view: that of its international users and that of Egypt. The shortened route for voyages from Europe to the Gulf and the Far East and the volume of traffic using it testify to its international significance.

The impact of the canal upon the Egyptian economy has been substantial. Canal dues from this shipping form a significant part of Egypt's total revenues. Except for Suez itself, all the towns and settlements along the canal have grown up since and as a result of its construction, so that an essentially barren area has been turned into one of growth and development that supports a sizable population. This development, as well as the settlements, were greatly damaged as a result of the Six Day War, though by 1978, after the re-opening of the canal, most of the people returned and the settlements were rebuilt.

GUY ARNOLD

See also: **Egypt: Nasser: Foreign Policy: Suez Canal Crisis to Six Day War, 1952–1970.**

Further reading

Kyle, Keith. *Suez*. London: Weidenfeld and Nicolson, 1991.
Love, Kennet. *Suez. The Twice-Fought War: A History*. New York: McGraw-Hill, 1969.
Nutting, Anthony. *No End of a Lesson: The Story of Suez*. London: Constable, 1967.
Whetten, Lawrence L. *The Canal War: Four-Power Conflict in the Middle East*. Cambridge, Mass.: Massachusetts Institute of Technology, 1974.

Sufism: *See* Abu Madian, al-Shadhili, and the Spread of Sufism in the Maghrib.

Sundiata: *See* Mali Empire, Sundiata and Origins of.

Swahili: Azania to 1498

The Swahili: People and Society

More than 400 Swahili towns and villages, many of them ancient ruins, lie perched on islands, inlets, and beaches along more than 3,000 kilometers (1864 miles) of the East African coast, from Somalia to Mozambique. Many Swahili are fishers and farmers, but others are urban traders, craftsmen, and Muslim clerics. Some live in simple timber and daub thatched houses in small villages, while others inhabit stone houses in large towns. Each local community has its own distinctive history, dialect, culture, and social structure, but all participate in a wider coastal culture and tradition, speak Swahili as their mother tongue, and are Muslim.

While Swahili communities are diverse, they are bound by common traditions and culture, language, and religion that often appear to owe their inspiration more to the Middle East than to Africa. Swahili have long traded with peoples around the Indian Ocean, and their urbane Muslim lifestyle contrasts dramatically with the lifestyles of their mainland neighbors. Many Swahili trace their descent from Persian forebears, and their dense urban settlements and elegant stone houses decorated with fine Persian, Arab, and Chinese pottery

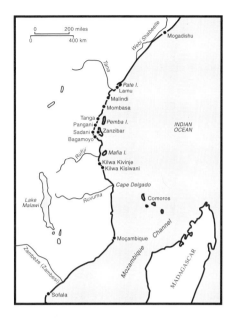

Swahili Coast to the fifteenth century.

all seem to derive from the Middle East. The Swahili language was first written in Arabic script, and it contains a large number of Arabic words. And Omani Arabs have exercised a dominant economic and political influence on the coast from their capital on Zanzibar.

Such appearances are deceptive, however. At the earliest archaeological levels, going back to the eighth century, Swahili towns were local fishing and farming communities, sharing a common culture widely spread among peoples of the coast and interior, and subsequent levels show a tradition of local cultural development to the present, with local pottery and building styles predominant throughout. While Middle Eastern Muslim influences clearly began to be felt by the tenth century, most Swahili remained farmers and fishers, living in small villages or in the mud and wattle sections of the stone towns. Similarly, Swahili is a Bantu language, closely related to the languages spoken by their closest neighbors, and it acquired most of its Arabic vocabulary and script only after the seventeenth century, when Omanis first began to assert their political and economic influence along the coast. There is little evidence of Persian cultural influence among the Swahili.

Focusing on foreign origins thus misses the complex economic, social, and cultural dynamics that marked the historical development of the Swahili. Rather, in settling on the coast, the Swahili slowly developed an urban, mercantile, maritime culture (the name Swahili comes from the Arabic for "people of the coast"). Abundant stocks of fish and shellfish allowed them to support concentrated settled populations, and marine transport allowed them to settle on remote islands and inlets and to travel quickly and easily among them, thus allowing them to maintain close contact among scattered settlements along thousands of kilometers of coastline. In this way, the Swahili have remained part of a widely dispersed, but tightly knit and relatively homogeneous culture for over 1,000 years.

Settling on the coast also facilitated trade: inland, with hunters, pastoralists, and farmers producing a variety of goods in different ecological zones; laterally, along the coast with other Swahili communities; and outward across the Indian Ocean with Arabia, Persia, and India. Gold, ivory, slaves, skins, copal, ambergris, timber, aromatics, spices, and dyes passed from East Africa through the Red Sea to the Mediterranean and traversed the Arabian Peninsula, Persian Gulf, and India as far as China.

Overseas trade was governed by the monsoons and existing maritime technology. Oceangoing dhows left Arabia and the Persian Gulf on the annual northeast monsoon between November and March to exchange pottery, cloth, beads, and iron tools for gold, ivory, timber, slaves, skins, dyes and perfumes in East Africa before catching the southeast monsoon home between April and September. Dhows were not able to sail farther south than the Lamu Archipelago, where the monsoon winds were more reliable and beyond which currents from the south and west restricted further progress, but over time, they sailed farther along the coast, eventually reaching as far as Kilwa on the southern Tanzanian coast early in the second millennium. Therefore, the earliest Swahili towns were concentrated on the northern Kenyan and Somali coasts, where local goods and those from farther south were gathered during the year in anticipation of the annual trading season. The most valuable single commodity, gold, was traded from the Zimbabwe plateau down to the Mozambique coast at Sofala and then slowly north along the coast until it reached northern Kenya and Somalia, while most other export goods were obtained locally.

Each Swahili town was the hub of its own commercial network, extending inland via its immediate neighbors into the interior, along the coast to other towns, and across the Indian Ocean. Thus, while the coastal towns were never incorporated into a larger state, each town was linked with a wide array of different peoples and cultures. As such, Swahili communities became classic "middleman" societies, serving as commercial and cultural brokers for those who traded with them. African hunters exchanged ivory, skins, and copal for meat and grain, iron arrowheads, and decorative beads, while herders and farmers traded meat and hides or grains and timber for beads, pottery, ironwork, and cloth. All could be found trading and living in Swahili towns, and most enjoyed extended social relations with different Swahili families and groups.

Similarly, Arab and Indian traders visited Swahili towns during the annual trading season and stayed with Swahili trading partners who brokered their trade with African suppliers and provisioned and serviced their boats. Some settled to become local agents themselves, marrying into local families and adopting local customs while also introducing their own customs, Islamic faith, and Arabic language.

As a result of such economic and social relations, early Swahili villages soon became sophisticated industrial and mercantile towns with diverse cosmopolitan populations. At their center, living in the stone town, were the old Swahili families, or *waungwana*, whose commercial and agricultural activities, urbane ways, stone houses, cultivated speech, and Islamic faith identified them as the social and political elite. Surrounding them were the local craftsmen, weavers, shipbuilders, farmers, and fishers who occupied mud and wattle dwellings and workshops in the adjacent ward. Arab and Indian merchants, ship owners, and financiers had their own ward as well. And mainland fishers, farmers, hunters, and herders who supplied many of the trade goods from the interior clustered among themselves on the outer edges of town. As trade increased and towns became more prosperous, newcomers were attracted by the economic opportunities. And as people became more economically specialized and differentiated, they also became more socially stratified. What distinguished the Swahili from their neighbors, then, was not alien origin, but settlement by the sea, trade, and urbanization, leading to social and cultural interaction, economic growth and differentiation, and social stratification.

Early Coastal Trade, Farming, and Ironworking (C.100BCE–800CE)

The earliest recorded trade in East Africa was Greco-Roman trade down the Red Sea and along the northern Somali coast to Rhapta (a site probably on the Tanzanian coast) from the first century BCE. It was followed by trade from the Persian Gulf from the second to the fifth centuries. Traders either camped on the shore or built temporary dwellings and traded with local peoples for frankincense, myrrh, and other fragrant gums and spices. Traders shifted their focus to Zanzibar Island from the fifth to the ninth centuries, but no permanent settlements were built there, either. Thus, trade throughout the first millennium was largely small-scale, coastal trade, conducted on the beach between scattered local peoples and visiting seafarers.

At the same time as foreign traders began to explore the Somali coast, however, important developments were taking place farther south, as the first Bantu-speaking farmers settled in the Kenyan-Tanzanian borderlands in the same areas where people were also beginning to smelt iron ore, forge iron, and produce Kwale Ware or Early Iron Ware (EIW) pottery (the two are part of the same tradition, termed Kwale Ware in Kenya and EIW in Tanzania). These two may have been the same people, settling alongside earlier stone tool using hunters, who continued to occupy the area. Over time, Bantu-speaking people began to expand north through eastern Kenya, where their speech slowly evolved into Sabaki, and by the end of the first millennium, they were speaking Swahili and the other Sabaki languages (such as Comorian, Mijikenda, and Pokomo) spoken in the area today.

The material culture of the area evolved as well, as Kwale Ware/EIW, which flourished from the first century BCE to the fifth century CE, slowly evolved into Tana Tradition (TT) or Triangular Incised Ware (TIW) (also the same tradition, with TT generally used in Kenya and EIW in Tanzania). TT/TIW had replaced Kwale/EIW and was widely distributed by the eighth century, indicating the development of a common regional culture along the Kenyan and Tanzanian coasts and their hinterlands. It was then that the Swahili began to establish their first coastal settlements and emerge as a distinctive maritime, urban culture, heirs to regional linguistic and cultural traditions extending at least eight centuries into the past.

Shanga: An Early Swahili Town (c.760–1425)

The town of Shanga, on Pate Island in the Lamu Archipelago, is an excellent example of the early development of such settlements. Shanga was first settled between 760 and 780 by a small group of local people who gathered shellfish and fished along the beach, produced early TT/TIW pottery typical of the region at the time, made shell beads and iron tools (probably for trade with their mainland neighbors), and lived in mud and wattle houses within a small enclosed area. They also traded with the Persian Gulf, exchanging ivory, mangrove poles, tortoise shell, ambergris, rock crystal, gum copal, and ironwork for Persian Sassanian-Islamic pottery and cloth. By 850, a few Muslims, probably foreign merchants, built the first small wooden mosque for their own use.

As iron production and trade increased from 850 to 1000, Shanga grew and people began to use carved porites coral to build a new town wall, a mosque, and household residences. By 1050, they had built a new Friday Mosque, the first that was large enough for all the adult men in the community. They also began to produce cloth, developed more refined versions of Tana Ware, and imported larger quantities of Persian pottery. Shanga was becoming a prosperous Muslim trading community.

The town was destroyed shortly thereafter, when the Friday Mosque was burned and the town leveled, but it quickly recovered. A new, larger mosque was built and new coral houses were constructed. By 1250, trade had shifted from the Gulf to southern Arabia, eclipsing local iron and textile production and turning Shanga into a mercantile town. Shanga reached its peak between 1325 and 1375, when people built large houses of coral rag and lime mortar and erected new mosques at either end of town. Subsequently, the town went into its final decline, and by 1425, it was a ruin, its Friday Mosque burned, its houses abandoned, and its inhabitants displaced to nearby Pate and Siyu, which then dominated area trade and production.

Thus, Shanga had slowly developed over nearly eight centuries from a small beachside fishing community to a large and prosperous mercantile town before it was overtaken by neighboring communities in the archipelago. Through it all, building styles evolved in situ, as people adapted new materials to older forms. The first coral houses were built on older mud foundations, their roofs continued to be pitched and thatched, and most people continued to live in timber and daub buildings throughout. Similarly, the overall town plan remained the same, even as individual mosques, tombs, and houses were slowly reoriented to face Mecca. And the first small timber mosques built by foreign merchants were repeatedly redesigned, rebuilt in coral, and enlarged to accommodate an expanding local Muslim population. The cultural foundations of the town were thus well established before foreigners began to exert much influence on the community, and local cultural patterns continued to coexist with Muslim ones throughout.

Early Swahili Towns (Ninth and Tenth Centuries)

Shanga was not the only Swahili town to emerge during the ninth and tenth centuries. Some 20 other towns also developed along the coast, including Mogadishu on the Somali coast, Manda and Pate in the Lamu Archipelago, Ungwana at the mouth of the Ozi River, Unguja Ukuu and Mkokotoni on Zanzibar Island, Kilwa on the southern Tanzanian coast, Dembeni and Sima in the Comoro Islands, and Chibuene on the Mozambique coast.

These early communities, arising almost simultaneously along the length of the coast, shared a great deal in common, forming a single emerging culture. Manda, Pate, and Ungwana were contemporary with Shanga, and all produced iron and copper work, timber, ivory, beads, and Tana Ware for local consumption and export. Contemporary finds at Kilwa, 800 kilometers

(497 miles) south of Shanga, are remarkably similar to those at the northern sites, including TT/TIW (termed "kitchen ware"), timber and daub houses, bead grinding, ironworking, weaving, and Persian pottery. Chibuene at the southern end of the coast, over 1,500 kilometers (932 miles) south of Kilwa, was first occupied at the same time, and the first settlements in the Comoro Islands also arose in the ninth century. While Comorians were not Swahili speakers, they spoke a closely related Sabaki language and their early communities were classic Swahili sites. People lived in rectangular pole and mud houses; fished with hook, line, and net; raised goats; cultivated rice, millet, coconut, legumes, and probably bananas and taro; produced iron; and made TT/TIW identical to that at Manda, Kilwa, and Chibuene. While the Comoros are 300 kilometers (186 miles) off the northern Mozambique coast, they lie astride the sailing routes north from Mozambique to Kilwa and were thus an integral part of the expanding Swahili commercial and cultural world.

Early Swahili towns were generally small, largely self-sufficient, non-Muslim communities. Few were larger than 40 acres or comprised more than a few thousand inhabitants. Located on beaches, inlets, and islands, they were not primarily sited for trade, and none had a good harbor. Rather, they were sited to take advantage of inshore fishing and gathering of shellfish, which comprised a large part of the local diet. People fished using spears, nets, hooks, and traps, using small dugout canoes and sewn planked boats for navigating inside the reefs. They also hunted wild game, including elephants, using spears and bows with poisoned arrows. They farmed, raising sorghum, millet, eleusine, rice, peas, beans, pumpkins, sugarcane, castor oil, coconuts, bananas, and taro. They cleared the bush with iron machetes and axes, cultivated and weeded with iron hoes, planted seeds with wooden digging sticks, threshed and winnowed grains, and pounded them in mortars with pestles. They also raised some chickens, goats and sheep, and a few cattle. Aside from fishing and trade, then, they differed little from their Sabaki-speaking, farming and ironworking neighbors, with whom they continued to trade and interact socially, and both continued to live alongside preexisting stone tool using hunters, gatherers, and herders. The Swahili were still predominantly non-Muslim, though small communities of foreign Muslim traders had begun to settle in the larger towns.

Mogadishu: A Northern Entrepôt
(Ninth to Fifteenth Centuries)

The expansion of overseas trade from the eleventh century led to the emergence of some towns as major regional trading centers, where traders bulked goods from smaller towns and villages along the coast in preparation for the annual trading season. Most of the early entrepôts were along the coast northeast of the Tana River, which dhows were easily able to reach, then returning to the Persian Gulf within the same year. Mogadishu was one of the earliest of these, based almost exclusively on its position and ability to bulk and break cargoes for other towns along the coast rather than on the wealth of its own hinterland. Among other things, Mogadishu was the primary supplier of gold from Zimbabwe, slowly amassed during local trading expeditions throughout the year.

Foreign visitors commented widely on Mogadishu's stature and wealth. Yaqut noted about 1220 that Mogadishu was the most important city of the coast, inhabited by local nomads as well as foreign Muslims. A Friday Mosque was built in 1269, and by the time of Ibn Battuta's visit in 1331, Mogadishu had grown into a large and prosperous Muslim town ruled by a pious shaykh. Mogadishu's merchants had become wealthy hosting overseas traders, producing cloth, and exporting sandalwood, ebony, ambergris, and ivory in addition to gold.

Expansion of Trade and Islam
(Eleventh to Thirteenth Centuries)

Like Shanga and Mogadishu, established Swahili communities grew rapidly between the eleventh and thirteenth centuries, and a large number of new ones emerged for the first time as Swahili continued to expand along the coast. While this was the peak period of trade with the Persian Gulf, however, there is little evidence of Persian cultural influence on Swahili artistic styles, culture, or language, and by the thirteenth century the focus of trade had shifted to southern Arabia.

Settlement by foreign Muslims and gradual adoption of Islam by local Swahili were among the most dramatic cultural developments of the period. Foreign traders had settled along the coast from the earliest days of Swahili trade, but Swahili communities remained largely non-Muslim until the eleventh century. While the first small wooden mosque appeared in Shanga in the ninth century, for example, one large enough for the local community was not built until the mid-eleventh century. But with the expansion of trade, the East African coast became progressively incorporated within an expanding Islamic world system, as traders and religious scholars journeyed from southern Arabia to the far reaches of the Muslim world and overseas Muslims made the pilgrimage to the homeland of the faith. By the thirteenth century, most Swahili communities were at least nominally Muslim. Increasing numbers of Muslim scholars, teachers, qadis (jurists), and sharifs (descendants of the Prophet

Muhammad) were settling in them, and local scholars were traveling to southern Arabia to study, but Swahili continued to live in a plural religious environment where beliefs in the powers of ancestral spirits also continued to hold sway.

At the same time, Swahili towns began to take on their characteristic layout and appearance. At the center was an open square containing the market and Friday Mosque, while radiating out from this were a series of residential wards, each containing people from a particular family or group, like so many residential village homesteads clustered within the larger town, the whole bound together by a town wall.

The most prominent central wards were occupied by the *waungwana*, the oldest and wealthiest families who were the first to build in stone. Stone houses all along the coast had the same basic design, with a series of long thin rooms the width of the house laid out parallel with one another from front to back. The outer vestibule and adjacent inner courtyard were for entertaining nonfamily members, while as one proceeded toward the rear one passed through progressively more private areas of the home inhabited by women.

Other wards were inhabited by craftsmen, fishers, newcomers to town, or people from surrounding towns or neighboring areas. In these, most people lived in rectangular timber and daub houses with thatched roofs, which usually combined residences and workshops where people produced ironwork, pottery, shell beads, cloth, furniture, boats, and fishing nets.

Kilwa, Sofala, and the Gold Trade (Ninth to Fifteenth Centuries)

Like Shanga and Mogadishu, Kilwa slowly grew from rural roots in the ninth century to become one of the most prominent towns of the coast. From about 800 to 1150, it was primarily a fishing and farming village whose inhabitants produced ironwork and beads, made TT/TIW pottery, and conducted local trade along the nearby coast. Kilwa began to come into its own around 1150 to 1300, however, when it became the main transshipment point for gold from Zimbabwe. Gold was mined on the Zimbabwe plateau and exchanged for cloth, ironwork, and beads at regional trade fairs with Swahili from Sofala and other Mozambique ports. From there, it was transshipped along the coast to Kilwa and beyond, eventually arriving in Lamu or Mogadishu in time to be shipped across the Indian Ocean to the Middle East and India during the annual trading season.

As people in Kilwa became more prosperous, they built large houses of coral rag and lime mortar, produced cloth to trade with their neighbors, minted their own copper coins, and imported increasing quantities of Persian and Chinese pottery, rich cloths, and expensive glass beads. Kilwa enjoyed its greatest prosperity around 1300 to 1500, however, when dhows became able to sail as far as Kilwa before having to catch the returning monsoon home, and it soon eclipsed Mogadishu in the gold trade. Imports of Chinese and Arabian pottery increased; extensive new buildings arose; dramatic new building and pottery styles emerged; but like Shanga, local iron and cloth production declined as Kilwa came to rely more on trade. During the fourteenth century, two of the architectural marvels of the Swahili coast—the Great Mosque and the huge complex known as Husuni Kubwa—were both built, and in the fifteenth century, an entirely new stone town was erected on the nearby island of Songo Mnara. Kilwa's end was near, however, and in 1505 it was sacked by the Portuguese, putting an end to seven hundred years of increasing trade and prosperity.

The first ruling dynasty of Kilwa was known as the Shirazi. These were not people from Shiraz in Persia, however, but Swahili from the northern coast who had adopted the name for its prestige. As an oral tradition of Kilwa relates, Kilwa was founded by three different groups of local people from the mainland, but one day Ali bin Selimani, a Shirazi, arrived by ship with his trade goods and children. He gave the local ruling elder, Mrimba, presents of cloth and beads and asked to be allowed to settle with his family. Mrimba agreed, and soon Ali married Mrimba's daughter while continuing to give trade goods to the local people. Then Ali persuaded his father-in-law to move to the mainland to avoid possible conflict, but Mrimba agreed only if Ali spread cloth all the way to the mainland so he could walk across.

Ali complied with Mrimba's wish, and Mrimba departed, but subsequently he changed his mind and made war on Ali. Ali retaliated by making sacrifices and reading a spell from the Qu'ran to prevent Mrimba from crossing back to the island. Ali then ruled on the island while Mrimba ruled on the mainland. Subsequently, Ali had a son by Mrimba's daughter, who then ruled on both the island and the mainland as the heir to both Mrimba and Ali. All of this happened before Kilwa became a trading town, for the people remained farmers and fishers, paid no taxes, and did not live within a town wall.

This oral tradition establishes with elegant simplicity the fundamental bases of Kilwa society. While the town was founded by local people, foreign traders arrived and gained the right to settle and trade by paying tribute in beads and cloth. Later, the two intermarried, with local people continuing to exercise authority over the land, while Shirazi gained control over the people of the town. Muslim Shirazi then consolidated their power through their superior wealth, religion and magic, but ultimately, the two groups became joined in their descendants, who were heirs to both the land and the people. Swahili society thus represented the fusion of local hunters, farmers, and fishers with immigrant Muslims and traders, each of whom played a distinctive role in the historical development of the wider town and society.

Wealth, Power, and Belief on the Swahili Coast (Fourteenth and Fifteenth Centuries)

The developments of the previous five centuries reached a peak in the fourteenth and fifteenth centuries, as Swahili societies became even richer, more socially diverse, and more culturally complex. In the process, different individuals and groups of people within each town struggled with one another to gain and retain dominance over others.

Swahili communities were relentlessly competitive. Each town was divided into two opposing halves (or *moieties*) that competed with one another in poetry competitions, religious festivals, and political power. Each descent group sought to expand its own status and power by negotiating wider kinship links, marrying well, and attracting new clients through patronage, and each residential ward sought to ally itself with other ward. Waungwana asserted their right to rule through their claims to prestigious "Shirazi" origins or to descent from the town's earliest residents, their control of the elaborate brass or carved ivory side-horns (*siwa*), flutes, drums, and cymbals that symbolized power, or their display of silk girdles, fine sandals, and turbans. As trade continued to expand, wealthy merchants used their wealth to build impressive stone houses, wear fine dress, and sponsor town festivals.

Claims to superior status and power were based on religious factors as well. Study with prominent Muslim scholars, sharif status, or patronage of religious scholars, schools, and mosques all contributed to one's social and religious status. In the process, local religious authorities, especially women, who acted as mediums of ancestral spirits and as healers, were challenged by Muslim teachers and healers, but Swahili continued to embrace religious pluralism in such ritual events as the annual circumambulation of the town or the competitive Maulidi celebrations of the birth of the Prophet, both of which merged Swahili rituals with Muslim ones. In the end, religious powers became widely distributed among different peoples and communities, as seen in the complex array of spirits, representing different peoples, powers, and rituals, to which most Swahili appealed in time of need. And the Swahili ritual calendar continued to combine the Persian solar calendar for local rituals, farming, fishing, monsoons, and navigation with the Arabic lunar one for Muslim religious celebrations.

Thus, as small fishing villages became prosperous trading towns, Swahili society and culture became progressively more economically diverse, socially complex, and culturally plural. Villages became ward within larger towns, lineage politics became the politics of patronage and alliance, egalitarian values gave way to values based on status and rank, and leadership became the politics of competing factions, classes, and religious powers.

Following their conquest of the coast between 1498 and 1505, the Portuguese established their main settlements on the Mozambique coast to control the gold trade from Zimbabwe. Trade declined elsewhere along the coast, and many prominent towns, like Kilwa, went into decline until Omani Arabs helped to drive the Portuguese out of the northern Indian Ocean between 1650 and 1698 and began to exert their own influence over the coastal towns from Zanzibar. While individual towns remained largely independent, Omani suzerainty led to an upsurge in trade and Arab influence in religion, law, commerce, architecture, dress, and vocabulary in the eighteenth and nineteenth centuries, such that many came to believe that Swahili was fundamentally an Arab culture, contrary to a thousand years of prior coastal history.

THOMAS SPEAR

Further Reading

Chami, Felix A. "A Review of Swahili Archaeology." *African Archaeological Review*, no. 15 (1998):199–218.

Helm, Richard M. *Conflicting Histories: The Archaeology of the Iron-Working, Farming Communities in the Central and Southern Coast Region of Kenya.* Bristol: Western Academic and Specialist Press, 2000.

Horton, Mark, and John Middleton. *The Swahili.* Oxford: Blackwell, in press.

Kusimba, Chapurukha M. *The Rise and Fall of Swahili States.* Walnut Creek, Calif: Altamira, 1999.

Mazrui, Alamin M., and Ibrahim Noor Shariff. *The Swahili: Idiom and Identity of an African People.* Trenton, N.J.: Africa World Press, 1994.

Middleton, John. *The World of the Swahili: An African Mercantile Civilization.* New Haven, Conn.: Yale University Press, 1992.

Nurse, Derek, and Thomas Spear. *The Swahili: Reconstructing the History and Language of an African Society, 800–1500.* Philadelphia: University of Pennsylvania Press, 1985.

Spear, Thomas, "Early Swahili History Reconsidered." Forthcoming.

———. "Swahili History and Society to 1900: A Classified Bibliography." *History in Africa*, no. 27 (2000): 339–373.

Swahili, Portuguese and: 1498–1589

When the first Portuguese vessels arrived along the coast of eastern Africa in 1498 under the command of Vasco da Gama, the Swahili city states were ill-prepared to defend themselves. While a few towns probably had acquired rudimentary firearms, they were not proficient in their use. Those towns protected by stone walls often were fortified only on their landward side as defense against mainland neighbors rather than any seaborne invaders. In any case, there are suggestions that the power of Swahili states was based more on socioreligious factors than on politicomilitary ones. While foreign "magic" might have intimidated the peoples of the hinterland, it made no impression on the Portuguese, however. In addition, there are indications that a new, perhaps more orthodox, Muslim mode of dominance was spreading through some Swahili towns, exacerbating already existent commercial rivalries, and working against the formation of effective alliances among them.

Gama's expedition essentially was an armed reconnaissance to establish a sea route to India, where, it was hoped, the Portuguese could supplant Venetian and Genoese traders who were monopolizing Asian imports into Europe. Finding that the inhabitants of the Swahili towns were Muslims (the Portuguese called them *Moors*) who were determined to defend their commercial and political integrity, friction quickly developed. Gama's ships bombarded Mozambique and Mogadishu, but one town, Malindi, whose trade was being captured by Mombasa to the south and whose very political survival was threatened by Pate to the north, saw the Portuguese as potential allies, and gave the fleet a cordial reception.

Other expeditions followed. In a subsequent voyage in 1502, Gama established the basic approach the Portuguese would use in their dealings with Swahili towns for the next two centuries. The submission of each state and the payment of annual tribute were demanded; any who refused were attacked and plundered. Larger flotillas, including one under Francisco D'Almeida in 1505, and the combined fleets of Tristao da Cunha and Affonso de Albuerque the following year, ravaged the coast in their turn. Some towns, including Mombasa and Barawa, offered determined resistance, only to suffer orgies of looting by the vengeful Portuguese after their capture. In some instances, Portuguese soldiers chopped the hands and ears off their victims to get their jewelry. The invaders established forts and garrisons at Mozambique, Sofala, and Kilwa, and, helping in quarrels with rival towns, solidified their alliance with Malindi. Other Portuguese forays, such as that by Ruy Lourenço Ravsco in 1503, were conducted without official sanction and amounted to open acts of piracy.

Distressed by their loss of Indian Ocean commerce, several states tried to reverse the growing Portuguese domination. Aided by Venetian shipbuilders, Egypt assembled a fleet to regain its position in the Red Sea and Indian Ocean. The Egyptians joined forces with Indians and Persians, but their combined naval forces were smashed at a climatic battle off Diu in 1509. The Portuguese had gained unrivaled control of the sea-lanes.

Albuerque, now viceroy of India, established a strategy of constructing fortified naval bases along the various coasts of the Indian Ocean to support his warships and merchantmen. The East African coast was accorded low priority, however. In fact, he ordered the station at Kilwa abandoned in 1512. The Portuguese retreated south to Mozambique and many Swahili city states now entered a period of abysmal decline. Under tight restrictions, their formerly vibrant commerce stagnated. For awhile, a few, including Kilwa, tried to continue the gold trade with the interior by bypassing coastal regions under Portuguese control. Others resisted as best they could through smuggling, noncooperation and flight. Most towns atrophied, however, and some disappeared altogether. When they appeared at all, Portuguese vessels called at the ports merely to extort or pillage. Most interactions entailed blatant greed, corruption and violence, and all too often they resembled those of gangsters engaged in a protection racket.

While superior in terms of naval technology and the science of fortification, the Portuguese lacked the weaponry, tactical sophistication, and logistical organization to permit any significant penetration of the African interior, except up the Zambezi River where they seized control of trading posts at Sena and Tete in the 1530s. Therefore, some towns, including Kilwa and especially Mombasa, developed important commercial relations with their hinterlands from which they continued to derive surprising vitality. Despite the Portuguese presence at Malindi, towns along northern parts of the coast, such as Mogadishu, remained unconquered and defiant.

Major expeditions against the Swahili towns abated after about 1530, but political tensions and a sense of instability steadily increased. By about 1580, the Portuguese had suffered several major reversals that appeared to threaten the very continuation of their dominance along the coast. As early as about 1570, a widespread conspiracy among various peoples of the Indian Ocean Empire who had long suffered Portuguese oppression flared up. A few years later, Portuguese attempts to push further up the Zambezi to gain control of the Monomotapa gold mines ended in failure and unleashed increasing ferment in the interior. In 1578, a disastrous Portuguese invasion of Morocco resulted in the death of her young king, paving the way for Spain to seize control of Portugal in the period of "Spanish Captivity" from 1580. Many Portuguese garrisons in Asia and Africa were sharply reduced.

Meanwhile, an outside force was abetting the growing Portuguese insecurity. From about 1540, the Ottoman Turks had extended their control over Egypt. More of a naval power than their Mamluk predecessors, the Turks began a determined drive down the Red Sea and into the Indian Ocean. Battling Portuguese galleons and disrupting shipping, they even besieged naval bases on the Indian coast. Sensitive to the deep animosity of Swahili towns after long years of Portuguese tyranny and neglect, the Turks presented themselves as potential liberators. By the 1570s they were poised to support the rebellious Indian Ocean peoples in their conspiracy, but were thwarted temporarily by their own catastrophic naval defeat at the battle of Leponto.

Turkish vessels were soon back in East African waters, however. In about 1585, a single Turkish ship promising support was sufficient to bring on a general revolt of Swahili towns, which the Portuguese promptly quelled. A couple of years later, Amir Ali Bey—whom some sources picture as an Ottoman official, but others as a mere buccaneer—appeared with a small force. Again, several city states immediately broke away from Portuguese control. At Pemba, the townspeople annihilated the occupying garrison, and an attack was mounted against Malindi, Portugal's staunchest ally. Again a Portuguese fleet from India restored control with appalling brutality. At Faza, they slaughtered the entire population, destroyed its vessels and plantations, and sent the head of its king as a grizzly trophy to Goa.

Ali Bey returned with a somewhat larger force two years later and took possession of Mombasa. Another Portuguese relief force was dispatched, and sailed into the harbor to find the Turks had come under siege by invaders they called *Zimba*, reportedly a savage people who had already destroyed Kilwa. The Portuguese fleet attacked and pillaged the city, and then, as they departed, the Zimba rushed in to complete the devastation. Advancing farther north, the Zimba finally were defeated at Malindi by a force of warlike pastoralists whom the Portuguese called *Masseguejos*, perhaps identifiable as elements of Bantu-speaking Segeju.

The Turkish incursions had pointed out, once and for all, the inherent weakness of Portuguese control along the East African coast. Obviously a strong naval station was needed along the northern coast to complement those farther south. In 1594, therefore, on the instruction of the Viceroy of India, construction of a powerful citadel, Fort Jesus, was begun at Mombasa to house a permanent garrison. With this stronghold anchoring Portuguese rule, the Swahili city states would continue to endure repression and brutality for another century.

JOHN LAMPHEAR

See also: **Portugal: Exploration and Trade in the Fifteenth Century.**

Further Reading

Allen, James de Vere. *Swahili Origins.* London: James Currey, 1993.

Alpers, Edward A. *Ivory and Slaves.* Berkeley and Los Angeles: University of California Press, 1975.

Boxer, C. R. *The Portuguese Seaborne Empire 1415–1825.* London: Hutchinson, 1969.

Freeman-Grenville, G. S. P. (ed.). *The East African Coast: Select Documents.* Oxford: Oxford University Press, 1962.

Gray, John Milner. "Portuguese Records Relating to the Wasegeju." *Tanganyika Notes and Records,* no. 29 (1950): 85–97.

Nurse, Derek, and Thomas Spear. *The Swahili: Reconstructing the History and Language of an African Society.* Philadelphia: University of Pennsylvania Press, 1985.

Prins, A. H. J. *The Swahili-Speaking Peoples of Zanzibar and the East African Coast.* London: International African Institute, 1961.

Strandes, J. *The Portuguese Period in East Africa,* edited by J. S. Kirkman, translated by J. F. Wallwork. Nairobi: East African Publishing, 1961.

Swahili: Mombasa, Fort Jesus, the Portuguese, 1589–1698

In 1589, Mombasa was sacked by the Portuguese for the fourth time in less than a century, this time in punishment for the hospitality shown to a fleet of Turkish raiders. This sacking was particularly destructive as it coincided with conflicts on the hinterland, improbably reported by Portuguese sources as the ingress of a wandering cannibal horde from Mozambique and perhaps more usefully understood as a period of exceptional violence in agropastoralist relationships. Having reestablished their dominance on the East African coast, the Portuguese made Mombasa the center of their new and reinforced presence, moving to this superior harbor the erstwhile ruling family of Malindi, who had been close allies of the Portuguese.

The period from 1593 to 1631 was the apogee of Portuguese power on the Kenya coast. Basic work on the impressive new fortress of Fort Jesus at Mombasa was begun in 1593 and completed in 1596. The Fort commanded the channel which led to the harbor on the north side of the island, and its guns also dominated the town, which lay around this harbor. Early seventeenth-century Mombasa also boasted a monastery and a Portuguese town of 70 houses; regrettably we have little idea of what these settlers might have been growing or how far they were engaged in trade. The most comprehensive account of Mombasa in the early seventeenth century was a semi-retrospective piece, written in 1635, that suggested that in terms of the ivory and other luxury goods the commerce of Mombasa was of limited value and that the considerable investment made in building the fortress was intended to provide a forward defense for Portugal's other possessions and to guarantee the supply of foodstuffs in the region.

These foodstuffs were not grown on the island, much of which was not cultivated. Supplies of grain, which from Mombasa fed into a complex coasting trade that varied in direction and intensity with the vagaries of weather and politics, were drawn partly from the immediate hinterland of Mombasa, from which grain might easily be transported on the little network of creeks around the island. The island and immediate hinterland were settled by a population described both as "Moors" and "Cafres." The term *Swahili* was not used in Portuguese records of this period, but the Moorsof their accounts were surely African Muslims, people who would later be called Swahili, living among a non-Muslim population. These Muslim and pagan settlements were considered to be part of the domain of Mombasa, to which they paid tax. Beyond them, farther inland, lived Mozungullos, to whose leaders tribute was paid to secure a degree of peace. The Portuguese never exercised authority beyond the narrow domain of Mombasa itself, and indeed seem hardly to have ventured off the island, in contrast to their policies in Mozambique. But there was considerable interaction between the peoples of the hinterland and the African populace of Mombasa. Tribute to the Mozungulloswas paid through "headmen" in Mombasa, so there may already have existed at this time the pattern recorded in the nineteenth century, according to which each Swahili kin group claimed a political and economic relationship with a particular hinterland ethnic group.

A member of the Malindi family brought to Mombasa by the Portuguese was installed as king. It is not clear how far this post was an invention of the Portuguese: sixteenth-century accounts of Mombasa mentioned a king, but this may well have been a misinterpretation, and Mombasan society has shown a remarkable historical tendency to political decentralization along kinship lines. The Portuguese were in effect trying to build a protectorate at Mombasa, and initially the king was allotted a portion of the duties on trade collected by the Portuguese. By 1630 he was a kind of tax farmer, paying the Portuguese crown for permission to tax trade, and collecting a tax in produce from his subjects. The Portuguese tried to Catholicize and integrate this new "kingdom," and in 1626 a new king, a Catholic educated in Goa, with a Portuguese wife, was enthroned. But the relationship between the kings and the Portuguese captains of the Fort was an unhappy one: each captain sought to enrich himself through trade and tax,

and in doing so infringed upon the king's privileges. In 1631 this tense relationship exploded when the king, Dom Jeronimo, massacred the Portuguese garrison and population. This abrupt annihilation revealed very clearly the fragility of Portuguese power in the region, a fragility underlined when an attempt to retake Mombasa was successfully repelled. But it revealed too that there was no immediate contender for domination. Without the support of the Portuguese, Dom Jeronimo was unable or unwilling to continue as king of Mombasa, and he sailed off to pursue a brief career as a pirate. When a small Portuguese force arrived to retake Mombasa in 1632, there was no resistance.

The fort was strengthened, but the Portuguese presence never regained the pretensions of the early seventeenth century. A handful of settlers were concentrated at Mombasa and a system of direct rule was introduced, with the captain of the fort as a waged administrator responsible for collecting duties and tax, and for enforcing the onerous restrictions which were intended to privilege Portuguese trade. But the trade was negligible, and the revenue very much less than the cost of maintaining the fort and its garrison. By the 1660s the captains were collecting tax on their own behalf and conducting private trade, but here, as elsewhere, the effect of Portuguese attempts to tax and monopolize was the destruction of commerce. Mombasa must have seemed a singularly unattractive post for officials bent on profit, and it is perhaps unsurprising that when Omani forces began to pursue their conflict with the Portuguese into East Africa, they met little effective resistance. The Portuguese town was sacked in an Omani raid in 1661. The Omanis returned in 1696, and Fort Jesus was besieged for 30 months, holding out for so long more because of the desultory nature of the siege and the ambivalent attitude of the populace of Mombasa than because of the half-hearted attempts at relief by fleets sent from Goa. When the fort fell in 1698 Portuguese power on the coast north of Mozambique was effectively ended; and the coast fell under an Omani hegemony that, while fragile and divided, was to persist for the next two centuries.

JUSTIN WILLIS

See also: **Zanzibar.**

Further Reading

Boxer, Charles, and C. de Azevedo. *Fort Jesus and the Portuguese in Mombasa, 1593–1729.* London, 1960.

Gray, John. "Rezende's Description of East Africa in 1634." *Tanganyika Notes and Records,* no. 23 (1947): pp.2–28.

Kirkman, James. *Fort Jesus. A Portuguese Fortress on the East African Coast.* Oxford: Clarendon Press, 1974.

Pearson, Michael. *Port Cities and Intruders: The Swahili Coast, India and Portugal in the Early Modern Era*. Baltimore: Johns Hopkins University Press, 1998.

Strandes, Justus. *The Portuguese Period in East Africa*, translated by J. Wallwork. Nairobi: East African Literature Bureau, 1961.

Swahili Language

Kiswahili, the most widely spoken African language on the continent, has a long and complex history that interweaves with that of the development of long-range trading networks throughout East Africa. Over the last ten centuries, the language spread from its East African coastal origins to become a lingua franca for both East and Central Africa. Today, mainland coastal Tanzanians and those who live on the island of Zanzibar speak Kiswahili as their mother tongue, while English and numerous other local languages besides Kiswahili continue to be spoken throughout mainland Tanzania. Kiswahili shares official state language status with English, and is considered the language of education and administration. Kiswahili, written in Arabic script until early in the twentieth century, represents a significant literary tradition. It stood as one of Africa's few written languages before the colonial period.

Historians trace the beginnings of a distinct Swahili language to the ninth century. Although related to other Bantu languages of the region, and especially to the Sabaki subgroup of languages, Kiswahili has a distinct grammatical structure that incorporates numerous loanwords from Arabic, Portuguese, German, English, and Hindi. The presence of these foreign words reflects not only the Swahili people's significant involvement in the ancient Indian Ocean trading system, but also the later period of European colonial rule. Swahili settlements along the East African coastline stretched from the southern Somali coast to the southern Tanzania coast. Mainly Muslim, the inhabitants of these settlements engaged in both inland and maritime trade. Around 1800, expanded trading networks developed by Yao and Nyamwezi traders from the interior of Tanzania resulted in permanent connections with coastal Swahili peoples.

During the 1820s, European and Zanzibari demand for ivory and slaves stimulated the further development of long-distance caravan routes between the Mrima coast opposite the island of Zanzibar and the interior of Tanzania. Permanent Swahili trading settlements in the interior grew during this period as well, with the most famous located at Ujiji, on Lake Tanganyika. By 1860, a complex central trading system existed, linking important interior trading towns across Tanzania with Swahili coastal towns. As this network became more entrenched in Tanzania, Kiswahili spread along the same paths. By the 1880s, peoples of the interior who lived near the trading routes used Kiswahili as a lingua franca for the purposes of conducting business with coastal Swahili. Besides the practical impetus to speak the language to facilitate trade, evidence also indicates that interior peoples may have also begun to speak the language as a means of enhancing their personal prestige and status. The coastal Swahili had achieved quite a high standard of living, and some non-Swahili sought to emulate them by acquiring some of their cultural attributes, such as adherence to Islam and command of the Kiswahili language.

When European missionaries and explorers began to arrive in Tanzania in the 1840s, they found that command of Kiswahili improved their ability to function in East Africa. They could, for example, reduce the need for interpreters, who the Europeans sometimes deemed untrustworthy. Thus, explorers like Sir Richard Burton sought to learn the language well enough to take advantage of its capacity as a lingua franca in furthering their own selfish goals. Europeans sometimes even used Kiswahili among themselves when they could not communicate in European languages.

Missionaries set about the work of writing dictionaries and grammars in order to improve communication between themselves and potential converts. The linguistic work done by these early missionaries and their successors resulted in the first formalized European renditions of the language. Their efforts became the foundation of later colonial educational and administrative plans to educate an African elite as colonial functionaries, and their dictionaries and grammars became the standard. Missionaries also employed converted Africans who spoke both Kiswahili and the local language to act as intermediaries between themselves and their converts. Many of these mission-educated and Christianized Africans later became educators and administrators in the colonial apparatus.

Germany established its claim to Tanganyika at the Berlin Conference of 1884–1885. By 1903 it split the colony into 28 districts, with a German administrator at the head of each. The small number of resident Germans in the colony available for administrative duties made necessary the training of a cadre of African civil servants. Although students in government schools received instruction in German, and the German government encouraged German language instruction by offering monetary incentives, the primary language taught to Africans was Kiswahili. In this way, and with the partial cooperation of Christian missions operating schools in the colony, the Germans built an efficient and flexible colonial apparatus of Kiswahili-speaking civil servants, teachers, and soldiers who easily navigated the language barrier between the German rulers and their subject peoples.

As an increasing number of Africans learned Kiswahili during the German colonial period, they spread the language to all corners of Tanzania. Because the Germans often posted their employees far away from their homes, Kiswahili spread widely as a medium of expression among diverse African ethnic groups, and its status as a lingua franca became further entrenched throughout polyglot Tanzania, reaching beyond the traditional trading routes and missionary communities.

When the British took over the colony as a mandate in 1918, they praised this aspect of German colonial rule and followed suit. However, the British also began educating African secondary school students in English. English came to be perceived, at least among Africans who wanted to succeed within the colonial structure, as the superior language, and Kiswahili correspondingly came to be viewed by those same elites as inferior and potentially limiting during the mandate period.

Tanzanians reversed this assumption during the independence movement of the 1950s. Recognizing the potential nationalist benefits of a language so widely spoken across Tanzania, leaders used Kiswahili to communicate their politics to the masses. Taking pride in the distinguished and rich written literary tradition of Kiswahili, and touting its attributes as a lingua franca, Tanzania's postindependence leaders sought to imbue the language with a status at least equal to English. In fact, as a young man, former Tanzanian President Julius Nyerere translated several of William Shakespeare's works into Kiswahili in order to show the peoples of Tanganyika, and arguably the former colonial rulers, the aesthetic quality of this African language.

Later government efforts to make Kiswahili the medium of instruction for secondary and university-level education have not, however, been very successful. Some scholars express concern that Kiswahili cannot accommodate the highly technical terminology of the twentieth and twenty-first centuries, and thus will not serve Tanzanians well as they try to further integrate their nation into the global system. Yet the language continues to expand as a true lingua franca for East and Central Africa, and surpasses English as the most spoken language in Tanzania. It stands as a living and meaningful symbol of African heritage and history to millions of Africans.

MICHELLE MOYD

See also: **Language, Colonial State and; Nyerere, Julius.**

Further Reading

Allen, James de Vere. *Swahili Origins.* Athens, Ohio: Ohio University Press, 1993.

Buchert, Lene. *Education in the Development of Tanzania 1919–1990,* Athens, Ohio: Ohio University Press, 1994.

Mazrui, Alamin, and Ibrahim Noor Shariff. *The Swahili: Idiom and Identity of an African People.* Trenton, N.J.: Africa World Press, 1994.

Mazrui, Ali A. and Alamin M. Mazrui, *Swahili State and Society: The Political Economy of an African Language.* London: James Currey, 1995.

Middleton, John. *The World of the Swahili: An African Mercantile Civilization.* New Haven, Conn.: Yale University Press, 1992.

SWAPO: *See* Namibia: SWAPO and the Freedom Struggle.

Swazi Kingdom: *See* Swaziland: Swazi Kingdom, Survival of, 1839–1879.

Swaziland: Sobhuza I, Foundation of Ngwane Kingdom

Sobhuza I was born around 1800 at Ngetfwese, near modern Mlosheni. His biological mother was Lojiba Simelane, the sister and junior wife (*inhlanti*) to Somnjalose Simelane, his legal mother, who was barren. His father was Ndvungunye (alias Zigode). Sobhuza's birth is shrouded in some mystery. His father Ndvungunye is reputed to have had a short and violent reign. He died unexpectedly after being struck

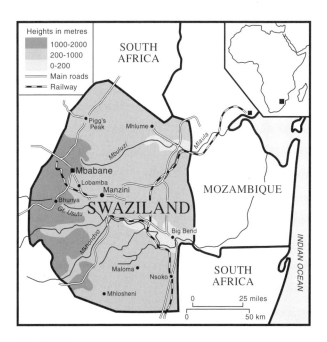

Swaziland.

by lightning in a thunderstorm. Few adult sons survived. In one account Lojiba was still pregnant with Somhlolo at this point. After his birth Sobhuza was given the additional name of Somhlolo (The Wonder) because the top of his head remained soft. Somhlolo is reputed to have been taken away to the Vryheid district by Ndvungunye's *sicile* (body servant) Lohija Nsibandze to protect him from jealous rivals. Little is known of this early period of Sobhuza's reign. His mother, Somjalose, who had earned the gratitude and respect of the Ngwane people by persuading Ndvungunye to "cool down," acted as leading regent and her personal stature may well have cemented the "dual monarchy" of king and queen mother, for which the Swazi have become renowned.

The first decade of the nineteenth century was politically turbulent. Large numbers of people resided in and around the king's residence (*Hhohlo*), all sharing homes. The *amabutho* (age regiments) that had been initiated by Ndvungunye were often under arms and residing in the vicinity. These two features of the Ngwane kingdom probably facilitated the rapid incorporation and acculturation of conquered and refugee groups. The main threat to the Ngwane kingdom came from the Ndvandwe under their king Zwide, whose capital was across the Phongola River near modern Nongoma. When Sobhuza was in his teens a diplomatic marriage was arranged between Sobhuza and Zwide's daugther Tzandile. The objective on the Ngwane part was to preempt attack by their powerful neighbor. This proved unrealistic. At some point around 1818 Zwide executed a sequence of violent attacks against his in-law. The trigger of conflict was control over the fertile banks and floodplain of the Phongola, whose value may have become suddenly heightened by a period of acute drought. In one of the first of these attacks the royal capital Zombodze was burned—its charred ruins being given the name of *eShselweni* (place of ashes).

Sobhuza fled first to Ephungalekazi near Hlatikhulu, in the southwestern region of modern Swaziland, but thereafter was pushed farther north by repeated attacks from Zwide's forces. Ultimately he was forced to seek refuge with a Sotho chief named Magoboyi living around the Dlomodlomo Mountains far to the northwest. Sobhuza was accompanied by a relatively small band of soldiers during these wanderings. Some of his military officers and subchiefs were instructed to remain behind to protect his former domain against Zwide's marauding troops. Others remained behind of their own accord. Among these was Sobhuza's brother Nkwekazi, who before long decided to assume the mantle of kingship. Many of Sobhuza's subjects were reluctant to accept Nkwekazi's elevation, Maloyi Nkhosi (later Mamba) among them. When Zwide was finally routed by Shaka Zulu in 1820 and forced to flee

across the Phongola River to the northern tributary of the Nkomati River, Maloyi Nkhosi sent an army to fetch him back. Their combined forces returned along the headwaters of the Phongola, and routed Nkwekazi. Zombodze and other royal villages were resuscitated near to their old sites.

After Zwide's flight to the northwest, Sobhuza continued to be threatened from the south, this time by Shaka. To counter this he entered into marriage alliances with the Zulu king, and probably became tributary at the same time. Some oral traditions speak of him actually visiting Shaka at his capital. As with Zwide, there was little to assure Sobhuza that he would remain immune from Zulu attacks, which ultimately materialized in the late 1820s. Soon after his return from the south he therefore took the momentous decision to colonize the Zulwini Valley (near modern Mbabane) and the region farther to the north, which among other things offered the sanctuary of near impregnable cave fortresses in the Mdzimba Mountains. Sobhuza began this exercise cautiously entering into a marriage alliance with and recognizing the autonomy of the Maseko chief Mgazi, who controlled the cave fortress of Nqabaneni. Besides Mgazi, his most powerful adversaries in the region were Mnjoli and Moyeni Magagola. He conquered both, the second with external (possibly Portuguese) support. With these subdued Sobhuza gradually extended his control to the Lebombo mountains in the east, the Dlomodlomo mountains in the northwest, and Simakade (Piet Retief) in the southwest.

For much of this time Sobhuza's kingdom remained a nation under arms. Little of the conquered territory was settled, and the bulk of the Ngwane core clustered for security in military towns. Only relatively late in his reign did Sobhuza begin "placing" his brothers and leading indunas in their own chiefdoms in this new domain. The bulk of the newly conquered population thus remained partially unassimilated, a situation that would continue until the reign of his successor Mswati.

After the assassination of Shaka and the installation of Dingane, in 1828, Sobhuza gained some respite from Zulu attacks. These resumed in 1836 in what the missionary Brownlee described as "an exterminating mission against the Swazies." This failed in its main intention due to a lack of coordination between the three invading groups. Warfare resumed in earnest after Dingane's defeat at Blood River in 1938. Now Dingane sought to acquire new territory in southern Swaziland, at a greater distance from the Boers. The plan was to set up villages and colonize. Realizing the gravity of the situation the Ngwane mobilized their entire military strength, with which they succeeded in defeating Dingane's forces at the pivotal battle of Lubuya in 1839. It was at this point that Sobhuza died.

His final legacy were the envoys he dispatched shortly before his death to seal an alliance with the trekkers. With that a framework of domestic governance and foreign policy was set in place on which his successor Mswati could build.

PHILIP BONNER

See also: **Mfecane; Shaka and Zulu Kingdom, 1810–1840.**

Further Reading

Bonner, P. L. *Kings, Commoners and Concessionaires: The Evolution and Dissolution of the Nineteenth Century Swazi State.* Cambridge: Cambridge University Press, 1983.
Matsebula, J. S. M. *A History of Swaziland.* Cape Town: Longman, 1972.

Swaziland: Swazi Kingdom, Survival of, 1839–1879

When Sobhuza died in 1839, he bequeathed a territory with roughly delimited borders, a rudimentary political and administrative structure, and a brief moratorium on external threats. His heir apparent was Mswati III, son of Zwide's daughter Tzandile, and still a boy of 13. Mswati's inner circle of supporters was soon engulfed in a sea of troubles. His regents (Tzandile, his brother Malambule, and his uncle Malunge Dlamini) were immediately confronted with a regional rebellion in the south, led by Mswati's elder brother Fokoti. Even after this was crushed, other elder brothers continued to eye his position covetously, and would conspire against him on at least three more occasions.

Mswati's regents quickly sought to reestablish their authority. They posted wives and sons of Sobhuza to govern chiefdoms all over the conquered territory, thereby strengthening and deepening Swazi administration. They overhauled the military system of the *amabutho* (age regiments), and they reformed the annual *incurala* (first fruits) ceremony, thereby strengthening the military and ideological powers of the king.

Swaziland's respite from external pressures was relatively short-lived. At the beginning of 1842, Dingane's brother and successor Mpande gave notice of his intention to launch a new attack on Swaziland. The new British colony of Natal acted as a brake on Mpande's ambitions until 1846. Then, renewed restiveness among several southern chiefs following a series of raids that accompanied Mswati's circumcision and a further princely revolt led by Malambule, the most senior brother to Mswati, gave Mpande the opportunity to intervene. When Malambule was defeated and fled toward the headwaters of the Phongola, Mswati's armies followed on their heels. This provided Mpande with the pretext he needed to launch a massive attack in the first half of 1847. The Swazi weathered the

attack by taking refuge in caves, and seeking sanctuary with the Boers of the neighboring Ohrigstad Republic.

The Ohrigstad Republic was founded in August 1845, and quickly became a pivot of Swaziland's external relations. In the early part of 1846 sharp factional cleavages emerged within the ranks of the Ohrigstad Boers between the followers of commandant general A. H. Potgeiter and the Volksraad Party. When Swazi envoys arrived in Ohrigstad seeking support against Mpande and offering the cession of a massive tract of land (on which no Swazi lived) between the Crocodile and Olifants Rivers, the Volksraad party jumped at the opportunity to out maneuver their rivals (who themselves claimed to have obtained a treaty of cession from the Pedi paramount Sekwati) by offering cattle and protection in return for the land. Shortly after this setback Potgeiter retired to the north.

The Volksraad treaty had been negotiated by another of Mswati's elder brothers, Somcuba. Somcuba's ambitions, possibly along with Mswati's suspicions, seem to have induced Somcuba to indulge in acts of defiance to Mswati, leading to an attack on Somcuba late in 1849. Upon this Somcuba promptly sought sanctuary with the Ohrigstad Boers, where he would remain until 1855.

The offer of asylum to Somcuba ruptured the relations that had been developing between Mswati and the Ohrigstad (now renamed Lydenburg) Republic. It also removed a major check on Mpande's ambitions in the north. In July 1852 he embarked on a new invasion of Swaziland, which proved so destructive that Mswati at one point even contemplated seeking sanctuary with the British in Natal. Had Mpande been able to press home the advantage, Swaziland might well have fractured and collapsed. In the end, Swazi diplomacy and renewed divisions in Zululand saved the day. In an inspired gambit Mswati dispatched his sister to marry the chief *induna* of Theophilus Shepstone, Natal's secretary for native affairs. This both reinforced and symbolically highlighted Natal's commitment to Swazi independence. At the same time, Zululand began to polarize into two camps led by Mpande's sons Cetshwayo and Mbuyazi. Now most of Mpande's political energies were absorbed at home.

Mswati took advantage of the political space that this opened up by invading the Lydenburg Republic and finally dispatching Somcuba, probably in July 1855. Any possible reprisal was apparently preempted by a new and even more massive cession of land negotiated in the same month, in which Swaziland's current borders were roughly laid down. Neither the Swazi nor the Boers abided by its terms. The Lydenburgers were too destitute and weak even to hand over all the cattle specified in its terms. Mswati, who by now had consolidated his domestic position, raided extensively in the north and west and continued to occupy and administer notionally ceded land. The Transvaal civil war of 1862–1864 further weakened the Boer position, to a point at which they enlisted the aid of the Swazi auxiliaries in campaigns against other African chiefdoms.

Mswati died in August 1865, and this immediately plunged the country into a new succession dispute. The eight-year-old Ludvonga was recognized as heir. Mswati's eldest son Mbilini staged a revolt, and once this failed sought refuge first with Lydenburg and then with Cetshwayo. In 1866 the republic took advantage of Swazi weakness by extracting a new treaty which for the first time provided a detailed border delimitation.

By the late 1860s the balance of power in the region shifted sharply against the Swazi. Boer society to the east of the Transvaal was consolidating politically and economically. In Zululand, Cetshwayo was likewise strengthening his position, one index of which was Zulu colonization on the north side of the Phongola River. Finally, two major military reverses against the Pedi and the Lowveld chiefdoms further undermined the Swazi position.

From the early 1870s the South African Republic stepped up its efforts to secure concessions from the Swazi kingdom including political suzerainty, a strip of land along the Phongola and the right to build a railway to Delagoa Bay. The Swazi regents warded off these demands with increasing difficulty. In March 1874 Ludvonga inexplicably took ill and died, prompting a witch hunt in which many leading Swazi figures were killed. After a period of uncertainty Mbandzeni, a political unknown, was installed. Taking advantage of the situation, Zulu and Republican pressure continued to mount. By 1875 Cetshwayo was proposing an invasion of Swaziland. The South African Republic responded by dispatching a military expedition to Swaziland that wrung out of the Swazi their subjection to Republican suzerainty, a railway crossing to the sea, and other concessions. After the departure of the expedition the Swazi repudiated the treaty, successfully invoking the support of the British in this regard. They nevertheless were unable to resist Republican pressure to provide a large force of auxiliaries in the unsuccessful 1876 war against the Pedi.

The Swazi were spared these increasingly insistent pressures from the Zulu and the Boers by the British annexation of the Transvaal in 1876. Following annexation, the British were quickly embroiled in wars with the Zulu and Pedi in 1878–1879. The Swazi provided limited support in the first and a huge army of 8,500 men in the second. The latter act created a huge debt of gratitude on the part of the British toward the Swazi, and this would be exploited to great affect after the retrocession of the Transvaal in 1881. The last act of the British before leaving the Swazi to face an

independent Boer republic in the Transvaal was finally to delimit the border between the two states.

PHILIP BONNER

See also: **Natal, Nineteenth Century; South Africa: Confederation, Disarmament and the First Anglo-Boer War, 1871–1881.**

Further Reading

Bonner, P. L. *Kings, Commoners and Concessionaires: The Evolution and Dissolution of the Nineteenth Century Swazi State*. Cambridge: Cambridge University Press, 1983.

Matesbula, J. S. M. *A History of Swaziland*. Cape Town: Longman, 1972.

Swaziland: Concessions, Annexation, 1880–1902

In the late nineteenth century, nearly all the African communities surrounding the Swazi were subjugated to European rule by force. The British defeated the Zulu at the Battle of Ulundi in July 1879, overran the Pedi in 1879–1881, and, following the prolonged war between the Boer communities of the Orange Free State and Moshoeshoe's Basotho, had annexed Lesotho. In Swaziland's case, however, the Europeans accomplished conquest as a direct outcome of the numerous concessions granted by King Mbandzeni (1875–1889). It was his failure to exert any real control over the English-speaking and Afrikaner concession-seeking whites flocking to his court that finally led to the country's annexation.

From 1882, the discovery of gold in northwestern Swaziland saw the beginning of a major rush of concession seekers to the Swazi court. While seeking the king's favor, however, the concessionaires were reluctant to obey his political or judicial authority. Mbandzeni therefore requested Sir Theophilus Shepstone, previously diplomatic agent of the native tribes in Natal (1845–1853) and secretary for native affairs (1853–1875), as an adviser. Shepstone duly sent his own son, Offie Shepstone, who took the title of resident adviser and agent of the Swazi nation. In this role, Offie became Mbandzeni's adviser in all matters concerning white settlers in Swaziland. A fluent Zulu speaker, he was an enthusiastic confidante of the Swazi nation, based on the strength of his father's influence on the ruling house rather than his own ability. His duties were to curb the concessions that were beginning to overwhelm Mbandzeni; in fact, however, he approved the largest number of concessions ever in the two-year period from 1887 to 1889. Moreover, Offie personally acquired six concessions in his own name and witnessed several others for various white concessionaires. The discovery that he had been encouraging concessions soon soured his relationship with the Swazi ruling house. Offie Shepstone knew fully well that the more concessions the king awarded, the more he would personally gain from the Swazi nation, for at the start of his employment, the two sides had agreed that the Swazi would pay him half the nation's entire income. As the bulk of this income came from the concessions, it was no surprise that far from helping control concessions granting at Mbandzeni's court, Offie Shepstone abetted the activities of the concessionaires. He was dismissed in February 1889, only to be reinstated later in October. He already had earned large sums of money from the Swazi royal house. By the time of his second dismissal in 1894, his payment had accumulated to as much as US$30,645.

The Swazi repeatedly told the late Hilda Kuper, doyenne of Swazi studies, that "the concessions killed us." It was only a short step from the concessions era to the formal imposition of European colonial rule over the nation. Although the Swazi rulers later argued that King Mbandzeni had never granted any permanent concessions and that Swazi sovereignty had never been forfeited, the whole country had in fact been handed over to the concessionaires. The rights so granted to European individuals and companies in the late 1890s included those that governments ordinarily exercised. The king had ceded posts, telegraphs, railways, customs, land rights, farming, grazing, and mineral rights to foreigners during the concessions rush. Realizing the dangers posed by the concessions-seekers, Mbandzeni later bitterly complained that they were disrupting the peace in his country and threatening his independence. Britain and the South African Republic, the two foreign powers involved in southeastern Africa at the time, signed the Conventions of Pretoria (1881) and London (1884), seeking to guarantee Swazi independence and sovereignty. By then, however, white intrusion into the kingdom had so eroded the nation's social and economic integrity as to render the conventions completely meaningless.

An interim period of joint rule in Swaziland by the two powers followed from 1890 to 1894. However, this arrangement was far from satisfactory as a solution to the concessions squabble at Mbandzeni's court. The continuing confusion led directly to the two white powers' decision to conclude a third agreement, the convention of 1894, by which the South African Republic (alias Transvaal) assumed "the protection, legislation, jurisdiction and administration" of Swaziland. The document pointed out that this "control" by Transvaal did not mean the incorporation of Swaziland. As Noel Garson (1957) has argued, however, this convention did nothing to guarantee or salvage Swazi independence or sovereignty. The convention of 1894, like the two previous ones, had been concluded by the two imperial rivals (Britain and Transvaal) without taking into account the Swazi people's views.

The outbreak of the Anglo-Boer War in 1899 signaled the end of Transvaal's five-year control of Swaziland. The next three years were a period of uncertainty concerning the country's future. The Swazi interpreted both powers' abandonment of their country in 1899 as marking the end of Transvaal control. They saw the Boers' defeat at the hands of the British in the war as a signal for the return of their own independence and sovereignty. However, the British assumed control of Swaziland soon after the end of the war; the first British Special Commissioner for the country, F. Enraght-Moony, arrived in June 1902. Since the country's old administrative headquarters, Bremersdorp (modern-day Manzini), had been destroyed during the war, the new British administration was now established at Mbabane. As elsewhere in British colonial Africa, the colonial state here was initially quite feeble: the special commissioner had at his disposal a small force of the South African Constabulary and a skeleton support staff of administrators. Thus, the European involvement in Swaziland, attributable largely to the concessions saga, had culminated in the annexation of the country by the British.

BALAM NYEKO

See also: **South Africa: Confederation, Disarmament and the First Anglo-Boer War, 1871–1881.**

Further Reading

Bonner, Philip. *Kings, Commoners and Concessionaires: The Evolution and Dissolution of the Nineteenth-Century Swazi State*. Johannesburg: Ravan Press/Cambridge: Cambridge University Press, 1983.

Garson, Noel George. "The Swaziland Question and a Road to the Sea, 1887–1895." *Archives Yearbook for South African History*, no. 2 (1957): 263–434.

Jones, Huw M. *Biographical Register of Swaziland to 1902*. Pietermaritzburg: University of Natal Press, 1993.

Kuper, Hilda. *An African Aristocracy: Rank among the Swazi*. London: Oxford University Press, 1947.

Nyeko, Balam. "Prenationalist Resistance to Colonial Rule: Swaziland on the Eve of the Imposition of British Administration, 1890–1902." *Transafrican Journal of History 5*, no. 2 (1976): 66–83.

Simelane, Hamilton Sipho. "Swazi Resistance to Boer Penetration and Domination, 1881–1898." *Transafrican Journal of History*, no. 18 (1989): 117–146.

Swaziland: Colonial Period: Land, Labor, Administration

The expansion of Western imperialism into southern Africa was manifested by the struggle for land between the incoming whites and the indigenous population. In Swaziland this process was highlighted by an influx of concession seekers of both British and Boer origin. They crowded the palace of King Mbandzeni, who in collaboration with his councilors issued numerous concessions which covered almost the whole country. The Swazi indigenous leadership, especially that of Queen Labotsibeni, contested the validity of the concessions arguing that the Swazi only gave occupancy rights to the whites.

When the British assumed control over Swaziland in 1903 they were faced with the difficult task of determining the validity of the concessions. In 1904 they established a commission to determine which concessions were valid. The work of the commission culminated in the Crown Lands Order, and the Concession Partition Proclamation of 1907. These proclamations legitimated most of the concessions such that approximately two-thirds of the land area of the country was alienated and shared between the British crown and concessionaires. The Swazi objected, claiming that the British government did not take cognizance of traditional Swazi systems of land allocation under which the concessions were given. Nevertheless, the British government appointed George Grey as special commissioner to demarcate the land; his work resulted in the creation of 32 reserves for Swazi occupation. The Swazi resident on land designated as private land were given a grace period of five years, after which they had to vacate the land.

From 1914 to the 1940s the negative impact of land alienation became evident. The number of landless peasants rose to over 20,000 by 1914; they were forced to enter into tenancy arrangements with the white owners. By the 1930s the majority of the reserves experienced overstocking, soil erosion, population congestion, and decline in land productivity. At the same time, most landowners were forcing peasants out of their farms in response to the capitalization of settler agriculture.

The British government was forced to address the problem of landlessness. This led to the establishment of the Native Land Settlement Scheme in the 1940s. By 1950 a little more than 50 per cent of the total land area was in the hands of the Swazi.

The land question in Swaziland remained problematic throughout the colonial period. The problem continued into the postcolonial period and the leadership of an independent Swaziland has failed to find a lasting solution.

The imposition of British colonial rule had a fundamental impact on labor relations in Swaziland as well: it intensified the process of labor migration to South African mines. The main focus of policy was to satisfy the labor demands of the South African mining industry while attempting not to upset the supply for local employers.

From the beginning of the colonial period the Swazi labor market was dominated by South African recruiting agents. The Swazi colonial state attempted to regulate the recruitment of labor with the aim of protecting the interests of the recruits and those of local employers.

However, colonial labor relations were not completely a matter of migration to South African mines. From the 1920s there was a growing local demand for labor which complicated the Swazi labor market. This local dimension was manifested after World War II, when the Swazi economy became more capitalized. The development of agroforestry industries on the Highveld and the sugar industries in the Lowveld opened up employment opportunities locally.

The concentration of labor in local enterprises was accompanied by a growing level of labor organization and labor militancy. This resulted in the formation of the first labor union in the country, among the workers at Usuthu Forests at Bhunya in 1962. Labor organization was received with displeasure by both the colonial government and the indigenous leadership. The outbreak of strikes between 1962 and 1963 intensified such negative attitudes. Official attempts to frustrate the unionization of labor became a characteristic of labor relations in colonial and postcolonial Swaziland.

After the conclusion of the South African War, the British took over the administration of Swaziland. They were reluctant to set up an independent colonial administration, thus Swaziland was administered as part of the Transvaal. In 1906 Swaziland, Basutoland, and the Bechuanaland Protectorate were placed under the British high commissioner and referred to as the High Commission Territories.

The type of colonial administration that emerged was structurally confusing, because it appeared to be largely dualistic, though power relations were unequal. There was the colonial government, the daily administration of which was carried out by a resident commissioner who was responsible to the high commissioner. There was also an assistant government secretary and a financial secretary. At the same time, the indigenous Swazi political structure was not destroyed but enjoyed administrative privileges on all matters pertaining to Swazi law and custom. The Swazi were administered through the monarchy and local authorities. The initial aim of preserving the indigenous hierarchies was to make sure that the Swazi were encouraged to establish internal self-government to suppress crimes and settle intertribal disputes. The first colonial officials were instructed to respect any Swazi laws provided they did not conflict with British sovereignty or were not injurious to the welfare of the Swazi population.

This type of administrative structure was sometimes referred to as "parallel rule" or "dual rule." The British government was determined to keep the cost of administration to a minimum and thus confined the functions of colonial officials to maintaining law and order, leaving actual administrative responsibility for Swazi affairs to the indigenous leadership. This created power centers which at times did not work to a common purpose. The Swazi king was expected to implement colonial polic, while at the same time, his subjects regarded him as king and turned to him for protection against the colonial administration. The structure left the colonial government less effective, because the traditional leadership remained in control of the areas occupied by the Swazi.

Parallel rule characterized colonial administration in Swaziland up to independence. Even though revisions were made from time to time, the general framework of the administrative structure remained the same. One of the major additions which took place was the establishment of the European Advisory Council in 1921. The main purpose of this body was to advice the colonial government on matters concerning the white population. This body grew to play a very prominent role in the administration of the country because it was consulted by the colonial government on most issues. It gave the settlers a political muscle especially for the purposes of lobbying for settler interests. Its establishment gave the administrative structure of the country a tripolar character, which continued up to independence.

HAMILTON SIPHO SIMELANE

See also: **Labotsibeni.**

Further Reading

Bonner, Philip. *Kings, Commoners and Concessionaires: The Evolution and Dissolution of the Nineteenth Century Swazi State*. Johannesburg: Ravan Press, 1983.

Crush, J. S. "The Colonial Division of Space: The Significance of the Swaziland Land Partition." *International Journal of African Historical Studies* 13, no. 1(1980): 71–86.

Crush, Jonathan, Alan Jeeves, and David Yudelman. *South Africa's Labor Empire: A History of Black Migrancy to the Gold Mines*. Boulder, Colo.: Westview Press, 1991.

Jeeves, Alan. *Migrant Labor in South Africa's Mining Economy: The Struggle for the Gold Mines's Labor Supply*. Kingston, Ont.: Queens-McGill University Press, 1985.

Simelane, Hamilton Sipho. "Capitalism and the Development of the Swazi Working Class, 1947–1962." In *Social Transformation: The Swazi Case*, edited by Nomthetho G. Simelane. Dakar: CODESRIA, 1995.

———. "Labor Mobilization for the War Effort in Swaziland, 1941–1942," *International Journal of African Historical Studies* 26, no. 3 (1993): 541–574.

———. "Landlessness and Imperial Response in Swaziland, 1938–1950." *Journal of Southern African Studies* 17, no. 4 (1991): 717–740.

Spence, J. E. "British Policy toward the High Commission Territories." *Journal of Modern African Studies* 11, no. 2 (1964): 220–246.

Wilson, F. *Labor in the South African Gold Mines, 1911–1969*. Cambridge: Cambridge University Press, 1972.

Youe, C. P. "Imperial Land Policy in Swaziland and the African Response." *Journal of Imperial and Commonwealth History* 7, no. 1 (1978): 56–70.

Swaziland: Kingship, Constitution, Independence

When Swaziland regained its independence from Britain in October 1968, King Sobhuza II was recognized as both *Ngwenyama* ("Lion," the Swazi traditional ruler) and the new head of state. The new constitution gave Sobhuza executive authority and allotted him complete political power in the country. Since 1968, Swaziland has seen a steady entrenchment of the king's position in the political development of the country, and a general consolidation of the power of the chiefs and other traditional rulers over the Swazi people. At the same time, the modern political parties' role has shrunk. In April 1973 the late Sobhuza II repealed the constitution and assumed all judicial, executive and legislative powers. Shortly after this, the king dissolved parliament and abolished party politics. He introduced a new system of rule through the Swazi *tinkhundla* (local traditional government structures), a mechanism that secured royal hegemony in the country even more firmly. In the postindependence period, Swazi kingship has thrived, while the prospects for multiparty politics have receded into the background.

The critical role of Swazi kingship and its centrality in Swaziland's social and political history in the twentieth century is best reflected in the Swazi saying that "without a king, we are no longer a people," and that in Swazi politics "kingship is the father, the people are the children." From precolonial times, the Dlamini ruling clan acquired for themselves a preeminent position through a variety of claims. During the early part of the nineteenth century, these included their ability to extract tribute from the surrounding peoples and to provide them with protection from the more powerful neighbors such as the Zulu. Having survived the social and political upheavals known as the *mfecane* (crushing, or forced migration), affecting the entire African population of the region from the 1830s to the 1850s, the Swazi kings continued to occupy this dominant role in Swazi affairs up to the period of European conquest and beyond. Throughout colonial rule, the Swazi royal house remained the focus of the nation, forging for itself a special position as both the champion and the protector of Swazi interests. One such key interest was the land question, which dated from the late nineteenth century and remained a major theme running through the country's history until the time of independence. During the first decade of the twentieth century, the British colonial state formally declared that two-thirds of Swaziland belonged to the white concessionaires (mining prospectors, land speculators and Boer farmers) who had arrived in the 1880s and 1890s and later settled in the country. Under the 1907 Land Partition Scheme, only one-third of the country would be reserved for the Swazi. This was clearly inadequate. From the early colonial period, therefore, the royal house led the "purchase back land" campaign, started by Queen Labotsibeni, and continued later by King Sobhuza II himself. This campaign earned the ruling house a fair measure of popularity among the ordinary Swazi, who began to regard the king and his adherents as their true leaders in the anticolonial struggle. A second area where the royal house seems to have played an equally outstanding role during the colonial period was in the Swazi resistance to the prospects of transfer from being controlled by the British to the Union of South Africa. From the formation of Union in 1910 up to the 1950s, transfer seemed a distinct possibility. Just like their counterparts in the other two former High Commission Territories of Botswana and Lesotho, the Swazi adamantly opposed the idea of their being incorporated into South Africa. Again, from Queen Labotsibeni's regency to Sobhuza II's reign in later years the Swazi ruling house always spearheaded the Swazi protest against this move. Throughout the colonial period, the Swazi "traditional" hierarchy successfully retained its separate identity and, in the eyes of its followers, was never really associated with the colonial authority. The royal house was therefore able to command a strong sense of loyalty from the country's largely rural and intensely conservative population.

A striking feature of the decolonization of Swaziland, then, was that the monarchy not only played a prominent role in the nationalist politics by directly participating in the leadership of the independence-winning party, the Imbokodvo National Movement (INM), but survived to take over political power from the departing colonialists. The INM, based upon the ideology of traditionalism, sought to mobilize the Swazi through a network of chiefs that paid allegiance to the king. By mid-1965 it had emerged as the prime mover in Swazi preindependence politics. Sobhuza maintained that this movement was not a political party but merely an extension of the "traditional" Swazi National Council, to be used as a weapon in political struggles. By stressing that it was an institution open to all Swazi, the only qualification for joining being "Swaziness," the INM appealed to the conservative elements in Swazi society, which meant the bulk of the Swazi populace. It was prepared to collaborate, if only temporarily, with the European settlers in Swaziland and the Republic of South Africa to crush the political parties. The INM strove for Swazi unity above all else and set about fighting the trade unions and the modern parties. Of all

these political parties, Ambrose Zwane's Ngwane National Liberatory Congress (NNLC) was probably the strongest. Swazi traditionalists regarded it as their archenemy. The NNLC espoused militant Pan-Africanism and commanded considerable support from the working class. In the end, King Sobhuza II successfully outmaneuvered not only the NNLC but also smaller political organizations such as J. J. Nquku's Swaziland Progressive Party, Allen Nxumalo's Swaziland Democratic Party, and Dr. George Msibi's short-lived Mbandzeni National Convention. Besides these African-dominated parties, a white settler political organization, the United Swaziland Association also emerged in the early 1960s. Starting as a social organization seeking to preserve the privileged position of the Europeans in Swaziland, the United Swaziland Association initially opposed the idea of independence for Swaziland, arguing that the choice here was—as in South Africa—between "white control and black nationalism." It wanted parity with the Africans in the parliament, despite their being overwhelmingly outnumbered by the Swazi population. Although the INM at first agreed to work with the United Swaziland Association and even accepted their idea of preserving a special position for whites, Sobhuza later changed his mind and pressed for a universal franchise. In the last preindependence elections held in Swaziland, the INM swept into power by winning all 24 seats in the parliament. At independence, therefore, both the European settlers and the African political party leaders had been either incorporated into Sobhuza's government or otherwise rendered completely ineffectual. The modern elite had been outwitted and political control had remained in the hands of the "traditional" authorities, the old elite, who had enjoyed access to some administrative power over the Swazi even under colonialism. The triumph of "tradition" over "modernity" had been achieved, but this victory had clearly sown the seeds of what was to be a continuing interfactional conflict in Swaziland's politics in subsequent years.

BALAM NYEKO

See also: **Swaziland: Sobhuza II, Life and Government of.**

Further Reading

Davies, Robert H., Dan O'Meara, and Sipho Dlamini. *The Kingdom of Swaziland: A Profile*. London: Zed, 1985.

Kuper, Hilda. *Sobhuza II: Ngwenyama and King of Swaziland*. London: Duckworth, 1978.

Macmillan, Hugh. "Swaziland: Decolonization and the Triumph of 'Tradition.'" *Journal of Modern African Studies* 23, no. 4 (1985): 643–666.

Matsebula, J. S. M. *A History of Swaziland*. Cape Town: Longman, 1987.

Potholm, Christian P. "The Ngwenyama of Swaziland: The Dynamics of Adaptation." In *African Kingships in Perspective: Political Change and Modernization in Monarchical Settings*, edited by R. Lemarchand. London: Cass, 1977.

———. *Swaziland: The Dynamics of Political Modernization*. Berkeley and Los Angeles: University of California Press, 1972.

Stevens, Richard P. "Swaziland Political Development." *Journal of Modern African Studies* 1, no. 3 (1963): 327–350.

Swaziland: Sobhuza II, Life and Government of

Nkhotfotjeni or Mona—later King—Sobhuza II of Swaziland was born on July 22, 1899. He was chosen as heir to the Swazi throne in 1899 and was installed as king in 1921. The choice of Sobhuza as heir to the Swazi throne was controversial, as his father left behind six widows with one child each—all with a legitimate claim to the throne. The council of princes given the responsibility to appoint the heir failed to make the final decision; it was left to Labotsibeni Mdluli, his grandmother, to decide. The selection followed Swazi law and custom, and because Sobhuza was still a minor, Labotsibeni ruled the country as queen regent. The British accepted that Sobhuza was the rightful heir to the Swazi throne but they felt that the title of king should be reserved for the British crown and that Sobhuza should be addressed as paramount chief.

Sobhuza was the first Swazi king to have a formal education. During World War I the high commissioner and the queen regent concluded that he should be sent to a school outside the country. In February 1916 he was sent to Lovedale in South Africa, where he stayed until 1918 when he was called back home following the death of Labotsibeni's daughter Ntongontongo. At the same time Labotsibeni's health began to deteriorate and she recommended that Sobhuza should not go back to school, but should be prepared to take over the leadership of the state.

Sobhuza took over from Labotsibeni in 1921 at a time when the Swazi were still bitter about land alienation suffered at the hands of the British. His first action was to continue Swazi requests for the restoration of the land alienated through the 1907 proclamation. The request for more land was made urgent by a growing problem of landlessness among the Swazi. Most of his attempts were not successful except for the establishment of the Native Land Settlement Scheme in the 1940s.

Sobhuza devoted a significant effort to the preservation of political institutions. He was aware that in most of Africa colonialism had destroyed traditional systems of governance. Preserving and strengthening the monarchy was the main priority of his leadership. He insisted that colonial officials had no authority to deal directly with the Swazi population in the reserves; he wanted the Swazi in the reserves to pay allegiance to the traditional power structure and operate through traditional institutions. He also insisted that the traditional land tenure system should prevail in the reserves.

Sobhuza's determination to preserve traditional political institutions was demonstrated in the 1940s, when he resisted attempts by the British to revise some aspects of the traditional authority. They proposed that the paramount chief and the chiefs in general should be appointed as opposed to inheriting the position. This proposition was rejected by Sobhuza; he insisted that Swazi law and custom should continue to govern the selection of Swazi kings and chiefs.

During the process of decolonization, Sobhuza continued to show his determination to preserve traditional political structures. The emergence of modern political parties was viewed by the traditionalists as a threat to the monarchy. Sobhuza reacted by forming his own political movement to contest for elections in the movement toward independence. He was successful in these attempts. The traditionalists inherited power from the British in 1968.

Sobhuza oversaw the Swazi state up to 1982. His reign was eventful partly because of its longevity and partly because of the aggressiveness with which traditional institutions were made operational in a predominantly volatile regional political atmosphere. The period from 1968 to 1982 was characterized by contradictions of an economically modernizing state and an undemocratic political organization.

From 1968, Sobhuza entrenched the traditional political structure while at the same time systematically eliminating all political opposition. The management of the state was divided into a traditional structure and a modern one. Sobhuza emphasized the primacy of Swazi tradition in conducting the affairs of the state.

Another important characteristic of Sobhuza's reign and government was personal rule. Modern political parties could only be tolerated as long as they upheld the authority of the king. The centralization of power in the king was reinforced by the independence constitution, which gave the king executive and legislative powers: Sobhuza had the power to make the final decision on all matters of the state. Such powers were even incorporated in his praise songs, which stated that he was "the mouth that spoke no lie." He enjoyed the power to appoint the cabinet, and loyalty to the king was central in such appointments. Up to his death in 1982, the political institutions of

Swaziland were a direct reflection of Sobhuza's thinking.

Sobhuza's reign can also be identified with intolerance of opposition, an intolerance presumably justified by tradition. He argued that political parties had no place in Swazi tradition and, therefore, could not play a role in the political organization of the Swazi state. He argued that the Swazi leadership was not a matter to be contested, because tradition was clear as to who should form the leadership. He pointed out that political parties were foreign entities and were unsuitable for Swaziland. He urged the Swazi to follow their traditional institutions in all their attempts to bring about change. His negative attitude regarding political parties led him to take steps to eliminate all forms of opposition.

The first such assault came through the overthrow of the constitution incorporated at independence through a decree in 1973. It was argued that the constitution did not allow the Swazi to be governed through their traditional institutions, as it allowed for the existence of political parties which could contest for leadership of the state. With the overthrow of the constitution, subsequent governments of Swaziland were handpicked by Sobhuza. From 1973 the traditional oligarchy reigned supreme, as opposition was suppressed.

This development was followed by the implementation of laws that generally deprived the Swazi of their freedoms of expression and association. It became illegal to hold demonstrations, and to have gatherings of more than five people without the permission of the commissioner of police. Those who violated these laws were subjected to detention for sixty days without trial. The majority of those opposed to Sobhuza were forced into silence; thus, the country appeared to be enjoying peace and stability.

While the opposition was being silenced, the traditionalists moved further to attempt to give legitimacy to the traditional political order. This was done through the activation of the *Tinkhundla* system of political organization. This system began operating in 1978 and it became one of Swaziland's versions for democracy; it was a system in which the parliamentarians are elected in rural localities called Tinkhundla and are expected to represent their specific regions in parliament. It was a continuation of the strategy of entrenching the power of the traditional oligarchy, and more particularly, that of the king.

When Sobhuza died in 1982, political organization and state management were still characterized by the supremacy of traditional institutions, as embodied by Sobhuza. The ministers who formed the government paid allegiance to the king, as he enjoyed the power to appoint cabinet ministers. Labor organizations, and political formations were suppressed as they were seen to be a threat to the monarchy.

HAMILTON SIPHO SIMELANE

See also: **Labotsibeni.**

Further Reading

Booth, Alan R. *Swaziland: Tradition and Change in a Southern African Kingdom.* Boulder, Colo.: Westview Press, 1983.

Daniel, John, Gladys Simelane, and Vusani Simelane (eds.). *Politics and Society in Swaziland.* Kwaluseni, University of Botswana, Lesotho and Swaziland, 1975.

Kuper, Hilda. *Sobhuza II, Ngwenyama and King of Swaziland: The Story of a Hereditary Ruler and His Country.* London: Duckworth, 1978.

Macmillan, Hugh. "Swaziland: Decolonization and the Triumph of Tradition." In *Historical Perspectives of the Political Economy of Swaziland: Selected Articles*, edited by John Daniel and Michael Stephen. Kwaluseni, Social Science Research Unit, 1986.

Potholm, C. "Changing Political Configurations in Swaziland." *Journal of Modern African Studies* 4, no. 3 (1966): 313–322.

———. *Swaziland: The Dynamics of Political Modernization.* Berkeley and Los Angeles: University of California Press, 1972.

Swaziland: Mswati III, Reign of

The Death of King Sobhuza II in 1982 left the nation of Swaziland in a state of uncertainty, as the entire government machinery had revolved around him. Some individuals in the royal family began to fight for supreme authority and they managed to gain support from some members of the Swaziland National Council. People such as Prince Mfanasibili wanted to impose themselves as the final decision makers in the absence of a substantive king.

The infighting was promoted by the rise of a political body called the Liqoqo, which had existed before colonial rule and was reconstituted in the colonial period into the Swaziland National Council. Its main responsibility was to advise the king on all matters of the state. It was made up of selected princes and regional chiefs, all of whom were appointed by the king. The confusion that resulted after 1982 arose from the fact that in the same year Sobhuza issued a decree elevating the Liqoqo to supreme council of state. His aim was to ensure the continuity of traditional rule. Although the decree defined the powers of the king and the manner of succession to the throne, it did not clarify the authority of the Liqoqo in the absence of a king, nor harmonize the relationship between the Liqoqo, as a supreme council of state, and the cabinet.

On Sobhuza's death, the queen regent Dzeliwe assumed her role, the 15 members of the Liqoqo were appointed by the queen regent, and Prince Sozisa was appointed as "authorized person," which meant he was to perform the functions of regent when she was not able to perform those functions. In this setup, the Liqoqo regarded itself as above all the other organs of the state including the office of the regent. Members of the Liqoqo also saw themselves as above the office of the prime minister. They accused the prime minister, Prince Mabandla, of organizing a coup to eliminate traditional leadership. This began a vicious struggle between the prime minister and the Liqoqo. Prince Mabandla was dismissed, and Prince Bhekimpi, a puppet of the Liqoqo, was appointed in his place.

Upon Mabandla's dismissal, the Liqoqo began to purge the civil service and other institutions of all those suspected of anti-Liqoqo feelings. It dismissed the head of state, Queen Regent Dzeliwe in August 1983. In her place they installed Queen Ntombi, mother of Sobhuza's son Makhosetive. He was announced as the heir to the Swazi throne. The ousting of Dzeliwe provoked protests from the general public, especially university students. The response from the Liqoqo was decisive, as over 30 students were arrested. A number of popular democratic movements emerged, such as the People's United Democratic Movement (PUDEMO), to push for democratic reforms and good governance.

The crisis of the regency, and the manner in which civil society reacted, demonstrated that, in the absence of a king, the Swazi political system was on the verge of collapse. The traditionalists saw their political authority gradually slipping away. The only solution, according to those who supported the monarchical system of government, was to crown the heir as king, even at a tender age. On April 25, 1986, 18-year-old Prince Makhosetive was recalled from boarding school in England and crowned as King Mswati III. In the same year the Liqoqo was disbanded and a new prime minister was appointed.

The reign of Mswati III has not produced a fundamental departure from the reign of his father. The country is still in a state of emergency, as it has been since the 1973 decree. Mswati III's reign faced opposition from different sections of the Swazi population, especially workers and university students. The same kind of repressive mechanisms employed by Sobhuza have continued to be applied against opponents of the old order. For instance, in 1990 the executive leadership of the PUDEMO was charged with treason after seditious pamphlets were found by police in different parts of the country. It was alleged that PUDEMO wanted to overthrow Mswati III and his government.

Mswati III has realized the need to review certain political institutions. The first to come under review was the Tinkhundla system, a traditional form of political organization which rejects modern party politics. This followed widespread opposition to the system and a realization that the system was not efficient. In 1991 Mswati III established the Tinkhundla Review Commission, popularly known as Vusela, to gather general opinion from the regions as to how the system could be transformed. When the commission submitted its conclusions in 1992, almost all the views of the proponents of democratization were ignored. According to the findings of the commission, the majority of the people in Swaziland were in favor of the Tinkhundla system.

The call for political transformation continued to trouble Mswati III's reign into the 1990s. Of particular significance were the calls for the nullification of the 1973 decree, which prevented the citizenry from engaging in free political dialogue. Even though the traditionalists, especially advisors of the king, continued to argue against political change, it was clear that the voices of protest could not be ignored for long. The situation was made more volatile by the mushrooming of new political groupings claiming the right to political participation. For instance, the majority of political parties came together to form the Swaziland Democratic Alliance, aimed at pressing for the democratization of the political institutions of the country.

Mswati III was forced to address the issue of political transformation. He decided to give priority to the formulation of a constitution, and in 1996 established the Constitutional Review Commission (CRC). The first step was a major source of controversy. The conflict arose when the traditionalists insisted that the king should appoint the commissioners, while a large number of people argued that the political organizations should be represented in their own right. Political groupings also insisted that the review process should be preceded by the removal of the 1973 decree, but the traditionalists felt that the decree should remain in force. The king went ahead and appointed the commissioners.

In 2001, the chairman of the CRC, Mangaliso Dlamini, announced that the powers of the king would be expanded, though few details were provided. Soon thereafter, King Mswati III announced that a new commission would be formed to draft a new constitution. However, no concrete results, or new constitutions, have as yet been presented.

The post-Sobhuza era in Swaziland can be generally characterized as a period of confusion in which questions of the past have resurfaced, while answers have not been forthcoming. Civil society has increased its demand for political transformation and democratization, while these processes have continued to be seen as a threat to the monarchy, and there is a continued reluctance to allow political participation within the framework of a modern state apparatus. Mswati III has attempted to bring about political transformation, but only toward the goal of strengthening and perpetuating the traditional order. This has put Swaziland in a very precarious position in light of changing political configurations in Southern Africa, as the majority of Southern African Development Community states have moved decisively toward democratization.

HAMILTON SIPHO SIMELANE

Further Reading

Furnell, D. C. *Under the Shadow of Apartheid: Agrarian Transformation in Swaziland.* London: Avery Press, 1991.

Levin, R. "Is This the Swazi Way?" *Transformation*, no. 13 (1990).

———. *When Sleeping Grass Awakens: Land and Power in Swaziland.* Johannesburg: Witwatersrand University Press, 1997.

Simelane, Hamilton S. "The Post-Colonial State, Class and the Land Question in Swaziland." *Journal of Contemporary African Studies* 11, no. 1 (1992): 22–50.

Simelane, R. M. "Some Succession Disputes over Kingship in the History of the Swazi People from 1840–1899." B.Ed. thesis, University of Swaziland, 1985.

Vilakati, S. J. "Labour and Politics in Swaziland, 1960–1996," B.A. thesis, University of Swaziland, 1997.

T

Takedda: *See* **Tuareg: Takedda and Trans-Saharan Trade.**

Tanganyika (Tanzania): Early Nineteenth Century

The first half of the nineteenth century witnessed some of the most far-reaching changes in the history of Tanzania. During this period the two main regions of the territory—the coast and the interior—were economically, and to some degree culturally, united into one whole. The coast had long been an active participant in Indian Ocean trade, but from the late 1700s the interior was gradually incorporated into the world economy, initially under quite favorable conditions. The international price of ivory, the region's main export, continued to rise against that of cotton sheeting, the main import. By the 1850s along the internal trade routes it was rare to find people dressed in skins or bark cloth. At the same time guns were beginning to enter the region in large numbers. This, along with the slave trade, Ngoni migrations from southern Africa, and increasing commercial competition between Swahili and Arab traders and interior peoples such as the Nyamwezi, initiated a period of intermittent violence later in the century.

Until recently, the history of precolonial Tanzania was written in terms of outsiders initiating change, whether it was the putative introduction of *ntemi*-ship (chiefship) from the interlacustrine (Great Lakes) region to the Sukuma and others south of Lake Victoria, the military innovations of the Ngoni, or "Arab" initiative in the caravan trade. Such views no longer hold. The main dynamics have come from the people of Tanzania themselves. The most basic force up until the middle of the nineteenth century was gradual population growth. After that time increasing violence and—more important—the ravages of small pox, cholera, tick-borne fever, and other diseases, spread along the busy trade routes and checked the earlier advances. Population growth added to demand and hence further stimulated local, regional, and long-distance trade. Larger and mixed populations, and increased surplus production and trade in well-watered regions such as the northeast highlands (Pare, Kilimanjaro, and the Usambara Mountains), the southwest (Ubena, Usangu), the shores of Lakes Victoria and Tanganyika (Karagwe, Usukuma, Ufipa), and the western interior (Unyamwezi, Uha), stimulated processes of state building. In addition, further colonization and settlement of lowland bush country—by cultivators, elephant hunters, and warrior bands (*ruga ruga*), with their slaves and followers—took place, particularly along important trade routes such as in Unyamwezi, and in Uzigua in the northeast. In this regard the south remained exceptional. Here, slave raiding from Kilwa and other coastal towns combined with Ngoni predations began to empty large tracts of countryside.

Settlement of wilderness areas had another significant consequence. African cultivators living in permanent communities and with mutually beneficial relations with their political or ritual leaders carefully managed their environment, keeping at bay stock-infesting trypanosomes spread by the bush-loving tsetse fly. Active environmental control meant that livestock herds could be built up even in hostile areas, as farmers created islands of tsetse-free pasture and fields in the wilderness. This balancing act was as important as anything else in the settlement of large parts of Unyamwezi and the northeastern plains in the first half of the century. The collapse of these systems of environmental management, depopulation, and the spread of cattle diseases (East Coast fever, rinderpest) were to have a devastating effect later in the century.

If demographic growth underlay everything, the main motor of change was long-distance trade. In the eighteenth century local and regional trading networks were already well developed. In the far interior, the position of the Nyamwezi between the producers of salt and iron in the west and the consumers of iron to the east and south made them ideal intermediaries. In the northeast, trade among peoples occupying different environments, including highland peoples such as the Chagga, the pastoral Maasai, and the Dorobo hunter-gatherers, was also significant. Arrangements such as these stimulated and in turn were enriched by long-distance trade, which connected regional networks from the end of the eighteenth century. In the north, Arabs and Swahili from Tanga and Pangani were beginning to venture as far as Mount Kilimanjaro. In the central parts of the territory, the breakthrough had been made some time in the mid-eighteenth century, when Sagara highlanders from the east migrated to Unyamwezi, bringing news from the coast. By 1800 at the latest, Nyamwezi and Sumbwa pioneer caravan operators were carrying elephant tusks down to coastal towns such as Pangani and Mbwa Maji in response to the demand for ivory in India. In the first decades the caravan trade remained the preserve of interior peoples (except in the north), although in the 1820s coastal traders such as the Indian Musa Mzuri reached Unyamwezi. The trade was well established by the 1830s, and large caravans regularly arrived at the coast from the far interior, bringing ivory, gum copal, and other products for new, rapidly expanding markets in North America and Europe. In 1839 Seyyid Said, Omani ruler and the sultan of Zanzibar, sent his own exploratory expeditions into the interior, following earlier attempts to seek allies among the Nyamwezi. From that time coast-based Arabs and Swahili increasingly sent their own caravans up-country. A pattern developed of dry season travel along set routes by increasingly specialized traders and porters, often accompanied by their families. Entrepôts, market towns, and caravan stops soon emerged in a hierarchy of incipient urbanization along the main central trade routes. When in the late 1830s the line of the route moved north from the Great Ruaha River due to Sangu raiding and the great *Ilogo* famine, and passed instead through dry Ugogo in the center of the territory, the whole framework of the trading system altered. Established trading centers such as Zungomero declined while others, including Tabora and Ujiji, were founded. The older routes in the south converging on Kilwa and Lindi diminished in importance, even though Yao traders continued to be active, while the domination of the Nyamwezi and eventually the Arabs and Swahili of the northern (Mrima) coast was cemented.

By the middle of the century the long-distance trading system had reached maturity. Increasing commercialization along the routes familiarized people with the market, wage labor, and the profit motive. Peasants, including women, responded to market opportunities and sold provisions to the armies of porters. In the interior the rise of independent traders and elephant hunters undercut traditional routes to authority and power. In the most commercialized areas, accumulating strong men with access to trade goods and guns challenged hereditary chiefs recognized as descendants of founder settlers. One such was the Nyamwezi trader Kiringawana, described as a "usurper," who established himself at Kisanga in Usagara sometime before 1830. The increasing movement and intermixing of people, not only as traders and porters or slaves, but also within host communities, helped break down the old isolation. Innovations contributing to interethnic mixing and regrouping included joking relationships (*utani*) utilized for hospitality and aid in stranger communities, a common caravan work culture, the spread of trading languages—first Kinyamwezi, then Kiswahili, and the spread of religious cults.

The history of the Shambaa kingdom in the Usambara Mountains illustrates the new pressures. Mbegha, a wandering hunter, had founded the state, and in response to the threat presented by the arrival of the Cushitic-speaking Mbugu, united the Shambaa clans. The royal clan continued to dominate the state and the surrounding peoples, especially during the long rule of Kimweri, from 1815 to 1862. But even then the kingdom was being undermined, as neighboring Zigua lowlanders acquired guns from the 1830s, and were better placed to control trade along the Pangani Valley. When Kimweri died the kingdom collapsed amid chaos and slave raiding.

Change was also occurring at the coast and on the offshore islands. Seyyid Said made Zanzibar his permanent capital in 1840, and led the economic development of his dominions. Well before then an export economy based on clove plantations on Zanzibar and Pemba had been established. Wealth from cloves, ivory, and slaves led to the emergence on the islands of a landed elite, largely Arab but with Indian and Swahili elements. Indian merchants supplied capital and ran the Sultan's customs service, and labor came from the annual importation of about 10,000 slaves from the mainland. A much smaller number of slaves were exported to Oman and other Middle Eastern destinations from Kilwa, Zanzibar, and other ports. The British had already, by 1810, suppressed the French slave trade from East Africa to their Indian Ocean sugar islands. From early in the century the slave trade became subsidiary to the expanding ivory trade. European consuls, traders, and sailors were largely confined to Zanzibar during the 1830s and 1840s, but their presence foreshadowed increasing intervention later in the century. In the meantime Zanzibar, as the dominant commercial power in the region, was able to influence developments in the interior through its discriminatory customs duties and role as the region's central entrepôt.

STEPHEN J. ROCKEL

Further Reading

Feierman, Steven. *The Shambaa Kingdom: A History*. Madison: University of Wisconsin Press, 1974.

Gray, Richard, and David Birmingham (eds.). *Pre-colonial African Trade*. London: Oxford University Press, 1970.

Iliffe, John. *A Modern History of Tanganyika*. Cambridge: Cambridge University Press, 1979.

Kimambo, Isaria N. *A Political History of the Pare of Tanzania c. 1500–1900*. Nairobi: East Africa Publishing, 1969.

Kimambo, Isaria N., and A. J. Temu (eds.). *A History of Tanzania*. Nairobi: East Africa Publishing, 1969.

Koponen, Juhani, *People and Production in Late Precolonial Tanzania: History and Structures*, Jyväskylä, Finland: Scandinavian Institute of African Studies, 1988.

Nicholls, C. S. *The Swahili Coast: Politics, Diplomacy and Trade on the East African Littoral 1798–1856*. London: Allen and Unwin, 1971.

Roberts, Andrew (ed.). *Tanzania before 1900*, Nairobi: East African Publishing, 1968.

Sheriff, Abdul. *Slaves, Spices and Ivory in Zanzibar: Integration of an East African Commercial Empire into the World Economy 1770–1873*. London: James Currey/Athens, Ohio: Ohio University Press, 1987.

Shorter, Aylward. *Chiefship in Western Tanzania: A Political History of the Kimbu*. Oxford: Oxford University Press, 1972.

Tanganyika (Tanzania): Ngoni Incursion from the South

While migration in African history often was a gradual, peaceful process, that of the Ngoni from South Africa to Tanzania was quite different. In a mere 20 years, the Ngoni traveled nearly 2000 miles, raiding and absorbing other societies. In Tanzania, their impact was profound. In some places they brought devastation, but in others their administrative and military systems were closely emulated. Often they provided the catalyst for the tighter coalescence of local communities.

The migration began about 1820, following the victory of the Zulu over their Nguni-speaking rivals, the Ndwandwe. Zwangendaba, an Ndwandwe *induna* (commander) fled north with a band of refugees who became known as the Ngoni. Having clashed with another band of fugitives in Mozambique, the Ngoni entered Zimbabwe and shattered the Rozvi federation of Shona speakers before crossing the Zambezi in 1835. Zwangendaba then led his followers northward up the corridor between the Luangwa River and Lake Malawi until finally establishing himself on the Fipa plateau in southern Tanzania. En route the Ngoni had become a relentless predatory state, consuming resources and incorporating outsiders to swell their numbers. With a superior military system based on the revolutionary

Zulu model of Shaka, the Ngoni easily overwhelmed decentralized peoples in their path; even more centralized ones, including some who had acquired firearms, proved no match for them. Their age-class system, which provided Zwangendaba with corporate, well-disciplined regiments, also facilitated the assimilation of strangers. By 1840 his followers were essentially a multitribal nation, held together by a common subscription to a superior Ngoni military culture.

As the migration progressed, however, it proved impossible to maintain the old Zulu-inspired system intact. Central control over age regiments became weaker; younger warriors established greater independence from their indunas. During his lifetime, Zwangendaba had managed to hold the society together, but with his death in the 1840s, damaging quarrels tore it apart into five major segments. Three of these returned south to establish Ngoni kingdoms in Malawi. The other two, the Tuta and Gwangara, pushed ahead into other parts of Tanzania.

The Tuta, advancing northward, continued for a while the tradition of predatory migration. One band of them, penetrating through Unyamwezi to the shores of Lake Victoria, eventually settled in the area west of Kahama, where, unlike other Ngoni groups, they maintained a cohesive identity, until finally dislodged by the Germans in 1891. Elsewhere, Tuta raids were launched against many western Tanzanian societies and they temporarily disrupted commerce along the central trade route from the coast. Increasingly, however, most Tuta disintegrated into smaller autonomous communities, and it became clear they would not be able to establish the same easy dominance over local peoples as they had to the south. In 1858, Ngoni raiders were defeated at Ujiji on Lake Tanganyika by slave musketeers in the service of coastal traders. They were also repulsed by reinvigorated Tongwe, Ha, and Rundi communities. Some Nyamwezi chiefs were stimulated into improving their military systems to repel Ngoni raids. Other societies constructed stout fortifications against their attacks. Still others, such as the Holoholo and Lunga, adopted Ngoni military techniques and sometimes began to surpass the skill of the Tuta groups themselves.

Gradually, many of the Tuta bands were subsumed by local societies. Into the 1870s some kept a degree of autonomy by forming military alliances with Nyamwezi and other communities. From these alliances emerged *ruga ruga* mercenary bands upon whom emergent nineteenth-century leaders in western Tanzania, including Nyungu-ya-Mawe and Mirambo, built their power. But while derived from Ngoni military tradition, the disciplined order of the original Nguni system quickly gave way to a more individualistic military professionalism: firearms supplanted stabbing spears; fantastic costumes replaced prescribed regimental uniforms. Increasingly the ruga ruga comprised rootless brigands drawn from many different sources, the products, ironically, of the restlessness which Ngoni intrusion into the region had helped foster in the first place.

In the meantime, the Gwangara segment of the Ngoni had been raiding and advancing into southeastern Tanzania, eventually forming two separate kingdoms, Njelu and Mshope. Here they encountered yet another far-ranging group of Nguni speakers from South Africa, the Maseko. While Zwangendaba's Ngoni had advanced northward to the west of Lake Malawi, these Maseko had migrated up through Mozambique, conquering and absorbing elements of the societies they encountered, and crossing the Rovuma River in the 1840s. Reaching the Songea plains, they subdued such groups as the Ndendeuli, Ndonde, and Nindi, and, when the Njelu and Mshope Ngoni arrived from the northwest, subjugated them as well. Internecine quarrels rapidly developed, however, and most of the Maseko were pushed back across the Rovuma in the 1850s. The Ndendeuli and other subject peoples, having learned much from their conquerors, now began to emulate them. Proclaiming themselves Ngoni, they formed their own chiefdoms. So fearsome was their reputation that they sometimes intimidated their neighbors merely by threat. In a series of conflicts, the Njelu and Mshope Ngoni established domination over the Songea region. Much of southeastern Tanzania was in turmoil. Outsiders, finding it impossible to distinguish between "true" Ngoni and their imitators, called them collectively *maviti* (robbers). Raids pushed nearly to the present border of Kenya in the north, and to the south ravaged Yao, Makonde, and Makua societies well into Mozambique. To the east, forays reached the outskirts of coastal towns such as Kilwa and Lindi. At first disrupting commerce, some Maviti eventually took to slave and ivory trading, sending caravans of their own to the coast.

To the west, the picture was different. Peoples such as the Sangu and Hehe adopted aspects of the Ngoni system to form more centralized and powerful states. By 1878 the Hehe were strong enough to take the offensive against Ngoni chiefdoms. A new military balance was created by the establishment of an *utani* (joking relationship) between them by about 1882.

By then, however, the Ngoni and their imitators were attracting the attention of powerful outsiders. The raids on the coastal towns had brought an intervention from the Sultan of Zanzibar, in whose sphere of influence they lay. Then, in 1882, an Ngoni raid on the neighborhood of an English mission station at Masasi brought about a growing European involvement.

Many of the Ngoni communities were beginning to turn away from pillaging to more sedentary cultivation, and the ongoing process of political disintegration was resulting in ever smaller and more localized chiefdoms in many places. From the early 1890s the Germans sought to encourage such fragmentation by recognizing local *indunas* as independent "sultans" in their new colonial order. Although initial control over Songea was established without Ngoni resistance in 1897, some communities eventually rebelled in 1905, but were decimated by German forces.

Nevertheless, a powerful legacy of Ngoni cultural identity persisted in southeastern Tanzania through the eras of colonialism and independence. Peoples descended from Zwangendaba's migration, or, of equal significance, those who had been merely affected by it and subsequent Ngoni incursions, continued to take pride in traditions of a military and administrative sophistication hardly surpassed in this part of Africa.

JOHN LAMPHEAR

Further Reading

Burton, Richard F. *The Lake Regions of Central Africa*, vol. 2. London: Longman, 1860.

Gallacher, J. T. "The Emergence of an African Ethnic Group: The Case of the Ndendeuli." *International Journal of African Historical Studies* 7, no. 1 (1975): 1–26.

Gulliver, P. H. "History of the Songea Ngoni," *Tanganyika Notes and Records*, no. 41 (1955): 16–23.

Lamburn, R. G. P. "The Angoni Raid on Masasi in 1882." *Tanzania Notes and Records*, no. 66 (1966): 207–213.

Read, Margaret, "Tradition and Prestigue Among the Ngoni." *Africa*, 9 (1936).

Redmond, Patrick M., "Some Results of Military Contacts Between the Ngoni and Their Neighbors in nineteenth Century Southern East Africa." *Transafrican Journal of African History*, 5, no. 1 (1976).

Spear, Thomas T., *Zwangendaba's Ngoni, 1820–1890*, Madison: University of Wisconsin Press, 1972.

Stanley, H.M., *Through the Dark Continent*. London: George Newnes, 1899.

Thomson, Joseph, "Notes on the Basin of the River Rovuma, East Africa." *Proceedings of the Royal Geographical Society*, 2 (Feb. 1882): 65–99.

Tanganyika (Tanzania): Nyamwezi and Long-Distance Trade

From the beginning of the nineteenth century, Nyamwezi long distance trading caravans dominated the central routes through Tanzania, stretching from Mrima coast ports to Ujiji on Lake Tanganyika and beyond. The Nyamwezi carried prodigious quantities of ivory, hippopotamus teeth, and other products of the interior down to the coast to exchange for imported trade goods including cloth, firearms, wire, and beads. By the middle of the nineteenth century, East Africa had become the largest supplier of ivory in an international market rapidly expanding under the forces of industrialization. The terms of trade favored expansion of the system, as ivory prices increased, while the cost of imported mass-produced cloth declined. Despite the inroads of Omani Arab and Swahili trading enterprises from the middle of the century, the Nyamwezi maintained a position of strength, and their caravans ranged as far as Uganda, the eastern Congo, and Zambia.

The fortunes of Nyamwezi traders and porters (the latter were largely wage earners paid in cloth currency) were linked not just to trends on the coast and changes in the international economy, but also to adaptability in the face of these changes, and a favorable labor market. Developments within the Nyamwezi domestic economy facilitated long-distance trade and migrant labor. Like colonial migrant laborers, porters combined wage earning with continued access to household production on the land. In Unyamwezi, increased cultivation of *mbuga* marshlands and the adoption of white rice increased agricultural production. Many Nyamwezi traders and porters used their earnings and profits to invest in cattle and their farms, the more successful paying for additional labor in the form of wives, slaves, and client Tutsi cattle herders. In turn, access to these sources of labor made travel possible. Thus, the nature of gender and other social roles were crucial.

The Sagara migrations, the distribution of natural resources in western Tanzania, and the central position of the Nyamwezi in the regional trading system of western Tanzania were key factors leading to the rise of the caravan system. The Nyamwezi were essentially cultivators, producing among other crops various grains, pulses, potatoes, pumpkins, and tobacco. But because Unyamwezi is a little more forested than neighboring territories, they were able to exploit forest products such as honey; to make baskets, wooden utensils, and bark cloth; and to hunt wildlife. Lacking iron ore and good quality salt, the Nyamwezi exchanged their products for Sumbwa and Konongo iron, and salt from the Uvinza pans. Other neighbors, especially the Gogo, Sukuma, and Ha, kept large cattle herds. The Nyamwezi exchanged their grain, bark cloth, honey, and other products for the cattle and hides of the herders. The position of the Nyamwezi in the center of the regional trading system between the producers of salt and iron in the west, and the consumers of iron to the east and south, made them ideal intermediaries. The organization of the gender division of labor, the absence at first of large herds of cattle, and the utilization of immigrant Tutsi and slave labor, left them free to travel during the dry season when there was little work in the fields.

A further factor that may have encouraged long distance travel and caravan porterage was the prevailing condition of peace and stability. There is no evidence for attacks by outsiders until the mid-nineteenth century, when the migrating Ngoni invaded parts of Ukimbu, Unyamwezi, and Usumbwa. Prior to this, conflict was limited to occasional small-scale raiding of one Nyamwezi chiefdom by another. A long period of peace enabled the Nyamwezi to utilize other advantages that they possessed.

The Nyamwezi trading system developed its own unique cultural characteristics, shared among the people of the caravan and host communities. These included the institution of the caravan and its labor culture, common trading practices, joking relationships that facilitated trade and hospitality between various groups along the trade routes, the practice of blood brotherhood, and the spread of a lingua franca—first Kinyamwezi, then Kiswahili. The presence of women in the caravans was crucial for the penetration of this multiethnic caravan culture. The spread of cultural influences was multidirectional. Caravan culture, basically Nyamwezi in origin, influenced people from the coast, just as up-country porters were exposed to the values of coastal civilization. Nyamwezi social and cultural norms prevailed because the peoples of the western interior pioneered the caravan system, and the majority of porters and caravans working the central routes were Nyamwezi. Nyamwezi influence on the culture of caravan travel diminished only toward the end of the nineteenth century as the colonial invasions began, and as structural and political change associated with early colonial rule undermined the independence and economic vitality of the peoples of the western interior.

There was no single pattern of Nyamwezi caravan organization, though many porters preferred dry-season travel, with agriculture the priority during the wet season. A range of options existed between occasional journeys and full time specialization. Nyamwezi caravans could be small-scale ventures of a dozen or so traders and porters, or massive undertakings of a thousand or more people. Many Nyamwezi entrepreneurs were members of the ruling class, but lesser citizens, such as subordinate chiefs, hunters, medicine men, and ordinary people, also operated trading caravans. Often the caravans were formed by individuals carrying their own trade goods, and small employers who hired just a few porters each. These numerous petty traders banded together for protection, and selected a caravan leader from among themselves. In minor chiefdoms such as Ndala, where there were no indigenous traders as rich as those in Usumbwa, Unyanyembe, or Urambo, caravans remained cooperative affairs. A few weeks before harvest, in April, a drummer would tour the villages broadcasting the news that a caravan would soon depart. Porters would then gather at the appointed place. Some would have their own goods to trade at the coast or elsewhere.

During the period from about 1840 to 1890 the Nyamwezi also operated much larger caravans, representing the commercial status of the members of the trading elite of Unyanyembe and other large chiefdoms. The more powerful chiefs such as Mirambo, as members of the *vbandevba* (merchant elite), could mobilize a huge workforce, drawing on their status as chief, rich trader, and warlord. Caravans of 2,500–3,000 porters were not unusual.

After the merchants (*watongi*), the most important caravan officers were the *wanyampara* (literally, "grandfathers," but meaning "headmen" or "elders"). The title was also used in caravans of coast-based porters, and was therefore accepted in a multiethnic environment, where its original meaning was lost.

Another important caravan official, the *mganga*, or traditional doctor and diviner, acted as advisor and provided ritual protection against the dangers of the road. Apart from protecting caravan personnel the mganga also ritually cared for the ivory. The fourth important caravan functionary was the *kirangozi*, the guide or leader on the march. The kirangozi was usually elected by the porters. He was not necessarily from a special rank or section of society. Any individual with experience and some standing among the porters, and with good knowledge of the road, could be chosen. While on the march the kirangozi led the caravan along the correct route. He might also negotiate *hongo* (taxes, fees) with chiefs along the route. Men such as these were professional porters, familiar with caravan life and possessing a deep knowledge of the roads.

Caravan labor was arduous, and the daily march averaged about 15 miles. Porters carried loads of up to 100 pounds, including trade goods or ivory, weapons, sleeping mat, cooking pots, and rations. Large tusks were carried by the strongest men; double loads carried by two men were abhorred, as they were difficult to maneuver along the narrow paths. Frequently women and children accompanied their men, and carried camp equipment and extra provisions. Camp life was highly organized, with porters eating in messes, with each member allocated a task. The routine of hard work was frequently broken by the excitement of the hunt, skirmishes, and new adventures.

Nyamwezi long distance trade embodied a way of life opening new doors to commercial success, the market, and wage labor, but by the end of the nineteenth century it was over. Once coastal competition, the colonial economy, and railway construction undercut the Nyamwezi and the Germans imposed restrictions on independent caravans and trading activities, the Nyamwezi turned to migrant labor to the plantations of the northeast, and to railway construction, neither so remunerative or fulfilling.

STEPHEN J. ROCKEL

See also: **Tanganyika (Tanzania): Early Nineteenth Century.**

Further Reading

Burton, Richard F. *The Lake Regions of Central Africa*, 1860. Reprint, St. Clair Shores: Michigan Scholarly Press, 1971.

Cummings, Robert J. "A Note on the History of Caravan Porters in East Africa." *Kenya Historical Review*. 1, no. 4 (1973): 109–138.

Gray, Richard, and David Birmingham (eds.). *Pre-colonial African Trade*. London: Oxford University Press, 1970.

Iliffe, John. *A Modern History of Tanganyika*. Cambridge: Cambridge University Press, 1979.

Rockel, Stephen J. "'A Nation of Porters': The Nyamwezi and the Labour Market in Nineteenth-Century Tanzania." *Journal of African History*. 41, no. 2 (2000).

———. "Wage Labor and the Culture of Porterage in Nineteenth Century Tanzania: the Central Caravan Routes." *Comparative Studies of South Asia, Africa and the Middle East*. 15, no. 2 (1995): 14–24.

Sheriff, Abdul. *Slaves, Spices and Ivory in Zanzibar: Integration of an East African Commercial Empire into the World Economy 1770–1873*. London: James Currey/Athens, Ohio: Ohio University Press, 1987.

Shorter, Aylward. *Chiefship in Western Tanzania: A Political History of the Kimbu*. Oxford: Oxford University Press, 1972.

Unomah, Alfred C. *Mirambo of Tanzania*. London: Heinemann, 1977.

Tanganyika (Tanzania): German Invasion and Resistance

The German conquest of East Africa lasted over twenty years, from 1884 to 1907. Characterized by the gradual extension of rule over a large territory encompassing some 120 different ethnicities, Germany's initial goal was to gain control of trade and toll stations on the coast and secure caravan routes to Lake Tanganyika and Victoria Nyanza. The initial African goal with respect to German conquest was to preserve participation in the caravan trade.

German conquest began with the incorporation of the coastal strip ruled by the Sultan of Zanzibar, ceded to Germany by a treaty of 1888. The major German player in this period was the German East Africa Corporation (DOAG), a private charter company founded to gather treaties from African societies in order to assert German rule in accordance with the Berlin Conference of 1884–1885. As the DOAG's agents occupied coastal ports to control and tax caravan trade and to found cash crop estates, local societies reacted in 1888 with a two-year resistance led by influential traders and planters, especially Abushiri bin Salim and Bwana Heri bin Juma. DOAG trading stations and estates were burned, and German agents were killed or expelled from the coast. Abushiri was aided by inland societies, including the Mbunga, Zigua, and Yao, who offered a concerted resistance that necessitated the

Gogo with traditional weapons, Tanganyika, 1890s. © Sammlung Christoph/Das Ftotoarchiv.

intervention of German forces, leading to the transfer of authority from the DOAG to the German state. Formal colonial rule began in 1891 with coastal ports in German hands.

The new colonial state, dependent on caravan revenues, immediately sought to extend control into the interior to revive trade. The Germans created the *Schutztruppe* to conquer the inland, a military force of about 1000 *askari* (soldiers), employing largely Sudanese and Shangaan mercenaries led by about one hundred German officers and uncomissioned officers. Armed with cannons, machine guns, and modern rifles, German forces confronted Africans rarely armed with more than muskets, and often using spears and poison-tipped arrows. Africans typically used guerilla-style tactics, using the landscape to great advantage. Martial law, which included summary executions of resisters, was prevalent on the frontier of expansion.

German forces generally sought quick submission of opponents followed by co-optation and alliance, so that conquest often occurred without a fight. Alliance or defeat was usually followed by the establishment of a *boma* garrison or police outpost. Once allied with the Germans, African leaders could expect recognition of their authority, a formal role in the colonial power structure, and aid against their enemies. Germans demanded that African allies participate in the conquest of other peoples. Those who resisted had their villages burned, crops and livestock confiscated, and often women and children taken hostage until formal submission was made. Throughout the period of conquest the Germans exploited internal African divisions. The Shambaa of eastern Usambara, for example, had long been embroiled in civil war and internal struggles for power, and the Germans avoided direct military conflict by playing off rivals to the throne. On Mount Kilimanjaro the Germans absorbed the Chagga by supporting chief Marealle militarily against his rivals. Initial Arusha and Meru accommodation with the Germans gave way to armed resistance by 1896 as European settler and missionary encroachment began on the fertile slopes of Mount Meru. With massive Chagga aid, the Arusha and Meru were put down with great violence by 1900.

Aided by the rinderpest outbreak that devastated cattle-keeping societies of the interior, such as the Gogo and Maasai, the Germans moved to control the central caravan routes. German forces concentrated on breaking the power of Isike of Unyanyembe around the Tabora caravan entrepôt. After two years of sporadic conflict, Schutztruppe forces stormed Isike's fortress in 1892, whereupon Isike committed suicide by blowing up his gunpowder stores. The Germans appointed a compliant rival to the throne, as they typically did once a polity was defeated. Haya rulers west of Victoria Nyanza accepted the Germans as allies to ward off Baganda encroachment from the north. By 1895 German forces effectively controlled the trade routes of the western plateau.

Concerted resistance to German conquest came from militarized societies of the southwest. German control of the caravan route brought them into conflict with the Mbunga and Hehe, the latter who, under Mkwawa, had raided the route from a fortified base at Iringa. Mkwawa's destruction of a German military contingent in Usagara in 1891 dictated that the Germans confront the Hehe to recoup their prestige. In the next few years German forces secured the caravan route, forged alliances with Hehe military rivals among the Bena, Sangu, and Ngoni to the south, and defeated the Mbunga in 1893 in preparation for an assault on the more formidable Hehe. Politically isolated and unable to avoid conflict, Mkwawa refused a demand to allow a German military station at Iringa. German forces bombarded the Iringa boma and broke Hehe power, but were unable to subdue Mkwawa until 1898, when he committed suicide to avoid capture. The conquest of German East Africa was completed with the incorporation of the Great Lakes states. Rwanda was absorbed in 1897 when the Germans supported Musinga as king in exchange for acknowledgment of German rule. Although resisting German penetration until 1903, civil war among the *ganwa* elite of Burundi led the *mwami* (king) Mwezi Gisabo to accept German suzerainty under a residency system similar to British indirect rule.

New conflicts arose as Germany developed an administrative and economic infrastructure in the late 1890s. Germany implemented taxes and forced labor, claimed land for German settlement, and demanded labor for plantations and cash crops from villagers.

1537

As the meaning of colonial rule was demonstrated for many people for the first time, a new phase of resistance began. Collective grievances associated with German policies led to the Maji Maji rebellion (1905–1907), the last colonial war of conquest in German East Africa, bringing many peoples who had previously acquiesced to German rule into direct conflict with the colonial state for the first time. The defeat of the rebellion after two years opened up the colony for concerted economic development.

THADDEUS SUNSERI

See also: **Resistance to Colonialism; Rinderpest and Smallpox: East and Southern Africa; Tanganyika (Tanzania): German Rule: Land, Labor, and Economic Transformation; Tanganyika (Tanzania): Maji Maji Rebellion, 1905–1907.**

Further Reading

Glassman, Jonathon. *Feasts and Riot: Revelry, Rebellion, and Popular Consciousness on the Swahili Coast, 1856–1888.* Portsmouth, N.H.: Heinemann, 1995.

Gwassa, G. C. K. "The German Intervention and African Resistance in Tanzania." In *A History of Tanzania*, edited by I. N. Kimambo and A. J. Temu. Nairobi: East African Publishing, 1969.

Iliffe, John. *A Modern History of Tanganyika.* Cambridge: Cambridge University Press, 1979.

Kieran, J. A. "Abushiri and the Germans." In *Hadith*, vol. 2, edited by Bethwell A. Ogot. Nairobi: East African Publishing, 1970.

Koponen, Juhani. *Development for Exploitation: German Colonial Policies in Mainland Tanzania, 1884–1914.* Helsinki: Finnish Historical Society/Hamburg: Lit Verlag, 1995.

Müller, Fritz-Ferdinand. *Deutschland—Zanzibar—Ostafrika: Geschichte einer deutschen Kolonialeroberung.* Berlin: Rütten u. Loening, 1959.

Stoecker, Helmuth. (ed.). *German Imperialism in Africa.* London: C. Hurst, 1986.

Temu, A. J. "Tanzanian Societies and Colonial Invasion 1875–1907." In *Tanzania under Colonial Rule*, edited by M. H. Y. Kaniki. London: Longman, 1980.

Tanganyika (Tanzania): Maji Maji Rebellion, 1905–1907

Maji Maji is the name that German colonial rulers gave to a rebellion that broke out in the Matumbi-Kichi region of Tanzania in late July 1905, spreading in the next few months to much of southern Tanzania. Named after the *maji* water medicine that many African fighters believed would give them immunity to German bullets, the rebellion was led by *majumbe* (village headmen) who had become caught between onerous German economic policies and villagers who bore the brunt of German rule. Those policies included a massive campaign to grow export cash crops, especially cotton, on village fields and on German and Arab estates in some regions of the south. Germans and their appointed *maakida* required majumbe to send villagers to work on these estates for virtually no compensation. German rulers also curtailed African use of forests as a commons, the use of nets to hunt crop predators, and the use of fire to open up new fields for agriculture. The effect of these laws was to severely encumber African agriculture and to create an environment conducive to famine in the outbreak regions. Many majumbe who refused or were unable to implement German policies were whipped or jailed. Oral evidence has suggested that the rebellion was planned about a year in advance under the aegis of spirit mediums located on the Upper Rufiji River, especially Kinjikitile Ngwale, who distributed water medicine and sent out *hongo* messengers to encourage revolt among neighboring peoples. In this way, once fighting broke out, many majumbe were prepared to take up arms.

The rebellion began in the eastern Matumbi hills when a *jumbe* attacked the local German-appointed *akida*, who demanded that workers be provided for local cotton plantations and as porters for inland expeditions. As word of the conflict got out, other *majumbe* organized their forces to assault representatives of German rule, including missionaries, German settlers, Arab maakida and planters, *askari* police and soldiers, Indian traders, and German garrisons. Majumbe who did not rise up were also attacked. In some cases majumbe who heard rumors of war sent representatives to obtain water and commit themselves to fight. In this way the rebellion spread north of the Rufiji as far as the central caravan route, south to the Ruvuma River, and inland as far as Lake Nyasa, encompassing over twenty Tanzanian societies. For some people, such as the Mwera and Ngindo, Maji Maji was the first concerted resistance to German rule. In the southern highlands, patterns of patronage, alliance, and struggle over territory dating back to the nineteenth century determined whether leaders of militarized societies such as the Bena, Sangu, or Ngoni chose to aid the Germans or join the rebellion. Ngoni participation has been viewed as the effort by a chiefly class to reassert control over *sutu* common people who had experienced greater autonomy under German rule. Leaders of peoples who had only recently been defeated in German wars of conquest, including the Nyamwezi and Hehe, did not participate in the uprising and some aided the Germans. Rebels armed with muskets, spears and arrows confronted German forces, composed largely of African askari commanded by German officers, who put down the uprising with machine guns and modern rifles. While most of the fighting was over within a few months, the search for some rebel leaders continued until 1907. In localities of the uprising Germans confiscated food, burned villages and crops in the field, and sometimes took women hostage to prevent them from aiding rebels. As a direct result of these tactics, many thousands of civilians died through dislocation and famine, which engulfed some regions for two years. German officials put the number of African casualties at 75,000, while critics of colonial policies in Germany put the figure at over 200,000.

The uprising came on the heels of the Nama-Herero war in German southwest Africa, at a time when critics assailed the German colonial state for poor administration and abuse. Although the goal of Maji Maji majumbe to end German rule failed, German policy in East Africa underwent important changes after the rebellion. Most historians have viewed Maji Maji as a break between an era that favored European settler immigration and compulsory labor and one privileging African peasant production. Governor G. von Götzen, whose forced-labor policies created the grievances leading to the uprising, was removed from office. The new administration of Albrecht von Rechenberg emphasized the production of cash crops grown by African householders as the backbone of the new economy. German settlers and plantations were assisted only inasmuch as they were prepared to accept a free labor market, as forced labor was discouraged as a means of recruiting labor for plantations. Following the uprising, German officials combated the influence of spirit mediums in rural societies, viewed as instigators of dissent, opening the door to the wider dissemination of Islam and Christianity as forms of African religious expression and leadership.

Maji Maji is central to Tanzanian national identity. During the independence campaign of the 1950s, Julius Nyerere and his Tanganyika African National Union (TANU) political movement invoked Maji Maji as its predecessor. Much of the subsequent historical literature on Maji Maji has been shaped by the nationalist tradition inaugurated by Nyerere. Citing the rebellion as the first example of a concerted interethnic Tanzanian resistance to colonial rule, the TANU depicted itself as the heir of the earlier movement. In the 1960s the History Department of the University College at Dar es Salaam responded to this comparison by launching an oral-history research project to record the memories of Tanzanians who had participated in or observed the uprising. The Maji Maji Research Project has become an important source for African perspectives on the uprising.

THADDEUS SUNSERI

See also: **Resistance to Colonialism.**

Further Reading

Gwassa, Gilbert. "Kinjikitile and the Ideology of Maji Maji." In *The Historical Study of African Religion*, edited by T. O. Ranger and I. N. Kimambo. London: Heinemann, 1972.

Gwassa, Gilbert, and John Iliffe (ed.s) *Records of the Maji Maji Rising*. Nairobi: East African Publishing, 1968.

Iliffe, John. "The Organization of the Maji Maji Rebellion." *Journal of African History*, no. 8 (1967): 495–512.

Maji Maji Research Project: Collected Papers. Dar es Salaam: University College History Department, 1969.

Mapunda, O. B. and G. P. Mpangara. *The Maji Maji War in Ungoni*. Nairobi: East African Publishing, 1969.

Monson, Jamie. "Relocating Maji Maji: The Politics of Alliance and Authority in the Southern Highlands of Tanzania, 1870–1918." *Journal of African History*, no. 39 (1998): 95–120.

Redmond, Patrick. "Maji Maji in Ungoni: A Reappraisal of Existing Historiography." *International Journal of African Historical Studies*, no. 8 (1975): 407–424.

Sunseri, Thaddeus. "Famine and Wild Pigs: Gender Struggles and the Outbreak of the Maji Maji War in Uzaramo (Tanzania)." *Journal of African History*, no. 38 (1997): 235–59.

Wright, Marcia. "Maji Maji: Prophecy and Historiography." In *Revealing Prophets: Prophecy in Eastern African History*, edited by David M. Anderson and Douglas H. Johnson. Athens, Ohio: Ohio University Press, 1995.

Tanganyika (Tanzania): German Rule: Land, Labor, and Economic Transformation

Germany began its conquest of East Africa in 1884 with little idea of the resources in the region. During the first decade of rule the colonial state relied on export tolls on products of inland caravan networks—especially wild rubber, ivory, copal, wax, and hides. Tolls were also exacted on imported goods, particularly Indian cotton cloth. After 1885 much of the trade in the colony was controlled by the German East Africa Corporation (DOAG), a charter company that ruled the coast until the German state took control in 1891 following the Abushiri rebellion. Local marketing in the colony was largely in the hands of Indian traders, whose networks predated colonial rule.

As the paucity of mineral resources in German East Africa became known in the 1890s, German rulers focused on fostering cash crops of value to the German market. Hoping to liberate the German textile industry from American cotton supplies, cotton seed was distributed to Arab and Swahili plantation owners along the southern coast, and to village headmen. The DOAG experimented with rubber, tobacco, coffee, tea, and cotton on a handful of estates in the northeast, the region of increasing European settlement in the late 1890s. Sisal, introduced in 1893, emerged over the next two decades as the major plantation cash-crop export from the colony.

The cash-crop policy opened the door to European settlement between 1896 and 1906. In that period some 100 settler estates and about 20 large plantations were founded, concentrated in the northeast mountains. Banking on German settlement as the economic base of the colony, the Usambara Railway, begun from the port city of Tanga in 1891, was extended toward Arusha in the next two decades, and thousands of acres of land were appropriated for white settlement in the northeast. Although Africans were never completely expropriated of their lands, land given over to Europeans in the densely populated and fertile mountains necessitated changes in African farming methods, gendered uses of land, and crop mixes. Chagga, Shambaa, and Arusha peoples, for example, began their first efforts at coffee growing, which they integrated with banana and maize farming.

Labor policy paralleled white settlement. In the first decade of German rule estate owners forced local villagers to work on their estates, hired porters on the coast awaiting the departure of new caravans, imported Asian indentured laborers, and hired slaves of Arab and Swahili coastal estate owners. Even at this early stage labor scarcity created a bottleneck for cash-crop production. The state implemented taxation in 1898 to compel villagers to work periodically for a wage and to draw villagers into a cash economy. Taxation marked the waning of trade in natural products as the state moved to diversify colonial revenues.

By 1900, poor economic returns led German policy makers to begin a massive program to invigorate cash-crop production. The administration of Governor von Götzen began a cotton program that urged settlers and missionaries to take up the crop, and demanded that African villagers work for virtually no compensation on state-controlled fields. Meanwhile African agriculture was impaired by conservation ordinances that curtailed hunting, proscribed peasant use of forest reserves, and prohibited bush burning to open up new fields—the basis of peasant extensive agriculture for much of the colony. The pressures created by these measures led to the Maji Maji rebellion (1905–1907), which policy makers in Germany interpreted as stemming from the forced labor and agrarian policies of the previous decade.

With the appointment of Albrecht von Rechenberg as governor in 1906, economic priorities entered a new phase. European settlement, viewed as economically unpromising, was discouraged, though well-capitalized plantation corporations were welcomed, especially those that concentrated on the production of the industrial crops of sisal, cotton, and rubber. Forced labor, viewed as the cause of rebellion, was officially proscribed, and a free labor market was implemented with the labor ordinances of 1909. Rwanda and Burundi, where 40 per cent of the colony's population resided, were closed to labor recruitment. Tax levels remained essentially unchanged despite incessant settler pressure for significant increases. The new program banked on African peasant production of cash crops. The semiofficial Colonial Economic Committee fostered peasant cotton growing by distributing seed, setting up ginning and marketing centers, and guaranteeing a minimum market price. The Central Railway, begun in 1905, was extended into the interior to Lake Tanganyika to foster peasant cash crop production and draw trade away from the Uganda railway in Kenya.

As the Usambara and Central Railways advanced, more settlers and plantation corporations arrived, totaling some 700 estates by 1912, creating great competition for already scarce labor. A vociferous lobby in Germany kept settler interests in the public eye, while a humanitarian lobby publicized abuses of workers on plantations. Labor policy and the question of whether German East Africa would be a settler or peasant colony were at the core of policy struggles in the colony until the end of German rule, and were issues that were never conclusively resolved.

Many significant changes accrued under German colonial rule. From being a major exporter of grain to Indian Ocean trade networks, German East Africa became an importer of food as coffee, sisal, and cotton replaced millet and rice as cash crops. Labor migration patterns upset village economies as fewer men were engaged in agricultural pursuits and women produced less grain for the market. Such household disruptions led to a general population decline, and contributed to the spreading of the tsetse belt (a region of Sub-Saharan Africa particularly afflicted by the tsetse fly, where livestock are especially vulnerable to disease carried by the insect), impairing the cattle economies of the interior. German policies that were expanded under British and postcolonial rule included the peasant adoption of coffee as a cash crop west of Victoria Nyanza and in the northeast mountains and cotton south of Victoria Nyanza, the expansion of sisal as a plantation crop, especially along the Central Railway, and the opening up of the colony through construction of the Usambara and Central Railways. The Germans also created forest and wildlife refuges that far exceeded European plantations in extent, hemming in peasant and pastoral economies significantly.

THADDEUS SUNSERI

See also: **Colonial European Administrations: Comparative Survey; Tanganyika (Tanzania): German Invasion and Resistance; Tanganyika (Tanzania): Maji Maji Rebellion, 1905–1907.**

Further Reading

Iliffe, John. *A Modern History of Tanganyika.* Cambridge: Cambridge University Press, 1979.
———. *Tanganyika under German Rule 1905–1912.* Cambridge: Cambridge University Press, 1969.
Kimambo, Isaria. *Penetration and Protest in Tanzania: The Impact of the World Economy on the Pare, 1860–1960.* London: James Currey/Athens, Ohio: Ohio University Press, 1991.
Kjekshus, Helge. *Ecology Control and Economic Development in East African History: The Case of Tanganyika 1850–1950,* 1977. Reprint. London: James Currey 1996.

Koponen, Juhani. *Development for Exploitation: German Colonial Policies in Mainland Tanzania, 1884–1914*. Helsinki: Finnish Historical Society/Hamburg: Lit Verlag, 1995.

Rodney, Walter. "The Political Economy of Colonial Tanganyika 1890–1930." In *Tanzania under Colonial Rule*. edited by M. H. Y. Kaniki. London: Longman, 1980.

Sunseri, Thaddeus. *Vilimani: Labor Migration and Rural Change in Early Colonial Tanzania, 1884–1914*. Portsmouth, N.H.: Heinemann, forthcoming.

Tetzlaff, Rainer. *Koloniale Entwicklung und Ausbeutung: Wirtschafts- und Sozialgeschichte Deutsch-Ostafrikas 1885–1914*. Berlin: Duncker and Humblot, 1970.

Tanganyika (Tanzania): World War I

At the outbreak of World War I, the colonial officials in German East Africa (GEA; now Tanzania) were divided. Governor Heinrich Schnee wanted to remain neutral, but the *Schütztruppe* commander, Lieutenant Colonel (later Major General) Paul von Lettow-Vorbeck believed that a guerrilla campaign would force the British to move men and material away from the western front to East Africa.

The British resolved this dispute on August 8, 1914, when the Royal Navy shelled a German wireless station near Dar es Salaam. Governor Schnee responded by declaring Dar es Salaam and Tanga open towns. On August 15, 1914, Lettow-Vorbeck attacked and seized Taveta, a small settlement along the GEA–East Africa Protectorate (EAP; now Kenya) border.

Meanwhile, the British were making preparations to go on the offensive. However, these efforts initially floundered because officers and men lacked an appreciation of the difficulties of fighting in GEA. On October 16, 1914, the 8,000-man Indian Expeditionary Force "B," comprised of two Indian army brigades and commanded by Major General (temporary) Arthur Edward Aiken, sailed from Bombay for East Africa. On November 2, 1914, the ill-prepared Force "B" attempted to land at Tanga. However, the better-trained Schütztruppe repulsed the attack. Force "B," which suffered 359 killed and 310 wounded, reembarked and withdrew to Mombasa. German casualties included only 71 killed and 76 wounded. Another British setback occurred on November 3, 1914, when a 1,500-man force failed to dislodge some 200 German troops and 200 to 300 *askaris* from Longido, an area near the GEA-EAP border.

These victories were vitally important to the Germans insofar as they stimulated recruitment into the Schütztruppe, which numbered 3,007 Europeans and 12,100 Africans at its peak in March 1916. From the British perspective, Tanga and Longido underscored their military ineptitude. On November 22, 1914, the War Office sought to improve the situation by assuming control of East African operations. However, the Schütztruppe, at least in the short term, maintained its superiority over its hapless foe by repeatedly attacking the Uganda Railway and preventing the British from establishing a significance in GEA.

The next phase of the East African campaign began on February 6, 1916, when Lieutenant General Jan Smuts became commander of the British East African Expeditionary Force. Unlike his predecessors, Smuts had considerable combat experience in Africa, having fought the British during the Boer War and, more recently, having defeated the Germans in Southwest Africa (Namibia) in 1915. Initially, Smuts planned to envelop the Schütztruppe by advancing on either side of Kilimanjaro, the area from which Lettow-Vorbeck launched cross-border raids in the EAP. However, by the time British forces arrived in Moshi, German troops already had started withdrawing south toward the central railway to link up with Schütztruppe units in Tabora.

Smuts thwarted this scheme by deploying mounted troops to Dodoma, which cut off the escape route to Tabora. On September 19, 1916, allied soldiers from the Congolese Force Publique occupied Tabora, but the town's German garrison escaped to the southeast. By December 1916, the Schütztruppe was concentrated on Mahenge and the Rufiji Valley in southeastern GEA. Troop contributions from the Gold Coast (now Ghana), Nigeria, Rhodesia (now Zimbabwe), South Africa, and the West Indies had increased allied strength to 98,800, while the Schütztruppe had dwindled to approximately 11,000 soldiers. Lettow-Vorbeck's reliance on guerrilla tactics ensured that this numerical disparity had little impact on the fighting.

However, both sides suffered tremendously from food and supply shortages. Also, bad weather, coupled with rampant diseases like dysentery, malaria, and sleeping sickness, took a tremendous toll on military effectiveness. Some 3,400 Schütztruppe personnel were unfit for service, while during the February–October 1916 period, the Ninth South African Infantry lost 90 per cent of its men.

In July 1917, the British launched a simultaneous attack from the coastal towns of Lindi and Kilwa to encircle the Schütztruppe from the south. However, Lettow-Vorbeck already had moved his troops south to confront the British coming from the east. Nevertheless, the war in GEA was drawing to an end. On October 9, 1917, Belgian soldiers from the Force Publique occupied Mahenge; shortly afterward, the Schütztruppe personnel who remained in the area surrendered to avoid starvation.

From October 15 through 18, 1917, British and German forces clashed at Mahiwa on the Mwera Plateau. It was the most savagely fought battle of the East African campaign. Of the 4,900 African, British, Indian, and South African soldiers who fought at Mahiwa, some 2,700 were killed or wounded. The Schütztruppe suffered 519 killed, wounded, missing, or captured.

In mid-November 1917, Germany sought to resupply Lettow-Vorbeck with 50 tons of arms, ammunition, and supplies. The scheme, codenamed the China Show, involved flying the 740-foot long Zeppelin airship L-59 nonstop from Europe to eastern Africa. The dirigible, which was aloft for four days, flew 4,180 miles before being recalled. The order to return supposedly came from the German admiralty. According to British sources, the wireless communication had been sent by British intelligence. With the failure of China Show, Lettow-Vorbeck had no option but to abandon GEA.

On November 25, 1917, the Schütztruppe, which was out of ammunition and low on supplies, crossed the Ruvuma River into Portuguese East Africa (now Mozambique). Lettow-Vorbeck and his remaining troops became nomadic foragers who only succeeded in mounting a few low-level operations against the Portuguese. On September 28, 1918, he crossed back into GEA, but before he could launch a new offensive, the war ended.

The human cost was staggering. In more than four years of fighting, the Germans lost 439 killed in action and 874 wounded, while British forces suffered 3,443 combat deaths and 7,777 wounded in action. Disease claimed 256 German soldiers and 6,558 British troops. African losses on the German side included 1,290 askaris killed in action and about 7,000 carriers dead from disease; 3,669 Africans sustained wounds. British forces lost 376 African carriers in combat and 1,645 wounded; 44,911 died of disease. The Belgians and their Congolese troops lost approximately 3,000, killed or wounded. Portugal and its African soldiers lost 1,734 killed and several hundred wounded.

The most significant political ramification on the East African campaign concerned the British takeover of GEA, which they renamed the Tanganyika Territory on February 1, 1920. The British ruled the country as a mandated territory under the League of Nations.

THOMAS P. OFCANSKY

See also: **World War I: Survey.**

Further Reading

Hornden, Charles. *Military Operations, East Africa*, vol. 1. London: HMSO, 1941.

Hoyt, Edwin P. *The Germans Who Never Lost: The Story of the Königsberg*. New York: Funk and Wagnalls, 1968.

——. *Guerrilla: Colonel Von Lettow-Vorbeck and Germany's East African Empire*. New York: Macmillan, 1981.

Lettow-Vorbeck, Paul von. *My Reminiscences of East Africa*. London: Hurst and Blackett, 1920.

Miller, Charles. *Battle for the Bundu*. London: Macdonald and Jane's, 1974.

Moyse-Bartlett, H. *The King's African Rifles: A Study in Military History of East and Central Africa, 1890–1945*. Aldershot, England: Gale and Polden, 1956.

Tanganyika (Tanzania): Colonial Period, British: "Indirect Rule"

German rule over Tanganyika was terminated in 1918 after a protracted military campaign, and, following the Versailles peace settlement, responsibility for making new administrative arrangements over it was vested in the new League of Nations. Considering its peoples "not yet able to stand by themselves under the strenuous conditions of the modern world" (Article 22 of the League Covenant), the league awarded Britain the mandate to administer Tanganyika on its behalf in 1920, with the not very onerous requirement to furnish an annual report to a Permanent Mandates Commission.

In Tanganyika itself, the new district administration saw the indirect rule as the most effective way of meeting the objectives of the mandate, replacing what was rather generally regarded as the directive (and by implication coercive) German system. However, aside from introducing the necessary legislation permitting the establishment of native authorities (1923), the first governor, Sir Horace Byatt, took few steps to put an indirect-rule system in place. It was left to his successor, Sir Donald Cameron (1925–1931), one of Britain's most effective and innovative governors of the interwar years, to implement proposals put forward by his senior district officials and establish full-fledged indirect rule. In his various policy circulars, Cameron stressed the need to move away from the concept of *rule* altogether, preferring the term *indirect administration*, to be a means for training traditional leaders to become modern and progressive, working toward the advancement of their people under the overall supervision of (white) district officials.

Between 1925 and 1929, the structures of indirect rule were established: native authorities (NAs) would made up usually of one, sometimes more, chiefs responsible for law and order and making regulations in fields that would be increased as their overall "competence" was demonstrated; native treasuries would collect tax on behalf of the government; and native courts would exercise relatively minor civil and criminal jurisdiction, with channels for appeal limited (after 1929) to the executive elevel (up to the level of governor) and excluding the territory's high court. In return, the NAs received a "rebate," varying between 20 and 33 per cent of tax collections at the end of the 1930s—amounts that tended to be swallowed up in chiefs' salaries and allowances. The actual implementation of the new system ran into several difficulties: first, there was the old problem of "finding the chief." On the coast, the *akida* system had submerged or fatally undermined indigenous authority; in other places "tribes" were manufactured and placed under chiefs; and the Maasai—who had had no chiefs before European rule—eventually had councils of elders recognized as the official NA. The existence of many small chieftaincies, especially in the north of the country, was a second difficulty, resolved by encouraging the formation of tribal federations: the Sukuma federation, set up in 1946, comprised 51 chiefs. Finally, the more powerful chiefs tended to become autocratic and/or resistant to change, a danger Cameron had recognized as inherent in the system, but to which his successors seem to have been oblivious.

However, the main shortcoming of indirect rule in practice was its failure to address the central issue of the link between local and national political development. Cameron had referred to the long-term possibility of a central native council, sending delegates to some kind of joint council with Legislative Council members, but had seen this, together with popular elections, as a distant goal, though one that had to be kept in sight. Thus, when his first Legislative Council was set up in December 1926, he restricted the selection of his nominated representatives to the European and Asian minority communities, arguing that the territory lacked any African of standing who had the necessary command of English to participate in debates. Cameron's even more cautious successors maintained this policy of African administration at the exclusively local level, allowing indirect rule to become a generally unprogressive dogma, marked by a paternalistic defence of the "old tribal order," supplemented by a growing hostility to the Westernized African elite emerging outside NA structures and a general distrust of "nationalist agitators." NAs became agencies of the central government, carrying out the instructions of district officials, while the administration in turn, envisaging a timescale of generations or even centuries before Tanganyikans would be ready for independence, was reluctant to force the pace of political change.

The new world order that emerged after World War II led to a reappraisal of administrative policy, starting with the appointment of two educated chiefs to the Legislative Council (1945); a move to bring educated African commoners into chiefs' councils; a move to stimulate local development; and an increase in the level of resources available to NAs. In 1946, the United Nations introduced a new supervisory structure, the Trusteeship Council, for the former mandates (now called *trust territories*), with a wider range of international representation and the right to send visiting missions every three years to each of the trust territories. Both of these changes substantially tightened up the previous system and markedly accelerated the pace toward independence throughout the 1950s. Then, in

March 1947, Colonial Secretary Arthur Creech Jones replaced indirect rule with local government, consigning the former (a "static policy," as he put it) to the dustbin. He believed that a local government system based on British lines would prevent the emergence of an oligarchy at the center. In practice, local government was only slowly introduced into Tanganyika after 1947: it was not until 1954 that the necessary legislation was introduced that would enable NAs to become local authorities. Attempts to create a higher—county—tier fell victim to the administration's attempt to balance racial (African/European/Asian) interests and create a racial partnership at the district as well as the national level. All of these efforts to create a more effective system of local government were overshadowed and eventually eclipsed by the rapid growth of a nationwide body of Westernized and educated Africans, the Tanganyika African Association (the Tanganyika African National Union, after 1954), which concentrated its efforts on the winning of power at the level where it mattered, in the Legislative Council itself.

MURRAY STEELE

See also: **Nigeria: Lugard, Administration and "Indirect Rule."**

Further Reading

Bates, Margaret. "Social Engineering, Multi-racialism, and the Rise of TANU in the Trust Territory of Tanganyika, 1945–1961." In *History of East Africa*, vol. 3, edited by Donald Low and Alison Smith. Oxford: Clarendon Press, 1976.

Cameron, Sir Donald. *My Tanganyika Service and Some Nigeria*, 1939. Reprint, Washington, D.C.: University Press of America, 1982.

Chidzero, Bernard. *Tanganyika and International Trusteeship*. London: Oxford University Press, 1961.

Hailey, Lord William Malcolm. *An African Survey: a Study of Problems Arising in Africa South of the Sahara*, rev ed. London: Oxford University Press, 1957.

———. *Native Administration in the British Territories*, vol. 1, 1950 Reprint, Nendeln: Kraus Reprint, 1979.

Iliffe, John. "The Age of Improvement and Differentiation (1907–45)." In *A History of Tanzania*, edited by Isaria Kimambo and A. J. Temu. Nairobi: Heinemann, 1969.

Ingham, Kenneth. "Tanganyika: the Mandate and Cameron: 1919–1931" and "Tanganyika: Slump and Short-Term Governors, 1932–45." in *History of East Africa*, vol. 2, edited by Vincent Harlow and E. M. Chilver. Oxford: Clarendon Press, 1965.

Taylor, James Clagett. *The Political Development of Tanganyika*. London: Oxford University Press/Stanford, Calif.: Stanford University Press, 1963.

Tanganyika (Tanzania): Colonial Period, British: Economy

Tanganyika Territory's new colonial rulers inherited an economy devastated by the most intense conflict waged on African soil during World War I. By the mid 1920s the essential reconstruction tasks—feeding the hungry, reviving the plantation sector, and restoring the basic infrastructure—had been completed, but Tanganyika's root problem, that of extreme underdevelopment, defied solution and at independence the overwhelming majority of its people still lived at subsistence level.

Sisal had been the main export crop of the former German East Africa, and the authorities gave priority to the resumption of its production, though again under "immigrant" (Greek/Indian) management in place of the departed German plantation owners. It remained the principal export throughout the whole period, especially during and just after World War II, when Japanese victories cut off supplies from the Pacific area. However, the industry as a whole employed only small numbers, and immigrant communities were the main beneficiaries. The same remarks apply to other export crops, such as tea and coffee grown by the limited British settler population allowed in by the administration during the 1920s. The new government inherited also the beginnings of black peasant coffee production in northern Tanganyika, centered on the Bukoba district and the Chagga, who lived around Mount Kilimanjaro. Despite frequent settler protests emanating from Kenya as well as Tanganyika, the authorities continued to support Chagga farmers' attempts to produce higher grade arabica coffee for export, in preference to the less marketable robusta. By the mid-1920s, the Chagga had become the most commercially oriented African society in Tanganyika, although in comparative terms the (black) peasant sector represented only a small fraction of the total rural population, even after World War II.

Much of Tanganyika remained poor and underdeveloped throughout this period, in spite of Britain's stated commitment to the terms of the mandate, which called for the development of all its people. A major inhibitory factor was the physical nature of Tanganyika, a country with reasonably fertile fringes and corresponding population density but saddled with an infertile interior with a small and scattered population eking out a bare subsistence in a difficult environment. Other factors, more recent in provenance, included the effect of the East African Campaign, which had been fought through the interior into Mozambique; and the associated spread of the tsetse fly following wartime human and livestock depopulation and the resultant encroachment of brush and other secondary growth into grazing areas: between 1913 and 1937, infected regions increased from one-third to two-thirds of the territory's total area. The interior thus remained one of the most backward in British Africa with the most rudimentary of communications, little in the way of social services and few incentives for anything beyond production for own consumption.

The one major attempt to break through this cycle of underdevelopment, the Tanganyika Groundnut Scheme (1947–1950) has become a byword for starry-eyed optimism and undue haste in development strategies. Implemented by the British government through its Overseas Food Corporation, the scheme was designed to provide essential oils for British industry and consumers, and equivalent opportunities for the economic and social development for black societies in Southern and Central Tanganyika. It failed because of hurried and inadequate research in the field, the setting of unrealistic targets for bush clearance and groundnut production, and the use of machinery ill suited to the area's iron-hard soils. The cost of the failure was borne by the British taxpayer, not the territory, though as Cyril Ehrlich (1976) has pointed out, the total amount written off (£36 millions) nearly matched the total expenditure of the Tanganyika government between 1946 and 1950. The scheme similarly made little impact on either the local population it was supposed to help, or the Territory's economy.

While the scheme demonstrated the reality that capital investment alone could not guarantee results, the Tanganyika government lacked the resources to engage in major development programme, even at the basic infrastructural level. At independence, the territory's road system had the reputation for being the worst in British colonial Africa. Part of the reason lay in its status as a mandate which did not "belong" to Britain in the sense that Kenya and Uganda did: this made it difficult for Tanganyika to attract outside investment, especially in the later 1930s, when its return to Germany became a distinct possibility in the current climate of appeasement. Naturally, there were some gains: its status made Tanganyika less attractive than Kenya and Southern Rhodesia for white settlers, and saved it from the land problems that were to bedevil these countries after World War II. But Tanganyika's structural poverty in turn had a negative effect on official economic policy, which mirrored the subsistence expectations of the majority of its people: self-sufficiency, balanced budgets, and general conservatism in the estimation of available local revenue became the order of the day. Only one interwar governor deviated from this policy: Sir Donald Cameron had increased expenditure of education and social services in the late 1920s to fulfill what he considered to be the terms of the mandate. The demerits of this extravagance had, in the opinions of a visiting commission (1932), been shown by the Great Depression, when the international price of sisal had collapsed: clearly the territory had to live within its means. Prudence became the watchword, prevailing through the war years when revenues (and prices) climbed steeply; and after the war, when the pace of development in British Africa generally quickened.

Government investment in social services, particularly education, certainly increased after 1945, but anticipated revenue was constantly underestimated in annual budgets by administrations wedded to the principle of financial caution. At independence in 1961, Tanganyika's economy was one of the least developed in British colonial Africa with an annual gross domestic product per head of only £21 (a quarter that of Ghana) and an infant mortality rate approaching 220 per thousand in parts of the country.

MURRAY STEELE

See also: **Tanganyika (Tanzania): German Rule: Land, Labor, and Economic Transformation.**

Further Reading

Ehrlich, Cyril. "The Poor Country: the Tanganyika Economy from 1945 to Independence." In *History of East Africa*, vol. 3, edited by D. Anthony Low and Alison Smith. Oxford: Clarendon Press, 1976.

Iliffe, John. "The Age of Improvement and Differentiation, 1907–45." In *A History of Tanzania*, edited by Isaria Kimambo and A. J. Temu. Nairobi: Heinemann, 1969.

Ingham, Kenneth. "Tanganyika: The Mandate and Cameron: 1919–1931" and "Tanganyika: Slump and Short-Term Governors, 1932–45." In *History of East Africa*, vol. 2, edited by Vincent Harlow and E. M. Chilver. Oxford: Clarendon Press, 1965.

Kjekshus, Helge. *Ecology Control and Economic Development in East African History: The Case of Tanganyika, 1850–1950*. London: Heinemann, 1977.

Wood, Alan. *The Groundnut Affair*. London: Bodley Head, 1950.

Tanganyika (Tanzania): African Association, 1929–1948

In British colonial territories administered through "indirect rule," Africans who felt that their interests were not well served by the chiefs routinely formed organizations to represent their interests. Usually these associations were small in scale, limited in membership, and did not last long, but some had more enduring legacies. In Tanganyika clerks, traders, urban residents, and rural dissidents formed the principal social base of the African Association. While it never fully overcame regional and sectarian differences among its members, and never articulated a coherent nationalist agenda, the African Association was the institutional progenitor of the party of mass nationalism and eventual independence, the Tanganyika African National Union (TANU).

The African Association was founded in the context of a proposed "closer union" among Uganda, Kenya, and Tanganyika (1929–1931). Disturbed by the prospect of the greater settler influence that would have accompanied integration with Kenya, both the government of Tanganyika and politically aware Africans opposed the plan. Of the latter, civil servants in government employment were an important constituency. In 1922 leading

African civil servants had formed the Tanganyika Territory African Civil Services Association (TTCSA). The TTCSA was an elitist organization that sought to protect its relatively privileged members from the type of racial discrimination that forced them to suffer such indignities as riding in third-class rail carriages. The African Association, on the other hand, claimed to speak for the interests of all Africans and aspired to represent African opinion in debates over government policy. Because they were on the same side of the "closer union" issue, the government showed some early signs of sponsoring the African Association, donating a plot of land for its first headquarters, for example. But the guardians of "indirect rule" were inevitably suspicious of any African group formed by voluntary association and aspiring to represent the African public: officially, Africans were members of tribes, properly represented by their chiefs.

Even lukewarm government patronage undercut the political potential of the organization. Civil servants were not allowed to join "political" associations. In order for African civil servants to be members, therefore, any taint of politics had to be avoided. For much of the 1930s the African Association, at least in the capital city Dar es Salaam, functioned as little more than a social club for Western-educated civil servants and urban notables. In the second half of the decade a radical faction under Erica Fiah attempted to move the African Association in a more activist direction. Fiah was unsuccessful, but to the extent that the African Association articulated an ideology, it was more Pan-African than nationalist, emphasizing the unity of all Africans across lines of social class and religion.

While the central office in Dar es Salaam was divided and ineffective during the 1930s, there were active branches in other parts of the country where the African Association had more of an impact. In Dodoma the association was relatively well organized, but remained primarily a social club for civil servants. In 1937 in Bukoba, however, it became involved in a large scale protest movement led by Muslim traders. Bukoba exemplified in extreme form a common pattern: African traders were both more radical and more connected to the rural areas than were the more educated members of the African Association. Lacking strong ties to the central organization, however, the radicalism of the Bukoba branch had no territorial effect.

A turning point came in 1939, when for the first time a national conference was held in the capital. Five such conferences were held over the next six years, as the war brought both austerity and greater exposure to radical ideas. This is the period when the African Association moved from being a social club to a political organization, formally recognizing the need to bring together the masses and the educated elite. There was still no talk of independence, but there was a stronger emphasis on African participation in government. A branch of the organization was formed at Makerere University in Uganda in 1945, with a young Julius Nyerere as branch president.

After the war the African Association did not fulfill the promise of this more activist stance. Conservative civil servants once again dominated the main urban branches. The political initiative passed to local and "tribal" organizations such as the Sukuma Union, the Pare Union, and the Kianja Labor Association. While politics became increasingly localized, the organizational center was once again in disarray. In 1948 a dispute between the Dar es Salaam and Zanzibar branches led the former to break away and rename itself the Tanganyika African Association (TAA), and the annual conference for that year was canceled.

As the political pace quickened in the provinces, the need for stronger leadership was increasing. In the early 1950s a new generation of activists reinvigorated the TAA. The earlier Pan-African emphasis was being replaced by an emphasis on Tanganyikan nationalism. It became a more professional and effective territorial organization, with stronger links and better communications between the provinces and the center. When the British attempted to relocate some Meru villages to make room for European farmers, the TAA effectively made the connection between a local issue and territorial politics. The TAA also brought the Meru Land Case to the attention of the United Nations Trusteeship Council: for the first time, Tanganyikan nationalism had an international dimension. By 1954 Julius Nyerere, Kirilo Japhet, Oscar Kambona, and other young nationalists had set the stage for the creation of the TANU, the party that would lead Tanganyika to independence.

KENNETH R. CURTIS

See also: **Nyerere, Julius; Tanganyika/Tanzania: Nationalism, TANU, Independence.**

Further Reading

Iliffe, John. *A Modern History of Tanganyika.* Cambridge: Cambridge University Press, 1979.

Kaniki, H. M. Y. (ed.). *Tanzania under Colonial Rule.* London: Longman, 1980.

Maguire, G. Andrew. *Toward "Uhuru" in Tanzania: The Politics of Participation.* Cambridge; Cambridge University Press, 1969.

Tanganyika (Tanzania): Nationalism, TANU, Independence

A mere seven and a half years elapsed between the formation of the Tanganyika African National Union (TANU) in July of 1954 and the independence of Tanganyika in December of 1961. During that brief period the party went from a small initial base to a mass membership of over one million; established Julius Nyerere as a figure of continental importance; swept several elections; and helped make Tanganyika the first independent nation of East Africa.

A prenationalist tradition of political organization in Tanganyikan history was represented by the African Association. Founded in 1929, the African Association was more often a social club for urban elites than a rallying point for political protest. Nevertheless, the African Association did create a foundation on which the TANU could later build by bringing together members of such key social groups as African civil servants, professional men, and traders, and by organizing national conferences (between 1939 and 1945) that brought together representatives from around the territory.

In Tanganyika, as elsewhere, World War II was a political watershed. Returning soldiers brought fresh political energy, and the impact of the first cadre of Makerere University graduates was soon to be felt. Wartime privations, though generally accepted before 1945, created a general sense of dissatisfaction. The constitutional future of Tanganyika, formerly a mandate of the now defunct League of Nations, was open to debate. And rural political protest was on the rise, in the northeast as well as in the economically important Lake Province.

The African Association (renamed the Tanganyika African Association after a split with the Zanzibar branch in 1948) was initially incapable of profiting from these conditions. Centrifugal tendencies had long characterized the African politics of the territory, and these increased in the postwar period. Politics remained local. In Pare, widespread popular resistance to the imposition of a graduated tax, the *mbiru* controversy of 1946, was led by the Pare Union, with no connection to any territorial organization. On Kilimanjaro, the Chagga Union based its politics on the selection of a paramount chief, also in isolation from territorial politics. Governor Edward Twining's policy of emphasizing local government reform through a new council system reinforced these parochial political tendencies. Coping with rapid change, it seemed that Tanganyikans were opting for an inward-looking neotraditionalism rather than a more expansive territorial nationalism.

However, important changes were occurring. In the Lake Province in the late 1940s, a nascent cooperative union brought together educated men with territorial connections and peasants resisting enforced agricultural schemes and the mandatory culling of cattle. For the first time, local grievances were combined with a call for political independence. The government reacted by prohibiting African civil servants from joining either the Tanganyika African Association. The Lake Province remained tense for most of the rest of the colonial period.

Meanwhile, another local African grievance gave the TAA an issue which it used to gain not only territorial but international publicity. An ill-conceived plan to consolidate settler landholdings in the northeast led the government to dispossess two Meru villages in the early 1950s. The local TAA secretary, Kirilo Japhet, coordinated an antigovernment campaign with the newly formed Meru Citizens Union: an effective interface between a postwar "tribal" society and territorial nationalism had been established.

Two other factors heightened the importance of the Meru Land Case. First, Japhet went to New York and carried the Meru complaint to the United Nations Trusteeship Council. The Trusteeship Council, particularly in the form of Visiting Missions, would present the nationalists with an important forum in the coming years. Second, on a trip to London Japhet met with Julius Nyerere, who was soon to return to Tanganyika and become president of the TAA.

The centrality of the role played by Julius Nyerere in the 1950s can hardly be overstressed. Educated at Makerere and the University of Edinburgh, and a member of the Fabian Bureau, he could articulate grassroots grievances in a language comprehensible to the British. From both his student days at Makerere and his stint as a teacher at Tabora, Nyerere knew virtually the entire rising generation of his educated countrymen. He was familiar with the trends of mass nationalism elsewhere in Africa and the world. And perhaps most important he was a charismatic figure around whom Tanganyikans could unite, since he was not associated with any particular region or social group. In 1950 the TAA had been reinvigorated in Dar es Salaam by the participation of ex-servicemen and former Makerere students. In 1953 Julius Nyerere became president of the TAA, and the transfer of control to a new generation was complete.

Tanzanians would later celebrate Saba Saba Day (Seven Seven Day) in commemoration of the TAA annual conference held on July 7, 1954. On that day a new constitution was approved, and the name of the organization was changed to the Tanganyika African National Union (TANU). The new constitution both enhanced central control over policy by creating a National Executive Council which would meet between annual delegates' conferences and facilitated greater contact with the provinces by making a provision that trade unions, cooperative societies and tribal unions could join as affiliates. Youth and women's sections were formed, with the leader of the women's section, Bibi Titi Muhammad, proving a powerful organizing force at the territorial level. The goal of the organization was now explicitly stated: to fight for independence.

It was a time of great possibilities, but also of potential danger. The Mau Mau emergency in neighboring Kenya made mass nationalism in East Africa a high-stakes game. Official policy in both Kenya and the Central African Federation was to reconcile colonialism with nationalism through "multiracialism." This ideology was represented in Tanganyika by Twining (1949–1958). Portraying the TANU and Nyerere as "racialist," the administration appointed ten unofficial members from each race (European, Asian, and African) to the Legislative Council, and from this nucleus sponsored the creation of the United Tanganyika Party (UTP) as an alternative to the TANU. Nyerere's counterformulation was that Tanganyika, while indeed multiracial in population, was "primarily African."

In the mid-1950s the TANU quickly developed its mass base. The government responded by scaling back some of its more unpopular schemes of agricultural compulsion and seeking allies for its "multiracialist" policy. The inevitable confrontation between government "multiracialism" and the TANU's nationalism came when Governor Twining announced that a semi-representative Legislative Council would be formed in 1958, with each eligible voter to cast one ballot for a candidate of each race. The question was whether the TANU should participate in elections conducted in a format to which it was opposed on principal. Although there was a great deal of disagreement about that question at the conference held in Tabora in January 1958, Nyerere carried the day with his argument that participation was necessary. The TANU agreed to support (though not to nominate) Asians and Europeans in the election. To balance this concession, the delegates voted to mount a "positive action" campaign unless responsible government were implemented before the end of 1959. A dissident faction which disapproved of participation in the elections broke away to form the African National Congress. This party, under Zuberi Mtemvu, had virtually no electoral impact.

In the first phase of the voting in October 1958, The TANU won 68 per cent of the vote and thirteen of fifteen seats. By the time the second phase was completed in February of the next year, the UTP had collapsed and the TANU won all fifteen seats. The TANU's power was now a *fait accompli*, and it was clear that the country could not be ruled without Nyerere's cooperation. By now the Suez Crisis had come and gone, Ghana was independent, Harold MacMillan was sensing the "winds of change," and Richard Turnbull had replaced Edward Twining as governor of Tanganyika. In a concession that would have been unthinkable a few years earlier, the 1959 East Africa Governors Conference approved of responsible government for Tanganyika in 1963–1964 and independence by 1970. But events were moving too quickly for the British to control. Riots in Nyasaland helped bring an end to official insistence on gradualism and multiracialism. The colonial secretary acceded to the demand for responsible government after the 1960 elections, and on December 9, 1961, Tanganyika became independent, with the TANU as the party of government and Julius Nyerere as prime minister.

In 1964, a union with postrevolutionary Zanzibar produced the new nation of Tanzania. In 1967, a TANU conference passed Julius Nyerere's Arusha Declaration, transforming the country from a de facto to a de jure one-party state. The end of the Tanganyika African National Union came in 1977 when it was integrated with the Afro-Shirazi Party on Zanzibar to form the Chama Cha Mapinduzi (Revolutionary Party).

KENNETH R. CURTIS

See also: **Nyerere, Julius.**

Further Reading

Iliffe, John. *A Modern History of Tanganyika.* Cambridge: Cambridge University Press, 1979.

Kaniki, H. M. Y. (ed.), *Tanzania under Colonial Rule.* London: Longman, 1980.

Lisotwel, Judity. *The Making of Modern Tanganyika.* London: Chatto and Windos, 1965.

Maguire, G. Andrew. *Toward "Uhuru" in Tanzania: The Politics of Participation.* Cambridge: Cambridge University Press, 1969.

McHenry, Dean. *Limited Choices: The Political Struggle for Socialism in Tanzania.* Boulder, Colo.: Lynne Rienner, 1994.

Pratt, Cranford. *The Critical Phase in Tanzania, 1945–1968: Nyerere and the Emergence of a Socialist Strategy.* Cambridge: Cambridge University Press, 1976.

Tangier

Tangier, a city in Morocco situated on the Atlantic coast, on the southern side of the entrance to the Straits of Gibraltar, was called Tingis in Roman times and was the capital of the Roman province of Mauritania Tingitana. It was ruled by Muslim dynasties from the early eighth century to 1471. In Arabic, the town is called Tanjah. From 1471 it was ruled by Spain and Portugal until 1662, when it was ceded to England as part of the dowry of Catherine of Braganza, Charles II's Portuguese wife. In 1684 England returned Tangier to the Sultan of Morocco.

In the nineteenth century, Tangier, a seaport close to Europe, became the main base for European commercial and diplomatic activity in Morocco. By then it had a medina, an old Muslim quarter enclosed by fifteenth-century ramparts, dominated by the Casbah. The sultan had a palace there and was represented by a Pasha. Consuls of several European countries were posted in Tangier; in 1860 they became heads of legations. They

had extensive power because of the large numbers of Moroccans who were given consular protection under the then common system of capitulations. The consuls worked together to play a role in local administration, to deal with sanitary problems for example. During the nineteenth century a European trading community grew up and many European travelers went to Tangier. By the turn of the century there were about 10,000 foreigners in Tangier; there had for long been an important Jewish community, and Tangier was already becoming the cosmopolitan city that it was to be famously later on.

Tangier was a center of political intrigue, negotiations, and conflicts in the early twentieth century, when European powers gradually encroached on the independent Sultanate. The Rif Berber chieftain Raisuli held a wealthy American resident of Tangier, Ion Perdicaris, to ransom in 1904 and was then appointed Pasha of Tangier for a time. In 1905, after the Anglo-French Entente Cordiale had given French ambitions in Morocco the go-ahead, Kaiser Wilhelm II of Germany visited Tangier to declare support for Moroccan independence. After the subsequent Algeciras Conference (1906), Spain occupied the northern strip of Morocco but not Tangier, which was also not occupied by the French when they took over the greater part of the country. Tangier remained separate under the collective control of the Western consuls. A special neutral status for Tangier had been discussed for some time, and the idea was revived after World War I. The three Western countries most interested in Morocco for decades, France, Spain and Britain, agreed in talks in London in 1923 on a Statute of Tangier, which came into force on June 1, 1925.

Tangier was recognized as being under the authority of the Sultan of Morocco, who was represented there by an official with the title of *Mendoub*, responsible for administering traditional Moroccan law and collecting taxes from the Muslims; however, the Sultan was completely under French control. Within the Tangier International Zone, covering about 150 square kilometers, a Committee of Control and an International Legislative Assembly were in charge. The committee consisted of eight European consuls, the assembly of 26 members including six Muslims and three Jews. In the International Zone, foreign trading powers had economic equality, Moroccan francs and pesetas were legal tender, and the official languages were French, Spanish, and Arabic. Foreign control was asserted even more fully after an amendment to the statute in 1927.

Under this unusual arrangement, modern development proceeded in Tangier, including the building of new houses and roads. The newly developed European areas were very much segregated from the districts where Muslim Moroccans lived (including a famous resident, the Salafi reformist scholar Abdullah bin Idris al-Sanusi, from 1910 to his death in 1931) and generally endured great deprivation. Elegant buildings filled the foreigners' districts; streets like the Boulevard Pasteur, the main street, and social landmarks like the Café de Paris were filled with both resident and visiting Westerners. In the early 1930s the population was estimated at around 50,000 (30,000 Muslim Moroccans, 8,000 Jews, and 12,000 "Tangerinos" of various nationalities). Tangier became a fashionable stopover for tourists from western countries, staying at the Hotel Rif (1937) and other modern hotels; 43,000 tourists called in 1934, two-thirds of them British.

During World War II, Spanish troops occupied the International Zone on June 14, 1940. Under Francisco Franco's effective rule, German influence increased, but the international administration continued to some extent, as did a British presence and the city was a center for espionage and intrigue, as it had been before. Spain withdrew its military and police forces by October 1945, when the Mendoub returned and the Committee of Control resumed charge. The Moroccan nationalist movement, encouraged by a speech made by Sultan Mohammed V in Tangier on April 10, 1947, won support in Tangier, where nationalists benefited from the uncensored postal services operated by three countries under Tangier's special arrangements. There was rioting against foreign rule in 1952, and later arms were smuggled through Tangier for resistance in French Morocco in the mid-1950s. But the international administration went on for some years, and under its light rule—characterized by low taxation and little regulation—the city became famous as a center for various sorts of business, including some that were direputable and/or criminal. There was a building boom, while the city's population expanded, reaching 160,000–180,000 by 1952, including 100,000 Moroccans. Tourism also flourished again, with 100,000 visitors in 1952.

Following the independence of French and Spanish Morocco in March 1956, the Statute of Tangier was abrogated on October 29, 1956, and Tangier was fully integrated into Morocco once again. The special features that had made Tangier famous or infamous did not disappear quickly. Mohammed V issued a royal charter, giving Tangier a free money market and the right of unrestricted imports and exports from August 29, 1957 on. Speculators and entrepreneurs flourished again for a time, but when notice was given of abrogation of the charter in October 1959, merchants left, money was moved out, and many business collapsed. The government started municipal projects to employ some of those thrown out of work; a carpet industry has since grown up in the city. On April 19, 1961, Tangier was fully integrated into the Moroccan state.

Tangier had acquired a worldwide reputation as a raffish and disreputable place. While some of the business activities that had fed that reputation now declined or stopped, the city remained for long after 1961 a haven for Western expatriates—especially artists, writers, and intellectuals, including Paul Bowles, Truman Capote, William S. Burroughs, and Allen Ginsberg.

Tangier is still one of the most important cities of Morocco, its population now being about 500,000. Although the King of Morocco has a palace there, Tangier lies in a deprived region neglected by the government. Prominent natives of Tangier include the writer Tahar Ben Djelloun, the comedian Bachir Skiredj, and Mohammed Choukri, another writer, whose autobiography published in translation as *For Bread Alone* (Peter Owen, 1973) described the wretched life of Tangier's indigenous people, far removed from the seedy glamour of its formerly notorious expatriate society.

JONATHAN DERRICK

See also: **Maghrib; Morocco.**

Further Reading

Finlayson, I. *Tangier: City of the Dream.* London: Flamingo, 1993.
Landau, R. *Portrait of Tangier.* Robert Hale, 1952.
Stewart, A. *Tangier: A Writer's Notebook.* London: Hutchinson, 1977.

Tanzania (Tanganyika): Arusha Declaration

In the Arusha Declaration, approved by Tanganyika African National Union's (TANU's) National Executive Committee on February 5, 1967, Julius Nyerere set out a blueprint for a future Tanzanian socialism. Section 1 of the declaration summed up his objectives for Tanzania: socialism, equality, and an end to poverty. Section 2 then defined socialism as the control of the means of production and exchange by workers and peasants; and Section 3 qualified this by emphasizing the primary role of peasants, criticizing the emphasis that had been placed on industrialization to date.

While Section 4 called upon the TANU members to accept these principles, it was in the Leadership Code (Section 5) that Nyerere strove to embed socialism in the political structure. According to the code, leaders (party and state) should be either peasants or workers, not associated with "the practice of capitalism or feudalism." They should not own shares nor hold directorships in private companies. They should receive one salary only, and should not be in receipt of rentals from property.

In a subsequent policy paper, "Socialism and Rural Development" (1967), Nyerere spelled out his concern about the social consequences of unrestricted urbanization, and advocated a policy of rural development

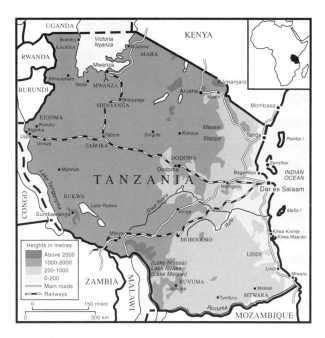

Tanzania.

based on the *ujamaa* village, which would start with communal, as well as individual plots, but evolve gradually into a single agricultural commune. Replacing the existing small village, the much larger ujamaa village's "economy of scale" would provide opportunities for the establishment of a wide range of technical and social services, helping to raise the peasant's overall standard of living.

Nyerere's socialist program grew out of the concept of *ujamaa* (familyhood), which harked back to what he believed were the guiding precepts of traditional, precolonial African society: respect, common property, and the obligation to work. He felt that these principles had been undermined by the colonial experience, which had encouraged individual enterprise at the expense of the common good, and had continued to flourish after the securing of independence with the emergence of a privileged elite operating in a neocolonialist milieu. Nyerere now sought to arrest this trend with the implementation of ujamaa socialism, emphasizing a number of related principles: mutual cooperation and public control; mass participation in the political process; self-reliance and self-sufficiency (with an end to reliance on foreign aid that he believed was trapping his country in a cycle of dependency); an emphasis on a socialist pattern of rural development (building on the foundations laid with the nationalization of land in 1962); an exhortation to Tanzanians (especially male peasants) to work harder; and the creation of a leadership oriented toward the public, rather than their own, interest. It was a socialism significantly different from the Marxist-Leninist model coming into fashion in the late 1960s, which sought to transplant from the Soviet system the industrial and urban route to development, with a select, carefully screened ("vanguard") party membership.

In practice, the ujamaa village experiment succeeded in consolidating rural settlement: at the end of the process, in 1976, some 13 million Tanzanian peasants lived in 7684 villages, according to Nyerere's figures. However, as early as 1973, the communal principle had been dropped in response to peasant hostility. More seriously, in some areas at least, overzealous party and state officials had coerced peasants into moving to the new villages, particularly after 1973, when the TANU leadership had called for an increase in the pace of village development, an error of judgment that Nyerere later admitted to. The development aims of ujamaa were frustrated by a shortage of resources to meet villagers' requests, leading to their eventual disillusionment; this was aggravated by a policy change in 1972, which moved decision making from the village level, where peasants could negotiate with officials, to regional headquarters. Peasants could send in requests for projects, but little else, and thus became dependent on the wishes of regional bureaucrats.

The ujamaa experiment thus failed in its main objective—namely, to make a breakthrough in rural production. The image of the typical ujamaa village was that of poverty and low expectations. Ironically, most of the main beneficiaries had been the black commercial farmers, who were tolerated by the administration provided that they made no public criticism of ujamaa, whose expertise and existing farming capital enabled them to make good use of official technical assistance.

Analysts have been divided between those who seek to account for the ujamaa experiment's failure in terms of the operation of external factors, essentially beyond the control of Nyerere's government, and those who would attribute it to inherent weaknesses in the experiment as a whole. From 1973, Tanzania, like much of Africa, was exposed to the ravages of the Organization of Petroleum Exporting Countries price rises and declining terms of trade in primary products, with the added local circumstance of a series of crippling droughts in the early 1980s and Tanzania's war against Idi Amin in Uganda. But ujamaa itself seems to have been undermined economically by a pricing policy for crops that benefited the country's parastatal purchasing organizations at the expense of peasant producers, and a national environment of mismanagement, overmanning, and overspending that left state corporations heavily in debt by the mid-1980s. Less easy to demonstrate is the impression of a utopian experiment fatally weakened by a bureaucracy operating at a remove from the peasantry, which feared making decisions that might rebound against it. The result was a growing conservatism, and an unwillingness to entertain innovation, much less radical change.

Whether its failure was inherent, or caused by extrinsic events, Tanzania's peasants became increasingly disaffected with ujamaa socialism, and cut back their production of cash crops in response to the fall in real producer prices. By the early 1980s, Tanzania had become more, rather than less, reliant on external aid. The country's increasingly precarious economic position gradually pushed its leadership into more pragmatic policies, with the symbolic decision in 1986 (after several years of refusal) to accept the conditions laid down by the International Monetary Fund for financial assistance. The Leadership Code, increasingly flouted by leaders forced to find supplementary sources of income in a deteriorating economy, survived until the reforms of the 1990s, when Tanzania moved toward a multiparty democracy.

MURRAY STEELE

See also: **Nyerere, Julius; Socialism in Postcolonial Africa.**

Further Reading

Coulson, Andrew. *Tanzania: a Political Economy.* Oxford: Clarendon Press,: Oxford University Press, 1982.

Hatch, John, *Two African Statesmen: Kaunda of Zambia and Nyerere of Tanzania.* London: Secker and Warburg/Chicago: Regnery, 1976.

Hyden, Goran. *Beyond Ujamaa in Tanzania: Underdevelopment and an Uncaptured Peasantry.* London: Heinemann/ Berkeley and Los Angeles: University of California Press, 1980.

McHenry, Dean. *Limited Choices: The Political Struggle for Socialism in Tanzania.* Boulder, Colo.: Lynne Rienner, 1994.

Nyerere, Julius. *The Arusha Declaration Ten Years After.* Dar es Salaam: Government Printer, 1977/

———. *Freedom and Socialism. Uhuru na Ujamaa; A Selection From Writings And Speeches.* Dar es Salaam: Oxford University Press, 1968.

Tanzania (Tanganyika): Chama Cha Mapinduzi (CCM), One-Party Politics

Popular votes created a virtual one-party state in Tanganyika, the mainland part of Tanzania, in 1960, when the Tanganyika African National Union (TANU) led the mainland to independence. The Afro-Shirazi Party (ASP) created a de facto one-party system on Zanzibar following their 1964 revolution. A presidential commission established on the mainland in 1964 to explore the desirability of a one-party system recommended that Tanganyika become a de jure, or legal, one-party state following the 1966 elections. Tanganyika was already a virtual one-party state. Although the law permitted multiparty democratic electoral politics, the TANU regularly won elections in 1958, 1960, and 1962. In fact, the TANU won all

parliamentary seats except one. Julius Nyerere, the father of Tanzania's independence, did not think that multiparty politics were good for Africa; he stated that "a struggle for freedom from colonialism is a patriotic struggle which leaves no room for differences." Nyerere believed that the Westminster model was divisive in an African context.

A small handful of people could pose a threat to the state, in Nyerere's mind, and a well-organized faction—or, worse yet, an opposition party—posed a more substantial risk for creating unrest. Each party, in his opinion, might become associated with one candidate, and his tribe would dominate that party. This might eventually lay the foundation for "a state of potential civil war." Where differences between parties were inconsequential, a multiparty system promoted "a spirit of purely artificial rivalry, like that which exists between a couple of soccer teams." Where the differences between parties were "fundamental," the potential for internal unrest was great.

Nyerere believed that democracy could thrive within a one-party system by encouraging vigorous competition within the party for nomination and office. He defended his position by arguing that overwhelming support of the TANU meant that opposing candidates stood a negligible chance of election. Nyerere believed that a one-party system whereby candidates belonging to the same party competed for election restored the principle of meaningful choice. Moreover, if all of the political tensions within the nation were contained within one party, then religious, regional, and ethnic groups would have to discuss their differences. Argument would lead to understanding and shared values. Nyerere elevated Kiswahili, making it the national language, so that members of parliament, like Bibi Titi, who did not speak English, could participate in national debate on important issues of the day. The TANU members would communicate in a common language, and tribalism, religious discrimination, and racism would be discouraged. Every Tanzanian would be accommodated within one system through the one-party state.

Nyerere was not alone in viewing new African states as fragile, and he was not merely rationalizing prolonged tenure in office for himself. He believed in freedom of choice, competition, and individual rights within the one-party state.

The one-party system did allow voters to express dissatisfaction. In successive elections between 1966 and 1980, many members of the Tanzanian parliament were voted out of office. Voters elected candidates who supported the Arusha Declaration of "socialism and self-reliance," launched in 1967. Tanzanian voters also elected leaders who supported the Leadership Code, which limited leaders to owning one house, one farm, and one directorship on a corporate board in order to combat corruption and elitism. Voters had some choices within this system, and they took advantage of them.

Although the two one-party states of Tanganyika and Zanzibar merged to form the United Republic of Tanzania in 1964, the two political parties, the TANU and the ASP, did not merge until the Chama Cha Mapinduzi (Party of the Revolution), or CCM, was officially formed in 1977.

Tanzania was a de jure one-party State from 1977 to 1992. Throughout this time, the National Conference was the highest organ of the CCM. The National Election Commission (NEC), however, appointed candidates and reserved the power to remove members of parliament by revoking their party membership. In 1988, seven members of parliament were dismissed from the party, thereby also losing their seats in parliament. This demonstrated the power of the NEC.

When the Soviet Union disintegrated in 1990–1991, this opened debate on the advisability of one-party States, and the CCM organized a national conference to discuss Tanzania's political culture. Conferences, workshops, and seminars provided other forums for discussing one-party vs. multiparty politics. In Kiswahili, these discussions are called *mageus* (the turning point). After more than a year of discussion, then President Ali Hassan Mwinyi appointed a presidential commission to consolidate the views of the nation and to offer recommendations. At the 1992 CCM conference a 16-page document, the Report of the Extraordinary National Conference on the Recommendation of the National Executive Committee to Change the Political System in Tanzania, recommended that CCM's monopoly of power end. Subsequently, President Mwinyi implemented a new multiparty democratic system, despite the fact that 80 per cent of Tanzanians polled favored a one-party state. Political pluralism, a strong civic society, and a market economy replaced the old system. This trend reflected broader international reforms, as well as the conditionality of international donors who linked foreign aid to adoption of the new culture. A third of Tanzania's gross domestic product was conditionally underwritten by Western donors. Former head of state Nyerere found such international pressure "contemptible" and "hypocritical," but recognized the need to change to a multiparty system so long as new parties were not forced to adopt external conditions.

Tanzania made a smooth transition from a one-party to a multiparty state. The CCM has since undergone profound changes. CCM branches in the armed forces and workplaces were abolished in 1992; CCM members in the armed forces had contributed $700,000 annually, and the loss of this money was a painful one. Moreover, party chairpersons, both national and local, now no longer receive salaries; theirs are now part-time volunteer positions. CCM offices have a smaller staff. Party officials, on loan to CCM offices from state owned corporations, have had to either return to their former jobs or retire. To reduce operating cost party secretariats fired many employees. Of the seven ideological colleges, only Kivukoni College in Dar es Salaam remains operational. Currently the Kivukoni Academy of Social Sciences functions like a private college. It offers courses on law, public administration, communications, development, management, and international relations, as well as a little ideological and political education. Students pay fees to attend.

It must be noted that the privatization of state companies, implementation of harsh economic reforms demanded by the International Monetary Fund and the World Bank, and the switch to a free market economy occurred with little or no tribalism or communal violence. CCM candidates promise voters many more years of peace and stability. Thirty years of socialist policies and Julius Nyerere's idealism maintained harmony among Tanzania's 120 ethnic groups. It minimized class divisions, openly fought public corruption, and encouraged religious tolerance. With a grassroots organization envied by rivals and a divided opposition, the CCM's hold on power seems secure.

DALLAS L. BROWNE

See also: **Nyerere, Julius.**

Further Reading

Halimoja, Yusuf J. *Chama Cha Mapinduzi*. Dar es Salaam: Mwangaza, 1977.

———. *Miongozo ya CCM*. Dar es Salaam: Mwangaza Publishers, 1980.

Hellman, Bruce. "Who Are the Indigenous Tanzanians? Competing Conceptions of Tanzanian Citizenship in the Business Community." *Africa Today* 45, nos. 3–4 (1998): 369–389.

Hussein, Tabasim. "End of Tanzanians One-Party Rule." Africa Report, July–August 1992, 122–124.

Mmuya, Maximilian. *Toward Multiparty Politics in Tanzania: A Spectrum of the Current Opposition and the CCM Response.* 1992.

Ngasongwa, Juma. "Tanzania Introduces a Multi-Party System." *Review of African Political Economy*, July 1992, 112–117.

Nyerere, Julius K. *Five-Years of CCM Government: The Address Given to the National Conference of the CCM.* Dar es Salaam: Government Printers, 1982.

———. *Freedom and Unity: 1952–1965.* Oxford: Oxford University Press, 1967.

———. *Man and Development.* Oxford: Oxford University Press, 1974.

———. *Moyo wa Kujitolea: Silaha ya Maendeleo: The Human Heart and Self Sacrifice: The Weapon of Progress.* 1988.

———. *Uhuru Na Ujamaa: Freedom and Socialism: 1965–57.* Oxford: Oxford University Press, 1970.

Potholm, Christian P. *Four African Political Systems*. Englewood Cliffs, N.J.: Prentice-Hall, 1970.

Randsell, Eric. "A Bright Spot in Africa." *U.S. News and World Report* 119, no. 16 (1995): 73.

Tanzania (Tanganyika): Uganda, Relations with

Uganda invaded Tanzania and attempted to annex the Kagera Salient in 1978. Tanzania protested this naked aggression and asked the international community to force Uganda to return its territory. Neither the United Nations, the Organization of African Unity, nor any nation-state came to Tanzania's aid. To make matters worse, landlocked Uganda threatened to seize a huge corridor of Tanzania's land, containing railroad, road, and harbor facilities and ending at the Indian Ocean port city of Tanga. In self-defense, Tanzania first forced the Ugandan army out of Tanzania. Then, to end the chronic threat of invasion and illegal annexation of territory, the Tanzanian army invaded Uganda. The Tanzania Expeditionary Force captured Uganda's capital, Kampala, and drove Uganda's then ruler Idi Amin into permanent exile in Saudi Arabia. Once Amin was removed, amicable relations between Tanzania and Uganda were restored.

On October 30, 1978, Idi Amin Dada sent an invasion force of 3,000 Ugandan troops across the border into neighboring Tanzania. A primary target was the Taka Bridge, which had been used by anti-Amin Ugandans living in Tanzania to invade Uganda. The Ugandan army falsely accused the Tanzanian army of invading Uganda in early October 1978. This propaganda was meant to confuse Tanzania and divert attention from the impending Ugandan invasion.

Ugandan troops killed 10,000 Tanzanian civilians and stole 12,000 cattle as well as other livestock, household effects, cars, furniture, and any other valuables that they could find. An estimated 485 Tanzanians were held captive at the Ugandan army base at Mutukulu, just across the Tanzania border. Uganda is landlocked, and Amin felt that Uganda needed assured access to the Indian Ocean.

Julius Nyerere, then Tanzanian head of state, asked Amin to withdraw Uganda's troops from Tanzanian territory on the grounds that they had violated Tanzania's sovereignty. Amin refused and instead challenged Nyerere to a "boxing duel." Needless to say, no fight took place; rather, Nyerere asked the United Nations and the Organization of African States to mediate the dispute. But Amin would not permit this.

Consequently, Tanzania sent several squadrons of modern jets to intercept and stop the Ugandan invaders. Other nations refused to stop Uganda, so Tanzania decided to defend itself. In spite of being among the world's poorest countries, Tanzania spent over $1 million a day to fund the war. Inflation grew rapidly, and Tanzania felt that it could not afford to fight for more than one month. Massive force was used to repel the Ugandan army and rapidly depose Amin.

Tanzania trained every adult Tanzanian to use modern weapons. The Tanzanian government was not afraid of its own people, but Amin, however, feared the Ugandans he ruled. Tanzania's army had veterans who were former military advisors in a variety of African conflicts. Uganda's army's only experience fighting was against unarmed Ugandan civilians, whom they intimidated; the outcome was determined before the two armies engaged in battle. Aided by Ugandans who sought to liberate their country from Amin's brutal dictatorship, the Tanzanians easily defeated and demoralized Amin's forces. By Christmas Tanzania had captured Uganda and turned the governance of the country over to Ugandans loyal to Uganda's first elected leader, Milton Obote. This brief war marked a turning point in modern African history for it established the principal that one African nation could invade another independent African nation if it had "sufficient cause."

Upon independence, Ugandans elected Milton Obote president, who promoted Idi Amin to general of the Ugandan army. Eventually, Amin overthrew Obote and reassumed leadership. Faced with dissent within the military and the civilian populace, Amin attempted to divert attention from this situation by invading Tanzania on October 30, 1978.

Although Tanzania was the 27th poorest country on earth, it committed a huge proportion of its meager resources to the liberation of Africans in other countries. Cynical observers note that Nyerere was a leader of the "Front Line States": Tanzania, Zambia, Botswana, Angola, and Mozambique. In 1978, these countries were embroiled in civil wars. Some scholars thus believe that it was not an accident that the Uganda-Tanzania war erupted during a critical moment in negotiations between liberation forces and Ian Smith's white minority government in Rhodesia. Tanzania sacrificed improvement in the standard of living of its citizens so that its support for African liberation forces would not be in jeopardy. Antiliberation forces therefore wanted to undermine Nyerere by any means possible. They argued that he retaliated against Amin for personal reasons. He was accused of building a political empire at the expense of African unity. The Uganda-Tanzania war came close to costing Nyerere his credibility. If Tanzania could be discredited, then millions of Africans would be forced to suffer oppression for an untold number of decades. In 1978 Rhodesia, Namibia, Mozambique, and Angola had won independence with Tanzania's help.

Thus, the Uganda-Tanzania border war reflected the complexities of internal conflict within Uganda. It also reflected regional tensions in eastern and southern Africa. Escalating Cold War tensions played a role, though the conflict never escalated into a war by proxy on the scale of Vietnam or Afghanistan. Tanzania invaded Uganda to defend itself and to rid Africa of Idi Amin (who eventually fled invading Tanzanian and Ugandan liberation forces and found refuge first in Libya and later in Saudi Arabia).

Uganda's invasion of Tanzania established a new precedent in African international relations. This incident highlighted the continuing significance of ethnicity and the tensions between groups that can result in civil war. It also underscored international tensions and conflicts associated with the birth of new states and nationalism.

The Tanzanian invasion of Uganda and its removal of a dictator whom Tanzania found intolerable establish a second precedent: African heads of state could now remove other African leaders whose policies and practices they found repugnant, and influence those who come to power. The Tanzanian invasion of Uganda created bold new possibilities for African relations. Africans could now create regional spheres of influence and use violence to maintain or expand them. The invasion was a turning point in African history.

DALLAS L. BROWNE

See also: **Museveni, Yoweri Kaguta; Nyerere, Julius; Obote, Milton; Uganda: Amin Dada, Idi: Coup and Regime, 1971–1979; Uganda: Tanzanian Invasion, 1979–1980.**

Further Reading

Avirgan, Tony. *War in Uganda: the Legacy of Idi Amin.* Dar es Salaam: Tanzania Publishing, 1983.

Kiwanuka, Semakula. *Amin and the Tragedy of Uganda.* Munich: Weltforum Verlag, 1979.

Richardson, Michael Lewis. *After Amin, the Bloody Pearl.* Atlanta: Majestic, 1980.

Smith, George Ivan. *Ghosts of Kampala.* New York: St. Martin's Press. 1980.

Tanzania and the War against Amin's Uganda. Dar es Salaam: Government of the United Republic of Tanzania, 1979.

Uganda 30 Years, 1962–1992. Kampala: Fountain, 1992.

Tanzania (Tanganyika): Democracy and Capitalism: 1990 to the Present

In the late 1980s, Tanzania's one-party political system—with Chama Cha Mapinduzi [CCM] renamed from the Tanganyika African National Union [TANU] in 1977, as the only permitted party—came under increasing criticism from a younger generation of Western-educated economists and financial technocrats within the ruling elite. Their views were shaped by a combination of considerations, such as the manifest inanition of CCM institutions, the move of

Forestry in Tanzania. © Charlotte Thege/Das Fotoarchiv.

Africa generally toward multipartyism, and reforms in Eastern Europe. The "Young Turks" received unexpected support from ex-president and now CCM head Julius Nyerere, who in February 1990 remarked that the one-party system "[tended] to go to sleep." Following a public consultation, a CCM conference unanimously supported a proposal to restore multiparty democracy, and Tanzania's constitution was amended accordingly in 1992. To safeguard national unity, it was stipulated that to be registered, political parties should reflect a national, and not a regional or religious, constituency. An array of political parties quickly emerged, but they were fragmentary, often led by erstwhile establishment figures, and in any case found themselves trying to operate in an environment in which the CCM had usurped the reformist agenda. As a result, they found it difficult to mount a convincing challenge to the ruling establishment. The CCM easily won the first multiparty election in 1995, and won a similarly sweeping victory in 2000, securing 244 of the 275 National Assembly seats. Significantly, the only really substantial opposition party on the mainland, the National Convention for Construction and Reform, or Mageuzi (Change) was led by a former CCM minister who had been dismissed a few months earlier for "indiscipline."

The growing domination of the reform movement was also reflected at the highest level—namely, the presidency. Nyerere's successor Ali Hassan Mwinyi (1985–1995) had introduced a measured program of economic liberalization, including some relaxation of the republic's very tight exchange control regulations from 1896 onward, but the final years of his presidency were overshadowed by charges of corruption and financial mismanagement. His successor, Benjamin Mkapa, campaigned on an anticorruption platform in the 1995 presidential election, and after winning a clear mandate (62 per cent of the popular vote), accelerated the pace of political and economic reform. However, as in Mwinyi's second term, his current tenure (2000–2005) has witnessed renewed allegations of corruption, nepotism and—following disputed election results and unrest on the island of Zanzibar—abuse of authority.

In the 1990s Tanzania finally turned its back on socialism. President Mkapa acknowledged its failure, while claiming its success as a guarantor of social stability and a mechanism for building the Tanzanian nation. A declining number of diehard socialists predicted the replacement of Nyerere's utopian vision by a capitalist dystopia, pointing to the rampant corruption of Mwinyi's last presidency as evidence. The reformers disagreed, attributing the crisis of 1992–1995 to the atmosphere of disillusion and structural dissolution that had characterized the final years of socialism, an interpretation owing much to contemporary events in the Soviet Union and its successors. The new Tanzania would be one in which the state would ensure that modernization continued, the conditions for entrepreneurship and economic growth maximized, foreign investment welcomed, and trade liberalized, with the State taking a direct role safeguarding equal opportunities and the provision of social welfare for all people.

The most obvious sign of its departure from socialism has been the program to privatize its 350+ parastatals, few of which were making a profit when the privatization legislation was enacted in 1992. Implementation was slow at first, with the government testing the water and seeking to protect various interests. Some prodding from world financial institutions, notably the International Monetary Fund (IMF), speeded up the process, helped after 1995 by Mkapa's wholehearted endorsement of modernization: by 2002, some 80 per cent of Tanzania's state corporations had passed into private hands. Recent proposed privatizations, involving sensitive areas such as public utilities (water, electricity), have led to charges of favoritism and corrupt practices, and the deadline of December 2003 for the winding up of the whole sector may not be achieved.

Similar allegations had been made earlier about the first beneficiaries of privatization and the move toward a freer market. The ability of Tanzania's Asian community to take advantage of these new commercial opportunities led to violence, attacks on Asian stores, and rioting in 1993–1994, and suggestions that only "indigenous" (i.e., non-Asian) Tanzanians should be able to buy into privatized parastatals. But young black would-be entrepreneurs were confronted by other obstacles, including a state bureaucracy that was reluctant to simplify regulations and procedures; a banking system that, albeit no longer a state monopoly, was inflexible and inefficient; and an environment in which established entrepreneurs had the wherewithal to grease palms when this proved necessary, a particular feature of the Mwinyi's second term. To these obstacles should be added the foreign investor, wooed by the state and encouraged by a number of inducements, including partial or total exemption from taxation for which local firms were liable. At the same time, trade liberalization exposed Tanzania's infant industries to the full blast of competition from foreign imports, further curbing the country's development.

Tanzania's program of economic liberalization and reform has won it plaudits from the World Bank and the IMF, as well as other foreign donors, and by the turn of the decade had created an economic growth rate of 4.5 to 5 per cent per year, higher than the African average. The costs of these reforms have been high: a stagnating rural sector, beset by low and falling world commodity prices for Tanzania's main export crops; a growing urban/rural economic divide; a continuing dependence on external aid, with a third of public spending in 2002 coming from this source; the decline in social services—which had started in the later *ujamaa* period—continuing with cuts in state expenditure in years of financial stringency; and reports of increasing social tension, especially since the start of the new millennium.

MURRAY STEELE

See also: **Nyerere, Julius; Tanzania (Tanganyika): Arusha Declaration.**

Further Reading

Barkan, Joel (ed.). *Beyond Capitalism vs. Socialism in Kenya and Tanzania.* Boulder, Colo.: Lynne Rienner, 1994.

Kaiser, Paul. "Structural Adjustment and the Fragile Nation: the Demise of Social Unity in Tanzania," *Journal of Modern African Studies.* 34, no. 2 (1996): 227–237.

Kennedy, Paul. "Political Barriers to African Capitalism," *Journal of Modern African Studies* 32, no. 2 (1994): 191–213.

Legum, Colin, and Mmari, Geoffrey (eds.). *Mwalimu: The Influence of Nyerere.* London: James Currey, 1995.

McHenry, Dean. *Limited Choices: the Political Struggle for Socialism in Tanzania.* Boulder, Colo.: Lynne Rienner, 1994.

Yeager, Rodger. *Tanzania, an African Experiment.* London: Dartmouth/Boulder, Colo.: Westview Press, 1989.

Taxation

Taxation turned indigenous peoples into a "governable" population, although controlling and containing them was fundamental to colonial administration. Direct taxation, in various forms of "hut," "head" or poll taxes on adult males, and consumption taxes on imports, ensured that Africans paid for the "benefits" of colonial rule. Although philosophies of imperial administration differed throughout Africa, taxation, backed up by colonial law and policing, was used as a "soft" coercive force, pushing Africans into labor for whites or cash-crop production. There was no single revenue policy, and thus tax burdens varied from colony to colony. During the 1930s Africans were further "squeezed" to compensate for the declining coffers of the colonial governments. However, even in the depths of economic depression, African colonies serviced their debts and balanced budgets as tax-collecting became more efficient. Africans thus saw little benefit from taxation, which became a focus of grievances articulated by African nationalist organizations.

In Britain (the major imperial power in Africa), the prevailing economic orthodoxy was that colonies should be self-supporting. An imperial subsidy was borne by British taxpayers, but defense constituted the largest component of this subsidy. The government also financed loans for imperial development, paid for primarily by African taxpayers, and made direct grants for public works and native education. Most colonial revenues came from taxes, but 30 per cent came from nontax sources such as licenses, fees, and mining royalties levied on private companies. European companies paid no taxes in the colonies in which they operated. In nonsettler colonies, consumption taxes and customs revenues on foreign trade, ultimately paid for by colonial consumers, constituted a major source of revenue. The burden of taxation fell almost wholly on the poor, as local middlemen were able to skim off profits on imports, widening the class and gender inequalities in African societies. Because of government dependence on customs revenues there was also less opportunity for import substitution than in the "white settler" colonies, perpetuating economic dependency.

The impact of taxation was most intense in the "white settler" colonies, where it was combined with land dispossession. In South Africa, all adult males, including urban migrants, paid poll tax, and in the "native reserves" such as the Transkei, the salaries of white administrators, "native" education, prisons, and policing were charged to Africans. In the 1930s, however, only 14.5 per cent was spent on education, as opposed to 29 per cent on prisons. Men had to travel to distant places to pay taxes (in a lump sum), involving loss of earnings, and, until 1939, default was a criminal offense punishable by fines or imprisonment. In the British South African High Commission Territories of Swaziland, Bechuanaland (Botswana), and Basutoland (Lesotho), and in Portuguese Mozambique, low levels of development and taxation created a dependency on migrant remittances from the South African mines which endured well into the postcolonial era.

The role of taxation in coercing African labor into the cash economy has been well documented, but its centrality to the wider culture of colonialism has received less attention. Taxation, suggests Sean Redding (1996), "imbued the colonial state with supernatural powers" that echoed widespread beliefs in witchcraft and drew Africans into participation in state rituals. Colonial censuses collected ethnographic information but also

facilitated the organization and extension of taxation. The connection between taxation and the wider "civilizing" project was clearly articulated by Frederick Lugard, the guru of British "native administration" in the 1920s. Lugard visualized an Africa where "horrible cruelties" were replaced by "order and justice." For Lugard, taxation was a "common burden" and "universal necessity of civilisation" that African communities had to share. The moral foundation of "native development," taxation stimulated individual enterprise and responsibility, emancipated Africans from slavery and forced labor (but also from "indolence"), enhanced "self-respect," and promoted "pride" in progress. Taxes were to be paid only in cash and it was the duty of colonial officers to energetically encourage trade.

In keeping with the principle of ruling through existing African political and legal structures, native treasuries, supposedly managed by native authorities, were set up to finance administration and development, though they were carefully audited by white officers. This reflected a general lack of trust in placing even more "civilized" Africans in positions of authority. Colonial officials and white "friends of the native" alike saw Africans as financially naive or inherently corrupt, unable to comprehend Western principles of taxation and accountancy. However, from an African perspective, taxation arguably represented a deep cultural imposition of alien accounting practices and concepts of individual agency that assumed that African societies were incapable of self-management of resources.

In West Africa, tax-collecting often provoked strong resistance and hostility and proved a disagreeable business. In more remote areas, widespread resistance was encountered and colonial officers would only travel with an armed escort. Resistance to taxation was punished by fines, imprisonment, or severe reprisals in the case of threats to colonial officers' lives. The imposition of direct taxation was particularly problematic in the Gold Coast. The British only finally crushed the powerful Asante military resistance in 1895, and the Asante and Fanti peoples continued to assert their traditional democratic practices, refusing to accept the principle of direct taxation and white-controlled native treasuries. Gold Coast Africans favored duties on export products where part of the burden fell on the foreign purchaser. New forms of urban taxation, such as the 1934 Waterworks Ordinance, which levied a rate for water from street taps, were deeply resented. In the ongoing struggle to impose direct taxation, an ordinance was passed in 1935 authorizing the raising of revenue by "annual levies" and depriving Africans of any control over local revenues.

After 1929 the extension of taxation to untaxed regions to compensate for reduced budgets, combined with deteriorating economic conditions, resulted in a sharp growth of unrest. In Nigeria and the Gold Coast women were actively involved in antitax protests as colonial interventions threatened to undermine their marketing activities, an economic sector in which they traditionally dominated. During the 1929 riots in Southern Nigeria, which Africans called the "Women's War," female protesters were shot dead by the colonial authorities. However, women's grievances were part of a more generalized unrest resulting from the introduction of a new Native Revenue Ordinance, hostility toward collaborative African chiefs, and a drop in the price of palm oil, the main export crop. After the riots, punitive fines were imposed, houses burned down, and expeditions sent out to administer a severe lesson to the local population.

Conflict between Africans and white authorities also emerged over taxation and control of alcohol. Despite international humanitarian conventions to control liquor imports into Sub-Saharan Africa, colonial governments regarded duties levied on imported alcohol as a valuable source of revenue. However, import taxes on alcohol merely increased the number of illegal stills, threatening government revenues and raising the specter of crime, disorder, and prostitution. From the 1930s on, popular struggles in the expanding urban townships increasingly centered around government control of alcohol and impinged on nationalist politics. Beer boycotts were launched in urban centers in South Africa and Northern Rhodesia, where municipal beer halls provided a healthy revenue for city councils but threatened the livelihoods of African women, who survived in urban areas by brewing and selling beer.

During World War II, new forms of taxation were introduced, food costs rose, and there was greater direction of labor. African protest grew and the rapid development of trade unionism and mass nationalism accelerated changes in French and British colonial policy. In recognition of the increasing importance of the African empire, the British government passed the Colonial Development and Welfare Act in 1940, which made available extra finances. However, development funds were firmly linked to capitalist interests and the expansion of the modern cash-crop economy and the colonized were still expected to pay for their own development through taxation. Order and profit thus remained at the heart of the imperial mission throughout the colonial era, and colonial revenue, accounting, and auditing are fundamental to debates around the profitability of the imperial enterprise and relations between government and business. But fiscal policies were also underpinned by cultural values that had irreversible impact on African societies and the established circles of poverty, debt, and dependency that have persisted into the postcolonial era.

BARBARA BUSH

See also: **Alcohol: Popular Culture, Colonial Control.**

Further Reading

Akyeampong, E. K. "What's in a Drink? Class Struggle, Popular Culture and the Politics of *Akpeteshie* (Local Gin) in Ghana, 1930–67." *Journal of African History.* 37, no. 2 (1996): 215–236.

Ambler, Charles. "Alcohol, Racial Segregation and Popular Politics in Northern Rhodesia." *Journal of Imperial and Commonwealth History.* 31, no. 3 (1990): 295–313.

Asechemie, D. P. S. "African Labour Systems, Maintenance Accounting and Agency Theory." *Critical Perspectives on Accounting.* 8, no. 3 (1997): 373–392.

Bush, Barbara. *Imperialism, Race and Resistance: Africa and Britain 1919–1945.* London: Routledge, 1999.

Cooper, F. *The Decolonisation of African Society: The Labour Question in French and British Africa.* Cambridge: Cambridge University Press, 1997.

Gorer, Geoffrey. *Africa Dances.* London: Faber and Faber, 1935.

Hopkins, A. G. *An Economic History of West Africa.* London: Longman, 1973.

Huttenback, R. A., and L. E. Davis. *Mammon and the Pursuit of Empire: The Political Economy of British Imperialism, 1860–1912.* Cambridge: Cambridge University Press, 1986.

Lugard, Frederick. *Political Memoranda; Revision of Instructions to Political Officers on Subjects Chiefly Political and Administrative, 1913–1918,* edited and with an introduction by A. H. M. Kirk Greene. London: Frank Cass, 1970.

Neu, Dean. "Discovering Indigenous Peoples: Accounting and the Machinery of Empire," *Accounting Historians Journal.* 26, no. 1 (1999): 53–82.

Redding, Sean. "Government Witchcraft: Taxation, the Supernatural, and the Mpondo Revolt in the Transkei, South Africa, 1955–1963." *African Affairs.* 95, no. 4 (1996): 555–579.

Suret-Canale, Jean. *French Colonialism in Tropical Africa, 1900–1945.* London: C. Hurst, 1971.

Taylor, Charles (*c*.1948–)
Former President of Liberia

Charles Taylor, the 21st president of the Republic of Liberia, has the singular honor of starting a bloody civil war on Christmas Eve 1989 and subsequently winning both the presidential and parliamentary vote in an election declared free and fair by the international community.

To appreciate the dynamics of this paradoxical transformation, one must trace the "rebellious" career of Taylor both as a student activist and in national politics. These activities formed the background that led him to plunge his country into a brutal seven-year civil war, an odyssey that resulted in the total destruction of Liberia and the displacement of large populations either internally or as refugees. Taylor is an Americo-Liberian from Arthington, one of the established settler communities along the St. Pauli River near Monrovia. He is a member of the elite group that ruled Liberia since its foundation in 1822 until the Armed Forces of Liberia overthrew the monolithic True Whig Party (TWP) on April 14, 1980.

Taylor's nascent rebel activities started in the United States where he was a student first at Chamberlain

Junior College in Boston, Massachusetts. He subsequently studied economics at Bentley College, also in Massachusetts. As part of his political activities he joined the Union of Liberian Associations in the Americas, becoming the chairman of its board of directors. Characteristic of the later insurgent movement of which he consequently became leader, Taylor was one of a few Americo-Liberians among an otherwise predominantly indigenous association.

In the aftermath of the coup d'état that overthrew the TWP, Taylor exploited his marriage to Tupee Taylor, niece of Thomas Quiwonkpa, who was then the army chief of staff, to secure an appointment as the director general of the General Services Agency (GSA), the government procurement agency. It is widely believed that the contacts established during the performance of his duties helped him during his recruitment drive and search for finances and weapons. Taylor was replaced as head of the GSA in November 1983 and eventually demoted to the position of deputy minister of commerce. Closely related to Taylor's demise was the escape of his mentor to the United States and a widespread assumption that he had used a transaction with a company to embezzle almost a million U.S. dollars. In the aftermath of the outcry that met this discovery, Taylor escaped to the United States only to be arrested and imprisoned awaiting extradition to Liberia after a request from the government of Samuel K. Doe.

The exact time and detail of Taylor's "escape from prison" in the United States and arrival in West Africa remain controversial. What is known for certain is that when Taylor arrived in West Africa, some time between November 1985 and April 1986, he went on an extensive tour of the subregion seeking support to overthrow the Doe government. Burkina Faso, Côte d'Ivoire, Ghana, and Libya are known to have extended diverse kinds of patronage ranging from finance, training grounds, and the supply of traveling documents and armaments to Taylor's embryonic group. Sierra Leone is one of the few countries that denied Taylor active support because of an earlier bungled attempt to overthrow Doe by Liberian exiles in November 1985.

Further controversy surrounds the issue of why and how Taylor became the leader of exiled Liberian opposition groups. One school of thought argues that with his knowledge of procurement procedures and his extensive contacts he was seen by the exiled Liberian opposition groups as a good choice. Another argues that with the disarray of the exiled opposition groups, it was easy for Taylor to manipulate himself into a position of influence and power. With the leadership question resolved and political support secured, Taylor eventually led his men, who now constituted the

National Patriotic Front of Liberia (NPFL), into Libya, where they were trained in guerrilla tactics and the use of weapons at the Wheeler Base in Tajura and also at the Mataba base outside Tripoli. After months of preparation, the NPFL insurgents, numbering about 150, invaded Nimba County, Liberia, through Burkina Faso and Côte d'Ivoire on an odyssey that lasted eight years.

Taylor's guerrilla strategy, from the initiation of rebel activities on December 24, 1989 until August 2, 1997, when he was inaugurated as president of Liberia, underwent several changes. First, the NPFL managed, through an effective strategy of exploiting the natural resources of the territories under their control, to gain enough international credibility to dispose of these resources. Second, he managed to manipulate the media into presenting his side of the story. Third, Taylor's aims for starting this war were initially projected in a regional and to some extent international context as resisting Nigerian hegemony. Finally, through his extraordinary political acumen, he established the quasi-state of Greater Liberia under a National Patriotic Reconstruction Assembly Government (NPRAG) headquartered at Gbarnga. From this secure base, he launched different waves of attack against the West African monitoring group, ECOMOG. The most famous of these was what in popular parlance came to be known as Operation Octopus in October 1992, in which the NPFL launched a concerted attack to wrest Monrovia from its international protectors. Failure to militarily succeed and an increasing rapprochement with Nigeria facilitated through Ghanaian diplomacy convinced Taylor to join the political search for peace. As a result, the NPFL was converted into the National Patriotic Party (NPP), which convincingly won the national elections of July 19, 1997.

Upon his inauguration as president of Liberia, Taylor promised that no recriminations would be carried out against his opponents. His government made national reconciliation the key to rebuilding the nation. Two years after his inaugural reassurances, the NPP government proved unable to fulfill its campaign promises; it failed to introduce a national political program of inclusion, while several former opponents were driven into exile. While there were verbal promises of international support for the economic reconstruction scheme, concrete measures were not taken. Finally, the vexed question of reintegration of former combatants and the creation of a new armed force for Liberia was discontinued. In the aftermath of these problems, there were increasing insurgency attacks in Liberia, especially in Lofa County and from Guinea.

In 1999, African nations including Ghana, Nigeria, and others accused Taylor of lending assistance to rebels in Sierra Leone. In return, Taylor charged Guinea with supporting Liberian rebels in the north. In 2000, government forces battled rebels, as well as

Guinean forces in skirmishes on the border. Thousands of people were displaced.

International pressure on Taylor to step down increased as the conflict came to a head in Monrovia and thousands suffered from starvation and displacement. In August 2003 Charles Taylor stepped down and went into exile in Nigeria. Moses Blah, the former vice president, has acted as Liberia's interim leader.

EMMANUEL KWESI ANING

Biography

Born *c.*1948. Studied in the United States at Chamberlain Junior College and Bentley College, Boston, Massachusetts. Imprisoned in the United States, returned to Africa in 1985 or 1986. Inaugurated as president, August 2, 1997. Stepped down from office and entered exile in Nigeria, August 2003.

Further Reading

Alao, Abiodun. *The Burden of Collective Goodwill: The International Involvement in the Liberian Civil War.* London: Aldergate Press, 1998.

Aning, Emmanuel Kwesi. "Ghana, Liberia and ECOWAS: An Analysis of Ghana's Policies in Liberia." *Liberian Studies Journal 21, no. 2* (1996).

Aning, Emmanuel Kwesi. "Eliciting Compliance from Warlords: The ECOWAS Experience in Liberia, 1990–1997." *Review of African Political Economy 26,* no. 81 (1999).

Hubband, Mark. *The Liberian Civil War.* London: Frank Cass, 1998.

Reno, William. *Warlord Politics and African States.* London: Lynne Reinner. 1998.

Teke: *See* Kongo, Teke (Tio) and Loango: History to 1482.

Tewodros II: *See* Ethiopia: Tewodros II, Era of.

Thuku, Harry (*c.*1895–1970)
Anticolonial Activist

Harry Thuku was probably born in 1895 in the Githunguri administrative division of the Kiambu District in central Kenya. His father died in 1897, leaving him in the care of his mother and elder brother. He spent his early childhood taking care of his brother's sheep and goats. However, his fortunes changed dramatically when his subclan, Mbari mya Gatirimu, granted a hundred acres of land to the Gospel Missionary Society for the establishment of a mission center at Kambui. In 1907, young Thuku was employed by the missionaries as a herd and house boy. His time at Kambui Mission and interaction with the missionaries enabled him to learn how to read and write. He next went to Nairobi, the headquarters of the colonial administration, in 1911 to seek his fortune. However, he was caught forging a check, and was sentenced to a two-year prison term.

His fortune changed for the better thereafter. The leading colonial newspaper, *Leader of British East Africa,* employed him as compositor and machine operator. This was a unique opportunity for keeping up to date with current affairs. In particular, he learned about the political battles then taking place between the Indian community and European settlers over the control and future of Kenya.

In 1918, he was employed at the treasury as a telephone operator. This was a good job that enabled him to widen his circle of friends and rent living quarters in Pangani among wealthy Africans drawn from different East African tribes.

During this period, several issues were causing tension and controversy. The Kikuyu community was chafing over their alienated land. The Carrier Corps, which took part in World War I, had experienced appalling casualties. Influenza was taking its toll, and settlers were threatening to reduce African wages by a third. In August 1920, Kikuyu chiefs from Kiambu District formed an organization called the Kikuyu Association (KA). Its purpose was to articulate their grievances, especially concerning land issues. It also joined in the chorus of protestation against the threatened wage cut.

These developments were not lost on Thuku. Moreover, he interacted with leaders of the East African Indian National Congress an Young Baganda Association. Barely a month later, he renamed it the East African Association (EAA) in order to embrace the multiethnic character of the African population then residing in Nairobi. In short, he was cognizant of the fact that the battle against the colonial system needed a joint effort of the oppressed, irrespective of their origin. He was thus prepared to cooperate with likeminded comrades. For example, he joined the KA leaders when they met with the colonial administration on June 24, 1921, at Dagoretti. Indeed, he played a prominent part in the discussions, having directly forwarded to the Colonial Office the memorandum that KA presented to the Kenyan colonial authorities for transmission on to London. In the cable he used the treasury's address and singled out missionaries and the Indians as special friends of the African, thereby infuriating the settlers. Finally, he kept in touch with prominent African Americans, such as Marcus Garvey, whose influence was suspect in colonial circles.

In his tour of Kikuyuland, Nyanza, and Ukambani he denounced the colonial government for its neglect of African welfare. In particular, he encouraged women not to participate in the hated soil conservation projects then in vogue. Women were so grateful for this unexpected support that they named Thuku *Munene wa Nyacing'a* (leader or chief of the women).

People flocked to Thuku's meetings in large numbers, which alarmed the government, chiefs, missionaries, and settlers. The government mobilized chiefs against him but he outsmarted the officials by employing divide-and-conquer tactics. He, too, mobilized the Nyeri and Murang'a chiefs against those from Kiambu, who were his main protagonists. Eventually, chiefs and missionaries swore affidavits in order to create the legal grounds for arresting and deporting him. He was arrested on March 14, 1922.

Thuku's supporters viewed the new turn of events with dismay. Consequently, they went on strike as a mark of solidarity with their arrested leader. Moreover, they went to the central police station to demand his release. On March 16, they surged forward toward the station. The police panicked and opened fire. It is also alleged that European customers on the veranda of the hotel joined in the skirmish. The official report was that 21 people died, a figure that is disputed by eyewitnesses.

The aftermath of the shooting was that Thuku was immediately exiled to Kismayu, where he remained from 1922 to 1925. Thereafter, he was transferred to Lamu, Witu, and finally Marsabit. In Marsabit he struck a rapport with a Major Sharpe, the local district commissioner, and with his assistance was able to while away the time in minor farming activities. This became a lucrative pastime, and Thuku was able to accumulate some funds before he was finally released in December 1930.

The government watched him carefully when it realized that he was in touch with members of the Kikuyu Central Association, the successor to his EAA. This did not deter him from becoming its president in 1932. Wrangling within the party, and disagreement over its policies, led him to form Kikuyu Provincial Association (KPA) in 1935. Significantly, he distanced himself from the independent schools and churches movement that was sweeping through central Kenya in the aftermath of the female circumcision crisis of 1929 to 1931. Above all, the constitution of the organization pledged its loyalty to the British crown and vigorously supported colonial policies, such as soil conservation, which were anathema to many rural people. Rightly or wrongly, the political fire in his belly seemed to have been quenched by his detention in the far off and god-forsaken places. His later activities seemed to confirm this view.

In 1944, the Kenya African Study Union was formed to support Eliud Mathu, the first African member of the Legislative Council. Thaku joined it for only three months. He even refused to have anything to do with its successor, the Kenya African Union. He reconciled with his nemesis, Chief Waruhiu, the pillar of colonial administration in Kiambu District. The KPA was reprieved from proscription like the other African political parties that were banned during World War II. He seemed to be only interested in personal and *Mbari ya Gathirimu* affairs. And finally, he denouced Mau Mau, which was spearheading the freedom struggle from 1952.

The upshot of this was that he was shunned by his former colleagues, and thus played no role in subsequent political developments. It is very telling that on independence day he celebrated it privately by planting coffee trees to signify his economic liberation. And in good measure, the independent Kenya government could only honor him by bestowing his name on the street that runs along the Norfolk Hotel, the scene of the confrontation between his supporters and the police in 1922.

And yet, Thuku towers over the history of the struggle for freedom. He had the courage to challenge the indomitable colonial system when very few would have dared to do so. He sacrificed a lucrative career in the civil service in order to articulate the grievances of his people. He thus became a symbol, an example, and pioneer of the nationalist movement in Kenya.

GODFREY MURIUKI

See also: **Kenya.**

Biography

Born *c*.1895 in the Githunguri administrative division of the Kiambu District in central Kenya. Moved to Nairobi, 1911. Met with the colonial administration on June 24, 1921, playing a prominent role in the discussions. Arrested on March 14, 1922. Riots resulting in deaths ensued. Exiled to Kismayu, 1922 to 1925. Released from prison, 1930. Named president of the Kikuyu Central Association, 1932. From 1944, increasingly alienated himself from the African political establishment. Died in 1970.

Further Reading

Abuor, C. Ojwando. *White Highlands No More*. Nairobi: Pan African Researchers, 1970.

Murray-Brown, J. *Kenyatta*. London: George Allen and Unwin, 1972.

Rosberg, Carl G., and John Nottingham. *The Myth of Mau Mau*. Nairobi: East African Publishing, 1966.

Thuku, Harry. *An Autobiography*. Nairobi: Oxford University Press, 1970.

Timbuktu

Timbuktu is a city located approximately 20 kilometers north of the River Niger, to which it is connected by a (now dry) channel. It is situated in the north of the modern Republic of Mali.

The origins of Timbuktu are obscure. According to local tradition and an indigenous chronicle written in

Timbuktu, a view of the city in the 1930s. © SVT-Bild/Das Fotoarchiv.

the seventeenth century, the *Tarikh es Soudan*, the city was founded in approximately 1100 as a seasonal nomad camp. This was centered around a well maintained by a group of slaves, under the charge of an old woman, Buktu. *Tin Buktu* or *Timbuktu* translates as "the place of Buktu." This seasonal camp then evolved into a more permanent entity owing to the town's placement at the junction of riverine and land transportation routes. Archaeology has, as yet, to confirm this folkloric account of Timbuktu's origin.

Following its original foundation, Timbuktu remained one among a number of trade centers scattered through the region. The city came under the control of the empire of Mali, a period (1325–1433) during which it appears to have grown significantly. This was a time of increasing prosperity and political stability, and this is reflected in a phase of monumental building that occurred in the fourteenth century. Both the Sankore (*c.* fourteenth century) and Djinguereber mosques (1327) were built, structures that stand to this day, along with a fabled royal palace, the Madougou, now lost.

After the collapse of the empire of Mali, Timbuktu fell under nomadic Berber control for a short period between 1433 and 1468, and the fortunes of the city declined. This process was exacerbated by the capture of Timbuktu by the Songhai ruler Sonni Ali in 1468 and its incorporation into the Songhay empire. According to historical sources, the capture of the city was accompanied by considerable bloodshed; Sonni Ali was severely castigated in the *Tarikh es Soudan*. Sonni Ali died in 1492, and following a brief and unsuccessful reign by his son, Timbuktu came under the control of a new Songhay dynasty, that of the Askias. Timbuktu entered what has been termed its "golden age," when scholarship and trade flourished.

The Askias were devout Muslims, and Timbuktu developed into the most important center for Islamic learning in Sub-Saharan Africa. The Qur'an, Hadith, Shari'a, and the Islamic sciences were studied and copied at the university, which was centered around the Sankore mosque. Trade likewise boomed, with gold and ivory exchanged for items obtained via trans-Saharan trade, such as beads, glazed ceramics, paper, books, and textiles.

The tales of the wealth of Timbuktu, and West Africa in general, which had been trickling northward across the desert for many years along with the traders, excited the interests of the Moroccans to the north. Thus, in 1590, an army was assembled under the leadership of Judar Pasha, and following an arduous trek across the desert, these forces defeated the Songhay armies at the battle of Tondibi in 1591.

Timbuktu soon came under the control of the Moroccans, with severe repercussions. Many leading Muslim scholars were exiled. Nevertheless, maintaining control south of the Sahara was costly for the Moroccans, and in 1618 this policy ended. The Moroccan garrison in Timbuktu was left to its own devices, with a living legacy of their presence being the Arma, a Songhai group who claim Moroccan descent.

From this point until the early nineteenth century, Timbuktu entered a quiet period, playing an insignificant role in historical terms. While it seems likely (although uncertain) that its intellectual and economic developments stagnated, its image in Europe was far from diminished. There, the vision of a proverbially "gold-plated" city was perpetuated, something that had persisted since the writings of Leo Africanus, a Spanish Moor, who probably visited the city in the early sixteenth century, were translated for a European audience (including an English translation in 1600). Various missions were dispatched in an attempt to reach Timbuktu. Individuals, notably Robert Adams, Shabeeny the Moor, and Mungo Park, also attempted to enter the city. It was not until August 1826, however, that a European, Major Alexander Gordon Laing, entered the city and left a verifiable account, which consists of a single, terse letter; his other papers were destroyed or lost after he was murdered on his homeward journey.

More fortunate was a Frenchman, René Caillié, who arrived in Timbuktu in 1828 disguised as an Arab (in contrast to Laing, who drew attention to himself in his European dress). Interestingly, Caillié was disappointed with the city; the reality did not match the preconceived image of Timbuktu that had been nurtured in Europe since the writings of Africanus were published. He found it had a "dull appearance" and its inhabitants were "indolent." Many other European adventurers and travelers have since visited Timbuktu, with the German Heinrich Barth providing one of the most comprehensive accounts of the city, providing information on mosques, trade, markets, manufactures, and the people following his eight-month sojourn in and around Timbuktu in the mid-nineteenth century.

With the exposure of Timbuktu through the writings of Caillié, Barth, and others and the expansion of French colonial rule in the region, the conquest of Timbuktu by this European power was only a matter of time. French troops first reached the city in December 1893, but part of the force and the relief column were killed by the Tuaregs; occupation was finally achieved the following year. Sixty years of colonial rule of the region then called French Sudan was initiated, with independence for Timbuktu and the new nation of Mali achieved in 1960. Since 1960 Timbuktu has continued to function both as a center of regional administration and of trade, serving the needs of both the nomadic and sedentary populations in the area. It is also increasingly a destination of "adventurous" tourists, and this aspect of the infrastructure is being developed as a potential source of income.

TIMOTHY INSOLL

See also: **Africanus, Leo; Europe: Explorers, Adventurers, Traders.**

Further Reading

Barth, H. *Travels and Discoveries in North and Central Africa.* London: Frank Cass, 1965.

Caillié, R. *Travels through Central Africa to Timbuctoo.* London: Frank Cass, 1968.

Insoll, T. "Archaeological Research in Timbuktu, Mali." *Antiquity,* no. 72 (1998): 413–417.

Saad, E. N. *Social History of Timbuktu: The Role of Muslim Scholars and Notables 1400–1900.* Cambridge: Cambridge University Press, 1983.

Tio: *See* Kongo, Teke (Tio), and Loango: History to 1483.

Tippu Tip (Muhammed bin Hamed)
East African Entrepreneur

Muhammed bin Hamed, commonly known as Tippu Tip, was the most prominent member of a group of East African entrepreneurs who extended Swahili Arab commercial and political influence into the eastern Congo. Tippu Tip was born near Zanzibar around 1840. His father, Mohammed ben Juma, was a wealthy Swahili merchant whose commercial and political dealings extended well into the interior of modern-day Tanzania. Already by the age of 12, along with his brothers and uncles, Tippu Tip began trading gum copal. As a teenager, he accompanied his father on an ivory trading expedition to Ujiji. Returning to Tabora, Hamed and his father became involved in a conflict that pitted the Swahili Arabs against the indigenous chief Manua Sera who had increased taxes on merchants passing through his territory.

By the age of 20, Tippu Tip had launched out on his own, traveling to the areas near the southern tip of Lake Tanganyika. It is possible that he reached the Mulongo region on the Lualaba River in the Congo before 1860. Borrowing capital, initially from relatives and then from Indian financiers in Zanzibar, he steadily increased his trade stock and weapon supply. At first, Tippu Tip followed the usual Swahili pattern of traveling to the interior, advancing trade goods to traders and chiefs, and later returning to collect the ivory acquired by his local suppliers. Although generally committed to peaceful trade, Tippu Tip was willing to resort to violence to protect his interests. For example, in 1867 he attacked and captured the Tabwa village of chief Nsama, who then granted Tippu Tip the right to trade and travel freely in the area. It was here, because of such violent encounters, that he gained the nickname Tippu Tip, which recalled the "tip-tip" sound of his guns.

By the end of the 1860s, Tippu Tip had made a number of trips to the Congo. His enterprise had become so large that he was able to attract the backing of Tarya Topan, head of one of the richest Indian financial houses in Zanzibar. While the interior trade in ivory and slaves was extremely lucrative, it was also a high-risk venture, both financially and physically. Disease, famine, war, and commercial ruin were common hazards. In about 1870, Tippu Tip set out from Zanzibar on an expedition that lasted 12 years. When he eventually returned to the coast, he had become the most powerful man in the Maniema area between Lake Tanganyika and the Lomani River.

In 1872, on his way to Maniema, Tippu Tip fought and defeated the forces of Kazembe's Lunda warriors. Sometime early in 1873, he arrived at the village of the Songye chief Kasongo Lushi, a man Tippu Tip claimed transferred power in his favor. In 1874, he managed to assert his authority over the large group of Swahili traders who had established an important slave and ivory market at Nyangwe on the Lualaba River. Early in 1875, Tippu Tip moved north to Kasongo, which became his permanent center of operations in central Africa. Increasingly, instead of traveling to engage in direct trade, he supervised agents stationed along the Lomami and Lualaba Rivers. These men collected ivory that they sent either to Kasongo or directly to Tarya Topan in Zanzibar. Some of the ivory was obtained through trade, some though organizing bands of professional elephant hunters, and some (at least in more remote areas) by raiding and holding villagers hostage until they paid a ransom in ivory. Tippu Tip's agents also procured slaves who were used as porters to transportation ivory to the coast.

Tippu Tip's headquarters at Kasongo soon took on the characteristics of a state. When the explorer Henry Morton Stanley arrived in the region in October 1876, Tippu Tip provided the large escort that enabled Stanley to proceed downstream along the Lualaba. Tippu Tip used this voyage as an opportunity to extend his own domain farther north into the forest region. In the territories near Kasongo, he installed or removed chiefs, imposed taxes, maintained roads, encouraged the cultivation of extensive fields, regulated elephant hunting, and supported the expansion of Islam. By the early 1880s, his control reached downstream as far as Stanley Falls. During the 1880s, Tippu Tip conducted political and diplomatic relations with other powers. Recognized as the most prominent figure in Maniema, he gained the allegiance not only of other Swahili traders but also of powerful African leaders such as the Songye chief Lumpungu. In 1882, while back in Zanzibar, he agreed to administer his territories as a representative of the Sultan of Zanzibar. Returning to Maniema, he and his subordinates attempted to extend their control in the region. Thus, in August 1886, Swahili forces attacked and defeated the International Association of the Congo post at Stanley Falls. Tippu Tip, himself en route back to the coast at the time, was not involved in the skirmish.

In spite of some initial Afro-Arab victories, it soon became clear that European forces would control central Africa. As a result, Tippu Tip elected to ally with the Congo Free State. In Zanzibar, where he worked through Stanley, he entered into a contract to serve the Belgian king, Leopold II, as Congo Free State governor at Stanley Falls. According to the 1887 treaty, Tippu Tip agreed to stop acquiring slaves below the falls. In addition, he promised to assist Stanley with the mission to relieve Emin Pasha in Sudan. Therefore, in February 1887, Stanley and Tippu Tip sailed from Zanzibar to the Congo via the Cape of Good Hope. From Matadi, traveling by land and river, they reached the base on the Aruwimi River where Stanley hoped to launch his rescue effort. Because it took Tippu Tip until March of 1888 to assemble a party of porters, Stanley blamed the Swahili leader for the eventual failure of the Emin Pasha venture.

In 1890, Tippu Tip left Maniema for the last time. Although a wealthy man, he recognized the fact that neither he nor any other Swahili Arab would be able to withstand the advances of the Europeans. For his part, because he was under increasing international pressure to avoid alliances with slave traders, Leopold II turned against the "Arabs" and defeated them in a conflict lasting from 1892 to 1895. Nyamgwe fell in March 1893 and Kasongo capitulated in April. Sefu, Tippu Tip's own son and deputy was killed in November of 1893. Tippu Tip, who never again returned to the Congo, lived out his final years in Zanzibar, where he wrote his memoirs. He died of malaria in 1905.

JOHN C. YODER

See also: **Stanley, Leopold, "Scramble."**

Biography

Tippu Tip was born near Zanzibar around 1840. He was trading by the age of 12, and struck out on his own at age 20. He died of malaria in 1905.

Further Reading

Bhacker, M. Reda. *Trade and Empire in Muscat and Zanzibar: Roots of British Domination.* London: Routledge, 1992.

Brode, Heinrich. *Tippu Tip: The Story of His Career in Central Africa Narrated by His Own Accounts.* London: Arnold, 1909.

Gray, Sir John. "Stanley versus Tippoo Tib." *Tanganyika Notes and Records,* December, 1944.

Mangat, J. S. *A History of the Asians in East Africa: c.1886 to 1945.* Oxford: Clarendon Press, 1969.

Hamed bin Muhammed, "Maisha ya Hamed bin Muhammed el Murjebi yaani Tippu Tip," Supplement to *East African Swahili Committee Journals* 28, no. 2 (1958) and 29, no. 1 (1959). This autobiography is translated into English.

Hinde, Sidney Langford. *The Fall of the Congo Arabs.* New York: Thomas Whittaker, 1897.

Stanley, Henry M. *The Congo and the Founding of the Free State, A Story of Work and Exploration.* London: Sampson Low, Marston, Searle, and Rivington, 1886.

Swann, Alfred J. *Fighting the Slave-Hunters in Central Africa: A Record of Twenty-Six Years of Travel and Adventure Round the Great Lakes and of the Overthrow of Tip-pu-Tib, Rumaliza and Other Great Slave Traders.* Philadelphia: J. B. Lippincott, 1910.

Turner, Thomas. "'Batetela,' 'Baluba,' 'Basonge': Ethnogenesis in Zaire," *Cahiers d'Études africaines* 132, 33, no. 4 (1993): 587–612.

Togo: German Colonial Rule

During its 30-year occupation by the Germans, Togo was upheld by many European imperialists as a "model colony" primarily because the German regime produced balanced budgets after a limited period of "pacification" devoid of any major wars. In the eyes of these imperialists, impressive railway and road systems were also constructed. These achievements were realized, however, through a combination of forced labor and excessive and arbitrary taxation imposed on the native population of Togo.

Since British imperial efforts were focused on the largely Akan areas to the west, while the French were preoccupied with Dahomey to the east, part of the area known in European sources as the Slave Coast escaped the immediate attention of these would-be European colonizers. This situation provided an opportunity for Germany, the latecomer into the "scramble," to seize a

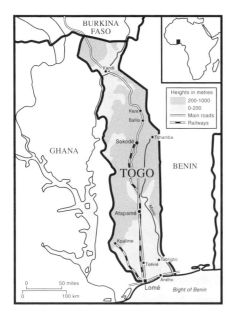

Togo.

31-mile (50-kilometer) stretch of the West African coast between the Volta River estuary (controlled by the British) and the mouth of the Mono River (occupied by the French).

In February 1884, a group of soldiers from the German warship *Sophie*, led by the explorer Gustav Nachtigal, kidnapped chiefs in Aného and forced them into negotiations. Farther west, a protectorate was proclaimed over the Lomé area in a treaty signed in July by Hans Gruner, a German imperial commissioner, and Chief Mlapa III of the town of Togo, after which the new colony was named by the Germans.

It was not until the early 1890s that the German regime began expanding its occupation from the coast. Through the Heligoland Treaty of July 1890 between Germany and Great Britain, part of the Peki Ewe state, including the important towns of Ho, Kpandu, and Hohoe, were transferred to German rule from the neighboring Gold Coast (present-day Ghana). Through so-called scientific expeditions farther north, German agents negotiated treaties of protection, many of which were later disputed and dismissed as fraudulent by African leaders, extending German territorial claims about 156 miles (250 kilometers) inland.

The Germans never established a formal military but instead relied on a police force, never exceeding 500 members, to forcibly occupy new areas. The native population of Togo resisted these campaigns, particularly in the north, where the Dagomba and the Konkomba, sometimes in alliance, fought several wars with the Germans until the turn of the century.

The borders of Togo were formally established by the European imperial powers by the end of the nineteenth century. In the east, Togo shared the Mono River with the French colony of Dahomey (present-day Benin) up to the seventh parallel, where the river fell entirely into German-occupied territory. Togo bordered the French Sudan (in the area of what was to become Burkina Faso) in the north, while the Gold Coast was situated to the west. Although these boundaries were ratified in the Treaty of Paris in 1897, the Germans effectively occupied only about 10 per cent of the colony at that time.

The German regime attempted to link, both administratively and economically, northern Togo with the coast, especially by redirecting trade. In the southern part of the colony it pursued aggressive policies to expand the cultivation of cash crops. The Germans were especially interested in promoting increased cotton cultivation in order to reduce Germany's dependence on imports from the United States. In January 1901, they enlisted the services of African American scientists from the Tuskegee Institute, who operated several experimental farms, distributed seeds of new cotton species, and instructed farmers in Togo. The Germans also encouraged (and sometimes sought to force) the cultivation of cocoa, coffee, coconut, rubber, and sisal, but palm oil and palm kernels consistently remained the top export crops.

The Germans strove to control trade and labor in the colony. African merchants were prohibited from exporting produce and manufactured goods and were restricted to the retail trade. In 1907, the German regime decreed that compulsory labor should be salaried and used exclusively for public works projects, yet flogging was still employed as the primary means of coercing the colonized population of Togo into forced labor.

Crucial in the process of imposing the new colonial order were the government-recognized chiefs, who received a minimal share of the taxes collected and were allowed to maintain a small police force. While they had jurisdiction over civil cases, criminal matters were handled by the German regime.

The German district commissioners exercised nearly complete administrative, judicial, and military powers. The colony's penal code of April 1896 granted them absolute authority over the population they ruled and allowed district officers to punish the Africans by flogging, delivering sentences of hard labor, or imposing fines.

Both direct and indirect taxes were exacted, ranging from import duties, which remained the regime's main source of income throughout the occupation, to income, urban, emigration, and dog taxes, as well as a levy for flying the German flag.

The Germans invested minimally in social services for Africans. Health care was outrageously expensive, if at all accessible, since only a few hospitals provided services to Africans. The regime mostly relied on missionary groups, notably the North German

Missionary Society, to provide schooling at their stations. Toward the end of the occupation, the regime established several governmental schools, but educational opportunities remained extremely limited. Children were often sent by their families to the Gold Coast for postprimary education. Many other Africans emigrated to the British colony to escape the harshness of the German occupation.

An extensive infrastructure was built, mostly through the use of forced labor, in order to facilitate the delivery of agricultural goods to the coast. Between 1900 and 1914, three railways and 766 miles of roads were constructed. Lomé, the capital of the colony since 1897, became a commercial center boasting an efficient port.

This development, however, was mostly limited to the southern third of the colony and was vitiated by the violence and burdens which characterized German rule. When World War I began, the native population of Togo welcomed the combined forces of the British and the French, who had invaded from their neighboring colonies, as liberators. The Germans quickly surrendered, after only a few skirmishes, on August 26, 1914.

DENNIS LAUMANN

See also: **World War I: Survey.**

Further Reading

Amenumey, D.E.K. "German Administration in Southern Togo." *Journal of African History* 10, no. 4 (1969): 623–639.

Asamoa, Ansa. "On German Colonial Rule in Togo." In *Studien zur Geschichte des deutschen Kolonialismus in Africa: Festschrift zum 60. Geburtstag von Peter Sebald*, edited by Peter Heine and Ulrich van der Heyden, Pfaffenweiler, Germany: Centaurus, 1995.

Knoll, Arthur J. *Togo under Imperial Germany 1884–1914.* Stanford, Calif.: Hoover Institution Press, 1978.

Maier, Donna J. E. "Persistence of Precolonial Patterns of Production: Cotton in German Togoland, 1800–1914." In *Cotton, Colonialism, and Social History in Sub-Saharan Africa*, edited by Allen Isaacman and Richard Roberts. Portsmouth, N.H.: Heinemann, 1995.

———. "Slave Labor and Wage Labor in German Togo, 1885–1914." In *Germans in the Tropics: Essays in German Colonial History*, edited by Arthur J. Knoll and Lewis H. Gann. Westport, Conn.: Greenwood Press, 1987.

Sebald, Peter. "Togo 1884–1900" and "Togo 1900–1914." In *German Imperialism in Africa: From the Beginnings until the Second World War*, edited by Helmuth Stoecker. London: C. Hurst, 1986.

Togo: Colonial Period: Dual Mandate, 1919–1957

World War I was fatal for the German colony of Togo. From August 1914, French and British occupation troops took possession of the territory and divided it, giving one-third to Great Britain and two-thirds to France. At the end of the war, the administration of occupied territories was entrusted to the League of Nations, more particularly to its Commission of Mandates. This situation lasted until the eve of the territory's independence in 1960, since, after World War II, the mandate was handed over to the United Nations.

The partition line in Togo was definitely fixed by the Simon-Milner agreement in London in 1919. This line would undergo only a few modifications later on—namely, in 1920 and then in 1929. The party put in charge by the French agreed upon the actual territory. The mandate for Togoland, the British trust territory, was integrated de facto into the Gold Coast, today's Ghana, after a local referendum organized in 1956. Lomé, the capital (the main connection point for all principal communications lines of the territory), and Kpalimé (the principal city of the rich cocoa zone), first located within the British occupation zone, were incorporated into French Togoland only on October 1, 1920.

In fact, the League of Nations only intervened after the coup in 1922. The distribution negotiations in Togo were rather fully led by the victorious Allied forces. The obligation of the representatives to account for their administration vis-à-vis the Commission of Mandates (after World War II the Commission of Protection), as well as the consciousness of autochthonous people of the particularity of their status, profoundly marked the evolution of the territory, which in several respects distinguished itself from other ex-colonies.

To begin with, the text of 12 articles, establishing France's mandate over the territory, prefigured the particular character of the mission: to increase, by every possible means, the material and moral well-being of the colony's inhabitants. This mission stood in contrast to the situation of simple colonies for which no charter defined objectives, and where everything happened without control or professional ethics; each metropolis had its own practices and exigencies. In addition, the text expressly foresaw the taking into account of indigenous laws and customs, respect of the law, and the protection of autochthonous interests. The instituted control, in the form of an annual report to be sent to the League of Nations, did not foresee any restricting sanctions. But the very context of the postwar period sharpened the sense of responsibility among the successive administrators of the territory to take into account the statutory limitations of the mandate. Thus an opportunity was given to the autochthonous people, who on many occasions have inundated with petitions the Commission of Mandates/Protection in the name of the particularity of their territory, and have even sent representatives to legislative meetings to express their grievances in person.

In the economic realm, the equality of treatment of all nationals of the member states of the League of

Nations (and later of the United Nations) favored commercial competition and prevented France from establishing a de facto monopoly. The United African Company (UAC), a subsidiary of Unilever (a consumer goods company), was the biggest commercial company in Togo during this period.

Togo nationals did not hide their sympathy for British culture. Traditionally, residents had gone to the British colony of the Gold Coast (Ghana) to study, work, or shop. A significant number of laborers from French Togo landed regularly in either the urban centers of the Gold Coast or the cocoa plantations.

The migratory stream was even more important during the Great Depression of the 1930s and World War II. Between 1920 and 1945, the territory has benefited only very little from investments. The facilities inherited from the German period remained useful for a long time; some were refurbished or replaced, including the wharf, replaced by a new facility, which was set up in 1928, and the railway line, extended by 70 miles (112 kilometers) between 1930 and 1932. The majority of the work was financed by a budget surplus coming from customs duties. The territory had thus specialized itself as a transit country.

After World War II, the Fonds d'Investment pour le Développement Economique et Social (FIDES) invested heavily in the nation, and numerous economic and social infrastructures were realized. But, as everywhere, the raising of the standard of life of the population is relative, and the colonial administration—and even more so, urban commercial and industrial interests—benefited most. Nonetheless, an indigenous elite was doubtlessly emerging, ready to take the destiny of the territory into their own hands.

A. N. GOEH-AKUE

Further Reading

Cornevin, Robert. *Le Togo: des origines à nos jours*, 4th ed. Paris, 1988.

Decalo, Samuel. *Historical Dictionary of Togo*, 2nd ed. Metuchen, N.J., 1987.

———. Togo. World Bibliographic Series. Oxford, 1995.

Gayibor N. L. (ed.). *Le Togo sous domination coloniale (1884–1960)*. Lomé: les Presses de l'UB, 1997.

———. (ed.). *Les Togolais face à la colonisation*. Lomé: Presses de l'UB, 1994.

Goëh-Akué, N. Adovi. *Finances publiques et dynamique sociale au Togo sous influence française (1920–1980)*. Thesis, University of Paris VII, 1992.

Togo: Eyadéma, Gnassingbé, Life and Era of President of Togo

The fate of Togo from long "transition periods" to rather short "stable" phases can be reflected along the lines of the life of its president, Gnassingbé Eyadéma.

Eyadéma has played and continues to play a key role in the history of Togo. He has been president since seizing power in a 1967 coup d'état, and is in the meantime the longest serving ruling leader in Africa—and second worldwide only to Fidel Castro.

Born in the northern part of Togo, he joined the then colonial army. As a veteran of various colonial wars, he left the colonial troops and returned to Togo in 1962. At that time, Togo was under the leadership of Sylvanus Olympio and the Comité de l'Unité Togolaise (CUT), in alliance with the Justice, Union, Vigilance, Éducation, Nationalisme, Ténacité, Optimisme Party.

Apparent irregularities in the payment of military pensions from the French army, as well as the political discrimination and unemployment of the former soldiers, provoked unrest among them. The first African postcolonial coup d'état in 1963, in which Eyadéma took part, was built both on an increasing discontent about the growing authoritarianism of the government of Sylvanus Olympio and on international—especially French—fears about its economic and diplomatic orientations.

After some days under a state of emergency, the junta handed power back to a civilian government under the leadership of two prominent personalities from a moderate and pro-French party, the Union Démocratique du Peuple Togolais. Antoine Méatchi and Nicolas Grunitzky were representing the two founding parties of this new union, the Union des Chefs et des Populations du Nord, a colonial creation for the northern part of Togo and its "traditional" authorities, and the Parti Togolais du Progrés, a French creation for the southern pro-French elites of the country. However, personal differences between the two ambitious leaders, combined with growing interference from the army and the French government as well as an economic crisis, led to a political crisis of the institutionalized system of "bicephalism." Once again, the army seemed to be the ultimate solution for the resolution of the political emergency.

A second coup then was attempted in November 1966 by former CUT leaders, but the army intervened in the end in favor of the Grunitzky government. After a few months of political crisis the army took power itself, naming Gnassingbé Eyadéma as president on January 13, 1967.

The subsequent major change in the orientation of the regime were the so-called authenticité politics (borrowed from Mobutu Sese Seko's Zaire), which looked to strengthen and deepen the power of the president, the ruling elite, and the state, on the basis of an essentialist and protofascist political mythology. The subsequent nationalization of the lucrative phosphate mining industry posed an economic threat to international and colonial capital. The following international criticism against the regime lent its genuine political tone and motive to an accident officially known as the "assault of Sarakawa": Eyadéma's plane crashed in the north of Togo, near his home village of Pya. He managed to escape safely and was magnified as the "miraculé de Sarakawa," "great leader," and *timonier* (enlightened guide) of the Togolese people, who was by divine will saved—according to the regime's mythology—from an attempt to end his life by an alliance of international capitalist and imperial powers and allies to the late Olympio.

In the wake of this event, the core elements of a totalitarian—but still relatively liberal in economic terms—corporatist state were established. The broad politicization of the country and the population was spearheaded by the Rassemblement du Peuple Togolais (RPT), the single political party at that time, created in 1971. The Eyadéma regime initiated a broad political mass mobilization and a mythologization of the founding events of the regime, which was supported by an extensive use of violence and widespread delation to strengthen its hold on the country: January 13 was celebrated as a national holiday, equal in importance to Togo's Independence Day, as well as the anniversary of the "assault of Sarakawa." Every Togolese person had to take up an "authentic" non-Christian first name. The "animation" (dancing and praise-singing sessions in honor of Eyadéma) was made part of the scholar curricula. The *école nouvelle* (new school) was established as a would-be contrast to the colonial school programs, aiming at large mass education and eradicating illiteracy.

This resulted in underground and informal networks becoming the only means of influencing politics from the bottom up, or of building top-down influence channels parallel to the official ones: Togo developed all the political characteristics of the African "postcolony" (Mbembe 2001), and became a paradigmatic "rhizome-state" (Bayart 1993). The regime was sustained by underground (and apparently apolitical) networks of support, an authoritarian leader ideology and by arbitrary imprisonments and extrajudicial executions. In this situation, a significant portion of the elite found a middle ground between cooperation with and overt opposition to the regime: it found refuge in public administration and the parastatal sector that for both ideological and practical reasons became the most desirable source of employment and status for highly skilled members of the elite, at least to those returning from studying or working overseas.

When it came under its first major economic threat and thus received major incentives to transformation, Togo, paradoxically, formalized and institutionalized the permanency of the "transition." The Eyadéma regime decided to stabilize the political life of the country by proclaiming, on January 13, 1980, a formal rule of law based on single-party rule (as laid out in the constitution) and a renewed economic liberalism. Soon after this, the third republic found itself facing a crisis. The government, in its attempts to establish a "controlled" pluralism within the single party, instituted a national and independent Human Rights Commission, froze salaries, and cut most public sector recruitment, thus denying the educated elite its largest and most desired source of employment.

Under growing popular pressure and discontent, 1991 saw the establishment of a national conference, which took over governmental duties and proclaimed itself ruler, actually stripping Eyadéma of his powers. The national conference nominated J. K. Koffigoh, one of the founders of the Human Rights League, as prime minister of the transitional government. The ensuing state of crisis—characterized by a "strategy of tension" marked by riots, marches, executions, and army assaults on the transition government and opposition parties—deepened the economic crisis, with a 20 per cent decrease in gross domestic product in the two years after the general strike in 1992. This almost destroyed the project of one of the most promising free trade zones in Africa (planned and promoted by U.S. agencies). But unpaid salaries in the public sector, the flight of foreign investment, and an interruption of pension payments are only some of the most important problems the Togolese population faced during this time (and still faces today).

In September 1992 a new liberal constitution was voted into law in a referendum. Eyadéma was nevertheless reinstated as head of the government, which was composed primarily of RPT-affiliated ministers. During this period, marked by conservative restoration, popular unrest, and a national general strike that lasted for nine months, Togo was in a state of emergency. More than 300,000 persons fled to Ghana and Benin. The existing north-south divide was exacerbated by being portrayed as a discourse of ethnic rivalry, almost leading in some parts of the country to ethnic cleansing, especially in some southern agricultural areas where the (northern) Kabyè traditionally worked as *métayers* (agricultural workers).

The legislative elections in 1994 were won by the (moderate) opposition, though they were boycotted by some opposition parties. However, Eyadéma succeeded in dividing the opposition by nominating internationally renowned politician and former Organization of African Unity (OAU) secretary general E. E. Kodjo as prime minister, even though he was leader of a minority party. It was believed that some stability could be regained under his direction. Kodjo remained in power until partial legislative elections in 1996 brought back a full-fledged RPT government. After the highly contested and unfair presidential elections in 1998, Togo became even more of a pariah of the international community, although Eyadéma succeeded in being elected OAU president in 2000. Western nations and the European Union (with the notable exception of France) froze, or reduced to a minimum, assistance to Togo. This had the unintended consequence of enhancing the general political apathy of a population now essentially dedicated to survival, and furthered the spread of petty corruption and nepotism in a public sector whose employees go unpaid for six months or more.

Near the end of 2002, the RPT-dominated parliament voted in favor of removing a constitutional clause that would have restricted Eyadéma from running for a third (constitutional) term in 2003. In June 2003, Eyadéma was declared the winner of the most recent presidential elections. Nevertheless, the signs of decay of the regime become more and more obvious, since former RPT prime minister A. Kodjo and former RPT president of parliament D. Péré declared in 2002 their refusal to further support the regime as it is. Even if they were excluded from the party, Péré's electoral results—according to civil society sources—threatened the RPT's electoral ethnoregional basis in the north and within the army. Irrespective of the formal legalism of the regime, international cooperation is not on the agenda of neither (but France) cooperation partners: Togo's narrow political and economic future seems to be rather dark, despite the regime's efforts to build up an internationally respectable face.

PATRICK F. A. WURSTER

See also: **Olympio, Sylvanus.**

Further Reading

Agbobli, A. K. *Sylvanus Olympio: Un destin tragique.* Lomé, 1978.

Bayart, J.-F. *The State in Africa: The Politics of the Belly.* London/New York, 1993.

Decalo, S. *Historical Dictionary of Togo.* Portland, Ore.

Kourouma, A. *Waiting for the Wild Beasts to Vote.* London: Heinemann, 2003.

Lange, Marie-France *L'école au Togo.* Paris, 1999.

Massina, P. *Droits de l'homme, libertés publiques et sous-développement au Togo.* Lomé, 1997. Mbembe, A. *On the Postcolony.* Berkeley, 2001.

Piot, Charles. *Remotely Global: Village Modernity in West Africa.* Chicago, 1999.

Tete, T. *Démocratisation à la togolaise.* Paris, 1998.

Toulabor, C. *Le Togo sous Eyadéma.* Paris, 1986.

Wurster, P. *From Postcolony to Postdictature.* Evaluation Paper for the Research Project Auf dem Weg zur marktwirtschaftlichen Demokratie of the Bertelsmann Foundation and CAP-Centrum für Angewandte Politikforschung. Osnabrück, 2003.

Yagla, W.O. *L'édification de la nation togolaise*, Paris, 1978.

Togoland: *See* British Togoland.

Toivo ya Toiva, Andimba (1924–)
Namibian Liberationist

Born in Umungundu in Ovamboland in northern Namibia in 1924, Andimba Toivo ya Toivo received a few years of primary education at St. Mary's Anglican Mission School at Odibo in Ovamboland. Thanks to his remarkable mother (who died in June 2000 at the age of 103), he was able to enroll in the Ongwediva teachers' training school. In World War II, he volunteered for the Native Military Corps of the South African Defence Force, and guarded military stores in regional southwest Africa and in South Africa. After returning to school in Ovamboland and completing standard 8 (grade 10), he taught briefly before going to work in the mines on the Witwatersrand. He moved to the more liberal Cape Town in the early 1950s, where he found work in a furniture store, and was befriended by Jack and Ray Simons, members of the Communist Party, who encouraged him to organize the Ovambo contract workers in the city. At a meeting in a barbershop on Somerset Road, Green Point, in 1957 he was one of the founders of the Ovambo People's Congress (OPC), the forerunner of the South West African People's Organization (SWAPO). The OPC sought to bring Southwest Africa under United Nations authority and to end the contract labor system in the territory.

When in December 1958 the South African authorities found out that he had mailed a petition, critical of South African rule in southwest Africa (hidden in a copy of *Treasure Island*), to Mburumba Kerina, a Namibian student then in New York, Toivo ya Toivo was told to leave South Africa. Arrested for entering the Tsumeb mine compound without a permit, he was restricted to Ondongwa in Ovamboland. There he continued his political work, much of which was carried out from a shop he opened. He helped the first SWAPO guerrillas who returned to the territory, though he had doubts about the wisdom of taking up arms against the powerful South Africans. After the launch of the armed struggle in mid-1966 he was arrested, and with others was taken to Pretoria. They were tortured, then tried under the Terrorism Act of 1967, made to apply retroactively, charged with attempting to overthrow the existing government and install a SWAPO-led government. Before being sentenced in February 1968, the charismatic Toivo ya Toivo made an extremely eloquent speech from the dock, in which he challenged the right of a South African court to try the Namibians, and spoke of their struggle for freedom and justice. His speech would long be an inspiration to those working for Namibian independence.

Sentenced to twenty years imprisonment, Toivo ya Toivo was sent to Robben Island, off Cape Town. There he learned much from Nelson Mandela. After serving sixteen years, he was released in March 1984, in the context of apparent advances in the negotiations relating to Namibian independence. He was released against his wishes, for he did not want to be free while other Namibians remained in apartheid jails. He was taken secretly to Windhoek and freed there. There was speculation at the time that the South African government hoped that his release would help split SWAPO and bring a moderate wing of the organization into the political process in Namibia. But as soon as he was free, Toivo ya Toivo stressed his loyalty to SWAPO and its leadership, and was soon appointed as SWAPO's secretary general.

Although he could have remained in Namibia, he chose to live abroad. Representing SWAPO, he spoke at the opening and closing of a major conference in London in September 1984, "Namibia, 1884–1994." Mainly involved in diplomatic work in the late 1980s, he kept a relatively low profile. He returned to live in Namibia in 1989, the year a film entitled *Toivo: Child of Hope* was made about his life. As Namibia moved toward independence, he explained that SWAPO's goal of socialism was a very long-term one, and that the new Namibia would have to proceed very cautiously. He was elected a member of the Constituent Assembly in November 1989, and then became minister of mines and energy in President Nujoma's first cabinet, which took office on March 21, 1990. He ran this key ministry competently, and was a voice of reason in his party and in the National Assembly. No longer believing in nationalizing the mines, he worked to encourage new foreign investment in the mineral sector. An arrangement was reached with the De Beers diamond company for joint ownership of the lucrative production of diamonds. Another controversial issue he had to deal with was the scheme to build a new hydroelectric power scheme at Epupa on the Cunene River, which would mean the relocation of large numbers of Himba people. Toivo ya Toivo managed to retain the respect of most people, and was one of the best-liked members of the government. He remained somewhat aloof from the daily round of politics, and outside the innermost circles of SWAPO. In December 1991, he gave up his post as secretary-general to devote his full attention to his ministry. His new wife, Vicki Erenstein, was in 1999 appointed government attorney. In that year he was moved sideways in a cabinet reshuffle, being made minister of labor at a time when some thought he

might, at 75, look forward to retirement. He is currently Honorable Minister of the Ministry of Prisons and Correctional Services.

CHRISTOPHER SAUNDERS

See also: **Namibia (Southwest Africa): South African Rule.**

Biography

Born in Umungundu, in Ovamboland in northern Namibia in 1924. Volunteered for the Native Military Corps of the South African Defence Force during World War II. Taught briefly, then worked in the mines on the Witwatersrand. Moved to Cape Town in the early 1950s. Cofounded the Ovambo People's Congress (OPC), the forerunner of the Southwest African People's Organization (SWAPO), in 1957. Assisted SWAPO guerillas and was arrested in 1966. Sentenced to twenty years imprisonment, and sent to Robben Island, off Cape Town. Released in 1984. Subsequently appointed SWAPO's secretary general. Involved in diplomatic work throughout the late 1980s. Returned to Namibia, after a period of living abroad, in 1989. Elected a member of the Constituent Assembly in 1989. Named as Minister of Mines and Energy in President Nujoma's first cabinet, which took office on March 21, 1990. Named Minister of Labor in 1999.

Further Reading

Bauer, G. *Labor and Democracy in Namibia*. Athens, Ohio: Ohio University Press, 1998.

Department of Information and Publicity, SWAPO of Namibia. *To Be Born a Nation*. London, 1981.

ja [*sic*] Toivo, T. "Namibia is Free. What Next?" *World Marxist Review*, March 1990.

Soggot, D. *Namibia: The Violent Heritage*. New York, 1986.

ya Toivo, T., Review of Nelson Mandela's *Long Walk to Freedom*. *Southern African Review of Books*, 1995.

Tolbert, William: *See* Liberia: Tolbert, William Richard, Life and Era of.

Tombalbaye, F. Ngarta (1919–1975)
President of Chad

In his youth, F. Ngarta Tombalbaye developed an interest in civic life. He frequented political discussion groups and led a youth movement inspired by the Social Christian traditions of French scouting.

By 1946 Tombalbaye had become the president of the Syndicat Autonome du Tchad, an independent trade union based in Sarh. The next year he was instrumental in launching the Parti Progrèssiste Tchadien (PPT), the Chadian branch of the Rassemblement Démocratique Africain, established to fight for independence in French Africa. The leader of the PPT was

Gabriel Lisette, an expatriate French citizen born and educated in the Caribbean. Tombalbaye was in charge of the party in Sarh and used his influence to gather support throughout the south, especially among his own clan. The French administration responded to these political activities by curtailing his employment as a teacher in public service, obliging him to take other work, including the manual fabrication of bricks.

Tombalbaye's political prospects flourished throughout the 1950s as the African nationalist PPT eroded support for Muslim and European parties, despite the divide-and-conquer tactics of the colonial administration. Elected as a deputy to the Territorial Assembly in 1952, he would be reelected in 1957, 1959, and 1962. Between 1957 and 1959 he was elected to serve as a member of the Grand Council of French Equatorial Africa in Brazzaville. December 1958 saw the formation of the first of four—preponderantly African—provisional governments in which the PPT played the leading role. At the same time, antagonism toward Lisette's foreign background and rivalry within the party saw the leadership transferred to Tombalbaye. Following victory at the polls in March 1959, he formed a permanent government. He became prime minister in June 1959, and assumed the presidency of newly independent Chad in August 1960.

Contrary to Lisette's intentions, the PPT had come to be seen as essentially a Sara party. Concern in the north that the Sara, dominated by the north for centuries, would exploit their control of government in order to exact revenge seemed justified following an extensive reallocation of middle-ranking southern administrators to the north. The urge to consolidate power led to dictatorship and repression. By 1962, Tombalbaye had reconstituted the National Assembly and banned competitive politics. The new assembly officially ratified this de facto one-party system in June 1964. Immediately following independence a thorough purge of the civil service and political opponents was initiated. Starting with political rivals in his own party, each stratum of Chadian society was sifted in turn. Lisette was stripped of citizenship, and refused residency in Chad. Despite comprehensive purges in the south, the image of southern domination of the north persisted. The impression was reaffirmed in May 1963. Following the discovery of an alleged plot, three ministers and the president of the assembly, all Muslim, were jailed on charges of conspiracy.

Popular disaffection in peripheral areas increased. In 1963 there were riots in N'Djaména and Am Timmam, in the east of the country. A rise in taxes and a new levy on cattle compounded a growing distrust of the bureaucracy, which was seen as corrupt and, especially in the case of southern tax officers acting in the north, high-handed and disdainful of local customs.

In late 1965 a peasant revolt erupted in Malgamé in central Chad. In retaliation for the murder of ten government officials several hundred local people were killed. As the unrest spread north a rebellion coalesced behind the Front de Libération Nationale (FROLINAT), founded in Sudan by exiled Chadians in June 1966. The scale of rebellion in the inaccessible Borkou-Ennedi-Tibesti (BET) region in the north was such that in 1968 and, again in 1969, Tombalbaye was forced to seek help from France under military assistance agreements concluded at independence. The price of assistance was a critical appraisal of Chad's administration by the French Mission for Administrative Reform. As a result, the percentage of Muslim troops in the national army was increased, a number of former political detainees incorporated into the central government organ, and a measure of administrative capacity sacrificed to traditional chiefs.

The early 1970s saw Tombalbaye embark on a series of ill-judged policies. He struck a secret deal with Libya, in which he seemed to renounce possession of the Aouzou strip between the two countries, in return for money and a loosening of links between Libya and FROLINAT. Unrealistic policies stymied the economy. Operation Agriculture sought to raise the cotton yield by 600 per cent in one year through a massive mobilization and relocation of farmers and town dwellers. Although the scheme was discontinued following Tombalbaye's defeat, wider cultivation laid the foundations for Chad's modern cotton industry.

In 1973, Chad underwent a "cultural revolution" called "authenticity" and based on Africanization policies developed in Mobutu Sese Sekou's Zaire. African names replaced European titles for people and places. Tombalbaye chose the name Ngarta, meaning "chief." The PPT was dissolved and a new party, the Mouvement National pour la Révolution Culturelle et Sociale (MNRCS), based on his personal rule was put in its place. Sara *yondo* initiation rites, including circumcision, were introduced for male government employees—even elderly noninitiates and those who had converted to Islam.

By the mid-1970s Tombalbaye faced armed opposition in all parts of the country. The repressive mechanisms of the security services and the extension of yondo to the wider southern population crystallized opposition among the Sara elite. In 1973, France withdrew much of its garrison in the country leaving a limited armored and air presence to support Chadian forces in the battle against FROLINAT. Nonetheless, by this time the rebellion held 90 per cent of the BET. On April 13, 1975, following a rumor of renewed purges in the army, junior officers from the south effected a coup d'état. Tombalbaye was either killed in crossfire, or possibly summarily executed. A man whom he had incarcerated as a political prisoner, General Félix Malloum, replaced him. Tombalbaye's reputation was reestablished during the Sovereign National Conference held in N'Djaména in 1993. In April 1994, his body was disinterred from its secret grave and returned to Bessada for reburial.

SIMON MASSEY

See also: **Chad.**

Biography

Born in Bessada, in the southern prefecture of Moyen Chari in 1918. Received primary and secondary education in Sarh and Brazzaville. As a teacher in the late 1940s, developed an interest in public life. In 1946 became president of an independent trade union. A year later, helped to found the Parti Progressiste Tchadien, assuming senior positions in the south. Despite discrimination from the French colonial authorities that followed his entry into the political sphere, Tombalbaye was elected as a deputy in the Territorial Assembly in 1952, and reelected in 1957, 1959 and 1962. After ousting the increasingly isolated secretary-general of the PPT, Gabriel Lisette, Tombalbaye assumed the presidency of the provisional government in March 1959, and in June of the same year was chosen as prime minister of the newly elected Legislative Assembly. On August 11, 1960, he became the first president of independent Chad. After almost fifteen turbulent years in power Tombalbaye was killed during a coup d'état in April 1975.

Further Reading

Azevedo, Mario J., and Emmanuel U. Nnadozie. *Chad: A Nation in Search of Its Future.* Boulder, Colo.: Westview Press, 1998.

Bah, Thierno. "Soldiers and 'Combatants': The Conquest of Political Power in Chad 1965–1990." In *The Military and Militarism in Africa,* edited by Eboe Hutchful and Abdoulaye Bathily. Dakar: CODESRIA, 1998.

Decalo, Samuel. *Historical Dictionary of Chad,* 3rd ed. Lanham, Md.: Scarecrow Press, 1997.

Kelley, Michael P. *A State in Disarray: Conditions of Chad's Survival,* Boulder, Colo.: Westview Press, 1986.

Nolutshungu, Sam C. *Limits of Anarchy: Intervention and State Formation in Chad,* Charlottesville: University Press of Virginia, 1996.

Tonga, Ila, and Cattle

It has been suggested (Langworthy 1972) that in the southern province of Zambia there was strong political power during the precolonial period, and that because of the relative lack of political organization among the Tonga and Ila, there was little significant history remembered. Most early studies emphasized this aspect and generally discussed the Tonga and Ila from the perspective of their raiders, particularly the Lozi and the Ndebele from across the Zambezi River in the south, who raided for slaves and cattle. It is generally acknowledged that because the Tonga and the Ila lacked a strong central authority they became easy target for outside raiders who found it easier to play off one headman against another by encouraging local wars.

The Tonga and the Ila people are considered distant descendants of the Early Iron Age people who had developed new ways of community life, such the Kalolo culture. These Early Iron Age people had also embarked on long distance trade, and laid foundations for the future expansion. After 1500 they lived in scattered communities and developed a village economy under headmen or chiefs in settlements that rarely numbered more than a few hundred people. They grew millet and a few other crops, raised cattle, and hunted for many kinds of game. They had plenty of land to move around despite tsetse fly in their area. They were not involved in much trade, whether local or long distance.

The Tonga and Ila practiced agriculture and kept cattle. The plateau where the Tonga and the Ila settled was an area that was prone to famine and hunger. There were usually periods of hunger just before the next harvest, when labor demands were highest. To cushion themselves against hunger the Tonga and Ila resorted to keeping livestock, hunting, and even gathering. Cattle was the most important livestock kept, and these were generally shorthorn Sanga, which were small in size. They are believed to have weighed a maximum of about 350 pounds and were described by the missionary explorer David Livingstone as beautiful. The cattle were carefully corralled at night and were carefully herded during the rains so that they did not damage crops.

Elizabeth Colson (1962) has noted that several households often banded together to form a *kraal* group, which cooperated in the work of cattle keeping. The Tonga and the Ila also developed an elaborate system of tending cattle lent to them by others, and also lent out cattle themselves. The system was developed to minimize the risk of losing cattle through raids, which were very common among the plateau people. Despite this threat during the dry season cattle were usually allowed to roam freely. They could also be driven to areas where water and pasture were available during the dry season.

In the Tonga and Ila societies, herding cattle was not a strictly gendered activity. Although young boys often did the herding, it was not uncommon to find men or women herding cattle. In Tonga and Ila communities, most economic activities were carried out by all. Cultivation, for example, was not an exclusively female domain in Tonga and Ila culture. This was also true in cattle herding, which was not solely a male activity. In Tonga and Ila cultures the dichotomy typical of most of southern Africa did not exist. Adam Caper, for example, describes a fundamental opposition between men and cattle on the one hand and women on the other. In such societies cattle were identified with men, and women were usually prohibited from coming into contact with such animals. Among the Tonga and Ila women not only herded cattle, but owned and handled them as well.

Possession of cattle in the Tonga and Ila cultures held great social and psychological importance. Cattle were also valued as a movable source of food and as insurance against famine. In theory cattle were something that could be exchanged in the form of a dowry, or lent out to other people. Most men in the Tonga and Ila communities strove to build up their herd in good times because it was the highest form of *lubono*, a symbol of wealth, social importance, and status. Those with large herds of cattle gained influence and control over others, especially their wives.

At the start of the twentieth century, cattle were very scarce due to warfare and disease. Kenneth Vickery (1986) has pointed out that on the eve of the European occupation of the area there were very few animals in the region; the large herds had been depleted in raids. The greatest blow, however, was the rinderpest epidemic of the mid-1890s, which swept through eastern and southern Africa. Despite this, the situation changed rapidly as the Tonga transformed the old and new utility of cattle. As stocks built up there was a reestablishment of cattle as an integral part of Tonga social fabric, particularly as a form of dowry.

Because cattle had numerous uses, they enabled the Tonga to participate in both the imperial and indigenous economies. Cattle were the Tonga's currency in a capitalist economy. They represented the wealth accumulated from income earned in wage employment, yielding interest, and were available when needed. Consequently, from the earliest years of the twentieth century the Tonga consciously strove to increase both the quantity and quality of their cattle, succeeding in this due to the fact that they always saw cattle as belonging to three separate spheres of their livelihood—subsistence, prestige, and human rights, particularly related to women and marriage. At all levels the aim was to convert whatever was earned into cattle which was then easily converted into status.

The importance of cattle among the Tonga led them to develop herding techniques that generally made efficient use of the soil, pasture, and water resources of the plateau. These techniques enabled the herds to stay in good condition and propagate rapidly. Cattle were usually allowed to roam freely during the dry season because this maximized the available grazing land, and because cattle were considered better judges of the whereabouts of dwindling food sources than any herder could be. The care of cattle that were already acquired contributed to the building up of cattle herds.

By the end of the second decade of the twentieth century, the Tonga had begun to improve their herd by acquiring graded stock from George Horton, colonial Zambia's premier cattle breeder. In some cases Tonga herders deliberately herded their cattle onto European farms to be serviced by pedigree bulls. This practice was widespread, and goes to show that the Tonga not only valued the numbers of their cattle but were equally conscious of their quality.

BIZECK JUBE PHIRI

See also: **Lozi Kingdom and the Kololo; Zambia: Early Nineteenth Century: Survey.**

Further Reading

Colson, Elizabeth. "The Role of Cattle among the Plateau Tonga of Mazabuka District." In *The Plateau Tonga of Northern Rhodesia: Social and Religious Studies.* Manchester: Manchester University Press, 1962.

Colson, Elizabeth, and Mark Chona, "Marketing of Cattle among the Plateau Tonga." *Rhodes-Livingstone Journal,* no. 37 (1965): 42–50.

Langworthy, Harry W. *Zambia before 1890: Aspects of Pre-Colonial History.* London: Longman, 1972.

Roberts, Andrew. *A History of Zambia.* London: Heinemann, 1976.

Vickery, Kenneth P. *Black and White in Southern Zambia: The Tonga Plateau Economy and British Imperialism, 1890–1939.* New York: Greenwood Press, 1986.

Torwa, Changamire Dombo, and the Rovzi

From the late fifteenth to the early eighteenth centuries, southwestern Zimbabwe was home to two powerful states. The region is essentially grassland; it merges with the Kalahari Desert margins, once occupied by people identified in archaeology with the Toutswe State (*c.*900–1200). The indigenous population is defined archaeologically by the Leopard's Kopje culture (*c.*950–1250), which is associated with the settlements of Mapela and Mapungubwe in the Limpopo Valley and at Ntabazingwe near Bulawayo. This region is probably the Guruuswa ("tall grass"), referred to as *Butua* in Portuguese sources of the sixteenth and seventeenth centuries. It is currently used for cattle ranching, an economic activity that is more than four centuries old. The low rate of rainfall and the common droughts dictate the growth of traditional drought-resistant crops such as millet and sorghum. These are supplemented by cattle, which rely on mopane leaves during the dry seasons. There is a rich gold belt, mentioned in Portuguese accounts, but it is cattle that formed the basis of the rulers' wealth and power. Cattle were easy to manage, multiplied quickly, and could be exchanged for other items. Rulers used cattle to reward the army, the miners, metal workers, and traders in addition to providing security in case of crop failure. The first of these states is identified as

Torwa, and its capital was Khami (*c.*1450–1660s). It was succeeded by the Rozvi State (*c.*1680–1830), founded by Changamire Dombo (*d.*1695).

The Torwa state was probably founded by rebels or outsiders (*vatorwa*) of the Mutapa state during the second half of the fifteenth century. By around 1494 a dynasty called Torwa broke away and established itself in Guruuswa in the southwestern periphery of the state. Between 1490 and 1547, a rebellion occurred in the Mutapa state, which is linked with the Torwa. From 1547 onward there is no evidence of their activity, until the middle of the seventeenth century,, when their capital was destroyed during a civil war. A political dispute occurred in the early 1640s in the area controlled by the Torwa; one of the Torwa rulers was defeated in a power struggle and forced to flee. The Portuguese intervened in this conflict by sending a small Portuguese army led by Sismundo Dias Bayao. This event is linked to the fall of Khami. The capital area shifted about 150 kilometers east, where the Torwa continued to rule until the early 1680s.

Between the 1640s and 1680s, a military transformation occurred in response to the growing threat of the Portuguese *prazo* holders and traders from the northeast. There was concern about the politically unstable conditions in the Mutapa State and the increased Portuguese presence on the Zimbabwe Plateau. After 1684 the Karanga, led by Dombo Changamire, replaced the Torwa dynasty. Their followers were called the Rozvi. Dombo Changamire founded a powerful state whose influence reached the areas formerly controlled by the Mutapa State such as Mukaranga, Mbire, and Manyika. Information about Dombo Changamire is sketchy but historical sources suggest he was a descendant of one the Torwa leaders who built his political career through cattle wealth. He is also linked with the Mutapa State, where Portuguese documents say he was a herdsman for the king. Oral traditions associate him with special powers such as rain making; and he was also renowned for his other magical powers and bravery. The Portuguese regarded him as a wizard, probably because of his military accomplishments; he seems to have transformed his army into such a powerful force that it managed to defeat and expel the Portuguese from the Zimbabwe Plateau in the 1680s.

Archaeological evidence shows the existence of stone buildings in southwestern Zimbabwe dating at least from the fifteenth century. These buildings are characterized by retaining walls built with well-shaped rectangular blocks, on top of which are platforms accommodating circular houses. The walls are profusely decorated with checkered, herringbone, dentelle, and other linear patterns. The biggest settlement is at Khami, near Bulawayo. Stone buildings of various sizes are located in the area once controlled by the Torwa. The Rozvi continued to build in stone in the same style and made polychrome incised, band and panel decorated pottery. Their capital was at Danangombe and other important centers include Naletale, Zinjanja, and Manyanga. This cultural continuity between Torwa and Rozvi suggests they were the same people. The stone building architecture in the southwest represents an expansion of the culture once based at Great Zimbabwe.

The succession disputes that occurred after the death of Dombo Changamire undermined the power of the state. Many Rozvi migrated elsewhere, with some setting up chiefdoms in the areas they subsequently settled. One son of Dombo Changamire moved to Hwange in the northwest and established a polity among the Nambya and the Tonga. Another son crossed the Limpopo River and conquered the territory of the Venda, establishing a capital at Dzata, in the Zoutpansberg. This is the Thovhela State that is mentioned by the Dutch traders based at Delagoa Bay (*c.*1730). Among both the Nambya and the Venda, the Zimbabwe culture system has been identified, indicating continuity and expansion of the culture.

Torwa-Rozvi rule lasted almost 400 years in southwestern Zimbabwe. The Rozvi declined following the arrival of the *mfecane* groups from the south of the Limpopo. Direct attacks by the Sotho and Nguni and the subsequent Ndebele settlement saw the demise of the Rozvi in the 1850s.

INNOCENT PIKIRAYI

See also: **Great Zimbabwe: Origins and Rise; Manyika of Eastern Zimbabwe; Mfecane; Sena, Tete, Portuguese, and Prazos; Zimbabwe: Incursions from the South, Ngoni and Ndebele.**

Further Reading

Beach, D. N. *The Shona and Zimbabwe, A.D 900–1850: An Outline of Shona History.* Gweru, Zimbabwe: Mambo Press, 1980.

Mudenge, S. I. G. "An Identification of the Rozvi," *Rhodesian History*, no. 5 (1974): 19–31.

———. *A Political History of the Munhumutapa.* Harare: Zimbabwe Publishing, 1988.

Pikirayi, Innocent. "Precolonial Towns of Zambezia." In *Encyclopedia of Precolonial Africa: Archaeology, History, Languages, Cultures and Environments*, edited by Joseph O. Vogel. London: Altamira Press, 1997.

Robinson, K. R. *Khami Ruins.* Cambridge: Cambridge University Press, 1959.

Summers, R. *Ancient Ruins and Vanished Civilisations of Southern Africa.* Cape Town: Baulpin, 1971.

Touré, Samori (*c.*1830–1900) and His Empire

Samori Touré is generally considered as one of the main opponents to the French during their occupation of the future French Sudan. However, the formation of Samori's empire should not be studied as a reaction to

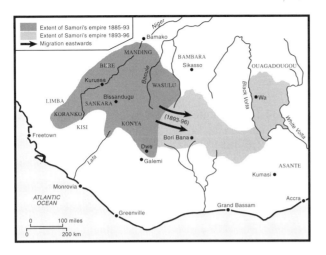

Samori Touré's empire, 1865–1898.

French imperialism. It is generally accepted that his warfare tactics were superior to those of France, and that only inferior armature led to his defeat.

Samori was born in approximately 1830 in the village of Sanankaro, southeast of Kankan in the present-day Republic of Guinea. Information on his early life is scarce. He is reported to have liberated his mother, who was captured in a slave raid, by serving in the army of Sori Birama, his mother's captor. After having served in the armies of various warlords, his personal political career started in the 1860s when he led increasingly bigger armies, thus being able to rule over increasingly larger areas.

Although Samori's empire was called Maninka (Malinké), Mandingue, or Mandinka (not to be confused with the Mandenka who live in Gambia), it did not have an ethnic base. It only took some ideological inspiration from the medieval Mali/Mandingue empire, the foundation of which has been attributed to Sunjata, as well, as it covered an area where the Maninka have been living. The organization of the empire followed patterns well-known in the region. However, the area occupied by Samori was relatively large, and his tactics where innovative. He set up networks of subjugated or collaborating rulers with regional power, resulting in structures that favored trade, which did not exclude small-scale banditry nor cooperation for major military expeditions. Collaboration between Samori and other rulers was never entirely voluntary; often Samori took the sons of collaborating rulers hostage, thus guaranteeing their loyalty and, at the same time, training their sons in warfare. Moreover, fortresses (called *tata*) were often built close to political centers to watch over allies.

Samori's "empire" was not the result of resistance against the French, who became his major adversaries after 1882, when they penetrated the Sudan. Samori's realm grew impressively in the 1870s; in 1881 it stretched from the limits of Bamako southward into to the forests of present-day Guinea, and the borders of Sierra Leone and Liberia, eastward almost to Sikasso; in the middle of this realm was Kankan. At first, the French made treaties with Samori, accepting the Niger River as a border, but when, in 1887, Samori moved his armies to the rising "state" of Kenedougou (with its strong fortified town of Sikasso as its political center), the French occupied the area that had been abandoned (and burned and depopulated) by Samori.

Equipped with some modern armature (often acquired with British aid), and skillfully exploiting the political rivalry between the French and the British, Samori forced the French to increase their military efforts during their occupation of the Sudan. Yet, partially because weakened by the siege of Sikasso, Samori had to cede from his territory; around 1892–1823 Samori and his troops moved eastward, thus creating, a few years later, a second empire in present-day northern Côte d'Ivoire, this time as a "foreign" ruler. In order to accomplish this new empire, the famous kingdom of Kong was occupied. The French persisted in their goal to occupy the entire Sudan, and after several battles (several of which won by Samori's armies) Samori was finally caught, in 1898, and exiled to the island of Missanga in the Gabon. He died there on June 2, 1900.

Samori is remembered in the area of his first empire as *lalmami*, the imam. This title he took at the end of his career; it invokes his spiritual leadership and his connection to Islam. To what extent Samori's wars can be seen as inspired by religious motivations is a point of ongoing discussion. In the beginning of his career he was a *kèlètigi*, an army leader. An intermediary stage was *faama*, an established ruler without hereditary rights to his realm. This three-step career also represents Samori's changing roles; first he was actively involved in warfare, but later his "younger brothers" led the armies, and Samori himself did not appear on the battle scene.

Historiographically, Samori's name is connected to Yves Person, whose detailed three-volume thesis (followed by many additional or popularized studies on Samori) is still the primary source for study. Person's analysis brought to the foreground the connections among warfare, trade, and Islam that characterized Samori's empire, thus setting the paradigm for later historical studies in the Southern part of the Sudan. A new and important field of study is being formed regarding the oral traditions on Samori; these traditions demonstrate his increasing importance in West African history. In particular, since the end of the 1950s when the former French colonies acquired independence,

Samori is celebrated as a resistance hero against French oppression, and his Maninka empire is pictured as a predecessor of such African republics as Guinea and Mali. In particular, under Sekou Touré, Guinea's first president, Samori gained a foothold in popular historical imagination: Touré himself even claimed to be a descendant of Samori, which he actually only is in a symbolic sense. Nowadays, extended epic narratives on Samori are recorded in Guinea and Southern Mali; these popular narratives mix data from the schoolbooks with local or regional models for heroic behavior. In some regions the traditions do not focus on Samori, but on his brothers who functioned as army leaders, which demonstrates how his empire was organized.

JAN JANSEN

See also: **Mali (Republic of): Economy and Society, Nineteenth Century.**

Further Reading

Mande Studies, no. 3 (2001), Special issue on Samori.
Person, Yves. *Samori: une révolution Dyula*. 3 vols. Dakar: IFAN, 1968–1975.

Tourism

In 1889, the German Hans Meyer was the first European to reach the top of Mount Kilimanjaro. Today, 15,000 tourists, assisted by some 35,000 guides and porters, attempt to climb the mountain each year. Approximately 40 to 50 per cent do reach the summit. It is one of Tanzania's major tourist attractions and exemplifies one of today's types of tourism in Africa: trekking. Others are culture, beach (in both summer and winter), and safari (photography and hunting) tourism.

In 1869, the year the Suez Canal was opened, Cook organized the first tour to Egypt (Gamble 1989, pp.26). The Cook family was also responsible for laying out the modern town of Luxor, today one of Egypt's major attractions due to its temples and tombs. Otherwise, tourism to Africa was mainly restricted to a small number of well-off Europeans interested in hunting big game. It was not until after World War II that tourist flows to Africa increased significantly. Commercial air transportation, improved tourism infrastructure, and increasing numbers of wealthy people stimulated holiday travel to distant countries (Popovic 1972, 188). In 1998, Africa (excluding Egypt's 3.7 million visitors) witnessed some 25 million tourists. This is equivalent to the United Kingdom figure for that same year, and is 4 per cent of global tourism arrivals of over 625 million, making US$ 445 billion. By comparison, in 1950

international tourism stood at 25 million arrivals and US$ 2 billion receipts (WTO 1994, 1). From 1970 to 1998, Africa more than doubled its share of arrivals (from 1.5 to 4 per cent), but its share in receipts fell from 2.7 to 2.2 per cent.

Among the top 40 tourism destinations for 1998 are four African countries: South Africa (5,981,000 arrivals—position 25), Tunisia (4,718,000—position 29), Egypt (3,766,000—position 34) and Morocco (3,241,000—position 38). Whereas the position of the latter three is rather stable, South Africa stood at position 55 in 1990. The abolition of the apartheid regime is among the major causes to explain this rise.

In 1998 almost 40 per cent of tourist arrivals originated in Africa itself (9.8 million). Europeans visiting Africa (8.9 million) constituted another major share at about 35 per cent. France (2.6 million), Germany (1.7 million), United Kingdom (1 million) and Italy (0.7 million) provided the bulk of European tourists in 1997. The total number of European tourist increased by 6.2 per cent annually in the last decade. The table below shows international tourist arrivals in Africa for the 1980–1998 period.

The northern Africa region includes destinations with relatively well-established tourism industries, such as Tunisia and Morocco. Among the major tourist attractions are Tunisia's sun-covered beaches and the Sahara to the south, Africa's oldest rock paintings at Tassili (Algeria) and the Moroccan Atlas Mountains. National residents working abroad and returning home for annual holidays are a major group among the tourists to this region (e.g., more than 1 million in Morocco and half a million in Algeria). In addition to the often once-in-a-life-time cultural visit to the pyramids, Egypt tries to develop beach tourism along the Red Sea shores in order to press tourists to return to the country.

The southern African (Botswana, Lesotho, Namibia, South Africa, Swaziland) share of arrivals in the African continent increased from 13 to 31 per cent in the 1989–1998 period. The mass of tourism flows in southern Africa arises from movements between countries in this subregion, as well as arrivals of tourists coming from Eastern African countries. Non-African tourists took a share of slightly over 26 per cent in 1997. The region offers beautiful scenery such as the Etosha National Game Park and Fish River Canyon (Namibia), Chobe National Park northeast of the Okavango Delta (Botswana) and Kruger National Park (South Africa). Lately the Peace Park Foundation Initiative attempts to link Kruger National Park (900,000 visitors per annum) with parks in Mozambique (5,000 visitors only) and Zimbabwe (*African Business* 1999).

In Eastern Africa the share of total arrivals rose from 18 to 23 per cent. In 1992, Kenya lost its position as main destination in favor of Zimbabwe. However, tourism in Kenya is much more profitable in terms of receipts, whch reflects the predominance of European tourism there. For the whole of eastern Africa, non-African tourists accounted for over 60 per cent of tourism in 1997. This part of Africa is richly endowed with a wide variety of spectacular views such as the wildebeest trek in Serengeti National Park (Tanzania), Victoria Falls on the Zambezi (Zimbabwe/Zambia), the source of the White Nile (Rwanda/Uganda), the Ruwenzori and Virunja Mountain gorillas (Uganda/Rwanda), the ruins of Great Zimbabwe, and Ethiopia's St. George Church in Lalibella.

The western African share has remained stable from 9.4 to 9.5 per cent between 1989 and 1998, and tourists of non-African origin had a share of 47 per cent. The region's attractions are long sandy beaches in Gambia, castles and forts in Ghana, the tomb of Ahmadu Bamba in Touba (Senegal), the "Our Lady of Peace" basilica in Yamoussoukro (Côte d'Ivoire), the Bandiagara Plateau of the Dogon and the mosque in Djenné (Mali), among others.

Finally, central Africa (Angola, Cameroon, CAR, Chad, Congo, DR Congo, Equatorial Guinea, Gabon, São Tomé, and Príncipe) market share is the weakest of all subregions. Tourist arrivals have remained practically unchanged, with an average annual growth rate of only 3.8 per cent, whereas receipts show a decrease of 4.5 per cent per annum.

Tourism is the fastest growing industry in the world (4.5 per cent annually in the last decade). Moreover, it now holds the number one position in world trade, ahead of the automobile and oil industries. In 1997 the tourism sector had a share of over 8 per cent of total world exports of goods consumed and almost 34 per cent of the total world exports of services. For Africa these figures stood at 8 and 45 per cent, respectively. However, there are huge regional differences.

Looking at Africa's place in international tourism receipts (excluding transportion), only Egypt (27th, US$ 3,838 million) is in the Top 40 earners in 1998 (WTO 1999a). South Africa (US$ 2,366 million) might soon enter this category as its annual growth was in the order of 15.5 per cent in the 1989–1998 period (WTO 1999b, 18). Other major African earners are Morocco (US$ 1,600 million) and Tunisia (US$ 1,550 million). Tourism's share in receipts of services increased from 35.1 to 45.4 per cent from 1989 to 1997, illustrating the importance of tourism for Africa. By investing in the tourist sector, African countries hope to create jobs and earn hard currencies. It is forecasted that total tourist arrivals in Africa will triple and reach 75 million by the year 2020 (Cleverdon 1998).

Besides positive effects, however, negative aspects in the social, cultural, environmental, and economic spheres should be mentioned. Wildlife is Africa's greatest natural asset, though, according to Western conservation organizations, it is in constant danger of extinction.

Pollution is another negative environmental effect. Trekking routes, including some of Mount Kilimanjaro's, are increasingly littered. Even the smallest hotels generate daily waste and sewage while making demands on land, water, and energy.

The problem of leakage of foreign exchange to international companies and airlines also deserves attention. For example, foreign companies, sometimes in collaboration with the local elite, reap most of the economic benefits of beach tourism at the expense of the local population's commercial activity (e.g., fishing). Investments in roads and hotels are directed to tourist areas. Yet, the tourist sector operates in a risky market. The preferences of tourists fluctuate constantly, and an economic decline affects travel abroad. The outbreak of a disease or local conflicts may also affect the tourism sector. These often unexpected and uncontrollable events could weaken the local tourist sector and force a large number of (small) entrepreneurs into bankruptcy virtually overnight.

MARCEL RUTTEN

Further Reading

African Business, no. 247 (1999).

Ardito, S. *Trekking in Africa: A Guide to the Finest Routes.* White Star, 1996.

Cleverdon, R. "Trends and Forecasts Worldwide and by Region." In: *CAF Seminar on Africa and Global Ttourism Prospects to the Year 2020: Challenges and Opportunities, Grand-Baie, Mauritius, 30 April–1 May 1998.* Madrid: World Tourism Organization, 1998.

Gamble, W. P. *Tourism and Development in Africa.* London: John Murray, 1989.

Panos. "Ecotourism—Paradise Gained, or Paradise Lost?" London: Panos, 1995.

Popovic, V. *Tourism in Eastern Africa.* Munich: Weltforum Verlag, 1972.

Rutten, M. M. E. M. S*elling Wealth to Buy Poverty: The Process of the Individualization of Landownership among the Maasai Pastoralists of Kajiado District, Kenya, 1890–1990.* Saarbrücken: Verlag Breitenbach, 1992.

World Tourism Organization (WTO). *Global Tourism Forecasts to the Year 2000 and Beyond.* Regional Forecasting Studies Series, vol. 2. Madrid: World Tourism Organization, 1994.

———. *Tourism Highlights 1999.* Madrid: World Tourism Organization, 1999(a).

———. *Tourism Market Trends, Africa 1989–1998.* Madrid: World Tourism Organization, 1999(b).

Toutswemogala: *See* **Iron Age (Later): Southern Africa: Toutswemogala, Cattle, and Political Power.**

Trade: *See* **Ghana (Republic of): Colonial Period: Economy.**

Trade Unions: Postcolonial

After independence, some legal impediments to free labor organization that existed under colonialism were removed, yet in the postcolonial era trade unions across Africa continued to suffer repression. Nationalist trade union alliances that were formed during independence struggles dissipated as political leaders sought to control labor and restrict wages to attract investment, stimulate capital accumulation, and prevent rival power bases from gaining influence and support. Governments appealed to national, not class, interests, a trend encapsulated by Kenyan leader Tom Mboya's comment that "the trade union and the national movement are almost invariably linked in independent territories."

Low rates of union membership in Africa reflected limited industrialization and the effects of antilabor state policies, while repression and military conflict made union organizing hazardous. Agricultural and informal sectors, which predominated in Africa (the latter comprised 61 per cent of urban workers in 1990) remained largely outside unions, although efforts were made to enroll domestic and farm workers, who included many women. In 1995, total estimated union numbers in Sub-Saharan Africa were ten million, often reflecting the size of economies. Figures were low in Gabon (5,000), Mauritania (15,000), Eritrea (18,000) and Guinea (13,000), but high in Nigeria (3.5 million in 1990), South Africa (3.15 million) and Egypt (3.3 million). The medium-sized economies of Kenya, Côte d'Ivoire, Cameroon, Morocco, Tanzania, and Ghana had between 250,000 and 700,000 unionists. Membership tended to decline from 1985 to 1995, falling in Uganda by 38 per cent and in Kenya by 29 per cent, although rising in South Africa (by 131 per cent), Zimbabwe (54 per cent), and Egypt (29 per cent). In this period, democratization helped boost union membership, which rose in Ethiopia from 4,000 to 152,000 and in South Africa from 1.4 to 3.15 million. Yet democratization often came with the shedding of state sector jobs and this reduced union membership. Despite multiparty elections, Zambian union numbers declined from 320,000 to 273,000. Other problems included high unemployment and low wages, which made unions unattractive, and their exclusion from the export processing zones that flourished with globalization.

Globalization also encouraged unions to expand their ties. There were instances of international trade union solidarity. In 1997, South African unions supported Swazi union demands, and unions in many countries opposed the Abacha regime in Nigeria. The Cold War, and political and religious differences, created divisions, and African unions affiliated to rival international labor federations. Nevertheless, the African Trade Union Confederation (founded in 1962) accepted a range of different groups and the Organization of African Unity supported the All-African Trade Union Federation (founded 1961) and its sequel, the Organization of African Trade Union Unity (founded 1973).

Unionists across Africa faced victimization. In Tunisia, unauthorized strikes became illegal in 1967. In Algeria, where the right to strike was restricted, many died in conflicts between the state and Islamic fundamentalists after 1992. In Morocco, unions participated in national policy making in the first years of independence but thereafter suffered harassment, though in 1999 King Mohammed VI signaled a liberalization of society. In Egypt and Libya unions remained firmly under state control, with no right to strike.

Successive Nigerian regimes sought to repress unions. In Ghana, Kwame Nkrumah and subsequent state leaders sought to subordinate them. In Niger, Mauritania, Senegal, and Zaire unionists were subject to arbitrary arrest. Civil war in Liberia in the 1990s saw increased restrictions on union rights. In Equatorial Guinea, only ruling party members could obtain certain jobs. Unions in the Central African Republic were excluded from politics, in Benin the right to strike was restricted, and in Cameroon government refused to register some unions.

South Africa recorded a rapid growth in union membership until the late 1990s when there were substantial job losses, especially in mining. The powerful Congress of South African Trade Unions formed a strategic, albeit critical, alliance with the African National Congress and gained recognition of union rights in the 1994 constitution. Madagascar and Mauritius restricted union rights in export processing zones. In Swaziland, the monarchy sought to crush free unions. Botswana prevented public, agricultural, and domestic workers from joining unions. The Banda regime in Malawi brutally repressed unions, and while democratization in 1994 brought more freedom, police continued to harass unionists. Tanzania and Zambia sought to place unions under ruling party hegemony, but in the 1990s the monolithic state-controlled union center was dismantled in the former and in the latter, ex-unionist Frederick Chiluba ended the UNIP's rule. Zimbabwe's ZANU-PF installed party-dominated workers' committees to maintain hegemony, but the Zimbabwe Congress of Trade Unions rejected the regime's harsh economic policies and led labor and popular protests over rising prices and the lack of democracy. By 1998 its leader, Morgan Tsvangirai, emerged as a rival to Robert Mugabe.

Similar restrictions on unions were imposed in eastern Africa. Kenyan public service workers could not join unions, and the state had the power to remove labor leaders. Ugandan unions had to belong to a single union center. Repression in Djibouti was fierce, with many unionists dismissed or detained. In Ethiopia, successive regimes sought to control unions, although the 1994 constitution allowed freedom of organization. Chad's new labor code in the 1990s ended long-standing violations of union rights, at least in principle. In the Sudan, a strong union movement developed after independence but was decimated by coups in 1958, 1969, and 1989, with independent unions abolished and many labor leaders detained.

After independence in 1974–1975, socialist-oriented one-party states developed in Mozambique, Angola, and Guinea-Bissau, emphasizing nation building, and with production councils given greater attention than unions. Where unions (such as the Organization of Workers of Mozambique, formed in 1983) emerged, they were state-controlled. Democratization in the 1990s saw changes: the formation of independent unions, a tendency toward industry unionism, legalization of the right to strike written into Mozambique's new constitution, and, in Guinea-Bissau, union activity against the PAIGC regime.

Overall, African unions remained weak in the postcolonial era. Yet, their actions could ignite government crises, as in the Sudan in 1964, Ghana in 1971, Madagascar in 1972, and Ethiopia in 1974, and they continually fought repression. Unions were prominent in prodemocracy actions in Mali and Swaziland, a prominent source of opposition to the Abacha regime in Nigeria and the 1997 Sierra Leone coup, and thwarted attempts at greater state authoritarianism in Cameroon and Zimbabwe. By the 1990s, fewer regimes were able to use unions as their mouthpieces, and some improvements in labor rights were apparent. In 1993, Kenyan unions cut ties with government, and the 1999 demise of Abacha in Nigeria allowed unions greater freedom. In postcolonial times, unions occasionally provided input to national policy making, but in general, their influence was limited. International labor standards often were ignored by governments and employers, while working conditions for many continued to deteriorate.

PETER LIMB

See also: **Algeria: Islamic Salvation Front, Military Rule, Civil War, 1990s; Mboya, Tom J.; Nkrumah, Kwame; South Africa: Industrial and Commercial Workers Union; Trades Unionism and Nationalism;**

Zimbabwe (Southern Rhodesia): African Political and Trades Union Movements, 1920s and 1930s.

Further Reading

Ananaba, Wogu *The Trade Union Movement in Africa: Promise and Performance.* London: C. Hurst/New York: St. Martin's Press, 1979.

Davies, Ioan. *African Trade Unions.* Harmondsworth, England: Penguin, 1966.

Freund, Bill. *The African Worker.* Cambridge: Cambridge University Press, 1988.

International Confederation of Free Trade Unions (ICFTU). *Annual Survey of Violations of Trade Union Rights, 1998.* Geneva: ICFTU, 1998.

International Labour Office (ILO). *ILO Activities in Africa: 1994–99.* Abidjan, Côte d'Ivoire: ILO, 1999.

Kester, Gerard, and Ousmane O. Sidibe (eds.). *Trade Unions and Sustainable Democracy in Africa.* Aldershot, England: Ashgate, 1997.

Meynaud, Jean, and Anisse Salah Bey. *Trade Unionism in Africa: A Study of Its Growth and Orientation,* translated by Angela Brench. London: Methuen, 1967.

Sandbrook, Richard, and Robin Cohen (eds.). *The Development of an African Working Class: Studies in Class Formation and Action. London:* Longman, 1975.

Southall, Roger (ed.). *Labour and Unions in Asia and Africa: Contemporary Issues,* Basingstoke, England: Macmillan/New York: St. Martin's Press, 1988.

Paul Tiyambe Zeleza. "Pan-African Trade Unionism: Unity and Discord," *Transafrican Journal of History,* no. 15 (1986): 164–90.

Trades Unionism and Nationalism

African trade unionists and African nationalists both generally opposed colonial rule, but their relations were complex and uneven. Their growth roughly coincided, a congruence that aided the interpenetration of class and national consciousness among workers but also alarmed colonial rulers. Concerned with the militancy of an emergent African industrial labor force, especially among transportation, mining, and state-sector workers who occupied a strategic position in colonial economies, and at the prospect of their uniting with nationalists, colonial officials sought to stifle unions. They were harshly repressed in Portuguese, Italian, and German colonies, unable to operate freely in the Belgian Congo until 1957, and tardily legalized by France (in Algeria and Tunisia in 1932, West Africa in 1944, Equatorial Africa in 1947) and Britain (authorized in 1930 but not implemented until later: 1938 in Nigeria). South African black unions achieved legal recognition only in the 1970s. Those unions that did emerge were strongly discouraged from supporting national liberation (Uganda outlawed "political unionism" in 1952) and had their strikes suppressed. Nevertheless, these measures did not prevent the emergence of unions or their forging of links with nationalists.

African workers initially had little formal organization beyond kin-based groups, and their access to European craft unions operating in Africa was barred. Into this vacuum stepped African nationalists and their predecessors, claiming to speak on behalf of workers: in Mozambique, Grêmio Africano tried to mobilize laborers in 1911, while the Transvaal Native Congress defended strikers in 1918. From the 1920s on, African workers began to organize, at first in general associations such as the Industrial and Commercial Workers' Union in South Africa and Rhodesia and then, gradually, in trade-based unions. Limited industrialization spawned a small proletariat, and early unions were ephemeral due to inexperienced officials, low incomes, and migrant labor instability. Isolated African labor federations formed in Tunisia in 1924 and South Africa in 1928, but were short-lived.

Unionization accelerated during and after World War II, stimulated by rising industrialization and heightened class-consciousness. Trade unionists became more involved in nationalist movements that now sought a mass base and began to incorporate union demands in their programs. By the late 1950s, unionists such as Tom Mboya in Kenya, Sékou Touré in Guinea, and Joshua Nkomo in Rhodesia were prominent nationalists.

The attractions of nationalism were several. Unionists were inclined toward political action by repression of their right to organize. Workers in the state sector were likely allies as their industrial discontent invariably turned against their employer, the colonial state, while those with rural ties were attracted to nationalist agendas highlighting land reform. Independence appeared to offer the prospect of an improved life, while discriminatory colonial housing and labor policies pushed together diverse African social strata, temporarily masking class differences. Finally, unionists had few viable alternative political allies, as social democratic parties in Africa were largely ineffective.

Trade unions were useful to nationalists because they could be a conduit for nationalism among workers and, with their organization and militancy, act as a battering ram against government opposition to African demands. In Guinea, Benin, South Africa, Kenya, and Nigeria, unions were important strategic allies of nationalists. The Sudan Workers Trade Union Federation actively supported nationalism. In Zanzibar, unions formed only in the last decade of colonial rule, simultaneous with rising nationalism, yet became a driving force in nationalist demonstrations. Strikes in Lagos (1945); Mombasa, Dar es Salaam, and French West Africa (1947); and Accra and Nairobi (1950) protested not only economic grievances but also colonialism, and catalyzed support for nationalists. A 1948 general strike in Rhodesia boosted nationalism and a 1950 wage dispute in Ghana grew into a proindependence general strike aiding Nkrumah's subsequent election victory. In return, nationalist leaders in many countries, including Morocco, Senegal, Nigeria, and Guinea, pledged support for labor rights. This extended to the international arena. The Namibian nationalist movement SWAPO officially represented Namibian workers in the International Labor Organization (ILO).

However, the nature and extent of cooperation greatly varied. In Ethiopia, Somalia, Botswana, Seychelles, Libya, Mauritania, and Rwanda-Burundi, unions were weak and played a minor role in nationalism: Libyan unions formed only after independence. Some unions saw their primary duty to members, were ambivalent, and did not affiliate to nationalist parties. This inclined writers of the 1960s to stress labor's passive role in nationalism, a claim challenged by recent research: Egyptian unions, once seen as politically quiescent, had vigorous if contradictory ties with nationalists. Formal agreements were concluded in a few countries. South Africa, with greater industrialization, had a strong union movement with close unity between union federations and nationalists. Pacts also emerged briefly in Nigeria (1944–1950), Ghana (1950), and Kenya (1960), but these were between national bodies. More often, the pattern was informal alliances of varying intensity: in French West Africa—notably, in Guinea—these tended to be close; in Nigeria after 1950 they were more distant. Relations were more complex when rival nationalist parties wooed unions, or rival union federations adopted different approaches. In the 1950s in Uganda, the dominant Trades Union Congress took an apolitical position while the Federation of Labor sought alliance with nationalists. In French Cameroon, overlapping membership of the nationalist Union des Populations du Cameroun and trade unions induced a more radical nationalism, whereas colonial officials in British Cameroon successfully encouraged apolitical associations among plantation workers. Splits in Zimbabwean unions in the 1960s and 1970s reflected political divisions among nationalist parties as well as rivalries between international labor federations. Unionists tended to oppose conservative nationalists: in Swaziland, they backed the modernist Ngwane National Liberatory Congress against the monarchy, while in Côte d'Ivoire, they criticized President Félix Houphouët-Boigny. There were othe reasons for rifts. Mine workers in Northern Rhodesia supported independence, yet their leaders remained aloof regaging nationalist parties partly due to personal rivalries.

A basic contradiction existed between the class orientation of trade unions and the broader policies of nationalist elites. As decolonization proceeded, the latter increasingly sought to co-opt the labor movement. In 1955 in Tanganyika, Nkrumah clashed with striking miners and thereafter demanded loyalty from unions. In Algeria, the National Liberation Front in the 1950s marginalized the main labor federation. In 1960, the Tanganyika African National Union moved to control the labor movement in Tanganyika. Such moves prompted trade unions in many countries to redefine their relationship to nationalist parties. Overall, African unionists and nationalists found common cause against colonialism, but this was not without tensions and contradictions between them, which deepened as independence beckoned.

PETER LIMB

See also: **Colonial European Administrations: Comparative Survey; Colonialism: Impact on African Societies; Guinea: Touré, Ahmed Sekou, Era of; Mboya, Tom J.; Nkomo, Joshua.**

Further Reading

Ananaba, Wogu. *The Trade Union Movement in Africa: Promise and Performance*. London: C. Hurst/New York: St. Martin's Press, 1979.

Berger, Elena L. *Labour, Race, and Colonial Rule: The Copperbelt from 1924 to Independence*. Oxford: Clarendon Press, 1974.

Cooper, Frederick. *Decolonization and African Society: The Labor Question in French and British Africa*. Cambridge: Cambridge University Press, 1996.

Coquery-Vidrovitch, Catherine. "Trade Unionism and Nationalism: The Slow Growth of Sociopolitical Movements." In *Africa: Endurance and Change South of the Sahara*. Berkeley and Los Angeles: University of California Press, 1988.

Davies, Ioan, *African Trade Unions*. Harmondsworth, England: Penguin, 1966.

Meynaud, Jean, and Anisse Salah Bey. *Trade Unionism in Africa: A Study of Its Growth and Orientation,* translated by Angela Brench. London: Methuen, 1967.

Sandbrook, Richard, and Robin Cohen (eds.). *The Development of an African Working Class: Studies in Class Formation and Action*. London: Longman, 1975.

Transportation: *See* **Ghana (Republic of): Colonial Period: Economy.**

Transportation Infrastructure

Until the middle of the nineteenth century, modern transportation infrastructure in Africa was largely nonexistent. Travel occurred on centuries-old bush paths or caravan routes, major rivers such as the Nile, Zambezi, Congo, and Niger, or followed the coastline. Before the era of colonialism, Europeans were restricted largely to the coastal areas because of the reputed inaccessibility of much of the interior and by their susceptibility to endemic diseases. Those few Europeans who did venture further followed long-established routes used by African or Arab traders.

European communications methods were introduced to Africa in the form of steamships, railroads,

Transportation problems in early colonial east Africa, c.1927–1930. © SVT Bild/Das Fotoarchiv.

and telegraph cables in the nineteenth century, and macadamized roads and airplanes in the twentieth century. They also took the form of such large engineering projects as the Suez Canal and dams. The growth of European technology in Africa played a decisive role in the "Scramble" for Africa in the late nineteenth century and in the ability of the European powers to administer and derive economic benefit from Africa during the colonial era.

As the preeminent maritime power of the nineteenth century, Britain played the biggest role in introducing Africa to modern technology. Steamships first appeared in African waters as early as the 1830s in the Royal Navy's West Africa Squadron used to suppress the slave trade. Others were employed in the delta of the Niger River in the 1840s. Steamships gradually came to dominate trade between Europe and North Africa and Egypt in the 1850s and 1860s. Reliance on coal led to the establishment of a string of coaling stations at key points along the African coast. Many of these, especially Freetown, Cape Town, Durban, and Mombasa, came to support a permanent Royal Navy presence that frequently acted as an agent of the British government in dealing with African rulers. The strategic importance of South Africa on the sea route to India and China, as well as its uniqueness as a place of European settlement, ensured it a higher level of technological development than any other part of Africa.

Maritime traffic around Africa was altered by the opening of the Suez Canal in 1869, which dramatically increased trade through the Red Sea and to the east coast of Africa as coaling stations were opened to support the trade to Asia and Australia. British companies such as P and O, the Orient Line, and Union Castle maintained substantial facilities along the routes, and the canal also spurred the construction of subsidiary canals, roads, and railways in Egypt. By the mid 1890s, four million tons of British shipping passed through the canal annually.

The perceived need to defend the canal profoundly affected British policy toward Africa; according to Ronald Robinson and John Gallagher's (1961) thesis of imperial expansion, defense of the canal led to a permanent British occupation of Egypt, necessitated the reconquest of the Sudan (1898), and required British preeminence in East Africa and Uganda.

As steamship trade with Africa expanded in the late nineteenth century, demand increased for improved port and passenger facilities. Some ports, such as those of Algiers, Lagos, and Mombasa, were expanded, while others (Dakar, Tema, and Port Harcourt) were newly constructed and quickly became major urban areas. This naturally had a significant social and economic impact on all the territories concerned. By 1900 ironclad steamships were a common feature in Africa, even plying far up the major rivers. Although natural routes for exploration, major rivers such as the Zambezi and Congo were only marginally useful for navigation and trade because of natural obstacles such as gorges, falls, and rapids.

An equally significant maritime development was the laying of submarine telegraph cables around Africa. Apart from one line under the Mediterranean to Algiers, this was an entirely British undertaking. Between 1879 and 1889 submarine cables were laid around the length of the African coast, connecting all major ports. No land lines were constructed, however. Most of these cables were owned and operated by the Eastern Telegraph Company and its subsidiaries.

Railroads were the most substantial transportation development of the colonial era. The first railway line in Africa was a short line built in Cape Colony in the 1850s, and from there South Africa quickly became the leader for railroad construction on the continent. The discovery of diamonds in Kimberley and gold in the Witswatersrand provided the incentive for rapid rail construction from the 1870s. By 1919 South Africa had 10,000 miles of railroad. Southern Africa's rail demands provided a huge boon for the development of the Rhodesias, and for branch lines through Portuguese Angola and Mozambique. In all parts of the continent, railroads permitted the penetration of colonial rule and economic activity. They provided the easiest way to move troops to trouble spots, and proved decisive in the Ndebele uprising (1896–1897), the reconquest of the Sudan (1898), and the Boer War (1899–1902).

Railroads were crucial to the economic development of Africa by the colonial powers. In many places their construction overcame difficult geographic and financial odds and often involved a heavy loss of life for the African (and in East Africa, Asian) labor force. The most common pattern was a rail line from the coast to the interior to expedite the extraction of raw materials such as copper, cotton, and groundnuts. There was little effort outside South Africa to provide lateral or intercolonial rail links. Modern Africa is still strongly affected by the trade flows created by the colonial railway systems.

Automobiles were introduced to Africa during and after World War I. However, modern roads were few and far between during the colonial era. They were concentrated in major cities and colonial capitals and tended not to go much farther. Only in South Africa the 1930s and 1940s were roads built to connect the major cities. Road construction that did occur in the colonial period tended to follow the existing rail lines, although many territorial governments had ambitious plans for the expansion of their road systems during the last phase of colonial development in the 1950s.

Commercial civil aviation came to Africa as imperial airline systems were gradually established. Virtually all were subsidized by the home governments. Britain was the primary aviation country in Africa, and the national flag carrier, Imperial Airways, developed routes to Egypt by 1921 and down the Nile Valley through East Africa to Cape Town in 1932 (a trip that took nine days). East and Central Africa were the most concentrated areas of aviation activity for Britain in Africa and included operators linked to Imperial Airways, such as Wilson Airways and Rhodesia and Nyasaland Airways. Air routes to West Africa were opened after World War II. Only Air France and KLM Royal Dutch Airlines operated comparable air service to Africa, especially to North and West Africa. Internal aviation in individual colonies did not begin in a substantial way until the 1940s and 1950s, and many of these small local airlines formed the basis of national airlines after independence.

DAVID R. DEVEREUX

See also: **Railways.**

Further Reading

Arnold, Guy, and Ruth Weiss. *Strategic Highways of Africa.* New York: St. Martin's Press, 1977.

Higham, Robin. *Britain's Imperial Air Routes, 1918–1939; The Story of Britain's Overseas Airlines.* London: G. T. Foulis, 1961.

Kennedy, P. M. "Imperial Cable Communications and Strategy, 1870–1914." *English Historical Review.* no. 86 (1971): 728–752.

McCormack, R. L. "Imperialism, Air Transport and Colonial Development: Kenya 1920–1946." *Journal of Imperial and Commonwealth History.* 17, no. 3 (1989): 374–395.

Munro, J. Forbes. "Shipping Subsidies and Railway Guarantees: William Mackinnon, Eastern Africa and the Indian Ocean, 1860–1893." *Journal of African History.* 28, no. 2 (1987): 209–230.

Olukoju, Ayodeji. "Elder Dempster and the Shipping Trade of Nigeria during the First World War," *Journal of African History.* 33, no. 2 (1992): 255–271.

Porter, Andrew. *Victorian Shipping, Business and Imperial Policy: Donald Currie, the Castle Line, and Southern Africa.* Royal Historical Society Studies series no. 49. New York: St. Martin's Press, 1986.

Robinson, Ronald, and John Gallagher with Alice Denny. *Africa and the Victorians: The Official Mind of Imperialism.* London: Macmillan, 1961.

Suret-Canale, Jean. *French Colonialism in Tropical Africa 1900–1945.* New York: Pica Press, 1971.

Transportation: Postcolonial Africa

During the postcolonial period in Africa, transportation has been associated with socioeconomic progress and decline. Changes in transportation have been geographically uneven; they have benefited some people and places but have disadvantaged others. The urban and rural poor have gained little from new transportation technologies and services. New transportation strategies are being put in place to tackle these and other failures.

In the last half of the twentieth century the African continent shared in the worldwide extension of motor vehicle use and ownership, and the elaboration of aviation services. As elsewhere, this technological modernization was accompanied by gradual decline in the significance of rail and shipping services, which had been the workhorses of the colonial period. Even so, the pace of technological development in global transportation in the last half-century has contributed to the marginalization of Africa. In the 1990s the formation of powerful global airline marketing and operating alliances weakened the viability and long-term survival of African civil aviation.

Increased motorization and flight in Africa in the 1950s and 1960s occurred at the same time as political decolonization. The transportation sector was used to express modernization and independence. Newly elected African leaders marked their ascension by building glamorous and prestigious urban motorways and airports, many of which bore their names. New flag-carrying national airlines were hived off from larger regional entities that had previously served

The Niger River. Segu, Mali, 1976. Photograph © David C. Conrad.

jointly several colonial territories in eastern and central Africa. In both the new and the old transportation sectors, employment profiles changed as expatriate managers, technicians, and workers departed, and as colonial hiring and contracting practices were abandoned in favor of Africanization of the entire transportation workforce rather than just laborers. Beyond the parastatal sector, African ownership and management of private road transportation companies increased quickly, becoming a prominent route into the middle class and to capital accumulation. On a larger scale, the assertion of "Africanness" in transportation was evident in the creation of multinational African shipping and aviation organizations to represent the continent on the world stage, to coordinate African transportation, and to negotiate favorable fuel purchase prices and vessel or aircraft purchasing and leasing.

The ending of colonialism was associated with other shifts in transportation. As the map of independent African states filled out, interest grew in Pan-African transportation projects. There were ambitious proposals to build international highways among countries that, in colonial times, were better connected to European metropoles than to other African colonies. Similarly, there were plans were to develop better flight connections among African capitals. These schemes were complemented by trade and transportation realignments that linked newly independent African states to new socialist partners in the USSR and eastern Europe. The most prominent case involved Chinese funding, construction, equipping, and operating the new Uhuru Railway, giving Zambia an outlet to the sea via Tanzania. This project reflected the new political and economic conditions in which transportation was used to distance Africa from its colonial past. Political realignments in transportation also featured purchases of transportation equipment such as road vehicles and aircraft from nontraditional sources beyond western Europe.

In southern Africa, strenuous efforts were made by landlocked states to end reliance on the transportation networks of neighboring countries that were still under white minority rule: Zambia sought to avoid Rhodesian transportation and, in turn, Zimbabwe sought to avoid South Africa. Transportation was being used as a lever to force political accommodation or change. By denying hostile black African governments rail access to South Africa's ports for vital raw material exports and imports (including food), the apartheid government hoped to curb antiapartheid protest and cross-border military action. In a cycle of retaliatory sanctions, independent African governments prevented South Africa's state-owned airline from flying over or landing in their countries.

The transportation plans and starter projects that emerged in postcolonial Africa have been hard to manage, sustain, and extend in a context of increasing economic stress. Transportation has had to compete with the military, education, housing, and health sectors for funds from a devaluing public purse. Political instability has deterred foreign investors. National budgetary, personnel, and material resources have failed to respond to the challenges, and in several instances transportation has been corrupted by nepotism and fraud. Lax regulation (notably of driver and vehicle licensing) has contributed to chaos. Aging taxi, truck, and lake-ferry fleets endanger personal and environmental safety. Roads have crumbled while the backlog of maintenance projects lengthens. Airline safety has been put at increasing risk by aging fleets and outdated navigational systems: in 1997, the average fleet age of airlines in Africa was the highest in the world. Only five African countries met international navigation standards.

Persistent mismanagement and underinvestment has meant that the quality of Africa's transportation infrastructure and services has worsened in the last 20 years. Transportation networks remain geographically sparse. Vehicles are butchered and recycled. Service is erratic. This is not least in countries where domestic warfare (including urban gangsterism) has decimated hardware and personnel; transportation infrastructure is very vulnerable to disruption. The Benguella railway in war-torn Angola has been nonoperational for 20 years. Fragile road infrastructure and services in the Great Lakes region, and in Liberia and Sierra Leone, have been damaged by persistent civil unrest. After a brief interlude when Mozambique's shattered inland transportation capacity was starting to revive after sixteen years of civil war, floods in 1999 set back the recovery program.

In the last two decades of the twentieth century, the United Nations made the restoration of transportation an African priority. In conventional manner, transportation investment was intended to promote economic development by speeding internal circulation and facilitating trade, and to allow social uplifting by facilitating access to schools and health clinics. In an era of neocolonial aid, international financial assistance for African transportation was made conditional on general economic reforms such as market liberalization and privatization of parastatal air, rail, road, and shipping services. Regulating urban passenger transportation was to be done alongside deregulation of long-distance road haulage and international aviation. Transportation monopolies and subsidies, and opaque contracting, licensing, and rate fixing, were to stop. Commercialization of transportation extended to infrastructure construction and operation. Several African airlines have survived only by agreeing to joint management, servicing and operating with a larger non-African carrier. User pricing was contemplated in the road transportation sector. In shipping and aviation, reform was also to standardize diverse national transportation technologies and administrative operations. Country by country, fragmentation of transportation was extended rather than ended by the national vanity which succeeded colonialism; early postcolonial Africa was a transportation seller's market.

In the first proud flush of postcolonialism, African transportation policy focused on new transportation installations. Now the emphasis lies on making better use of existing local and regional transportation capacity through integration and improved management. Technical modernization no longer has an innately higher priority than organizational reform. The financial affordability, social desirability, and environmental sustainability of transportation projects and solutions are also emerging as key criteria. Nonexploitative facilities and services that meet Africa's needs will include transportation for the delivery of emergency relief aid to refugee populations and to zones of food insecurity. Deaths following natural disasters and civil insurrection have been higher because of transportation undercapacity, remoteness, and transportation inaccessibility. Transportation geared to ecotourism could capitalize on the continent's scenic beauty and wildlife; deregulating African skies to accommodate foreign charter airlines would be a notable step forward. There is potential also to exhibit the transportation history of a continent whose ports and railways were central to the operation of extractive colonial economies, were sites of cultural and racial contrasts and clashes, labor strikes, slave shipping, overland labor migrancy, racial labor practices and racial segregation.

During colonialism, African transportation was geared to enriching and empowering places and people beyond Africa's shores. The immediate postcolonial reaction was to emulate inward-looking national transportation systems overseas. Capital-intensive, showcase projects have proved unsustainable and inappropriate to many of Africa's requirements and resources. For local travel and transportation in and between towns and villages, nonmotorized transportation (including bicycles and animal-drawn carts) emerges as a technology that matches the needs and capabilities of many (female-headed) households and communities. Transportation is needed that is affordable, maintainable, and does not use costly energy. Instead of constructing expensive tarred roads designed to foreign standards, earth roads are being built whose surfaces and inclines are better suited to pedestrians, head loaders, and animal-drawn vehicles. Road construction and maintenance is in several instances being organized through a food-for-work program which alleviates local unemployment and poverty.

GORDON H. PIRIE

Further Reading

Abeyratne, R. "Global Issues Confronting African Civil Aviation." *Aviation Quarterly*. no. 3 (1999): 2–16.

Gibb, R. A. "Imposing Dependence: South Africa's Manipulation of Regional Railways." *Transport Reviews*. no/11 (1991): 19–39.

Hoyle, B. S., and J. Charlier. "Inter-port Competition in Developing Countries: An East African Case Study." *Journal of Transport Geography*. no. 3 (1995): 87–104.

Iheduru, O.C. "1996: Post-apartheid South Africa and its Neighbors: a Maritime Transport Perspective." *Journal of Modern African Studies*. no. 34 (1996): 1–26.

Khosa, M. M. "Transport and Popular Struggles in South Africa." *Antipode*. no. 27 (1995): 167–88.

McCutcheon, Robert. "Labour Intensive Road Construction in Africa," *Habitat International*. no. 13 (1988): 109–123.

Mwase, N. "The Liberalisation and Deregulation of the Transport Sector in Sub-Saharan Africa." *African Development Review*. no. 5 (1993): 74–86.

———. "Road and Bridge Maintenance Strategies in Eastern and Southern Africa: Opportunities and Challenges." *International Journal of Transport Economics*. no. 22 (1995): 65–84.

———. "Zambia, TAZARA and Alternative Outlets to the Sea," *Transport Reviews*. no. 7 (1987): 191–206.

Njoh, A. J. "Gender-based Transportation Planning in Sub-Saharan Africa with Special Reference to Cameroon." *Journal of Asian and African Studies*. no. 34 (1999): 216–34.

Pirie, G. H. "Transport, Food Insecurity and Food-Aid in Sub-Saharan Africa." *Journal of Transport Geography*. no. 1 (1993): 12–19.

Poonoosamy, V. "Challenges Facing African Countries in the Field of Civil Aviation and the Impact of European Aeropolitical Developments on African Countries." *European Transport Law*. no. 29 (1994): 245–56.

Porter, G. "Mobility and Inequality in Rural Nigeria: the Case of Off-Road Communities," *Tijdschrift voor Economische en Sociale Geografie*. no. 88 (1997), 65–76.

Turner, J., and E. Kwakye. "Transport and Survival Strategies in a Developing Economy: Case Evidence from Accra, Ghana." *Journal of Transport Geography*. no. 4 (1996): 161–168.

Turton, B. J. and C. C. Mutambirwa. "Air Transport Services and the Expansion of International Tourism in Zimbabwe." *Tourism Management*. no. 17 (1996): 453–462.

Transvaal: *See* Afrikaans and Afrikaner Nationalism, Nineteenth Century; Boer Expansion: Interior of South Africa; Jameson Raid, Origins of South African War, 1895–1899; Pedi Kingdom, and Transvaal, 1822–1879; South Africa: Gold on the Witwatersrand, 1886–1899; South African War, 1899–1902.

Traoré, Moussa: *See* Mali (Republic of): Traoré, Moussa, Life and Era of.

Treason Trials: *See* South Africa: Defiance Campaign, Freedom Charter, Treason Trials.

Tripoli

With a population of 1.5 million (1994), Tripoli is the capital of present-day Libya. The city, located on the northern fringe of the Sahara, acquired fame in the past due to its entrepôt status and for its political significance. In ancient times, Tripoli experienced Phoenician, Carthaginian, Roman, and Vandal conquests. Its more recent history also recorded rule by the Arabs and the Ottoman Empire, as well as the French, Italians, and British. In spite of these invasions, the population and the pattern of existence in the city retained an overwhelmingly Arabic and Islamic characteristic.

A significant political development in the history of Tripoli was the creation in the sixteenth century of the Regency of Tripoli by the Ottoman sultan. From that period onward, the sultan usually appointed a pasha, who was in turn assisted by a body of janissary officers who helped in the supervision of the local administration. Turkish pashas continued to be sent to Tripoli until 1711, when the office became hereditary in the local oligarchy, the Karamanli family. This dynasty was to shape the history of Tripoli in the eighteenth and early nineteenth centuries.

With the ascendancy of the Karamanli family, Tripoli became a significant factor in the development of the trans-Saharan trade route, which provided a major link between North and West Africa. From the eighteenth century on, the route from Tripoli via Fezzan and Bilma to Lake Chad, Bornu, and Hausaland became one of the most important caravan routes of the trans-Saharan trade. Via this route came a consistent supply of Sudanese slaves who were distributed by the merchants of Tripoli to Istanbul, Damascus, Cairo. and other regions of the Muslim world.

The mercantilist spirit of Tripoli was, however, extended into illegal activities and piracy. On the Barbary Coast of North Africa the rulers of Tripoli, just like those of Morocco, Algeria, and Tunis, had for years promoted piracy and extortion. After the American Revolution, shipping fell prey to Tripoli's machinations. In May 1801, the Pasha of Tripoli not only demanded protection money from American ships, but also declared war on the United States. An exasperated Thomas Jefferson sent warships to blockade Tripoli, and a wearisome war dragged on till 1805. The plundering of American ships and the demand for tributes did not cease until 1815, when the U.S. Congress authorized a naval expedition against the Mediterranean pirates.

Tripoli became a distributing center for the leatherworks from Hausaland well known in Europe as "Morocco leather." Tripoli's exports to the Sudan consisted mainly of arms, armor, mercenary soldiers who served as bodyguards to Sudanese rulers, and Arab horses. This rich and rewarding relationship continued until political upheavals disturbed the administration of the territory. After the death of Yusuf Pasha Karamanli in 1830, the disputed succession that followed led to several years of confusion. The Ottoman government thereafter decided to reassert its direct political control over Tripoli. It also took this step to counter Muhammed Ali's ascendancy in Egypt and the French presence in Algeria.

On May 25, 1835, an Ottoman squadron of 22 vessels, together with Turkish troops, stormed the Tripoli harbor. The reigning pasha was deposed and Tripoli was taken over on behalf of the Ottoman sultan.

The occupation of Tripoli by the Ottoman Empire had important consequences. First, the trans-Saharan trade suffered gravely. It also meant the abolition of the Karamanli dynasty. The overthrow of the dynasty marked the beginning of the second Ottoman occupation of Tripoli, and this continued till 1911, when the Italians replaced the Turks as the colonial rulers. However, World War II eroded Italian control of this territory.

In 1949, the United Nations General Assembly passed a resolution proposing to combine the three provinces of Tripolitania, Cyrenaica, and Fezzan into the independent state of Libya. The nation was formally pronounced as independent on December 24, 1951, with King Idris as ruler. The king ruled an impoverished land that had a population of slightly less than a million people at independence.

In 1969, a military coup led by Colonel Moammar Gaddafi overthrew the king. Upon assuming power, Gaddafi took it upon himself not only to challenge what he regarded as Western imperialism, but also to champion the cause of those he believed were oppressed by capitalism. His suspected implications in various terrorist plots, and support of terrorist activities, has earned him international condemnation, which has had grave implications for Tripoli, culminating in the American bombing of the city in 1986.

In Tripoli, as in the other principal cities of Libya, the cult of the leader is highly venerated. Social mores are relatively relaxed, though polygamy and the restriction and subordination of women in social and political affairs remain a reality. The desire of young Libyans to partake of the good life, brought about by the country's oil wealth, has led to rural-urban drift and this has put a lot of pressure on housing and social infrastructures. In what could also be regarded as the practical manifestation of the philosophy of Jahamariya, a regime officially based on grassroots democracy, every family in Tripoli, with the personal approval of Gaddafi and the official approval of the government, has at least one AK-47 assault rifle in its possession.

OLUTAYO ADESINA

See also: **Libya.**

Further Reading

Folayan, K. *Tripoli during the Reign of Yusuf Pasha Qaramanli.* Ile-Ife, University of Ife Press, 1979.

Irwin, R. W. *The Diplomatic Relations of the United States with the Barbary Powers, 1776–1816*, Durham, N.C., 1931.

Khadduri, M., *Modern Libya: A Study in Political Development.* London, 1963.

Tuareg: Takedda and Trans-Saharan Trade

Trans-Saharan trade between North Africa and the West African Sudan predated Carthaginian and Roman settlement in North Africa. It was the introduction of the camel to the Sahara in the first centuries that made regular and extensive trade possible.

Expansion of the trans-Saharan caravan trade, with the Arab conquest of North Africa in the seventh and eighth centuries, was a major stimulus to the creation of political organization south of the Sahara. The main commodities were gold, slaves, spices, leather, and (later) ostrich feathers going north; and weapons, horses, textiles, and paper going south. From the eighth century on, North African Arabic writers make increasingly precise references to kingdoms in the Western Sudan straddling the Sahel-Saharan fringes: Takrur in the far west, on the Senegal, Ghana farther east in the open Sahel, and Gao, the nucleus of the later Songhay empire, on the Niger bend. Farther south, on the upper Niger and tributaries, an incipient kingdom of the Malinke people, the likely forerunner of the Mali empire, was mentioned in the eleventh century. These polities were to form the matrix of the western

A nineteenth-century Tuareg engraving. Hoggar, Algeria. © Das Fotoarchiv.

Sudanese politicocommercial empires until the 1590s (Curtin et al. 1984). Also significant were permanent settlements in Saharan pastoral nomadic areas such as Aoudaghost in Mauritania, Tadamakkat-Es-Suk in Mali, and Takadda-Azelik in Niger, which were vital centers of commerce, religious scholarship, and the arts. Timbuktu, Jenne, Takedda, and Gazargamu were among the centers of Islamic learning from where Islamic scholars emerged during the fourteenth to sixteenth centuries as influential leaders serving as ministers, scribes, envoys, and peacemakers. The scholars and mystics in the Mali Adrar and the Air massif established cells and hermitages there. Of diverse Shaharan origins, many came from Arab and Berber clans who had been settled in these districts for many centuries. They included the Massufa Sahhaja, who were reputedly ancestors of the Inessufa Icherifan. These latter, centered today around the town of In Gall in Niger, around Takadda (Azelik), and also in Agadez itself, formed the ruling class in the medieval copper and salt complex of Takadda. They were also citizens of the "town of scholars," Anu Samman, the ruins of which lie west of Agadez. Before the rise of Agadez to prominence, Takadda held status as a town of commerce and Islamic scholarship (Norris 1990).

These settled centers and their infrastructures, as well as the organization of caravan trade, encouraged—indeed, enabled—commerce to occur between political parties that were sometimes in armed conflict. The point of contact with the trans-Saharan trade was the desert's edge. A sedentary state near the desert would seek to control the desert ports and to control as long a section of the desert-savanna frontier as possible. With an exchange like that of gold for salt, bargaining was open, without a multiplicity of buyers and sellers to establish a market price. Salt could be monopolized because the Saharan deposits were few and easily controlled. Gold could also be monopolized in the same way, but no state south of the Sahara ever came to control the three principal gold fields in West Africa. The Saharan populations benefited from this trade by providing marketplaces in the oases, or by collecting toll and protection money from foreign traders. These revenues could be transformed into political capital, because the group that controlled the trade route could also control its neighbors. The revenues could also be invested in agricultural production in the desert-side regions.

The most important commodity in local and regional trade has been salt, which has been exchanged for millet or other foodstuffs in the south. Notable deposits deposits are found in the deserts of Mauritania and Mali, the Saharan Tenere of eastern Niger, near Fachi, and Bilma in the Kawar region. The earliest-known rock salt mine was in Idjil (present-day Mauritania), where laborers exploited the deposits from the tenth to the fifteenth centuries. Taghaza (in present-day Mali) was also in full production in the fifteenth century. After the destruction of Taghaza in the sixteenth century, Taodeni (Taghaza al Ghizlan) took its place and in the mid-twentieth century was still producing several thousand tons of salt a year.

In prosperous times, profits from salt and date sales enabled the Tuareg (who were active in the salt trade) to purchase many savanna products: indigo cloth, spices, household utensils, and tools. The large annual caravans of several thousand camels each carried salt and dates to urban commercial centers in the Sahelian periphery. Unlike other trans-Saharan business, however, Tuareg merchants reaped most of the profits from the salt trade. Originally, there were three trans-Saharan caravan routes for this trade; later, only two routes persisted in importance: the route east to Bilma and Fachi for salt and dates. Men from the Air region take leave in October or November, trade millet for salt and dates there, and then return briefly to the Air before proceeding on south to trade in millet, salt, and dates in Kano. Caravanners usually remain in the Hausa Southlands for five to seven months of the year, and bring back millet, utensils, tools, pottery, cloth, and spices. Before departure, camels were grazed in pastures to the west. One camel transported three sacks of millet from Hausaland; when trucks began crossing the Sahara, they did not replace camel caravans, but did diminish their importance, for one truck can take a load comparable to twenty camels' loads. Some camel caravanners go in person, and some send relatives or former servile persons still attached commercially to the caravanner's family. The caravanner who takes one camel is entitled to keep one-half a sack of millet; if, for example, he takes six camels, he keeps three sacks, and the owner who sent him received fifteen sacks, and so on. Formerly, nobles brought back one sack of millet for the smith/artisan client families. In the past, slaves accompanied the caravans to cook and watch over animals. Although traditionally Tuareg noble women have not gone on caravan trading expeditions (only slave women went, in the past, to cook and gather firewood), women may participate in the caravan trade indirectly, through sending camels with male relatives (Rasmussen 1998).

The Tuareg participated in the trans-Saharan trade primarily as transporters, guides, and hired security forces, and they also controlled a sizable proportion of desert-edge production destined for trans-Saharan export. Exports of ostrich feathers from the Sudan increased rapidly in the 1870s, declined again in the 1880s, and by the 1890s accounted for about half the total value of exports. The finance of the feather trade was largely in the hands of North African expatriates, most of whom came from Ghadames. Few nomads possessed the capital needed to invest directly in the trans-Saharan trading; instead, camel owners received a payment for each load they carried and left organization to North Africans who had more specialized knowledge of market conditions and more financial connections. Trade was the driving force of the Mali and Songhay kingdoms. Once new regions of commerce were discovered, particularly in the Americas, the volume and importance of trade declined. Gold, for example, could be obtained from the trans-Atlantic trade, and by the middle of the fifteenth century the adoption of the lateen sail and the stern-post rudder allowed ships to sail to the West African coast and return to Europe. There was no need to cross the desert anymore to trade with West African entities. As a result, the focus of long-distance trade shifted to the coasts of Africa and away from the Sahelian areas.

SUSAN RASMUSSEN

See also: **Sahara.**

Further Reading

Alexander, J. "The Salt Industries of West Africa." In *The Archaeology of Africa: Food, Metal and Towns,* edited by T. Shaw, P. Sinclair, B. Andah, and A. Okpoko. London: Routeledge, 1993.

Baier, Steven, and Paul Lovejoy. "The Desert-Side Economy of the Central Sudan." In *The Politics of Natural Disaster: The Case of the Sahel Drought,* edited by Michael Glantz. New York: Praeger, 1977.

Brett, Michael, and Elizabeth Fentress. *The Berbers.* Oxford: Blackwell, 1996.

Curtin, Philip, Steven Feierman, Leonard Thompson, and Jan Vansina. *African History.* London: Longman, 1984.

Meillassoux, Charles, (ed.). *The Development of Indigenous Trade and Markets in West Africa.* Oxford: Oxford University Press, 1971.

Nicolaisen, Johannes. *Ecology and Culture of the Pastoral Tuareg.* Copenhagen: Royal Museum, 1963.

Norris, H. T. *Sufi Mystics of the Niger Desert.* Oxford: Clarendon Press, 1990.

Tuareg: Traders, Raiders, and the Empires of Mali and Songhay

The Tuareg first came to prominence as nomadic stock-breeders and caravanners in the Saharan and Sahelian regions at the beginning of the fourteenth century, when trade routes to the lucrative salt, gold, ivory, and slave markets in North Africa, Europe, and the Middle East sprang up across Tuareg lands. As early as the seventh century BCE there were extensive migrations of pastoral Berbers, including the two important groups related to contemporary Tuareg, the Lemta and the Zarawa. Invasions of Beni Hilal and Beni Sulaym Arabs into Tuareg Tripolitania and Fezzan pushed

many Tuareg southward into the Aïr massif (Nicolaisen 1963, 411). The sedentary cultivators of the Sudan south of the Sahara depended on the salt of the desert; whereas the nomadic Tuareg of the Sahara had to supplement their diet with grains imported from the Sahel, those Sudanic lands immediately bordering the desert. Thus, the successful operation of the trans-Sharan trade required the cooperation of Berbers and Sudanese.

Steven Baier and Paul Lovejoy (1977) argue that the Tuareg and their neighboring societies cannot be treated in isolation, that distinctions between them are not fixed but fluid, closely related to economic specialization and interdependence, and that movement across cultural and political boundaries was frequent and necessary to the economy. The Tuareg and their neighboring peoples interacted within a large, composite society and economy in which cultural distinctions often reflected degrees of specialization. Tuareg society, constructed in a pyramid fashion with nobles on top and various levels of dependents and servile groups below, was dominated by a few aristocratic leaders who in effect acted as managers of large "firms." They invested in diverse activities, ranging from stock breeding to transportation; trade in salt, dates, and grain; manufacturing; land ownership; slave labor; finance of artisanal production; and commercial brokerage. Investments crossed cultural boundaries, however defined, so that Tuareg firms were heavily committed to the economic well-being of the whole Sudan, not just the desert edge of the nomads. Personnel for the firms was drawn from those on both sides of the Saharan-Sudanic frontier, including the Songhay, Hausa, Kanuri, Tubu, and North African peoples. Movement across the Saharan frontier was continuous and at times accelerated by droughts and economic cycles. A strong correlation existed between nomadic life and Tuareg cultural affiliation on the one hand, and sedentary life and non-Tuareg identification, on the other (Baier and Lovejoy 1977).

Climatic cycles of drought were of chief importance in the direction and extent of trading and raiding relations with neighbors. There were limits to the growth of the desert-side sector, which was always more severely affected by drought than the savanna. Since the desert sector could not grow beyond a certain point, the forging of close links with the Sudanic Sahelian savanna border zone and ever-expanding investments there were inevitable. The commercial networks uniting desert and savanna assumed a particularly critical importance in ecological disaster, serving as a safety value for migrating nomadic desert Tuareg in their escape from an environment temporarily unable to support them. Even in prosperous years, however, the desert and savanna were bound together through commerce, for the Tuareg secured a living from the harsh environment of the Sahara and Sahel through special-ization. During July and August, when some rain fell in the southern desert, herders took their animals to the areas with the best pastures. Rainfall in the Air massif of the Sahara was greater than in the surrounding countryside, so pastures there held up long enough for a large contingent of Air Tuareg, as well as others from the south and west, to make an annual trek across the arid Tenere in late October or November to Bilma and Fachi, two oases north of Bornu. Here they purchased salt and dates and sold grain.

The Tuareg sometimes raided and enslaved seden-tary people, but the dominant mode of interaction was that of cooperation and peaceful trade. Although they obtained some grain and dates through taxation of sedentary oases peoples, the Tuareg traded for well over half of their requirements. Evidence suggests that raiding may have occurred more frequently on the eastern and western fringes of the desert economy (Baier and Lovejoy 1977). For in these peripheral ar-eas, economic interaction between pastoralists and sedentary people was less intense than in the central area, so that Tuareg had less of a stake in the welfare of their western sedentary Songhay neighbors than they did in the case of more central Sudanic neighbors such as the Hausa, with whom they traded intensively on caravans, and where they resided for longer time peri-ods on those caravans. Yet the Tuareg often promoted their commercial interests by alliances with the Song-hay, whose authority during most the sixteenth century extended over the Sahara as far as the salt mines of Taghaza due to the collaboration of the Tuareg. As al-lies, the Tuareg chiefs were given daughters of the *askiya* (the ruling dynasty of the Songhai empire) in marriage and became more involved in the internal conflicts of the royal family of Songhay.

Peoples at the interface of desert and savanna there-fore often interacted in complementary and mutually beneficial exchange: in markets centers such as Agadez, Timbuktu, Gao, and Kano; in caravan trading expeditions; and in marriage alliances. There were also, however, conflicts. Political hegemony oscillated between the nomads of the desert and the kingdoms of the Sudan. Whenever the states of the Sudan controlled the southern termini of the Saharan trade, they extended their influence into the Sahara. The nomads, by their own choice, became incorporated into the hegemonic state. But when the power of the state declined and it was unable to protect trade in the desert-Sahel interface, the nomads pressed south into the Sahel. Military conquest beyond the interface was almost im-possible, however, as Sudanese troops were no match for the Tuareg in the desert, and as the camels of the nomads became ineffective as they advanced to the more humid climate in the south. Thus, there was a

delicate military balance between the Tuareg and the Songhay, as each side had the advantage in its own ecological zone.

The institutions of slavery and the slave trade were also common to almost all the states of both the Sahara and the Sudan. Tuareg raids on their neighbors were al-together different from raids on other Tuareg groups, for here new wealth could be created, particularly in slaves. Once these slaves had become integrated into Tuareg society, however, social mobility was possible and identity was negotiable and flexible (Nicolaisen 1963; Rasmussen 1997 and 1999). Within each cul-tural division, furthermore, other distinctions were rec-ognized; for example, Hausa and Songhay societies also were organized into hereditary, stratified group-ings cross-cut by occupations.

In response to military and commercial concerns in relations with their neighbors, the Sahel developed a tradition of a Sudanic imperial system from the eighth to the sixteenth centuries. Two early empires or states in the region of present-day Mali and Niger were Mali (1100–1700BCE) and Songhay (1335–1591BCE). Mali, originally a small kingdom located at the head-waters of the Upper Niger River at Kangaba, gradu-ally expanded so that at its apogee in the fourteenth century it included most of the area of modern Mali as well as Senegal, Gambia, and parts of Mauritania. Songhay developed first around Gao, but it too ulti-mately extended its reach throughout most of the whole of present-day Mali and also into what is now Niger and Burkina Faso. In the Mali Empire, Sundiata's work as a military leader and lawmaker was considerable. He created a system of alliance both among Malinke clans and between Malinke clans and others, and converted to Islam. Mansa Musa (reigning 1312–1337BCE) shaped the Islamic outlook of the empire and gave it international fame, and developed the Niger River as a waterway between Timbuktu and Jenne, from where trade was carried to the edge of the forest. The rise of Mali was also crucial to the Islamization of the western Sudan (Curtin et al. 1984). At its peak, the authority of Mali extended into the desert. Berbers of the desert paid tribute to Mali and were recruited into its armies. Before the end of the fourteenth century, however, Mali lost its political influence over the Sahara.

The Tuareg, who had earlier acknowledged the au-thority of Mali, now took advantage of Mali's weak-ness, raided Timbuktu, and then captured Walata, and much of the northern portion of the Mali domain. During the 40 years that the Tuareg ruled Timbuktu, they did not extend their authority beyond the Niger River, as they were unable to rule lands farther south in the Sahel. As Malian power shrank in the fifteenth century, Timbuktu's economic advantage remained.

Three contestants emerged, seeking to control the strategic Niger bend: the Mossi states within the bend south of Timbuktu; the riverain Songhay; and the Tuareg nomads to the north. Songhay won militarily, and the reign of Sonni Ali (r.1464–1492) marked the passage of Songhay from a small riverain state to a great empire.

The Songhay leader Sonni Ali was succeeded by his son, whose rule only lasted a few months before one of Sonni Ali's generals, who became known as Askia Mohammed, usurped the crown. He divided the state into administered provinces, instituted a tax system, and standardized weights and measures. He encouraged Islamic scholarship and conversions in Timbuktu, Jenne-jeno, and Walata. Askia Mohammed eventually took all land that had once belonged to Mali. He then attacked the Hausa states to the east, and by 1515, he successfully defeated the Tuareg and took their stronghold at Agadez in the Air region. The Tuareg gave him control over the trade routes leading to Tunis, Tripoli, and Egypt. Sonni Ali initiated the conquests of the Songhay empire from the Middle Niger region and chased the Tuareg from Timbuktu, but was unable to pursue them overland to the oasis town of Walata (in modern-day Mauritania), some 250 miles to the west.

In the first decade of the sixteenth century, Songhay extended its lateral control westward to the Senegal, thus blanketing Mali's access to the Saharan trade and establishing once more the dominance of the desert-savanna fringe, to last nearly to the end of the sixteenth century, when troops of musketeers, sometimes called *arma*, under Ahmad al-Mansur (1578–1603) and the Sa'adis or Saadian rulers of Morocco, in 1591 marched across the Sahara to establish themselves in Timbuktu. The structure was fragile, however, and crumbled within a few years of the conqueror's death in 1603.

SUSAN RASMUSSEN

See also: **Mali Empire; Songhay Empire; Timbuktu.**

Further Reading

Baier, Steven, and Paul Lovejoy "The Desert-Side Economy of the Central Sudan." In *The Politics of Natural Disaster: The Case of the Sahel Drought*, edited by Michael H. Glantz. New York: Praeger, 1977.

Claudot-Hawad, Helene. *Touareg: Portrait en fragments.* Aix-en-Provence: Edisud, 1993.

Curtin, Philip, Steven Feierman, Leonard Thompson, and Jan Vansina. *African History*. London: Longman, 1984.

Nicolaisen, Johannes. *Ecology and Culture of the Pastoral Tuareg*. Copenhagen: Royal Copenhagen Museum, 1963.

Rasmussen, Susan. *The Poetics and Politics of Tuareg Aging: Life Course and Personal Destiny in Niger*. DeKalb, Ill.: Northern Illinois University Press, 1997.

———. "The Slave Narrative in Life History and Myth, and Problems of Ethnographic Representation of the Tuareg Cultural Predicament." *Ethnohistory* 46, no. 1 (1999): 67–108.

Tuareg: Twentieth Century

Toward the end of the nineteenth century, the Tuaregs began to gradually lose control over the vast area that they occupied. Once the French had set foot in North Africa and begun to expand from Senegal into West Africa, these nomads found themselves trapped between two branches of the same alien power, which was seeking to link its possessions on either side of the continent. Determined to retain their independence and their freedom, the Tuaregs were among those who resisted colonial penetration with the greatest ferocity and tenacity.

Nevertheless, in February 1894, following the massacre of Bonnier's troops by the River Tuaregs at Takoubao, Colonel Joffre seized control of the city of Timbuktu. Farther East, Madidou, the *amenokal* of the Iwllemmedan, signed a treaty in 1896 with Lieutenant Hourst of the French Navy, who was coming down the River Niger, and Madidou's group submitted to the French authorities in 1902. Thus, by the first decade of the twentieth century the French had control of both banks of the Niger.

Meanwhile, Saharan troops from Algeria had slowly been moving southward. The city of In Salah was occupied on December 28, 1899, by the Flamand-Pein mission, while the Eu mission established itself in the oases of Tidikelt and Touat. In 1901, Lieutenant Colonel Laperrine was appointed commander of the Saharan Oases and founded the Saharan Companies. In 1902, Lieutenant Cottenest penetrated the Hoggar and defeated the Tuaregs in the Battle of Tit (May 7). Shortly after this battle, Moussa ag Amastane, the prestigious warlord of the Kel Ahaggar, submitted to the French. The Sudanese and Algerian forces combined for the first time in April 1904, when Laperrine, coming from the north, met Captain Théveniaud, who had set out from the banks of the Niger, at Timiawin. However, the occupation of the Adrar des Ifoghas did not really begin until 1908, and the frontier between Algeria and French Sudan was not officially established until 1909, with the convention of Niamey.

The Tuaregs had not been truly suppressed, however, as the French still had to combat major uprisings. One was led by Firhun, the amenokal of the Iwllemmedan, in 1916, and another, in 1917, was led by Kaocen of the Kel Air, who was allied by way of the Sanussiyya brotherhood to the Ottoman Turks and the Germans. Finally, it was only in 1920 that the city of Djanet was taken from Kel Ajjer.

Since the French never maintained more than a minimal physical presence in this enormous territory, colonial administration was conducted through the traditional chiefs, who were made responsible for gathering their subjects together for census enumeration and using that data to apportion taxes among their peoples. Similarly, justice was usually a matter of customary law. The territory saw few reforms and little development, while education remained no more than embryonic throughout the colonial era. The primary goal of the French administration was to maintain order, both internally and externally. During the first decades of colonization, its chief concerns were the struggle against the *rezzous*, coming mainly from Morocco to the south, and the settlement of internal disputes by the imposition of arbitration.

Nevertheless, colonization did have some significant effects. The Tuareg lands, which had formed the framework not only for economic activities and relationships but also for social and political bonds, were broken up by the creation of administrative frontiers across the Sahara, with profound consequences for the internal coherence of Tuareg society. Traditional relations between rulers, internal relations of dependence, and external relations of domination over the sedentary peoples of the Sudanese Sahel were all torn apart as new power relations were established. The marginalization of an entire people in relation to the new economic systems being introduced by colonization, and their continuing lack of adaptation to the new social and political arrangements of the settled population (who were being educated and opened up to influences from outside), imposed on the Tuaregs a time lag that was difficult to overcome. This was the fateful situation in which the French left them when, at the time of decolonization, a marginalized Tuareg population found itself having to face an expanding black society.

In 1963, the Tuaregs of the Adrar of the Ifoghas rebelled against the new government of Mali, but other Tuareg groups did not join in this first uprising and it was defeated, with considerable bloodshed, by the new Malian army. As a result, distrust of government spread throughout the Tuareg groups in the Sahel, while in both Mali and Niger the new regimes, having inserted themselves into the administrative and military structures inherited from the French, launched a new, African kind of colonization among the nomad populations. The Tuaregs were not integrated into the structures of these states: few Tuaregs joined the military or administrative elites. Their regions saw few development projects and were governed by the military.

This difficult situation was greatly exacerbated by the recurrent droughts of the 1970s and 1980s, which caused the disappearance of a large proportion of the livestock and the undermining of pastoral nomadism. Hundreds of thousands of Tuaregs took refuge in neighboring countries (Algeria, Mauritania, and Libya), where they were forced to settle, without resources and in precarious conditions, on the peripheries of cities in the Sahel. Large numbers of young men went to Libya, knowing that they would be able to find work there. Many of them joined the army of Colonel Moammar Gaddafi, and were used in Libya's external campaigns, notably in Lebanon and Chad. Young Tuaregs took advantage of these experiences to acquire military training, with a view to future rebellion, and organized themselves politically, forming the Front populaire de libération du Sahara arabe central (FPLSAC) in September 1980.

The FPLSAC launched its rebellion in 1990. International public opinion was aroused by the army massacres at Tchin Tabaraden in Niger, but the revolt in fact began in Mali, in June 1990, with an armed raid led by Iyad ag Ghali on the city of Menaka. This was followed by dozens of attacks on Malian military bases in the Adrar of the Ifoghas. The Malian dictator, President Moussa Traoré, was already engaged in a confrontation with democratic opponents in the south of the country, and on January 6, 1991, he signed the Tamanrasset accords with the Mouvement populaire de l'Azawad and the Front islamique arabe de l'Azawad in order to give himself a free hand there. However, these accords, which had been drawn up all too hastily, had no effect. Moussa Traoré was overthrown in Banako on March 26, 1991, while in the North of the country there were continual confrontations between the army and the various movements and fronts into which the Tuaregs were divided. These internal divisions reflected a range of complex factors: differences over the ultimate goals of the struggle, individual strategies and personal rivalries, regional and kinship divisions, internal social struggles, and rejection of the traditional structures of chieftaincies and dominant lineages.

On April 11, 1992, after several months of negotiations, the new government of Mali, the Comité transitoire de salut public, headed by Amadou Toumani Touré, succeeded in signing an agreement with the Mouvements et Fronts unifiés de l'Azawad, known as the Pacte national (National Pact), just before the inauguration of Alpha Omar Konaré, the first democratically elected president of Mali. The Pacte national provided for the integration of the rebel fighters into Malian society and gave a special status to the north, which was transformed by a significant measure of decentralization. As a result, insecurity gradually diminished, and the return of peace to Mali was symbolized by the ceremony of the Flamme de la Paix (Flame of Peace) on March 27, 1996, when the rebel movements proclaimed that they were dissolving themselves.

Events unfolded in a similar manner in Niger. After numerous attacks in the north of the country, notably in the Air massif, the Front de libération de l'Aér et de l'Azawakh signed an initial cease-fire with the state of Niger on May 15, 1992. This did not hold, and was followed by a second cease-fire in March 1993. The rebel movement broke up into several different fronts, but these were eventually successfully united in the Coordination de la résistance armée, led by Mano Dayak, who set out his political program in February 1994. Following lengthy negotiations conducted under the auspices of Burkina-Faso, France, and Algeria, a peace agreement was signed on April 24, 1995. However, the last remaining Tuareg dissidents in the Union des forces de la résistance armée, who were allied to the Toubou rebels, did not sign an accord with the government of Niger until November 28, 1997.

The Tuareg revolts did not raise the question of the national frontiers inherited from colonial times in either Mali or Niger. Instead, they demanded better political, economic, and social integration of the nomad communities that had been marginalized since decolonization. In both countries, such integration required the transformation of the Tuaregs into citizens in the fullest sense, with their identity being considered as one of the cultural components of the nation, and the genuine opening up of the Tuareg regions. By the end of the 1990s, with hundreds of Tuaregs having joined the regular armies of the two states and with the populations in the South beginning to take account of the existence of nomad societies as integral parts of their nations, it seemed that these goals were on their way to being realized.

PIERRE BOILLEY

Further Reading

Ag Yussuf, I., and R. E. Poulton. A Peace of Timbuktu: Democratic Governance, Development and African Peacemaking. New York and Geneva: UNIDIR, 1998.

Boilley, Pierre. Les Tuaregs Kel Adagh. Dépendances et révoltes, du Soudan français au Mali contemporain. Paris: Karthala, 1999.

Tubman, William V. S.: *See* Liberia: Tubman, William V. S., Life and Era of.

Tukolor Empire of al-Hajj Umar

The Tukulor empire of Al Hajj Umar (*c.*1796–1864) was formed in western Africa in the middle of the nineteenth century, against the background of major jihads (holy wars) and the beginning of colonial penetration. It was an era of political upheavals, during which some remarkable individuals, appealing both to Islam and to certain specific social groups, undertook large-scale conquests and founded political entities that amounted to states, complete with administrative structures. Umar Tal, who was to be one of these individuals, was born in 1796 or 1797 at Halvar (now in Mali) on the Senegal River. This was shortly after an initial wave of jihad had been launched in western Africa, notably under the leadership of the *almamy* (ruler) Ibrahim Sori, who founded the Islamic state of Futa Jalon; and some years before Usman dan Fodio (1754–1817) and his successor Mohammed Bello (1817–1837) established the caliphate of Sokoto farther to the East.

Umar Tal was born a member of the Tukulor people (a name derived from the Wolof *Tekkrur*) and of a family of *hal-pularen* (speakers of the Pular dialect of Fulfulde) that had links to a clerical caste. This meant that he received a form of religious instruction that was enhanced by a long journey to the Qadiriyah brotherhood's *zawiya* (monastic settlement) of Walata and, above all, to the holy places of Islam in the Arab Hejaz. In the course of this journey he passed through Bornu and Egypt, where he made contact with the literary men of the university of Al Ahzar. He stayed in Mecca for three years, residing with Muhammad al-Ghali, the Caliph of the Tijaniyah brotherhood, who made Umar a *muqaddam* (headman) within the brotherhood, and commissioned him to destroy paganism in Sudan, upon which al-Ghali made Umar the Tijaniyah caliph.

After his return from Mecca, Umar remained in Sokoto for seven years (1830–1837), forming an alliance with Mohammed Bello, who arranged for Umar to marry his daughter. It was also in Sokoto that Umar wrote his most important book, *Suyuf al Saïd*, in which he expounds his teachings. He was then received in the capital of Massina, in the home of Seku Ahmadu at Hamdalahi, and finally by the almamy of Futa Jalon. With the authorization of this ruler, he founded his own monastic settlement at Jegunko in 1840. This is where Umar wrote *Ar Rimah* (*The Spears*), the work that became the basis for the Umarian branch of the Tijaniyah brotherhood.

Al Hajj Umar's jihad began in 1852–1853 with the siege of Tamba, where the movement scored its first victory. New disciples, drawn by Umar's prestige, flocked to Dinguiraye, where he established himself next. Using the booty collected thus far, Umar reinforced his army and armed the troops with English shotguns bought in Sierra Leone. Following the conquest of the gold-mining region of Bambuk, they took Nioro, the capital of the animistic Bambara state of Kaarta, on April 11, 1855; it became the center of Umar's government. Next, Umar turned west, toward Futa Toro, but he came up against the hostility of the Qadiriyah zawiyas and, more important, of the French, based in Saint-Louis at the mouth of the Senegal, who had strengthened their position by building fortifications at points along the river. In 1856 the French Governor Louis Faidherbe responded to the threat by ordering the construction of the fort at Médine, which allowed the French to drive a wedge between Umar's two main possessions, Kaarta and Dinguiraye. Faidherbe entrusted the command to Paul Holle and made a series of agreements with local chiefs that began to change the pattern of regional alliances, undermining Al Hajj Umar's position.

Umar first repressed the Jawara revolt, which caused his movement significant losses, and then launched an attack on Médine in April 1857. His army, 15,000 strong, encircled the French fort, which was defended by a much smaller number of troops. However, the French were armed with cannons and were well protected by the steep fortifications. Following a series of unsuccessful assaults, Umar besieged the fort for two months, but in July the rising of the river waters permitted Faidherbe to send two gunboats, with several hundred men, up close to Médine. They succeeded in liberating the fort.

The caliph then launched a large-scale migration of his supporters toward the East, modeled on the Prophet Mohammed's *hejira* (journey from Mecca to Medina), in order to put some distance between his movement and the French. In October 1859, however, Faidherbe took the offensive once more, attacking and razing Gemu, Umar's main fortress in northern Senegal. With his expansion to the west blocked by the French, Al Hajj Umar moved east once again, to assault the Bambara kingdom of Segu. With this goal in mind, but also to protect himself, he entered into negotiations with Faidherbe, assuring him that he renounced all claims on Senegal.

Umar's armies then conquered the Marka cities of Nyamina and Sinsani, and in the battle of Woïtala, in September 1860, they triumphed over the forces of the Bambara empire. Thus, Umar's influence was extended over the most important cities on the Middle Niger. He reached Segu on March 9, 1860, had the Bambara ruler executed and the animist fetishes destroyed, and made the city his capital.

In 1862, Umar's jihad took a new turn as he led his armies against the caliphate of Hamdalahi in Massina, which, like his own realm, was both Fulani and Moslem. This action was criticized by many Muslims on precisely these grounds, and it was not easy to justify it. On May 17, 1862, Al Hajj Umar entered Hamdalahi in triumph, after winning a battle, but he proved to be unable to maintain control of the country. An insurrection soon broke out, and the rebels won several of their battles with Umar's armies. By the end of 1863, Hamdalahi was under siege. On February 6, 1864, Umar succeeded in escaping from the city, but the insurgents caught up with him, and he met his death on February 10, among the cliffs of Degembere, near Bandiagara.

The succession to Umar was contested, and as a result his empire did not long survive him. His nephew Tijani initiated the reconquest of the territories that had gone over to the insurgents, an undertaking that lasted for several years and resulted in the devastation of Massina. Matters were not made any easier for him by his quarrels with Umar's son Ahmadu Seku, who could not accept Tijani's claim to be Umar's successor. Meanwhile, conquests by the French as they advanced eastward reduced what was left of Umar's possessions. Nioro was conquered in 1891, and Ahmadu fled to Bandiagara, where he had himself recognized as "commander of the faithful." However, he was compelled to flee still further to the East when the French approached that city too. He died in 1897.

Nonetheless, at its peak Umar's empire, a military theocracy that took the law of the Quran as its principle of government, had succeeded in establishing an administrative structure on the Egyptian or Turkish model, with a separation of powers between civilian pashas and military beys under the authority of the spiritual leader, who was assisted by a council. However, the empire did not last long enough for this attempted structure to become stabilized, while Umar laid himself wide open to criticism by transforming jihad into a war of conquest. His endeavors, coming too late, clashed with European imperialism, which struck the fatal blow against them.

PIERRE BOILLEY

See also: **Futa Jalon; Senegal: Faidherbe, Louis and Expansion of French Senegal, 1854–1865; Sokoto Caliphate: Hausa, Fulani and Founding of; 'Uthman dan Fodio.**

Further Reading

Fortes, M., and E. E. Evans-Pritchard. *African Political Systems.* London: International African Institute and Oxford University Press, 1940.

Hiskett, M. *The Development of Islam in West Africa.* London: Longman, 1984.

Ki-Zerbo, J. *Histoire de l'Afrique noire*, Paris: Hatier, 1978.

Last, M. *The Sokoto Caliphate.* London: Longman, 1967.

Martin, B. G. *Muslim Brotherhoods in Nineteenth-century Africa.* Cambridge: Cambridge University Press, 1976.

Oloruntimehin, B. O. *The Segu Tukulor Empire.* London: Longman, 1972.

Robinson, D. *The Holy War of Umar Tall.* Oxford: Oxford University Press, 1985.

Trimingham, J. S. *A History of Islam in West Africa.* Oxford: Oxford University Press, 1962.

Tulunids: *See* Egypt: Tulunids and Ikhshidids, 850–969.

Tunis

The capital and largest city of Tunisia lies on the western bank of the Lake of Tunis, a shallow lagoon linked to the Mediterranean Sea by a narrow channel. A settlement already existed on the site in the ninth century BCE, when Phoenician merchants founded Carthage on the coast some ten miles away. The Romans destroyed

Tunis along with Carthage after their victory in the Third Punic War (146BCE). Although the revival of Tunis preceded that of Carthage itself, the city existed in the shadow of its more famous neighbor throughout the early Christian era.

The Arab invaders of the seventh century at first avoided the area around Carthage, focusing their attention on the steppes and deserts that were less well defended by the region's Byzantine rulers. In 698, Ibn Numan did capture Carthage, but ignored it in favor of Tunis, a site less susceptible to seaborne counterattacks. Tunis remained the second city (after Qayrawan) of the province the Arabs called Ifriqiya (Africa) until 1160, when the al-Muwahhid dynasty acknowledged its growing orientation toward the Mediterranean by making Tunis the capital. The Hafsid dynasty, which came to power half a century later, elevated Tunis to the rank of a first class Mediterranean urban center, creating a golden age by lavishing vast sums, generated by a flourishing maritime and trans-Saharan commerce, on the city's physical appearance and cultural atmosphere. The importance of Tunis was reflected in the increasing use of the word *Tunisia*, rather than *Ifriqiya*, to designate the whole territory.

Hafsid's deterioration in the sixteenth century exposed Tunis to a variety of external pressures. In 1534, the Muslim corsair Khair al-Din Barbarossa seized the fortress guarding the entrance to the Lake of Tunis at La Goulette, only to be ousted in the following year by the Hapsburg emperor Charles V, whose victory inaugurated a Spanish protectorate over the city and its immediate vicinity. The Turkish ruler of Algiers occupied Tunis in 1569, but failed to dislodge the La Goulette garrison. This failure enabled Spain to regain Tunis in 1573, but in the next year Ottoman troops compelled the Spaniards to relinquish both positions for the last time.

Direct Turkish rule over Tunis lasted only until 1591, when a military coup replaced Istanbul's governor with a succession of military officers, the *deys*. Their inability to exercise control beyond Tunis and a few other urban centers enabled the *beys*, soldiers responsible for the security of the countryside, to seize power. Murad Bey and his descendants made the city their headquarters, carefully cultivating links with its prominent families. Rivalries among Murad's heirs triggered a civil war in which the rulers of Algiers intervened, occupying Tunis in 1686 and again in 1694–1695. Until the middle of the seventeenth century, the city thrived on the corsair raiding that had been a mainstay of its economy since Hafsid times. When the mercantilist philosophy of the European powers prompted them to take steps to limit such activities in the latter half of the century, Tunis's entrepreneurs compensated by increasing their participation in legitimate, if not always equally remunerative, commerce.

An upsurge in corsair activity during the Napoleonic Wars led to a British naval bombardment of Tunis in 1816 that brought the maritime raids launched from the city to an end. For the remainder of the nineteenth century, European influences in Tunis became increasingly apparent as Western commercial and political institutions proliferated. European speculators also promoted infrastructural development projects that included the construction of railway and telegraph lines expediting contacts between Tunis and Europe.

Although French troops entered the city in May 1881 and established a protectorate over the country, the policy of maintaining an appearance of continuity with the precolonial regime enabled Tunis to retain its position as the country's political and economic center of gravity. In the years that followed, the city underwent considerable physical expansion, as the mile or so of marshland between its walls and the lake was reclaimed to become the European residential and commercial quarter. Neighborhoods that already existed outside the walls were gradually incorporated into the capital, but the lake on one side of the city and several dry lake beds on the other severely limited its prospects for physical expansion.

The 1994 national census placed the population of Tunis and the governorates of Ariana and Ben Arous, which comprise its modern suburbs, at just over 1.8 million, or more than a fifth of the country's total population. In 2000, the population of Tunis proper passed the one million mark. These figures indicate that the capital is the overwhelmingly dominant urban center of the country. Industrialization has concentrated in and around Tunis, where the best-educated and most highly skilled members of the workforce live. Its easy access to European markets offers another valuable asset. The potential benefits of this process have been blunted by the city's magnet effect on the unemployed and underemployed elsewhere in Tunisia. Internal migration to Tunis has placed a great strain on the city's infrastructure, particularly in terms of housing and essential public services. While less acute than in many cities of the developing world, these issues nonetheless pose a serious ongoing challenge.

The temporary relocation to Tunis of several regional political organizations raised the city's international profile in the 1980s. To protest Egypt's peace treaty with Israel, the Arab League moved its secretariat from Cairo to Tunis in 1979. Its offices remained there until Egypt was reintegrated into the Arab world, making a return to Cairo feasible in 1990. When the 1982 Israeli invasion of Lebanon drove the Palestine Liberation Organization (PLO) out of Beirut, the Tunisian government, at the urging of the United States, proposed its capital as the new site of the PLO's headquarters. In the years that followed, Tunis became the center of

Palestinian political and diplomatic activity and the home of several thousand PLO officials and their families. Pursuant to the terms of the 1993 peace treaty between the PLO and Israel, the Palestinian Authority was formed to administer territory recovered from Israeli occupation. Thereafter, a steady stream of PLO administrators, led by Yasser Arafat, left Tunis to take up residence in Palestine.

KENNETH J. PERKINS

See also: **Barbary Corsairs and the Ottoman Provinces: Algiers, Tunis, and Tripoli in the Seventeenth Century; Carthage; Maghrib: Ottoman Conquest of Algiers, Tripoli, and Tunis; Tunisia.**

Further Reading

Bachrouch, Taoufik. *Formation sociale barbaresque et pouvoir à Tunis au XVIème siècle*. Tunis: University of Tunis, 1977.

Chérif, Mohammed. "Tunis de la fin du XVIIè siècle à 1956." In *Hasab wa nasab—Parenté, alliance et patrimoine en Tunisie*, edited by Sophie Ferchiou. Paris: Centre National de la Recherche Scientifique, 1992.

Cleveland, William. "The Municipal Council of Tunis," *International Journal of Middle East Studies*. no. 9 (1978): 33–61.

Daoulatli, Abd al-Aziz. *Tunis sous les hafsides: évolution urbaine et activité architecturale*. Tunis: Institut National d'Archéologie et d'Art, 1976.

Doumerc, Bernard. "La ville et la mer: Tunis au XVème siècle." *Cahiers de Tunisie*. no. 34 (1986): 111–30.

Lancel, Serge. *Carthage: A History*. Oxford: Blackwell, 1995.

Lawless, Richard. "Social and Economic Change in North African Medinas: The Case of Tunis." In *Change and Development in the Middle East: Essays in Honor of W. B. Fischer*, edited by John I. Clarke and Howard Bowen-Jones. London: Methuen, 1981.

Lawless, Richard, and Allan Findlay. "Tunis." In *Problems and Planning in Third World Cities*, edited by M. Pacione. London: Croom Helm, 1981.

Revault, Jacques. *Palais, demeures et maisons de plaisance à Tunis et dans ses environs du XVIe au XIXe siècle*. Aix-en-Provence: Edisud, 1984.

Sebag, Paul. *Tunis au XVIIè siècle: une cité barbaresque au temps de la course*. Paris: L'Harmattan, 1989.

Woodford, Jerome S. *The City of Tunis: Evolution of an Urban System*. Wisbech, England: Middle East and North African Studies Press, 1990.

Tunisia: Ahmad Bey and Army Reform

Ahmad Bey (*r.* 1837–1855), the tenth ruler of the Husyanid dynasty, came to power shortly after the French occupation of Algeria in 1830 and the Ottoman occupation of Libya in 1835, both of which posed threats to Tunisia's autonomy. While the Ottomans envisaged an occupation of Tunisia, Ahmad Bey sought French diplomatic support to counter the Ottomans. The French supported Ahmad Bey because an alliance between Tunisia and France provided security for the

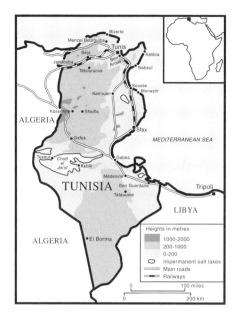

Tunisia.

eastern border of Algeria during the Algerian war of resistance between 1830 and 1848. To mark the alliance, Ahmad Bey made an official state visit to France in 1846, the first such visit made by an African head of state to Europe.

An essential part of Ahmad's policy to secure Tunisia's autonomy was the reform of the army. Husayn Bey (*r.* 1824–1835) began reform along the lines adopted by the Ottoman army in 1826, which was referred to by the Ottomans and the Tunisians as the "new order" (*nizam-i cedid*). Ahmad Bey's reforms showed the influence of Ottoman reform, yet Tunisia had been impressed by the French defeat of the Ottoman *dey* (governor) in Algiers. Thus, upon assuming power in 1837, Ahmad Bey declared himself commander in chief of the army and sought French assistance for military reform. The size of the army was rapidly expanded by conscription to 26,000. While the highest ranks in the army continued to be filled by *mamluk* (slave) recruits from Istanbul, conscription of native Tunisians had a revolutionary impact upon Tunisian society. Conscription fell upon the agrarian population. Each family was obliged to furnish one adult male between 15 and 40 years of age, whose service in the army was of indefinite, and possibly of lifelong, duration. Resistance was intense, and fines and imprisonment were imposed on entire families to ensure that conscripts were made available for service. By such brutal methods a new social order was created. Ahmad Bey's government portrayed service in the army as a religious and patriotic duty, the latter indicating a major shift in cultural attitudes toward national patriotism.

The mamluk elite was not immune from the new order, either. In 1831 French officers began instruction of troops and officers at the military base at Muhammadiya;

in 1840 a military academy at Bardo was founded. An official French military mission arrived in 1842 to assist in training the officers. The impact this had on the mamluk officers is evident in the career of Khayr al-Din. Purchased in 1839 and trained in the military academy, Khayr al-Din was afterward renowned for his dedication to modernization of the administration as well as the system of government. In this way the reform of the military was instrumental in creating a new political cadre, trained in modern technologies, administrative methods, and political thought. This was perhaps the most enduring legacy of military reform, as the army itself was decimated at the end of Ahmad Bey's reign in the Crimea and the French military mission at Bardo disbanded.

The economy was also transformed by Ahmad Bey. Although already integrated into the Middle Eastern and European economies, Tunisia in the era of Ahmad Bey increased its trade with Europe to raise revenue for military reforms. Olive oil exports became the basis of a new, state-led commercial venture by which the *bey* (governor) endeavored to monopolize revenues by demanding olive oil as payment of state taxes. However, foreign investors also demanded olive oil in return for cash advances, which ruined many merchant and agrarian notables. The agrarian economy of Tunisia was thus drawn into an expansive international economy, increasingly controlled by the developing financial institutions of Europe. Likewise, in the free market system imposed by France in the treaty of 1830, Tunisian industries could not compete with European imports. Nor could Tunisians produce for the international market without borrowing from European financiers. For instance, the previously very profitable production of the fez (*shashiyya*), which was exported to Middle Eastern markets, declined with competition from European producers. Likewise, when factories were built to produce armaments and gunpowder, European speculators profited at Tunisia's expense. Much of the armaments purchased in Europe were second-rate, in some cases dating from the late eighteenth century, while the suppliers and contractors filling government orders made huge profits. Even more ominous for Tunisia's autonomy was the proposal by the bey to secure loans from European financiers to continue the development of the military and navy, as well as the construction of a series of palaces, which were draining the treasury of its reserves of gold and silver. This trend indicated that while Tunisia had made a positive response to new circumstances by developing the export economy, the necessary reorientation to Europe had weakened the national economy relative to Europe.

Before the European loan was proposed, Ahmad Bey had sought revenue by a reorganization of tax collection, which transformed the customary relations between state and society. State involvement in agrarian society increased with the imposition of new taxes and tax collectors under a tax-farming regime, presided over by the state banker and supplier, Mahmud Ibn al-'Ayyad, and the treasurer, Mustafa Khaznadar. Tax reform increased the amount, as well as the number of different types, of taxes. New taxes were imposed on olive and palm trees, as well as on the sale of livestock, which brought nomadic pastoralists under the sway of the tax collector for the first time. Yet, the greatest burden fell upon the agrarian population. Khaznadar was committed to centralization of the regime to facilitate tax collection therefore tax-farming privileges were concentrated in the hands of his supporters, which broke the power of the hereditary, agrarian notables, such as the Jalluli family of Sfax. In Tunis new taxes were resisted when initially imposed in the 1840s. Revolts occurred in Tunis, its port La Goulette, and at Kabis. Tunis was thus exempt from the new tax regime. But this only increased the burden on the rural population, while tax-farmers, such as Ibn al-'Ayyad, made fortunes. Although a general inquest into the tax system was begun in the 1850s, the purpose was to consolidate the reformed tax system and increase state revenue.

The impulse of military reform had been straightforward. It was designed to increase the powers of the Husaynid dynasty against external threats, and to win from the Ottomans recognition of Ahmad Bey as an independent sovereign. But the methods Ahmad Bey employed to modernize the army and increase revenue had complex and multiple ramifications. The new practice of army conscription, as well as tax reform, increased the role of the state, which had a revolutionary impact upon relations between state and society. One important symbol of political and social change came in 1846, when Tunisia became the first North African state to abolish slavery, two years before slavery was abolished in French Algeria. Not only were domestic servants freed; abolition also meant an end to the practice of purchasing mamluks for military and administrative service. On the other hand, the development of the modern state brought with it commercialization of the economy, which opened the door to Europe's imperial expansion. This ultimately undercut the initial impulse of reform to strengthen Tunisia against foreign threats and secure its political independence.

JAMES WHIDDEN

See also: **Tunisia: French Protectorate, 1878–1900; Tunisia: Khayr al-Din and Constitutional and Administrative Reform, 1855–1878.**

Further Reading

Abun-Nasr, Jamil M. *A History of the Maghrib.* London: Cambridge University Press, 1971.

Anderson, Lisa. *The State and Social Transformation in Tunisia and Libya, 1830–1980.* Princeton, N.J.: Princeton University Press, 1986.

Brown, Leon C. *The Tunisia of Ahmad Bey.* Princeton, N.J.: Princeton University Press, 1974.

Micaud, Charles A., with Leon Carl Brown and Clement Henry Moore. *Tunisia: The Politics of Modernization.* London: Pall Mall Press, 1964.

Morsy, Magali. *North Africa 1800–1900: A Survey from the Nile Valley to the Atlantic.* New York: Longman, 1984.

Valensi, Lucette. *Tunisian Peasants in the Eighteenth and Nineteenth Centuries,* tranlsated by Beth Archer. New York: Columbia University Press, 1985.

Tunisia: Khayr al-Din and Constitutional and Administrative Reform, 1855–1878

At the end of the reign of Ahmad Bey in 1855, Khayr al-Din had already established his reputation as an administrative reformer. With the accession of Muhammad Bey (1855–1859) a reform law was passed in 1857, known as the "fundamental pact," that instituted judicial and political reform. Khayr al-Din participated in committees formed afterward to modernize the judiciary, particularly to reform criminal, commercial, and agricultural law, as well as sitting on a committee to draft the first Tunisian political constitution (*dustur*). The constitution of 1861 reiterated the declarations of the fundamental pact, which guaranteed equal rights for all subjects, as well as setting up a system of state tribunals which superseded the Islamic courts. In addition it created a supreme council, a new legislative body composed of 60 Tunisian notables, which limited the historic, autocratic powers of the *bey* (governor).

The reforms were supported by the French and British consuls as a means to bring about a market economy favorable to European commercial expansion. Thus, when Khayr al-Din opposed Tunisian loans from European financiers in 1862, the European consuls entered Tunisian politics on the side of the autocratic *bey* against the reformers, led by Khayr al-Din. Muhammad al-Sadiq Bey (1859–1882) and the prime minister, Mustafa Khaznadar, saw this as an opportunity to reestablish the hereditary powers of the ruler and therefore forced Khayr al-Din from office in 1862, with European support. The loan made by European financiers in 1863 imposed particularly excessive interest, which meant the bey was compelled to double the rate of the *majba* (capitation) tax. The result was the great insurrection of 1864. Initially a rural movement against the tax collector, the insurrection spurred the political reaction against the reformers. Such reaction had the support of the religious class, which

resented the imposition of state tribunals and laws above the Islamic courts. With this as a ready justification, Muhammad al-Sadiq Bey and Khaznadar suspended the constitution.

These events influenced Khayr al-Din's political thought as expressed in his political treatise, *The Surest Path to Knowledge of the Conditions of Kingdoms* (1867), which argued that modern institutions and principles of government, such as parliamentary consultation, were the equivalent of original, Islamic political concept. The treatise also appealed to the religious class to take an active role in politics, which he described as compatible with original Islamic, if not customary, practice. He also argued that there was nothing in Islamic law that impeded modern finance, technology, and science as initiated in Europe, because knowledge and truth did not recognize cultural boundaries. Beside this attempt to reformulate Islamic ideology, he made an analysis of modern imperialism when he predicted that Europe's industrial economy would make North Africa a target for European expansion.

Khayr al-Din sat as the sole Tunisian alongside British and French representatives on an international financial commission founded in 1869 after Khaznadar's corrupt regime had bankrupted the country. Designed to reorganize Tunisia's finances with European advice and supervision, the findings of the commission resulted in the dismissal of Khaznadar in 1873. In that year Khayr al-Din became the prime minister, beginning a period of administrative reform, which laid the foundations of the modern Tunisian state. His reorganization of rural administration reduced the executive authority of the provincial governors (*qa'ids*) by legally defining their revenue rights, which had been subject to abuse under Khaznadar. A law of 1860 regulating the provinces was revived, along with supplementary laws, which limited the governor's share of taxes to 10 per cent of the total, as well as making the governor responsible for delivering the tax to the state treasury. As a result, what had formerly been an aristocratic sinecure was transformed into a bureaucratic office under tight supervision. The reform also reversed a trend under Khaznadar of appointing members of his clique, normally of *mamluk* (Ottoman slave official) origin, to these lucrative provincial seats.

In accordance with his political thought, Khayr al-Din sought the support of the religious class in his administrative reform. The elementary (*kuttab*) schools and the Zaytuna university mosque were placed under state administration, while a modern university, al-Sadiqiyya, was created to instruct civil servants. The government committees convened to bring about these reforms were staffed by moderate religious scholars, who inspected the application of reforms that touched upon issues of Islamic personal status. Khayr al-Din's measures were designed to reduce the autonomy of the religious class and thereby decrease the potential for opposition, while bringing the jurisdiction of the Islamic courts under bureaucratic supervision. By incorporating the religious leadership into the bureaucracy, new opportunities were opened to native-born Tunisians; consequently, old distinctions between mamluk aristocracy and subjects, Turks and Tunisians, were broken down, engendering a more unified national elite. In sum, Khayr al-Din was responsible for the formation of Tunisia's modern, bureaucratic institutions, which was the first step toward creating a national community.

Khayr al-Din's relationship to Europe is complex. As the executive minister between 1869 and 1873, he worked with European commissioners to consolidate the national debt and reorganize Tunisia's finances. After 1873, as prime minister, his reforms increased the area under cultivation, which raised national productivity by perhaps as much as a third. Yet, by removing land from indigenous and peasant sharecropping systems to a private market economy, his agricultural reforms tended to play into larger financial interests. He became essentially an absentee landlord. Likewise, treaties with European powers ensured the relative weakness of Tunisia's economy, such as provisions that kept tariffs low—to the detriment of Tunisian commerce and industry. However, even while some of his reforms favored European interests, Khayr al-Din resisted European encroachments where he could. He limited the number of concessions made to Europeans, guarding against the kind of collusion between European financiers and Tunisian statesmen that had characterized the era of Khaznadar. As European competition for contracts and concessions grew intense in the late 1870s, Khayr al-Din resisted concessions for railways, ports, utilities, and mines, which were largely designed to enrich concessionaires and facilitate French imperial expansion in the region.

Nevertheless, Khayr al-Din's resistance to European influence brought about a coalition of interests against him in 1877, similar to those that brought about his isolation in 1862. In this case, however, it was the first step toward French colonial occupation in 1881. After his dismissal from office and exile in 1877, Khayr al-Din was forced to observe from Istanbul the spectacle of Britain, France, Italy, and Germany bargaining away Tunisia's independence at the Congress of Berlin in 1878. While the sale of his properties made him wealthy, as well as establishing a foothold for colonial speculators, his historical legacy as the founder of constitutional government, as an Islamic modernist and as

a statesmen dedicated to Tunisia's independence, has made him a hero of the Tunisian nationalist movement.

JAMES WHIDDEN

See also: **Tunisia: Ahmad Bey and Army Reform; Tunisia: French Protectorate, 1878–1900.**

Further Reading

Ganiage, Jean. *Les Origines du protectorat francais en Tunisie (1861–1881)*. Paris: Presse universitaires de France, 1959.

Green, Arnold. *The Tunisian Ulama, 1873–1915*. Leiden: E. J. Brill, 1978.

Khayr al-Din. *The Surest Path: The Political Treatise of a Nineteenth Century Statesman*, translated by L. Carl Brown. Cambridge, Mass.: Harvard University Press, 1967.

Kraiem, Mustapha. *La Tunisie precolonial: Etat, gouvernement, administration*. Tunis: Societe Tunisienne de Diffusion, 1973.

Krieken, G. S. van. *Khayr al-Din et la Tunisie*, Leiden: E. J. Brill, 1976.

Morsy, Magali *North Africa 1800–1900: A Survey from the Nile Valley to the Atlantic*. London: Longman, 1984.

Smida, Mongi. *Khereddine: Ministre reformateur 1873–1877*. Tunis: Maison Tunisienne de l'Edition, 1970.

Tunisia: French Protectorate, 1878–1900

At the Congress of Berlin in 1878, the European powers acknowledged France's special interest in Tunisia because of its political assimilation of neighboring Algeria. Three years later, raids by Tunisians into Algerian territory provided the excuse to dispatch French soldiers across the frontier. Encountering only sporadic resistance, they marched on to Tunis. With this formidable force at the doorstep of his capital, Muhammad al-Sadiq Bey had little choice but to accede to French demands, which were embodied in the Treaty of the Bardo. Although the *bey* (governor) kept his throne, he was compelled to accept a French resident minister to oversee Tunisian contacts with foreign powers. In addition, the commander of the French troops, which remained in Tunisia, took charge of the Tunisian armed forces.

Significant resistance to the French occupation developed only among the groups of central and southern Tunisia. In the coastal cities, whose prosperity was linked to the maintenance of order, even foreign rule was preferable to tribal insurrection. French and Tunisian troops crushed the rural resistance in short order, but as many as 120,000 rebels (10 per cent of the total population) escaped the clutches of the government by fleeing to Tripolitania. Since neither the bey nor the French wanted large numbers of disgruntled Tunisians beyond their reach in an adjacent territory, the government issued a general pardon that induced most of the exiles to return within a few years.

Ali Bey, who followed Muhammad al-Sadiq to the throne in 1882, signed the La Marsa Convention formally establishing a French protectorate over Tunisia in 1883. Obliged by its terms to implement administrative, judicial, and financial reforms dictated by France, the bey now lost control over many domestic matters, as well as over foreign affairs. Responsibility for applying these reforms fell to Paul Cambon, the French resident general after 1882. Cambon carefully maintained the appearance of Tunisian sovereignty while reshaping the administrative structure in order to give France complete control of the country and render the beylical government a hollow shell devoid of real power.

French officials employed various tactics to assure their dominance of the beylical government. They urged the bey to place in key posts members of the precolonial ruling elite whose personal loyalty would cause them to follow his lead in offering no opposition to French plans, while those Tunisians who had supported the 1881 rebellion or had otherwise opposed the extension of French influence were dismissed from government posts. A Frenchmen became the secretary general to the Tunisian government, an office created in 1883 to advise the prime minister and oversee and coordinate the work of the bureaucracy. French experts responsible to the secretary general and the resident general managed and staffed the government's technical services, which dealt with finances, public works, education, and agriculture. The resident general also had the power to promulgate executive decrees.

France also left the framework of local government in place, while devising similar mechanisms of control. Before the protectorate, *qaids*, or provincial governors, maintained order and collected taxes in jurisdictions defined either by tribal membership or geography. The central government appointed them and, on their recommendation, the shaykhs who constituted the next level of leadership. Because most of these men grasped the futility of resisting the French, as well as the possibility of benefiting from collaboration with them, most were able to retain their posts. To keep a close watch on developments outside the capital, however, the resident general relied on *contrôleurs civils*, French officials who closely supervised the qaids and shaykhs throughout the country, except in the extreme south. There, military officers assigned to a *service des renseignements* (intelligence service) performed the same task. Successive residents general, fearful of the soldiers' tendency toward direct rule, which belied the myth of continued Tunisian governance, strove to bring the service des renseignements under their control, finally succeeding late in the century.

Shoring up the debt-ridden Tunisian treasury headed Cambon's list of immediate priorities. In 1884, France guaranteed the Tunisian debt and abolished the International Debt Commission, a multinational agency that had overseen the country's finances since 1869. Responding to French pressures to create a more equitable tax system that would stimulate a revival in productivity and commerce and would generate additional revenues for the state, the beylical government lowered taxes, including a particularly hated personal assessment, the *majba*.

In 1883, the introduction of French courts and French law, which subsequently applied to all foreigners, induced the European powers to abandon the consular courts that had been designed to shelter their nationals from the Tunisian judiciary. The protectorate authorities made no attempt to alter the system of Muslim religious courts in which judges, or *qadis*, tried cases in accordance with Islamic law. Under the watchful eye of the French, a beylical court handling Tunisian criminal cases operated in the capital and similar courts functioned in the provinces after 1896.

Persuaded that modern education would foster harmonious Franco-Tunisian relations by bridging the gap between Arab and European cultures, as well as creating a cadre of Tunisians with skills needed in the growing government bureaucracy, the protectorate authorities created a Directorate of Public Education, headed by a Frenchman, to oversee all Tunisian schools, including religious ones. The directorate set up a unitary Franco-Arab school system for French and Tunisian pupils in which French was the medium of instruction, the curriculum replicated that of schools in metropolitan France, and French-speaking students studied Arabic as a second language. In urban areas, even in such schools, racial mixing rarely occurred, because private religious schools, both Christian and Muslim, continued to flourish. Although they met with greater success in rural areas, the Franco-Arab schools never enrolled more than a fifth of Tunisia's eligible students. At the summit of the modern education system was Sadiqi College. Highly competitive examinations regulated admission, but Sadiqi graduates were almost assured of a government position by virtue of their advanced training in modern subjects and their mastery of the increasingly important French language.

KENNETH J. PERKINS

See also: **Tunisia: Nationalism, Growth of, 1881–1938.**

Further Reading

Ganiage, Jean. *Les origines du protectorat français en Tunisie (1861–1881)*. Paris: Presses Universitaires de France, 1959.

Green, Arnold. "The Tunisian Ulama and the Establishment of the French Protectorate, 1881–1882." *Revue d'Histoire Maghrébine*. 1, no. 1 (1974): 14–25.

Macken, Richard. "Louis Machuel and Educational Reform in Tunisia during the Early Years of the French Protectorate," *Revue d'Histoire Maghrébine*, no.3 (1975): 45–55.

Mahjoubi, Ali. *L'établissement du protectorat français en Tunisie*. Tunis: Université de Tunis, 1977.

Tunisia: Immigration and Colonization, 1881–1950

European speculators had begun purchasing land around Tunis and in the Majarda Valley even before the inauguration of the French protectorate in 1881. To facilitate colonization, the protectorate government introduced voluntary land registration procedures in 1885. It also decreed that French, not Islamic, courts would adjudicate property disputes, but high fees limited the area registered. An 1886 beylical decree allowed foreigners to acquire *habus* lands (the revenues of which traditionally supported religious and charitable foundations or individual family trusts) through a system of permanent rental. When Europeans acquired property, they often charged Tunisians high rents to remain on the land or forced them into sharecropping arrangements.

Even after a decade of the protectorate, only about 1500 French, a minority of whom worked the land, lived in rural regions. Italians, who were more numerous, owned less land but more often farmed it themselves. Concern over the size of the Italian community prompted protectorate officials to take steps to attract French settlers. Tunisian state-owned lands were parceled into lots for sale at minimal cost to French citizens. To make still more land available, protectorate officials required the Habus administration to earmark at least 5,000 acres annually for purchase by French buyers. Consequently, the number of French settlers, or *colons*, on the land increased. Colon agriculture

Plowing a field, Tunisia, 1922. © SVT Bild/Das Fotoarchiv.

centered around olive cultivation, especially in the Sahel, the region along the east coast.

Colons enjoyed numerous privileges. The protectorate government expended considerable sums to develop a transportation and communication network geared to their needs. A road system expedited the movement of their produce to market. Railways linking Tunis with the Sahel and Bizerte with the Majarda Valley, both areas with large settler populations, branched off the main line between Tunis and Algeria. Another railroad served the phosphate mines in the south. Improvements to the ports of Tunis, Bizerte, and Sfax during the 1890s benefited European commercial interests. Protectorate fiscal policy also worked to colon advantage. Farmers who utilized modern equipment, which included virtually all Europeans and almost no Tunisians, enjoyed a 90 per cent tax exemption on cereals. No taxes were levied on grapes, prompting settlers (but not Tunisians) to plant vineyards. Nor did colons pay the *majba*, a personal tax. Such concessions absolved the colons of all but minor assessments, placing the brunt of the tax burden on Tunisians, who, despite widespread impoverishment, often accounted for as much as four-fifths of the protectorate's revenues. The colons exercised political power through the Consultative Conference, an advisory body to the resident general created in 1891. Since Tunisians were not permitted to sit in the Conference until 1907, it served as a vehicle for the expression and protection of colon interests.

By 1900, French citizens owned 1.25 million acres, a fourfold increase during the 20 years of the protectorate. Only about 12 per cent of the French population worked the land, however, with most French residents still living in urban areas. By World War I, French property totalled 1.75 million acres, while all other Europeans in the country owned only 300,000 acres. Even with the steady growth of the French population, Italians remained more numerous until the 1930s.

The settlers' economic impact belied their numbers. Employing modern techniques on the rich land, they produced surpluses of exportable wheat and olive oil. To guarantee a market for Tunisian products, France granted them duty-free entry after 1890. A further integration of the two economies occurred in 1898 when French goods gained duty-free entry to Tunisia. In addition to their agricultural pursuits, the colons also built factories and mills, many for processing or packaging crops, and developed mines. But their hope that exporting Tunisia's substantial phosphate reserves would correct the country's trade imbalance was shattered when the mineral's value plummeted early in the twentieth century. In the mines and factories of the protectorate, as in its fields, the French acted as managers; Italians or other Europeans provided skilled labor; and Tunisians were relegated to menial jobs at the bottom of the economic ladder.

The colons continued to prosper after World War I and an increasing number of French worked an increasing proportion of the land. As part of its effort to augment the French population, the government made easy credit available to prospective settlers and continued to promote the sale of Tunisian products in France. The high price of and steady demand for wheat in the metropole encouraged capital intensive agricultural enterprises. Many Tunisian tenant farmers and sharecroppers lost their access to land, forcing them into day labor, the exploitation of marginal tracts, or migration to the cities. In search of large profits, the colons also sowed previously uncultivated lands used for pasturage, thus endangering the livestock on which many Tunisians depended for their survival.

The depression of the 1930s hit Tunisia hard. The market value of its most important products reached its nadir in 1934 and French quotas on imported wines hurt vintners. The price of olive oil fell drastically just as new trees, planted in the postwar boom, began bearing fruit. Most assistance programs were tailored to the needs of the export-dependent colons. To avert their total ruin, the government imposed a debt moratorium in 1934 and also intervened to stabilize the price of wheat. In another attempt to shore up settler agricultural interests, the government financed the uprooting of grape vines and their replacement with potentially more profitable fruit trees. The colons' plight improved after 1936, when the Spanish Civil War and League of Nations sanctions on Italy reduced the agricultural exports of two of Tunisia's main competitors.

World War II disrupted the recovery. Following the Allied liberation of the country in 1943, the colons' prospects brightened, but a surge in nationalist sentiment during the decade after the war created an uncertain political and economic environment unattractive to new settler projects. Even so, the relatively pacific nature of the Tunisian nationalist movement (at least until the very eve of independence) meant that there was no massive settler flight, with many Europeans choosing to remain in the country even after the termination of the protectorate.

KENNETH J. PERKINS

See also: **Tunisia: French Protectorate, 1878–1900; World War I: Survey; World War II: North Africa.**

Further Reading

Baduel, Pierre-Robert. "Politique tunisienne de développement hydro-agricole (1881–1943)." In *L'homme et l'eau en Méditerranée et au Proche-Orient*, edited by Pierre Louis, Jean Metral, Françoise Metral, and Paul Sanlaville. Lyon: Presses Universitaires de Lyon, 1987.

Dougui, Nourredine. "La naissance d'une grande entreprise coloniale: la Compagnie des Phosphates et du Chemin de Fer de Gafsa." *Cahiers de Tunisie*. 30, no. 119–20 (1982): 123–164.

Harber, Charles C. "Tunisian Land Tenure in the Early Protectorate," *Muslim World*. no. 63 (1973): 307–315.

Jerad, Mustapha. "La politique fiscale du gouvernement de la Régence de Tunisie et la crise des années trente." *Revue d'Histoire Maghrébine*. 18, nos. 63–64 (1991): 289–94.

Mahjoubi, Azzam. "La crise des années trente ou le développement du sous-développement en Tunisie." In *Les mouvements politiques et sociaux dans la Tunisie des années trente*, edited by Monchef Chenoufi. Tunis: Ministère de l'Education, de l'Enseignement et de la Recherche Scientifique, 1987.

Poncet, Jean, *La Colonisation et l'agriculture européennes en Tunisie depuis 1881*. Paris: Mouton, 1962.

———. "La crise des années 30 et ses répercussions sur la colonisation française en Tunisie." *Revue Française d'Histoire d'Outre-Mer*. no. 63 (1976): 622–627.

Taieb, Jacques. "Le commerce extérieur de la Tunisie aux premiers temps de la colonisation (1881–1913)." *Revue de l'Institut des Belles Lettres Arabes*. 43, no. 145 (1980): 79–115.

Tunisia: Nationalism, Growth of, 1881–1934

The earliest calls for changes in the French protectorate came from a small group of loosely organized reformers who urged France to honor its unfulfilled pledge to introduce reforms liberalizing the beylical government and enhancing its subjects' well-being. At the same time, these Young Tunisians, as they were known, also insisted on protecting the country's Arabo-Islamic heritage. In the late 1880s they began publishing *al-Hadira*, a newspaper that stressed the need for social change within an Islamic context but also urged the selective adaptation of western ideas. In 1896, the movement organized the *Khalduniyya*, an educational society offering Arabic-language instruction in a variety of modern subjects to students in traditional Islamic institutions.

The Young Tunisians' efforts to straddle the cultural divide elicited strong criticisms. Conservative Tunisians attacked their enthusiasm for the West while European settlers, especially the poorer among them, feared the implications of the equitable relationship the Young Tunisians advocated. To disseminate accurate information about the movement's goals to French readers, Ali Bash Hamba, one of its most active members, established the newspaper *Le Tunisien* in 1907. Despite such efforts, the settlers sabotaged the expansion of modern education for Tunisians, severely restricting Tunisians' social, economic, and political opportunities and creating acute frustrations. As the Young Tunisians grew more strident, they alienated those protectorate officials who had at one time seen their movement as a potential link between the two cultures. Although their Muslim opponents accused the Young Tunisians of abandoning Islamic traditions, they demonstrated their commitment to their religious heritage in their opposition to French plans to desecrate one of Tunis's Muslim cemeteries in 1911.

Soon thereafter, the Young Tunisians clashed with the government. When a tram driven by an Italian ran down a Tunisian child, the movement launched a boycott, demanding the removal of Italian workers and a pledge that French and Tunisian workers would receive equal pay for equal work. The Young Tunisian leaders who ignored the government's order to cancel the boycott were arrested. The government's subsequent declaration of a state of emergency, which remained in effect through World War I, brought an end to the Young Tunisians' activities.

Seeking a French commitment to apply the principle of self-determination to Tunisia, a delegation composed primarily of former Young Tunisians attended the Versailles Peace Conference in 1919. Its failure prompted one of its members, Abd al-Aziz Thaalbi, to write *La Tunisie Martyre*, a work asserting that Tunisia had enjoyed a "golden age" in the nineteenth century, which the imposition of foreign rule had cut short. As evidence of Tunisia's precolonial accomplishments, Thaalbi cited the 1861 constitution, which he urged the *bey* to restore. Thaalbi soon assumed the leadership of the newly created Destour (Constitution) Party. Its program called for an elected assembly with real legislative powers; the formation of a government responsible to the assembly; elected municipal councils; equal pay for equal work; freedom of the press; and educational opportunities for all Tunisians. In 1922, the party attempted to strengthen its hand by enlisting the support of Nasir Bey, who announced he would abdicate if France ignored the Destour's demands. The ruler retreated, however, when protectorate officials made it clear they would not tolerate such threats. The Destour's attempt to co-opt the bey cost it the support of French moderates, who took the incident as a prelude to troublesome future behavior.

In 1922, France created a Grand Council with Tunisian and European sections. Reflecting political, if not demographic, realities, the council's European members outnumbered their Tunisian counterparts. Settlers elected the European representatives, but local advisory councils controlled by French officials or carefully chosen Tunisians appointed the Tunisian members. The Destour rejected this arrangement. Fearing a repetition of the harsh measures taken to muzzle critics of French policy after the 1912 tram boycott, Thaalbi fled the country in 1923. Although the repression did not materialize, the most effective subsequent opposition to the French came from labor organizations, not the party.

When European workers refused to support striking Tunisian longshoremen's demands for equal pay for equal work in 1924, the dockworkers formed their own union, the Confédération Générale des Travailleurs Tunisiens (CGTT) and sought to forge links with the Destour. But it proved difficult to align the two groups' agendas. The protectorate had economically and politically devastated the traditional Tunis bourgeoisie that formed the core of the Destour. Its adherents were interested in restoring their lost power and privileges, while the workers clamored for social justice, an issue in which few Destourians showed any interest. Moreover, party leaders, reflecting an ideal of public restraint and moderation on which the bourgeoisie prided itself, disliked any form of protest other than petition and supplication. Mass demonstrations were deemed vulgar and distasteful. Despite CGTT attempts to rally Tunisian workers behind the party, most Destourians were never comfortable with the support of the masses. A collective sense of class consciousness prevented the party from turning worker discontent to its benefit. When the French cracked down on the CGTT following a wave of strikes in 1925, the Destour distanced itself from the union to avoid being crushed along with it. In the following year, a series of decrees restricted press freedoms and criminalized a broad range of political activity, forcing the weakened and increasingly ineffectual Destour to adopt a low profile.

By the early 1930s a younger generation with more populist views and a more militant philosophy had risen to prominence in the party. Their demand that the protectorate be terminated led the authorities to threaten the party with dissolution, opening a rift in Destour ranks between its old guard, which had no stomach for a full scale confrontation with the French, and its younger militants, who believed their goals could be achieved in no other way. Many of the latter either resigned or were expelled from the party. Led by Habib Bourguiba, they formed a new party in 1934. The Neo-Destour Party completely eclipsed the older organization and its less parochial leadership subordinated class identification to opposition to foreign control, laying the basis for a far more formidable anticolonial movement.

KENNETH J. PERKINS

See also: **Tunisia: French Protectorate, 1878–1900; Tunisia: Immigration and Colonization, 1881–1950; Tunisia: Neo-Destour and Independence, 1934–1956.**

Further Reading

Ayadi, Taoufik. *Mouvement réformiste et mouvements populaires e Tunis (1906–1912).* Tunis: Université de Tunis, 1986.

Julien, Charles-André. *L'Afrique du nord en marche: nationalismes musulmanes et souveraineté français.* Paris: Julliard, 1972.

———. "Colons français et Jeunes Tunisiens (1882–1912). *Revue Française d'Histoire d'Outre-Mer*, no. 54 (1967): 87–150.

Le Tourneau, Roger. *L'Evolution politique de l'Afrique du nord musulmane, 1920–1961*. Paris: Armand Colin, 1962.

Mahjoubi, Ali. *Les origines du mouvement national en Tunisie (1904–1934)*. Tunis: Université de Tunis, 1982.

Sammut, Carmel. *L'Impérialisme capitaliste français et le nationalisme tunisien (1881–1914)*. Paris: Publisud, 1983.

Sraieb, Noureddine. *Le Collége Sadiki de Tunis, 1875–1956. Enseignement et nationalisme*. Paris: Centre National de la Recherche Scientifique, 1994.

Tlili, Béchir. *Nationalismes, socialisme et syndicalisme dans le Maghreb des années 1919–1934*. Tunis: Université de Tunis, 1984.

Tunisia: Neo-Destour and Independence, 1934–1956

In the early 1930s, Destour Party dissidents grew increasingly frustrated by their leaders' failure to win concessions from the protectorate authorities. Unlike the Tunis bourgeoisie that dominated the Destour, most of these maverick party members were Western-educated young men from middle-class families of the Sahel (the coastal region between Sousse and Sfax). Because of their Western education, which in some cases included studying at French universities, they considered themselves more politically sophisticated than the party's conservative elders. They recognized, for example, the importance of disseminating their ideas at the grassroots level and building a popular base of support, processes the elitist leadership disdained. Despite their immersion in Western culture, however, they valued Tunisia's Arab-Islamic identity, which they feared French assimilationist policies would undermine.

One of their number, Habib Bourguiba, became the editor of the party newspaper, *L'Action Tunisienne,* in 1932. His outspoken attacks on the protectorate challenged the tentative approach of the Destour leaders. When *L'Action Tunisienne* called for independence in 1933, the French ordered the dissolution of the Destour. Bourguiba's vigorous opposition to a French offer to allow the reconstitution of the Destour in return for a moderation of its policies ended in his expulsion from the party. In 1934, Bourguiba convened a meeting in Ksar Hellal at which the Neo-Destour Party was formed. Its founding members included Bourguiba's brother M'hammad, Mahmoud Matari (its first president), Tahar Sfar, and Bahri Guiga. Its principal demands were independence, an end to official colonization, the promulgation of a constitution, and a larger role for Tunisians in the political process.

The party's first goal was to create a countrywide organization. Copying the tactics of communist organizers Bourguiba had observed as a student in France, the Neo-Destour established local cells linked to a central command in a pyramidal structure. The party benefited from its ability not only to organize Destour malcontents but also to garner support in regions the older party had largely ignored. While the urban-based Destour had had little involvement with the rural population, which had been especially hard hit by the deteriorating economy of the 1930s, the Neo-Destour worked assiduously to build party cells in Tunisia's small towns and villages. Within a few months, Bourguiba and most other Neo-Destour leaders were jailed, but the party structure proved its worth by functioning in their absence. The decision of the French Popular Front government to release Bourguiba and his colleagues in 1936 paved the way for a resumption of Neo-Destour activity. In the following year, the return to Tunisia from a self-imposed exile of Abd al-Aziz Thaalbi, the Destour's founder, presented a dilemma for the Neo-Destour. Despite an initial show of respect for Thaalbi, it quickly became apparent that the Neo-Destour's secular, populist strategy precluded a permanent accommodation and party militants systematically disrupted Thaalbi's public appearances. The Neo-Destour also experienced disagreements within its own ranks. Bourguiba's insistence that the party not compromise on its demands alienated some prominent party members who wanted to endorse a reform program proposed by France in 1937. Mahmoud Matari, the party president, resigned in protest.

With the Popular Front no longer in power, the French authorities responded vehemently to renewed Neo-Destour demonstrations in 1938, imprisoning party leaders and disbanding the organization. Once again, the Neo-Destour's highly developed organization enabled it to continue to operate, albeit at a much reduced level. The outbreak of World War II again divided the party, with some of its members regarding collaboration with the Axis powers as the surest route to achieving their objectives. But Bourguiba, steeped in the traditions of liberalism, decried such an alliance. From his prison cell in France, he urged his followers to stand by that country in its confrontation with fascism.

The incarceration of the party's strongest leaders and a bid by Tunisia's monarch, Moncef Bey, to gain control of the nationalist movement rendered the Neo-Destour quiescent in the early years of World War II. Bourguiba's return to Tunisia just before its liberation by the Allies in 1943, Moncef's deposition shortly thereafter and Thaalbi's death in 1944 foreshadowed the party's resurgence. By helping labor leaders to organize a new union in 1944 and 1945, the party not only reaffirmed its links with the workers' movement but also assured itself of influence in an important group that could be employed to mobilize public opinion. As soon as the war ended, Bourguiba left Tunisia to solicit international support for the Neo-Destour.

Inside the country, party secretary general Salah Ben Yusuf continued to stress its demand, supported by virtually all politicized Tunisians, for complete and immediate independence.

Bourguiba returned in 1949. In contrast to the more fiery Ben Yusuf, he counseled a policy of negotiation and gradualism that became the Neo-Destour's official strategy for resolving conflicting French and Tunisian views on the protectorate's future. In 1951, France officially recognized the party, whose membership had been steadily increasing since the end of the war. Prominent Neo-Destour members served in Tunisian governments that sought to define a mutually acceptable formula of cosovereignty, but settler resistance to even minor concessions invariably thwarted these efforts. In early 1952, when the frustrated Neo-Destour leaders took steps to bring the Tunisian issue to the United Nations, the equally frustrated French authorities ordered their arrest, triggering a new wave of riots. After an abortive search for credible interlocutors among Tunisians unaffiliated with the Neo-Destour, the French government initiated talks that finally produced, in 1955, an accord granting internal autonomy. Party radicals, led by Ben Yusuf, denounced Bourguiba's assertion that such a status would inevitably lead to full independence. A bitter struggle between the two factions took place at the Neo-Destour Congress in October 1955. Following his victory there, Bourguiba expelled Ben Yusuf from the party, creating a monolithic political environment that endured for the next quarter of a century. When France agreed to terminate the Moroccan protectorate in 1956, Tunisian demands for similar treatment could not be denied. Full independence was granted in March 1956 and in the ensuing elections for a constituent assembly, Bourguiba loyalists within the Neo-Destour won a substantial majority.

KENNETH J. PERKINS

See also: **Tunisia: Bourguiba, Presidency of: Economic and Social Change; Tunisia: Bourguiba, Presidency of, Government and Opposition; Tunisia: French Protectorate, 1878–1900; Tunisia: Immigration and Colonization, 1881–1950; Tunisia: Nationalism, Growth of, 1881–1938.**

Further Reading

Hamza, Hassine Raouf. "Eléments pour une réflexion sur l'histoire du Mouvement national pendant l'entre-deux-guerres: la scission du Destour de mars 1934." In *Les mouvements politiques et sociaux dans la Tunisie des années trente,* edited by Monchef Chenoufi. Tunis: Ministére de l'Education, de l'Enseignement et de la Recherche Scientifique, 1987.

———. "Les émeutes du 9 avril 1938 à Tunis: Machination policière, complot nationaliste ou mouvement spontané?" In *Révolte et Société.* Paris: Histoire au Présent, 1989.

———. "Le mouvement national tunisien de 1945 à 1950: hégémonie et institutionalisation du Néo-Destour." In *La Tunisie de l'aprés- guerre.* Tunis: Institut Supérieur d'Histoire du Mouvement National, 1991.

Hassan, Abdelhamid. "Moncef Bey et le Mouvement moncefiste (1942–1948)." *Revue d'Histoire Maghrébine* 15, nos. 49–50 (1988): 25–46.

Kraiem, Mustapha. "Contribution à l'étude de l'histoire du mouvement national tunisien pendant la seconde guerre mondiale." *Revue d'Histoire Maghrébine* 5, nos. 10–11 (1978): 25–66.

———. "Le Néo-Destour: cadres, militants et implantation pendant les années trente." In *Les mouvements politiques et sociaux dans la Tunisie des années trente,* edited by Moncef Chenoufi. Tunis: Ministére de l'Education, de l'Enseignement et de la Recherche Scientifique, 1987.

Le Tourneau, Roger. *L'évolution politique de l'Afrique du nord musulmane, 1920–1961.* Paris: Armand Colin, 1962.

Tunisia: Bourguiba, Presidency of: Government and Opposition

The Tunisian Constituent Assembly deposed Amin Bey, the country's monarch, and established a republic in 1957, the year after independence. Habib Bourguiba, the popular nationalist hero, became the country's first president, a position endowed by the constitution with considerable powers. He was twice reelected without opposition and in 1974 the National Assembly made him president for life. From 1956 until 1970, Bourguiba also held the post of prime minister. In addition to these state offices, he presided over the country's only legal political party, the Neo-Destour or, as it was known after 1964, the Socialist Destour Party (PSD).

Many Tunisian political elites interpreted Bourguiba's appointment of Ahmad Ben Salah to direct the critical Planning Ministry in 1961 as the designation of a political heir. Ignoring warnings that Ben Salah's socialist agenda was breeding widespread resentment and antagonism, Bourguiba gave the minister complete and unequivocal support until he unveiled plans in 1969 to bring all private agricultural land under state control. The ensuing furor was so virulent that Bourguiba broke with his protégé, whom he accused of deliberate deception and misconduct. Ben Salah was imprisoned, but escaped and went abroad in 1973. In Europe, he formed the Mouvement d'Unité Populaire (MUP), a socialist party consisting primarily of exiled Tunisian intellectuals.

The Ben Salah affair prompted a small but growing contingent of critics within the PSD who demanded curbs on Bourguiba's extraordinary powers. They also pleaded for a liberalization of party procedures in order to break the monopoly on decision making enjoyed by the old guard that had crystallized around the chief executive. Bourguiba's recurrent bouts of ill health gave his adversaries yet another reason to urge that he loosen his grip on both the party and the government. Bourguiba weathered this storm of protest, but fully grasped its significance. With his health restored in 1974, he strengthened his control over the party by expelling his most outspoken challengers and engineering his appointment as party president for life.

This reaffirmation of personal authority made it difficult for Bourguiba to dissociate himself from unpopular policies or shield himself from public resentment over economic conditions, which in the 1970s were affecting lower- and middle-class Tunisians particularly adversely. Rather than allowing a reprise of the challenges that had followed the Ben Salah debacle, Bourguiba condoned stiff measures against protestors. The failure of the leaders of the national labor union, most of whom were veteran party activists, to impress upon the president the seriousness of workers' grievances resulted in a general strike on January 26, 1978. In attempting to formulate an appropriate response to these "Black Thursday" demonstrations, the PSD leadership split between advocates of reforms to correct social and economic ills and proponents of a vigorous crackdown on the government's critics. Ahmad Mistiri, the leader of the PSD's liberal wing, tried to establish a loyal opposition party, but hardliners thwarted his plans. Bourguiba chose to address the situation by punishing protestors while making minimal concessions that did little to alter the status quo.

An armed uprising in the southern city of Gafsa on the second anniversary of Black Thursday, however, revealed the need for a more diligent approach. Bourguiba appointed a new prime minister, Muhammad Mzali, whom he charged with opening up the political environment and strengthening the economy. Mzali initially enjoyed some success in both endeavors. Mistiri's Mouvement des Démocrates Sociales was granted recognition as a political party in 1983, as was the Tunisian Communist Party and the Mouvement d'Unité Populaire–2, a splinter group of Ben Salah's MUP. These first legal opposition parties, however, were enjoined from attacking the president personally.

Despite his increasing infirmity, Bourguiba monitored the political scene attentively and intervened at will. In January 1984, the bloodiest rioting since independence erupted when Mzali yielded to pressure from international creditors to remove subsidies from basic foodstuffs as a condition of continuing economic assistance (the so-called Bread Riots). Bourguiba's order to reinstate the subsidies severely undercut Mzali's influence. When the president suffered a heart attack later in the year, Mzali reasserted himself, but in 1986 a coterie of Bourguiba's closest associates, who resented the political pluralism Mzali had tentatively introduced, persuaded him not only to dismiss the prime minister but also to divorce his wife Wassila and break

with his son Habib, both of whom had backed Mzali. For the next year, Bourguiba endorsed the heavy-handed efforts of Prime Minister Rashid Sfar to contain the opposition, which now centered on the unions, the opposition parties, and the increasingly active Mouvement de la Tendance Islamique (MTI), which had first appeared in the 1970s.

Bourguiba despised the Islamic militants, viewing them as reactionaries and a threat to the progress Tunisia had made under his leadership. In September 1987 scores of MTI members were tried on charges of conspiring to overthrow the government. Much to Bourguiba's satisfaction, several death sentences and many lengthy prison terms were meted out. But Interior Minister Zine el-Abidine Ben Ali convinced Bourguiba to commute the death sentence of MTI leader Rashid Ghannouchi to avoid giving the movement a martyr. The president accepted this advice and promoted Ben Ali to prime minister in October. Within weeks, however, Bourguiba seemed about to reverse his decision. Attributing this and other erratic behavior to poor health and senility, Ben Ali had the president examined and on November 7, 1987, had him declared medically incapable of executing his duties. In accordance with the constitution, Ben Ali succeeded him as chief executive.

The new president assured Tunisians that Bourguiba would receive the respect to which his long public career had entitled him. Responsibility for the worst abuses of the former president's last years in office was attributed to members of his entourage, several of whom were tried and sent to prison. Nonetheless, Ben Ali set about dismantling the cult of personality that had developed around Bourguiba. The concept of a lifetime presidency was abolished, the statues of Bourguiba that were fixtures in virtually every town in the country were quietly removed, and the many thoroughfares, public buildings, and institutions named in his honor were given new designations.

KENNETH J. PERKINS

See also: **Tunisia: Ahmad Bey and Army Reform; Tunisia: Ben 'Ali, Liberalization; Tunisia: Bourguiba, Presidency of: Economic and Social Change; Tunisia: Neo-Destour and Independence, 1934–1956.**

Further Reading

Bessis, Sophie, and Souhayr Belhassen. *Bourguiba. Un si long régne (1957–1987).* Paris: Jeune Afrique, 1989.
Entelis, John. "Ideological Change and an Emerging Counter-Culture in Tunisian Politics." *Journal of Modern African Studies*, no. 12 (1974): 543–568.
Hermassi, Abdelbaki. "The Islamist Movement and November 7." In *Tunisia: The Political Economy of Reform*, edited by I. William Zartman. Boulder, Colo.: Lynne Rienner, 1991.

Hopwood, Derek. *Habib Bourguiba of Tunisia: The Tragedy of Longevity*. New York: St. Martin's Press, 1992.

Moore, Clement Henry. "Tunisia and Bourguibism: Twenty Years of Crisis." *Third World Quarterly*, no. 10 (1988): 176–190.

Ruf, Werner. "Tunisia: Contemporary Politics." In *North Africa: Contemporary Politics and Economic Development*, edited by Richard Lawless and Allan Findlay. London: Croom Helm, 1984.

Stone, Russell. "Tunisia: A Single Party System Holds Change in Abeyance." In *Political Elites in Arab North Africa*, edited by I. William Zartman. New York: Longmans, 1982.

Tessler, Mark. "Political Change and the Islamic Revival in Tunisia," *Maghreb Review*, no. 5 (1980): 8–19.

Vandewalle, Dirk. "Bourguiba, Charismatic Leadership and the Tunisian One Party System." *Middle East Journal*, no. 34 (1980): 149–159.

Tunisia: Bourguiba, Presidency of: Economic and Social Change

After Tunisian independence, Habib Bourguiba shifted his prioritics from political issues to social change and economic development. Because the success of both endeavors hinged on an educated citizenry, schooling was free. Within 20 years, three-quarters of all children at the primary level and 40 per cent of those at the secondary level were enrolled, and the national literacy rate exceeded 60 per cent.

The 1956 Personal Status Code unambiguously established Bourguiba's commitment to social change. It outlawed polygamy, imposed minimum marriage ages, required women to consent to marriages, replaced the right of a husband to divorce his wife by oral declaration with court proceedings that either spouse could instigate, ended restrictions on interfaith marriages, and revised traditional Quranic inheritance laws. Efforts were also made to discourage veiling and other forms of traditional clothing. Although such apparel never entirely disappeared, Western dress became increasingly common, especially in urban areas and among the young.

In 1962, the government introduced a Ten Year Plan based on socialist development strategies. Despite some resistance, small farms were consolidated into cooperatives that, by the end of the decade, included more than a third of Tunisia's cultivable land and employed almost a third of the rural population. The plan also promoted capital intensive industrialization projects that fostered the image of a burgeoning modern economy but created relatively few jobs. A proposal to bring all cultivable land under state control in 1969 encountered such staunch opposition that Bourguiba personally rejected it and allowed disgruntled farmers to withdraw from the cooperatives entirely, leaving the socialist experiment in disarray.

A reorganization of the economy, directed by Prime Minister Hadi Nouira ensued. In rural areas, an almost immediate increase in productivity and profits accompanied the restoration of private property. Legislation in 1972 appealed to private, particularly foreign, investors by offering tax exemptions and rebates as well as duty free import privileges, for companies manufacturing for export. Jobs were the major benefit of such ventures, since their products never reached Tunisian consumers and their owners paid few, if any, taxes. The economic liberalization sparked a dramatic growth spurt. By 1978, over 500 foreign-owned factories had been built and the industrial sector provided 20 per cent of all jobs. Gross domestic product rose steadily and national revenue doubled during the 1970s, partly because of these policies, but also because the value of petroleum exports registered a tenfold increase during the same period.

Severe socioeconomic traumas accompanied the shift from socialism to liberalism, however. Average income rose almost 4 per cent annually, but consumer prices climbed at twice that rate. Class disparities widened, with the wealthiest 20 per cent of the population accounting for over half of all expenditures and the poorest 20 per cent accounting for only one twentieth of expeditures. As unemployment hovered around 13 per cent, educated young men and women found few opportunities in the stagnant economy. In the agricultural sector, few small farmers had sufficient capital to survive in the transformed economy and the heads of many rural families migrated in search of work. Despite the official prohibition of strikes, workers frequently walked off the job. The use of force to end these protests fueled the conviction that the political leadership did not care about the problems Nouira's economic policies had created. In 1978, when the national workers' union launched the first general strike since independence, the protest degenerated into violent clashes with the police and army.

The unstable environment of the 1970s invited criticisms of the regime not only from an emerging political opposition, but also from a religiously based one. Islamist organizations asserted that Bourguiba's economic and social policies had supplanted traditional Arabo-Islamic concepts with imported ideologies that failed to meet the country's needs. Muslim leaders' dissatisfaction with Westernization and secularization had been simmering since the late 1950s, when Bourguiba had pushed through reforms undermining the religious establishment. The state had gained control over mosques and schools by seizing lands whose revenues supported these religious enterprises and assuming direct financial responsibility for them. Islamic courts were abolished and a unified national judicial system with civil, commercial, and criminal codes derived from Western models was established. The most serious opposition to these moves had erupted in 1961 when Bourguiba encouraged Tunisians to ignore the

Muslim obligation to fast during the month of Ramadan because of the decline in productivity its observance occasioned. Religious leaders strenuously objected to this suggestion, which they considered the last straw in a succession of government infringements on religion. Protest demonstrations in Kairouan were crushed, however, and critics in the religious establishment removed from their posts. The virulence of the government's response eliminated any religiously based opposition for the moment, but engendered feelings of bitterness and animosity that resurfaced in the deteriorating conditions of the 1970s.

When Nouira resigned in 1978, Bourguiba ordered his successor, Muhammad Mzali, to pursue an economic middle course between the socialism of the 1960s and the liberalism of the 1970s. Recurrent droughts, the residual impact of declining oil and phosphate sales, and an elaborate system of government subsidies on basic foodstuffs impeded development plans during the early years of Mzali's tenure. In 1983, the government reluctantly bowed to demands by the International Monetary Fund and other aid donors to withdraw some subsidies and reduce many others. The 115-per-cent rise in the price of bread and semolina, staples of the Tunisian diet, stimulated riots that paralyzed the country for almost two weeks in 1984. Unemployed workers formed the core of the demonstrators, but many factions, including the Islamists, participated in the hope that the disorders might topple the government.

The remaining years of Bourguiba's presidency were scarred by repeated confrontations with both secular and religious opposition groups, and by internal disputes within the national political leadership over how best to deal with the diverse threats to the Bourguibist tradition of secularization and Westernization. The enfeebled president's inability to provide effective leadership during this crisis resulted in his removal from office in 1987. His successor, Zine el-Abidine Ben Ali, vowed to continue Bourguiba's social and economic policies, but to loosen the political restrictions that had characterized his years in power.

KENNETH J. PERKINS

See also: **Tunisia: Neo-Destour and Independence, 1934–1956.**

Further Reading

Ennaceur, Mohamed. "La politique sociale de la Tunisie depuis l'indépendance et sa place dans le développement." In *Le développement en question*, edited by Abdelwahab Bouhdiba. Tunis: Centre d'Etudes et de Recherche Economiques et Sociales, 1990.

Ferchiou, Ridha. "The Social Pressure on Economic Development in Tunisia." In *Tunisia: The Political Economy of Reform*, edited by I. William Zartman, Boulder, Colo.: Lynne Rienner, 1991.

Findlay, Allan, "Tunisia: The Vicissitudes of Economic Development." In *North Africa: Contemporary Politics and Economic Development*, edited by Richard Lawless and Allan Findlay. London: Croom Helm, 1984.

Hermassi, Abdelbaki. "La société tunisienne au miroir islamiste." *Maghreb-Machrek*, no. 103 (1984): 39–56.

Jedidi, Mohamed. "L'expansion du tourisme en Tunisie et ses problémes." *Revue Tunisienne de Géographie*, no. 18 (1990): 149–80.

Marzouki, Ilhem. *Le mouvement des femmes en Tunisie au Xxéme siécle: féminisme et politique*. Paris: Maisonneuve et Larose, 1993.

Payne, R. M. *Language in Tunisia*. Cambridge: Heffer, 1983.

Salem, Norma. "Islam and the Politics of Identity in Tunisia," *Journal of Arab Affairs*, no. 2 (1986): 194–216.

Stone, Russell, and John Simmons. *Change in Tunisia. Studies in the Social Sciences*. Albany: State University of New York Press, 1976.

Tessler, Mark, Janet Rogers, and Daniel Schneider. "Women's Emancipation in Tunisia." In *Women in the Muslim World*, edited by Lois Beck and Nikki Keddie. Cambridge, Mass.: Harvard University Press, 1978.

Waltz, Susan. "Islamist Appeal in Tunisia." *Middle East Journal*, no. 40 (1986): 651–670.

Zussman, Mira. *Development and Disenchantment in Rural Tunisia: The Bourguiba Years*. Boulder, Colo.: Westview Press, 1992.

Tunisia: Ben 'Ali, Liberalization

Prime Minister Zine al-Abidine Ben 'Ali took power from President Habib Bourguiba in the constitutional coup of November 7, 1987. As a director of Tunisia's security forces, Ben 'Ali was well placed to stage a coup and secure his hold on power afterward. Ben 'Ali had a military education, including training in France and the United States, and was the director of military security through the troubled years between 1978 and 1987. With his succession to the presidency, Ben 'Ali implemented a policy of economic and political liberalization. The new regime thus appeared to follow the dominant trends of the late twentieth century, which favored liberal economic and political reforms. Indeed, the Tunisian administration was reformed to better manage economic change, however Ben 'Ali's government did not favor political liberalization. Instead, a new council for national security was created in November of 1987 that secured the powers of the police and military personnel in the government.

Economic liberalization had the support of Tunisian reformers as well as the International Monetary Fund and the World Bank, who supported an adjustment of the economy from socialist to liberal models. Known as the "tranquil revolution," the reforms brought about financial and trade reform, privatization, and foreign investment in new export industries. The government therefore began to withdraw from industry to concentrate instead upon social services such as welfare, education, and health. The state-operated enterprises of the Bourguiba era were dismantled, along with labor laws, price and currency controls, and import restrictions. Financial reform reduced inflation and trade reform opened foreign markets to Tunisian industry. However, the reforms also deepened Tunisia's integration into the European economy, forcing Tunisian producers to compete with foreign imports and adjust to fluctuations in European demand. Nevertheless, the new economic regime sustained economic growth and stability into the twenty-first century.

Ben 'Ali's coup was championed as a restoration of Tunisia's political institutions, which had been subverted by Bourguiba's authoritarianism. Political prisoners were released, including trade union activists and Islamists, while Bourguiba's closest associates were forced to resign from public life. Ben 'Ali used the language of democracy and reconciliation to build a broad base of support for his reforms. In a symbolic move, the word *Social*, implying socialism, was dropped altogether from the ruling Social Democratic Party, which was renamed the Constitutional Democratic Rally. The political system was reformed in the National Pact of November 1988. Conceived as a social contract of important national organizations, the pact declared a national commitment to multiparty politics, which ended the political monopoly of the ruling party. The party was also reformed to bring new, younger recruits into the party, reducing the influence of the old guard. At the same time the pact attempted to reduce the appeal of the Islamist opposition by asserting that the state was the guardian of the Arabic and Islamic character of Tunisian society. Ben 'Ali thus distanced his government from Bourguiba's uncompromising secularism, however, at the same time the pact prohibited the formation of political parties on racial, religious, or regional foundations while underlining the principle of women's emancipation, scientific advancement, and Islamic reform. In this way the pact indicated that the new government would continue the political tradition of a reformist Tunisian state, which dated to the mid-nineteenth century.

In the presidential elections of April 1989, Ben 'Ali took 99.27 per cent of the votes. In the parliamentary elections conducted at the same time, the Constitutional Democratic Rally took over 80 per cent of the votes, while the Islamist-oriented parties took 13 per cent of the votes, more than double that of the remaining secular parties. Although the elections indicated that the Islamists were the government's main opponents, the electoral system ensured that the Constitutional Democratic Rally took all of the 141 seats in the parliament. The elections disenchanted the secular and Islamic opposition. Yet the rise of the Islamic Salvation Front in Algeria rallied support for a more authoritarian style of government, particularly among Tunisia's

business and political classes, The Algerian civil war also insulated Ben 'Ali from pressures for full-scale democratization from the West. At the same time that the Algerian government clamped down on Islamists in 1990, Ben 'Ali unleashed the security apparatus upon Islamic groups in Tunisia, with the complicity of the secular opposition. In a move away from the parliamentary system, the technocratic elite that stood behind the presidency withdrew from party politics. As a result, the government became increasingly dependent upon the military and the security apparatus. Marking the new style of politics, a referendum in May 2002 amended the constitution to extend Ben Ali's tenure in office. Due to step down in 2004, Ben 'Ali may now remain in office for an additional two terms after 2004. These events demonstrated that the presidential palace was the real source of political power, not the parliament.

The economic and political adjustments of the 1980s and 1990s brought stability, while at the same time increasing class distinctions between the upper 20 per cent of the population profiting from privatization and the lower 20 per cent. Stability depended upon the affluence of the middle class. From 1988 to 1998, Tunisia's average income doubled; it was the highest in North Africa. The size of the middle class increased as a result of annual growth rates of five to six per cent through the 1990s. The living standards of the middle class improved with industrial growth, particularly in the textile industry, as well as tourism and remittances from migrant workers in Europe and the Middle East. Foreign income, along with a reformed tax system, enabled the government to improve health standards. For instance, life expectancy increased by five years in the 1990s. In addition, the government increased educational and employment opportunities for women. Significantly, the number of unmarried women in the workforce increased. Such improvements highlighted the liberal character of the regime. The lower classes also profited from the social reforms of the regime, with the construction of modern, affordable housing for the poor. Relative affluence and improved living conditions were indicators of the success of Ben 'Ali's Tunisia, which enabled the government to head off possible resistance from Islamist groups.

The social and economic accomplishments of Ben 'Ali's government were remarkable, but at the cost of political and civil freedoms. Ben 'Ali relentlessly pursued his opponents, both among Islamist groups and human rights militants. The police force was dramatically expanded and the autonomy of the legal opposition, media, and unions was reduced. Nevertheless, the political class remained united behind Ben 'Ali's combination of authoritarianism and liberal social and economic reforms. Ben 'Ali's supporters, both domestic and foreign, justified his policies by claiming that gradual social and economic development laid the foundations for more liberal political institutions. In the short term, therefore, those forces that threatened the gradual process of modernization, such as the Islamists, were suppressed. Further justification was found in the fact that international creditors and investors regarded Tunisia as one of Africa's most successful liberal economies.

JAMES WHIDDEN

See also: **Tunisia: Bourguiba, Presidency of: Economic and Social Change.**

Further Reading

Anderson, Lisa. "Political Pacts, Liberalism and Democracy: The Tunisian National Pact of 1988." *Government and Opposition* 26, no. 2 (1991): 245–260.

Murphy, Emma C. *Economic and Political Change in Tunisia: From Bourguiba to Ben Ali*. London: Macmillan, 1999.

Reudy, John (ed.). *Islamism and Secularism in North Africa*. New York: St. Martin's Press, 1994.

Vandewalle, Dirk (ed.). *North Africa:Development and Reform in a Changing Global Economy*. New York: St. Martin's Press, 1996.

Zartman, I. William (ed.). *Tunisia: The Political Economy of Reform*, Boulder, Colo.: Lynne Rienner, 1991.

Tunisia: Educational Policy and Development Since Independence

When independence from France was achieved in 1956, 25 per cent to 28 per cent of the Tunisian population was literate, thanks to the educational system set in place by the French during the Protectorate period. Tunisia's first president, Habib Bourgiba, believing it was necessary to create a strong workforce, put a strong emphasis on public education, working to make it available and free to all Tunisians. He felt that in order to modernize and instill nationalism, the population had to be well educated. One of the first steps Bourgiba took upon entering office in 1956 was to nationalize the schools. In order to extend education to the masses, in 1958, a law was passed that made public education free to all children. However, attendance was not made compulsory.

One of the primary emphases in educational policy was to expand the number of schools available to the Tunisian people. During the 1960s, in order to add more educational facilities, a double-shift school day was instituted. It has been estimated that this policy allowed about 75 per cent of children between the ages of 6 and 12 to enter the primary level of education. In the age bracket of 12 to 17 years, 40 per cent enrolled in secondary education. In these two categories, female attendance in Tunisian schools increased to 40 per cent. However, parents in rural areas tended to pull their daughters out of school before the educational cycle ended, as tradition held that education for females was not as important as for males.

With the new open enrollment policy, Tunisian schools became overcrowded and it became necessary to place a limit on how many times a child could repeat a grade. In a related move, admission standards for secondary schools were raised. This eventually brought about a decline of school enrollments during the mid-1970s. The decline in enrollment forced the government to start implementing technical training programs in agriculture and industry. This pattern of education has led to an unequal standard of education, as young people from rural lower socioeconomic areas are not able to compete with those from the urban areas and higher socioeconomic levels.

Even with the inequity in education, by the mid-1980s attendance rose in primary education (ages 6–12) to 90 per cent and to 30 per cent for those (ages 13–19) receiving secondary education. There was also an enrollment of about 6 per cent of those (ages 20–25) receiving higher education. In 1988, there were over two million children receiving primary education and over 1.3 million receiving secondary education.

At independence, Habib Bourguiba and his colleagues maintained the French system of education that had been established during the Protectorate period, as they felt it would best support their goal of secularizing the educational program and removing religion from the curriculum. Therefore, Tunisia implemented a bilingual educational program, which is still used today. All children study the Arabic language alone until the third year of primary school, when French is introduced. One-half to three-fourths of all language instruction in secondary schools is in the French language. In universities, the majority of instruction is carried out in French, especially in technological and scientific subjects. Religion, literature, and many of the humanities are today taught primarily in Arabic. French-language instruction continues today primarily due to increased interest in scientific and technological fields of study. Therefore, the original goal of eventually conducting all teaching in Arabic has not been achieved. However, the Tunisian presence in the schools has become more pronounced, as teachers themselves are predominantly Tunisian.

Higher education has been improved upon since independence. Tunisia's only university, the University of Tunis, was founded in 1958 in a merger of other existing higher educational institutions. In 1979, the Ministry of Higher Education and Scientific Research was set up to manage the university. In 1984, there were 12 faculties or divisions at the University of Tunis, and many additional affiliated institutions and schools. There are today also various other schools of higher education that confer degrees equivalent to those offered by the university. In total, there are fifty-four schools of higher education.

One of the most important schools is the National School of Administration, which specializes in graduate courses in the civil service discipline. In 1985, approximately 40,000 students were admitted to higher learning institutions. Admission to higher education programs has historically been, and still is, conducted as it was under the French Protectorate.

Originally the educational system relied on teachers from France, especially during the protectorate period and following independence. By the mid-1980s, however, the greatest number of teachers were Tunisian. On the primary level, most positions were filled by Tunisians. Out of 76,634 teachers on the secondary level, 19,000 (25 per cent) were still French in 1988. On the university level, however, the majority of the faculty was and still is foreign, being mostly French.

The success of education is in many ways illustrated through the rate of literacy. In Tunisia, literacy has increased significantly since independence. In 1980, it was estimated that the literacy rate had risen to 50 per cent for the population over the age of 15. The rising literacy reflects the push the Tunisian administration has made in not only educating men, but women as well. If broken down, the 1980 figures reflect that of that 50 per cent, 67 per cent were male, while 33 per cent were female.

BARBARA DEGORGE

Further Reading

Anderson, Lisa. *The State and Social Transformation in Tunisia and Libya*. Princeton, N.J.: Princeton University Press, 1986.

Perkins, Kenneth J. *Tunisia, Crossroads of the Islamic and European Worlds*. Boulder, Colo.: Westview Press, 1986.

Tunisia, A Country Study. Foreign Areas Study. Washington, D.C., 1988

_____ Berry, LaVerle, and Robert Rhinehart. "The Society and Its Environment."

_____ Rhinehart, Robert. "Historical Setting."

Tunisia: Modern International Relations
The Maghrib

Tunisia's constitution advocates Maghrib unity, but the divergent political and economic systems of its North African neighbors have impeded this goal. The Algerian revolution created a diplomatic dilemma for newly independent Tunisia. Tunisia attempted to maintain good relations with France, which continued to provide economic and technical assistance, but was also sympathetic to Algeria's governing FLN. Some Algerian troops operated from sanctuaries inside Tunisia and French planes bombed a border village in 1958,

causing extensive damage and civilian casualties. The bonds between Tunisia and Algeria eroded in the 1960s and 1970s as each embraced quite different economic and political philosophies. Relations improved with the advent of a more liberal leadership in Algeria in 1979, and in 1983 the two countries signed the Maghrib Fraternity and Cooperation Treaty establishing the framework for a Maghrib union. At the time, only Mauritania joined them in adhering to the accord.

Libya, with its oil-based economy and small population, provided jobs for thousands of Tunisians before Colonel Moammar Gaddafi's 1969 coup, but his regime's radicalism soon created problems. After President Habib Bourguiba refused to unify the two countries in 1974, Gaddafi began supporting the Tunisian opposition. In 1980, Libyan-backed dissidents briefly seized control of the southern city of Gafsa. When Tunisia expelled numerous Libyans on espionage charges in 1985, Gaddafi delivered a staggering blow to the country's economy by forcing 30,000 Tunisians working in Libya to return home. This rift was healed only in 1987 when Libya agreed to indemnify the deported workers. Two years later, Libya and Morocco joined the other North African states in forming the Union of the Arab Maghrib (UAM).

Despite strong Tunisian support for the UAM, it enjoyed limited success in the 1990s. This stemmed in part from serious disagreements among its members, particularly over the future of the Western Sahara, and in part from its members' need to concentrate on critical domestic issues. Some of the latter, such as the Islamist insurgency in neighboring Algeria and the United Nations ban on international air travel to and from Libya, had a significant impact on Tunisia, requiring the formulation of policies that protected the national interests while honoring regional commitments.

The Eastern Arab World

In the decade after its independence, Tunisia acknowledged the justice of the Palestinian struggle, but questioned the Arab League's confrontational approach to Israel. Like other Arabs, however, Tunisians found Israel's stunning victory in the June 1967 war humiliating. Thereafter, relations with the countries of the eastern Arab world improved dramatically. The 1970 death of Gamel Abdel Nasser, whom Bourguiba had regarded as a demagogue, further facilitated Tunisia's integration into the Arab fold. The country assumed a central role in Middle Eastern affairs in 1979, when the Arab League transferred its secretariat from Cairo to Tunis as part of a campaign to punish Egypt for making peace with Israel. The League offices remained in Tunis until 1990.

When Israel's 1982 assault on Beirut forced the Palestine Liberation Organization (PLO) to withdraw from Lebanon, it selected Tunis as its new headquarters. PLO officials remained until 1994, when successful negotiations with Israel enabled them to take up residence in Gaza. Soon afterward, Tunisia moved to normalize its own relations with Israel. Following a series of exploratory contacts, formal diplomatic links were established in 1996. Tunisian perceptions of Israel's dealings with the Palestinian authority determined the enthusiasm with which interstate ties were pursued, however, and a generally cautious atmosphere prevailed.

Tunisia's warmer relationship with the Arab East afforded opportunities for Tunisians to work in the Arabian Peninsula, thereby easing the country's unemployment problems. Economic aid from the oil producing states also increased, accounting for more than 30 per cent of all foreign assistance by the mid-1980s. Tunisia's condemnation of the dispatch of American and European military forces to Saudi Arabia following the Iraqi invasion of Kuwait in 1990 soured relations with the Persian Gulf states, however, and it was the middle of the decade before Tunisia found its way back into their good graces.

Europe

French control of the Bizerte naval base after independence complicated bilateral relations. Tunisian demonstrators blockaded the base in 1961, prompting France to deploy paratroops who captured large parts of the city, inflicting thousands of casualties on the civilians and paramilitary units defending it. Tunisia demanded an immediate evacuation, but France postponed discussions until after the Algerian War, finally ceding the base to Tunisia in 1963. Despite some bitterness over the Bizerte affair, France helped Tunisia attain associate membership in the European Economic Community in 1969. The experiment with a more open economy in the 1970s led to improved ties with other Western European countries whose economic and military aid and investments contributed significantly to Tunisia's development. In 1995, the country became the first Middle Eastern or North African state to sign an economic association agreement with the European Union.

The United States

From independence until the Gulf War, the United States was Tunisia's largest source of aid. American military assistance was expanded substantially in the late 1970s in response to Tunisian appeals for more advanced equipment to defend against neighbors, such as Libya, that were intent on meddling in its affairs. Opposition leaders argued that the acquisition of American weaponry diverted funds from important social and economic programs, but also worried that weapons ostensibly acquired to defend Tunisia's frontiers might be turned against critics of the regime. The United States terminated military aid during the 1991 Gulf War, while economic assistance dwindled to a tiny fraction of its former levels. By 1995 many economic assistance programs had been restored, although military aid remained considerably below earlier levels.

Africa

Tunisia's traditional economic and political connections with Sub-Saharan Africa deteriorated during the protectorate. Although few strong ties existed at independence, Tunisia played an active role in the founding of the Organization of African Unity (OAU) in 1963. Since his accession to office in 1987, President Zine al-Abidine Ben 'Ali has taken a particular interest in African affairs, serving as the OAU's chairperson in 1994 and speaking forcefully on behalf of African issues in international forums.

KENNETH J. PERKINS

See also: **Libya: Foreign Policy under Qaddafi.**

Further Reading

Deeb, Mary Jane, and Ellen Laipson. "Tunisian Foreign Policy: Continuity and Change under Bourguiba and Ben Ali." In *Tunisia: The Political Economy of Reform*, edited by I. William Zartman, Boulder, Colo.: Lynne Rienner, 1991.
Renaud, P. C. *La bataille de Bizerte*. Paris: L'Harmattan, 1996.

Turabi: *See* **Sudan: Turabi's Revolution, Islam, Power.**

Turco-Egyptian Sudan: *See* **Sudan: Turco-Egyptian Period, 1820–1885.**

Ture, Muhammad: *See* **Songhay Empire: Ture, Muhammad and the Askiya Dynasty.**

Tutu, Desmond (1931–)
Archbishop of the Anglican Church of South Africa

Archbishop Desmond Mpilo Tutu became the first African head of the Anglican Church of South Africa. He won the Nobel Peace Prize in 1984 for his leadership of nonviolent resistance to apartheid. For much of the 1980s, Tutu played a leading role in the internal campaign to end apartheid peacefully, at great personal risk. A churchman, not a politician, Tutu commanded moral authority, calling for a nonracial society in which race would no longer matter. His tireless Christian witness to the dilemma of a powerless black majority ruled by a powerful white minority helped end a system that Tutu said was "as evil as Nazism."

Tutu became a deacon in 1960 and was ordained an Anglican priest in 1961. He joined Father Trevor Huddleston's Mirfield Fathers and assumed their devotion to social justice. A brilliant student, he earned a scholarship to study at the University of London from 1962 to 1966, earned his M.A. there. Upon returning to South Africa he taught theology and became chaplain at Fort Hare University. He served a similar role at the National University of Lesotho at Roma from 1969 to 1972. Throughout the next three years, he acted as associate director of the Theological Education Fund for the World Council of Churches scholarship program in Bromley Kent, England.

Tutu returned to South Africa to become the first black dean of Johannesburg, in 1975. Consecrated Bishop of Lesotho in 1976, promoted to secretary general of the ecumenical South African Council of Churches in 1978, then bishop of Johannesburg in 1985, Tutu became archbishop of Cape Town in 1986. While serving as the dean of Johannesburg, he impressed the African population. Declining a huge house in a wealthy section of town, Tutu chose to live in Soweto, to be close to the common people. Weeks before the Soweto uprising, Tutu wrote an open letter to Prime Minister B. J. Vorster, warning him that racial tensions were dangerously high and volatile, a warning Vorster did not heed.

Tutu increasingly confronted the evils of apartheid and violence. Remaining committed to Christian principles of nonviolence, he openly admired and praised Mahatma Gandhi and Martin Luther King Jr. Like his heroes, Tutu advocated peaceful civil disobedience, demonstrations, and racial reconciliation. His international reputation and stature grew. He was elected secretary general of the South African Council of Churches (SACC) in 1978, a group opposed by the South African government because, while refusing to supply freedom fighters with arms, the SACC openly sent them money for food, clothing, and medicine. Tutu's support of this policy brought him under suspicion of supporting "terrorism."

Furthermore, endorsing economic sanction against South Africa was a crime, but on a trip to Denmark in 1979 Tutu called on the world to divest it-self of investments in, and impose economic sanctions against, South Africa. The South African government confiscated his passport and revoked his right to travel abroad for two years. Following recovery of his passport, he went on a world tour. Defiantly, Tutu again called for sanctions. Confiscating Tutu's passport a second time, the government then issued him a travel document stamped with the phrase "nationality undetermined." Denying Tutu citizenship was part of a larger pattern of racism. Only Tutu's international renown protected him from harm as he fought apartheid.

Tutu won the Nobel Peace Prize in 1984. He donated the $193,000 prize money to scholarships for underprivileged South Africans. The South African synod of 23 Anglican bishops appointed Tutu the first black Anglican Bishop of Johannesburg shortly thereafter. An appointment as chancellor of the University of the Western Cape in Cape Town followed in 1988. Throughout this time, racial turmoil escalated and the government banned so-called political funerals; Tutu defied this ban and preached at these events. Always an independent peacemaker, he avoided any political affiliation. Tutu demanded that churches demonstrate their social commitment. He was influential in persuading members of the U.S. Congress to adopt legislation that imposed sanctions on South Africa. The effect was profound, and gradually, apartheid unraveled. Tutu's efforts were critical in this transformation. His fierce advocacy of punitive international sanctions against apartheid helped South Africa avoid a bloodbath.

In 1995, Tutu was appointed as chair of the Truth and Reconciliation Commission, which sought to deal with grievances arising from violations of human rights during the apartheid era. The commission had the power to grant amnesty for politically motivated acts committed before May 10, 1994. While many South Africans viewed this commission as a positive step on the long road to national healing and forgiveness, critics charged it with impeding justice (especially relatives of those killed by security forces).

Tutu played an instrumental role in South Africa's decision to ban the death penalty. Encouraged by this ban, former security officers confessed to many crimes they committed. Whatever its limitations, Tutu's commission has contributed to a broader understanding of the violence that plagued apartheid-era South Africa and reinforced his role in his country's racial reconciliation and peace.

DALLAS L. BROWNE

See also: **South Africa: Antiapartheid Struggle, International; South Africa: Antiapartheid Struggle:**

Townships, the 1980s; South Africa: Transition, 1990–1994; South Africa: 1994 to the Present.

Biography

Born in Klerksdorp on October 7, 1931. Moved with family to Sophiatown, Johannesburg, in 1943. Met Father Trevor Huddleston, a mentor figure. Contracted tuberculosis as a teenager. After regaining health, earned money selling peanuts at railway stations and caddying at white golf courses. In 1953, earned a diploma from the Bantu Normal College in Pretoria, and completed a correspondence B.A. in education from the University of Johannesburg. Taught high school in Johannesburg and Krugersdorp from 1954 to 1957. Married Leah Nomalizo Shenxane in 1955. Enrolled at St. Peter's Theological College in Johannesburg. Played key role in the antiapartheid struggle. Awarded the Nobel Peace Prize in 1984. Appointed chair of the Truth and Reconciliation Commission in 1995.

Further Reading

Bunting, Brian. *The Rise of the South African Reich.* Cambridge, Massachusetts: International Defense and Aid Fund, 1986.

DuBoulay, Shirley. *Tutu: Voice of the Voiceless.* Grand Rapids, Mich.: William B. Eerdmans, 1988.

Hope, Marjorie, and James Young. *The South African Churches in a Revolutionary Situation.* Maryknoll, New York: Orbis Books, 1981.

Johns, Sheridan, and R. Hunt Davis, Jr. *Mandela, Tambo and the African National Congress: The Struggle Against Apartheid, 1948–1990.* New York: Oxford University Press, 1991.

Lodge, Tom. *Black Politics in South Africa Since 1945.* New York: Longman, 1983.

Murray, Martin. *South Africa: Time of Agony, Time of Destiny.* London: Verso, 1987.

Nolutshungu, Sam. *Changing South Africa: Political Considerations.* New York: Africana, 1982.

Tutu, Desmond. *Crying in the Wilderness: The Struggle for Justice in South Africa.* Grand Rapids, Mich.: William B. Eerdmans, 1982.

Tutu, Desmond. *Hope and Suffering.* Johannesburg: Skotaville Press, 1983.

U

Uganda: Early Nineteenth Century

The early nineteenth century saw the end of Uganda's lack of direct contact with the outside world. Yet the dramatic consequences of these new contacts would not become evident until later in the century. The first half of the nineteenth century was a period of remarkable change, but the changes were essentially endogenous, resulting from expanding systems of trade, migration, and military and administrative innovations.

In 1800, southern and western Uganda was dominated by long-established kingdoms of varying size, the populations of which were relatively stable. Much of northern and eastern Uganda, by contrast, was still experiencing large-scale immigration and ethnic consolidation. Yet these two regions were not zones of separate development. Rather, they were becoming increasingly linked by exchange, warfare, and ideology.

There was a clear trend in the nineteenth century toward consolidation of power within states by central political leaders. The control of labor, trade goods, and military might became increasingly centralized, while state structures became increasingly institutionalized. There was another, related trend, one that saw centers of local opposition to growing pressure from major kingdoms of the region develop and eventually collapse. Internal rebellions and external resistance both flowed from increasing demands for tribute and clearer acknowledgment of sovereignty from the most powerful royal governments.

The kingdoms that dominate southern and western Uganda are of considerable antiquity, but they were relatively loosely ruled until the nineteenth century. It appears that it was the growing desire of kings in this region to expand their territories and to intensify their control of the peripheries of the states that prompted the rebellions and secessions of the late eighteenth and early nineteenth centuries. The creation of Tooro and the rebellions of princes in Palwoland and eastern Buganda were not the result of the decay of ancient empires. Rather, they were primarily the consequence of local resistance to growing demands from the central royal governments. The kingdoms required ever greater collections of foodstuffs, livestock, and labor to sustain the growing chiefly and royal courts. These needs were fulfilled not only by the subjects of the particular states but also by those of nearby tributary chiefdoms. As the century wore on, the competition between the major kingdoms for regional preeminence became focused on the control of trade routes and formerly autonomous and highly productive areas such as Bugerere. As the needs of royal governments changed, so did their structures and strategies.

Kings Kamanya and Suna, who made Buganda the most powerful state in Uganda in this period, are remembered for their ferocity at home and their aggression abroad. Within Buganda, kings employed the new institution of the *bitongole*, administrative departments with military functions, to ensure that products of the royal court system dominated Buganda's peripheries. The transformation of the Ganda state appears to have been a reaction to the devastating series of princely rebellions in the late eighteenth century. The threat that rebel princes and their foreign allies posed to royal rule encouraged Buganda's leaders' drive toward despotic government and unceasing aggression against centers of opposition on the western and eastern borderlands. The power of Nkore and its kings also expanded from the late eighteenth century, partly as a result of the collapse of the kingdom of Mpororo, but also because of the creation of trained regiments (*emitwe*) under the command of officers appointed by Nkore's king. These military developments enabled an essentially pastoralist kingdom to incorporate large, densely settled agriculturalist areas to the west. The growing power of the state permitted greater exploitation of the labor of subject

Uganda.

peoples and an expansion of slave labor for agricultural production. Above all, however, it was extraction from foreign territories that underlay the growing concentration of power within Uganda's kingdoms in this period. Buganda's quest for territorial expansion was abandoned as it was realized that it was more profitable to mount raids against neighboring peoples in order to capture slaves, livestock, and other goods.

The early nineteenth century was a period of relative decline for Bunyoro, as military defeats resulted from ambitious kings overreaching themselves. Yet, while Bunyoro suffered territorial losses, it consolidated its position as the dominant economic and political power in most of northern and eastern Uganda. Bunyoro's iron and salt drew Lango and northern Busoga closely into the Lake Kyoga trading network that Bunyoro dominated. In part this was facilitated by the arrival of traders from the East African coast in Buganda in 1844, that focused Buganda's attention on the trading networks of the Victoria Nyanza basin. The expansion of agriculture among Iteso, Langi, and related peoples in this period was fostered by the importation of iron hoes and the introduction of sweet potatoes and groundnuts from Bunyoro. Nyoro mainly received sesame, ivory, and livestock in exchange.

Eastern Uganda was dominated by population movements in the early nineteenth century, just as it had been for some centuries. The most significant migrations of this period were those of the Iteso. Traditions state that the Iteso were still leaving modern Karamoja and colonizing well-watered areas to the west around Lakes Salisbury and Kioga early in the nineteenth

century. As population densities rapidly increased, pastoralist immigrants increasingly turned to cultivation, and new generations of farmers pushed farther south and west. It appears that pressure from immigrants such as the Iteso encouraged Bantu groups to move westward across the Mpologoma River, where they sought to take advantage of the opportunities available in the newer states and more open areas of northwestern Busoga.

The main development in northern Uganda was the consolidation of large ethnic groups, such as the Lugbara, Alur, and Acoli. Atkinson argues that this process was accelerated by the long drought of the 1830s that increased raiding and population movements, which in turn heightened people's identification with nearby chiefdoms and increased a sense of identification with neighboring groups. In Acoli, the early nineteenth century also saw the emergence of military confederacies and alliances, and the growing primacy of the Payira chiefdom, whose distance from Langi and Jie raiders and plentiful rainfall provided its subjects with greater security than her rivals could offer. As in the southern kingdoms, the most significant forces of change were the enlargement of scale, the concentration of power, and the increasing centrality of violence.

SHANE DOYLE

See also: **Buganda: To Nineteenth Century; Bunyoro; Kabarega and Bunyoro; Great Lakes Region.**

Further Reading

Atkinson, R. The Roots of Ethnicity: *The Origins of the Acholi of Uganda before 1800*. Philadelphia: University of Pennsylvania Press, 1994.

Cohen, D. Womunafu's Bunafu: *A Study of Authority in a Nineteenth-Century African Community*. Princeton, N.J.: Princeton University Press, 1977.

Cohen, D. *"Food Production and Food Exchange in the Precolonial Lakes Plateau Region."* In Imperialism, Colonialism and Hunger: East and Central Africa, edited by R. Rotberg, Lexington, D.C. Heath, 1983.

———. "Peoples and States of the Great Lakes Region" in General History of Africa VI: *Africa in the Nineteenth Century until the 1880s, edited by I. F. Ade Ajayi.* Oxford: Heinemann, 1989.

Cohen, D. "The Cultural Topography of a Bantu Borderland: Busoga, 1500–1850." *Journal of African History 29*, no. 1 (1988): 57–79.

Karugire, S. A History of the Kingdom of Nkore in Western Uganda to 1896. Oxford: Oxford University Press, 1971.

Kiwanuka, S. A History of Buganda from the Foundation of the Kingdom to 1900. London: Longman, 1971.

Lawrence, C. The Iteso: *Fifty Years of Change in a Nilo-Hamitic Tribe of Uganda.* London: Oxford University Press, 1957.

Nyakatura, J. Anatomy of an African Kingdom: *A History of Bunyoro-Kitara, edited by G. N. Uzoigwe.* New York: NOK, 1973.

Southall, A. *Alur Society.* Cambridge: Heffer and Sons, 1953.

Tosh, J. "The Northern Interlacustrine Region" in Pre-colonial African Trade: *Essays on Trade in Central and Eastern Africa Before 1900, edited by R. Gray and D. Birmingham.* London: Oxford University Press, 1970.

Uganda: Mwanga and Buganda, 1880s

In 1884, Mwanga succeeded his father, Mutesa, as *kabaka* (king) of Buganda. He was 18 years old, and like other young Baganda of his generation he had been a *musomi* (reader) at the Lubiri (the royal enclosure). However, he lacked that sustained commitment and intense passion with which many of his contemporaries (the *bagalagala*, or pages) had adopted the literacy introduced by the representatives of Islam and Christianity. Islam had been an important force within Buganda since the 1840s. Christianity, in its rival British Protestant and French Catholic versions, had been present since the late 1870s. Like his father, Mwanga was aware of the power and utility of these religions in the creation of a modern state. But, equally, he was acutely conscious of the interconnection between the new religions and the strategic geopolitical developments occurring in Eastern Africa and the Nile Valley, and of the dangers they posed for the independence and integrity of the Ganda state. Whereas in Mutesa's time those dangers had seemed largely to come from an Islamic imperialism emanating from Egypt, by the time of Mwanga's accession it was increasingly European activity on the East African coast which appeared threatening. Mwanga was consequently suspicious of the Christian missionaries at his court, and of the increasing number of converts who flocked to the mission compounds for literacy and catechism classes and baptism. In 1885 the anticipated arrival of the first Anglican bishop, James Hannington, was treated with great suspicion, as possibly the first step in the European takeover of the interior of East Africa (the Germans were already attempting to assert control at the coast). Hannington's insistence on approaching Buganda by a new eastern route traditionally associated with invaders gave plausibility to these fears. The execution of the bishop on September 29, 1885, just before he crossed the Nile to enter Buganda, confirmed the estimate of missionaries that Mwanga was a cruel, unpredictable tyrant. But Hannington's death did not stem from the whim of Mwanga alone, and was a reasoned act of state taken on the advice of senior statesmen in Buganda. In 1886, reprisals were taken against the Christian communities within Buganda, with the massacre of nearly 50 Catholic and Protestant Christians at the traditional execution site of Namugongo (where ten years earlier young Muslim converts had been killed by Mutesa), and an unknown number of victims in other parts of the country. One of the subsidiary causes triggering this persecution

was the desire of the Christian communities to protect their younger members from the homosexual attentions of the Kabaka, but homosexuality was not the only or the main cause of the massacres, which was primarily related to a need for the young and untried king to assert his authority, and, internationally, a fear that the Christians were acting as agents of the invaders. The massacres were limited in duration and scope, and many Christians were protected by the chiefs. However much they shared Mwanga's political fears, the chiefs also valued the Christian converts as their own children and kinsfolk.

The martyrs went to their deaths bravely, expressing both the traditional stoicism in the face of death that Baganda had long been expected to endure, but also with confidence in a universal God who was above all earthly rulers, and a belief in a bodily resurrection. One of the consequences of the victimization of the Christian groups was a growing realization of the need for self-protection through the procurement of arms. The next few years saw the emergence of Muslim, Protestant, and Catholic regiments whose access to weapons allowed them to assert themselves and to be accused of arrogance (*ekyeejo*). Mwanga, understanding the futility of attempting to inhibit these powerful armed factions and his own vulnerability in the absence of fire power, endeavored to co-opt the religious leaders, promoting his Muslim and Christian age-mates into positions of power. Mwanga soon found that he was unable to control the forces so unleashed, and in 1888 an alliance of all the religious groups resulted in Mwanga's deposition; he fled south by boat and found refuge among the very missionaries whom he had previously despised.

The coalition soon broke up, with the Christians suspicious of the Muslim's attempts to set up a state organized strictly along Muslim lines, with a brother of Mwanga as kabaka. The Christians felt compelled to make overtures to the exiled Mwanga, agreeing to restore him as titular kabaka, if he supported their endeavors. In an alliance with traditionalist forces, the Christians were able to recapture the state from the Muslims, whose army fled and whose kabaka, Kalema, subsequently died of smallpox. The Christians were aided in their consolidation of power by the Imperial British East Africa Company, led by Captain Frederick Lugard, who arrived at the capital in December 1890, to begin a process that would eventually wrest sovereignty from the Kabaka and put it in the hands of the British. Lugard also intervened in internal disputes between Catholics and Protestants. These had broken out soon after the Christian takeover, eventually supporting the numerically weaker Protestant faction led by Apolo Kaggwa in 1892. Lugard's arrival by the route pioneered by Bishop Hannington, indicates that

Mwanga's fears had not been illusory. The close connection of religion, power, and violence was an embarrassing one for the missionaries, as were the theological disagreements between the missionary societies. For the Baganda converts, the debates between Alexander Mackay of the Anglican Church Missionary Society and Fr. Simeon Lourdel of the French White Fathers, and the vigor with which they defended their respective versions of their faith was intellectually exciting, and replicated in the self-definition and identity of the new religious communities within Buganda. The extension of religious conflict into the political arena was, to a certain extent, a continuation of the traditional factionalism that was a strong feature of life at court. But the new situation created by the advent of colonialism helped to turn evanescent factions into more persistent and clearly defined ideological and political parties. Mwanga, who had hoped to control and use these groups, found himself the victim. Under the new regime he had little alternative but to identify himself with the Protestant faction. But it was only after he was deposed in 1897, after a failed attempt to throw off British rule, that he was baptized, some time after his infant son and successor, Daudi Cwa, had been baptized by the Protestants. Mwanga died in 1904, still in exile in the Seychelles.

KEVIN WARD

See also: **Buganda: To Nineteenth Century; Missionary Enterprise: Precolonial; Religion, Colonial Africa: Conversion to World Religions.**

Further Reading

Ashe, Robert. *Chronicles of Uganda*, 1894. Reprint, Cass, 1971.
————. *Two Kings of Uganda*, 1889. Reprint, Cass, 1970.
Kiwanuka, Semakula. *A History of Buganda: From the Foundation of the Kingdom to 1900*. London: Longmans, 1971.
————. *The Kings of Buganda*. Nairobi: East African Publishing, 1971. The book is a translation of Apolo Kaggwa's *Ekitabu kya Basekabaka be Buganda*.
Ray, Benjamin. *Myth, Ritual, and Kingship in Buganda*. Oxford: Oxford University Press, 1991.
Twaddle, Michael. *Kakungulu and the Creation of Uganda*. London: James Currey, 1993.
Wright, M. *Buganda in the Heroic Age*. Nairobi, 1971.

Uganda: Colonization, Resistance, Uganda Agreement, 1890–1900

The Partition of East Africa, where Uganda is located, was carried out by two European powers, Britain and Germany. The British, who had occupied Egypt in 1882, feared that the Germans, who were advancing inland from Tanganyika (Tanzania) would occupy Uganda, the source of Nile River. The British initiated negotiations with the Germans, which culminated in the signing of the Anglo-German Agreements of July 1890. This agreement left Uganda in the British sphere of influence in East Africa; the British colonization of Uganda therefore started that same year. Apart from the desire to protect the source of the Nile, the British colonized Uganda because of its agricultural potential as a site where raw cotton needed by the British textile mills would be produced. The British also thought that Uganda would serve as a market for manufactured goods from Britain.

The first British colonial administrator to go to Uganda was Captain Frederick Lugard. Lugard went to Uganda in 1890 as a representative of the Imperial British East African Company. Formed in September 1888 under the chairmanship of William Mackinnon, the company was given permission by the British government to administer Uganda on behalf of Britain. Due to financial constraints and administrative problems, however, the company relinquished its control over Uganda in 1893 and henceforth the British government assumed direct control.

The reaction of the people of Uganda to the imposition of British colonial rule was twofold. Some African rulers collaborated with the British, while others resisted. For example, King Mwanga of Buganda, who had succeeded his father Mutesa I in October 1884, initially collaborated with the British. He gave Buganda warriors to Captain Lugard to help the British fight Kabarega, the King of Bunyoro in western Uganda, who was the traditional enemy of Buganda. Mwanga and the British signed the 1894 Protectorate Agreement, which formally established British rule over Buganda. Mwanga thought that by allying with the British he would be able to preserve his position as King of Buganda and secure the military support of the British to fight Bunyoro.

However, when the British colonial rulers stopped him from receiving tribute from Busoga in eastern Uganda, enacted a law to end his prerogative as the only giver of land to his subjects, and continued to erode his powers, Mwanga led an armed resistance against the British in 1897. The British colonial forces defeated Mwanga at Kabuwoko Hill, in southwestern Buganda. Mwanga then escaped to Tanganyika where he was captured by the Germans and imprisoned at Mwanza. In 1898 Mwanga escaped from prison, returned to Uganda, and went to Lango in northern Uganda and joined Kabarega in a joint guerrilla war against the British. These two resisters were finally captured by the British Colonial forces in 1899 and deported to the Seychelles Islands in the Indian Ocean, where Mwanga died.

After Mwanga's deportation to the Seychelles in 1899, his infant son Daudi Chwa was crowned King of Buganda. Since Chwa was a minor, three leading Buganda chiefs were made his regents. Sir Harry Johnston, who arrived in Uganda in 1900 as the new British commissioner, signed an agreement on March 10, 1900, with a group of Buganda chiefs led by the three regents.

Although the agreement was referred to as the Uganda Agreement, it only dealt with issues concerning Buganda. The agreement defined the position of Buganda in the Uganda protectorate; the Kingdom of Buganda became a mere province within Uganda, and Buganda thus lost its original political status as an independent kingdom. The agreement reduced the personal authority of the King of Buganda; henceforth he became an agent of the British Colonial administration. However, the King of Buganda was given permission to appoint his subordinate chiefs. The agreement also recognized the Lukiiko (Buganda's traditional parliament) as Buganda's legislature and allowed it to continue to operate.

The 1900 agreement further reduced the King of Buganda's powers by preventing him from receiving tribute from communities outside Buganda. This provision particularly affected the tribute that the king had hitherto received from some parts of Busoga in eastern Uganda where he had territorial claims, thus reducing the king's revenue.

The new land tenure system that was introduced by the 1900 agreement also eroded the King of Buganda's powers. Before the imposition of British Colonial rule over Uganda, all land in Buganda belonged to the king (*kabaka*), who had the power to distribute it to chiefs for the duration of their office. However, according to the Uganda Agreement of 1900, about 9003 square miles of land in Buganda were to be allocated to the king and about a thousand chiefs of Buganda on the basis of freehold. This freehold came to be known as *Mailo* land, a Luganda version of the English word *mile*, because the plots of land that were distributed were measured in square miles.

The 1900 agreement prolonged the enmity between Bunyoro and Buganda, as it confirmed Buganda's right to control all the territories that it had acquired from Bunyoro through the wars of the second half of the nineteenth century. Bunyoro became bitter and struggled to regain what it termed the "lost countries."

SEWANYANA SENKOMAGO

See also: **Johnston, Harry H.; Kagwa, Apolo; Kakungulu and the Creation of Uganda; Nyabingi Cult and Resistance.**

Further Reading

Karugaire, S. R. *A Political History of Uganda.* Nairobi: Heinenmann 1980.

Kiwanuka, M. S. M. *A History of Buganda.* Longman, 1971.
Lugard, F. D. *The Rise of Our East African Empire*, vol. 1. London: Longman, 1893.
Ogot, B. A. and I. Kieran (eds.). *Zamani: A Survey of.* Nairobi: East African Publishing, 1972.
Oliver, R. A. *Sir Harry Johnston and the Scramble for Africa.* London: Longman, 1957.
Were, G. *East Africa through a Thousand Years.* Nairobi: Longman, 1980.

Uganda: Colonial Period: Administration, Economy

Administration

Uganda was declared a British protectorate in 1894. From then on, the British embarked on the task of establishing effective control of the area, starting from Buganda. From 1895 to 1896, the protectorate was extended through the signing of agreements with Busoga, Toro, Bunyoro, and Ankole. It was not until 1900 that an agreement was signed with the kingdom of Buganda to regularize its affairs. In 1902, the Uganda Order in Council brought Buganda, Busoga, Toro, Bunyoro, Ankole and Bukedi (which included Teso, Bugisu, and Bukedi) under British rule. Kigezi was added to the protectorate in 1911, Acholi and Karamoja in 1913, and West Nile in 1914. By 1918, the British Protectorate of Uganda had attained its present shape and limits.

The country was divided into the Northern, Eastern, and Western Provinces and Buganda. Buganda was the only kingdom that was given provincial status; its provinces were divided up into seventeen districts. Except for West Nile, Kigezi, and Bukedi Districts, each of the districts was inhabited by a single ethnic group. At the local government level, the colonial administrators decided to use the Buganda model of

"The Prince of Wales inspecting the King's Royal African Rifles" (original caption), 1930s. © SVT Bild/Das Fotoarchiv.

local government whereby the king ruled the counties through chiefs. This was not only cheap but also akin to the "indirect rule" system, which was widely used by the British in Africa. Initially, chiefsfrom Buganda were posted to most districts but the move proved unpopular and district chiefs were replaced with local ones. In the segmentary and quasi-segmentary societies, the administrators created artificial chiefs or gave the existing chiefs powers they did not previously possess. Their position was enhanced by the 1919 Native Authority Ordinance, which gave them wide-ranging powers to enable them to keep law and order. Although the 1900 Uganda Agreement had greatly reduced the powers of the *kabaka* (king) and greatly altered the relationship between him and his chiefs, in theory he continued to rule his people through the chiefs. Compared to the other provinces, Buganda enjoyed a special relationship with the colonial government.

After World War II, the imperial government decided on the policy of democratizing the organs of local governments and to give them wider responsibilities. In 1949, the Local Government Ordinance was passed. It gave corporate powers and responsibilities to the district councils of those areas where no agreements had been signed. The governor was empowered to establish a district or provincial council in any part of the protectorate. Although the people were now empowered to elect their representatives to the district councils, these parliaments fostered ethnic particularism. The impact of this was the nurturing of ethnic nationalism with untold consequences for the future.

In 1921, a legislative council was set up to be the parliament of Uganda, but it was not until 1946 that the first Africans were added to it. Because of the decolonization process that had began following the war, rapid steps were taken to strengthen the legislative council, and by 1956 the number of African representatives had grown to 30. However, these attempts at democratizing local government institutions and creating a national parliament were overtaken by the activities of the political parties that were formed in the 1950s.

Economy

In 1895, just one year after Uganda became a British protectorate, the colonial government approved the construction of a railway to link Uganda and the coast. The rail line, which was completed in 1901, was intended to ease communication as well as administrative difficulties. It would enable Ugandans to meet the expenses of colonial administration; it would also cut the transportation costs and make the production of the new cash crops profitable. In most parts of Uganda, land was rich and plentiful, and rainfall was sufficient.

From the commencement of colonial rule, emphasis was on agricultural production. In Buganda, major changes in the land tenure system produced private land ownership. In the rest of Uganda, each ethnic group had its defined territory exclusively for use by its occupants. There was to be no private land ownership except in Buganda. The policy of the colonial power was to develop the colony's economy so as to complement its own. This meant the introduction of crops required by the British industry. The revenue collected from the sale of these crops would then meet the administrative costs. The chief cash crops introduced in Uganda were cotton, coffee, rubber, sugarcane, and tobacco. Agricultural production was encouraged in Buganda, the Eastern Province and the Western Province (excluding Kigezi District). The Northern Province and Kigezi District were to produce labor for the coffee and cotton farms and sugar plantations in Buganda, as well as recruits for the security forces. This policy produced uneven development in Uganda by dividing it into productive regions and labor regions.

In order to increase production and to ensure labor supply, a cash economy was introduced in 1901 when the Indian rupee became Uganda's currency. Cotton and coffee remained the chief cash earners for the country throughout the colonial period, with coffee surpassing cotton in the 1950s. These were grown mainly by peasants, along with food crops. Between 1945 and 1960, coffee and cotton contributed over 75 per cent of export earnings. Buganda and the Eastern Province produced 75 per cent of the African monetary income. The colonial administration ensured the exclusion of the Africans from the commercial sector by introducing a license tax of £10 in 1901. This was more than the majority of Africans could pay. Attempts by Africans to enter the retail trade were blocked by government restriction. On the other hand, Asians were denied the right to lease or purchase land. Only a total of 0.6 per cent of land was allotted to non-Africans. Settler agriculture was tried but was abandoned by about 1920 due in part to the high transportation cost, inadequate subsidies as well as lack of support by the colonial administration.

From 1907 on, financial institutions including banks were established to carry out financial transactions. In 1919 the East African Currency Board was established and the East African shilling replaced by the rupee as Uganda's currency. By 1930 Uganda's traditional economy had been transformed and incorporated into the world economy. Africans were relegated to the labor and production sectors, while Asians and whites controlled marketing and processing. In the 1940s African economic frustration led to unrest and forced the protectorate government to establish the Lint Marketing Board, which took over marketing from the expatriates.

After World War II, colonial officials took steps to increase production by expanding the production of existing cash crops, diversifying production by introducing new cash crops, stimulating the progressive farmers to greater efforts, introducing tractor service, instituting land registration, and encouraging large-scale farming. Unfortunately none of these efforts succeeded. Although Uganda's gross domestic product grew markedly between 1945 and 1960, no noticeable change took place in the country's economic structure.

Initially, the colonial administration did not encourage industrialization, mainly because it would reduce revenue from import duties. European investors and financiers were also opposed to it. This attitude to industrialization changed after 1940 as a result of wartime developments. The 1946 Ten Year Development Plan permitted the establishment of processing industries, and the expansion of education and health facilities. Because Uganda had neither coal nor oil, it was decided that hydroelectric power be provided to give investors an incentive. Between 1948 and 1954 the Owens Falls Dam was constructed, but the expected dramatic growth of industries around Jinja did not take place. The obstacles included Uganda's distance from the coast, lack of purchasing power of the indigenous population, failure to create a permanent labor force, and failure to attract additional foreign industry. By 1962, the main customers for the Uganda Electricity Board were a copper smelting industry, textile mill, a cement factory, and Kenya. The government therefore set up the Uganda Development Corporation (UDC) to sponsor industrial projects. The UDC owned cement, textile, metal, chemical, fertilizer, and distilling companies. By 1962, the level of industrialization in Uganda was still very low, and the country depended on foreign markets for a limited variety of crops, thus making the economy very fragile. From 1954 to 1960 the share industrial sector increased to an average of 10 per cent, of which 50 per cent came from cotton production, sugar processing, and coffee curing.

Apart from the British expatriates, the colonial administration used Asians for skilled and semiskilled labor for Uganda. As a result, the administration neglected education and left it to the missionaries, who on the whole provided an irrelevant system of education unsuited for the Ugandan situation. The mission schools were not only few but were also unevenly distributed in Uganda, with the majority located in Buganda. The few Africans that joined the skilled labor force were paid much less than their British and Asian counterparts. With a fragile economy, unequal economic development and a scarce skilled labor, Uganda's postindependence history was bound to be stormy.

FILDA OJOK

See also: **Uganda: Education.**

Further Reading

Brett, E. A. *Colonialism and Underdevelopment in East Africa.* London: Heinemann, 1973.
IBRD, *The Economic Development of Uganda.* Baltimore: Johns Hopkins University Press, 1962.
Ingham, K. *The Making of Modern Uganda.* London: Allen and Unwin, 1958.
Kaberuka, Will. *The Political Economy of Uganda 1890–1979: A Case Study of Colonialism and Underdevelopment.* New York: Vantage Press, 1990.
Karugire S. R. *A Political History of Uganda.* Nairobi: Heinemann, 1980.
Lury, D. "Dayspring Mishandled? The Uganda Economy 1945–1960." In *History of East Africa*, vol. 3, edited by D. A. Low and S. Smith. Nairobi: East African Literature Bureau, 1976.
Zwanneberg, P. M. A. *An Economic History of Kenya and Uganda,* London: Macmillan, 1977.

Uganda: Colonial Period: Northern Uganda

Uganda was declared a British protectorate in 1894, but it was not until 1911 that any serious concern was directed toward integrating Northern Uganda into the protectorate. In fact, when Sir Hesketh Bell was made commissioner of the Uganda Protectorate in 1906, he demoted the province to the status of a district. In August 1911, however, Lango district was created and a military force made to patrol Karamoja, Acholi, and West Nile. By 1913, East and West Acholi had been integrated into the protectorate administration. West Nile was added to the province in 1914, following readjustments of territorial boundary involving Uganda and Sudan. Although a military station was established in Karamoja in 1913, it was in 1921 that a civilian district officer was appointed for the area. The province had thus become the last province to be integrated into the protectorate.

When the British established their rule over Northern Uganda, the Buganda model of administration was applied to the area. This model, which centered on the appointment of chiefs either from the cadre of preexisting chiefs or Baganda agents, was vehemently resisted, partly because the affected, segmented societies considered as alien the imposition of single-person authority in the place of their elders and traditional chiefs. The result was that in Lango, for example, between 1910 and 1911, skirmishes occurred between the Baganda agents and the indigenous peoples in which lives were lost. Among the Acholi, antipathy toward the government by civil servants heralded the deposition of the *rwot* (chief) of Atyak in 1927 because he ostensibly failed to carry out colonial orders. In Karamoja, so long as the protectorate government restricted its dealings to road construction and occasional taxation, the relationship between the Karamojong and the protectorate government remained amicable. When, however, the government began restricting cattle movement and replacing elders with protectorate-appointed chiefs, there were skirmishes. In 1923, such a conflict led to the death of a protectorate-appointed chief, Achia.

As a result of the hatred by the indigenous peoples of the alien system, the protectorate government resorted to force in order to enforce the peace in Northern Uganda. Subsequently, the colonial government became more discreet in their actions and the official position in regard to Baganda agents was to withdraw them as quickly as the occasion warranted.

The establishment of councils in the various districts of Northern Uganda was another component of protectorate administrative mechanism. In Acholi, a Central Native Council was formed in Gulu in 1914 (composed of prominent Acholi) with the aim of exercising judicial and executive powers. In Lango, a similar council was established in 1919. The councils were in reality a means of control because they established vertical relationships with the protectorate administration. But it was also the councils that later became the loci of anti-colonial agitations.

Northern Uganda during the colonial period became a province that was ignored in the protectorate colonial scheme of development partly because of the belief on the part of protectorate officials that the province had no economic viability. Instead, West Nile, Madi, Acholi, and Lango were considered labor reserves for the cash-crop economy of the south, where adult males went to acquire money for paying poll taxes. Partly due to the labor policy—which by 1925 entailed discouraging or not supporting cash crop production in the "outlying areas"— of the 162,000 acres of cash crops in Uganda in 1919–1920, 137,000 acres were in Buganda and the Eastern Province; and by 1928, 29,576,000 out of 699,000 acres were in those two areas. In 1925, the director of agriculture informed an agricultural officer in West Nile that the discouragement of cash-crop production in West Nile was a policy to be adhered to if labor was to be available for the support of essential services in the "producing districts."

Until the 1940s, attempts by the colonial government to develop disease control measures in the province were insignificant. In both Lango and Karamoja, for instance, no attempt was concretely made to control the cattle diseases there. As a result, no marketing facilities for livestock developed during much of the colonial period, and sales that occurred were purely dictated by individual need for money to pay poll taxes or sales occasioned by famine.

Social development in Northern Uganda before independence equally demonstrated the subservient position of the province in relation to others in Uganda. By 1920,

for example, the report of the Colonial Office reflected so few schools that the statistics for Northern Uganda were simply not given. By 1938, the situation had not significantly changed, and according to the report of A. Warner, the provincial commissioner for the province, Acholi, West Nile, Madi, and Lango had neither a full secondary school nor an institute for vocational education. It was not until the 1950s that the first secondary school was built.

In the era leading up to Uganda's independence in 1972, northern politicians were primarily occupied with the concerns of the people over the protectorate government's oppressive policy, which discouraged economic and social development in Northern Uganda. In Lango, support was given to the Uganda National Congress (UNC) in the belief that the it could address the problem of inequality and promote education and rapid development. In Acholi, the chiefs were seen as tools of the protectorate government, and the congress acquired ready support in Acholi. As a result of lopsided development, Milton Obote challenged the UNC's position in regard to the introduction of education and social services in the north in a letter addressed to the *Uganda Herald* of April 24, 1952.

CYPRIAN B. ADUPA

See also: **Obote, Milton; Uganda: Buganda Agreement, Political Parties, Independence; Uganda: Obote's First Regime, 1962–1971.**

Further Reading

Jorgensen, J. J. *Uganda: A Modern History*. London: Croom Helm, 1981.

Kabwegyere Tarsis, B. *The Politics of State Formation: The Nature and Effects of Colonialism in Uganda*. Nairobi: East Africa Literature Bureau, 1974.

Karugire Samwiri, R. *A Political History of Uganda*. Nairobi: Heinemann, 1980.

Mamdani, Mahmood. *Politics and Class Formation in Uganda*. London: Heinemann, 1976.

Nabudere Wadada, D. *Imperialism and Revolution in Uganda*. London: Onyx Press/Dar es Salaam: Tanzanian Publishing, 1980.

Zwanenberg, R. M. A. and Anne King. *An Economic History of Kenya and Uganda 1800–1970*. London: Macmillan, 1972.

Uganda: Education

After independence in 1963, Ugandans confronted an educational system that had been dominated by foreign teachers and materials. They also debated the role of education in a free African country and the legacy of the colonial period. The issue of the relationship between education and society was one that stretched back nearly a century, when the informal education of the precolonial era was joined by formal education based on literacy.

All societies in precolonial Uganda had some type of informal social education and vocational training. Social and cultural education took place in the home, as did early training in subsistence activities, while oral traditions were a means of instructing children about their history and society. There were definite gender distinctions in education; girls learned from their mothers and boys from their fathers, and boys were at times apprenticed to craft specialists or learned about politics from elders, and in centralized states in the compound of a chief or the court of a king.

The introduction of formal education in the mid- to late nineteenth century is traced to the appearance of foreign traders and missionaries. During the reign of *Kabaka* (King) Mutesa I of Buganda, coastal Muslim traders taught Swahili using an Arabic alphabet, which became the first written language in Uganda. They attempted to convert people to Islam and taught the Qu'ran. Christian missionaries arrived in Buganda in the 1870s and applied an alphabet to Luganda to create a written form of the language. This was used to teach Christianity to converts thus spreading literacy in an African language. African converts were required to learn to read a catechism, and the connection between religion and literacy (and by extension all formal education) was very strong. Later in the nineteenth century other European Christian missionaries extended education to include more general education and some vocational training, but the core remained preparation for baptism, and the majority of the formal schools were run by African catechists of either the Protestant or Catholic missions.

The establishment of Uganda as a British protectorate brought no immediate changes in education. The religious organizations maintained control over schools, with the protectorate government providing supportive grants to the mission bodies and an increasing level of oversight. Under the British protectorate there were a range of schools from basic, village-level schools to postsecondary teacher colleges, technical schools, and Makerere College (later, Makerere University), which originated in 1922 as a technical school but gradually became a college of general higher education. The creation of a protectorate department of education in 1925 meant direct government involvement in education, including over materials and subjects, but not direct control. While religious groups ran the schools, African elites, the missions, and the government debated about the proper balance between academic and technical curricula. Government officials wanted education to prepare Ugandans for a village life and felt the schools offered instruction that was too literary. Many Ugandans, on the other hand, sought a literary education for their children as a means of obtaining high-paying jobs in government, teaching, and commerce.

The first decade of the twentieth century saw the establishment of the first secondary schools offering a general education in Uganda. These were boarding schools designed to educate the sons of chiefs, to help develop a Christian, Western-educated ruling elite. The first secondary boarding school for girls opened in 1905 with the intention that graduates would become the wives of the graduates of the boys' schools. Educated African women were limited to positions as teachers, nurses, midwives, and homemakers. By the late 1930s a more academic curriculum for girls was introduced, but the students numbered only in the dozens. The first young women entered Makerere College in 1945, but were limited in their fields of study.

The Muslim population lacked equal educational opportunities, in part because Muslims rejected the Christian-centered teaching at the mission schools and instead taught children in Qu'ranic schools. The growth of secular schools for Muslims was slow, and by the 1950s there were only two junior secondary schools for Muslims, though they also began attending the government nondenominational schools that were established in 1952. Muslim girls were the least educated segment of the population, with only a few attending the secondary schools in the 1950s.

Ugandans since independence have been actively struggling with molding an educational system to fit the needs of the new state, including early efforts at Africanizing and secularizing both curricula and faculty. By the mid-1970s the government had taken over the schools formerly under religious control, introduced Africa-centered curricula and producing most school materials at home in Uganda. But the progress made was halted and even reversed under the rule of Idi Amin Dada and the succeeding regime of Milton Obote. Makerere University was hard hit, losing both material and human resources, and while the primary and secondary schools continued operating they too deteriorated.

All sectors of the country, including the schools, were rebuilt in the 1990s, though the process was hampered by a relatively weak economy. Several contentious points were addressed, including access to schools, the form and cost of education, and the continuing appropriateness of a university specializing in a liberal arts education. The governments of independent Uganda have taken successive steps at remaking a school system to meet the needs of a country that requires indigenous expertise in agriculture and veterinary science, engineering, and education. At Makerere University, resources have been focused on the sciences and the medical school, and a new university was founded at Mbarara with a mission to support rural development.

The government of Museveni recognizes the importance of an educated, literate populace for the rebuilding of the country. After taking over in the mid-1980s, the government had a program of political and civic education to create a civilian population engaged in the nation-building process, and programs to promote adult literacy. The government has also struggled with how to make education accessible for all citizens. A regional imbalance continues, with most schools—including the universities—located in the south, and in or near urban areas. The Museveni administration has been promoting a program of universal primary education but it remains to be seen how it can fund the massive expansion of schools that would be required. One option suggested is the implementation of fees at Makerere University, which has been historically free, and an increase in fees for primary and secondary education. Understandably, there has been great resistance to new or higher fees, and although international aid has helped the education budget hard choices must still be made.

MICHAEL W. TUCK

See also: **Education; Uganda: Reconstruction: Politics, Economics.**

Further Reading

Dinwiddy, Hugh, and Michael Twaddle. "The Crisis at Makerere." In *Uganda Now: Between Decay and Development*, edited by Hölgar Bernt Hansen and Michael Twaddle. London: James Currey, 1988.

Furley, Oliver. "Education in Post-independence Uganda: Change Amidst Strife." In *Uganda Now: Between Decay and Development*, edited by Hölgar Bernt Hansen and Michael Twaddle. London: James Currey, 1988.

Hansen, Hölgar Bernt. *Mission, Church and State in a Colonial Setting, Uganda 1890–1925*. London: Heinemann, 1984.

Kajubi, W. Senteza. "Educational Reform during Socio-economic Crisis." In *Changing Uganda: The Dilemma of Structural Adjustment and Revolutionary Change*, edited by Hölgar Bernt Hansen and Michael Twaddle. London: James Currey, 1991.

Kwitonda, Aloysius. "A Century of School and Education in Uganda." In *Uganda: A Century of Existence*, edited by P. Godfrey Okoth, Manuel Muranga, and Ernesto Okello Ogwang. Kampala, Uganda: Fountain, 1995.

Musisi, Nakanyike B. "Colonial and Missionary Education: Women and Domesticity in Uganda, 1900–1945." In *African Encounters with Domesticity*, edited by Karen Tranberg Hansen. New Brunswick, N.J.: Rutgers University Press, 1992.

Pirouet, M. Louise. "Education" and "Makerere College." In *Historical Dictionary of Uganda*. Meuchen, N.J.: Scarecrow Press, 1995.

Ssekamwa, J. C. *History and Development of Education in Uganda*. Kampala, Uganda: Fountain, 1997.

Tiberondwa, Ado K. *Missionary Teachers as Agents of Colonialism in Uganda*, 2nd ed. Kampala, Uganda: Fountain, 1998.

Uganda: Buganda Agreement, Political Parties, Independence

The genesis of political-party activities in Uganda is rooted in the Bataka Association, which was formed in 1921. Its purpose was to fight the Asian monopoly on the processing and marketing of cotton, and to wage war against the oligarchy in Buganda, which had seized power in the 1890s, their predominance guaranteed by the Buganda Agreement of 1900. Unfortunately for the association, their attempt to seek a revision of the Buganda Agreement of 1900 with specific reference to the land settlement failed.

During the interwar years, the official protectorate government position was opposed to the development of representative institutions for Africans. Representative institutions were partly opposed because it was believed that the institutions would shift the loyalty of educated Africans away from their tribal institutions and would also bring them into greater prominence. In spite of the protectorate position, in May 1938, an organization was formed, the Sons of Kintu, with the purpose of directing the complaints of the farmers and merchants to the protectorate political establishment. The Sons of Kintu marked the beginning of regular political organization and signified the establishment of modern nationalism in Uganda.

The precursor to the establishment of a Uganda-wide political party was the Uganda African Farmers' Union (UAFU), which was formed in April 1941. The union was intended to be an organization for various growers in Buganda, led by Ignatius Musazi, who had also been at the helm of Sons of Kintu. The riots of 1945 and 1949 led to the collapse of the UAFU, but they also paved the way for the formation, in 1952, of the first Uganda-wide political party, the Uganda National Congress (UNC).

From the beginning, the UNC was socialist, cosmopolitan, and interracial and had Pan-African objectives. The party was dominated by former students of King's College–Budo and was predominantly Protestant. While the UNC was intensely nationalist, with its main demand of "self-government now," its effectiveness was determined in many areas of Uganda by the degree of success with which it handled local issues. In Mbale, for instance, the UNC branch was strongly anti-Asian. In Northern Uganda, the differences among members of the Acholi Congress over religious and clan disputes made it a party of local preoccupation. The dilemma of the congress was that the party was compliant with the protectorate government and had representation in the Legislative Council while Buganda, the root of the congress itself, was at odds with the protectorate government.

In 1953, the *Kabaka* (King) of Buganda was deported to Britain, precipitating the climax of the first stage of political party organization generally and that of the UNC specifically. In June 1953, the colonial secretary, Oliver Lyttleton, had remarked that the Federation of East Africa was likely to soon become a reality. The remark resulted in a showdown between the kabaka and the governor of Uganda, Sir Andrew Cohen. The kabaka insisted that Buganda should not be made part of the proposed Federation of East Africa. It was not until the Namirembe Conference of 1954 that the impasse was resolved, and the kabaka returned to his kingdom in October 1955. The Buganda Agreement of 1955 was then signed between the kabaka and the governor, an agreement that made recommendations for the reform of the Buganda government, the Legislative Council, and the Executive Council.

Another political party of a smaller stature was established in 1955, the Progressive Party (PP). Founded before the kabaka's return, the PP was a party of influential individuals, led by E. M. K. Mulira. The party comprised important members of the Lukiiko (Buganda parliament), prominent businessmen, leaders of the Uganda Teachers' Association, and those who had served in public bodies and church organizations. Unfortunately for the party, it sunk into oblivion after the return of the kabaka, partly because it was essentially a party of intellectuals without mass support. Moreover, the conflict between the chiefs in Buganda and the party helped seal its fate.

In 1956 another political party, the Democratic Party (DP), was born; it was founded mainly by Catholics. What prompted the formation of the DP was Bugandan Catholic dissatisfaction over the award of chieftaincies in Buganda. The defeat of Matayo Mugwanya in the elections of 1955 for the post of *katikiro* (prime minister) of Buganda signaled the establishment of the party. The most crucial objective of the DP was Africanization of the civil service.

The politics of Uganda over the next six years, in the period prior to independence, were marked by the Buganda government's change of position regarding participation in the Legislative Council. Buganda withdrew its representatives from the council in 1957. Despite Buganda's withdrawal, direct elections were held in other parts of Uganda in 1958, with the UNC acquiring five seats and the DP one seat; four seats were taken by independent candidates. The first meeting of the new Legislative Council marked the establishment of another political party in Uganda, the Uganda People's Union (UPU), comprised exclusively of African members of the Legislative Council.

In the wake of Buganda intransigence, the UNC split in January 1959, with one section led by Milton Obote and the other by Ignatius Musazi, denoting further conflict between Buganda and the rest of Uganda. It was the Obote wing of Congress that merged with the UPU to form the Uganda Peoples' Congress (UPC) in March 1960. In the meantime, the year 1961 signified the establishment of the Kabaka Yekka (KY) party (a Buganda party) and in the same year, Uganda attained self-government led by the DP

with Benedicto Kiwanuka as chief minister. In the April 1962 elections, UPC and KY formed an alliance, and in October 1962 Uganda became independent under Prime Minister Obote.

CYPRIAN B. ADUPA

See also: **Obote, Milton.**

Further Reading

Apter, David T. *The Political Kingdom in Uganda: A Study of Bureaucratic Nationalism.* Princeton, N.J.: Princeton University Press, 1967.

Karugire Samwiri, R. *A Political History of Uganda.* Nairobi: Heinemann, 1980.

Low Anthony David Pratt Cranford R. *Buganda and British Overrule 1900–1955.* London: Oxford University Press, 1960.

Mamdani, Mahmood. *Politics and Class Formation in Uganda.* London: Heinemann, 1976.

Mutibwa, Phares. *Uganda since Independence: A Study of Unfulfilled Hopes.* Kampala, Uganda: Fountain, 1992.

Nabudere Wadada, D. *Imperialism and Revolution in Uganda.* London: Onyx Press/Dar es Salaam. Tanzania Publishing, 1980.

Uganda: Obote's First Regime, 1962–1971

The first nine years of Uganda's independence illustrate the complexities of nation building in a former colony with a fragile statehood from the outset. We can best understand the instability characterizing this period in the context of the country's colonial history and the slow and uncertain path it followed toward independence from Britain in October 1962. The crisis in which Uganda found itself four years after gaining independence was born of a combination of factors. Apart from the absence of any strong nationalist sentiment embracing the whole country, there was also the lack of a charismatic, universally accepted leadership. Furthermore, the question of ethnic diversity and regional differences compounded Uganda's colonial history. Finally, the emergent Ugandan political elite of the 1950s and 1960s displayed a strong attachment to district politics. Uganda's ex-colonial overlord, Britain, had bequeathed to the new rulers a country that was politically disunited and economically weak.

On the eve of independence, no single political party had emerged as the dominant political organization in the various regions of the country. The Democratic Party (DP), which had won the elections of 1961 and led Uganda into self-government under Chief Minister Benedicto Kiwanuka from May 1961 to April 1962, lost the last preindependence elections. These were won by the alliance of Milton Obote's Uganda People's Congress (UPC) and the neotraditionalist, conservative Kabaka Yekka (King Only; KY) party. KY was committed to the preservation of the kingship and their kingdom within greater Uganda, an alliance that had brought together unlikely bedfellows. Obote's UPC was a comparatively radical and socialist party comprising leaders mainly, though not exclusively, from outside Buganda. On the other hand, KY naturally commanded overwhelming support within Buganda, but it had no ambition whatever to become a Uganda-wide political party. The alliance had led the country into independence and formed the government with Milton Obote as prime minister and the *Kabaka* (King) of Buganda as nonexecutive president and head of state. However, tension developed between these two partners right from the outset; Obote dissolved the alliance in August 1964. This "divorce" became one important ingredient of the crisis that soon engulfed the country.

Yet the two sides had tried to accommodate each other in the years leading up to independence. For his part, Obote had attempted to achieve the integration of Buganda and the rest of the country by insisting that, contrary to the predominant view within his party, the Kabaka of Buganda be elected president in November 1963. He had hoped this would help placate Buganda and thus lead to better cooperation between it and the rest of the country. On the other hand, the kabaka himself had shown a positive attitude toward the leader of the UPC. As the kabaka pointed out in his own account of the events leading up to the 1966 crisis, Obote seemed to be someone he could work with. This apparent mutual trust, however, began to be eroded by the machinations of both sides in the period 1963–1966. The antireferendum riots in and around Kampala in late November 1964 provoked the central government into overreacting by sending irresponsible and overzealous troops to quell the disturbances. This could only further antagonize the Baganda.

The Gold Allegations Motion of early 1966, introduced by a KY member of the National Assembly, accused Idi Amin Dada, then the commander of the army, of stealing a massive amount of gold from neighboring Congo. It also implicated Prime Minister Obote and two of his cabinet ministers. This was soon followed by Obote's arrest and the detention of five ministers suspected of being involved in a plot to oust the prime minister. In May 1966 the central government clashed with the Buganda kingdom administration. The abolition of kingship in Uganda as a whole and the introduction of the Republican Constitution followed in 1967. Four years later, the Amin coup of January 1971 took place. All these were in many ways the outcome of Uganda's difficulties dating from the years before independence. By the middle of 1967, the Kabaka of Buganda had fled into exile. The UPC had established a strong central government under a new republican constitution, with Milton Obote as executive president.

These changes, however, had not resolved Uganda's fundamental problems. National unity remained elusive, as did economic development and political stability. In the next three years, the UPC government embarked on what Ali Mazrui described as a program of "documentary radicalism." In its "move to the left" the party sought to change Uganda's ideology from "capitalism, feudalism and tribalism," to a radical socialist one. It thus introduced the Common Man's Charter in 1969, intended to pave the way for a revolution in Ugandan society that would vastly improve the position of the ordinary Ugandan. Other documents followed, this setting out a new socialist program that included the nationalization of major enterprises and banks and the introduction of a new system of elections to the National Assembly. These proposed changes stimulated a great deal of reaction among the main political parties, including the ruling UPC itself, the civic society, and the wider Ugandan community. While some elements in society welcomed such changes, clearly a fair amount of disenchantment with the program manifested itself even within the ruling circle. It was hardly surprising, therefore, that this dissatisfaction, combined with the discontent that had been simmering in Buganda since 1964, the disquiet within the military, and the personal ambitions and anxieties of army chief Amin, all culminated in the January 1971 coup coup d'état that overthrew Obote's first government. By this stage, however, the Ugandan nation-state was still as weak and fragile as ever. Its ruin and almost complete disintegration under Amin's military dictatorship from 1971 to 1979 most graphically demonstrated this.

BALAM NYEKO

See also: **Obote, Milton; Uganda: Amin Dada, Idi: Coup and Regime, 1962–1979.**

Further Reading

Gertzel, Cheryl. "Leadership and Institution Building in Uganda." *African Review*. 2, no. 1 (1972): 175–187.

Gingyera-Pinycwa, Anthony G. G. *Apolo Milton Obote and His Times*. New York: NOK, 1978.

———. "A Decade of Independence in Uganda: The Political Balance-Sheet." *Africa Quarterly*. 12, no. 2 (1972): 75–90.

Hancock, Ian. "The Buganda Crisis of 1964." *African Affairs*. 69, no. 275 (1970): 109–123.

Ingham, Kenneth. *Obote: A Political Biography*. London: Routledge, 1994.

Mudoola, Dan M. *Religion, Ethnicity and Politics in Uganda*. Kampala, Uganda: Fountain, 1993.

Nyeko, Balam. "Introduction." In B. Nyeko, *Uganda*, rev. ed. Oxford: Clio Press, 1996.

Sathyamurthy, T. V. *The Political Development of Uganda, 1900–1986*. Aldershot, England: Gower, 1987.

———. "The Social Base of the Uganda People's Congress, 1958–70." *African Affairs*. 74, no. 297 (1975): 442–460.

Uzoigwe, Godfrey N. (ed.). *Uganda: The Dilemma of Nationhood*. New York: NOK, 1982.

Uganda: Amin Dada, Idi: Coup and Regime, 1971–1979

As president of Uganda from 1971 to 1979, the rule of Idi Amin Dada (1924–2003) was synonymous with personalization of power, disregard for human rights, unpredictability, and overall socioeconomic and political disintegration.

Born between 1924 and 1927 in Koboko (former West Nile province), Amin had humble but diverse origins. His father was a Kakwa, of the ethnic group found in the Democratic Republic of the Congo, Sudan, and Uganda. His mother, who influenced his early childhood, was a Lugbara, of the largest ethnic group in West Nile.

As a result of his mother's separation from his father, he left his homeland at an early age; he and his mother left West Nile and settled at the Lugazi sugar estate in Buganda. Amin worked several odd jobs to make ends meet and constantly changed residences to follow wherever his mother went. Due to these circumstances, he acquired only a fourth grade education.

The British colonial rulers were impressed with Amin. He was strong, he spoke Kiswahili, and his lack of a formal education led them to believe that he would be subservient. Joining the army as a private in 1946, he was promoted to corporal in 1949. Amin fought against the Mau Mau nationalists, who opposed British rule in Kenya, in the 1950s and 1960s. The British promoted him to sergeant in 1951, lance corporal in 1953, *effendi* (a rank invented for outstanding African noncommissioned officers) in 1959, and in 1961 Amin and Shaban Opolot became the first Ugandan commissioned officers with the rank of lieutenant.

Before Uganda's independence in 1962, Amin's brutality surfaced. He overstepped his orders to stop cattle rustling between the neighboring ethnic groups in Karamoja (Uganda) and Turkana (Kenya), and instead engaged in gross violations of human rights. The British recommendation to prosecute Amin for his atrocities soon after independence was politically unpalatable to Apolo Milton Obote (Uganda's new prime minister), who instead reprimanded him. Despite his opposition to Obote's recruitment of educated Ugandans into the armed forces, Amin was still promoted to captain in 1962, major in 1963, and was selected in 1963 to participate in the commanding officers' course at the Wiltshire School for infantry in Britain.

An army mutiny of 1964 catapulted the armed forces into political prominence in general, and Amin in particular. At issue was the desire by Ugandan soldiers to improve their overall working conditions. For his role in ending the crisis, Amin was promoted to the rank of colonel and commanding officer of the First Battalion.

Obote's desire to assist followers of Patrice Lumumba (the murdered prime minister of Congo, now the Democratic Republic of the Congo) in 1965 presented an opportunity for Amin to become close to Prime Minister Obote. Without the knowledge of the chief of staff of the army, Obote instructed Amin to establish military camps in the Congo. Additionally, Amin became involved in procuring coffee, gold, and ivory from the Congo for Uganda in order to raise money for arms.

Opponents of Obote, including the *Kabaka* (King) of Buganda (Edward Mutesa) wanted to launch an investigation into the illegal entry of gold and ivory into Uganda. Obote circumvented the affair by appointing a commission of inquiry, arresting five cabinet ministers, suspending the constitution, firing the kabaka, and promoting Amin to commander of the armed forces. Amin ruthlessly attacked the kabaka's palace, forcing Mutesa to flee to Britain, where he died in exile in 1969.

The overall political conditions between 1966 and January 25, 1971, when Amin successfully staged his coup d'état against Obote's government, were unstable. In addition to the political wrath from Baganda (the largest ethnic group in Uganda), Obote faced ideological conflicts within the ruling party, the Uganda People's Congress.

It is unclear why Obote promoted Amin in 1970 to the rank of chief of general staff, a position that gave him access to every aspect of the armed forces and subsequently enabled him to overthrow Obote's government on January 25, 1971.

Amin's eight years in power were characterized by a lack of any orderly policy making, the presence of sycophants, and the use of terror as a means of control. There was a total administrative breakdown resulting from Amin's inefficient leadership. Amin convinced many Ugandans and the world at large that he was a simple man who had intervened in politics to save the country. Between 1971 and 1972, Amin freely interacted with ordinary people, disbanded Obote's secret police, granted amnesty to political prisoners, allowed the return of the kabaka's body for a royal burial, appointed a cabinet of technocrats, and promised Ugandans that he would hand power back to the civilians.

Amin's real personality (that of a consummate liar who was capricious, cunning, ruthless, and shrewd) eventually emerged. During the euphoric period (1971–1972), Amin systematically eliminated Obote's supporters (mainly the Acholi and Langi) in the armed forces, promulgated a decree reintroducing detention without trial, and, despite his friendly relationship with the West at the time, ordered the murder of two

Americans (Nicholas Stroh and Robert Siedle) who were investigating massacres that had occurred at the Mbarara barracks in western Uganda.

In 1972, Amin suddenly turned against Britain and Israel, two countries that had been his close allies, due to their reluctance to provide funds and arms. Faced with their hesitancy, Amin found Libyan leader Muammar Gaddafi's willingness to assist him appealing.

The quid pro quo between Amin and Gaddafi was clear: rid Uganda of Western interests in return for Libya's financial assistance. On March 27, and again on August 5, 1972, Amin ordered Israelis to leave the country in three days' time, and Asians holding British passports were ordered to do the same within three months. Amin justified his actions by claiming that he wanted to rid the country of "imperialists and Zionists" and replace Asians with African entrepreneurship. Amin's "economic war" (as the expulsion of 50,000 Asian traders came to be known), together with his anti-Western position, plunged Uganda into problems from which it has yet to recover.

Amin entrusted the economy to Nubians and a few Ugandans, all of whom lacked business experience. Consequently, Uganda's once prosperous economy was ruined. The immediate impact was the scarcity of basic consumer goods such as bread, butter, milk, sugar, and salt. Those in positions of economic power created artificial shortages and later sold the items under a system popularly known as *magendo* (illegal or underground economy). Corruption became characteristic of the economic system. The departure of foreigners also led to a loss of tax revenue and jobs, for many Ugandans once employed by the foreigners were unable to find alternative employment.

Amin looked for scapegoats to account for the failure of his "Economic War." Through his secret police (the State Research Bureau and the Public Safety Unit) and the rest of the armed forces, Amin used institutionalized violence to control and intimidate Ugandans. He eliminated anyone he considered a potential threat.

The human cost of Amin's rule was devastating. The few remaining educated Ugandans fled the country, fearing for their lives. With most national funds devoted to the armed forces and Amin's personal security, education and the industrial and manufacturing sectors were neglected.

The domestic situation was exacerbated by Uganda's inability to receive sufficient international aid. A number of able foreign ministers tried to dispel the international opinion that Amin lacked the necessary intelligence and expertise to lead the country. Their partial success in this regard was reflected by Tanzania's signature of the Mogadishu (Somalia) agreement with Uganda in 1972, Amin's election to the position of chairman of the Organization of African Unity (OAU) in 1975, and the 1977 success of African countries in blocking a United Nations resolution that would have condemned Amin for gross violation of human rights.

Rather than using African support to improve Uganda's tarnished image, Amin's unpredictable personality produced one embarrassment after another. Soon after the sudden expulsion of Asians in 1972, Amin oversaw the murders of chief justice Benedicto Kiwanuka in 1972, foreign minister Michael Ondoga in 1974, and Archbishop Janani Luwum in 1977. He also supported Palestinians who hijacked a 1976 Air France flight to Entebbe airport.

In response, the United States closed its embassy in Uganda in 1973, as did Britain in 1976. All Ugandan economic transactions with other nations were carried out on a short-term or cash basis, except for those made with Libya and Saudi Arabia. The nation acquired a negative image internationally due to its economic dealings, which in turn adversely affected the entire economy. The tourism industry was especially badly hurt.

By the late 1970s, the economy was in ruins. Coffee (Uganda's main export) prices had plummeted from a high of $3.18 (U.S.) per pound to $1.28 per pound. The situation was exacerbated when the United States stopped purchasing Ugandan coffee in 1978. Arab nations that had generously donated funds became concerned with Amin's inability to Islamize Uganda, and worried by his involvement in the murder of fellow Muslims. The deteriorating economic situation made it difficult for Amin to import luxury items for his armed forces.

To divert attention from this crisis, Amin ordered an invasion of Tanzania in October 1978, allegedly because the latter planned to overthrow his government. Tanzania, which at the time was preoccupied with the "Rhodesian questions" and had all along assumed that the Mogadishu Agreement signed in 1972 had ended any hostilities between the two countries, was taken unawares. Consequently, Amin's soldiers easily occupied the country, systematically killing Tanzanians and destroying their property.

Despite pressure from the OAU, Amin refused to renounce his territorial claims over Tanzania. Julius Nyerere (president of Tanzania, 1961–1985) was forced to order the Tanzania People's Defense Forces to repel the Ugandan forces. Tanzanians and exiled Ugandan soldiers continued their pursuit of Amin until his government was overthrown on April 11, 1979.

Amin fled to Libya. He later moved to Jeddah, Saudi Arabia, where, according to recent information, he led a comfortable life. He died on August 16, 2003. The continuing problems Uganda faces attest to the enormous drain that Amin's rule had upon the political, economic, social, and cultural life of that country.

PETER F. B. NAYENGA

See also: **Luwum, Janani; Museveni, Yoweri Kaguta; Obote, Milton; Tanzania (Tanganyika): Uganda, Relations with.**

Biography

Born in West Nile Uganda, *c.*1924; received a formal education only to the fourth grade. Enlisted as a private in 1946. Distinguished himself as a good soldier and became one of the two commissioned officers when Uganda became independent in 1962. Between 1962 and 1966, served in a number of capacities as a military officer in Milton Obote's government (1962–1971). Close association with Obote earned him the rank of commander of the Uganda army in 1966, a position he held until his differences with Obote caused him to stage a coup d'état on January 25, 1971. Invaded Tanzania in 1978, prompting that country to send troops into Uganda, thus overthrowing Amin's government on April 11, 1979. Fled first to Libya, and then settled in Jeddah, Saudi Arabia. Died August 16, 2003.

Further Reading

Nayenga, Peter F. B. "Amin." In *Encyclopedia of World Biography*. Palatine, Ill.: Jack Heraty, 1987.

Pirouet, Louise M. *Historical Dictionary of Uganda*. Metuchen, N.J.: Scarecrow, 1995.

Turyahikayo-Rugyema, Benoni. *Idi Amin Speaks: An Annotated Selection of His Speeches*. Madison, Wisconsin: University of Wisconsin African Studies Program, 1998.

Uganda: Tanzanian Invasion, 1979–1980

The Tanzanian incursion into Uganda that resulted in the removal of the Amin regime in April 1979 was the culmination of long-standing friction between the two countries dating from the overthrow of the first administration of Milton Obote by the army in January 1971. From the outset, Tanzanian president Julius Nyerere's government had immediately offered Ugandan ex-president Obote political asylum, roundly condemned the coup makers, and totally refused to recognize the new order of Idi Amin Dada in Kampala. For his part, at his first public meeting after the takeover, Amin countered that Nyerere was conspiring to invade Uganda and restore the fallen president to power. The Tanzanian bogey thus became the military regime's constant cry whenever it faced any internal crisis. The regime portrayed Obote and Nyerere as Uganda's major threat throughout Amin's rule. In September 1972, Amin's claims seemed to be vindicated when exile troops loyal to Obote crossed into Uganda from Tanzania with Nyerere's backing and attempted to overthrow the military junta. Yet it was, in fact, Amin's army that first invaded Tanzanian territory six years later in October 1978, occupied the Kagera region in the north of the country, and declared it Ugandan land. The Tanzanian intervention that followed immediately was a counterattack to drive the Ugandans out. Initially, as Nyerere declared, the aim was merely to protect Tanzania's sovereignty. At the time, however, Ugandan exile opposition forces accompanied the Tanzanian troops; together they waged a joint war that lasted barely five months and finally removed the Amin dictatorship in April 1979.

In early March, with the imminent collapse of the Amin junta, President Nyerere realized that Uganda would soon urgently require a new administration to replace it. A political leadership vacuum in Kampala would have been unthinkable, and would have merely exacerbated the country's crisis. The Tanzanian government therefore set about bringing together Uganda's political opposition groupings, then scattered all over eastern and central Africa, Europe, and the United States. However, though the various Ugandan opposition organizations all agreed on the one purpose of removing the Amin regime, they were exceptionally weak and as fragmented and disunited as ever over the kind of government to establish once they had accomplished this goal. As the anti-Amin war came threateningly close to Kampala, the various Ugandan exile groups assembled, under the Tanzanian government's sponsorship, in the northern town of Moshi in late March 1979 to work out a political program for the post-Amin period. The country's two major political parties, the Democratic Party led by Paul Semogerere and Milton Obote's Uganda People's Congress (UPC) were still in existence. However, both had become all but moribund through inactivity during the Amin years. Both organizations sent a number of individuals to the Moshi Conference. The Dar es Salaam–based Ugandan Delegates Credentials Committee in charge of the meeting, however, was extremely reluctant to admit the old parties for fear of reopening past political wounds. The committee, headed by Dan Nabudere and comprising other Ugandan academics such as Yash Tandon and Omwony Ojwok, were themselves really self-appointed and clearly lacked any political base of their own inside the country. They argued vehemently against a return to the old political party politics of the 1960s. The committee preferred to work with some small exile organizations—numbering 28 in all—from Tanzania itself, Zambia, Kenya, Europe and the United States. Some of these existed in name only, but all were recognized as representatives at the Moshi meeting. They varied enormously in strength. Only two of these groups could legitimately claim to be actively engaged in the ongoing anti-Amin war—those paying allegiance to Milton Obote and Yoweri Museveni. Most of the others were little more than welfare societies, or mere discussion groups with hardly any claim to political support inside the country.

Amid some controversy as to who qualified to attend, and subsequently over the exact meaning of some of the minutes of the meeting, the Moshi Conference established a broad body, the Uganda National Liberation Front (UNLF). This brought the different groups present into a single organization. Given Uganda's immediate past history of conflict, the delegates decided that the politically inexperienced but noncontroversial and seemingly amiable 67-year-old Yusufu Lule should lead the new organization. An ex-minister in the British colonial administration in Uganda during the 1950s, Lule was a soft-spoken former principal of Makerere College and chairman of Uganda's Public Service Commission. He was viewed as a compromise candidate who would be acceptable to the majority of the Ugandan populace. Moreover, as Kenneth Ingham (1994) points out, Lule's candidature was strongly underwritten by Britain, which apparently made such a condition for its support for any post-Amin administration in Uganda. Thus, though unknown and with no recognizable political constituency of his own, Lule was "elected" the chairman of the Executive Council of the newly launched UNLF. The UNLF also had a National Consultative Council (NCC), the equivalent of an interim parliament and by some accounts the organization's supreme body. Several committees assisted the council. Lule returned to Uganda on April 13, 1979, two days after the capture of Kampala by the Ugandan exile forces fighting alongside the Tanzanian troops.

Throughout the period of transition from 1979 to 1980, controversy, dispute, and argumentation dogged the UNLF administration. Before flying out to Kampala, Lule had announced the formation of a new government and named a cabinet, with himself as the new president under the 1967 constitution. This immediately sparked off disagreement as certain members of the UNLF argued that Lule had overstepped the bounds of his power. They claimed the Moshi Conference had merely authorized Lule to act as chairman of an interim administration comprising the 11-member Executive Council of the UNLF and the larger NCC. As the minutes of the Moshi meeting had never been presented to the NCC, however, the UNLF was unable to resolve the question. An even more burning issue was the exact relationship between the NCC and the Executive Council. The chairman of the former body, Edward Rugumayo, who had spent his exile years in Zambia, argued that under the Moshi agreement the NCC *was* supreme. In his view, this made him take precedence over Lule in the overall operation of the UNLF administration. Lule countered that the 1967 Uganda Constitution clearly recognized the supremacy of the president. This kind of constitutional dispute

seemed to be aggravated by the long and futile debates in the NCC itself. NCC members, most of whom were middle-class professionals such as lawyers, medical doctors, university academics, and school teachers with little or no political experience, discussed issues in the minutest of details. Government work, particularly in the urgent areas of the country's reconstruction and rehabilitation, was almost at a standstill as the NCC members carried on with their exchanges. At the same time, President Lule became increasingly isolated as he lost the support of the NCC. The council members claimed that he had become dictatorial and had refused to present his ministerial appointments to them for ratification. Moreover, those members of the NCC who still supported Milton Obote's UPC accused Lule of being blatantly anti-Obote when he dismissed or demoted some ministers who were his sympathizers. In the event, the radicals within the NCC combined with the UPC supporters and other dissatisfied members to vote Lule out of power in late June 1979. Lule claimed later that his dismissal had been supported by Nyerere to pave the way for Obote's reinstatement to the presidency of Uganda. The evidence, however, points to Lule's fall having been more the result of internal political differences rather than any outside intervention.

Godfrey Binaisa's presidency (June 1979 to May 1980) saw the continuing contest for power and supremacy between the executive and the parliamentary wings of government. Uganda's state and economy had disintegrated, yet the UNLF seemed unable to move forward. The conflict between the NCC and the new president finally led to the latter's downfall. Once again, disagreement centered initially on the extent to of presidential powers to appoint cabinet ministers. Although Binaisa had apparently resigned himself to the Moshi Conference's resolution that the country should have a relatively weak presidency vis à vis the NCC, he subsequently began to challenge this—if not in words, at least in some of his actions. The final straw was his decision to ban the political parties and his insistence on elections under the UNLF "umbrella" rather than through open party competition. In May he attempted to dismiss the army chief of staff, Brigadier David Oyite Ojok, formerly a commander of the guerrilla forces loyal to Milton Obote in the anti-Amin war. The army reacted by taking over a radio station and announcing the dismissal of Binaisa himself. It reversed his original proposal of holding elections under a no-party system, a move warmly welcomed by both Obote's UPC and the DP. Uganda had just undergone the third government change in the space of only one year. The country was no nearer the social and economic recovery or political stability it so badly needed.

BALAM NYEKO

See also: **Museveni, Yoweri Kaguta; Nyerere, Julius; Tanzania (Tanganyika): Uganda, Relations with.**

Further Reading

Avirgan, Tony, and Martha Honey. *War in Uganda: The Legacy of Idi Amin*. Dar es Salaam: Tanzania Publishing, 1982.

Gertzel, Cherry. "Uganda after Amin: The Continuing Search for Leadership and Control." *African Affairs* 79, no. 317 (1980): 461–489.

Ingham, Kenneth. *Obote: A Political Biography*. London: Routledge, 1994.

Mamdani, Mahmood. *Imperialism and Fascism in Uganda*. London: Heinemann, 1983.

Museveni, Yoweri K. *Sowing the Mustard Seed: The Struggle for Freedom and Democracy in Uganda*, edited by Elisabeth Kanyogonya and Kevin Shillington. Basingstoke, England: Macmillan, 1997.

Nyeko, Balam. "The Background to Political Instability in Post-Amin Uganda." *Ufahamu* 15, no. 3 (1986–1987): 11–32.

———. "Exile Politics and Resistance to Dictatorship: The Ugandan Anti-Amin Organizations in Zambia, 1972–79." *African Affairs* 96, no. 382 (1997): 95–108.

Omara-Otunnu, Amii. *Politics and the Military in Uganda, 1890–1985*. Basingstoke, England: Macmillan, in association with St Antony's College, Oxford, 1987.

Uganda: Obote: Second Regime, 1980–1985

In May 1980, Milton Obote returned home after nine years' exile in neighboring Tanzania, where he had lived since Idi Amin's overthrow of his first regime in January 1971. As Uganda prepared to go to the polls, Obote visited nearly every corner of the country, delivering a series of campaign speeches for his political party, the Uganda People's Congress (UPC). In December 1980 he made history by becoming the first African ex-president to be returned to office through a general election. However, the actions of the incumbent Military Commission government in handling the elections results were highly questionable. In this the role of Paulo Muwanga, the Military Commission chairman and a staunch UPC member who later became Obote's vice president, was paramount. He virtually dismissed the officially appointed Uganda Elections Commission and undertook personally to screen and then announce the election results himself. The Commonwealth Observer team later declared that "despite a number of irregularities . . . the overall conduct of the elections themselves had been fair and . . . the outcome probably represented the views of the people of Uganda" Nevertheless, Obote's opponents seemed to have reasonable grounds for charging that the UPC had rigged the elections.

Yoweri Museveni's guerrillas launched a campaign in February 1981 to remove the government by force of arms. Museveni had lost the contest for a seat in his home area to a candidate of the Democratic Party (DP). His own recently formed political party, the Uganda Patriotic Movement (UPM), had done dismally against the two more established parties, the DP and Obote's UPC. The UPM, which had in fact secured only one seat in the parliament, further accused Obote of dictatorship and tyranny. Museveni vowed to fight for democracy and "fundamental change" in the country. Throughout its four-and-a-half-year life, then, the Obote government had to contend with this military challenge to its very existence and with the worsening lawlessness in much of the country as the civil war escalated. In addition, Uganda had undergone staggering social and economic decay in the period of Idi Amin's anarchic rule from 1971 to 1979. Following the removal of the Amin regime, the country's old political differences, suspended by the various groups during the anti-Amin campaign, had reappeared. The two main traditional political parties had renewed their old political rivalries. The Baganda's suspicions of Obote's intentions toward them had never really died; memories of his bitter clash with their late *Kabaka* (King) Mutesa II in 1966 were still fresh. The Uganda to which Obote had returned was a country in a state of utter collapse, both physically and morally. His second presidency was therefore destined to be one of the most difficult periods in the postcolonial history of Uganda.

An early source of worry for Obote was the inadequacy of the Uganda National Liberation Army (UNLA). This comprised the survivors of the anti-Amin campaign who had come in from Tanzania and had been joined by hastily recruited and virtually untrained individual volunteer soldiers. In fact, Uganda possessed no truly *national* army. The UNLA had been merely a combination of various forces paying allegiance to individual warlords during the transition period of 1979–1980. This recently created army singularly lacked discipline and proved completely unequal to the task of fighting off the rebel forces of Yoweri Museveni's National Resistance Army (NRA). For several years the two sides locked horns in the Luwero Triangle in what was a most costly war; each side blamed the loss of hundreds of civilian lives on the other. When the UNLA's chief of staff, Major General Oyite Ojok, died in a helicopter crash in December 1983, this became an important turning point in the Obote regime's fortunes. Ojok was a highly trained and widely respected officer who had begun to instill some discipline in the troops. This had begun to pay off in the government's antiinsurgency operations, at least in the areas around Kampala and Luwero. His death was followed by a prolonged and agonizing search by Obote for his replacement. When the president finally announced the name of the new chief of staff, who happened to be from his own ethnic group, some senior Acholi officers who claimed to have been overlooked for this appointment felt disgruntled, accusing Obote of tribalism. The growing discontent clearly contributed to the internal division and conflict within the UNLA that eventually resulted in the coup that removed Obote's second regime on July 27, 1985. Again, he was forced into exile.

The explanation for his overthrow by his own army for the second time in his political career is similar in some ways to the reasons for his first fall in 1971, for, as in 1971, the 1985 army was divided. A prolonged anti-Museveni campaign had led to considerable war-weariness in a large section of the army. Moreover, the split in the army seemed to be ethnically based: Tito Okello, the army commander and himself an Acholi, had claimed that the Acholi soldiers in the UNLA had incurred the greatest number of casualties in the war against Museveni. Whether this was a correct interpretation or not, the effect was to sow division within the ranks of the whole army and to weaken both it and the government considerably. His collaborator, Bazilio Okello (no relation), was another senior Acholi officer. He was particularly dismayed that Obote had not appointed him the new chief of staff, although it is not certain that he qualified for the position. The two Okellos' coup of July 1985 was therefore clearly an Acholi coup that arose partly from the two officers' disgruntlement with the government. Parallel to this split in the army, a serious crack also occurred within the ruling party itself. By early 1985, with the prospects of another general election later in the year, factions emerged in the UPC between the "radical" wing and the "moderate" members. The former perceived Obote as too temperate in his political outlook. According to Obote's biographer, Kenneth Ingham, this group feared that the party might exclude them from its list of candidates for the impending elections. Consequently, they decided to side with the army officers who were conspiring to overthrow the government. Although the party never conclusively proved it, Obote's own vice president, Paulo Muwanga, seemed to have been in this camp. At any rate, he soon became part of the new military government set up by the Okellos.

From 1980 to 1985, government troops were often ruthless and were responsible for numerous deaths among the civilians. Overall, however, the picture that emerges is one of a government overwhelmed by the immensity of the social, economic, political, and military challenges it faced. Obote genuinely seemed to want to help his country; he undertook a thorough reassessment of Uganda's economic recovery program. In this he received the support of the World Bank as well as the International Monetary Fund for some of his rather radical fiscal policies. These included the novel but bold decision to "float" the Ugandan currency, the shilling, in the regime's battle against inflation. The government focused extensively on rural development, including such areas as water supply and the reintroduction of cash-crop farming. Given the complexity of the country's myriad problems and Obote's own nine years' absence from the country, however, he was quite clearly unequipped to find the solutions to these difficulties. In July 1985, the military set his government aside and brought his political career to an end.

BALAM NYEKO

See also: **Museveni, Yoweri Kaguta; Obote, Milton.**

Further Reading

Gupta, Vijay. *Obote: Second Liberation*. New Delhi: Vikas, 1983.

Hansen, Hölgar Bernt, and Michael Twaddle (eds.). *Changing Uganda: The Dilemmas of Structural Adjustment and Revolutionary Change*. London: James Currey 1991.

———. *Uganda Now: Between Decay and Development*. London: James Currey, 1988.

Ingham, Kenneth. *Obote: A Political Biography*. London: Routledge, 1994.

Museveni, Yoweri K. *Sowing the Mustard Seed: The Struggle for Freedom and Democracy in Uganda*, edited by Elisabeth Kanyogonya and Kevin Shillington. Basingstoke, England: Macmillan, 1997.

Nyeko, Balam. "A. M. Obote Revisited: A Review Article." *Uganda Journal*, no. 44 (1997), 73–91.

Omara-Otunnu, A. *Politics and the Military in Uganda, 1890–1985*. London: Macmillan, 1987.

Tindigarukayo, Jimmy K. "Uganda, 1979–85: Leadership in Transition." *Journal of Modern African Studies* 26, no. 4 (1988): 607–622.

Uganda: National Resistance Movement (NRM) and the Winning of Political Power

The National Resistance Movement (NRM) had its origins in agroup of individuals who gathered around Yoweri Museveni in the early 1970s in Dar es Salaam, Tanzania, to form an organization called the Front for National Salvation (Fronasa). The group consisted mainly of young idealistic exiles from Uganda who, like Museveni, hoped to topple the regime of Idi Amin. Many individuals within Fronasa, like James Wapakhabulo and Eriya Kategaya, would later become prominent within the NRM government. Fronasa was also one of the many exile organizations that would eventually form the Ugandan National Liberation Front (UNLF), which invaded Uganda in April 1979 with the help of the Tanzanian army and ousted Idi Amin Dada.

The first UNLF government was headed by Yusufu Lule. Museveni. The UNLF coalition government under

Lule did not last long, however. After only 68 days in office, Lule was overthrown on June 19, 1979 in favor of Godfrey Binaisa. Binaisa's reign was short-lived as well. In March 1980 General Tito Okello and Paulo Muwanga staged a coup that overthrew the Binaisa government. This paved the way for the reemergence of Milton Obote. In December 1980 elections were held and Milton Obote emerged victorious as head of the UPC. However, the election was regarded as fraudulent by Museveni and his allies within Uganda; they contested the election. At this point, Museveni, who had campaigned with the Uganda Patriotic Movement, began a guerilla campaign against the Obote regime in the southern part of Uganda, north of Kampala, known as the Luwero Triangle. It was during this period that the NRM began to cohere.

With an incipient core group of about 27 individuals that included later NRM stalwarts Sam Magera, Ahmed Seguya, Fred Rubereza, Sam Katabarwa, Elly Tumwine, and Museveni's brother Salim Saleh, Museveni began to build the structures that would evolve into the NRM. A failed attack on Kabamba baracks to secure arms on February 6, 1981 signaled the start of the war that would last approximately five years.

Initially, the insurgents were called the Popular Resistance Army (PRA). A National Resistance Council (NRC) acted as the civilian wing of the movement. The NRC supported the PRA through a network of civilian committees that provided intelligence support, recruitment and also food for the army.

In June 1981, Museveni's PRA merged with the anti-UNLF group Uganda Freedom Fighters, headed by the ousted Yusufu Lule, to form the NRM. Lule was designated chairman, and Museveni vice chairman. The NRM would serve as the civilian political wing of the National Resistance Army (NRA).

Between 1981 and 1983, the NRA lacked adequate equipment and arms, relying on guerrilla tactics to conduct the war against the UNLF. During this phase of the war, the NRA employed ambush and sabotage tactics against specific targets to either acquire arms or destroy enemy equipment and morale.

The problem of acquiring food was always a serious problem for the NRA, one that led them to rely heavily upon the peasant population in the Luwero Triangle. The NRA was able to gain much support from the peasants, however, by treating them with respect. This included paying for goods commandeered from the peasants. To facilitate good civilian relationships with the peasantry the NRA also adopted a code of conduct that governed relationships between the NRA soldiers and the civilian population. An operational code of conduct was also instituted to deal with offenses during the operation of a battle. As a result, the NRA was able to rely on the peasantry for help in providing both food and intelligence.

In January 1983 the UNLA launched a major offensive against the NRA in the Luwero Triangle. This offensive, in which the UNLA concentrated 75 per cent of its troop strength against the NRA, followed the pattern of a similar offensive in June 1982 and was designed to overwhelm the guerrillas with superior force and numbers. The overwhelming UNLA force, coupled with an inadequate supply of arms, forced the NRA to retreat into the more remote upper reaches of the triangle. The retreat, however, occasioned a reorganization of the NRA's tactics and strategy.

During the second phase of the war (1983–1985), the NRA began to incorporate a policy of so called mobile warfare. This entailed more attacks against entrenched enemy positions. The NRA formed a mobile brigade to facilitate these attacks with Museveni as first commander. With this reorganization, the original brigades became zonal brigades responsible for protecting or carrying out attacks in a specific zone or locality, while the mobile brigade carried out attacks far afield from a specific zone. With the emphasis on mobile warfare the NRA increased their attacks on UNLA targets during June and July of 1983.

In December 1983 the chief of staff of the UNLA, David Oyite-Ojok, was killed in a helicopter crash. This had a negative ripple effect on the UNLA and set in motion a chain of events that would ultimately lead to the ousting of Obote. Ojok's death caused confusion and a leadership vacuum that led to conflict within the UNLA ranks. On July 27, 1985 Obote was overthrown in favor of a military council headed by the Generals Bazilio Okello and Tito Okello Lutwa.

Steady advances by the NRA allowed them to open up a second front in the southwestern region of Uganda, at the base of the Rwenzori mountains, in March and April. By August 1985 peace talks had begun between the NRM and the UNLA; a tenuous peace accord was signed on December 17. However, fighting continued and the NRA advanced on Kampala, capturing it on January 26, 1986. Museveni was sworn in as president three days later.

The NRM attempted to implement the political objectives of its so-called Ten Point Program, which sought to establish popular democracy, encourage national unity, and rebuild the economy. As part of this course of action, the NRM extended amnesty to guerrilla groups. Museveni created a coalition government consisting of members of the Democratic Party, the Uganda Peoples Congress and the Federal Democratic Movement, plus several other organizations. Eventually most of these parties left the coalition. The most notable defection was Paul Ssemogerere of the DP, who would become Museveni's strongest opponent in the elections of 1996.

The NRM saw political parties as historically divisive in Uganda because they promoted sectarianism along ethnic lines. As part of the Ten Point Program, political parties were eschewed under the banner of "no partyism." Political parties were allowed to operate but could not enjoy official status.

Despite attempts at coalition building, the NRM was not able to bring in dissident groups from the north. The vacuum created by the defeat of the Acholi-led military commission was filled by the insurgency of Alice Lakwena and the Holy Spirit Movement. After the defeat of the Holy Spirit Movement by the NRA, the Lord's Resistance Army initiated a program of guerrilla warfare. The winning of political power by the NRM has come, to some extent, at the expense of northern integration.

OPOLOT OKIA

See also: **Museveni, Yoweri Kaguta.**

Further Reading

Amaza, Godfrey Ondoga ori. *Museveni's Long March: From Guerrilla to Statesman.* Kampala, Uganda: Fountain, 1998.

Hansen, Hölgar Bernt, and Michael Twaddle (eds.). *From Chaos to Order: The Politics of Constitution-Making in Uganda.* Kampala, Uganda: Fountain Press/London: James Currey, 1995.

Museveni, Yoweri K. *Sowing the Mustard Seed: The Struggle for Freedom and Democracy in Uganda,* edited by Elisabeth Kanyogonya and Kevin Shillington. Basingstoke, England: Macmillan, 1997.

———. *What is Africa's Problem? Speeches and Writings on Africa.* Kampala, Uganda: NRM, 1992.

Ociti, Jim. *Political Evolution and Democratic Practice in Uganda, 1952–1996.* Lewiston, Edwin Mellon Press, 2000.

Uganda: Reconstruction: Politics, Economics

Following years of misrule and civil conflict in Uganda, power was achieved by Yoweri Museveni and his National Resistance Movement (NRM) government in January 1986 following a guerrilla war with, successively, the second government of Milton Obote (1980–1985) and then the government of Generals Bazilio Okello and Tito Okello. On coming to power, Museveni proclaimed that his top priorities were national conciliation, economic development, and army discipline. While the latter aim was swiftly achieved, with the army gaining much respect from most ordinary Ugandans, the country embarked on a managed transition to an unusual form of democracy in the early 1990s. Heading an elected "no-party" government, president Museveni attacked the concept of multiparty democracy with both vigor and eloquence. He claimed that it was inappropriate for Uganda to have a political system based on divided and divisive political parties. He noted—with some justification—that, when tried in the past, a fundamental cause of the country's societal

and political problems had been the ethnic and religious divisiveness caused by the competition of multiparty politics. In Uganda, there are four main religious divides—Protestants, Catholics, Muslims, and followers of African traditional religions—and some 40 distinct ethnic groups.

Museveni and his government inherited a shattered economy, heavily dependent on foreign loads and investment if it were soon to recover. Encouraged by Museveni's determination to rebuild the country's political, social, and economic stability, Uganda was the recipient of billions of dollars of foreign aid from the late 1980s on. A condition for its disbursement, however, was the adoption of major economic reforms via a structural adjustment program, with terms dictated by the International Monetary Fund and the World Bank. Surprisingly, the international financial institutions did not try to link the granting of financial assistance to political conditionality, especially progress to a multiparty political system. The chief reason, it appears, is that there was admiration for the way that Museveni and his government had managed to install a fair level of stability after decades of turmoil.

The centerpiece of political reform in Uganda after 1986 was the proclaimed policy of fundamentally shifting power to the mass of ordinary people, especially in the rural areas, where the majority of Ugandans live. Museveni claimed to have created a government of national unity drawn from as many effectively autonomous or semiautonomous political forces as possible, in order to bring the country's internal wars to a close. Balancing (and to some extent constraining) the resultant broad-based but weak central government were resistance councils (RCs), strong representations of the multifarious political grassroots of the country. These bodies were established initially in the early 1980s in the "liberated areas" then under Museveni's control. Small-scale, face-to-face support groups, they were examples, he claimed, of grassroots, popular democracy. Following the achievement of power, RCs spread throughout Uganda as an important NRM policy.

The RCs were not seen by the country's political leaders as an inferior substitute for other kinds of representative institutions. Rather, they were defended as being fundamentally more democratic institutions than earlier political parties operating in the country. Traditional parties—including the Democratic Party, the Uganda Peoples' Congress, and the Kabaka Yekka (King Alone) movement in Buganda—had collectively made Uganda's transition to independence from Britain in 1962 an intensely pressured and divisive affair. Their maneuvers and strategies to achieve power had the counterproductive result of strongly encouraging ethnic, regional and "sectarian" differences (what Museveni's government called the country's "politicoreligious cleavages") still dividing Uganda today.

After its seizure of power, the NRM installed an intricate structure of "nonparty" RCs from village to district level. Elections to the various levels were held in 1989 and 1992. The October 1995 constitution provided for a 276-member unicameral parliament and an autonomous, independently elected president. The constitution formally extended Uganda's one-party "movement system" form of government for five years and severely restricted political party activities.

In what was widely interpreted as a step toward political normalization, separate generally peaceful and orderly presidential and parliamentary elections were held in June and July 1996. Museveni was elected president by a wide margin (70 per cent) over his nearest challenger, Paul Ssemogerere, joint candidate of the Democratic Party and the Ugandan People's Congress. NRM supporters won an overwhelming majority of seats in the new parliament. Overall, popular participation in the three sets of elections was widespread, providing positive evidence of the NRM's commitment to its own kind of no-party democracy.

During the 1990s, political reforms were paralleled by economic reforms. Despite the regime's disavowal of multiparty democracy and a questionable human and civil rights record, there was considerable financial support for the NRM government from external sources. The government relied heavily on foreign aid to support its development program, with foreign assistance accounting for approximately 51 per cent of government spending. Rebuilding the country's export base after years of decline, there were economic reward: between 1985 and 1997 average annual growth of gross domestic product per capita averaged 2.7 per cent. Overall, in the 1990s the economy grew, albeit from a low base, at over 7 per cent a year. While much of this growth was no more than rebuilding after years of civil strife, it was nonetheless a good record.

Museveni has been able to bring political stability and economic steadiness to most of a country that has hardly experienced either since independence in 1962. He was reelected in 2001, and in 2003 he proposed lifting the ban on multiparty politics, subject to a referendum. Surrounded by politically volatile countries (including the Democratic Republic of Congo [Zaire], Sudan, Ethiopia, and Rwanda), Uganda is seen by Western governments as an island of stability in an increasingly turbulent East African region. However, despite undoubted successes, significant problems remain. While national reconstruction and economic growth and reconstruction have forged ahead in the south of the country, the government is embroiled in a civil war in the north with rebels with bases in southern Sudan and eastern Congo.

JEFF HAYNES

See also: **Museveni, Yoweri Kaguta.**

Further Reading

Hansen, Hölgar Bernt and Michael Twaddle (eds.). *Changing Uganda: The Dilemmas of Structural Adjustment and Revolutionary Change.* London: James Currey, 1991.
———. *Developing Uganda.* Oxford: James Currey, 1998.
———. *From Chaos to Order: The Politics of Constitution-Making in Uganda.* Kampala, Uganda: Fountain/London: James Currey, 1995.
———. *Uganda Now: Between Decay and Development.* London: James Currey, 1988.
Kasfir, Nelson, "'No-Party Democracy in Uganda." *Journal of Democracy* 9, no. 1 (1998): 49–63.
Museveni, Yoweri. *What is Africa's Problem? Speeches and Writings on Africa.* Kampala, Uganda: NRM, 1992.

Uganda: Conflict, Regional Since 1990

During the 1990s, Uganda's efforts at recovery from the internal upheavals of the 1970s and 1980s were striking. By the beginning of the new millennium, some parts of the country had made appreciable social and economic progress. Overall, a fair degree of political stability had returned to the south.

Yet the country has been mired in one conflict after another throughout the period since 1990. Apart from cases of internal strife, such as the war in the north and east and the rebellion in the west, Uganda was embroiled in the armed conflicts raging in neighboring Sudan, Rwanda, and the Democratic Republic of the Congo (DRC) under the auspices of the National Resistance Movement (NRM).

Yoweri Museveni's NRM regime was faced with serious internal rebel activity almost from the moment it assumed power in January 1986. Following the defeat of the forces of Tito Okello and Bzilio Okello, some soldiers of the Uganda National Liberation Army (the previous government's fighting force) joined the newly formed rebel Uganda People's Democratic Army (UPDA) operating in northern Uganda. In August they attacked Gulu town. This marked the formal start of the internal rebel war in opposition to the NRM government.

Although the UPDA itself did not score any spectacular victory, the arrival of the Holy Spirit Mobile Forces (HSMF) on the political scene in late 1986 compounded the situation considerably. The HSMF, which succeeded in recruiting large numbers of ex–government soldiers in a comparatively short period, was led by Alice Lakwena, described as a prophet or spiritual leader. The HSMF's declared principal objective was to fight evil and remove the central government. In late 1987, it was defeated on the outskirts of Iganga, a town barely 80 kilometers from Kampala, Uganda's seat of government. Despite the administration's persistent claim over the years that the antigovernment war was being stamped out, the violence and insecurity arising from this rebellion continued to destabilize Uganda well into and beyond the 1990s.

Historically, relations between Uganda and Sudan have been particularly important because they have had similar internal problems over the years. Both the northern Ugandans and southern Sudanese are on the periphery of their respective countries, and both have been involved in rebel activities against their central governments. From the late 1980s, Sudanese troops allegedly crossed into Ugandan territory in search of Sudanese rebels. Uganda even claimed that Sudanese military aircraft had bombed parts of northern Uganda several times.

From 1992 to 1995, hostilities between the two nations increased, with over 100,000 Sudanese refugees reportedly crossing into Uganda. Each side accused the other of supporting rebel groups to attack it. The arrival of the Lord's Resistance Army (LRA) on the political scene complicated matters further, as it reportedly received military backing from the Sudan government. At the same time, the Ugandan government threw its support behind the Sudan People's Liberation Army in its rebel war against the Khartoum administration.

From the early 1990s, the LRA stepped up its fight by not only attacking military targets in northern Uganda but also kidnapping children, both boys and girls, and forcibly recruiting them into their army. The NRM government also accused them of torturing civilians and carrying them into Sudan. In response, the LRA charged that Museveni had betrayed the Acholi following his abrogation of the December 1985 peace agreement with the previous administration of Tito Okello; his NRM had overturned the government in January 1986, and later occupied Acholi land. The NRM had carried out serious human rights abuses on the Acholi in its abortive campaign to bring about a military solution to the conflict. The NRM's decision to remove over 200,000 individuals by force and place them in so-called protected villages from 1990 onward, coupled with the LRA's own attacks on civilians, only caused the civilian population further suffering as they inevitably became victims of the two warring sides. Quite often the operations resulted in rapes, abductions and even summary executions.

The growing tension between Uganda and Sudan in the mid-1990s led to the two breaking diplomatic relations in 1995. This situation seemed to be improving, however, when the presidents of the two countries signed the Nairobi Agreement in December 1999. This accord mapped out a detailed plan for ending the conflict between the two nations. Both nations agreed to disarm rebel groups on their own soil and to stop supporting them. They also promised to restore full diplomatic relations by early 2000. This, however, did not happen.

The regionalization of Uganda's involvement in conflict was further carried forward by the alleged support it lent to the Rwanda Patriotic Front's (RPF) invasion of Rwanda in late 1990. Since the 1959 upheavals in Rwanda, thousands of Rwandans had flocked to Uganda. By the late 1980s approximately 250,000 such refugees had settled in the country. Several generations had taken up Ugandan citizenship and some had in fact become involved in the country's politics at the highest levels. One such Rwandan exile was Major General Fred Rwigyema, who not only had risen to the position of deputy commander of the national army, but had even previously worked as Uganda's deputy minister of defense. In October 1990 he led a group of approximately 4000 Uganda-based Rwandan rebel troops in an incursion into northern Rwanda. Rwigyema was killed by Rwandan government soldiers in the attack, and the invasion worsened relations between the two countries significantly. Although an agreement was reached in early 1991 in which the Rwandan administration extended an amnesty to all exiled Rwandans on condition of their observing a cease-fire, rebel activities continued unabated in northern Rwanda from 1991 to 1993. This caused the displacement of thousands of Ugandans living in the border area in early 1994. At the same time, Rwanda was experiencing internal civil strife involving the genocidal massacre of up to a million people, all of which complicated relations with neighboring countries, including Uganda.

The turning point came with the RPF's military victory over the Rwandan government soldiers in mid-1994. The new vice president and minister of defense, Paul Kagame, had been a high-ranking officer in the Ugandan national army. Thereafter, relations between Uganda and Rwanda improved dramatically. Museveni paid an official visit to Rwanda the following year (1995), and the two countries agreed to strengthen economic and social cooperation. In 1996 and 1997, it became an open secret that the two administrations had both lent their support to the then Zairean (now DRC) rebel organization led by Laurent Kabila that toppled the Mobutu government in May 1997.

Of the regional conflicts in which Uganda was involved since 1990, the crisis in the DRC has lasted the longest and produced the most severe ramifications. The roots of the conflict date back to the late 1980s, when groups of Ugandan anti-Museveni rebels based in Zaire began to attack western Uganda, allegedly with the support of Zairean soldiers. The most prominent of these disparate Ugandan rebel organizations was the Allied Democratic Front (ADF), which posed a major threat to security and peace in Uganda's Ruwenzori region. In retaliation, Ugandan troops often pursued these rebels into eastern Zaire and occupied the territory. There were, additionally, persistent reports (later confirmed) that the Ugandan government had been arming Kabila's rebel movement and giving it tactical support in its fight against the Mobutu regime. Kabila took power in May 1997. Later, however, Uganda withdrew its support for Kabila as he seemed unable (and unwilling) to stop the anti-Museveni rebel forces from using eastern DRC as their launching pad for attacks on western Uganda.

In August 1998 Museveni's government, in collaboration with the Rwandan regime, sent troops into eastern DRC, ostensibly to protect Ugandan and Rwandan security interests. The two countries formed a joint military command. The Kabila government's response was to charge (with some justification, it seems) that both Uganda and Rwanda's real intentions were to expand Tutsi domination in the Great Lakes region and to exploit the enormous mineral wealth of the DRC.

Amid such accusations and counteraccusations the conflict continued. In July 1999 the parties to the conflict signed the Lusaka Accord. They agreed to observe a cease-fire monitored by a joint military commission. The Kabila government also agreed to accept United Nations (UN) peacekeeping troops in the DRC after all foreign forces had withdrawn from the country.

The implementation of the Lusaka Accord, however, proved quite problematic almost from the outset. There were frequent violations of the cease-fire. Additionally, tense relations developed between Uganda and Rwanda when the main DRC rebel group they had backed broke up into two rival factions. This not only resulted in the two countries giving support to two opposing groups, but also to a major military confrontation in Kisangani between Ugandan and Rwandan troops in late 1999 and early 2000. In the clash, the Ugandan troops were humiliated when the Rwandans drove them out of Kisangani, while the main victims of this unsightly contest between two foreign African countries outside their own respective territory were the DRC people. Later, the two sides agreed to withdraw their troops from Kisangani. In May 2000, the DRC agreed to the deployment of 500 UN military observers, supported by some 5000 troops, to monitor the cease-fire.

The assassination of DRC president Kabila in January 2001 removed one of the perceived major stumbling blocks to the implementation of the Lusaka Accord. His replacement by his 29-year old son, Joseph, seemed to give the quest for a peaceful settlement of the DRC conflict a new lease of life. In April 2001 a UN panel published a damning report that concluded that "the governments of Uganda, Rwanda and Burundi, whose troops occupied parts of eastern DRC, were profiting from the conflict by looting gold and other precious minerals . . . [and] elephant tusks."

Under international pressure, Uganda was forced to institute its own commission of inquiry into the reported misdeeds. While it had been expected by many observers that Uganda's role in the DRC war had seriously eroded the president's popularity, Ugandans went to the polls in March 2001 and elected Museveni for another five-year term as president. In the campaign leading up to the controversial elections, questions had been raised about the negative effects of the armed conflicts on Uganda's economy and the possibility that a large section of the population had become thoroughly disenchanted with Museveni during his fifteen-year rule. However, his most effective challenger in the presidential elections, retired army colonel Kiiza Besigye, was unable to stop Museveni, despite a strong showing. By mid-2001 there were indications that the conflict in the DRC might begin to abate as the various countries embroiled there began to withdraw their troops. In December 2002 a peace deal was signed, appearing to end the conflict.

BALAM NYEKO

See also: **Congo (Kinshasa), Democratic Republic of/Zaire: Post-Mobutu Era; Museveni, Yoweri Kaguta.**

Further Reading

African Rights. "Northern Uganda: Justice in Conflict." Report, 20 January 2000; www.unimondo.org/AfricanRights/html/ugand0001.htm/

Gakwandi, Arthur. "Foreign Relations." In *Uganda's Age of Reforms,* edited by Justus Mugaju. Kampala, Uganda: Fountain, 1999.

Westbrook, David. "The Torment of Northern Uganda: A Legacy of Missed Opportunities." *OJPCR: The Online Journal of Peace and Conflict Resolution* 3, no. 2 (2000); *www.trinstitute.org/ojpcr/*

Uganda Agreement: *See* **Uganda: Colonization, Resistance, Uganda Agreement, 1890–1900.**

Uganda Railway: *See* **Kenya: East African Protectorate and the Uganda Railway.**

Umzila: *See* **Soshangane, Umzila, Gungunhane and the Gaza State.**

Undi: *See* **Maravi: Phiri Clan, Lundu and Undi Dynasties.**

Union Douanière et Economique de L'Afrique Central (UDEAC)

The Union Douanière et Economique de L'Afrique Central (UDEAC) was established in 1968, but its origins date back to 1959, when France, in an effort to achieve an easy administration within its colonies in central Africa, created the Afrique Equatorial Francaise (AEF). The countries that made up the AEF were the Central African Republic (CAR), Chad, Congo, and Gabon. With the demise of French colonial rule, the leaders of the AEF decided to transform it into the Union Douanière Equatorial (UDE), or Equatorial Custom Union. This was achieved through a treaty that was signed in Brazzaville, Congo, on June 23, 1959. The objectives of the UDE were to establish a common external tariff and import duties among its members, to obtain a harmonized fiscal policy, and to coordinate the economic and social development plans of member states.

In 1961, the UDE was transformed into the Union Douanière Equatorial et du Cameroun (UDE-Cameroun) when Cameroon, which was not part of the French union (AEF) signed a treaty with UDE, setting the stage for exchange control and providing for regional cooperation. However, the UDE-Cameroon Treaty did not provide for a total harmonization of custom duties between Cameroon and the UDE countries, though it did provide for Cameroon's adoption of most of the integration measures of UDE. Consequently, Cameroon opted for full membership in UDE.

It was this eagerness by Cameroon to create unity that culminated in the signing of the Treaty of Brazzaville in 1964, establishing the UDEAC. The treaty became effective on January 1, 1966. In 1984, Equatorial Guinea joined the Union (UDEAC), making it the only member that is not a former French colony.

The transformation of UDE-Cameroun into UDEAC paved the way for a broader economic union. The objectives include an eventual economic union between member states and the creation of a regionally balanced industrial structure. The Treaty of Brazzaville advocated the elimination of restrictions on commodity movement between member states, the institution of a common external tariff against third countries, and the removal of intra union trade barriers, including some degree of harmonization of national economic policies, especially in the areas of industrial, investment, and transportation development. No member country can unilaterally impose import duties or taxes on another member except when such a measure is instituted as a safeguard. A single tax system was established in order to promote the creation of a regional manufacturing base and trade in manufacture goods. The treaty also encourages free movement of capital, goods and services within UDEAC's territory.

The UDEAC is made up of three primary organs. The supreme decision-making body is the Council of Heads of States, which is comprised of the six heads of states of the member countries. It meets annually and makes decisions affecting the union on the basis of consensus among all its members. Next is the Management Committee, which is comprised of two ministers from each member state—usually the minister of finance and the minister of economic development. This committee meets biannually and derives its power from the Council of Heads of States. It is charged with making decisions on the rates of the common tariff, fiscal harmonization and coordination of industrial policy, the single tax, custom legislation, and regulation. Prior to its meeting, a committee of experts meets and makes recommendations to the Management Committee, most of which are accepted. The Secretariat, the administrative body of the UDEAC, is located in Bangui, CAR, and is headed by a secretary general. It is composed of two divisions: the first deals with foreign commerce, fiscal policies, and statistics while the second carries out industrial planning and harmonizes transportation policies.

The UDEAC has taken several steps toward economic integration. It operates a central bank, Banque de l'Etats d'Afrique Central, which issues a common currency (the francs CFA) used by the six member countries. A complete unification of most taxes has been achieved. A common external tariff applies to all imports entering the member countries. On the other hand, goods circulating within the UDEAC are exempt from any import duties, except where there is a differential in the rate of supplementary tax between the countries of final consumption. Goods manufactured within the UDEAC are under the single tax system, which was designed to eliminate the tendency of members to either lose important fiscal resources (if they industrialize) or continue to import from foreign countries. All industries whose products are sold in more than one member state are regulated by the single tax. These industries are exempt from all import duties with respect to their raw materials including the items that they use in packing. The single tax varies from one country to the other for the same item. Member states sometimes demand higher rates for an item produced in another member state compared to the rates they demand for the item produced in their own country. This is due to the fact that each country wants to protect its industries against competition from the same industries in the other partner's state.

Common custom offices have been established throughout the union, and the sharing and settlement of proceeds of custom duties takes place every three months. A Solidarity Fund exists, the purpose of which is to help reduce the level of economic disparity between the more developed member states, such as Cameroon and Gabon, and the less developed ones, such as the CAR and Chad.

Since its creation, the UDEAC has not been without problems. In 1968 Chad and the CAR, dissatisfied with the union's policy, withdrew to form a parallel union with the Democratic Republic of Congo. However, this did not work as the CAR returned to the UDEAC shortly after it left, while Chad returned in 1984. Against a background of persistent economic crisis that has been plaguing the UDEAC, the Treaty of Brazzaville was revised in 1974 because of declining trade among the union's members. In 1994 a new custom and fiscal regime, intended to effect broad economic changes within the union, was created.

PETER J. TESI

See also: **Banking and Finance; Colonial Federations: French Equatorial Africa; Communauté Financière Africaine; Economic Community of West African States (ECOWAS).**

Further Reading

Aryeetey, Ernest. "Sub-Saharan African Experiences with Regional Integration." In *Trade Reform and Regional Integration in Africa*, edited by Zubair Iqbal and Mohsin S. Khan. Washington, D.C.: International Monetary Fund, 1998.

Asante, S. K. B. *Regionalism and Africa's Development: Expectations, Reality, and Challenges.* Basingstoke, England: Macmillan Press/New York: St Martin's Press, 1997.

Elbadawi, Ibrahim A., and Francis M. Mwega. "Regional Integration, Trade, and Foreign Direct Investment in Sub-Saharan Africa." In *Trade Reform and Regional Integration in Africa*, edited by Zubair Iqbal and Mohsin S. Khan. Washington, D.C.: International Monetary Fund, 1998.

General Agreement on Tariffs and Trade (GATT). *Trade Policy Review: Cameroon*, vols. 1 and 2. Geneva: GATT, 1995.

International Trade Centre, UNCTAD/GATT. *Cameroon: The Market for Selected Manufactured Products from Developing Countries.* Geneva, International Trade Centre, 1969.

Jalloh, Abdul Aziz. "Foreign Private Investment and Regional Political Integration in UDEAC." In *Economic Cooperation and Integration in Africa*, edited by Wilfred A. Ndongko. Dakar: CODESRIA, 1985.

UNITA: *See* Angola: MPLA, FNLA, UNITA, and the War of Liberation, 1961–1974.

United Nations: *See* Mandates: League of Nations and United Nations; Namibia (Southwest Africa): League of Nations, United Nations Mandate.

Upare, Usambara, Kilimanjaro

Mount Kilimanjaro and the mountains of Upare and Usambara form the northeastern highlands of Tanzania, which stretch almost to the East African coast. The history of the former inhabitants of this region, like the earlier history of the peoples living there today, remains largely unknown because of the scantiness of available materials. Most of the current inhabitants of the highlands are Bantu peoples, such as the Chagga at Kilimanjaro,

the Upare in the Upare Mountains, and the Shambala in the Usambara Mountains. Additionally, some clans of the Southern Cushitic Mbugu still live in the Usambaras, and scattered Eastern Nilotic Masai groups can be found throughout the area.

Knowledge of the early history of this region is based mainly on archaeology, and less on linguistic reconstructions and oral traditions. Unfortunately, archaeological Stone Age sequences attesting to the introduction of pottery or to techniques of food production are completely lacking; the same is true of sites that might document the transition from the Later Stone Age to the Iron Age. The few pottery findings of the Later Iron Age tell us little, as they do not involve detailed sequences, comprehensively analysed assemblages, or well-dated sites; nor can they be linked with any people living there today.

The best-documented period by far is the Early Iron Age, represented mostly by pottery of the so-called Kwale style. Kwale pottery has been found exclusively in South Upare and the Usambaras, with finds dating from the third to the ninth centuries. Iron and iron slag are frequently found associated with this pottery style, and there are clear indications of agriculture and a cattle economy. Pottery strongly resembling the Kwale type has been found throughout the highlands and near Mombasa. In the Kwale region a local diversification of pottery styles took place as early as the fourth century, in such a way that often no clear relation can be established among the various styles. Conclusions drawn from this picture in regard to ethnic history are thus problematic: ethnic continuity may have prevailed while the pottery style was diversified, or else the original population may have been replaced by several unidentified groups.

From 870, there appeared in South Upare a new pottery style called Maore, independent of Kwale and only rarely to be found at Kwale sites. Maore ware was also in use in Northern Upare, but here often along with Kwale ware; the Northern Upare evidence can be dated from the sixth to the tenth centuries. In the Kilimanjaro region both styles can again be found in the same sites, and are dated from 250. The makers of Maore ware presumably subsisted on hunting and stockraising; they may, however, also have practiced agriculture and maintained trade contacts with the coast, as reflected in the beads and shell ornaments found. In the Usambaras the Kwale ware of the second and third centuries was replaced by the so-called Tana ware of the fifth and sixth centuries, which differs too strongly from Kwale to have evolved from it. In tandem with the change in ceramic style, a change in settlement patterns can also be recognized. The Kwale settlements in the Usambaras were situated on mountain ridges, a settlement scheme that can still be found today at

Kilimanjaro among the Chagga. With the emergence of the Tana ware this settlement pattern came to an end in the Usambaras. The few lexical roots reconstructed linguistically for this period appear to confirm these archaeological results.

The oral traditions of the Upare, Chagga, and Shambala do not shed much light on the history of the Early and Late Iron Ages. They report that the Upare migrated from the Taita Hills to their present territories about 600 years ago, and that the ancestors of the Chagga immigrated from many directions and/or descended from various ethnic groups. The Upare and Chagga do, however, mention small groups of hunters whom they met at their arrival and subsequently drove off or absorbed.

The Kwale ware is frequently associated with the Bantu populations now found in the region, inasmuch as Kwale is part of an early Iron Age complex that includes the dimple-based ware of the interlacustrine region and almost certainly the channelled wares found in Zambia and present-day Zimbabwe. Some scholars have therefore constructed a cultural connection between the manufacturers of these pottery styles. The geographical distribution of these related styles coincides with that of the hypothetisized Bantu expansions. However, this alignment of relatively recent linguistic distributions with archaeological distributions often showing an age of at least a millennium, is highly questionable in methodological terms, and is based only on the similarity of geographical distribution. Thus the above hypothesis can by no means be considered as proven. It does, however, receive some support from the local agricultural traditions. These characterize the immigrating Bantu as farmers who made use of Iron Age technologies. The regions economically suitable for such agriculturalists correspond well with the dispersal area of Kwale pottery; indeed, the Kilimanjaro, Upare, and Usambara regions resemble each other in respect to rainfall quantities and native vegetation. Though oral traditions indicate that agriculture—for example, on the western and northern slopes of the Kilimanjaro—is a recent phenomenon, botanical evidence militates against this. The evidence that agriculture was carried out at a much earlier period on the northern slopes of Mount Kilimanjaro consists partly in the existence of a forest belt of wild olive trees, which generally regrow naturally in the Mount Kilimanjaro forest in the regeneration phase after the forest has been burned. Further, the vegetation of the forest clearings, in which most of the fields lie, displays features that can be interpreted as vestiges of very old agricultural traditions.

The Upare have traditionally maintained an iron industry of supraregional importance; this might indicate a link to the early Iron Age findings.

REINHARD KLEIN-ARENDT

See also: **Iron Age (Later): East Africa.**

Further Reading

Ehret, Christopher. *An African Classical Age: Eastern and Southern Africa in World History, 1000 B.C. to A.D. 400.* Charlottesville: University Press of Virginia/Oxford: James Currey, 1998.

Kimambo, Isaria N. *A Political History of the Upare of Tanzania, c1500–1900.* Nairobi: East African Publishing, 1969.

Odner, Knut. "A Preliminary Report of an Archaeological Survey on the Slopes of Kilimanjaro." *Azania.* no. 6 (1971): 131–151.

———. "Usangi Hospital and Other Archaeological Sites in the North Upare Mountains, North-Eastern Tanzania." *Azania.* no. 6 (1971): 89–131.

Soper, Robert. "Iron Age Sites in North-Eastern Tanzania." *Azania.* no. 2 (1967): 19–37.

Upper Volta: *See* Burkina Faso (Upper Volta).

Urabi Pasha: *See* Egypt: Urabi Pasha and British Occupation, 1879–1882.

Urbanization and Site Hierarchy: West Africa: Savannah and Sahel
The Concept of Urbanism

Our current understanding that urbanism was an indigenous and recurrent phenomenon in West African savanna and the Sahel dates largely to the postcolonial period. In the colonial imagination, Africa was predominantly rural in character, composed of small, undifferentiated villages of mud and thatch huts. The walled cities and towns of the Sahel (Kano province alone had 170 in 1900) were, consequently, a colossal surprise to Europeans. Frederick Lugard commented in 1902 before his assault on Kano that "I have never seen, nor even imagined, anything like it in Africa" (quoted in Connah 2000, 43). Colonial era historians and archaeologists accommodated this urban anomaly by "medievalizing" the Sahel and conceptualizing it as an economic and cultural dependent of the Islamic world. Cultural and political achievements in the Sahel were attributed to influences from the north. This diffusionist paradigm formalized the belief that urbanism was not native to Africa.

Farther south, European administrators and anthropologists did not recognize the large, densely populated, nucleated Yoruba settlements as urban in character. Why was this? One of the main obstacles to the recognition of precolonial African urbanism was that all the conceptual tools available for investigating this topic had been developed with reference to Western sequences of historical development. The bulk of the ideas on what cities are and how they have changed through time dealt with European urban transformations from classical antiquity through the Middle Ages and the Industrial Revolution. Thus, many nineteenth- and early-twentieth-century attempts to define the term *urban* proceeded by constructing ideal types that identified essential features differentiating Western urban society from pre- or nonurban society.

The archaeologist V. G. Childe constructed a list of essential features of urban civilization, including writing and monumental architecture, thereby excluding much of black Africa from consideration. The West has long thought of cities as centers of despotic power, with impressive architecture reflecting that power. It is now recognized that monumentality, while a common strategy employed by rulers of early city-states in Mesoamerica and Mesopotamia (among others), was not an inevitable accompaniment of early urbanism. The Bronze Age cities of China, for example, had no monumental architecture. Among the reasons for the lack of investment in monuments in much of Sub-Saharan Africa are lack of suitable building materials (such as stone) in some areas and the prevalence of extensive, slash-and-burn agricultural systems that required settlement relocation after several decades, thus working against permanent installation of populations at one location for long periods. In many areas, the location of the capital city shifted with every accession of a new ruler. Ecological constraints linked to a value system that conceived of space as social (rooted in kin groups and genealogical proximity), rather than as a particular physical place, produced African urban configurations that looked quite different than the cities of the West.

All of this helps explain why European observers failed to recognize African towns and cities: because they did not conform to concepts of urbanism derived from Western historical sequences. The postcolonial period has seen a reorientation of research that has exposed the ethnographic assumptions and ideological underpinnings of many of the earlier theories of urbanism. Emphasis has shifted from what a city is (widely agreed to be a futile pursuit in view of the tremendous range of urban forms) to what a city does. We owe to geographers the important realization that urban centers never exist in isolation; they are always articulated with a regional hinterland. Whatever else a city may be, it is a unit of settlement that performs specialized functions in relation to a broader hinterland. The specialized functions may be of an economic nature, such as production and export of goods and services, or they have a more social aspect, such as the elaboration of power and new social institutions or the exchange of information. Urbanism thus represents a novel kind of relationship among sites in a region involving the emergence of specialization and functional interdependence. The symbiosis characteristic of the urban system emerges out of the circulation of commodities essential to subsistence (food, iron used to produce food) within it. Urban systems are predicated upon the exchange of agricultural surplus. Their characteristic spatial signature is a hierarchy of higher and lower order settlements in which higher order sites are larger and more populous and fill a wider range of specialized functions than lower order settlements.

Urbanism and Site Hierarchies in West Africa

The systematic study of the earliest manifestations of precolonial urban growth in West Africa is still in its infancy. Although archaeological research undertaken in the late 1960s and 1970s demonstrated the antiquity and indigenous character of very large-scale agglomerations on the margins of the southern Sahara at Tichitt and along the Middle Niger River at Jenne-jeno, West Africa remains underserved by archaeologists interested in urbanism.

There are four "urban zones" of West Africa wherein urbanism is a recurrent feature of the indigenous cultural landscape with considerable time depth. In order of apparent chronological appearance, these are the Tichitt-Walata escarpment in southeastern Mauritania; the Inland Niger Delta and Méma regions of Mali; the southern Nigerian savanna and forest; and Hausaland, in the northern Nigerian Sahel. These areas are easily identifiable due to the prominent physical remains of walls, settlement mounds, or earthworks associated with the towns. Other "urban zones" with less prominent features probably await discovery by archaeologists. The diversity of "nontypical" urban forms (as defined by Western historical experience) in West Africa has great potential to broaden our comparative understanding of the forms and circumstances of early urban development.

Tichitt-Walata—Along the 60- to 100-meter-high escarpment that stretches 400 kilometers from Tichitt to Walata and Nema, agglomerations of stone-walled circular or oval compounds occur in considerable numbers; they were erected from 3500 to 2300 years ago, during the Neolithic period. Some are extremely large, measuring 30 to 95 hectares (a hectare is a unit of land 100 meters by 100 meters in size; it equals 2.5 acres), with 200 to 600 compounds. Questions have been raised as to whether these represent early towns, with an urban hierarchy of a very few large, some medium, and many small settlements. Or are these the remains of a seasonal settlement system of agropastoralists organized into an early chiefdom? One of the difficulties in evaluating these interpretations is the lack of agreement by different researchers over the interpretation of chronology at these settlements. Identification of site hierarchies presupposes some way of determining which settlements and compounds within settlements were occupied contemporaneously. This has proven elusive. Until more chronologically oriented research is done, the nature of the apparent hierarchies at Tichitt must remain in a suspense account.

Inland Niger Delta, Méma—Archaeological research indicates that the clustering of settlement mounds is characteristic of the "urban zone" in the basin of the Middle Niger, where people lived within the floodplain. Commonly, a cluster comprises a large, central settlement mound of up to 10 meters in height and 20 to 80 hectares in area, surrounded by intermediate and smaller size mounds at distances of 100 to 1000 meters. Excavation and survey at the vast mound of Jenne-jeno revealed that the site expanded to its maximum size of over 30 hectares by 850, soon after which a city wall of unfired mud brick was built. Regional survey indicated that of the 65 mounds located within four kilometers of Jenné-jeno, 32 were actively occupied in the period 850–1000. At this time, a clustered pattern of truly large settlements, plus a host of smaller ones in what seems to be a three-tier hierarchy, was a significant feature of the settlement system. The functional interdependence of these mounds was indicated by surface distributions of iron-smithing debris and fishing equipment that were restricted to only a few of the sites within the cluster. Interregional trade in local staples for raw materials such as stone and iron, unavailable on the floodplain, appears to have fueled this growth. The population of the entire urban cluster is estimated to have been between 10,000 and 25,000 people. Roderick McIntosh has suggested that clustered, functionally integrated settlements such as these may have been a common form of early urbanism in Africa as well as China, in cases where a powerful centralized authority had not yet emerged. Large, clustered mounds dating to the first millennium have also been investigated in the Méma region to the northwest of the Inland Delta, where there is some evidence that this pattern may extend back into the first millennium BCE or even earlier.

Nigerian Savanna and Forest—The typical form of the precolonial cities of the Yoruba and Edo peoples was a vast system of earthworks or earthen walls encircling both habitations and agricultural land. Roads ran like spokes on a wheel toward the palace of the *oba* (divine king), who was the spiritual center of the city-state. The great terra cotta, copper alloy, and stone sculptural traditions associated with forest city-states

such as Ife and Benin indicate the high level of craftsmanship and specialization that developed. Old Oyo (Oyo Ile), which was abandoned in the nineteenth century, was the most important Yoruba city-state located within the savanna zone. Seventy kilometers of enclosing earthen walls have been mapped and the area of the palace alone exceeds 200 hectares. Survey indicates that earthworks began to be erected in the later first millennium.

Hausaland, Northern Nigeria—The large fortified cities and towns of Hausaland were well-established by the sixteenth century, but their antiquity has not been investigated archaeologically. Fired brick city walls up to 20 kilometers in length enclosed urban domiciles and agricultural land, offering protection from raiders. Archaeological research may show that urban growth in this region was as early as in the Inland Niger Delta, and similarly linked to the growth of regional and indigenous long-distance trade.

SUSAN KEECH MCINTOSH

See also: **Iron Age and Neolithic: West Africa.**

Further Reading

Agbaje-Williams, Babatunde. "Oyo Ruins of NW Yorubaland, Nigeria." *Journal of Field Archaeology* 17, no. 3 (1990): 367–373.

Connah, Graham. "African City Walls: A Neglected Source?" In *Africa's Urban Past*, edited by David A. Anderson and Richard Rathbone. Oxford: James Currey, 2000.

———. *African Civilizations: Precolonial Cities and States in Tropical Africa.* Cambridge: Cambridge University Press, 1987.

Coquery-Vidrovitch, Catherine. "The Process of Urbanization in Africa (From the Origins to the Beginning of Independence)." *African Studies Review* 34, no. 1 (1991): 1–98.

Davidson, Basil. *The Lost Cities of Africa.* Little, Brown, 1959.

Holl, Augustin. "Background to the Ghana Empire: Archaeological Investigations on the Transition to Statehood in the Dhar Tichitt Region." *Journal of Anthropological Archaeology*, no. 4 (1985): 73–115.

Hull, Richard. *African Cities and Towns before the European Conquest.* New York: W. W. Norton, 1976.

Mabogunje, A. L. *Urbanization in Nigeria.* London: University of London Press, 1968.

McIntosh, Roderick. "Clustered Cities of the Middle Niger: Alternative Routes to Authority in Prehistory." In *Africa's Urban Past*, edited by David A. Anderson and Richard Rathbone. Oxford: James Currey, 2000(a).

———. "Western Representations of Urbanism and Invisible African Towns." In *Beyond Chiefdoms: Pathways to Complexity in Africa*, edited by Susan Keech McIntosh. Cambridge: Cambridge University Press, 2000(b).

McIntosh, Susan Keech, and Roderick McIntosh, "The Early City in West Africa: Toward an Understanding." *African Archaeological Review*, no. 2 (1984): 302–319.

Munson, Patrick. "Archaeology and the Prehistoric Origins of the Ghana Empire," *Journal of African History* 21 (1980): 457–466.

Munson, Patrick, "About 'Economie et société Néolithique du Dhar Tichitt (Mauritanie),'" *Sahara*, no. 2 (1989): 106–108.

Togola, Téréba. "Iron Age Occupation in the Méma Region, Mali." *African Archaeological Review* 13, no. 2 (1996): 91–110.

Wheatley, Paul. "The Concept of Urbanism." In *Man, Settlement and Urbanism*, edited by P. J. Ucko, R. Tringham and G. W. Dimbleby. London: Duckworth, 1972.

Winters, Christopher. "The Classification of Traditional African Cities." *Journal of Urban History* 10, no. 1 (1983): 3–31.

Urbanization: Colonial Context

The effervescence of the Hausa city-states and the Swahili ports, the prestige of the Sudanese capitals, the cultural influence of Timbuktu and Cairo, the fortifications of Great Zimbabwe, the architectural beauties of Zanzibar: these all bear witness to the diffusion of the urban phenomenon in precolonial Africa.

In North Africa, Arab Muslim civilization has long been largely urban, and over a long period the numerous urban centers of the Maghrib and the Mashriq, from Cairo to Marrakech, have accumulated political, economic, cultural, and residential functions. However, while urbanization was an ancient phenomenon to the North of the Sahara, many of the cities in Sub-Saharan Africa have developed much more recently, and, in general, partly as a result of colonial penetration. Whether in the north of the continent or the south, the older cities have themselves been greatly transformed by colonists.

As a result, urbanization in Africa has generally been characterized by external constraints connected with the logic of colonialism. Created, or refounded, in response to the expectations of metropolitan powers and made into pivots of imposed administrative structures, locations of European power, and indispensable synapses in colonial economies, they acquired characteristics that, in many respects, have still not been eliminated even now.

One of the most obvious ways in which colonization has influenced urbanization is through the far-reaching reorganization of urban networks. In West Africa, for example, the precolonial cities were generally hinterland cities, controlling the trade routes across the Sahara. A more dispersed organization of urban networks began to be put in place during the sixteenth century in line with the establishment of trading posts along the coasts; these formed the earliest zones of European settlement. Following the military conquests of the nineteenth century, there was a relative shift in the balance in favor of the urban centers of the interior, which were chosen—or created—for their strategic or economic worth according to the logic of the colonists. In parallel with this tendency, however, the development of ports and transportation infrastructure during the first half of the twentieth century helped to accentuate the distortion of urban networks toward the exterior, for their function was to siphon off African products to Europe.

Numerous cities were founded by the colonists, motivated either by strategic considerations or economic ones; indeed, many colonial cities started out with military and/or commercial functions. In central and southern Africa, for example, mining cities appeared, bringing thousands of workers together in compounds. Elsewhere, colonial capitals, such as Niamey (in Niger) or Nouakchott (in Mauritania), were created from scratch, and attempts were made to attract merchant ventures to them. The construction of railways also contributed to the development of certain centers that had previously been enclaves—for example, Nairobi in Kenya.

In their African cities, the colonists applied principles of development that they derived from the urban planning theories of their day, but they also adapted them to the needs and concerns of colonialism. One can observe throughout the continent the effects of their desire to rationalize and control space through the registration of plots of land, the imposition of symmetry and regular layouts, and the creation of subdivisions, all of which frequently led to the authoritarian displacement of populations. For most of the colonial period, nineteenth-century principles of public health and then, in the 1930s and 1940s, the practices of zoning (planning urban spaces according to function) legitimized, de facto or de jure, the separation of the "white city" from the "native city" according to a logic of spatial segregation that was taken to the extreme in South Africa, northern Rhodesia (now Zambia), and southern Rhodesia (now Zimbabwe). The ideal of the garden city was dominant in the European quarters of the cities in the British colonies. As for the Africans, they had to adapt themselves to the constraints of planning regulations, which favored "concessions"—plots of land on which several dwellings were grouped around a courtyard, a type of horizontal housing arranged in loose networks that took up a great deal of urban space. In North Africa—for example, in Cairo—certain dilapidated districts became much more densely populated.

In general, there was little regard for precolonial buildings. In Algeria the medinas were systematically destroyed over the course of the nineteenth century. Forms of "colonial" architecture emerged that were syncretic inventions by European architects or adaptations of models developed in the West Indies; these included, among many other examples, houses with verandas, buildings in "Moorish" or "neo-Sudanese" styles, and the farms of the Kenyan highlands.

Modern infrastructure such as electricity systems, street cleaning, water supplies or public services was financed mainly from local resources—whether customs dues, tax receipts, or borrowed funds—and was concentrated in the "white cities," while the native quarters on their peripheries were significantly underequipped. The first "shantytowns" (in the modern sense of the term) appeared in the major cities of northern Africa during the crisis of the 1930s. In southern Africa and northern Rhodesia, segregationist rules, which were reinforced after 1945, contributed to the strictly separate development of white cities and black "townships."

The urban growth that began in the late 1930s and continued after World War II presented difficult problems for colonial developers. Many of the development and urbanization plans of the 1950s were characterized by a new concern for improving the housing of Africans and increasing the range of urban services. Throughout Africa, however, the massive influx of country people seeking work, as well as the rapid natural growth of the city-dwelling populations, largely undermined the efforts undertaken in most of the colonies toward the end of the colonial period. The obvious marks of underdevelopment were already visible in the conurbations that formed the legacy of colonialism to the newly independent states.

SOPHIE DULUCQ

Further Reading

Coquery-Vidrovitch, Catherine. *Histoire des villes d'Afrique Noire*. Paris: Albin Michel, 1993.

———. "Villes coloniales et histoire des Africains." *Vingtième siècle*, no. 20 (1988): 49–73.

Gugler, J., and W. G. Flanagan. *Urbanization and Social Change in West Africa*. Cambridge: Cambridge University Press, 1978.

Poinsot, Jacqueline, Aain Sinou, and Jaroslav Sternadel. *Les villes d'Afrique Noire. Politiques et opérations d'urbanisme entre 1650 et 1960*. Paris: La Documentation Française, 1989.

Skinner, Edward P. "Urbanization in Francophone Africa." *African Urban Quarterly* 1, nos. 3–4 (1986): 191–195.

Soulillou, Jacques (ed.). *Rives coloniales: architectures, de Saint-Louis à Douala*. Marseille: Parenthèses-ORSTOM, 1993.

Southall, V. "The Impact of Imperialism upon Urban Development in Africa." in *Colonialism in Africa*, edited by V. Turner. Cambridge: Cambridge University Press, 1971.

Urbanization, Housing and Employment

Urbanization has not been a purely modern development in Africa; the capitals of some precolonial kingdoms date back to the tenth and eleventh centuries. However, many of Africa's major urban centers developed only during the colonial era, with the pace of urbanization accelerating markedly in the postcolonial era.

Africa is the world's least urbanized region, in terms of the proportion of the population living in urban centers. Only 30.5 per cent of the total population are presently living in such centers; this proportion ranges from 6 per cent in Rwanda to 82.5 per cent in Djibouti. Despite the generally low levels of urbanization, Africa is experiencing the highest rates of urbanization in the world, averaging about 4.4 per cent per annum. In the 1970s and 1980s, the population growth was in the range of 4.3 to 4.9 per cent, which was twice the rate of more developed countries' (MDCs) average. Moreover, whereas urban growth rates have been falling both in the world as a whole and in less developed countries (LDCs) in general, this is not the case in Africa.

The urban population in Africa increased from 14.7 per cent in 1950 to 30.5 per cent in 1994, and is likely to reach 50.5 per cent by 2025. In 1950, eight of every ten urban Africans resided in small and intermediate urban centers. By 2015 it is expected that more than half of the urban population will still be residing in such urban centers. Low levels of urbanization characterize most of Africa except for northern and southern Africa. By 1980, 25 per cent of Africa's population lived in urban areas; this figure was just behind Asia (27 per cent), but much less than half that of Latin America (65 per cent) and that of the MDCs (71 per cent). The rate of growth in Africa reached a peak of 4.9 per cent per annum in 1960–1965 and has started to taper off rather slowly.

Until the 1990s, Africa was characterized by the absence of any large urban center with 10 million or more inhabitants. The first urban center to achieve this size was Lagos, in 1995. The second class of urban centers, those with a population of 5 million to 10 million, held 6.4 per cent of the African urban population in 1970. After the expected disappearance of the second-level urban centers, through movement into the group of 10 million or more, the number of the latter is expected to reach 11 by 2015. At that time, they will contain 11.9 per cent of the urban population, or 68 million persons. The percentage of Africans living in urban centers with 1 million to 5 million inhabitants rose from 10.5 per cent in 1950, to 21.3 per cent in 1990 and is expected to remain at about that level until 2015 (20.8 per cent). Beginning from the relatively modest 84 million urban residents in 1970, Africa had 240 million urban dwellers in 1995, expected to increase to 804 million by 2025. Due to the extremely large population base in rural areas, countries have to absorb large numbers of rural migrants while struggling with rapid urbanization.

The degree of urbanization and the rate of growth of urban population in Africa vary considerably from country to country and from region to region. Except for northern and western Africa, urbanization is essentially a twentieth-century phenomenon and basically a product of Africa's colonial history. Southern Africa has the highest rate of urbanization; western Africa and parts of central Africa have the longest trend of African-initiated urbanization processes. Eastern Africa is the least urbanized region, while Northern Africa has the longest history of urbanization processes.

Although the level of urbanization in Africa is still relatively low, the continued growth of the urban population poses serious developmental problems. The high rate of urban growth is mainly due to rural-to-urban migration, a high natural increase in urban areas, an arbitrary expansion of urban boundaries, and ethnic conflicts. In addition, nonspatial factors have had significant impacts on the form, rate, nature, and extent of urban growth; these include fiscal, industrial, defense, equalization, agricultural, and immigration policies.

The rate of growth of the urban population of Africa has continued to increase, even as the rate of growth of gross national product per capita declined from 1.3 per cent in the 1960s to 0.7 per cent in the 1970s, and even further in the 1980s and 1990s. Migration has been fuelled by planning policies that have favored urban dwellers.

The development of Africa's small and intermediate urban centers will be the focus of urbanization in the twenty-first century because they link urbanization with rural development. The interdependence of urban and rural populations in Africa is striking. An estimated 70 per cent of urban residents maintain strong links to the rural sector; that figure may increase to 90 per cent in some urban areas. Small and intermediate urban centers have begun to grow very rapidly in Africa because the surrounding agricultural areas are prospering. More attention should be given to the role of these centers in agricultural processing, marketing, storage, bulking, and distribution. It is important to understand the nature of urban-rural linkages of small and intermediate urban centers considering, among other factors, the demand by the rural population for nonfood goods, inputs, and services needed by the agricultural sector and demand for agricultural output, which is highly income sensitive. In fact, increasing the demand for the last two is necessary for an appropriate supply response by farmers to price increases for farm inputs. Increases in rural incomes brought about by improved accessibility to markets and rising agricultural productivity lead to higher levels of activity in small and intermediate urban centers. The low-income households consume products and services produced locally rather than in distant urban centers. Therefore, increased rural consumption due to increased income will tend to diversify the economic activities of nearby urban centers and create substantial off-farm employment opportunities.

Africa's share of megacities and large urban centers is expected to increase from 14 per cent in 1950 to 56 per cent in 2015; the continent will contain more megacities and large urban centers than any other continent during the twenty-first century. Although in 1990 only 1 of the 33 large urban centers were in Africa, the large urban centers are growing faster than those in MDCs historically have.

The problems related to the high rates of urban growth in Africa are often accentuated by the concentration of population in the megacities and large urban centers. To the extent that these are the focus of development, they act as a magnet for migrants from both rural and other urban areas. The result is to increase the concentration of the urban population in one large metropolitan area to form what as been called a *primate urban pattern*. The growth of megacities and large urban centers and the prospects of their continued expansion rank among the most pressing urban problems of the twenty-first century. In addition, the size of megacities and large urban centers magnifies the problems of income and development discrepancies inherent in urbanization and suburbanization.

The megacities and large urban centers in Africa face increasing problems as population growth outruns investment in urban infrastructure. In most African megacities and the large urban centers, households spend over 40 per cent of their income on food. In Kinshasa and Johannesburg, at least two-thirds of the households lack water or electricity; for Lagos and Cape Town the figure is over 40 percent. In most African megacities and large urban centers there is less than one telephone for every ten persons. In Johannesburg and Lagos, at most one-third of residents aged 14 to 17 are in school; the percentages of school enrollment among that age group is higher in some other megacities. In terms of infant mortality, Cape Town and Johannesburg have reached relatively low levels (18 and 22 infant deaths per 1,000 live births, respectively). The two African megacities or large urban centers with the highest infant mortality (over 80 infant deaths per 1,000 live births) are Lagos and Kinshasa.

Over 60 per cent of urban dwellers in Africa live in poverty. With the current rates of urban growth and the inability of housing delivery systems to cope with the demand for affordable housing, the housing crisis is likely to increase in the future. If we move beyond the issue of population growth to the increase in the number of households, we get a better impression of the challenges ahead in terms of housing needs. Household sizes are declining in Africa. The result is that the need for new housing units is considerably higher than that indicated by the rate of population growth. In absolute terms, the increase in the number of households in MDCs are actually larger than population increase. From 1990 to 2000, 1.10 new households were created for each person added to the population. This stands in contrast with the situation in the Africa, where the corresponding figure was 0.31. This figure is expected to increase between 2000 and 2010 to 1.63 in MDCs and

0.38 in Africa. In the following decade (2010–2020), the figures are projected to reach 1.7 and 0.4 for MCDs and Africa, respectively.

In every year between 2000 and 2010, Africa will have to accommodate some 21 million additional urban households; for the following decade (2010–2020) this figure will increase to some 25 million. If all households that are currently homeless or living in inadequate housing units are to be adequately housed by the year 2020, that implies an additional requirement of some 14 million housing units each year over the next two decades. A rough estimate of the total average annual housing need in Africa during the next decade is thus 35 million units. In the following decade (2010–2020) this figure will increase to 39 million units. The total demand on national housing supply systems in urban areas is thus truly staggering. Roughly 11 per cent, it is estimated, will occur in Africa.

The need for a clearly formulated national urban policy arises, precisely because of the importance of ensuring an appropriate role for urban centers in regional and national development in Africa. It is against this background that productive investments must be placed in those urban centers that are most efficient and have already proved to have high economic potential, whatever their size. A crucial need is to develop links between the economic activities of the megacities, large urban centers, small and intermediate urban centers and the national development strategies.

The new planning strategy for urban Africa is to move beyond isolated projects that emphasize housing and residential infrastructure and more toward integrated urban-wide efforts that promote productivity and reduce constraints on efficiency; increase the demand for labor, stressing the generation of jobs for the urban poor; improve access to basic infrastructure; and increase our understanding of urban issues through research. These efforts should promote the role of urban centers as engines of growth for rural areas, and hence for national economies as a whole, while the population is properly housed and employed.

R. A. OBUDHO

Further Reading

Baker, Jonathan (ed.). *Small Town Africa: Studies in Rural-Urban Interaction.* Philadelphia: Coronet, 1990.

Baker, Jonathan, and Paul O. Pedersen (eds.). The *Rural-Urban Interface in Africa: Expansion and Adaptation.* Uppsala, Sweden: Scandinavian Institute of African Studies, 1992.

El-Shakhs, Salah, and R. Obudho (eds.). *Urbanization, National Development, and Regional Planning in Africa.* New York: Praeger, 1974.

Hance, William A. *Population, Migration, and Urbanization in Africa.* New York: Columbia University Press, 1970.

Kuper, Klaas. "Urbanization in Sub-Saharan Africa: Issues and Policies." *ITC Journal*, no. 2 (1992): 1–12.

O'Connor, A. *The African City.* New York: Africana, 1983.

Obudho, R. A. "The Development of Urbanization, Slum and Squatter Settlements in Africa: Toward A Planning Strategy." in *The Changing Geography of Urban Systems: Perspecting of the Developed and Developing Worlds*, edited by Larry S. Bourne et al. Navarra: Universidad de Navarra, 1989.

———. "Population Distribution in Africa; Urbanization under Process and as Weak Economic Conditions." In *Population Distribution and Migration*, edited by the UNFPA. New York: United Nations, 1999.

———. "The Growth of Africa's Urban Population." In *Urbanization in Africa: A Handbook*, edited by James Tarver. Westport, Conn.: Greenwood Press, 1994.

Obudho, R. A., and Salah El-Shakhs (eds.). *Development of Urban Systems in Africa.* New York: Praeger, 1979.

Obudho, R. A., and Constance C. Mlhanga (eds.). *Slum and Squatter Settlements in Sub-Saharan Africa: Toward a Planning Strategy.* New York; Praeger, 1988.

Stren, Richard E., and Rodney A. White (eds.). *African Cities in Crisis: Managing Rapid Urban Growth.* Boulder, Colo.: Interview, 1989.

Tarver, James D. *Urbanization in Africa: A Handbook.* Westport, Conn.: Greenwood Press, 1994.

Usambara: *See* Upare, Usambara, Kilimanjaro.

'Uthman dan Fodio (1754–1817)
Religious Leader

'Uthman dan Fodio (also known as Shehu Usman/Usumanu Dan Fodiyo, Shehu Usman, or Shehu) was a preacher, scholar, and statesman of the late eighteenth and early nineteenth centuries, known among the Fulbe as Usman bii Foduye. He established the Sokoto empire and become the first *sarkin musulmi* (*amir al-mu'minin*, "commander of the faithful") in Hausaland. The name Fodio is a Fulbe variant of the Arabic word meaning "ransomed," and was popular in Fulbe society at the time.

'Uthman dan Fodio began his career as an itinerant preacher in places such as Kebbi and adjacent areas including Gobir, Zamfara, and Degel. By 1788–1789, his influence had become so marked that the ruler of Gobir, Bawa Jan Gwarzo, plotted to eliminate him. But 'Uthman managed to obtain the right to preach, and the independence of his Muslim community.

In 1804 Yunfa dan Nafata, a new *sarki* (commander) of Gobir, sent his army to overtake a part of 'Uthman's community. It led to encounters between the forces of Gobir and the community. Yunfa ordered 'Uthman to move out of Degel. On February 21, 1804 'Uthman made his hejira. The Muslims of Gobir moved toward Gudu. (This emigration from Degel to Gudu was associated by 'Uthman with the hejira of the Prophet Muhammad). The community persuaded 'Uthman to assume leadership; it because of this that he came to be known as the *amir al-mu'minin* (commander of the faithful).

In his early life and works, 'Uthman claimed to be a Malikite, which is evident by the way he signed his name ('Uthman b. Muhammad b. 'Uthman al-Fallati nasaban al-Maliki madhaban al-Ash'ari i'tiqadan). But apparently he did not hold to a strict Malikite position. For instance, he permitted the use of musical instruments, generally forbidden by Malikite law. There are further examples of authorities other than the Malikite permitted by 'Uthman: recognition of two imams (leaders); fighting in holy months; the use of traditional African troops; and the use of silver and gold. He stressed the flexibility and latitude of Islam and Islamic law.

The fact that he was often called simply by the title Shehu indicates that he was a special shaykh, and that he was primarily identified by the general population through his connection with the Qadiriyya order. He appears to have held the top leadership position of the Qadiriyya brotherhood in the central Sudan.

In his early writings, 'Uthman dan Fodio made oblique statements suggesting that he saw himself as the *Mahdi* (guided leader, infallible guide, a restorer of the faith in the last days). Later, he claimed only to be the last *mujaddid al-islam* (reviver of Islam). He was convinced that his own jihad (holy war) would precede the coming of the Mahdi. The need for such a rejuvenation of the faith was based on an assumption that the Muslim community would stray from the true, ideal path of Islam. It is this tendency which became the driving force behind jihad and which led to jihad leaders being called *mujaddid*.

Although the Sufi order is associated with a nonmilitant brand of Islam, 'Uthman is recognized for his military leadership. However, he was 50 years old when the jihad started, and not strong enough to take an active part in military raids. His major role was to instruct and consult in matters affecting jihad and to ensure that administration of the new community was carried out according to Islamic law.

In addition to heading the scholarly community, 'Uthman dan Fodio was called to the task of forming, directing, and educating a revolutionary force within Hausaland. Military strategy, political propaganda, and apologetic writings for the jihad were all components of his work. The idealistic scholar and theologian became a forceful and commanding leader, who paid the necessary attention to the practical details of running an army and of establishing an empire.

DMITRY BONDAREV

See also: **Sokoto Caliphate: Hausa, Fulani and Founding of.**

Biography

Born on December 15, 1754 in the village of Maratta in the city-state of Gobir. Started preaching in 1774. Demanded Sultan Bawa grant him the freedom to propagate Islam in 1788. Cut himself and his community off from the jurisdiction of the Hausa Sultans in 1795. Sultan Nafata decreed sanctions against Uthman's community in 1802.

Made a hejira to Gudu with his followers in February 1804. Attacked at Kwotto by Sultan Yunfa in June 1804 (the sultan was unsuccessful). Led an attack on the Hausa states from 1805 to 1808. Wrote to justify jihad and advised followers on administrative and religious matters from 1810 to 1816. Died April 20 1817, and is buried in Sokoto.

Further Reading

Balogun, S. U. "Arabic Intellectualism in West Africa: The Role of the Sokoto Caliphat." *Journal of Institute of Muslim Minority Affairs* 6, no. 2 (1985): 394–411.

Graham, Christopher (comp.). *The Slave Raid that Failed and Other Stories*. Ibadan, Nigeria: Oxford University Press, 1966.

Martenson, Robert Raymond. *The Life and Work of Usmaanu bii Fooduye, with Special Reference to the Religious Nature of the Encounter between the Hausa Muslim and Muslim Communities*. St. Paul, Minn.: Hartford Seminary Foundation, 1978.

Usman, Y. B. (ed.). *Studies in the History of the Sokoto Caliphate: The Sokoto Seminar Papers*. Zaria: Department of History, Ahmadu Bello University, 1979.

V

Vandals and North Africa, 429–533

Most scholars believe the Vandals originally migrated south from the northernmost part of Jutland during the first centuries of the common era. From 406 to 408 they followed the route along the Danube through northern and southern Gaul into the Iberian Peninsula.

In 429 the Vandals, estimated at 80,000, crossed the Strait of Gibraltar, led by Geiseric. The Roman governor in North Africa, Bonifacius, for some time managed to hold on to the larger cities (Carthage; Hippo Regius, today Bone; and Cirta, today Constantine), but in the end was forced to return to Italy. When it reached Hippo Regius, the Vandal army besieged the city for 14 months without success. Later, however, the Romans evacuated Hippo Regius and Geiseric resided there for some time. In 431–432 the Romans unsuccessfully attempted to retake north Africa. In 435 Rome was forced to make a treaty with Geiseric. The Vandals were allowed to retain an area on the border between present day Algeria and Tunisia, including the cities Hippo Regius and Cirta. In October 439, Geiseric suddenly broke the treaty and took Carthage, which was then the second greatest city of the West Roman empire.

Over the course of the following three years Geiseric consolidated the Vandal kingdom in North Africa, which he ruled 430–77, which was to last almost a century. The Vandals controlled the former Roman provinces of Africa Proconsularis, Byzacena, and Tripolitania. The king built a powerful fleet, which came to dominate the waters of the western Mediterranean; he also raided Sicily and southern Italy. The Balearic islands, Corsica, Sardinia and the part of Sicily closest to the kingdom were also taken.

A treaty of 442 confirmed King Geiseric's sovereignty over Roman Africa, which included most of present-day Tunisia and northern Algeria. The Vandals settled in the region and made no further attempts at enlarging the state. The Vandals now controlled the main source of grain in the west, which to a great degree made Rome dependant on the Vandal state.

In 455 the Vandal army occupied the city of Rome and subjected it to weeks of plunder. The city's buildings and infrastructure were relatively unharmed, but King Geiseric returned to Carthage with many prominent Roman hostages, including the empress Eudoxia and two daughters of Emperor Valerianus, who had been executed earlier that year. One of the daughters was later married to Geiseric's son Huneric.

In return, Emperor Majorianus planned a naval attack on the kingdom from Spain in 458. Geiseric, however, learned of the plan, and the Vandals destroyed the invading fleet in its harbor. Two years later, however, Geiseric signed a treaty with Rome and promised not to let the Vandal fleet plunder Roman territory in the west.

Still, the empire in the west feared Geiseric and turned to Byzantine for help. A large fleet was sent against Carthage in 468, but Geiseric managed to stop the attack.

Geiseric was succeeded by his son Huneric (477–484). Huneric's successor, in turn, was Gunthamund (484–496), a nephew of Geiseric. During his reign Gunthamund battled the local Maurians, but was unsuccessful. Thrasamund ruled next (496–523), and was followed by the son of Huneric, Hilderic (523–530). He was deposed after attempting a reconciliation with the Byzantines.

The Vandals converted to Arianism, an eastern sect of Christianity. This led to extensive conflicts in the kingdom between the Catholic and Arian churches. Hilderic was favorably inclined toward the Catholic Church, which led to his deposal in 530. He was replaced by the last Vandal king, Gelimer (53–533), who was a nephew of Thrasamund and a strong believer in Arianism.

In 533 Emperor Justinian I sent a strong Byzantine fleet with an army under General Belisarius against Carthage. King Gelimer had sent his brother Tzazo and others to quell a revolt on Vandal Sardinia; this considerably weakened the Vandal forces left to oppose the Byzantine attack. The Vandals met the Byzantines at Dekimon on the road to Carthage on September 13, 533, and Gelimer retreated. Carthage, having no city wall, capitulated to Belisarius. Gelimer fled but was later captured and brought to Constantinople. After that the Vandals disappeared from history, as did several of the Germanic peoples who formed kingdoms in the western Mediterranean.

The Vandal administration in the kingdom was based on three groups: the Arian clergy, the warriors, and the optimates (the nobility). The Arian church received some of the property of the Roman Catholic church. The warriors and the nobility received land, which was expropriated from the Roman owners, who were to a great extent absentee landlords. Many Roman aristocrats, however, stayed on and were left in peace.

There are signs of some neglect by the Vandal rulers, as testified to by archaeologists, but according to classical literature the Vandals lived a luxurious life. The two harbors in Carthage, one commercial and one military, were kept in use, although some neglect is apparent. Most of the churches also show neglect dating from the time of Vandal rule.

Around 425, during the Roman period, a wall with a ditch had been built around the city, but the city defenses were neglected during Vandal rule, which proved fatal in 533, ensuring the Vandals' demise. Vandal silver and bronze coinage circulated and minting started during the reign of Gunthamund. There is little other information available about the Vandal economy and trade.

BERTIL HÄGGMAN

See also: **Byzantine Africa, 533–710; North Africa: Roman Occupation, Empire.**

Further Reading

Clover, F. M. *The Late Roman West and the Vandals.* Aldershot, England: Variorum, 1993.

Evans, James A. S. *The Age of Justinian: The Circumstances of Imperial Power.* London: Routledge, 1996.

Goffart, Walter. *Barbarians and Romans, AD 418–584: The Techniques of Accommodation.* Princeton, N.J.: Princeton University Press, 1984.

Randers-Pehrson, Justine Davis. *Barbarians and Romans: The Birth Struggle of Europe, A.D. 400–700.* Norman: University of Oklahoma Press, 1983.

Vitensis, Victor. *Victor of Vita: History of the Vandal Persecution,* translated by J. Moorhead. Liverpool: Liverpool University Press, 1990.

Verwoerd, H. F. (1901–1966)

Prime Minister of South Africa

H. F. Verwoerd was the key political figure, as minister of native affairs and later prime minister, in the construction of the apartheid state in South Africa in the 1950s and 1960s; it was his political legacy that dominated the country's history up to 1994.

Biographies of Verwoerd have tended to fall into one of two strict categories, hagiography or outright condemnation, which is not surprising considering the highly contentious nature of his policies and the passionate reactions they stirred. Moreover, many earlier studies of apartheid (by both supporters and opponents) presented Verwoerd as doggedly implementing a ready-made set of apartheid policies, according to a long-term blueprint already drafted by the Sauer Commission, which reported on the National Party's "color policy" in 1947. More recent studies have questioned such monolithic interpretations, arguing that the content and direction of apartheid policies were contested within the National Party and the bureaucracy, and that Verwoerd and others shaped apartheid in response to these conflicts. Some accounts stress Verwoerd's pragmatism, while others portray him as an arrogant, self-righteous bully who would brook no dissent. All agree, however, that he was an ambitious, and talented, politician.

Verwoerd was born in the Netherlands in 1901, but came to South Africa in 1903. His family had Afrikaner sympathies and was a member of the Dutch Reformed Church. Verwoerd was educated in both English and Afrikaans in Cape Province, Southern Rhodesia (Zimbabwe), and the Orange Free State until 1917. A gifted student, he studied psychology and philosophy at the University of Stellenbosch and obtained a doctorate in psychology in 1924. After further studies at the Universities of Leipzig, Hamburg, and Berlin, he was appointed professor of applied psychology and psychotechnics (applied individual psychology) at the University of Stellenbosch in 1928.

His early career was taken up with his academic work, and with involvement in social welfare issues in the Cape. His appointment as professor of sociology and social work was an indirect consequence of the Carnegie Commission's report into the "poor white problem," which recommended the establishment of a social studies department at a South African university. The 1934 *Volkskongres* (National Congress) to consider white poverty, which followed the Carnegie Report, gave Verwoerd a place on the national stage. He served as chairman of its Socioeconomic Committee and presented a paper on combating poverty and the reorganization of welfare work. He condemned the Anglicization of Afrikaners and argued that Africans should be sent back to the native reserves rather than be allowed to compete for work with whites in the cities.

In 1937, Verwoerd was appointed chief editor of the Gesuiwerde (purified) National Party's new newspaper, *Die Transvaler,* and moved to the Transvaal. He became an officer in the Transvaal Party. Despite the expectation of the party's Cape establishment that Verwoerd would be a restraining influence on the "extremism" of J. G. Strijdom, the Transvaal Party leader, Verwoerd became Strijdom's close friend and political ally. They, with others, opposed J. M. B. Hertzog's leadership of the Herenigde (reunited) National Party in 1940. Verwoerd campaigned against the Ossewa Brandwag (Ox-Wagon Sentinels), a fascist-inclined movement that competed with the National Party, particularly as executive committee member of the secret Afrikaner Broederbond. In 1947, he and Strijdom opposed the election pact between the National Party and N.C. Havenga's Hertzogite Afrikaner Party.

Defeated at the parliamentary election for Alberton in 1948, Verwoerd was appointed to the senate, where he became leader of government business. In his maiden speech, he strongly defended the party's "color policy." This has allowed admirers and detractors alike to present Verwoerd as somehow destined to become minister of native affairs. In fact, the new Prime Minister, D. F. Malan, refused to invite this "Transvaal extremist" into his cabinet in 1948, and Verwoerd's subsequent appointment in 1950 came as a surprise—not least to Verwoerd, who had neither desired nor expected this selection. Malan had originally offered the native affairs post to Paul Sauer, the chairman of the Sauer Commission; Sauer refused and suggested Verwoerd.

Verwoerd threw himself into his new job, and by the mid 1950s he had piloted through the parliament many of the measures that later came to define the apartheid state. Nevertheless, his career in native affairs almost ended abruptly in 1957; he offered to resign his position, although Strijdom, now prime minister, persuaded him to remain. Verwoerd had made many enemies within Nationalist Party ranks; he had orchestrated Strijdom's campaign for the premiership in 1954, against Malan's preference for Havenga as his successor, and further alienated the party's Cape establishment. Some within the party thought his ideas of "separate development" too liberal, while others were suspicious of his ambitions and his creation of a native affairs "superministry" under his exclusive control. Following his rejection, in 1956, of the recommendations of the government's Tomlinson Commission for a thoroughgoing development of African reserves, influential Nationalist Party intellectuals within the South African Bureau for Racial Affairs (SABRA), who had previously supported his policies, now judged that they had lost their moral basis.

In 1958, after Strijdom's death, Verwoerd won the party leadership, his victory largely due to the votes of Nationalist members of the Senate, his main powerbase. It took him three years, however, to dominate government, party, and state. Consciously pursuing a high-risk political strategy, he began the process of establishing "independent" African "homelands" to assuage external criticism of South Africa's racial policies and to divert internal African opposition. Shortly afterward he announced a referendum on the establishment of a republic, that long-cherished goal of Afrikaner nationalism.

After surviving an assassination attempt in April 1960, in the aftermath of the Sharpeville crisis, Verwoerd presided over an increasingly repressive state. He adopted the persona of the *Volksleier* (national leader). saved by divine providence during the referendum campaign, which he won by a slim majority in October 1960, enhancing his popular support among Afrikaners. Increasingly confident, he soon promised to erect "walls of granite" around the apartheid state. He withdrew South Africa from the British Commonwealth in March 1961. He used his Broederbond connections and his domination of the Transvaal Party as a counterbalance to Cape opposition. By 1961, he had managed to silence critics in the Dutch Reformed Church and purge SABRA of his opponents. Having called an early election in October 1961, he won a decisive victory, after which he was unassailable in the political sphere for five years, until he was assassinated in September 1966 by an apparently deranged parliamentary messenger.

ROBERT MCINTOSH

See also: **South Africa: Apartheid, 1948–1959; South Africa: Defiance Campaign, Freedom Charter, Treason Trials: 1952–1960; South Africa: Homelands and Bantustans: South Africa: Rural Protest and Violence: 1905s; South Africa: Sharpeville Massacre.**

Biography

Born in the Netherlands in 1901. Moved to South Africa in 1903. Obtained a doctorate in psychology in 1924. Appointed professor of applied psychology and psychotechnics at the University of Stellenbosch in 1928. Appointed chief editor of the National Party's newspaper, *Die Transvaler*, and moved to the Transvaal in 1937. Appointed to the senate in 1948. Named minister of native affairs in 1950. Won party leadership in 1958. Survived assassination attempt in 1960. Elected prime minister in 1961. Assassinated in September 1966.

Further Reading

Evans, Ivan. *Bureaucracy and Race: Native Administration in South Africa*. Berkeley and Los Angeles: University of California Press, 1997.

Lazar, John. "Verwoerd versus the 'Visionaries': The South African Bureau of Racial Affairs (Sabra) and Apartheid, 1948–1961." In *Apartheid's Genesis, 1935–1962*, edited by Philip Bonner, Peter Delius, and Deborah Posel. Johannesburg: Ravan Press and Witwatersrand University Press, 1993.

Miller, Roberta Balstad. "Science and Society in the Early Career of H. F. Verwoerd," *Journal of Southern African Studies* 19, no. 4 (1993): 634–661.

Schrire, Robert (ed.). *Leadership in the Apartheid State: From Malan to De Klerk*. Cape Town: Oxford University Press, 1994.

Scholtz, G. D. *Dr Hendrik Frensch Verwoerd, 1901–1966*. 2 vols. Johannesburg: Perskor, 1974.

Wadai: *See* **Bagirmi, Wadai, and Darfur; Chad, Nineteenth Century: Kanem/Borno (Bornu) and Wadai.**

Wafd: *See* **Egypt: Nationalism, World War I and the Wafd, 1882–1922.**

Wallace-Johnson, I. T. A. and Radical Politics: West Africa: 1930s

Isaac Theophilus Akunna Wallace Johnson (1894–1965) came from the Creole people of Freetown. He had an early start in education, Christianity, modern-style work and trade, and politics among West Africans. Political activity was already flourishing among the Creoles when he was born. However, he forged a new path, becoming in the 1920s one of the first of a new band of radical African anticolonial campaigners. They were the precursors to nationalism, largely forgotten today.

Wallace Johnson worked first for the customs in Sierra Leone. He was dismissed for helping lead a strike but was later reinstated. He then worked as a clerk with the British Army's Carrier Corps, with which many Africans served during World War I. Later, working for the Freetown City Council, he organized workers' campaigns and incurred the authorities' hostility. In the later 1920s Johnson is said to have worked as a seaman and traveled overseas, but documentation of that part of his life is obscure. At some point he made contact with left-wing activists linked to the Comintern and the Soviet Communist regime, which were campaigning against Western colonialism in the 1920s and early 1930s.

Johnson was working at Sekondi in Gold Coast as a clerk in 1929. The following year he went to Nigeria, where he worked as a journalist (as he continued to do in many countries for several years) and also helped establish the Nigerian Workers' Union, becoming its general secretary. Most accounts of his life accept that he attended, under a pseudonym, the communist-organized First International Conference of Negro Workers in Hamburg in 1930; he certainly became an associate editor of the campaigning newspaper founded then, the *Negro Worker*. In 1932–1933 Johnson traveled to Europe and possibly spent some time in the Soviet Union, where he may have gone earlier and may perhaps have attended the communist University of the Toilers of the East (*Kutvu*), though this is uncertain.

Wallace Johnson returned to Nigeria in 1933 but left after a police raid on his home later that year. He then worked in Gold Coast, where he founded the West Coast Youth League (WAYL). He corresponded with left-wing anticolonial figures in Britain and was considered by the British to be a dangerous "agitator" working for the communists. An active journalist, in Gold Coast he wrote for newspapers including the *African Morning Post*, a daily edited in 1935–1936 by the Nigerian Nnamdi Azikiwe. He wrote an article— "Has the African a God?"—that was published on May 15, 1936, and led to a celebrated case in which he and Azikiwe were charged with sedition. He was fined, and then left for Britain in 1937.

In Britain he met leading radical anti-imperialists, some of whom he had contacted or met before. The most celebrated was George Padmore from Trinidad; others included Jomo Kenyatta, the future president of Kenya, the Guyanese Ras Makonnen, and another Trinidadian, C. L. R. James. A number of these activists, having lived in several countries (including the USSR) in previous years, were now living in Britain, in contact with British sympathizers. Having been communists or close to communism before, they were now independent and critical of communists. They formed the International African Friends of Abyssinia, which protested against the Italian occupation of Ethiopia in 1935–1936, and later, in 1937, the International African Service Bureau, of which Johnson became the secretary general. It aimed to raise awareness about the colonies' conditions in Britain and arouse support for needed reforms.

In April 1938 Johnson returned to Sierra Leone. Soon afterward he founded the West African Youth League (WAYL) and became its secretary general; the following January a new newspaper, the *African Standard*, was founded to publicize the views of the WAYL. Those views were strongly critical of the colonial government, but the WAYL won widespread support and four of its candidates were elected to the Freetown City Council in November 1938. The leading African politician in Sierra Leone at that time, Dr. H .C. Bankole-Bright, was strongly opposed to Johnson, but the newcomer to the Freetown political scene had enormous popularity. Johnson, not a member of the top elite of Freetown, appealed to ordinary people and started to build the first mass political organization in Sierra Leone. As in Gold Coast earlier, he took up ordinary people's complaints and grievances, especially those of workers, and exposed bad labor conditions. He aimed ultimately at independence, but sought above all to organize protests at the way things were.

In 1938–1939 Johnson also founded the West African Civil Liberties and National Defence League, and resumed his trade union work, setting up several new unions. A series of strikes in 1939, and Johnson's writings, confirmed the British view of him as an intolerable troublemaker, and led to the introduction of six new laws to curb opposition to British rule; these in turn aroused a strong protest campaign in 1939.

Upon the outbreak of World War II, Wallace Johnson was arrested. He served a one-year sentence for criminal libel and in all spent five years under detention or restriction; he was held first at a temporary internment camp; then (1940–1942) at Pademba Road Prison in Freetown, the conditions of which led him to write poems in protest; and then at Bonthe on Sherbro island until 1944. In February 1945 Johnson went to Paris to attend the founding congress of the World Federation of Trade Unions. In October 1945 he took part with Padmore, Kenyatta, Makonnen, Kwame Nkrumah, and W. E. B. DuBois in the Fifth Pan-African Conference in Manchester, England.

Johnson's brief preeminence on the political scene in Sierra Leone did not last. He became a leading member of the National Council of the Colony of Sierra Leone (NCCSL), and was elected to the Legislative Council, in 1951; that body, defending the narrow

interests of the privileged colony (i.e. Freetown) when the mass of the people of the protectorate were being enfranchised, had little impact on the nationalist movement and the progress toward independence. Johnson soon left the NCCSL and later joined the United Progressive Party; expelled from that, he later founded the Radical Democratic Party. In 1960 he was one of the delegates to the London Constitutional Conference, which led to agreement on independence for Sierra Leone. He held no office after independence came in 1961, but the high regard in which he was held as a pioneer nationalist was shown by widespread mourning when he died, following a road accident in Ghana, on May 10, 1965.

JONATHAN DERRICK

See also: **Azikiwe, Nnamdi; Diaspora: Colonial Era; Ethiopia: Italian Invasion and Occupation: 1935–1940; Sierra Leone: Protectorate: Administration and Government.**

Biography

Born Isaac Theophilus Akunna Wallace Johnson in 1894 in Freetown. Made contact with leftist activists connected with the Soviet Union in the 1920s and 1930s. Traveled to Europe and possibly the Soviet Union in 1932 and 1933. Returned to Nigeria, but left later that year for Gold Coast, where he was tried for sedition. Left for Britain in 1937. One of the founding members of the International African Friends of Abyssinia (IAFA). Returned to Sierra Leone, and founded the West African Youth League. Founded the West African Civil Liberties and National Defence League and set up several new unions in 1938 and 1939. Arrested at outbreak of World War II, and served one year, for libel. Took part in the Fifth Pan-African Conference in Manchester, England, in 1945. Eelected to the Legislative Council in Sierra Leone in 1951. Joined the United Progressive Party; was expelled, then founded the Radical Democratic Party. Died on May 10, 1965.

Further Reading

Cartwright, John R. *Politics in Sierra Leone 1947–67*. Tornoto: University of Toronto Press, 1970.

Langley, J. Ayodele. *Pan-Africanism and Nationalism in West Africa 1900–1945*. Oxford: Oxford University Press, 1973.

Makonnen, Ras. *Pan-Africanism from Within*, as told to Kenneth King. Nairobi: Oxford University Press, 1973.

Padmore, George. *Pan-Africanism or Communism?* Dennis Dobson, 1956.

Wyse, A. J. *H. C. Bankole-Bright and Politics in Colonial Sierra Leone, 1919–1958*. Cambridge: Cambridge University Press, 1958.

Wassa: *See* **Akan States: Bono, Dankyira, Wassa, Akyem, Akwamu, Fante, Fifteenth to Seventeenth Centuries.**

Water Supplies and Schemes

Shortages of fresh water supplies are one of the major problems to be faced during the twenty-first century, and Africa is especially vulnerable. Large parts of the continent are arid or semiarid while other regions are subject to regular droughts. The continent's two most advanced economic powers, Egypt and South Africa, both require more water than they have under their own control. More generally, the indications are that water will increasingly become the subject of bitter disputes.

There are four great river systems on the continent: the Nile, the Niger, the Congo, and the Zambezi. The demand for their waters, whether for irrigation or power, threatens to outstrip their capacity to meet the demands.

There exist a number of agreements between Egypt and Sudan to govern the control of the Nile waters and a treaty between the two countries allocates the water on a ratio of 55.5 billion cubic meters to Egypt and 18.5 billion cubic meters to Sudan annually. During the 1990s friction mounted between Egypt, the biggest user of Nile waters, and Ethiopia. A meeting of the Nile Basin states was held in Tanzania in March 1998, at which Ethiopia rejected Egypt's share of the waters. Ethiopia is determined to have a greater share of the waters so that it may implement its own large-scale irrigation projects and is demanding (with Uganda) that an additional 18 billion cubic meters of water be taken from Egypt's current allocation. The upstream Nile riparian countries look set to claim their full share of Nile waters. Egypt, meanwhile, has set in motion a large-scale plan, the Toshka Scheme, to irrigate its Western Desert, which will require 5,500 million cubic meters of water from Lake Nasser, and did so without consulting the other Nile users.

In 1998 the Ethiopian foreign minister, Seyoun Mesfin, said, "The time has come to erect dams and build reservoirs at the source of the Nile in Ethiopia." Indeed, it may well turn out that Ethiopia holds the trump card for the Blue Nile, which rises in Ethiopia, and accounts for 68 per cent of the high water discharge at Aswan. Should Ethiopia embark upon major irrigation and hydro-schemes in its highlands, this could have a devastating impact on the flow of water to Egypt.

The Congo is the world's second largest river, after the Amazon, and this vast resource is more than adequate to meet the needs of all the Congo Basin countries while providing surplus power and water for export. The Congo's hydroelectric potential, an estimated 132 million kilowatts, is equivalent to one-sixth of known world resources. The Inga Dam complex on the Lower Congo is one of the world's largest water projects, and though much of the planned development has been delayed, because of political instability in the Democratic Republic of Congo (Kinshasa), Inga still produces some of the cheapest electricity in the world. Plans now exist for major power exports; among these are projects in Egypt (yet to begin), the neighboring People's Republic of Congo (Brazzaville), while the state electricity board (SNEL) is linked into the Zambian grid. In 1996 South Africa's state electricity corporation, ESKOM, in collaboration with Angola and Namibia, began an investigation into connecting their power grids to Inga and channeling power through Zambia and Zimbabwe to South Africa so as to create a southern Africa grid system. Given peace and stability in Congo (Kinshasa), the country could well become a principal source of hydroelectric power for much of central and southern Africa.

South Africa is chronically short of water and sources of hydroelectric power. The huge Lesotho Highlands Water Scheme to harness the waters from the Maluti Mountains is designed to supply both power and fresh water to Gauteng Province, the industrial heartland of South Africa. However, by the end of the twentieth century there were growing signs that Lesotho regretted having mortgaged almost its entire water resource, which is the country's only major resource, to South Africa. Meanwhile, South Africa has been exploring the possibility of tapping the Zambezi waters to supply the Johannesburg region.

The idea is to move Zambezi waters 1100 miles through a system of canals, pipelines, and tunnels to augment the Vaal River system, which supplies the Gauteng industrial and residential complex that includes Johannesburg. The diverted waters of the Zambezi would also be used for agricultural, domestic, and industrial purposes in the water-short regions of western Zimbabwe, eastern Botswana, and northwestern South Africa while providing Zambia with income from foreign sources. This scheme, which is the most ambitious of its kind in the world, would take 10 per cent of the river's annual flow.

The possibility of disputes over Zambezi waters became apparent in 1998 with the proposal for a pipeline from the Zambezi to Bulawayo, which is chronically short of water, in Zimbabwe. Known as the Matabeleland Zambezi Water Project (MZWP), the pipeline is to be 280 miles in length. The project includes the construction of the Gwayi-Shangani Dam. However, a regional agreement to cover siphoning water from the river has yet to be determined. Botswana, South Africa, and Zambia are each short of water, though South Africa is not a riparian state of the Zambezi. Zambia is uneasy about the project, which could jeopardize its own development prospects while diverting the waters to benefit the countries to the south because a reduced flow could harm the tourist attraction of Victoria Falls, downstream, and reduce output from the Livingstone power station. As of 2003, a loan of $50 million (U.S.) by the Export-Import Bank of Malaysia suggested that work on the long-delayed project would soon move forward.

African countries have an obvious vested interest in working together to share their precious water resources. The Congo waters are so vast that, politics permitting, there should be no problem about the Democratic Republic of the Congo exporting power or, indeed, water. Sharing the Zambezi waters, however, presents more complex political and economic problems, while the issue of demands on Nile waters could prove explosive within the first decade of the twenty-first century.

GUY ARNOLD

Further Reading

Arnold, Guy, and Ruth Weiss. *Strategic Highways of Africa.* London: Julian Friedmann/New York: St. Martin's Press, 1977.
Atlas Jeune Afrique, The African Continent. Paris: Jeune Afrique, 1973.
Barbour, K. Michael, et al (eds.). *Nigeria in Maps.* London: Hodder and Stoughton/New York: Africana, 1982.
Hurst, H. E. *The Nile.* 1952.
Huybrechts, A., *Transports et structures de developpement au Congo. Etude de progres economique de 1900 a 1970.* Paris: Editions Mouton, 1970.
Lander, John, and Richard Lander,. *Journal of an Expedition to Explore the Course and Termination of the Niger.* 1832.

Welensky, Roy (1907–1991)

Trade Union Leader, Politician and Statesman

Roy Welensky became involved in trade unionism while working on the Rhodesian Railways, and eventually became the head of the Rhodesian Railways Union. In 1930 he helped to organize an ill-fated strike at the Wankie (Hwang) colliery. Welensky's role in the strike angered the rail's management, and he was eventually sent to work in Northern Rhodesia as punishment. There he revived the dormant branch of the Railway Worker's Union. As a union organizer he earned a reputation as a hard bargainer and a champion of the rights of lower-class whites. By 1938 he was the colony's leading union leader, and his popularity among white workers helped him to become a member

of the Northern Rhodesian Legislative Council. When World War II broke out in 1939, he became the director of manpower for the Northern Rhodesian government. By the end of the war Welensky was one of the most well-known and influential politicians in the region.

After the war, Welensky became a proponent of a scheme to amalgamate Northern and Southern Rhodesia. Amalgamation promised to combine the mineral wealth of the Northern Rhodesian copper belt with the agricultural resources of Southern Rhodesia to create a wealthy, settler-dominated state. However, the British Colonial Office feared amalgamation would leave Africans in Northern Rhodesia at the mercy of the settlers of Southern Rhodesia. At the suggestion of Sir Godfrey Huggins, the prime minister of Southern Rhodesia, Welensky began lobbying instead for the federation of the two Rhodesias. Working together, Huggins and Welensky argued that a federation could create a viable political and economic entity while still protecting the interests of Africans in Northern Rhodesia. Their plan became increasingly attractive after the Afrikaner Nationalist Party took power in South Africa in 1948. In the wake of the South African elections the British government agreed to permit the two Rhodesias to federate if they would included the small and impoverished colony of Nyasaland (modern Malawi). In 1953 the Federation of the Rhodesias and Nyasaland was formed, with Huggins as its first prime minister and Welensky as the federation's minister for transportation and posts. In the same year Welensky received a knighthood. When Huggins retired to a peerage in 1956, Welensky succeeded him as prime minister.

During Welensky's first four years in office, a series of crises combined to threaten the future of the federation. In 1956 the British government suffered a humiliating diplomatic defeat in the Suez Crisis. The following year the Gold Coast became the first British colony in Africa to achieve independence. Then in 1960 the Belgian government in Congo, the federation's neighbor to the north, suddenly abandoned the colony, precipitating a crisis that threatened to destabilize the region. Against this backdrop, African national consciousness within the federal territories developed rapidly. In 1958 Dr. Hastings Banda in Nyasaland, and Kenneth Kaunda in Northern Rhodesia, began organizing protests against the federation. The following year Josh Nkomo led similar demonstrations in Southern Rhodesia. Clashes between supporters of Banda's Congress party and Federal troops resulted in the declaration of a state of emergency in Southern Rhodesia and Nyasaland. Shortly thereafter Northern Rhodesian authorities arrested Kaunda and banned his party. Government repression soon reestablished colonial authority in all three territories. However, the spectacle of colonial troops fighting to preserve the federation severely undermined the credibility of Welensky's government. A British report on the disturbances issued in 1960 characterized Nyasaland as a "police state" and turned opinion in Britain against the federation. The British government stepped in and granted Nyasaland and Northern Rhodesia the right to secede, and in 1964 they became the independent nations of Malawi and Zambia.

Welensky vehemently opposed the dissolution of the federation. During the late 1950s he had been pushing the British to grant his state independence, and was bitterly disappointed when Prime Minister Harold MacMillan's government gave Malawi and Zambia their freedom. Shortly after the federation's demise Welensky published a memoir titled *4000 Days*, which chronicled his tenure as prime minister. In it he blamed the British Conservative Party for the betrayal of its British subjects in Central Africa.

Welensky returned to Southern Rhodesia. There the white settler regime of Ian Smith was moving toward declaring independence from Britian. Welensky stood for election in the Rhodesian parliament, only to be defeated by one of Smith's closest allies. Welensky then retired from politics but remained in Rhodesia. In 1965, when Smith proclaimed independence, both Welensky and his old ally Huggins opposed it. In 1969, Welensky's wife Elizabeth died. He remarried, to Valerie Scott, an English woman 30 years his junior, in 1972. The Welenskys moved to London in 1981, and Roy Welensky died in Dorset in 1991, at the age of 84.

Welensky was a combative politician whose tactics owed much to his impoverished upbringing and his career in the ring. He enjoyed his greatest support among the blue-collar workers and artisans who flocked to the Rhodesias from South Africa and Britian after World War II. However, settlers and politicians on both ends of the political spectrum viewed him as unreliable. White supremacists considered him a dangerous liberal, while proponents of African equality and independence viewed him as a reactionary.

JAMES BURNS

See also: **Kaunda, Kenneth; Malawi (Nyasaland): Colonial Period: Federation; Nkomo, Joshua; Zambia (Northern Rhodesia): Federation, 1953–1963. Zimbabwe (Southern Rhodesia): Federation.**

Biography

Born in Salisbury, Southern Rhodesia (modern Harare, Zimbabwe) on January 20, 1907. Largely self-educated. Worked in a variety of menial positions before joining the Rhodesian Railways. In 1926, became the boxing champion of Northern and Southern Rhodesia, a title he held for two years. In 1928, married Elizabeth Henderson, a waitress from Bulawayo. Became a member of the Northern Rhodesian Legislative Assembly in 1938, and director of manpower for the Northern Rhodesian government in 1939. Knighted in 1953, became the Central African Federation's minister for Transportation in the same year, and its prime minister three years later. Despite his opposition, the Central African Federation was dissolved in 1963, and he retired from politics shortly thereafter. Remained in Rhodesia until 1980, and died in England in 1991.

Further Reading

Baker, C. A. *State of Emergency: Crisis in Central Africa, Nyasaland 1959–1960.* London: Tauris Academic Studies, 1997.

Taylor, Don. *The Rhodesian: The Life of Sir Roy Welensky.* London: Museum Press, 1955.

Welensky, Roy. *4000 Days.* London: Collins, 1964.

Wood, J. R. T. *The Welensky Papers: A History of the Federation of Rhodesia and Nyasaland.* Durgan: Graham, 1983.

"Sir Roy Welensky" (obituary). *New York Times*, December 6, 1991.

Western Africa: *See* Stone Age, Later: Western Africa.

Western Nilotes: *See* Nilotes, Eastern Africa: Western Nilotes: Luo; Nilotes, Eastern Africa: Western Nilotes: Shilluk, Nuer, Dinka, Anyuak.

Western Sahara: Nineteenth Century to the Present

The parched wastes of Western Sahara, beyond the nineteenth-century frontier of Moroccan rule, were dominated by nomadic Saharawi camel herders. Based on complex tribal loyalties, kinship factions, subordinate castes, and tributary relationships, each tribe had its own assembly of notables who selected a shaykh and imposed its own laws. Politics consisted of ever-shifting feuds and alliances.

In 1859–1860, Spain attacked Morocco, imposed a heavy indemnity, and secured the rights to expand its fortified enclaves at Melilla and Ceuta, and for the "restoration" of Santa Cruz on the Saharan coast, from which it had been expelled by Saharawi tribesmen in 1524. However, Morocco could not cede what it did not control, and Santa Cruz evaporated in Spanish indecision.

In 1882, Sultan Moulay Hassan of Morocco led a military expedition into the Anti-Atlas and consulted

Western Sahara.

with local Saharawi chieftains for their support in thwarting European penetration. Stung by the loss of its American empire, a perceived threat to the Spanish Canaries from French and English traders on the Saharan coast and dreams of a new African empire, Spain countered by claiming the Atlantic coastal strip of Rio de Oro in 1884, based on its lone coastal trading garrison at Villa Cisneros. In 1887, Spain decreed the territory between Cape Bojador and Cape Blanco, to a distance of 150 kilometers inland, under the authority of the governor general of the Canary Islands; Saharawi control, however, remained unchallenged.

The southern and interior frontiers with French spheres were delineated by French-Spanish treaties of 1886 and 1900. Under the Franco-Spanish conventions of 1904, Spain acquired vast expanses of desert comprising Rio de Oro (71,000 square miles) and Saguia el Hamra (31,650 square miles). The Franco-Spanish convention of 1912 formalized the Spanish protectorate of Southern Morocco (a narrow strip of 9,900 square miles south of the Draa) and the Spanish enclave of Ifni (580 square miles).

In 1900, the Sufi *marabout* Sheikh Ma el-Ainin forged a Saharawi alliance and, from his base at Smara, proclaimed jihad (holy war) against the French in Morocco and Algeria while confining the Spanish to their coastal garrison. Following el-Ainin's death in 1910, the Saharawi continued to harass the French, unimpeded by the Spanish. Captain Francisco Bens Argandoña, the Spanish governor from 1903 to 1925, adopted a policy of appeasing the Saharawi tribe while

establishing garrisons at Tarfaya (1916) and La Guera (1920) at Cape Blanco. But the Spanish Foreign Legion was fighting the Rif rebellion, led by Abdel Karim, in northern Spanish Morocco, which was not finally suppressed until 1926.

In 1934 the French mounted a major campaign against the Saharawi and pressured Spain into occupying strategic interior outposts, such as Smara. However, the Spanish Sahara remained a neglected wasteland until the discovery of rich phosphate deposits in the 1940s and iron ore in the 1950s.

Moroccan independence in 1956 inspired nationalists in French Algeria and Mauritania, as well as the Spanish Sahara. A Saharawi uprising was put down by a combined French-Spanish military operation in 1958, while both Morocco and Mauritanian nationalist pressed claims to the Spanish Sahara. Spain, which continued to repress Saharawi nationalism, rejected a United Nations–proposed referendum on self-determination in 1966. In 1973, Saharawis abroad formed the Polisario Front to wage guerrilla resistance for full independence.

In July 1974, Spain proposed local Saharawi autonomy leading to an independence referendum, which was promptly denounced by Morocco. "Great Morocco" nationalist aspirations were viewed as threatening by Algeria and Mauritania as well as the Polisario. Spain vacillated between oppression and negotiations with the Polisario; the United Nations (UN) was mired in indecision. In 1975, the case went before the International Court of Justice, which rejected the claims of both Morocco and Mauritania. King Hassan of Morocco seized the opportunity to win nationalist support as well as the phosphate-rich territory by temporarily sending 350,000 "volunteers" on the "Green March" across the northern frontier, under a secret agreement with Spain.

In the dying days of the Franco regime, the Spanish government was otherwise preoccupied and wanted a speedy settlement, irrespective of Saharawi aspirations. Colonial rule formally ended on February 28, 1976, whereupon Moroccan and Mauritanian troops entered the region. Polisario, which had proclaimed the Saharan Arab Democratic Republic (SADR) on February 27, put up determined resistance. With Algerian support, the SADR was admitted to the Organization of African Unity, despite Moroccan opposition, in 1982. Economically weak and militarily ill equipped, Mauritania withdrew. The United States supported its Cold War ally Morocco, branding the Polisario as communist. The Soviet Union, dependent upon Moroccan phosphate supplies, equivocated. Morocco established defensive positions around the towns and mining sites, severely restricting the Polisario's operations.

Polisario claimed that a free and fair referendum on self-determination could not be held with Moroccan troops in Western Sahara, while Morocco refused direct negotiation with Polisario. Indirect talks in 1986 failed, but on August 30, 1988, both sides accepted a UN initiative calling for a cease-fire and referendum for the territory's indigenous people. Polisario declared a unilateral truce, but heavy fighting soon resumed, reflecting growing impatience with the slow pace of the UN-sponsored peace efforts.

A 1991 UN peace plan was undermined when Morocco moved 37,000 people into the territory, sparking accusations of vote-tampering, and held a constitutional referendum in August 1992 endorsing King Hassan's plan for the integration of Western Sahara into Morocco. Simultaneously, Algeria decided to drop its backing of the Polisario Front in order to improve relations with Morocco. Polisario called on the UN Security Council and the international community to take steps to end what it termed Morocco's violation of the UN-planned referendum.

The UN became embroiled in a dispute over voter registration lists, leading to repeated delays in the proposed referendum. Morocco has tried to have thousands of Moroccans registered as Saharans, while holding hundreds of suspected Polisario supporters in prison. The war has created a Saharawi refugee crisis, largely ignored by the outside world. Since the end of the Cold War, Morocco has continued its obfuscation, hoping to wear down UN opposition to its seizure of the territory. It is a war neither side can militarily win, but neither can politically afford to lose.

DAVID DORWARD

See also: **Maal'-Aynayn; Morocco: International Relations since Independence; Polisario and the Western Sahara.**

Further Reading

Damis, John. *Conflict in Northwest Africa: The Western Sahara Dispute.* Stanford, Calif.: Hoover Institute, 1983.

Hodges, Tony, *Western Sahara: The Roots of a Desert War.* Westport, Conn.: Lawrence Hill/London: Croom Helm, 1983.

Hodges, Tony, and Anthony Pazzanita. *Historical Dictionary of Western Sahara*, 2nd ed. Metuchen, N.J.: Scarecrow, 1994.

Kamil, Leo. *Fueling the Fire: U.S. Policy and the Western Sahara Conflict.* Trenton, N.J.: Red Sea Press, 1987.

Lawless, Richard, and Laila Monahan (eds.). *War and Refugees: The Western Sahara Conflict.* London: Pinter, 1987.

Rezette, Robert. *The Western Sahara and the Frontiers of Morocco.* Paris: Nouvelles Editions Latines, 1975.

Thompson, Virginia, and Richard Adloff. *The Western Saharans: Background to Conflict.* London: Croom Helm/Totowa, N.J.: Barnes and Noble, 1980.

White Settlement: *See* Cape Colony: Khoi-Dutch Wars.

White Settler Factor: Economic and Political

Few white settlers came to Africa without sponsorship. In low-lying tropical areas malaria, yellow fever, and a host of other diseases deterred private individuals from establishing themselves on the continent except as traders. All the important historical examples of white settlement were the product of state action.

In 1652 the Dutch East India Company founded a settlement at the Cape of Good Hope for the purpose of supplying their ships with fresh provisions. When the use of company employees to farm and herd animals proved expensive, the company imported so-called free burghers to take their place. Once settled on the land, the white settlers and their descendants defied efforts to confine them to the immediate vicinity of Cape Town. They spread northward and eastward with their flocks and herds. As they expanded, they used their command of horses and firearms to decimate the indigenous Khoi and San peoples. Only when they encountered the Bantu-speaking agriculturists at the Great Fish River was their progress slowed, late in the eighteenth century. The wars between the expanding settlers and the Xhosa people of the eastern Cape frontier lasted for a century.

When the wars of the French Revolution brought the Netherlands under French rule, the British seized the Cape in 1795 to prevent it being made a stronghold for their enemy's navies. In 1820 the British launched their own experiment in white settlement. Fearing that their island home was in danger from large populations of vagrants and unemployed people, various schemes of overseas settlement were devised. South Africa's "1820 settlers" were located in the areas adjacent to Grahamstown in the Eastern Cape. After initial periods of hardship and stress, they adjusted to their new African environment. Frustrating official hopes that they might serve as a counterweight to the Dutch-speaking Boer population, the 1820 settlers soon espoused similar attitudes. They denounced missionaries, defended policies designed to force Africans to work for them, and advocated extension of the Cape frontier into the Transkei and the southeastern interior regions. When Boers moved up into the South African High Veld regions and Natal in the course of their so-called Great Trek in 1836, English-speaking settlers followed close behind. The spread of white settlers throughout South Africa complicated and embittered relations with African peoples. The settlers insisted on democratic rights for themselves, but resisted the extension of similar rights to Africans. As they gradually seized control of colonial governments from British officials, they established racially stratified and discriminatory regimes. The rise of apartheid in South Africa in the twentieth century was the most pernicious product of Dutch and British sponsorship of white settlement.

The next large-scale experiment in white settlement was sponsored by France after its invasion of Algeria in 1830. Seeking to multiply loyal supporters of their rule and to stimulate economic development, France used grants of conquered land, exemptions from taxation, and other incentives to attract settlers. After the revolution of 1848 in France, the government exported more than 20,000 French workers to Algeria, where they were provided with houses, farming machinery, livestock, food, and spending money. After the Franco-Prussian War of 1870, 8000 refugees from Alsace-Lorraine were granted 100,000 hectares of Algerian land. Successive waves of settlers did aid the French effort to subdue Algerian resistance to their invasion, but in the longer run they created problems similar to those spawned by the white settlers of South Africa. They, too, insisted on all the political rights enjoyed by citizens of metropolitan France, while denying similar rights to the Algerian people, and they, too, devised schemes of taxation and forced labor. In Algeria the pretext for segregation was a law of 1865 that declared indigenous Algerians French subjects without according them citizenship. To become citizens with rights equal to those of the settlers, Algerians were required to renounce their Muslim civil status, an act regarded as a virtual renunciation of their religion. Very few Algerians were willing to take such a step; even fewer were accepted as full citizens. By the end of World War II, the settler population had risen to about a million. Because settlers had the right to vote for members of the National Assembly in Paris, their votes could make or break French governments. After the outbreak of the Algerian Revolution in 1954, settler representatives used their vital votes to block attempts to end the conflict through negotiation or conciliation. Charles de Gaulle's coup d'état of 1958 finally broke their hold on power and paved the way for Algerian independence in 1962—and the flight of nearly the entire French population.

A century after the French invasion of Algeria, Portuguese dictator Antonio Salazar embarked on a program to bolster white settlement in Angola and Mozambique. Like the French in Algeria, Salazar aimed to provide opportunities for the poor among his people and at the same time erect a bulwark against the threat of African insurrection. As in Algeria, the Portuguese employed an artificial distinction between "assimilated" and "nonassimilated" people to preserve the position of the white settlers as a ruling class. That did nothing to stave off a war of independence. As in France, the commitment of blood and treasure required to combat the insurrection brought a new government to power and a rapid transition to independence in 1974.

The first experiment in white settlement under commercial sponsorship occurred in Zimbabwe in 1890. The British South Africa Company, under the direction of Cecil Rhodes, recruited a "pioneer column" of settlers from South Africa and Britain to spearhead a drive into the lands of the Mashona. Under the pretext of a concession to prospect for minerals granted by the Ndebele King Lobengula, the settlers streamed into the land they were later to call Southern Rhodesia. In fact, they had been promised large tracts of land in return for their participation in Rhodes's venture. The company expected a war with Lobengula and counted on the weight of the settler population to ensure their victory. This came in due course with the war of 1893. A subsequent rebellion was suppressed in 1897. When company rule ended in 1924 and Southern Rhodesia was granted "responsible government" as a British colony, settlers dominated that government. Very few Africans were allowed to qualify as voters. Schemes of racial segregation confined Africans to the less-productive and rugged parts of the colony. Settler agriculture was protected from African competition in a variety of ways.

After World War II, Southern Rhodesia was joined to Northern Rhodesia and Nyasaland in the so-called Central African Federation. As the wave of decolonization swept southward through the continent, African nationalists in the territories then known as Nyasaland and Northern Rhodesia denounced the federation as a scheme to keep them under the thumb of Southern Rhodesian settlers. When those territories withdrew from the federation and were granted independence as the new nations of Malawi and Zambia, the white-dominated government of Southern Rhodesia demanded its own independence. When told by the British government that it must first guarantee unimpeded progress toward majority rule, it unilaterally declared independence under the leadership of Ian Smith. A long and bitter war of liberation ended in the Lancaster House Agreement of 1979 and the independence of Zimbabwe under President Robert Mugabe in 1980.

In other parts of Africa white settlers were introduced to speed the development of a cash economy based on agricultural commodities. When Britain took over Kenya from the bankrupt British East Africa Company, the territory badly needed a dependable source of revenue. Unwilling to wait until Africans adapted to a market economy, the government used grants of land to entice white settlers in the hope that they would generate enough taxes to defray the costs of administration. Attracted by the romantic possibilities of owning a farm in Africa, a collection of European aristocrats, wealthy speculators, and adventurers flocked to what were then known as the "white highlands." For a time a colorful, if notorious, clutch of settlers made "Happy Valley" a by-word for a way of life that featured living fast and dying young. This high living flourished at the expense of African farmers and pastoralists, whose lands were expropriated to attract the settlers. When depression and other afflictions imperiled the profitability of settler agriculture, the state stepped in with laws that protected white farmers against competition from Africans who had, in spite of expectations, adapted rapidly to market opportunities. The settler population of Kenya (like the settler populations of Tanganyika, Northern Rhodesia, and Nyasaland) never attained a critical mass. When an African rising, known to the Europeans as Mau Mau, proved too difficult for Britain to contain without unacceptable costs to taxpayers at home, Kenya was granted independence.

The last stand of the white settlers against the unstoppable movement toward majority rule occurred in South Africa, where guerilla warfare, urban insurrection, economic problems, and international pressure brought about a transition to democracy with the elections of 1994, which resulted in the election of an African president, Nelson Mandela.

NORMAN A. ETHERINGTON

See also: **Boer Expansion: Interior of South Africa; Kenya: Mau Mau Revolt; Rhodes, Cecil J.; South Africa: Apartheid, 1948–1959; South Africa: 1994 to the Present; Zimbabwe (Southern Rhodesia): Colonial Period: Land, Tax, Administration.**

Further Reading

Berman, Bruce, and John Lonsdale. *Unhappy Valley: Conflict in Kenya and Africa.* London: James Currey, 1992.

Cell, John. *The Highest Stage of White Supremacy: The Origins of Segregation in South Africa and the American South.* Cambridge: Cambridge University Press, 1982.

Denoon, Donald. *Settler Capitalism: The Dynamics of Dependent Development in the Southern Hemisphere.* Oxford: Clarendon Press, 1983.

Horne, Alistair. *A Savage War of Peace: Algeria, 1954–1962.* London: Macmillan, 1977.

Lorcin, Patricia. *Imperial Identities: Stereotyping, Prejudice and Race in Colonial Algeria.* London: I. B. Tauris, 1995.

Mason, Philip. *Birth of a Dilemma: The Conquest and Settlement of Rhodesia.* London: Oxford University Press, 1958.

Phimister, Ian. *An Economic and Social History of Zimbabwe, 1890–1948.* London: Longman, 1988.

Wilson, Monica, and Leonard Thompson (eds.), *The Oxford History of South Africa,* vol. 1, *South Africa to 1870.* Oxford: Clarendon Press, 1969.

Witwatersrand: *See* **South Africa: Gold on the Witwatersrand, 1886–1899.**

Wolof and Jolof Empires

The Wolof people form the single largest ethnic group in Senegal and are one of the major groups in the Gambia. Wolof traditions trace their origins to the lower Senegal and the Jolof Empire, *c.*1200 to 1550. The Jolof empire was a successor state to Ghana and Takrur and dominated the Senegambian region for several centuries. Its territories included the Wolof provinces of Jolof, Waalo, Kajoor, and Bawol, and the Sereer provinces of Siin and Saalum, all of which later became independent kingdoms. Wolof traditions date the end of the empire to the battle of Danki in 1549, when the ruler of Kajoor led a rebellion that broke up the empire and created six successor kingdoms. The enrichment of the coastal provinces through Atlantic commerce hurt Jolof, which was located inland to the south of the Senegal River.

The Wolof share a hierarchical social order with 15 other societies of West Africa that divide society into three orders: free farmers, including the nobility; "caste" groups (bards, blacksmiths, and leather workers); and slaves. Based on linguistic evidence, the Wolof are one of three societies for whom this system of stratification is most ancient. Political power was monopolized by matrilineal dynasties, which based their power on their military strength and on slavery. Slaves served the monarchy as agricultural workers, as soldiers and as administrators. Caste groups were important political and economic clients of the nobility.

During the Atlantic slave trade, the Wolof kingdoms exported 300–500 slaves per year to the Americas; these slaves were exchanged for firearms, textiles, iron bars, alcohol, and an assortment of manufactured goods. At the same time, the Wolof kingdoms maintained an active trade with the Saharan region to the north, exporting slaves and grain in exchange for horses and other livestock. The scale of slave exports in both sectors was relatively small by comparison with other regions, but the export slave trade had important domestic consequences. Wolof Muslims condemned the monarchy for the enslavement of fellow Muslims and the consumption of imported alcohol. In the eyes of Wolof Muslims the king and the court were "pagans," a charge that was at odds with reality, but accurately reflected Muslim opposition to the monarchy. Alongside the export slave trade the Wolof kingdoms maintained an active trade in foodstuffs and other provisions with European forts on the coast. As a result of the grain trade with the Atlantic and the desert, the Wolof kingdoms retained as many slaves as they exported and the expansion of internal slavery was one of the most important consequences of the era of Atlantic commerce.

Islam played an important role in Wolof society. Dynastic traditions gave an Islamic identity to the Jolof empire from its foundation. The Wolof populations living near the Senegal River, in Waalo and northern Kajoor, were the first to convert to Islam. Wolof populations in southern Kajoor and Bawol lived interspersed with Sereer communities that resisted Islam until the contemporary era. As a result, Islam was well established in the north, but remained a proselytizing religion in the south. By 1700 the monarchy in Kajoor and Bawol granted local autonomy to Muslim communities by giving land grants and titles to Muslim leaders, who were called *sëriñ* in Wolof, a term translated as *marabout* in both French and English. Within their domains marabouts distributed land to their following, collected taxes and rents, and served as religious councilors, judges, and educators. They were required to aid the monarchy in the defense of the kingdom and served as intermediaries between their followers and the state. The recognition given to Islam patched over the differences between the monarchy and Muslims, but in the long run Muslims were not satisfied with their autonomous status. Titled marabouts led a major rebellion against the monarchy in Kajoor in the 1790s; similar movements continued in the nineteenth century. Alongside the titled marabouts, there were many lesser Muslim scholars who served as teachers, judges, and prayer leaders in Muslim villages. Islam steadily gained ground as a counterforce to the monarchy.

During the eighteenth century, the European trading settlements on Gorée island and at Saint-Louis, at the mouth of the Senegal River, gave birth to important urban, commercial communities. The majority of the inhabitants were slaves who worked in the river trade or provided domestic labor to maintain European trading operations and feed the slaves held in transit on the coast. Women slaves, in particular, pounded millet and cooked food for slaves awaiting ships for the Americas. The slave owners were free women from the mainland called *signares* by French merchants. Male children of the signares and male merchants were referred to as *habitants*. Because most of the free migrants to the European settlements were Wolof speakers from Kajoor and Waalo, Wolof became the dominant language and culture in the new coastal cities. The African merchant communities of Gorée and Saint-Louis, which included some important families of mixed African-European ancestry, played an important role in the river and coastal trade of the eighteenth century. They supplied French merchants with slaves, gold, ivory, gum arabic, grain, and other provisions. There were frequent conflicts between the habitants and European merchants,

in spite of a close working relationship. The pattern of urbanization that emerged in the eighteenth century, with Wolof as the dominant urban language and culture, and with Wolof speakers serving as intermediaries between Europeans and Africans, continued in subsequent centuries. Its legacy is still evident in contemporary Senegal.

By 1800 the Wolof played a leading role in the trade between northern Senegambia and the Atlantic world. Wolof kings taxed Europeans for the right to trade and sold slaves captured in war or enslaved as a punishment for rebellion or failure to pay tribute. The Wolof kingdoms carried on an active trade in grain, fresh produce, cattle, and other provisions with French merchants based in Saint-Louis and Gorée. During the gum boom of the early nineteenth century the Wolof increased their grain exports to the Saharan region. After 1840, Wolof peasants and slaves began growing peanuts as a new export crop. The speed with which Wolof farmers adapted to the changing demands of the Atlantic economy reflected the influence of the habitant merchants, who were always looking for new opportunities as French merchants used colonial power to force them out of established branches of trade.

JAMES SEARING

See also: **Sahara: Trans-Saharan Trade; Slavery: Atlantic Trade: Effects in Africa and the Americas.**

Further Reading

Barry, Boubacar. *Muslim Revolutions and the Atlantic Slave Trade: Senegambia before the Colonial Conquest.* Cambridge: University of Cambridge Press, 1998.

Boulègue, Jean. *Le Grand Jolof (XIIIe–XVIe siècle).* Paris: Harmattan, 1987.

Searing, James. *West African Slavery and Atlantic Commerce: The Senegal River Valley, 1700–1860.* Cambridge: Cambridge University Press, 1993.

Tamari, Tal. "The Development of Caste Systems in West Africa." *Journal of African History* 32, no. 2 (1991): 221–250.

Women: History and Historiography

The history of African women has emerged since 1970 as a vibrant and steadily expanding area of research and study motivated, as with other areas of women's history, by the development of the international feminist movement. African women's history also paralleled the expansion of African history following World War II, as scholars inside and outside of Africa began to focus on historical transformations on the African continent.

Before the 1970s, there was little available research on African women's history. Information on women in Africa was more often found in anthropological and ethnographic studies. This focus has continued in the preponderance of research on African women appearing in development studies rather than history per se. The first publications in the 1970s dealt with women and economic change and with women as political activists. By the mid-1980s there were a number of important extended studies that began to appear. Soha Kader's *Egyptian Women in a Changing Society* (1987), Nina Mba's *Nigerian Women Mobilized* (1982), Claire C. Robertson's *Sharing the Same Bowl* (1984), and Margaret Strobel's *Muslim Women in Mombasa* (1979) still primarily focused on women's public lives. However, with Kristin Mann's *Marrying Well* (1985), Fatima Mernissi's *Beyond the Veil* (1975), and Luise White's *The Comforts of Home* (1990), studies of family and sexuality were also emerging. Only in the 1990s did a substantial number of monographs on specific topics begin to appear, though the bulk of new research is still found in journal and anthology articles.

Earlier historical eras were initially neglected, in part a result of the difficulty in obtaining historical sources that dealt with women before the nineteenth century. Because many African communities were decentralized and nonliterate, written materials on earlier eras, especially from an African woman's perspective, were scarce. While some historians have turned to women's life histories and the use of oral testimony to fill lacunae in published sources, as Susan Geiger (1986) has noted, this has limitations in researching earlier periods. Topics that have archival source materials include elite women such as Queen Nzinga, a sixteenth-century ruler in what became Angola, and market women along the West African coast who interacted with European traders. Julia Wells has written about Eva, a seventeenth-century African woman who settled in the early Dutch community on the Cape in South Africa. Because she married a European colonist, many aspects of her life were documented in settler accounts, providing an unusual amount of contemporary data. Egypt was exceptionally strong in sources concerning women in earlier centuries.

African women's history has been taken further into the past by scholars such as David Schoenbrun, who use historical linguistics to examine changing patterns in women's roles as wives and mothers within pastoralist and agricultural communities. Archeologists have also retrieved information about women's activities. Heidi Nast's investigation of the fifteenth-century royal palaces in Kano, Nigeria, demonstrates the increasing seclusion of elite women as Islam spread, and David Beach's description of sixteenth- century Great Zimbabwe suggests that as firewood was depleted, women's reluctance to travel long distances in search of fuel sources might have been a factor in the demise of that large centralized settlement.

Source availability influenced the large number of studies on slave women in the nineteenth century, which is an important issue but did not represent the experience of most women. As Claire Robertson and Martin Klein's *Women and Slavery in Africa* (1983) has demonstrated, slaves within Africa were more likely to be women, a reflection of their productive and reproductive contributions to their communities. With creative use of sources, scholars have retrieved information on other aspects of the lives of women in the nineteenth century, as exemplified by Elizabeth Eldredge on women's work in Lesotho, Nakanyike Musisi on elite women in Buganda, Marcia Wright on women's vulnerability in Central Africa, Edward Alpers on Swahili women's spirit possession cults, Agnes Aidoo on Asante queen mothers' political influence, Judith Tucker on women's access to property in Egypt, and Jean Boyd and Murray Last on religious Muslim women in West Africa.

Turning to more nontraditional sources has enabled historians to retrieve further details about women's experiences. Leroy Vail and Landeg White analyzed Tumbuka women's songs from Malawi to suggest a new periodization of history. For those women the late nineteenth century was marked by a loss of power resulting from a shift away from matrilineal descent patterns, an issue ignored in the conventional regional histories of Ngoni raids. Colleen Kriger's analysis of weaving techniques found in nineteenth century fabrics from Sokoto in West Africa suggests that women's weaving was more varied, had a higher value, was more organized, and was better known than earlier studies indicated.

Reexamining familiar issues from a woman's perspective has altered African history more generally. For example, many of the initial studies of women's work during the colonial period showed how they had lost power and economic autonomy with the arrival of cash crops and their exclusion from the global marketplace, in contrast to men, who were more likely to benefit from these economic changes. The emphasis of labor history in Africa on the formal sector of the economy eclipsed women's actual economic activity, which centered on agricultural work. Studying women's economic contributions meant paying attention to rural agricultural work as well the urban efforts of market vendors, both sectors previously neglected in African labor history. The research on women also revealed a tension between women as victims and women as powerful agents within their communities. Female agricultural innovations were described by Margaret Jean Hay and Maud Muntemba as essential to community survival, and according to Cora Ann Presley, women became politically active because of their work experiences. Women's changing position in arenas formerly seen as only male has been researched by Jane Parpart writing on mining compounds in Zambia, Lisa Lindsey on railway communities in Nigeria, and Beth Baron on journalism in Egypt.

Studies of women's involvement in political activism changed previously accepted ideas of women's passivity in the face of such changes. Judith Van Allen demonstrated in an influential article that women drew on precolonial practices to express their displeasure with the colonial powers. Susan Geiger's study of the leadership role played by illiterate Muslim women in Dar es Salaam fundamentally changed the view that the Tanzanian anticolonial movement was led solely by men who were products of Christian mission education (1987). Souad Bakalti and Alison Baker showed how Muslim women in North Africa were also active in anticolonial movements. Analysis by Martin Chanock of the development of legal systems under colonialism has shown that women were at a disadvantage as "customary" laws were established based on male testimony that gave men, especially elite men, advantages over women in issues of marriage and divorce.

Studies of women and religion have included work by Bennetta Jules-Rosette on the role of women in developing local churches that were often offshoots of larger denominations, Iris Berger on female spiritual power in local religions, and Margaret Badran on the intersection of Islam and politics in Egypt's nationalist movement. Research in the 1990s also included a focus on women and missions with researchers such as Deborah Gaitskell and Birgitta Larsson demonstrating that the introduction of European ideas about marriage and family simultaneously brought new oppressions and new opportunities for women.

Although a 1987 overview by Claire Robertson suggests that African women's history had shifted to include a more economic perspective—or, as Margaret Jean Hay argues, had moved from the study of elites to the study of more ordinary women—the most notable change has been an increasing level of analysis. The earliest works, with some exceptions, tended to be descriptive, as scholars worked to prove that African women were there, and had made an impact on their societies. More recently studies have provided much more nuanced descriptions of the complexities of women's lives, of the changes over time, and of local and outsider ideologies about women in Africa. Cheryl Johnson did not simply describe the market women's associations in Lagos, but discussed why three different organizations formed, serving different groups of women. A recent reanalysis of the role of the adolescent girl Nongqawuse in the Xhosa cattle killing of the 1870s has demonstrated that taking women's testimony seriously and centering women's experience and expression of history can fundamentally change the explanation of an event. Helen Bradford convincingly suggests that issues of changing sexuality and possibly abuse or incest were of central importance to understanding people's motivations, and conventional reliance on broader economic and political reasons for the upheaval is not completely satisfactory.

Among the issues continuing to appear in writings on African women's history are those of representation (who is writing this history and for what audience), sources and methodology, and periodization, as well as the usual areas of productive work, family life, and public activities such as politics and religion. Tiyambe Zeleza has described the enduring marginalization of African women's history, as the information that has been recovered is omitted from textbooks or included in very limited ways. The absence of African women historians is frequently commented on, as there are regrettably few who publish regularly (Tabitha Kanogo, Makanyike Musisi, Kenda Mutongi, and Bolanle Awe are among them). Often work by African scholars is not published, or is only available in African publications, which can be difficult to obtain in Europe and North America. Recently work has expanded on gender, masculinity, and ideologies, as in Timothy Burke's examination of ideas about consumption and cleanliness in Zimbabwe and as noted in Nancy Rose Hunt's overview of gender in Africa, which refers to a number of important French studies. The history of women in precolonial Africa continues to be a weak point, while the history of the colonial era (c.1880 to the 1960s for most of the continent) has shifted from examining the impact of colonialism on women (assessed as mostly negative) to investigating African communities and history from their own perspective. This includes an emphasis on African women's agency and efforts to present African women's own voices, as in Jean Allman, Fatima Mernissi, Jane Turrittin, and in collections edited by Karen Tranberg Hansen and Kathleen Sheldon. These approaches both reexamine territory already covered and open new topics while infusing the research with the voices of African women as both subjects and scholars, indicating the direction African women's historical scholarship will take in the near future.

KATHLEEN SHELDON

See also: **Colonialism, Overthrow of: Women and the Nationalist Struggle; Historiography of Africa.**

Further Reading

Aidoo, Agnes. "Asante Queen Mothers in Government and Politics in the Nineteenth Century." In *The Black Woman Cross-Culturally*, edited by Filomina Chioma Steady. Cambridge, Mass.: Shenkman, 1981.

Allman, Jean. "Rounding Up Spinsters: Gender Chaos and Unmarried Women in Colonial Asante," *Journal of African History*, no. 37 (1996): 195–214.

Alpers, Edward A. "'Ordinary Household Chores': Ritual and Power in a Nineteenth-Century Swahili Women's Spirit Possession Cult." *International Journal of African Historical Studies*, no. 17 (1984): 677–702.

Awe, Bolanle (ed.). *Nigerian Women in Historical Perspective*. Lagos, 1992.

Badran, Margot. *Feminists, Islam, and Nation: Gender and the Making of Modern Egypt*. Princeton, N.J.: Princeton University Press, 1995.

Bakalti, Souad. *La femme tunisienne au temps de la colonisation (1881–1956)*. Paris: L'Harmattan, 1996.

Baker, Alison. *Voices of Resistance: Oral Histories of Moroccan Women*. Albany: State University of New York Press, 1998.

Baron, Beth. *The Women's Awakening in Egypt: Culture, Society, and the Press*. New Haven, Conn.: Yale University Press, 1994.

Beach, David, and others,. "Cognitive Archaeology and Imaginary History at Great Zimbabwe," *Current Anthropology*, no. 39 (1998): 47–72.

Berger, Iris. "Fertility as Power." In *Revealing Prophets: Prophecy in Eastern African History*, edited by David M. Johnson and Douglas H. Anderson. London: James Currey, 1995.

Boyd, Jean, and Murray Last. "The Role of Women as 'Agents Religieux' in Sokoto." *Canadian Journal of African Studies*, no. 19 (1985): 283–300.

Bradford, Helen. "Women, Gender, and Colonialism: Rethinking the History of the British Cape Colony and its Frontier Zones, *c.*1806–70," *Journal of African History*, no. 37 (1996): 351–370.

Brooks, George, Jr. "The *Signares* of Saint-Louis and Gorée: Women Entrepreneurs of Eighteenth-Century Senegal." In *Women in Africa*, edited by Nancy Hafkin and Edna Bay, Stanford, Calif.: Stanford University Press, 1976.

Burke, Timothy. *Lifebuoy Men, Lux Women: Commodification, Consumption, and Cleanliness in Modern Zimbabwe*. Durham, N.C.: Duke University Press, 1996.

Chanock, Martin. "Making Customary Law: Men, Women, and Courts in Colonial Northern Rhodesia." In *African Women and the Law: Historical Perspectives*, edited by Margaret Jean Hay and Marcia Wright. Boston: African Studies Center, Boston University, 1983.

Eldredge, Elizabeth A. "Women in Production: The Economic Role of Women in Nineteenth-Century Lesotho," *Signs*, no. 16 (1991): 707–731.

Gaitskell, Deborah. "Hot Meetings and Hard Kraals: African Biblewomen in Transvaal Methodism, 1924–60." *Journal of Religion in Africa*, no. 30 (2000): 277–309.

Geiger, Susan. *TANU Women: Gender and Culture in the Making of Tanganyikan Nationalism, 1955–1965*. Portsmouth, N.H.: Heinemann, 1997.

———. "Women's Life Histories: Method and Content." *Signs*, no. 11 (1986): 334–351.

Hansen, Karen Tranberg (ed.). *African Encounters with Domesticity*. New Brunswick, N.J.: Rutgers University Press, 1992.

Hay, Margaret Jean. "Queens, Prostitutes and Peasants: Historical Perspectives on African Women, 1971–1986." *Canadian Journal of African Studies*, no. 22 (1988): 431–447.

Hunt, Nancy Rose. "Introduction." *Gender and History*, no. 8 (1996): 323–337. Special issue, "Gendered Colonialisms in African History."

———. "Placing African Women's History and Locating Gender." *Social History*, no. 14 (1989).

Johnson, Cheryl. "Class and Gender: A Consideration of Yoruba Women during the Colonial Period." In *Women and Class in Africa*, edited by Claire Robertson and Iris Berger. New York: Holmes and Meier, 1986.

Jules-Rosette, Bennetta (ed.). *The New Religions of Africa*. Norwood, N.J.: Ablex, 1979.

Kader, Soha Abdel. *Egyptian Women in a Changing Society, 1899–1987*. Boulder, Colo.: Lynne Rienner, 1987.

Kanogo, Tabitha. "Kikuyu Women and the Politics of Protest: Mau Mau." In *Images of Women in Peace and War*, edited by Sharon Macdonald, Pat Holden, and Shirley Ardener. Cambridge, 1987.

Kriger, Colleen, "Textile Production and Gender in the Sokoto Caliphate." *Journal of African History*, no. 34 (1993): 361–401.

Larsson, Birgitta. *Conversion to Greater Freedom? Women, Church and Social Change in North-Western Tanzania under Colonial Rule*. Stockholm: Almqvist and Wiksell, 1991.

Lindsey, Lisa. "Domesticity and Difference: Male Breadwinners, Working Women, and Colonial Citizenship in the 1945 Nigerian General Strike." *American Historical Review*, no. 104 (1999): 783–812.

Mann, Kristin. *Marrying Well: Marriage, Status, and Social Change Among the Educated Elite in Colonial Lagos*. New York, 1985.

Mba, Nina. *Nigerian Women Mobilized: Women's Political Activity in Southern Nigeria, 1900–1965*. Berkeley: Institute of International Studies, University of California, 1982.

Mernissi, Fatima. *Beyond the Veil: Male-Female Dynamics in a Modern Muslim Society*. New York: John Wiley, 1975.

———. *Doing Daily Battle: Interviews with Moroccan Women*, trans. May Jo Lakeland. London: Women's Press, 1988.

Miller, Joseph. "Nzinga of Matamba in a New Perspective." *Journal of African History*, no. 16 (1975): 201–216.

Muntemba, Maud Shimwaayi. "Women and Agricultural Change in the Railway Region of Zambia: Dispossession and Counterstrategies, 1930–1970." In *Women and Work in Africa*, edited by Edna Bay. Boulder, Colo.: Westview Press, 1982.

Musisi, Nakanyike B. "Women, 'Elite Polygyny,' and Buganda State Formation," *Signs*, no. 16 (1991): 757–786.

Mutongi, Kenda. "'Worries of the Heart': Widowed Mothers, Daughters and Masculinities in Maragoli, Western Kenya, 1940–60." *Journal of African History*, no. 40 (1999): 67–86.

Nast, Heidi J. "Islam, Gender, and Slavery in West Africa Circa 1500: A Spatial Archaeology of the Kano Palace, Northern Nigeria." *Annals of the Association of American Geographers*, no. 86 (1996): 44–77.

Parpart, Jane L. "Sexuality and Power on the Zambian Copperbelt: 1926–1964." In *Patriarchy and Class: African Women in the Home and the Workforce*, edited by Sharon B. Stichter and Jane L. Parpart. Boulder, Colo.: Westview Press, 1988.

Presley, Cora Ann. "Labor Unrest among Kikuyu Women in Colonial Kenya." In *Women and Class in Africa*, edited by Claire Robertson and Iris Berger. New York: Holmes and Meier, 1986.

Robertson, Claire. "Developing Economic Awareness: Changing Perspectives in Studies of African Women, 1976–1985." *Feminist Studies*, no. 13 (1987): 97–135.

Robertson, Claire C. "Never Underestimate the Power of Women: The Transforming Vision of African Women's History." *Women's Studies International Forum*, no. 11 (1988).

———. *Sharing the Same Bowl: A Socioeconomic History of Women and Class in Accra, Ghana*. Bloomington: Indiana University Press, 1984.

Robertson, Claire, and Martin Klein. *Women and Slavery in Africa* (1983). Reprint, Portsmouth, N.H.: Heinemann, 1997.

Schoenbrun, David L. "Gendered Histories Between the Great Lakes: Varieties and Limits." *International Journal of African Historical Studies*, no. 29 (1996).

Sheldon, Kathleen (ed.). *Courtyards, Markets, City Streets: Urban Women in Africa*. Boulder, Colo.: Westview Press, 1996.

Strobel, Margaret. *Muslim Women in Mombasa: 1890–1975.* New Haven, Conn.: Yale University Press, 1976.

Thornton, John. "Legitimacy and Political Power: Queen Njinga, 1624–1663." *Journal of African History*, no. 32 (1991): 25–40.

Tucker, Judith E. *Women in Nineteenth-Century Egypt.* Cambridge: Cambridge University Press, 1985.

Turrittin, Jane. "Aoua Kéita and the Nascent Women's Movement in the French Soudan." *African Studies Review*, no. 36 (1993).

Vail, Leroy, and Landeg White. "The Possession of the Dispossessed: Songs as History among Tumbuka Women." In *Power and the Praise Poem: Southern African Voices in History*, edited by Leroy Vail and Landeg White. Charlottesville: University Press of Virginia, 1991.

Van Allen, Judith. "'Aba Riots' or Igbo 'Women's War'? Ideology, Stratification, and the Invisibility of Women." In *Women in Africa*, edited by Nancy J. Hafkin and Edna Bay. Stanford, Calif.: Stanford University Press, 1976.

Wells, Julia. "Eva's Men: Gender and Power in the Establishment of the Cape of Good Hope, 1652–74." *Journal of African History*, no. 39 (1999): 417–437.

White, Luise. *The Comforts of Home: Prostitution in Colonial Nairobi*. Chicago: Chicago University Press, 1990.

Wright, Marcia. "Women in Peril: A Commentary on the Life Stories of Captives in Nineteenth-Century East Central Africa." *African Social Research*, no. 20 (1975): 800–819.

Zeleza, Tiyambe. "Gender Biases in African Historiography." In *Engendering African Social Sciences*, edited by Ayesha M. Imam, Amina Mama, and Fatou Sow. Dakar: CODESRIA, 1997.

World Bank, International Monetary Fund, and Structural Adjustment

The postcolonial development crisis that had grown acute by the early 1980s saw the introduction of a new development paradigm in Africa. It marked the ascendancy of neoliberal analysis, both in terms of causes and solutions to the crisis. This neoliberal analysis is championed by the International Financial Institutions (IFIs)—that is, the World Bank and the International Monetary Fund—as well as Western creditor nations and liberal scholars. However, the IFIs have become the primary instruments for the implementation of the neoliberal prescriptions that are embodied in the structural adjustment programs (SAPs) of these institutions. The IFIs and Western creditor nations collaborate in ensuring that African countries accept and implement the adjustment programs; as a result, the IFIs make the implementation of these programs a condition for further loans and debts rescheduling, while the Western creditor nations require African countries to reach agreements with the IFIs before they can receive further loans and have their debts rescheduled.

The core of the SAPs is the minimization of the role of the state while granting ascendancy to market forces. This is based on the argument that the main cause of the development crisis is the excessive state regulation of African economies, a situation inimical to the unfettered operation of market forces. Some of the issues singled out by the IFIs were the overvaluation of African currencies, state regulation of the import licensing system, subsidization of petroleum products and various social sectors of the economy, inefficient state-owned enterprises, and corruption. These were seen as the negative outcome of the overregulation of African economies. The SAPs are therefore aimed at redressing these issues through the promotion of the unfettered operation of market forces.

Massive devaluation of African currencies occupies a central position in the adjustment policies of the IFIs; it is regarded as crucial for ending import dependency in Africa while at the same time promoting an export orientation. The argument is that the overvalued nature of African currencies led to a situation where imports were considerably cheaper than exports, thereby encouraging massive importation of various goods, with many of them being irrelevant consumer goods, while discouraging production for exports. In the case of trade liberalization, it is argued that by removing all bureaucratic control over the foreign exchange markets, African businesses would be able to import the necessary inputs for their industries while more foreign investments would be attracted into the continent. Moreover, the abolition of marketing boards that would remove government control and direct participation in the marketing of agricultural products would make the increased income from agricultural products to be passed on to the farmers, thereby increasing rural incomes. This would encourage increased production for exports by the rural dwellers.

Other related policies are the reduction in public expenditures and the privatization of public enterprises. The idea behind the reduction in public expenditure is based on the argument that the huge subsidization of petroleum products, and social services like health, education, social infrastructure, and other services, constitute a phenomenal drain on the resources of African countries while at the same time benefiting only the urban elites to the detriment of rural dwellers, who need to be encouraged to increase their agricultural outputs. With regard to the privatization of public enterprises, the argument is based on their poor performance necessitating regular subsidies that constitute a further drain on government resources. It is argued that privatization would expose these enterprises to market-determined competition and therefore make them operate more efficiently if they want to remain in business. At the same time, budgetary allocations that used to go to them would be released for carrying out more beneficial economic activities.

The SAPs are hardcore neoliberalism, and constitute mere reformulations of the modernization policy that was the main paradigm that influenced the failed postcolonial economic development policies in Africa. It should be noted that, theoretically, policies like those of massive devaluation and trade liberalization are situated within the neoclassical economic policy of comparative advantage. This emphasis on comparative advantage constitutes a continuation of the unfair and unequal international division of labor that assigns African countries to the disadvantageous position of continuing to produce agricultural raw materials for advanced capitalist industries and, therefore, continuing to be dependent on the importation of industrial products.

Massive devaluation has had untold negative effects on Africa. It is now generally agreed that from a perceived position of overvaluation, African currencies have become so devalued that they are virtually worthless. The effects of this situation have been disastrous for African economies. As has already been noted, the main argument for devaluation is that it would discourage imports while encouraging exports and therefore help in reallocating resources to farmers. But in practice, the debilitating effects of devaluation on the wages of farmers have made them flood the world market with their products, thereby further lowering prices and increasing their woes. In addition, in the face of the phenomenal decrease in the purchasing power of African currencies, the reduction in wages, and retrenchment of government workers advocated by SAPs, most urban dwellers can no longer afford to purchase agricultural products. Furthermore, devaluation has negatively affected the industrial sector. The import substitution strategy of industrialization that has been adopted in postcolonial African countries is highly import-dependent in terms of machines, raw materials, and other inputs. Since devaluation has made the prices of these inputs astronomically high and beyond the reach of many indigenous industries, the prices of the products of even the few industries that manage to afford the inputs are so high that they are more expensive than imported alternatives. As a result, most of the small-scale and medium-scale industries have gone out of production while the few industries that have remained in production are producing at very reduced capacity.

The poor performance of many state-owned enterprises provides some justification for the privatization of some of the industries. But the prescription for privatization of all state-owned enterprises irrespective of the functions they perform does not appear desirable.

There are those enterprises that perform socially relevant services for the vast majority of the people and therefore have to remain government owned in order to continue to perform these functions. Moreover, experience with privatization in many African countries has shown that the process is leading to the concentration of the countries' resources in the hands of very few wealthy individuals and also increasing foreign control of African enterprises, yet the enterprises are sold to these individuals at very low rates. This has therefore resulted in discrimination against the poor in the disposition of collectively owned wealth. Even then, a major contradiction with the privatization policy is that while most of the reforms have to be carried out and ensured by the state, adjustment policies call for the minimization of the state. It would therefore be counterproductive to expect the much maligned African state to effectively and efficiently carry out the privatization process.

Given the fact that the rescheduling of African debts and the getting of more loans are conditioned on the acceptance and implementation of SAPs, the desperate African countries have no choice but to accept the programs. Yet SAPs have serious implications for African autonomy. As a program that is fully designed by the IFIs without any inputs from African countries that are forced to implement them, SAPs represent external *diktat* and a clear loss of autonomy for the African countries concerned. A good example is Ghana, touted as the star pupil of SAPs in Africa, which has almost lost its autonomy to the officials of the IFIs and their "experts" who have virtually taken over the management of the economy of Ghana to the chagrin of many Ghanaians.

Indeed, all over Africa, SAPs have caused untold hardships. The massive devaluation of national currencies and the resultant spiraling inflation, sharp reduction in public expenditure, retrenchment, cuts in wages, unprecedented level of unemployment, and removal of subsidies from social sectors, among other similar measures, have caused widespread poverty and misery. One of the worst hit areas is the social sector. The removal of subsidies from this sector and the huge decline in government allocations have led to a significant deterioration and virtual collapse of areas like health and education, which are very crucial for the development of any country. These are clearly manifested in the poor conditions of service for staff and the consequent extremely low level of morale, lack of facilities, libraries that are devoid of current books and journals, and hospitals that have become glorified consulting clinics and virtual mortuaries. In addition, the debilitating effects of SAPs have virtually discouraged any form of productive activities, promoting massive brain drains from African countries, capital flight, disinvestment, and, worst of all, the flooding of African markets with used goods from various Western capitalist countries. Thus, apart from the fact that SAPs have discouraged production, they are not only reinforcing and sustaining the existing emphasis on distribution, but are in fact doing so at the worst level. While previous distribution efforts have concentrated primarily on the importation of new goods, the current emphasis on the importation of used goods and the primary concern with foreign exchange speculation by African banks are promoting the worst form of "buccaneer" capitalism in Africa.

It is important to note that although in theory SAPs are calling for the minimization of the state, in practice the IFIs promote authoritarian and interventionist states because it is only under such conditions that the harsh policies of SAPs can be carried out. Since adjustment programs are helping to worsen the African crisis while further entrenching neocolonial dependency, what African countries need are structural transformation programs, not programs that merely adjust the neocolonial structures as prescribed by SAPs.

J. I. DIBUA

See also: **Development, Postcolonial: Central Planning, Private Enterprise, Investment.**

Further Reading

Callaghy, T. M., and J. Ravenhill (eds.). *Hemmed In: Responses to Africa's Economic Decline.* New York: Columbia University Press, 1993.

Cornia, G. A., and G. K. Helleiner (eds.). *From Adjustment to Development in Africa: Conflict, Controversy, Convergence, Consensus.* New York: St. Martin's Press, 1994.

Dibua, J. I. "Journey to Nowhere: Neo-Liberalism and Africa's Development Crisis." *Comparative Studies Of South Asia, Africa and the Middle East* 18, no. 2 (1998).

Economic Commission for Africa (ECA). *African Alternative Framework to Structural Adjustment Programme for Economic Recovery and Transformation.* Addis Ababa: United Nations Economic Commission for Africa, 1989.

Hussain, I., and R. Faruqee (eds.). *Adjustment in Africa: Lessons From Country Case Studies.* Washington, D.C.: World Bank, 1994.

Onimode, B. (ed.). *The IMF, the World Bank and the African Debt.* 2 vols. London: IFAA and Zed Books, 1989.

Sahn, D. E. (ed.). *Adjusting to Policy Failure in African Economies.* Ithaca, N.Y.: Cornell University Press, 1994.

World Bank. *Adjustment in Africa: Lessons from Country Case Studies.* Washington, D.C.: World Bank, 1994.

———. *Sub-Saharan Africa: From Crisis to Sustainable Growth, A Long-Term Perspective Study.* Washington, D.C.: World Bank, 1989.

World History, Africa in

By any measure, Africa's contribution to world history is immense and diverse. From the monumental pyramids of ancient Egypt to the towering twentieth-century figures of Nelson Mandela and Kofi Annan, continental Africa has produced innumerable cultural and political moments and people of great historical importance. As part of the many world systems that have ebbed and flowed over millennia, Africa has also made its mark. From the earliest geological and fossil remains; through ancient civilizations in Nubia; to the slave trade, imperialism, colonialism, and the Third World Non-Aligned Movement, African men and women actively participated in the establishment of new ideas, concepts and movements. And aside from the historical record, the role of African history looms large in the development of a body of scholarship known as "world history."

On the African continent archaeologists have found the earliest evidence of the evolution of humans. Several sites in Ethiopia, Kenya, and South Africa have produced fossils of human ancestors, known as *hominids*, enabling anthropologists to trace the history of humans back to primates living between four and one million years ago. The earliest group, known as *australopithicus*, was succeeded by a larger species with tool-making skills, *Homo habilis*. Besides these earliest hominids, skeletal remains of *Homo erectus* have demonstrated that this more humanlike ancestor was responsible for the migration of primates out of Africa and into Asia and Europe. Modern man, *Homo sapiens*, is believed to have first appeared in Africa c.200,000 to 100,000. From tropical Africa, humans spread to all major regions of the world by 10,000. But while the basic physiology of this species is evident from fossils, direct links to the many variations of skin color and appearance of Africans and other peoples today is impossible. Because of this extensive archaeological record, continental Africa, and in particular the Great Rift Valley running through Tanzania and Kenya, is often referred to as the "cradle of humankind."

Stone Age cultures developed in Africa as they did throughout the world, sometimes in tandem, other times at vastly divergent speeds. Hunter-gatherer societies flourished throughout the continent by c.10,000 and detailed documents of their lifestyles are depicted in rock art in the savannah regions. The movement and settlement of these peoples was marked by changes in the environment over millennia. Africa in 7000 was much wetter and more densely forested than it is now. The Kho-San peoples are one of the last remaining traditional hunter-gather communities, and many of their practices bear striking similarity to information collected from archaeological deposits in southern and south central Africa. *Neolithic* culture eventually gave way to regularized agriculture and pastoralism, which foreshadowed the rise of the first organized farming communities along the riverine systems of northeast Africa in Egypt and Nubia.

During the mid-fourth millennium the first centralized agricultural kingdoms arose along the Nile River. Small towns consolidated into two regions, Upper and Lower Egypt. In approximately 3100 Narmer (also known as Menes) conquered the lower region of the Nile Delta and established the first dynasty of ancient Egypt. The kings, known as pharaohs, ruled with divine authority over an authoritarian and bureaucratic state. The wealth for the kingdom came from trade and peasant labor along the Nile Valley and gold in Nubia (present-day Ethiopia). The Egyptians constructed monumental tombs for their kings, including possibly the largest single building constructed by hand, the Great Pyramid at Giza (c.2500BCE). Among the many legacies of ancient Egypt are the hieroglyphic script, a panoply of religious, mathematical, and scientific texts, and an early form of monotheism attributed to the pharaoh Akhenaton.

While Egyptian politics looked toward the Mediterranean, the empire was deeply African; several generations of kings and important civilizations, such as the Meroë, came from the highlands of Nubia. By 500BCE much of West Africa became part of a much larger African-European network of trade in textiles, slaves, and precious commodities. In central Nigeria, "Nok culture" established a powerful influence over the Niger-Benuë River network. Copper, iron, and bronze working came early to Africa, and large deposits of these metals meant that north and east Africa became quickly the center of Afro-Asiatic trade in metal goods. With gold, plentiful grain supplies, and other valuable commodities, Egypt and Libya became major players in the evolving Mediterranean civilizations. First Asia Minor, and then Greece, Carthage and Rome, drew on Egyptian and Nubian culture and bounty. North African civilizations, such as Carthage and other Phoenician cities, penetrated into the Sahara Desert and West Africa. Early trans-Saharan trade routes exchanged iron products for salt and gold. With the rise of Christianity, Egyptian Christians challenged the authority of Rome and founded the independent Coptic Church. St. Augustine of Hippo, a north African, fought against their variations in doctrine and practice.

The next 1000-year period was marked by important changes in the relationship between North and Sub-Saharan Africa and the outside world. A slow but steady movement of Iron Age peoples from the forested regions in the center westward and southward put pressure on Stone Age cultures. To the north the brief ascendancy of the Christian church was displaced by Islam from the seventh century. To the south civilizations arose around the Great Lakes region, and in the west the kingdom of Ghana grew replete on the gold and salt trade. By 711 all of north Africa had come under Muslim rule, and Islam began to spread up the Nile, along the east coast, and across the Sahara. First as an army of conquest, and slowly over many decades, Islamic identities permeated and mixed with indigenous African cultures. By the mid-twelfth century, trans-Saharan trade routes were controlled by Islamized Berber communities, and Arabic writers told of untold wealth. Ghana declined as the Almoravids from North Africa encroached on the trade routes. Other powerful states arose in its place, including Mali and Songhay. The region maintained strong ties with the northern Islamic states, and after the reign of Sundiata (c.1250) Mali also became Islamic. During this period Timbuktu rose to prominence as a center of Islamic scholarship. To the east, Christianity maintained a firm hold in Ethiopia despite the incorporation of much of the Swahili coast in Islamic Indian Ocean trading networks. Elsewhere, the kingdom of Zimbabwe extended its political control over much of the southeast.

By the sixteenth century, all of coastal Africa and much of the interior was part of one or several internationalized trading networks. In the 1470s the first European forts were built along the Fanti coast to control metal and cloth trading. Soon after, São Tomé and Principe were colonized for slave-run sugar plantations. In 1498 Portuguese navigators sailed around the Cape of Good Hope and met Chinese, Arab and Indonesian merchants operating in the commercial infrastructures of Madagascar, Pemba, and Zanzibar. Portuguese raids along the Swahili coast were to some extent a continuation of the Crusader wars of the European Middle Ages. Plantations, manufacturing, and mining industries along both coasts were soon manned exclusively by slave labor. The arrival of Columbus in the Western Hemisphere created further opportunities for plantations and mines, and thus began the trans-Atlantic slave trade. The first slaves came from the Gambia River; the first slave cargo to be taken directly across the Atlantic dates to 1532. But with Portuguese infiltration of the Kingdom of Kongo and Dutch settlement in Cape Town, the entire western seaboard was drawn into the trade.

Until the mid-nineteenth century only Algeria and South Africa were sites of European colonization. White settlement grew rapidly and the pressures put on local African communities by the French invasion (1830) and Boer Treks (1830s–1840s) resulted in massive displacement and violence. Elsewhere European and Arabic merchants and military bases controlled small frontier enclaves. In the mid-1800s, however, Europeans took a renewed interest in Africa. Peanut farming in the Senegal River Valley and Christian missionary activity throughout the continent were two new activities that shifted the world's attention away from Africa as a source of slaves to a new site for "legitimate commerce." Powerful African states arose on the fortunes of the slave trade, including Dahomey and the Asante kingdom. Others, such as the British colony Sierra Leone and the independent state of Liberia (1847), were built by freed slaves. Europe's fascination for luxuries such as ivory and its insatiable demand for gold as a base for its currencies drew investment and interest as part of wider European imperialism.

European imperial designs on Africa were both internal and external in origin. European and North American economies urgently needed raw materials for their industrializing economies. Moreover, the continent was increasingly viewed from outside as a battleground among the Christian, Islamic, and pagan religions. Within the continent various events fueled European concerns, including the Mahdist empire (from the 1870s on) in Sudan threatening the Suez Canal, the discovery of huge deposits of diamonds (1870s) and gold (1880s) in southern Africa, and various powerful Islamic and non-Islamic kingdoms in West Africa. From the 1840s on, the British and French governments increased their presence along the western coast, and by the 1880s European rivalries eventually gave way to real competition. After French and Belgian forces began to encroach farther into Senegal and the Congo Rivers regions, a conference was convened in Berlin (1884) at which the ground rules for the European "Scramble" were established. Between 1880 and 1895 the greater part of Africa was partitioned and violently conquered. Ethiopia, however, valiantly withstood an Italian invasion in 1896 at the Battle of Adowa.

Over the next several decades much of Sub-Saharan Africa was drawn into the evolving world economic system. In southern Africa, gold and diamond deposits were exploited with black and white labor. In the Congo and elsewhere, rubber was harvested in slavish conditions resulting in the deaths of tens of thousands. In South Africa the British, African, and Boer settlers went to battle in the first imperial war enjoining support from Australia, Canada, and New Zealand. Throughout the continent millions of Africans resisted and engaged colonial rule; the Maji Maji rebellion in Tanganyika and the formation of the African National Congress (1912) in South Africa are two important examples. Railways, often built by forced labor, paved the way for the extraction of raw materials. During World War I the European powers, using African troops, fought throughout Africa, with Tanzania and Cameroon being sites of particularly violent clashes. Many thousands of Africans also fought in Europe and Asia. After Germany was expelled from its African colonies (1914–1919), the League of Nations administered these territories via Britain, France, and Belgium; both Liberia and Abyssinia were admitted as members of the Geneva-based organization. The 1920s–1940s witnessed the most developed and exploitative years of colonial rule, but Africans also turned their hands to economic opportunities and developed cash crops of cotton, peanuts, coffee, and cocoa.

The Great Depression inflicted immense misery on Africa; by 1931 salaried Africans were receiving 50 per cent of their 1929 income. This economic disaster was fundamental for the mobilization of organized labor and politics, and Africans formed welfare associations, political parties, and unions as part of a continent-wide movement that was to develop into a full-fledged independence struggle. African politics was deeply influenced by the politics of the African diaspora in the Western Hemisphere and Europe. W. E. B. DuBois, Marcus Garvey, and Blaise Daigne, among others were instrumental in the development of a Pan-African political and cultural identity. The independence of Egypt, the rise of Afrikaner nationalism, and the 1936 Italian invasion of Abyssinia were important moments that helped this ideology crystallize into a continent-wide movement, uniting North Africans, their southern cousins, and even Indian migrant workers in South Africa. North Africa was a major battlefield of World War II; the Allied invasion of Europe began after Morocco and Algeria were retaken from Axis control. While Libya, Egypt, Ethiopia, and Somalia also saw significant fighting, the rest of continental Africa was belabored by unparalleled European demands for raw materials.

World War II unleashed tremendous opposition to colonial rule, and Europe began to lose control of its empire. In 1944 the Brazzaville Conference heralded a change of direction for French colonies. In 1945 Anglophone Pan-Africanists met in Manchester, England, to plan a concerted campaign for independence. The independence struggle (1945–1960) was at times bloody and at other times negotiated. In Kenya, South Africa, and Algeria guerrilla wars began in earnest; Ghana blazed a trail in peaceful transition; and Guinea unleashed the wrath of France by rejecting closer ties with its colonial master. The 1958 All African People's Conference in Accra brought together independence leaders from throughout the continent. Although in 1960 Belgian and French governments simply pulled out and African elites slid into the reigns of power, to the south white supremacists held sway for many years in the Portuguese colonies, Southern Rhodesia, and South Africa.

The African independence struggle drew world attention and was part of much larger anticolonial protest. Although Ethiopia, Egypt, and Liberia were founding members of the United Nations (1945), it was not until 1960 that dozens of newly independent African nations tipped the balance away from Europe and America, making it a truly world body. Following the Bandung conference (1955) in Indonesia, many African governments joined to form the Non-Aligned Movement (1961). Also known as the Third World, these nations positioned themselves apart from the United States and the Soviet Union and their respective allies. Despite this maneuver Africa was a site of great Cold War tension, especially in Angola, Ethiopia, and Somalia. While many of Africa's democracies faltered in the late 1960s and 1970s, the Zimbabwean war of liberation and the antiapartheid struggle in South Africa kept alive hopes for a continent free of foreign domination. During the same period, African scholarship, diplomacy, and culture made daring and important contributions to world movements. Two Africans have served as secretary general of the United Nations; Africans have been awarded ten Nobel Prizes (three in literature, two in medicine, and five for peace) and many other distinctions. With the 2001 United Nations Conference on Racism in Durban, South Africa, and the anti–child labor, "blood diamonds," AIDS medications, and debt cancellation campaigns, Africa today continues its role as the progenitor of popular international movements.

African historical writing has played an important role in the development of the historiography of world history, and this final section considers this body of scholarship. While Africa was the location of important advances in anthropological and archaeological scholarship from the 1920s, African history, as distinct from imperial history, only established itself as an independent subfield in 1960. Since then there has been an ever-increasing interest in African historical traditions. Early researchers recorded oral histories and nationalist historians focused on important moments such as anticolonial revolts as part of the nation-building project. In spite of these developments, in the academy the canon of Western history remained relatively unchallenged.

With the growth of multiculturalism, scholars and students began to dispute Western constructions of the historical past as well as profoundly one-sided "Western civilization" undergraduate programs. The first calls for change erupted in the United States during the era of the Black Power movement (1965–1975), as students demanded classes on African and African American cultures and history, as well as increased placement of people of color in the academy. Many Black Power advocates drew on the powerful black consciousness ideology of the South Africa militant Steve Biko. Biko himself drew on the experience of Pan-Africanism, *Négritude*, and the virulent racism of South Africa's apartheid.

By the early 1980s, this struggle over the nature of knowledge and the shape of its transmission entered a new phase. Students and teachers, as well as governments and legislators, began to discuss openly the implications of teaching policies. The most important scholarly development was the growth of "subaltern studies": scholarship that investigated the previously unknown "other," the silenced voices of history, the dispossessed, and the displaced. Much of this scholarship focused on South Asia; it strove to recover the lives of people forgotten in narratives of global exploitation and national mobilization. In so doing, scholars called into question the very narratives themselves, the source material, theoretical frameworks, and the subject positions of historians. One view interprets this scholarship as demonstrating that all histories of colonized regions, Africa included, as they are written, exist in the shadow of Europe, not solely because of the powerful intrusion of colonization into other continents, but also because Europe's self-perceived movement toward state-building, capitalist development, and modernity marked—and still mark—a vision of historical progress against which African history is a failure.

Responding to the changing political and social fabric of the United States and elsewhere, historians embraced this vision, and multiculturalism's challenge to "Western culture" for greater minority inclusion was paralleled by a shift away from the study of Western civilization to world history. Instead of one Western culture, students explored many world cultures; and instead of one Western civilization, teachers professed many world civilizations. Thus it was argued that incorporating underrepresented minorities in a set of analytical categories that remain unchanged only left intact a cultural and political architecture of the study of the past that privileged certain forms of cultural and intellectual expression. Echoing Cheikh Anta Diop in linguistic scholarship, people like Martin Bernal have even argued for the African origins of Western classical cultures. Furthermore, teachers of history have attempted to move beyond the restricting organizing concepts of the term *civilization*. Some have chosen to abandon the "West" altogether in an effort to permit students to appreciate the great diversity of human responses to common problems. With increasing frequency, universities advertise studies in World History. In each of these pedagogical moves to de-Westernize the center, and to de-center the West, African history continues to play a fundamental role.

BENJAMIN NICHOLAS LAWRANCE

See also: **History, African: Sources of.**

Further Reading

Bernal, Martin. *Black Athena: The Afroasiatic Roots of Classical Civilization*. London, 1987.

Curtin, Philip, Steven Feierman, Leonard Thompson, and Jan Vansina. *African History: From Earliest Times to Independence*, 2nd ed. New York: Longman, 1995.

Reader, John. *Africa: A Biography of the Continent*. London: Hamish Hamilton, 1997.

Roberts, Richard. "Teaching Non-Western History at Stanford." In *Learning History in America: Schools, Cultures, and Politics*, edited by Donald Reid Kramer and William L. Barry. Minneapolis: University of Minnesota Press, 1994.

Shillington, Kevin. *History of Africa*. New York: St. Martin's Press, 1989.

World War I: Survey

The Great War of 1914–1918 was the major imperialist war of the twentieth century, and the first truly total war of the industrial era, an essentially European conflict in which distant colonial command of African human and material resources formed a significant element in the war effort of several belligerent states. While Africa as a region was fairly marginal to actual Allied strategy and purpose, it could not help but become caught up in the war, simply because virtually all of it was under the thumb of European imperialism. Inevitably, therefore, seizing Germany's African colonies of Togoland, Kamerun, Ostafrika, and Sudwestafrika was an obvious British and French war aim. Equally, wartime control of vital raw materials, food, manpower, deep-water ports, radio stations, and transportation arteries, and their denial to the enemy, was of considerable importance to European campaigning and to the balance of military capability among London, Paris, Berlin, and Vienna.

Without ample Nigerian groundnuts and palm produce, Senegalese cocoa and dried bananas, Algerian tobacco, or strategic South African mineral reserves, European Allied forces and their supplying economies would have had a far rougher time. Equally, without skilled white settler volunteers, motivated by imperial patriotism, and the mass recruitment of African troops for war service, industrial powers would have had fewer fighting tools. At the same time, the level of African contribution to, and involvement in, the war varied enormously across the continent. In parts of East and Central Africa, the impact of labor recruitment bit deeply into peasant societies, while the dominant experience elsewhere was that of a remote conflict that barely touched the lives of ordinary inhabitants.

The effects of global war on African economies was mixed. In general terms, war dislocated colonial production by choking off European investment, disorganizing normal shipping routes and trading connections, increasing tax burdens, and creating a run of fiscal crises for various rickety colonial administrations. In the early years of the war there was a drastic decline in exports of cash crops and other commodities, and falling prices seriously worsened terms of trade for exchange economies. Shortages of basic commodities and soaring prices for imported goods saw the living standards of many workers decline, especially in urban areas that became pinched by scarcity and inflation. Confronting growing wartime impoverishment, many workers grew rebellious, and by 1918 towns across Africa were experiencing regular outbreaks of labor militancy.

At the same time, there were major differences between the economic experiences of Africans in different parts of the continent. Once shipping lanes had been reopened and transportation links secured by 1916, regions like West Africa recovered as Allied demand for cash crops and other raw materials boosted colonial production and drove up export prices. Nigerian groundnut producers benefited from favorable trade terms for African producers. Others who did well included African workers in the Gold Coast, whose skills and job prospects were improved as they replaced skilled whites who were drawn off to war duties. Moreover, from the beginning, Africa's most advanced industrial economy was effectively reoriented to meet strategic wartime priorities. South African supply of minerals, food, and other agricultural commodities aided its accumulation, fostering a new burst of industrialization and market expansion. Here, too, for a time the transfer of whites into overseas war service opened up job mobility for Africans in a range of sectors, from mining to transportation. In effect, for the great majority of African men and women, the experience of World War I was felt through prices, market shortages or opportunities, and through changed work conditions rather than through military participation and combat.

Such economic change was naturally not the only variable in considering the repercussions of the war for the inhabitants of Africa. Colonial campaigns against the Germans meant that a European war was fought across African land, burdening local inhabitants with the costs of sprawling bush warfare, fought mainly with African troops. France, in particular, also raised many thousands of African soldiers for service in theaters of war beyond the continent, in areas such as the Western Front and the Dardenelles. As in the earlier Franco-Prussian War, France again exploited African manpower to try to make good its military deficiency against its powerful European opponent. In all, some 600,000 men from French North Africa and West Africa were conscripted into French colonial fighting forces, along with 140,000 labor conscripts, mostly North Africans. The cost paid by African regiments was not negligible. Over 70,000 soldiers died in French service, some of these in a Moroccan regiment that ended up as the most-decorated unit of the entire French Army.

Unlike France, Britain was more politically nervous about deploying African troops in European hostilities, fearing the possible effects of this on the social and political consciousness. But within the continent itself, white South African, Rhodesian, and other settler forces were too small to settle affairs with Germany on their own, and the British had no option but to "Africanize" their local war effort. Approximately 50,000 African troops were raised in East, West, and Central Africa in a recruiting campaign accompanied by a massive drive to snare the labor needed to maintain communication and supply lines over huge distances. In all, Britain engaged over one million African porters, carriers, laborers, and other camp followers as a vast labor army. Well over half this number of able-bodied men were forcibly conscripted or otherwise muscled into service, where arduous foot marches and exceptionally harsh conditions produced a death rate of over 10 per cent in British carrier corps by the end of the war.

The impact of war-related mortality, illness, and disability was by no means restricted to army service and auxiliary work. Food shortages and even famine in some areas as a result of the seizure of cattle and other food resources for the war effort took a toll, as did severe population dislocation caused by British, French, Belgian, German, and Portuguese demands for labor and goods. Vulnerable rural populations in areas such as Central and East Africa also faced a debilitating combination of epidemic disease and ecological disaster as a consequence of war demand. In Tanganyika, for example, the sudden depletion of a customary agricultural labor supply checked the clearing of bush, creating conditions for the rapid spread of tsetse pestilence. Finally, toward the end of hostilities, the penetrative effects of the war carried the Spanish influenza epidemic from Europe and the United States into Africa, leading to hundreds of thousands of deaths. In response to this demographic upheaval and to the general instability that marked the end of the conflict, many Christian and Muslim Africans turned to millenarian religious beliefs, and anticolonial sentiment influenced by charismatic notions of deliverance from European mastery.

Africans generally earned little by way of reward for wartime loyalty to European empire. That notwithstanding, their experience of World War I has sometimes been associated with the emergence of a more "modern," assertive nationalist consciousness, based on exposure to new kinds of European realities. Yet aside from white South Africa, where the war encouraged a drift toward greater autonomy within the imperial system, colonial African territories achieved nothing by way of any strengthening of an independent political position. Post-1918 repartitioning of Africa by the victorious Allied powers took no heed of local aspirations, and this new division of African territory actually led to a level of European control even more dense than that of 1914.

BILL NASSON

See also: **Egypt: Nationalism, World War I and the Wafd, 1882–1922; Kenya: World War I, Carrier Corps; Senegal: World War I; South Africa: World Wars I and II; Tanganyika (Tanzania): World War I.**

Further Reading

Crowder, Michael. "The First World War and its Consequences." In *General History of Africa*, vol. 7, *1880–1935*, edited by A. Adu Boahen. London: James Currey, 1990.

Echenberg, Myron. *Colonial Conscripts: The Tirailleurs Senegalais in French West Africa, 1875–1960*. London: James Currey, 1991.

Grundlingh, Albert. *Fighting Their Own War: Black South Africans and the First World War*. Johannesburg: Ravan, 1986.

Journal of African History 19, no. 1 (1978). Special Issue on Africa and World War I.

Killingray, David. "The War in Africa." In *The Oxford Illustrated History of the First World War*, edited by Hew Strachan. Oxford: Oxford University Press, 1998.

Lettow-Vorbeck, Paul von. *My Reminiscences of East Africa*. Nashville: Battery, 1993.

Nasson, Bill. "Le Zulu Blanc: South African Infantry in Flanders." In *Passchendaele in Perspective*, edited by Peter Liddle. London: Leo Cooper, 1997.

———. "War Opinion in South Africa." *Journal of Imperial and Commonwealth History* 23, no. 2 (1995).

Page, Melvin (ed.). *Africa and the First World War*. London: Macmillan, 1987.

Waites, Bernard. "Peoples of the Underdeveloped World." In *Facing Armageddon: The First World War Experienced*, edited by Hugh Cecil and Peter H. Liddle. London: Leo Cooper, 1996.

World War I: North and Saharan Africa

In the half century preceding the outbreak of World War I, vast tracts of North Africa and the Sahara had fallen under European rule. The French expanded from initial bases in the coastal regions of Algeria and Senegal into Morocco and Tunisia, the Algerian Sahara, and what became Mauritania, Mali, Niger, and Chad. The British moved into Egypt, the Sudan, and the Saharan entrepôts of northern Nigeria. The Italians entered Libya, and the Spanish laid claim to enclaves both north and south of French Morocco.

These campaigns met with resistance, and, in the case of the British at Khartoum in 1885, a stunning defeat. Shortly before the war, in 1911, the Italians had invaded Libya, where they encountered resistance led by the Sanusiya, an Islamic Sufi order based in Cyrenaica, with networks reaching throughout the central Sahara. With colonial conquest, peoples living in remote mountain and desert areas came under control of a central state often for the first time. Many suffered economic dislocations and environmental degradation as European armies passed through, requisitioning food and pack animals.

German and Ottoman strategists sought to exploit the grievances of the population, and to harness their military skills to draw off French, British, and Italian military personnel and resources. They also sought to undermine the loyalty of troops recruited from the region, above all from French North Africa, who were serving on the Western Front. Toward this end they recruited Algerian and Tunisian exiles living in the Ottoman Empire, including the Tunisian Mohamed Bach Hamba, who carried on propaganda efforts from a base in Lausanne, Switzerland.

The success of these efforts was limited. Early in the European war there were incidents of French North African troops refusing orders on the front, and occasional desertions. In French Morocco, Abd al-Malik, a son of Algerian resistance leader Abd al-Qadir, who had grown up in Syria and served as an Ottoman army officer, was involved in anti-French rebellions. There were localized revolts in Algeria, sparked mainly by military conscription.

The most serious and widespread threat came from the Sanusiya, working with help from the Germans and Ottomans who brought money, arms, and military personnel across the Mediterranean by submarine. In early 1915 the Italians suffered a major reversal in the Misurata region of Libya, losing a large quantity of arms to rebels. Prompted by their German and Ottoman allies, the Sanusiya struck at the British in Egypt in late 1915 but were defeated early the next year. Authority in Cyrenaica then shifted from Sayyid Ahmad to Sayyid Idris al-Sanusi, who was on cordial terms with the British. With the British as intermediaries he negotiated a truce with the Italians and gained recognition as emir of Cyrenaica.

In 1916 Sanusi forces advanced in French Saharan territories, taking the post of Djanet in southeastern Algeria, and then launching an attack on Agades in the center of Niger. Thanks to the astuteness of the local French commander, and the support of the British in Nigeria, the rebels were defeated. The French exacted brutal revenge on all they perceived as enemies in the area.

To the east, in the Anglo-Egyptian Sudan, the British governor Sir Reginald Wingate, faced a challenge from Sultan Ali Dinar, whose kingdom of Darfur on the western frontier had never been brought under direct control from Khartoum. In 1915, as military activity was escalating to the north, Ali Dinar opened contacts with the Sanusiya, signaling his defiance of the British. In February 1916 Wingate launched an attack on Darfur, defeating Ali Dinar's army and, by November, killing the sultan himself. Wingate was careful to maintain cordial relations with leaders of Sudan's principal Sufi orders, a policy paralleling that of the French in North Africa. Also, thanks to Sudan's proximity to the Hijaz, Wingate had a role in promoting British support for the Arab revolt against the Turks launched there in June 1916, and later in monitoring the revolt's development.

The failure of German-Ottoman efforts in North Africa and the Sahara might be contrasted with the success of the British with the Arab Revolt in the Hijaz. The Germans and Ottomans provided little in the way of material aid to the rebels—Saharan people who, in the wake of a devastating drought in 1912–1913, desperately needed food as well as arms. There was neither a clear strategic goal, nor a German or Ottoman conventional force to combine efforts with the rebels.

The French not only survived the assorted rebellions, but recruited hundreds of thousands of troops and workers from their North African territories. Their success owed in part to their cultivating the loyalty of traditional leaders, from the Moroccan sultan to local leaders of Sufi orders, policies associated with Marshal Lyautey, then French resident in Morocco. Another factor, however, was that young North African men faced poverty and repression at home. In France they were treated with greater respect and were decently paid. Some, like the future Algerian nationalist leader Messali Hajj, began their acquaintance with radical political ideas at this time. As the French recruited troops for the European war in North Africa they brought West African troops to help maintain order there. The Italians followed a similar policy bringing Eritrean troops to Libya.

World War I left a complex heritage in North Africa and the Sahara. Romantic images of desert warriors notwithstanding, the war demonstrated the importance of modern military training. The most effective rebellions had a leavening of officers trained in the Ottoman army. But far more North Africans served under colonial powers than fought under rebel flags. Loyal service in the war would ultimately do more to force a redefinition of the colonial order than any of the rebellions, for it laid the foundations for new political demands, such as those voiced by Emir Khaled in Algeria.

New external factors also came to bear on North Africa. U.S. president Woodrow Wilson's promotion of self-determination inspired demands for independence or autonomy in Egypt, Tunisia, and Algeria. The Communist International and Mustafa Kemal's Turkey both inspired anticolonial movements, including the revolt of Abd al-Krim in the Moroccan Rif, and renewed conflict in Libya. Yet for peoples who lived deep in the Sahara, the devastation of the initial conquest, followed by drought and the turmoil of war, left them struggling to survive.

ALLAN CHRISTELOW

See also: **Egypt: Nationalism, World War I and the Wafd, 1882–1922.**

Further Reading

Daly, Martin W. *The Sirdar: Sir Reginald Wingate and the British Empire in the Middle East.* Philadelphia: American Philosophical Society, 1997.

Evans-Pritchard, Edward E. *The Sanusi of Cyrenaica.* Oxford: Oxford University Press, 1963.

Fuglestad, Finn. *A History of Niger, 1850–1960.* Cambridge: Cambridge University Press, 1983.

Hoisington, William. *Lyautey and the French Conquest of Morocco.* New York: Saint Martin's Press, 1995.

Porch, Douglas. *The Conquest of the Sahara.* New York: Alfred A. Knopf, 1984.

World War II: French West Africa, Equatorial Africa

The Federation of French West Africa (FWA) was formally established in 1904 and included seven territories: Senegal, Côte d'Ivoire, Niger, Dahomey, French Sudan, French Guinea and Mauritania, and the mandate of Togo. The neighboring federation of French Equatorial Africa (FEA) was established in 1910 and included four territories: Chad, Gabon, Oubangui Chari and French Congo, and the mandate of Cameroon.

As of the beginning of World War II, France and Britain decided to cooperate across the globe. French Black Africa had a strategic importance for the fighting parties in Europe. The port of Dakar was the third biggest port after Marseilles and le Havre, and both Niger and Chad had joint borders with the Italian colony of Libya (Tripolitania). Chad also enabled access to Anglo-Egyptian Sudan and the British colonies of East Africa.

This atmosphere of friendly cooperation between the two major colonial powers in Africa changed dramatically when France was occupied by Germany and its newly appointed head of state, Marshal Petain, signed an armistice with Germany. The conditions of the armistice allowed France to keep its empire intact as long as the colonies stayed neutral and the armies in them reduced. Following the fall of France, the French Empire in Sub-Saharan Africa split in two. Pierre Boisson, the general governor of FEA, announced his support of Petain, and was immediately transferred by the Vichy government to Dakar, the capital of the more valuable federation. In the meantime, the governor of Chad, Felix Eboue, contacted Charles de Gaulle and

was appointed by him to serve as the general governor of FEA, which was now controlled by the Free French Forces.

The alignment of FWA with Vichy caused frictions between France and Britain. The British feared that this territory would fall into the hands of the Germans. The relations between the two countries deteriorated even further following the British attack on Mers-el-Kebir in Algeria on July 3–4, 1940. The final blow came with the British-Gaullist attempt to conquer Dakar by attacking it on September 23 and 25, 1940, during which around 200 people (mostly Africans) were injured. After the failure of the British-Gaullist attack on Dakar, and a Vichist failure to take control of Gabon, hostilities in both federations ceased.

Although the FEA was not perceived as important by the French, it offered de Gaulle what he lacked most: territory. During the war years, Eboué introduced certain reforms that aimed to train Africans for positions in the administration.

When Boisson took over the federation of FWA he declared that his aim was to defend the territory that was vested in his hands from the Germans and from the British. During the Vichy period in FWA there was only one visit by a German official, and he was forced to disguise himself as a Frenchman. The Vichy colonial regime was deeply worried about the African reactions to the defeat of France and was prepared for large-scale revolts. These, however, never occurred. Apart from a few incidents such as a murder of Europeans in Bobo-Dioulasso (Upper Volta in North Côte d'Ivoire) and the "defection" of the king of the Abrons with a thousand members of his court to the British-ruled Gold Coast, the federation remained relatively calm.

In most areas there was a large degree of continuity in the colonial policy of the Vichy regime. Most changes in policy stemmed from the special circumstances of the war. However, there were two changes introduced by the Vichy colonial regime. The first new development was the unprecedented network of propaganda that was aimed not only at the African elite but at the entire African population. This propaganda diffused the main messages of the Vichy "national revolution" and tried to retain the respect of the population to France in spite of its defeat. Another major change was in the area of education and youth. The importance that was assigned to youth by the Vichy regime in France was also dominant in the colonial policy in the FWA. The reform in education in France was also implemented in the FWA. For the first time, the colonial regime attempted to organize African youth from all social strata in youth movements and youth centers.

Following the Allies' landing in North Africa on November 7, 1942, Boisson declared that he would protect the FWA from the Americans. By the end of

November, however, he had signed an agreement with U.S. General Dwight D. Eisenhower, according to which the FWA would change its allegiance to the Allies but would remain free from any American or French domination. Only on July 7, 1943, did Boisson leave the federation. It was then formally transferred to the Free French Forces.

During the Free French period, no reforms were introduced. Africans were forced to work even harder in order to contribute to the war effort. The most serious incident that occurred during the war in the FWA was the mutiny of African soldiers in a military camp near Dakar, Thiaroye, on December 1, 1944. The soldiers, whose demobilization had been postponed, protested their living conditions. The French reacted severely, and 35 soldiers were killed. This tragic event, marked in the Senegalese collective memory as the first anti-colonial act, demonstrated the large measure of continuity in the colonial policy of the prewar, Vichy, and Free French periods. The importance of World War II as a turning point in the decolonization process in French Africa is related more to the international consequences of the war than the internal ones.

The main result of the war in the French territories was the Brazzaville Conference, which was organized by de Gaulle on January 30, 1944. The reforms that were suggested in this conference, in which no African delegates took part, were meant to save the French Empire from dissolving. but actually paved the way for decolonization.

RUTH GINIO

See also: **Colonial Federations: French West Africa; Senegal: World War II.**

Further Reading

Ageron, Charles-Robert. "Vichy, les français et l'Empire." In *Le Regime de Vichy et les français*, edited by Jean-Pierre Azéma and François Bédarida. Paris: Fayard, 1992.

Akpo-Vaché, Catherine. *L'AOF pendant la deuxième guerre mondiale*, Paris: Karthala, 1996.

Blanchard, Pascal, and Gilles Boëtsch. "La France de Pétain et l'Afrique: Images et propagandes coloniales." *Canadian Journal of African Studies* 28, no. 1 (1994): 1–31.

Crowder, Michael. "The 1939–1945 War and West Africa." In *History of West Africa*, edited by Michael Crowder and J. F. A Ajayi. London: Longman, 1987.

Echenberg, Myron. "Morts pour la France; The African Soldier in France during the Second World War." *Journal of African History* 26, no. 4 (1985): 363–380.

Lanne, Bernard. "Chad the Chadians and the Second World War, 1939–1945." *Africana Journal, no.* 16 (1991): 311–325.

Lawler, Nancy. "The Crossing of the Gyaman to the Cross of Lorraine: Wartime Politics in West Africa, 1941–1942" *African Affairs* (London), 96, no. 382 (1997): 53–72.

———. "Reform and Repression under the Free French: Economic and Political Transformation in the Côte d'Ivoire, 1942–1945." *Africa* (London) 60, no. 1 (1990): 88–110.

Shaka, Femi Okiremuete. "Vichy Dakar and the Other Story of French Colonial Stewardhip in Africa: Ousmane Sembène and Thierno Faty Sow's Camp de Thiaroye." *Research in African Literatures* 26, no. 3 (1995): 67–77.

Thomas, Martin. "The Anglo-French Divorce over West Africa and the Limitations of Strategic Planning, June–December 1940." *Diplomacy and Statecraft* 6, no. 1 (1995): 252–278.

World War II: North Africa

For the Allied powers, North Africa was an important strategic field in World War II. Indeed, the landings of November 1942 might be said to be a crucial turning point in the war. For the colonized peoples of North Africa, the war itself, rather than any single military event, was a vital stage in their nations' evolution. After 1945, colonial regimes in Algeria, Tunisia, Morocco, Libya, and Egypt were no longer able to resist the tide of nationalism. Though not solely a product of the war, the united, organized, politically astute, and internationally supported nationalist movements in North Africa were the most significant consequence of the war in the region. North Africa was not a very high priority for the Axis powers, but Germany realized the value of propaganda undermining France and Britain aimed at native populations, and Benito Mussolini had territorial claims on Tunisia.

After the fall of France in 1940, the government briefly considered moving to North Africa and continuing the war effort from there. The authorities in French North Africa, however, remained loyal to the Vichy government, a decision that pleased most settlers and subjected Jews to discrimination. For nationalists, France's humiliation was a source of encouragement and many, for a short time, looked hopefully to Germany. The only fighting in the early stages of the war in North Africa took place on the Egyptian-Libyan border following Italy's entry into the war. Many Libyan

French tanks in North Africa, November 1942. © SVT Bild/Das Fotoarchiv.

exiles in Egypt took this opportunity to express anti-Italian sentiment, while Egypt attempted to tread a path between its obligations to Britain and encirclement by Axis forces. Fighting continued in the region through 1941, as German reinforcements arrived.

The colonial powers' prestige diminished as the war continued. Discontent grew along with hardship in the French territories as supplies were requisitioned and rationed; anti-British feeling was widespread in Egypt as Britain obtained a favorable government with the threat of military force; in Libya the Italian infrastructure was ruined by the fighting and many Italian settlers were evacuated, returning land to the native Bedouin. On November 8 1942, the relative calm that had prevailed in the western regions was broken by the Anglo-American landings in Morocco and Algeria known as Operation Torch, under U.S. commander in chief Dwight D. Eisenhower. With complete strategic surprise achieved and only minor losses sustained in the taking of Casablanca and Algiers, the chief problem the occupying forces had to deal with was political. The Allies agreed to a cease-fire with Admiral Darlan, commander in chief of the Vichy armed forces, but this led the collaborationist government in France to accept German air support in the form of air raids and troop movements into Tunisia. Darlan was appointed high commissioner for French North Africa by the Allies, to the annoyance of Charles de Gaulle's Free French. Though Darlan was assassinated in December 1942, the French settlers in North Africa were gradually won over to the Allied side.

By the end of 1942, substantial German reinforcements had been deployed in Tunisia, halting the Allied advance short of Tunis. Erwin Rommel's forces made significant gains in the mountains, but by April 1943, the Allies were able to regroup and regain ground. The Allied naval blockade and aerial bombardment seriously affected Axis supply lines, and in May 1943 Allied forces under Alexander and Montgomery forced a German surrender. The Allies' control of North Africa now gave them a solid base from which to launch their campaign in Southern Europe. The civilian consequences of the Allies' campaign were equally important. The Jews of French North Africa were liberated from anti-Semitic laws and the Vichy regime was discredited, to the benefit of the Free French, who established a provisional government in Algiers by the end of 1943. In Libya, conditions improved as the country came under American, British, and French control. In Morocco, Franklin D. Roosevelt is reported to have promised postwar independence to the Sultan, Sidi Mohammed, at this stage. The Tunisian nationalist leader Habib ibn Ali Bourguiba was released from arrest in France by Axis forces, supposedly to cooperate with Italy, but proceeded instead to order support for

de Gaulle and continue to champion his country's cause.

The improvement in nationalist fortunes was short-lived, however. De Gaulle's administration had no time for independence demands, and de Gaulle was a more valuable ally than the nationalists for the Americans. In Tunisia, the new monarch, Moncef Bey, demanded representation and equality, but was exiled by the French and replaced with another, loyal, figure. The newly formed Moroccan independence party, Istiqlal, was repressed by the French, with no American intervention to support earlier encouragement. In Libya, it was decided that the country's future should be determined by talks involving France, Britain, America, and the Soviet Union, but independence was not thought to be a viable option. Indeed, the French seemed interested in incorporating the southern Fezzan province into Algeria. Only in Egypt, with both Britain and the government discredited, did nationalism continue to thrive, as radical movements seeking a complete departure from the European rule that had led to war became more popular.

The final year of the war saw North African troops make a large contribution to the French forces in the Italian campaign. Recognizing that their loyalty and sacrifice must be recompensed, de Gaulle announced a program of reform, moving away from the colonial policy of assimilation, and instituting economic modernization, social progress, and representation for colonial subjects. Nationalists, however, encouraged by the Atlantic Charter that enshrined the right to self-determination, demanded nothing short of independence. Contact with the Americans during the war led nationalist leaders such as Bourguiba to take their case to the United States and the newly formed United Nations. Egyptian nationalists, meanwhile, also looked abroad, but to the more radical examples of the Soviet Union and Asian communism. Libya provided the ultimate example of independence being decided by the international community, as no decision at all on its future was taken in 1945, the issue being put on hold until a peace treaty with Italy could be concluded. The most tragic demonstration of the European powers' struggle to retain control of their North African colonies after the war came in Algeria, where nationalist demonstrations on May 8, 1945, were violently repressed by French forces, with several thousand casualties. The next 15 years were to be dominated by the consequences of World War II's blow to European prestige and awakening of nationalist hopes in North Africa.

STEPHEN TYRE

See also: **Libya: World War II and the Kingdom of Libya, 1942–1969.**

Further Reading

Hosington, W. A. *The Casablanca Connection: French Colonial Policy, 1936–1943.* Chapel Hill: University of North Carolina Press, 1984.

Marshall, D. Bruce. "Free France in Africa: Gaullism and Colonialism." In *France and Britain in Africa: Imperial Rivalry and Colonial Rule,* edited by P. Gifford and W. Roger Louis. New Haven, Conn.: Yale University Press, 1971.

McGuirk, D. *Rommel's Army in Africa.* London: Stanley Paul, 1987.

Moorehead, A. *African Trilogy: the North African Campaign, 1940–43.* London: Cassell, 1998.

Vatikiotis, P. J. *The History of Modern Egypt: From Muhammad Ali to Mubarak.* London, Weidenfeld and Nicolson, 1991.

World War II: Sub-Saharan Africa: Economic Impact

It was impossible for Sub-Saharan Africa to avoid the economic impact of World War II. By the outbreak of the war in 1939, the economies of Britain, France, Belgium, Portugal, and Spain and their colonies in this region formed part of a single economy. In addition, many of the strategic mineral and agricultural resources that were demanded by the nations at war were found in Sub-Saharan Africa.

The period 1939 to 1942 was a time of hardship for the agricultural sector in the region. In French West Africa for example, farmers in the colonies that remained loyal to the Vichy regime suffered because the naval blockade of the Allied forces brought trade to a virtual standstill. This was also a difficult period for the producers of agricultural commodities, who were either heavily or completely dependent on the export market for their livelihood. Included among them were citrus farmers in southern Mozambique; coffee growers in Angola; cocoa farmers in Nigeria and Ghana, and most oilseed producers. The notable exceptions to this trend were cotton growers in Nigeria, whose surplus was absorbed on the domestic market, and their counterparts in Mozambique, who were beneficiaries of the added impetus given by the war to Portugal's drive for imperial autarky.

The Japanese victory over the Allied forces in the Far East in February of 1942 eliminated a major source for Allied supplies of agricultural produce and strategic minerals. As a result, Sub-Saharan Africa became a vitally important alternative source for Allied requirements of these commodities, and a concerted effort was made to expand their production for export. In the case of agricultural products, a lot of emphasis was placed on commodities such as groundnuts, palm oil, palm kernels, copra, and cotton. The expansion in their production led to an increase in economic activity in Sub-Saharan African states. However, the economic circumstances of African producers did not improve because the prices they received for their produce were well below the ones prevailing on the world market. Further, in places such as Mozambique, export maximization sometimes took precedence over food production, areas completely unsuited to cash crop production were brought under cultivation and forced labor was used to expand export production.

The major mineral exports of Sub-Saharan Africa were strategically important to the forces involved in the war; they were therefore not adversely affected by it. The Belgian Congo, for instance, was one of the principal sources for the copper, cobalt, industrial diamonds, tin, gold, silver, and uranium needs of the United States and Britain. Thus, to facilitate wartime production, the mining industry received major capital injections from the United States. In Zambia, the most important African source of copper, the demand that was generated by the rearmament program of the late 1930s continued during the war years, and a number of innovations in copper extraction were introduced. The war also led to the rise of the bauxite industry in Ghana and the revival of tin mining in Nigeria. Overall however, in most of the mineral-producing Sub-Saharan African states the development and expansion of mineral production during the war years did not lead to any significant economic growth. In many of them it resulted in the creation of small enclaves within colonial economies, the seasonal migration of workers in and out of the mining areas, and the repatriation of a large percentage of the profits made by mining companies to metropolitan countries. The severe restrictions imposed on goods imported into Sub-Saharan Africa during World War II caused severe shortages and steep price increases. The price of a bicycle in Brazzaville increased from 700 francs in 1939 to 2,700 francs in 1944. In Nigeria the Lagos Cost of Living Committee, appointed in January 1944, found that the cost of living index had increased by over 70 points between 1939 and 1943. Inadequacies in the food supplies in Sub-Saharan Africa reached crisis proportions in places such as Senegal and Mozambique. Many states sought to expand domestic food production in order to satisfy local needs. For example, compulsory rice production was introduced in Mozambique in 1941 and by 1946 it was self-sufficient in rice. In Nigeria, even though the demand for food outstripped its production during the war years, major improvements were made in the production of rice, wheat, sugar, potatoes, and onions.

The shortages in imported goods was also a powerful incentive for industrialization throughout Sub-Saharan Africa. In South Africa, the manufacturing sector expanded rapidly and significantly, creating a huge demand for industrial labor. By 1945, the urbanization of all races had increased substantially. In addition, the foundation was created for manufacturing to supersede mining as the dominant sector in the South African economy. In Nigeria increases in wheat production in parts of Bornu, Sokoto, Katsina, and Kano led to the establishment of a flour mill at Kano. Industries were also established or revived to enable the production of roofing shingles, soap, cigars, boot polish, belting, and shoe leather. In Angola and Mozambique the Portuguese government abandoned its opposition to industrialization and allowed companies for the manufacture of cotton textiles and other commodities to be established.

There was also an acceleration in the pace of economic reform in some Sub-Saharan African states during the war years. In the British colonies, for example, after the Japanese victory in the Far East in 1942, the Colonial Office acknowledged that it needed to adopt a more organized approach to colonial economic planning, and by the middle of 1943 the concept of planning was established as an important feature of its colonial development policy. In recognition of their loyalty and contribution to its war effort, France rewarded its colonies in Tropical Africa with the creation of the Fonds d'Investissement pour le Developpment Economique et Sociale, an investment fund for their social and economic development. By 1945 the economic measures that were introduced into the colonial dependencies during the war years had produced an unprecedented level of state intervention in colonial economic affairs in Sub-Saharan Africa and enhanced the economic links between colonial economies in the region and the economies of metropolitan countries.

ALLISTER HINDS

See also: **Fonds d'Investment pour le Développement Economique et Social (FIDES).**

Further Reading

Clarence-Smith, Gervase. "The Impact of the Spanish Civil War and The Second World War on Portuguese Africa." *Journal of African History* 26, no. 4 (1985): 309–326.

Crowder, M. "The 1939–45 War and West Africa." In *History of West Africa*, vol. 2, edited by J. Ajayi and M. Crowder. London: Longman, 1987.

Dumett, Raymond. "Africa's Strategic Minerals during the Second World War." *Journal of African History* 26, no. 4 (1985): 381–408.

Gifford, P., and W. R. Louis (eds.). *The Transfer of Power in Africa: Decolonization 1940–1960.* New Haven, Conn.: Yale University Press, 1982.

Havinden, M., and D. Meredith. *Colonialism and Development: Britain and Its Tropical Colonies, 1850–1960.* London: Routledge, 1993.

Newitt, Malyn. *Portugal in Africa.* London: C. Hurst, 1981.

Y

Yaoundé

The geographical site of Yaoundé is quite unusual for an African capital: Cameroon's administrative center is situated over 200 kilometers from the country's coast in the midst of (now rapidly disappearing) tropical rainforest. Until 1992, Yaoundé was the only capital south of the Sahara without an international airport; the road and rail systems that link it with the port of Douala, the country's largest city and economic center, were only extended in the 1980s. The city center is characterized by a number of administrative buildings (some of them very bizarre pieces of architecture) now rapidly dilapidating. Poverty, growing slums, and pollution are dominant features of Yaoundé today. According to André Franqueville (1984), two-thirds of the ethnic groups in Cameroon were represented in the Yaoundé population already by 1957. The local Beti people and the immigrant groups of Bassa and Bamiléké are numerically the most important groups today. In recent years ethnic tensions and clashes have increased, often over access to urban land.

Founded in 1888 by a civilian, the botanist and explorer Georg August Zenker, Yaoundé was run during the German period as a military and administrative post. The name *Jaunde*, given to the settlement by the Germans, probably resulted from a linguistic misunderstanding, as the new colonial rulers meant to name this site after the local ethnic group Ewondo. The relatively densely populated area soon attracted some German merchants. In 1895, the first trading post was opened for purchasing rubber, palm oil, and ivory. German administrators in Yaoundé experienced recurrent difficulties feeding the military post, in spite of the abundance of food in the surrounding region. Forced requisitions of food led to military confrontation and loss of life. By the time the Germans lost Cameroon at the end of World War I, Yaoundé consisted of a military enclosure, some formal buildings, and a stately avenue of mango trees, but a very small population. In 1914 the military and police forces included 2,700 men and 215 officers. Other occupations were probably limited to trade and transportation.

During World War I, the French set up their headquarters in Yaoundé, because of its comparatively pleasant climate and its secluded location, favorable to military defense. In 1921, they made the town the administrative center for both Yaoundé circumscription and the national government, headed by the high commissioner. The area was one of the most important administrative regions of French Cameroon. Its population of about 400,000 comprised 18 per cent of the total population. In 1935 it was the major indigenous producer of palm kernels, coffee, and sesame, and the second most important producer of cocoa, palm oil, and groundnuts.

However, between the wars, Yaoundé remained a fairly small town in the cocoa belt. The urban population consisted of 5,500 Cameroonians and 365 foreigners in 1926, and 6,190 and 261, respectively, in 1933. In addition, there was an average daily workforce on *corvée* labor duty of 800 to 1,000, a prison population of 300 to 400, and a hospital population of at least 200. Many more people came into Yaoundé as porters, workers for private traders, litigants in court cases, and a variety of other capacities. In 1927, the completion of the Transcamerounais Railway considerably improved the city's traffic connections.

The abolition of the *indigénat* in Cameroon in 1946 led to a new mobility of labor. In Yaoundé workers were needed for a number of new public building projects launched under the FIDE development scheme. The city's population increased from 9,080 in 1939 to 17,311 in 1945 and 36,786 by 1953, thereby tripling within a 15-year period. Around the time of independence, Yaoundé experienced a second growth increase.

Civil war and massive violence in the Bassa and Bamiléké regions drove parts of the rural population out of these areas into the big urban centers of Douala and Yaoundé, and the fast-growing administration in Yaoundé attracted many college graduates. Between 1957 and 1962 the urban population of Yaoundé rose from 54,343 to 89,969. Since then the rate of growth has sped up, resulting in a population of 313,706 in the mid-1970s, about 700,000 in the late 1980s, and more than a million inhabitants by the end of the twentieth century.

Federal capital of independent Cameroon since 1961, Yaoundé became seat of the united republic in 1972. Yaoundé's growing importance was also enhanced by the establishment of the university. This institution grew rapidly, from 213 graduates in 1961, to 10,000 in 1982, to 41,000 in 1992. A high proportion of the population in Yaoundé was employed in the civil service and in salaried occupations associated with government and education. In comparison, the industrial sector remained small, and industrial employment was dominated by very few enterprises: a cigarette factory, a beer factory, and printing. Many of the civil service positions were held by the local Beti people, while the Bamiléké dominated commerce, transportation, and "artisanal activities." Following the deep economic crisis that started in the early 1980s, many urban jobs were discontinued and state salaries severely cut in order to meet demands from the International Monetary Fund. Graduating students found an increasingly competitive labor market. It was these frustrated graduates, together with their teachers and professors, who started to agitate for a process of democratization.

While in the 1990s students and teachers, like lawyers and journalists, tried to create a civil society, the elite continued to flaunt their ostentatious consumption of luxuries such as champagne and expensive villas and cars. This lifestyle was displayed in Yaoundé in a particularly flamboyant way. The Cameroonian sociologist Frances Nyamnjoh noted ironically in his book *Mind Searching* (1991),

> They have built little prisons for themselves in an attempt to imitate fences in Europe! Some of my folks in Briqueterie [a poor area in Yaoundé] might wonder . . . what residents of Bastos [the neighboring district, the richest residential area in the capital] have done wrong against their people and the rest of the world, that they have chosen to live behind barbed wire, protected by pieces of broken beer and champagne bottles?

ANDREAS ECKERT

See also: Cameroon.

Further Reading

Franqueville, André. *Yaoundé. Construire une capitale*. Paris: Èditions de l'ORSTOM, 1984 Guyer, Jane I. "Feeding Yaoundé, capital of Cameroon." In *Feeding African Cities: Studies in Regional Social History*, edited by Jane I. Guyer. Bloomington: Indiana University Press, 1987.
Laburthe-Tolra, Philippe. *Yaoundé d'après Zenker*. Extrait des Annales de la Faculté des Lettres et Sciences Humaines de Yaoundé, no. 2. Yaoundé.

Yeke: *See* Msiri: Yeke Kingdom.

Yoruba-Speaking Peoples

Located in southwestern Nigeria, Ile-Ife (Ife) is regarded by an overwhelming Yoruba majority as the source and heart of the Yoruba nation. This fact, coupled with its impressive culture as demonstrated by its famous brass, stone, and clay sculpture, placed it in a position of preeminence among the Yoruba. The belief that Oduduwa (Oodua) was the first king at lle-Ife and that he was the father of the founding princes of other Yoruba kingdoms has inspired the description of the Yoruba as the *Omo Oodua* (offspring of Oodua). This would partially explain why Yoruba history, culture, and religion have centered on lle-Ife.

Structured as a mini-state in the pre-Oduduwa period, lle-Ife comprised territorially distinct but related settlements including Oke Oja, Oke Awo, and Iraye, among others. The arrival of Oduduwa heralded the reorganization of lle-Ife and the existing states. Equipped with iron and superior weapons, Oduduwa, through force and diplomacy, wrested power from Obatala and transformed the semiautonomous settlements into a megastate.

lle-Ife, as the "father kingdom" and Yoruba national headquarters, so to speak, had a unique type of constitutional and historical growth. Completely surrounded by other Yoruba kingdoms that acknowledged its supremacy, it had no fear of attack from its neighbors. It therefore did not possess any arms and the *onis* (kings) were not known to be great military leaders. Ile-Ife concentrated its attention on religious, artistic, and cultural matters.

If lle-Ife is understandably regarded as the spiritual center of the Yoruba, it is with many justifications that Oyo is widely recognized as the political focal point of the Yoruba. Situated in the southern fringe of the savanna and close to Nupeland, Oyo grew from a petty principality to become the most powerful of all Yoruba kingdoms. Oranmiyan, the founder of Oyo, was the youngest son of Oduduwa.

Frequent attacks from the Nupe and the Bariba compelled Oyo to reorganize its army into cavalry and infantry. The ruler Sango is credited with transforming the small polity into a kingdom; widely acknowledged among the Yoruba as a magician and warrior, he built up the cadre of slave officials who played a significant role in Oyo's administration. However, Robin Law (1978) has categorized Sango, along with Oduduwa and Oranmiyan, as "humanized deities."

The king whose reign actually launched Oyo on the path of greatness was, according to Samuel Johnson (1973), Obalokun. Under him, Oyo expanded to Egbado and southwestward to the coast. It became involved in the Atlantic trade, thereby generating the much-needed foreign exchange with which horses were purchased.

Ajagbo, who succeeded Obalokun, created the *Are-Ona Kakanfo* (generalissimo) title and instituted the system of sending out four expeditions at a time under four titled holders. Oyo expanded westward between the seventeenth and eighteenth centuries, when it brought Dahomey under its rule. In the agreement of 1730, Dahomey's tributary status was regularized. For the rest of the eighteenth century, Dahomey remained a dependent of Oyo. Oyo's vassal states were ruled by Oyo's appointees (*ajele*). Paradoxically, its expansion bred weakness and division, and Oyo was on the brink of collapse.

While Ile-Ife and Oyo occupy the central and northern Yorubaland, respectively, southeast Yorubaland is the homeland of the Ijebu, Ondo, Itsekiri, and Ikale. Their political history is connected to the better-known centers of Ijebu Ode, Ondo, Idanre, and Ode Itsekiri and the smaller towns of Ikale and Ilaje.

The second largest of the Yoruba polities was Ijebu, which, according to Elizabeth Isichei (1983), was less a unitary kingdom than a federation of states where the king, with his capital at Ijebu Ode, enjoyed an acknowledged supremacy over his brother Ijebu Obas. Obanta, the first Awujale, was one of the sons of Oduduwa.

East of Ijebu are Ondo and Ile-Oluji, whose traditions ascribe the origin of their dynasties to the descendants of Oduduwa. One of the distinguishing characteristics of Ondo area is the institution of women chiefs. The installation of the *osemawe* (king) of Ondo is performed by the female chief, the *lisa olobun*. Farther to the east of the Ijebu and along the coast in the areas of the Ikale and the Ilaje, no central or dominant dynasty emerged.

To the northwest of the Ijebu were the Egba who, before the nineteenth century, occupied the sites later inhabited by the Ibadan and Ijaye. Like the Ijebu, the Egba were heterogeneous until the first *alake* (king), who was the son of Oduduwa, organized them into a loose federation.

Along the Atlantic coast are the Awori and the Ogu, with the principal towns of Lagos and Badagry. The Awori claimed descent from Ile-Ife, although some Aworis became more culturally influenced by Benin upon their conquest. The Ogu, on the other hand, are

the offshoot of migrants from Whydah and Allada (Porto Novo).

The rest of the Yoruba-speaking peoples—the Ijesa, Ekiti, Akure, and Akoko—have affinities with Ile-Ife, even though the latter three share many cultural traits with the Edo-speaking peoples of Benin. Among the Ekiti, Akure, and Akoko are stories that traced their origins to Ile-Ife. The Ekiti kingdoms, totaling more than sixteen, are territorially small, as a result of the influence of the hilly terrain. Ado Ekiti, the largest, is given a certain preeminence in the Ekitit area. Like Ile-Ife, the Ijesa, Ekiti, and Akure emphasize the importance of nonmilitary factors in the growth of kingdoms.

In the northeast Yorubaland live the Ibolo, Igbomina, and Okun Yoruba-speaking peoples. Established by migrants from Ile-Ife and Oyo, their settlements included Ila Orangun, Ajase, Omu Aran, Isanlu Iwo, Oro, Eku Apa, Ora, Ikosin, and Igbaja. The most northeasterly of the Yoruba kingdoms is Owo. Its location in a cultural frontier zone, so to speak, opened it to influences from Benin and other Yoruba groups. Established by an Ile-Ife prince, Owo extended to Kabba and Akoko.

One basic feature of the Yoruba-speaking peoples is urbanism. Each town was an entity in itself. Government in each town was based on the unwritten constitution of the people in which the spiritual was inextricably bound up with the physical. At the head of the government was the *oba* (ruler) assisted by a council called differently in various towns. Known as Oyo Mesi in Oyo, it was headed by the *basorun* (prime minister) who was responsible to the *alafin* (king of Oyo).

In addition, there was the custodian of the cult, the *ifa* (soothsayer). The ifa priest, together with the principal councilors, belonged to the Ogboni society, a secret society. The society discussed political, economic, and social affairs and its decisions were binding on all members. Government at Oyo, as well as several Yoruba towns, was a delicate balance of power between the oba and his palace administration on the one hand, and the council and the more representative Ogboni society on the other.

MODUPEOLU FASEKE

See also: **Ife, Oyo, Yoruba, Ancient: Kingship and Art.**

Further Reading

Ajayi, J. F. A, and M. Crowder. (eds.). *History of West Africa*, vol. 1. London: Longman, 1981.

Deji, Ogunremi, and Adediran Abiodun (eds.). *Culture and Society in Yorubaland*. Ibadan: Rex Charles, 1998.

Ikime, Obaro (ed.). *Groundwork of Nigerian History*. Ibadan, Nigeria: Heinemann 1981.

Isichei, Elizabeth. *A History of Nigeria*. London: Longman, 1983.

Johnson, Samuel. *The History of the Yorubas from the Earliest Times to the Beginning of the British Protectorate* (1921). Reprint, Lagos: CMS 1973.

Smith, R. S. *Kingdoms of the Yoruba*. London: Methuen, 1969.

Yoruba States: Oyo

The Yoruba are one of the three major ethnic groups in modern day Nigeria along with the Hausa and Igbo. The Yoruba are also one of the largest ethnic groups in all of West Africa, primarily living in western Nigeria, but also in Benin and Sierra Leone. Their language is part of the Benue–Congo family and is divided into several distinctive but mutually intelligible dialects. The Yoruba have been very influential in the development of modern culture in West Africa and the African diaspora. Gods from the traditional Yoruba religion provide the basis for deities in Western Hemisphere belief systems, such as Santeria in Cuba and Vodun in Haiti. In contemporary Nigeria, Yoruba-language books and films are major sources of entertainment for both Yoruba and non-Yoruba audiences.

Historically, the Yoruba were also a major influence on the development of West African history. According to oral tradition, the Yoruba migrated from the east. In *The History of the Yorubas* (1921), Samuel Johnson states the region of origin as Arabia. Modern historians believe that the Yoruba did migrate to their current home, but the actual point of origin is unknown. Yoruba-speaking regions of West Africa were among the first of that region to undergo the process of urbanization that is such a distinctive aspect of forest and savanna populations in West Africa. Apparently urbanization began in the forest zone between the ninth and tenth centuries CE.

The city that is traditionally regarded as the home of the Yoruba people is Ife (Ile-Ife). Since Ife was the oldest of Yoruba cities, it rulers were accorded preeminence within the *ebi* system, which conceptualized the relations between the elites of various Yoruba cities as the equivalent of sibling relations within a family, with Ife as the parent. According to oral tradition, the first leader, or *oba*, of Ife was Oduduwa. Oduduwa was the father of Oranyan, who became the first ruler of Oyo, the most politically and economically important of the Yoruba cities in the later precolonial era. Oranyan, also known as Oranmiyan in Edo, is credited with being the father of the ruler Benin in that society's oral tradition.

In addition to being the traditional home of the ruling class of traditional Yoruba society, Ife was very important as the point of dissemination for major forms of West African art. In particular, sculptures of busts and other naturalistic figures were created in Ife and a similar style of artwork was adopted by neighboring peoples, especially the Edo of Benin. Many researchers assume that the Ife style bronzes were a continuation of the forms of brass work that were first seen in Nigeria in Nok around 500BCE.

Traditional Yoruba life was centered on cities, but many of the residents of these cities worked as farmers outside the walls of town. The principal crops that were produced were yams in the forest regions, and millet, sorghum, and cowpeas in the savanna regions. Bananas, which are of Asian origin, would also eventually become a major food crop in the forest region, along with maize, which was introduced after the sixteenth century by European traders. Kola nuts, which were produced in Yoruba areas, were a valuable export crop that was sold to buyers in the Sahelian regions. In addition to agriculture, the Yoruba were heavily involved in many traditional crafts and industries. These included brass and iron working, but the most noteworthy was textile production. Yoruba women were particularly noted for the production of finely patterned cloth. This traditional production would continue into the twentieth century. It should also be noted that women in general figured very prominently in the commercial world; they were often the largest and most successful merchants in the markets. Women were also responsible for a large percentage of agricultural production.

By the year 1300, Ife had reached its peak as the dominant city of Yorubaland. By 1400, Oyo, which was farther to the north at the margins of the forest and savanna, became the dominant commercial and political city of the Yoruba. Oyo began to rise as a major power

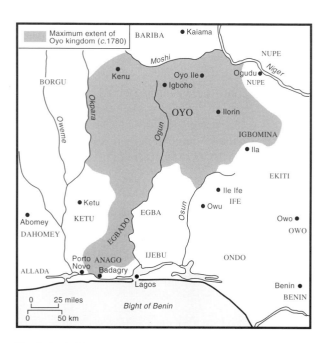

Yorubaland, fifteenth–eighteenth centuries.

after the leadership adopted the use of cavalry as the foundation of their army. This change meant that Oyo would always be dependent on routes from the north for a fresh supply of horses because Oyo was too far south for the successful breeding of large horses that were suitable for battle.

The political system of Oyo was at once arranged with checks and balances, but it was also quite hierarchical and was designed to maintain power within the hands of Oyo's elite. At the head of the system was the *alafin*, or king. In addition to the alafin there was a council known as the *Oyo mesi* that was headed by an official known as the *bashorun*. The king was very powerful and was considered to be a demigod by the general population; however, the Oyo mesi had the right to command the king to commit suicide if they deemed him unfit for office. Within the Oyo mesi, there was also a secret society known as the *ogboni* that also was at the center of struggles for power within Oyo.

Apparently, Oyo began to expand in the sixteenth century in response to an invasion by the Nupe in 1531, which destroyed the city. The leaders of Oyo would eventually inflict serious defeats upon the Nupe while also making the northern Yoruba town of Ilorin part of the Oyo empire. Oyo, however, found that its expansion to the south was limited by its dependence on cavalry. In heavy forests, the horse had difficulties not only with the pestilence of tsetse fly, but also with the lack of fields, which minimized advantages for mounted soldiers. Because of these strategic difficulties, Benin would remain the dominant power in the southeastern regions while Oyo sought to expand in the west and southwest. Eventually, Oyo controlled territory spreading from the Niger River in what is now Nigeria to present-day Togo. As Oyo gained suzerainty over territory on the Atlantic coast, the empire became involved in the supplying slaves to Europeans for transatlantic trade.

Oyo would eventually begin to decline as a result of a protracted period of civil war and invasion. These wars were stimulated by a number of factors. The system of Oyo government in which the alafin was exalted yet could be ordered to commit suicide naturally lead to tension between its respective components. In 1770, the alafin Abiodun came to power and he had the bashorun Gaha and his family put to death since Gaha had ordered the suicide of a number of alafins prior to Abiodun. In addition to the disruption caused by the killing of Gaha and his family, some scholars feel that Abiodun alienated the military by reducing the focus on them and concentrating on commercial activities. This largely meant emphasizing the slave trade with the Europeans. Oyo's increased emphasis on slave trading increased resentment and resistance to Oyo.

The result being a series of revolts by regions like Nupe and Borgu. In addition to these problems, the Fon of present-day Benin Republic had begun to organize and acquire firearms from European traders. This made them a formidable opponent on the fringe of the Oyo state. In addition to these internal pressures, Oyo came under pressure from the Fulani-led jihads (holy wars) of the eighteenth century which resulted in the permanent loss of the northern Yoruba territory of Ilorin after 1800. The loss of Ilorin served to emphasize the general strife that developed between Yoruba states. The preeminence of Oyo was always somewhat in contradiction to the principal Ebi system that emphasized familial relations among Yoruba ruling elites with Ife as the center. Once Oyo began to destabilize, it allowed other Yoruba states to break away, which exacerbated this period of civil strife.

By the 1835, Oyo had been destroyed and the stage was set for increasing influence of Western influences in Yoruba culture. The leading social group behind this change were the Saro, Yoruba who had been enslaved in the transatlantic slave trade who were able to return to Nigeria. Most of the Saro were the recaptive African who were rescued by British antislave patrols and brought to Sierra Leone as refugees, There the Saro became a major component of the Krio (Creole) community that would provide late precolonial and early colonial Africa with much of its Western-educated population. It is, notably, from this group that Samuel Johnson, the author of *The History of the Yorubas* (1921) would arise.

ANTHONY CHEESEBORO

See also: **Ife, Oyo, Yoruba, Ancient: Kingship and Art.**

Further Reading

Byfield, Judith. *The Bluest Hands*. Portsmouth, N.H.: Heinemann, 2002.

Davidson, Basil. *West Africa before the Colonial Era*. Upper Saddle River, N.J.: Longman, 1998.

Johnson, Samuel. *The History of the Yorubas from the Earliest Times to the Beginning of the British Protectorate* (1921). Reprint, Lagos: CMS 1973.

Murphy, E. Jefferson. *History of African Civilization*. New York: Dell, 1978.

Yoruba States (Other Than Ife and Oyo)

By the eighteenth century, the Yoruba had distinguished themselves by their well-established traditions of sacred kingship, urbanism, and sculptural arts. These aspects of Yoruba culture are epitomized by in historical development of Ile-Ife (Ife) and Oyo. However, besides these famous kingdoms, other states flourished in Yorubaland. The most notable among these were established among the Ijesa, Ekiti, Egba, Ijebu, Igbomina, Ibolo, Awori, Ondo, Akoko, and Okun Yoruba-speaking dialectal groups. Many of these states achieved varying degrees of power and influence in the Yoruba country before the nineteenth century. The earliest of these was the kingdom of Owu, which grew to such prominence that it competed with Oyo for the dominance of central and northern Yorubaland, until the reign of the third *alafin* (king), Sango, who broke Owu's stranglehold over Oyo and effectively terminated its temporary paramountcy in northern Yorubaland. The next to achieve prominence was the kingdom of Ijesa in east central Yorubaland. Established by Ajibogun, a son of Oduduwa and father of the Yoruba people, Ijesa grew to incorporate several polities east of Ile-Ife, such as Ilemure, ruled by the Ita, and Ilesa, ruled by the Onila. Under the reign of Atakunmosa (*c*.1500) and the series of warlike Owa who succeeded him, the kingdom expanded to the Osun, Ekiti, and Igbomina areas.

South of Oyo and west of Ife lay the country of the Egba people, who did not form a united kingdom. Instead they were organized into a loose confederacy of four autonomous but interdependent groups. These were the Egba Gbagura, ruled by the *agura* based in Ido; the Egba Oke Ona, ruled by the *osile* based at Oko; the Egba Ake ruled by the *alake* headquartered at Ake; and finally the Egba Ageyin headed by the *ojoko* of Kesi. The most powerful of these rulers was the alake, who, after absorbing the Agbeyin group, was on his way to emerging as the paramount ruler when the Egba came under the imperial control of Oyo empire in the late seventeen century. Under the leadership of Lisabi, the Egba successfully asserted their independence of Oyo during the closing years of the eighteenth century.

To the west of the Egba was the kingdom of Ijebu. Established by three successive waves of migrants from Ile-Ife, Ijebu was known to European visitors by the fifteenth century. Though large in size and homogenous in culture and dialect, the Ijebu were not fully integrated politically before the nineteenth century. While the majority recognized the paramountcy of Awujale based at Ijebu Ode, a group known as the Remo instead acknowledged the akarigbo of Ofin Sagamu as their leader. By virtue of its location, Ijebu had to fight continuously for its independence from the imperial designs of Oyo and Benin. Along the Atlantic Coast and south of Ijebu were the kingdoms of Lagos and those of the Ikale and Ilaje people. Established like Ijebu by successive waves of Awori-Yoruba migrants from central Yorubaland, Lagos soon came under the imperial tutelage of Benin. This imperial connection, however, did not prevent its emergence and prosperity as a major entrepôt of the transatlantic slave trade.

In western Yorubaland, a number of kingdoms flourished before the nineteenth century. The most notable of these were Ketu, Sabe, and Idaisa; of these, Ketu became the most important. Located between hostile and more aggressive neighbors, Ketu had to contend for its independence for much of its history. Its massive and impressive fortifications notwithstanding, Ketu came under Oyo's imperial rule some time during the eighteenth century. In 1789, a rampaging Dahomey army invaded and sacked the town, taking most of its inhabitants into slavery. South of Ketu lay the country of the Egbado. Loosely organized into numerous and autonomous mini-states such as Ilobi, Erinja, Ado, Ipokia, Igan, Egua, and Aiyetoro, the Egbado were soon conquered by Oyo, whose economic and strategic interests led it to reshape the political map of this region from the seventeenth century on.

The rugged topography of the land of the Ekiti, in eastern Yorubaland, allowed for the emergence and proliferation of several centers of power, many of which eventually developed into kingdoms. Of the 16 traditionally accorded primacy in oral traditions, the most notable were Ado, Ijero, Otun, Aye, and Akure. All these kingdoms claimed royal ancestry from Ile-Ife, while their proximity to Benin brought them at different times and to varying degrees under the imperial and cultural dominance of the Benin empire. Southeast of the Ekiti were the kingdoms of Owo and Ondo, whose locations in a cultural frontier zone opened them to considerable cultural and political influences from Benin and other Yoruba groups. The establishment of Owo by a prince of Ile-Ife involved the conquest and integration of several preexisting groups, the most notable of these were the seven autonomous settlements of Idasin, ruled by the Alale, as well as Iyare and Iso. Similarly, the emergence of Ondo occurred at the expense of the indigenous groups, namely the Idoko, Oka, and Ifore, who had to be subdued and forcibly integrated into the nascent state.

North of Ekiti and east of Oyo lived the Ibolo, Igbomina, and Okun-Yoruba groups. By the early eighteenth century, many independent state structures could be identified in this region. Among the Igbomina these included Ila, Ajase, Omu, Aran, Isanlu-isin, Iwo, Oro Ora, and Igbaja. The Ibolo states included Ofa, Igosun, Ijagbo, Ipee, and Igbonna. Peopled by migrants of diverse origins, including the non-Yoruba speaking Nupe, Edo, and Igala, the Okun-Yoruba were divided into five major subgroups—namely, the Owe, Yagba, Bunu, Ijumu, and Oworo. Although considerable interaction occurred between them, and while the Orangun of Ila and the Olofa of Ofa were accorded some respect, none of these groups ever formed a single political entity. Apart from a few notable exceptions, the sociopolitical organization was characterized by the mini-states, made up of independent villages in which no right or authority was acknowledged beyond the confines of each of the autonomous settlements. This decentralized sociopolitical existence rendered these northeastern Yoruba groups particularly vulnerable to constant military pressures, imperial conquest, and human depredations by their more powerful and imperious neighbors, such as Oyo, Nupe, and Benin, who did not hesitate to make short work of their nebulous independence.

FUNSO AFOLAYAN

See also: **Benin Kingdom: Nineteenth Century.**

Further Reading

Adediran, Biodun. *The Frontier States of Western Yorubaland, circa 1600–1889.* Ibadan, Nigeria: French Institute for Research in Africa, 1994.

Afolayan, Funso, "Kingdoms of the Yoruba: Socio-political Development before 1800," in *Culture and Society in Yorubaland,* edited by G. Ogunremi and Abiodun Adediran. Ibadan, Nigeria: Rex Charles, 1998.

Ajayi, J. F. A. and Robert S. Smith. *Yoruba Warfare in the Nineteenth Century.* London: Cambridge University Press, 1971.

Biobaku, Saburi O. *The Egba and Their Neighbours, 1842–1872.* Ibadan, Nigeria: University Press PLC, 1991.

Johnson, Samuel. *The History of the Yorubas Yorubas from the Earliest Times to the Beginning of the British Protectorate* (1921). Reprint, Lagos: CMS 1973.

Pemberton, John, and Funso S. Afolayan. *Yoruba Sacred Kingship: A Power like That of the Gods.* Washington, D.C.: Smithsonian Institution Press, 1996.

Smith, Robert S. *Kingdoms of the Yoruba.* London: James Currey/Madison: University of Wisconsin Press, 1988.

Yoruba States: Trade and Conflict, Nineteenth Century

For the Yoruba, the nineteenth century was a period of warfare and change. Prior to this the Yoruba people were organized into several states, of which the most powerful was the Oyo empire. While it lasted, Oyo was a bastion of law and order. Its collapse ushered in a period of chaos and instability that lasted until the end of the nineteenth century. Internal dissension, debilitating power struggles between the *alafin* (king) and his principal chiefs, economic decline associated with the abolition of the Atlantic slave trade, and the Fulani jihadist (holy war) invasion from the north hastened the collapse of the empire. The Fulani jihadists seized control of Ilorin, sacked the capital of Oyo, and proceeded to devastate and destroy many northern Yoruba towns. Thousands of refugees began to pour into central and southern Yorubaland. Many settled in already existing towns not yet ravaged. Others established new settlements. Some organized themselves into marauding hordes, extending the zone of pillage and carnage to southern Yorubaland. The Oyo refugee soldiers descended on the Owu and Egba, destroying their towns.

From the ruins of Oyo and in response to other pressures, new states emerged competing to fill the vacuum and gain control of the trade routes to the coast, from whence were obtained European firearms and other goods. The struggle for power and supremacy among these successor states, such as Ibadan, Ijaye, Ilorin, New Oyo, Abeokuta, and Oke Odan, resulted in intermittent warfare. At the battle of Osogbo in 1839, Ilorin's ambition to conquer and bring much of Yorubaland under the Sokoto caliphate was checked by the rising power of Ibadan. Thereafter Ibadan proceeded to extend its hegemony over much of eastern and central Yorubaland, incorporating parts of Ijesa, Ekiti, Igbomina, and Akoko. The defeat and elimination of Ijaye by Ibadan in 1862 left Ibadan as the leading Yoruba state. But the imperial ambition of Ibadan soon provoked widespread reactions. Ibadan became embroiled in wars on several fronts, fighting against the Ijesa, Ekiti, Ilorin, and others in the north and against Ijebu and Egba to the south. These wars resulted in chaos and instability and a pervasive state of fear and insecurity that lasted until the end of the century.

The consequences of these crises were far-reaching. The wars resulted in massive population movement, the destruction and desertion of old towns, and the establishment of new ones. Intensive urbanization also resulted as refugees flocked together to establish major settlements and maximize the advantages of their numerical strength at a time when numbers were important to security and victory in war. Yoruba society became highly militarized; professional armies and warriors emerged. Slavery and the slave trade intensified as more hands were needed to serve as soldiers, farm hands, trade agents, wives, and followers and to enhance the power and prestige of the *ologun*, or war leaders. More Yoruba were also sold into the Atlantic slave trade now than at any other period before this time, and in greater number than that of any other African group during this period. Their large number as well as their late arrival ensured a dominant and permanent Yoruba cultural imprint in the New World of the Americas.

The endemic state of warfare and the perennial need for security gave preeminence to the military in politics. In the most important of the new towns, the monarchical institution characteristic of traditional Yoruba political system was discarded for new forms of government that evolved to cope with the exigencies of the time. In Ibadan, a republican system in which career was made open to talent was established. The new republic was dominated by a military oligarchy, in which leadership was collective. Appointment of chiefs was not hereditary. Status was determined by the command of "men and means," and new titles were created to reward brave warriors. The intense and dangerous rivalry for power among the ologun kept Ibadan in a state of turmoil and Yorubaland unstable for much of the century. In Ijaye, Kurunmi, the *are ona kakanfo* (commander) of the Oyo empire, after suppressing and eliminating all his rivals established a personal autocracy that brooked no rival until its demise at the hand of Ibadan in 1862. In Abeokuta and Oke Odan, a loose federal system in which power was shared among several quasi-autonomous communities and their notable war chiefs was established.

The state of crisis was further accentuated and complicated by pressures from outside the Yoruba country. Islam, a foreign religion whose advent well predated the nineteenth century, took advantage of the crises of this era to penetrate into much of Yorubaland. From the south, missionaries, made up of Europeans, Americans, and freed slaves (or recaptives) from Sierra Leone, brought Christianity. Beginning at Badagry in 1841, the Christian religion made successful inroads into southern and western Yorubaland by the end of the century. Similarly, from the north, the Nupe, now reinvigorated by their new dynasty of Fulani rulers, conquered the Okun-Yoruba, parts of Igbomina, and Ekiti. From the southeast, Benin's army reached Otun-Ekiti in northeastern Yorubaland. From the west, the Dahomey army ravaged Ketu and Egbado and on several occasions (1851, 1864, 1873, and 1874) lay siege to Abeokuta. In addition to the efforts of its soldiers, Abeokuta's successive victories were facilitated by the assistance it received from the British on the coast.

The need for raw materials such as cotton and palm oil to feed its industries and for markets to sell its manufactures had forced Britain to actively engage in the political economy of the West African coast. Determined to stimulate legitimate trade, open up the Yoruba country to civilizing missionary influence, and put an end to the slave trade (which had increased in Yorubaland in spite of the official abolition of the transatlantic slave trade), the British bombarded and conquered Lagos in 1851. Ten years later, Lagos became a crown colony of the British. Thereafter, tension over the control of the trade routes to the interior repeatedly brought the British into conflict with Ijebu, Egba, and Ibadan. In the meantime, the British became involved in the efforts to resolve the nearly century-old fratricidal civil wars in the Yoruba country. Stalemate and war-weariness among the combatants led to the success of British and Christian missionary diplomacy and the signing of a peace agreement in 1886. However, with the onset of the European "Scramble" for and partition of Africa, the British did away with all pretense and in 1892 Ijebu was invaded and annexed. The lesson of this defeat was not lost on Abeokuta and Ibadan, both of which surrendered without a fight. Only New Oyo and Ilorin had to be compelled by force of arms to submit to the colonial forces. However, the memory of the stirring events of the nineteenth century and their consequences has continued to exercise a powerful influence on modern Yoruba historical consciousness, as well as on its intra- and intergroup relations and politics.

FUNSO AFOLAYAN

See also: **Ife, Oyo, Yoruba, Ancient: Kingship and Art.**

Further Reading

Adediran, Biodun. *The Frontier States of Western Yorubaland, circa 1600–1889.* Ibadan, Nigeria: French Institute for Research in Africa, 1994.

Afolayan, Funso. "Warfare and Slavery in Nineteenth Century Yorubaland." In *War and Peace in Yorubaland 1783–1893,* edited by Adeagbo Akinjogbin. Ibadan, Nigeria: Heinemann, 1998.

Ajayi, J. F. A., and Robert S. Smith. *Yoruba Warfare in the Nineteenth Century.* London: Cambridge University Press, 1971.

Akintoye, S. A. *Revolution and Power Politics in Yorubaland, 1840–1893.* London: Longman, 1971.

Awe, Bolanle. "The Rise of Ibadan as a Yoruba Power, 1851–1893." Ph.D. diss., Oxford University, 1964.

Falola, Toyin, and Dare Oguntomisin. *The Military in Nineteenth Century Yoruba Politics.* Ile-Ife: University of Ife Press, 1984.

Gbadamosi, T. G. O. *The Growth of Islam among the Yoruba.* London: Longman, 1978.

Pemberton, John, and Funso S. Afolayan. *Yoruba Sacred Kingship: A Power like That of the Gods.* Washington, D.C.: Smithsonian Institution Press, 1996.

Yusuf ibn Tashfin: Almoravid Empire: Maghrib: 1070–1147

After the death of their ideologue, Ibn Yasin, in 1059, the Almoravids ceased to be simply a reform movement bent on religious proselytism and gradually took the shape of a dynastic state. The loose ties that kept the movement together were replaced by new political alliances between the Almoravid leadership and subject groups, such as non-Sanhaja Berbers and Andalusian Muslims. The power structure of the nascent state was hierarchical; it contrasted greatly with the absence of a centralized authority and lack of tribal cohesion that characterized the formative period of the movement. Political power was monopolized by Lamtuna chiefs from whose ranks both rulers (known as *emirs*) and court dignitaries were selected. The title of *murabit* (Almoravid) was reserved for members of the three constituent communities of the movement: the Lamtuna, Guddala, and Massufa, who filled the

Almoravids, c.1050–1147.

main administrative posts. The bottom echelons were occupied by tribes such as the Jazula and Lamta that, though grudgingly at first, had finally embraced the Almoravid reformist program. They formed the backbone of the army and were known as "the followers" (al-hasham).

The rise of Yusuf ibn Tashfin to political prominence was somehow fortuitous. While Abu Bakr bin 'Umar, nominal ruler, was busy trying to bring restive tribes in the south back to the fold, Yusuf had served as his deputy, actually in absolute charge of the territories north of the High Atlas. Aware that any attempt to oppose Yusuf's political ambitions would result in the fragmentation of the state, Abu Bakr decided to abdicate in favor of his protégé in 1072.

Most of the Almoravid conquests took place during Yusuf's reign (1061–1107). Marrakech, the new capital founded by Abu Bakr in 1070 because of its strategic location, constituted an ideal springboard for future campaigns in the north. Fez was taken in 1075 and the occupation of the Rif, the mountain range that runs parallel to the Mediterranean coast, was completed within less than a decade. Although Almoravid troops reached the mountains of Kabylia, the extent of their rule did not go beyond present-day Oran, in western Algeria. Ceuta, taken in 1083, served as the gateway to the annexation of the Iberian Peninsula (Al-Andalus).

Yusuf ibn Tashfin is favorably portrayed in Muslim sources. The fact that he abstained from adopting the title of *amir al-mu'minin* (XXXX, theoretically reserved for the Abbasid caliph in Baghdad), thus

avoiding a religious schism in Sunni Islam, enhanced his reputation among contemporary chroniclers as a pious and selfless ruler. The adoption of Malikism as the state legal doctrine was also one of Yusuf's main policies. At his behest, Maliki scholars were allocated official stipends and granted numerous privileges, such as access to his privy council. The monopoly exerted by Maliki jurists (*fuqaha'*) over legal matters is often regarded as a mixed blessing by later authors. The existence of an officially sponsored school of law helped homogenize legal proceedings in a vast geographical area that included Muslim Spain and North Africa. It gave too much power, however, to a single category of legal experts, thus opening the way to nepotism, abuse of office, and other pernicious practices commonly associated with corporate-like institutions. Reliance on a single legal code is blamed, moreover, for the "intellectual impoverishment" and rigidity that, according to most modern scholars, marked the Almoravid period. The excessive use of manuals of legal casuistry (*furu'*) and the subsequent neglect of the traditional sources of Islamic law (Qur'an and prophetic traditions), a propensity to follow existing legal precedents (*taqlid*) rather than exercise individual powers of jurisprudence (*ijtihad*), and, finally, the use of literal Qur'anic exegesis even when the latter might engender anthropomorphic views, are some of the most frequently mentioned signs of this alleged ideological decline.

The influence of Maliki jurists became even more overpowering during the reign of Yusuf's successor, 'Ali ibn Yusuf ibn Tashfin (1107–1143). Although his asceticism and piety are not in dispute, chroniclers are unanimous in their portrayal of this ruler as a well-meaning but cowardly monarch, unfortunate enough to be faced with the task of tackling three simultaneous dangers: the resurgence of the Christian kingdoms in Spain (a constant drain in terms of financial and military resources), the rebellion of Ibn Tumart from 1125 onward, and the increasing stranglehold of the Maliki establishment on the Almoravid state. The surge of military activity in Al-Andalus forced 'Ali ibn Yusuf to increase the amount of troops dispatched there and to impose dubious taxes on his Maghribi subjects. This latter measure caused considerable discontent and it was viewed as a betrayal of the Almoravid programme of abolishing non-Qur'anic taxes. To compound matters, military shortages in Morocco were offset by recruiting Christian mercenaries. This unpopular decision benefited the Almohads, Ibn Tumart's followers, as it confirmed their claims that the ruling elite no longer enjoyed religious legitimacy. Almohad pressure became ever more intense and the walls of Marrakesh had to be reinforced in 1129.

Among the criticisms against 'Ali ibn Yusuf's rule, none seems more damaging than his incapacity to rein in the excesses of the Maliki legal establishment. Jurists took advantage of their position to extract more privileges and financial perks from the Almoravid court. Although anti-Maliki propaganda must be treated with caution, it seems certain that some judiciary-instigated measures such as the ban on Al-Ghazali's mystical works, the official clampdown on Sufi circles and, more generally, the endorsement of heavy fiscal policies caused widespread popular discontent.

'Ali ibn Yusuf spent most of the second half of his reign (from 1125 to his death in 1143) combating both the Christians of the Iberian Peninsula and the fledgling Almohad movement. A series of military setbacks in Spain weakened the Almoravid army. This, coupled with growing restiveness among the populace due to heavy taxation, explains his inability to subdue the Almohad rebels before they were numerically superior. His two successors, Tashfin (1143–1145) and Ishaq (1145–1147), inherited a kingdom that would inevitably disappear.

FRANCISCO RODRIGUEZ-MANAS

See also: **'Abd Allah ibn Yasin: Almoravid: Sahara.**

Further Reading

Abun-Nasr, J. M. *A History of the Maghrib in the Islamic Period.* Cambridge, 1987.
Laroui, A. *The History of the Maghrib: An Interpretive Essay,* Princeton, N.J.: Princeton University Press, 1977.
Norris, H. T. *The Berbers in Arabic Literature.* London, 1982.

Yusuf Pasha Karamanli: *See* **Libya: Yusuf Pasha Karamanli and the Ottoman Reoccupation, 1795–1835.**

Z

Zaire: Politics, Regional

The country known today as the Democratic Republic of Congo (DRC) was christened the Republic of Zaire in 1971. In 1997, President Laurent Kabila changed it back to the DRC. From 1960 to 1971, Zaire had no independent foreign policy, as this was a period of pervasive international involvement in its domestic politics. After gaining power in November 1965, President Mobutu Sese Seko was able to consolidate the political authority of the new regime and to reduce external interference by projecting a nationalist and Pan-African image of his regime. Nonetheless, the country remained dependent on American and French goodwill to prevent bankruptcy during the Cold War, and this had a marked effect on Mobutu's regional policy orientation. In the early years of his presidency, he followed a fairly independent course of policy. Thus, he undertook his first major initiative in 1968 with the creation of the Union of States of Central Africa, which included the Central African Republic (CAR), Chad, and Zaire. Under French pressures, the CAR later withdrew from the union; it would, however, maintain friendly ties with Zaire throughout Mobutu's presidency. Also, relations with Sudan were generally cordial. Mutual interest dictated cooperation for the purpose of controlling cross-border activities by various rebel groups along common borders.

The only western neighboring state with which relations were periodically troubled during Mobutu's presidency was Congo-Brazzaville, which had backed the 1964 rebellion in Zaire. After that, the situation between the two countries had fluctuated considerably. Ideological differences played a role in the often tense relations as well, because Congo-Brazzaville claimed to be a Marxist state.

Mobutu's regional diplomacy with his eastern colleagues was more amicable. He always had good relations with Rwanda, except in 1967, when Zairean army units mutinied over the lack of pay. They were joined by foreign mercenaries and tried to bring down the Mobutu regime. Government troops succeeded in driving the rebels into Rwanda. Mobutu's request for their extradition was denied, leading to a break in diplomatic relations in January 1968. Relations were reestablished in February 1969 and were further strengthened in September 1976 when Juvenal Habyarimana of Rwanda joined Mobutu of Zaire and Michel Micombero of Burundi in forming the Economic Community of the Great Lakes (CEPGL).

Relations with Burundi also remained strong until November 1976, when Micombero was overthrown in a bloodless coup led by Lieutenant Colonel Jean-Baptiste Bagaza. Bagaza's personal dealings with Mobutu were always difficult. The overthrow of Bagaza in September 1987 by Major Pierre Buyoya led to improved Zaire-Burundi relations. The annual summit of the CEPGL in January 1988 provided a pretext for Mobutu to pay an official visit to Bujumbura, his first since the 1976 creation of the community. Mobutu often offered himself as a conciliator of conflicts among his eastern neighbors. He was instrumental in the establishment of a formal relationship between Idi Amin Dada of Uganda and Julius Nyerere of Tanzania after Amin had overthrown the administration of Milton Obote. The diplomatic situation between Tanzania and Zaire was generally good, but it became strained in the 1980s when Mobutu accused the Tanzanian government of harboring Zairian dissident guerillas who had attacked the city of Moba on Lake Tanganyika in 1984 and 1985.

Zaire encountered more problems with its southern neighbors, Zambia and Angola. Border disputes between

Zambia and Zaire as well as competition for markets for their principal exports, copper and cobalt, had caused occasional strains. The most difficult situation occurred during the Katanga invasions in 1977 and 1978, when the Front National for the Liberation of Congo guerillas used the Zambian territory to attack southern Katanga. Tensions eased when it became evident that they did so without the consent of the Zambian government. Relations were also strained in 1983 and 1984 by a series of border clashes in southern Katanga involving smugglers and acts of banditry by hungry and unpaid soldiers. In 1985, the two governments responded with a joint commission to settle disputes and announced their intention to observe an agreement to prevent prices for cobalt from falling below certain levels. The two countries contained most of the known cobalt reserves in the free world before 1989.

The situation with Angola hadn't been cordial since the mid-1970s. After Zaire obtained its independence in June 1960, it supported Angolan independence movements and allowed many Angolan refugees to live in Western Zaire. Mobutu's subversive behavior toward Angola started when the Popular Movement of the Liberation of Angola took control of Luanda in June 1975 and installed a Marxist regime, which received substantial Cuban and Soviet military support during the Cold War. However, the National Front for the Liberation of Angola and the National Union for the Total Independence of Angola (UNITA), which were backed by the United States through Zaire and South Africa, continued a guerilla war against the Angolan government.

With the decline of Zaire's strategic importance at the end of the Cold War, Western willingness to overlook the Mobutu regime's record of economic mismanagement, corruption, and human-rights abuse was also on the wane. His mediating role in the Angolan civil war was increasingly viewed as irrelevant by all parties. Nonetheless, relations between Zaire and Angola remained hostile as Angola continued to accuse Mobutu of assisting UNITA's destabilizing efforts.

The post–Cold War era also changed Mobutu's role in eastern Africa. In early 1990s, his efforts to mediate between the Rwandan government and the Rwanda Patriotic Front (RPF) met with little success. As hopes of a negotiated settlement waned, however, Mobutu's support for Habyarimana's embattled regime was maintained until Habyarimana was killed in an airplane crash in April 1994. A few months later, the RPF took power in Rwanda. The result was the outflow of more than 1.2 million Hutu refugees to Zaire, and among these were thousands of former soldiers who had been responsible of the 1994 genocide in Rwanda. Soon after crossing the borders, these soldiers began launching armed attacks into Rwanda from bases in refugee camps, with the aim of making Rwanda ungovernable.

In September 1996 the RPF attacked the refugee camps and forced the repatriation of more than half a million Hutu back to Rwanda. Having gained partial control of its borders, the Rwandan government decided to help a coalition of Banyamulenge and other Zairean insurgents, called the Alliance of the Democratic Forces for the Liberation of Congo, to topple Mobutu. They were joined by Uganda and Angola. The coalition entered the capital city of Kinshasa in May 1997.

The involvement of Angola, Rwanda, and Uganda in toppling Mobutu was motivated by their desire to have a friendly government in Kinshasa capable of securing their borders with Zaire. In conclusion, the withdrawal of Zaire's two major patrons—the United States and France—after the collapse of the Soviet Union weakened Mobutu's regional position and precipitated his downfall.

KISANGANI EMIZET

See also: **Congo (Kinshasa), Democratic Republic of/Zaire.**

Further Reading

Emizet, K. "Rebels vs. Democrats in Power: How to Establish Regional Security Cooperation in Central Africa." *International Journal on World Peace* 15, no. 1 (1998): 51–83.

Young, C. and T. Turner. *The Rise and Decline of the Zairian State.* Madison: University of Wisconsin Press, 1985.

Zambia: Early Nineteenth Century: Survey

Zambia (or Northern Rhodesia, as the country was known during the colonial period, from 1890 to 1964) is roughly in the middle of Africa. It is a landlocked country with no direct access to either the east or west coasts. In the early nineteenth century the country had very limited contacts with Europeans because of its geographical location. The country also had very limited contacts with the Arab and Muslim world. Zambia therefore was largely influenced in its early social, economic, and political developments by African peoples who migrated into the region during this period. Indeed, the lasting influences were those engineered by the peoples associated with Bantu migrations.

The influences that shaped Zambia's future were therefore largely demographic. The early migrants spread into the area now encompassing Zambia and introduced new economic, political, and cultural systems. These newcomers also spread chieftainships. In the area of economy, the country developed strong links with the east-west trade routes across the continent that developed into the long distance trade.

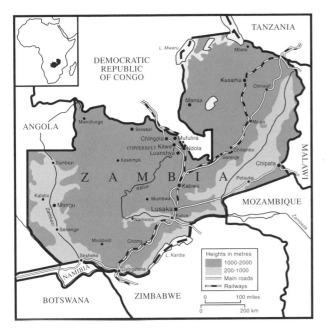

Zambia.

The nineteenth-century history of Zambia was shaped by its geography and its river system. To the south Zambia is bounded by the Zambezi River, which forms the boundary between Zambia and Zimbabwe, and to the northwest, the Zambezi River forms the boundary with Angola in some places. To the east, Zambia is bounded by the highlands that run along the west coast of Lake Malawi, while to the north the country continues to be bounded by the continuation of the same highlands between Lake Malawi and lake Tanganyika. During the nineteenth century these geographic features provide security for the local people against invaders, much as they proved to be obstacles for the movement of the people and traders from outside the region.

Most of the people in nineteenth-century Zambia originated from the Congo, under the Bantu migrations. As a result of this, as early as the nineteenth century the people of Zambia displayed a great deal of cultural uniformity, speaking the same Bantu languages, possessing shared knowledge of the use of iron, and practicing some form of agriculture. There were three main groups of people during this early period: the southern Tonga and Ila, who were cattle keepers and traced their descent matrilineally; the northeastern cattle-keeping Mambwe, Iwa, and Namwanga, who traced their descent patrilineally; and the the Congolese Bemba, Bisa, Lamba, and Kaonde, who practiced matrilineal records of descent.

During the early nineteenth century the political organization of the Zambian people varied. Some, like the Tonga, did not have chiefs. Even in those societies where there were chiefs, their status differed from one community to another. Some were only respected as ritual leaders with little real political authority, let alone military power. In other tribes the chiefs had real political power, and in others they combined political and military power. This diversity affected the way in which Zambian tribes responded to European intrusion in the country in the late nineteenth century.

The early nineteenth century in Zambia witnessed wave after wave of interference and invasion. The result was that traditional civilizations were either damaged or submerged in the rising tide of newcomers. The end of the eighteenth century in many respects signified the end of a great period in the history of Africa. It was the end of centuries of Iron Age growth, during which period most peoples of Zambia were little touched by outside political and economic developments. The start of the nineteenth century was characterized by events that were to forever revolutionize the entire region, including Zambia.

One of the major revolutionary changes after the early Bantu migrations was the invasion from the south. In 1818, some 2,000 miles away in southeastern Africa two groups of the Ngoni people, the Mutetwa and Ndwandwe, fought each other in one of the decisive battles that were to affect Zambia's early nineteenth century history. The events in South Africa during this period sent the Ngoni and other groups north in search of refuge. In 1835 the Ngoni, led by Zwangendaba, crossed the Zambezi River in to Zambia and caused a great deal of havoc, defeating local people along the way and taking men as soldiers and women as wives. The impact of the Ngoni invasion was felt in a wide area of Zambia, from the south to the northern border with Tanzania, before the Ngoni finally settled in the eastern province of Zambia.

In the west, the Lozi kingdom was strong and prosperous at the center, but was quite fragile at its edges. This made its ruler, Lewanika, grow increasingly anxious about the potential threats to his kingdom from the Portuguese in the west and the Ndebele in the south. His fears were worsened by warring internal factions, which led to increased instability. In response to such threats, Lewanika was forced to sign a concessionary treaty with the British South Africa Company in 1890.

Meanwhile, in the south, because no centralized kingdom existed, the Tonga and Ila were frequently raided as sources of slaves and cattle by outside peoples. The raiders included the Lozi from the west, the Ndebele from the south across the Zambezi River, and the Portuguese Chikunda from around Chirundu and the Kafue confluence with the Zambezi, who traded in slaves. In Central Zambia the Lenje showed a remarkable political unity and strength. They were generally involved in trade with the Swahili from the northeast, the Mbari from the west, and the Chikunda from the south.

Throughout most of the nineteenth century, Zambia was characterized by interaction and external influences. External actors connected with long-distance trade became active in the interior, causing some kingdoms to decline. Nineteenth-century Zambia was marked by constant change resulting from both internal and external forces.

BIZECK JUBE PHIRI

See also: **Lozi Kingdom and the Kololo; Tonga, Ila, and Cattle.**

Further Reading

Fagan, B. M. (ed.). *A Short History of Zambia*, 2nd ed. Nairobi: Longman, 1968.

Langworthy, H. W. *Zambia before 1890.* London: Longman, 1972.

Ranger, T. O. (ed.). *Aspects of Central African History.* London: Heinemann, 1968.

Rennie, J. K. "The Ngoni States and European Intrusion." In *The Zambezian Past: Studies in Central African History,* edited by Eric Stokes and Richard Brown. Manchester: Manchester University Press, 1966.

Roberts, Andrew. *A History of Zambia.* Nairobi: Heinemann, 1976.

Zambia: Long-Distance Trade, Nineteenth Century

Jan Vansina (1962) has identified three types of trade in precolonial Africa. The first of these was local trade, which was conducted by people living within easy reach of one another; this trade was conducted in local markets, from village to village catering for goods from local industry. The second type of trade is what Vansnia termed "regional trade"; it was conducted over greater distances either among culturally different peoples within a single state, or among neighboring peoples. Regional trade was conducted at marketplaces located closer to the borders of the trading peoples or at the capitals of the states involved in the trade. The third type of trade that Vansina identified is long-distance trade.

In order appreciate the nature and character of long-distance trade, it is necessary to examine the development of local trade. It used to be supposed that trade in Africa only began when gold, ivory, and slaves were exported out of Africa. Yet on closer examination it becomes clear that these items were only the most glamorous—and horrific—results of the economic interaction between African societies on the one hand and between Africa and the outside world on the other. Local trade was centered on items that met everyday

needs, such as foodstuffs, metalwork, pottery, and clothing. Although there was no money involved in the exchange of goods, items like wire, copper crosses, beads and cloth were sometimes used as currency because they were in general demand.

There were no permanently established markets for local trade, but chiefs' palaces sometimes served as centers where redistribution of goods took place. The process assisted chiefs in that they were able to enhance their power and authority over their people. This local trade determined the capacity of Zambian precolonial nineteenth-century societies to participate in long distance trade. As a result of the patterns of the local exchange and industry, trade routes were shaped and sustained between the African interior and the coast. While the growth of coastal trade stimulated the production of goods that were consumed within African communities, it also stimulated growth of goods produced for export overseas. Early European visitors like the missionary David Livingstone left behind vivid descriptions of the kind of trade that they found taking place in Africa.

Long distance trade was unknown in Central Africa before the arrival of Europeans. It only became a common feature in nineteenth-century Zambia. Long-distance trade was direct trade, and consisted mainly of European goods. Several other items, including slaves and iron, featured prominently in this early form of exchange between communities in the region. By 1840, the Luvale of northwestern Zambia were busy exchanging slaves for guns with the Mbundu of Bihe. Sibetwane of the Kololo, who had settled in the Upper Zambezi, maximized his trading fortunes from there. During much of the nineteenth century the economic life of Zambian societies were affected by trade in ivory and slaves. Starting in 1852, for two decades traders from Angola known as the Mambari constantly visited Barotseland selling guns and cloth for ivory and a few slaves from the Kololo.

By 1800 Zambia had been drawn into the trading systems of the Nyamwezi from Tanzania and the Arabs on Zanzibar Island and the east coast. The Nyamwezi had reached as far as the Katanga copper mines. In 1855 a Nyamwezi caravan reached Kazembe's capital. Another important Arab trader was Msiri who was active in northern Zambia. These traders changed the focus of long distance trade.

Some long-distance traders defeated local chiefs to enhance their trading activities in nineteenth-century Zambia. For example, in 1867 Tippu Tip defeated the Tabwa to ensure a monopoly on ivory trade. The presence of Arab long-distance trade had a destabilizing influence. Some local people formed alliances with Arab traders for support in their succession disputes. A good example is the 1872 case of a Lunda prince who sought Arab support in his quest to displace the Kazembe; he succeeded in taking over the kingship with the help of Arab traders. The process amounted to a revolution in the Kazembe kingdom. Since then Lunda princes are closely guarded at the capital and are denied political office.

Long-distance trade covered a large area of part of colonial Zambia that was also part of the Luba Lomani empire. Luba Lomani was the largest of the Luba kingdoms that were founded by Kongolo and Kalala Ilunga. With the help of long-distance trade, the kingdom expanded to the land of the Bisa and linked the trade through them to east coast. This trade was well established by 1780. As the trade increased, goods were also transported from the west coast through Luanda. By 1800 the Bisa began to extend their trade beyond Kazembe with whom they had began to trade about 1760. They are believed to have conducted trade in ivory and slaves.

It is generally believed that the establishment of Kazembe Kingdom and the introduction of long-distance trade goods stimulated the traditional economy. This in turn strengthened subregional specialization in trade goods for communities in precolonial Zambia, which participated in the long-distance trade. The Lamba, for example, specialized in iron working and this enhanced their involvement in long-distance trade. Their experience in regional trade made it easier for them to participate in long-distance trade. The Ushi of present day Luapula Province specialized in making iron and copper weapons. This gave them advantages over other societies that took part in long-distance trade.

The Shila and Tabwa who lived around Lake Mwelu specialized in making salt. Through these commodities, Luba Lomani was linked with the Kazembe kingdom through several trade routes. Copper crosses that were made in the Kazembe kingdom were used as a currency in Luba Lomani. Consequently, every year Luba Lomani traders traveled long distances to Kazembe country to purchase copper crosses. During the period of the Luba Lomani expansion the pace of long-distance trade increased as new trading groups came on the scene. They included the Nyamwezi, who are believed to have reached Kazembe Kingdom around the second or third decades of the nineteenth century. They were followed by Arabs.

The growth of long-distance trade in precolonial Zambia facilitated the growth and expansion of some kingdoms while others were defeated. Msiri was the first long-distance trader to seize political power in about 1860 in the tributary copper state of the Katanga and Mpande. He established a direct trade route with both the east and the west coasts, and in the process he increased his political power. Long-distance trade was

major contributing factor to the coming of foreign rule in Zambia.

BIZECK JUBE PHIRI

See also: **Msiri: Yeke Kingdom.**

Further Reading

Gray, Richard, and David Birmingham (eds.). *Pre-Colonial African Trade*. London: Oxford University Press, 1970.

Roberts, Andrew. *A History of Zambia*. Nairobi: Heinemann, 1976.

———. "Pre-Colonial Trade in Zambia." *African Social Research*, no. 10 (1970): pp.715–746.

Vansina, Jan. "Long Distance Trade Routes in Central Africa," *Journal of African History* 3, no. 3 (1962): 375–390.

Wilson, Anne. "Long Distance Trade and the Luba Lomani Empire." *Journal of African History* 13, no. 4 (1972): 575–589.

Zambia: Ngoni Incursion from the South

The Ngoni migrated North from South Africa in the early nineteenth century. These migrations introduced new state systems unlike those from the Luba and Lunda in the early period. The Ngoni were a product of the rise of Shaka of the Zulu people in South Africa. Their history began about 1818 when the Zulu, led by Shaka, defeated the Ndandwe of Zwide. A group of the Jere people led by Zwangendaba fled from Natal and later became known as the Ngoni. On their long migration to the north they brought with them their newly developed social and political systems. The rise of the Ngoni state in Zambian precolonial history was a quick one.

From Natal the Ngoni briefly settled in southern Mozambique, but they were forced to move on because the area was already occupied by Shoshangane, who had earlier fled from Shaka. Zwangendaba led his people through Rhodesia where he did not settle, although the area was rich in cattle. He took his people northward and crossed the Zambezi near Zumbo on November 19, 1835.

After crossing the Zambezi, the Ngoni settled among the Nsenga of Petauke, whom they defeated, taking their women for wives. The Ngoni completely changed the way of life of the Nsenga people and disturbed their trade. By 1840, Zwangendaba decided to move farther north into the Malawi and Tanzania territories, finally settling in Fipa country. Zwangendaba died in 1845 while the Ngoni were in Fipa country. After his death, the Ngoni state began to break up over succession disputes. This division reflected the lack of a clear successor to Zwangendaba. Two of Zwangendaba's sons, Mpezeni and Mbelwa, struggled for the leadership of the Ngoni after the death of their father. Because at the time of his death the two were both too young to take over, a period of regency was required and struggle resulted from the supporters of Mpezeni and Mbelwa. This resulted into a split of the state. The Mbelwa group went into Bemba country and the Bemba wars started. The two Ngoni groups never united again.

When Mpezeni was old enough he led his people southward, first settling in northern Malawi. From here Mpezeni's Ngoni made frequent raids into the lands of the Tumbuka and Senga people in Lundazi, who were forced to accept a type of tributary status to Ngoni *indunas*. Mpezeni's final settlement area, after unsuccessfully failing to defeat the Bemba, was Chipata.

Mpezeni passed through the Mpika and Serenje districts and finally settled in Nsenga country, where his father had settled 30 years earlier. Mpezeni and his people assimilated large numbers of Nsenga people, a process that almost led to the extinction of the Nsenga people. At the same time, Mpezeni's continued raid of the Chewa, led by Undi, virtually led to the collapse of Undi's kingdom. Undi was never really defeated and in the 1870s, Mpezeni finally moved his people to their final destination in Chipata. It was in the Chipata area that the Ngoni came in direct contact with Europeans, who actually halted Mpezeni's raids of the surrounding people.

The Ngoni raids brought them into direct contact with the Chikunda, Arab or Swahili slave caravans. Since these were well armed, Mpezeni avoid conflict with them and entered into trade relations instead. It was the Europeans who were to change the history of the Ngoni in the 1890s; this was a period when European explorers were consolidating territorial claims on behalf of their European countries through treaties.

The region, which is today the Eastern Province of Zambia, was part of what was initially known as Northeastern Rhodesia. Before that, the area was also known as East Luangwa District and covered part of what is today the Northern Province. A German trader named Carl Wiese led to its establishment as a colonial entity following his 1892 visit to the paramount chief of the Ngoni, Mpezeni. During the visit, Wiese is believed to have won Mpezeni's friendship and trust. He therefore obtained from Mpezeni a concession whose terms were vague. Nonetheless, the concession was the basis for the North Charterland Exploration Company's (NCEC's) claim of the whole region.

However, the NCEC was not yet in control of the territory and could not administer the territory without Mpezeni's consent. This notwithstanding, an administrative station was established at Chinunda (Old Fort Jameson) and a Mr. Morringham was appointed by the company in charge of the post. His administration

was ineffective because the administrative post was outside Ngoni territory. However, with the permission of Mpezeni, the NCEC established their headquarters at Fort Young. Despite Mpezeni's permission, the NCEC were nervous, believing the Ngoni would attack the station. Residents of Fort Young applied to the Nyasaland Protectorate for an armed force. The response was immediate: the protectorate administration at Zomba dispatched troops to Fort Young.

The Ngoni were caught unprepared for the impending attack. They were preparing for the Ncwala ceremony, which was interpreted as preparation for war by the residents of Fort Young. The Ngoni became uneasy with the arrival of troops at Fort Young. Mpezeni's eldest son, Nsingu, became aggressive and began preparation for war. The troops attacked the Ngoni in January 1898. The Ngoni were defeated very quickly and lost almost all their cattle, which were taken as booty. Nsingu was captured and executed. This suppression of the Ngoni paved the way for the actual occupation of the territory by the NCEC administration. An administrative station was built at Chimpinga, close to the site of Mpezeni's village, and was placed under a collector who was charged with the responsibility of enforcing the NCEC's control of the region. To prevent any trouble in the future, a military station was also established on the protectorate's border, from which Mpezeni was banished for a year.

After the defeat of the Ngoni by the Europeans they remained under European rule, and this effectively brought colonial rule to the area. It is in this respect that it is argued that colonial rule in Northeastern Rhodesia was brought through defeat and not by peaceful agreement, as was the case in Northwestern Rhodesia. Today the paramount chief of the Ngoni plays an important role in the politics of the Eastern Province. The Ngoni are the sixth largest ethnic group in Zambia.

BIZECK JUBE PHIRI

See also: **Zambia (Northern Rhodesia): British Occupation, Resistance: 1890s.**

Further Reading

Barnes, J. A. *Politics in a Changing Society: Political History of the Fort Jameson Ngoni.* London: Oxford University Press, 1954.

Langworthy, Harry W. *Zambia before 1890: Aspects of Precolonial History.* London: Longman, 1972.

Needham, D. E., E. K. Mashingaidze, and N. Bhebe. *From Iron Age to Independence: A History of Central Africa.* London: Longman, 1988.

Omer-Cooper, John D. *The Zulu Aftermath: A Nineteenth-Century Revolution in Bantu Africa.* London: Longman, 1966.

Poole, E. H. L. *Native Tribes of the Eastern Province of Northern Rhodesia.* Lusaka, Northern Rhodesia: 1949.

Rennie J. K. "The Ngoni States and European Intrusion." In *The Zambesian Past*, edited by E. Stokes and R. Brown. Manchester: Manchester University Press, 1966.

Roberts, Andrew D. *A History of Zambia*. London: Heinemann, 1976.

Zambia (Northern Rhodesia): British Occupation, Resistance: 1890s

British occupation of Zambia was preceded by the activities of European explorers, hunters, traders, and missionaries. George Westbeech is believed to have been one of the leading white traders who contributed to the founding of the country. He established himself at Pandamatenka, south of Victoria Falls. It is believed that between 1871 and 1876 he exported 30,000 pounds of ivory.

Further, it is surmised that Westbeech introduced the missionaries Francois Coillard and F. C. Arnot to the Lozi chief Lewanika. Another who had great influence in the opening up of Central Africa to other Europeans was the Scottish missionary David Livingstone. In 1851 he crossed the Zambezi River, and by arrangement with a hunter, William Oswel, he reached Bulozi, where he established friendship with the Kololo chief Sebetwane. At the time he decided to concentrate his work on the area north of the Zambezi, making three exploratory journeys into the area between 1851 and 1873; his main aim was to explore the area for later missionary work. It is in this respect that Livingstone is acknowledged to have been more successful as a writer and scientific observer than a missionary. After his death in 1873 at Chitambo in the Bisa area, those who followed in his footsteps put his ideas into practice.

Lewanika's land was brought under colonial rule through the work of concession seekers. In 1889 Henry Ware obtained a concession that he later sold; it was eventually bought by Cecil Rhodes. In 1890 Rhodes sent his agent to obtain the Lochner Concession, which effectively brought Lewanika's kingdom under the domain of the British South Africa Company (BSAC).

While Livingstone was conducting his journeys, the Plymouth Brethren missionary F. S. Arnot was also carrying out his explorations among the Yeke under Chief Msili. Just as Lewanika was impressed by the medical skills of Livingstone, Msili was impressed by the medical skills of Arnot. The Plymouth Brethren Mission therefore established itself in Lake Mwelu area. Another missionary society that established itself during this period was the London Missionary Society. These missionary activities were taking place at a time when European governments were not formally interested in the area.

However, toward the end of the nineteenth century, European powers abandoned the concept of informal empire and formally partitioned Africa into a number of colonial states. It was during this period that the cluster of various tribes in Northern Rhodesia, each with its own history, were brought under one overall authority and the territory became British. British people in South Africa, through the BSAC, gained control of the territory by way of treaties. The BSAC's charter was signed on October 29, 1889, and its field of operation was vaguely defined as "the region of South Africa lying immediately to the north of British Bechuanaland, and to the north and west of the South African Republic, and to the west of the Portuguese Dominions."

Lewanika wanted British protection from both his internal and external adversaries. Chief Khama of the Bamangwato, who had sought and obtained British protection in 1883, largely influenced him in this decision. This wish from protection led Lewanika to sign treaties with the British. In June 1890 he signed the Lochner Concession, which eventually made it possible for the BSAC to acquire Northern Rhodesia. In 1900 the Coryndon Treaty was signed and this, together with previous treaties, was responsible for directly bringing the British government into the affairs of the territory. This marked the beginning of British imperial influence in Buloziland and much of what was known as Northwestern Rhodesia. Colonial occupation of Northwestern Rhodesia was peaceful.

That of Northeastern Rhodesia, however, was not. It was characterized by a number of bloody wars because of resistance from the local people in the area. Apart from this, malaria also frustrated attempts in 1890 and 1892 to set up administrative posts at Chiengi, northwest of Lake Mwelu, and on the Kalungwishi River. Consequently, from 1895 on, Northeastern Rhodesia was administered from Zomba in Nyasaland. The first British administrator was Patrick Forbes, who was succeeded by Robert Codrington.

In the meantime, the Ngoni, Bemba, and Swahili continued to resist colonial occupation. The deployment of British armed forces was necessary to establish colonial rule in the areas they populated. The Bemba gave in more easily than expected after several skirmishes and negotiations. The Ngoni, to the southeast, put up a more determined fight; their warriors were led by Nsingo, Mpezeni's son. Fighting between the Ngoni and the British began in December 1897. Thousands of Ngoni warriors armed with spears proved ineffective against the British soldiers, armed as they were with guns. The resisting Ngoni were brutally subdued, and by January 25, 1898, when Mpezeni's palace was captured, several Ngoni villages had been burned down. Nsingo was tried by a British court-martial. He was found guilty and was executed in front of his warriors. As further punishment, Ngoni herds were taken as loot to cover the expenses of the war. Mpezeni was imprisoned, although he was later released. The defeat of the Ngoni was significant because it allowed the establishment of the capital of Northeastern Rhodesia, which was named Fort Jameson.

Having defeated the people of Northeastern Rhodesia, the British government went ahead to establish actual colonial administration of the territory. As the founders were motivated by external designs, they did not observe any political, economic or social systems as had existed prior to the creation of Northern Rhodesia. Consequently, tribes were split into two or even three by artificial boundaries, which were demarcated to separate one colonial state from another.

BIZECK JUBE PHIRI

See also: **Lewanika I, the Lozi and the BSA Company; Msiri: Yeke Kingdom.**

Further Reading

Barnes, J. A. *Politics in a Changing Society: A Political History of the Fort Jameson Ngoni*. Manchester: Manchester University Press, 1967.

Gann, L. H. *A History of Northern Rhodesia: Early Days to 1953*. London: Chatto and Windus, 1964.

Hall, Richard. *Zambia, 1890–1964: The Colonial Period*. London: Longman, 1976.

Langworthy, Harry W. *Zambia before 1890: Aspects of Precolonial History*. London: Longman, 1972.

Meebelo, Henry S. *Reaction to Colonialism: A Prelude to Independence in Northern Zambia 1893–1939*. Manchester: Manchester University Press, 1971.

Needham, D. E, E. K. Mashingaidze, and N. Bhebe. *From Iron Age to Independence: A History of Central Africa*. London: Longman, 1988.

Oliver, R. A. *Sir Harry Johnston and the Scramble for Africa*. London: Chatto and Windus, 1957.

Zambia (Northern Rhodesia): Colonial Period: Administration, Economy

Northern Rhodesia was occupied by Britain during the late nineteenth-century "Scramble" for Africa. The initial inroads were made in Barotseland, through the 1890 Barotse Concession to Cecil Rhodes's British South Africa Company (BSAC), ostensibly as a representative of Queen Victoria. Through a series of dubious treaties by BSAC representatives, the company gained the rest of Northern Rhodesia by the end of 1891. Although other European powers had by the end of 1891 recognized the BSAC's right to occupy and exploit areas north of the Zambezi River, actual occupation was slow and at times violent. At the request of the BSAC, Northern Rhodesia was split into Northeastern Rhodesia and Northwestern Rhodesia. They were linked to the outside world by different routes and had different origins. From its inception, Northern Rhodesia was conceived as a tropical dependency and not a settler colony.

The imperial government assumed greater powers in Northwestern Rhodesia than it did in Northeastern Rhodesia. This was reflected through the government's control over the appointment of the administrator and his officials. These were appointed by the high commissioner at the BSAC's recommendation and not by the BSAC. By contrast, however, Northeastern Rhodesia was directly under an administrator and officials appointed by the BASC, only subject to approval by the secretary of state. While the administrator of Northeastern Rhodesia could legislate subject to the approval of the commissioner of British Central Africa, his counterpart needed the assent of the high commissioner of South Africa before he could act. In either case, however, the secretary of state retained the right to disallow all legislation while ensuring certain safeguards for Africans. Here we see the idea of the trusteeship policy already in place, though not clearly conceptualized.

Arguably, therefore, the imperial government had considerable powers on paper and in theory. Yet in practice, the imperial government exerted very limited influence. Consequently, the elaborate constitutional differences between Northeastern and Northwestern Rhodesia proved to be of little value. This was largely because there was no close supervision on the ground since the imperial government did not have any officer in Northern Rhodesia until 1911. Furthermore, there was no staff in either Zomba or Pretoria to deal specifically with the affairs of Northern Rhodesia.

Thus, in both Northeastern Rhodesia and Northwestern Rhodesia, the imperial government relied entirely on information supplied by its commissioners, who themselves were preoccupied with the affairs of South Africa and Nyasaland. Decisions were therefore based on reports submitted by the BSAC administrators.

Northern Rhodesia was officially created in 1911, when the separate administrations of Northwestern Rhodesia and Northeastern Rhodesia, first divided by the Kafue River and then by the rail line, were amalgamated by the BSAC to economize. In that year a resident commissioner who was answerable to the high commissioner was appointed. The territory was controlled from Livingstone, near Victoria Falls. The BSAC ruled the vast region with financial support from Cecil Rhodes. However, its powers in Northern Rhodesia were in theory limited because of the negative effects of the Jameson Raid. The Colonial Office felt that it was not advisable to strengthen the company's hand in Northern Rhodesia. In practice, the BSAC local administrator was left with a great deal of independence. This was in part due to the fact that the board of directors in London left much of the administrative work to their administrators. The directors were more concerned with commercial matters and issues affecting the BSAC's land and mineral rights. For almost three decades, therefore, the BSAC, through its man on the spot, ruled Northern Rhodesia for the British Crown.

Initially, the BSAC had little interest in Northern Rhodesia. Despite the company's encouragement to settle white farmers in the territory, it was never envisaged that Northern Rhodesia would develop into a white colony in the same way as in Kenya, where European settlement was adopted as an official colonial policy as early as 1902. Nonetheless, between 1904 and 1911 a total of 159 farms had been established between Kalomo in the south and Broken Hill (Kabwe) in the north. Yet, Northern Rhodesia's original role was to serve as a labor reserve for the developing white areas of Southern Rhodesia and South Africa at least up to the mid-1920s (Henderson 1974).

The BSAC faced financial problems during much of its administration of the territory. To address this problem it introduced a "hut tax" in 1900 and 1904 in Northeastern and Northwestern Rhodesia, respectively. Initially, Africans resisted paying; but because the company involved chiefs in the enforcement and collection of tax, a considerable number of people paid their taxes regularly. It should be pointed out, however, that there existed much coercion in the collection of tax.

By the 1920s Northern Rhodesia's position began to shift from that of a purely black colony like British colonies in West Africa to the uncomfortable middle position of a multiracial colony. It was in this respect that the development of the mining industry led to significant political and administrative changes in Northern Rhodesia. Mining, therefore, became the backbone of Northern Rhodesia's social, economic, and political development.

Northern Rhodesia did not have as much gold as Southern Rhodesia. Instead, it had copper, which was not as valuable, but was soon to become an indispensable raw material in the electrical industry. By 1906 mining was already the most important export industry of the country. Initially, the availability of African cheap labor made mining less expensive. Inexperienced Africans could perform much of the work. Most Africans worked for short periods to earn enough money with which to pay their taxes. Consequently, African labor remained, for the most part, unskilled and marked by low productivity.

Although mining in Northern Rhodesia had started at Broken Hill around the turn of the century and by 1906 minerals had become the colony's chief export, copper production started slowly and only picked up after 1924. The growth of the mining industry coincided with the development of the railway from the south to the north. By 1906 the railway had reached Broken Hill; it linked with the Belgian Congo railway system in 1909. Besides improving mining prospects, the railway also helped in the development of agriculture in the colony. As a result, an increasing number of white immigrants set up farms on land alongside the line of rail.

The discovery of large quantities of copper sulphide ores in 1925 at Ndola in the area just to the south of the Belgian Congo border and the rise in copper prices in the 1920s made investment in the copper mines of Northern Rhodesia economically feasible. Large mining companies were attracted to the area, which developed into Northern Rhodesia's Copperbelt.

Africans near the mines preferred to sell grain to raise tax money instead of working in the mines. To assist the mines acquire the much need African labor, in 1909 taxation was raised from 5s to 10s in the Copperbelt area. Thus, political pressure instead of economic incentives was used to force Africans into wage labor in the mines and elsewhere. Because the system never really benefited Africans, shortage of African labor was a major constraint in the early years.

The demand for skilled and semiskilled labor, with competition from neighboring mines, led to labor stabilization in the Copperbelt. J. W. Davidson (1967) estimates that about 30,000 Africans worked in the mines in 1930. The urbanization process had begun. Women and children were part of the Copperbelt population.

With insufficient white workers in Northern Rhodesia during this period, some African workers had better opportunities in skilled and clerical work than was the case in the countries to the south. African participation on the labor market, both in the mines and in the clerical ranks of the civil service, led to the eventual emergence of a small elite with the education to understand modern political methods, and ready to take a lead in the development of modern African nationalism.

BIZECK JUBE PHIRI

See also: **Livingstone, David; Rhodes, Jameson, and the Seizure of Rhodesia; Zambia (Northern Rhodesia): Copperbelt.**

Further Reading

Davidson, J. W. *The Northern Rhodesia Legislative Council.* London: Faber and Faber, 1967.

Gann, L. H. *The Birth of a Plural Society: The Development of Northern Rhodesia under the British South Africa Company.* Manchester: Manchester University Press, 1958.

———. *A History of Northern Rhodesia: Early Days to 1953.* London: Chatto and Windus, 1964.

Henderson, I. "The Limits of Colonial Power: Race and Labour Problems in Colonial Zambia 1900–1953." *Journal of Imperial and Commonwealth History* 2, no. 3 (1974): 294–307.

Roberts, A. *A History of Zambia*. London: Oxford University Press, 1976.

Vickery, K. P. "Saving Settlers: Maize Control in Northern Rhodesia," *Journal of Southern African Studies* 11, no. 2 (1985): 212–234.

Zambia (Northern Rhodesia): Copperbelt

The Copperbelt's arrival on the international mining scene in the 1920s was facilitated by the growth of the electrical industry and the technical breakthrough of the flotation process (1911), which enabled the relatively low-grade, sulphide ores located in most Copperbelt mines to be refined cheaply. The high development costs involved created a mining system similar to that of the Rand: two large companies, the Anglo-American Corporation (AAC) and Rhodesian (later Roan) Selection Trust, invested sizable amounts of capital, operating several workings and employing a small skilled (white) labor force supervising a large number of unskilled (black) laborers. However, no sooner had the Copperbelt reached full production than the Great Depression caused a collapse in prices, forcing two mines (Nchanga and Mufulira) to close and the laying off of 80 per cent of the black workers.

Although the industry recovered in the later 1930s, black wage levels, reduced in the Depression years, remained low, and helped to contribute to a growing worker consciousness, exemplified in the 1935 and 1940 strikes. In response, white workers, many originally from South Africa, formed their own (Northern Rhodesia) Mineworkers' Union, which the mining companies recognized in 1937. World War II underlined the importance of the Copperbelt as the empire's main producer of a strategically vital metal, and gave the union the opportunity to secure a virtual "closed shop" for its (exclusively white) members, formalized in 1946, and underwritten by a commitment to "the rate for the job." White miners won a de facto system of job reservation that kept Africans out of all skilled and semiskilled jobs, and showed their determination to safeguard this by rejecting all suggestions for African advancement, however gradual.

Following instructions from the government of Clement Attlee, the Lusaka authorities announced in November 1946 that they would help black workers form unions. While in part a reaction to white worker racism, it was more fundamentally an attempt to divert black worker activism away from political channels. The Northern Rhodesia African Mineworkers' Union (AMU), led by Lawrence Katilungu, was set up in 1949 with 19,000 members, and quickly established a pattern that was to be followed up to independence and beyond: pressing the mining companies to release an ever-widening range of jobs to black workers, securing steady increases in pay for all its members, but keeping

out of the political arena. The AMU won several victories, including the progressive dismantling of "job reservation" from 1955 onward, the opening up of apprenticeships to all races (1959), and the ending of the European workers' closed shop in 1963. Unskilled workers also benefited from a steady increase in basic wages, obtained through the measured use of strike action and negotiation, to the point that by 1960, they were significantly higher than those prevailing in the South African mining industry.

The buoyant postwar economy (with the additional boost of the Korean War) enabled the companies to deliver higher wages to both black and white workers, and to open up new mines to supplement the original "big four" (Nkana, Roan Antelope, Mufulira, and Nchanga). Prices dropped by more than half in 1957–1958 (from a £437 per ton peak), but the Vietnam War renewed demand, and the Copperbelt reached its record output (756,000 tons) in 1970. The African union, now the Zambia Mineworkers' Union, continued to win successive pay increases, and was now sufficiently powerful to withstand the ruling party's attempt to install its nominees within the union structure (1965–1966). However, there were already signs of strain in the industry as a whole: production costs were significantly higher than the world average, as a result of high wage levels and transportation costs, aggravated by the effect of the Rhodesian Unilateral Declaration of Independence (UDI).

As part of its move toward state ownership, the government of Kenneth Kaunda secured a 51 per cent stake in the two main mining groups in 1970, and signed a management and sales contract with them (it terminated in 1975). Finally, in 1982, control of the whole industry was vested in one large parastatal concern, Zambia Consolidated Copper Mines (ZCCM), with 60 per cent state share ownership. Nationalization took place in times of mounting difficulty for the industry, beset by extreme price fluctuations in the international market, increasing costs as older mines began to run out, and ever-mounting wage bills. The situation was worsened by the government's habit of treating ZCCM as an apparently limitless source of funds for social expenditure in the country as a whole, to the extent that ZCCM was starved of capital to explore and develop new prospects: by the mid-1990s it had a debt of about $800 million (U.S.).

Meanwhile, a more direct attempt to curb union power was answered by the Copperbelt strike of 1980, which helped to launch the political career of trade union leader Frederick Chiluba, who was to displace Kaunda in the first multiparty election of 1991. By this stage, the industry, like Zambia itself, had reached crisis point, with annual production down to 300,000 tons and some mines operating at a loss. The setting in place of arrangements for a phased privatization of state enterprises became a precondition for foreign donor aid to rescue the Zambian economy, which led to the Chiluba government's approval in principle for ZCCM privatization in 1996. Implementation was delayed for four years as both sides, government and potential investors, tried to get the best deal. Finally, in March 2000, the AAC group returned, at the head of a consortium, Konkola Copper Mines, which undertook to make a substantial investment at Konkola Deep, and provide Zambia with an estimated 30 years' supply of copper; another international group, Mopani Cooper Mines, took over other mines. This restructuring was accompanied by another feature of denationalization, the large-scale shedding of labor, organized in conjunction with the Mineworkers Union of Zambia (as it was now called), and funded by the World Bank. Prospects for the Copperbelt now seem brighter, but privatization has created new problems, preeminently massive unemployment.

MURRAY STEELE

See also: **Mining.**

Further Reading

Berger, Elena. *Labour, Race and Colonial Rule: The Copperbelt from 1924 to Independence.* Manchester: Manchester University Press, 1974.

Burawoy, Michael. *The Colour of Class on the Copper Mines: from African Advancement to Zambianization.* Manchester: Manchester University Press, 1972.

Gupta, Anirudha. "Trade Unionism and Politics on the Copperbelt." In *Politics in Zambia,* edited by William Tordoff. Manchester: Manchester University Press, 1974.

Perrings, Charles. *Black Mineworkers in Central Africa: Industrial Strategies and the Evolution of the African Proletariat in the Copperbelt.* London: Heinemann/New York: Africana Publishing, 1979.

Sklar, Richard. *Corporate Power in an African State: the Political Impact of Multinational Mining Companies in Zambia.* Berkeley and Los Angeles: University of California Press, 1975.

Zambia (Northern Rhodesia): Mineworkers' Strikes: 1935, 1940

Black mineworkers on the Zambian Copperbelt took industrial action in the form of strikes in May 1935 and again in March 1940. It was met with an official resistance that resulted in loss of life and injury at Roan Antelope (Luanshya) in 1935 (with 6 killed, 22 wounded) and Nkana in 1940 (with 13 killed, 71 wounded, of whom 4 died later). The 1935 and 1940 strikes, taking place in what was then the periphery of the southern African industrial system, formed an important landmark in imperial labor history. They also contributed to a growing awareness of colonial issues in Britain that ultimately led to the postwar Labour Party government

placing emphasis on the economic and social advancement of the African colonies.

The Copperbelt mines (Nkana, Mufulira, Roan Antelope, and Nchanga) developed at spectacular speed from 1926 on. By September 1930, nearly 32,000 black workers were employed on all mining operations in Northern Rhodesia (Zambia), with the overwhelming majority at these four mines. The Bemba, from Zambia's Northern Province, made up the largest contingent of the workforce, and were to provide much of the leadership in both strikes. The concentration of so many miners working for common employers in what amounted to "company towns" and the previous industrial experience of a substantial part of that labor force in other territories such as Southern Rhodesia (Zimbabwe), South Africa, and the Belgian Congo (Democratic Republic of the Congo) led to an equally spectacular growth of a worker consciousness, culminating in an embryonic trade union leadership that, prior to the 1940 strike, put forward wage demands on behalf of fellow workers.

Sudden changes in economic circumstances provided the spark that led to strike action. In 1935, it was the government decision to raise the level of "native tax" on the Copperbelt from 12s 6d to 15s per annum. The 1940 strike was caused by the failure of wage levels to match wartime price inflation, influenced by the success gained by white miners in their own industrial action earlier that month.

But beneath these immediate causes lay deeper, more structural factors. First, the steep differentials between white and black mineworkers, with the lowest-paid white worker earning £1 per shift in 1940, and black underground workers starting at 22s 6d per ticket (= 30 shifts, equivalent to six weeks' work), just prior to the 1940 strike, was a key factor. Second, the steady imposition of a de facto industrial color bar that progressively shut black mineworkers out of skilled and many semiskilled jobs effectively reserved for whites played a role. By the end of World War II, the Copperbelt had developed many of the racially restrictive employment practices of the South African Rand. Third, there was the stagnation of basic wage levels for black workers, even after the postdepression recovery: the 2s 6d per ticket cost of living increase conceded by the mining companies just prior to the 1940 strike was the first increase to black pay scales since 1932. Fourth, working conditions in the mainly underground Copperbelt mines were appalling, with high incidence of silica-based diseases. Living conditions for single men were cramped, very basic, and uncomfortable. Finally, physical abuse took place both in the workplace and the mine compounds; one instance, reported by the Russell Commission appointed after the 1935 strike, involved a compound manager who habitually "boxed" Africans' ears.

As a strike notice posted at Nkana put it,

> Know how they cause us to suffer, they cheat us for money, they arrest us for loafing, they persecute us and put us in gaol for tax. . . . See how we suffer with the work and how we are continually reviled and beaten underground. Many brothers of us die for 22s 6d, is this money that we should lose our lives for?

The colonial state chose to highlight a cause that it believed was central to the 1935 strike: the assumed "detribalization" of black workers who had been permitted to live for long unbroken periods in urban areas. Influenced by contemporary social anthropologists and the practice of "indirect rule" in British tropical Africa, government officials called for the compulsory repatriation of mineworkers every 18 to 24 months to prevent what they perceived to be the breakdown of wholesome and necessary tribal sanctions that included, preeminently, the authority of chiefs as traditional leaders over the younger generation of migrant laborers. They contended that unless such remedial action was taken, the 1935 strike was likely to be the first in a mounting wave of unrest, with the certainty of further violence.

However, the government's stance was dictated by other, less altruistic, considerations: a desire to improve tax collections in rural areas; the fear that a large stabilized urban population might be infected by the type of industrial activism that had been a feature of South African life in the 1920s; and the determination, shared by mining company officials, that the bulk of black social welfare costs should be borne by the "tribal system," not the modern sector. The government's hostility to black labor stabilization effectively led to its abdication from its possible role as an agent of social and economic improvement until after World War II, when indirect rule policies were eventually abandoned. By this stage, white mineworkers had taken advantage of the war situation to build up a position of considerable privilege within the industry, frustrating attempts to secure African advancement until the later 1950s.

Although the 1935 and 1940 strikes failed, they were harbingers of future industrial activism in the 1950s and 1960s, when the African Mineworkers' Union, led by Lawrence Katilungu and John Chisata, won significant reward for their members. By the time Zambia won its independence in 1964, they had become some of the most highly paid black industrial workers in the entire continent.

MURRAY STEELE

See also: **Labor, Migrant; Mining.**

Further Reading

Berger, Elena L. *Labour, Race, and Colonial Rule: The Copperbelt from 1924 to Independence.* Oxford: Clarendon Press, 1974.

Northern Rhodesia Government, *Report of the Commission Appointed to Inquire into the Disturbances in the Copperbelt of Northern Rhodesia.* Lusaka, Northern Rhodesia, 1941.

Perrings, Charles. *Black Mineworkers in Central Africa: Industrial Strategies and the Evolution of the African Proletariat in the Copperbelt.* London: Heinemann/New York: Africana Publishing, 1979.

Roberts, Andrew. *A History of Zambia.* London: Heinemann/New York: Africana Publishing, 1976.

United Kingdom Government, *Report of the Commission Appointed to Enquire into the Disturbances in the Copperbelt, Northern Rhodesia.* London, 1935.

Zambia (Northern Rhodesia): Federation, 1953–1963

The Central African Federation, also known as the Federation of Rhodesia and Nyasaland, was a semiautonomous British dependency created in October 1953 amid African opposition. It came into being after many years of campaigning by Europeans in the self-governing colony of Southern Rhodesia (Zimbabwe), and the protectorates of Northern Rhodesia (Zambia), and Nyasaland (Malawi). Settlers in Southern Rhodesia were attracted by the copper wealth of the north, while settlers in Northern Rhodesia and Nyasaland sought increased security by associating with the settlers in Southern Rhodesia. In Northern Rhodesia, Sir Roy Welensky was the key player, while in Southern Rhodesia Godfrey Huggins was the major player in the establishment of the federation.

The federation was ruled through an act passed by the British Parliament in May 1953 and approved by Queen Elizabeth I on August 1, 1953. The federal parliament was based in Salisbury (Harare), in Southern Rhodesia, and was headed by a prime minister. Each of the three members had it own legislatures.

The idea of federation or amalgamation in British Central Africa was as old as Rhodesia itself. It was the protectorate status of Northern Rhodesia and Nyasaland that proved to be the stumbling block in its establishment. The British South Africa Company had articulated the economic advantages of contiguous territorial expansion as early as 1905 when the company sought permission to amalgamate Northwestern and Northeastern Rhodesia. This request was not granted until 1911, when both the Colonial Office and the paramount chief of the Lozi (particularly the latter) accepted the company's assurances that the Barotse Valley would be reserved against white settlement. There is a sense, therefore, that the Colonial Office established a tradition of consulting (however defined) the indigenous community before granting requests by the local settler administration.

The federation was a Colonial Office attempt to give self-government to the local people at a time when white settlers were calling for self-government while maintaining a limited measure of political control. Africans had learned through experience that a settler dominated-federation would not be in their best interests. Consequently, African chiefs joined modern nationalists in opposing federation, and on April 20, 1953, sent a petition to the British government. Federation was unacceptable to both African chiefs and modern nationalists. Africans nationalists also petitioned the secretary general of the United Nations over federation. Yet despite these protests and petitions by Africans, federation was imposed on the three British territories.

The British government ignored African opposition, and imposed federation under the belief that federation would be economically beneficial to both whites and Africans. The British government was more concerned with economic interests, and therefore, ignored the political injustice that federation would bring to the larger population of the region. While federation brought economic growth in the three territories, and lured many Europeans overseas to settle and invest in various enterprises, the economic well-being of Africans only improved marginally.

Because the federal system heavily benefited Southern Rhodesia and the policy of partnership appeared to undermine African political interest, Africans continued to oppose federation and worked hard to see it dismantled. Nationalists in Zambia continued to seek ways to secede from the federation; this opposition persisted throughout its life. In view of this opposition, the Monckton Commission noted that despite economic advantages, the political aspirations of Africans were not met. The future of the federation was seriously in question.

By January 1960, when Kenneth Kaunda was released from jail, the British government had realized that there would have to be rapid constitutional advance in Northern Rhodesia. It also seemed increasingly doubtful whether the federation could be held together. African pressure against it was rising fast in Northern Rhodesia and Nyasaland. In southern Rhodesia, where many Europeans had always opposed any form of union with the north, there was growing white support for the Dominion Party, which aimed at a fully independent Southern Rhodesia. In Northern Rhodesia, there were powerful economic reasons why at least the more farsighted Europeans were ready to see the end of federation.

On September 28, 1960, Iain Macleod, the colonial secretary, undoubtedly influenced by the Monckton Report, announced that constitution changes were planned for Zambia. The Macleod announcement was a landmark in Zambian history. For the first time, African pressure had scored a political victory over the white settler population. The country had taken a further step toward independence.

In December 1960 a conference was held, but no agreement was reached. There were further conferences in 1961. The Colonial Office proposed a constitution for Northern Rhodesia that would make possible an African majority in the Legislative Council, even though this was bound to lead before long to Northern Rhodesia's seceding from the federation. Britain, under pressure from the federal prime minister, Sir Roy Welensky, revised this plan in favor of the Europeans. This angered the United National Independence Party (UNIP), which staged a campaign of civil disobedience throughout the northern and eastern Provinces. The campaign involved a good deal of violence against government property rather than Europeans. In 1962, the constitution was revised once again, and this time UNIP agreed to participate. It was under this new constitution that elections were held in November 1962. The United Federal Party (UFP) won 15 seats, and the UNIP 14 seats. In a by-election held soon afterward in an effort to fill some more of the national seats, the UFP total rose to 16. Throughout November 1962, both the UFP and UNIP courted the African National Congress (ANC), which had acquired seven seats. In the end, ANC decided to form a coalition with UNIP.

During 1963, there were further negotiations in Northern Rhodesia toward independence. In July 1963 talks began that led to the acceptance of a constitution that would grant the country independence under a prime minister, cabinet, and a parliament of 75 members. On December 31, 1963, the federation was formally ended. In January 1964, there were elections, in which the UNIP won 55 seats, the ANC 10 seats, and the National Progress Party (the new name for the UFP) 10 seats. The UNIP ascended to power, with Kaunda becoming the first prime minister on January 23, 1964. On October 24, 1964, Zambia became a republic within the British Commonwealth.

BIZECK JUBE PHIRI

See also: **Malawi (Nyasaland): Colonial Period: Federation; Welensky, Roy; Zimbabwe (Southern Rhodesia): Federation.**

Further Reading

Franklin, Harry. *Unholy Wedlock: The Failure of the Central African Federation.* London: George Allen and Unwin, 1963.
Gifford, Prosser. "Misconceived Dominion: The Creation and Disintegration of Federation in British Central Africa." In

Transfer of Power in Africa: Decolonization, 1940–1960, edited by Prosser Gifford and William R. Louis. New Haven, Conn.: Yale University Press, 1982.

Hyam, Ronald. "The Geopolitical Origins of the Central African Federation: Britain, Rhodesia and South Africa, 1948–1953" *Historical Journal* 30, no. 1 (1987): 145–172.

Phiri, Bizeck J. "The Capricorn Africa Society Revisited: The Role and Impact of 'Liberalism' in Zambia's Colonial History 1949–1963." *International Journal of African Historical Studies* 24, no. 1 (1991): 65–83.

Rotberg, Robert I. *The Rise of Nationalism in Central Africa: The Making of Malawi and Zambia, 1873–1964*. Cambridge, Mass.: Harvard University Press. 1965.

Virmani, K. K. *Zambia: The Dawn of Freedom*. Delhi: Kalinga, 1989.

Wood, J. R. T. *The Welensky Papers: A History of the Federation of Rhodesia and Nyasaland*. Oxford: Oxford University Press, 1984.

Zambia: Nationalism, Independence

Protest against colonialism in Zambia did not have a definitive starting point, because colonial rule was imposed gradually. Early African resistance to colonial rule was manifested through resistance to taxation and the demands for wage labor by the colonial government. Other forms of early African resistance were through independent African religious movements, such as the Watchtower movement, especially in the period 1918–1935. Welfare Societies and labor organizations also took modern and political outlook. On the Copperbelt and in Broken Hill (now Kabwe), labor formed a nucleus of protest against some of the features of colonial rule. African miners on the Copperbelt twice challenged colonial authority. In 1935 and 1940, Africans went on strike over wages; in 1949, the African Mineworkers' Union (AMU) was formed with Lawrence Katilungu as its leader.

Zambian nationalism suffered from lack of educated leadership in the early years because the colonial government neglected African education. (Munali School, which provided secondary education, was only founded in 1939.) Because of this, Europeans dominated politics in Northern Rhodesia until the late 1940s. They first demanded a share in the territory's government in 1910. An order in council in 1924 established Northern Rhodesia's first Legislative Council, with nine officials and five unofficial elected members who were all Europeans. The order also established an Executive Council. Although officials controlled both councils, settlers and officials alike assumed that Northern Rhodesia was going to receive responsible government.

Modern nationalism was ushered in by the formation of the Federation of African Societies at Broken Hill (now Kabwe) in 1946, with Dauti Yamba as president. This was a direct response to European challenge in politics, and settler drive for political power. African

Welfare Societies in Zambia started in 1912, when Donald Siwale and David Kaunda, the father of Zambia's first president, formed the Mwenzo Welfare Association to bring African views to the attention of the government. In 1914, when World War I broke out, there was fighting with the Germans near the border. Mwenzo Mission, established by the Scottish Livingstonia Mission in 1894, was evacuated, and the Mwenzo Welfare Association was disbanded. It was revived in 1923, only to fail once again in 1927. However, between 1929 and 1931, African Welfare Societies were formed in several towns along the rail line. From 1942, African Welfare Society branches were formed in the mining towns on the Copperbelt.

In 1948, the Federation of Welfare Societies changed its name to the Northern Rhodesia African Congress (NRAC); Godwin Mbikusita Lewanika was elected its first president. For the next few years, the NRAC was a very moderate body; it affirmed its loyalty to the British Crown and its officials and very politely asked for some minor reforms. The NRAC even tried to establish good relations with the government and European settlers, but this achieved very little and did not win the NRAC government recognition. In these first few years, the NRAC mainly represented the African elite and had nothing to do with the masses.

From 1948 to 1951, the NRAC began to oppose the scheme for a federation of the Rhodesias and Nyasaland, first mentioned in October 1948 at a meeting of Northern and Southern Rhodesia white settler politicians. It was further discussed in February 1949, at a secret meeting of white settler representatives of the three territories at Victoria Falls, under the chairmanship of Sir Miles Thomas. The meeting unanimously passed a resolution in favor of federation, but the resolution marked the start of a period of controversy in all the Central African territories. In spite of African opposition to federation, the Conservative Party (which came to power in Britain in October 1951) created the Federation of Rhodesia and Nyasaland in October 1953.

In July 1951 Harry Mwaanga Nkumbula succeeded Lewanika as president of the NRAC, which changed to the Northern Rhodesia African National Congress (ANC). Under Nkumbula the ANC grew into a large organization covering the country and commanding great support. Many members of the AMU supported the ANC, which had taken an active part in opposing the introduction of the federation, but the African trade unions did not become subordinate to the ANC. This was shown by the fact that when Nkumbula called for a two-day period of national prayer to fall on April 1–2, 1953, to show opposition to federation and the strength and unity of the ANC, the leader of the AMU, Katilungu, did not cooperate and refused to allow

African miners to observe these days by staying away from work. The failure of the plan for national prayer, and the introduction of the federation discredited the ANC, and affected the growth of African nationalism in Zambia.

The ANC temporarily lost political direction. This led to the rapid growth between 1954 and 1958 of a new religious movement in the Northern Province, the Lumpa Church, which was founded by Alice Mulenga Lenshina, who was more concerned with eradicating witchcraft than with federation. The ANC was also weakened by its disagreements with the AMU. By 1958, however, the ANC was revived, partly as a response to the Benson Constitution (named after Arthur Benson, then governor of Northern Rhodesia). It provided for fairly radical change. Nkumbula agreed to take part in elections to be held under this constitution, but radicals in the ANC opposed him. Consequently, the ANC split in 1958. The Zambia African National Congress (ZANC) was formed on October 24, 1958, with Kenneth Kaunda (who had been general secretary of the ANC) as president. Elections under the Benson Constitution took place in March 1959, but the satisfaction of the white settlers through their own organ, the United Federal Party (UFP) at the curbing of African nationalism was marred by its failure to win any measure of nonwhite support at the polls or an outright majority of the thirty seats in the Legislative Council.

After the ZANC was banned, new political parties were immediately formed to fill the political vacuum. Paul Kalichini formed the African National Independence Party (ANIP), which also joined the United National Freedom Party (UNFP) led by Dixon Konkola in September 1959, to form the United National Independence Party (UNIP). It was also in September 1959 that UNIP held its first party conference at Broken Hill (now Kabwe). Kalichini defeated Solomon Konkola for the presidency during the elections that took place at the conference. The other office bearers were Kalulu as secretary general, Frank Chitambala as assistant secretary general, and Sykes Ndilila as information secretary. Konkola resigned from UNIP after his defeat by Kalichini.

There was considerable rivalry between the ANC and the UNIP during 1960, amid British Prime Minister Harold Macmillan's "wind of change" speech in Cape Town at the end of his African tour, in which he implied that African independence could not be stopped. The Monckton Commission was appointed to review the federation. African nationalists in Northern Rhodesia and Nyasaland boycotted it. Yet it was this commission that recommended the dismantling of the federation.

Conferences and negotiations from 1960 through 1963 would lead the formal dissolution of the federation on December 31, 1963. On October 24, 1964, Zambia became a republic within the British Commonwealth. Kenneth Kaunda became head of state.

BIZECK JUBE PHIRI

See also: **Gore-Browne, Stewart; Kaunda, Kenneth; Nkumbula, Harry Mwaanga.**

Further Reading

Gann, L. H. *The Birth of a Plural Society: The Development of Northern Rhodesia under the British South Africa Company, 1894–1914.* Manchester: Manchester University Press, 1958.

———. *A History of Northern Rhodesia: Early Days to 1953.* London: Chatto and Windus, 1964.

Hall, R. *Zambia 1890–1964: The Colonial Period.* London: Longman, 1976.

Mulford, David C. *The Northern Rhodesian General Election, 1962.* Nairobi: Oxford University Press, 1964.

———. *Zambia: The Politics of Independence 1957–64.* London: Oxford University Press, 1967.

Roberts, Andrew. *A History of Zambia.* London: Heinemann, 1976.

Sikalumbi, Wittington K. *Before UNIP: A History.* Lusaka, Zambia: NECZAM, 1977.

Tordoff, William (ed.). *Politics in Zambia.* Manchester: Manchester University Press, 1974.

Zambia: Religious Movements

The history of Zambia's religious movements is closely linked to that of the country's political struggles. In the last years of the nineteenth century, the direct challenge to colonial rule fizzled out and the new regime of Christianity, British South Africa Company (BSAC) rule, tax collection, and migrant labor had taken root. Once-mighty village despots, kings, and empire builders were reduced to junior partners of the colonial state. Most historians agree that taxation was imposed not only to raise government revenue for financing the administration of the colony but to force subsistence farmers into wage labor. When people could sell cattle or some other commodity they avoided wage labor, but for the great majority, taxes could only be paid after working for the Europeans, who needed cheap labor to transport their goods, build telegraph lines and roads, and work on the farms and in the mines. Forced labor and taxation were two of the main features of colonial rule that provoked the anger of the Africans. The other was the Europeans' irresponsible attitude toward witchcraft.

Witchcraft

When the colonial authorities imposed their modernist view of witchcraft on the society and declared it a mere superstition while at the same time outlawing the construction of new villages, they must have appeared thoroughly cruel in the eyes of their bewildered colonial subjects. After all, how could the Europeans say witchcraft did not exist when their own Bible said it did? Why did the colonial authorities punish the accuser/victim while protecting those accused of witchcraft? How could the Europeans fail to see that many of the chemicals they introduced were potent instruments of witchcraft and sorcery? These questions have still not been addressed, as the postcolonial state has retained the same legal framework on witchcraft matters as its colonial predecessor. Generally, witchcraft movements have blossomed during periods of crisis.

During the influenza, rinderpest, and sleeping sickness epidemics; World War I; and the mass unemployment and HIV/AIDS pandemic of the 1990s traditional healers and witch finders have tended to become more active than usual.

The first witchcraft eradication movement to attract the attention of the colonial authorities was the *mcape*. Coming close on the heels of the 1930 Great Depression and 1933 crop failure caused by drought and locusts, the mcape found an eager audience wherever they went in northeastern parts of Zambia. Their use of Christian notions of purification and resurrection earned them the title "modern witch finders." The desire to bring harmony to a society ravaged by illness, political oppression, and economic crises by religious means is an ever-present one: only the methods, sects, and cults change.

The Watchtower

Although Africans had always been migrants (as witnessed by the movement of various groups across central Africa), labor migration was an entirely new experience that removed young men from their rigidly controlled villages and brought them into contact with Europeans, Africans from other countries and introduced them to the hardships of colonial capitalism, as well as the politics of liberation.

The Scottish missionaries who were based at Mwenzo opposed the mistreatment of the local population at the hands of the BSAC officials. Mission schools trained many of the leaders of the anticolonial nationalist movement that led the country to independence. Initial attempts to mobilize against British rule, however, were not always well organized. Mission-educated men were the most frustrated colonial subjects when they discovered that their knowledge of the Bible, English, or industrial skills did not win them respect, as the colonial society in which they lived and worked was inherently racist.

Between 1914 and 1918, labor migrants who had come into contact with the ideas of the millenarian Watchtower Bible and Tract Society in South Africa and Southern Rhodesia organized what was the first religious opposition to colonial rule in northeastern Rhodesia. Although they used the tracts of the American sect operating from Cape Town, the latter disowned it and preferred to work only with its European followers.

The war against the Germans in Tanganyika provided an eager audience for the message of apocalyptic change. The leader of the Watchtower movement, Hanoc Shindano, preached a message centered on berating the Europeans for their sins and their refusal to share the goodness of the earth with Africans. After the Watchtower had stirred rebellion among the population, the colonial authorities arrested the leaders and sentenced them to short terms in jail. Other preachers took their place, however, and the anticolonial preaching continued as an oppressed people eagerly accepted the message of redemption, believing that Africans in America would return to liberate them from bondage, as the preachers promised.

In 1935, the violent strikes on the Copperbelt region were blamed on the influence of the Watchtower, and the sale of Watchtower tracts was banned until 1946. The movement's message of liberation continued to have the support of many Africans. Only with a stabilization of colonial rule and the improvement in workers' lives after World War II was the militant African faction brought under the control of the main American body.

Tomo Nyirenda and the Mwanalesa Movement

The leader of the Mwanalesa antiwitchcraft movement was a man from Nyasaland called Tomo Nyirenda. *Mwana Lesa* literally means "child of God," and clearly reflects Nyirenda's messianic claims. After acquiring knowledge of the basic Watchtower teachings anticipating the end of the world and the establishment of a new Kingdom, Nyirenda started preaching and conducting baptisms, promising his converts that the baptized would never die. He also used baptism to identify witches; those who floated or could not be completely immersed were deemed witches.

Nyirenda's desire to rid Lala country (Mkushi and Serenje) of witchcraft was not unusual. However, his campaign was marked by its extreme violence. Whereas others cleansed witches, Nyirenda killed them because, he believed, "God is coming and before God comes the witches must be killed to keep the villages clean" (quoted in Rotberg 1965, 145). In 1925, after he had killed 16 people in Mkushi, he moved to Ndola, where he killed 6 more. He then crossed the border into Katanga, where he killed over a hundred "witches." Escaping the wrath of the Belgian authorities, Nyirenda crossed back into Northern Rhodesia, but was eventually arrested and executed.

Not all African Christianities or religious nationalists were concerned with witchcraft. In the urban areas, especially in the Copperbelt, Ernest Muwamba founded the Union Church in the 1920s not as an act of religious nationalism, but simply because there were no missionaries in the Copperbelt at that time. The Nyasa elite were prominent in both church and welfare association matters and established cooperative relationship between the Union Church and several local Protestant missions. The Union Church would eventually develop into the United Church of Zambia.

In the late 1990s, new religious groups, often influenced by American television evangelists and preaching prosperity theology, grew increasingly popular in urban areas. These Christians were influential during the the administration of Frederick Chiluba (1991–2001), at which time the Zambian constitution was amended to declare Zambia a "Christian nation."

OWEN SICHONE

See also: **Lenshina, Alice; Religion, Colonial Africa: Independent, Millenarian/Syncretic Churches.**

Further Reading

Meebelo, Henry S. *Reaction to Colonialism: A Prelude to the Politics of Independence in Northern Zambia, 1893–1953.* Manchester: Manchester University Press, 1971.

Roberts, Andrew. *A History of Zambia.* London: Heinemann, 1981.

Rotberg, Robert I. *The Rise of Nationalism in Central Africa: The Making of Malawi and Zambia 1873–1964.* Cambridge, Mass.: Harvard University Press, 1965.

Willis, A. J. *An Introduction to the History of Central Africa.* London: Oxford University Press, 1964.

Zambia: First Republic, 1964–1972: Development and Politics

Zambia had a mixed inheritance upon independence in October 1964. In terms of skilled personnel, whether in terms of formal education and training or senior managerial and political experience, the inheritance was very poor. There were fewer than 1,200 people who had attended secondary school, and only about 100 university graduates. The country may have been colonized in a political sense by Britain, but commercially and economically it had been colonized from the south. There was, therefore, a rigid color bar in the economic sector prior to independence, even in the mines, which provided more than 90 per cent of foreign exchange earnings.

In financial terms, in contrast, independence coincided with a remarkable increase in the availability of both foreign exchange and government revenue. The price of copper doubled between 1963 and 1966, and stayed at historically high levels because of need for it during the Vietnam War and other external factors favorable to Zambia. The new government acquired the mineral royalties from the British South Africa Company for an *ex gratia* payment of £2 million a few hours before independence, having offered £50 million only a year previously. (Research revealed that the company's legal claim to the royalties was dubious). The royalty formula was based on the price of copper, and had therefore risen to a large annual payment abroad, amounting to 16 per cent of government revenue in 1965. Second, a large part of the tax on copper profits that accrued domestically had been spent by the government of the Federation of Rhodesia and Nyasaland in Southern Rhodesia. This outflow ceased when the federation folded in 1963.

Economic management of a mineral boom would have been difficult in any context; in the Zambian case, it was made much more so by circumstances. A year after independence, Southern Rhodesia made a Unilateral Declaration of Independence (UDI). The British government persuaded the new Zambian government to impose sanctions on Southern Rhodesia, arguing that they would only be needed for a few months, and offering to meet the cost to Zambia out of British aid. This promise was not kept, but Zambia did impose sanctions, at great cost to the economy. Within three years, the proportion of imports from Southern Rhodesia was reduced from 40 per cent to 7 per cent, almost all of which was electricity from the jointly owned hydroelectric plant at the Kariba Dam. Because of oil sanctions against Southern Rhodesia, Zambia was forced to import oil products along 1,300 miles of mud road from Tanzania. Perhaps even more serious than the direct financial cost was that the new government had to manage a crisis from an early stage, which made sound and thoughtful economic policies more difficult to implement. The need for crisis management was increased by political problems on Zambia's borders—not just the border with Southern Rhodesia, but also the borders with Angola, the Congo, and Mozambique. These conflicts also generated internal problems; for example, in 1966 it was found that senior members of the Zambian Special Branch were working on behalf of the UDI government.

A positive aspect of the financial boom was that the government had the resources to start redressing the colonial neglect of public services—in particular, that of health and education. The imposition of sanctions against Southern Rhodesia created a high degree of protection in the manufacturing sector. As a result, the sector grew extremely fast, further stimulated by tariff protection. Real gross domestic product, also stimulated by government spending, increased by 55 per cent between 1964 and 1972; less positively, employed increased by only 15 per cent in that same period.

Zambia has been widely accused of mismanaging the copper boom of this period, but the evidence does not support the accusation. The central government budget was in surplus from 1964 to 1966, and was balanced in 1967 (if net government lending is excluded). There was a deficit in 1968, to which the government reacted by reducing its own spending and net lending by 11 per cent in real terms in 1969, which resulted in a budget surplus in that year and in 1970. Only in 1971 and 1972 did substantial budget deficits begin to appear, and yet the foreign exchange reserves continued to increase in terms of the number of months of imports covered (there were 15 months of imports covered in 1972). The available evidence suggests responsible economic management.

During this period the government reacted to the domination of the private sector by foreigners, or by resident ethnic minorities (Asians and whites), by introducing a series of measures to increase Zambia's economic independence. The rhetoric was a mixture of socialism and Zambian humanism, with the goal of the pursuit of economic nationalism present as well. President Kaunda's Mulungushi Speech in 1968 announced the government's intention to acquire 51 per cent of 26 industrial firms. The takeovers were negotiated successfully, without outright conflict with the foreign owners. The government also announced, effective January 1, 1969, that a wide range of trading licenses would be reserved for Zambian citizens.

Later in 1969, in the Matero Speech, the president announced that the government would acquire 51 per cent of the copper mines. Again, this was negotiated, not imposed. The mining takeover had been widely expected, and the ending of uncertainty, combined with the fact that the foreign shareholders regarded the settlement as fair, led to investment plans that would have increased annual production from 750,000 tons to 900,000 tons. Because of a mining disaster in 1970, and a renegotiation of the takeover agreement, the target of 900,000 tons was never reached. Further takeovers followed, together with government investment in a number of new, protected-monopoly manufacturing companies. It was announced in 1970 that the commercial banks would be taking over 51 per cent, but agreement was never reached.

The ruling United National Independence Party (UNIP) won the 1968 general election comfortably, in part assisted by the booming economy. The government dealt with ethnic rivalries with continuing success (in the sense that political stability was maintained) by constantly shuffling senior political and civil service personnel. This "solution" reduced the efficiency of the public sector, however. In 1970, Vice President Simon Kapwepwe started a new party claiming that the northern ethnic groups had been neglected. This

was followed by the declaration of a one-party state in 1972, and the dissolution of the First Republic.

CHARLES HARVEY

See also: **Kaunda, Kenneth; Nkumbula, Harry Mwaanga; Zambia: Second Republic, 1973–1991.**

Further Reading

Bostock, Mark, and Charles Harvey (eds.). *Economic Independence and Zambian Copper: A Case Study of Foreign Investment.* New York: Praeger, 1972.

Burdette, Marcia. *Zambia: Between Two Worlds.* Boulder, Colorado: Westview Press/London: Avebury, 1988.

Elliott, Charles (ed.). *Constraints on the Economic Development of Zambia.* Oxford: Oxford University Press, 1971.

Government of the Republican Zambia. *First National Development Plan 1966–70,* Lusaka: Government Printer, 1966.

International Labour Office (ILO). *Narrowing the Gaps: Planning for Basic Needs and Productive Employment in Zambia,* Addis Ababa, Ethiiopia: ILO/JASPA, 1977.

Roberts, Andrew. *A History of Zambia.* London: Heinemann, 1977.

Tordoff, William (ed.). *Politics in Zambia.* Manchester: Manchester University Press, 1976.

Zambia: Second Republic, 1973–1991

The "welfare state" that seemed to emerge soon after independence in Zambia quickly turned into a system based on patronage. The ruling elite, far from being in charge of impartial redistribution, promptly became a machine of patronage. The politicoeconomic organization tended toward an extreme concentration of power in the hands of the architects of independence. It aimed at eliminating any potential opposition by way of the systematic co-optation of any leader with some importance, arbitrary arrests, and many other manipulations.

The regime was to set up a one-party state system from the first of January 1973, for "peace, progress, and stability." President Kenneth Kaunda's prerogatives became so extended that, for the most part, Zambian political life during this period was organized from the presidential palace. Kaunda transformed himself into an autocrat able to monopolize the distribution of the main resources; he incarnated both the supreme head whose munificence reinforced his legitimacy and the fickle leader with whom it would be particularly advisable not to fall into disgrace.

Many studies emphasize the manifest absence of merit-based criteria in official appointments, which were more than ever linked to loyalty bargaining. Continually increasing the number of his counselors, practicing a subtle game of musical chairs among his ministers so as to master them better, Kaunda asserted himself as the one orchestrating all power relations. Observers from this period consider that qualified political actors easily lost interest in their respective tasks at the head of governmental offices or nationalized companies, obsessed as they were with the factional game and their personal lot. The opposition, or what remained of it, was hardly worthy of credibility insofar as it did not have anything really solid to hand out. Everything seemed connected to the one-party state, of which one had to be a loyal supporter to obtain anything at all.

These dynamics proved to be functional for the stalwarts of the regime but equally for those holding the slightest bit of power, who often acted the role of crucial intermediaries. More precisely, this system was able to last as long as it remained possible to draw from the copper revenue to finance it. But the combination of the drop in prices from 1975 and a tendency to sacrifice economic capital for political favoritism was to gradually ruin Zambia. In spite of a considerable proliferation in governmental bodies, institutionalization was very limited. Relations remained extremely personalized, essentially linked with exchanges, be they of a nepotistic or clientelist nature.

Right to the end, Katinda proved to be little inclined to draw inferences from this alarming spiral. While the country's indebtedness reached a disturbing level, for a long time he refused to call into question the subsidy of food products, one of the pillars of his popularity. The malfunctions, which were more and more evident from the beginning of the 1980s, were invariably attributed to the heritage from colonialism and to indiscipline. On the other hand, the purely internal logics of the decline were completely ignored. For many years, Kenneth Kaunda and his lieutenants could ascribe the internal difficulties to hindrances linked to the wars in Rhodesia, Angola, and Mozambique, but the independence of Zimbabwe (in 1980) and the evolution of regional conflicts no longer gave them leave to do it in such a convincing way. The ambiguous relations with South Africa and other neighbors, the pragmatic denial of foreign affairs displayed dogma were also to disconcert quite a number of the regime supporters.

From an ideological point of view, the 1980s were to appear very uncertain, characterized by many steps backward. At one time the president would seem to give in, a little reluctantly, to the neoliberal injunctions of the indispensable donors. At another time he would attack the capitalist structure and claim to be the advocate of scientific socialism (as in 1982), then of a national recovery program (after the 1987 break with the International Monetary Fund). However, with the economic and social situation constantly deteriorating (Zambia had one of the worst growth rates in the world), disillusion increased. The weak institutionalization of political power is the reason why the malcontents tended to personally attack the leaders and their representatives. The trade unions did not hesitate

to denounce the practice of personal enrichment. As early as 1980, the government was compelled to introduce an anticorruption bill to its parliament, but faced with the rise in protests against the one-party state, the regime had to grow tougher while the great dogma did not seem to be respected anymore by its promoters.

Political violence has always prevailed in Northern Rhodesia and then in Zambia, one authoritarian system having succeeded another. However, Zambia was not going to reach the level of atrocity perpetrated by the most woefully bloody dictatorships of the continent. It must nevertheless be emphasized that the practice of torture seemed established under the Second Republic, along with all kinds of repressive practices that became more pronounced as the regime was contested. Generally speaking, the deprivation of freedom to opponents on all sides proved to be a weapon used very much by Kaunda.

Kaunda's downfall was hastened by the extreme crisis of the redistribution system. If a non-negligible fraction of the population had originally benefited from Zainbianization and other such advantages, the combined effect of the fall in revenues, accumulated indebtedness, bad management of resources, and diverse misappropriations ended up ruining the prestige that the regime might have accumulated. A sort of general disillusionment settled in and grew stronger as hospitals lacked medicines and schools fell into decay. Unpaid salaries and retrenchments were synonymous with the rapid deterioration of means of subsistence. Even the purchasing power of those managing to maintain steady employment was brought down to reduced material wealth. A good deal of the population could not afford to eat properly, while the majority of town and city residents were exasperated by the desperately empty stalls and the endless queues that had to be endured in order to obtain food.

While average citizens increasingly resented Kaunda, so did the elite, who were often forced to undergo humiliations by Kaunda so as to retain their position. Although the president tried to divert the anger of the people toward the IMF and World Bank, his decline and overthrow seemed irreversible. Contrary to previous hunger riots that were tied to the doubling of the price of maize in 1990, Kaunda's removal from office was driven by a focused and organized opposition. He fought to retain power, but was forced to make concession after concession under pressure from the populace, finally accepting the principle of multipartyism and free elections. The enormous gatherings of the new Movement for Multiparty Democracy must essentially be interpreted as a sign of exasperation mixed with disproportionate expectations, in line with the frustrations endured.

JEAN-PASCAL DALOZ

See also: **Kaunda, Kenneth; Nkumbula, Harry Mwaanga; Zambia: 1991 to the Present.**

Further Reading

Bratton, Michael. *The Local Politics of Rural Development: Peasant and Party-State in Zambia,* Hanover, N.H.: University Press of New England, 1980.

Burdette, Marcia M. *Zambia: Between Two Worlds*, Boulder, Colo.: Westview Press, 1988.

Chan, Stephen. *Kaunda and Southern Africa: Image and Reality in Foreign Policy*. London: British Academic Press, 1992.

Good, Kenneth. "Debt and the One-Party State in Zambia." *Journal of Modern African Studies* 27, no. 2 (1989): 297–313.

Mwanakatwe, John M. *End of Kaunda Era*, Lusaka, Zambia: Multimedia, 1994.

Osei-Hwedie, Kwaku, and Muna Ndulo (eds.). *Issues in Zambian Development*. Boston: Omenana, 1985.

Tordoff, William (ed.). *Administration in Zambia*. Manchester: Manchester University Press, 1980.

Zambia: 1991 to the Present

Following the peaceful electoral removal of Kenneth Kaunda in 1991, Zambia was commonly viewed as a model of smooth political transition in Africa. The opposition Movement for Multiparty Dernocracy (MMD), let by the trade unionist Frederick Chiluba, had managed successfully to gain wide support from those who were discontented politically or dissatisfied with the economy (and, in particular, food shortages). From the outset, the MMD was a variegated coalition that included landholders and businessmen supporting financial and trading liberalization, intellectuals favoring radical change, the bulk of the trade union movement, young graduates in search of employment, and a large number of former members of the Kaunda regime. It quickly appeared that the 1991 ballot was much more of a referendum on the Kaunda regime's performance after so many years of personal domination, than a reflective adhesion to a precise program.

The clear-cut victory of Chiluba and his MMD gave the victors an imposing legitimacy. Despite dubious dealings during the electoral campaign as well as many controversies relating to the neutrality of the observers, the peaceful and fair nature of the ballot itself was widely welcomed. The electoral verdict was reluctantly accepted by the country's former leader and his supporters, but the fact that he acknowledged the rules of the game and his defeat also gave him back a certain legitimacy (at least from a Western viewpoint). The main strategy of the new regime was to incessantly denounce the defects of the Kaunda era, on which all the ills affecting the country were imputed. Having no links with the former system, president Chiluba made the utmost use of this legitimacy. He knew well how to take advantage of an international context favoring neoliberal values of which he became the advocate. Nevertheless, if the latter could appear to make up a true political resource, they would rapidly prove to be incompatible not only with the populations' aspirations but also with those of Chiluba's own entourage, awaiting immediate spin-offs. The Zambian case very clearly illustrates the contradictions in legitimacy that the actors having advocated democracy, while accepting the structural adjustment, had to face. It was obligatory for them to stake their position of power rather quickly, when the drastic measures to be taken for the improvement of the economy could only be unpopular and a potential source of delegitimation. Torn between the necessity to meet the donors' expectations on which his position depended and that of ensuring his political survival on a short-term basis (that is to say, his reelection), the new president was obliged to constantly switch from one register to another, not only at the risk of inconsistency but also that of displeasing everybody—especially as the opposition vied in demagogic outbidding.

The sensitive issue of freedom of the press appears as one of the most symptomatic: How could one succeed in reconciling the right to free expression, justly considered as the major achievement of the change in regime, with the need to control newspapers that regularly exposed new scandals? The government was torn between the desire to silence those who systematically discredited them and their fear of giving off an antiliberal image discordant with its proclaimed ideals. One may also question the relation with the opposition. Once he was elected, Chiluba advocated a certain reconciliation, even if his argumentation remained deliberately hostile to his predecessor. As the latter's return became increasingly possible, Chiluba was finally to organize Kaunda's disqualification (through constitutional reform) and even his temporary detention.

Furthermore, like those of most other African countries drawing a crucial revenue from a strategic product, many Zambian leaders seemed reluctant to precipitate restructuring in the "red gold" sector of copper (even if some could profit from the privatization). The need for large investments to modernize an obsolete production tool would suppose prompt decisions, but copper represented 90 per cent of the country's jobs and revenues (directly or indirectly) throughout the 1990s.

Outside aid donors deplored the continued presence in government of incompetent or corrupt ministers (some implicated in drug trafficking). Even if Chiluba (who was reelected in 1996) knew for a fact that an enormous amount had been invested in the Zambian experiment and that it could not be totally abandoned, he badly needed foreign financial aid and would not be able to displease those spending it. But the rifts within the coalition in power, the prominence in Chiluba's regime of "recycled" elites, and the use of well-worn governing practices to ensure a continuous hold on power cast doubt on the reformist potential of the administration. In 2001, Chiluba's vice president, Levy Mwanawasa, was elected as the new president. He removed Chiluba's aids from their government posts, and approved an investigation into corrupt practices under Chiluba.

JEAN-PASCAL DALOZ

See also: **Kaunda, Kenneth; Zambia (Northern Rhodesia): Copperbelt.**

Further Reading

Bratton, Michael. "Economic Crisis and Political Realignment in Zambia." In *Economic Change and Political Liberalization in Sub-Saharan Africa*, edited by Jennifer A. Widner. Baltimore: Johns Hopkins University Press, 1994.

———. "A Focus Group Assessment of Political Attitudes in Zambia." *African Affairs*, no. 93 (1994): 535–563.

Daloz, Jean-Pascal "'Can We Eat Democracy?' Perceptions de la "démocratisation" zambienne dans un quartier populaire de Lusaka." In *Transitions démocratiques africaines dynamiques et contraintes*, edited by Jean-Pascal Daloz and Patrick Quantin. Paris: Karthala, 1997.

Daloz, Jean-Pascal, and John D. Chileshe (eds.). *La Zambie contemporaine*, Paris: Karthala, 1996.

Kees Van Donge, Jan. "Reflections on Donnors, Opposition and Popular Will in the 1996 Zambian General Elections." *Journal of Modem African Studies* 36, no. 1 (1998): 71.

Sichone, Owen, and Bornwell C. Chiluko (eds.). *Democracy in Zambia: Challenges for the Third Republic*. Harare: SAPES, 1996.

Zanzibar (City)

The principal port and commercial center of the islands bearing the same name, Zanzibar is situated just off the East African coast. Zanzibar's heyday was in the nineteenth century, when its economic influence extended deep into the heart of the African mainland.

The town originated as a Swahili fishing village in the twelfth century, on the Shangani Peninsula on the west side of Unguja Island. In the mid-sixteenth century it was visited by the Portuguese, who by 1591 had established a base there. Over the following century Zanzibar was governed by local rulers under Portuguese hegemony. During the late seventeenth century it was caught up in Portuguese-Omani rivalry, as a result of which the town itself was twice razed. Zanzibar eventually succumbed to the ascendant Omanis in about 1698. They built a fort on the ruins of the old Portuguese chapel (which remains a prominent landmark to this day) in order to house a small garrison of troops. The indigenous ruler of northern Unguja, Queen Fatuma, was forced into exile until 1709.

Soon after these developments, the town began to grow. Around 1725, Fatuma's successor, Sultan Hassan, remembered as the true founder of Zanzibar, cleared the Shangani Peninsula of bush, thus laying the foundations for its development. Over subsequent years Arab merchants and plantation owners from Pate, and Shatiri Arabs from Mafia, settled there. Buoyed by profits earned from the slave trade to the French plantation islands of Ile-de-France (Mauritius) and Ile Bourbon (Réunion), in the latter half of the eighteenth century the town slowly expanded, though at this time only a handful of the houses were constructed in stone.

By the beginning of the nineteenth century, the value of the East African trade in slaves and ivory had become increasingly apparent to the Busa'idi rulers of Oman. In 1840, this, along with political and strategic considerations, led Sultan Seyyid Said to transfer his capital from Muscat to Zanzibar. The shift coincided with Zanzibar's rise to regional predominance. From its Zanzibar base the Busa'idi dynasty sought to exploit the growing Western demand for tropical products and as such became a major entrepôt. Trading caravans funded and/or led by Zanzibar merchants penetrated the African interior as far inland as present-day Zambia and Congo in search of ivory and slaves. By mid-century, Zanzibar hegemony stretched throughout East Africa as far as Lake Tanganyika, though it was predominantly commercial in form. Annual exports passing through Zanzibar grew from $765,000 worth of goods in 1843 to $3,734,845 in 1864. This consisted mainly of re-export goods from the mainland—principally ivory, but also copal, cowrie, and hides. Meanwhile, in response to growing international demand from the 1820s, Zanzibar Arabs had established clove plantations on Unguja and Pemba, worked by slave labor from the mainland. By 1859, five million pounds of cloves were passing through the port. The mid-nineteenth century was also the time when the East African slave trade reached its peak. In the 1850s and 1860s up to 20,000 slaves arrived in the town annually. The majority of these probably remained on the island, the remainder being exported to plantations on the East African littoral or to India and the Middle East.

The prosperity generated through Zanzibar's role as regional entrepôt, and to a lesser extent as a producer of cloves, was reflected in the town's architecture. The Stone Town was largely a product of this era, as wealthy merchants invested profits in constructing large houses of Arabic design. Their plain facades were embellished by the incorporation of elaborately carved doors, which served to indicate the status of the owner. The Sultans themselves were also great builders—notably Bargash (1870–1888), who built the massive *Beit al-Ajaib*, or House of Wonder (completed

1883), which has dominated the Zanzibar seafront up to the present day.

Zanzibar's rise to prominence attracted other groups to the town, including Indian Muslims. The Indian community grew from just 214 in 1819 to over 3000 in the 1870s. By the late nineteenth century Indian Muslims had largely supplanted Arabs as financiers of the caravan trade to the interior and in the export/import trade. They too plowed profits into the construction of grand houses in the expanding Stone Town; these are characterized by their elaborate wooden balconies and Indian-influenced carved doors. Less wealthy Indians took up residence along the central thoroughfares of the town, living above shops from which they engaged in minor trade.

Another feature of Zanzibar's nineteenth-century development was the emergence of Ng'ambo ("the other side"), which became the principal African residential area. As the Stone Town expanded in midcentury, Africans living to the south of the Shangani Peninsula began building across the creek that divided the peninsula from the island proper. Prior to 1850 Ng'ambo was a small community, comprised predominantly of African slaves, and surrounded by cultivated land. After this it grew rapidly. By 1895 it consisted of 15 *mitaa* (wards), and was home to over 15,000. Slaves had been joined by an equal number of free laborers, and smaller immigrant communities including Indian traders and Malagasy settlers. In 1922 Ng'ambo's population had grown to over twice that of the Stone Town.

By the second half of the nineteenth century there was also an embryonic European community. Diplomatic links with the West had been established as far back as 1837, when the United States appointed a consul to Zanzibar. A British consul followed soon after, and as representative of the principal world power, he exercised considerable influence over the Sultan. From the 1860s explorers such as Richard Francis Burton, James Hanningtton Speke, David Livingstone, and Henry Morton Stanley used the town as a base from which to launch expeditions into the African interior. A decade later the Anglican Universities Mission to Central Africa established their regional headquarters in the town, building a church on the site of the old slave market in 1879. In the following decade, European encroachment on the mainland undermined the regional hegemony of the Sultan. This culminated in the declaration of a British protectorate over Zanzibar in 1890.

The British colonial period was one of relative decline. In 1896 Zanzibar suffered the ignominy of British bombardment as a result of a succession dispute after the death of Sultan Hamid. Meanwhile, as European administrations established themselves on the mainland and modern ports were built there, Zanzibar's importance as regional entrepôt diminished.

A new wharf, constructed in 1929, was reliant on the trade in home-produced cloves and coconut products, and imported goods for the restricted domestic market. In the early colonial period the British constructed a number of large official buildings to grace their new capital, introducing "Saracenic" architectural influences to Zanzibar (the best example of which being the High Court building). They were also responsible for the reclamation of the creek that divided the Stone Town from Ng'ambo, which was completed by 1950. Meanwhile, the town continued to expand. Ng'ambo stretched ever farther west and by the time of independence the total population had grown to almost 80,000.

Independence was conceded by the British in December 1963, when Sultan Jamshid regained sovereignty over the islands. Within a month the sultanate had been overturned and Jamshid sent into exile thanks to an uprising famously led by an itinerant Ugandan, John Okello. The key events of the revolution occurred in the streets of the capital as Okello and his followers successfully besieged the Ziwani, Mtoni, and Malindi police stations. In the wake of the revolution many Arabs, and later Indians, left Zanzibar. Houses in the Stone Town were nationalized by the incoming Afro-Shirazi Party, and were either occupied by officials or left abandoned. Shops closed down and as the area was deserted by its former residents Stone Town fell into decline. Ng'ambo, on the other hand, continued to grow, through the construction of traditional Swahili housing, as well as the ill-conceived erection of huge blocks of flats of East German design at Michenzani in 1972. By 1978 Zanzibar's population had reached 111,000.

In 1988, in an attempt to reverse the decline of Stone Town, it was declared a conservation area by the Zanzibar government. Its conservation and development has been aided by its announcement as a United Nations World Heritage site. More important still has been the growth of private ownership of housing and an increase in commercial activity. In addition, money from tourism—an ever more important source of income—has assisted conservation activities, although the growing number of tourists has also placed strains on the urban infrastructure.

Zanzibar today is a city with architectural riches and a cosmopolitan population that provide a constant reminder of its former importance. It remains a bustling center of regional commerce, and migrants from both the rural areas of Zanzibar as well as farther afield continue to settle in the town. Having weathered the lean postindependence decades, future prospects for the city are now somewhat brighter.

ANDREW BURTON

See also: **Swahili; Zanzibar.**

Further Reading

Burton, Richard Francis. *Zanzibar: City, Island, and Coast.* London: Tinsley Brothers, 1872.

Clayton, A. *The Zanzibar Revolution and its Aftermath.* London: C. Hurst, 1981.

Martin, E. B. *Zanzibar: Tradition and Revolution.* London: Hamish Hamilton, 1978.

Sheriff, A. *Slaves, Spices and Ivory in Zanzibar.* London: James Currey, 1987.

Sheriff, A. (ed.). *The History and Conservation of Zanzibar Stone Town.* London: James Currey, 1995.

Zanzibar: Busaidi Sultanate in East Africa

The origins of the Busaidi sultanate in East Africa predate the sultanate itself. Led by the Ya'rubi imams, the Arabs of Uman shook off control by the Portuguese in 1652 and gradually drove them from all their East African possessions north of Mozambique. Civil wars in Uman gave the Busaidi control over their homeland in 1744. However, opposition to their rule in Uman prevented them from asserting their claims in East Africa throughout the eighteenth century. Coastal peoples under local ruling dynasties exercised almost complete freedom of action without Busaidi interference. Most notable among these local clans were the Mazrui family, who exercised control over Mombasa and surrounding smaller city-states like Vumba. On the northern coast, the Nabahany of Pate rivaled the Mazrui. Only Zanzibar appears to have remained completely loyal to the distant sultans of Uman.

Sayyid Said bin Sultan began avowing Busaidi claims in East Africa in 1813 when, following an invitation from the town elders seeking protection from Mazrui and Nabahany aggression, he succeeded in placing a garrison in Lamu. Pate soon became home to a contingent of the Sultan's loyal Baluchi troops, too, but permanent control over that place and Pemba was not fully resolved in Said's favor until 1822, when the last of the Mazrui and their followers and slaves were driven out. The sultanate did not come formally into existence in East Africa until 1840, the year Said permanently relocated his capital to Muscat to Zanzibar.

As international interest in regional exports developed in the nineteenth century, it was Arab and Indian planters and traders, led by the sultans themselves, who led in linking local economies more closely to international finance and trade. Plantation farming increasingly provided the international market with cloves and grains. At the same time, new trade routes linking the coast to the deep interior brought a host of products like ivory and skins to market. During the decades after Said's move, consequently, Umani influences on East Africans grew in importance and strength.

Underpinning this were noticeable developments in the East African economy. The Sultanate both benefited from and helped foster more intense interaction with, and dependence on, international markets. Subsistence agriculture soon gave way to plantations growing cloves and grains for export. Likewise, international appetites for animal products like iron and skins, as well as local need of slaves for the plantations, opened caravan routes linking the far interior with the coast. In all of this, the sultans led the way. Sayyid Said and his successors maintained extensive plantations and engaged in the caravan trade.

The Busaidi had enemies in East Africa as well as Uman, and their ascendance there did not escape challenges. The Harthi clan of Zanzibar sided with malcontents within the Busaidi family to challenge the sultanate during both Said's and Majid's reigns. The Mazrui were not removed from power in Mombasa until 1837, and they continued making trouble for the Sultans and their British allies long afterward. At Takaungu, Mbarak bin Rashid Mazrui alternately swore allegiance, then rebelled, until Mazrui power was broken by Hamid bin Thuwayn's British-led forces in 1895. In similar fashion, the Nabahany family, long the Sultans of Pate, were driven to the mainland. At Witu, Ahmad Simba Nabahany declared an independent sultanate and, for some time, enjoyed German protection. However, like the Mazrui of Takaungu, the Witu sultanate was crushed finally in 1896.

The fundamental weakness of the sultanate was its reliance on Britain. British-controlled India was Uman's greatest trading partner, and British support for Said against his enemies in Uman and the Gulf enabled him to secure his position there sufficiently to shift his residence to Zanzibar. The British saw the Ba-Saidi as a stabilizing force in the Gulf and East Africa and as a compliant host willing to control the slave trade. For the Busaidi, this support was purchased at the price of growing dependence and a willingness to brook interference from their allies. Treaties gradually restricting slave trafficking were signed in 1822, 1847, and 1873. An 1876 treaty banned all slave trade, and in 1897 a compliant Sultan Hamud bin Muhammad issued a decree making slavery itself illegal in Zanzibar.

Such treaties inevitably worsened relations between the sultans and their Muslim subjects, who resented "infidel" interference. Caught between their subjects and the more powerful British, the sultans had to yield to the latter. Some, like Barghash, Khalifa, and Ali, tried to resist European pressures, and to avoid further concessions. However, a series of occurrences forced them to yield, which further alienated their subjects, and so reinforced their dependence on the British. The crucial role played by British consuls in settling succession disputes was one such occurence. More critical still was the attempt by Khedive Ismail of Egypt to seize East African ports for himself. Only British intervention saved the situation. Finally, open claims to Tanganyika and Witu by the Germans after 1884 forced the sultans to accept British "protection" and to cede Kenya to the British. By the time of the reign of Hamud bin Muhammad, British control was almost absolute. Thereafter, and until Zanzibar achieved independence, the Busaidi sultans ruled under colonial consul generals and residents as little more than figureheads. Independence, once achieved, proved a disaster for the Busaidi: the revolution in 1964 saw the massacre of 5,000 Arabs, and the last sultan, Abdullah bin Khalifa, was forced to flee into exile.

RANDALL L. POUWELS

See also: **Livingstone, David; Malawi: Long-Distance Trade, Nineteenth Century; Slavery, Plantation: East Africa and the Islands.**

Further Reading

Bennett, Norman R. *A History of the Arab State of Zanzibar.* London: Methuen, 1978.
Coupland, Sir Reginald. *The Exploitation of East Africa, 1856–1890.* London: Fisher Unwin, 1934.
Hollingsworth, L. W. *Zanzibar under the Foreign Office.* London: MacMillan, 1952.
Nicholls, Christine. *The Swahili Coast.* New York: Africana, 1971.

Table 1:   The Sultans of Zanzibar

Said b. Sultan	(1806–1856)
Majid b. Said	(1856–1870)
Barghash b. Said	(1870–1888)
Khalifa b. Said	(1888–1890)
Ali b. Said	(1890–1893)
Hamid b. Thuwayn	(1893–1896)
Hamud b. Muhammad	(1896–1902)
Ali b. Hamud	(1902–1911)
Khalifa b. Harub	(1911–1960)
Abdullah b. Khalifa	(1960–1964)

Zanzibar: Trade: Slaves, Ivory

For the last two millennia, the East African coast has been part of a far-flung commercial system spanning vast areas of the Indian Ocean. Until the nineteenth century the role of the coast was confined mainly to trade and was concerned less with the production of goods. The Roman Empire may well have satisfied its demand for ivory partly in eastern Africa, with the assistance of southern Arabian merchants. After the collapse of Rome, China and India emerged as customers for ivory in the seventh century. Exactly when slaves became an essential factor in commerce is not known. Several scholars regard the rebellion of African slaves in Iraq between 868 and 892 as evidence that slaves were already being exported from East Africa at this time; others, however, doubt that these slaves were of East African origin.

Only at the beginning of the eighteenth century did Zanzibar enter the scene as an important trading center with supraregional significance, dealing in ivory from the hinterland; slaves from southern Tanganyika, Malawi, and Mozambique; and gold from Zimbabwe and Mozambique. By this time Oman was starting to replace Portugal as a hegemonic power in this part of the Indian Ocean, and the coastal towns, including Zanzibar, soon came under the control of the Omani rulers. Oman was already a full-fledged mercantile state by around 1700, and slaves were needed for its date plantations and for its army; these were acquired at various towns along the East African coast.

Around 1770, a labor-intensive plantation economy developed in the French possessions Mauritius and Réunion, which led to an unprecedented increase in demand for slaves. The second half of the eighteenth century thus saw the emergence of Zanzibar in particular as a trading center for slaves, though Kilwa and Mozambique Island were the main collecting points for slave transportation from the hinterland. Kilwa lies on the edge of the monsoon area; thus, navigating a large sailing ship there could be difficult at times, so that slaves had to be transported from Kilwa to Zanzibar partly in small boats. At Zanzibar the slaves were exchanged for imported goods, which in turn were redistributed throughout East Africa. The Napoleonic Wars, however, interrupted this lucrative trade. The result was the economic collapse of Oman, so that some of the rich Omani merchants moved to Zanzibar. In 1804 Sayyid Sa'id ascended the throne of Oman, and in the coming years he was forced to confront the strong opposition to slave trade on the part of the British, who represented the new hegemonic power in the region. The British pressure on Sayyid Sa'id resulted in a series of treaties from 1822 on, in which Sa'id agreed first to the restriction and finally to the official abolition of slave trading. The loss of profits from the slave trade forced the Arabs of Zanzibar to develop new sources of income after 1830—notably, the cultivation of cloves on large plantations. This again fueled the demand for slaves, since the plantations' heavy manpower needs could not be met by the recruitment of free laborers alone. Dodging the treaties against slavery, an average of perhaps 10,000 to 15,000 slaves annually were brought to Zanzibar in the 1830s and 1840s, only part of which were meant for export. The demand continued to mount toward the end of the

1850s, in part because the mortality rate among the plantation slaves was very high. The antislavery pressure by the British remained rather ineffective, partly because it was concentrated mainly on the Atlantic slave trade, but probably also because a flourishing and cost-effective clove-raising economy netted the British obvious advantages.

Under Sa'id's successor Majid the slave trade continued to grow between 1859 and 1872, with the import reaching an average of some 20,000 to 25,000 slaves annually. Majid's successor Bargash further encouraged the import of slaves, particularly because of cholera epidemics raging among the slave population. By 1870 the British had brought their antislavery campaign on the Atlantic coast to a successful conclusion and could now turn to the Indian Ocean. The pressure upon Bargash became so strong that by 1877 the slave trade had collapsed, though the most basic need for plantation slaves could still partially be met by smuggling. In 1890 Zanzibar became a British protectorate. The British now had direct influence on the sultan's policy, so that the slave trade was effectively wiped out by the turn of the century.

Before the nineteenth century the main customer for ivory was India, and the demand was relatively light. Only around 1820 did the demand begin to grow, as the prosperous bourgeoisie in the United States and Western Europe came to desire fancy articles made of ivory. The raw material was routed by preference via Zanzibar, where customs duties were kept low. The ivory came from areas controlled by Zanzibar, such as the hinterlands of Mombasa, Lamu, or Kilwa, where it was taken in hand by Arabian middlemen. Increasingly, however, traders of the Nyamwezi tribe began bringing ivory tusks all the way to the coast, which had been hunted particularly around Lakes Victoria and Tanganyika. Ivory from this area was subject to a heavy tax at Zanzibar, so as to encourage Arabian traders to penetrate these territories for themselves and to drive the Nyamwezi away from the ivory trade. Their increasing economic power enabled the Zanzibarians, from the 1860s on, to send well-equipped caravans all the way to Unyamwezi, which ultimately led to their seizing the monopoly on the intermediate trade.

The ivory from Lake Victoria was carried across the Kilimanjaro region to Pangani and Mombasa. Along this route a network of Swahili-Arabian trading posts was established, linked directly with Zanzibar. During the 1870s and 1880s European companies began to appear in the East African interior, and tried to interrupt the supply of ivory to Zanzibar by diverting it to their own trading posts. At the beginning of the 1880s Sultan Bargash had to summon all his influence to prevent Africans and Arabs from selling their ivory to European competitors. What he could not anticipate was the partition of East Africa between Britain and Germany. This meant the end of his control over the ivory transshipment ports and thus the loss of most of his customs revenues.

REINHARD KLEIN-ARENDT

See also: **Livingstone, David; Malawi: Long-Distance Trade, Nineteenth Century; Slavery: East Africa: Eighteenth Century; Slavery, Plantation: East Africa and the Islands; Tanganyika (Tanzania): Nyamwezi and Long-Distance Trade.**

Further Reading

Bennett, Norman R. *A History of the Arab State of Zanzibar.* London: Methuen, 1978.

Cooper, Frederick. *Plantation Slavery on the East Coast of Africa.* New Haven, Conn.: Yale University Press, 1977.

Gray, John Milner. *History of Zanzibar.* London: Oxford University Press, 1962.

Martin, Esmond Bradley, and Chryssee Perry Martin. *Cargoes of the East.* London: Elm Tree, 1978.

Said-Ruete, Rudolph. *Said bin Sultan.* London: Alexander-Ouseley, 1929.

Sheriff, Abdul. *Slaves, Spices and Ivory in Zanzibar: Integration of an East African Commercial Empire into the World Economy, 1770–1873.* London: James Currey, 1987.

Zanzibar: Britain, Germany, "Scramble"

During the first three quarters of the nineteenth century, the peoples of East Africa became more closely linked to the Indian Ocean system of trade. Increasingly, this contact was channeled through Arabs from Oman who were encouraged to settle in Zanzibar by Seyyid Said, who reigned from 1806 to 1856. Financed by Indian capitalists, many became clove plantation owners on Zanzibar and Pemba or began to travel inland for ivory and slaves. By 1870, when Barghash became Sultan, Zanzibar had economic, and even a vague political hegemony over the mainland. The Sultanate itself had come under British Indian sway and then increasingly strong Foreign Office influence. The Consul, John Kirk, was able to persuade Barghash to do what Britain wanted, namely provide reasonable facilities for traders and abolish the slave trade—the latter occurred in 1873. Through Zanzibar, Britain exercised an indirect control over East Africa.

Change came in the late 1870s. Intense interest created by explorers, and the response to Livingstone's death, made the region a theater for a series of missionary and other initiatives from Britain often incompatible with Arab trading activities. Europeans responded to explorers' reports of the Great Lakes region—not least that of King Leopold II of Belgium, who set up the International African Association. This sent several expeditions to East Africa and stimulated initiatives by

German, French, and British "national committees." Meanwhile, Egypt had been trying to extend its trade and control up the Nile Valley to Uganda. Many Africans reacted with new political or economic arrangements. Zanzibar's suzerainty became more difficult to sustain during the rise of the "Scramble."

Late in 1884, Zanzibar's (and therefore Britain's) position was directly challenged when Carl Peters of the German Society for Colonization secured treaties from some African chiefs ceding sovereignty to his society and Germany. Certainly, neither the British nor the German governments were anxious to become directly involved in East Africa in 1884, but the increasing competition on the international scene in the 1880s and 1890s made it difficult for them to disengage. The most obvious victim was likely to be Zanzibar.

For much-debated reasons, German Chancellor Otto von Bismarck was not disposed to leave Britain's position in East Africa unchallenged. On February 25, 1885, he issued the Schutzbrief, accepting the Peters treaties. To British Prime Minister William Gladstone's dismay, certain figures tried to arrange treaties for Britain in the Kilimanjaro area, while Barghash sent expeditions to make Zanzibar's political claims more tangible in mainland areas.

Negotiations in Europe now led Britain, France, and Germany to agree in October 1885 to set up a Delimitation Commission to define Zanzibar's territory on the mainland and therefore, by implication, indicate how much was left for Europeans. The German commissioner's view was the most unfavorable to Zanzibar, but had to be accepted as the minimum agreed. The commission's report provided the basis for the Anglo-German Agreement of November 1886. (France opted to concentrate on Madagascar.) The sultan was accorded a ten-mile-wide strip of territory along the coast. The mainland was divided into spheres for Germany around Witu and south of a line running from near Vanga, around the north side of Kilimanjaro to the east coast of Lake Victoria, and for Britain north of this line as far as Witu.

The 1886 treaty created more problems than it solved. The chartered companies both governments set up to operate in their respective spheres became embroiled in disputes with Africans or Arabs. The purchase and occupation in 1888 of the Sultan's ten-mile strip adjacent to the southern German sphere provoked a major revolt. Italy made claims on the northern coast. Most problematic was the region beyond Lake Victoria that was not covered by the treaty. Egyptian forces cut off near Lake Albert by the Mahdist revolt seemed to offer a tempting piece of ready-made empire. Leopold was now anxious to extend his Congo Free State to the Nile. In Buganda itself, Muslim, Catholic, and Protestant factions vied for control of the state. Farther south

Tippu Tip (Hamed bin Muhammad) had created a trading empire west of Lake Tanganyika linked to, if not really under the control of, Zanzibar. Various expeditions were launched by Europeans anxious to force issues in such areas. The most important of these was the 1886–1889 expedition jointly organized by Leopold, which sent the explorer Henry Morton Stanley to "relieve" Emin Pasha and take over the territories he was assumed to control.

Such expeditions became irrelevant when, following the fall of Bismarck in 1890, Chancellor von Caprivi decided to reach an accommodation with Britain on African questions. Again, official motives have been much debated including whether, for strategic reasons to do with defending Egypt and the Suez Canal, Britain was determined to hold the Nile source area. The new Anglo-German Treaty extended the boundary westward as far as Leopold's territory, so making Uganda a British territory, while Germany gave up any claims to Zanzibar (in return for Heligoland, an island off the Hamburg estuary in the North Sea) or to Witu. Further British arrangements were made with Italy and Portugal in 1891 and details settled with Leopold in 1894. Essentially, however, the whole of East Africa now gained either German or British overlords. In 1894 in Uganda and in 1895 in what is now Kenya, the British government felt obliged to take over direct control from the Chartered Company. Germany had done the same in its sphere in April 1890. Colonial rule, which was to last a mere 70 years, had now begun. It was inaugurated with a period of turmoil as "effective occupation" measures exacerbated the ecological catastrophe. Zanzibar became a British protectorate with an entirely nominal residual sovereignty over the coast strip in the Kenya sector. Now manifested as only a couple of rather insignificant islands in the British Empire, the Sultanate's brief period of great importance was at an end.

ROY BRIDGES

See also: **Berlin West Africa Conference, 1884–1885.**

Further Reading

Bridges, Roy. "Toward the Prelude to the Partition of East Africa." In *Imperialism, Decolonization and Africa*, edited by Roy Bridges. Basingstoke, England: Macmillan, 1999.

Collins, Robert O. "Origins of the Nile Struggle: Anglo-German Negotiations and the Mackinnon Agreement of 1890." In *Britain and Germany in Africa: Imperial Rivalry and Colonial Rule*, edited by Prosser Gifford and Wm. Roger Louis. New Haven, Conn.: Yale University Press, 1967.

Coupland, Reginald. *The Exploitation of East Africa 1856–1890: The Slave Trade and the Scramble.* London: Faber, 1939.

Flint, John E. "The Wider Background to Partition and Colonial Occupation." In *History of East Africa*, edited by Roland Oliver and Gervase Mathew. Oxford: Clarendon Press, 1963.

Galbraith, John S. *Mackinnon and East Africa, 1878–1890: A Study in the "New Imperialism"*. Cambridge: Cambridge University Press, 1972.

Müller, Fritz F. *Deutschland, Zanzibar, Ost-Afrika. Geschichte einer deutscher Kolonialeroberung, 1884–1890*. Berlin, 1959.

Robinson, Ronald E., and John Gallagher with Alice Denny. *Africa and the Victorians*. London: Macmillan, 1961.

Wesseling, H. L. *Divide and Rule: The Partition of Africa, 1880–1914*, translated by Arnold J. Pomerans. Westport, Conn.: Praeger, 1996.

Zanzibar: Colonial Period

Zanzibar was declared a British protectorate in November 1890. This was preceded by an increase in European influence upon the island state, which until then had been governed autocratically by a sultan and an elite, originally of Omani extraction. The island's prosperity resulted first and foremost from the traditional role of Zanzibar as intermediary in the trade for raw materials and slaves from the African mainland, and for luxury goods from overseas. Increasing antislavery pressure on the part of Great Britain in the first half of the nineteenth century impelled the rulers to turn to the cultivation of cloves on large plantations as their main source of income, together with trade in raw materials. The influence of the United States, Great Britain, and France upon Zanzibar was formalized between 1833 and 1844 in "amity and commerce" treaties, which awarded these countries the status of "most-favored nations." The establishment of European consulates followed; these were meant chiefly to safeguard the commercial interests in the region. The new plantation economies on Zanzibar and Pemba, however, had quite the reverse effect of what British antislavery policy had intended. In fact, tens of thousands of slaves were imported annually from the mainland for plantation labor, a practice that was tacitly tolerated by the British, in part because the Royal Navy was underrepresented in East African waters. In 1873, however, the British pushed through an agreement that banned the slave trade within the Sultan's sphere of influence.

Even so, the British hoped to maintain the power of the Sultan, for they regarded the Arabs as the only group able to rule the islands and to guarantee political stability and hence economic prosperity, from which the British of course profited. While stripping the Sultan of his control over foreign relations, they left him sovereignty over home affairs. Already in 1891, however, the British intervened massively in Zanzibarian domestic policy because they had finally come to regard the political system as too corrupt and inefficient. Though the prohibition of slaveholding on Zanzibar and Pemba in April 1897 further weakened the Arab economic position, the British stuck to their plan of integrating the Arabs and Indians, but no other ethnic groups, into the political and administrative system; Indians and Arabs were trained as public employees and obtained important positions. Moreover, the British had formulated the decree of 1897 in favor of the Arab plantation enterprises. Slaves were obliged to sue for their freedom in open court, while slaveholders could claim compensation for the loss in manpower. Since harvesting cloves required a certain degree of training, former slaveholders frequently made efforts to keep their workers by offering them improved working conditions. The British administration, however, despite its demonstrative and vocal antislavery policy, had its eye primarily on productivity and did not stand by the plantation workers.

Economic conditions for the plantation owners deteriorated further at the turn of the century, as the railway construction in Kenya drew away tens of thousands of workers. Starting in 1904–1905, the labor shortage was dealt with by compelling the inhabitants of Zanzibar to work on the plantations. For the British, this forced labor system had not only economic, but also political advantages: they thereby gained firm control over the labor system. Until 1925 the clove exports of Zanzibar and Pemba continued to grow—especially to Europe and the United States, where the useful chemical substance vanillin was distilled from cloves. After 1925, however, the monoculture on the islands was plunged into crisis, as cheaper synthetic substitutes for vanillin were discovered. The worldwide economic depression at the end of the 1920s exacerbated the situation; an attempt to increase the production of copra served only to postpone the catastrophe. The Arab landowners sank ever deeper into debt, while the rural population was impoverished not only through shrinking profits for cloves and copra, but also because, in the years of the export boom, their small fields had literally been squeezed out by the expansion of the plantations. The British administration's more favorable treatment of the Arabs and Indians drove the wedge between them and the African residents deeper and deeper. The Indians were further divided into Muslims and Hindus; the Africans were divided, roughly speaking, into the *Shirazi*, a term often used for the long-established residents of Zanzibar, and the descendants of the former slaves. As late as 1926 the political franchise was granted only to British and Arabs via an Executive Council and a Legislative Council. The British resident, particularly through the Legislative Council, could exercise strong control over the political fate of the islands. Only in the mid-1950s did a reform of the two councils take place. However, for the local political circles, which were becoming increasingly emancipated in the context of the decolonization in Asia and Africa, this reform was not far-reaching enough. Subsequently, political parties were formed. The first was the mainly Arab Zanzibar Nationalist Party (ZNP) in 1955, whose political program was modeled on the Marxist/Pan-Arabist regime in Egypt; the ZNP elected Sheikh Barwani as its leader. In 1957 the more moderate Afro-Shirazi Party (ASP) was founded; their leader was Shaykh Abeid Karume. Subsequently the Zanzibar and Pemba Peoples' Party (ZPPP) splintered off from the ASP. The British finally agreed to free elections for six of the seats in the Legislative Council. The elections took place in July 1957; five seats were won by the ASP, one by the small Muslim League. The ethnic and political hostility among the parties, however, continued to grow, manifesting itself especially in the form of mutual boycotting of the one party by the other.

The elections of January 1961 produced a deadlock, since, of the 22 seats, ASP and ZNP each occupied 11. New elections took place in June, with the ZNP and ZPPP forming an election coalition. Favored by the voting system, this coalition won 13 seats and the ASP only 10, even though the ASP had the most votes. The ASP smelled electoral fraud; turmoil broke out, leaving 68 people dead. The last preindependence elections, which took place in June 1963, confirmed the results of 1961, even though the ASP again topped the list. In December 1963 Zanzibar became independent under a ZNP/ZPPP government.

REINHARD KLEIN-ARENDT

See also: **Tanganyika (Tanzania): Colonial Period, British: "Indirect Rule."**

Further Reading

Ayani, Samuel G. *A History of Zanzibar: A Study in Constitutional Development 1934–1964*. Nairobi: Kenya Literature Bureau, 1983.

Clayton, Anthony. "The General Strike in Zanzibar, 1948." *Journal of African History* 17, no. 3 (1976): 417–434.

Cooper, Frederick. *From Slaves to Squatters: Plantation Labor and Agriculture in Zanzibar and Coastal Kenya, 1890–1925*. New Haven, Connn.: Yale University Press, 1977.

Iliffe, John. "Tanzania under German and British Rule." In *Zamani: A Survey of East African History*, edited by Bethwell A. Ogot and John A. Kieran. Nairobi: East African Literature Bureau/Longmans of Kenya, 1969.

Lofchie, Michael F. *Zanzibar: Background to Revolution*. Princeton, N.J.: Princeton University Press, 1965.

Sheriff, Abdul, and Ed Ferguson (eds.). *Zanzibar under Colonial Rule*. London: James Currey, 1991.

Zanzibar: Revolution and Union (Tanzania)

The revolution in Zanzibar occurred on the night of January 11, 1964, just over a month after the transfer of sovereignty from Britain to an independent Zanzibar ruled by the sultan and an elected government. The revolution was ostensibly led by John Okello, a Ugandan who had arrived in Zanzibar in 1959 via Kenya. In his autobiography, written from a Kenyan prison after the revolution, Okello attributes his action to an internal "voice" that had commanded him, as a Christian, to undertake the mission of freeing Africans from Arab domination.

Arab contact with Zanzibar spans centuries, the first recorded testimony being that of the anonymous Greek traveler who wrote *The Periplus of the Erythrean Sea* (*c.*200CE). Such sustained contact, resulting in trade and intermarriage, forged a bond that was made all the stronger with the introduction of Islam on the East African coast, most probably in the eighth century. Arab and Swahili cultures intermingled, and Islam itself was "Swahilized" and made part of Swahili identity and way of life. But Arabs also ruled the coastline, the latest dynasty being the Busaidi, whose first sultan settled in Zanzibar, establishing it as his capital in 1840. While Arab rule brought prosperity to Zanzibar as a thriving port and commercial center and later as an exporter of cloves, it also set in motion political and socioeconomic trends that eventually proved to be detrimental to its own existence. Not least among these was reliance on slave labor in the plantations; another was the cosmopolitan nature of the city and its attraction to mainland workers and laborers, the bulk of whom were employed on clove plantations, as menials in government departments, as domestic servants in the city, as dock workers, and, perhaps most significant of all, in the police. By 1957, when the first elections took place in Zanzibar, the number of registered, known mainlanders was around 25,000. By that year, too, political consciousness on the islands had begun to freeze racial attitudes. The British had encouraged a division of the people along racial lines, a feature well reflected in the administrative hierarchy, with Europeans at the top, "Arabs" and Indians in the middle, and mainland as well as indigenous Africans at the bottom. Whereas on the mainland (in Tanganyika) political consciousness was clear-cut in its source and direction—as against the British from the African population—the situation on the islands was somewhat more complex. The Sultan, Sayyid Khalifa bin Harub, had been on the throne since 1911. By all accounts, Khalifa was held in genuine affection by the majority of the population; moreover, the sultanate itself had by now become ethnically mixed, like the majority of the so-called Zanzibari Arabs. The identity of the "Arab," the "Swahili," and the "African" was blurred, and yet local politics, overseen by the British, were conducted along ethnic lines. Thus, the Zanzibar Nationalist Party (ZNP) was considered an Arab organ and the Afro-Shirazi Party (ASP) as African, though both had members who belonged to more than one of the island's ethnic groups. The situation became even more complex with the subsequent emergence of two other political parties: the Zanzibar and Pemba People's Party (ZPPP) and the Umma Party; the latter was said to have leftist, communist leanings and support, and was represented as such in the media.

Events between 1957 and 1963 took the islands further down the road of communal divisions. The ASP had emerged relatively strong from the 1957 elections; it repeated its performance in the elections of January 1961, gaining ten seats to the ZNP's nine. But a tie developed when three members of the third party, the ZNNP, divided their support, two for the ZNP and one for the ASP. The British then enacted a new seat in Pemba and fresh elections were held in June 1961. The ZPPP and the ZNP joined forces and had 13 seats between them to ASP's 10 seats. Shamte of the ZNNP became chief minister, a post he retained even after the election of July 1963, when the ASP gained more votes than the other two parties combined (54 per cent of the electorate to 46 per cent) and had 13 seats to the ZNP's 12 and the ZPPP's 6. The latter two formed a coalition government, taking Zanzibar to independence on December 12, 1963. Okello seized power a month later, toppled the government, and dissolved the sultanate.

The events of the day itself only took a few hours to unfold. Three police stations were captured and their arms taken; the radio station was occupied and Okello made a broadcast as "Field Marshall." Shamte resigned as chief minister and was arrested along with other ZNP ministers. The young Sultan Jamshed, who had succeeded his father six months previously, went into exile with his family. Okello initiated and organized a rule of terror, induced through broadcasts. His position, however, became increasingly precarious as his colleagues began to question his dictatorial behavior, the excesses of terror, and, perhaps most significant, his identity. Just over a month after installing himself as field marshal, Okello had to leave the island permanently on February 20, 1964, ousted by the revolutionary government that was itself now settling into power.

The immediate achievement of the revolution was to revamp the social structure of Zanzibar: most of the British, Indians, and Arabs departed. Some Arabs were eligible to take refuge in Oman, where they were well received; in turn, they served Oman by providing a much-needed middle-level human resource that was well educated and had a good command of English. Left on its own, Zanzibar became inward-looking for a time despite its formal link to Tanganyika. On April 26, 1964, Abeid Karume and Julius Nyerere, as presidents of Zanzibar and Tanganyika respectively, signed the Articles of Union, creating the United Republic of Tanzania. Under the agreement, Zanzibar retained its revolutionary government but also participated in the union government, an arrangement that has intermittently been subjected to intense debate in both parts of the union. In proposing the union and in offering to Zanzibar what now seems a generous arrangement, Nyerere's aim might have been to assert the independence—or, one might say, the "African-ness"—of Zanzibar. The islands, however, have had their own ethnic dynamics, forged for centuries, which are accommodated within the larger framework of being "Swahili." In this regard, Anthony Clayton's observations are relevant:

> The Revolution should not be viewed solely in either class or race terms as an African rising against an Arab establishment. It also manifested a striving for a new identity, neither wholly Arab nor wholly African. In this quest for a Zanzibari identity there is a thread of continuity from Sultan Khalifa to Abeid Karume and in some measure even Ali Muhsin. All had very different concepts of what that Zanzibari identity should be, but all can lay some claim to patriotism. (1981, 115)

FAROUK TOPAN

See also: **Nyerere, Julius; Tanganyika (Tanzania): Chama Cha Mapinduzi (CCM), One-Party Politics.**

Further Reading

Clayton, Anthony. *The Zanzibar Revolution and Its Aftermath.* London: C. Hurst, 1981.
Lofchie, Michael F. *Zanzibar: Background to Revolution.* London: OUP, 1965.
Mapuri, Omar R. *Zanzibar: The 1964 Revolution, Achievements and Prospects.* Dar es Salaam: TEMA, 1996.
Martin, E. B. *Zanzibar: Tradition and Revolution.* London: Hamilton, 1978.
Okello, John. *Revolution in Zanzibar.* Nairobi: East African Publishing, 1967.

Zawila: *See* **Sijilmasa, Zawila: Trans-Saharan Trade.**

Zimba: *See* **Maravi: Zimba "Invasions."**

Zimbabwe: Nineteenth Century, Early

The late eighteenth and early nineteenth centuries were a period of decentralization and fragmentation for the mostly Shona-speaking people of the Zimbabwean plateau. The two large states of the area, the Mutapa and Changamire Rozvi, were already in decline. Mutapa, a once centralized state that had suffered under Portuguese exploitation in the seventeenth century, had transformed into a more federal type of government. During the eighteenth century, the Changamire Rozvi, a state that had emerged in the 1680s and 1690s to drive out the Portuguese, had shifted its base to the southwest,

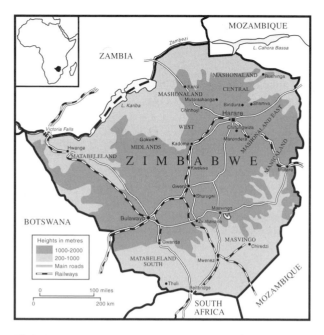

Zimbabwe.

(c.1200–1450), continued to survive in a fragmented form but lost considerable ground to the Njanja, who were moving in from the lower Zambesi Valley. One of the first new and large polities in that area was the Duma Confederation, a loose collection of small states each of which retained considerable autonomy, which had settled the fertile land of the Bikita Highlands. However, Duma quickly came' under pressure from other new Shona-speaking arrivals and began to loose the fringes of its territory. Around 1800, the Tsonga-speaking Hlengwe pushed up the lowland rivers of the southeast and absorbed Shona people already living there. In the far south, at roughly the same time, groups of Venda speakers were crossing north of the Limpopo River to settle on the Zimbabwean Low Veld, and to the southwest, various Sotho people were doing the same thing. The political landscape of the south became dominated by many small chiefdoms; this was reflected by the dropping of the prestigious royal title of *mambo* in favor of the less pretentious *ishe*. This decentralization meant that the large capital town, typical of previous Shona states, became less common in the south. The practice of giving tribute to rulers also declined—except in Duma, where it survived to a limited extent. In addition, the old practice of granting ward to royal wives and sisters was discontinued.

In the early nineteenth century, Shona religion, particularly in the south, began to develop new complexities involving combinations of old and new beliefs. Previously, the Shona had revered ancestral spirits with religious organization centered on the spirits of former rulers. Around the turn of the eighteenth and nineteenth centuries, mediums of spirits (such as Chaminuka, Kaguvi, and Nehanda) not all connected to local ruling lineages, began to gain popularity. This might be explained by the decline of the more powerful royal families. In the eighteenth century, Shona speakers from Rozvi had moved south of the Limpopo River to set up the new Singo state among the Venda. There, the Rozvi belief in a high god called Mwari syncretized with the Venda cave cult of Raluvhimba. In the early nineteenth century, Singo collapsed and its Shona rulers were assimilated into Venda society. Subsequently, when the Venda began to move north, they brought with them a new set of religious beliefs, and the cave shrines of the Matopo Hills were established, which gradually became popular throughout the south and southwest. Additionally, religious organizations based on rain charms began to spread that might have been related to the droughts of the period.

In the early 1830s, a series of invasions by Ngoni speakers from the far south passed through the Zimbabwe plateau area. While the Ngoni of Zwangendaba and others damaged the Rozvi state, they moved north of

conquered the old Torwa state, established a capital at Danangombe, and begun to absorb the local Kalanga people. However, by the 1820s, the Rozvi were loosing territory in their new area to Tswana people arriving from farther to the southwest. In the highlands of the east, the Rozvi withdrawl meant more autonomy for the Manyika Shona who began to move north into the mountainous Nyanga area in the late eighteenth and early nineteenth centuries.

Two major droughts, one from 1795 to 1800 and another from 1824 to 1829, contributed to political instability and disrupted long established trade with the Portuguese posts of Sena and Tete along the Zambezi River. As the Portuguese demand shifted from gold to slaves, the people of the eastern part of what is now Zimbabwe began to experience the horrors of slave raiding. The early nineteenth century saw the decline of the long established tradition of gold mining in the Zimbabwe area. With the decline of central governments, the many small states of the Shona people concentrated primarily on agriculture and some ivory trading.

The movement of the Changamire Rozvi to the southwest resulted in a power vacuum in the south and a subsequent land grab in that area. In the early eighteenth century, many small groups of Karanga Shona had begun to move from their homes in the northeast to establish themselves in the south. Later in the eighteenth century, other Shona peoples from various areas moved into the southern region once controlled by the Rozvi. The old state of Buhera, which might have dated back to the time of Great Zimbabwe the Zambesi in 1835. The Ndebele of Mzilikazi, however, broke Rozvi power by settling in the southwest around the Mutopos in the late 1830s. Rozvi resistance to the expansion of the Ndebele Kingdom continued up to the 1860s. Nguni raiders under Shoshangane, who actually drove out earlier Ngoni intruders under Nxaba, set up a similar state in the eastern highlands in 1836 but after suffering from smallpox they moved to the southeast in 1838 to establish the Gaza state between the Sabi and Limpopo Rivers. Unlike the Ndebele, who absorbed many of the local Kalanga people of the southwest and stayed in that area, the Gaza state could never achieve the same type of stability because it moved around a number of times in the mid- to late nineteenth century.

TIMOTHY J. STAPLETON

See also: **Torwa, Changamire Dombo, and the Rovzi.**

Further Reading

Beach, D. N. *The Shona and Zimbabwe, 900–1850.* Gweru, Zimbabwe: Mambo Press, 1980.
———. *Zimbabwe before 1900.* Gweru, Zimbabwe: Mambo Press, 1984.
———. *A Zimbabwean Past: Shona Dynastic Histories and Oral Traditions.* Gweru, Zimbabwe: Mambo Press, 1994.
Bhila, H. H. K. *Trade and Politics in a Shona Kingdom: The Manyika and Their Portuguese African Neighbours, 1575–1902.* Harlow, England: Longman, 1982.
Mudenge, S. I. G. *A Political History of Munhumutapa, c.1400–1902.* Harare: Zimbabwe Publishing, 1988.

Zimbabwe: Incursions from the South, Ngoni and Ndebele

Up to the 1830s, the southwest region of present-day Zimbabwe was dominated by a long succession of Shona-speaking cultures and states. Until this period, the main population group of the area was the Kalanga branch of the Shona. By the late 1600s, the Changamire Rozvi, a Shona state based in the northeast, had taken over this area, with the immigrants gradually being absorbed into the Kalanga population. In the 1820s the Rozvi were losing territory in the southwest to the expanding Tswana and to the southeast to the expanding Tsonga. To add to these troubles, in the mid- to late 1830s this area experienced repeated invasions by Nguni- and Sotho-speaking groups originating south of the Limpopo River in what is now South Africa.

The causes of these incursions in southern Africa during the 1820s and 1830s have been hotly debated by historians. An expanding Zulu state, drought, and colonial-sponsored raiding have all be identified as possible reasons why large groups of people went north in this period, moving as far as present-day Malawi and southern Tanzania.

Ngoni refers to groups of northern Nguni (Zulu)-speaking people under leaders such as Zwangendaba, Ngwana Maseko, and Nyamazana that moved north of the Limpopo sometime in the early 1830s. The main advantage of the Ngoni was their military system of age regiments that cut across local affiliations and made it easier to assimilate conquered people. Using their short, stabbing spears and shock tactics, the Ngoni raided the Rozvi for cattle and other types of food. They even killed the Rozvi *mambo* (ruler) Chirisamhuru. While the Ngoni raiders did do damage, Rozvi resistance ultimately pushed them farther north and east, and their main body of several thousand crossed the Zambesi River in 1835.

The arrival of the Ndebele, another group of northern Nguni speakers from south of the Limpopo, had a more lasting impact on the area. Under the leadership of Mzilikazi, what would become the nucleus of the Ndebele state left the Pongola River area in the early 1820s and moved north of the Drakensberg Mountains. For at least a decade the Ndebele were the major power of the South African Highveld and assimilated many Sotho speakers into their ranks. In 1836 and 1837 they were defeated by parties of Boer trekkers moving north from the Cape Colony; at this point they moved farther north across the Limpopo. During this move the Ndebele split into two groups, the smaller under Mzilikazi and the larger under Gundwane, with the intention of meeting up again. In 1838–1839, Gundwane's group arrived in the Umzingwani Valley and faced stiff resistance from the local Rozvi. However, when reinforced by the arrival of Mzilikazi's group, the Ndebele came to dominate the area. Unlike the Ngoni, the Ndebele did not terrorize and raid the Kalanga people, who they came to rely on for supplies of grain. Mzilikazi took over from the Rozvi as the ruler of the local Kalanga population. Since a large number of Rozvi cattle had been taken by the Ngoni, the Rozvi even agreed to provide the Ndebele with young men, who would be incorporated into their regiments, in exchange for borrowed livestock, which they cared for in exchange for milk. This relationship obviously favored the Ndebele, as they could reclaim their cattle if the Rozvi displeased them, but the Rozvi could not reclaim their young men.

Frustrated by the loss of their young men to Mzilikazi, the Rozvi in the early 1850s attempted to regain their power in the region by raiding Ndebele territory. The Ndebele counterattacked and ravaged the Rozvi state during the great raids of 1854–1855 that ultimately led to the Rozvi surrender of 1857. However, because Mzilikazi had found it difficult to storm the Rozvi mountain strongholds he could not extend his power to the northeast. Throughout the 1860s the Ndebele continued to raid Shona groups, and in 1866 they once again defeated the Rozvi, who were now a spent force. This gave the Ndebele a strong position over the regional trade network, and during the 1870s they were at the height of their power, with many Shona tributary states.

By 1879, various Shona states had acquired a significant number of guns through the ivory trade and through working in the diamond mines south of the Limpopo. As the Portuguese began to expand west from Mozambique, they also supplied the Shona with firearms. This made the Shona hill strongholds much more easily defensible against Ndebele raids, and from that point on the regional power of the Ndebele state, now under Mzilikazi's son Lobengula, declined. By the late 1880s the Ndebele could no longer raid far to the northeast into the central Shona country.

Colonial writers falsely claimed that the Ndebele dominated and raided the Shona throughout the mid- to late 1800s. This theory orginated from propaganda by the British South Africa Company (BSAC), Cecil Rhodes's chartered company, which fraudulently obtained a concession from Lobengula in 1888 that gave it the right to occupy Mashonaland. Although the Ndebele king had no authority over most of this area save a few tributary states on his border, the BSAC position in what became the colony of Southern Rhodesia was based on the belief that he did. Colonial propaganda also sought to legitimize the colonization of Mashonaland by claiming that it saved the Shona people from the depredations of Ndebele raids.

TIMOTHY J. STAPLETON

See also: **Difaqane on the Highveld; Lozi Kingdom and the Kololo; Shaka and Zulu Kingdom, 1810–1840; Torwa, Changamire Dombo, and the Rovzi; Zambia: Ngoni Incursion from the South.**

Further Reading

Beach, D. N. "Ndebele Raiders and Shona Power." *Journal of African History* 25, no. 4 (1974).
———. *War and Politics in Zimbabwe 1840–1900.* Gweru, Zimbabwe: Mambo Press, 1986.
Bhebe, N. "Some Aspects of Ndebele Relations with the Shona." *Rhodesian History*, no. 4 (1973), 31–38.
Cobbing, Julian. "The Ndebele under the Khumalos." Ph.D. diss., University of Lancaster, 1976.
Summers, R., and C. W. Pagden. *The Warriors.* Cape Town: Balkema, 1970.

Zimbabwe: 1880s

The history of Zimbabwe in the 1880s has been clouded by a number of potent myths. Contemporary descriptions by imperialists, arguing the supposed benefits of the Pax Britannica, propounded the myth of the warlike Ndebele state in the west parasitically raiding the agriculturally productive but cowardly Shona to the east. Postindependence accounts by cultural nationalists have sought to bolster the project of nation building by asserting a precolonial unity for the Shona, an organic totality of religion and politics. But precolonial Zimbabwean identities were far more complex than these simple caricatures, and they interacted with equally diverse regional economies.

The Shona, who comprised two-thirds of the population, lived predominantly on the plateau. The term *Shona* had no tribal meaning at this stage; there was neither a Shona consciousness prior to the twentieth century, nor a single Shona political entity. The term thus makes more sense as the delineation of a cultural and linguistic zone whose members shared a common language and attitude to religion and politics. Shona speakers were oriented in different directions by military and trading links and adherence to different territorial cults, such as the Mwari cult in the west or the Dzivaguru/Karuva cult in the northeast. The Shona understood themselves as members of polities with shifting boundaries. There were 200 or more of these polities, of varying sizes and strengths. Territories like Nhowe or Maungwe were 43 miles (70 kilometers) across, while the smallest were as little as 6 miles (10 kilometers) wide, composed of no more than a few settlements. While some were relatively new and fragile, others could be two or three centuries old.

The plateau and surrounding lowlands were overshadowed by two African superpowers, the Gaza state in the east, in what is today Mozambique, and the Ndebele in the southwest, who were the second largest Zimbabwean language group. Although the Ndebele state was larger and more organized than any Shona polity, its identity was no less fluid. The Ndebele had come into existence through the assimilation of various peoples migrating from the extended political and military conflict in southern Africa, often termed *mfecane*. Sixty per cent of Ndebele were of Shona origin, the rest being Nguni and Sotho.

There were also other smaller, but important, language groups living in the tsetse-infested lowlands beyond the plateau, such as the Zambezi Tonga, Tavara, and Chikunda in the north, the Sena in the northeast, the Hlengwe and Tsonga in the southeast, and the Venda in the south.

The Ndebele, whose territory was too arid for dependence on agriculture, relied more on pastoralism. Although the Ndebele did raid, a large portion of the Zimbabwean plateau lay outside the range of either Ndebele or Gaza warriors. More important, by the 1880s Ndebele power over its tributaries, such as the Chivi and Hwata, had begun to diminish as these peoples acquired guns and asserted their independence. Nevertheless, the Ndebele culture held a remarkable appeal for their Shona neighbors—particularly young men, who preferred a life of raiding, beef-eating, and increased access to women to a more circumscribed existence under their own patriarchs. But, given that political power lay in controlling cattle, women and trade as a means of amassing male clients, the "big men" who dominated Zimbabwean politics, all engaged in raiding. Raids by the independent Shona polities in the east such as the Makoni, Mutasa, and Mutoko—on each other and their neighbors—were a common occurrence. Hence, the majority of Zimbabwean settlements sought the added security of hilltop locations, or behind wooden stockades on the lowlands.

The varied pattern of cultures, resources, and technologies created specific regional economies. On the Save River were the Njanja iron workers and hoe traders. This renowned group of Shona craftsmen had developed a complex trading network that closely mirrored their marriage links. To the west, the Shangwe sold tobacco. Their home area, the Mafungabusi Plateau, was also famous for salt production. The Banyubi who lived in the Matopos hills produced a grain surplus for trade with the Ndebele. But these specializations were not of a scale to support whole communities. Diversification was the key to survival, and these trades were important supplements to agriculture and pastoralism, particularly in time of drought.

By the 1880s, Zimbabwe's regional economies were integrated into the wider network of British and Afrikaner economies to the south and those of the Portuguese to the east. From the late 1860s the Ndebele were trading cattle with the Kimberly mines, and this trade increased with the rise of the Transvaal mines in the 1880s. By 1880, the Shona near Chivero had begun to craft iron for tourists. Other goods drew European traders into Zimbabwe. In the east, the Portuguese had a well-established network of trading posts for the purchase of quills filled with gold dust, though this trade in alluvial gold was declining. To the south, other Europeans came in search of ivory, known as "white gold." Ivory trading proved so lucrative that the Ndebele organized state ivory hunts. But excessive hunting by whites and blacks meant that this trade was also in decline. The cloth, beads, copper wire, and guns received in exchange for Zimbabwean commodities were important sources of power, status, and social mobility. A young man with a gun could kill an elephant and use the ivory to circumvent bride price or bride service.

Mercantilism was being supplemented by capitalist relations. As men in the south migrated to the South African mines, the Shona in the east worked as regular carriers for Portuguese traders and adventurers. By the 1880s, governments and companies were taking an active interest in the region. Concession hunters flooded across the Limpopo, attempting to secure a stake in what they hoped would be a "second Rand." In 1889 the Portuguese Companhia de Moçambique attempted to secure the allegiance of the central Shona by giving them guns and ammunition when they flew the Portuguese flag. This short-lived attempt at Portuguese colonization was thwarted a year later by the arrival of Cecil Rhodes's British South Africa Company on the Zimbabwean Plateau.

DAVID MAXWELL

See also: **Rhodes, Jameson, and the Seizure of Rhodesia; Rudd Concession, 1888.**

Further Reading

Beach, David. *The Shona and their Neighbours.* Oxford: Blackwell, 1994.
———. *War and Politics in Zimbabwe 1840–1900.* Gweru, Zimbabwe: Mambo, 1986.
———. *Zimbabwe before 1900.* Gweru, Zimbabwe: Mambo, 1984.
Maxwell, David. *Christians and Chiefs in Zimbabwe. A Social History of the Hwesa People, c. 1870s–1990s.* Edinburgh: International Africa Library, 1999.
Mudenge, Stanislas. *A Political History of the Munhumutapa c.1400–1902.* Harare: Zimbabwe Publishing, 1988.
Ranger, Terence O. *Voices from the Rocks: Nature, Culture and History in the Matopos Hills of Zimbabwe.* London: James Currey, 1999.

Zimbabwe (Southern Rhodesia): Ndebele and Shona Risings: First Chimurenga

Despite the victory of the European settlers and British South Africa Company forces over the Ndebele in 1893, the white grip on Southern Rhodesia (Zimbabwe) remained weak. The years between 1893 and 1896 were fraught with difficulties. Whites, operating on the assumption that almost all cattle in the Ndebele kingdom belonged to the king, seized the herds as "reparations" for the war. Perhaps as many as 200,000 cattle, 80 per cent of all the Ndebele herds, were appropriated in this way. Plans were formed to resettle the Ndebele into two reserves, Gwai and Shangani, which were areas of poor soil with very little water resources. Although this resettlement never actually took place, many Ndebele were dispossessed of their land by white settlers. Bulawayo became a European town, soon to be a railhead and a very important center of white power. Tensions between the Ndebele and the Shona were heightened by the manner in which Shona men were recruited into the police force and, perhaps not unnaturally, sometimes roughly handled their former Ndebele masters. Moreover, both Ndebele and Shona were pressed into forced labor gangs both for public works and to help white farmers develop their farms. Violent reprisals were also carried out against villages, mainly in Mashonaland, whose inhabitants were alleged to have harbored thieves.

In addition to all of these grievances, a sequence of environmental disasters hit the region. There were seasons of drought. Locusts swarmed to an extent not seen for many years. Rinderpest, a cattle disease brought by Europeans to northeastern Africa, ravaged both the cattle and the game of the territory. Europeans attempted to control the disease by shooting healthy cattle, a measure that had little effect and naturally seemed preposterously destructive to the Africans. In time of famine, Africans had been accustomed to turn to game for relief, but European hunters and settlers had destroyed most of the game near human settlements, and rinderpest had a devastating effect on buffalo and all the larger antelopes, the most important sources of meat. In the midst of all of this distress, the Ndebele in early 1896 heard the news that the administrator, Dr. L. S. Jameson, had withdrawn almost all of the British South Africa police to Bechuanaland in preparation for what would be his notorious raid upon the Transvaal.

Frederick Selous, a celebrated hunter and author who had been the guide for the Pioneer Column in 1890, had acquired a vast estate called Essexvale, south of Bulawayo. He recounted how the Ndebele induna, Umlugulu, who was a neighbor, visited him and took a particular interest in Jameson's raid and his arrest in the Transvaal in January 1896. By March of that year some Ndebele communities rose in revolt. Many Europeans were killed and the others rapidly retreated to laagers in the towns. In June the revolt spread to Mashonaland. This was unexpected, and devastating to the whites who assumed that the Shona people were relieved at being released from the Ndebele yoke. Imperial troops arrived both from the south, via Bechuanaland, and from the east, via Mozambique, to help save the company and its beleaguered settlers. Cecil Rhodes and the new administrator, Albert (the future Earl) Grey, met in Rhodesia and a series of indabas was held with the Ndebele indunas in the Matopos Hills in September and October of 1896. Peace was made, as were concessions to the Ndebele, but the Shona revolt continued into 1897 and was extinguished without similar peace negotiations. One in every ten of the settlers had been killed and the entire future of white Rhodesia seemed to be in doubt.

The Colonial Office appointed the commissioner of Swaziland, Sir Richard Martin, to conduct an enquiry into the Ndebele revolt and his report turned out to be a searching and lengthy document. Martin's report suggested that the Ndebele political and regimental system had not been adequately destroyed (from the white point of view) in the 1893 war, but went on to condemn the company's methods with regard to forced labor, concessions, and policing, as well as suggesting that the native administration under Jameson had been totally inadequate. Grey did his best to defend the company and in doing so chose to create what for him was an irrational explanation for the revolt. He suggested that it had been stimulated by the *Mlimo*, the Shona supreme being who had been incorporated into the Ndebele cosmology, and priests (whom he called "witch doctors") and mediums associated with these religious systems.

Subsequent historians have developed these two aspects of the Martin Report. It has been suggested that the supposed unity demonstrated in the revolt had its origins in the emergence of new religious figures who were able to substitute for the inadequacies of the political systems and forge joint action between the Ndebele and the Shona. Others have argued that patterns of disunity are just as important. Some Ndebele indunas and their regiments remained loyal to the whites, facilitating the arrival of the imperial troops from the south. The Shona rose in a very patchy way, connected with their former relations with the Ndebele and with the degree to which white oppression had hit them. Following Martin, it has been argued that traditional Ndebele political networks remained in place, that one of the key moments was the inauguration in the Matopos of Nyamanda, son of Lobengula, as king during the revolt. The religious dimensions thus sanctified rather than stimulated or led the revolt.

The effects of the revolt were to be widespread and highly significant. The hands of the enemies of the company, among the missionary and humanitarian factions in London, as well as the settlers themselves, were to be greatly strengthened. But the company survived, albeit under stricter controls from London. The settlers were given representation on a legislative council and this can be seen as the origins of white rule that secured responsible government in 1923 and ultimately led to a unilateral declaration of independence by Ian Smith in 1965. For Africans, the revolt remained a potent memory. Its brutal suppression in many areas helped to channel politics into new forms, but when the guerrilla resistance to Smith developed in the 1970s, it was seen as a second *chimurenga* in direct succession to the first. Modern politicians sought to connect themselves to the earlier revolt and after independence in 1980; the heroes of resistance were seen as embracing both those of the 1890s and the 1970s. The historical record is more complex, and patterns of collaboration with—as much as those of resistance to—the whites need to be understood.

JOHN M. MACKENZIE

See also: **Jameson Raid, Origins of South African War: 1895–1899; Resistance to Colonialism; Rhodes, Cecil J.; Rhodes, Jameson, and the Seizure of Rhodesia.**

Further Reading

Beach, D. N. *The Shona and Zimbabwe, 900–1850: An Outline of Shona History*. London: Heinemann, 1980.

Palley, Claire. *The Constitutional History and Law of Southern Rhodesia, 1888–1965*. Oxford: Oxford University Press, 1966.

Ranger, T. O. *Revolt in Southern Rhodesia, 1896–7*. London: Heinemann, 1967.

Ranger, Terence. *Voices from the Rocks: Nature, Culture and History in the Matopos Hills of Zimbabwe*. London: James Currey, 1999.

Selous, F. C. *Sunshine and Storm in Rhodesia*. London: Rowland Ward, 1896.

Zimbabwe (Southern Rhodesia): Colonial Period: Land, Tax, Administration

The colonization of Zimbabwe began with the signing of infamous Rudd Concession of 1888. Charles Rudd and his party had been sent by the diamond magnate and imperialist Cecil Rhodes to compel Lobengula, the King of Amandabele, to sign a treaty giving exclusive rights for Rhodes to take over Lobengula's country. Soon after the signing of the Rudd Concession, Rhodes obtained a royal charter from England to administer, on behalf of the queen, the colony of Rhodesia—so named after him. He called this administration the British South Africa Company (BSAC).

The colonial period of Zimbabwe therefore can be divided into four phases, that of the British South Africa Company (1890–1923); responsible government (1953–1963), the federation (1953–19]3), and the Unilateral Declaration of Independence (1965–1980). During all these phases the white settler community of colonial Zimbabwe was in control of all aspects of the country, land economy, and politics.

Having established itself in 1890, the BSAC administration proceeded to appropriate African land, when the rumored El Dorado (land of riches), the premise upon which southern Rhodesia had been "founded," became illusory. The Pioneer Column, having hoisted the Union Jack in northeast Zimbabwe, started to appropriate Vashona lands when hopes of gold findings turned into frustrations and dreams. The year 1893 saw a war between Amandebele and the BSAC. When settlers turned to Amandebele country for minerals and found none or few, they nonetheless appropriated Amandebele land. Realizing the loss of their country to BSAC through trickery by the Rudd Concession, the Amandebele went to war with the settlers; the Amandebele lost.

From 1893 to 1923 the BSAC appropriated more African land, both in Amandebele and Vashona territories. The company also took African cattle, demanded African labor to work in the farms that had been pegged out by settlers, and demanded tax that had to be paid in European currency, thereby forcing the Africans to provide wage labor. The company further proceeded to demarcate African land, shelving Africans into reserves—generally areas that were less fertile and tsetse-infested, resulting in overcrowdedness and the further depletion of soils. The reserves generally impoverished Africans, placing them under wage labor in order to pay the required tax. Hut and poll taxes were required from Africans and had to be paid in monetary terms and not in kind.

Some Africans were encouraged to stay on European farms as "tenants," but this would mean that they had to offer free labor to the landlords in return for staying in settler-owned land. Generally, the era of the company was exploitative and oppressive culminating in the first *chimurenga* wars of 1896–1897, ostensibly fought because Africans were against land appropriation, labor demands, and exorbitant taxes.

When responsible government replaced company rule in 1923, it inherited an administration, land, and tax systems that discriminated against Africans. It did very little to redress the situation. In fact, it compounded the problem by not only keeping the tax system but by introducing and legislating the infamous Land Apportionment Act of 1930. This act was a result of the Morris Carter Commission of 1925, charged with the responsibility of determining the "practicability of limiting the rights of acquisition of land to [natives] and Europeans." The commission set the stage for a racially divided society because it recommended a racial division of land in the country. The Land Apportionment Act did not protect the interests of the Africans, as was often argued; rather, it entrenched what the settlers often wanted—a racial division of land and eventually division of the whole country along racial lines.

Of the 96 million acres in the colony, 10 million were set aside as national land; 40 million were set aside for Africans and dubbed "tribal" trust lands; 4 million were designated as "native purchase areas"; 6 million were open to all races in the country; and 36 million were open exclusively to Europeans. The tribal trust lands were often infertile and the 4 million acres of native purchase land desperately failed to take account of the population of Africans.

Throughout the era of responsible government to the time of federation, the administration was based on racial lines that for the most part favored the settlers, as predicated by the Land Apportionment Act. In fact, the settlers exerted pressure on the government to institute a legislation that made it impossible for individual land to be sold to "Asiatics" and "natives" within exclusive settler communities. The result was that the Land Apportionment Act was reenacted in 1941 with even more rigid conditions for Africans. The Animal

Husbandry Act of 1951, stipulating the restricted number of livestock Africans had to own and the amount of land they should occupy, simply compounded the problem of land ownership in Zimbabwe.

The federation of the two Rhodesias and Nyasaland did very little to change administration, land, and tax issues. During this era, exceptions were made whenever Europeans saw fit and when convenience suited their situations. Africans were, for example, allowed to reside on European farms, mines, and even homesteads because labor could be conveniently accessed. Towns fell within European areas but because African labor was so much needed, townships or "locations" were set aside for Africans so that labor could easily be available.

Throughout the federation period, the settlers tried to pursue policies that appeared to accommodate African interests, but still the general administration of southern Rhodesia, land reforms and tax issues continued to be dictated by the settlers. The Africans rose and opposed the federation because it had failed to address African interests, particularly land and the general politics of the country.

The Unilateral Declaration of Independence (UDI), made in 1965 by Ian Smith and the Rhodesia Front reversed whatever mild changes the federation had intended. The Rhodesia Front ticket endorsed a racially divided society and saw to it that old acts such as Land Apportionment and Industrial Conciliation Act (which discouraged Africans from competing for jobs with Europeans) were reinstated. In 1967 the leader of the Rhodesia Front, Ian Smith, declared that his government strove for a system that acknowledged different community rights, interests, and freedoms. He was in fact proclaiming a racially divided country, with all aspects of the society, economy, land, tax, administration, and politics dictated by the minority settler community. This state of affairs was bitterly challenged by African nationalists and liberation movements until independence in 1980. At the end of the century, the disproportionate division of land along racial lines remained the most contentious issue in Zimbabwean politics.

P. T. MGADLA

See also: **White Settler Factor: Economic and Political.**

Further Reading

Banana, Canaan (ed.). *Turmoil and Tenacity: Zimbabwe 1890–1990.* Harare: College Press, 1989.

Bull, T. (ed.). *Rhodesian Perspective.* London: Michael Joseph, 1963.

Mlambo, Eshmael. *Rhodesia: The Struggle for a Birthright.* London: C. Hurst, 1972.

Palmer, Robin. *Land and Racial Domination in Southern Rhodesia.* Berkelkey and Los Angeles: University of California Press, 1977.

Van Onselen, Charles. *Chibaro: African Labour in Southern Rhodesia 1900–1933.* Braamfontein, Raven Press, 1980.

Williams, Richard-Hodder. *White Farmers in Rhodesia 1890–1965.* London: Macmillan, 1983.

Zimbabwe (Southern Rhodesia): African Political and Trades Union Movements, 1920s and 1930s

Mainly urban-based black political and industrial organizations, developed steadily in Southern Rhodesia in the 1920s and early 1930s, suffered significant setbacks during the Great Depression (1931–1934), but rallied with the establishment of the Bantu Congress, progenitor of the first truly nationalist party, the Southern Rhodesia African National Congress (ANC), in 1938.

Initial postwar political activity was stimulated by economic inequality and the exemplar provided by the white settler campaign to secure self-government, which was achieved in 1923. Three predominantly urban-based associations emerged: the Rhodesian Bantu Voters Association (RBVA), the (Southern) Rhodesia Native Association (RNA) and the Gwelo (later Southern Rhodesia) Native Welfare Association. All three were moderate politically, and tiny in membership terms: the RBVA spoke for a constituency of about 50 registered black voters, mostly of South African origin. The RNA, based in Harare, had a predominantly local Shona, membership, comprising "advanced" farmers and teachers. Although all three bodies took up popular grievances such as taxation and cattle dip fees, they were essentially elitist in character and advocated what Terence Ranger has termed "the politics of participation." An investigation of the very few occasions when the various association leaders apparently overstepped the mark shows that it was often the result of overreaction by unduly sensitive or innately suspicious Native Department officials, rather than some conscious design.

The overwhelming majority of black Zimbabweans were little affected by the activities of these predominantly urban-based organizations. Much more significant for the Ndebele was the campaign for the restoration of the Ndebele monarchy, abolished upon occupation in 1894, and an amelioration of the land problem in Matabeleland. In 1929 the Matabele Home Society was formed, bringing together the traditional and modern Ndebele elite. Christian and non-Christian chiliastic movements emerged at sporadic intervals from World War I onward, and at various stages articulated the political and economic grievances, as well as the fears and expectations, of their followers. In 1923, Watchtower adherents at Hwange spread rumors that

"America" (perceived to be a black nation) would defeat Britain and liberate Africa. Apart from occasional millenniarian prophecies, and complaints to officials at meetings about taxation, low cattle prices, and other such grievances, the rural areas as such seemingly remained quiescent in the interwar period.

In contrast, urban trade union activity took a much more radical turn. The Shamva gold mine, located to the north of Harare, became a prime center of black industrial militancy, with a boycott of European-owned stores in 1920, a work stoppage in 1922, and the first major strike by black workers in September 1927, which the authorities suppressed with the use of force. The presence of non-Zimbabwean miners, many with South African experience, seems to have been an important precipitating factor.

Similarly, South Africa provided the inspiration for the biggest black trade union/political association operating between the wars, the Independent Industrial and Commercial Workers' Union of Rhodesia (IICU). This was launched by Robert Sambo, a relative of its founder in South Africa, Clements Kadalie, in early 1927. Two local personalities, destined to become important figures in Zimbabwean labor history, Masotsha Ndhlovu and Charles Mzingeli, took over control after Sambo's deportation. In contrast to its South African parent, the IICU called no strikes and concentrated instead on developing black awareness and mass support. It held regular meetings each weekend in the black townships of Bulawayo and Harare, attended on average by about 500, at which speakers denounced Native Department officials as oppressors and condemned the way black people were being treated by employers and white people generally. The government retaliated by charging its leaders with "criminal slander" of officials, but otherwise did not intervene, a comparative tolerance that evaporated when the IICU began to filter into rural areas and take up local grievances, especially in Ndebele districts like Flilabusi. At length, Native Department officials put pressure on local traditional leaders to outlaw union activity, and Ndhlovu was imprisoned in 1932 for holding an unauthorized meeting in a black reserve. The onset of the Great Depression severely weakened the IICU; membership fell away as people were unable to pay their dues, and after an argument about the use of funds it became defunct in 1936.

Although Mzingeli managed to revive the union as the Reformed ICU after the war, a more lasting contribution to political development was made by other leaders in the late 1930s. In 1928, the first meeting of the Missionary Conference of Native Christians had taken place. Influenced by radical white missionaries like Arthur Shearly Cripps and John White, the conference became an important mouthpiece for "respectable" African opinion, expressing views, couched in temper-

ate language, on a variety of matters affecting ordinary Africans. By the mid-1930s, a generation of local, Christianized Africans, often based in the new black purchase areas, had emerged, with individuals such as Thompson Samkange, Aaron Jacha, and Solomon Chavunduka. Many were members of such organizations as the RNA and RBVA, a consideration that persuaded them to advocate unity at a meeting of organizations that met in 1936. The outcome of this was the creation of the Bantu Congress in April 1938. By fits and starts, this became the first truly nationalist party, the Southern Rhodesia ANC, in the later 1950s.

By the outbreak of war, some progress had been made in establishing an African voice in Southern Rhodesia, although with a few exceptions such as the IICU, that voice was essentially deferential. Most black leaders were in effect trying to win acceptance from white society, operating from the standpoint that those who had become "civilized" men (as defined by the Colony's founder, Cecil Rhodes, at the end of the previous century) could reasonably expect to be accepted by that society. This hope was to be disappointed with the move of colonial Zimbabwe toward fuller segregation in the 1930s. However, it was only after 1945 that political (and in particular trade union) activity became militant in deed as well as in word.

MURRAY STEELE

See also: **Trades Unionism and Nationalism.**

Further Reading

Phimister, Ian. "The Shamva Strike of 1927: An Emerging African Proletariat." *Rhodesian History*, no. 2 (1971): 65–88.

Ranger, Terence. *The African Voice in Southern Rhodesia, 1898–1930.* London: Heinemann/Evanston, Ill.: Northwestern University Press, 1970.

———. *Are We Not Also Men? The Samkange Family and African Politics In Zimbabwe, 1920–1964.* London: James Currey/Portsmouth, N H: Heinemann, 1995.

Ranger, Terence (ed.). *Aspects of Central African History.* London: Heinemann, 1968.

Van Onselen, Charles. *Chibaro: African Mine Labour in Southern Rhodesia, 1900–1933.* London: Pluto Press, 1976.

Zimbabwe (Southern Rhodesia): Urbanization and Conflict, 1940s

During the 1940s, rapid urbanization in Southern Rhodesia attracted a large African population into the colony's cities for the first time. Forced off of their rural homelands by overcrowding, and drawn to the cities by the economic development that accompanied World War II, these new urban immigrants found themselves confronted with segregation and economic exploitation. African protests against the problems of urban living culminated in rallies against racial segregation in 1946 and a general strike in 1948.

The large-scale migration of Africans from rural to urban areas during the 1940s had its roots in the Land Apportionment Act of 1931. This legislation divided the colony into "European" and "native" areas. It had the dual effect of expropriating large tracts of arable land from African farmers while denying Africans the legal right to establish residency in the "European" urban areas.

However, by the early 1940s the provisions of the Land Apportionment Act had become unenforceable. The reserves set aside for African communal farming proved inadequate to support the growing population, driving many landless workers to the expanding urban areas of Salisbury and Bulawayo. The outbreak of World War II in 1939 provided a tremendous boost to the colony's urban economy. The capital, Salisbury, became a major training ground for the Royal Air Force, and the war economy encouraged the development of light industry there and in other major cities. After the war the boom continued, as European immigrants poured into the colony. These new settlers brought capital and skills, further spurring economic growth and providing employment for many Africans in domestic service. The booming colonial cities drew thousands of African workers off of the reserves. Between 1936 and 1946 the African populations of the colony's largest cities grew from 45,000 to over 99,000. According to the provisions of the 1931 act, however, these new immigrants were in the cities illegally. In 1941 the Southern Rhodesian government amended the Land Apportionment Act in recognition of the fact that African workers were a permanent fixture of the urban economy. The amendment encouraged local authorities to develop "native" urban areas for the growing African workforce. In 1946 the passage of the Native (Urban Areas) Accommodation and Registration Act required urban employers to provide free housing for their African employees within the native urban areas. This act also included provisions for stringent pass laws designed to control the influx of Africans into urban areas. Though the act recognized the rights of African workers to live in the cities, legally urban Africans remained transients, and were permitted to remain in urban areas only so long as they were employed. If fired, or upon retirement, they were expected to return to the rural areas. While working in the cities Africans were required to live in designated neighborhoods such as Highfields in Salisbury or Mzilikazi in Bulawayo. Segregated from the European sections of the cities, these areas suffered from overcrowding, few social services, poorly developed infrastructure, and frequent harassment from the police.

The 1946 act proved widely unpopular among urban Africans; in response to its passage of the act the trade union leader Charles Mzingeli convened a rally against the measure in the Harare township of Salisbury. Though the provisions of the act were ultimately carried out with little or no regard to African opinion, the rallies of 1946 marked a watershed in the history of the colony. They represented the first organized protest against government policy since the conquest of the colony in the 1890s. The Salisbury rallies were followed in April of 1948 by a general strike among workers in the largest cities of the colony. The strike was organized by two trade union leaders, Benjamin Burumbo and Jasper Savanhu, and began among the African municipal workers of the city of Bulawayo. Though the immediate grievance of the workers was the low wages paid by the city government, the generally dire conditions of urban Africans throughout the colony encouraged workers throughout the city, and in Salisbury, to strike as well. The strike lasted several days, and involved African workers from many professions in both Bulawayo and Salisbury. It ultimately ended in defeat for the strikers, as the wage gains promised by the government were viewed by most workers as inadequate. However, like the Harare protests of 1946, the general strike of 1948 set a precedent for concerted action against the state that foreshadowed the political conflict that would characterize the late 1950s.

By the end of the 1940s the Southern Rhodesian government had recognized that the Land Apportionment Act of 1931 had become unworkable. The overcrowding of the reserves and the agitation of the African urban population convinced the settler government to take further steps to resolve the land issue. In the late 1940s the government began drafting legislation intended to stabilize the urban population and to ameliorate the overcrowding and environmental degradation that plagued rural areas. Passed in 1951, the Native Land Husbandry Act sought to alleviate the problems of the reserves by transforming communally held lands into private property and destocking African herds. This act also attempted to end the migration to and from the cities by requiring urban workers to abandon any claims to property in rural areas. With this one piece of legislation the Southern Rhodesian government managed to threaten the livelihood of people on the reserves and in the cities. The act rescinded the rights of urban workers to hold land in the rural areas, which had provided a needed supplement to low urban wages and offered the only hope for social security in old age. The passage of the act inspired tremendous resistance among urban and rural Africans, and inaugurated a new phase in nationalist politics in the colony.

JAMES BURNS

See also: **Nkomo, Joshua; Samkange, Rev. D. T.; Urbanization: Colonial Context.**

Further Reading

Bowman, Larry W. *Politics in Rhodesia: White Power in an African State*. Boston: Harvard University Press, 1973.

Mnyanda, B. J. *In Search of Truth: A Commentary on Certain Aspects of Southern Rhodesia's Native Policy*. Bombay: Hind Kitabs, 1954.

Phimister, I. R. *An Economic and Social History of Zimbabwe, 1890–1948: Capital Accumulation and Class Struggle*. London: Longman, 1988.

Phimister, Ian, and Brian Raftopolous (eds.). *Keep on Knocking: A History of the Labour Movement in Zimbabwe, 1900–1997*. Harare: Baobab, 1997.

Rakodi, Carole. *Harare: Inheriting a Settler-Colonial City: Charge or Continuity?* Chichester, England: John Wiley and Sons, 1995.

Vambe, Lawrence. *From Rhodesia to Zimbabwe*. Pittsburgh: University of Pittsburgh Press, 1976

Zimbabwe (Southern Rhodesia): Federation

Between 1953 and 1963, the British government united the colonies of Northern Rhodesia, Southern Rhodesia, and Nyasaland into the Central African Federation. Though the federation proved a boon for white settlers in the Rhodesias, it profited its African subjects very little. In 1963 the British government dissolved the federation after Africans in the Northern Rhodesia and Nyasaland voted overwhelmingly for independence.

Settlers in Northern and Southern Rhodesia began seriously discussing amalgamating their territories during the 1930s. Their aim was to combine the mineral wealth of the Northern Rhodesian Copperbelt with the agricultural resources of Southern Rhodesia to create a wealthy, settler-dominated state. In 1945, after the conclusion of World War II, Roy Welensky, the leader of the Northern Rhodesian Legislative Assembly, and Sir Godfrey Huggins, the prime minister of Southern Rhodesia, began lobbying the British Colonial Office to support amalgamation. However the Labour Party government in London feared that the creation of a unitary state would place Africans in the Protectorate of Northern Rhodesia at the mercy of the settler-ruled government of Southern Rhodesia, and rejected the suggestion. Proponents of amalgamation then began promoting the confederation of the two Rhodesias, arguing that a federation could create a strong state and still protect the interests of Africans in Northern Rhodesia. Their plan became increasingly attractive to the British government after Daniel F. Malan's Afrikaner National Party took power in South Africa in 1948. Fearing the absorption of Southern Rhodesia into the apartheid state to its south, in 1953 the British government agreed to permit the two Rhodesias to federate if they would include the small and impoverished colony of Nyasaland (modern Malawi). Later in the same year the Federation of the Rhodesias and Nyasaland was formed, with Sir Godfrey Huggins as its first prime minister. The new state had a parliament, with representatives elected from all three of the territories. Though whites dominated the legislature, the federal constitution reserved a handful of seats for African representatives. The federal government took control of a variety responsibilities that affected all three colonies, including defense, immigration and emigration, external affairs, customs, income tax, and the postal service. The territorial governments retained control of all other responsibilities, including, significantly, "native affairs" and law and order.

Colonial officials made little effort to consult African opinion on the subject of federation. While a few African leaders, including Southern Rhodesia's Joshua Nkomo, voiced lukewarm support for federation, most boycotted the conferences leading up to its creation, fearing that it would allow the segregationist policies of Southern Rhodesia to take root in their colonies. In 1949 Hastings Banda, a Nyasa doctor, and Northern Rhodesian Trade Union leader Harry Nkumbula prepared an influential memo outlining their objections to federation.

Proponents of federation promised that it would benefit Africans and white settlers alike. In the eyes of many settlers this promise was fulfilled. The early years of federation saw the continuation of an economic boom in the region that had begun during the late 1940s. Prosperity continued to attract white colonists from South Africa and Great Britain, especially to Southern Rhodesia. Though economic growth slowed during the final years of the 1950s, most of the settlers associated federation with an increase in material prosperity. Economic growth allowed the new government to develop the region's infrastructure, and between 1953 and 1963 the federal government built the Kariba Dam, the National Archives, and expanded the rail and road networks within the three colonies.

The benefits for Africans were less apparent. Supporters of federation insisted that it would introduce partnership between blacks and whites in the region. The federation did bring some improvements to the position of Africans in colonial society, particularly in Southern Rhodesia; there some segregationist laws were relaxed, and the government established the University of Rhodesia and Nyasaland in Salisbury, Southern Rhodesia, as a multiracial institution. But such advances were largely cosmetic: de facto segregation continued in Southern Rhodesia, and the university only admitted eight African students in its first class. Otherwise the federal government upheld the colonial social and economic orders, and made little effort to include Africans in the political process. It took no steps to curb the inexorable process of land alienation by the Southern Rhodesian government or to encourage wage equality among black and white workers in the Northern Rhodesian copper mines.

After 1956 a series of crises combined to threaten the future of the federation. In 1956 the British government suffered a humiliating diplomatic defeat in the Suez Crisis, which revealed the limitations of imperial power. The following year the Gold Coast became the first British colony in Africa to achieve independence. Then, in 1960, the Belgian government in Congo, the federation's neighbor to the north, suddenly abandoned the colony, precipitating a crisis that threatened to destabilize the region. Against this backdrop, African national consciousness within the federal territories developed rapidly. In 1958, Banda in Nyasaland, and Kenneth Kaunda in Northern Rhodesia, began organizing protests against the federation. The following year Nkomo led similar protests in Southern Rhodesia. Clashes between supporters of Banda's Congress party and federal troops resulted in a state of emergency in Southern Rhodesia and Nyasaland. Shortly thereafter Northern Rhodesian authorities arrested Kaunda and banned his party. Government repression soon reestablished colonial authority in all three territories. However, the spectacle of colonial troops fighting to preserve the federation severely undermined the credibility of the federal government. A British report on the disturbances issued in 1960 characterized Nyasaland as a police state and turned public opinion in Britain against the federation. The British government stepped in and granted Nyasaland and Northern Rhodesia the right to vote on the future of the federation. Africans in both colonies voted overwhelmingly to become independent nations. In 1964 they achieved independence as the new states of Malawi and Zambia. Faced with pressure from the British government to grant the franchise to Africans, the following year Southern Rhodesia (or simply Rhodesia, as it now called itself) declared independence.

JAMES BURNS

See also: **Malawi (Nyasaland): Colonial Period: Federation; Mugabe, Robert; Nkomo, Joshua; Welensky, Roy; Zambia (Northern Rhodesia): Federation.**

Further Reading

Baker, C. A. *State of Emergency: Crisis in Central Africa, Nyasaland 1959–1960.* London: Tauris Academic Studies, 1997.

Banda, H. Kamuzu, and Harry Nkumbula. *Federation in Central Africa.* Harlesden, England: Leveridge, 1951.

Franklin, Henry. *Unholy Wedlock: The Failure of the Central African Federation.* London: G. Allen and Unwin, 1963.

Hargreaves, J. D. *Decolonization in Africa.* London: Longman, 1988.

Welensky, Roy. *Welensky's 4000 Days; the Life and Death of the Federation of Rhodesia and Nyasaland.* New York: Roy, 1964.

Zimbabwe (Southern Rhodesia): Nationalist Politics, 1950s and 1960s

The 1950s and 1960s witnessed the development of a national consciousness among the African peoples of Southern Rhodesia, and the concomitant rise of nationalist political parties committed to the end of colonial rule. However, as these parties grew in strength they suffered from political infighting and severe repression at the hands of the Rhodesian government. Despite these impediments, by the end of the 1960s nationalists had launched the guerilla war that would ultimately bring majority rule to Zimbabwe in 1980.

Political activism in Southern Rhodesia remained moderate until the late 1950s. Before World War II the colony's largest political association, the Bantu Congress of Southern Rhodesia, remained committed to reforming the colonial system. The first challenge to the colonial order appeared shortly after the war when African workers staged a series of strikes to protest urban segregation and low wages. The settler regime ultimately broke the strikes and imposed further restrictions on Africans through such legislation as the 1946 Urban Areas Act. This early political activity established a pattern of African protest and severe government repression that would characterize politics in the colony until independence.

Nationalist politics developed more slowly in Southern Rhodesia than it did in neighboring Northern Rhodesia or Nyasaland. In these colonies the first stirrings of a nationalist consciousness arose in response

African women lead a large crowd in an attempt to break through a police cordon at a meeting of the Zimbabwe African People's Union (ZAPU) at Harare. September 20, 1962. © SVT Bild/Das Fotoarchiv.

to the British government's plans to create the Central African Federation in 1953. Leaders in these colonies feared that federation would allow the segregationist policies of Southern Rhodesia to take root in their more liberally administered protectorates. For precisely this reason federation inspired less resistance in Southern Rhodesia, where some African politicians hoped that it might encourage greater liberalization.

In Southern Rhodesia the issue that awakened national consciousness was the passage in 1951 of the Native Land Husbandry Act. By the end of World War II the Rhodesian government had expropriated the colony's most valuable lands and relegated Africans to marginal, overcrowded reserves. The act sought to alleviate the problems of overcrowding and erosion by transforming communally held lands into private property, and by destocking African herds. These provisions threatened the livelihood of people on the reserves, and therefore did more than any other piece of legislation to inspire opposition to the Southern Rhodesian government.

In 1955 the creation of the Salisbury City Youth League signaled a new era in nationalist politics. The league was organized by several leaders who would go on to play important roles in the nation's liberation struggle, including James Chikerema, George Nyandoro, and Edson Sithole. Among its first acts was the organization of a bus strike in 1956 to protest fare hikes in Salisbury. The following year the league merged with the Bulawayo branch of the African National Congress to form the Southern Rhodesian National Congress (SRNC), which chose Joshua Nkomo as its first president. Nkomo had made a name for himself as a moderate opponent of federation during the early 1950s. The SRNC was initially reformist, and devoted its energy to encouraging the Southern Rhodesian government to live up to the rhetoric of racial equality and partnership that supposedly underpinned the creation of the Central African Federation. However as neighboring African colonies began achieving independence, and as the Southern Rhodesian government moved to repress even the most moderate political opposition, the SRNC became committed to a more radical program.

By 1959 politicians in Nyasaland and Northern Rhodesia were agitating for an end to federation and complete independence from Britain. Inspired by their example the SRNC began organizing protests in favor of democracy in Southern Rhodesia. In response the Southern Rhodesian government banned the SRNC, interned 500 of its members, and enacted several laws to suppress political activity. The SRNC then re-formed as the National Democratic Party (NDP). Faced with growing government repression, the NDP's followers staged demonstrations in the hopes of forcing Britain or the United Nations to pressure the Southern Rhodesian

government into negotiating with them. When the Southern Rhodesian government banned the NDP in 1961 its leadership re-formed as the Zimbabwe African People's Union (ZAPU). However the government banned the ZAPU shortly after its formation, and this time the leadership decided to go underground.

Shortly after the ZAPU's banning the party experienced a split that had devastating consequences for the future. In 1963 Ndabaninigi Sithole and several followers, including the future prime minister of Zimbabwe, Robert Mugabe, split off to form the Zimbabwe African National Union (ZANU), while Nkomo remained the leader of the ZAPU. The two parties were divided by some differences in methods: the ZANU was perhaps more militant, and anxious to wage a guerilla campaign, while the ZAPU was more focused on gaining the support of the international community. The party differences developed an ethnic component as well, with the ZAPU enjoying greater support among the colony's Ndebele peoples and the ZANU remaining under the leadership of a predominantly Shona group. But the goals of the organizations were essentially the same, and the divisions between them stemmed in large part from personality conflicts. Shortly after the split, fighting broke out between ZANU and ZAPU supporters. The conflict, which lasted for years, had a disastrous effect on the nationalist movement. It undermined many people's faith in the two parties, taxed the patience of foreign leaders sympathetic to the struggle, and allowed the Rhodesian security forces play the two sides off of one another.

By 1964 the parties were organizing a guerilla insurrection. When the Rhodesian government declared its Unilateral Declaration of Independence from Britain in 1965 both the ZANU and the ZAPU intensified their commitment to overthrowing the colonial government. By 1966 both parties were training guerillas in neighboring nations, and the decade ended with ZANU and ZAPU forces staging raids throughout the country. Within a decade these fighters would liberate much of the country and force the Rhodesian government to hold national elections. Upon independence many of the new leaders of Zimbabwe were veterans of these early nationalist movements.

JAMES BURNS

See also: **Mugabe, Robert; Nkomo, Joshua; Zimbabwe (Southern Rhodesia): Federation.**

Further Reading

Bhebe, Ngwabi. *Burombo: African Politics in Zimbabwe, 1947–1958.* Harare: College Press, 1989.
Bowman, Larry W. *Politics in Rhodesia: White Power in an African State.* Boston: Harvard University Press, 1973.
Blake, Robert. *A History of Rhodesia.* New York: Alfred A. Knopf, 1978.

Phimister, I. R. *An Economic and Social History of Zimbabwe, 1890–1948: Capital Accumulation and Class Struggle.* London: Longman, 1988.

Ranger, T. O. *Are We Not Also Men? The Samkange Family and African Politics in Zimbabwe, 1920–64.* Portsmouth, N.H.: Heinemann, 1995.

Vambe, Lawrence. *From Rhodesia to Zimbabwe.* Pittsburgh: University of Pittsburgh Press, 1976

Zimbabwe (Rhodesia): Unilateral Declaration of Independence and the Smith Regime, 1964–1979

Once the Central African Federation (CAF) was dissolved by Britain on December 31, 1963, it became clear that the white minority in Southern Rhodesia would attempt to prolong their rule by any means in their power. Already in 1958 the gradualist leader of the United Federal Party (UFP) and prime minister, Garfield Todd, who was seen as too conciliatory, had been pushed aside to be replaced by Sir Edgar Whitehead. Whitehead negotiated a new constitution with Britain, though it was rejected by the two African nationalist groups, the Zimbabwe African National Union (ZANU), led by the Rev. Ndabaningi Sithole, and the Zimbabwe African People's Union (ZAPU), led by Joshua Nkomo. A breakaway group of dissident whites opposed to any concessions to the African majority now split the UFP to form the Rhodesia Front (RF). In the elections of 1962 they won 35 seats (to 30 for the UFP), so Whitehead resigned and Winston Field became prime minister on December 16, 1962. He, too, was seen as too moderate by the RF hardliners and on in April 1964 he was forced out in favor of Ian Smith. The stage was thus set for the Unilateral Declaration of Independence (UDI).

On becoming prime minister, Smith said, "I cannot see in my lifetime that the Africans will be sufficiently mature and reasonable to take over . . . our policy is one of trying to make a place for the white man." On November 11, 1965, the Smith government proclaimed its independence unilaterally via the UDI and the issue of Rhodesia sparked off 15 years of pressures—from the Organization of African Unity (OAU), the British Commonwealth, and the United Nations—upon Britain to prevent it from allowing the Smith regime to make its UDI permanent. An emergency session of the OAU held in November 1965 called upon its members to break diplomatic relations with Britain if it did not take strong action against the Smith regime. In January 1966 a special meeting of Commonwealth heads of government was held in Lagos, Nigeria, to consider further action against Rhodesia. Britain then instituted a naval blockade of Beira to prevent oil being delivered to Rhodesia through the Lonrho pipeline; in fact, Rhodesia received its oil through South Africa

throughout the UDI years. At the Lagos meeting Harold Wilson, Britain's prime minister, declared that sanctions would work in a matter of weeks rather than months.

At the Commonwealth Heads of Government Meetings of 1966, 1969, and 1971, other members of the commonwealth exerted pressures upon Britain to regain control of Rhodesia, and in 1966 and again in 1968 Wilson held talks with Smith but failed to make him give way. In May 1968 the United Nations imposed mandatory sanctions upon Rhodesia.

Meanwhile, nationalist guerrilla actions against the Smith government were steadily increasing and in August 1967, ZAPU guerrillas from Zambia came within 60 miles of Bulawayo. This induced the Smith government to ask Pretoria for help, and from that time on South African paramilitary units were to be stationed in Rhodesia as a backup to the Rhodesian security forces. In 1970 guerrilla action increased sharply, with the main thrust coming from ZANU forces in the eastern part of the country.

In June 1969 the white population held a referendum and voted to make Rhodesia a republic, which it became on March 2, 1970. In Britain, the general election of June 1970 brought the Conservative Party to power under Edward Heath. The new foreign secretary, Sir Alec Douglas Home, visited Salisbury to negotiate a new settlement; his terms, had they been accepted, would only have produced majority rule by 2035. However, Britain insisted upon a test of opinion and a commission under Lord Pearce, a British judge, went to Rhodesia and conducted meetings with all shades of opinion over several months: of 120,730 people interviewed, 107,309 Africans said no to the Home proposals.

The situation was to change dramatically at the end of 1972, when ZANU guerrillas escalated the war in northeast Rhodesia by launching an attack on Altena Farm. From then on white farms were potential targets and the government found, for the remainder of the decade, that more and more of its resources had to be diverted to the security forces and fighting the guerrilla war, until in 1977 the Rhodesian commander of combined operations, Lieutenant General Peter Walls, was to argue publicly that the whites could not win the war. The independence of Mozambique in 1975 meant that Rhodesia had lost a sympathetic neighbor (the Portuguese) and instead faced a 700-mile border that was ideal for guerrilla activities now controlled by the ZANU's allies, the new FRELIMO government of Samora Machel.

During 1974, following the military coup that toppled the government of Marcello José das Neves Alves Caetano in Portugal, an attempt at detente was pushed by John Vorster, the prime minister of South Africa, in the hope of finding a peaceful solution to the UDI and the escalating guerrilla war. The attempt failed, but one result was the release of Robert Mugabe from detention. He promptly went to Maputo to replace Ndabaningi Sithole as leader of the ZANU. The war again escalated, and in 1976, the ZANU and the ZAPU agreed to form the Patriotic Front to coordinate their war against the Smith government.

In 1978, Smith attempted to bring about an internal settlement with Bishop Abel Muzorewa of the Rhodesian African National Congress, but this made no difference to the guerrilla war in the northeast of the country. Elections were held under the terms of the internal settlement constitution in April 1979 and on June 1 Bishop Muzorewa became prime minister of Zimbabwe-Rhodesia. Meanwhile, divisions had split the PF leadership between Mugabe and Nkomo. In Britain, Margaret Thatcher had come to power at the head of a new Tory administration. She attended the Commonwealth Heads of Government Meeting (CHOGM) at Lusaka, Zambia, on August 1, 1979, and the summit agreed to a constitutional conference to be held in London that September. In a temporary alliance, Britain, South Africa, and the front line states jointly put pressure upon the leaders of the Patriotic Front to end the war and upon Smith to concede defeat. In December 1979 Zimbabwe-Rhodesia (as it now called itself) renounced the UDI and an agreement was signed that would lead to elections in March 1980 in which 20 seats out of 100 would be reserved for whites.

The first three months of 1980, leading to the March elections, were a fraught time in Rhodesia, with 20,000 guerrillas coming into assembly points to accept the cease-fire, threats of a white military coup in the background, and a British governor, Lord Soames, dependent upon the existing machinery of government to oversee the change. In the elections the ZANU-PF (Mugabe) won 57 seats, the ZAPU-PF (Nkomo) won 20, the renamed United African National Congress (Muzorewa) won 3, while all 20 reserved seats were won by the RF. On April 18, 1980, Zimbabwe became independent, with Robert Mugabe as prime minister.

GUY ARNOLD

See also: **Mugabe, Robert; Nkomo, Joshua; White Settler Factor: Economic and Political.**

Further Reading

Charlton, Michael. *The Last Colony in Africa: Diplomacy and the Independence of Rhodesia.* Oxford: Basil Blackwell, 1990.

Kriger, Norma J. *Zimbabwe's Guerrilla War: Peasant Voices.* Cambridge: Cambridge University Press, 1991.

Legum, Colin. *The Battlefronts of Southern Africa.* New York: Africana Publishing, 1991.

Weiss, Ruth. *Zimbabwe and the New Elite.* London: British Academic Press, 1994.

Zimbabwe: Second Chimurenga, 1966–1979

The sceond *chimurenga* (Chimurenga II) derived its inspiration from the first unified Shona and Ndebele war (Chimurenga I) against British colonialism of 1896–1897, which the Africans lost despite their invocation of guidance from heroic indigenous spirit mediums such as Mbuya Nehanda, Chaminuka, and others. For over 70 years the Shona and Ndebele suffered landlessness, disenfranchisement, Britain's apathy, various diplomatic failures to achieve universal suffrage, and the settlers' Unilateral Declaration of Independence (UDI) in 1965, which was accompanied by the banning of black political parties. This state of affairs precipitated African nationalism and peasant radicalism by the mid-1960s. Chimurenga II was a war of liberation in which freedom fighters were to reclaim their land by resisting the UDI and colonialism while achieving democratic self-governance. The war was unevenly waged by the Zimbabwe African National Union (ZANU) and Zimbabwe African Peoples Union (ZAPU), through their military wings, the Zimbabwe National Liberation Army (ZANLA) and the Zimbabwe People's Liberation Army (ZIPRA), respectively. The ZANU-ZANLA, representing 80 per cent of the population, dominated Chimurenga II, with the ZAPU-ZIPRA increasing its military activity in the mid-1970s. The political leadership mostly consisted of university graduates; commanders and cadres generally had high school educations or less. Banned in Rhodesia, nationalist politicians formed governments in exile in 1964, with the ZANU and ZAPU headquarters in Tanzania and Zambia, respectively, from which Chimurenga II was organized.

Initially, the ZANU proclaimed socialism and radical revolutionary strategies contrary to the ZAPU's communism, but in the end they both advocated for scientific socialism. The ZANLA forces originally trained in China, Cuba, Ethiopia, Mozambique, North Korea, Tanzania, Romania, and Yugoslavia were persistently deficient in military resources as compared to the ZIPRA cadres, trained in Algeria, China, Czechoslovakia, Ghana, North Korea, and Russia.

Chimurenga II evolved in three phases. The first phase, which lasted from 1966 to 1970, was a turning point of the liberation struggle and focused on disrupting law and order. In 1966 a fierce Senoia battle took place in which ZANLA warriors, intending to sabotage the Kariba Dam's hydroelectricity output, were inadvertently ambushed by Rhodesian forces, instigating conventional warfare with a more superior military force. The ZIPRA followed suit, simulating the Shona and Ndebele unity of Chimurenga I. While avoiding detection from police dogs, air searches and notorious government trackers (Selous Scouts) masquerading as guerillas, early freedom fighters faced thirst and hunger while carrying heavy weaponry loads across the treacherous and crocodile-infested Zambezi River, and the survival of the ruggedness of the Zambezi escarpment. The ZIPRA, commanding most guerrillas at the time, registered record setbacks due to the conventional warfare strategy of the Rhodesian forces, whose counterinsurgency entailed ruthless massacres of guerrillas, showcasing their mutilated corpses, and torturing survivors and peasants considered Chimurenga allies. Such was Rhodesia's practice in the aftermath of the 1968 Wange battle of 70 ZIPRA and African National Congress (ANC)–South Africa guerrillas in which there was one survivor. This alliance legitimized South Africa's military intervention in Rhodesia throughout the war, taxing Chimurenga heavily. Costly experiences of the first phase taught the freedom fighters to win the hearts and minds of peasants while avoiding conventional warfare.

The second phase of Chimurenga II (1971–1973) prioritized clandestine countryside infiltration; raising peasant awareness; self-reliance in recruitment, training, and logistics; establishing the process of seizing power; constitutional development; and preparing for a protracted hit-and-run war to exhaust and liquidate the Rhodesian regime, ultimately liberating Zimbabwe. The effort of gaining mass support for the revolution was aided by traditional spirit mediums' articulation of people's concerns, promotion of principles of *hunhu* (virtue), and effective guerrilla warfare. The Rhodesian government became aware of the second phase of Chimurenga II after the ZANLA's battalion of 60 had mounted a cutting-edge offensive in December 1972 and responded by installing barbed wire–protected villages, with nightly floodlights, in Mtoko, the base for the Rhodesian Security Forces and Joint Operations Command for Operation Hurricane in northeastern Mashonaland. The Shona, particularly Karanga staffing the majority of the government's African troops also dominated the rank and file of the ZANLA.

At the end of this phase, the ZANLA had developed an elaborate system of partyorganization and liberation support structure, with committees and officers responsible for logistics, political commissar, record-keeping, food supplies, and finance. Parents' committees (*vabereki*) worked with messengers of guerrillas (*mujiba,* male messengers) and (*chimbwido,* female messengers) numbering 50,000 by 1979 to provide a transportation and intelligence communication network. Camaraderie was monitored through *pungwes* (nightly political meetings) interjected with revolutionary songs.

The third phase of Chimurenga II (1974–1979) entailed a protracted intensification of military action, with Mozambique's 1975 independence improving the ZANLA's geopolitical situation and ability to expand the war, institutionalize ethos of purposeful transformation in its liberated zones, and access the midlands where the ZIPRA was already operating. An upsurge of peasants to front line states overwhelmed refugee camps, pressuring the ZANLA and the ZIPRA to shorten guerrilla-training periods. Rhodesia, having reinforcements from South African and U.S. troops and total control of the airfield, used fearsome force, claiming a "kill ratio" of 14 to 1 in the Operation Hurricane zone around Mtoko, with Selous Scouts murdering approximately 1,800 peasants by the end of 1979.

When the 1978 Zimbabwe-Rhodesia internal settlement excluded the ZANU-ZAPU alliance (Patriotic Front [PF]), the armed wings of which were attacking Rhodesia-South Africa forces, Chimurenga intensification forced all the parties concerned to include the PF at the Lancaster House independence talks. At the peak of the revolution (1978–1979), there were 22,000 guerrillas, with 13,000 operating within Rhodesia-Zimbabwe. Rhodesia–South Africa cross-border air bombings killed 1,000 refugees in Zambia alone and inflicted the highest refugee-camp deaths in front line states. Death rates of guerrillas, civilians, and security forces escalated at unprecedented proportions. In liberated zones, Chimurenga warriors blended with villagers in everyday activities while subversively planting explosives, slaughtering settler livestock, destroying government-operated veterinary services and schools, transmitting messages, and moving military reinforcements. These tactics were supported by the guerrillas' ability to live in the forest, especially during the rainy season, when Chimurenga inflicted its most devastation while camouflaged by thriving bush cover. The ZANLA, responsible for 80 per cent of Zimbabwe's guerrilla warfare between 1972 and 1979, dominated the armed struggle with impressive results.

Chimurenga's successes were often disrupted by frequent leadership and tribal squabbles between Ndebele and Shona within the ZANU and the ZAPU, and the Front Line States' push for détente with South Africa-Rhodesia, having a domino effect on ZANLA and ZIPRA forces. Despite the ZANLA's triumph, an imposed 1976 joint ZANLA and ZIPRA military force, the Zimbabwe Peoples Army, led to a mutiny accentuated by the tendency of the front line states to overlook factionalism. Front line states also coerced liberation movements to form the Patriotic Front (PF), an alliance among the ZANU, the ZAPU, and the ANC, and engage in detente with Rhodesia–South Africa or face mass extradition.

When the PF was formed, many peasants were alienated by the ruthless fighting and recruitment strategies. A pattern of intimidation, coercion, kidnappings, selective assassinations, massacres, and armed confrontations emerged among both guerrilla and Rhodesian forces. These catastrophes drove entire communities off their lands, causing widespread homelessness and social disruption contrary to the original Chimurenga principles of *hunhu* proclaimed by spirit mediums. The war reduced Rhodesia's economic viability by disrupting businesses, schools, and farming and inflating the defense budget when the tax base sustaining the expensive war had been shrunk through settler depopulation from 278,000 to 230,000.

In 1979—known as *gukurahundi* (the year of the peoples' storm)—the ZANLA had 20,000 fighters, and Rhodesian Marshall Law had been expanded to cover 95 per cent of the country. Between December 1972 and January 1977, 3,845 peasants, 760 security forces, 310 white civilians, and 6,000 freedom fighters were reported killed. In 1979 alone, death rates increased by 45 per cent among peasants, 60 per cent among civilian whites, 50 per cent among ZANLA forces, and 37 per cent among Rhodesian forces. By the time of the December 1979 cease-fire, there were approximately 40,000 dead consisting of 7,000 black civilians, 10,000 guerrillas, 700 black security forces and 350 whites (the rest murdered in exile). There were approximately 22,000 ZANLA and 8,000 ZIPRA forces operating in Zimbabwe-Rhodesia who were placed in assembly points under external pressure from front line states, the United Nations, Britain, and the United States, even before the Lancaster Agreement leading to the end of Chimurenga II and subsequent the ZAPU-ZANU (PF) independence victory of 1980 was achieved.

SALIWE M. KAWEWE

See also: **Mugabe, Robert; Nkomo, Joshua.**

Further Reading

Astrow, Andre. *Zimbabwe: A Revolution That Lost Its Way.* London: Zed, 1983.

Bhebe, N. and T. Ranger (eds.). Soldiers *in Zimbabwe's Liberation War.* Harare: University of Zimbabwe, 1995.

Davidson, Basil, Joe Slovo, and Anthony R. Wilkinson (eds.). *Southern Africa: the New Politics of Revolution.* New York: Pelican, 1977.

Gann, H. Lewis. *The Struggle for Zimbabwe: Battle in the Bush.* New York: Praeger, 1981.

Kriger, Norma J. *Zimbabwe's Guerrilla War: Peasant Voices.* New York: Cambridge University Press, 1992.

Lan, David. *Guns and Rain: Guerrillas and Spirit Mediums in Zimbabwe.* Berkeley and Los Angeles: University of California Press, 1985.

Martin, David, and Phyllis Johnson. *The Struggle for Zimbabwe: The Chimurenga War.* London: Faber and Faber, 1981.

Masipula, Sithole. *Zimbabwe; Struggles within the Struggle.* Salisbury, Rujeko, 1979.

Ranger, Terence. *Peasant Consciousness and Guerrilla War in Zimbabwe: A Comparative Study.* Berkeley and Los Angeles: University of California Press, 1985.

Shamuyarira, Nathan. *National Liberation through Self Reliance in Rhodesia 1956–1972.* Ann Arbor, Mich.: University Microfilms International, 1989.

Zimbabwe: Zimbabwe-Rhodesia, Lancaster House and Independence: 1978–1980

The Lancaster House Conference (September-December 1979) in London was the final step in a long-awaited transition to legal independence from Britain and majority rule in Southern Rhodesia. The delegations participating in the talks included both factions of the Patriotic Front (PF)—Robert Mugabe's ZANU (Zimbabwe African National Union) and Joshua Nkomo's ZAPU (Zimbabwe African Patriotic Union)—and a joint Bishop Abel Muzorewa–Ian Smith delegation representing the Zimbabwe-Rhodesia government that had resulted from the so-called internal settlement. British foreign secretary Lord Carrington played the decisive mediating role in the negotiations on behalf of the British government.

Earlier attempts at diplomatic settlement of the Rhodesia conflict—Smith-Home (1971), Lusaka (1975), and Geneva (1976)—had failed. In 1979, U.S. president Jimmy Carter and secretary of state Cyrus Vance began to work with the government of Margaret Thatcher in Britain in an effort to bring all conflicting parties back to the table for another round of negotiations. A turning point came shortly after the Commonwealth Conference in Lusaka in March of that year.

Up to then, Rhodesia appeared no closer to majority rule and independence from Britain than it had at any time since Ian Smith's Unilateral Declaration of Independence (UDI) in November of 1965. Britain had made two early attempts to bring the rebel UDI regime back to legality via diplomacy on HMS *Tiger* (1966) and HMS *Fearless* (1968) while making it clear that military intervention was not an option.

Whites represented less than 5 per cent of the population. Many supported the RF's increasingly harsh measures to preserve minority economic and political power in the face of significant African nationalist challenges.

These challenges took on a military dimension after 1966. A full-scale civil war was on by 1973–1974, when a new front was opened in the northeast by ZANU guerrilla forces, the ZANLA. ZAPU fighters, the ZIPRA, based in Zambia, continued to make incursions from the north. After 1975, the Rhodesian counterinsurgency military campaign was increasingly overstretched and stalemated by a large, effective

ZANLA force, based in newly independent, front-line Mozambique. Public opinion was turning against the war. International sanctions against Rhodesia had been in effect for nearly a decade. In 1976, Ian Smith was pressed by U.S. secretary of state Henry Kissinger and South African president John Vorster to announce a two-year timetable leading to some form of qualified majority rule.

Mugabe and Nkomo refused to accept anything short of full sovereign independence and majority rule and, after the failed Geneva talks, intensified the military campaign. Military pressure eventually forced the Smith regime to reconsider its political position and enter talks with ZANU and ZAPU leaders over the issue of majority rule. Faced with a combination of international diplomatic pressure, damaging economic effects of sanctions, and escalating guerrilla activity, Smith announced an "internal settlement" with Bishop Muzorewa's new party, the United African National Council (UANC), in March 1978. PF leaders condemned the agreement and refused to participate in the April 1979 elections under a new constitution that gave whites 28 per cent of the parliamentary seats.

By the time of the elections, 85 per cent of the country was under martial law, 10 per cent of the African population was interred in "protected villages," and nearly 50,000 guerrilla fighters had swelled the ranks of the ZANLA and the ZIPRA with arms and external military support from China and the Soviet Union. Muzorewa's UNAC took a majority of the African seats and in June 1979 he became prime minister of Zimbabwe-Rhodesia. The war continued to escalate to the point where leaders of African front line states launched a diplomatic initiative that soon engaged the British, who organized a new round of negotiations between the PF and the Zimbabwe-Rhodesia government at Lancaster House in London, leading to an independence agreement.

Several entrenched provisions—particularly the demand by Muzorewa-Smith for reserved Parliamentary seats (20 of 100) for whites for seven years under the new constitution and a ten-year stipulation prohibiting compulsory government acquisition of land—made PF agreement doubtful right up to the last minute, when collapse of talks was averted by powerful lobbying by key leaders of the front line states, particularly Zambian president Kenneth Kaunda and Mozambican president Samora Machel, whose states hosted exile headquarters of the ZAPU and the ZANU, respectively, and threat of a separate agreement between Britain and the Zimbabwe-Rhodesia government.

The agreement, signed on December 21, 1979, laid out the principles for a Westminster-style democratic constitution, a transition period leading to British-supervised, common-role elections, and a cease-fire between government forces and the military wings of the PF: the ZANLA (ZANU) and the ZIPRA (ZAPU). Britain assumed direct control of the colony under governor Lord Soames, who enacted an amnesty and unbanned the ZANU and the ZAPU as a first step toward general elections. A Commonwealth Monitoring Force was deployed under British command to supervise the implementation of a cease-fire. Rhodesian Army units and guerilla fighters of the ZANLA and the ZIPRA were ordered to barracks or designated assembly points. International sanctions against Rhodesia were lifted by the United Nations Security Council.

General elections for 80 of the 100 seats of the House of Assembly and a separate white roll for the remaining 20 seats were held in February 1980. The RF party swept all 20 white seats. The ZANU–PF, which contested the election separately from the PF alliance, won 57 of the 80 contested seats with 63 per cent of the vote. The ZAPU–PF won 20 seats and 24 per cent of the popular vote. Bishop Muzorewa's UNAC party won 3 seats on 8 per cent of the African vote.

On March 3, 1980, Robert Mugabe was appointed first prime minister of the Republic of Zimbabwe, and a coalition cabinet with ZAPU leader Nkomo as home affairs minister was named. Zimbabwe independence was granted formally on April 18, 1980.

Emphasizing national reconciliation, the Mugabe government immediately faced immense problems, including assassination attempts; restarting the war-ravaged economy; integrating the guerrilla armies of the ZANLA and the ZIPRA with the Rhodesian army; South African sabotage; and satisfying high expectations of the African majority, particularly for land, education, and Africanization of government and private sector employment. Ethnic and political factionalism persisted. Within a year the coalition cabinet began to come apart and the ZANU–PF was on the way toward de facto one-party rule.

JAMES J. ZAFFIRO

See also: **Mugabe, Robert; Nkomo, Joshua.**

Further Reading

Baumhogger, Goswin. *The Struggle For Independence: Documents on the Recent Development of Zimbabwe*, vols. 6–7. Hamburg: Institute for African Studies, 1984.

Charlton, Michael. *The Last Colony in Africa: Diplomacy and Independence in Rhodesia*. Cambridge, Mass: Oxford University Press, 1990.

Commonwealth Observer Group. *Southern Rhodesia Elections*. London: Commonwealth Secretariat, 1980.

Davidow, Jeffrey. *A Peace in Southern Africa: The Lancaster House Conference on Rhodesia, 1979*. Boulder, Colo.: Westview Press, 1984.

Great Britain, Secretary of State for Foreign and Commonwealth Affairs, *Report of the Constitutional Conference*. London: HMSO, 1980.

Journal of Southern African Affairs, 4, no. 4 (1979) Special issue, with key Lancaster House Conference documents reprinted.

Martin, David, and Phyllis Johnson. *The Struggle for Zimbabwe.* London: Faber and Faber, 1981.

Newhouse, John. "Profiles (Lord Carrington)." *New Yorker*, February 14, 1983.

"Rhodesian Settlement Initiatives," *Southern African Record*, no. 18 (1979): 1–46.

Soames, Lord Christopher. "Rhodesia to Zimbabwe." *International Affairs* 56, no. 3 (1980): 405–419.

Stedman, Stephen John. *Peacemaking in Civil War: International Mediation in Zimbabwe.* Boulder, Colo.: Westview Press, 1991.

Wiseman, Henry. *From Rhodesia to Zimbabwe: The Politics of Transition.* New York: Pergamon Press, 1981.

Zimbabwe: Conflict and Reconstruction, 1980s

During the Rhodesian bush war of the 1970s, the Zimbabwe liberation movement had developed two very different camps. The Zimbabwe African People's Union (ZAPU) received assistance and ideology from the Soviet Union and had planned to use its largely conventional army, based in Zambia, to seize power. The membership of this organization came mostly from Matabeleland, in western Zimbabwe, and their lingua franca became Sindebele (the language of the Ndebele people of that region.) In contrast, the Zimbabwe African National Union–Patriotic Front (ZANU–PF), had gravitated to China, adopted a Maoist ideology, and waged a guerrilla war against the British regime of Ian Smith from its bases in Mozambique. Because of its emphasis on politicizing the rural people of eastern Zimbabwe, most of its support came from the predominantly Shona-speaking area. (Shona people made up roughly 75 per cent of the entire population.) This division would have an impact on Zimbabwe in the 1980s.

After the Lancaster House agreement of December 1979 in which government and liberation movement forces declared a cease-fire, Zimbabwe-Rhodesia held its first free and fair elections in February 1980. ZANU–PF won a strong victory and its leader, Robert Mugabe, became prime minister of an independent Zimbabwe in April 1980. The ZANU-PF had won most of the seats throughout the country except in the predominantly Ndebele region of Matabeleland where the other prominent liberation movement, the ZAPU, under Joshua Nkomo, received most of its support. However, ZANU–PF gained more than three times the number of seats in Parliament than ZAPU. Upon his victory, Mugabe announced a policy of national reconciliation and tried to transcend regional divisions by forming a coalition government in which Nkomo and several ZAPU members held cabinet posts.

Relations between the ZANU–PF and the ZAPU deteriorated in the early 1980s. In 1982, in a township of Bulawayo, the capital of Matabeleland, there was a major battle between ex-combatants of the Zimbabwe African National Liberation Army (ZANLA), the ZANU's armed wing during the war, and the Zimbabwe Independent People's Revolutionary Army (ZIPRA), the ZAPU's armed wing. The ZANU–PF–dominated government began to fear that arms caches on Nkomo's farms were to be used for a coup and that the ZAPU had begun to receive assistance from the apartheid government in South Africa, which wanted to destabilize its black-ruled neighbors. (It should be noted that Nkomo was later brought to trail on charges of treason but that the judge dismissed them.) In any case, in 1982 Nkomo and other ZAPU members were dismissed from the government.

In an effort to crush dissident activities, Mugabe's government sent the Zimbabwean army's Fifth Brigade into Matabeleland in early 1983. The Fifth Brigade was predominantly Shona speaking, and made up mostly of ex-ZANLA fighters. Unlike other Zimbabwean military units, it was North Korean–trained and equipped. It was given the name Gukurahundi, which is a Shona term meaning "the rain that washes away rubbish." (The Ndebele people of Matabeleland would come to believe that they were the "rubbish" that was to be washed away.) Utilizing the same state-of-emergency powers that had been implemented by the Rhodesian government of Ian Smith, the Fifth Brigade terrorized the rural people of Matabeleland in an effort to prevent them from supporting "dissidents." In 1984 a 24-hour curfew was imposed on Matabeleland South Province that closed schools and stores, and control of access to food was used to coerce rural communities. In 1985, ZAPU officials and ex-ZIPRA combatants were abducted, and after the parliamentary elections of July 1986 some 200 ZAPU supporters were detained without charge. The Fifth Brigade employed the strategy of "collective punishment"—ironically, implemented by the Smith regime—on entire communities suspected of secretly supporting "dissidents." They were spurred on by the belief that they were heroes of the national liberation struggle who were combating counterrevolutionary forces.

With the Unity Accord between the ZANU–PF and the ZAPU in 1987, the later organization was merged into the governing party, and some of its members were absorbed into the government. In 1988 the government declared an amnesty for all ex-ZIPRA fighters who were in hiding or who had fled the country. Nkomo became one of two deputy presidents in 1990. After 1986 the conditions of the Lancaster House agreement, which guaranteed Zimbabwean whites 20 seats in the parliament, expired, and Ian Smith, who had continued to serve as a member of parliament, officially retired from politics. At this time Mugabe combined the positions of prime minister and president and became president.

Whites owned most of the best agricultural land, and the ZANU, from the days of the liberation war, had promised to redistribute this to the majority of African rural people who lived in communal reserves. However, by the late 1980s, the ZANU government had come under criticism for not moving swiftly enough to redistribute land and for allocating available land to wealthy government ministers. On the other hand, the white farming community began to use the courts to challenge government expropriation of their land and claimed that this program would destroy the country's primarily agricultural economy. This controversy would continue well into the 1990s.

TIMOTHY J. STAPLETON

See also: **Mugabe, Robert; Nkomo, Joshua.**

Further Reading

Hebst, Jeffrey. *State Politics in Zimbabwe*. Berkeley and Los Angeles: University of California Press, 1990.

Mandaza, Ibbo (ed.). *Zimbabwe: The Politics of Transition, 1980–86*. Dakar: CODESRIA, 1986.

Werbner, Richard. *Tears of the Dead: The Social Biography of an African Family*. London: Edinburgh University Press, 1991.

Zimbabwe: Since 1990

In the 1990s Zimbabwe faced a host of multifaceted and complex economic crises rooted in its inherited colonial structure, exacerbated by exogenous forces leading to the government's undertaking of far-reaching economic reforms. Difficulties confronting Zimbabwe were formidable, and the progress of the 1980s was clearly being eroded in the early 1990s due to internal and external elite confluence as globalization of markets surfaced as one of the country's greatest challenges. The crisis situation reached alarming proportions with the intensification of declining exports; mounting foreign debts and foreign debt servicing; underemployment and unemployment exacerbated by retrenchment; indigenous agriculture marginalization; poor economic growth; falling per capita incomes; accelerating ecological degradation; increased food imports and prices leading to urban civil disturbances; widespread misuse of political and economic power for individual gain; and human rights abuses. These were compounded by problems with refugees; rapid population growth; impoverishment; declining quality of education, social services, and health care and exacerbated by the devastation of the HIV/AIDS pandemic reaching its peak in Zimbabwe during the 1990s.

Zimbabwe entered the 1990s soon after the amalgamation of Robert Mugabe's Zimbabwe African National Union–Patriotic Front (ZANU–PF) and Joshua Nkomo's Zimbabwe African People's Union–Patriotic Front (ZAPU–PF) into one organization, the ZANU-PF, at the end of 1988, making the lingering prospect of a one-party state in the forthcoming presidential elections of 1990 eminent but controversial. The ruling party's fixation with a one-party state based on Marxist-Leninist ideology was thwarted by opposition from a former ZANU–PF secretary general's formation of the Zimbabwe Unity Movement (ZUM) in 1989. The ZANU–PF systematically marginalized opposition by harassment, occasional patronage, and co-opting white settlers whose colonial ethos continued under the Conservative Alliance of Zimbabwe. It was not surprising, therefore, that after the 1990 elections there was minimal opposition to the ZANU–PF as the ZUM claimed 17 per cent of the presidential vote (with the ZANU–PF claiming 117 seats out of a total of 120).

Eight opposition parties participated in the 1995 elections, but the ZUM and five other parties boycotted the elections on grounds of government corruption. Overall, Mugabe's popularity continued to decline during this decade, as shown by dwindling voter turnouts from over 94 per cent in 1980; to 84 per cent in 1985, to 54–65 per cent in 1990, representing only 31.7 per cent of all those eligible to vote. Whites' political influence in the parliament had been reduced since the 1980s, but the political process was also removed from the parliament at the same time that the president gained a combination of executive and ceremonial roles as the office of the prime minister was merged with that of the president, making the president more powerful than ever and allowing interest groups to deal directly with the executive branch outside of electoral politics.

Although Zimbabwe's independence of 1980 was achieved after a protracted civil war prompted by racism, sexism, infringement of blacks' fundamental human rights, and persistent inequities in resource distribution, no radical changes were introduced after independence and the racial tension continued through the 1990s. Despite presidential and the ZANU–PF leadership's rhetoric threatening national reformative action (which was barely enforced), such complacence left the white in their privileged position unabated. Further, in 1999 the Zimbabwean Supreme Court reversed two decades of women's human rights gains by ruling Zimbabwean women as minors to men and without inheritance rights. Zimbabwe's Constitution Commission embarked on drafting a new constitution in late 1999, claiming the inclusion of a Bill of Rights guaranteeing fundamental human rights and freedoms of individuals regardless of race, sex, color, creed, religion, sexual orientation, economic or social status, or ethnicity, and limiting presidential terms.

A combination of the elite's inexperience and vested interests led in the 1990s to some policies that were part of a systematic framework, but others (those regarding liberalization) were adopted *ad hoc*. Structural change posed a threat to a variety of entrenched interests in society, but Zimbabwe's reversal of economic development strategy without the expertise and corresponding change in government compounded by authoritarianism, entrenched in African leadership, rendered the black government a mismatch for white settlers' administrative and economic expertise. Even though the economy was in no serious danger then, top level government technocrats, strong white interest groups, and the World Bank converged with the adoption of structural adjustment programs (SAPs). White lobbyists, technocrats, and International Monetary Fund (IMF)/World Bank interests lay in deregulation of prices, imports and foreign exchange. Additionally, the brain drain from public to the private sector weakened the government's ability to do business with the experienced economic groups. Economic discussions and agreements between the ministries and white interest groups were carried out in quiet diplomacy and unknown to voters. Thus, transforming economic development strategy from that of the 1980s was done smoothly with whites, ensuring the protection of their interests and preventing redistribution of their assets through their use of overwhelming influence and expertise in economic policy formulation. Certain aspects of structural adjustment reform—trade, foreign exchange, price and financial sector liberalization—were carried out swiftly, but public expenditure and tax reforms were developed slowly.

The national policy of indigenization and land reform endorsed by the Land Acquisition Act of 1993, aimed at eliminating racial and class disparity in wealth through the government's purchase of settler-owned farms to resettle peasants, was barely successful as whatever little land acquired was grabbed by the black elite. By 1996 the state had resettled only 72,000 black peasants in 21 government-purchased farms since independence. The skewed land distribution in favor of whites continued despite government claims of some progress in redressing the land equation. The CFU steadfastly resisted land redistribution by also co-opting the black elite in the mid-1990s. Thus, minimal strides were made in rural resettlement, extensive agricultural services, education and health services, food aid during cyclic droughts, and pricing policies for communal farmers. Historically, government initiatives geared toward satisfying the rural peasantry are announced just before the elections in order for the government to retain and garnish electoral votes. By August 1999 the government had bought 94,000 hectares (on 47 farms) worth over $95 million (U.S.) from commercial farmers and intended to acquire another 120 uncontested farms for the resettlement of landless peasants.

An intricate relationship between the internal elite and the international interests of Britain, the United States, and South Africa affected the countries in the region. Zimbabwe was caught in a quandary of attempting to retain political legitimacy while at the same time abiding by the externally imposed and monitored SAPs intended to ensure economic growth. The external interests and their convergence with those of the elite was paramount in curbing Zimbabwe's predicament, since independence and Zimbabwe's domestic policy making had been subject to the dictates of foreign ideologies since colonial times. These constraints were compelling in limiting the leadership's ability to successfully achieve economic changes, especially as the globalization of world markets surfaced as one of the greatest challenges facing Zimbabwe and exposed limitations of statehood autonomy, particularly during the post–Cold War era, as Africa lost its geopolitical strategic value. The early 1990s marked a turning point in the Zimbabwean government's ability to shape economic policy autonomously. The emerging order of SAPs was based on shock treatments of mercantilism and monetarism, which failed to create an environment conducive for poor nations to win concessions from the global markets or affect the deployment of power and resources. The fear of marginalization through unfair global competition was real because production in Africa is more costly than in other developing regions like Asia, and a shortage of investment opportunities also limited foreign and domestic investment. More African countries have become classified as least developed nations, with none becoming classified as a developed nation due to efforts by the United States and Russia or the United Nations. The adverse effects of trade restrictions and protectionism in Zimbabwe increased in the 1990s with further marginalization of the masses from political and decision-making processes.

Exceeding the expectations of even the most powerful private sector white interest groups, in 1990 the Zimbabwean government, in a reversal of position, backpedaled on its Marxist-Leninist approach, development strategy, and the repudiation of SAPs by abruptly adopting and proceeding with the previously unacceptable conditions of liberalization of trade, including civil service cuts. Although the economy was showing signs of stress and increasing debt servicing, it was not in such a state of crisis to warrant the abrupt imposition of SAPs. Economic growth was sought through deregulation, import liberalization, devaluation of the exchange rate of the Zimbabwean dollar, privatizing state enterprises, and the removal of state controls. SAPs were never intended to punish or reward the poor, yet in order to reduce public expenditures and state controls in imports and prices, and shift resources to those who could use them more productively in the economic sense, in practice SAPs led to hardship and discontent among Zimbabweans—particularly urbanites, because these reforms were directly linked to the urban economy. The closure of industries and retrenchment of middle- to low-income earners in the public and private sectors most devastated urbanites. The situation was compounded by the 1991–1992 drought, which increased borrowing, leading to a debt service ratio of 30 per cent, which declined to 22 per cent in 1995. The Grain Marketing Board deficit alone reached 5 per cent of the gross domestic product (GDP), with the government subsidies becoming larger than the wage bill for most years since the mid-1980s. In 1993, total imports were US$1.8 million and US$1.5 million total exports with a 13.4 per cent of GDP budget deficit. The government failed to cut public expenditure, partly due to the drought and partly due to its reluctance to offset it political constituency.

As a result, when Zimbabwe increased its indebtedness and dependence on foreign aid, the government's ability to determine economic policies independently was thwarted. In 1995, the IMF and World Bank suspended a balance of payments of $120 million (U.S.) when the government failed for the second time, after 1993–1994, to meet the target of a budget deficit reduction of 7 per cent, but reached 14 of the GDP per cent instead. The European Union also announced in March 1996 that it would suspend other disbursements to Zimbabwe until the IMF/World Bank conditions—particularly fiscal targets—were met, but would allocate US$32 million for Zimbabwe's education, health, and drought relief.

Although shifting from a state-led to a fully market-based economic management system was bound to be difficult, SAPs, regardless of their merits, were an external imposition that relied on preexisting discredited domestic power structures for its implementation. SAPs led to Zimbabwe's greater dependence on external forces while increasing the hardship of the disadvantaged majority. Because they were never products of initial consultations and open debate before adoption, the implementation of SAPs translated into accountability of the government to the donors instead of to the people, who make the sacrifice needed for the programs' success. Resistance to foreign-imposed political conditions generated some friction between the World Bank and donor agencies on one hand and the government on the other regarding reformist attention being given to human rights, empowerment, and the protection of vulnerable groups (especially women and children).

Zimbabwe's foreign debt increased from 45 per cent of the GDP in 1990 to 75 per cent in 1994 and then fell to 67 per cent in 1995. Ninety-five per cent of the debt is by government and its parastatal organizations. Zimbabwe continued to be vulnerable to external forces potentially increasing external borrowing into the twenty-first century. The 1995–1996 budget and subsequent budgets have reflected a deficit in excess of 10 per cent of the GDP. Services claimed 46.4 per cent of the GDP during the early 1990s, while expenditure in defense declined, but the government involvement in the Republic of Congo war in 1998 inflated the Zimbabwean military expenditure again. The second phase of SAPs, beginning in 1996, was to focus particularly on privatization. Mugabe's attempts to reimpose some price controls and cap tariffs in 1996 (with increased tariffs to as high as 75 per cent) were thwarted as a contravention of the IMF conditionality. The social dimension program was introduced in an attempt to tackle the social cost of SAPs by assuming the burdens of food and other subsidies previously shouldered by the government. Redistributive policies inevitably have an adverse effect on those groups that are politically and economically the strongest. In 1999, after two years of waiting, the IMF approved $193 million (U.S.) in stand-by credit to be disbursed over a 14-month period and dependent on meeting performance goals and completing program evaluations for Zimbabwe's second phase of ESAP.

Whereas Zimbabwe was internationally considered to have political growth potential at independence, two decades later that economic potential has not been realized with the country entering the twenty-first century with per capita incomes lower than they were in 1980; a rapidly increasing number of impoverished people; inability of the state to design and implement sustained poverty-eradication development schemes; and incapability to handle peaceful resolution of conflicts. For example, in December 1998, after the price of corn meal (the staple food) and other commodities had escalated, culminating in to urban civil disturbances, the government responded with brutal force, resulting in record hospitalizations of the injured and eight lives lost. This government brutality set a precedent for bloodshed, because revolutions are often prompted when an existing framework fails to mediate fundamental discontent among existing organizations over institutional change.

SALIWE KAWEWE

See also: **Mugabe, Robert; Nkomo, Joshua; World Bank, International Monetary Fund, and Structural Adjustment.**

Further Reading

Beach, D. N. *A Zimbabwean Past: Shona Dynastic Histories and Oral Traditions*. Gweru, Zimbabwe: Mambo Press, 1994.

Bello, W. *Dark History: The U.S. Structural Adjustment and Global Poverty*. Oakland, Calif.: Institute for Food and Development Policy, 1993.

Mandaza, I., and L. M. Sachikonye (eds.). *The One Party State and Democracy; The Zimbabwe Debate*. Harare: SAPES, 1991.

Moyo, N. Jonathan. *Voting for Democracy: Electoral Politics in Zimbabwe*. Harare: University of Zimbabwe, 1992.

Moyo, Sam. *The Land Question in Zimbabwe*. Harare: SAPES, 1995.

O'Flaherty, M. "Communal Tenure in Zimbabwe: Divergent Models of Collective Land Holding in the Communal Areas." *Africa, Journal of the International African Institute* 68, no. 4 (1998): 536–557.

Potts, D., and C. Mutambirwa. "'The Government Must Not Dictate': Rural-Urban Migrants Perspectives of Zimbabwe's Resettlement Program." *Review of African Political Economy* 24, no. 74 (1997): 549–566.

Wanmali, S., and Y. Islam. "Rural Infrastructure and Agricultural Development in Southern Africa: A Centre-Periphery Perspective." *Geographical Journal* 163, no. 3 (1997): 259–269.

Zimbabwe-Rhodesia: *See* Zimbabwe: Zimbabwe-Rhodesia, Lancaster House and Independence, 1978–1980.

Ziyanids: *See* Maghrib: Marinids, Ziyanids, and Hafsids, 1235–1359.

Zulu Kingdom: *See* Anglo-Zulu War, 1879–1887; Cetshwayo; Mfecane; Shaka and Zulu Kingdom, 1810–1840.

CONTRIBUTORS

Abaka, Edmund. Department of History, University of Miami. Articles contributed: Asante Kingdom: Osei Tutu and Founding of; Collaboration as Resistance; Ghana (Republic of) (Gold Coast): Colonial Period: Economy; Ghana: Revolution and Fourth Republic, 1981 to Present; Songhay Empire: Sunni Ali and the Founding of Empire; Songhay Empire: Ture, Muhammad and the Askiya Dynasty.

Abdullahi, Mohamed Diriye. Somali scholar, Ontario, Canada. Articles contributed: Cushites: Northeastern Africa: Stone Age Origins to Iron Age; Mogadishu; Somalia: 1990 to the Present; Somalia: Nineteenth Century ; Somalia: Barré, Muhammad Siad, Life and Government of; Somalia: Pastoralism, Islam, Commerce, Expansion: To 1800.

Abubakar, Tanimu. Department of History, University of Ahmadu Bello, Nigeria. Article contributed: Literature, Western: Africa in.

Adejumobi, Saheed A. Department of Africana Studies, Wayne State University, Michigan. Articles contributed: Awolowo, Obafemi; Community in African Society.

Adesina, Olutayo. Department of History, University of Ibadan, Nigeria. Articles contributed: Benin, Republic of (Dahomey): Democratization, National Conference and, 1990s; Benin, Republic of (Dahomey): Kérékou, Mathieu; Carthage; Mali Empire: Economy; Mauritania: Ethnicity, Conflict, Development, 1980s and 1990s; Tripoli.

Adhikari, Mohamed. Department of History, University of Cape Town, South Africa. Articles contributed: South Africa: Colored Identity; South Africa: Defiance Campaign, Freedom Charter, Treason Trials: 1952–1960; South Africa: Sharpeville Massacre.

Adi, Hakim. School of Humanities and Cultural Studies, Middlesex University, England. Articles contributed: Colonialism, Overthrow of: Nationalism and Anticolonialism; Ethiopia: 1991 to the Present.

Adupa, Cyprian B. Department of History, Institute of Teacher Education, Kyambogo, Uganda. Articles contributed: Uganda: Buganda Agreement, Political Parties, Independence; Uganda: Colonial Period: Northern Uganda.

Afolayan, Funso. Department of History, University of New Hampshire. Articles contributed: Benue Valley Peoples: Jukun and Kwarafa; Historiography of Africa; Macauley, Herbert;

Yoruba States (Other Than Ife and Oyo); Yoruba States: Trade and Conflict, Nineteenth Century.

Aghrout, Ahmed. European Studies Research Institute, University of Salford, England. Articles contributed: Algeria: Conquest and Resistance, 1831–1879; Maghrib Unity, European Union and; Morocco: Nationalism, Muhammad V, Independence, 1930–1961.

Ahanotu, Austin Metumara. Department of History, California State University–Stanislaus. Article contributed: Religion, Postcolonial Africa: Church and State Relations.

Ahazuem, J. O. History Department, University of Nigeria. Articles contributed: Benin Kingdom: Nineteenth Century; Nigeria: Gowon Regime, 1966–1975.

Ajayi, S. Ademola. Department of History, University of Ibadan, Nigeria. Articles contributed: Anti-Slavery Squadron, Decline of Export Slave Trade, Nineteenth Century; Borno (Bornu), Sultanate of: Mai Idris Alooma; Diop, Cheikh Anta; Egypt: Urabi Pasha and British Occupation, 1879–1882; Haile Selassie I; Ibadan; Iron Age (Later): Southern Africa: Peoples; Luthuli, Albert John Mavumbi; Maghrib: Arab Conquest of, 650–715; Mauritania: Domestic and International Politics and Conflict, 1980s and 1990s; Organization of African Unity (OAU) and Pan-Africanism.

Alagoa, E. J. Department of History, University of Port Harcourt, Nigeria. Articles contributed: Niger Delta and its Hinterland: History to Sixteenth century; Niger Delta and its Hinterland: Peoples and States to 1800.

Alao, Akin. Department of History, Obafemi Awolowo University, Nigeria. Articles contributed: Economic Community of West African States (ECOWAS); North Africa: Roman Occupation, Empire; Sanhaja.

Anthony, Douglas A. Department of History, Franklin and Marshall College, Pennsylvania. Article contributed: Nigeria: Federalism, Corruption, Popular Discontent: 1960–1966.

Anyake, Joseph B. C. Department of History, University of Nigeria. Article contributed: History, African: Sources of.

Arnold, Guy. Writer and lecturer, London, England. Articles contributed: Algeria: Ben Bella, Boumédienne, era of, 1960s and 1970s; Beira Corridor; Civil War: Postcolonial Africa; Commonwealth, Africa and the; Congo (Kinshasa), Democratic Republic of/Zaire: Civil War, 1960–1965; Diamonds; East

CONTRIBUTORS

AFRICAN COMMUNITY, THE, 1967–1977; ETHIOPIA: CIVIL WAR AND LIBERATION; INDUSTRIALIZATION AND DEVELOPMENT; KAUNDA, KENNETH; LIBERIA: DOE, SAMUEL K., LIFE AND ERA OF; LIBYA: FOREIGN POLICY UNDER QADDAFI; LUMUMBA, PATRICE; NIGERIA: MILITARY RULE, 1983–1999; PAN-AFRICAN TECHNICAL ORGANIZATIONS AND ASSOCIATIONS; POLISARIO AND THE WESTERN SAHARA; SUEZ CANAL; WATER SUPPLIES AND SCHEMES; ZIMBABWE (RHODESIA): UNILATERAL DECLARATION OF INDEPENDENCE AND THE SMITH REGIME, 1964–1979.

Awasom, Nicodemus Fru. Faculty of Humanities and Social Sciences, University of the Gambia. Article contributed: CAMEROON: REBELLION, INDEPENDENCE, UNIFICATION, 1960–1961.

Azevedo, Mario J. Department of African American Studies, University of North Carolina. Articles contributed: CHAD, NINETEENTH CENTURY: KANEM/BORNO (BORNU) AND WADAI; CHAD: COLONIAL PERIOD: FRENCH RULE.

Bangura, Abdul Karim. School of International Service, American University, Washington, D.C. Articles contributed: EGYPT: SADAT, NATIONALISM, 1970–1981; FREETOWN; FUTA JALON TO 1800; SIERRA LEONE: MOMOH, JOSEPH SAIDU: REGIME, 1986–1992.

Banyata, Bundjoko. Assistant Curator. Ethnographic Section, Musee National de Lubumbashi. Article contributed: KASAI AND KUBA: CHIEFDOMS AND KINGDOM.

Barham, Lawrence. Department of Archaeology, University of Bristol, England. Article contributed: STONE AGE (LATER): CENTRAL AND SOUTHERN AFRICA.

Barry, Ismael. Faculté des Lettres et Sciences Humaines, Université de Conakry, Guinea. Articles contributed: FUTA JALON: NINETEENTH CENTURY; GUINEA: DECOLONIZATION, INDEPENDENCE.

Bayer, Gerd. Department of Modern Languages and Literatures, Case Western Reserve University, Ohio. Articles contributed: ACHEBE, CHINUA; NGUGI WA THIONG'O.

Beauregard, Erving E. Professor Emeritus of History, University of Dayton, Ohio. Article contributed: SENEGAL: FAIDHERBE, LOUIS AND EXPANSION OF FRENCH SENEGAL, 1854–1865.

Bechhaus-Gerst, Marianne. Institute of Afrikan Studies, Universität zu Köln, Germany. Articles contributed: EGYPT, ANCIENT, AND AFRICA; NUBIA: BANU KANZ, JUHAYNA AND THE ARABIZATION OF THE NILOTIC SUDAN; OROMO: MIGRATION AND EXPANSION: SIXTEENTH AND SEVENTEENTH CENTURIES; OROMO: ORIGINS, SOCIAL AND ECONOMIC ORGANIZATION.

Bennison, Amira K. Faculty of Oriental Studies, University of Cambridge, England. Articles contributed: MOROCCO: MAWLAY 'ABD AL-RAHMAN, LIFE AND ERA OF; MOROCCO: MAWLAY ISMA'IL AND EMPIRE OF; MOROCCO: MAWLAY SULAYMAN, LIFE AND ERA OF.

Berliner, David. Faculté des Sciences sociales, politiques et économiques/Ecole de commerce Solvay, Université Libre de Bruxelles, Belgium. Article contributed: GUINEA: 1984 TO THE PRESENT.

Beswick, Stephanie. Department of History, Ball State University, Indiana. Article contributed: NILOTES, EASTERN AFRICA: WESTERN NILOTES: SHILLUK, NUER, DINKA, ANYUAK.

Beyan, Amos J. Department of History, West Virginia University. Articles contributed: BLYDEN, E. W.; MANE: MIGRATIONS, SIXTEENTH CENTURY, HISTORY OF.

Bhana, Surendra. Department of History, University of Kansas. Article contributed: SOUTH AFRICA: GANDHI, INDIAN QUESTION.

Boahen, A. Adu. Historian, Ghana. Articles contributed: AKAN STATES: EIGHTEENTH CENTURY; AKAN STATES: BONO, DANKYIRA, WASSA, AKYEM, AKWAMU, FANTE, FIFTEENTH TO SEVENTEENTH CENTURIES; GHANA (REPUBLIC OF): COLONIZATION AND RESISTANCE, 1875–1901; NKRUMAH, KWAME.

Boilley, Pierre. Professor of contemporary African history, Université Paris 1—Panthéon Sorbonne et Directeur du laboratoire CNRS/U-PARIS 1 (UMR 8054) MALD (Mutations africaines dans la longue durée), France. Articles contributed: MALI, REPUBLIC OF: KEITA, MODIBO, LIFE AND ERA OF; MALI, REPUBLIC OF: NATIONALISM, FEDERATION, INDEPENDENCE; MALI, REPUBLIC OF: POLITICS, ECONOMICS: 1990s; MOROCCO: AHMAD AL-MANSUR AND THE INVASION OF SONGHAY; TUAREG: TWENTIETH CENTURY; TUKOLOR EMPIRE OF AL-HAJJ UMAR.

Bondarev, Dmitry. University of St. Petersburg, Russia. Articles contributed: BORNO (BORNU), SULTANATE OF, SEVENTEENTH AND EIGHTEENTH CENTURIES; BORNO (BORNU), SULTANATE OF: ORIGINS AND RISE, FIFTEENTH CENTURY; 'UTHMAN DAN FODIO.

Bonner, Philip. Department of History, University of the Witwatersrand, South Africa. Articles contributed: SOUTH AFRICA: AFRICAN NATIONAL CONGRESS (ANC); SOUTH AFRICA: INDUSTRIAL AND COMMERCIAL WORKERS UNION; SWAZILAND: SOBHUZA I, FOUNDATION OF NGWANE KINGDOM; SWAZILAND: SWAZI KINGDOM, SURVIVAL OF, 1839–1879.

Bradshaw, Richard. Department of History, Centre College, Kentucky. Articles contributed: BOGANDA, BARTHÉLEMY; CENTRAL AFRICAN REPUBLIC: NINETEENTH CENTURY: GBAYA, BANDA, AND ZANDE.

Bridges, Roy. Professor emeritus of history, University of Aberdeen, Scotland and president of the Hakluyt Society. Articles contributed: EUROPE: EXPLORERS, ADVENTURERS, TRADERS; ZANZIBAR: BRITAIN, GERMANY, "SCRAMBLE."

Brinkman, Inge. Ghent University, Belgium. Articles contributed: ANGOLA: MPLA, FNLA, UNITA, AND THE WAR OF LIBERATION, 1961–1974; NETO, ANTÓNIO AGOSTINHO.

Browne, Dallas L. Department of Anthropology, Southern Illinois University–Edwardsville. Articles contributed: AJA-SPEAKING PEOPLES: DAHOMEY, RISE OF, SEVENTEENTH CENTURY; EGYPT, ANCIENT: PTOLEMAIC DYNASTY: HISTORICAL OUTLINE; EGYPT: ARAB CONQUEST; LIBERIA: TOLBERT, WILLIAM, RICHARD, LIFE AND ERA OF; LIBERIA: TUBMAN, WILLIAM V. S., LIFE AND ERA OF; ODINGA, A. OGINGA; TANGANYIKA (TANZANIA): CHAMA CHA MAPINDUZI, ONE-PARTY POLITICS; TANZANIA (TANGANYIKA): UGANDA, RELATIONS WITH; TUTU, DESMOND.

Burns, James. Department of History, Clemson University, South Carolina. Articles contributed: PRESS: TROPICAL AFRICA; WELENSKY, ROY; ZIMBABWE (SOUTHERN RHODESIA): FEDERATION; ZIMBABWE (SOUTHERN RHODESIA): NATIONALIST POLITICS, 1950s AND 1960s; ZIMBABWE (SOUTHERN RHODESIA): URBANIZATION AND CONFLICT, 1940s.

Burton, Andrew. British Institute in Eastern Africa, Kenya. Articles contributed: DAR ES SALAAM; ZANZIBAR (CITY).

Bush, Barbara. Article contributed: TAXATION.

Butanko, Muya. Musée National de Lubumbashi and Université de Lubumbashi, Democratic Republic of Congo. Articles contributed: IRON AGE (LATER): CENTRAL AFRICA; IRON AGE (LATER): CENTRAL AFRICA: PEOPLES, FOREST; IRON AGE (LATER): CENTRAL AFRICA: UPEMBA BASIN.

Calvert, John. Department of History, Creighton University, Nebraska. Articles contributed: 'ABOUH, MUHAMMAD; EGYPT: FATIMID CALIPHATE; EGYPT: SALAFIYYA, MUSLIM BROTHERHOOD; IBN KHALDUN: CIVILIZATION OF THE MAGHRIB; IBN KHALDUN: HISTORY OF THE BERBERS; LIBYA: MUHAMMAD AL–SANUSI (c.1790–1859) AND THE SANUSIYYA.

1742

Campbell, Gwyn R. PRATIC, University of Avignon, France. Articles contributed: MADAGASCAR: COLONIAL PERIOD: FRENCH RULE; MADAGASCAR: FRENCH CONQUEST, COLONIZATION; MADAGASCAR: MALAGASY KINGDOMS, EVOLUTION OF; MADAGASCAR: MERINA KINGDOM, NINETEENTH CENTURY; MADAGASCAR: PREHISTORY AND DEVELOPMENTS TO c.1500; SLAVERY: EAST AFRICA: EIGHTEENTH CENTURY.

Carton, Ben. Department of History, George Mason University, Virginia. Article contributed: SOUTH AFRICA: CAPITALIST FARMING, "POOR WHITES," LABOR.

Chabal, Patrick. Department of Portuguese and Brazilian, King's College, England. Article contributed: POLITICAL SYSTEMS.

Chafer, Tony. School of Languages and Area Studies, University of Portsmouth, England. Articles contributed: EDUCATION: FRENCH WEST AFRICA; SENEGAL: NATIONALISM, FEDERATION, AND INDEPENDENCE; SENEGAL: WORLD WAR II.

Cheeseboro, Anthony. Department of Historical Studies, Southern Illinois University–Edwardsville. Articles contributed: BUTHELEZI AND INKATHA FREEDOM PARTY; DIASPORA: HISTORIOGRAPHICAL DEBATES; SOBUKWE, ROBERT AND THE PAN-AFRICANIST CONGRESS; SUDAN: CONDOMINIUM PERIOD: ECONOMY; SUDAN: COTTON, IRRIGATION, AND OIL, 1970s; YORUBA STATES: OYO.

Christelow, Allan. Department of History, Idaho State University. Articles contributed: ALGERIA: MUSLIM POPULATION, 1871–1954; ALGERIA: ARABISM AND ISLAMISM; ALGERIA, COLONIAL: ISLAMIC IDEAS AND MOVEMENTS IN; ALGERIA: ISLAMIC SALVATION FRONT, MILITARY RULE, CIVIL WAR, 1990s; ALGERIA: MUSLIM POPULATION, 1871–1954; ALGIERS; LAW, ISLAMIC: POSTCOLONIAL AFRICA; WORLD WAR I: NORTH AND SAHARAN AFRICA.

Chuku, Gloria Ifeoma. Department of History and Political Science, South Carolina State University. Articles contributed: IGBOLAND, NINETEENTH CENTURY; PORT HARCOURT.

Clark, Andrew F. Department of History, University of North Carolina–Wilmington. Articles contributed: DIOUF, ABDOU; FULBE/FULANI/PEUL: ORIGINS; FUTA TORO; GAMBIA, THE: NINETEENTH CENTURY TO INDEPENDENCE; GAMBIA, THE: INDEPENDENCE TO PRESENT; GAMBIA, THE: RELATIONS WITH SENEGAL; SENEGAL: NINETEENTH CENTURY; SENEGAL: CASAMANCE PROVINCE, CONFLICT IN; SENEGAL: INDEPENDENCE TO THE PRESENT; SENEGAL: WORLD WAR I.

Clark, John F. Department of International Relations, Florida International University. Articles contributed: COLD WAR, AFRICA AND THE; CONGO (BRAZZAVILLE), REPUBLIC OF: INDEPENDENCE, REVOLUTION, 1958–1979; CONGO (BRAZZAVILLE), REPUBLIC OF: LIBERALIZATION, REBELLION, 1980s AND 1990s; SASSOU-NGUESSO, DENIS.

Clark, Nancy L. Department of History, California Polytechnic State University. Articles contributed: SOUTH AFRICA: INDUSTRY, LABOR, URBANIZATION, 1940–1946; SOUTH AFRICA: SEGREGATION, POLITICAL ECONOMY OF.

Cleaver, Gerry. School of International Studies and Law, Coventry University, England. Articles contributed: ARMS, ARMIES: POSTCOLONIAL AFRICA; PEACEKEEPING: POSTCOLONIAL AFRICA.

Cobley, Alan Gregor. Faculty of Humanities and Education, University of the West Indies. Article contributed: PROFESSIONS, AFRICANS IN: COLONIAL.

Cockerton, Camilla. Department of Geography, University of Canterbury, New Zealand. Articles contributed: AFRICAN DEVELOPMENT BANK; AID, INTERNATIONAL, NGOs AND THE STATE; EDUCATION IN COLONIAL SUB-SAHARAN AFRICA; EDUCATION IN POSTCOLONIAL SUB-SAHARAN AFRICA; GENDER AND MIGRATION: SOUTHERN AFRICA; POPULATION AND DEMOGRAPHY.

Cole, Jennifer. Committee on Human Development, University of Chicago. Article contributed: MADAGASCAR: GREAT REBELLION, 1947–1948.

Collins, Robert O. Department of History, University of California–Santa Barbara. Articles contributed: BAGIRMI, WADAI, AND DARFUR; CHAD: LIBYA, AOUZOU STRIP, CIVIL WAR; EGYPT, NORTH AFRICA: SCRAMBLE; KANEM: DECLINE AND MERGE WITH BORNO; KHARTOUM; MASSASSI AND THE KAARTA STATE; RABIH IBN FADL ALLAH; SALAH AL-DIN/SALADIN; SUDAN: SADIQ AL-MAHDI REGIME, 1980s.

Conrad, David C. Department of History, State University of New York–Oswego. Articles contributed: MALI EMPIRE, SUNDIATA AND ORIGINS OF; MANSA MUSA, MALI EMPIRE AND; SEGU: ORIGINS AND GROWTH OF A BAMANA KINGDOM.

Coquery-Vidrovitch, Catherine. Professeur émérite, Université Paris 7–Denis Diderot. Article contributed: DROUGHT, FAMINE, DISPLACEMENT.

Crummey, Donald. Department of History, University of Illinois–Urbana. Articles contributed: ETHIOPIA: EIGHTEENTH CENTURY; ETHIOPIA: EARLY NINETEENTH CENTURY; ETHIOPIA: TEWODROS II, ERA OF.

Curtis, Kenneth R. Department of History, California State University–Long Beach. Articles contributed: TANGANYIKA (TANZANIA): AFRICAN ASSOCIATION, 1929–1948; TANGANYIKA (TANZANIA): NATIONALISM, TANU, INDEPENDENCE.

Daftary, Farhad. Department of Academic Research and Publication, Institute of Ismaili Studies, England. Article contributed: EGYPT: FATIMIDS, LATER: 1073–1171.

Daloz, Jean-Pascal. Chercheur au CNRS, Centre d'étude d'Afrique Nord, France. Articles contributed: POLITICAL ELITES AND PATRONAGE: POSTCOLONIAL AFRICA; ZAMBIA: 1991 TO THE PRESENT; ZAMBIA: SECOND REPUBLIC, 1973–1991.

Darkwah, R. H. Kofi. Department of History, University of Botswana. Articles contributed: ETHIOPIA: c.1550–c.1700; ETHIOPIA, PORTUGUESE AND, SIXTEENTH–SEVENTEENTH CENTURIES; ETHIOPIA: JOHANNES IV, ERA OF; EUROPE: INDUSTRIALIZATION AND IMPERIALISM; MASSAWA, ETHIOPIA, AND THE OTTOMAN EMPIRE.

Davidson, John. Department of History and Welsh History, University of Wales–Aberystwyth (retired). Articles contributed: MARTIAL RACES; SIERRA LEONE: PROTECTORATE: ECONOMY; SIERRA LEONE: TEMNE, MENDE, AND THE COLONY.

Degefa, Terefe. Visiting Research Fellow, African Studies Centre, Leiden, The Netherlands. Article contributed: ADDIS ABABA.

Degorge, Barbara. Director of institutional effectiveness, American University, Dubai, United Arab Emirates. Articles contributed: MOROCCO: EDUCATION SINCE INDEPENDENCE; TUNISIA: EDUCATIONAL POLICY AND DEVELOPMENT SINCE INDEPENDENCE.

Derrick, Jonathan. Articles contributed: ALGERIA: INTERNATIONAL RELATIONS, 1962–PRESENT; ALGERIA: NATIONALISM AND REFORM, 1911–1954; CENTRAL AFRICAN REPUBLIC: COLONIAL PERIOD: OCCUPATION, RESISTANCE, BAYA REVOLT, 1928; DIAGNE, GUEYE, AND POLITICS OF SENEGAL, 1920s AND 1930s; DOUALA; JOURNALISM, AFRICAN: COLONIAL ERA; KOUYATE, TIEMOKO GARAN; MOROCCO: RESISTANCE AND COLLABORATION, BU HMARA TO ABDLEKRIM (IBN 'ABD EL-KRIM); NYERERE, JULIUS; TANGIER; WALLACE-JOHNSON, I. T. A. AND RADICAL POLITICS: WEST AFRICA: 1930s.

Devereux, David R. Department of History, Canisius College, Buffalo, New York. Articles contributed: COLONIAL FEDERATIONS: FRENCH EQUATORIAL AFRICA; COLONIAL FEDERATIONS: FRENCH WEST

AFRICA; FEDERATIONS AND UNIONS, POSTCOLONIAL; TRANSPORTATION INFRASTRUCTURE.

Dibie, Robert. Department of Government, Western Kentucky University. Article contributed: NIGERIA: ARMY.

Dibua, J. I. Department of History and Geography, Morgan State University, Maryland. Articles contributed: NIGERIA: CONFERENCES, COMMISSIONS, NIGERIAN CONSTITUTION: 1956–1960; NIGERIA: MURTALA MUHAMMED, OBASANJO AND RETURN TO CIVILIAN RULE, 1975–1979; NIGERIA: OPPOSITION, 1990S, TO THE FOURTH REPUBLIC; NIGERIA: SECOND REPUBLIC, 1979–1983; WORLD BANK, INTERNATIONAL MONETARY FUND, AND STRUCTURAL ADJUSTMENT.

Digre, Brian. Department of History and Geography, Elon University, North Carolina. Articles contributed: COLONIALISM, OVERTHROW OF: SUB-SAHARAN AFRICA; GHANA (REPUBLIC OF): NATIONALISM, RISE OF, AND THE POLITICS OF INDEPENDENCE; SOUTH AFRICA: WORLD WARS I AND II.

Dimier, Véronique. Université Libre de Bruxelles, Belgium. Articles contributed: LOMÉ CONVENTIONS, THE; RÉUNION: 1946 TO THE PRESENT.

Dioka, Leo C. Department of History, University of Lagos, Nigeria. Article contributed: NOK CULTURE: TERRA-COTTA, IRON.

Dodson, Aidan. Department of Archaeology, University of Bristol, England. Articles contributed: AKHENATEN; EGYPT, ANCIENT: ARCHITECTURE; EGYPT, ANCIENT: CHRONOLOGY; EGYPT, ANCIENT: ECONOMY: REDISTRIBUTIVE: PALACE, TEMPLE; EGYPT, ANCIENT: FUNERAL PRACTICES AND MUMMIFICATION; EGYPT, ANCIENT: HIEROGLYPHICS AND ORIGINS OF ALPHABET; EGYPT, ANCIENT: MIDDLE KINGDOM: HISTORICAL OUTLINE; EGYPT, ANCIENT: OLD KINGDOM AND ITS CONTACTS TO THE SOUTH: HISTORICAL OUTLINE.

Domergue-Cloarec, Danielle. Université Paul Valéry, Montpellier III, France. Articles contributed: CÔTE D'IVOIRE (IVORY COAST): COLONIAL PERIOD: ADMINISTRATION AND ECONOMY; CÔTE D'IVOIRE (IVORY COAST): PARTI DÉMOCRATIQUE DE LA CÔTE D'IVOIRE; NIGER: COLONIAL PERIOD TO INDEPENDENCE.

Donkoh, Wilhelmina Joseline. Department of General and African Studies, University of Science and Technology, Ghana. Articles contributed: CLOTHING AND CULTURAL CHANGE; KUMASI.

Dorward, David. African Research Institute, La Trobe University, Australia. Articles contributed: LIBERIA: FIRESTONE; WESTERN SAHARA: NINETEENTH CENTURY TO THE PRESENT.

Doyle, Shane. British Institute in East Africa, Kenya. Articles contributed: BUNYORO; KABAREGA AND BUNYORO; UGANDA: EARLY NINETEENTH CENTURY.

Driver, Thackwray. Independent scholar, Trinidad and Tobago. Articles contributed: LESOTHO (BASUTOLAND): COLONIAL PERIOD; LESOTHO (BASUTOLAND): PEASANTRY, RISE OF.

Dubois, Colette. Institut d'Etudes africaines, La Maison Méditerranéenne des Sciences de l'Homme, France. Article contributed: DJIBOUTI: NINETEENTH CENTURY TO THE PRESENT: SURVEY.

Dulucq, Sophie. Department of Modern History, Université de Toulouse-le Mirail, France. Articles contributed: BAMAKO; FONDS D'INVESTISSEMENT POUR LE DÉVELOPPEMENT ECONOMIQUE ET SOCIAL; URBANIZATION: COLONIAL CONTEXT.

Dumbuya, Peter A. Department of Social and Behavioral Sciences, Fort Valley State University, Georgia. Article contributed: MANDATES: LEAGUE OF NATIONS AND UNITED NATIONS.

Dumett, Raymond E. Department of History, Purdue University, Indiana. Articles contributed: AKAN AND ASANTE: FARMERS, TRADERS, AND THE EMERGENCE OF AKAN STATES; ANTI-SLAVERY MOVEMENT; BYZANTINE AFRICA, 533–710; GOLD: AKAN GOLDFIELDS: 1400 TO 1800; GOLD: MINING INDUSTRY OF GHANA: 1800 TO THE PRESENT.

Dunn, Kevin C. Department of Political Science, Hobart and William Smith Colleges, Geneva, New York. Articles contributed: CONGO (KINSHASA), DEMOCRATIC REPUBLIC OF/ZAIRE: EVOLUÉS, POLITICS, INDEPENDENCE; CONGO (KINSHASA), DEMOCRATIC REPUBLIC OF/ZAIRE: MOBUTU, ZAIRE, and MOBUTUISM.

Duperray, Anne-Marie. Articles contributed: BURKINA FASO (UPPER VOLTA): NINETEENTH CENTURY; BURKINA FASO (UPPER VOLTA): COLONIAL PERIOD.

Eckert, Andreas. Zentrum Moderner Orient, Humboldt Universität, Germany. Articles contributed: CAMEROON: NINETEENTH CENTURY; COLONIAL ADMINISTRATIONS, AFRICANS IN; COLONIAL EUROPEAN ADMINISTRATIONS: COMPARATIVE SURVEY; YAOUNDÉ.

Ekechi, Felix K. Department of History, Kent State University, Ohio. Article contributed: MEDICAL FACTOR IN CHRISTIAN CONVERSION.

Emizet, Kisangani. Department of Political Science, Kansas State University. Article contributed: ZAIRE: POLITICS, REGIONAL.

Erlank, Natasha. Department of History, Rand Afrikaans University, South Africa. Articles contributed: BOTSWANA: MISSIONARIES, NINETEENTH CENTURY; IRON AGE (LATER): SOUTHERN AFRICA: ETHNICITY, LANGUAGE, IDENTITY; IRON AGE (LATER): SOUTHERN AFRICA: HIGHVELD, EMERGENCE OF STATES ON; IRON AGE (LATER): SOUTHERN AFRICA: LEOPARD'S KOPJE, BAMBANDYANALO, AND MAPUNGUBWE; IRON AGE (LATER): SOUTHERN AFRICA: TOUTSWEMOGALA, CATTLE AND POLITICAL POWER.

Esedebe, Peter Olisanwuche. Department of History, University of Nigeria. Article contributed: DIASPORA: COLONIAL ERA.

Etherington, Norman A. Department of History, University of Western Australia. Articles contributed: BOER EXPANSION: INTERIOR OF SOUTH AFRICA; DIFAQANE ON THE HIGHVELD; LESOTHO: TREATIES AND CONFLICT ON THE HIGHVELD, 1843–1868; MISSIONARY ENTERPRISE: PRECOLONIAL; MOSHOESHOE I AND THE FOUNDING OF THE BASOTHO KINGDOM; NATAL, NINETEENTH CENTURY; WHITE SETTLER FACTOR: ECONOMIC AND POLITICAL.

Falola, Toyin. Department of History, University of Texas–Austin. Articles contributed: LAGOS; NIGERIA: COLONIAL PERIOD: FEDERATION; NIGERIA: WORLD WAR I; OBASANJO, OLUSEGUN.

Fanthorpe, Richard. Department of Anthropology, University College London. Articles contributed: FOREST PEOPLES: SIERRA LEONE, LIBERIA, AND CÔTE D'IVOIRE (IVORY COAST): HISTORY OF TO 1800; SIERRA LEONE: DEVELOPMENT OF THE COLONY, NINETEENTH CENTURY.

Faseke, Modupeolu. Department of History and International Studies, Lagos State University, Nigeria. Article contributed: YORUBA-SPEAKING PEOPLES.

Filatova, Irina. Department of History, University of Durban–Westville, South Africa. Article contributed: SOVIET UNION AND AFRICA.

Finneran, Niall. Department of Archaeology, University of Southampton, England. Articles contributed: PERMANENT SETTLEMENT, EARLY; ROCK ART: EASTERN AFRICA; STONE AGE (LATER): EASTERN AFRICA.

Fleisch, Axel. Visiting scholar, Department of Linguistics, University of California–Berkeley. Articles contributed: ANGOLA: AMBAQUISTA, IMBANGALA, AND LONG-DISTANCE TRADE; ANGOLA: CHOKWE, OVIMBUNDU, NINETEENTH CENTURY; ANGOLA: "SCRAMBLE"; ANGOLA: SLAVE TRADE, ABOLITION OF.

Fomin, E. S. D. Yaoundé University, Cameroon. Article contributed: SLAVERY IN AFRICAN SOCIETY.

Fuller, Dorian Q. Institute of Archaeology, University College London. Articles contributed: CROP CULTIVATION: THE EVIDENCE; FARMING: STONE AGE FARMERS OF THE SAVANNA; FARMING: TROPICAL FOREST ZONES.

Fyfe, Christopher. Articles contributed: HORTON, JAMES AFRICANUS BEALE; SIERRA LEONE: CHRISTIANITY, EDUCATION, KRIO DIASPORA.

Gadzekpo, Leonard. Black American Studies Program, Southern Illinois University. Articles contributed: COLONIALISM: IDEOLOGY OF EMPIRE: SUPREMACIST, PATERNALIST; SLAVERY: ATLANTIC TRADE: TRANSATLANTIC PASSAGE.

Gaillard, Gérald. Centre Lillois d'Etudes et de Recherches Sociologiques et Economiques, Université des Sciences et Technologies de Lille, France. Articles contributed: GUINEA-BISSAU: NINETEENTH CENTURY TO 1960; GUINEA-BISSAU: CABRAL, AMÍLCAR, PAIGC, INDEPENDENCE, 1961–1973.

Gardinier, David E. Department of History, Marquette University, Wisconsin. Articles contributed: GABON: BONGO, OMAR, AND THE ONE-PARTY STATE, 1967 TO THE PRESENT; GABON: COLONIAL PERIOD: SOCIAL TRANSFORMATION; GABON: DECOLONIZATION AND THE POLITICS OF INDEPENDENCE, 1945–1967.

Gearon, Eamonn. Independent researcher, Hanover, New Hampshire. Articles contributed: BURKINA FASO (UPPER VOLTA): INDEPENDENCE TO THE PRESENT; BURUNDI: 1988 TO PRESENT; CENTRAL AFRICA, NORTHERN: ARAB PENETRATION, RISE OF CAVALRY STATES; CENTRAL AFRICA, NORTHERN: CENTRAL SUDANIC PEOPLES; CENTRAL AFRICA, NORTHERN: CHADIC PEOPLES; CENTRAL AFRICA, NORTHERN: ISLAM, PILGRIMAGE; HUNTING, FORAGING; MAGHRIB: EUROPEAN EXPANSION INTO, 1250–1550; MOROCCO: ECONOMICS AND SOCIAL CHANGE SINCE INDEPENDENCE; MOROCCO: INTERNATIONAL RELATIONS SINCE INDEPENDENCE; NORTH AFRICA, ANCIENT: URBANIZATION; RWANDA: TO 1800; SAHARA: SALT: PRODUCTION, TRADE.

Gimode, Edwin. Department of History, Kenyatta University, Kenya. Article contributed: MBOYA, TOM J.

Ginio, Ruth. Institute of Asian and African Studies, Hebrew University of Jerusalem, Israel. Article contributed: WORLD WAR II: FRENCH WEST AFRICA, EQUATORIAL AFRICA.

Gocking, Roger. Division of Civic and Cultural Studies, Mercy College, Dobbs Ferry, New York. Articles contributed: ACCRA; CASELY HAYFORD, JOSEPH EPHRAIM; GHANA (REPUBLIC OF) (GOLD COAST): COLONIAL PERIOD: ADMINISTRATION.

Goeh-Akue, N. Adovis. Université de Togo. Articles contributed: LOMÉ; TOGO: COLONIAL PERIOD: DUAL MANDATE, 1919–1957.

Goerg, Odile. Professeure d'historie contemporaine, Université des Sciences Humaines de Strasbourg, France. Articles contributed: CONAKRY; GUINEA: COLONIAL PERIOD; GUINEA: TOURÉ, AHMED SEKOU, ERA OF.

Goldschmidt, Arthur, Jr. Department of History and Religious Studies, Pennsylvania State University. Articles contributed: EGYPT: NATIONALISM, WORLD WAR I AND THE WAFD, 1882–1922; EGYPT: PRINTING, BROADCASTING.

Gondola, Charles Didier. Department of History, Indiana University–Purdue University at Indianapolis. Articles contributed: BRAZZAVILLE; CONGO (BRAZZAVILLE), REPUBLIC OF: COLONIAL PERIOD: MOYEN-CONGO; CONGO (BRAZZAVILLE), REPUBLIC OF: DE BRAZZA AND FRENCH COLONIZATION; CONGO (BRAZZAVILLE), REPUBLIC OF: NINETEENTH CENTURY: PRECOLONIAL; CONGO (KINSHASA),

DEMOCRATIC REPUBLIC OF/ZAIRE: BELGIAN CONGO: ADMINISTRATION AND SOCIETY, 1908–1960; CONGO (KINSHASA), DEMOCRATIC REPUBLIC OF/ZAIRE: BELGIAN CONGO: COLONIAL ECONOMY, 1908–1960; KIMBANGU, SIMON, AND KIMBANGUISM.

Goodridge, Richard A. Department of History, University of the West Indies–Barbados. Articles contributed: LABOR: DECLINE IN TRADITIONAL FORMS OF EXPLOITATION; PLANTATIONS AND LABOR, COLONIAL.

Goodwin, Stefan. Professor of Anthropology, Morgan State University, Maryland (retired). Article contributed: STONE AGE (LATER): NILE VALLEY.

Gordon, Robert J. Department of Anthropology, University of Vermont. Articles contributed: NAMIBIA (SOUTHWEST AFRICA): LEAGUE OF NATIONS, UNITED NATIONS MANDATE.

Häggman, Bertil. Swedish Writer's Union. Article contributed: VANDALS AND NORTH AFRICA, 429–533.

Hamblin, William J. Department of History, Brigham Young University, Utah. Articles contributed: EGYPT: AYYUBID DYNASTY, 1169–1250; EGYPT: FATIMIDS, LATER (1073–1171): ARMY AND ADMINISTRATION; EGYPT: MAMLUK DYNASTY (1250–1517): ARMY AND IQTA' SYSTEM.

Hanlon, Joseph. Department of Development Policy and Practice, Open University, England. Articles contributed: DEBT, INTERNATIONAL, DEVELOPMENT AND DEPENDENCY; MOZAMBIQUE: RENAMO, DESTABILIZATION; SOUTH AFRICA: ANTIAPARTHEID STRUGGLE, INTERNATIONAL.

Hargreaves, John D. Faculty of Social Sciences, Open University, England. Articles contributed: BERLIN WEST AFRICA CONFERENCE, 1884–1885; BOUNDARIES, COLONIAL.

Hartmann, Wolfram. University of Namibia. Articles contributed: NAMIBIA: NINETEENTH CENTURY TO 1880; NAMIBIA (SOUTHWEST AFRICA): NAMA AND HERERO RISINGS.

Harvey, Charles. Botswana Institute for Development Policy Analysis. Articles contributed: BANKING AND FINANCE; BOTSWANA: INDEPENDENCE: ECONOMIC DEVELOPMENT, POLITICS; ZAMBIA: FIRST REPUBLIC, 1964–1972: DEVELOPMENT AND POLITICS.

Haynes, Jeff. Department of Law, Governance, and International Relations, London Metropolitan University. Articles contributed: ALGERIA: BENDJEDID AND ELECTIONS, 1978–1990; ARAB AND ISLAMIC WORLD, AFRICA IN; BENIN (REPUBLIC OF)/DAHOMEY: INDEPENDENCE, COUPS, POLITICS; CONGO (KINSHASA), DEMOCRATIC REPUBLIC OF/ZAIRE: NATIONAL CONFERENCE AND POLITICS OF OPPOSITION, 1990–1996; CONGO (KINSHASA): POST-MOBUTU ERA; GHANA, REPUBLIC OF: SOCIAL AND ECONOMIC DEVELOPMENT: FIRST REPUBLIC; HUMAN RIGHTS: POSTCOLONIAL AFRICA; MAURITIUS: 1982 TO THE PRESENT; RAWLINGS, JERRY JOHN; RELIGION, COLONIAL AFRICA: CONVERSION TO WORLD RELIGIONS; RELIGION, COLONIAL AFRICA: PROPHETIC MOVEMENTS; RELIGION, COLONIAL AFRICA: RELIGIOUS RESPONSES TO COLONIAL RULE; RELIGION, POSTCOLONIAL AFRICA: AFRICAN THEOLOGY, INDIGENIZATION; RELIGION, POSTCOLONIAL AFRICA: INDEPENDENCE AND CHURCHES, MISSION-LINKED AND INDEPENDENT; RELIGION, POSTCOLONIAL AFRICA: ISLAM; RESISTANCE TO COLONIALISM; UGANDA: RECONSTRUCTION: POLITICS, ECONOMICS.

Herbert, Eugenia W. Department of History, Mount Holyoke College, Massachusetts. Articles contributed: METALWORKING: ORIGINS OF IRONWORKING.

Hinds, Allister. Department of History, University of the West Indies–Jamaica. Articles contributed: COLONIAL IMPORTS VERSUS INDIGENOUS CRAFTS; WORLD WAR II: SUB-SAHARAN AFRICA: ECO-

NOMIC IMPACT.

Hoover, Jeff. University of Lubumbashi, Democratic Republic of Congo. Articles contributed: KAZEMBE'S EASTERN LUNDA; LUNDA: KINGDOMS, SEVENTEENTH AND EIGHTEENTH CENTURIES; LUNDA: MWAANT YAAV (MWATA YAMVO) AND ORIGINS; LUNDA: TITLES.

Hymans, Jacques Louis. Department of History, San Francisco State University. Articles contributed: NÉGRITUDE; SENGHOR, LÉOPOLD SÉDAR.

Ijoma, J. Okoro. Department of History, University of Nigeria. Article contributed: IGBO AND IGALA.

Ikram, Salima. Department of Egyptology, American University, Egypt. Articles contributed: EGYPT, ANCIENT: AGRICULTURE; EGYPT, ANCIENT: LITERACY; EGYPT, ANCIENT: SOCIAL ORGANIZATION.

Insoll, Timothy. Department of Art History and Archaeology, University of Manchester, England. Articles contributed: RELIGION: ISLAM, GROWTH OF: WESTERN AFRICA; SONGHAY EMPIRE, GAO AND ORIGINS OF; TIMBUKTU.

Isaac, Tseggai. Department of History and Political Science, University of Missouri–Rolla. Article contributed: ERITREA: 1941 TO THE PRESENT.

Jaggar, Philip J. Department of Africa, School of Oriental and African Studies, University of London. Article contributed: LANGUAGE CLASSIFICATION.

Jansen, Jan. Department of Cultural Anthropology, University of Leiden, Netherlands. Articles contributed: MALI (REPUBLIC OF): ECONOMY AND SOCIETY, NINETEENTH CENTURY; TOURÉ, SAMORI AND HIS EMPIRE.

Jennings, Christian. University of Texas–Austin. Articles contributed: EASTERN SAVANNAH, POLITICAL AUTHORITY IN; GEOGRAPHY, ENVIRONMENT IN AFRICAN HISTORY; HUNTING, COLONIAL ERA; NILOTES, EASTERN AFRICA: MAASAI.

Johnson, Amy J. Department of History, Berry College, Georgia. Articles contributed: 'ABD AL-QADIR; ALEXANDRIA; ALGERIA: WAR OF INDEPENDENCE, 1954–1962; CAIRO; COLONIALISM: IMPACT ON AFRICAN SOCIETIES; EGYPT: CROMER ADMINISTRATION, 1883–1907: IRRIGATION, AGRICULTURE, AND INDUSTRY; EGYPT, WORLD WAR II AND; IBN BATTUTA, MALI EMPIRE AND; MOROCCO: FRENCH AND SPANISH PROTECTORATES, 1903–1914; MOROCCO: HAY, EDWARD AND JOHN DRUMMOND, BRITISH DIPLOMATIC PROTECTION, 1829–1903; MOROCCO: IMMIGRATION AND COLONIZATION, 1900–1950; MOROCCO: MAWLAY HASAN AND THE MAKHZEN; NORTHERN AFRICA; RELIGION, COLONIAL AFRICA: ISLAMIC ORDERS AND MOVEMENTS; SUDAN: OMDURMAN AND RECONQUEST.

Jok, Jok Madut. Department of History, Loyola Marymount University, California. Articles contributed: GARANG, JOHN, AND THE SUDAN PEOPLES' LIBERATION PARTY (SPLA); SUDAN: CIVIL WAR: 1990S.

Jones, James A. Department of History, West Chester University, Pennsylvania. Articles contributed: DAKAR; MALI (REPUBLIC OF): COLONIAL SOUDAN FRANÇAIS; SENEGAL: COLONIAL PERIOD: RAILWAYS.

Jusu, Michael J. Department of History, University of the Gambia. Articles contributed: MANDINKA STATES OF GAMBIA; SIERRA LEONE: MARGAI, SIR MILTON: INDEPENDENCE, GOVERNMENT OF; SIERRA LEONE: PROTECTORATE: ADMINISTRATION AND GOVERNMENT; SIERRA LEONE: STEVENS, SIAKA AND THE ALL PEOPLE'S CONGRESS.

Kahera, Akel Ismail. College of Architecture, Texas Tech University. Article contributed: MOSQUE, SUB-SAHARAN: ART AND ARCHITECTURE OF.

Kalinga, Owen J. M. Department of History, North Carolina State University. Articles contributed: BANDA, DR. HASTINGS KAMUZU; BLANTYRE; MALAWI: INDEPENDENCE TO THE PRESENT; MALAWI: NATIONALISM, INDEPENDENCE.

Kallaway, Peter. Faculty of Education, University of the Western Cape, South Africa. Article contributed: SOUTH AFRICA: APARTHEID, EDUCATION AND.

Kanduza, Ackson M. Department of History, University of Swaziland. Article contributed: LABOTSIBENI.

Katanekwa, Nicholas. National Heritage Conservation Commission, Zambia. Articles contributed: INGOMBE ILEDE; IRON AGE (LATER): CENTRAL AFRICA: LUANGWA TRADITION.

Katzenellenbogen, Simon. Department of History, University of Manchester, England. Articles contributed: CONGO (KINSHASA), DEMOCRATIC REPUBLIC OF/ZAIRE: MINERAL FACTOR; MINING; MOZAMBIQUE: COLONIAL PERIOD: LABOR, MIGRATION, ADMINISTRATION; RAILWAYS; SOUTH AFRICA: GOLD ON THE WITWATERSRAND, 1886–1899.

Kawewe, Saliwe M. School of Social Work, Southern Illinois University–Carbondale. Articles contributed: ZIMBABWE: SECOND CHIMURENGA, 1966–1979; ZIMBABWE: SINCE 1990.

Kerr-Ritchie, Jeffrey R. Department of History, Wesleyan University, Connecticut. Article contributed: SLAVERY, ATLANTIC BASIN IN THE ERA OF.

Killingray, David. Department of History, Goldsmiths College, University of London. Articles contributed: DUBOIS, W. E. B. AND PAN-AFRICANISM; MILITARY: COLONIALISM, CONQUEST, RESISTANCE.

King, Lamont DeHaven. Department of History, James Madison University, Virginia. Article contributed: SOKOTO CALIPHATE: HAUSA, FULANI AND FOUNDING OF.

Kitchen, K. A. Professor emeritus, School of Archaeology, Classics, and Oriental Studies, University of Liverpool, England. Article contributed: PUNT AND ITS NEIGHBORS; RAMSES II.

Kiyaga-Mulindwa, David. Teacher Training College, Uganda. Articles contributed: BUGANDA: TO NINETEENTH CENTURY; EDUCATION, HIGHER, IN POSTCOLONIAL AFRICA; GREAT LAKES REGION: KITARA AND THE CHWEZI DYNASTY; KAMPALA; MUSEUMS, HISTORY OF: POSTCOLONIAL; MUTESA; NYABINGI CULT AND RESISTANCE.

Klein, Martin A. Professor emeritus, Department of History, University of Toronto. Articles contributed: FUTA TORO: EARLY NINETEENTH CENTURY; "LEGITIMATE COMMERCE" AND THE EXPORT TRADE IN THE NINETEENTH CENTURY; SENEGAL: COLONIAL PERIOD: ADMINSITRATION AND "ASSIMILATION"; SLAVERY; MEDITERRANEAN, RED SEA, INDIAN OCEAN.

Klein-Arendt, Reinhard. Institute for African Studies, University of Cologne, Germany. Articles contributed: BANTU CULTIVATORS: KENYAN HIGHLANDS; MALAWI: LONG-DISTANCE TRADE, NINETEENTH CENTURY; MALAWI: NGONI INCURSIONS FROM THE SOUTH, NINETEENTH CENTURY; MARAVI: KALONGA MASULA: EMPIRE, TRADE; MARAVI: PHIRI CLAN, LUNDU AND UNDI DYNASTIES; MARAVI: ZIMBA "INVASIONS"; RWANDA: COLONIAL PERIOD: GERMAN AND BELGIAN RULE; SIRIKWA AND ENGARUKA: DAIRY FARMING, IRRIGATION; SLAVE TRADE: ARMS, IVORY, AND (EAST AND CENTRAL AFRICA); UPARE, USAMBARA, KILIMANJARO; ZANZIBAR: COLONIAL PERIOD; ZANZIBAR: TRADE: SLAVES, IVORY.

Kleinitz, Cornelia. Institute of Archaeology, University College London. Article contributed: ROCK ART: WESTERN AND CENTRAL AFRICA.

Krieger, Milton. Department of Liberal Studies, Western Washington University, Bellingham, Washington. Article contributed: CAMEROON: INDEPENDENCE TO THE PRESENT.

Kwesi Aning, Emmanuel. Institute for Security Studies, South Africa. Articles contributed: LIBERIA: CIVIL WAR, ECOMOG, AND THE RETURN TO CIVILIAN RULE; TAYLOR, CHARLES.

Labode, Modupe G. Department of History, Iowa State University. Articles contributed: MAKEKE, CHARLOTTE MAKHANYE; SOUTH AFRICA: MISSIONARIES: NINETEENTH CENTURY.

Lame, Danielle de. Royal Museum for Central Africa, Belgium. Articles contributed: RWANDA: PRECOLONIAL, NINETEENTH CENTURY; RWANDA: CIVIL UNREST AND INDEPENDENCE, 1959–1962.

Lamphear, John. Department of History, University of Texas–Austin. Articles contributed: NILOTES, EASTERN AFRICA: EASTERN NILOTES: ATEKER (KARIMOJONG); NILOTES, EASTERN AFRICA: SOUTHERN NILOTES: KALENJIN, DADOG, POKOT; SWAHILI, PORTUGUESE AND: 1498–1589; TANGANYIKA (TANZANIA): NGONI INCURSION FROM THE SOUTH.

Lane, Paul. British Institute in Eastern Africa, Kenya. Articles contributed: IRON AGE (EARLY) AND DEVELOPMENT OF FARMING IN EASTERN AFRICA; IRON AGE (LATER): EAST AFRICA: SALT; IRON AGE (LATER): EAST AFRICA: TRADE; NILOTES, EASTERN AFRICA: ORIGINS, PASTORALISM, MIGRATION; NILOTES, EASTERN AFRICA: WESTERN NILOTES: LUO; PRODUCTION AND EXCHANGE, PRECOLONIAL.

Laumann, Dennis. Department of History, University of Memphis. Articles contributed: AJA-SPEAKING PEOPLES: AJA, FON, EWE, SEVENTEENTH AND EIGHTEENTH CENTURIES; TOGO: GERMAN COLONIAL RULE.

Lawal, Babatunde. Department of Art History, Virginia Commonwealth University. Articles contributed: ART AND ARCHITECTURE, HISTORY OF AFRICAN.

Lawal, Kunle. Department of History, Lagos State University, Nigeria. Articles contributed: ALLADA AND SLAVE TRADE; BALEWA, ALHAJI SIR ABUBAKAR; BELLO, ALHAJI (SIR) AHMADU; HAILEY: AN AFRICAN SURVEY; IFE, OYO, YORUBA, ANCIENT: KINGSHIP AND ART.

Lawrance, Benjamin Nicholas. Department of History, University of California–Davis. Articles contributed: OLYMPIO, SYLVANUS; WORLD HISTORY, AFRICA IN.

Leaver, David. Article contributed: GREAT ZIMBABWE: COLONIAL HISTORIOGRAPHY.

Lester, Alan. Department of Geography, University of Sussex, England. Articles contributed: CAPE COLONY: BRITISH OCCUPATION, 1806–1872; HUNDRED YEARS' WAR, 1779–1878.

Levtzion, Nehemia. Department of History, Hebrew University of Jerusalem. Article contributed: EGYPT AND AFRICA: 1000–1500.

Lewis-Williams, J. D. Professor emeritus, Department of Geography, Archaeology, and Environmental Studies, University of the Witwatersrand, South Africa. Article contributed: ROCK ART: SOUTHERN AFRICA.

Liesegang, Gerhard. Department of History, Eduardo Mondlane University, Mozambique. Articles contributed: MOZAMBIQUE: NINETEENTH CENTURY, EARLY; MOZAMBIQUE: YGUNI/NGONI INCURSIONS FROM THE SOUTH; SOSHANGANE, UMZILA, GUNGUNHANE AND THE GAZA STATE.

Limb, Peter. Department of History, Michigan State University; Africana bibliographer. Articles contributed: MATTHEWS, Z. K.; MPHAHLELE, EZEKIEL; SOUTH AFRICA: MINING; TRADE UNIONS: POSTCOLONIAL; TRADES UNIONISM AND NATIONALISM.

Locatelli, Francesca. Ph.D. candidate, School of Oriental and African Studies, University of London. Articles contributed: ERITREA: OTTOMAN PROVINCE TO ITALIAN COLONY; ETHIOPIA: ITALIAN INVASION AND OCCUPATION: 1935–1940.

Lodge, Tom. Department of Political Studies, University of the Witwatersrand, South Africa. Articles contributed: ANGOLA: REVOLTS, 1961; PRETORIA.

Luig, Ute. Institut für Ethnologie, Germany. Article contributed: CÔTE D'IVOIRE (IVORY COAST): COLONIZATION AND RESISTANCE.

Lwamba Bilonda, Michel. Université de Lubumbashi, Democratic Republic of Congo. Article contributed: LUBUMBASHI.

MacKenzie, John M. Professor emeritus of imperial history, Lancaster University; honorary professor, University of Aberdeen. Regional Survey: RHODES, JAMESON, AND THE SEIZURE OF RHODESIA; SOUTHERN AFRICA: ZIMBABWE (SOUTHERN RHODESIA): NDEBELE AND SHONA RISINGS: FIRST CHIMURENGA.

MacKinnon, Aran S. Department of History, State University of West Georgia. Articles contributed: ANGLO-ZULU WAR, 1879–1887; DURBAN; PEDI KINGDOM, AND TRANSVAAL, 1822–1879; SHAKA AND ZULU KINGDOM, 1810–1840.

MacLean, Rachel. School of Art History and Archaeology, University of Manchester, England. Articles contributed: IRON AGE (EARLY): FARMING, EQUATORIAL AFRICA; IRON AGE (LATER): EAST AFRICA: CATTLE, WEALTH, POWER; IRON AGE (LATER): EAST AFRICA: LABOR, GENDER, PRODUCTION; IRON AGE (LATER): EAST AFRICA: SOCIETIES, EVOLUTION OF.

Mafela, Lily. Department of Language and Social Science Education, University of Botswana. Article contributed: PHELPS-STOKES COMMISSION.

Mahoney, Michael. Department of History, Yale University, Connecticut. Articles contributed: BHAMBATHA REBELLION, 1906; SOUTH AFRICA: PEASANTRY, AFRICAN.

Maloba, Wunyabari O. Department of History, University of Delaware. Articles contributed: COLONIALISM, OVERTHROW OF: WOMEN AND THE NATIONALIST STRUGGLE; KENYA: MAU MAU REVOLT.

Mangut, Benedicta N. University of Ahmadu Bello, Nigeria. Article contributed: IGBO-UKWU.

Mangut, Joseph. University of Ahmadu Bello, Nigeria. Article contributed: CLIMATE AND VEGETATIONAL CHANGE IN AFRICA.

Marks, Shula. Professor emeritus, School of Oriental and African Studies, England. Articles contributed: CETSHWAYO; DUBE, JOHN LANGALIBALELE; RHODES, CECIL J.; SMUTS, JAN C.; SOUTH AFRICA: PEACE, RECONSTRUCTION, UNION: 1902–1910.

Marschall, Sabine. Department of Cultural and Heritage Tourism, University of Durban–Westville, South Africa. Article contributed: ART, POSTCOLONIAL.

Masonen, Pekka. Department of History, University of Tampere, Finland. Articles contributed: AFRICANUS, LEO; CARVAJAL, LUIS DEL MÁRMOL; GHANA EMPIRE: HISTORIOGRAPHY OF ORIGINS; HISTORIOGRAPHY OF WESTERN AFRICA, 1790s–1860s.

Massey, Simon. African Studies Centre, Coventry University, England. Articles contributed: CHAD: INDEPENDENCE TO THE PRESENT; GUINEA-BISSAU: INDEPENDENCE TO THE PRESENT; TOMBALBAYE, F. NGARTA.

Máthé-Shires, Lászlo. Articles contributed: BENIN KINGDOM: BRITISH CONQUEST, 1897; HAUSA POLITIES: URBANISM, INDUSTRY AND COMMERCE; LAGOS COLONY AND OIL RIVERS PROTECTORATE; NIGERIA: BRITISH COLONIZATION TO 1914; NIGERIA: LUGARD, ADMINISTRATION, AND "INDIRECT RULE"; SOKOTO CALIPHATE, NINETEENTH CENTURY.

Mathews, K. Department of African Studies, University of Delhi, India. Articles contributed: REFUGEES; SOMALIA: INDEPENDENCE, CONFLICT, AND REVOLUTION.

Maxon, Robert. Department of History, West Virginia University.

Articles contributed: KENYA: COLONIAL PERIOD: ADMINISTRATION, CHRISTIANITY, EDUCATION AND PROTEST TO 1940; KENYA: COLONIAL PERIOD: ECONOMY, 1920S–1930S; KENYA: EAST AFRICAN PROTECTORATE AND THE UGANDA RAILWAY.

Maxwell, David. Department of History, Keele University, England. Articles contributed: RELIGION, COLONIAL AFRICA: INDEPENDENT, MILLENARIAN/SYNCRETIC CHURCHES; RELIGION, POSTCOLONIAL AFRICA: NEO-PENTECOSTALISM; ZIMBABWE: 1880S.

May, Timothy. Department of History, University of Wisconsin–Madison. Article contributed: EGYPT: MAMLUK DYNASTY: BAYBARS, QALAWUN, MONGOLS, 1250–1300.

Maylam, Paul. Department of History, Rhodes University, South Africa. Articles contributed: BOTSWANA: BECHUANALAND PROTECTORATE, FOUNDING OF: 1885–1899; SOUTH AFRICA: APARTHEID, 1948–1959; SOUTH AFRICA: SOWETO UPRISING.

M'bayo, Tamba. Department of History, Michigan State University. Article contributed: BENIN (REPUBLIC OF)/DAHOMEY: COLONIAL PERIOD: SURVEY.

McAllister, Patrick. Department of Sociology, University of Canterbury, New Zealand. Article contributed: LABOR: COOPERATIVE WORK.

McIntosh, Robert. Department of English, Mary Ward Centre, England. Articles contributed: SOUTH AFRICA: HOMELANDS AND BANTUSTANS; VERWOERD, H. F.

McIntosh, Susan Keech. Department of Anthropology, Rice University, Texas. Articles contributed: STONE AGE, LATER: WESTERN AFRICA; URBANIZATION AND SITE HIERARCHY: WEST AFRICA: SAVANNAH AND SAHEL.

McLaughlin, Glen W. Drake University, Iowa. Articles contributed: MA'AL-'AYNAYN; MAGHRIB: MUSLIM BROTHERHOODS; MAURITANIA: COLONIAL PERIOD: NINETEENTH CENTURY; MAURITANIA: INDEPENDENCE AND WESTERN SAHARA, 1960–1979; MOROCCO: SPAIN IN MOROCCO AND THE SAHARA, 1900–1958.

McNulty, Mel. Foreign and Commonwealth Office, Africa Research Group, England. Article contributed: RWANDA: 1962–1990.

Mendel, Daniela. Seminar für Ägyptologie der Universität zu Köln, Germany. Article contributed: EGYPT, ANCIENT: RELIGION.

Messier, Ronald A. Department of History, Middle Tennessee State University. Article contributed: SIJILMASA, ZAWILA: TRANS-SAHARAN TRADE.

Mgadla, P. T. Department of History, University of Botswana. Articles contributed: BOTSWANA: NINETEENTH CENTURY: PRECOLONIAL; COLONIAL FEDERATIONS: BRITISH CENTRAL AFRICA; KHAMA III; MOZAMBIQUE: COLONIAL PERIOD: RESISTANCE AND REBELLIONS; ZIMBABWE (SOUTHERN RHODESIA): COLONIAL PERIOD: LAND, TAX, ADMINISTRATION.

Miers, Suzanne. Professor emerita of African History, Ohio University. Articles contributed: BRUSSELS CONFERENCE AND ACT, 1890; SLAVERY, COLONIAL RULE AND.

Miller, James A. Department of History and Geography, Clemson University, South Carolina. Articles contributed: BERBERS: ANCIENT NORTH AFRICA; CASABLANCA; MARRAKECH; MOROCCO: HASSAN II, LIFE AND GOVERNMENT OF; SAHARA: TRANS-SAHARAN TRADE.

Mojuetan, B. A. Department of History, University of Ibadan, Nigeria. Articles contributed: ABU MADIAN, AL-SHADHILI, AND THE SPREAD OF SUFISM IN THE MAGHRIB; MOROCCO: ECONOMY AND SOCIETY, NINETEENTH CENTURY; MOROCCO: MARABOUTIC CRISIS, FOUNDING OF THE 'ALAWITE DYNASTY; MOROCCO: SA'DIANS.

Morgan, Kenneth. Department of American Studies and History, Brunel University, England. Articles contributed: SIERRA LEONE: ORIGINS, 1787–1808; SLAVERY: ATLANTIC TRADE: ABOLITION: PHILANTHROPY OR ECONOMICS?

Moyd, Michelle. History Department, Cornell University, Ithaca, New York. Articles contributed: LANGUAGE, COLONIAL STATE AND; SWAHILI LANGUAGE.

Mufuka, Kenneth. Department of History and Political Science, Lander University, South Carolina. Article contributed: GREAT ZIMBABWE: ORIGINS AND RISE.

Mukhtar, Yakubu. Department of History, University of Maiduguri, Nigeria. Articles contributed: BORNO (BORNU), SULTANATE OF: SAIFAWA DYNASTY: HORSES, SLAVES, WARFARE; NIGERIA: COLONIAL PERIOD: RAILWAYS, MINING, AND MARKET PRODUCTION.

Mulindwa, Barbara. Division of History, Staffordshire University, England. Article contributed: TAXATION.

Munslow, Barry. Center for African Studies, University of Liverpool, England. Articles contributed: ANGOLA: CIVIL WAR: IMPACT OF, ECONOMIC AND SOCIAL; ANGOLA: COLD WAR POLITICS, CIVIL WAR, 1975–1994; ANGOLA: PEACE BETRAYED, 1994 TO THE PRESENT; LUANDA; MAPUTO; MONDLANE, EDUARDO; MOZAMBIQUE: CHISSANO AND, 1986 TO THE PRESENT; SAVIMBI, JONAS.

Muriuki, Godfrey. Department of History, University of Nairobi, Kenya. Articles contributed: KENYA: KENYATTA, JOMO: LIFE AND GOVERNMENT OF; THUKU, HARRY.

Muzzolini, Alfred. Articles contributed: GARAMANTES: EARLY TRANS-SAHARAN TRADE; HERDING, FARMING, ORIGINS OF: SAHARA AND NILE VALLEY; ROCK ART, SAHARAN; STONE AGE (LATER): SAHARA AND NORTH AFRICA.

Nasson, Bill. Department of Historical Studies, University of Cape Town, South Africa. Articles contributed: SOUTH AFRICAN WAR, 1899–1902; WORLD WAR I: SURVEY.

Nayenga, Peter F. B. Department of History, St. Cloud State University, Minnesota. Article contributed: UGANDA: AMIN DADA, IDI: COUP AND REGIME, 1971–1979.

Ndege, George Oduor. Department of History, St. Louis University, Missouri. Articles contributed: COLONIALISM, INHERITANCE OF: POSTCOLONIAL AFRICA; ETHNICITY, TRIBALISM: COLONIAL EXPERIENCE; IDENTITY, POLITICAL; KENYA: INDEPENDENCE TO THE PRESENT; LABOR, MIGRANT; POLITICAL IDENTITY.

Nelson, Samuel. Department of History, United States Naval Academy, Annapolis, Maryland. Articles contributed: CONCESSIONARY COMPANIES; CONGO (KINSHASA), DEMOCRATIC REPUBLIC OF/ZAIRE: CONGO FREE STATE, 1885–1908; EPIDEMICS: MALARIA, AIDS, OTHER DISEASE: POSTCOLONIAL AFRICA.

Newitt, Malyn. Department of Portuguese and Brazilian Studies, King's College, England. Articles contributed: COMOROS/MAYOTTE: NINETEENTH CENTURY TO 1975; COMOROS/MAYOTTE: INDEPENDENCE TO THE PRESENT; COMOROS: BEFORE 1800; SENA, TETE, PORTUGUESE, AND PRAZOS.

Ngalamulume, Kalala J. Department of History, Bryn Mawr College, Pennsylvania. Articles contributed: HEALTH: MEDICINE AND DISEASE: COLINIAL; MAKENYE KALEMBA; STANLEY, LEOPOLD II, "SCRAMBLE."

Ngoh, Victor Julius. Department of History, University of Buea, Cameroon. Article contributed: CAMEROON (KAMERUN): COLONIAL PERIOD: GERMAN RULE.

Ngolet, François. Department of History, College of Staten Island, New York, New York. Articles contributed: GABON: NINETEENTH CENTURY: PRECOLONIAL; GABON: COLONIAL PERIOD: ADMINISTRATION, LABOR AND ECONOMY; LIBREVILLE; RESETTLEMENT OF RE-

CAPTIVES: FREETOWN, LIBREVILLE, LIBERIA, FRERETOWN, ZANZIBAR.

Ngwa, Canute A. Department of History, University of Nigeria. Article contributed: CAMEROON: COLONIAL PERIOD: BRITISH AND FRENCH RULE.

Niane, Djibril Tamsir. Articles contributed: JUULA/DYULA; MALI EMPIRE: DECLINE, FIFTEENTH CENTURY.

Njoku, Onwuka N. Department of History, University of Nigeria. Articles contributed: NIGERIA: AGRICULTURE, IRRIGATION, RURAL DEVELOPMENT; NIGERIA: INDUSTRY, OIL, ECONOMY; NIGERIA: WORLD WAR II; ROYAL NIGER COMPANY, 1886–1898; SLAVERY: TRANS-SAHARAN TRADE.

Nwaubani, Ebere. Department of History, University of Colorado–Boulder. Articles contributed: EGYPT: MUHAMMAD ALI, 1805–1849: IMPERIAL EXPANSION; EGYPT: MUHAMMAD ALI, 1805–1849: STATE AND ECONOMY; SUDAN: MAHDIST STATE, 1881–1898.

Nyeko, Balam. Department of History, University of Swaziland. Articles contributed: OBOTE, MILTON; SWAZILAND: CONCESSIONS, ANNEXATION, 1880–1902; SWAZILAND: KINGSHIP, CONSTITUTION, INDEPENDENCE; UGANDA: CONFLICT, REGIONAL SINCE 1990; UGANDA: OBOTE: SECOND REGIME, 1980–1985; UGANDA: OBOTE'S FIRST REGIME, 1962–1971; UGANDA: TANZANIAN INVASION, 1979–1980.

Obi-Ani, Paul O. Department of History, University of Nigeria. Article contributed: NIGERIA: BIAFRAN SECESSION AND CIVIL WAR, 1967–1970.

Obiyo Mbanaso Njemanze, Paul. History Department, University of Lagos, Nigeria. Articles contributed: ENVIRONMENT, CONSERVATION, DEVELOPMENT: POSTCOLONIAL AFRICA; MULTINATIONALS AND THE STATE; SLAVERY, ABOLITION OF: EAST AND WEST AFRICA.

Obudho, R. A. Centre for Urban Research, University of Nairobi, Kenya. Article contributed: URBANIZATION, HOUSING AND EMPLOYMENT.

Ochwada, Hannington. Article contributed: CORRUPTION AND THE CRIMINALIZATION OF THE POSTCOLONIAL STATE.

Ofcansky, Thomas P. Articles contributed: KENYA: WORLD WAR I, CARRIER CORPS; SOMALIA: HASSAN, MUHAMMAD ABDILE AND RESISTANCE TO COLONIAL CONQUEST; TANGANYIKA (TANZANIA): WORLD WAR I.

Ogbogbo, C. B. N. Department of History, University of Ibadan, Nigeria. Articles contributed: ABUJA; MONROVIA; SONGHAY EMPIRE: MOROCCAN INVASION, 1591.

Ogunsiji, Ayo. Department of English, University of Ibadan, Nigeria. Article contributed: SOYINKA, WOLE.

Ojok, Filda. Department of History, Institute of Teacher Education, Kyambogo, Uganda. Articles contributed: KAKUNGULU AND THE CREATION OF UGANDA; LUWUM, JANANI; UGANDA: COLONIAL PERIOD: ADMINISTRATION, ECONOMY.

Okeny, Kenneth. Department of History, Salem State College, Massachusetts. Articles contributed: SUDAN: CIVIL WAR, INDEPENDENCE, MILITARY RULE, 1955–1964; SUDAN: CONDOMINIUM PERIOD: ADMINISTRATION, LEGACY IN SOUTH; SUDAN: TURCO-EGYPTIAN PERIOD, 1820–1885.

Okia, Opolot. Department of History, University of Tennessee. Articles contributed: SLAVERY: ATLANTIC TRADE: EFFECTS IN AFRICA AND THE AMERICAS; UGANDA: NRM AND THE WINNING OF POLITICAL POWER.

Oliver, Roland. Professor emeritus, School of Oriental and African Studies, University of London. Article contributed:

JOHNSTON, HARRY H.

Olukoju, Ayodewi. Department of History, University of Lagos, Nigeria. Articles contributed: CURRENCIES AND BANKING; NIGERIA: COLONIAL PERIOD: CHRISTIANITY AND ISLAM.

Oluwatoki, Jamiu A. Department of History, Lagos State University. Article contributed: EGYPT: ARAB EMPIRE.

Ombongi, Kenneth Samson. Department of History, Nairobi University, Kenya. Article contributed: KENYA: NINETEENTH CENTURY: PRECOLONIAL.

Orwin, Caroline. Independent scholar, England. Articles contributed: ADAL: IBRAHIM, AHMAD IBN, CONFLICT WITH ETHIOPIA, 1526–1543; ETHIOPIA: MUSLIM STATES, AWASH VALLEY: SHOA, IFAT, FATAGAR, HADYA, DAWARO, ADAL, NINTH TO SIXTEENTH CENTURIES; ETHIOPIA: SOLOMONID DYNASTY, 1270–1550.

Owusu-Ansah, David. Department of History, James Madison University, Virginia. Articles contributed: GHANA (REPUBLIC OF) (GOLD COAST): GUGGISBERG ADMINISTRATION, 1919–1927; GHANA, REPUBLIC OF: COUPS D'ÉTAT, SECOND REPUBLIC, 1966–1972.

Papini, Robert. Former research officer, KwaMuhle Museum, City of Durban Local History Museums, South Africa. Articles contributed: ETHIOPIANISM AND THE INDEPENDENT CHURCH MOVEMENT; HUMANKIND: HOMINIDS, EARLY, ORIGINS OF; OLDUWAN AND ACHEULIAN: EARLY STONE AGE.

Parpart, Jane L. Department of International Development Studies, Dalhousie University, Nova Scotia. Article contributed: BULAWAYO.

Parsons, Neil. Department of History, University of Botswana. Article contributed: KHAMA, SERETSE.

Parsons, Timothy. African and Afro-American Studies Program and Department of History, Washington University, Missouri. Articles contributed: MALAWI (NYASALAND): COLONIAL PERIOD: LAND, LABOR, AND TAXATION; SOLDIERS, AFRICAN: OVERSEAS.

Pearce, Robert. Department of History, University College of St. Martin, England. Articles contributed: AZIKIWE, NNAMDI; NIGERIA: COLONIAL PERIOD: INTELLIGENTSIA, NATIONALISM, INDEPENDENCE.

Percox, David A. Researcher and writer. Article contributed: KENYA: NATIONALISM, INDEPENDENCE.

Perkins, Kenneth J. Department of History, University of South Carolina. Articles contributed: AGHLABID AMIRATE OF IFRIQIYA; ARAB BEDOUIN: BANU HILAL, BANU SULAYM, BANU MA'QIL; FATIMID EMPIRE: MAGHRIB, 910–1057; QAYRAWAN; TUNIS; TUNISIA: BOURGUIBA, PRESIDENCY OF: ECONOMIC AND SOCIAL CHANGE; TUNISIA: BOURGUIBA, PRESIDENCY OF: GOVERNMENT AND OPPOSITION; TUNISIA: FRENCH PROTECTORATE,1878–1900; TUNISIA: IMMIGRATION AND COLONIZATION, 1881–1950; TUNISIA: MODERN INTERNATIONAL RELATIONS; TUNISIA: NATIONALISM, GROWTH OF, 1881–1934; TUNISIA: NEO-DESTOUR AND INDEPENDENCE, 1934–1956.

Petit, Pierre. Belgian National Funds for Scientific Research and Free University of Brussels, Belgium. Articles contributed: CONGO (KINSHASA), DEMOCRATIC REPUBLIC OF/ZAIRE: NINETEENTH CENTURY: PRECOLONIAL; LUBA: SEVENTEENTH AND EIGHTEENTH CENTURIES; MSIRI: YEKE KINGDOM.

Phillips, Jacke. McDonald Institute for Archaeological Research, University of Cambridge, England. Articles contributed: EGYPT, ANCIENT: NEW KINGDOM AND THE COLONIZATION OF NUBIA; EGYPT, ANCIENT: PREDYNASTIC EGYPT AND NUBIA: HISTORICAL OUTLINE; EGYPT, ANCIENT: UNIFICATION OF UPPER AND LOWER: HISTORICAL OUTLINE; EGYPTOLOGY: FROM HERODOTUS TO THE TWENTIETH CENTURY; KERMA AND EGYPTIAN NUBIA.

Phillipson, David W. Cambridge University Museum of

Archaeology and Anthropology, England. Articles contributed: AKSUM, KINGDOM OF; IRON AGE AND NEOLITHIC: WEST AFRICA; NEOLITHIC, PASTORAL: EASTERN AFRICA; STONE AGE, MIDDLE: CULTURES.

Phiri, Bizeck J. Department of History, University of Zambia. Articles contributed: ASIANS: EAST AFRICA; GORE-BROWNE, STEWART; LOZI KINGDOM AND THE KOLOLO; LUSAKA; NKUMBULA, HARRY MWAANGA; TONGA, ILA, AND CATTLE; ZAMBIA (NORTHERN RHODESIA): BRITISH OCCUPATION, RESISTANCE: 1890S; ZAMBIA (NORTHERN RHODESIA): COLONIAL PERIOD: ADMINISTRATION, ECONOMY; ZAMBIA (NORTHERN RHODESIA): FEDERATION, 1953–1963; ZAMBIA: EARLY NINETEENTH CENTURY: SURVEY; ZAMBIA: LONG-DISTANCE TRADE, NINETEENTH CENTURY; ZAMBIA: NATIONALISM, INDEPENDENCE; ZAMBIA: NGONI INCURSION FROM THE SOUTH.

Phiri, Government Christopher. Department of Economic History, University of Zimbabwe. Article contributed: HARARE.

Pikirayi, Innocent. Department of History, University of Zimbabwe. Articles contributed: MANYIKA OF EASTERN ZIMBABWE; MUTAPA STATE, 1450–1884; TORWA, CHANGAMIRE DOMBO, AND THE ROVZI.

Pirie, Gordon H. University of Salford, England. Article contributed: TRANSPORTATION: POSTCOLONIAL AFRICA.

Pouwels, Randall L. Department of History, University of Central Arkansas. Articles contributed: ISLAM IN EASTERN AFRICA; KENYA: ISLAM; ZANZIBAR: BUSAIDI SULTANATE IN EAST AFRICA.

Pwiti, Gilbert. Department of History, University of Zimbabwe. Article contributed: IRON AGE (LATER): SOUTHERN AFRICA: CHARACTERISTICS AND ORIGINS, SOUTH OF ZAMBEZI.

Rajaonah, Faranirina. Articles contributed: ANTANANARIVO; MADAGASCAR: DEMOCRACY AND DEVELOPMENT, 1990S TO THE PRESENT; MADAGASCAR: INDEPENDENCE TO 1972; MADAGASCAR: RECONCILIATION, REFORM AND INDEPENDENCE, 1948–1960; MADAGASCAR: REFORM AND REVOLUTION, 1972–1989.

Rasmussen, Susan. Department of Anthropology, University of Houston. Articles contributed: AIR, SULTANATE OF; SAHARA: PEOPLES OF THE DESERT; TUAREG: TAKEDDA AND TRANS-SAHARAN TRADE; TUAREG: TRADERS, RAIDERS, AND THE EMPIRES OF MALI AND SONGHAY.

Reid, Andrew. Institute of Archaeology, University College London. Articles contributed: GREAT LAKES REGION: GROWTH OF CATTLE HERDING; GREAT LAKES REGION: KARAGWE, NKORE, AND BUHAYA; GREAT LAKES REGION: NTUSI, KIBIRO, AND BIGO.

Reid, Richard. Department of History, Durham University, England. Articles contributed: EASTERN AFRICA: REGIONAL SURVEY; ETHIOPIA: SHOAN PLATEAU, FIFTEENTH AND SIXTEENTH CENTURIES; ETHIOPIA: ZAGWE DYNASTY, 1150–1270.

Reynolds, Edward. Department of History, University of California–San Diego. Articles contributed: ALL-AFRICAN PEOPLE'S CONFERENCE, 1958; GHANA (REPUBLIC OF): 1800–1874; GHANA, REPUBLIC OF: ACHAEMPONG REGIME TO THE THIRD REPUBLIC, 1972– 1981; GOLD: PRODUCTION AND TRADE: WEST AFRICA; PORTUGAL: EXPLORATION AND TRADE IN THE FIFTEENTH CENTURY.

Robinson, W. Frank. Department of History, Vanderbilt University, Tennessee. Article contributed: NUJOMA, SAM.

Rockel, Stephen J. Department of Humanities (History), University of Toronto–Scarborough. Articles contributed: TANGANYIKA (TANZANIA): EARLY NINETEENTH CENTURY; TANGANYIKA (TANZANIA): NYAMWEZI AND LONG-DISTANCE TRADE.

Rodriguez-Manas, Francisco. Articles contributed: 'ABD ALLAH IBN YASIN: ALMORAVID: SAHARA; 'ABD AL-MU'MIN: ALMOHAD EMPIRE, 1140–1269; IBN TUMART, ALMOHAD COMMUNITY AND;

YUSUF IBN TASHFIN: ALMORAVID EMPIRE: MAGHRIB: 1070–1147.

Ross, Andrew C. School of Divinity, University of Edinburgh. Articles contributed: LIVINGSTONE, DAVID; MALAWI (NYASALAND): COLONIAL PERIOD: FEDERATION; MALAWI: MISSIONARIES AND CHRISTIANITY, NINETEENTH CENTURY.

Rowe, John. Professor emeritus, Department of History, Northwestern University, Illinois. Article contributed: KAGWA, APOLO KAFIBALA GULEMYE.

Rutten, Marcel. African Studies Centre, Netherlands. Articles contributed: ADDIS ABABA; KENYA: NINETEENTH CENTURY: PRECOLONIAL; TOURISM.

Salamone, Frank A. Department of Sociology, Iona College, New Rochelle, New York. Articles contributed: FULBE/FULANI/PEUL: CATTLE PASTORALISM, MIGRATION, SEVENTEENTH AND EIGHTEENTH CENTURIES; HAUSA POLITIES: ORIGINS, RISE; HAUSA POLITIES: WARFARE, NINETEENTH CENTURY; KANO; AL-MAGHILI; RELIGION, HISTORY OF; RELIGION: INDIGENOUS BELIEFS: SUB-SAHARAN AFRICA; RUMFA, MUHAMMAD.

Salm, Steven J. Department of History, Xavier University, Louisiana. Articles contributed: ALCOHOL: POPULAR CULTURE, COLONIAL CONTROL; MUSIC: POSTCOLONIAL AFRICA.

Sanders, James. Articles contributed: ANGOLA: INDEPENDENCE AND CIVIL WAR, 1974–1976; MANDELA, NELSON; SOUTH AFRICA: 1994 TO THE PRESENT.

Sandomirsky, Natalie. Formerly of the Departments of French and African Studies, Southern Connecticut State University. Articles contributed: BENIN, EMPIRE: OBA EWUARE, TRADE WITH THE PORTUGUESE; BENIN, EMPIRE: ORIGINS AND GROWTH OF CITY-STATE; DAHOMEY: EIGHTEENTH CENTURY; HAMDALLAHI CALIPHATE, 1818–1862; MALI (REPUBLIC OF): ALLIANCES AND WARS; MALI, REPUBLIC OF: TRAORÉ, MOUSSA, LIFE AND ERA OF; NIGER: NINETEENTH CENTURY: SURVEY; NIGER: FRENCH OCCUPATION AND RESISTANCE; NIGER: INDEPENDENCE TO PRESENT.

Saucier, Paul Khalil. Department of Sociology and Anthropology, Northeastern University, Massachusetts. Article contributed: CAPE VERDE, HISTORY OF.

Saul, John S. Department of Political Science, York University, Toronto. Articles contributed: COLONIALISM, OVERTHROW OF: THIRTY YEARS WAR FOR SOUTHERN AFRICAN LIBERATION; MOZAMBIQUE: FRELIMO AND THE WAR OF LIBERATION, 1962–1975; MOZAMBIQUE: MACHEL AND THE FRELIMO REVOLUTION, 1975–1986; NAMIBIA: SWAPO AND THE FREEDOM STRUGGLE; SOCIALISM: POSTCOLONIAL AFRICA; SOUTH AFRICA: TRANSITION, 1990–1994.

Saunders, Christopher. Department of Historical Studies, University of Cape Town, South Africa. Articles contributed: CAPE LIBERALISM, NINETEENTH CENTURY; MADIKIZELA-MANDELA, WINNIE; NAMIBIA (SOUTHWEST AFRICA): SOUTH AFRICAN RULE; NAMIBIA: INDEPENDENCE TO THE PRESENT; NAMIBIA: STRUGGLE FOR INDEPENDENCE, 1970–1990; RAMPHELE, DR. MAMPHELA ALETTA; SOGA, TIYO; SOUTH AFRICA: AFRICA POLICY; SOUTH AFRICA: ANTIAPARTHEID STRUGGLE: TOWNSHIPS, THE 1980S; TOIVO YA TOIVO.

Scarr, Deryck. Formerly of the Institute of Advanced Studies, Australian National University. Articles contributed: BOURBON, ILE DE FRANCE, SEYCHELLES: EIGHTEENTH CENTURY; MAURITIUS: SLAVERY AND SLAVE SOCIETY TO 1835; SEYCHELLES: INDEPENDENCE, REVOLUTION, RESTORATION OF DEMOCRACY; 1960 TO PRESENT; SEYCHELLES: 1770 TO 1960.

Schmitt, Deborah. Pikes Peak Community College and Metropolitan State College, Colorado. Articles contributed:

ARMIES, COLONIAL: AFRICANS IN; BOTSWANA: COLONIAL PERIOD.

Schmitz, Christopher. Department of Modern History, University of St. Andrews, Scotland. Articles contributed: JOHANNESBURG; MINING, MULTINATIONALS, AND DEVELOPMENT.

Schraeder, Peter J. Department of Political Science, Loyola University, Illinois. Articles contributed: DEMOCRACY: POSTCOLONIAL; FRANCOPHONIE, AFRICA AND THE; NATIONALISM(S): POSTCOLONIAL AFRICA; POLITICAL PARTIES AND ONE-PARTY STATES.

Schroeter, Daniel J. Department of History, University of California–Irvine. Article contributed: MOROCCO: SIDI MUHAMMAD AND FOUNDATIONS OF ESSAWIRA.

Schubert, Benedict. Africa Desk, Mission 21, Switzerland. Article contributed: ANGOLA: NEW COLONIAL PERIOD: CHRISTIANITY, MISSIONARIES, INDEPENDENT CHURCHES.

Schuerkens, Ulrike. Ecole des Hautes Etudes en Sciences Sociales, Paris, France. Article contributed: BRITISH TOGOLAND.

Schultz, Warren C. Department of History, DePaul University, Illinois. Articles contributed: EGYPT: MAMLUK DYNASTY (1250–1517): LITERATURE; EGYPT: MAMLUK DYNASTY (1250–1517): PLAGUE.

Searing, James F. Department of African American Studies, University of Illinois–Chicago. Articles contributed: SENEGAL: COLONIAL PERIOD: ECONOMY; SENEGAL: COLONIAL PERIOD: FOUR COMMUNES: DAKAR, SAINT-LOUIS, GORÉE, AND RUFISQUE; SENEGAL: COLONIAL PERIOD: ECONOMY; WOLOF AND JOLOF EMPIRES.

Seibert, Gerhard. Instituto de Investigação Científica Tropical, Centro de Estudos Africanos e Asiáticos, Portugal. Articles contributed: SÃO TOMÉ AND PRINCIPE, TO 1800; SÃO TOMÉ AND PRINCIPE, 1800 TO THE PRESENT.

Senkomago, Sewanyana. Faculty of Arts, Kyambogo University, Uganda. Articles contributed: GHANA, EMPIRE OF: HISTORY OF; UGANDA COLONIZATION, RESISTANCE, UGANDA AGREEMENT, 1890–1900.

Shantz, Jeff. Department of Sociology, York University, Toronto. Articles contributed: ANGOLA: NEW COLONIAL PERIOD: ECONOMICS OF COLONIALISM; CABINDA; SPORTS: POSTCOLONIAL AFRICA.

Shapiro, David. Department of Economics, Pennsylvania State University. Article contributed: KINSHASA.

Sheldon, Kathleen. Center for the Study of Women, University of California–Los Angeles. Article contributed: WOMEN: HISTORY AND HISTORIOGRAPHY.

Shillington, Kevin (volume editor). Independent scholar, England. Articles contributed: KIMBERLEY, DIAMOND FIELDS AND; MUSEVENI, YOWERI KAGUTA.

Sichone, Owen. Department of Social Anthropology, University of Cape Town, South Africa. Articles contributed: LENSHINA, ALICE; PEASANT PRODUCTION, POSTCOLONIAL: MARKETS AND SUBSISTENCE; ZAMBIA: RELIGIOUS MOVEMENTS.

Simba, Malik. Department of History, California State University–Fresno. Articles contributed: DRAMA, FILM: POSTCOLONIAL; LAW AND THE LEGAL SYSTEM: POSTCOLONIAL AFRICA.

Simelane, Hamilton Sipho. Department of History, University of Swaziland. Articles contributed: SWAZILAND: COLONIAL PERIOD: LAND, LABOR, ADMINISTRATION; SWAZILAND: MSWATI III, REIGN OF; SWAZILAND: SOBHUZA II, LIFE AND GOVERNMENT OF.

Smith, Andrew B. Department of Archaeology, University of Cape Town, South Africa. Articles contributed: DOMESTICATION, PLANT AND ANIMAL, HISTORY OF; NEOLITHIC NORTH AFRICA.

Smith, Benjamin. School of Geography, Archaeology and Environmental Studies, University of the Witwatersrand, South Africa. Articles contributed: MALAWI: COLONIZATION AND WARS OF RESISTANCE, 1889–1904.

Smith, Lawrence. McDonald Institute for Archaeological Research, University of Cambridge, England. Article contributed: NUBIA: RELATIONS WITH EGYPT (SEVENTH TO FOURTEENTH CENTURIES).

Smythe, Kathleen R. Department of History, Xavier University, Ohio. Articles contributed: LITERACY: VEHICLE FOR CULTURAL CHANGE; MONOPHYSITISM, COPTIC CHURCH, 379–640; RELIGION, COLONIAL AFRICA: INDIGENOUS RELIGION.

Soper, Robert. Department of History, University of Zimbabwe. Article contributed: NYANGA HILLS.

Spaulding, Jay. Department of History, Kean University, New Jersey. Article contributed: FUNJ SULTANATE, SIXTEENTH TO EIGHTEENTH CENTURIES.

Spear, Thomas. Department of History, University of Wisconsin-Madison. Article contributed: SWAHIL: AZANIA TO 1498.

Senkomago, N. Department of History, Institute of Teacher Education, Uganda. Articles contributed: GHANA, EMPIRE: HISTORY OF; UGANDA: COLONIZATION, RESISTANCE, UGANDA AGREEMENT, 1890–1900.

Stapleton, Timothy J. Department of History, Trent University, Ontario. Articles contributed: JABAVU, JOHN TENGO; NONQAWUSE AND THE GREAT XHOSA CATTLE-KILLING, 1857; SOUTH AFRICA: RURAL PROTEST AND VIOLENCE: 1950s; ZIMBABWE: NINETEENTH CENTURY, EARLY; ZIMBABWE: CONFLICT AND RECONSTRUCTION, 1980s; ZIMBABWE: INCURSIONS FROM THE SOUTH, NGONI AND NDEBELE.

Steele, Murray. Former head of Afro-Asian studies, Edge Hill College of Higher Education; honorary research fellow, Keele University, England. Articles contributed: AFRIKAANS AND AFRIKANER NATIONALISM, NINETEENTH CENTURY; ALGERIA: ALGIERS AND ITS CAPTURE, 1815–1830; ALGERIA: EUROPEAN POPULATION, 1830–1954; ALGERIA: GOVERNMENT AND ADMINISTRATION, 1830–1914; ANGOLA: NEW COLONIAL PERIOD: WHITE IMMIGRATION, MESTIÇOS, ASSIMILATED AFRICANS; CENTRAL AFRICAN REPUBLIC: 1980s AND 1990s; CENTRAL AFRICAN REPUBLIC: COLONIAL PERIOD: OUBANGUI-CHARI; CENTRAL AFRICAN REPUBLIC: NATIONALISM, INDEPENDENCE; EQUATORIAL GUINEA: COLONIAL PERIOD, NINETEENTH CENTURY; EQUATORIAL GUINEA: INDEPENDENCE TO THE PRESENT; EQUIANO, OLAUDAH; KRUGER, PAUL; MALAWI (NYASALAND): COLONIAL PERIOD: CHILEMBWE RISING, 1915; RELIGION, COLONIAL AFRICA: MISSIONARIES; SAMKANGE, REV. D. T.; SCHREINER, OLIVE EMILIE ALBERTINA; SOUTH AFRICA: AFRIKANER NATIONALISM, BROEDERBOND AND NATIONAL PARTY, 1902–1948; SOUTH AFRICA: CONFEDERATION, DISARMAMENT AND THE FIRST ANGLO-BOER WAR, 1871–1881; TANGANYIKA (TANZANIA): ARUSHA DECLARATION; TANGANYIKA (TANZANIA): COLONIAL PERIOD, BRITISH: "INDIRECT RULE"; TANGANYIKA (TANZANIA): COLONIAL PERIOD, BRITISH: ECONOMY; TANZANIA (TANGANYIKA): DEMOCRACY AND CAPITALISM: 1990 TO THE PRESENT; ZAMBIA (NORTHERN RHODESIA): COPPERBELT; ZAMBIA (NORTHERN RHODESIA): MINEWORKERS' STRIKES: 1935, 1940; ZIMBABWE (SOUTHERN RHODESIA): AFRICAN POLITICAL AND TRADES UNION MOVEMENTS, 1920s AND 1930s.

Sundelin, Lennart. Princeton University, New Jersey. Articles contributed: EGYPT: FATIMIDS, LATER: WORLD TRADE; EGYPT: TULUNIDS AND IKHSHIDIDS, 850–969.

Sunseri, Thaddeus. Department of History, Colorado State University. Articles contributed: TANGANYIKA (TANZANIA): GERMAN INVASION AND RESISTANCE; TANGANYIKA (TANZANIA): GERMAN RULE: LAND, LABOR AND ECONOMIC TRANSFORMATION; TANGANYIKA

(Tanzania): Maji Maji Rebellion, 1905–1907.

Tamari, Tal. Centre National de la Recherche Scientifique, France. Article contributed: Literacy and Indigenous Scripts: Precolonial Western Africa.

Teelock, Vijaya. University of Mauritius. Articles contributed: Mascerene Islands Prior to the French; Mauritius: Indentured Labor and Society, 1835–1935; Mauritius: Nationalism, Communalism, and Independence, 1935–1968; Slavery, Plantation: East Africa and the Islands.

Tesi, Moses K. Department of Political Science, Middle Tennessee State University. Articles contributed: Ahidjo, Ahmadou; Communaute Financière Africaine; Coups d'État and Military Rule: Postcolonial Africa; Development, Postcolonial: Central Planning, Private Enterprise, Investment; Oil; Southern African Development Community.

Tesi, Peter J. University of Virginia School of Law. Article contributed: Union Douanière et Economique de L'Afrique Centrale.

Thabane, Motlatsi. Department of History, National University of Lesotho. Articles contributed: Jonathan, Chief Joseph Leabua; Lesotho (Basutoland): Colonization and Cape Rule, 1868–1884; Lesotho: Independence to the Present; Lesotho: Nationalism and Independence; Mokhehle, Ntsu.

Thornton, John K. Department of History, Millersville University of Pennsylvania. Articles contributed: Angola, Eighteenth Century; Kongo Kingdom, 1543–1568; Kongo Kingdom: Seventeenth and Eighteenth Centuries; Kongo Kingdom: Afonso I, Christianity, and Kingship; Kongo Kingdom: Jaga Invasion to 1665; Kongo, Teke (Tio), and Loango: History to 1483; Loango: Slave Trade; Ndongo, Kingdom of; Njinga Mbande; Ovimbundu States; Slavery: Atlantic Trade: Opposition, African.

Tibebu, Teshale. Department of History, Temple University, Pennsylvania. Articles contributed: Ethiopia: Aksumite Inheritance, c.850–1150; Ethiopia: Famine, Revolution, Mengistu Dictatorship, 1974–1991; Ethiopia: Land, Agriculture, Politics, 1941–1974; Ethiopia: Menelik II, Era of; Lalibela and Ethiopian Christianity.

Tignor, Robert L. Department of History, Princeton University, New Jersey. Articles contributed: Egypt: Nasser: Foreign Policy: Suez Canal Crisis to Six Day War, 1952–1970; Egypt: Nasser: High Dam, Economic Development, 1952–1970.

Topan, Farouk. Department of the Languages and Cultures of Africa, School of Oriental and African Studies, England. Article contributed: Zanzibar: Revolution and Union (Tanzania).

Truschel, Louis W. Department of History, Western Washington University. Articles contributed: Namibia (Southwest Africa): German Colonization, 1893–1896; Plaatje, Sol T.; Rudd Concession, 1888.

Tuck, Michael W. Department of History, Northeastern Illinois University. Articles contributed: Health: Medicine and Disease: Postcolonial; Uganda: Education.

Tuck, Steven L. Department of Classics, Miami University, Oxford, Ohio. Article contributed: Egypt, Ancient: Roman Conquest and Occupation: Historical Outline.

Tyre, Stephen. Department of Modern History, University of St. Andrews, Scotland. Articles contributed: Morocco: Lyautey, General Hubert, and Evolution of French Protectorate, 1912–1950; World War II: North Africa.

Wagner, Michele. Department of History, University of Minnesota–Twin Cities. Articles contributed: Burundi to c.1800; Burundi: Nineteenth Century: Precolonial; Burundi: Colonial Period: German and Belgian; Burundi: Independence to 1988; Rwanda: Genocide, 1994; Rwanda: Genocide, Aftermath of.

Wainaina, Michael. Literature Department, Kenyatta University, Kenya. Articles contributed: Policing, Colonial.

Walker, Ezekiel. Department of History, University of Central Florida. Articles contributed: Agriculture, Cash Crops, Food Security; Kanem: Origins and Growth; Mai Dunama Dibalami; Peasant Production, Colonial: Cash Crops and Transport.

Walker, Iain. Department of Anthropology, University of Sydney. Articles contributed: Mauritius: Ramgoolam, Seewoosagur, Government of; Réunion: Nineteenth Century to 1946.

Waller, Richard. Department of History, Bucknell University, Pennsylvania. Articles contributed: Rinderpest and Smallpox: East and Southern Africa.

Walls, Andrew F. Centre for Study of Christianity in the Non-Western World, University of Edinburgh. Article contributed: Alexandria and Early Christianity: Egypt.

Ward, Kevin. Department of Theology and Religious Studies, University of Leeds, England. Article contributed: Uganda: Mwanga and Buganda, 1880s.

Wariboko, Waibinte Elekima. Department of History, University of the West Indies–Jamaica. Article contributed: Delta States, Nineteenth Century.

Waziri, Ibrahim Maina. Department of History, University of Maiduguri, Nigeria. Article contributed: Peasant Production, Colonial: Food, Markets: West Africa.

Weeks, John. Department of Development Studies, School of Oriental and African Studies, England. Article contributed: Globalization, Africa and.

Welch, Ashton Wesley. Department of History and Program in Black Studies, Creighton University, Nebraska. Articles contributed: Crowther, Reverend Samuel Ajayi and the Niger Mission; Harris, Prophet William Wade.

Welsby, Derek. Department of Egyptian Antiquities, British Museum, England. Articles contributed: Kush; Meroe: Meroitic Culture and Economy; Napata and Meroe; Nobadia, Makurra and 'Alwa; Soba and Dongola.

Whidden, James. Department of History, Murray State University, Kentucky. Articles contributed: Barbary Corsairs and the Ottoman Provinces: Algiers, Tunis, and Tripoli in the Seventeenth Century; Colonialism, Overthrow of: Northern Africa; Education: North Africa (Colonial and Postcolonial); Egypt: Monarchy and Parliament, 1922–1939; Egypt: Mubarak, Since 1981: Agriculture, Industry; Egypt: Mubarak, Since 1981: Politics; Egypt: Ottoman, 1517–1798: Historical Outline; Egypt: Ottoman, 1517–1798: Mamluk Beylicate; Egypt: Ottoman, 1517–1798: Napoleon and the French in Egypt; Egypt: Ottoman, 1517–1798: Nubia, Red Sea; Egypt under the Ottomans, 1517–1798: Trade with Africa; Maghrib: Algiers, Tunis, and Tripoli Under the Deys, Husaynids, and Quaramanlis in the Eighteenth Century; Maghrib: Marinids, Maghrib: Ottoman Conquest of Algiers, Tripoli, and Tunis; Press: Northern Africa; Tunisia: Ahmad Bey and Army Reform; Tunisia: Ben 'Ali, Liberalization; Tunisia: Khayr al-Din and Constitutional and Administrative Reform, 1855–1878.

Wilburn, Kenneth. Department of History, East Carolina University, North Carolina. Article contributed: Jameson Raid,

ORIGINS OF SOUTH AFRICAN WAR: 1895–1899.

Willis, Justin. Department of History, University of Durham, England. Articles contributed: KENYA: MEKATILELE AND GIRIAMA RESISTANCE, 1900–1920; SWAHILI: MOMBASA, FORT JESUS, THE PORTUGUESE, 1589–1698.

Wilmsen, Edwin N. Department of Anthropology, University of Texas–Austin. Articles contributed: IRON AGE (EARLY): HERDING, FARMING, SOUTHERN AFRICA; SLAVE TRADE: ARMS, IVORY, AND (SOUTHERN AFRICA).

Woods, Dwayne. Department of Political Science, Purdue University, Indiana. Articles contributed: HOUPHOUËT-BOIGNY, FÉLIX; CÔTE D'IVOIRE (IVORY COAST): INDEPENDENCE TO THE PRESENT.

Woodward, Peter. Department of Politics, University of Reading, England. Articles contributed: SUDAN: NIMEIRI, PEACE, THE ECONOMY; SUDAN: OCTOBER REVOLUTION, 1964; SUDAN: TURABI'S REVOLUTION, ISLAM, POWER.

Worden, Nigel. Department of History, University of Cape Town, South Africa. Articles contributed: CAPE COLONY: KHOI-DUTCH WARS; CAPE COLONY: ORIGINS, SETTLEMENT, TRADE; CAPE COLONY: SLAVERY; CAPE TOWN.

Wright, David. Divinity School, University of Edinburgh. Articles contributed: AUGUSTINE, CATHOLIC CHURCH: NORTH AFRICA; DONATIST CHURCH: NORTH AFRICA.

Wright, John. Department of Historical Studies, University of Natal, South Africa. Articles contributed: CENTRAL AFRICA, NORTHERN: SLAVE RAIDING; IRON AGE (LATER): SOUTHERN AFRICA: SOUTHEASTERN LOWVELD, EMERGENCE OF STATES ON; KANEM: SLAVERY AND TRANS-SAHARAN TRADE; LIBYA: GADDAFI (QADHDHAFI) AND JAMAHIRIYYA (LIBYAN REVOLUTION); LIBYA: ITALIAN COLONIZATION AND ADMINISTRATION; LIBYA: ITALIAN INVASION AND RESISTANCE 1911–1931; LIBYA: OIL, POLITICS, AND OPEC; LIBYA: WORLD WAR II AND THE KINGDOM OF LIBYA, 1942-1969; LIBYA: YUSUF PASHA KARAMANLI AND THE OTTOMAN REOCCUPATION, 1795–1835; MFECANE.

Wurster, Patrick F. A. Department of Social Sciences, University of Osnabrueck, Germany. Article contributed: TOGO: EYADÈMA, GNASSINGBE, LIFE AND ERA OF PRESIDENT OF TOGO.

Yoder, John C. Department of Politics and History, Whitworth College, Washington. Articles contributed: KASAI AND KUBA: CHIEFDOMS AND KINGDOM; LIBERIA, NINETEENTH CENTURY: POLITICS, SOCIETY, AND ECONOMY; LIBERIA, NINETEENTH CENTURY: ORIGINS AND FOUNDATIONS; LUBA: ORIGINS AND GROWTH; TIPPU TIP (MUHAMMED BIN HAMED).

Youé, Chris. Department of History, Memorial University of Newfoundland. Articles contributed: LAND AND "RESERVES," COLONIAL; LEWANIKA I, THE LOZI AND THE BSA COMPANY.

Zack-Williams, Alfred. Editorial board, *Review of African Political Economy.* Articles contributed: SIERRA LEONE: DIAMONDS, CIVIL WAR, 1990S.

Zaffiro, James J. Department of Political Science, Central College, Iowa. Articles contributed: COMMUNICATIONS; MEDIA AS PROPAGANDA; MUGABE, ROBERT GABRIEL; NKOMO, JOSHUA MGABUKO; PRESS: SOUTHERN AFRICA; ZIMBABWE: ZIMBABWE-RHODESIA, LANCASTER HOUSE AND INDEPENDENCE, 1978–1980.

Zoungrana, Guy. Article contributed: RURAL DEVELOPMENT, POSTCOLONIAL.

INDEX

INDEX

Au: it
is 1st
or 2nd
Entry?

INDEX

INDEX

Ludvonga, 1522
Lugard, Frederick, 95, 731, 1095–1098, 1202, 1556, 1615,
1616, 1638
Lugbara, 1257
Lukonzolwa, 856
Lule, Yusufu, 1053, 1628, 1630–1631
Lumpa Church, 805–806, 1250, 1257, 1272, 1703
Lumumba, Patrice, 70, 253, 271, 310–311, 858–859, 1625
Lunda, 303, 304, 738, 851, 859–863, 1692–1693, *See also*
Katanga
Eastern Lunda, 741–742
"love story," 860, 862
Ovimbundu and, 1184
Lundu, 944–946
Luo, 179, 743–744, 756, 1127, 1132–1134
Luo Union, 1172
Lusaka, Zambia, 864–865
Lushi, Kasongo, 1562
Luthuli, Albert, 865–866, 1448, 1449, 1457
Lutoko, 1125
Luwum, Janani, 866–867
Luyhia, 743–744
Lwo, 594, 1127, 1296–1297
Lyautey, Louis-Hubert-Gonzalves, 1013–1014, 1016–1017,
1020–1021, 1672

M

M'siri, 304, 741, 1047–1048
Ma'al-'Aynayn, 869–870, 957, 1016, 1656
Ma Ba, 1330
Maa language, 1129
Maa-speaking people, 385–386, 1125
Maasai, 743–744, 1125, 1129–1130, 1131
environmental history, 560
Loikop Wars, 1129–1130
pastoralism, 1130
rinderpest epidemic, 1284, 1537
Sirikwa and, 1368
War of Morijo, 1130
Maay, 1404
Maba, 228
Maban, 226
Mabhudu, 705
Mabude, Saul, 1448
Macapi, 1252
Macarico, 939
Macaulay, Herbert, 117, 330, 870–871, 1103, 1104–1105
Macaulay, Zachary, 1273, 1353
MacCarthy, Charles, 537, 565, 1355
MacDonald, Claude, 341
Macequece, 1032
MacGregor, William, 1096
Machar, Riek, 557, 1506
Machel, Samora, 992, 1039–1040, 1044, 1053, 1455
Macheng (Kgosi), 763
Macina, 614–615, 922, 924
Mackay, Alexander, 729, 1616
MacKay, Claude, 1080
Mackenzie, C. F., 906
Mackenzie, John, 165
Mackinnon, William, 1616
Maclean, George, 566, 567
Maclean, Sir Harry, 1011
Macleod, Iain, 754, 1701
Macpherson, 131
MacQueen, James, 561
Madagascar (Malagasy Republic), 872–887
Antananarivo, 92–94
Christianity, 886

coffee production, 879
Comoros and, 290, 291
democracy and development 1990s to present, 885–886
forced labor (*fanompoana*), 875–876, 877
French conquest and rule, 876–882
gold, 877
great rebellion (1947–1948), 879–881
independence to 1972 (Tsiranana government), 882–883
Islamic-Swahili economy and culture, 873
labor movement, 1577
Malagasy identity, 875
Malagasy kingdoms, 873–875
Malagasy language, 797, 872
Mascarene Islands economy and, 874, 875, 877
Merina Kingdom, 19th century, 875–878
nationalist revolts, 875–876, 878
prehistory to 1500, 872–873
reform and revolution (1972–1989), 884–885
slavery and slave trade, 872, 874, 905, 1384, 1386–1387
World War II and, 880
Madanda, 1416
Madani, Abassi, 63
Madeira, 1221
Mademba Sy, 1337
Madi, 1128
Madikizela-Mandela, Winnie, 887–888, 936
Mafeking, 1199
Mafia, 382
Maghrawa, 1
Maghrib, 889–899, 996, 1149, *See also* Algeria; Libya; Mauritania;
Morocco; North Africa; Sahara; Tuareg; Tunisia
Abbasids, 1151
Almohads, *See* Almohad dynasty
Almoravids, *See* Almoravid dynasty
ancient Berber culture, 145–146
Arab conquest and Islamization, 889–890, 1151
Bedouin invasions, 98–99
Byzantine rule, 889
European expansion (1250–1550), 892–893
Fatimid rule, 524–525, 1151–1152, *See also* Fatimids
historical sources, 641
historiography, 628, 637
Ibadi Islam, 801
Ibn Khaldun's writings, 665–668
Islam in, 890
later Stone Age culture, 1484
Marinids, Zivanids, and Hafsids (1235–1359), 890–891
mineral resources, 985
Ottoman conquest and rule, 893–896
Qayrawan, 1237–1238
Sufi movement, 7–8, 891, 896–897, *See also* Sufism
trans-Saharan trade, Garamantes, 554–555
unity, European Union and, 897–899
unity, Tunisia and, 1609
Zirids, 98, 525, *See also* Zirids
Magigwane Khosa, 1417
Magomi, 157
Magopa, 687
Magude Khosa, 1417
Maguire, James Rochfort, 1294
Maharero, Sam, 1065
Mahdi, Sadiq al, 556
Mahdi and Mahdism, 120, 459, 765, 1101, 1253, 1257,
1490–1493
defeat at Omdurman, 1491–1493
Christian Ethiopia and, 507
Gordon's demise at Khartoum, 459, 765, 1253,
1491–1492
"Mad Mullah," 1258, 1276, 1405–1407

INDEX

Mahdiyya, 524, 525, 1238
Maherero, Samuel, 1063, 1064
Mahmud, Muhammad, 470
Mahmud al-'Araki, 1160
Maïnassara, Baré, 1094–1095
Maize, 1463–1464
Majdhubiyya, 897
Maji Maji rebellion (1905–1907), 266, 383, 1251, 1257, 1275, 1276, 1277, 1538–1539
Majid, Seyyid, 336
Majjawi, Abd al-Qadir al-, 56
Makanjira, 909
Makeba, Miriam, 1056
Makenye Kalemba, 901–903
Makerere University, 1621
Makgatho, S. M., 1229
Makhzen, 894, 1010, 1023
Makhzumi, 492
Makkura, 229
Makonnen, T. Ras, 350, 611, 1651
Makua, 699, 905, 1369, 1370
Makurra, 535, 1141–1143, 1158–1159, 1392–1393
Makwakwas, 1032
Malagasy identity, 875
Malagasy kingdoms, 873–875
Malagasy language, 797, 872
Malagasy people, origins of, 872–873
Malagasy Republic, *See* Madagascar
Malambule, 1521
Malan, D. F., 1442, 1447, 1649
Malaria, 321, 329, 482–483, 621
  indigenous African immunity, 528–529, 852
  quinine and, 329, 621, 792, 1096
Malawi (Nyasaland), 903–918
  access to the sea (Beira), 129–130
  arms, ivory, and slave trade, 1368–1369
  Banda and, 123–124
  Beira corridor, 130
  Blantyre, 149–150
  British Central Africa, 909
  British Commonwealth and, 282
  British protectorate and colonization, 907–910
  Central African Federation, 1468
  Chilembwe's mission, 907
  Chilembwe's uprising of 1915, 912–913
  Christianity and missions, 906–908, 913, 914
  colonial administration, underfunded, 1202
  colonial administration and Rhodesia federation, 913–916
  colonial boundaries, 169
  colonial economy and land policies, 910–912
  colonial legacy, 256
  development approach, 345
  famine, 370
  Federation, 259, 1654–1655, 1658, 1700–1702, 1724, 1727–1729
  food production, 23
  independence, 124, 916, 1728
  Kilimanjaro Johnston and, 719
  labor movement, 1577
  long-distance trade, 19th century, 905–906
  Maravi kingdom (16th-17th century), 944–948
  nationalism and independence, 914–916
  Native Associations, 913–915
  Ngoni and Yao resistance, 909–910
  Ngoni incursions (19th century), 903–905, 1694
  Ngoni kingdoms, 1533–1534
  postindependence history, 124, 916–918
  press, 723, 1225
  public health spending, 622
    Rhodes and, 1281, *See also* Rhodes, Cecil
    salt production, 697
    slave trade, 905–906
    Southern Africa Development Coordination Conference, 1469
    thangata labor system, 909, 911–912
    World War II and, 914
Malawi Congress Party (MCP), 124, 916
Malebo Pool, 172, 297, 304
Mali, 923–933
  alliances and wars (19th century), 924–925
  anticolonial nationalism, 927–929
  Bamako, 122–123
  coup and military regime, 930–931
  economy and society (19th century), 923–924
  Egyptian trade, 440
  Federation, 261, 262, 925, 928–929, 1334, 1342, *See also* French West Africa
  French administration (Soudan Français), 925–929
  French colonialism, 923–929
  French franc zone (CFA), 282
  Ghana-Guinea union, 1139
  gold, 440, 588, 920, 940
  Islam, 230
  Islam, Muslim brotherhoods, 926–927
  Konaré, 1590
  missionary activity, 926
  music, 1056
  oral traditions, 643
  postindependence history, 929–933
  precolonial literacy, 840
  rock art, 1291
  Sa'di rule, 1153
  salt production, 1586
  Samori Touré and, *See* Touré, Samori
  strikes, 927
  Timbuktu, *See* Timbuktu
  transition to democracy, 932
  Traoré and, 1590
  Tuareg disaffection and rebellion, 931–932, 961, 1590
  warrior states, 19th century, 923
Mali empire (13th-15th centuries), 230–231, 664–665, 918–922, 940
  economy, 920–921
  Gao and, 1413, *See also* Gao
  Juula and, 922
  Mansa Musa, *See* Mansa Musa
  merchant caste, 724
  Moroccan relations, 941
  mosques, 1030
  Segu, a Bamana kingdom, 1327–1328
  Sundiata, 231, 643, 918–919, 937, 1314, 1588
  trans-Saharan trade, 1314
  Tuareg and, 1588
  Timbuktu, 1561, *See also* Timbuktu
Malik Sy, 1338
Maliki school of Islam, 20, 803, 1645, 1687–1688
Malindi, 744
Malinké, 604, 1588
Mallemtis, 160
Malloum, Félix, 1571, 244
Mambo, 162
Mambwe, 1691
Mamluks, 199, 950, 1152–1153
  beylicate, 449–450
  Egypt, 438–447, 950, 1152–1153, 1158–1159
  literature, 443–444
  military system, 444–445, 950
  Tunisia, 1594–1595
Mammeir, Mouloud, 368

INDEX

INDEX

Tunisia, 1157, 1594–1610, *See also* Ifriqiya; Tunis *(continued)*
  Spanish rule, 893
  tax revolts, 1595, 1596
  tourism, 1575
  World War II and, 1156, 1602, 1674, 1675
Tunni, 1404
Turabi, Hasan al-, 802, 1503–1505
Ture, Muhammed, 1414
Turkana, 385, 744, 1125, 1128–1129
Turner, Henry, 349
Turshain, Khalifa 'Abd Allahi Muhammad, 459
Tuta, 1533
Tutsi, 1273, *See also* Hutu-Tutsi violence and genocide; Rwanda
  colonial history, 189–190, 1299–1300
  Hutu conflict, Burundi, 190–193
  Hutu conflict, cattle herding origins, 590
  Hutu conflict and genocide, 248, 384, 1246–1247, 1303–1308
  postindependence Rwanda, 1302
  precolonial history, 381, 1296–297
  precolonial history, Hutu relationship, 1297, 1298
  Rwandan independence and, 1300–1301
Tutu, Desmond, 1256, 1273, 1610–1611
Tutu, Osei, 780
Twa, 1296, 1301
Twagiramungu, Faustin, 1306
Twi, 31
Twifo, 32, 33
Twining, Edward, 1546, 1547
Typhoid fever, 621

U

Uasin Gishu, 1129
Ubangi, 298
Ubangi-Shari, *See* Oubangi-Shari
Ubangi Liberal Intergroup (ILO), 155
Ubayd Allah, 431
UDEAC, *See* Union Douanière et Economique de l'Afrique Central
Uganda, 1613–1635
  African Association (1929–1948), 1545
  Alice Lakwena's Holy Spirit Movement, 1257, 1632, 1633
  Anglo-German Agreement, 1615, 1714
  Angolan civil war and, 92
  anti-colonial Nyabingi resistance movement, 1162–1163
  Asians in, 112, 1626, *See also* Indians in Africa
  British Commonwealth and, 282
  Bunyoro, 178–180, *See also* Bunyoro
  cash crops, 1188
  cattle herding, Great Lakes region, 590–591
  Christianity, 1267, 1615–1616
  colonial rule, 282, 383
  colonial rule, administration and economy, 1617–1619
  colonial rule, sociocultural legacies, 277, 279
  Congo and, 315, 316, 1054, 1634–1635
  Cwezi, 694, 696
  debt, 339
  East African Community, 377–378, 1054, 1167, 1171
  East African Protectorate, 745–746
  economy, postindependence, 1632
  education, 392, 393, 1619, 1620–1622
  Federation of East Africa, 1622–1623
  Gaddafi's Libya and, 1626
  history, Buganda to 19th century, 176–177
  Idi Amin and, 384, 867, 1172, *See also* Amin Dada, Idi
  independence, 384, 1623
  indigenization policy, 757
  indigenous states, early 19th century, 1613–1614
  industrialization, 1619
  Iron Age, cattle and pastoralism, 693, 695

Iron Age, development of farming, 682
Iron Age, salt production, 697
Islam and, 711
Janani, archbishop of, 866–867
Kabarega, 727–728
Kagwa and, 728–730
Kakungulu and, 730–731
Kampala, 731–732
Karimojong, 1127–1129
Kilimanjaro Johnston and, 719
labor movement, 1578
later Stone Age culture, 1482
military rule, 326
missionary activity, 1059
Museveni administration, 1621–1622
Museveni and National Resistance Army, 1053–1054
Mutesa and Buganda monarchy (1856–1884), 176, 1058–1059, 1615
Mutesa II, Edward, 176, 732, 1625
National Resistance Movement and Museveni regime. 1630–1635
nationalism, 1950s, 1171
Nilotes, 1125, *See also* Nilotic peoples
Northern Uganda, colonial, 1619–1620
Nyabingi cult, 1162–1164, 1251
Obote and, 1170–1172, *See also* Obote, Milton
Obote and, first regime (1962–1971), 1623–1624
Obote and, second regime and overthrow (1980–1985), 1629–1631
Partitition and Anglo-German Agreement, 1616
political parties and independence, 1622–1623
post-Amin government and politics (1979–1980), 1627–1628
postindependence, 384
precolonial history, 380–381
precolonial states, Great Lakes region, 591–596
press, 723, 1227
professional class, 1235
prophetic movements, 1257
public health, 623
railways, 1618
rinderpest epidemic, 1284, 1285
Rwanda and, 1303, 1634–1635
socialism and nationalization program, 1624
Sudan and, 1633
Sudanic peoples, 226–227
Tanzania conflict and relations, 101, 1166–1167, 1553–1554, 1626–1627
Yakan cult, 1257, 1277
Uganda African Farmers Union (UAFU), 1622
Uganda Agreement of 1900, 1617, 1618, 1622
Uganda Development Corporation (UDC), 1619
Uganda National Congress (UNC), 1171, 1620, 1622, 1623
Uganda National Liberation Army (UNLA), 1629–1631, 1633
Uganda National Liberation Front (UNLF), 1628, 1630
Uganda Patriotic Movement (UPM), 1629
Uganda People's Congress (UPC), 1171, 1623, 1627, 1629
Uganda People's Democratic Army, 1633
Uganda People's Union (UPU), 1171
Uganda Railway, 744, 745–746
Ugba ibn Nafi, Sidi, 889
Ugweno, 386
Ujamaa, 22, 783, 1166, 1209, 1395, 1549–1551
Ujiji, 382
Ukerewe, 593
Ulama, 55, 57, 58, 1253, 1267
Ulduwan, 1175–1176
Ulumu, 135
'Umar bin Idris, 156
'Umar Tal (al-Hajj), *See* Hajj 'Umar, al-

1818